ALMANAC

Compiled and Edited by
Craig T. and Peter G. Norback
and
the Editors of *TV Guide*® Magazine

BALLANTINE BOOKS • NEW YORK

Acknowledgments

First of all, we are most grateful to Walter Annenberg and Merrill Panitt of Triangle Publications for allowing us to do the book in the first place, and to Harold Clemenko for working so hard on the development of the project from the beginning as well as his continued editorial assistance.

In addition, we would like to offer our special thanks to Travis Whitlow of A.C. Nielsen & Company for his patience and total willingness to help us with our innumerable requests for information.

Thanks as well to all of the networks for their cooperation and in particular to Betty Jane Reed and Natalie Tiranno of NBC, Peggy Rienow of CBS, and Dan Rustin and Anne Riccitelli of ABC.

Library of Congress Cataloging in Publication Data

Norback, Craig T.
   TV guide almanac.

   Includes index.
   1. Television broadcasting—United States—
Handbooks, manuals, etc. I. Norback, Peter G.,
joint author. II. TV guide. III. Title.
PN1992.3.U5N6   384.55'4'0973   79-15240
ISBN 0-345-28566-2
ISBN 0-345-27688-4 pbk.

Manufactured in the United States of America

First Ballantine Books Edition: January 1980

1 2 3 4 5 6 7 8 9

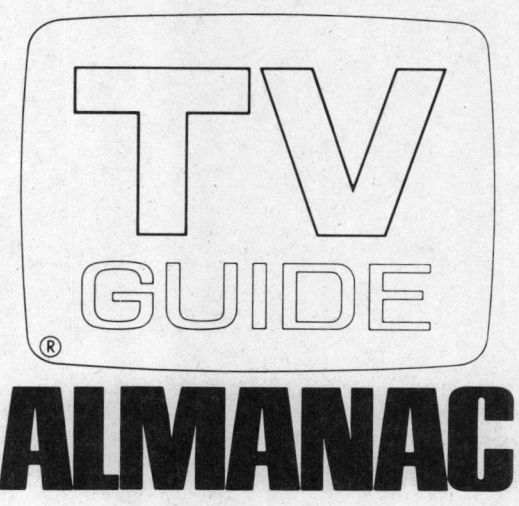

Contents

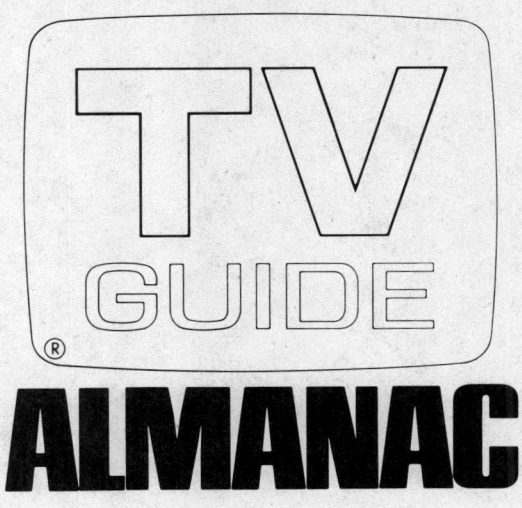

ADVERTISING

What follows is a listing of 1978's top-100 television advertisers, along with a product-classification summary based on combined network and spot-advertiser investments, as reported by Broadcast Advertisers Reports (BAR). Also included are expenditures by product classification in spot television. Spot-TV figures are based on monitoring in 75 markets. Network figures are based on continuous monitoring of the three networks. This information was provided by the Television Bureau of Advertising, 1345 Ave. of the Americas, New York, NY 10019 (212-397-3462). Other detailed information about the corporations, along with a partial listing of products, is from the *Standard Directory of Advertisers* and is reproduced with permission of the National Register Publishing Company, 5201 Old Orchard Rd., Skokie, IL 60076 (312-966-8500).

TOP 100 TELEVISION ADVERTISERS

1. Procter & Gamble
P. O. Box 599
Cincinnati, OH 45201
(513) 562-1100
J.G. Smale, president

Products: *Soaps, detergents and household cleaners*—Bold, Bonus, Camay, Coast, Dawn, Downy, Dreft, Duz, Cascade, Blue Cheer, Comet, Dash, Ivory soap, Ivory Flakes, Ivory Snow, Ivory Liquid, Joy, Lava, Mr. Clean, Oxydol, Safeguard, Salvo, Spic and Span, Thrill, Tide, Top Job, Zest, Biz, Gain, Era, Bounce. *Food products*—Crisco, Crisco Oil, Duncan Hines prepared baking mixes, Fluffo, Jif peanut butter, Pringle's potato chips. *Toilet goods*—Crest, Gleem, Head & Shoulders, Lilt, Prell, Scope, Secret, Sure. *Household paper products*—Charmin bathroom tissue, White Cloud bathroom tissue, Puffs facial tissues, Bounty paper towels, Pampers diapers

Total TV expenditures:	$421,023,300
Total spot-TV expenditures:	159,308,000
Total network-TV expenditures:	261,715,300

2. General Foods Corp.
250 North Ave.
White Plains, NY 10625
(914) 683-2500
J.L. Ferguson, chairman and chief executive

Products: Bird's Eye quick frozen vegetables, Orange Plus, Tang, Kool Aid, Country Fine lemonade mix, Gaines dog meal, Gravy Train, Gaines Burgers, Log Cabin syrup, Jell-O Brand desserts, coffee (Maxwell House, Yuban, Sanka, Maxim, Brim, Max-Pax)

Total TV expenditures:	$246,724,200
Total spot-TV expenditures:	77,235,200
Total network-TV expenditures:	169,489,000

3. American Home Products Corp.
685 3rd Ave.
New York, NY 10017
(212) 986-1000
William F. Laporte, chairman of the board

Products: Chef Boy-Ar-Dee Italian foods, Jiffy popcorn

Total TV expenditures:	$149,857,300
Total spot-TV expenditures:	38,721,100
Total network-TV expenditures:	111,136,200

4. General Mills, Inc.
9200 Wayzata Blvd.
Minneapolis, MN 55440
(612) 540-2311
E. Robert Kinney, president

Products: Gold Medal flour, Betty Crocker products, Bisquick, Cheerios, Wheaties, Country corn flakes, Total, Hamburger Helper

Total TV expenditures:	$134,968,000
Total spot-TV expenditures:	50,986,300
Total network-TV expenditures:	83,981,700

5. General Motors
General Motors Bldg.
Detroit, MI 48202
(313) 556-5000
Elliott M. Estes, president

Products: Chevrolet cars and trucks, Buick, Cadillac, Oldsmobile, Pontiac, GMC trucks, AC spark plugs, Delco batteries

Total TV expenditures:	$132,952,000
Total spot-TV expenditures:	25,087,200
Total network-TV expenditures:	107,864,800

6. Bristol-Myers Co.
345 Park Ave.
New York, NY 10022
(212) 644-2100
R. L. Gelb, chairman of the board, president

Products: Ban deodorant, Bromo Quinine, Bufferin, Congespirin, Datril, Excedrin, Excedrin P.M., Feminique, 4 Way cold tablets, 4 Way nasal spray, Minit-Rub, Multi-Scrub, NoDoz, Pals chewable vitamins, Sal Hepatica, Score hair products, Silence Is Golden, Softique bath beads and oil, Vitalis

Total TV expenditures:	$127,363,300
Total spot-TV expenditures:	17,021,900
Total network-TV expenditures:	110,341,400

7. McDonalds Corp.
McDonalds Plaza
Oak Brook, IL 60521
(312) 887-3200
Paul D. Schrage, executive vice-president—marketing

Products: hamburger restaurant chain

Total TV expenditures:	$114,866,800
Total spot-TV expenditures:	66,319,500
Total network-TV expenditures:	48,547,300

8. Ford Motor Co.
The American Road
Dearborn, MI 48121
(313) 322-3000
Lee A. Iacocca, president

Products: Fords and Mercurys, Pinto, Granada, Maverick, Ford LTD., Mustang II, Thunderbird, Mercury Cougar, Comet, Ford trucks

Total TV expenditures:	$110,812,000
Total spot-TV expenditures:	31,301,400
Total network-TV expenditures:	79,510,600

9. Lever Brothers Co.
390 Park Ave.
New York, NY 10022
(212) 688-6000
Thomas S. Carroll, president

Products: All cold water liquid and powder, Rinso, Wisk, Dove, Lux dishwashing liquid, Caress soap, Lifebuoy, Lux beauty soap, Phase III, Pepsodent, Close-up toothpaste, Aim, Twice as Nice shampoo, Imperial margarine, Promise margarine, Mrs. Butterworth's syrup

Total TV expenditures:	$99,586,300
Total spot-TV expenditures:	39,060,400
Total network-TV expenditures:	60,507,900

10. Chrysler Corp.
P. O. Box 1919
Detroit, MI 48231
(313) 956-5252
E.A. Cafiero, president

Products: Plymouth, Dodge, Chrysler; Dodge trucks

Total TV expenditures:	$93,663,700
Total spot-TV expenditures:	32,675,700
Total network-TV expenditures:	60,988,000

11. PepsiCo, Inc.
Purchase, NY 10577
(914) 253-2000
Andrall E. Pearson, president

Products: Pepsi-Cola soft drink, Frito-Lay, Wilson sporting goods

Total TV expenditures:	$92,500,500
Total spot-TV expenditures:	47,236,700
Total network-TV expenditures:	45,263,800

12. Sears Roebuck & Co.
Sears Tower
Chicago, IL 60684
(312) 875-2500
A. Dean Swift, president

Products: department stores and mail-order houses

Total TV expenditures:	$92,458,300
Total spot-TV expenditures:	21,090,800
Total network-TV expenditures:	71,367,500

13. Coca-Cola Co.
310 North Ave. NW
Atlanta, GA 30318
(404) 897-2121
John Ogden, president

Products: soft drinks

Total TV expenditures:	$84,537,400
Total spot-TV expenditures:	44,433,500
Total network-TV expenditures:	40,103,900

14. Colgate-Palmolive Co.
300 Park Ave.
New York, NY 10022
(212) 751-1200
Keith Crane, president

Products: Ajax cleaner, laundry detergent, and window cleaner, Axion, Baggies, Cashmere Bouquet soap, Cold Power, Colgate dental cream, Colgate 100 mouthwash, Fab, Halo shampoo, Handi Wipes, Hour After Hour deodorant, Irish Spring, Palmolive Gold, Rapid Shave, Ultra Brite toothpaste, Wildroot hair groomer, Stretch 'n Seal, Curad bandages, Dynamo, Wilkinson blades

Total TV expenditures: $84,479,600
Total spot-TV expenditures: 34,801,400
Total network-TV expenditures: 49,678,200

15. Warner-Lambert Pharmaceutical Co.
201 Tabor Rd.
Morris Plains, NJ 07950
(201) 540-2000
Ward S. Hagan, president

Products: Rolaids, Dentyne and Trident gum, Dentyne Dynamints, Certs, Adams gums and Halls cough drops and syrup, Efferdent, Effergrip, Listerine antiseptic, lozenges, and breath fresheners, Sloan's liniment, Anahist tablets and spray, Schick hot-lather machine, Schick razors and blades, Clorets, Smith Brothers cough drops, Cool Ray sunglasses

Total TV expenditures: $84,020,600
Total spot-TV expenditures: 28,248,600
Total network-TV expenditures: 55,772,000

16. Philip Morris Inc.
100 Park Ave.
New York, NY 10017
(212) 679-1800
Hugh Cullman, president (international)

Products: *Cigarettes* — Marlboro, Benson & Hedges, Parliament, Virginia Slims, Philip Morris, Merit, English Ovals

Total TV expenditures: $82,331,900
Total spot-TV expenditures: 15,165,300
Total network-TV expenditures: 67,166,600

17. American Telephone & Telegraph Co.
195 Broadway
New York, NY 10007
(212) 393-9800
Charles L. Brown, president

Products: telecommunications products

Total TV expenditures: $75,314,800
Total spot-TV expenditures: 34,111,400
Total network-TV expenditures: 41,203,400

18. Ralston Purina Co.
Checkerboard Square
St. Louis, MO 63188
(314) 982-0111
W.M. Shapleigh, president

Products: Chicken of the Sea seafoods, Chex cereals, Van Camp canned food, Ry Krisp, Purina cat food, Tender Vittles, Chuck Wagon, Puppy Dinner, Fit & Trim dog food

Total TV expenditures: $71,865,400
Total spot-TV expenditures: 14,792,000
Total network-TV expenditures: 57,073,400

19. Johnson & Johnson
George & Hamilton
New Brunswick, NJ 08901
(201) 524-0400
J.E. Burke, chairman of the board

Products: Johnson baby products, band-aids, Micron oral antiseptic

Total TV expenditures: $71,544,400
Total spot-TV expenditures: 6,565,300
Total network-TV expenditures: 64,979,100

20. Nabisco, Inc.
East Hanover, NJ 07936
(201) 884-0500
Val B. Diehl, president

Products: Ritz, Premium Saltines, Sugar Honey Maid Grahams, Oreos, Sugar Wafers, Fig Newtons, Shredded Wheat, 100% Bran, Team Flakes, Cream of Wheat cereal, Milk-Bone dog food, Rival dog food, Dromedary cake mix, Chuckles candy

Total TV expenditures: $68,200,700
Total spot-TV expenditures: 11,694,600
Total network-TV expenditures: 56,506,100

21. Nestle Co., Inc.
100 Bloomingdale Rd.
White Plains, NY 10605
(914) 946-6400
David E. Guerrant, president

Products: instant coffee and tea, chocolate products, Crosse & Blackwell products, Taster's Choice coffee, cookie mixes

Total TV expenditures: $66,712,400
Total spot-TV expenditures: 29,846,300
Total network-TV expenditures: 36,866,100

22. Kellogg Co.
Battle Creek, MI 49016
(616) 962-5151
W.E. LaMothe, president

Products: *Cereals*—Corn Flakes, Pep, Rice Krispies, 40% Bran Flakes, Raisin Bran, Sugar Pops, Cocoa Krispies, Sugar Smacks, All-Bran, Sugar Frosted Flakes, Special K, Froot Loops, etc.

Total TV expenditures: $65,465,800
Total spot-TV expenditures: 22,244,200
Total network-TV expenditures: 43,221,600

23. Pillsbury Co.
608 Second Ave. S
Minneapolis, MN 55402
(612) 330-4966
William H. Spoor, chairman of the board

Products: cake mixes, flours, frosting, pancake mix, pie-crust mix, dessert mixes

Total TV expenditures: $63,498,100
Total spot-TV expenditures: 23,649,000
Total network-TV expenditures: 39,849,100

24. Sterling Drug, Inc.
90 Park Ave.
New York, NY 10016
(212) 972-4141
G.W. Johnston, president

Products: Bayer aspirin, cold tablets, Bayer cough
syrup, Phillips Milk of Magnesia, Midol, etc.

Total TV expenditures: $61,341,400
Total spot-TV expenditures: 6,298,100
Total network-TV expenditures: 55,043,300

25. Kraftco Corp. (Kraft)
(US Retail Food Group)
500 Peshtigo Ct.
Chicago, IL 60690
(312) 222-4600
H. Keith Ridgway, president

Products: Kraft cheese, jellies and preserves, salad
dressings, confections, barbecue sauce

Total TV expenditures: $59,329,900
Total spot-TV expenditures: 33,350,300
Total network-TV expenditures: 25,979,600

26. Anheuser-Busch, Inc.
721 Pestalozzi
St. Louis, MO 63118
(314) 577-0577
August A. Busch, III, president

Products: Budweiser, Busch, and Michelob beer

Total TV expenditures: $57,882,000
Total spot-TV expenditures: 11,041,200
Total network-TV expenditures: 46,840,800

27. Gillette Co.
Prudential Tower Bldg.
Boston, MA 02199
(617) 421-7000
Colman M. Mockler, Jr., chairman of the board,
president

Products: Gillette razors and blades, Cricket light-
ers, Paper Mate ball pen

Total TV expenditures: $57,414,800
Total spot-TV expenditures: 14,653,700
Total network-TV expenditures: 42,761,100

28. Esmark, Inc.
55 E. Monroe
Chicago, IL 60603
(313) 431-3600
Donald P. Kelly, president

Products: Playtex apparel

Total TV expenditures: $51,153,800
Total spot-TV expenditures: 17,564,600
Total network-TV expenditures: 33,589,200

29. Richardson Merrell, Inc.
10 Westport Rd.
Wilton, CT 06897
(203) 762-2222
John S. Scott, president

Products: *Proprietary Medicines and Toiletries—*
Lavoris mouthwash, Clearasil ointment, Oil of Olay
lotion and cream, Vicks cough drops, Vicks cough
syrup, Vicks Formula 44, Nyquil nighttime cold
medicine

Total TV expenditures: $50,079,400
Total spot-TV expenditures: 10,366,700
Total network-TV expenditures: 39,712,700

30. J. C. Penney Co., Inc.
1301 Ave. of the Americas
New York, NY 10019
(212) 957-4321
Walter J. Neppi, president

Products: chain department stores

Total TV expenditures: $48,897,500
Total spot-TV expenditures: 19,223,200
Total network-TV expenditures: 29,674,300

31. Heublein, Inc.
Farmington, CT 06032
(203) 677-4061
Hicks B. Waldron, Jr., president

Products: wines and liquors, Harvey's Bristol
Cream

Total TV expenditures: $47,245,300
Total spot-TV expenditures: 20,121,100
Total network-TV expenditures: 27,124,200

**32. International Telephone and Telegraph
Corp.**
320 Park Ave.
New York, NY 10022
(212) 752-6000
Francis J. Dunleavy, president

Products: telecommunications equipment, consumer products, hotels, motels

Total TV expenditures: $44,603,000
Total spot-TV expenditures: 27,657,600
Total network-TV expenditures: 16,945,400

33. Mobil Oil Co.
150 E. 42nd St.
New York, NY 10017
(212) 883-4242
W.P. Tavoulareas, president

Products: gasoline, oil, tires, batteries, heating oils

Total TV expenditures: $44,240,400
Total spot-TV expenditures: 33,294,400
Total network-TV expenditures: 10,946,000

34. Mars, Inc.
1651 Old Meadow Rd., Westgate Park
McLean, VA 22101
(703) 821-4900
G.M. Conklin, president

Products: M&M's, Milky Way, Snickers, 3 Musketeers, Mars Almond Bar, Munch Peanut, Marathon Snik Snak Stiks, Uncle Ben's converted, quick and flavored rice, Stuff 'n' Such, Kal Kan dog and cat food

Total TV expenditures: $41,557,500
Total spot-TV expenditures: 18,102,800
Total network-TV expenditures: 23,454,700

35. Jos. Schlitz Brewing Co.
235 W. Galena
P. O. Box 614
Milwaukee, WI 53201
(414) 224-5000
E.B. Peters, president

Products: Schlitz beer, Schlitz malt liquor, Old Milwaukee beer, Primo beer

Total TV expenditures: $40,622,900
Total spot-TV expenditures: 8,387,200
Total network-TV expenditures: 32,235,700

36. The Clorox Co.
1221 Broadway
Oakland, CA 94612
(415) 271-7000
R.B. Shetterly, president

Products: Clorox liquid bleach, Liquid Plumber, Litter Green cat box fillers

Total TV expenditures: $39,836,100
Total spot-TV expenditures: 5,711,700
Total network-TV expenditures: 34,124,400

37. Chesebrough Ponds, Inc.
33 Benedict Pl.
Greenwich, CT 06830
(203) 661-2000
R.E. Ward, president

Products: Cutex products, Pond's products, Vaseline petroleum jelly and other products, Q-Tips cotton swabs and balls, Pertussin cough syrup, Prince Matchabelli perfume and related products, Ragu spaghetti sauce, Adolph's meat tenderizer

Total TV expenditures: $39,372,000
Total spot-TV expenditures: 5,341,400
Total network-TV expenditures: 34,030,600

38. William Wrigley, Jr., Co.
410 N. Michigan Ave.
Chicago, IL 60611
(312) 644-2121
William Wrigley, president

Products: Wrigley's Spearmint, Doublemint, Juicy Fruit, Big Red, Freedent, and P.K. chewing gum

Total TV expenditures: $39,004,500
Total spot-TV expenditures: 32,426,500
Total network-TV expenditures: 6,578,000

39. H.J. Heinz Co.
1062 Progress
Pittsburgh, PA 15212
(412) 237-5757
A.J.F. O'Reilly, president

Products: ketchup, Star-Kist tuna, Ore-Ida potatoes

Total TV expenditures: $38,007,300
Total spot-TV expenditures: 8,520,000
Total network-TV expenditures: 29,487,300

40. Schering-Plough Corp.
Galloping Hill Rd.
Kenilworth, NJ 07033
(201) 931-2000
Richard J. Bennett, president

Products: St. Joseph aspirin, Musterole, Solarcaine products, Coppertone suntan products, Di-Gel, Maybelline cosmetics, Aspergum, Sardo bath oils, Sudden Tan bronzing foam by Coppertone, etc.

Total TV expenditures: $36,629,000
Total spot-TV expenditures: 8,141,200
Total network-TV expenditures: 28,487,800

41. Revlon, Inc.
767 5th Ave.
New York, NY 10022
(212) 758-5000
Michel Bergerac, chairman of the board, president and chief executive officer

Products: *Cosmetics and Toiletries*—Mitchum, Colorsilk, Love Pat, Young Blush, Revlon eye makeup, Charlie, Revlon lipstick and nail enamel, Moon Drops, Milk Plus

Total TV expenditures: $36,388,900
Total spot-TV expenditures: 13,264,200
Total network-TV expenditures: 23,124,700

42. Eastman Kodak Co.
343 State
Rochester, NY 14650
(716) 325-2000
Walter A. Fallon, president

Products: cameras, projectors, film, etc.

Total TV expenditures: $35,448,200
Total spot-TV expenditures: 4,237,000
Total network-TV expenditures: 31,211,200

43. Miles Laboratories, Inc.
1127 Myrtle
Elkhart, IN 46514
(219) 264-8111
George W. Orr, Jr., president

Products: Alka-Seltzer, Alka-Seltzer Plus, One-A-Day vitamins, Flintstones vitamins, Bactine antiseptic, SOS scouring pads, etc.

Total TV expenditures: $35,328,100
Total spot-TV expenditures: 7,535,400
Total network-TV expenditures: 27,792,700

44. Toyota Motor Distributors, Inc.
2055 W. 190th St.
P. O. Box 2991
Torrance, CA 90509
(213) 532-5010
I. Makino, president

Products: Toyota cars and trucks

Total TV expenditures: $35,218,300
Total spot-TV expenditures: 20,195,700
Total network-TV expenditures: 15,022,600

45. Quaker Oats Co.
Merchandise Mart Plaza
Chicago, IL 60654
(312) 222-7111
Kenneth Mason, president

Products: Quaker oats, puffed wheat, puffed rice, Life cereal, Cap'n Crunch cereal, Quaker shredded wheat, Aunt Jemima pancake mix & syrup, Aunt Jemima products, Burry cookies, Flako baking mixes, Celeste frozen pizza, Fisher-Price toys, Ken-L Ration canned dog food, Puss'n Boots canned cat food

Total TV expenditures: $34,065,600
Total spot-TV expenditures: 13,985,300
Total network-TV expenditures: 20,080,300

46. Nissan Motor Corp. U.S.A.
18501 S. Figueroa St.
Carson, CA 90744
(213) 532-3111
Hiroshi Majima, president

Products: Datsun cars and trucks

Total TV expenditures: $33,151,100
Total spot-TV expenditures: 13,840,200
Total network-TV expenditures: 19,310,900

47. Norton Simon, Inc.
277 Park Ave.
New York, NY 10017
(212) 832-1000
David J. Mahoney, chairman of the board, president

Products: Canada Dry soft drinks, Max Factor cosmetics, McCall patterns, Hunt's tomato products, Wesson oil, Reddi-Wip, Manwich

Total TV expenditures: $32,659,300
Total spot-TV expenditures: 14,400,300
Total network-TV expenditures: 18,259,000

48. CPC International, Inc.
International Plaza
Englewood Cliffs, NJ 07632
(201) 894-4000
James W. McKee, Jr., president

Products: Hellmann's mayonnaise, Skippy peanut butter, S.B. Thomas English muffins, H-O instant oatmeal

Total TV expenditures: $31,884,100
Total spot-TV expenditures: 13,433,600
Total network-TV expenditures: 18,450,500

49. Polaroid Corp.
549 Technology Sq.
Cambridge, MA 02139
(617) 864-6000
William McCune, president

Products: cameras and film

Total TV expenditures: $31,861,000
Total spot-TV expenditures: 3,721,100
Total network-TV expenditures: 28,139,900

50. American Express Co.
American Express Plaza
New York, NY 10004
(212) 480-2000
Howard L. Clark, chairman of the board

Products: credit cards, traveler's checks

Total TV expenditures: $31,133,300
Total spot-TV expenditures: 8,248,500
Total network-TV expenditures: 22,884,800

51. RCA Corp.
30 Rockefeller Plaza
New York, NY 10020
(212) 598-5900
Edgar H. Griffiths, president

Products: radios, televisions, records, Random House books, Hertz Rent A Car, Banquet foods

Total TV expenditures: $30,476,200
Total spot-TV expenditures: 9,683,900
Total network-TV expenditures: 20,792,300

52. Mattel, Inc.
5150 Rosecrano Ave.
Hawthorne, CA 90250
(213) 644-0411
Raymond P. Wagner, president

Products: toys

Total TV expenditures:	$29,689,200
Total spot-TV expenditures:	18,352,900
Total network-TV expenditures:	11,336,300

53. American Motors Corp.
American Center
27777 Franklin Rd.
Southfield, MI 48034
(313) 827-1000
William V. Luneburg, president

Products: Pacer, Gremlin, Hornet, Matador, Jeep

Total TV expenditures:	$29,186,600
Total spot-TV expenditures:	11,254,100
Total network-TV expenditures:	17,932,500

54. Time, Inc.
Time & Life Bldg.
Rockefeller Center
New York, NY 10020
(212) 586-1212
Andrew Heiskell, chairman of the board

Products: *Time, Fortune, Sports Illustrated, Money* and *People* magazines, Time-Life Books, Time-Life records, Time-Life films, Forest products

Total TV expenditures:	$29,129,300
Total spot-TV expenditures:	23,078,300
Total network-TV expenditures:	6,051,000

55. Volkswagenwerk A.G.
818 Sylvan Ave.
Englewood Cliffs, NJ 07632
(201) 894-5000
J. Stuart Perkins, president

Products: Volkswagen station wagons, trucks, automobiles, Porsche–Audi automobiles

Total TV expenditures:	$28,746,200
Total spot-TV expenditures:	9,976,500
Total network-TV expenditures:	18,769,700

56. Morton-Norwich Products Inc.
110 N. Wacker Dr.
Chicago, IL 60606
(312) 621-5200
John W. Simmons, chairman of the board, president

Products: Morton salt, Pepto Bismol

Total TV expenditures:	$28,701,000
Total spot-TV expenditures:	5,253,200
Total network-TV expenditures:	23,447,800

57. Gulf & Western Industries, Inc.
1 Gulf & Western Plaza
New York, NY 10023
(212) 333-7000
David N. Judelson, president

Products: movies, paper products, apparel, food products, records, books

Total TV expenditures:	$28,233,100
Total spot-TV expenditures:	13,895,600
Total network-TV expenditures:	14,337,500

58. Hanes Corp.
630 5th Ave.
New York, NY 10020
(212) 582-3025
J.R. Hobert, president

Products: Hanes and L'Eggs hosiery

Total TV expenditures:	$28,100,200
Total spot-TV expenditures:	2,902,100
Total network-TV expenditures:	25,198,100

59. Squibb Corp.
40 W. 57th St.
New York, NY 10019
(212) 489-2000
Dr. D. Barry Davis, president

Products: Life Savers roll candy, Beechnut gum, Care-Free gum, Pine Bros. cough drops; Arpege, Jean Nate, Rive Gauche, My Sin, etc., perfumes; Squibb drugs and pharmaceuticals

Total TV expenditures:	$27,356,300
Total spot-TV expenditures:	2,465,800
Total network-TV expenditures:	24,890,500

60. General Electric
3135 Easton Turnpike
Fairfield, CT 06431
(203) 373-2211
Reginald H. Jones, chairman of the board

Products: light bulbs, refrigerators, televisions, radios, stereos, stoves

Total TV expenditures:	$27,299,800
Total spot-TV expenditures:	8,215,400
Total network-TV expenditures:	19,084,400

61. Noxell Corp.
11050 York Rd.
Baltimore, MD 21203
(301) 666-1661
George L. Bunting, Jr., president

Products: Lestoil, Noxzema cream, Cover Girl makeup

Total TV expenditures:	$27,029,000
Total spot-TV expenditures:	3,591,400
Total network-TV expenditures:	23,437,600

62. Campbell Soup Co.
Camden, NJ 08101
(609) 964-4000
H.A. Shaub, president

Products: soups, V-8 cocktail juice, Franco-American spaghetti products, Swanson frozen prepared foods

Total TV expenditures:	$25,932,900
Total spot-TV expenditures:	9,711,100
Total network-TV expenditures:	16,221,800

63. American Cyanamid Co.
Wayne, NJ 07470
(201) 831-1234
J.G. Affleck, president

Products: Pinesol, Copper Glo, Formica Floor Shine

Total TV expenditures:	$25,162,300
Total spot-TV expenditures:	6,576,500
Total network-TV expenditures:	18,585,800

64. A.H. Robins Co., Inc.
1407 Cummings Dr.
Richmond, VA 23220
(804) 257-2000
W.L. Zimmer, III, president

Products: pharmaceuticals

Total TV expenditures:	$24,937,600
Total spot-TV expenditures:	24,937,600
Total network-TV expenditures:	—

65. Beecham Group, Ltd.
Church Hill Rd.
P. O. Box 1467
Pittsburgh, PA 15230
(412) 787-5250
R.A. Fallon, president

Products: Calgon bath products, Calgonite, B.F.I., Bo-Car-Al, Cuprex, Fruit-Fresh, Melozets, S.T. 37, Sucrets, Thermotabs, Cling Free, Hold cough suppressant, Brylcreem hairdressing, Macleans toothpaste, Massengill feminine hygiene products

Total TV expenditures:	$24,617,400
Total spot-TV expenditures:	3,886,100
Total network-TV expenditures:	20,731,300

66. Warner Communications, Inc.
75 Rockefeller Plaza
New York, NY 10019
(212) 484-8000
Steven J. Ross, chairman of the board

Products: diversified entertainment and communications operations

Total TV expenditures:	$24,500,100
Total spot-TV expenditures:	8,682,300
Total network-TV expenditures:	15,817,800

67. Kresge Co.
3100 W. Big Beaver
Troy, MI 48084
(313) 643-1000
E.E. Wardlow, president

Products: Kresge, K-Mart, and Jupiter chain stores

Total TV expenditures:	$24,037,300
Total spot-TV expenditures:	15,045,100
Total network-TV expenditures:	8,992,200

68. Borden, Inc.
277 Park Ave.
New York, NY 10017
(212) 573-4000
Eugene J. Sullivan, president

Products: Cracker Jacks, cheese and milk products, Harvard beets, Campfire marshmallows, Pet Milk, Drake's cakes, Wise potato chips, Melba toast, Wyler instant bouillon cubes, Mystik tapes, Joy dishwashing liquid, Borden ice cream

Total TV expenditures:	$23,782,600
Total spot-TV expenditures:	10,672,400
Total network-TV expenditures:	13,110,200

69. S.C. Johnson & Son, Inc.
1525 Howe
Racine, WI 53403
(414) 554-2000
W.K. Eastham, president

Products: cleaning agents, Glory rug shampoo, Pledge, Klean 'n Shine, Shout laundry soil and stain remover, Glade Mist air fresheners, Raid insecticides, etc.

Total TV expenditures:	$22,657,400
Total spot-TV expenditures:	2,108,800
Total network-TV expenditures:	20,548,600

70. Scott Paper Co.
Scott Plaza
Philadelphia, PA 19113
(215) 521-5000
C.D. Dickey, Jr., president

Products: ScotTissue, Waldorf, Soft-Weve, Lady Scott and Cottonelle bathroom tissue; ScotTowels; Cut-Rite wax products; Viva; Scotkins Napkins; Lady Scott Facial Tissue; Confidets sanitary napkins

Total TV expenditures:	$22,631,100
Total spot-TV expenditures:	17,845,300
Total network-TV expenditures:	4,785,800

71. Alberto Culver Co.
2525 Armitage Ave.
Melrose Park, IL 60160
(312) 531-2000
Leonard H. Lavin, president

Products: *Toiletries*—Alberto VO5 hair care products, Get Set hair setting lotion and gel, Command Holding hair spray, New Dawn 2 hair color, FDS feminine hygiene products, For Brunettes Only Shampoo-In hair color. *Household and Grocery Products*—SugarTwin, Kleen Guard furniture and rug care products, Milani salad dressings, sauces and seasonings, Smithers gourmet foods, Static Guard

Total TV expenditures:	$22,497,800
Total spot-TV expenditures:	14,872,100
Total network-TV expenditures:	7,625,700

72. Kimberly Clark Corp.
N. Lake St.
Neenah, WI 54956
(414) 729-1212
Darwin E. Smith, chairman of the board and chief executive officer

Products: Kleenex tissues, table napkins and towels, Teri towels, Kotex feminine hygiene products, Delsey bathroom tissue, Kimbies disposable diapers, newsprint, mimeograph and xerography papers

Total TV expenditures:	$22,359,700
Total spot-TV expenditures:	5,904,300
Total network-TV expenditures:	16,455,400

73. North American Philips Corp.
100 E. 42nd St.
New York, NY 10017
(212) 697-3600
Pieter C. Vink, president

Products: electronics, Norelco razors and appliances, Magnavox televisions, games

Total TV expenditures:	$22,182,000
Total spot-TV expenditures:	10,884,300
Total network-TV expenditures:	11,297,700

74. Smithkline Corp.
1500 Spring Garden
Philadelphia, PA 19101
(215) 854-4000
Henry Wendt, president

Products: medical products

Total TV expenditures:	$22,064,200
Total spot-TV expenditures:	5,226,100
Total network-TV expenditures:	16,838,100

75. Beatrice Foods Co.
120 S. LaSalle
Chicago, IL 60603
(312) 782-3820
Wallace N. Rasmussen, president

Products: dairy and grocery goods

Total TV expenditures:	$21,693,800
Total spot-TV expenditures:	16,254,800
Total network-TV expenditures:	5,439,000

76. Avon Products, Inc.
9 W. 57th St.
New York, NY 10019
(212) 593-4017
David W. Mitchell, president

Products: cosmetics

Total TV expenditures:	$21,218,400
Total spot-TV expenditures:	1,103,900
Total network-TV expenditures:	20,114,500

77. Carnation Co.
5045 Wilshire Blvd.
Los Angeles, CA 90036
(213) 931-1911
D.L. Stuart, president

Products: Carnation evaporated milk, instant milk, ice cream, Instant Breakfast, Breakfast Bars, Coffee-Mate, Slender diet food, Friskies dog and cat food, Contadina tomato products, hot cocoa mix

Total TV expenditures:	$20,892,300
Total spot-TV expenditures:	3,196,600
Total network-TV expenditures:	17,695,700

78. Royal Crown Cola Co. (Soft Drink Div.)
1000 10th Ave.
P. O. Box 1440
Columbus, GA 31902
(404) 322-4431
Edward F. O'Reilly, president

Products: Royal Crown Cola soft drink

Total TV expenditures:	$20,484,200
Total spot-TV expenditures:	18,550,500
Total network-TV expenditures:	1,933,700

79. MCA, Inc.
100 Universal City Plaza
Universal City, CA 91608
(213) 985-4321
Lew R. Wasserman, chairman of the board

Products: motion pictures, TV programs and phonograph record production and distribution, music publishing, gift mail orders and retail stores; recreational activities; book publishing

Total TV expenditures: $20,177,600
Total spot-TV expenditures: 12,686,600
Total network-TV expenditures: 7,491,000

80. Federated Dept. Stores, Inc.
222 W. 7th St.
Cincinnati, OH 45202
(513) 852-3000
Harold Krensky, president

Products: Abraham & Strauss, Bloomingdales, and other department-store chains

Total TV expenditures: $20,109,900
Total spot-TV expenditures: 20,109,900
Total network-TV expenditures: ——

81. Exxon Corp.
1251 Ave. of the Americas
New York, NY 10020
(212) 974-3000
H.C. Kauffman, president

Products: petroleum products

Total TV expenditures: $19,471,600
Total spot-TV expenditures: 6,803,600
Total network-TV expenditures: 12,668,000

82. Consolidated Foods Corp.
135 S. La Salle
Chicago, IL 60603
(312) 726-6414
John J. Cardwell, president

Products: *Consumer goods and services*—Abbey Rents & Sells, Gant shirtmakers, Shasta beverages, Popsicle industries, Sara Lee, etc.

Total TV expenditures: $19,050,200
Total spot-TV expenditures: 12,582,400
Total network-TV expenditures: 6,467,800

83. Wendy's Old Fashioned Hamburgers
Box 256
4288 W. Dublin Granville
Dublin, OH 43017
(614) 889-0900
R. David Thomas, chairman of the board

Products: hamburger restaurant chain

Total TV expenditures: $18,992,800
Total spot-TV expenditures: 10,448,200
Total network-TV expenditures: 8,544,600

84. Standard Brands, Inc.
625 Madison Ave.
New York, NY 10022
(212) 759-4400
E. Ross Johnson, president

Products: Planters peanuts, Blue Bonnet margarine, Fleischmann's corn oil, Egg Beaters, Royal gelatins, Fleischmann's yeast, Chase & Sanborn coffee, Baby Ruth bars, Butterfinger candy, Sun-Maid raisins, Planters peanut butter, etc.

Total TV expenditures: $18,901,700
Total spot-TV expenditures: 9,480,000
Total network-TV expenditures: 9,421,700

85. Block Drug Co.
257 Cornelison Ave.
Jersey City, NJ 07302
(201) 434-3000
James A. Block, president

Products: Polident powder, Poli-Grip, Py-co-Pay toothbrushes and powder, Tegrin shampoo, Romilar, Nytol sleeping tablets

Total TV expenditures: $18,703,200
Total spot-TV expenditures: 4,879,300
Total network-TV expenditures: 13,823,900

86. E. & J. Gallo Winery
P. O. Box 1130
Modesto, CA 95353
(209) 521-3111
Julio Gallo, president

Products: wines, champagne, brandy and vermouth

Total TV expenditures: $18,541,000
Total spot-TV expenditures: 2,967,600
Total network-TV expenditures: 15,573,400

87. Pabst Brewing Co.
917 W. Juneau Ave.
Milwaukee, WI 53201
(414) 347-7300
Frank C. DeGuire, president and chief executive officer

Products: Pabst Blue Ribbon Beer, Andeker Supreme Beer, Red White & Blue Beer, Eastside Old Tap Lager, Burgermeister, Pabst Extra Light, Burgie Light Golden Beer

Total TV expenditures: $17,949,000
Total spot-TV expenditures: 12,480,500
Total network-TV expenditures: 5,468,500

88. Honda Motor Co., Inc.
100 W. Alondra
Gardena, CA 90247
(213) 321-8680
K. Yoshizawa, president

Products: Honda motorcycles and automobiles

Total TV expenditures: $17,845,900
Total spot-TV expenditures: 1,121,000
Total network-TV expenditures: 16,724,900

89. Hershey Foods Corp.
19 E. Chocolate Ave.
Hershey, PA 17033
(717) 534-4200
H.S. Mohler, chairman of the board

Products: cocoa, chocolate and confectionary products

Total TV expenditures: $17,835,600
Total spot-TV expenditures: 5,381,000
Total network-TV expenditures: 12,454,600

90. UAL, Inc. (United Air Lines)
1200 Algonquin Rd.
Mt. Prospect, IL 60056
(312) 952-4000
Edward Carlson, chairman of the board and chief executive officer

Products: air transportation

Total TV expenditures: $17,780,000
Total spot-TV expenditures: 8,378,500
Total network-TV expenditures: 9,401,500

91. Union Carbide Corp.
270 Park Ave.
New York, NY 10017
(212) 551-2345
Warren M. Anderson, president

Products: Prestone antifreeze, Eveready flashlights and batteries, Glad plastic bags and wrap, Simonize waxes and polishes

Total TV expenditures: $17,070,400
Total spot-TV expenditures: 1,469,800
Total network-TV expenditures: 15,600,600

92. Liggett Group, Inc.
4100 Roxboro Rd.
Durham, NC 27702
(919) 471-7511
Raymond J. Mulligan, president

Products: tobacco products, breakfast foods, pet foods, Alpo canned dog food, household cleaning products

Total TV expenditures: $17,064,100
Total spot-TV expenditures: 4,678,800
Total network-TV expenditures: 12,385,300

93. Milton Bradley Co.
1500 Main St.
East Longmeadow, MA 01028
(413) 525-6411
James J. Shea, Jr., chairman of the board and president

Products: toys, games, puzzles

Total TV expenditures: $16,828,200
Total spot-TV expenditures: 16,226,200
Total network-TV expenditures: 602,000

94. Goodyear Tire & Rubber Co.
1144 E. Market
Akron, OH 44316
(216) 794-2121
J.H. Gerstenmaier, president

Products: tires and other rubber products

Total TV expenditures: $16,670,600
Total spot-TV expenditures: 3,793,900
Total network-TV expenditures: 12,876,700

95. Firestone Tire & Rubber Co.
1200 Firestone Pkwy.
Akron, OH 44317
(216) 379-7000
Richard A. Riley, chairman and chief executive officer

Products: Firestone tires, tubes, camelback and repair materials, molded and extruded rubber products, natural and synthetic rubber, steel and aluminum stampings, steel rims and wheels, stainless steel containers, aluminum beverage cases, seat belts and shoulder harnesses, synthetic fibers, textiles, coated fabrics

Total TV expenditures: $16,336,400
Total spot-TV expenditures: 6,510,400
Total network-TV expenditures: 9,826,000

96. CBS, Inc.
51 W. 52nd St.
New York, NY 10019
(212) 975-4321
William S. Paley, chairman

Products: radio, television, records, musical instruments, toys, book publishing

Total TV expenditures: $16,222,700
Total spot-TV expenditures: 13,384,400
Total network-TV expenditures: 2,838,300

97. Tandy Corp.
1800 One Tandy Center
Fort Worth, TX 76102
(817) 335-2551
Charles D. Tandy, chairman of the board

Products: consumer electronics

Total TV expenditures: $16,209,100
Total spot-TV expenditures: 4,734,200
Total network-TV expenditures: 11,474,900

98. Safeway Stores, Inc.
4th & Jackson Sts.
Oakland, CA 94660
(415) 891-3000
W.S. Mitchell, chairman of the board, president and chief executive officer

Products: Retail food stores

Total TV expenditures:	$16,029,700
Total spot-TV expenditures:	16,029,700
Total network-TV expenditures:	——

99. IC Industries, Inc.
111 E. Wacker Dr.
Chicago, IL 60601
(312) 565-3000
William B. Johnson, chairman of the board

Products: commercial and consumer products, financial services, real estate, rail transportation

Total TV expenditures:	$15,695,200
Total spot-TV expenditures:	9,014,000
Total network-TV expenditures:	6,681,200

100. Transamerica Corp.
600 Montgomery St.
San Francisco, CA 94111
(415) 983-4000
John R. Beckett, chairman of the board and president

Products: diversified service organization

Total TV expenditures:	$15,501,200
Total spot-TV expenditures:	8,292,900
Total network-TV expenditures:	7,208,300

THE TELEVISION BUREAU OF ADVERTISING

The Television Bureau of Advertising is a national consulting firm uniting television stations and advertisers throughout the world, from Australia and Nigeria to Illinois and California. TvB is a forum for the exchange of concepts, the updating of methods, the dissemination of information, and the solving of problems.

TVB OFFICERS

Roger D. Rice, president
Norman E. Cash, vice-chairman
George Huntington, executive vice-president—operations
Robert A. Lefko, executive vice-president—sales
Harvey Spiegel, senior vice-president—research
Richard Severance, vice-president—national sales
Beverly Keene, vice-president—creative services
Walter Vetter, vice-president—technical services

John Sheehan, vice-president—member services
Barbara Ann Zeiger, manager—public relations

Headquarters: 1345 Ave. of the Americas, New York, NY 10019

The executives of branch offices include the following:
Will Dougherty, vice-president—Southeast sales
  3340 Peachtree Rd., NE, Suite 1415, Tower Pl., Atlanta, GA 30326
Chuck Hanson, vice-president—Southwest sales
  3141 Hood St., Suite 220, Dallas, TX 75219
Dick O'Donnell, vice-president—Detroit
  1017 Fisher Bldg., Detroit, MI 48202
Dave Michels, vice-president—Chicago
  410 N. Michigan Ave., Chicago, IL 60611
Robert Fairbanks, vice-president—Western sales
  3700 Wilshire Blvd., Los Angeles, CA 90010

THE CLIO AWARDS

The Clio Awards
30 E. 60th St.
New York, NY 10022
(212) 593-1900
Bill Evans, president

Each year since 1960 the advertising industry has engaged in competition for awards not unlike the Oscar and Emmy competitions. The award—"for advertising excellence worldwide"—everyone seeks is called a Clio. As with most awards in the field of entertainment or communication, the judging is done by panels of professionals, in this case members of the advertising community from all over the world. They choose a winner, or more precisely a "best," in each of about 25 categories in all media.

"Clio," by the way, is derived from the Greek

Kleo, the muse who was the proclaimer, glorifier, and celebrator of history and accomplishment.

We have listed here the winners, from 1959 to 1978, in the TV competition. You will no doubt recognize your favorites. In some cases, the judges could not agree on a "best" in a specific category, and therefore none is listed. The first entry in each category is the title of the award-winning commercial. If other information about the commercial—the ad agency or production company responsible, for example—is not listed, it is because the information is either unavailable or not applicable.

What the Clio award signifies is that the TV commercials many viewers like or admire are thought highly of by others as well, and that some of them are not only effective but also innovative and artistic.

1959–1960

Best Apparel
Don't forget your nylons
Product: Nylon stockings
Sponsor: Chemstrand
Ad Agency: Doyle Dane Bernbach, New York
Production Co: Elliot, Unger & Elliot, New York

Best Appliances
Elaine May and Mike Nichols
Product: refrigerator and freezer
Sponsor: General Electric
Ad Agency: Young & Rubicam, New York
Production Co: NBC, New York

Best Automotive
Easy aces
Product: Mercury cars
Sponsor: Ford Motor Company
Ad Agency: Kenyon & Eckhardt, New York
Production Co: Filmways, New York

Best Auto Accessories
Five-car salute
Product: Delco car batteries
Sponsor: United Motors Service
Ad Agency: Campbell-Ewald, New York
Production Co: NBC, New York

Best Baked Goods
Movie set
Product: Taystee Brown 'N Serve rolls
Sponsor: American Bakeries
Ad Agency: Young & Rubicam, Chicago
Production Co: Quartet, California

Best Beers and Wines
Golf
Product: Falstaff beer
Sponsor: Falstaff Brewing Corp.
Ad Agency: Dancer-Fitzgerald-Sample, New York
Production Co: MPO, New York

Best Breakfast Cereal
Board meeting
Product: Post Sugar Crisp
Sponsor: General Foods
Ad Agency: Benton & Bowles, New York
Production Co: Ray Favata, New York

Best Cigarette and Cigar
Haydn
Product: Dutch Master cigars
Sponsor: Dutch Master Cigar Company
Ad Agency: Erwin Wasey, Ruth & Ryan, New York
Production Co: ABC-TV, California

Best Coffee and Tea
Lowest prices
Product: Instant Maxwell House Coffee
Sponsor: General Foods
Ad Agency: Benton & Bowles, New York
Production Co: Television Graphics, New York

Best Consumer Service
Number One
Product: Institutional advertising
Sponsor: Albuquerque National Bank
Ad Agency: Ward Hicks, Albuquerque
Production Co: KGGM-TV, Albuquerque

Best Cosmetics and Toiletries
Pinkissimo
Product: Lipstick and nail enamel
Sponsor: Revlon
Ad Agency: Warwick & Legler
Production Co: CBS, New York

Best Dairy Product
More milk for the weekend
Product: milk
Sponsor: American Dairy Association
Ad Agency: Campbell-Mithun, Chicago
Production Co: Cascade, California

Best Gasoline and Oil
Stop-sign of 76
Product: 76 gasoline
Sponsor: Union Oil
Ad Agency: Erwin Wasey, Ruth, & Ryan, Los Angeles
Production Co: Playhouse Pictures, Los Angeles

Best Household Cleanser and Detergent
Penetrating agent
Product: Lestoil
Sponsor: Lestoil
Ad Agency: Jackson, Mass.
Production Co.: Robert Lawrence, New York

Best Home Furnishings and Maintenance
Snoring
Product: Acrilan blankets
Sponsor: Chemstrand
Ad Agency: Doyle Dane Bernbach, New York
Production Co: MPO, New York

Best Institutionals—Public Service
Who owns American industry?

Sponsor: General Electric
Ad Agency: BBDO, New York
Production Co: Transfilm-Caravel, New York

Best Jewelry, Sports, and Toys
Grand Central
Product: Westclox self-winding watch
Sponsor: General Time
Ad Agency: BBDO, New York
Production Co: Telestudios, New York

Best Meat Product
Peter Fish
Product: Fish and shellfish
Sponsor: Bureau of Commercial Fisheries, U.S. Dept. Interior
Production Co: De Frenes, Philadelphia

Best Paper and Wraps
CF 501
Product: aluminum foil
Sponsor: Kaiser Aluminum
Ad Agency: Young & Rubicam, San Francisco
Production Co: Freberg (with Playhouse)

Best Pet Food
New puppy
Product: Ken-L-Ration
Sponsor: Quaker Oats Company
Ad Agency: J. Walter Thompson, Chicago
Production Co: Fred A. Niles, Chicago

Best Pharmaceutical
Sounds No. 1268
Product: Sheer Strip band-aid
Sponsor: Johnson & Johnson
Ad Agency: Young & Rubicam, New York
Production Co: On Film, Princeton

Best Prepared Foods and Mixes
Bisquick
Product: Bisquick
Sponsor: General Mills
Ad Agency: Knox-Reeves, Minneapolis
Production Co: NBC, New York

Best Program Billboards, Openings, Closings
Forgetful . . . light bulb
Product: Ernie Ford Show (Opening)
Sponsor: Ford Motor Company
Ad Agency: J. Walter Thompson, New York
Production Co: Playhouse, California

Best Soft Drink
Old movie kitchens
Product: Seven-Up
Sponsor: Seven-Up
Ad Agency: J. Walter Thompson, Chicago
Production Co: Ray Patin, California

Best Travel and Transportation
Abernathy
Product: coach and tour service
Sponsor: Greyhound
Ad Agency: Grey Advertising, New York
Production Co: Klaeger, New York

Best 8-10 Second ID
Bowling
Product: Schaefer beer
Sponsor: F. & M. Schaefer Brewing Company
Ad Agency: BBDO, New York
Production Co: Lars Calonius, New York

1961

Best Apparel
Modern art
Product: DuPont Westbury fashions
Sponsor: E.I. DuPont
Ad Agency: BBDO, New York
Production Co: Videotape Productions of New York

Best Appliances
Tango
Product: G.E. refrigerators
Sponsor: General Electric
Ad Agency: Young & Rubicam, New York
Production Co.: VPI, New York

Best Automobiles
Oasis
Product: Chevrolet Corvair
Sponsor: Chevrolet Div., General Motors
Ad Agency: Campbell-Ewald, Detroit
Production Co: American Films, St. Louis

Best Auto Accessories
Dynamo
Product: Delco-Remy replacement parts
Sponsor: United Motors Service
Ad Agency: Campbell-Ewald, Detroit
Production Co: Arco, New York

Best Baked Goods
Follow the leader
Product: Drake's Ring Dings
Sponsor: Drake Bakeries
Ad Agency: Young & Rubicam, New York
Production Co: Sarra, New York

Best Bath Soap
Laurie
Product: Praise soap
Sponsor: Lever Brothers, Ltd.
Ad Agency: Cockfield, Brown, Toronto
Production Co: B. L. Associates, New York

Best Beer and Wine
Kangaroo
Product: Jax beer
Sponsor: Jackson Brewing, Jacksonville
Ad Agency: Doherty, Clifford, Steers & Shenfield, New York
Production Co: Pelican Films, New York

Best Breakfast Cereal (Tie)
Typewriter
Product: Post Toasties
Sponsor: General Foods
Ad Agency: Benton & Bowles, New York
Production Co: Craven Films, New York

What to buy
Product: Kellogg's Snack-Pak
Sponsor: Kellogg
Ad Agency: Leo Burnett, Chicago
Production Co: Filmfair, Los Angeles

Best Cake Mix
Datenut cake mix
Product: Duncan Hines Early American cake mix
Sponsor: Procter & Gamble
Ad Agency: Gardner, St. Louis
Production Co: Wilding, Chicago

Best Cigarette and Cigar
Match
Product: Lucky Strike cigarettes
Sponsor: American Tobacco Company
Ad Agency: BBDO, New York
Production Co: MPO Videotronics, New York

Best Coffee and Tea
Iced coffee
Product: Instant Maxwell House coffee
Sponsor: General Foods
Ad Agency: Benton & Bowles, New York
Production Co: TV Graphics, New York

Best Consumer Service
Cat
Product: Esso oil heat
Sponsor: Imperial Oil, Ltd.
Ad Agency: MacLaren, Toronto
Production Co: Elektra, New York

Best Cosmetic and Toiletry
Documentary
Product: Ban deodorant
Sponsor: Bristol-Myers
Ad Agency: Ogilvy, Benson & Mather, New York
Production Co: WCD Productions, New York

Best Dairy Product and Margarine
Squeeze
Product: Blue Bonnet margarine
Sponsor: Standard Brands
Ad Agency: Ted Bates, New York
Production Co: Transfilm-Wylde, New York

Best Dentifrices
Cheryl Clapham
Product: Crest toothpaste
Sponsor: Procter & Gamble
Ad Agency: Benton & Bowles, New York
Production Co: TV Graphics, New York

Best Gasoline and Lubricant
Little girl—tricycle
Product: Texaco oil
Sponsor: Texaco petroleum products
Ad Agency: Cunningham & Walsh, New York
Production Co: Craven, New York

Best Gift Item
Take a picture
Product: Kodak film
Sponsor: Eastman Kodak
Ad Agency: J. Walter Thompson, New York
Production Co: MPO Videotronics, New York

Best Hair Preparation
Fur
Product: Prell Concentrate
Sponsor: Procter & Gamble
Ad Agency: Benton & Bowles, New York
Production Co: Transfilm-Caravel, New York

Best Home Furnishings
Customer support—traffic
Product: Colorib panels
Sponsor: Aluminum Company of America
Ad Agency: Fuller & Smith & Ross, New York
Production Co: TV Graphics, New York

Best Household Cleansers and Waxes
99 squeezes Calypso
Product: Brillo soap pads
Sponsor: Brillo Manufacturing
Ad Agency: J. Walter Thompson, New York
Production Co: Elektra, New York

Best Institutional
Man and wife
Product: Alcan aluminum
Sponsor: Aluminum Limited
Ad Agency: J. Walter Thompson, New York
Production Co: Group, Detroit

Best Laundry Soaps and Detergents
We suggest
Product: Ivory Flakes
Sponsor: Procter & Gamble
Ad Agency: Grey Advertising, New York
Production Co: MPO Videotronics, New York

Best Packaged Foods
Elevator
Product: Chun King Chow Mein
Sponsor: Chun King Enterprises, Inc.
Ad Agency: BBDO, Minneapolis
Production Co: Freberg Ltd. & Jacmar, Los Angeles

Best Paper Products
Picnic
Product: Scott (all brands)
Sponsor: Scott Paper
Ad Agency: J. Walter Thompson, New York
Production Co: MPO Videotronics, New York

Best Pet Foods
Dog and cat
Product: Gaines Gravy Train
Sponsor: General Foods
Ad Agency: Benton & Bowles, New York
Production Co: TV Graphics, New York

Best Pharmaceuticals
Headache-heartbeat
Product: Bufferin
Sponsor: Bristol-Myers
Ad Agency: Young & Rubicam, New York
Production Co: On Film, Princeton

Best Public Service
One little hand
Sponsor: United Cerebral Palsy Associations
Ad Agency: Direct
Production Co: Newsfilm USA, New York

Best Retail Stores
Party
Product: Boys' clothing
Sponsor: Barney's
Ad Agency: Mogul Williams & Saylor, New York
Production Co: CBS Television, New York

Best Soft Drink
Old movie–harried housewife
Product: Seven-Up
Sponsor: Seven-Up
Ad Agency: J. Walter Thompson, Chicago
Production Co: Sarra, Chicago

Best Travel
Polo . . . Japanese girls (2)
Product: Northwest Orient Airlines
Sponsor: Northwest Orient Airlines
Ad Agency: Campbell-Mithun, Minneapolis
Production Co: Desilu, Los Angeles

Best 8-10 Second ID
Mannequin
Product: Liquid Mist Reddi-Starch
Sponsor: Union Starch & Refining
Ad Agency: Baer, Kemble & Spicer, Cincinnati
Production Co: Format Films, Los Angeles

Best Billboards, Openings and Closings
Peanuts–phonograph
Product: Ernie Ford Show (Opening)
Sponsor: Ford Motor Company
Ad Agency: J. Walter Thompson, New York
Production Co: Playhouse Pictures, Los Angeles

Best Integrated By Program Cast
Fugitive father
Product: Post Grape Nuts
Sponsor: General Foods
Ad Agency: Benton & Bowles, New York
Production Co: Marterto, Los Angeles

Best Premium Offer
Band–record offer
Product: Lucky Strike cigarettes
Sponsor: American Tobacco Company
Ad Agency: BBDO, New York
Production Co: NBC Telesales, New York

Best Canadian Market
Masquerade
Product: Puss 'N Boots cat food
Sponsor: Quaker Oats
Ad Agency: Spitzer, Mills & Bates, Toronto
Production Co: Elektra, New York

Best Single Market (Service)
Daddy's new car
Product: auto loans
Sponsor: Manufacturers Trust
Ad Agency: Young & Rubicam, New York
Production Co: Animotion Associates, New York

Best Single Market (Product)
Upside down
Product: Trewax
Sponsor: Trewax Company
Ad Agency: Tilds & Cantz, Los Angeles
Production Co: KTTV Commercial Tape, Los Angeles

Best Single Market (Store)
Shoes . . . ready to wear
Product: shoes
Sponsor: ZCMI, Salt Lake City
Ad Agency: David W. Evans, Salt Lake City
Production Co: KSL-TV, Salt Lake City

1962

Best Series
Qualities of aluminum
Product: Alcoa aluminum
Sponsor: Aluminum Company of America
Ad Agency: Fuller & Smith & Ross, New York
Production Co: On Film, Princeton

Best Apparel
Sweaters of orlon
Product: DuPont products
Sponsor: E. I. DuPont
Ad Agency: BBDO, New York
Production Co: Elliot, Unger & Elliot, New York

Best Appliances (Home)
Peek a brew
Product: G.E. coffeemaker
Sponsor: General Electric
Ad Agency: Maxon, New York
Production Co: Elektra, New York

Best Appliances (Office)
Little girl
Product: Xerox 914 copier
Sponsor: Xerox Corp.
Ad Agency: Papert, Koenig & Lois, New York
Production Co: Elliot, Unger & Elliot, New York

Best Automobile
Swamp
Product: Chevrolet Corvair
Sponsor: Chevrolet Div., General Motors
Ad Agency: Campbell-Ewald, Detroit
Production Co: Woodburn & Walsh, Coral Gables

Best Auto Accessories
Micro-interior
Product: Autolite batteries
Sponsor: Electric Autolite Div., Ford Motor
Ad Agency: BBDO, New York
Production Co: Sarra, New York

Best Baked Goods and Confections
Little girls have pretty curls
Product: Oreos
Sponsor: National Biscuit
Ad Agency: McCann-Erickson, New York
Production Co: Morris Engel, New York

Best Baking Mixes
Fun
Product: Pillsbury yellow cake mix
Sponsor: Pillsbury
Ad Agency: Leo Burnett, Chicago
Production Co: On Film, Princeton

Best Banks
Symphony
Product: Bankamericard
Sponsor: Bank of America
Ad Agency: Johnson & Lewis, San Francisco
Production Co: Film-Fair, Hollywood

Best Beer and Wine
Beach
Product: Piel's beer
Sponsor: Piel Brothers
Ad Agency: Young & Rubicam, New York
Production Co: Screen Gems, Hollywood

Best Cereal
Package reader
Product: Kellogg's corn flakes
Sponsor: Kellogg
Ad Agency: Leo Burnett, Chicago
Production Co: MPO, Los Angeles

Best Cigar and Cigarette
Match folders
Product: Winston cigarettes
Sponsor: R. J. Reynolds
Ad Agency: William Esty, New York
Production Co: Pelican, New York

Best Cleansers and Waxes
John, Mary, and George
Product: Windex cleaner
Sponsor: Drackett
Ad Agency: Young & Rubicam, New York
Production Co: MPO, New York

Best Coffee and Tea
Cup and a half
Product: Instant Maxwell House coffee
Sponsor: General Foods
Ad Agency: Benton & Bowles, New York
Production Co: TV Graphics, New York

Best Cosmetics and Toiletries
Ooh la California
Product: Factor nail polish and lipstick
Sponsor: Max Factor
Ad Agency: Carson/Roberts, Los Angeles
Production Co: Filmfair, Hollywood

Best Dairy and Margarines
Butter crust pie
Product: American Dairy products
Sponsor: American Dairy Assoc.
Ad Agency: Campbell-Mithun, Chicago
Production Co: Sarra, New York

Best Gasoline and Lubricant
Man who wears the star
Product: Texaco gasoline
Sponsor: Texaco
Ad Agency: Benton & Bowles, New York
Production Co: Filmways, New York

Best Gift Items
Turn around
Product: Kodak film
Sponsor: Eastman Kodak
Ad Agency: J. Walter Thompson, New York
Production Co: Filmways, New York

Best Home Furnishings
Photography
Product: steel sinks
Sponsor: United States Steel
Ad Agency: BBDO, New York
Production Co: Ferro, Mogubgub & Schwartz, New York

Best Institutional
Workability
Product: Alcoa aluminum
Sponsor: Aluminum Company of America
Ad Agency: Fuller & Smith & Ross, New York
Production Co: On Film, Princeton

Best Insurance
Angleton, Texas
Product: Allstate insurance
Sponsor: Allstate
Ad Agency: Leo Burnett, Chicago
Production Co: WFAA-TV, Dallas

Best Laundry Soap and Detergent
Surprise
Product: Ivory Snow
Sponsor: Procter & Gamble
Ad Agency: Benton & Bowles, New York
Production Co: On Film, Princeton

Best Media
Sunday Bosley
Product: New York Herald Tribune
Sponsor: New York Herald Tribune
Ad Agency: Papert, Koenig, Lois, New York
Production Co: Videotape Productions, New York

Best Metals and Materials
Pilferproof wine caps
Product: Alcoa products
Sponsor: Aluminum Company of America
Ad Agency: Ketchum, MacLeod & Grove, Pittsburgh
Production Co: Producing Artists, New York

Best Packaged Foods (Tie)
Documentary
Product: Chun King Chow Mein
Sponsor: Chun King
Ad Agency: BBDO, Minneapolis
Production Co: Freberg, Hollywood

Elephants
Product: Skippy peanut butter
Sponsor: Best Foods Div., Corn Products
Ad Agency: Guild, Bascom & Bonfigli, San Francisco
Production Co: Quartet, Hollywood

Best Paper Products and Foils
Thank goodness
Product: All Scott products
Sponsor: Scott Paper
Ad Agency: J. Walter Thompson, New York
Production Co: On Film, Princeton

Best Pet Product
Drug store
Product: Sergeant's Flea & Tick Spray
Sponsor: Polk Miller Products
Ad Agency: N. W. Ayer, Philadelphia
Production Co: Group, Detroit

Best Pharmaceuticals
Breathing bandage
Product: Band-Aid Sheer Strips
Sponsor: Johnson & Johnson
Ad Agency: Young & Rubicam, New York
Production Co: On Film, Princeton

Best Public Service
Sponsor: Southern California Cancer Center
Ad Agency: Foote, Cone & Belding, Los Angeles
Production Co: Cascade Pictures of California

Best Soft Drink
Masquerade
Product: Pepsi-Cola
Sponsor: Pepsi-Cola Company
Ad Agency: BBDO, New York
Production Co: TeleVideo, New York

Best Toy
Blaze
Product: Mattel talking horse
Sponsor: Mattel
Ad Agency: Carson/Roberts, Los Angeles
Production Co: Lou Lilly, Hollywood

Best Travel
Visitors
Product: Greyhound bus
Sponsor: Greyhound
Ad Agency: Grey Advertising, New York
Production Co: WCD, New York

Best Utilities
It's great to phone
Product: AT&T communications services
Sponsor: AT&T
Ad Agency: N. W. Ayer & Son, Philadelphia
Production Co: Pintoff, New York

Best 8-10 Second ID
Call softly
Product: Culligan water softeners
Sponsor: Culligan, Inc., Northbrook, Illinois
Ad Agency: Alex T. Franz, Chicago
Production Co: Dallas Williams, Hollywood

Best Program Openings and Billboards (Tie)
Wonderful world of color
Product: Walt Disney Show
Sponsor: Eastman Kodak
Ad Agency: J. Walter Thompson, New York
Production Co: Walt Disney, Hollywood

Peanuts dinner
Product: The Ford Show
Sponsor: Falcon Div., Ford
Ad Agency: J. Walter Thompson, New York
Production Co: Playhouse Pictures, Hollywood

Best Premium Offer
Soap box camera offer
Product: Chevron gasoline
Sponsor: Standard Oil of California
Ad Agency: BBDO, New York
Production Co: Elektra, New York

Best Local Retail (Tie)
Smallest olds dealer
Product: Brady Olds
Sponsor: Oldsmobile Div., General Motors
Ad Agency: Bozell & Jacobs, Minneapolis
Production Co: Studio One, Minneapolis

Watermelons
Product: 7-Eleven food stores
Sponsor: 7-Eleven Food Stores
Ad Agency: Stanford, Dallas
Production Co: WFAA-TV, Dallas

Best Children's Market
Pop goes the cookie
Product: Arnold Cookie Pops
Sponsor: Arnold Bakers
Ad Agency: Donahue & Coe, New York
Production Co: MGM Telestudios, New York

Best Midwest Market
Beef
Product: National food stores
Sponsor: National Tea Company
Ad Agency: Lillienfeld, Chicago
Production Co: Sarra, Chicago

Best Southwest Market
Watermelons
Product: 7-Eleven food stores
Sponsor: 7-Eleven Food Stores
Ad Agency: Stanford, Dallas
Production Co: WFAA-TV, Dallas

Best West Coast Market
Bankamericard—No. One
Product: Bankamericard
Sponsor: Bank of America
Ad Agency: Johnson & Lewis, San Francisco
Production Co: Film-Fair, Hollywood

Best Canadian Market
A shine should shine
Product: Success liquid wax
Sponsor: Success Wax Company Ltd.
Ad Agency: Cockfield, Brown, Toronto
Production Co: B. L. Associates, Toronto

Best Canadian Market (French)
Two sisters
Product: Dash soap
Sponsor: Procter & Gamble of Canada
Ad Agency: Dancer-Fitzgerald-Sample
Production Co: Robert Lawrence Ltd., Toronto

1963

Best Overall Series
Go, go
Product: Goodyear snow tires
Sponsor: Goodyear Tire & Rubber Company
Ad Agency: Young & Rubicam, New York
Production Co: VPI Productions, New York

Best Automobile
Box
Product: Volkswagen station wagon
Sponsor: Volkswagen of America
Ad Agency: Doyle Dane Bernbach, New York
Production Co: VPI Productions, New York

Best Auto Accessories
Go, go
Product: Goodyear snow tires
Sponsor: Goodyear Tire & Rubber Company
Ad Agency: Young & Rubicam, New York
Production Co: VPI Productions, New York

Best Apparel
Raincoat
Product: Scotchgard
Sponsor: Minnesota Mining & Manufacturing
Ad Agency: MacManus, John & Adams, New York
Production Co: MGM Telestudios, New York

Best Appliances (Home)
Demo
Product: G.E. can opener
Sponsor: General Electric
Ad Agency: Maxon, New York
Production Co: Elektra, New York

Best Baked Goods and Confections
Old lady
Product: Laura Scudder potato chips
Sponsor: Laura Scudder Div., Pet Milk Co.
Ad Agency: Doyle Dane Bernbach, New York
Production Co: Elliot, Unger & Elliot, New York

Best Baking Mixes
White on white
Product: Pillsbury pancakes
Sponsor: The Pillsbury Company
Ad Agency: McCann-Marschalk, New York
Production Co: Robert Lawrence, New York

Best Banks
NY is people
Product: Chase Manhattan Bank services
Sponsor: Chase Manhattan Bank
Ad Agency: Ted Bates, New York
Production Co: Sarra, New York

Best Bath Soaps and Deodorants
Best for Judy
Product: Ivory bar soap
Sponsor: Procter & Gamble
Ad Agency: Compton, New York
Production Co: On Film, Princeton

Best Breakfast Cereals
Wind-up Wanda
Product: Raisin`Bran
Sponsor: Kellogg
Ad Agency: Leo Burnett, Chicago
Production Co: Hanna & Barbera, Los Angeles

Best Building Products (Tie)
Light construction schools
Product: Alcoa aluminum
Sponsor: Aluminum Company of America
Ad Agency: Fuller & Smith & Ross, New York
Production Co: Pelican Films, New York

Box
Product: U.S. Plywood products
Sponsor: U.S. Plywood Corp.
Ad Agency: Kenyon & Eckhardt, New York
Production Co: MPO Videotronics, New York

Best Beers and Wines
Whats its
Product: Jax beer
Sponsor: Jackson Brewing, New Orleans
Ad Agency: Doherty, Clifford, Steers, Shenfield,
  New York
Production Co: Pelican Films, New York

Best Cleansers, Waxes, Polishes
Line-up
Product: Windex cleaner
Sponsor: The Drackett Company
Ad Agency: Young & Rubicam, New York
Production Co: Elliot, Unger & Elliot, New York

Best Coffee and Tea
Not just a little
Product: La Touraine coffee
Sponsor: La Touraine Coffee Company
Ad Agency: Hichs & Greist, New York
Production Co: On Film, New York

Best Cosmetics and Toiletries
Five women
Product: Trushay
Sponsor: Bristol-Myers Company
Ad Agency: Grey Advertising, New York
Production Co: Norman Gaines, New York

Best Dairy, Margarine, Drinks
Drop for drop
Product: Foremost milk
Sponsor: Foremost Dairies
Ad Agency: Guild, Bascom & Bonfigli, San Francisco
Production Co: Fred Niles, Hollywood

Best Gasolines and Lubricants
The long pullback
Product: Sinclair gasoline
Sponsor: Sinclair Refining Company
Ad Agency: Geyer, Morey & Ballard, New York
Production Co: Paramount, Hollywood

Best Gifts, Cameras, Watches
Boy with trumpet
Product: Polaroid cameras
Sponsor: Polaroid Corporation
Ad Agency: Doyle Dane Bernbach, New York
Production Co: Pelican Films, New York

Best Hair Preparations
Mother and baby
Product: Ozon hair spray
Sponsor: Ozon Products Inc.
Ad Agency: Sudler & Hennessey, New York
Production Co: On Film, Princeton & New York

Best Home Furnishings
Sound of safety
Product: Rubbermaid bathtub mat
Sponsor: Rubbermaid, Inc.
Ad Agency: Ketchum, MacLeod & Grove, New York
Production Co: Van Praag, New York

Best Institutionals
Christopher Columbus
Product: Hallmark cards
Sponsor: Hallmark Cards
Ad Agency: Foote, Cone & Belding, Chicago
Production Co: Robert Lawrence, New York

Best Insurance
Welder
Product: Liberty Mutual business lines
Sponsor: Liberty Mutual Insurance
Ad Agency: BBDO, New York
Production Co: WCD, New York

Best Laundry Soaps and Detergents
Mother cares
Product: Ivory Flakes
Sponsor: Procter & Gamble
Ad Agency: Grey Advertising, New York
Production Co: Mickey Schwarz, New York

Best Media and Entertainment
Madame
Product: movie starring Sophia Loren
Sponsor: Embassy Pictures
Production Co: Ferro, Mohammed & Schwartz, New York

Best Pet Foods and Products
Dane and ducks
Product: Gaines Gravy Train
Sponsor: General Foods
Ad Agency: Benton & Bowles, New York
Production Co: Filmways-Sutherland, New York

Best Packaged Foods
Noodles Italiano
Product: Betty Crocker foods
Sponsor: General Mills
Ad Agency: Doyle Dane Bernbach, New York
Production Co: TeleVideo, New York

Best Paper Products, Foils
King
Product: Zee napkins
Sponsor: Crown Zellerbach Corp.
Ad Agency: Doyle Dane Bernbach, New York
Production Co: Producing Artists, New York

Best Pharmaceutical (Tie)
Testimonials
Product: Excedrin
Sponsor: Bristol-Myers
Ad Agency: Young & Rubicam, New York
Production Co: Audio, New York

Weeds
Product: Allerest
Sponsor: Pharmacraft
Ad Agency: Papert, Koenig, Lois, New York
Production Co: Elliot, Unger & Elliot, New York

Best Public Service
Rose
Product: teenage VD prevention
Sponsor: Public Health Dept., NYC
Ad Agency: Grey Advertising, New York
Production Co: Klaeger, New York

Best Retail Stores
Back to school
Product: Sears, Roebuck
Sponsor: Sears, Roebuck Company
Ad Agency: Ogilvy, Benson & Mather, New York
Production Co: WCD, New York

Best Soft Drink
Spice pak
Product: Sprite
Sponsor: Fanta Beverage
Ad Agency: McCann-Marschalk, New York
Production Co: VPI, New York

Best Toy
Elephant
Product: Goofer gun
Sponsor: Marx Toys
Ad Agency: Ted Bates, New York
Production Co: Filmways of California

Best Travel, Transportation
Suzy Parker out West
Product: Hertz services
Sponsor: Hertz Rent-A-Car
Ad Agency: Norman, Craig & Kummel, New York
Production Co: Filmex, New York

Best Utilities
Between planes
Product: long distance telephoning
Sponsor: AT&T
Ad Agency: N. W. Ayer, Philadelphia
Production Co: TeleVideo Productions, New York

Best Premium Offers
Glass blower
Product: Yuban coffee
Sponsor: General Foods
Ad Agency: Benton & Bowles, New York
Production Co: MPO Videotronics, New York

Best 8-10 Second ID
Hot sandwich
Product: Gulden's Diablo mustard
Sponsor: Charles Gulden
Ad Agency: Richard K. Manoff, New York
Production Co: Farkas Films, New York

Best Program Openings
Lively ones
Product: Ford cars
Sponsor: Ford Div., Ford Motors
Ad Agency: J. Walter Thompson, New York
Production Co: Filmways of California

Best Children's Market
School bus and candy store
Product: Cracker Jacks
Sponsor: The Cracker Jack Company
Ad Agency: Doyle Dane Bernbach, New York
Production Co: Rose-Magwood, New York

Best Program Cast
Sid Caesar, waiting room
Product: Dutch Masters cigars
Sponsor: Consolidated Cigar Company
Ad Agency: Papert, Koenig, Lois, New York
Production Co: ABC-TV, New York

1964

Best Overall Series
European dishes
Product: Betty Crocker rice
Sponsor: General Mills Gourmet Foods
Ad Agency: Doyle Dane Bernbach, New York
Production Co: TeleVideo, New York

Best Automobile
Snowplow
Product: Volkswagen sedan
Sponsor: Volkswagen of America
Ad Agency: Doyle Dane Bernbach, New York
Production Co: Film Contracts, London

Best Apparel
Car wash
Product: Van Heusen shirts
Sponsor: Phillips-Van Heusen Corp.
Ad Agency: Grey Advertising, New York
Production Co: Rose-Magwood, New York

Best Office Appliance
Ordinary paper
Product: Xerox 914 copier
Sponsor: Xerox Corporation
Ad Agency: Papert, Koenig, Lois, New York
Production Co: Farkas Films, New York

Best Home Appliance
Cowboy
Product: G.E. automatic toothbrush
Sponsor: General Electric
Ad Agency: Maxon, New York
Production Co: Videocrafts, New York

Best Auto Accessories
Landmine
Product: Goodyear tires
Sponsor: Goodyear Tire & Rubber Co.
Ad Agency: Young & Rubicam, San Francisco
Production Co: VPI of California

Best Baked Goods and Confections
Pledge
Product: Laura Scudder's potato chips
Sponsor: Laura Scudder Div., Pet Milk
Ad Agency: Doyle Dane Bernbach, New York
Production Co: Wylde Films, New York

Best Baking Mixes
Yellowbird
Product: Aunt Jemima pancakes
Sponsor: Quaker Oats Company
Ad Agency: J. Walter Thompson, Chicago
Production Co: Elliot, Unger & Elliot, New York

Best Banks and Financial
Armored car
Product: Great Western savings banks
Sponsor: Great Western Savings & Loan
Ad Agency: Doyle Dane Bernbach, Los Angeles
Production Co: Gerald Schnitzer, Los Angeles

Best Bath Soaps and Deodorants
Beach
Product: Princess Dial soap
Sponsor: Armour & Company
Ad Agency: Foote, Cone & Belding, Chicago
Production Co: FilmFair, Los Angeles

Best Beers and Wines
Crushed can
Product: Country Club malt liquor
Sponsor: Pearl Brewing
Ad Agency: John W. Shaw, Chicago
Production Co: MGM Telestudios, New York

Best Building Products and Home Maintenance
Screen door
Product: Kaiser screening
Sponsor: Kaiser Aluminum
Ad Agency: Young & Rubicam, San Francisco
Production Co: Don Fedderson, Hollywood

Best Breakfast Cereals (Tie)
Headache
Product: Cheerios
Sponsor: General Mills
Ad Agency: Dancer-Fitzgerald-Sample, Hollywood
Production Co: Freberg Ltd., Hollywood

Proper grip
Product: Kellogg's Frosted Flakes
Sponsor: Kellogg
Ad Agency: Leo Burnett Company, Chicago
Production Co: Gerald Schnitzer, Hollywood

Best Cigars and Cigarettes
Sidewalk cafe
Product: White Owl cigars
Sponsor: General Cigar Company
Ad Agency: Young & Rubicam, New York
Production Co: MPO Videotronics, New York

Best Cleansers, Polishes, Waxes
Penny
Product: Twinkle copper cleaner
Sponsor: Drackett Company of Canada, Ltd.
Ad Agency: Young & Rubicam, Toronto
Production Co: Rabko TV, Toronto

Best Women's Cosmetics and Toiletries
Body sings
Product: Cashmere Bouquet talc
Sponsor: Colgate-Palmolive Company
Ad Agency: D'Arcy, New York
Production Co: Elliot, Unger & Elliot, New York

Best Men's Toiletries
Slap
Product: Mennen High Sierra
Sponsor: The Mennen Company
Ad Agency: Grey Advertising, New York
Production Co: TeleVideo, New York

Best Dentifrices
Apple
Product: Poligrip
Sponsor: Block Drug Company
Ad Agency: Grey Advertising, New York
Production Co: Gray O'Reilly, New York

Best Coffee and Tea
Edward G. Robinson
Product: Instant Maxwell House coffee
Sponsor: General Foods
Ad Agency: Benton & Bowles, New York
Production Co: 'MPO Videotronics, Hollywood

Best Corporate–Institutional
SIMCA
Product: Chrysler Corporation products
Sponsor: Chrysler Corporation
Ad Agency: Young & Rubicam, New York
Production Co: Filmex, New York

Best Dairy Products, Drinks
Don't kid around
Product: Eversweet orange juice
Sponsor: Eversweet Foods, Inc.
Ad Agency: Doyle Dane Bernbach, New York
Production Co: VPI, New York

Best Gasolines and Oils
Snow scene
Product: Clark gasoline
Sponsor: Clark Oil & Refining
Ad Agency: Papert, Koenig, Lois, New York
Production Co: Audio Productions, New York

Best Gift and Recreation Items
Mine once more
Product: Kodak movie cameras
Sponsor: Eastman Kodak Company
Ad Agency: J. Walter Thompson, New York
Production Co: Sutherland Associates, New York

Best Hair Preparations
Night ride
Product: Breck shampoos
Sponsor: John H. Breck, Inc.
Ad Agency: Young & Rubicam, New York
Production Co: Ansel-Shaw, New York

Best Home Furnishings
Bull in china shop
Product: Centura tableware
Sponsor: Corning Glass Works
Ad Agency: N. W. Ayer & Son, Philadelphia
Production Co: Rose-Magwood, New York

Best Insurance
Burning house
Product: Traveler's insurance
Sponsor: Traveler's Insurance Company
Ad Agency: Young & Rubicam, New York
Production Co: Audio Productions, New York

Best Laundry Soaps, Detergents
Lullaby
Product: Downy fabric softener
Sponsor: Procter & Gamble
Ad Agency: Grey Advertising, New York
Production Co: Robert H. Klaeger, New York

Best Media and Entertainment
Tense generation
Product: Reader's Digest Services
Sponsor: Reader's Digest
Ad Agency: J. Walter Thompson, New York
Production Co: MPO Videotronics, New York

Best Oils, Dressings, Toppings
Shower
Product: Hunt's tomato catsup
Sponsor: Hunt Foods, Inc.
Ad Agency: Young & Rubicam, Los Angeles
Production Co: Signet, Hollywood

Best Packaged Foods
Rice Valenciana
Product: Betty Crocker foods
Sponsor: General Mills
Ad Agency: Doyle Dane Bernbach, New York
Production Co: TeleVideo, New York

Best Paper, Foils, Containers
Two sponges
Product: Kaiser foil
Sponsor: Kaiser Aluminum
Ad Agency: Young & Rubicam, San Francisco
Production Co: Signet, Hollywood

Best Pet Foods
Self trainer
Product: Milk Bone Flavor Snacks
Sponsor: National Biscuit Company
Ad Agency: Kenyon & Eckhardt, New York
Production Co: Storyboard Inc., New York

Best Pharmaceuticals
Animals
Product: Allerest
Sponsor: Pharmacraft Laboratories
Ad Agency: Papert, Koenig, Lois, New York
Production Co: Elliot, Unger & Elliot, New York

Best Public Service
Read
Product: National Library Week
Sponsor: American Library Assoc.
Ad Agency: Doyle Dane Bernbach, New York
Production Co: Wylde Films, New York

Best Retail Outlets
Ford has changed
Product: Ford dealers
Sponsor: Ford Dealers of So. California
Ad Agency: J. Walter Thompson, New York
Production Co: Ansel-Shaw, New York

Best Soft Drinks
Beach
Product: Coca-Cola
Sponsor: Coca-Cola Company
Ad Agency: McCann-Erickson, New York
Production Co: Wylde Films, New York

Best Toys and Games
Western guns
Product: Mattel toys
Sponsor: Mattel, Inc.
Ad Agency: Carson/Roberts, Los Angeles
Production Co: Lou Lilly, Los Angeles

Best Travel and Transportation
Waterfall
Product: Jamaica travel services
Sponsor: Jamaica Tourist Board
Ad Agency: Doyle Dane Bernbach, New York
Production Co: Rose-Magwood, New York

Best 8-10 Second ID
Old lady
Product: L.A. Dodge dealers
Sponsor: Dodge Dealers of Los Angeles
Ad Agency: Cole Fischer Rogow, Beverly Hills
Production Co: Sandler Films of Hollywood

Best 20-Second ID
Delicatessen
Product: Levy's rye bread
Sponsor: Henry S. Levy & Son
Ad Agency: Doyle Dane Bernbach, New York
Production Co: Elliot, Unger & Elliot, New York

Best Program Opening
IX Winter Olympics
Product: Olympics TV coverage
Sponsor: Participating stations
Ad Agency: ABC-TV and Sports Programs, Inc.
Production Co: Paul Kim & Lew Gifford, New
   York

Best Children's Audience
Boardwalk
Product: Cracker Jacks
Sponsor: Cracker Jack Company
Ad Agency: Doyle Dane Bernbach, New York
Production Co: Rose-Magwood, New York

Best Premium Offer
Baby parade
Product: Ivory Flakes
Sponsor: Procter & Gamble
Ad Agency: Grey Advertising, New York
Production Co: Pelican, New York

1965

Best Overall Series
No man around
Product: Goodyear tires
Sponsor: Goodyear Tire & Rubber
Ad Agency: Young & Rubicam, San Francisco
Production Co: FilmFair, Hollywood

Best Apparel
Beach
Product: Cole swimsuits
Sponsor: Cole of California
Ad Agency: R. M. Klosterman, Los Angeles
Production Co: John Urie, Los Angeles

Best Automobiles and Trucks
Mitty
Product: Ford Mustang
Sponsor: Ford Motor
Ad Agency: J. Walter Thompson, New York
Production Co: Sandler Films, Los Angeles

Best Auto Accessories (Tie)
Airport flat
Product: Goodyear tires
Sponsor: Goodyear Tire & Rubber
Ad Agency: Young & Rubicam, San Francisco
Production Co: FilmFair, Studio City

Rolling tire
Product: Gulf Cruisemaster tire
Sponsor: Gulf Oil
Ad Agency: Erwin Wasey, Pittsburgh
Production Co: MPO, New York

Best Baby Products
Growing baby
Product: Pet Formil
Sponsor: Pet Milk
Ad Agency: Needham, Harper & Steers, New York
Production Co: VPI, New York

Best Baked Goods and Confections
Bloop, bloop
Product: Premium Saltines
Sponsor: National Biscuit Company
Ad Agency: McCann-Erickson, New York
Production Co: VPI, New York

Best Banks and Finance
Sponge
Product: Manufacturer's Hanover Trust
Sponsor: Manufacturer's Hanover Trust
Ad Agency: Young & Rubicam, New York
Production Co: VPI, New York

Best Bath Soaps, Talcs, Deodorants
Starts something
Product: L'Aimant dusting powder
Sponsor: Coty
Ad Agency: West, Weir & Bartel, New York
Production Co: Pelican, New York

Best Beers and Wines
On the rocks
Product: Byrrh
Sponsor: Heublein
Ad Agency: Benton & Bowles, New York
Production Co: PGL, New York

Best Cake Mixes and Toppings
Cookies
Product: Bakers Coconut
Sponsor: General Foods
Ad Agency: Young & Rubicam, New York
Production Co: Audio, New York

Best Breakfast Cereals
Split screen
Product: Instant Quaker Oats
Sponsor: Quaker Oats
Ad Agency: Doyle Dane Bernbach, New York
Production Co: Directors Group, New York

Best Childrens Foods and Drinks
Shake shake
Product: Borden's chocolate
Sponsor: Borden Company
Ad Agency: Young & Rubicam, New York
Production Co: Audio, New York

Best Cleansers, Waxes, Polishes
Gobbles up dirt
Product: Glass Wax spray
Sponsor: Gold Seal
Ad Agency: Campbell-Mithun, Minneapolis
Production Co: FilmFair, Hollywood

Best Coffee and Tea
Full line
Product: Salada tea
Sponsor: Salada Foods
Ad Agency: Carl Ally, New York
Production Co: Rose-Magwood, New York

Best Cosmetics and Toiletries
Fun begins
Product: Arpege
Sponsor: Lanvin
Ad Agency: Foote, Cone & Belding, New York
Production Co: Libra, New York

Best Dairy Products and Drinks
Grown larger
Product: Tang
Sponsor: General Foods
Ad Agency: Young & Rubicam, New York
Production Co: EUE-Screen Gems, New York

Best Dentifrices
Hard roll
Product: Poligrip
Sponsor: Block Drug
Ad Agency: Grey Advertising, New York
Production Co: VPI, New York

Best Gift Items
Zoo
Product: Polaroid cameras
Sponsor: Polaroid Corporation
Ad Agency: Doyle Dane Bernbach, New York
Production Co: EUE-Screen Gems, New York

Best Gasolines and Lubricants
Railroad mileage
Product: Super Shell gasoline
Sponsor: Shell Oil
Ad Agency: Ogilvy, Benson & Mather, New York
Production Co: Movietone and VPI, California

Best Hair Preparations
Cinderella
Product: Liquid Prell shampoo
Sponsor: Procter & Gamble
Ad Agency: Benton & Bowles, New York
Production Co: Directors Group, New York

Best Home Appliances
Girl
Product: Westinghouse Instant-On TV
Sponsor: Westinghouse Electric
Ad Agency: McCann-Erickson, New York
Production Co: EUE-Screen Gems, New York

Best Home Furnishings
Miniatures
Product: Acrilan carpets
Sponsor: Chemstrand
Ad Agency: Doyle Dane Bernbach, New York
Production Co: Pelican, New York

Best Household Items
Harry
Product: Westinghouse light bulbs
Sponsor: Westinghouse Electric
Ad Agency: McCann-Erickson, New York
Production Co.: EUE-Screen Gems, New York

Best Corporate or Institutional
Marsh amphibian
Product: Chrysler cars
Sponsor: Chrysler Corp.
Ad Agency: Young & Rubicam, New York
Production Co: EUE-Screen Gems, New York

Best Insurance
Burned-out house
Product: Hartford insurance
Sponsor: Hartford Insurance Company
Ad Agency: Marschalk, New York
Production Co: PGL, New York

Best Laundry Soaps and Detergents
Hello egg
Product: Swan
Sponsor: Lever Brothers
Ad Agency: BBDO, New York
Production Co: TeleVideo, New York

Best Media Promotion (Tie)
Central Park
Product: New York Herald Tribune
Sponsor: New York Herald Tribune
Ad Agency: Papert, Koenig, Lois, New York
Production Co: CBS-TV, New York

Tokyo Olympics
Product: NBC-TV 1964 Tokyo Olympics
Sponsor: NBC-TV 1964 Tokyo Olympics
Production Co: NBC-TV, New York

Best Men's Toiletries
Shower
Product: Sentry
Sponsor: Bristol-Myers
Ad Agency: Young & Rubicam, New York
Production Co: EUE-Screen Gems, New York

Best Oils, Dressings, Condiments
Muttering
Product: Heinz ketchup
Sponsor: H. J. Heinz
Ad Agency: Doyle Dane Bernbach, New York
Production Co: TeleVideo, New York

Best Packaged Foods
Turkey noodle
Product: Campbell's turkey soup
Sponsor: Campbell Soup Company
Ad Agency: BBDO, New York
Production Co: EUE-Screen Gems, New York

Best Paper Products, Foils
Sneeze-quake
Product: Kleenex man-size tissues
Sponsor: Kimberly-Clark
Ad Agency: Foote, Cone & Belding, Chicago
Production Co: Cascade, Hollywood

Best Pet Products
Beaverbrook
Product: Ken-L-Ration stew
Sponsor: Quaker Oats
Ad Agency: J. Walter Thompson, Chicago
Production Co: Sarra, Chicago

Best Pharmaceuticals
Stomach
Product: Alka-Seltzer
Sponsor: Miles Laboratories
Ad Agency: Jack Tinker & Partners, New York
Production Co: TeleVideo, New York

Best Public Service
Searchlight
Product: Radio Free Europe
Sponsor: Advertising Council
Ad Agency: Doyle Dane Bernbach, New York
Production Co: Directors Group, New York

Best Retail Stores
Charlie Hall
Product: Lawson's stores
Sponsor: Lawson Milk Company
Ad Agency: Wyse Advertising, Cleveland
Production Co: EUE-Screen Gems, New York

Best Soft Drinks
Miss America
Product: Pepsi-Cola
Sponsor: Pepsi-Cola Company
Ad Agency: BBDO, New York
Production Co: TeleVideo, New York

Best Tobacco Products
Erik is here
Product: Erik cigars
Sponsor: P. Lorillard
Ad Agency: Grey Advertising, New York
Production Co: TeleVideo, New York

Best Toys and Games
Hot rodder
Product: Vroom Engine
Sponsor: Mattel
Ad Agency: Carson/Roberts, Los Angeles
Production Co: Wilding-Fedderson, Los Angeles

Best Travel and Transportation
English countryside
Product: BOAC airlines
Sponsor: BOAC
Ad Agency: Pritchard, Wood, New York
Production Co: Wylde, New York

Best Utilities
Two boys
Product: Ontario hydroelectric power
Sponsor: Ontario Power Commission
Ad Agency: Foster Advertising, Toronto
Production Co: Peterson, Toronto

Best 20-Second ID
House
Product: Laura Scudder potato chips
Sponsor: Laura Scudder potato chips
Ad Agency: Doyle Dane Bernbach, Los Angeles
Production Co: John Urie, Los Angeles

Best 8-10 Second ID
Flip of the finger
Product: Knickerbocker beer
Sponsor: Jacob Ruppert Brewing
Ad Agency: Gumbinner-North, New York
Production Co: Audio, New York

Best Premium Offer
Cookbook
Product: Sweeta
Sponsor: E. R. Squibb
Ad Agency: Benton & Bowles, New York
Production Co: Videotape Productions of New
   York

1966—International

Best Automotive
Steps
Product: Standard Triumph cars
Sponsor: British Leyland Motor Company
Ad Agency: Ogilvy & Mather, London
Production Co: Pearl & Dean, London

Best Personal and Gift Items
River
Product: Kodak Instamatic camera
Sponsor: Eastman Kodak Company
Production Co: Peter Sims, London
Ad Agency: J. Walter Thompson, London

Best Apparel
Children
Product: Vonnel underwear
Sponsor: Mitsubishi Rayon
Ad Agency: Dai-Ichi Kikaku, Tokyo
Production Co: Gakushu Kenkyu-sha

Best Beverages and Tobacco
Voilier
Product: Aperitif Martini
Sponsor: Societe Martini & Rossi
Ad Agency: Publicis
Production Co: Cinima et Publicite, Paris

Best Cosmetics and Toiletries
Teen-ager
Product: pink Palmolive soap
Sponsor: Colgate-Palmolive
Ad Agency: Norman, Craig & Kummel, San Juan,
   Puerto Rico
Production Co: Delta Films, San Juan

Best Housekeeping
Dinner party
Product: Crown Vinyl wallcovering
Sponsor: The Wall Paper Manufacturers
Ad Agency: Notley, London
Production Co: Keith Ewart, London

Best Services
Money talks
Product: Midlandbank, Ltd.
Sponsor: Midlandbank, Ltd.
Ad Agency: Charles Barker, London
Production Co: Cammell, Hudson & Brownjohn,
   London

Best Corporate
Plexiglas
Product: Plexiglas
Sponsor: Fa, Rohm & Haas
Ad Agency: Direct
Production Co: Domo Film, Munich

1966—National

Best Overall Campaign
Small things
Whole man
Offenders
Product: Alka-Seltzer
Sponsor: Miles Laboratories
Ad Agency: Jack Tinker & Partners, New York
Production Co: Harold Becker; Brillig

Best Automobiles
Circus
Product: VW station wagon
Sponsor: Volkswagen of America
Ad Agency: Doyle Dane Bernbach, New York
Production Co: TeleVideo, New York

Best Auto Accessories
Foggy road
Product: Goodyear tires
Sponsor: Goodyear Tire & Rubber
Ad Agency: Young & Rubicam, New York
Production Co: John Urie, Los Angeles

Best Beers and Wines
Beach
Product: Colt 45 malt liquor
Sponsor: National Brewing
Ad Agency: W. B. Doner, Detroit
Production Co: Craven Films, New York

Best Coffee and Tea
Sleeping man
Product: Maxwell House coffee
Sponsor: General Foods
Ad Agency: Ogilvy & Mather, New York
Production Co: TeleVideo, New York

Best Soft Drinks
Crazy
Product: Tab
Sponsor: Coca-Cola Company
Ad Agency: Marschalk, New York
Production Co: VPI, New York

Best Cosmetics and Toiletries
Riviera
Product: Noxzema Cover Girl
Sponsor: Noxzema Chemical
Ad Agency: SSC&B, New York
Production Co: Les Cineastes, Paris

Best Hair Preparations
Airport
Product: Vitapoint
Sponsor: Clairol Div., Bristol-Myers
Ad Agency: Doyle Dane Bernbach, New York
Production Co: TeleVideo, New York

Best Men's Toiletries
Stripper
Product: Noxzema shave cream
Sponsor: Noxzema Chemical
Ad Agency: William Esty, New York
Production Co: PGL, New York

Best Pharmaceuticals
Small things
Product: Alka-Seltzer
Sponsor: Miles Laboratories
Ad Agency: Jack Tinker & Partners, New York
Production Co: Harold Becker, New York

Best Major Appliances
Greatest
Product: Westinghouse Jet Set TV
Sponsor: Westinghouse Electric
Ad Agency: McCann-Erickson, New York
Production Co: Harold Becker, New York

Best Small Appliances
Nuts and bolts
Product: Westinghouse fry pan
Sponsor: Westinghouse Electric
Ad Agency: McCann-Erickson, New York
Production Co: VPI, New York

Best Home Furnishings
Love birds
Product: Simmons mattresses
Sponsor: Simmons
Ad Agency: Young & Rubicam, New York
Production Co: TeleVideo, New York

Best Laundry Soaps
Burlap
Product: Downy fabric softener
Sponsor: Procter & Gamble
Ad Agency: Grey Advertising, New York
Production Co: Wylde Films, New York

Best Household Items
Face
Product: Dow drain opener
Sponsor: Dow Chemical
Ad Agency: MacManus, John & Adams
Production Co: VPI, New York

Best Pet Products
Father and son
Product: Flavor Snacks
Sponsor: National Biscuit Company
Ad Agency: Kenyon & Eckhardt, New York
Production Co: John Hubley, New York

Best Corporate
Flower pot
Product: Campbell soups
Sponsor: Campbell Soups
Ad Agency: Leo Burnett, Chicago
Production Co: Swift-Chaplin, Los Angeles

Best Trade Association
Naked wool
Product: Wool Bureau
Sponsor: Wool Bureau
Ad Agency: Grey Advertising, New York
Production Co: Libra, New York

Best Public Service
49 people
Product: pedestrian safety
Sponsor: Mayor's Committee for Pedestrian Safety
Ad Agency: McCann-Erickson, New York
Production Co: PGL, New York

Best Main and Side Dishes
Furlough
Product: Jell-O
Sponsor: General Foods
Ad Agency: Young & Rubicam, New York
Production Co: MPO, Stone-Langley

Best Condiments
Relatives
Product: Hunt's tomato sauce
Sponsor: Hunt's Foods
Ad Agency: Young & Rubicam, Los Angeles
Production Co: FilmFair, Los Angeles

Best Breakfast Cereals
Funny cereal
Product: Nabisco shredded wheat
Sponsor: National Biscuit Company
Ad Agency: Kenyon & Eckhardt, New York
Production Co: On Film, New York

Best Dairy Case Products
Break this habit
Product: Chiffon margarine
Sponsor: Anderson Clayton
Ad Agency: Benton & Bowles, New York
Production Co: EUE-Screen Gems, New York

Best Baked Goods
Kids
Product: Toast 'Ems
Sponsor: General Foods
Ad Agency: Foote, Cone & Belding, New York
Production Co: EUE-Screen Gems, New York

Best Confections
Shuffle
Product: Teaberry gum
Sponsor: Philip Morris
Ad Agency: Leo Burnett, Chicago
Production Co: Lee Lacy, Los Angeles

Best Children's Audience
The big "L" candy family
Product: Luden's
Sponsor: Luden's
Ad Agency: Erwin Wasey, Philadelphia
Production Co: Gryphon, New York

Best Banks and Financial
New York woman
Product: Chemical Bank, New York
Sponsor: Chemical Bank, New York
Ad Agency: Benton & Bowles, New York
Production Co: Cahill, Kacine, Heimann

Best Insurance
Rififi
Product: Continental insurance
Sponsor: Continental Insurance
Ad Agency: Doyle Dane Bernbach, New York
Production Co: Brillig, New York

Best Utilities
Quick cuts
Product: electric power
Sponsor: American Electric Power Systems
Ad Agency: Handley & Miller, Indianapolis
Production Co: Film Makers, Chicago

Best Cameras, Watches, Personal Appliances
200 Strokes
Product: Broxodent electric toothbrush
Sponsor: Olin Matheson Chemical
Ad Agency: Doyle Dane Bernbach, New York
Production Co: TeleVideo, New York

Best Apparel
Laundromat
Product: Arrow shirts
Sponsor: Cluett Peabody
Ad Agency: Young & Rubicam, New York
Production Co: EUE-Screen Gems, New York

Best Toys and Games
Creepy crawlers
Product: Mattel toys
Sponsor: Mattel
Ad Agency: Carson/Roberts, Los Angeles
Production Co: R-TV, Los Angeles

Best Travel (Tie)
Lake couple
Product: American air service
Sponsor: American Airlines
Ad Agency: Doyle Dane Bernbach, New York
Production Co: EUE-Screen Gems, New York

Birds
Product: Eastern air service
Sponsor: Eastern Airlines
Ad Agency: Young & Rubicam, New York
Production Co: EUE-Screen Gems, New York

Best Media Promotion
Traveler wanted
Product: encyclopedia
Sponsor: Encyclopedia Britannica
Ad Agency: McCann-Erickson, New York
Production Co: Horn/Griner, New York

Best Premium Offers
Great songs of Christmas
Product: Goodyear tires
Sponsor: Goodyear Tire & Rubber
Ad Agency: Young & Rubicam, New York
Production Co: John Urie, Hollywood

Best 8-10 Second ID
Karate
Product: banking service
Sponsor: First Pennsylvania Bank
Ad Agency: N. W. Ayer & Son, Philadelphia
Production Co: Rose-Magwood, New York

Best 20-Second ID
Cigar
Product: Esskay franks
Sponsor: Schluderberg-Kurdle
Ad Agency: VanSant, Dugdale, Baltimore
Production Co: Freberg, Los Angeles

Best Northeast
Skateboard
Product: communications service
Sponsor: Southern New England Telephone
Ad Agency: BBDO, Boston
Production Co: Peterson

Best Southeast
Shout
Product: banking service
Sponsor: North Carolina Bank
Ad Agency: Cargill, Wilson & Acree
Production Co: Milner-Fenwick

Best Southwest
Man and wife
Product: Austex chili
Sponsor: Frito-Lay
Ad Agency: Tracy-Locke, Dallas
Production Co: Rose-Magwood

Best Midwest
Produce
Product: Sentry food stores
Sponsor: Sentry Food Stores
Ad Agency: Post, Keyes, Gardner
Production Co: EUE-Screen Gems

Best West Coast
Checker
Product: Blue Seal bread
Sponsor: Interstate Bakeries
Ad Agency: Doyle Dane Bernbach, New York
Production Co: Lou Lilly

1967

Best Overall Campaign
Disadvantages
Product: Benson & Hedges 100s
Sponsor: Philip Morris
Ad Agency: Wells, Rich, Greene, New York
Production Co: Howard Zieff, New York

Best Automobiles
The cars
Product: Volvo cars
Sponsor: Volvo
Ad Agency: Carl Ally, New York
Production Co: TeleVideo; Howard Zieff

Best Auto Accessories
Monster
Product: Uniroyal Raintire
Sponsor: Uniroyal
Ad Agency: Doyle Dane Bernbach, New York
Production Co: Bill Littlejohn, Los Angeles

Best Gasolines and Lubricants
Love-making
Product: Mobile gasoline
Sponsor: Mobil Oil
Ad Agency: Doyle Dane Bernbach, New York
Production Co: MPO, New York

Best Beers and Wines
Read a can
Product: Carling beer
Sponsor: Carling Black Label
Ad Agency: Jack Tinker, New York
Production Co: Rose-Magwood, New York

Best Soft Drinks
Airport
Product: Diet Pepsi
Sponsor: Pepsi-Cola
Ad Agency: BBDO, New York
Production Co: Libra and Take Five, New York

Best Coffee and Tea
Demanding man
Product: Savarin coffee
Sponsor: S. A. Schonbrunn
Ad Agency: Foote, Cone & Belding, New York
Production Co: VPI, New York

Best Bath Soaps
Subliminal
Product: Dial soap
Sponsor: Armour Grocery Products
Ad Agency: Foote, Cone & Belding, Chicago
Production Co: EUE-Screen Gems, Los Angeles

Best Dentifrices
Egg
Product: Polident
Sponsor: Block Drug
Ad Agency: Grey Advertising, New York
Production Co: Landis/Wolf, New York

Best Deodorants
Couple
Hunter
Product: Ban
Sponsor: Bristol-Myers
Ad Agency: Ogilvy & Mather, New York
Production Co: EUE-Screen Gems, New York

Best Hair Preparations
Children
Product: Toni
Sponsor: Toni Div., Gillette
Ad Agency: Jack Tinker, New York
Production Co: James Garrett, London

Best Men's Toiletries
Duke Snider
Product: Great Day
Sponsor: Clairol Div., Bristol-Myers
Ad Agency: Doyle Dane Bernbach, New York
Production Co: EUE-Screen Gems, New York

Best Pharmaceutical
Pie eaters
Product: Alka-Seltzer
Sponsor: Miles Laboratories
Ad Agency: Tinker, New York
Production Co: Howard Zieff, New York

Best Cleansers, Waxes, Polishes
Pow
Product: Dow oven cleaner
Sponsor: Dow Chemical
Ad Agency: MacManus, John & Adams
Production Co: Pelican, New York

Best Household Items
Splash
Product: RIT
Sponsor: Best Foods
Ad Agency: SSC&B, New York
Production Co: Illustra, New York

Best Paper and Foils
Many uses
Product: Dixie Cup
Sponsor: American Can
Ad Agency: Hicks & Griest, New York
Production Co: Harold Becker, New York

Best Home Furnishings
Wrestling
Product: Simmons mattress
Sponsor: Simmons
Ad Agency: Young & Rubicam, New York
Production Co: TeleVideo, New York

Best Major Appliances
Joe's
Product: Westinghouse dishwasher
Sponsor: Westinghouse Electric
Ad Agency: McCann-Erickson, New York
Production Co: VPI, New York

Best Small Appliance
Bakeware
Product: DuPont Teflon
Sponsor: E. I. DuPont
Ad Agency: N. W. Ayer, New York
Production Co: FilmFair, New York

Best Corporate
XB-70
Product: IBM computers
Sponsor: IBM
Ad Agency: Ogilvy & Mather, New York
Production Co: VPI, New York

Best Political
Product: Rockefeller for New York governor
Sponsor: Friends of Rockefeller
Ad Agency: Jack Tinker, New York
Production Co: Howard Zieff; Tempo, New York

Best Public Service
Breathing
Product: clean air
Sponsor: Citizens for Clean Air
Ad Agency: Carl Ally, New York
Production Co: Tempo, New York

Best Trade Associations
Mod shop
Product: International Coffee Organization
Sponsor: International Coffee Organization
Ad Agency: McCann-Erickson, New York
Production Co: Wylde Films, New York

Best Baked Goods and Mixes
Man and Wife
Product: Jell-O cheesecake mix
Sponsor: General Foods
Ad Agency: Young & Rubicam, New York
Production Co: Focus, New York

Best Cereals
Chuckwagon
Product: Post Honeycombs
Sponsor: General Foods
Ad Agency: Benton & Bowles, New York
Production Co: New Directions, New York

Best Dairy Products, Drinks
Calorie count
Product: Carnation Slender
Sponsor: Carnation
Ad Agency: Jack Tinker, New York
Production Co: TeleVideo, New York

Best Main and Side Dish
Maine
Product: Jell-O
Sponsor: General Foods
Ad Agency: Young & Rubicam, New York
Production Co: MPO, New York

Best Snacks
Devil
Product: Lay's potato chips
Sponsor: Frito-Lay
Ad Agency: Young & Rubicam, New York
Production Co: EUE-Screen Gems, New York

Best Children's Food and Drink
On his own
Product: Bosco
Sponsor: Best Foods
Ad Agency: Dancer-Fitzgerald-Sample, San Francisco
Production Co: Lee Lacy, Los Angeles

Best Apparel
Dance
Product: Burlington socks
Sponsor: Burlington Industries
Ad Agency: Doyle Dane Bernbach, New York
Production Co: MPO, New York

Best Gift Items
The way you look tonight
Product: Kodak cameras
Sponsor: Eastman Kodak
Ad Agency: J. Walter Thompson, New York
Production Co: Gerald Schnitzer, Los Angeles

Best Tobacco Products
Disadvantages
Product: Benson & Hedges 100s
Sponsor: Philip Morris
Ad Agency: Wells, Rich, Greene, New York
Production Co: Howard Zieff, New York

Best Toys
Kaboom
Product: Ideal's Kaboom
Sponsor: Ideal Toy
Ad Agency: Smith/Greenland, New York
Production Co: TeleVideo, New York

Best Recreation Equipment
Hands
Product: Lowrey organ
Sponsor: Lowrey Organ
Ad Agency: Doyle Dane Bernbach, New York
Production Co: Videotape Center, New York

Best Media Promotion
Newsstand
Product: World Journal Tribune newspaper
Sponsor: World Journal Tribune
Ad Agency: Carl Ally, New York
Production Co: Videotape Center, New York

Best Travel
Acapulco/New York
Product: Eastern air service
Sponsor: Eastern Airlines
Ad Agency: Young & Rubicam, New York
Production Co: Audio, New York

Best Local Market
Hudson's Pantry Shop
Product: Hudson's Pantry Shop
Sponsor: J. L. Hudson, Detroit
Ad Agency: Reilly Bird Assoc., Detroit
Production Co: Reilly Bird, Detroit

Best Insurance
Homeowners
Product: Continental insurance
Sponsor: Continental Insurance Company
Ad Agency: Doyle Dane Bernbach, New York
Production Co: MPO, New York

Best Utility
Circus
Product: communications service
Sponsor: American Telephone & Telegraph
Ad Agency: N. W. Ayer
Production Co: EUE-Screen Gems, New York

Best Banks
Auto loan
Product: banking services
Sponsor: First National City Bank
Ad Agency: BBDO, New York
Production Co: MPO, New York

Best 8-10 Second ID
Eloise
Product: Open Pit barbeque sauce
Sponsor: General Foods
Ad Agency: Ogilvy & Mather, New York
Production Co: Filmex, New York

Best 20-Second ID
Couple
Product: Ban
Sponsor: Bristol-Myers
Ad Agency: Ogilvy & Mather, New York
Production Co: EUE-Screen Gems, New York

Best Office Appliance
Words on paper
Product: IBM typewriter
Sponsor: IBM
Ad Agency: Benton & Bowles, New York
Production Co: Mark Shaw, New York

Best Regional Market
Tavern
Product: Fyfe & Drum beer
Sponsor: Genesee Brewing
Ad Agency: William Esty, New York
Production Co: Rose-Magwood, New York

1968

Best Overall Campaign
Silhouette
Tax audit
Dinner
Product: Excedrin
Sponsor: Bristol-Myers
Ad Agency: Young & Rubicam, New York
Production Co: Audio Productions; PGL

Best Overall Campaign
Super insulation
Sevin
Ocean systems
Laser surgery
Product: Union Carbide
Sponsor: Union Carbide
Ad Agency: Young & Rubicam, New York
Production Co: VPI, New York

Best Apparel
Kneeburst
Product: Burlington fabrics
Sponsor: Burlington
Ad Agency: Doyle Dane Bernbach, New York
Production Co: Take Two, New York

Best Appliances
Man talking
Product: Sylvania color television
Sponsor: General Telephone & Electronics
Ad Agency: Doyle Dane Bernbach, New York
Production Co: Tele-Tape, New York

Best Automobiles
Mr. Jones
Product: VW sedan
Sponsor: Volkswagen of America
Ad Agency: Doyle Dane Bernbach, New York
Production Co: EUE-Screen Gems, New York

Best Auto Accessories
Chain reaction
Product: Goodyear snow tires
Sponsor: Goodyear
Ad Agency: Young & Rubicam, New York
Production Co: Peterson, Hollywood

Best Banks, Financial
Wildlife
Product: banking services
Sponsor: Chemical Bank of New York Trust
Ad Agency: Benton & Bowles, New York
Production Co: K & P Enterprises, Los Angeles

Best Bath Soaps and Deodorants
Dreams come true
Product: Ban deodorant
Sponsor: Bristol-Myers
Ad Agency: Ogilvy & Mather, New York
Production Co: EUE-Screen Gems, New York

Best Beers and Wines
Thank you
Product: Piels beer
Sponsor: Piels Beer
Ad Agency: Papert, Koenig, Lois, New York
Production Co: Anglofilms, New York

Best Cake Mixes and Desserts
Magic faucet
Product: Betty Crocker products
Sponsor: General Mills
Ad Agency: Dancer-Fitzgerald-Sample, San Francisco
Production Co: MPO, New York

Best Family Cereal
Cop
Product: Kellogg corn flakes
Sponsor: Kellogg
Ad Agency: Leo Burnett, Chicago
Production Co: Wylde Films, New York

Best Cigarettes, Cigars
Great taste
Product: Tiparillo
Sponsor: General Cigar
Ad Agency: Young & Rubicam, New York
Production Co: Jerry Ansel, New York

Best Cleansers, Waxes, Polishes
Still looks wet
Product: non-scuff floor wax
Sponsor: Simoniz
Ad Agency: J. Walter Thompson, Chicago
Production Co: Harry Hamburg, New York

Best Coffee and Tea
Filter
Product: Max Pax
Sponsor: General Foods
Ad Agency: Ogilvy & Mather, New York
Production Co: Mark Shaw, New York

Best Confections, Snacks (Tie)
What is an egg roll?
Product: Chun King
Sponsor: R. J. Reynolds Foods
Ad Agency: J. Walter Thompson, Chicago
Production Co: Sarra Studios, Chicago

Show us your pizza roll pack
Product: Jeno's frozen pizza rolls
Sponsor: Jeno's, Inc.
Ad Agency: MacManus, John & Adams, St. Paul
Production Co: Freberg, Los Angeles

Best Corporate
Laser beam
Product: Union Carbide
Sponsor: Union Carbide
Ad Agency: Young & Rubicam, New York
Production Co: VPI, New York

Best Dentifrice
Kiss
Product: Speakeasy mouth spray
Sponsor: American Safety Razor
Ad Agency: Wells, Rich, Greene, New York
Production Co: Howard Zieff, New York

Best Gifts, Personal Items
Yesterdays
Product: Kodak cameras
Sponsor: Eastman Kodak
Ad Agency: J. Walter Thompson, New York
Production Co: MPO, New York

Best Gifts, Personal Items
Temper, Temper
Product: Parker 45
Sponsor: Parker Pen
Ad Agency: Doyle Dane Bernbach, New York
Production Co: Harold Becker, New York

Best Hair Preparations
Kindergarten
Product: Toni Innocent Color
Sponsor: Toni
Ad Agency: Jack Tinker, New York
Production Co: Airport, New York

Best Insurance
Egg and you
Product: State Farm auto insurance
Sponsor: State Farm
Ad Agency: Needham, Harper & Steers, Chicago
Production Co: Tempo, New York

Best Laundry Soaps, Detergents
Hand sawing
Product: Bold
Sponsor: Procter & Gamble
Ad Agency: Tatham-Laird & Kudner, Chicago
Production Co: Tempo, New York

Best Media Promotion
World watchers
Product: CBS news
Sponsor: CBS-TV
Ad Agency: CBS-TV, New York
Production Co: CBS-TV, New York

Best Media Promotion
Organization chart
Product: Wall Street Journal
Sponsor: Dow Jones
Ad Agency: BBDO, New York
Production Co: Stars & Stripes, New York

Best Men's Toiletries
Barber
Product: Gillette super stainless-steel blades
Sponsor: Gillette
Ad Agency: Doyle Dane Bernbach, New York
Production Co: J. H. Film Company, New York

Best Office Equipment
Aging office
Product: Xerox copier
Sponsor: Xerox
Ad Agency: Papert, Koenig, Lois, New York
Production Co: VPI, New York

Best Oils, Dressings, Condiments
Spinach
Product: Ac'cent
Sponsor: Accent
Ad Agency: Foote, Cone & Belding, Chicago
Production Co: N. Lee Lacy, Los Angeles

Best Packaged Foods
Sunsweet marches on
Product: Sunsweet pitted prunes
Sponsor: Sunsweet Growers
Production Co: Freberg, Los Angeles

Best Pharmaceuticals (Tie)
Tax audit
Product: Excedrin
Sponsor: Bristol-Myers
Ad Agency: Young & Rubicam, New York
Production Co: Audio, New York

Stomach talk
Product: Alka-Seltzer
Sponsor: Miles Laboratories
Ad Agency: Jack Tinker, New York
Production Co: Elektra, New York

Best Public Service
Guess who
Product: National Safety Council
Sponsor: Advertising Council
Ad Agency: Needham, Harper & Steers, Chicago
Production Co: Flagg, Hollywood

Best Retail Chains
Escape
Product: Kentucky fried chicken
Sponsor: Kentucky Fried Chicken Stores
Ad Agency: Noble, Dury, Nashville
Production Co: PGL, New York

Best Local Retail
Bug killer
Product: Rambler American
Sponsor: Harris County Rambler Dealers, Texas
Ad Agency: S. L. Brown, Houston
Production Co: AIE, Houston

Best Department Stores
Distant worlds
Product: Marshall Field stores
Sponsor: Marshall Field Department Store
Ad Agency: McCann-Erickson, Chicago
Production Co: Videotape Center, New York

Best Soft Drinks
Glass elevator
Product: Diet Pepsi
Sponsor: Pepsi-Cola
Ad Agency: BBDO, New York
Production Co: PGL; Audio, New York

Best Toys and Games
Product: Incredible Edibles
Sponsor: Mattel
Ad Agency: Carson/Roberts, Los Angeles
Production Co: Spungbuggy Works, Los Angeles

Best Trade Associations
Naming the baby
Product: coffee
Sponsor: International Coffee Organization
Ad Agency: McCann-Erickson, New York
Production Co: Wylde, New York

Best Travel and Transportation
Second summer
Product: Eastern air services
Sponsor: Eastern Airlines
Ad Agency: Young & Rubicam, New York
Production Co: Audio, New York

Best Travel and Transportation
Poor soul
Product: Hertz rentals
Sponsor: Hertz Rent-A-Car
Ad Agency: Carl Ally, New York
Production Co: TeleVideo, New York

Best Utilities (Tie)
Little more
Product: natural gas range
Sponsor: Natural Gas Companies
Ad Agency: Ketchum, MacLeod & Grove, Pittsburgh
Production Co: Drew Lawrence, New York

Dial "0"
Product: Pacific telephone services
Sponsor: Pacific Telephone & Telegraph
Ad Agency: BBDO, San Francisco
Production Co: Harry Dorsey, Los Angeles

Best 8-10 Second ID (Tie)
Duel
Product: Gulfspray insecticide
Sponsor: Gulf Oil
Ad Agency: Erwin Wasey, Pittsburgh
Production Co: Savage-Friedman, New York

Interview
Product: Roosevelt Raceway
Sponsor: Roosevelt Raceway
Ad Agency: Smith/Greenland, New York
Production Co: Dimension, New York

Best 20-Second ID
How to survive
Product: Hertz rentals
Sponsor: Hertz Rent-a-Car
Ad Agency: Carl Ally, New York
Production Co: TeleVideo, New York

Best Regional Market
Love is a funny game
Product: Zale diamond rings
Sponsor: Zale Jewelry Stores
Ad Agency: Bloom, Dallas
Production Co: Hanna-Barbera, Los Angeles

Best Locally Produced
Little problems
Product: banking services
Sponsor: Maryland National Bank
Ad Agency: VanSant, Dugdale, Baltimore
Production Co: BF&J, Baltimore

Best Canadian Market
Flies you to
Product: rail transportation
Sponsor: Canadian Pacific Railway
Ad Agency: McKim/Benton & Bowles, Toronto
Production Co: Don Wilder, Toronto

Best Canadian Market
Restaurant
Product: Gainesburgers
Sponsor: General Foods
Ad Agency: Young & Rubicam, Toronto
Production Co: Sebert Productions, Toronto

1969
Best Overall Campaign
You've come a long way baby
Product: Virginia Slims cigarettes
Sponsor: Virginia Slims
Ad Agency: Leo Burnett, New York
Production Co: Dick Miller Associates

Best Apparel
Torture test
Product: Penman's underwear
Sponsor: Penman's Underwear
Ad Agency: McConnell Eastman, Toronto
Production Co: Paul Herriott, Toronto

Best Small Appliances, Housewares
Locks
Product: Tupperware
Sponsor: Tupperware House Parties
Ad Agency: BBDO, New York
Production Co: Harold Becker, New York

Best Automobile
Driving school
Product: Rebel
Sponsor: American Motors
Ad Agency: Wells, Rich, Greene, New York
Production Co: Howard Zieff, New York

Best Auto Accessories
Flashlight
Product: Sears' Silent Guard tires
Sponsor: Sears, Roebuck & Company
Ad Agency: J. Walter Thompson, Chicago
Production Co: Petersen, Chicago

Best Baby Products
Pinless
Product: Scott disposable diapers
Sponsor: Scott Paper Company
Ad Agency: BBDO, New York
Production Co: Harold Becker, New York

Best Banks & Financial
Mr. Bender
Product: Manufacturer's banking services
Sponsor: Manufacturer's Hanover
Ad Agency: Young & Rubicam, New York
Production Co: Wylde, New York

Best Bath Soaps, Deodorants
Volkswagen
Product: Dial soap
Sponsor: Armour & Company
Ad Agency: Foote, Cone & Belding, Chicago
Production Co: N. Lee Lacy, Los Angeles

Best Beers & Wines
Name change
Product: Koehler beer
Sponsor: Erie Brewing Company
Ad Agency: Lando, Pittsburgh
Production Co: CPI, New York

Best Cigarettes & Cigars
A long way baby
Product: Virginia Slims cigarettes
Sponsor: Virginia Slims
Ad Agency: Leo Burnett, New York
Production Co: Dick Miller, New York

Best Cleansers, Polishes
Custodian
Product: Spic & Span
Sponsor: Procter & Gamble
Ad Agency: Young & Rubicam, New York
Production Co: Pelican, New York

Best Coffee and Tea
Jerky perks
Product: Maxim coffee
Sponsor: Maxwell House
Ad Agency: Ogilvy & Mather, New York
Production Co: Syncrofilm, New York

Best Confections & Snacks
Train
Product: Cracker Jacks
Sponsor: Cracker Jack Company
Ad Agency: Doyle Dane Bernbach, New York
Production Co: Rose-Magwood, New York

Best Corporate
Rodney
Product: Union Carbide
Sponsor: Union Carbide
Ad Agency: Young & Rubicam, New York
Production Co: VPI, New York

Best Cosmetics, Toiletries
Blonde line
Product: Clairol
Sponsor: Clairol Div., Bristol-Myers
Ad Agency: Foote, Cone & Belding, New York
Production Co: Tele-Tape, New York

Best Dairy Products
Surfer
Product: Carnation Bodybuild
Sponsor: Carnation
Ad Agency: Erwin Wasey, New York
Production Co: Pelican, New York

Best Desserts
Mrs. Tom Zak
Product: D-Zerta
Sponsor: General Foods
Ad Agency: Grey Advertising, New York
Production Co: Motion Associates, New York

Best Dentifrices
Sven
Product: Vademecum toothpaste
Sponsor: Consumer Goods International Inc.
Ad Agency: Carl Ally, New York
Production Co: Howard Zieff, New York

Best Gasoline Products
Loser
Product: Flying A gasoline
Sponsor: Flying A
Ad Agency: Smith/Greenland, New York
Production Co: Horn/Griner, New York

Best Gifts, Personal Items
Anticipating
Product: Kodak cameras
Sponsor: Eastman Kodak
Ad Agency: J. Walter Thompson, New York
Production Co: EUE-Screen Gems, Los Angeles

Best Home Furnishings
Programmed sleep
Product: Simmons mattress
Sponsor: Simmons
Ad Agency: Young & Rubicam, New York
Production Co: Horn/Griner, New York

Best Home Maintenance
House breathing
Product: Pittsburgh paint
Sponsor: Pittsburgh Paint
Ad Agency: Young & Rubicam, New York
Production Co: Cascade Pictures, Los Angeles

Best Insurance
Puzzle
Product: Hartford insurance
Sponsor: The Hartford Insurance Company
Ad Agency: LaRoche, McCaffrey, McCall
Production Co: Horn/Griner, New York

Best Laundry Soaps, Detergents
Second baby
Product: Ivory Snow
Sponsor: Procter & Gamble
Ad Agency: Benton & Bowles, New York
Production Co: Dimension, New York

Best Media Promotion
Eggs
Product: encyclopedia
Sponsor: World Book Encyclopedia
Ad Agency: Post-Keyes-Gardner, Chicago
Production Co: Wilding TV, Chicago

Best Men's Toiletries
Hustler
Product: Remington shaver
Sponsor: Sperry Rand Corp.
Ad Agency: Young & Rubicam, New York
Production Co: VPI, New York

Best Office Equipment
Forms
Product: Xerox telecopier
Sponsor: Xerox
Ad Agency: Needham, Harper & Steers
Production Co: Horn/Griner, New York

Best Oils, Dressings, Condiments
Great grandmother
Product: Buitoni sauce
Sponsor: Renfield Importers, Ltd.
Ad Agency: Doyle Dane Bernbach, New York
Production Co: TeleVideo, New York

Best Packaged Foods
Relay race
Product: Mrs. Pauls onion rings
Sponsor: Mrs. Pauls Kitchens, Inc.
Ad Agency: J. M. Korn & Son, Philadelphia
Production Co: BF&J Productions

Best Pharmaceuticals
Cold diggers of 1969
Product: Contac
Sponsor: Menley & James Laboratories
Ad Agency: Foote, Cone & Belding, New York
Production Co: Sokolskyfilm, New York

Best Paper Foils
Giggles
Product: Scotties Hanki-Pack
Sponsor: Scott Paper Company
Ad Agency: J. Walter Thompson, New York
Production Co: B.C.T.V., Vancouver

Best Pet Products
Park bench
Product: Purina dog meats
Sponsor: Ralston-Purina Company
Ad Agency: Gardner, St. Louis
Production Co: Pacific Commercials

Best Public Service Campaign
Give a damn
Send your kid to a ghetto
Slumlord
Kids
Sponsor: New York Urban Coalition
Ad Agency: Young & Rubicam, New York
Production Co: Horn/Griner, DVI

Best Political
The strap
Sponsor: Winthrop Rockefeller
Production Co: Shelby Storck, St. Louis

Best Retail Stores, Dealers
Leather look
Product: Sears, Roebuck stores
Sponsor: Sears, Roebuck & Company
Production Co: Advertel, Toronto

Best Soft Drinks
Washington
Product: Diet Pepsi
Sponsor: Pepsi-Cola Company
Ad Agency: BBDO, New York
Production Co: PGL

Best Toys and Games
Battling tops
Product: Ideal toys
Sponsor: Ideal
Ad Agency: Helfgott & Partners, New York
Production Co: Plus Two, New York

Best Travel, Transportation
Acapulco sun god
Product: Eastern air services
Sponsor: Eastern Airlines
Ad Agency: Young & Rubicam, New York
Production Co: Jenkins-Gomes, New York

Best Utilities
Sexton
Product: telephone services
Sponsor: Wisconsin Telephone
Ad Agency: Cramer-Krasselt, Milwaukee
Production Co: Sandler Films, Los Angeles

Best 8-10 Second ID
Baby shoes
Sponsor: National Safety Council
Ad Agency: Needham, Harper & Steers
Production Co: Sedelmaier, Chicago

Best 20-Second ID
Grinding wheel
Product: cutlery
Sponsor: Utica Cutlery
Ad Agency: Delehanty, Kurnit & Geller
Production Co: E. Burin/Tempo

Best Regional Market
Sexton
Product: telephone services
Sponsor: Wisconsin Telephone
Ad Agency: Cramer-Kasselt, Milwaukee
Production Co: Sandler Films, Los Angeles

Best Locally Produced
Nutty egg
Product: natural gas
Sponsor: Lone Star Natural Gas
Ad Agency: BBDO, Dallas
Production Co: Visual Presentations, Dallas

Best Canadian Market
Torture test
Product: Penman's underwear
Sponsor: Penman's Underwear
Ad Agency: McConnell Eastman, Toronto
Production Co: Paul Herriott, Toronto

1970

Best Overall Campaign (Tie)
Special sauce
Unfinished lunch
Politician
Product: Alka-Seltzer
Sponsor: Miles Laboratories, Inc.
Ad Agency: Jack Tinker, New York
Production Co: (1) Piggyback (2) Lee Lacy (3)
    Gomes Lowe, New York

Wedding
Star
Escapo
Product: Talon zippers
Sponsor: Talon Zippers
Ad Agency: DKG, New York
Production Co: (1) Dick Miller, New York (2-3)
    Wylde, New York

Best Apparel
Great Ocolo
Product: Talon Invisible zipper
Sponsor: Talon Zippers
Ad Agency: DKG, New York
Production Co: Howard Zieff, New York

Best Automobile (Tie)
Funeral
Product: Volkswagen sedan
Sponsor: Volkswagen of America
Ad Agency: Doyle Dane Bernbach, New York
Production Co: Howard Zieff, New York

Americans
Product: Volvo cars
Sponsor: Volvo
Ad Agency: Scali, McCabe, Sloves, New York
Production Co: Harold Becker, New York

Best Auto Accessories (Tie)
Glass rocks
Product: Firestone tires
Sponsor: Firestone
Ad Agency: J. Walter Thompson, New York
Production Co: Rita and Eddie's, New York

Can stabbing
Product: Zerex antifreeze
Sponsor: E. I. DuPont
Ad Agency: BBDO, New York
Production Co: Directors Group, New York

Best Baked Goods and Snacks
Attic
Product: Cracker Jacks
Sponsor: Cracker Jack Company
Ad Agency: Doyle Dane Bernbach, New York
Production Co: Rose-Magwood, New York

Best Banks and Financial
Birthday present
Product: Bankamericard
Sponsor: Bank of America
Ad Agency: D'Arcy, San Francisco
Production Co: Peter Cooper, New York

Best Bath Products
Active people
Product: Active deodorant
Ad Agency: Carl Ally, New York
Production Co: Alton/Melsky, New York

Best Beers and Wines (Tie)
Ella
Willie Mosconi
Product: Schaefer beer
Sponsor: Schaefer Brewing Company
Ad Agency: BBDO, New York
Production Co: Wylde, New York

Best Cereals
Vesti
Product: Kelloggs Rice Krispies
Sponsor: Kelloggs
Ad Agency: Leo Burnett, Chicago
Production Co: Screen Gems, Los Angeles

Best Cigarettes
Plaza
Product: Virginia Slims cigarettes
Sponsor: Virginia Slims
Ad Agency: Leo Burnett, Chicago
Production Co: Wylde, New York

Best Cigars
Theirs / ours
Product: White Owl cigars
Sponsor: Culbro Corp.
Ad Agency: Young & Rubicam, New York
Production Co: Dick Stone, New York

Best Coffee and Tea
Father El Exigente
Product: Savarin coffee
Sponsor: S. A. Schonbrunn & Company, Inc.
Ad Agency: Foote, Cone & Belding, New York
Production Co: Pelican, New York

Best Corporate (Tie)
What a day
Product: Hallmark cards
Sponsor: Hallmark
Ad Agency: Foote, Cone & Belding, Chicago
Production Co: Topel, Chicago

Nomex: Mario Andretti
Product: DuPont products
Sponsor: DuPont
Ad Agency: BBDO, New York
Production Co: Len Mandelbaum, New York

Best Cosmetics, Toiletries (Tie)
My girl's lips
Product: Lovesticks
Sponsor: Menley & James Labs., Inc.
Ad Agency: Wells, Rich, Greene, New York
Production Co: DVI, New York

Garden of love
Product: Love's Lemon Cleanser
Sponsor: Menley & James Labs., Inc.
Ad Agency: Wells, Rich, Greene, New York
Production Co: DVI, New York

Best Dairy Products
Zipper
Product: Carnation Slender
Sponsor: Carnation
Ad Agency: Jack Tinker, New York
Production Co: Gomes Lowe, New York

Best Dentifrices
Big family
Product: Crest toothpaste
Sponsor: Procter & Gamble
Ad Agency: Benton & Bowles, New York
Production Co: Van Praag; Audio Lex, New York

Best Home Appliances
Race, color, creed
Product: Sylvania TV
Sponsor: GTE Sylvania
Ad Agency: Doyle Dane Bernbach, New York
Production Co: Len Steckler, New York

Best Home Furnishings (Tie)
Water
Product: Alexander Smith carpets
Sponsor: Mohasco Corp.
Ad Agency: Smith/Greenland, New York
Production Co: Kaleidoscope, Los Angeles

Windsong
Product: Sears, Roebuck carpeting
Sponsor: Sears, Roebuck & Company
Ad Agency: Ogilvy & Mather, New York
Production Co: TeleVideo, New York

Best Home Maintenance (Tie)
Girl on rug
Product: Glamorene rug cleaner
Sponsor: Glamorene
Ad Agency: J. Walter Thompson, New York
Production Co: MPO, New York

Open cans
Product: Super Kem-Tone paint
Sponsor: Sherwin-Williams Company
Ad Agency: Griswold-Eshleman, Cleveland
Production Co: Stallion, New York

Best Insurance
Overeating
Product: Metropolitan life insurance
Sponsor: Metropolitan Life Insurance Company
Ad Agency: Young & Rubicam, New York
Production Co: Horn/Griner, New York

Best Laundry Soaps
Hockey
Product: Javex bleach
Sponsor: Wilbert Products Company, Inc.
Ad Agency: MacLaren, Toronto
Production Co: Rose-Magwood, Toronto

Best Media Promotion (Tie)
Memories
Product: Merv Griffin Show
Sponsor: CBS-TV
Ad Agency: Carl Ally, New York
Production Co: Mike Cuesta, New York

Senator
Hot dog
Football
Product: WABC Eyewitness News
Sponsor: WABC-TV
Ad Agency: Lampert, New York
Production Co: Audio, New York

Best Men's Toiletries
Swedish
Product: Mennen Tonik
Sponsor: Mennen
Ad Agency: Grey Advertising, New York
Production Co: East/West, New York

Best Office Equipment
Only human
Product: IBM Mag Card Selectric typewriter
Sponsor: IBM
Ad Agency: Carl Ally, New York
Production Co: Gomes Lowe, New York

Best Oils, Dressings
Italian lady
Product: Heinz spaghetti sauce
Sponsor: Heinz Foods
Ad Agency: Grey Advertising, New York
Production Co: Stan Lang, New York

Best Packaged Foods
Boy running
Product: Prince spaghetti
Sponsor: Prince
Ad Agency: Venet, New York
Production Co: PGL, New York

Best Paper Products, Foils (Tie)
Boiled egg
Product: Kimberly-Clark Teri-Towel
Sponsor: Kimberly-Clark
Ad Agency: Needham, Harper & Steers
Production Co: Wylde, New York

Wrap up
Product: Alcoa Wrap
Sponsor: Aluminum Company of America
Ad Agency: Ketchum, MacLeod, Grove
Production Co: Audio, New York

Best Personal and Gift Items
Father and son
Product: Remington shaver
Sponsor: Remington
Ad Agency: DKG, New York
Production Co: Zieff, New York

Best Pet Products (Tie)
Tom Sawyer
Product: Gaines Gravy Train
Sponsor: General Foods
Ad Agency: Benton & Bowles, New York
Production Co: TeleVideo, New York

Fashion show
Product: Purina Cat Chow
Sponsor: Ralston-Purina
Ad Agency: Gardner, St. Louis
Production Co: Directors Center, Los Angeles

Best Pharmaceuticals (Tie)
Groom's first meal
Product: Alka-Seltzer
Sponsor: Miles Laboratories
Ad Agency: Doyle Dane Bernbach, New York
Production Co: DSI, New York

Unfinished lunch
Product: Alka-Seltzer
Sponsor: Miles Laboratories
Ad Agency: Jack Tinker, New York
Production Co: N. Lee Lacy, Los Angeles

Best Public Service Campaigns
Funeral
Depression
Sponsor: New York Urban Coalition
Ad Agency: Young & Rubicam, New York
Production Co: Horn/Griner, New York

Best Political Campaigns
Lindsay
Product: Lindsay Mayoral Campaign, New York
Sponsor: Lindsay Mayoral Campaign
Ad Agency: Young & Rubicam, New York
Production Co: Dick Miller, New York; Stan Lang;
   Liberty; Video Editors, New York

Best Recreation Equipment (Tie)
Jennifer
Product: Kodak Instamatic cameras
Sponsor: Eastman Kodak
Ad Agency: J. Walter Thompson, New York
Production Co: Motion Associates, New York

Nice old ladies
Product: Sylvania flashcubes
Sponsor: GTE Sylvania
Ad Agency: Doyle Dane Bernbach, New York
Production Co: Wylde, New York

Best Soft Drinks
Portrait of America
Product: Pepsi-Cola
Sponsor: Pepsi-Cola
Ad Agency: BBDO, New York
Production Co: BFB; Libra, New York

Best Travel, Transportation
Cymbals
Product: TWA air service
Sponsor: Trans World Airlines
Ad Agency: Wells, Rich, Greene, New York
Production Co: Howard Zieff, New York

Best Utilities (Tie)
To stop a thief, light a light
Product: Con Edison of New York
Sponsor: Con Edison
Ad Agency: Dancer-Fitzgerald-Sample
Production Co: MPO, New York

Telephone poles
Saw
Product: C & P Telephone
Sponsor: C & P Telephone
Ad Agency: Cargill Wilson & Acree, Richmond
Production Co: Provence, Atlanta

Best 20-Second ID
Paper barrier
Product: VW Karmann Ghia
Sponsor: Volkswagen of America
Ad Agency: Doyle Dane Bernbach, New York
Production Co: East/West, New York

Best 8-10 Second ID
Ice cube
Gendarme
Product: Dubonnet
Sponsor: Dubonnet
Ad Agency: Gilbert, New York
Production Co: TeleVideo, New York

1970—Children's Audience

Best Food and Drink
Mr. Cow
Product: Tootsie Pops
Sponsor: Tootsie Roll
Ad Agency: W.B. Doner, Detroit
Production Co: Murakami-Wolf, Los Angeles

Best Toys, Games, Sports Equipment (Tie)
The chase
Product: AMF Roadmaster bicycles
Sponsor: AMF Wheel Goods Div.
Ad Agency: Niefeld, Paley, Kuhn, Chicago
Production Co: Sedelmaier, Chicago

Tiger paws
Product: Keds
Sponsor: Uniroyal, Inc.
Ad Agency: Doyle Dane Bernbach, New York
Production Co: Harold Becker, New York

1971

Best Overall Campaign
Better job
Product: Midas mufflers
Sponsor: Midas-International
Ad Agency: Wells, Rich, Greene, New York
Production Co: Flickers, New York

Best Apparel
Trial
Product: Fanfares Peek-a-Boo shoes
Sponsor: Brown Group, Inc.
Ad Agency: Daniel & Charles, New York
Production Co: Richards & Myers, New York

Best Automobiles (Tie)
Now that's a hardtop
Product: Volvo cars
Sponsor: Volvo
Ad Agency: Scali, McCabe, Sloves, New York
Production Co: Mike Cuesta, New York

49 auto show
Product: VW cars
Sponsor: Volkswagon of America
Ad Agency: Doyle Dane Bernbach, New York
Production Co: Zieff Films, New York

Best Auto Accessories
Edsel
Product: Midas mufflers
Sponsor: Midas-International
Ad Agency: Wells, Rich, Greene, New York
Production Co: Flickers, New York

Best Gasolines
Blind date
Product: ARCO gasoline
Sponsor: Atlantic-Richfield
Ad Agency: Needham, Harper & Steers (Benson Needham Univas Network)
Production Co: Wylde Films, New York

Best Banks, Financial (Tie)
Nick
Product: banking services
Sponsor: United California Bank
Ad Agency: Doyle Dane Bernbach, New York
Production Co: Richards & Myers, New York

Check bounce
Product: banking services
Sponsor: Bank of America
Ad Agency: Grey Advertising, Los Angeles
Production Co: Kaleidoscope, Los Angeles

Best Beers and Wines (Tie)
Truck driver
Front four
Product: Schaefer beer
Sponsor: Schaefer Brewing
Ad Agency: BBDO, New York
Production Co: 1) Brownstone, New York 2) Strawberry, New York

Best Soft Drinks
Young America
Product: Pepsi-Cola
Sponsor: Pepsi-Cola
Ad Agency: BBDO, New York
Production Co: Sokolskyfilm, New York

Best Coffee/Tea
Ernie's diet
Product: Diet Sanka
Sponsor: General Foods
Ad Agency: Young & Rubicam, New York
Production Co: Liberty Studios, New York

Best Corporate/Trade Association
Chameleon man
Product: 3M
Sponsor: 3M
Ad Agency: BBDO, New York
Production Co: Perpetual Motion, New York

Best Cosmetics/Toiletries (Tie)
Kissing
Product: Love lipsticks
Sponsor: Menley & James Labs., Inc.
Ad Agency: Wells, Rich, Greene, New York
Production Co: DVI Films, New York

Mona and cop
Product: Right Guard deodorant
Sponsor: Gillette Company
Ad Agency: BBDO, New York
Production Co: Wylde Films, New York

Best Dentifrice/Pharmaceuticals
Honor roll
Product: Pepto-Bismol liquid
Sponsor: Norwich Pharmacol Company
Ad Agency: Benton & Bowles, New York
Production Co: Focus Presentation, New York

Best Home Appliances
Flashlight
Product: Panasonic TV
Sponsor: Panasonic
Ad Agency: Ted Bates, New York
Production Co: Audio, New York

Best Home Furnishings
Argument
Product: Castro convertible sofas
Sponsor: Castro Convertible
Ad Agency: Dusenberry, New York
Production Co: Wylde, New York

Best Housewares
Scrambled eggs
Product: DuPont Teflon
Sponsor: E.I. DuPont
Ad Agency: N. W. Ayer, Philadelphia
Production Co: Petersen, Hollywood

Best Household Items
Time lapse
Product: Prolong
Sponsor: Texize Chemicals
Ad Agency: John Rockwell, New York
Production Co: John Rockwell, New York

Best Media Promotion
News spoof
Product: WLS-TV
Sponsor: WLS-TV
Ad Agency: Rink Wells, Chicago
Production Co: Sedelmaier, Chicago

Best Recreation
Ballet of the foals
Product: Big A and Belmont
Sponsor: Aqueduct and Belmont Race Tracks
Ad Agency: McCann-Erickson, New York
Production Co: EUE, New York

Best Packaged Foods
Anniversary waltz
Product: Cool Whip
Sponsor: General Foods
Ad Agency: Benton & Bowles, New York
Production Co: Brownstone, New York

Best Breakfast Cereals
Johnny Bench
Product: Wheaties
Sponsor: General Mills, Inc.
Ad Agency: Dancer-Fitzgerald-Sample, New York
Production Co: Wylde Films, New York

Best Personal Articles (Tie)
Blind date
Product: Foster Grant sunglasses
Sponsor: Foster Grant
Ad Agency: Geer, DuBois, New York
Production Co: Zieff, New York

Innovator
Product: Remington hot comb
Sponsor: Remington
Ad Agency: DKG, New York
Production Co: Zieff Films, New York

Best Pet Products (Tie)
Fred
Product: French's Dog Gravy
Sponsor: French's
Ad Agency: Rumrill-Hoyt, Rochester
Production Co: Garrett W. Brown, Philadelphia

Jody's home
Product: Purina Dog Chow
Sponsor: Ralston-Purina
Ad Agency: Gardner, St. Louis
Production Co: Directors Center, Los Angeles

Best Public Service (Tie)
Haves and have-nots
Product: National Hemophilia Foundation
Sponsor: National Hemophilia Foundation
Ad Agency: Della Femina, Travisano, New York
Production Co: Horn/Griner, New York

Lincoln
Product: College Level Exam Program
Sponsor: College Level Exam Program
Ad Agency: Daniel & Charles, New York
Production Co: Gomes Loew, New York

Best Recreation Equipment
Green, green grass of home
Product: Kodak cameras and film
Sponsor: Eastman Kodak
Ad Agency: J. Walter Thompson, New York
Production Co: MPO, New York

Best Retail
Men of destiny
Product: Barney's men's clothing
Sponsor: Barney's
Ad Agency: Jack Byrne, New York
Production Co: Horn/Griner, New York

Best Tobacco Products
Horses
Product: Marlboro cigarettes
Sponsor: Philip Morris, Inc.
Ad Agency: Leo Burnett, Chicago
Production Co: Filmfair, Los Angeles

Best Travel/Transportation
Two faces
Product: Greyhound bus services
Sponsor: Greyhound
Ad Agency: Grey Advertising, New York
Production Co: Gomes Loew, New York

Best Utilities (Tie)
Privacy
Product: telephone services
Sponsor: Illinois Bell Telephone Company
Ad Agency: N. W. Ayer, Chicago
Production Co: MPO, New York

Splattered spokesman
Product: telephone services
Sponsor: General Telephone Company of California
Ad Agency: Doyle Dane Bernbach, Los Angeles
Production Co: Time-Life, San Diego

1972

Best Overall Campaign
Restaurant
Whole thing
Party
Product: Alka-Seltzer
Sponsor: Miles Labs, Inc.
Ad Agency: Wells, Rich, Greene, New York
Production Co: Gomes Loew, New York

Best Apparel
Strangers
Product: Levi's apparel
Sponsor: Levi-Strauss
Ad Agency: Honig-Cooper & Harrington, San Francisco
Production Co: John Urie, Los Angeles; Snazelle, San Francisco; Ken Nordine, Chicago

Best Automobiles
Sun roof
Product: American Motors cars
Sponsor: American Motors
Ad Agency: Wells, Rich, Greene, New York
Production Co: Richards & Myers Films, New York

Best Auto Accessories
Big Jo
Product: Amoco gasoline
Sponsor: Amoco
Ad Agency: D'Arcy-MacManus-Intermarco, Chicago
Production Co: Sedelmaier, Chicago

Best Banks, Financial
Family
Brother-in-law
Internal Revenue
Product: H & R Block campaign
Sponsor: H & R Block
Ad Agency: Della Femina, Travisano & Partners, New York
Production Co: Shore Productions, New York

Best Beers and Wines
Leaf
Product: Miller High Life beer
Sponsor: Miller Brewing Company
Ad Agency: McCann-Erickson, New York
Production Co: Ampersand Prod. (Budin), New York

Best Coffee and Tea
Irwin and Yolanda
Product: Taster's Choice coffee
Sponsor: Nestle Company
Ad Agency: Leo Burnett, Chicago
Production Co: N. Lee Lacy, New York

Best Confections and Snacks
Bakery
Product: Drake's Devil Dogs
Sponsor: Borden, Inc.
Ad Agency: Grey Advertising, New York
Production Co: Horn/Griner, New York

Best Corporate
40 firemen
Product: communications services
Sponsor: AT&T
Ad Agency: N. W. Ayer, New York
Production Co: Tibor Hirsch, New York

Best Cosmetics and Toiletries
Voice over vignettes
Product: Avon products
Sponsor: Avon
Ad Agency: Dreher, New York
Production Co: Puddingstone, New York

Best Dairy Foods and Juices
Best effort
Product: Chiffon margarine
Sponsor: Anderson Clayton Foods
Ad Agency: Cunningham & Walsh, New York
Production Co: Wakeford-Orloff, Hollywood

Best Dentifrice and Pharmaceutical
Restaurant
Product: Alka-Seltzer
Sponsor: Miles Labs., Inc.
Ad Agency: Wells, Rich, Greene, New York
Production Co: Gomes Loew, New York

Best Home Furnishing
Wake up late
Product: Westclox clock
Sponsor: Westclox
Ad Agency: Della Femina, Travisano, New York
Production Co: Stan Lang, New York

Best Household Items
Industrial air tools
Product: Black & Decker power tools
Sponsor: Black & Decker
Ad Agency: VanSant Dugdale, Baltimore
Production Co: Lear Levin, New York

Best Insurance
Baby
Product: Blue Cross insurance
Sponsor: Blue Cross
Ad Agency: Richardson, Seigle Rolfs & McCoy, Seattle
Production Co: Mike Van Ackren, Seattle

Best Media Promotion/Entertainment
History
Product: Big A and Belmont
Sponsor: Aqueduct and Belmont Race Tracks
Ad Agency: McCann-Erickson, New York
Production Co: Dove Film, Los Angeles

Best Office Equipment
Son of little girl
Product: Xerox 4000 copier
Sponsor: Xerox
Ad Agency: Needham, Harper & Steers, New York
Production Co: Alton/Melsky, New York

Best Packaged Foods
Alice
Product: Braun's rye bread
Sponsor: ITT Continental Baking Co.
Ad Agency: Grey Advertising, New York
Production Co: Wylde Films, New York

Best Pet Product
Tunnel
Product: Chuckwagon
Sponsor: Ralston-Purina Company
Ad Agency: Gardner, St. Louis
Production Co: Excelsior, Dir. Center, Los Angeles

Best Personal Items and Gifts
Locomotive
Product: American Tourister
Sponsor: American Tourister
Ad Agency: Doyle Dane Bernbach, New York
Production Co: DSI, New York

Best Public Service
Little girl
Product: American Cancer Society
Sponsor: American Cancer Society
Ad Agency: Green Dolmatch, New York
Production Co: Harold Becker, New York

Best Retail
Cube radio
Product: Allied Radio Shack
Sponsor: Allied Radio Shack
Ad Agency: Bloom Agency, Dallas
Production Co: Wylde, New York

Best Soft Drinks
Test
Product: Canada Dry club soda
Sponsor: Canada Dry
Ad Agency: Grey Advertising, New York
Production Co: Richards & Myers, New York

Best Toys and Games
Skittle scoreball
Product: Aurora products
Sponsor: Aurora
Ad Agency: Grey Advertising, New York
Production Co: Donlee, Los Angeles

Best Travel and Transportation
Sun
Product: Bahamas tourism
Sponsor: Bahamas Ministry of Tourism
Ad Agency: McCann-Erickson, New York
Production Co: David Quaid Prod., New York

Best Utilities
Heart to heart
Product: AT&T long distance services
Sponsor: AT&T
Ad Agency: N. W. Ayer, New York
Production Co: Wylde, New York

1973

Best Overall Campaign
Old couple
Father and son
Sisters
Product: AT&T communications services
Sponsor: AT&T
Ad Agency: N. W. Ayer, New York
Production Co: Wylde, New York

Best Apparel
Yoga
Product: Cricketeer suits
Sponsor: Joseph & Feiss Company
Ad Agency: Leonard Sachs, New York
Production Co: Associates & Lofaro, New York

Best Automobile
Duke of Klaxon
Product: Audi automobiles
Sponsor: Audi
Ad Agency: Doyle Dane Bernbach, New York
Production Co: Howard Zieff, New York

Best Auto Accessories
Menace
Product: Midas muffler
Sponsor: Midas-International
Ad Agency: Wells, Rich, Greene, New York
Production Co: Howard Zieff, New York

Best Banks/Financial
Traffic jam
Product: banking services
Sponsor: Bank of America
Ad Agency: Grey Advertising, Los Angeles
Production Co: Wakeford/Orloff, Los Angeles

Best Bath Soaps/Deodorants
Perspiration can be expensive
Product: Ban roll-on deodorant
Sponsor: Bristol-Myers Company
Ad Agency: Daniel & Charles, New York
Production Co: Wakeford/Orloff, New York

Best Beers and Wines
Psychiatrist
Product: Blue Nun wine
Sponsor: Blue Nun
Ad Agency: Della Femina, Travisano, New York
Production Co: Ampersand, New York

Best Coffee and Tea
Sisters
Product: Maxwell House coffee
Sponsor: General Foods
Ad Agency: Ogilvy & Mather, New York
Production Co: Myers & Eisenstat, New York

Best Confections and Snacks
Azar the terrific
Product: Azar nuts
Sponsor: Azar
Ad Agency: Hoefer, Dieterich & Brown, San Francisco
Production Co: Topel & Associates, Chicago

Best Corporate
Education omnibus
Product: AT&T communications services
Sponsor: AT&T
Ad Agency: N. W. Ayer, New York
Production Co: Directions Visual, New York

Best Cosmetics and Toiletries (Men)
Champagne
Product: Gillette Dry Look
Sponsor: Gillette Company
Ad Agency: BBDO, New York
Production Co: Official Team Photographers, New York

Best Cosmetics and Toiletries (Women)
Jennifer's hair
Product: Alberto VO5
Sponsor: Alberto-Culver Company
Ad Agency: Rosenfeld, Sirowitz & Lawson, New York
Production Co: DVI, New York

Best Dairy Foods
Choice of the experts
Product: Del Monte pudding cup
Sponsor: Del Monte
Ad Agency: McCann-Erickson, San Francisco
Production Co: Associates & Lofaro, New York

Best Gift Items
Bus stop
Product: Polaroid Square Shooter 2 camera
Sponsor: Polaroid
Ad Agency: Doyle Dane Bernbach, New York
Production Co: D.S.I., New York

Best Home Furnishings
Pregnant woman
Product: DuPont Teflon
Sponsor: E.I. DuPont
Ad Agency: N. W. Ayer, Philadelphia
Production Co: Ampersand, New York

Best Home Maintenance
T'day's the day
Product: Cotoran Plus
Sponsor: Ciba-Geigy Corp.
Ad Agency: Keenan, Keane & McLaughlin, New York
Production Co: Liotta-Milan, New York

Best Household Items
Broderick to Broderick
Product: Brillo soap pads
Sponsor: Purex Corp.
Ad Agency: Hoefer, Dieterich & Brown, San Francisco
Production Co: Vern Gillum & Friends, Los Angeles

Best Insurance
Exchange scrapbook
Product: insurance
Sponsor: Auto Club of Michigan
Ad Agency: Stockwell-Marcuse, Southfield, Michigan
Production Co: May Day, New York

Best Media Promotion/Entertainment
'72 summer Olympics
Product: ABC-TV
Sponsor: ABC-TV
Production Co: ABC On-Air, Los Angeles

Best Packaged Foods
Baby sitter
Product: Campbell soup
Sponsor: Campbell Soups
Ad Agency: BBDO, New York
Production Co: Wylde Films, New York

Best Personal Items
Golf
Product: AMF Voit power plugs
Sponsor: AMF
Ad Agency: Cochran Chase, Fullerton
Production Co: Kaleidoscope, Hollywood

Best Pet Products
Neighbor
Product: Purina Tender Vittles
Sponsor: Ralston-Purina
Ad Agency: Wells, Rich, Greene, New York
Production Co: Apples Eye, New York

Best Pharmaceutical
Truisms
Product: Bayer aspirin
Sponsor: Sterling Drug Company
Ad Agency: Dancer-Fitzgerald-Sample, New York
Production Co: Sunlight Pictures, New York

Best Public Service
Alarm clock
Product: American Cancer Society
Sponsor: American Cancer Society
Ad Agency: Benton & Bowles, New York
Production Co: Z Productions, New York

Best Recreation Equipment
Hondaway
Product: Honda motorcycle
Sponsor: Honda
Ad Agency: Grey Advertising, Los Angeles
Production Co: FilmFair, Studio City

Best Retail/Auto
Harrison Fields
Product: Ford Dealers Association/Pinto
Sponsor: Ford
Ad Agency: J. Walter Thompson, San Francisco
Production Co: Snazelle, San Francisco

Best Retail/Foods, Restaurants
Tom Jones eating orgy
Product: Brown Derby restaurants
Sponsor: Brown Derby Restaurants
Ad Agency: Lang, Fisher & Stashower, Cleveland
Production Co: Shooting Gallery, Chicago

Best Retail/Stores, Services
Knits are neat
Product: Dayton's
Sponsor: Dayton's
Ad Agency: Grey Advertising, Detroit
Production Co: Twenty-Fifth Frame, Toronto

Best Soft Drink
Country sunshine
Product: Coca-Cola
Sponsor: Coca-Cola
Ad Agency: McCann-Erickson, New York
Production Co: Horn/Griner, New York

Best Tobacco Product
Eve
Product: Apple pipe tobacco
Sponsor: R. J. Reynolds Industries
Ad Agency: Della Femina, Travisano, New York
Production Co: Horn/Griner, New York

Best Toys and Games
Don of dons
Product: Aurora Skittle Bingo
Sponsor: Aurora
Ad Agency: Grey Advertising, New York
Production Co: Entertainment Concepts, Los Angeles

Best Travel/Transportation
Gypsy caravan
Product: Air Canada air services
Sponsor: Air Canada
Ad Agency: Foster, Montreal

Best Utilities
Brothers
Product: AT&T communications services
Sponsor: AT&T
Ad Agency: N. W. Ayer, New York
Production Co: Ampersand, New York

1974

Best Overall Campaign
Coffee and rolls
Nice buns
Bread City
Product: Old Home bread, buns and rolls
Sponsor: Old Home
Ad Agency: Bozell & Jacobs, Omaha
Production Co: Visual Presentations, Dallas

Best Apparel
Standing on my foot
Product: Thom McAn shoes
Sponsor: Thom McAn
Ad Agency: Carole Langer, New York
Production Co: Horn/Griner, New York

Best Automotive
Stunt driver
Product: Fiat cars
Sponsor: Fiat
Ad Agency: Carl Ally, New York
Production Co: Politecne Cinematografica, Milan, Italy

Best Auto Accessories
Old man
Product: B. F. Goodrich Lifesaver radials
Sponsor: B. F. Goodrich
Ad Agency: Grey Advertising, New York
Production Co: Camelot, New York

Best Banks/Financial
Account transfer
Product: banking services
Sponsor: Bank of America
Ad Agency: Grey Advertising, Los Angeles
Production Co: FilmFair, Los Angeles

Best Bath Products
Roommates
Product: Johnson's baby powder
Sponsor: Johnson & Johnson
Ad Agency: Young & Rubicam, New York
Production Co: Ampersand, New York

Best Beers/Wines
It certainly is
Product: Malt Duck
Sponsor: Carling National Breweries, Inc.
Ad Agency: W. B. Doner, Southfield, Michigan
Production Co: Sedelmaier Films, Chicago

Best Cereal
Three brothers
Product: Life cereal
Sponsor: Quaker Oats
Ad Agency: Doyle Dane Bernbach, New York
Production Co: D.S.I., New York

Best Coffee/Tea
Candlelight
Product: Sanka
Sponsor: General Foods
Ad Agency: Young & Rubicam, New York
Production Co: Ampersand, New York

Best Confection/Snack
Goddess
Product: M&M plain and peanut chocolate candies
Sponsor: Mars Inc.
Ad Agency: Ted Bates, New York
Production Co: EUE, New York

Best Corporate/Institution
Absent mother
Product: General Electric
Sponsor: General Electric
Ad Agency: BBDO, New York
Production Co: Gomes Loew, New York

Best Cosmetics and Toiletries/Men
Undercover agent
Product: Trac II razor
Sponsor: Gillette
Ad Agency: Benton & Bowles, New York
Production Co: Myers & Eisenstat, New York

Best Cosmetics and Toiletries/Women
Oh da flowers
Product: Eau de Love
Sponsor: Menley & James Labs, Inc.
Ad Agency: Wells, Rich, Greene, New York
Production Co: Wylde & Associates, New York

Best Dairy Products/Juices
Sweet-tart
Product: Ocean Spray Cranapple juice
Sponsor: Ocean Spray
Ad Agency: Ted Bates, New York
Production Co: Chance III, New York

Best Gasoline and Lubricants
Tortoise and the hare
Product: Texaco gasoline
Sponsor: Texaco
Ad Agency: Benton & Bowles, New York
Production Co: Weiner-Berman, New York

Best Personal/Gift Items
Memories
Product: Kodak film
Sponsor: Eastman-Kodak
Ad Agency: J. Walter Thompson, New York
Production Co: EUE, Los Angeles

Best Home Furnishing/Appliance
Tech center
Product: Frigidaire range
Sponsor: Frigidaire
Ad Agency: Needham, Harper & Steers, New York
Production Co: Weiner-Berman, New York

Best Household Item
Slurp
Product: the Slurp
Sponsor: Nylonge Corp.
Ad Agency: Project Group Inc., New York
Production Co: Wylde & Associates, New York

Best Insurance
Ring
Product: life insurance
Sponsor: Metropolitan Life Ins.
Ad Agency: Young & Rubicam, New York
Production Co: Wylde & Associates, New York

Best Media Promotion/Entertainment
Dance
Product: Pippin
Sponsor: Pippin
Ad Agency: Blaine Thompson, New York
Production Co: Fucci-Stone, New York

Best Office Equipment
Erasing typewriter
Product: IBM Correcting Selectric typewriter
Sponsor: IBM
Ad Agency: Carl Ally, New York
Production Co: Horn/Griner, New York

Best Packaged Foods
Bacon
Product: West Virginia Bacon
Sponsor: Hygrade Food Products Corp.
Ad Agency: W. B. Doner, Southfield, Michigan
Production Co: Lou Puopolo, New York

Best Pet Products
Singing cats
Product: Meow Mix
Sponsor: Ralston-Purina
Ad Agency: Della Femina, Travisano, New York
Production Co: David Langley, New York

Best Pharmaceutical
A day in the life
Product: Scope mouthwash
Sponsor: Procter & Gamble Co.
Ad Agency: Benton & Bowles, New York
Production Co: Jenkins-Covington, New York

Best Public Service
Ezzard Charles
Product: Muscular Dystrophy Assoc.
Sponsor: Muscular Dystrophy Assoc.
Ad Agency: Benton & Bowles, New York
Production Co: EUE, New York

Best Recreation Equipment
Snorkel
Product: Acushnet Titleist golf balls
Sponsor: Acushnet
Ad Agency: Humphrey Browning MacDougall, Boston
Production Co: Petersen Co., Los Angeles

Best Retail/Auto Dealers
Pontiac priest
Product: New England Pontiac Dealers Assoc.
Sponsor: Pontiac
Ad Agency: Hill, Holliday, Connors, Cosmopulos, Boston
Production Co: Videocom, Dedham, Mass.

Best Retail/Food Stores/Restaurant
Graduation
Product: Benihana of Tokyo
Sponsor: Benihana of Tokyo
Ad Agency: Kracauer & Marvin, New York
Production Co: Rick Levine, New York

Best Retail/Stores, Services
1923
Product: Barney's
Sponsor: Barney's
Ad Agency: Scali, McCabe, Sloves, New York
Production Co: Ampersand, New York

Best Soft Drink
Pepperettes
Product: Dr. Pepper soft drinks
Sponsor: Dr. Pepper
Ad Agency: Young & Rubicam, New York
Production Co: Ampersand, New York

Best Toys and Games
Excuses
Product: Tonka toys
Sponsor: Tonka
Ad Agency: Carl Ally, New York
Production Co: Horn Griner, New York

Best Travel
Friends
Product: United air travel services
Sponsor: United Airlines
Ad Agency: Leo Burnett, Chicago
Production Co: Denny Harris, Los Angeles

Best Utilities
Friends
Product: AT&T long-distance telephone service
Sponsor: AT&T
Ad Agency: N. W. Ayer, New York
Production Co: Jenkins/Covington, New York

1975

Best Overall Campaign
Orgy
Party
Bum
Product: Southern Airways services
Sponsor: Southern Airways
Ad Agency: McDonald Little, Atlanta
Production Co: Sedelmaier, Chicago

Best Automotive
Shell
Product: American Motors Pacer
Sponsor: American Motors
Ad Agency: Cunningham & Walsh, New York
Production Co: Dick Stone, New York

Best Auto Accessories
Richest man
Product: Midas mufflers
Sponsor: Midas International Corp.
Ad Agency: Wells, Rich, Greene, New York
Production Co: Kaleidoscope, Los Angeles

Best Apparel
Henry and Pa
Product: Hush Puppies
Sponsor: Wolverine World Wide Corp.
Ad Agency: Wells, Rich, Greene, New York
Production Co: Rick Levine, New York

Best Banks/Financial
I'm not an actor
Product: US Life Savings and Loan services
Sponsor: US Life
Ad Agency: Chiat/Day, Los Angeles
Production Co: Harvest, Los Angeles

Best Bath Products
Damaged
Product: No More Tangles
Sponsor: Johnson & Johnson
Ad Agency: Compton, New York
Production Co: Jerry Ansel Productions, New York

Best Beer and Wine
Kites
Product: Schaefer beer
Sponsor: Schaefer Brewing Co.
Ad Agency: BBDO, New York
Production Co: James Garrett & Partners, New York

Best Confection and Snack
Bang out of life
Product: Tic-Tac mints
Sponsor: Ferrero U.S.A., Inc.
Ad Agency: Chalek & Dreyer, New York
Production Co: Wylde Films & Sunlight Pictures, New York

Best Corporate
Bull in the Lexan shop
Product: GE Lexan
Sponsor: General Electric
Ad Agency: BBDO, New York
Production Co: May Day, New York

Best Cosmetic and Toiletry/Women
Lips
Product: Pure Magic Great Shine lipstick
Sponsor: Max Factor & Company
Ad Agency: Rosenfeld Sirowitz and Lawson, Beverly Hills
Production Co: N. Lee Lacy, Los Angeles

Best Dentifrice
Laura Baugh-love life
Product: Ultra-Brite toothpaste
Sponsor: Colgate-Palmolive
Ad Agency: William Esty, New York
Production Co: Filmco, New York

Best Gift and Personal Item
The first time ever I saw your face
Product: Kodak film
Sponsor: Eastman-Kodak
Ad Agency: J. Walter Thompson, New York
Production Co: MPO, Los Angeles

Best Home Furnishings/Appliances
Our song
Product: Sony components
Sponsor: Sony
Ad Agency: Rosenfeld, Sirowitz & Lawson, New York
Production Co: Lovinger, Tardio Melsky, Corless, New York

Best Home Maintenance
Rabbits
Product: Duracell batteries
Sponsor: Duracell
Ad Agency: Dancer-Fitzgerald-Sample, Maryland
Production Co: Lobel, New York

Best Insurance
Cabin
Product: MONY
Sponsor: MONY
Ad Agency: Marschalk, New York
Production Co: Steve Horn, New York

Best Media Promotion/Entertainment
Masterpiece Theatre
Product: Mobil Oil
Sponsor: Mobil
Production Co: Varied Directions, New York

Best Office Equipment
Exodus
Product: Xerox automatic typewriter
Sponsor: Xerox
Ad Agency: Needham, Harper & Steers, New York
Production Co: EUE/Screen Gems, New York

Best Packaged Foods
Catsup moon
Product: Del Monte catsup
Sponsor: Del Monte
Ad Agency: McCann-Erickson, San Francisco
Production Co: Denny Harris, Los Angeles

Best Pharmaceutical
Dance marathon
Product: Dr. Scholl shoe insole
Sponsor: Dr. Scholl
Ad Agency: N. W. Ayer ABH International, Chicago
Production Co: FilmFair, Los Angeles

Best Public Service
Toy soldiers
Product: National Alliance of Businessmen
Sponsor: National Alliance of Businessmen
Ad Agency: Grey Advertising, New York
Production Co: Ampersand, New York

Best Recreation Equipment
Garage
Product: Kawasaki motorcycles
Sponsor: Kawasaki
Ad Agency: Cunningham & Walsh, Los Angeles
Production Co: STF/Pytka, Los Angeles; Sandler, Los Angeles

Best Retail/Auto Dealers
Hubcaps
Product: Big 10 Ford dealers
Sponsor: Ford
Ad Agency: Mike Sloan, Miami
Production Co: A&R, Miami

Best Retail/Food Stores
Hit
Product: Burger King foods
Sponsor: Burger King
Ad Agency: BBDO, New York
Production Co: Dove, Los Angeles

Best Retail/Stores, Services
You're big enough
Product: Barney's
Sponsor: Barney's
Ad Agency: Scali, McCabe, Sloves, New York
Production Co: Steve Horn, New York

Best Soft Drinks/Coffee (Tie)
Zipper boutique
Product: Diet Pepsi
Sponsor: Pepsi-Cola
Ad Agency: BBDO/Michlin & Hill
Production Co: Sunlight Pictures/Michlin & Hill

Pied-piper
Product: Pepsi-Cola
Sponsor: Pepsi-Cola
Ad Agency: BBDO, New York
Production Co: James Garrett & Partners, New York

Best Toys and Games
Elephant
Product: Tonka Toy trucks
Sponsor: Tonka
Ad Agency: Carl Ally, New York
Production Co: Horn/Griner, New York

Best Travel and Transportation
Orgy
Product: Southern Airlines services
Sponsor: Southern Airlines
Ad Agency: McDonald & Little, Atlanta
Production Co: Sedelmaier, Chicago

Best Utilities
Teenager
Product: telephone services
Sponsor: Illinois Bell
Ad Agency: N. W. Ayer ABH International, Chicago
Production Co: Hil Covington, Los Angeles

1976

Best Overall Campaign
Traveling lady
Heartburn cafe
Product: Alka II
Sponsor: Miles Laboratories, Inc.
Ad Agency: J. Walter Thompson, New York
Production Co: Lovinger, Tardio, Melsky/Ampersand, New York

Best Apparel
Bankrobber
Product: Beautymist Panty Hose
Sponsor: Beautymist
Ad Agency: Long, Haymes & Carr, Winston-Salem
Production Co: Spungbuggy, Los Angeles

Best Auto Accessories
Joan Rivers
Product: B. F. Goodrich tires
Sponsor: B.F. Goodrich
Ad Agency: Grey Advertising, New York
Production Co: Griner/Cuesta, New York

Best Automotive
Breakthrough
Product: American Motors cars
Sponsor: American Motors
Ad Agency: Cunningham & Walsh, New York
Production Co: Wakeford/Orloff, Los Angeles

Best Bath Product and Deodorant
Shake hands
Product: Boraxo
Sponsor: U.S. Borax & Chemical Corp.
Ad Agency: McCann-Erickson, Los Angeles
Production Co: Ross McCanse, Los Angeles

Best Bank/Financial
Mel Blanc
Product: American Express credit card
Sponsor: American Express
Ad Agency: Ogilvy & Mather, New York
Production Co: Wakeford/Orloff, New York

Best Beer and Wine
The professionals
Product: Bartenders Instant Cocktail Mix
Sponsor: Brady Enterprises, Inc.
Ad Agency: Humphrey Browning MacDougall, Boston
Production Co: N. Lee Lacy, New York

Best Confection/Snack
Wedding
Product: Almond Joy and Mounds
Sponsor: Mars Inc.
Ad Agency: Dancer-Fitzgerald-Sample, New York
Production Co: Gomes Lowe, New York

Best Corporate
Rock bolts
Product: DuPont industries
Sponsor: E.I. DuPont
Ad Agency: BBDO, New York
Production Co: Gregg Kramer, New York

Best Coffee and Tea
Construction worker
Product: Red Rose tea
Sponsor: Brooke Bond Tea Company, Inc.
Ad Agency: Warwick, Welsh, Miller, New York
Production Co: Bob Giraldi, New York

Best Dairy Products and Juices
Deejay
Product: American Dairy Assoc. milk
Sponsor: American Dairy Assoc.
Ad Agency: D'Arcy, MacManus & Masius, Chicago
Production Co: Sunlight, New York

Best Dentifrice and Pharmaceutical
Bowling
Product: Alka-Seltzer
Sponsor: Miles Labs, Inc.
Ad Agency: Wells, Rich, Greene, New York
Production Co: Rick Levine, New York

Best Gasoline and Lubricant
Motor oil
Product: Sunoco products
Sponsor: Sunoco
Ad Agency: Wells, Rich, Greene, New York
Production Co: Rick Levine, New York

Best Home Appliances and Furnishings
Lamps
Product: Berkline Wall-Away Recliner
Sponsor: Berkline
Ad Agency: W. B. Doner, Baltimore
Production Co: The Movie House, New York

Best Home Maintenance
I'm a roof
Product: Celotex residential roofing
Sponsor: Celotex
Ad Agency: Mike Sloan, Miami
Production Co: Gomes Lowe, New York

Best Household Item
Squeak
Product: Ajax dishwashing liquid
Sponsor: Ajax
Ad Agency: Norman Craig Kummel, New York
Production Co: Filmco, New York

Best Insurance
Immunization
Product: Blue Cross/Blue Shield
Sponsor: Blue Cross/Blue Shield of New York
Ad Agency: J. Walter Thompson, New York
Production Co: Ampersand, New York

Best Media Promotion
A Chorus Line
Product: A Chorus Line
Sponsor: A Chorus Line
Ad Agency: Blaine Thompson, New York
Production Co: Bob Giraldi, New York

Best Men's Products
Revolving couple
Product: Canoe
Sponsor: Dana Perfumes Corp.
Ad Agency: DKG, New York
Production Co: Andreozzi, New York

Best Office Equipment
Dictation
Product: IBM cartridge system
Sponsor: IBM
Ad Agency: Carl Ally, New York
Production Co: Gomes Lowe, New York

Best Packaged Foods
Unartificial snack
Product: California grapes
Sponsor: California Grapes
Ad Agency: Botsford Ketchum, San Francisco
Production Co: Sedelmaier, Chicago

Best Personal and Gift Items
Bachelor
Product: BASF Tapes
Sponsor: BASF
Ad Agency: Young & Rubicam, New York
Production Co: Bob Giraldi, New York

Best Pet Products
All over the world
Product: Meow Mix
Sponsor: Ralston-Purina
Ad Agency: Della Femina, Travisano, New York
Production Co: Stan Lang, New York

Best Public Service
Bowling ball
Product: Alabama education
Sponsor: Alabama Education
Ad Agency: Luckie & Forney, Birmingham
Production Co: Helios, Tuscaloosa

Best Recreation Equipment
Durable DT
Product: Acushnet Titleist golf balls
Sponsor: Acushnet
Ad Agency: Humphrey Browning MacDougall, Boston
Production Co: Weiner/Berman, Los Angeles

Best Retail Foods
Peter Piper the pickle poker
Product: Burger King foods
Sponsor: Burger King
Ad Agency: BBDO, New York
Production Co: Gregg/Kramer

Best Retail Specialty
English room
Product: Barney's
Sponsor: Barney's
Ad Agency: Scali, McCabe, Sloves, New York
Production Co: Phil Kimmelman, New York/Steve Horn, New York

Best Soft Drink
Celebrities
Product: Canada Dry ginger ale
Sponsor: Canada Dry
Ad Agency: Grey Advertising, New York
Production Co: Lovinger, Tardio, Melsky, New York

Best Tobacco Product
John Weitz
Product: Capitan cigars
Sponsor: Consolidated Cigar Corp.
Ad Agency: David Oksner Mitchneck, New York
Production Co: RHA, New York

Best Travel, Transportation
General consumer
Product: Alitalia Airlines services
Sponsor: Alitalia Airlines
Ad Agency: DKG, New York
Production Co: Tibor Hirsch, New York

Best Utilities
Performance
Product: AT&T communications services
Sponsor: AT&T
Ad Agency: N. W. Ayer ABH International, New York
Production Co: Elliot Lawrence, New York

Best Women's Products
Aviance night
Product: Aviance
Sponsor: Prince Matchabelli
Ad Agency: Advertising to Women, New York
Production Co: Jerry Ansel, New York

1977

Best Overall Campaign
Running
Swimming
Gymnastics
Product: ABC-TV 1976 Summer Olympic Games
Sponsor: ABC-TV
Ad Agency: In-House, New York
Production Co: Camelot, New York

Best Apparel
Growing up
Product: Carter's childrens' clothing
Sponsor: William Carter Company
Ad Agency: BBDO, Boston
Production Co: Gregg Kramer, New York

Best Auto Accessories
Pops
Product: B.F. Goodrich radial tires
Sponsor: B.F. Goodrich
Ad Agency: Grey Advertising, New York
Production Co: Lovinger, Tardio, Melsky, New York

Best Automotive
Two halves
Product: AMC Pacer wagon
Sponsor: AMC
Ad Agency: Cunningham & Walsh, New York
Production Co: EUE/Screen Gems, Los Angeles

Best Banking and Financial
Alexander Hamilton's ghost
Product: Bank of New York banking services
Sponsor: Bank of New York
Ad Agency: Doremus, New York
Production Co: Dick Stone, New York

Best Bath Products
So beautiful, baby
Product: Camay soap
Sponsor: Procter & Gamble
Ad Agency: Leo Burnett, Chicago
Production Co: Swanson/Bailin, Studio City

Best Beer and Wine
Artist
Product: Busch beer
Sponsor: Anheuser-Busch Brewing
Ad Agency: Gardner, St. Louis
Production Co: Wakeford/Orloff, Los Angeles

Best Bicentennial
Bicentennial
Product: Coca-Cola
Sponsor: Coca-Cola
Ad Agency: McCann-Erickson, New York
Production Co: Steve Horn, New York

Best Confection and Snack
This long
Product: Bubble Yum bubble gum
Sponsor: Life Savers, Inc.
Ad Agency: BBDO, New York
Production Co: Bean/Kahn, New York

Best Corporate
Convention
Product: A&P supermarkets
Sponsor: A&P Supermarkets
Ad Agency: McCann-Erickson, New York
Production Co: N. Lee Lacy, New York

Best Dairy Product and Fruit Drink
Ice
Product: Breakstone sour cream
Sponsor: Kraftco
Ad Agency: Richard K. Manoff, New York
Production Co: Gomes Loew, New York

Best Dentifrice/Pharmaceutical
Before bed
Product: Alka-Seltzer
Sponsor: Miles Labs, Inc.
Ad Agency: Wells, Rich, Greene, New York
Production Co: Rick Levine, New York

Best Gasoline and Lubricant
Motor oil
Product: Chevron motor oil
Sponsor: Standard Oil Company of California
Ad Agency: BBDO, San Francisco
Production Co: Kurtz & Friends, Los Angeles

Best Home Furnishing and Appliances
Shower song/man
Product: Conair Waterfingers
Sponsor: Continental Hair Products
Ad Agency: Della Femina, Travisano, New York
Production Co: Bob Giraldi, New York

Best Home Maintenance
Skydiver
Product: Black & Decker cordless ¼" drill
Sponsor: Black & Decker
Ad Agency: BBDO, New York
Production Co: Wakeford/Orloff, Los Angeles

Best Household Item
Stick 'em up
Product: Airwick Stick Ups
Sponsor: Airwick Industries, Inc.
Ad Agency: Della Femina, Travisano, New York
Production Co: Bob Giraldi, New York

Best Insurance
Monkeys
Product: Blue Cross/Blue Shield of Northeast Ohio Hospital Insurance
Sponsor: Blue Cross & Blue Shield
Ad Agency: Carr Liggett, Cleveland
Production Co: Asch, Chicago

Best Media Promotion/Entertainment
Power sports
Product: ABC-TV 1976 Summer Olympic Games
Sponsor: ABC-TV
Production Co: Lou LaRose, New York

Best Office Equipment
Magician
Product: Xerox telecopier transceiver
Sponsor: Xerox
Ad Agency: Needham, Harper & Steers, New York
Production Co: Myers & Eisenstat, New York

Best Packaged Foods
Ingredients
Product: Arnold Brick Oven bread
Sponsor: Arnold Bakeries, Inc.
Ad Agency: W. E. Long, Chicago
Production Co: Goldsholl, Northfield

Best Personal and Gift Items
Genius
Product: Casio calculator
Sponsor: Casio
Ad Agency: Doremus, New York
Production Co: Gomes Loew, New York

Best Pet Products
Steak comparison
Product: Bonz snack food for dogs
Sponsor: Ralston-Purina
Ad Agency: Gardner, St. Louis
Production Co: Z, New York; Gardian, Los Angeles

Best Political
Carter for President
Sponsor: Carter for President
Ad Agency: Gerald R. Rafshoon, Atlanta

Best Public Service
Child abuse
Sponsor: Ad Council PTA
Ad Agency: The Bloom Agency, Dallas
Production Co: Pailsey, Los Angeles

Best Recreation Equipment
Blue Mondays
Product: AMF sporting goods
Sponsor: AMF
Ad Agency: Benton & Bowles, New York
Production Co: Kurtz & Friends, Hollywood

Best Retail Auto Dealers
Lotta bull
Product: A. D. Anderson Chevrolet
Sponsor: Chevrolet
Ad Agency: Mathis, Burden & Charles, Baltimore

Best Retail Food Chains
W. C. and kids
Product: Arthur Treacher's Fish and Chips
Sponsor: Arthur Treacher's Fish and Chips
Ad Agency: Ketchum, MacLeod & Grove, Pittsburgh
Production Co: Bill Hudson, New York

Best Retail Specialty Stores
History
Product: Barney's
Sponsor: Barney's
Ad Agency: Scali, McCabe, Sloves, New York
Production Co: N. Lee Lacy, New York

Best Soft Drink and Coffee
The exception
Product: A & W sugar-free root beer
Sponsor: A & W
Ad Agency: Humphrey, Browning, MacDougall, Boston
Production Co: Ampersand, New York

Best Tobacco Products
Shower curtain
Product: Sir Walter Raleigh pipe tobacco
Sponsor: Brown & Williamson
Ad Agency: Post-Keyes-Gardner, Chicago
Production Co: FilmFair, Studio City

Best Toys and Games
Adversary
Product: Adversary game
Ad Agency: Chiat/Day, San Francisco
Production Co: Rick Levine, New York

Best Travel and Transportation
Francophile
Product: Air France air services
Sponsor: Air France
Ad Agency: Kenyon & Eckhardt, New York
Production Co: Howard Zieff, New York

Best Utilities
Flames
Product: American gas
Sponsor: American Gas Assn.
Ad Agency: J. Walter Thompson, New York
Production Co: Dove/Forma, New York

Best Women's Products
Restaurant
Product: Faberge Babe
Sponsor: Faberge
Ad Agency: Nadler & Larimer, New York
Production Co: Gomes Loew, New York

1978

Best Overall Campaign
Drummer
Tuthill
Rollins
Product: Pioneer HiFi components
Sponsor: Pioneer Electronics Corp.
Ad Agency: Scali, McCabe, Sloves, New York
Production Co: Bob Giraldi, New York; Steve Horn, New York

Best Apparel
Moments
Products: Pro Keds
Sponsor: Uniroyal, Inc.
Ad Agency: Young & Rubicam, New York
Production Co: Rick Levine, New York

Best Automotive
Four generations
Product: Ford pick-up trucks
Sponsor: Ford Motor Company
Ad Agency: J. Walter Thompson, Detroit
Production Co: Ray Corwin, New York

Best Auto Accessories
Rich lady
Product: B.F. Goodrich tires
Sponsor: B.F. Goodrich Company
Ad Agency: Grey Advertising, New York
Production Co: Lovinger/Tardio/Melsky, New York

Best Banks/Financial
Auto loan
Product: Manufacturers Hanover Trust banking services
Sponsor: Manufacturers Hanover Trust Company
Ad Agency: Young & Rubicam, New York
Production Co: Gomes Loew, New York

Best Bath Products
Jury
Product: Right Guard antiperspirant
Sponsor: Gillette Company
Ad Agency: BBDO, New York
Production Co: Ansel, New York

Best Beers/Wines
Bubba Smith
Product: Miller Lite beer
Sponsor: Miller Brewing Company
Ad Agency: McCann-Erickson, New York
Production Co: Bob Giraldi, New York

Best Cereals
Ballet
Product: Kretschmer wheat germ
Sponsor: International Multifoods Corp.
Ad Agency: Della Femina, Travisano, New York
Production Co: Bob Giraldi, New York

Best Confection/Snacks
Singers No. 2
Product: Peter-Paul Mounds
Sponsor: Peter Paul, Inc.
Ad Agency/Music Production Co: Dancer-Fitzgerald-Sample, New York
Production Co: Bob Giraldi, New York

Best Corporate
Edison / outdoor lighting
Product: General Electric services
Sponsor: General Electric
Ad Agency: BBDO, New York
Production Co: Myers/Griner/Cuesta, New York

Best Dairy Products/Fruit, Drinks
Son of Russia
Product: Dannon yogurt
Sponsor: Dannon Milk Products
Ad Agency: Marstellar, New York
Production Co: Bob Gaffney, New York

Best Dentifrice/Pharmaceuticals
Sticks & doesn't
Product: Johnson & Johnson band-aids
Sponsor: Johnson & Johnson
Ad Agency: Young & Rubicam, New York
Production Co: Rick Levine, New York

Best Gasoline/Lubricants
Long line
Product: Mobil 1 oil
Sponsor: Mobil Oil
Ad Agency: Doyle Dane Bernbach, New York
Production Co: Independent Artists, New York

Best Entertainment Promotion
Shortcut
Product: Empire Stakes
Sponsor: New York State Lottery
Ad Agency: Smith/Greenland, New York
Production Co: Lovinger, Tardio, Melsky, New York

Best Home Furnishings/Appliances
Tuthill
Product: Pioneer sound systems
Sponsor: Pioneer Electronics Corp.
Ad Agency: Scali, McCabe, Sloves, New York
Production Co: Bob Giraldi, New York

Best Home Maintenance
Ruthless
Product: Rubbermaid refuse container
Sponsor: Rubbermaid, Inc.
Ad Agency: Ketchum, MacLeod & Grove, Pittsburgh
Production Co: Toni Ficalora, New York

Best Household Items
Stick 'em up
Product: Airwick Stick Ups
Sponsor: Airwick Industries, Inc.
Ad Agency: Della Femina, Travisano, New York
Production Co: Bob Giraldi, New York

Best ID—Corporate
Hello Federal
Product: Federal Express
Sponsor: Federal Express Corp.
Ad Agency: Ally & Gargano, New York
Production Co: Sedelmaier, Chicago

Best ID—Station
The music is the force
Product: WCOZ-FM radio
Sponsor: WCOZ-FM
Ad Agency: Skyway, Boston
Production Co: Lisberger, Boston

Best Insurance
Family dinner
Product: Blue Cross/Blue Shield health insurance
Sponsor: Blue Cross/Blue Shield
Ad Agency: N. W. Ayer ABH International, Chicago
Production Co: Jenkins-Covington, New York

Best Media Promotion
Block party
Product: WLS-TV Eyewitness News
Sponsor: WLS-TV
Ad Agency: N. W. Ayer ABH International, Chicago
Production Co: Bob Giraldi, New York

Best Men's Products
Max
Product: Mennen Trouble after-shave cologne
Sponsor: Mennen Company
Ad Agency: Case & McGrath, New York
Production Co: Mason/Stearns, New York

Best Office Equipment
Low overhead
Product: Fisher office furniture
Sponsor: Fisher Office Furniture
Ad Agency: Clinton E. Frank, Chicago
Production Co: Sedelmaier Film, Chicago

Best Oils/Dressings
Waiter
Product: Progresso seafood sauces
Sponsor: Progresso Foods Corp.
Ad Agency: Chalek and Dreyer, New York
Production Co: Bob Giraldi, New York

Best Packaged Foods
Did you forget?
Product: California strawberries
Sponsor: California Strawberries Advisory Board
Ad Agency: Botsford Ketchum, San Francisco
Production Co: Ampersand, New York

Best Personal/Gift Items
Samsonite vs. Steelers
Product: Samsonite luggage
Sponsor: Samsonite Corp.
Ad Agency: J. Walter Thompson, New York
Production Co: Myers & Griner/Cuesta, New York

Best Pet Products
Quiz show
Product: Meow Mix cat food
Sponsor: Ralston-Purina
Ad Agency: Della Femina, Travisano, New York
Production Co: Cooper, Dennis, Hirsch, New York

Best Public Service
Church
Product: American Cancer Society
Sponsor: American Cancer Society
Ad Agency: Benton & Bowles, New York
Production Co: DJM, New York

Best Recreation Equipment
Spectator
Product: AMF sporting equipment
Sponsor: AMF, Inc.
Ad Agency: Benton & Bowles, New York
Production Co: Perpetual Motion, New York

Best Recruitment
12 months to say goodbye
Product: U.S. Army
Sponsor: U.S. Army Recruiting Command
Ad Agency: N. W. Ayer ABH International, New York
Production Co: Myers & Eisenstat, New York

Best Retail Auto
Stop pretending
Product: Carousel Porsche–Audi–Renault
Sponsor: Volkswagen of America, Inc.
Ad Agency: Lunch Hour, St. Louis
Production Co: Maag & Knutson, Minneapolis

Best Retail Foods
Wipes
Product: Wendy's hamburgers
Sponsor: Wendy's International, Inc.
Ad Agency: Dick Rich, New York
Production Co: Rick Levine, New York

Best Retail Specialty
Out-of-towners
Product: Barney's
Sponsor: Barney's
Ad Agency: Ally & Gargano, New York
Production Co: Steve Horn, New York

Best Soft Drinks
Pied Pepper-cross country
Product: Dr. Pepper soft drinks
Sponsor: Dr. Pepper Company
Ad Agency: Young & Rubicam, New York
Production Co: Sunlight, New York

Best Coffee/Tea/Cocoa Mix
Big news
Product: Ovaltine hot cocoa mix
Sponsor: Ovaltine Products, Inc.
Ad Agency: TBWA—Baron, Costello & Fine, New York
Production Co: Merle Bloom, New York

Best Toys/Games
Bank
Product: Hangman Game
Sponsor: Milton Bradley Company
Ad Agency: MB Communications, Springfield, Mass.
Production Co: Peterson, Los Angeles

Best Transportation
Pass it on
Product: Federal Express
Sponsor: Federal Express Corp.
Ad Agency: Ally & Gargano, New York
Production Co: Sedelmaier, Chicago

Best Travel
People, places
Product: Pan Am air services
Sponsor: Pan American World Airways
Ad Agency: Ally & Gargano, New York
Production Co: Tibor Hirsch, New York

Best Utilities
Broken phone
Product: telephone services
Sponsor: Illinois Bell Telephone Company
Ad Agency: N. W. Ayer, Chicago
Production Co: Harvest, Los Angeles

Best Women's Products
Boat
Product: Revlon Jontue Fragrance
Sponsor: Revlon, Inc.
Ad Agency: Grey Advertising, New York
Production Co: Lipson Film, New York

Associations and Organizations

Academy of Television Arts & Sciences
4605 Lankersham Blvd.
Suite 800
North Hollywood, CA 91602
(213) 506-7880
Purpose: An organization seeking to promote excellence in all aspects of television.

Accuracy in Media
777 14th St., NW
Washington, DC 20005
(202) 783-4407
Contact: Reed Irvine
Purpose: A consumer group keeping tabs on the accuracy of news coverage.

Action for Children's Television
46 Austin St.
Newtonville, MA 02160
(617) 527-7870
Contact: Peggy Charren
Purpose: A consumer group seeking to promote quality children's programming on TV.

Actors' Equity Association
1500 Broadway
New York, NY 10036
(212) 869-8530
Contact: Theodore Bikel
Purpose: An actors' union.

American Advertising Federation College Chapters
1225 Connecticut Ave., NW
Washington, DC 20036
(202) 659-1800
Contact: Jonah Gitlitz
Purpose: An academic organization working with the American Advertising Federation to disseminate information about advertising and the media.

American Association of Schools and Departments of Journalism
School of Journalism and Mass Communication
University of Minnesota
Minneapolis, MN 55455
(612) 373-3172
Contact: Harold Wilson
Purpose: An educational organization of colleges and universities that have accredited journalism courses.

American Auto Racing Writers and Broadcasters Association
922 N. Pass Ave.
Burbank, CA 91505
(213) 842-7005
Contact: Dusty Brandel
Purpose: An organization seeking to improve auto-racing coverage and to provide improved facilities for writers.

American Baptist Churches in the U.S.A.
Division of Communication
Valley Forge, PA 19481
(215) 768-2216
Contact: Phillip E. Jenks
Purpose: An organization promoting religious broadcasting in the United States.

American Bible Society
Department of Information
1865 Broadway
New York, NY 10023
(212) 581-7400
Contact: Thomas S. Johnson
Purpose: A religious organization concerned with the dissemination of information about the Bible through media channels.

American Business Communication Association
317b David Kinley Hall
University of Illinois
Urbana, IL 61801
(217) 333-1007
Contact: Francis W. Weeks
Purpose: An educational organization of people interested in writing for the media in the business field.

American Cinema Editors
422 S. Western Ave.
Los Angeles, CA 90020
(213) 384-0588
Contact: John A. Martinelli
Purpose: A professional society of television and movie editors that seeks to improve film editing.

American Council for Better Broadcasts
120 E. Wilson St.
Madison, WI 53703
(608) 257-7712
Contact: Leslie Spence
Purpose: A consumer group seeking to promote quality in broadcasting.

American Federation of Television and Radio Artists
1350 Ave. of the Americas
New York, NY 10019
(212) 265-7700
Contact: Sanford I. Wolff
Purpose: A labor organization of artists in the radio and television industry.

American Film Institute
John F. Kennedy Center for the Performing Arts
Washington, DC 20566
(202) 833-9300
Contact: George Stevens, Jr.
Purpose: A cultural organization concerned with the development and preservation of our cultural resources in film and television.

American Guild of Variety Artists
1540 Broadway
New York, NY 10036
(212) 765-0800
Contact: Penny Singleton
Purpose: A labor union for variety artists.

American Society of Cinematographers
1782 N. Orange Dr.
Hollywood, CA 90028
(213) 876-5080
Contact: Linwood Dunn
Purpose: A professional society seeking to maintain high standards in cinematography.

American Society of Composers, Authors and Publishers
One Lincoln Plaza
New York, NY 10023
(212) 595-3050
Contact: Stanley Adams
Purpose: A professional organization that acts as a clearinghouse in the field of performers' rights.

American Society of TV Cameramen, Inc.
P.O. Box 296
Sparkill, NY 10976
(914) 359-5985
Contact: Robert M. Zweck
Purpose: A professional organization seeking to promote high standards in television camera work.

American Women in Radio & Television
1321 Connecticut Ave., NW
Washington, DC 20036
(202) 296-0009
Contact: Franchine P. Proulx
Purpose: An organization for the advancement of women in radio and television.

Arizona Broadcasters Association
Box 7429
Phoenix, AZ 85011
(602) 991-1700
Contact: Robert Allingham
Purpose: A state organization of broadcasters.

Armed Forces Communications and Electronics Association
Skyline Center
5205 Leesburg Pike
Falls Church, VA 20041
(703) 820-5028
Contact: Vice-Admiral (Ret.) John L. Boyes
Purpose: An organization seeking to promote better relations between the Armed Forces and the communications industry.

Artists' Representatives Association
1350 Ave. of the Americas
New York, NY 10019
(212) 586-5487
Contact: David C. Baumgarten
Purpose: A non-profit organization that includes in its membership most of the persons, firms, and corporations actively engaged in the agency business in the broadcast fields.

Associated Actors & Artists of America
1500 Broadway
New York, NY 10036
(212) 869-0358
Contact: Frederick O'Neal
Purpose: A union of actors and other artists.

Associated Press Broadcasters, Inc.
50 Rockefeller Plaza
New York, NY 10020
(212) 262-4000
Contact: Gerald Trapp
Purpose: An association of broadcast stations promoting journalism through radio and television.

Association for Broadcast Engineering Standards
1730 M St., NW, Suite 700
Washington, DC 20036
(202) 331-0606
Contact: William J. Potts
Purpose: A voluntary group of licensees and permittees of U.S. broadcast stations seeking to provide the best radio service possible to their listeners.

Association of Broadcast Executives of Texas
% Tracy Locke, Adv.
1407 Main St.
Dallas, TX 75202
(214) 742-3131
Contact: Lawrence Spiegel
Purpose: An association of Texas broadcasting executives.

Association of Cinema and Video Laboratories
P.O. Box 34932
Bethesda, MD 20034
(301) 469-8881
Contact: Dudley Spriull
Purpose: An association for the improvement of film procedures and the establishment of uniform standards among film laboratories.

Association for Educational Communications and Technology
1126 16th St., NW
Washington, DC 20036
(202) 833-4180
Contact: Howard Hitchens, Jr.
Purpose: An association seeking to promote the use of communications media in education.

Association for Education in Journalism, Division of Radio–Television
2120 Flint Hall
University of Kansas
Lawrence, KS 66045
(913) 864-2700
Contact: David Davy
Purpose: An educational organization seeking to advance the use of radio and television in journalism education.

Association of Federal Communications Consulting Engineers
Cohen & Zippell, P.Z.
527 Munsey Bldg.
Washington, DC 20004
(202) 783-0111
Contact: Donald D. Everist
Purpose: Radio engineers concerned with proper federal regulation and administration of radio.

Association of German Broadcasters
45 Rockefeller Plaza, Suite 554
New York, NY 10020
(212) 757-7911
Contact: David Berger
Purpose: An organization that distributes German radio programs in the United States.

Association of Independent Television Stations, Inc.
19 W. 44th St.
New York, NY 10036
(212) 575-0577
Contact: Herman W. Land
Purpose: An organization concerned with the needs of independent television stations.

Association of Maximum Service Telecasters
1735 DeSales St., NW
Washington, DC 20036
(202) 347-5412
Contact: Lester W. Lindow
Purpose: An organization serving as a spokesperson for television broadcasters in management matters.

Association of Media Producers
1707 L St., NW
Washington, DC 20036
(202) 296-4710
Contact: Maureen Kenney
Purpose: An organization seeking to promote the best possible use of media in education.

Association of Motion Picture & Television Producers, Inc.
8480 Beverly Blvd.
Los Angeles, CA 90048
(213) 653-2200
Contact: Edward P. Prelock
Purpose: A trade organization of major film- and television-producing companies.

Association of Regional Religious Communications
1100 W. 42nd St.
Indianapolis, IN 46208
(317) 926-5371
Contact: Rev. Fred H. Erickson
Purpose: An organization seeking to promote religious broadcasting.

Association of Theatrical Press Agents and Managers
268 W. 47th St.
New York, NY 10036
(212) 582-3750
Contact: Dick Weaver
Purpose: A labor union for press agents and theatrical managers.

Bedside Network of the Veterans Hospital Radio and TV Guild
1841 Broadway
New York, NY 10023
(212) 757-8657
Contact: Hope Martinez
Purpose: To provide recreational and rehabilitative programs for patients and help them produce their own programs.

Booker T. Washington Foundation
Cablecommunications Resource Center
2000 K St., NW
Washington, DC 20006
(202) 857-4852
Contact: Phil Watson
Purpose: An association interested in helping minority businessmen with the purchase and maintenance of cablecommunication and telecommunication broadcast facilities.

Broadcast Education Association
1771 N St., NW
Washington, DC 20036
(202) 293-3519
Contact: Dr. Harold Niven
Purpose: A group seeking to upgrade standards of teaching and improve the curriculum at schools offering radio and television broadcasting courses.

Broadcast Music, Inc.
40 W. 57th St.
New York, NY 10019
(212) 586-2000
Contact: Edward Cramer
Purpose: An association that collects license fees due
writers and composers from groups performing
their music.

Broadcast Pioneers
40 W. 57th St.
New York, NY 10019
(212) 586-2000
Contact: Kay Powers
Purpose: An organization of people who have been
in radio broadcasting 20 or more years or television broadcasting for 10 or more years.

Broadcast Pioneers Library
1771 N St., NW
Washington, DC 20036
(202) 223-0088
Contact: Joseph E. Baudino
Purpose: An organization that provides reference
material on all aspects of broadcasting.

Broadcast Rating Council
420 Lexington Ave., Room 2347
New York, NY 10017
(212) 687-7733
Contact: Hugh M. Beville, Jr.
Purpose: A council that sets minimum standards
for broadcast-rating surveys.

Broadcast-Television Recording Engineers
3518 Cahuenga Blvd. W, Suite 307
Hollywood, CA 90068
(213) 851-5515
Contact: Andrew J. Draghi
Purpose: A professional organization seeking to
improve broadcast-television recording.

Broadcasters Promotion Association, Inc.
P.O. Box 5102
Lancaster, PA 17601
(717) 626-4524
Contact: Patricia A. Evans
Purpose: An organization seeking to improve and
promote the broadcast industry.

Cable Communications Resource Center
2000 K St., NW, Suite 800
Washington, DC 20006
(202) 857-4800
Contact: Charles E. Tate
Purpose: An organization that helps minority
businessmen involved in cable television.

Cable Television Information Center
Suite 400, 4th floor
2100 M St., NW
Washington, DC 20037
(202) 872-8888
Contact: Harold Horn
Purpose: A non-profit advisory group created by
the Ford and Markle Foundations to help local
officials make decisions about cable television.

California Broadcasters Association
1107 9th St., Suite 907
Sacramento, CA 95814
(916) 444-2237
Contact: Howard J. Smiley
Purpose: A state organization of broadcasters.

Catholic Alliance for Communications
1011 1st Ave., Room 1920
New York, NY 10022
(212) 371-6100
Contact: John Curran
Purpose: An organization that provides schooling
in communications and conducts research
projects.

Children's TV Workshop
1 Lincoln Plaza
New York, NY 10023
(212) 595-3456
Contact: Joan Ganz Cooney
Purpose: A research organization seeking new
ways to use television for the instruction of
the young.

Christian Church (Disciples of Christ)
Office of Communication
P.O. Box 1986
Indianapolis, IN 46206
(317) 353-1491
Contact: Charles A. Hamilton
Purpose: A division of the Christian Church pro-
moting religious communications.

Church Women United
Radio-TV & Press Division
475 Riverside Dr., Room 812
New York, NY 10027
(212) 870-2346
Contact: Virginia Baron
Purpose: An organization of women seeking to
promote religious communication.

Citizens Communications Center
1914 Sunderland Pl., NW
Washington, DC 20036
(202) 296-4238
Contact: Nolan Bowie
Purpose: A law firm informing citizens of their
rights to be heard on radio or television.

Colorado Broadcasters Association
7138 W. Frost Dr.
Littleton, CO 80123
(303) 979-8787
Contact: Jack Miller
Purpose: A state organization of broadcasters.

Common Carrier Association for Telecommunications
% Telecommunications Systems
P.O. Box 28
Pasadena, MD 21122
(301) 685-3300
Contact: Richard Vega
Purpose: An association of common (cable) carriers.

Common Cause
2030 M St., NW
Washington, DC 20036
(202) 833-1200
Contact: John W. Gardner
Purpose: A consumer group seeking to make the government aware of and sympathetic to the needs of the nation, with heavy interest in television programming.

Communication Commission
475 Riverside Dr.
New York, NY 10027
(212) 870-2567
Contact: William F. Fore
Purpose: An organization of the National Churches of Christ that produces religious television and radio programs.

Communications
Church of the Brethren General Board
1451 Dundee Ave.
Elgin, IL 60120
(312) 742-5100
Contact: Kermon Thomason
Purpose: An organization that promotes religious broadcasting.

Communications Workers of America
1925 K St., NW
Washington, DC 20006
(202) 785-6700
Contact: Glenn Watts
Purpose: A union of communication workers.

Community Broadcasters Association
3219 W. State Rd.
Olean, NY 14760
(716) 372-0161
Contact: John R. Henzel
Purpose: An organization of owners and operators of class-IV radio stations.

Concert Music Broadcasters Association
Penthouse E, Terminal Tower
Cleveland, OH 44113
(216) 241-0900
Contact: C. K. Patrick
Purpose: An organization that promotes the broadcasting of concert music.

Conference of State Cable Agencies
Tower Bldg.
Empire State Plaza
Albany, NY 12223
(518) 474-4992
Contact: George A. Cincotta
Purpose: A conference of New York State cable agencies concerned with improvements in the cable-television industry.

Connecticut Broadcasters Association
15 Highland Park Rd.
North Haven, CT 06473
(203) 771-6433
Contact: Peter K. Orne
Purpose: A state organization of broadcasters.

Corporation for Public Broadcasting
1111 16th St., NW
Washington, DC 20036
(202) 293-6160
Contact: Henry Loomis
Purpose: An agency promoting noncommercial radio and television.

Council on Children, Media and Merchandising
1346 Connecticut Ave., NW, Suite 523
Washington, DC 20036
(202) 466-2583
Contact: Robert B. Choate
Purpose: An organization seeking the FTC's regulation of advertising directed at children.

Council for UHF Broadcasting
P.O. Box 23640
L'Enfant Plaza Station
Washington, DC 20024
(202) 488-5022
Contact: Daniel Wells
Purpose: An alliance of eight organizations that lobby for UHF broadcasting.

Directors Guild of America
7950 Sunset Blvd.
Hollywood, CA 90046
(213) 656-1220
Contact: Michael Franklin
Purpose: An independent union of radio, TV, and film directors.

Educational Broadcasting Corporation
356 W. 58th St.
New York, NY 10019
(212) 560-2000
Contact: John Jay Iselin
Purpose: The owner and licensee of WNET (Channel 13) television.

Educational Communication Association
960 National Press Bldg.
14th & F Sts., NW
Washington, DC 20004
(202) 393-6267
Contact: Ella F. Harlee
Purpose: An educational organization seeking to encourage multi-media programs to help society.

Educational Film Library Association
43 W. 61st St., 9th Floor
New York, NY 10023
(212) 246-4533
Contact: Nadine Covert
Purpose. An association that evaluates audiovisual educational materials.

Executive Council of the Episcopal Church
Radio-TV Division
815 2nd Ave.
New York, NY 10017
(212) 867-8400
Contact: McGee Anderson
Purpose: An organization promoting religious programming.

Federal Communications Bar Association
P.O. Box 32251
Washington, DC 20007
(202) 331-4520
Contact: Edgar W. Holtz
Purpose: An association of attorneys that practice before the Federal Communications Commission.

Film and Television Coordination Committee
Publicists Guild
1427 N. LaBrea Ave.
Los Angeles, CA 90028
(213) 851-1600
Contact: Mac St. Johns
Purpose: An organization seeking to reduce the number of reruns presented during prime time.

Florida Association of Broadcasters
3131 N.W. 13th St., Suite 37
Gainesville, FL 32601
(904) 372-0708
Contact: Gert Schmidt
Purpose: A state organization of broadcasters.

Forest Industries Telecommunications
Box 5446
Eugene, OR 97405
(503) 485-8441
Contact: James H. Baker
Purpose: An organization that informs the Federal Communications Commission of communications matters regarding the forest industries.

Foundation to Improve Television
50 Congress St., Room 925
Boston, MA 02109
(617) 523-5520
Contact: William S. Abbott
Purpose: A consumer group for quality television programming, especially for children.

Hawaiian Association of Broadcasters
1534 Kapiolani Blvd.
Honolulu, HI 96814
(808) 941-3011
Contact: Dick Weinea
Purpose: A state organization of broadcasters.

Health Sciences Communications Association
P.O. Box 79
Millbrae, CA 94030
(415) 666-1958
Contact: Thomas L. Banks
Purpose: A health organization that gathers and distributes information dealing with health-sciences communications.

Hollywood Radio and Television Society
1717 N. Highland Ave.
Hollywood, CA 90028
(213) 465-1183
Contact: Oliver H. Crawford
Purpose: A membership organization of people in radio, television and advertising.

Idaho State Broadcasters Association
Box 884
Boise, ID 83701
(208)
Contact: Harold Hirte
Purpose: A state organization of broadcasters.

Indiana Broadcasters Association
1111 E. 54th St.
Indianapolis, IN 46220
(317) 251-3704
Contact: Tom Hines
Purpose: A state organization of broadcasters.

Industrial Audio-Visual Association
Box 656, Downtown Station
Chicago, IL 60690
(312) 662-3460
Contact: Frederick J. Woldt
Purpose: A professional organization of audiovisual department managers concerned with raising the standards of industry operations.

Industrial Communication Council
P.O. Box 3970
Grand Central Post Office
New York, NY 10017
(212) 661-5080
Contact: Mariam Goldfine
Purpose: An organization for improving communications between its members and their customers, employees, and stockholders.

Institute of Broadcasting Financial Management
360 N. Michigan Ave.
Chicago, IL 60601
(312) 332-1295
Contact: Robert E. McAuliffe
Purpose: A business organization concerned with the financial management of the radio and television industry.

Institute for Education by Radio–Television
Ohio State University
Fawcett Center for Tomorrow
2400 Olentangy River Rd.
Columbus, OH 43210
(614) 421-2540
Contact: Liz Young
Purpose: An organization seeking the advancement of radio and television as educational tools.

Intercollegiate Broadcasting System
3107 Westover Dr., SE
Washington, DC 20020
(202) 582-7210
Contact: George Abraham
Purpose: An academic organization seeking to promote high standards among college radio stations.

Intermedia
475 Riverside Dr.
New York, NY 10027
(212) 870-2376
Contact: Vern Rossman
Purpose: To promote the use of radio, television, audiovisual aids, publishing houses, and bookstores for the advancement of the Christian ministry around the world.

International Communications Association
Box 836
Bellaire, TX 77401
(713) 666-3067
Contact: Roger Aude
Purpose: An organization seeking to advance communications.

International Council of the National Academy of Television Arts & Sciences
110 W. 57th St.
New York, NY 10019
(212) 765-2450
Contact: Bob Howard
Purpose: An organization seeking to promote international television and improve communications.

International Industrial Television Association
26 South St.
New Providence, NJ 07974
(201) 464-6747
Contact: Ms. Bobette Kandle
Purpose: An organization promoting the arts and sciences in non-broadcasting industrial television.

International Radio and Television Foundation, Inc.
420 Lexington Ave., Room 531
New York, NY 10017
(212) 867-6650
Contact: Stephen B. Labunski
Purpose: A professional organization promoting the radio and television industry.

International Telecommunication
Satellite Organization
490 L'Enfant Plaza East, SW
Washington, DC 20024
(202) 488-2300
Contact: S. Astrain
Purpose: An organization concerned with the development, maintenance, and operation of the space segment of the global communications satellite system.

Iowa Broadcasters Association
1230 Marston Ave.
Ames, IA 50010
(515) 294-4340
Contact: Jack Shelley
Purpose: A state organization of broadcasters.

Japan Broadcasting Corporation
850 3rd Ave.
New York, NY 10022
(212) 371-2772
Contact: Shoji Yoshino
Purpose: The New York news bureau of a Japanese television network.

Joint Council on Education Telecommunications
1126 16th St., NW
Washington, DC 20036
(202) 659-9740
Contact: Frank W. Norwood
Purpose: An educational committee designed to keep tabs on advancements in communication technology and make people aware of education's needs in the field of telecommunications.

Joint Media Committee on News Coverage Problems
Columbia Broadcasting System, Inc.
530 W. 52nd St.
New York, NY 10019
(212) 975-2781
Contact: William Small
Purpose: An organization concerned with solving news-coverage problems.

The Joint Telecommunication Advisory Committee
345 E. 47th St.
New York, NY 10017
(212) 644-7900
Contact: Audrey Mikel
Purpose: A committee that evaluates technical or engineering data relating to the radio industry.

Louisiana Association of Broadcasters
% WPRZ
Box 2906
Baton Rouge, LA 70893
(504) 387-2222
Contact: Jules Mayeaux
Purpose: A state organization of broadcasters.

Lutheran Church in America
Department of Press, Radio & Television
231 Madison Ave.
New York, NY 10016
(212) 481-9669
Contact: Marshall Stross
Purpose: A division of the Lutheran church concerned with promoting religious programming on radio and television, and in newspapers.

Maine Association of Broadcasting
Box 307
Augusta, ME 04330
(207) 623-3878
Contact: Norman Gallant
Purpose: A state organization of broadcasters.

Marketing Communications Executives International
2130 Delancey Pl.
Philadelphia, PA 19103
(215) 732-9340
Contact: A. O. Dietrich
Purpose: A business organization seeking to promote research in marketing communications.

Maryland–District of Columbia–Delaware Broadcasters Association
Rte. 1, Box 125
St. Michaels, MD 21665
(301) 745-5155
Contact: Bob Cockrin
Purpose: A regional organization of broadcasters.

Mass Communications History Center
State Historical Society of Wisconsin
816 State St.
Madison, WI 53706
(608) 262-3271
Contact: Janice O'Connell
Purpose: To collect and preserve primary resources relating to broadcasting, the press, advertising, film, theater, and public relations.

Media Research Directors Association
Parade Magazine
733 3rd Ave.
New York, NY 10017
(212) 953-7574
Contact: Morton M. Vitriol
Purpose: An organization of national newspaper, magazine, and broadcasting research directors.

Media Services Center
American Lutheran Church
TV/Radio/Films
1568 Eustis St.
St. Paul, MN 55108
(612) 645-9173
Contact: John Brekke
Purpose: An organization that produces television and radio programs for the national office of the American Lutheran Church and serves as a liaison between the church and public media.

Media Studies Program
66 5th Ave.
New York, NY 10011
(212) 741-8903
Contact: Dr. John Culkin
Purpose: A graduate program concerned with improving the use of media as educational tools.

Michigan Association of Broadcasters
Box 16015
Lansing, MI 48901
(517) 371-1729
Contact: Thomas M. Girocco
Purpose: A state organization of broadcasters.

Missouri Broadcasters Association
1800 Southwest Blvd.
Jefferson City, MO 65101
(314) 636-6692
Contact: Ted Griffin
Purpose: A state organization of broadcasters.

Morality in Media
487 Park Ave.
New York, NY 10022
(212) 752-7611
Contact: Morton A. Hill
Purpose: A consumer group concerned about the problem of pornography in the media and desiring to set up standards of censorship.

Motion Picture and Television Credit Association
1725 Beverly Blvd.
Los Angeles, CA 90026
(213) 483-4694
Contact: Fabian Berke
Purpose: An organization of credit executives of the movie and television industries.

Motion Picture and Television Fund
335 N. LaBrea Ave.
Los Angeles, CA 90036
(213) 937-7250
Contact: Jack E. Staggs
Purpose: A welfare organization seeking to provide hospital and medical care for its members in the film and television fields.

Museum of Broadcasting
1 E. 53rd St.
New York, NY 10022
(212) 475-7986
Contact: Robert Saudek
Purpose: A museum devoted to the history and technological development of broadcasting.

National Academy of Television Arts & Sciences
110 W. 57th St.
New York, NY 10032
(212) 586-8424
Contact: John Cannon
Purpose: An organization seeking to promote excellence in all facets of television.

National Alliance of Television and Electronic Service Associations
5906 S. Troy St.
Chicago, IL 60629
(312) 476-6363
Contact: Frank J. Moch
Purpose: An organization of businesses that repair and service TV, radio, hi-fi, and appliance equipment.

National Appliance and Radio-TV Dealers Association
2 N. Riverside Plaza, Suite 222
Chicago, IL 60606
(312) 454-0944
Contact: Jules Steinberg
Purpose: An organization designed to help dealerships become more profitable.

National Association for Better Broadcasting
P.O. Box 43640
Los Angeles, CA 90043
(213) 474-3283
Contact: James V. Bennett
Purpose: A consumer group seeking to promote quality radio and television programming.

National Association of Broadcast Employees and Technicians
1701 Wisconsin Ave.
Washington, DC 20014
(202) 657-8420
Contact: Edward M. Lynch
Purpose: A union of broadcast employees and technicians.

National Association of Broadcasters
1771 N St., NW
Washington, DC 20036
(202) 293-3500
Contact: Vincent T. Wasilewski
Purpose: An organization aimed at setting up voluntary codes for keeping high standards in radio and television broadcasting.

National Association of Educational Broadcasters
1346 Connecticut Ave., NW
Washington, DC 20036
(202) 785-1100
Contact: Jim Fillows
Purpose: An educational organization working to improve educational broadcasting.

National Association of Farm Broadcasters
P.O. Box 119
Topeka, KS 66601
(913) 272-3456
Contact: George Logan
Purpose: A group promoting more and better programs concerned with farming.

National Association of Independent Television Producers and Distributors
375 Park Ave.
New York, NY 10022
(212) 751-0600 ext. 236
Contact: Giraud Chester
Purpose: An association of independent television producers and distributors.

National Association of Media Women
157 W. 126th St.
New York, NY 10027
(212) 666-1320
Contact: Leona Brady
Purpose: A group of professional women seeking to promote the advancement of women in the field of mass communication.

National Association of State Educational Department Information Officers
Publications and Information
Georgia Dept. of Education
Atlanta, GA 30334
(404) 656-2476
Contact: Anne Raymond
Purpose: An educational organization seeking to improve the quality of public information in education.

National Association of Television Program Executives
Box 5272
Lancaster, PA 17601
(717) 626-4424
Contact: Pat Evans
Purpose: A trade organization seeking to improve television programming.

National Association of Television and Radio Announcers
3705 Liberty Heights
Baltimore, MD 21215
Contact: Al Germany
Purpose: A trade organization seeking to promote the educational and professional aspects of communications.

National Audio-Visual Association
3150 Spring St.
Fairfax, VA 22030
(703) 273-7200
Contact: Harry R. McGee
Purpose: A business organization of dealers, manufacturers, producers, and suppliers of audiovisual products.

National Broadcast Editorial Association
% KOMO-TV
100 4th Ave. N
Seattle, WA 98109
(206) 223-4000
Contact: Art McDonald
Purpose: A membership organization of those involved in both the preparation and the delivery of broadcast editorials.

National Cable Television Association
918 16th St., NW
Washington, DC 20006
(202) 457-6700
Contact: Robert L. Schmidt
Purpose: A business organization seeking to advance the cable television industry.

National Cable Television Institute
16075 W. Belleview Ave.
Morrison, CO 80465
(303) 697-4967
Contact: Roland D. Hieb
Purpose: An educational institution providing technical information and training materials to the cable-television industry.

National Center on Educational Media and Materials for the Handicapped
Ohio State University
Columbus, OH 43210
(614) 422-6446
Contact: S. C. Ashcroft
Purpose: An organization that distributes educational materials to handicapped students.

National Citizens Committee for Broadcasting
1028 Connecticut Ave., NW, Room 918
Washington, DC 20036
(202) 466-8407
Contact: Pat Scott
Purpose: A consumer group seeking to improve the quality of broadcasting.

National Committee for UHF Television
% CBN Television
P.O. Box 111
Portsmouth, VA 23725
(804) 499-8241
Contact: Scott Hessek
Purpose: A group seeking to increase UHF viewership and inform the public about UHF television.

National Council of Churches Communication Commission
475 Riverside Dr., Room 856
New York, NY 10027
(212) 870-2567
Contact: D. Williams McClurken
Purpose: A division of the National Council of Churches seeking to promote religious programming through radio, television, and the press.

National Education Association
1201 16th St., NW
Washington, DC 20036
(202) 833-4484
Contact: Terry Herndon
Purpose: An organization of educators that promotes American education, with interest in all media.

National News Council
1 Lincoln Plaza
New York, NY 10023
(212) 595-9411
Contact: William B. Arthur
Purpose: An organization protective of freedom of the press.

National Press Club
National Press Bldg.
529 14th St., NW
Washington, DC 20045
(202) 737-2500
Contact: Frank R. Aukofer
Purpose: An organization of reporters, writers, and other news people involved in all forms of news media.

National Religious Broadcasters
Box 2254R
Morristown, NJ 07960
(201) 540-8500
Contact: Dr. Abe C. Van Der Puy
Purpose: An organization seeking to promote religious broadcasting around the world.

Nebraska Broadcasters Association
Box 31802
Omaha, NB 68131
(402) 551-4360
Contact: John Howard
Purpose: A state organization of broadcasters.

Nevada Broadcasters Association
Box 2427
Reno, NV 89505
(702) 825-3465
Contact: James C. Herzig
Purpose: A state organization of broadcasters.

New Jewish Media Project
15 E. 26th St.
New York, NY 10010
(212) 689-0790
Contact: Eric Goldman
Purpose: Promoting the use of audiovisual materials in Jewish interest areas.

New Mexico Broadcasters Association
709 Fruit Ave.
Albuquerque, NM 87102
(505) 897-0692
Contact: Dick McKee
Purpose: A state organization of broadcasters.

Newswomen's Club of New York
52 E. 41st St.
New York, NY 10017
(212) 685-1347
Contact: Christiana Kich
Purpose: An organization of women in the news media that promotes professional, social, and charitable activities.

New York State Broadcasters Association, Inc.
9 Herbert Dr.
Latham, NY 12110
(518) 783-5821
Contact: Leavitt J. Pope
Purpose: A state organization of broadcasters.

North American Broadcast Section of World Association for Christian Communications
600 Palms Bldg.
Detroit, MI 48201
(313) 962-0340
Contact: Rev. Ed Willingham
Purpose: A division of the World Association for Christian Communications, seeking to promote religious broadcasting in North America.

North Carolina Association of Broadcasters
BB&T Bldg., Suite 300
Raleigh, NC 27602
(919) 821-7300
Contact: Jerry Oakley
Purpose: A state organization of broadcasters.

North Dakota Broadcasters Association
Box 5347, University Station
Fargo, ND 58102
(701) 237-8321
Contact: C. H. Logan
Purpose: A state organization of broadcasters.

Office for Film and Broadcasting
U.S. Catholic Conference
1011 1st Ave., Suite 1300
New York, NY 10022
(212) 644-1800
Contact: Rev. Patrick J. Sullivan, S.J.
Purpose: An organization that reviews films.

Ohio Association of Broadcasters
41 High St., S
Columbus, OH 43215
Contact: Thomas Sawyer
Purpose: A state organization of broadcasters.

Permanent Charities Committee of the Entertainment Industries
463 N. LaCienega Blvd.
Los Angeles, CA 90048
(213) 652-4680
Contact: William E. Arnold
Purpose: Administers an annual fund-raising campaign for health and welfare organizations in and around Los Angeles.

Prime Time School Television
120 S. LaSalle St., Room 810
Chicago, IL 60603
(312) 368-1088
Contact: William S. Singer
Purpose: A consumer group promoting prime time television viewing for educational purposes.

Producers Guild of America
8201 Beverly Blvd., Suite 500
Los Angeles, CA 90048
(213) 651-0084
Contact: Stanley Rubin
Purpose: An organization of TV and film producers.

Protestant Radio & Television Center
1727 Clifton Rd., NE
Atlanta, GA 30329
(404) 634-3324
Contact: William Horlock
Purpose: To provide syndicated religious programs to radio and television and to meet the religious needs of various groups.

Publi-Cable
1201 16th St., NW
Washington, DC 20036
(202) 833-4108
Contact: Ralph Lee Smith
Purpose: A consumer group seeking to promote interest in broadband communications.

Radio & Television Correspondents Association
% U.S. Capitol, Room S-312
Washington, DC 20510
(202) 224-6421
Contact: Joe Benton
Purpose: A professional organization covering Congressional activities for radio and television stations and networks.

Radio & Television News Directors Association
Station WKAR - Radio 310 Auditorium
Michigan State University
East Lansing, MI 48824
(517) 355-6540
Contact: Rob Downey
Purpose: An association seeking to improve broadcast journalism.

Rocky Mountain Broadcasters Association
Box 220
Pocatello, ID 83201
(208) 233-5020
Contact: Henry Fletcher
Purpose: A regional organization of broadcasters.

Screen Actors Guild
7750 Sunset Blvd.
Hollywood, CA 90046
(213) 876-3030
Contact: Chester L. Migden
Purpose. A labor organization for actors and actresses.

Society for the Advancement of Education
1860 Broadway
New York, NY 10023
(212) 265-6680
Contact: Stanley Lehrer ·
Purpose: An organization in behalf of education in relation to radio and television.

Society of Broadcast Engineers, Inc.
Box 50844
Indianapolis, IN 46250
(317) 842-0836
Contact: Glenn Lahman
Purpose: A membership organization of radio & television engineers.

Society of Cable Television Engineers
1100 17th St., NW, Suite 506
Washington, DC 20036
(202) 659-2131
Contact: Charles S. Tepfer
Purpose: A professional group seeking to raise standards in cable-television engineering and promote interest in the field.

Society of Data Educators
983 Fairmeadow Rd.
Memphis, TN 38117
(901) 761-0727
Contact: Dr. Dana H. Verry
Purpose: An educational society promoting computers in education.

Society of Motion Picture and Television Art Directors
7715 Sunset Blvd.
Hollywood, CA 90046
(213) 876-4330
Contact: Gene Allen
Purpose: An organization of art supervisors of movie and television set design.

Society of Motion Picture and Television Engineers
862 Scarsdale Ave.
Scarsdale, NY 10583
(914) 472-6606
Contact: Denis A. Courtney
Purpose: A group of engineers and technicians seeking to improve engineering technology in the motion picture industry.

Society of Television Pioneers
P.O. Box 1475
Lubbock, TX 79408
(806) 762-0404
Contact: W. D. Rogers, Jr.
Purpose: A membership organization of the first owners and executives of TV stations and networks.

Southern Baptist Radio & Television Commission
International Communications Center
6350 W. Freeway
Fort Worth, TX 76150
(817) 737-4011
Contact: Dr. Paul M. Stevens
Purpose: An organization of the Southern Baptist Church seeking to promote religious programming world wide.

Southern California Broadcasters Association
1800 N. Highland Ave., Suite 609
Hollywood, CA 90028
(213) 466-4481
Contact: Robert M. Light
Purpose: A regional organization of broadcasters.

Station Representatives Association
230 Park Ave., Room 1565
New York, NY 10017
(212) 687-2484
Contact: M. S. Keliner
Purpose: An association of sales representatives who sell spot advertising on radio or television.

Television Bureau of Advertising, Inc.
1345 Ave. of the Americas
New York, NY 10019
(212) 397-3456
Contact: Roger D. Rice
Purpose: A group promoting television for advertising.

Television Information Office
745 5th Ave.
New York, NY 10022
(212) 759-6800
Contact: Roy Danish
Purpose: A television organization seeking to promote understanding between the audience and the television industry.

Television Programmers Conference
%WTMJ
720 E. Capital Dr.
Milwaukee, WI 53201
(414) 332-9611
Contact: Jerry McGrath
Purpose: An organization that promotes quality programming on television.

Tennessee Association of Broadcasters
Box 2688
Nashville, TN 37219
(615) 254-5671
Contact: Harold Crump
Purpose: A state organization of broadcasters.

United Church of Christ
Office of Communication
289 Park Ave. South
New York, NY 10010
(212) 475-2127
Contact: Rev. Everett C. Parker
Purpose: A division of the United Church of Christ seeking to promote religious broadcasting.

United Methodist Church
Division of Public Media
475 Riverside Dr., Suite 1370
New York, NY 10027
(212) 663-8900
Contact: Nelson Price
Purpose: A division of the Methodist Church promoting religious broadcasting of quality.

United Nations Office of Public Information
Radio and Visual Services Division
1st Ave. at 42nd St.
New York, NY 10017
(212) 754-1234
Contact: Marcel Martin
Purpose: An organization seeking to produce news coverage of quality.

United Presbyterian Church in the U.S.A.
Dept. of Broadcasting
475 Riverside Dr., Room 1940
New York, NY 10027
(212) 870-3101
Contact: Robert Thomson
Purpose: A division of the United Presbyterian Church promoting religious broadcasting.

United Press International
220 E. 42nd St.
New York, NY 10017
(212) 682-0400
Contact: R. W. Beaton
Purpose: A wire service providing radio, television, and the press with news.

Variety Clubs International
Tower 58
58 W. 58th St., Suite 23-C
New York, NY 10019
(212) 751-8600
Contact: Morton Sunshine
Purpose: An organization concerned with sponsoring charity programs for children on television and other media.

Vermont Association of Broadcasters
Box 608
Burlington, VT 05401
(802) 658-6300
Contact: Peter Martin
Purpose: A state organization of broadcasters.

Veterans Hospital Radio & Television Guild
1841 Broadway
New York, NY 10023
(212) 757-8657
Contact: Alex F. Courtney
Purpose: A professional group teaching hospitalized veterans how to produce and air their own radio and TV programs over closed-circuit networks.

Videotape Production Association
63 W. 83rd St.
New York, NY 10024
(212) 935-2220
Contact: Morton Dubin
Purpose: A business group that promotes videotape as a means of communication.

Virginia Association of Broadcasters
301 E. Market St.
Charlottesville, VA 22901
(804) 977-3716
Contact: Peter Easter
Purpose: A state association of broadcasters.

Washington Area Broadcasters Association
4461 Connecticut Ave.
Washington, DC 20008
(202) 686-3000
Contact: Thomas Cookerly
Purpose: An association of broadcasters in and around the capital.

Washington State Association of Broadcasters
1411 4th Ave., Suite 1015
Seattle, WA 98101
(206) 622-2991
Contact: James A. Murphy
Purpose: A state organization of broadcasters.

West Virginia Broadcasters Association
1910 Parkview St.
Huntington, WV 25701
(304) 522-2905
Contact: Jack Williams
Purpose: A state organization of broadcasters.

Western Educational Society for Telecommunications (W)
KOCE-TV
P.O. Box 2476
Huntington Beach, CA 92647
(714) 897-0302
Contact: Ann Murdock
Purpose: A professional group promoting educational television and serving as a consulting service on telecommunications.

White House Correspondents Association
National Press Bldg.
Washington, DC 20045
(202) 737-2934
Contact: Aldo B. Beckman
Purpose: An organization of Washington television, radio, newspaper, and magazine correspondents that deal entirely in news work.

Wisconsin Broadcasters Association
Box 11725
Shorewood, WI 53211
(414) 332-8270
Contact: Joe Killeen
Purpose: A state organization of broadcasters.

Women in Communications
8305-A Shoal Creek Blvd.
Austin, TX 78758
(512) 452-0019
Contact: Mary E. Utting
Purpose: A society of women professionals in journalism and communications.

Worldwide TV-FM DX Association
Box 202
Whiting, IN 46394
(219) 659-2954
Contact: Frank Aden, Jr.
Purpose: A group that promotes long-distance TV and radio viewing and listening.

Writers Guild of America, East
22 E. 48th St.
New York, NY 10026
(212) 575-5060
Contact: Keith Johnson
Purpose: A labor union for writers from the radio, television, and motion picture industries.

Writers Guild of America, West
8955 Beverly Blvd.
Los Angeles, CA 90048
(213) 550-1000
Contact: Leonard Chassman
Purpose: A labor union for writers from the radio, television, and motion picture industries.

Young Audiences
115 E. 92nd St.
New York, NY 10028
(212) 831-8110
Contact: Warren Yost
Purpose: A group that seeks to present live programs in the performing arts to children in grades K–12.

Audience Research

A.C. Nielsen Company

A.C. Nielsen Company was founded in 1923. In the beginning, the company pioneered in "Performance Surveys" for manufacturers of industrial machinery and equipment. But this service proved to be very hard to produce and even harder to sell.

In 1933, the company launched a continuous marketing service known as the Nielsen Drug Index. This service used a standing panel of drug stores to provide measurements of sales and sales influencing factors for products sold through this type of outlet. Seven months later, a parallel service called the Nielsen Food Index was established for the food industry. These services, now known as the Retail Index Services, quickly became, by far, the world's largest marketing research operation—a position it has now held for over 40 years.

Efforts in the area of broadcast audience measurement commenced in 1936 with the acquisition, from Professors Robert F. Elder and Louis Woodruff of Massachusetts Institute of Technology, of an ingenious device known as the "Audimeter." This device was designed to provide a mechanical link between the tuning dial on a radio receiver and a moving roll of paper in such a way that a permanent record of dial position was produced.

After more than six years of costly technical research and pilot testing, the company launched, in 1942, a commercial audience measurement service applicable to radio. As is the case with nearly all advancements, the first service seems rudimentary by today's standards. But at the time, the service represented the application of the most advanced technological, statistical, and data-processing methods and equipment available.

The initial sample consisted of 1,000 Audimeter homes in nine Eastern and Central states. Each of these homes was visited once a month by a full-time fieldman who had the technical training necessary to change the tapes.

Owing to wartime restrictions on the manufacture of the Audimeter, NRI service covered an area that included about 25% of all U.S. radio homes. It is interesting to note, however, that the leading competitor at this time covered approximately 20% of U.S. homes and introduced the additional restriction of being able to contact only telephone homes.

By 1948, Audimeter design had been advanced to the point where they required very little in-field maintenance, and, more importantly, allowed the respondent to mail the permanent record of listening rather than requiring a visit by a technician. Though this step may not sound significant, it provided a basis for expanding home samples into areas that had previously been inaccessible (without introducing unacceptable costs), thus significantly broadening the projectability of the data gathered.

In addition, this development aided entering the field in which Nielsen is now best known—television-audience research. In September of 1950 the Nielsen Television Index, which measures the audiences of *network* television, was launched. In April of 1954 the Nielsen Station Index, which provides parallel information on *local* stations, began operation.

WHY AUDIENCE RESEARCH?

Nielsen audience measurements (including "ratings") were originally devised and developed as an index for the information and guidance of advertisers, advertising agencies, station and network business managers, and others concerned with broadcasting as a medium of advertising.

Their purpose is to report the approximate size and composition of audiences reached. They are roughly comparable in general character and application to the readership figures of newspapers and magazines.

One of the most often encountered misconceptions about ratings is that they are "popularity polls" designed to judge the intrinsic social or artistic value of television programs. There are, however, several factors beyond popularity that affect program ratings.

The first factor is the power and effectiveness of the station or the network on which the program is being broadcast—it is a matter of how well the transmission comes through the air to the antenna of a receiving set. This is sometimes affected by power failures, electrical interference, and other interruptions which can forcibly reduce an audience.

The second factor is the competing strength of programs that may be heard or seen at the same time on rival stations and networks. If a program's competition is weak, it will probably reach a larger audience than if it has very strong competition.

The third factor is the number of people who

are at home, awake, and available at the time the program is broadcast. Even the best program cannot reach the biggest audience if it is broadcast when a large part of the population is out of the home or otherwise occupied.

Therefore, such program qualities as popular appeal, cultural value, or artistic excellence may be insufficient to guarantee a large audience. They may be overcome by one or all of these three sets of circumstances.

The people for whom the ratings are made understand all these facts, but the public and many of the performers assume that the ratings are a critical measure of a program's intrinsic merit—and this mistaken idea produces emotional and personal reactions that blame the television ratings.

Furthermore, good programming requires a certain amount of willingness to venture, and to try new things. It is an art and not a science. As a result, each year brings new program series—some that succeed in reaching large and enthusiastic audiences; others that do not.

But it is important to realize that some programs are designed to reach certain segments of the audience, so mere audience size is not the important thing. There are many programs that are not anywhere near the top of the rating lists but remain on the air because they provide the most efficient vehicle for specific types of advertising.

For example, a manufacturer of a universally used product, such as toilet soap, would reach the greatest number of potential buyers through a program with broad appeal. On the other hand, if a guitar manufacturer were to use the same program, he would be paying to reach a great number of people who do not use his product.

It is therefore important to recognize that ratings are a record of the public's viewing habits, showing with useful accuracy the relative sizes of the different audiences reached by various programs and stations.

It is also important to recognize that a single rating, which shows the audience reached by a program on a given occasion, is seldom useful by itself. Programmers normally watch the trends of ratings over periods of weeks or even months. If this trend shows a clear improvement over a period, it is evidence enough that the program is winning more viewers. But if it shows a marked decline, it is a reasonable conclusion that people are losing interest or that they prefer something else.

MEDIA SERVICES TODAY

As mentioned earlier, Nielsen media services measure either network viewing (NTI) or local station viewing (NSI). Because measurement methods, report types, sampling techniques, etc., are different for the two services, we will describe each separately.

To begin, no television-audience-measurement service can produce audience estimates without an accurate sample—and NTI is no exception.

To do a proper job, a sample needs to reflect, with a proper degree of accuracy, the universe it measures. It is, in effect, a scale model of this universe. The Nielsen TV samples, for example, include all types of households and neighborhoods—in cities, towns, and farms—with and without telephones, geographically dispersed in over 600 counties.

Employing the latest U.S. Census listing of all households in the country and scientific sampling procedures, Nielsen statisticians pre-designate those neighborhoods and housing units that will eventually be providing NTI audience information. Then trained Nielsen in-field surveyors visit these neighborhoods and locate each sample housing unit. But the work doesn't end there. Every year the sample must be updated with new housing units to keep pace with population shifts and growth.

All of this—the design, implementation, and maintenance of the samples—is the responsibility of Nielsen's Statistical Research Department. They in turn work closely with the Field Department to see that the operating sample meets the specification of the sample design.

Most of the pre-designated Nielsen households agree to cooperate. By design, each household is replaced over a five-year period . . . long enough to provide continuity of trend information.

Once this sample has been constructed, and its validity demonstrated, the method used for collecting data becomes the crucial next step.

There are, of course, several techniques for obtaining viewing information from sample households. And while it's true that no technique is perfect, the primary objectives in data collection are accuracy, continuity, speed and objectivity. To achieve these objectives, no system devised to date can substitute for NTI's latest generation of fact-gathering systems—the Storage Instantaneous Audimeter (SIA®).

Installed out of sight in a closet, basement, or cabinet, the SIA home unit silently measures all TV set usage within a household. It stores in its electronic memory exactly when each TV set in the household is turned on, how long it stays on, the channel tuned, and all channel switchings. Even backyard and patio usage of battery portables can be recorded—by a transmitter mounted on the TV set and radio-linked to the Audimeter. The SIA home unit is designed to operate with crystal-controlled accuracy even in the event of temporary power outages. Each SIA home unit is connected to a special phone line used only by NTI. At least twice a day a Central Office computer dials up each home unit and retrieves the stored information. The entire process is automatic and requires no work on the part of the sample household. Two back-up Central Office computers (in two locations) serve as protection against electrical failure.

The Audimeter sample tells us whether a *household* is viewing and what is being viewed. To find out who in the family is watching TV by age and sex, Nielsen places diaries in a separate panel of National Audience Composition (NAC) households during 34 weeks per year, distributed through the four viewing seasons. (One-third of the sample is used in each NAC audit week.)

Each TV set in NAC sample households is equipped with a Recordimeter,® which records the amount of time that that set is in use, information which the diarykeeper enters once a day into the appropriate space on his Audilog®. The quarter-hour entries of viewing are compared with the actual record of elapsed time provided by the Recordimeter.

After the sample has been constructed and the data-collection method has been established, the final step is consolidating the data in ways most meaningful to broadcasters and advertisers. In the case of NTI, the data are present in the form of reports—each of which is designed to fill a particular need.

Filling these needs takes the form of providing "ratings" for specific areas of interest to broadcasters and advertisers. Among currently reported ratings are these:

Average audience rating is the estimated number of households tuned to each network program during the average minute of the telecast, expressed as a percentage of all U.S. TV-equipped households.

Total audience ratings are estimates of households tuned to a program for six or more minutes.

Persons ratings reinforce the evidence provided by household ratings with audience estimates in terms of people—by sex, age, and family role—to pinpoint the degree to which programs with similar household ratings may differ in the age/sex pattern of the persons who view.

These ratings are combined with other useful information, such as number of households using television, share of available audience reached by a program, and number of stations carrying a program, to produce a range of reports that include:

Nielsen national TV ratings ("The Pocketpiece"). The NTI pocketpiece provides the following information about the national TV audience:

1. Household audience estimates for all sponsored network programs.
2. Persons audience estimates ("audience composition") for a large array of persons categories.
3. Season-to-date averages of program performance.
4. Program type averages.
5. Overall TV usage comparisons versus year-ago.
6. TV usage by time periods.

Daily national ratings. Telephone lines link the Storage Instantaneous Audimeter (SIA®) in each NTI household to computer facilities in Dunedin, Florida, making available to clients for each day of the year network program audience estimates on data terminals in their own offices. Prime-time network program ratings are generally available on the morning of the second weekday following the telecast.

Fast weekly household (FWH) ratings. These compact reports provide audience estimates for all sponsored network programs, 52 weeks per year, and are generally available on the second Monday following the end of the report week.

Fast evening persons (FEP) audiences. This report is issued weekly during the first 22 (or more) weeks of the TV season. It provides persons-audience estimates (as 2-week moving averages) for evening programs and is available only 2 days after the Fast Weekly Household Ratings Report. It is NTI's fastest persons-audiences report.

Fast multi-network area ratings. This report recaps the 70-market Dailies on a weekly basis. It is generally available to clients on the Friday following the end of each report week.

Households and persons ranking (HPR) report. This report shows the ranking, rating, and projected audience of each network program, in terms of households and 15 persons categories. It is issued biweekly (17 times a year), concurrently with each pocketpiece which contains audience composition data.

In addition to these regular reports, NTI produces "Analysis Reports" to examine questions beyond per-telecast audience estimates. Among these reports are the following:

NTI/NAC audience demographics (NAD) report. For a multi-dimensional picture of the TV audience, NTI offers the NAD report. It provides comprehensive detail on household and persons audiences in terms of overall TV usage, program-type averages, and individual network programs. *Volume 1* is a compact summary of *Total U.S.* audiences—households and 32 persons categories—more age breaks than in any other NTI report. *Volume 2* provides households and persons audience estimates (for 16 persons categories) within a wide array of market sections (territories, household size, household income, education, etc.). Nearly 500 audience estimates describe the kind of viewers reached by each network program. Overall TV usage (by 38 day parts) is reported in similar detail.

Market section audiences (MSA) report. This report provides household audiences by market sections for overall TV usage, program type averages, and individual network programs. The market section data in this report are the earliest available estimates of audiences among particular categories of households.

Program and brand cumulative audiences reports. With today's advertising schedules spread across many programs, day parts, and networks, it is difficult to estimate an advertiser's reach and frequency for a brand's total schedule. Cumulative Audience reports provide advertisers with estimates of the number of households reached in four weeks, by brand and program, including frequency distribution by number of messages received and cost efficiency comparisons.

NAC cost supplement. Appraisal of a program as a "good" or "bad" buy depends not only on the size and demographic distribution of its audience but also on its cost. The NAC Cost Supplement relates cost to audience (in terms of "Estimated Cost per 1000 Commercial 30 Seconds Delivered"), among households and 13 categories of persons.

In addition to ratings and analysis reports, NTI provides the following summary reports simply as a convenience to clients who want to "get it all together" in a minimum of space.

Program tracking report. Issued monthly, each page chronicles a program's performance (in terms of household audience—and in the context of its competition during the preceding 13–24 months), so that trends can be readily evaluated.

Persons tracking report. A companion to the preceding report, issued eight times a year with trends for a year, plus multi-month averages and a wide range of persons data for each program including "specials."

HUT summary report. A program's performance is affected by TV usage levels in its time period. This report, issued quarterly, provides estimates of Total U.S. TV usage (sometimes called "the available audience") for each half-hour time period as weekly and monthly averages and for the four most recent quarters as quarterly and annual averages. In addition, TV usage is shown by major day parts.

INTERPRETATION

The data produced by NTI are, of course, subject to a wide range of applications and many of these would require a complete textbook to explain. What follows is a brief description of some of the more common uses, and is by no means exhaustive.

Three important concepts are involved in any analysis of ratings information: Average Audience, Total Audience, and Share of Audience. Average Audience is simply the program's audience during the average minute, which, in effect, shows the audience size during any one (average) commercial. Total Audience is the number of households tuned to at least six minutes of a program and provides an indication of the number of households that may be reached by at least one message in the course of a telecast. Share of Audience figures express the ratio of a telecast's audience to the total number of households viewing at the time of broadcast, to permit equating programs aired during low-television-usage periods to those broadcast during high-usage periods.

The applications of data can relate in many ways to the general marketing policies of the advertiser. For example, some advertisers feel that repetition of a commercial message is the quickest way to sell a product. Their research objective would then be to measure the number of households reached and the frequency with which they are reached and then to select programs with parallel audiences. Another advertiser might feel that his message is strong enough to make the sale the first time around. His research objective would then be to select programs with dissimilar audiences to provide the largest number of households reached.

For the majority of advertisers, however, the objective is to establish the best balance of reach and frequency. NTI's data are designed to permit users to determine which combination of programs and messages provides the best reach, frequency, or combination of both.

NIELSEN STATION INDEX

As noted earlier, NTI is designed to estimate national audience sizes for network programming. It does not provide local audience estimates for individual markets or for individual stations. These estimates are provided by NTI's companion service, the Nielsen Station Index (NSI).

NSI provides measurements of all television viewing within over 200 specific television markets at various intervals, depending on the size of the market. The larger the market, the more frequently it is measured.

The most significant difference between NTI and NSI lies in the method used to collect data. Where NTI uses the Audimeter in conjunction with a diary panel to provide raw data, NSI relies upon an Audimeter/diary panel only in the three largest metropolitan areas (New York, Chicago, and Los Angeles). The remaining metropolitan areas are measured through specially selected diary panels. These panels are chosen to reflect the relative importance of the business decisions made with local television audience research while taking into account any problems associated with measuring a particular market or market type (for example, a market with a high concentration of Spanish-language homes).

All NSI Viewers-In-Profile reports (which will be described in greater detail later) are based upon a sample of residential phone listings selected freshly for each measurement interval. These listings are provided by an organization that maintains a listing of approximately 51 million residential telephones compiled from approximately 4,000 alphabetical and street address telephone directories.

To identify the specific households to be contacted, a random-number technique is used. For example, assume a sampling area has 100,000 unduplicated residential telephone listings and the desired gross sample size necessary is 100. The sampling rate would then be one in 1,000. If a random number of 450 were generated, the computer would select the 450th telephone listing, the 1,450th, the 2,450th, etc., to the 99,450th listing.

In a number of markets, NSI also employs techniques (Total Telephone Frame) that make it possible to include samples of unlisted telephone households. This is accomplished by isolating gaps in the listings and dialing a sampling of those numbers that should be there.

Once the household has been identified, telephone calls are placed to the household to acquire television information and to enlist cooperation. Diaries are then mailed to the sample households. Based upon information gathered from households during the initial interview, additional diaries are sent to those having more than one television, and Spanish-language diaries are sent to those homes in which it was necessary to conduct the interview in Spanish. Simple basic instructions in the diary aid accurate and complete entries of stations, channels, and programs viewed for more than five minutes per quarter-hour and the individuals viewing.

The data gathered through this technique are compiled in NSI's basic information piece, Viewers In Profile. VIP reports include not only overall viewing levels but also pertinent demographic detail. For example, the current format presents ratings for TV households, total persons, total adults, women (by seven age groups), men (by five age groups), teens (12–17), children (2–11), total lady of house, and total working women.

Other data collected include CATV viewing, which is reported separately for those NSI areas having an estimated subscription level between 10% and 90% of all TV households.

Multi-set usage is also recorded in order to accurately report individual station ratings. In multi-set households, duplicate viewing entries are counted only once in compiling the Households Using Television (HUT) figures for the reports. Viewing entries for different stations, however, are counted for each station. As a result, the sum of reported station ratings may equal or exceed the HUT figure.

Supplementary reports. In addition to the regular VIP reports, NSI issues a number of supplementary reports that are based primarily on retabulations of VIP report data. Among them are the following:

Viewers-in-profile reference volumes. At the end of each measurement cycle in which all NSI markets are measured, all VIP reports are combined into the minimum number of volumes to permit rapid comparisons between markets.

Market day-part summaries. These reports include day-part audience summaries, geographic delineations, and appropriate market-data information to provide a quick overview of markets and for broad comparisons.

Network programs by markets. These reports also follow all-market measurement periods and show a station-by-station and Designated Market Area (DMA) audience profile for each qualifying program. The report is a valuable media planning tool in allocating network audiences or expenditures to local TV markets.

DMA test market profiles. Includes market statistics for every DMA in the country in one convenient volume. The volume contains detailed information relating to the media, the marketplace, and population characteristics.

DMA TV trends by season. After the summer all-market measurement, a trend report is issued showing seasonal viewing levels for all 200 DMA's.

DMA audience allocation. Provides information on viewing originating outside the DMA.

Report on syndicated programs. This report shows distributor, program type, household-and-viewer demographics, lead-in audiences, and competition for over 300 syndicated programs appearing in ten or more markets. The report also ranks the programs by demographics and program types.

DMA—CATV audience distribution. Provides a measure of CATV performance in terms of the number of CATV households and share of viewing.

Weekly preview. Eight times annually, Weekly Preview reports are issued and are mailed within fourteen days of the measured weeks. They are designed to provide an early opportunity to evaluate new programs, one-time specials, election coverage, sporting events, and individual movie titles.

In addition to these basic reports, NSI offers a wide range of NSI Plus special analyses and services to extend the usefulness of the data gathered.

© 1977 by A. C. Nielsen Company.

The Arbitron Company

The Arbitron Company was established in 1949 to provide information about the size and composition of the television audience. In 1965, Arbitron began measurement of radio audiences. The primary function of The Arbitron Company is to estimate the size and demographic composition (including an age–sex breakdown) of a television or radio audience. It would be impossible, because of the length of time and huge costs involved, to actually count the number of people watching a particular program at a given time. Thus, audience estimates of television programs are made on the basis of data received from a sample of households in every television coverage area (or television market) in the U.S.

These audience estimates are required by television and radio stations to determine how many persons have been exposed to their commercial message. Television and radio stations, advertisers and their agencies subscribe to Arbitron surveys. Stations use these estimates to decide which programs should be left on the air, which should be cancelled, and which programs should be moved to another time period. Advertisers use the estimates to decide which programs reach the audience most likely to buy their product. Arbitron makes no qualitative judgments; it simply provides data that will assist stations and advertisers in learning what the public is viewing or listening to.

In the production of Arbitron audience estimates, established sampling techniques are used. Sampling is required when it is impossible to survey every person in a specified area. It is the key to all audience measurement. It is also employed in widespread research at all levels of government, business, and industry. For example, the U.S. Census data are based on sampling. Other estimates, such as the monthly cost-of-living index or the daily stock market averages are also based on it. The fact is that almost all of the statistics we hear about each day are developed by sampling.

SELECTING THE SAMPLE

Arbitron employs the services of a company which has every residential telephone listing in the U.S. stored in a computer. These telephone lists are updated daily and are classified so that a sample can be provided representing any geographical area. A sampling quota is established for every county, and by a statistically sound random selection method a computer draws the proper number of sample households required for each survey.

Each household selected is first notified by letter that it will be asked to participate in a one-week survey. A few days later, each is phoned by an Arbitron field representative in regard to the diary Arbitron mails to those who agree to participate, and answers any questions concerning the procedure. The sample households receive one diary for every television set in the home. At the end of the survey week the diary is sealed and returned to Arbitron where the data are entered into computers and processed into audience estimates.

TAKING THE SURVEY

The Arbitron Company does not measure an audience per se, yet it does provide estimates of television viewing and radio listening. These estimates are based on the diary entries provided by the persons taking part in the survey. The data taken from these sample households, which can number anywhere from 800 to 2,000 homes depending on the size of the market and the number of stations to be measured, are then subdivided by computer to indicate audience size and demographic composition for every time period in every day of the survey period. (Demographic composition, as determined by Arbitron, shows the number of men and women by various age groups—e.g., total women, all women in the survey; women 18–49, only those women aged 18–49 who took part in the survey.)

METHODS OF MEASUREMENT

The principal sampling tool for Arbitron television and radio audience reports is the diary—one for each television set in the household for a television survey (since television viewing is considered a family activity), or one for each person aged 12 or over in a household for the radio survey (since radio listening is considered an individual activity).

In the television diary the persons in the sample households fill in the station call letters, the channel number, and the program title of every program viewed. Times for "set on" and "set off" are also noted. There is a page for every day of the survey week with spaces to indicate the age and sex of each person viewing in each time period.

Arbitron also provides audience estimates based on the Telephone Coincidental method. This is a survey made by telephone to get viewing (or listening) data at the exact time that the viewing or listening is taking place—hence the term *coincidental* survey.

Arbitron occasionally uses personal interviews to fulfill the need for certain types of specialized market information, or in the periodic check of its own methodology and procedures.

RATINGS

A rating is an approximation. Even though it is expressed as a number it does not have mathematical precision. A television rating of 20 (indicating that an estimated 20% of all television-equipped households in the survey area were viewing) means *about* 20, not *exactly*. There is a certain plus/minus range around that rating because in any estimate based on a sampling there is statistical imprecision (often termed *standard deviation*). The plus/minus range is also affected by other factors, such as the size of the sample and the number of stations being measured.

The important thing to remember, however, is

that the plus/minus range can be measured mathematically, and Arbitron provides the means by which the user of an Arbitron report can determine for himself the plus/minus range of any rating. He might find, for example, that the hypothetical rating of 20 we have just discussed has a plus/minus range of 3.6. This means that the true rating is somewhere between 16.4 (20−3.6) and 23.6 (20+3.6) with the greater probability of its being at or near the 20.0 mark. (If Arbitron took 100 surveys in the same area at the same time, 95 out of 100 estimates for a particular time period would range between two specific percentages, such as 16.4 and 23.6, with most of the estimates clustered near 20.0.) The same plus/minus factor applies to audience projections other than ratings. They are not intended to be absolute,

but are accurate enough to aid broadcasters and advertisers in making local business decisions.

Arbitron information provided by the Arbitron Company and used with their permission.

ARBITRON COMPARED WITH NIELSEN

The basic difference between Arbitron and Nielsen is the fact that Arbitron does not have a national network measurement system for determining the number of people watching a particular show. Arbitron is basically structured around local markets. It does not use an audiometer (an electronic device attached to a TV to indicate to a computer which shows are being watched).

TV Household Penetration Statistics

This section presents a comparison of Arbitron and Nielsen market analyses and TV household penetration statistics. The two charts indicate how many television households there are in a particular county against the total number of households. Each firm has also given the percentages of households with TV.

This comparison is meant only as a guideline. The figures are the most up-to-date available at the time this book was compiled. Of course, each firm updates its information annually and so the figures change from year to year.

A. C. NIELSEN COMPANY*

COUNTY	MARKET	HOUSEHOLDS	TV's	%
ALABAMA				
Autauga	Montgomery	9,200	9,010	98
Baldwin	Mobile-Pensacola	24,400	23,600	97
Barbour	Columbus, GA	9,200	8,800	96
Bibb	Birmingham, Anniston	4,500	4,340	96
Blount	Birmingham, Anniston	12,300	11,980	97
Bullock	Montgomery	3,500	3,220	92
Bulter	Montgomery	7,300	6,980	96
Calhoun	Birmingham, Anniston	38,800	38,140	98
Chambers	Columbus, GA	13,000	12,750	98
Cherokee	Atlanta	7,000	6,830	98
Chilton	Birmingham, Anniston	10,500	10,200	97
Choctaw	Meridian	5,800	5,390	93
Clarke	Mobile-Pensacola	9,400	8,950	95
Clay	Birmingham, Anniston	5,200	4,980	96
Cleburne	Birmingham, Anniston	4,100	3,950	96
Coffee	Dothan	12,700	12,270	97
Colbert	Huntsville-Decatur, Flornce	17,700	17,190	97
Conecuh	Mobile-Pensacola	5,100	4,830	95
Coosa	Birmingham, Anniston	3,700	3,530	95
Covington	Montgomery	13,300	12,850	97
Crenshaw	Montgomery	5,600	5,420	97
Cullman	Birmingham, Anniston	21,300	21,050	99
Dale	Dothan	13,500	13,160	97
Dallas	Montgomery	18,100	17,350	96
De Kalb	Huntsville-Decatur, Flornce	18,200	17,790	98
Elmore	Montgomery	12,700	12,450	98
Escambia	Mobile-Pensacola	11,500	11,100	97

*Nielsen information © 1978 by A.C. Nielsen Company.

COUNTY	MARKET	HOUSEHOLDS	TV's	%
ALABAMA—*Cont'd*				
Etowah	Birmingham, Anniston	34,100	33,410	98
Fayette	Birmingham, Anniston	6,100	5,910	97
Franklin	Huntsville-Decatur, Flornce	10,300	10,010	97
Geneva	Dothan	8,900	8,690	98
Greene	Birmingham, Anniston	3,200	2,840	89
Hale	Birmingham, Anniston	4,500	4,110	91
Henry	Dothan	5,300	5,180	98
Houston	Dothan	26,000	25,480	98
Jackson	Chattanooga	17,600	17,010	97
Jefferson	Birmingham, Anniston	232,200	227,730	98
Lamar	Columbus-Tupelo	6,400	6,100	95
Lauderdale	Huntsville-Decatur, Flornce	26,200	25,600	98
Lawrence	Huntsville-Decatur, Flornce	9,400	9,040	96
Lee	Columbus, GA	23,500	22,760	97
Limestone	Huntsville-Decatur, Flornce	14,500	14,290	99
Lowndes	Montgomery	3,700	3,460	94
Macon	Montgomery	8,500	8,150	96
Madison	Huntsville-Decatur, Flornce	58,400	57,590	99
Marengo	Meridian	7,800	7,290	93
Marion	Birmingham, Anniston	9,900	9,630	97
Marshall	Huntsville-Decatur, Flornce	21,900	21,450	98
Mobile	Mobile-Pensacola	112,700	110,010	98
Monroe	Mobile-Pensacola	6,800	6,430	95
Montgomery	Montgomery	63,300	61,840	98
Morgan	Huntsville-Decatur, Flornce	30,000	29,490	98
Perry	Birmingham, Anniston	3,900	3,570	92
Pickens	Columbus-Tupelo	7,200	6,940	96
Pike	Montgomery	8,600	8,220	96
Randolph	Atlanta	6,800	6,650	98
Russell	Columbus, GA	14,800	14,240	96
St Clair	Birmingham, Anniston	12,000	11,740	98
Shelby	Birmingham, Anniston	17,400	17,130	98
Sumter	Meridian	5,400	5,140	95
Talladega	Birmingham, Anniston	22,700	22,050	97
Tallapoosa	Montgomery	13,000	12,570	97
Tuscaloosa	Birmingham, Anniston	40,600	39,320	97
Walker	Birmingham, Anniston	23,400	22,900	98
Washington	Mobile-Pensacola	5,300	5,010	95
Wilcox	Montgomery	4,400	4,040	92
Winston	Birmingham, Anniston	7,600	7,440	98
	STATE TOTAL	1,261,900	1,228,570	97
ARIZONA				
Cochise	Tucson (Nogales)	25,800	24,770	96
Coconino	Phoenix, Flagstaff	20,700	18,010	87
Gila	Phoenix, Flagstaff	11,800	11,210	95
Graham	Phoenix, Flagstaff	6,500	5,950	92
Greenlee	Phoenix, Flagstaff	3,900	3,730	96
Maricopa	Phoenix, Flagstaff	455,800	445,480	98
Mohave	Phoenix, Flagstaff	15,600	14,890	95
Navajo	Phoenix, Flagstaff	16,800	13,740	82
Pima	Tucson (Nogales)	168,800	163,920	97
Pinal	Phoenix, Flagstaff	27,500	26,320	96
Santa Cruz	Tucson (Nogales)	5,700	5,310	93
Yavapai	Phoenix, Flagstaff	20,600	19,370	94
Yuma	Yuma-El Centro	24,000	22,670	94

COUNTY	MARKET	HOUSEHOLDS	TV's	%
ARIZONA—*Cont'd*				
Apache-N	Albuquerque, Farmington	8,600	6,190	72
Apache-S	Tucson (Nogales)	2,400	1,700	71
	STATE TOTAL	814,500	783,260	96
ARKANSAS				
Arkansas	Little Rock-Pine Bluff	7,900	7,630	97
Ashley	Monroe-El Dorado	8,700	8,480	97
Baxter	Springfield, MO	9,900	9,500	96
Benton	Joplin-Pittsburg	22,700	21,830	96
Boone	Springfield, MO	9,200	8,750	95
Bradley	Little Rock-Pine Bluff	4,800	4,590	96
Calhoun	Little Rock-Pine Bluff	1,800	1,720	96
Carroll	Springfield, MO	6,000	5,810	97
Chicot	Monroe-El Dorado	5,700	5,320	93
Clark	Little Rock-Pine Bluff	8,100	7,830	97
Clay	Jonesboro	8,100	7,830	97
Cleburne	Little Rock-Pine Bluff	5,600	5,460	98
Cleveland	Little Rock-Pine Bluff	2,500	2,420	97
Columbia	Shreveport	8,700	8,300	95
Conway	Little Rock-Pine Bluff	8,700	8,520	98
Craighead	Jonesboro	22,700	22,040	97
Crawford	Ft. Smith	11,600	11,130	96
Crittenden	Memphis	14,600	14,000	96
Cross	Memphis	6,100	5,880	96
Dallas	Little Rock-Pine Bluff	3,300	3,240	98
Desha	Little Rock-Pine Bluff	5,800	5,570	96
Drew	Little Rock-Pine Bluff	5,600	5,330	95
Faulkner	Little Rock-Pine Bluff	12,500	12,230	98
Franklin	Ft. Smith	4,400	4,230	96
Fulton	Springfield, MO	3,400	3,110	91
Garland	Little Rock-Pine Bluff	26,600	25,470	96
Grant	Little Rock-Pine Bluff	4,300	4,090	95
Greene	Jonesboro	11,300	11,100	98
Hempstead	Shreveport	7,100	6,840	96
Hot Spring	Little Rock-Pine Bluff	8,800	8,460	96
Howard	Shreveport	5,100	4,860	95
Independence	Little Rock-Pine Bluff	9,100	8,730	96
Izard	Springfield, MO	4,200	4,000	95
Jackson	Little Rock-Pine Bluff	8,100	7,800	96
Jefferson	Little Rock-Pine Bluff	27,600	26,710	97
Johnson	Little Rock-Pine Bluff	6,000	5,780	96
Lafayette	Shreveport	3,400	3,230	95
Lawrence	Jonesboro	7,900	7,370	93
Lee	Memphis	5,500	5,120	93
Lincoln	Little Rock-Pine Bluff	3,800	3,670	97
Little River	Shreveport	3,800	3,630	96
Logan	Ft. Smith	6,600	6,390	97
Lonoke	Little Rock-Pine Bluff	10,900	10,570	97
Madison	Springfield, MO	3,900	3,580	92
Marion	Springfield, MO	4,300	4,230	98
Miller	Shreveport	12,300	11,920	97
Mississippi	Memphis	20,400	19,690	97
Monroe	Little Rock-Pine Bluff	4,700	4,340	92
Montgomery	Little Rock-Pine Bluff	2,700	2,610	97
Nevada	Sheveport	4,000	3,870	97
Newton	Springfield, MO	2,600	2,380	92

COUNTY	MARKET	HOUSEHOLDS	TV's	%
ARKANSAS—*Cont'd*				
Ouachita	Little Rock-Pine Bluff	10,400	10,010	96
Perry	Little Rock-Pine Bluff	2,600	2,530	97
Phillips	Memphis	11,800	11,050	94
Pike	Little Rock-Pine Bluff	3,300	3,220	98
Poinsett	Memphis	9,300	8,950	96
Polk	Little Rock-Pine Bluff	6,300	5,930	94
Pope	Little Rock-Pine Bluff	13,100	12,680	97
Prairie	Little Rock-Pine Bluff	3,900	3,780	97
Pulaski	Little Rock-Pine Bluff	118,800	116,450	98
Randolph	Jonesboro	6,400	6,120	96
St Francis	Memphis	10,000	9,510	95
Saline	Little Rock-Pine Bluff	15,100	14,880	99
Scott	Ft. Smith	3,600	3,460	96
Searcy	Little Rock-Pine Bluff	3,200	2,910	91
Sebastian	Ft. Smith	33,200	32,440	98
Sevier	Shreveport	4,900	4,760	97
Sharp	Jonesboro	4,900	4,540	93
Stone	Little Rock-Pine Bluff	2,900	2,770	96
Union	Monroe-El Dorado	16,700	16,350	98
Van Buren	Little Rock-Pine Bluff	3,800	3,710	98
Washington	Tulsa	32,700	31,790	97
White	Little Rock-Pine Bluff	17,800	17,420	98
Woodruff	Little Rock-Pine Bluff	3,800	3,580	94
Yell	Little Rock-Pine Bluff	6,300	6,110	97
	STATE TOTAL	768,200	742,140	97
CALIFORNIA				
Alameda	San Francisco-Oakland	437,200	420,590	96
Alpine	Reno	500	470	94
Amador	Sacramento-Stockton	6,800	6,480	95
Butte	Chico-Redding	51,200	49,020	96
Calaveras	Sacramento-Stockton	6,700	6,520	97
Colusa	Sacramento-Stockton	5,400	5,190	96
Contra Costa-E	Sacramento-Stockton	20,500	20,180	98
Contra Costa-W	San Francisco-Oakland	201,400	197,960	98
Del Norte	Eureka	6,100	5,720	94
El Dorado-E	San Francisco-Oakland	13,600	13,170	97
El Dorado-W	Sacramento-Stockton	13,300	12,840	97
Fresno	Fresno (Visalia)	162,100	157,550	97
Glenn	Chico-Redding	7,500	7,300	97
Humboldt	Eureka	40,100	38,110	95
Imperial	Yuma-El Centro	29,300	27,550	94
Inyo	Los Angeles, Palm Springs	7,200	6,690	93
Kern-E	Los Angeles, Palm Springs	16,500	16,010	97
Kern-W	Bakersfield	107,000	103,950	97
Kings	Fresno (Visalia)	23,500	22,870	97
Lake	San Francisco-Oakland	13,000	12,420	96
Lassen	Reno	7,000	6,670	95
Los Angeles	Los Angeles, Palm Springs	2,742,200	2,660,430	97
Madera	Fresno (Visalia)	17,400	16,890	97
Marin	San Francisco-Oakland	84,800	81,940	97
Mariposa	Fresno (Visalia)	3,700	3,360	91
Mendocino	San Francisco-Oakland	23,100	21,630	94
Merced	Fresno (Visalia)	42,300	40,900	97
Modoc	Chico-Redding	3,400	3,180	94
Mono	Sacramento-Stockton	3,000	2,790	93

COUNTY	MARKET	HOUSEHOLDS	TV's	%
CALIFORNIA—*Cont'd*				
Monterey	Monterey-Salinas	85,500	82,550	97
Napa	San Francisco-Oakland	35,600	34,590	97
Nevada	Sacramento-Stockton	16,700	16,090	96
Orange	Los Angeles, Palm Springs	679,600	667,710	98
Placer	Sacramento-Stockton	36,500	35,710	98
Plumas	Sacramento-Stockton	5,700	5,270	92
Riverside	Los Angeles, Palm Springs	220,100	213,190	97
Sacramento	Sacramento-Stockton	270,200	263,930	98
San Benito	Monterey-Salinas	7,400	7,030	95
San Bernardino	Los Angeles, Palm Springs	267,500	259,950	97
San Diego	San Diego	646,700	627,720	97
San Francisco	San Francisco-Oakland	313,500	290,820	93
San Joaquin	Sacramento-Stockton	103,300	99,860	97
San Luis Obispo	Santa Barbara-Santa Maria	53,700	51,900	97
San Mateo	San Francisco-Oakland	225,700	220,670	98
Santa Barbara	Santa Barbara-Santa Maria	106,400	102,420	96
Santa Clara	San Francisco-Oakland	439,100	428,380	98
Santa Cruz	Monterey-Salinas	70,200	66,930	95
Shasta	Chico-Redding	36,600	35,310	96
Sierra	Sacramento-Stockton	1,300	1,250	96
Siskiyou	Medford-Klamath Falls	14,300	13,450	94
Solano-E	Sacramento-Stockton	37,400	36,660	98
Solano-W	San Francisco-Oakland	33,300	32,580	98
Sonoma	San Francisco-Oakland	101,900	98,310	96
Stanislaus	Sacramento-Stockton	88,000	85,390	97
Sutter	Sacramento-Stockton	17,800	17,360	98
Tehama	Chico-Redding	12,900	12,610	98
Trinity	Chico-Redding	4,400	4,010	91
Tulare	Fresno (Visalia)	77,100	75,110	97
Tuolumne	Sacramento-Stockton	11,000	10,850	99
Ventura	Los Angeles, Palm Springs	161,100	158,070	98
Yolo	Sacramento-Stockton	38,700	37,360	97
Yuba	Sacramento-Stockton	15,900	15,400	97
	STATE TOTAL	8,330,900	8,076,820	97
COLORADO				
Adams	Denver	73,000	72,020	99
Alamosa	Albuquerque, Farmington	4,100	3,960	97
Arapahoe	Denver	82,300	81,560	99
Archuleta	Albuquerque, Farmington	1,200	1,110	93
Baca	Colorado Springs-Pueblo	2,200	2,070	94
Bent	Colorado Springs-Pueblo	2,400	2,340	98
Boulder	Denver	64,400	61,760	96
Chaffee	Denver	4,600	4,490	98
Cheyenne	Colorado Springs-Pueblo	700	660	94
Clear Creek	Denver	1,800	1,760	98
Conejos	Albuquerque, Farmington	2,100	2,020	96
Costilla	Albuquerque, Farmington	1,000	890	89
Crowley	Colorado Springs-Pueblo	1,100	1,080	98
Custer	Colorado Springs-Pueblo	300	280	93
Delta	Grand Junction-Montrose	8,000	7,800	98
Denver	Denver	202,900	196,230	97
Dolores	Albuquerque, Farmington	600	530	88
Douglas	Denver	6,700	6,520	97
Eagle	Denver	3,400	3,220	95
Elbert	Denver	2,400	2,340	98

COUNTY	MARKET	HOUSEHOLDS	TV's	%
COLORADO—*Cont'd*				
El Paso	Colorado Springs-Pueblo	95,500	93,320	98
Fremont	Colorado Springs-Pueblo	10,200	9,890	97
Garfield	Denver	7,700	7,540	98
Gilpin	Denver	900	870	97
Grand	Denver	2,700	2,580	96
Gunnison	Colorado Springs-Pueblo	3,100	2,930	95
Hinsdale	Grand Junction-Montrose	600	600	100
Huerfano	Colorado Springs-Pueblo	2,600	2,560	98
Jackson	Denver	600	580	97
Jefferson	Denver	115,700	113,830	98
Kiowa	Colorado Springs-Pueblo	900	850	94
Kit Carson	Wichita-Hutchinson Plus	3,000	2,930	98
Lake	Denver	3,100	2,930	95
La Plata	Albuquerque, Farmington	8,400	8,030	96
Larimer	Denver	47,000	45,820	97
Las Animas	Colorado Springs-Pueblo	6,300	5,950	94
Lincoln	Colorado Springs-Pueblo	1,900	1,860	98
Logan	Cheyenne-Scottsblf-Sterling	7,300	7,130	98
Mesa	Grand Junction-Montrose	26,200	25,450	97
Mineral	Colorado Springs-Pueblo	200	180	90
Moffat	Denver	3,900	3,720	95
Montezuma	Albuquerque, Farmington	5,100	4,860	95
Montrose	Grand Junction-Montrose	7,600	7,410	98
Morgan	Denver	7,900	7,800	99
Otero	Colorado Springs-Pueblo	9,200	9,050	98
Ouray	Grand Junction-Montrose	800	740	93
Park	Denver	1,900	1,820	96
Phillips	Cheyenne-Scottsblf-Sterling	2,100	2,070	99
Pitkin	Denver	4,000	3,630	91
Prowers	Colorado Springs-Pueblo	5,000	4,870	97
Pueblo	Colorado Springs-Pueblo	44,700	43,890	98
Rio Blanco	Salt Lake City	2,000	1,950	98
Rio Grande	Albuquerque, Farmington	3,700	3,580	97
Routt	Denver	4,400	4,280	97
Saguache	Albuquerque, Farmington	1,300	1,240	95
San Juan	Grand Junction-Montrose	300	290	97
San Miguel	Grand Junction-Montrose	1,000	930	93
Sedgwick	Cheyenne-Scottsblf-Sterling	1,300	1,270	98
Summit	Denver	2,300	2,200	96
Teller	Colorado Springs-Pueblo	2,900	2,830	98
Washington	Denver	2,200	2,130	97
Weld	Denver	37,800	36,990	98
Yuma	Denver	3,600	3,510	98
	STATE TOTAL	964,100	939,530	97
CONNECTICUT				
Fairfield	New York	283,500	280,330	99
Hartford	Hartford & New Haven	288,400	284,490	99
Litchfield	Hartford & New Haven	55,300	54,470	98
Middlesex	Hartford & New Haven	43,700	42,950	98
New Haven	Hartford & New Haven	269,600	266,210	99
New London	Providence	81,100	79,800	98
Tolland	Hartford & New Haven	35,400	34,950	99
Windham	Boston, Manchester, Worcestr	34,800	34,200	98
	STATE TOTAL	1,091,800	1,077,400	99

COUNTY	MARKET	HOUSEHOLDS	TV's	%
DELAWARE				
Kent	Philadelphia	30,600	29,930	98
New Castle	Philadelphia	138,700	137,000	99
Sussex	Salisbury	33,200	32,380	98
	STATE TOTAL	202,500	199,310	98
DIST. OF COLUMBIA				
Dist of Columbia	Washington, DC, Hagerstown	282,200	272,500	97
	STATE TOTAL	282,200	272,500	97
FLORIDA				
Alachua	Gainesville	45,500	43,240	95
Baker	Jacksonville	3,900	3,840	98
Bay	Panama City	33,200	32,540	98
Bradford	Jacksonville	5,300	5,090	96
Brevard	Orlando-Daytona Beach	81,700	80,320	98
Broward	Miami-Ft. Lauderdale	367,800	363,590	99
Calhoun	Panama City	2,300	2,220	97
Charlotte	Ft. Myers	21,000	20,760	99
Citrus	Tampa-St. Petersbg, Sarasota	16,100	15,480	96
Clay	Jacksonville	18,200	17,950	99
Collier	Ft. Myers	27,000	26,050	96
Columbia	Jacksonville	10,300	10,070	98
Dade	Miami-Ft. Lauderdale	562,000	548,430	98
De Soto	Tampa-St.Petersbg, Sarasota	6,000	5,830	97
Dixie	Gainesville	2,400	2,170	90
Duval	Jacksonville	202,300	198,450	98
Escambia	Mobile-Pensacola	77,800	75,980	98
Flagler	Orlando-Daytona Beach	3,300	3,140	95
Franklin	Panama City	2,900	2,740	94
Gadsden	Tallahassee-Thomasville	9,900	9,510	96
Gilchrist	Gainesville	2,100	1,990	95
Glades	West Palm Beach, Ft. Pierce	1,800	1,660	92
Gulf	Panama City	3,500	3,390	97
Hamilton	Jacksonville	3,300	3,090	94
Hardee	Tampa-St. Petersbg, Sarasota	5,900	5,710	97
Hendry	Ft. Myers	5,700	5,540	97
Hernando	Tampa-St. Petersbg, Sarasota	12,800	12,410	97
Highlands	Tampa-St. Petersbg, Sarasota	16,000	15,620	98
Hillsborough	Tampa-St. Petersbg, Sarasota	220,200	215,380	98
Holmes	Panama City	5,300	5,190	98
Indian River	Miami-Ft. Lauderdale	18,700	18,150	97
Jackson	Dothan	13,900	13,330	96
Jefferson	Tallahassee-Thomasville	3,200	3,090	97
Lafayette	Tallahassee-Thomasville	1,300	1,190	92
Lake	Orlando-Daytona Beach	36,500	35,730	98
Lee	Ft. Myers	69,000	68,050	99
Leon	Tallahassee-Thomasville	47,200	45,230	96
Levy	Gainesville	6,200	5,810	94
Liberty	Tallahassee-Thomasville	1,600	1,490	93
Madison	Tallahassee-Thomasville	5,000	4,750	95
Manatee	Tampa-St. Petersbg, Sarasota	57,400	56,220	98
Marion	Orlando-Daytona Beach	37,600	36,480	97
Martin	West Palm Beach, Ft. Pierce	20,100	19,610	98
Monroe	Miami-Ft. Lauderdale	18,400	17,490	95

COUNTY	MARKET	HOUSEHOLDS	TV's	%
FLORIDA—*Cont'd*				
Nassau	Jacksonville	10,800	10,590	98
Okaloosa	Mobile-Pensacola	33,800	33,210	98
Okeechobee	West Palm Beach, Ft. Pierce	6,200	5,900	95
Orange	Orlando-Daytona Beach	154,100	150,880	98
Osceola	Orlando-Daytona Beach	16,500	16,280	99
Palm Beach	West Palm Beach, Ft. Pierce	195,100	190,740	98
Pasco	Tampa-St. Petersbg, Sarasota	66,200	64,840	98
Pinellas	Tampa-St. Petersbg, Sarasota	318,000	312,610	98
Polk	Tampa-St. Petersbg, Sarasota	103,000	100,440	98
Putnam	Jacksonville	16,400	15,800	96
St Johns	Jacksonville	15,800	15,490	98
St Lucie	West Palm Beach, Ft. Pierce	27,900	27,000	97
Santa Rosa	Mobile-Pensacola	17,100	16,610	97
Sarasota	Tampa-St.Petersbg, Sarasota	76,800	75,430	98
Seminole	Orlando-Daytona Beach	52,200	51,380	98
Sumter	Orlando-Daytona Beach	7,500	7,330	98
Suwannee	Jacksonville	6,700	6,230	93
Taylor	Tallahassee-Thomasville	4,800	4,530	94
Union	Jacksonville	2,500	2,360	94
Volusia	Orlando-Daytona Beach	90,100	88,470	98
Wakulla	Tallahassee-Thomasville	3,100	2,970	96
Walton	Panama City	6,900	6,660	97
Washington	Panama City	4,700	4,520	96
	STATE TOTAL	3,347,800	3,274,270	98
GEORGIA				
Appling	Savannah	4,900	4,610	94
Atkinson	Albany, GA	1,700	1,580	93
Bacon	Savannah	3,100	2,950	95
Baker	Albany, GA	1,100	1,040	95
Baldwin	Macon	7,600	7,380	97
Banks	Atlanta	2,200	2,150	98
Barrow	Atlanta	7,000	6,930	99
Bartow	Atlanta	12,100	11,880	98
Ben Hill	Albany, GA	5,200	4,930	95
Berrien	Albany, GA	4,400	4,260	97
Bibb	Macon	47,400	46,370	98
Bleckley	Macon	3,800	3,750	99
Brantley	Jacksonville	2,600	2,520	97
Brooks	Tallahassee-Thomasville	4,700	4,610	98
Bryan	Savannah	2,900	2,820	97
Bulloch	Savannah	10,900	10,470	96
Burke	Augusta	5,600	5,300	95
Butts	Atlanta	3,900	3,780	97
Calhoun	Albany, GA	2,100	1,960	93
Camden	Jacksonville	3,900	3,840	98
Candler	Savannah	2,300	2,210	96
Carroll	Atlanta	18,600	18,300	98
Catoosa	Chattanooga	11,900	11,760	99
Charlton	Jacksonville	2,000	1,930	97
Chatham	Savannah	63,100	61,530	98
Chattahoochee	Columbus, GA	2,200	2,190	100
Chattooga	Chattanooga	7,900	7,720	98
Cherokee	Atlanta	14,300	14,040	98
Clarke	Atlanta	23,700	22,950	97
Clay	Columbus, GA	1,200	1,150	96

COUNTY	MARKET	HOUSEHOLDS	TV's	%

GEORGIA—*Cont'd*

COUNTY	MARKET	HOUSEHOLDS	TV's	%
Clayton	Atlanta	43,900	43,600	99
Clinch	Jacksonville	1,900	1,820	96
Cobb	Atlanta	84,000	83,120	99
Coffee	Albany, GA	7,900	7,630	97
Colquitt	Albany, GA	11,400	11,140	98
Columbia	Augusta	10,200	10,080	99
Cook	Albany, GA	4,300	4,210	98
Coweta	Atlanta	12,400	12,040	97
Crawford	Macon	2,000	1,890	95
Crisp	Albany, GA	6,300	6,150	98
Dade	Chattanooga	3,900	3,810	98
Dawson	Atlanta	1,900	1,830	96
Decatur	Tallahassee-Thomasville	8,100	7,890	97
De Kalb	Atlanta	154,200	152,450	99
Dodge	Macon	5,900	5,770	98
Dooly	Columbus, GA	3,700	3,530	95
Dougherty	Albany, GA	29,200	28,470	98
Douglas	Atlanta	16,000	15,790	99
Early	Dothan	4,300	4,160	97
Echols	Tallahassee-Thomasville	500	480	96
Effingham	Savannah	4,900	4,720	96
Elbert	Greenville-Spart-Asheville	6,300	6,190	98
Emanuel	Augusta	7,100	6,870	97
Evans	Savannah	3,000	2,910	97
Fannin	Chattanooga	5,100	4,870	95
Fayette	Atlanta	6,200	6,040	97
Floyd	Atlanta	27,700	27,140	98
Forsyth	Altanta	7,500	7,340	98
Franklin	Greenville-Spart-Asheville	5,000	4,880	98
Fulton	Atlanta	209,600	205,020	98
Gilmer	Atlanta	3,700	3,570	96
Glascock	Augusta	700	680	97
Glynn	Jacksonville	15,300	14,880	97
Gordon	Atlanta	9,400	9,300	99
Grady	Tallahassee-Thomasville	6,500	6,330	97
Greene	Atlanta	3,300	3,200	97
Gwinnett	Atlanta	42,500	41,810	98
Habersham	Atlanta	8,200	7,970	97
Hall	Atlanta	23,400	22,790	97
Hancock	Augusta	2,800	2,680	96
Haralson	Atlanta	6,500	6,380	98
Harris	Columbus, GA	3,800	3,620	95
Hart	Greenville-Spart-Asheville	5,800	5,770	99
Heard	Atlanta	2,100	2,040	97
Henry	Atlanta	9,500	9,290	98
Houston	Macon	23,100	22,740	98
Irwin	Albany, GA	3,000	2,920	97
Jackson	Atlanta	8,300	8,080	97
Jasper	Atlanta	2,200	2,110	96
Jeff Davis	Savannah	3,700	3,540	96
Jefferson	Augusta	5,100	4,820	95
Jenkins	Augusta	2,800	2,690	96
Johnson	Augusta	2,300	2,200	96
Jones	Macon	5,200	5,080	98
Lamar	Atlanta	3,600	3,480	97
Lanier	Albany, GA	1,800	1,720	96
Laurens	Macon	11,800	11,210	95
Lee	Albany, GA	3,100	2,990	96

COUNTY	MARKET	HOUSEHOLDS	TV's	%
GEORGIA—*Cont'd*				
Liberty	Savannah	6,200	5,940	96
Lincoln	Augusta	1,900	1,840	97
Long	Savannah	1,000	960	96
Lowndes	Tallahassee-Thomasville	21,100	20,520	97
Lumpkin	Atlanta	2,700	2,570	95
McDuffie	Augusta	6,000	5,790	97
McIntosh	Savannah	2,700	2,590	96
Macon	Columbus, GA	3,600	3,450	96
Madison	Greenville-Spart-Asheville	5,500	5,390	98
Marion	Columbus, GA	2,200	2,070	94
Meriwether	Atlanta	6,000	5,800	97
Miller	Albany, GA	1,800	1,720	96
Mitchell	Albany, GA	6,100	5,870	96
Monroe	Atlanta	3,500	3,430	98
Montgomery	Savannah	1,900	1,790	94
Morgan	Atlanta	3,200	3,110	97
Murray	Chattanooga	5,900	5,810	98
Muscogee	Columbus, GA	55,600	54,650	98
Newton	Atlanta	10,700	10,410	97
Oconee	Atlanta	3,200	3,120	98
Oglethorpe	Atlanta	2,600	2,460	95
Paulding	Atlanta	8,200	7,930	97
Peach	Macon	6,200	6,040	97
Pickens	Atlanta	3,700	3,630	98
Pierce	Jacksonville	3,600	3,480	97
Pike	Atlanta	2,600	2,500	96
Polk	Atlanta	10,700	10,550	99
Pulaski	Macon	2,800	2,720	97
Putnam	Atlanta	2,500	2,410	96
Quitman	Columbus, GA	600	580	97
Rabun	Greenville-Spart-Asheville	3,500	3,380	97
Randolph	Columbus, GA	3,100	3,010	97
Richmond	Augusta	47,500	46,330	98
Rockdale	Atlanta	9,800	9,510	97
Schley	Columbus, GA	800	770	96
Screven	Augusta	4,100	3,970	97
Seminole	Dothan	2,800	2,710	97
Spalding	Atlanta	15,900	15,660	98
Stephens	Greenville-Spart-Asheville	8,500	8,430	99
Stewart	Columbus, GA	1,600	1,510	94
Sumter	Columbus, GA	9,000	8,680	96
Talbot	Columbus, GA	1,500	1,430	95
Taliaferro	Augusta	800	770	96
Tattnall	Savannah	4,800	4,630	96
Taylor	Columbus, GA	2,400	2,260	94
Telfair	Macon	3,800	3,630	96
Terrell	Columbus, GA	3,700	3,570	96
Thomas	Tallahassee-Thomasville	12,600	12,120	96
Tift	Albany, GA	10,200	9,900	97
Toombs	Savannah	7,300	6,910	95
Towns	Atlanta	1,500	1,460	97
Treutlen	Savannah	2,000	1,910	96
Troup	Atlanta	15,600	15,180	97
Turner	Albany, GA	3,100	3,050	98
Twiggs	Macon	2,100	2,010	96
Union	Atlanta	2,900	2,830	98
Upson	Atlanta	8,500	8,290	98
Walker	Chattanooga	19,400	19,030	98

COUNTY	MARKET	HOUSEHOLDS	TV's	%
GEORGIA—*Cont'd*				
Walton	Atlanta	9,900	9,690	98
Ware	Jacksonville	12,200	11,780	97
Warren	Augusta	1,900	1,820	96
Washington	Augusta	5,400	5,190	96
Wayne	Savannah	6,200	6,050	98
Webster	Columbus, GA	600	570	95
Wheeler	Macon	1,900	1,800	95
White	Atlanta	3,000	2,910	97
Whitfield	Chattanooga	19,600	19,260	98
Wilcox	Albany, GA	2,500	2,450	98
Wilkes	Augusta	3,500	3,310	95
Wilkinson	Macon	3,000	2,860	95
Worth	Albany, GA	5,500	5,280	96
	STATE TOTAL	1,676,500	1,637,680	98
HAWAII				
Hawaii	Honolulu	24,500	23,090	94
Honolulu	Honolulu	215,900	209,870	97
Kauai	Honolulu	10,900	10,180	93
Maui	Honolulu	19,100	18,030	94
	STATE TOTAL	270,400	261,170	97
IDAHO				
Ada	Boise	53,100	52,000	98
Adams	Boise	1,100	1,020	93
Bannock	Idaho Falls-Pocatello	20,200	19,760	98
Bear Lake	Salt Lake City	2,300	2,210	96
Benewah	Spokane	2,800	2,720	97
Bingham	Idaho Falls-Pocatello	10,100	9,790	97
Blaine	Boise	3,300	3,230	98
Boise	Boise	800	760	95
Bonner	Spokane	7,800	7,510	96
Bonneville	Idaho Falls-Pocatello	19,600	19,160	98
Boundary	Spokane	2,500	2,350	94
Butte	Idaho Falls-Pocatello	900	880	98
Camas	Twin Falls	200	200	100
Canyon	Boise	26,900	25,870	96
Caribou	Salt Lake City	2,500	2,400	96
Cassia	Twin Falls	6,300	6,030	96
Clark	Idaho Falls-Pocatello	500	470	94
Clearwater	Spokane	3,500	3,310	95
Custer	Idaho Falls-Pocatello	1,300	1,180	91
Elmore	Boise	6,700	6,510	97
Franklin	Salt Lake City	3,000	2,970	99
Fremont	Idaho Falls-Pocatello	3,400	3,320	98
Gem	Boise	3,900	3,720	95
Gooding	Twin Falls	4,200	4,070	97
Idaho	Spokane	4,500	4,270	95
Jefferson	Idaho Falls-Pocatello	4,500	4,300	96
Jerome	Twin Falls	5,700	5,530	97
Kootenai	Spokane	18,800	18,400	98
Latah	Spokane	9,800	9,280	95
Lemhi	Idaho Falls-Pocatello	2,200	2,000	91

COUNTY	MARKET	HOUSEHOLDS	TV's	%
IDAHO—*Cont'd*				
Lewis	Spokane	1,900	1,840	97
Lincoln	Twin Falls	1,400	1,340	96
Madison	Idaho Falls-Pocatello	4,100	3,990	97
Minidoka	Twin Falls	6,400	6,150	96
Nez Perce	Spokane	12,100	11,650	96
Oneida	Salt Lake City	1,200	1,160	97
Owyhee	Boise	2,600	2,520	97
Payette	Boise	6,000	5,750	96
Power	Idaho Falls-Pocatello	2,000	1,900	95
Shoshone	Spokane	6,600	6,320	96
Teton	Idaho Falls-Pocatello	700	690	99
Twin Falls	Twin Falls	17,900	17,310	97
Valley	Boise	1,600	1,510	94
Washington	Boise	3,400	3,160	93
	STATE TOTAL	300,300	290,510	97
ILLINOIS				
Adams	Quincy-Hannibal-Keokuk	25,600	25,120	98
Alexander	Paducah-C. Girardeau-Harrbg	5,500	5,290	96
Bond	St. Louis	5,400	5,270	98
Boone	Rockford	9,600	9,400	98
Brown	Quincy-Hannibal-Keokuk	2,500	2,450	98
Bureau	Davenport-R. Island-Moline	13,200	13,060	99
Calhoun	St. Louis	2,200	2,160	98
Carroll	Davenport-R. Island-Moline	7,200	7,030	98
Cass	Quincy-Hannibal-Keokuk	5,500	5,400	98
Champaign	Champaign & Springfld-Decatur	56,200	54,480	97
Christian	Champaign & Springfld-Decatur	14,300	14,100	99
Clark	Terre Haute	6,500	6,410	99
Clay	Terre Haute	5,800	5,640	97
Clinton	St. Louis	9,800	9,740	99
Coles	Champaign & Springfld-Decatur	17,400	17,110	98
Cook	Chicago	1,908,800	1,863,810	98
Crawford	Terre Haute	8,300	8,200	99
Cumberland	Terre Haute	3,900	3,830	98
De Kalb	Chicago	22,900	22,590	99
De Witt	Champaign & Springfld-Decatur	6,600	6,520	99
Douglas	Champaign & Springfld-Decatur	7,200	7,090	98
Du Page	Chicago	172,000	170,290	99
Edgar	Terre Haute	8,400	8,210	98
Edwards	Evansville	3,300	3,280	99
Effingham	Terre Haute	10,300	10,160	99
Fayette	St. Louis	7,800	7,490	96
Ford	Champaign & Springfld-Decatur	5,200	5,150	99
Franklin	Paducah-C. Girardeau-Harrbg	18,400	18,130	99
Fulton	Peoria	17,100	16,840	98
Gallatin	Paducah-C. Girardeau-Harrbg	2,500	2,460	98
Greene	St. Louis	6,200	6,070	98
Grundy	Chicago	10,300	10,140	98
Hamilton	Paducah-C. Girardeau-Harrbg	3,400	3,270	96
Hancock	Quincy-Hannibal-Keokuk	8,100	7,950	98
Hardin	Paducah-C. Girardeau-Harrbg	2,200	2,160	98
Henderson	Davenport-R. Island-Moline	3,100	3,100	100
Henry	Davenport-R. Island-Moline	21,000	20,850	99
Iroquois	Chicago	12,400	12,160	98
Jackson	Paducah-C. Girardeau-Harrbg	18,600	17,870	96

COUNTY	MARKET	HOUSEHOLDS	TV's	%
ILLINOIS—*Cont'd*				
	Terre Haute	4,100	4,040	99
Jasper	St. Louis	13,600	13,250	97
Jefferson	St. Louis	6,600	6,520	99
Jersey	Davenport-R. Island-Moline	7,600	7,490	99
Jo Daviess	Paducah-C. Girardeau-Harrbg	3,500	3,380	97
Johnson	Chicago	88,700	87,060	98
Kane	Chicago	31,500	30,960	98
Kankakee	Chicago	10,500	10,460	100
Kendall	Davenport-R. Island-Moline	22,600	22,120	98
Knox	Chicago	121,000	119,510	99
Lake	Chicago	38,800	38,110	98
La Salle	Terre Haute	6,700	6,540	98
Lawrence	Davenport-R. Island-Moline	11,300	11,040	98
Lee	Chicago	13,900	13,450	97
Livingston	Peoria	10,400	10,290	99
Logan	Quincy-Hannibal-Keokuk	12,300	12,080	98
McDonough	Chicago	43,500	42,880	99
McHenry	Peoria	42,500	41,640	98
McLean	Champaign & Springfld-Decatur	48,200	47,350	98
Macon	St. Louis	17,600	17,470	99
Macoupin	St. Louis	86,500	84,760	98
Madison	St. Louis	15,400	15,090	98
Marion	Peoria	4,900	4,810	98
Marshall	Peoria	7,700	7,590	99
Mason	Paducah-C. Girardeau-Harrbg	5,400	5,260	97
Massac	Champaign & Springfld-Decatur	4,300	4,250	99
Menard	Davenport-R. Island-Moline	6,600	6,530	99
Mercer	St. Louis	6,500	6,400	98
Monroe	St. Louis	12,000	11,780	98
Montgomery	Champaign & Springfld-Decatur	13,200	12,950	98
Morgan	Champaign & Springfld-Decatur	4,500	4,440	99
Moultrie	Rockford	15,100	14,840	98
Ogle	Peoria	75,200	73,710	98
Peoria	St. Louis	8,300	8,050	97
Perry	Champaign & Springfld-Decatur	6,100	6,020	99
Piatt	Quincy-Hannibal-Keokuk	7,700	7,550	98
Pike	Paducah-C. Girardeau-Harrbg	1,800	1,740	97
Pope	Paducah-C. Girardeau-Harrbg	3,800	3,670	97
Pulaski	Peoria	2,000	1,950	98
Putnam	St. Louis	11,300	11,120	98
Randolph	Terre Haute	6,300	6,050	96
Richland	Davenport-R.Island-Moline	61,500	60,660	99
Rock Island	St. Louis	96,400	93,880	97
St Clair	Paducah-C. Girardeau-Harrbg	11,900	11,610	98
Saline	Champaign & Springfld-Decatur	67,800	66,160	98
Sangamon	Quincy-Hannibal-Keokuk	3,100	3,010	97
Schuyler	Quincy-Hannibal-Keokuk	2,600	2,570	99
Scott	Champaign & Springfld-Decatur	8,800	8,700	99
Shelby	Peoria	3,000	2,970	99
Stark	Rockford	17,500	17,340	99
Stephenson	Peoria	45,300	44,490	98
Tazewell	Paducah-C. Girardeau-Harrbg	6,600	6,430	97
Union	Champaign & Springfld-Decatur	38,000	37,250	98
Vermilion	Evansville	5,400	5,250	97
Wabash	Davenport-R. Island-Moline	7,900	7,770	98
Warren	St. Louis	5,900	5,730	97
Washington	Evansville	7,100	6,900	97
Wayne	Evansville	6,800	6,640	98
White				

COUNTY	MARKET	HOUSEHOLDS	TV's	%
ILLINOIS—*Cont'd*				
Whiteside	Davenport-R. Island-Moline	22,800	22,590	99
Will	Chicago	97,700	96,410	99
Williamson	Paducah-C. Girardeau-Harrbg	20,900	20,530	98
Winnebago	Rockford	86,700	85,200	98
Woodford	Peoria	10,300	9,950	97
	STATE TOTAL	3,968,200	3,886,520	98
INDIANA				
Adams	Ft. Wayne	8,800	8,450	96
Allen	Ft. Wayne	98,000	96,520	98
Bartholomew	Indianapolis, Lafayette	20,600	20,140	98
Benton	Indianapolis, Lafayette	3,800	3,750	99
Blackford	Indianapolis, Lafayette	5,600	5,460	98
Boone	Indianapolis, Lafayette	12,000	11,810	98
Brown	Indianapolis, Lafayette	3,300	3,240	98
Carroll	Indianapolis, Lafayette	6,400	6,270	98
Cass	Indianapolis, Lafayette	13,800	13,630	99
Clark	Louisville	29,200	28,640	98
Clay	Terre Haute	9,000	8,750	97
Clinton	Indianapolis, Lafayette	11,300	11,090	98
Crawford	Louisville	3,300	3,120	95
Daviess	Terre Haute	9,000	8,570	95
Dearborn	Cincinnati	10,900	10,710	98
Decatur	Indianapolis, Lafayette	8,200	7,900	96
DeKalb	Ft. Wayne	10,600	10,430	98
Delaware	Indianapolis, Lafayette	42,600	41,840	98
Dubois	Evansville	9,800	9,650	98
Elkhart	South Bend-Elkhart	44,700	43,530	97
Fayette	Cincinnati	9,600	9,380	98
Floyd	Louisville	19,800	19,430	98
Fountain	Indianapolis, Lafayette	6,700	6,540	98
Franklin	Cincinnati	5,600	5,410	97
Fulton	South Bend-Elkhart	6,200	6,160	99
Gibson	Evansville	11,100	10,880	98
Grant	Indianapolis, Lafayette	28,800	28,160	98
Greene	Terre Haute	10,700	10,460	98
Hamilton	Indianapolis, Lafayette	25,100	24,850	99
Hancock	Indianapolis, Lafayette	14,300	14,000	98
Harrison	Louisville	8,200	8,070	98
Hendricks	Indianapolis, Lafayette	20,900	20,660	99
Henry	Indianapolis, Lafayette	18,600	18,270	98
Howard	Indianapolis, Lafayette	31,100	30,630	98
Huntington	Ft. Wayne	12,200	12,110	99
Jackson	Louisville	12,200	11,900	98
Jasper	Chicago	7,800	7,610	98
Jay	Indianapolis, Lafayette	8,600	8,350	97
Jefferson	Louisville	9,100	8,890	98
Jennings	Indianapolis, Lafayette	6,600	6,550	99
Johnson	Indianapolis, Lafayette	22,800	22,440	98
Knox	Terre Haute	15,100	14,800	98
Kosciusko	South Bend-Elkhart	18,700	18,280	98
Lagrange	South Bend-Elkhart	7,200	6,400	89
Lake	Chicago	176,700	173,180	98
La Porte	Chicago	34,700	34,310	99
Lawrence	Louisville	15,000	14,700	98
Madison	Indianapolis, Lafayette	48,900	48,240	99

COUNTY	MARKET	HOUSEHOLDS	TV's	%
INDIANA—*Cont'd*				
Marion	Indianapolis, Lafayette	275,400	270,680	98
Marion	Terre Haute	3,700	3,570	96
Marshall	SouthBend-Elkhart	13,100	12,800	98
Miami	Indianapolis, Lafayette	13,200	12,980	98
Monroe	Indianapolis, Lafayette	31,500	30,460	97
Montgomery	Indianapolis, Lafayette	12,200	12,090	99
Morgan	Indianapolis, Lafayette	15,800	15,390	97
Newton	Chicago	4,900	4,800	98
Noble	Ft. Wayne	11,300	11,120	98
Ohio	Cincinnati	1,700	1,660	98
Orange	Louisville	6,500	6,400	98
Owen	Indianapolis, Lafayette	4,500	4,300	96
Parke	Terre Haute	5,700	5,560	98
Perry	Evansville	6,200	6,130	99
Pike	Evansville	5,100	4,960	97
Porter	Chicago	32,000	31,600	99
Posey	Evansville	7,600	7,480	98
Pulaski	South Bend-Elkhart	4,500	4,450	99
Putnam	Indianapolis, Lafayette	9,400	9,220	98
Randolph	Indianapolis, Lafayette	10,600	10,440	98
Ripley	Cincinnati	7,900	7,700	97
Rush	Indianapolis, Lafayette	7,100	6,920	97
St Joseph	South Bend-Elkhart	80,200	79,270	99
Scott	Louisville	6,300	6,130	97
Shelby	Indianapolis, Lafayette	13,800	13,610	99
Spencer	Evansville	5,600	5,420	97
Starke	South Bend-Elkhart	7,200	7,050	98
Steuben	Ft. Wayne	8,300	8,170	98
Sullivan	Terre Haute	7,900	7,830	99
Switzerland	Cincinnati	2,500	2,460	98
Tippecanoe	Indianapolis, Lafayette	37,100	36,150	97
Tipton	Indianapolis, Lafayette	5,400	5,330	99
Union	Cincinnati	2,600	2,530	97
Vanderburgh	Evansville	57,200	56,540	99
Vermillion	Terre Haute	6,400	6,270	98
Vigo	Terre Haute	38,800	38,100	98
Wabash	Ft. Wayne	12,000	11,730	98
Warren	Indianapolis, Lafayette	2,800	2,750	98
Warrick	Evansville	11,900	11,750	99
Washington	Louisville	7,000	6,830	98
Wayne	Dayton	26,500	25,830	97
Wells	Ft. Wayne	8,500	8,220	97
White	Indianapolis, Lafayette	8,000	7,910	99
Whitley	Ft. Wayne	8,600	8,510	99
	STATE TOTAL	1,827,700	1,793,260	98
IOWA				
Adair	Des Moines-Ames	3,700	3,680	99
Adams	Omaha	2,500	2,460	98
Allamakee	Cedar Rapids-Watrloo, Dubuq	5,200	5,080	98
Appanoose	Des Moines-Ames	6,400	6,250	98
Audubon	Omaha	3,200	3,140	98
Benton	Cedar Rapids-Watrloo, Dubuq	8,500	8,390	99
Black Hawk	Cedar Rapids-Watrloo, Dubuq	45,400	44,860	99
Boone	Des Moines-Ames	9,700	9,660	100
Bremer	Cedar Rapids-Watrloo, Dubuq	8,100	8,020	99

COUNTY	MARKET	HOUSEHOLDS	TV's	%

IOWA—*Cont'd*

COUNTY	MARKET	HOUSEHOLDS	TV's	%
Buchanan	Cedar Rapids-Watrloo, Dubuq	7,300	7,160	98
Buena Vista	Sioux City	7,900	7,800	99
Butler	Cedar Rapids-Watrloo, Dubuq	6,500	6,370	98
Calhoun	Des Moines-Ames	5,200	5,190	100
Carroll	Des Moines-Ames	7,400	7,330	99
Cass	Omaha	6,300	6,190	98
Cedar	Cedar Rapids-Watrloo, Dubuq	6,500	6,470	100
Cerro Gordo	Mason City-Austin-Rochestr	18,100	17,930	99
Cherokee	Sioux City	5,800	5,760	99
Chickasaw	Cedar Rapids-Watrloo, Dubuq	5,400	5,270	98
Clarke	Des Moines-Ames	3,300	3,210	97
Clay	Sioux City	7,200	7,150	99
Clayton	Cedar Rapids-Watrloo, Dubuq	7,600	7,410	98
Clinton	Davenport-R. Island-Moline	20,600	20,350	99
Crawford	Omaha	7,000	6,920	99
Dallas	Des Moines-Ames	10,000	9,870	99
Davis	Ottumwa-Kirksville	3,300	3,210	97
Decatur	Des Moines-Ames	3,600	3,440	96
Delaware	Cedar Rapids-Watrloo, Dubuq	6,300	6,220	99
Des Moines	Davenport-R. Island-Moline	17,200	16,870	98
Dickinson	Sioux City	5,300	5,270	99
Dubuque	Cedar Rapids-Watrloo, Dubuq	28,700	28,330	99
Emmet	Mankato	5,100	5,020	98
Fayette	Cedar Rapids-Watrloo, Dubuq	9,400	9,250	98
Floyd	Mason City-Austin-Rochestr	7,700	7,610	99
Franklin	Mason City-Austin-Rochestr	5,200	5,150	99
Fremont	Omaha	3,600	3,510	98
Greene	Des Moines-Ames	4,800	4,750	99
Grundy	Cedar Rapids-Watrloo, Dubuq	5,200	5,080	98
Guthrie	Des Moines-Ames	5,200	5,110	98
Hamilton	Des Moines-Ames	6,700	6,630	99
Hancock	Mason City-Austin-Rochestr	5,400	5,320	99
Hardin	Des Moines-Ames	8,300	8,150	98
Harrison	Omaha	6,200	6,140	99
Henry	Davenport-R. Island-Moline	6,500	6,260	96
Howard	Mason City-Austin-Rochestr	4,000	3,900	98
Humboldt	Des Moines-Ames	4,500	4,440	99
Ida	Sioux City	3,200	3,170	99
Iowa	Cedar Rapids-Watrloo, Dubuq	5,300	5,220	98
Jackson	Davenport-R. Island-Moline	7,400	7,290	99
Jasper	Des Moines-Ames	13,400	13,220	99
Jefferson	Ottumwa-Kirksville	5,500	5,350	97
Johnson	Cedar Rapids-Watrloo, Dubuq	27,900	26,880	96
Jones	Cedar Rapids-Watrloo, Dubuq	6,800	6,710	99
Keokuk	Cedar Rapids-Watrloo, Dubuq	5,700	5,590	98
Kossuth	Mason City-Austin-Rochestr	7,900	7,750	98
Lee	Quincy-Hannibal-Keokuk	15,500	15,220	98
Linn	Cedar Rapids-Watrloo, Dubuq	58,800	57,940	99
Louisa	Davenport-R. Island-Moline	4,100	4,010	98
Lucas	Des Moines-Ames	4,200	4,130	98
Lyon	Sioux Falls (Mitchell)	4,500	4,310	96
Madison	Des Moines-Ames	5,000	4,900	98
Mahaska	Des Moines-Ames	8,300	7,970	96
Marion	Des Moines-Ames	9,900	9,680	98
Marshall	Des Moines-Ames	15,600	15,370	99
Mills	Omaha	4,900	4,860	99
Mitchell	Mason City-Austin-Rochestr	4,000	3,940	99
Monona	Omaha	4,700	4,660	99

COUNTY	MARKET	HOUSEHOLDS	TV's	%
IOWA—*Cont'd*				
Monroe	Des Moines-Ames	3,700	3,510	95
Montgomery	Omaha	5,400	5,300	98
Muscatine	Davenport-R. Island-Moline	14,400	14,250	99
O'Brien	Sioux City	6,400	6,330	99
Osceola	Sioux Falls (Mitchell)	2,900	2,790	96
Page	Omaha	7,800	7,600	97
Palo Alto	Sioux City	4,800	4,750	99
Plymouth	Sioux City	8,100	8,020	99
Pocahontas	Sioux City	4,300	4,270	99
Polk	Des Moines-Ames	110,300	108,470	98
Pottawattamie	Omaha	29,700	29,100	98
Poweshiek	Des Moines-Ames	7,200	7,000	97
Ringgold	Des Moines-Ames	2,600	2,550	98
Sac	Sioux City	6,000	5,940	99
Scott	Davenport-R. Island-Moline	53,000	51,960	98
Shelby	Omaha	5,100	5,030	99
Sioux	Sioux City	9,500	9,230	97
Story	Des Moines-Ames	22,800	22,220	97
Tama	Cedar Rapids-Watrloo, Dubuq	7,600	7,510	99
Taylor	Omaha	3,200	3,130	98
Union	Des Moines-Ames	5,300	5,190	98
Van Buren	Ottumwa-Kirksville	3,300	3,280	99
Wapello	Ottumwa-Kirksville	15,400	15,130	98
Warren	Des Moines-Ames	10,500	10,450	100
Washington	Cedar Rapids-Watrloo, Dubuq	6,700	6,390	95
Wayne	Des Moines-Ames	4,000	3,880	97
Webster	Des Moines-Ames	16,600	16,320	98
Winnebago	Mason City-Austin-Rochestr	5,300	5,270	99
Winneshiek	Cedar Rapids-Watrloo, Dubuq	6,600	6,530	99
Woodbury	Sioux City	37,800	37,350	99
Worth	Mason City-Austin-Rochestr	3,200	3,140	98
Wright	Des Moines-Ames	5,900	5,780	98
	STATE TOTAL	1,035,000	1,017,420	98
KANSAS				
Allen	Joplin-Pittsburg	6,100	5,980	98
Anderson	Kansas City	3,200	3,090	97
Atchison	Kansas City	6,800	6,670	98
Barber	Wichita-Hutchinson Plus	2,500	2,470	99
Barton	Wichita-Hutchinson Plus	11,500	11,400	99
Bourbon	Joplin-Pittsburg	7,000	6,780	97
Brown	Kansas City	5,000	4,820	96
Butler	Wichita-Hutchinson Plus	15,400	15,030	98
Chase	Wichita-Hutchinson Plus	1,400	1,350	96
Chautauqua	Tulsa	2,200	2,150	98
Cherokee	Joplin-Pittsburg	8,600	8,400	98
Cheyenne	Wichita-Hutchinson Plus	1,800	1,760	98
Clark	Wichita-Hutchinson Plus	1,100	1,080	98
Clay	Topeka	3,900	3,830	98
Cloud	Lincoln & Hstngs-Krny Plus	4,800	4,630	96
Coffey	Topeka	3,300	3,120	95
Comanche	Wichita-Hutchinson Plus	1,200	1,160	97
Cowley	Wichita-Hutchinson Plus	13,000	12,700	98
Crawford	Joplin-Pittsburg	15,200	14,900	98
Decatur	Wichita-Hutchinson Plus	1,900	1,850	97
Dickinson	Wichita-Hutchinson Plus	8,200	8,030	98

COUNTY	MARKET	HOUSEHOLDS	TV's	%

KANSAS—*Cont'd*

COUNTY	MARKET	HOUSEHOLDS	TV's	%
Doniphan	St. Joseph	3,500	3,490	100
Douglas	Kansas City	21,900	21,260	97
Edwards	Wichita-Hutchinson Plus	1,900	1,860	98
Elk	Tulsa	1,600	1,540	96
Ellis	Wichita-Hutchinson Plus	8,700	8,590	99
Ellsworth	Wichita-Hutchinson Plus	2,400	2,370	99
Finney	Wichita-Hutchinson Plus	8,100	7,930	98
Ford	Wichita-Hutchinson Plus	8,700	8,490	98
Franklin	Kansas City	8,000	7,820	98
Geary	Topeka	10,700	10,430	97
Gove	Wichita-Hutchinson Plus	1,400	1,350	96
Graham	Wichita-Hutchinson Plus	1,700	1,670	98
Grant	Wichita-Hutchinson Plus	2,200	2,150	98
Gray	Wichita-Hutchinson Plus	2,200	2,150	98
Greeley	Wichita-Hutchinson Plus	700	690	99
Greenwood	Wichita-Hutchinson Plus	4,400	4,280	97
Hamilton	Wichita-Hutchinson Plus	1,300	1,260	97
Harper	Wichita-Hutchinson Plus	3,900	3,800	97
Harvey	Wichita-Hutchinson Plus	11,000	10,680	97
Haskell	Wichita-Hutchinson Plus	1,600	1,570	98
Hodgeman	Wichita-Hutchinson Plus	900	880	98
Jackson	Topeka	4,600	4,530	98
Jefferson	Kansas City	4,900	4,820	98
Jewell	Lincoln & Hstngs-Krny Plus	2,200	2,170	99
Johnson	Kansas City	80,600	79,860	99
Kearny	Wichita-Hutchinson Plus	1,200	1,180	98
Kingman	Wichita-Hutchinson Plus	3,800	3,760	99
Kiowa	Wichita-Hutchinson Plus	2,000	1,910	96
Labette	Joplin-Pittsburg	10,000	9,760	98
Lane	Wichita-Hutchinson Plus	1,100	1,080	98
Leavenworth	Kansas City	18,200	17,870	98
Lincoln	Wichita-Hutchinson Plus	1,800	1,730	96
Linn	Kansas City	3,800	3,700	97
Logan	Wichita-Hutchinson Plus	1,500	1,450	97
Lyon	Topeka	12,500	12,130	97
McPherson	Wichita-Hutchinson Plus	9,700	9,270	96
Marion	Wichita-Hutchinson Plus	5,100	4,880	96
Marshall	Topeka	5,800	5,690	98
Meade	Wichita-Hutchinson Plus	2,000	1,990	100
Miami	Kansas City	7,700	7,590	99
Mitchell	Wichita-Hutchinson Plus	3,100	3,010	97
Montgomery	Tulsa	16,500	15,990	97
Morris	Topeka	2,900	2,830	98
Morton	Wichita-Hutchinson Plus	1,200	1,170	98
Nemaha	Topeka	4,000	3,880	97
Neosho	Joplin-Pittsburg	7,100	7,030	99
Ness	Wichita-Hutchinson Plus	2,000	1,950	98
Norton	Wichita-Hutchinson Plus	2,500	2,490	100
Osage	Topeka	5,400	5,310	98
Osborne	Wichita-Hutchinson Plus	2,600	2,500	96
Ottawa	Wichita-Hutchinson Plus	2,600	2,570	99
Pawnee	Wichita-Hutchinson Plus	2,800	2,770	99
Phillips	Lincoln & Hstngs-Krny Plus	3,300	3,230	98
Pottawatomie	Topeka	5,100	5,020	98
Pratt	Wichita-Hutchinson Plus	3,900	3,850	99
Rawlins	Wichita-Hutchinson Plus	1,500	1,460	97
Reno	Wichita-Hutchinson Plus	24,600	23,970	97
Republic	Lincoln & Hstngs-Krny Plus	3,400	3,320	98

COUNTY	MARKET	HOUSEHOLDS	TV's	%
KANSAS—*Cont'd*				
Rice	Wichita-Hutchinson Plus	4,900	4,870	99
Riley	Kansas City	17,800	17,420	98
Rooks	Wichita-Hutchinson Plus	3,100	3,080	99
Rush	Wichita-Hutchinson Plus	2,000	1,960	98
Russell	Wichita-Hutchinson Plus	3,700	3,670	99
Saline	Wichita-Hutchinson Plus	18,000	17,740	99
Scott	Wichita-Hutchinson Plus	2,300	2,250	98
Sedgwick	Wichita-Hutchinson Plus	125,800	123,260	98
Seward	Wichita-Hutchinson Plus	6,500	6,360	98
Shawnee	Topeka	55,600	54,720	98
Sheridan	Wichita-Hutchinson Plus	1,100	1,070	97
Sherman	Wichita-Hutchinson Plus	3,100	3,040	98
Smith	Lincoln & Hstngs-Krny Plus	2,400	2,360	98
Stafford	Wichita-Hutchinson Plus	2,900	2,840	98
Stanton	Wichita-Hutchinson Plus	800	780	98
Stevens	Wichita-Hutchinson Plus	1,700	1,630	96
Sumner	Wichita-Hutchinson Plus	9,300	9,150	98
Thomas	Wichita-Hutchinson Plus	3,500	3,430	98
Trego	Wichita-Hutchinson Plus	1,700	1,640	96
Wabaunsee	Topeka	2,500	2,430	97
Wallace	Wichita-Hutchinson Plus	900	880	98
Washington	Lincoln & Hstngs-Krny Plus	3,700	3,590	97
Wichita	Wichita-Hutchinson Plus	1,000	970	97
Wilson	Joplin-Pittsburg	5,000	4,870	97
Woodson	Joplin-Pittsburg	1,700	1,640	96
Wyandotte	Kansas City	65,200	63,810	98
	STATE TOTAL	850,100	832,640	98
KENTUCKY				
Adair	Louisville	5,200	4,830	93
Allen	Nashville, Bowling Green	5,100	4,970	97
Anderson	Lexington	4,100	4,040	99
Ballard	Paducah-C. Girardeau-Harrbg	3,500	3,440	98
Barren	Nashville, Bowling Green	11,100	10,720	97
Bath	Lexington	3,200	3,080	96
Bell	Knoxville	11,100	10,510	95
Boone	Cincinnati	12,000	11,840	99
Bourbon	Lexington	6,700	6,550	98
Boyd	Charleston-Huntington	18,200	17,950	99
Boyle	Lexington	8,400	8,160	97
Bracken	Cincinnati	2,900	2,850	98
Breathitt	Lexington	4,900	4,070	83
Breckinridge	Louisville	5,700	5,550	97
Bullitt	Louisville	10,700	10,390	97
Butler	Nashville, Bowling Green	3,800	3,710	98
Caldwell	Paducah-C. Girardeau-Harrbg	5,100	4,890	96
Calloway	Paducah-C. Girardeau-Harrbg	11,200	10,990	98
Campbell	Cincinnati	27,800	27,400	99
Carlisle	Paducah-C. Girardeau-Harrbg	2,300	2,260	98
Carroll	Cincinnati	3,100	3,060	99
Carter	Charleston-Huntington	7,800	7,580	97
Casey	Lexington	4,800	4,340	90
Christian	Nashville, Bowling Green	21,400	21,000	98
Clark	Lexington	9,700	9,550	98
Clay	Knoxville	6,300	5,630	89
Clinton	Nashville, Bowling Green	2,900	2,690	93

COUNTY	MARKET	HOUSEHOLDS	TV's	%
KENTUCKY—*Cont'd*				
Crittenden	Paducah-C. Girardeau-Harrbg	3,700	3,650	99
Cumberland	Nashville, Bowling Green	2,300	2,110	92
Daviess	Evansville	27,900	27,570	99
Edmonson	Nashville, Bowling Green	3,300	3,110	94
Elliott	Charleston-Huntington	1,800	1,750	97
Estill	Lexington	4,700	4,330	92
Fayette	Lexington	67,100	65,840	98
Fleming	Cincinnati	4,300	4,140	96
Floyd	Charleston-Huntington	13,900	13,240	95
Franklin	Louisville	13,700	13,470	98
Fulton	Paducah-C. Girardeau-Harrbg	3,400	3,310	97
Gallatin	Cincinnati	1,600	1,560	98
Garrard	Lexington	3,300	3,210	97
Grant	Cincinnati	4,900	4,760	97
Graves	Paducah-C. Girardeau-Harrbg	12,700	12,470	98
Grayson	Louisville	7,000	6,730	96
Green	Louisville	3,700	3,620	98
Greenup	Charleston-Huntington	11,100	10,880	98
Hancock	Evansville	2,400	2,310	96
Hardin	Louisville	19,800	19,450	98
Harlan	Knoxville	14,100	13,440	95
Harrison	Cincinnati	5,400	5,250	97
Hart	Louisville	5,700	5,480	96
Henderson	Evansville	13,300	13,150	99
Henry	Louisville	4,200	4,120	98
Hickman	Paducah-C. Girardeau-Harrbg	2,200	2,140	97
Hopkins	Evansville	16,500	16,000	97
Jackson	Lexington	3,300	2,970	90
Jefferson	Louisville	240,400	236,710	98
Jessamine	Lexington	8,000	7,830	98
Johnson	Charleston-Huntington	7,800	7,590	97
Kenton	Cincinnati	45,200	44,650	99
Knott	Tri-Cities; TN-VA	5,200	4,790	92
Knox	Knoxville	9,600	9,280	97
Larue	Louisville	4,000	3,830	96
Laurel	Knoxville	10,900	10,540	97
Lawrence	Charleston-Huntington	4,400	4,180	95
Lee	Lexington	2,600	2,290	88
Leslie	Knoxville	4,000	3,650	91
Letcher	Tri-Cities; TN-VA	9,200	8,840	96
Lewis	Charleston-Huntington	4,400	4,210	96
Lincoln	Lexington	6,300	6,000	95
Livingston	Paducah-C. Girardeau-Harrbg	3,600	3,550	99
Logan	Nashville, Bowling Green	7,900	7,760	98
Lyon	Paducah-C. Girardeau-Harrbg	2,000	1,930	97
McCracken	Paducah-C. Girardeau-Harrbg	23,000	22,570	98
McCreary	Knoxville	4,800	4,580	95
McLean	Evansville	3,900	3,790	97
Madison	Lexington	15,300	14,780	97
Magoffin	Charleston-Huntington	3,800	3,620	95
Marion	Louisville	4,800	4,660	97
Marshall	Paducah-C. Girardeau-Harrbg	8,600	8,510	99
Martin	Charleston-Huntington	3,400	3,260	96
Mason	Cincinnati	5,700	5,620	99
Meade	Louisville	5,200	5,140	99
Menifee	Lexington	1,300	1,230	95
Mercer	Lexington	6,500	6,380	98
Metcalfe	Nashville, Bowling Green	3,300	3,200	97

COUNTY	MARKET	HOUSEHOLDS	TV's	%

KENTUCKY—*Cont'd*

COUNTY	MARKET	HOUSEHOLDS	TV's	%
Monroe	Nashville, Bowling Green	4,400	4,250	97
Montgomery	Lexington	6,100	5,900	97
Morgan	Charleston-Huntington	3,800	3,480	92
Muhlenberg	Nashville, Bowling Green	11,900	11,590	97
Nelson	Louisville	7,400	7,170	97
Nicholas	Lexington	2,500	2,390	96
Ohio	Nashville, Bowling Green	7,800	7,560	97
Oldham	Louisville	6,300	6,200	98
Owen	Cincinnati	3,300	3,110	94
Owsley	Lexington	1,700	1,520	89
Pendleton	Cincinnati	3,700	3,650	99
Perry	Lexington	9,000	8,370	93
Pike	Charleston-Huntington	22,800	21,880	96
Powell	Lexington	2,700	2,460	91
Pulaski	Lexington	16,100	15,350	95
Robertson	Cincinnati	700	680	97
Rockcastle	Lexington	4,000	3,600	90
Rowan	Lexington	4,600	4,400	96
Russell	Knoxville	4,300	4,040	94
Scott	Lexington	6,700	6,550	98
Shelby	Louisville	7,200	7,100	99
Simpson	Nashville, Bowling Green	5,600	5,520	99
Spencer	Louisville	1,900	1,860	98
Taylor	Louisville	6,500	6,240	96
Todd	Nashville, Bowling Green	4,100	3,950	96
Trigg	Nashville, Bowling Green	3,000	2,880	96
Trimble	Louisville	1,900	1,860	98
Union	Evansville	5,000	4,970	99
Warren	Nashville, Bowling Green	22,100	21,490	97
Washington	Louisville	3,300	3,220	98
Wayne	Knoxville	5,300	4,830	91
Webster	Evansville	5,800	5,600	97
Whitley	Knoxville	10,700	10,280	96
Wolfe	Lexington	2,200	2,030	92
Woodford	Lexington	6,100	6,000	98
	STATE TOTAL	1,181,900	1,149,060	97

LOUISIANA

COUNTY	MARKET	HOUSEHOLDS	TV's	%
Acadia	Lafayette, LA	17,300	16,840	97
Allen	Lafayette, LA	6,500	6,280	97
Ascension	Baton Rouge	13,100	12,850	98
Assumption	Baton Rouge	5,900	5,840	99
Avoyelles	Alexandria, LA	12,500	12,090	97
Beauregard	Lake Charles	9,100	8,870	97
Bienville	Shreveport	5,900	5,690	96
Bossier	Shreveport	23,000	22,540	98
Caddo	Shreveport	86,300	84,370	98
Calcasieu	Lake Charles	52,300	51,470	98
Caldwell	Monroe-El Dorado	3,100	3,020	97
Cameron	Lake Charles	2,900	2,840	98
Catahoula	Monroe-El Dorado	3,600	3,430	95
Claiborne	Shreveport	5,800	5,590	96
Concordia	Monroe-El Dorado	6,300	6,030	96
De Soto	Shreveport	8,100	7,690	95
East Baton Rouge	Baton Rouge	112,300	110,510	98
East Carroll	Monroe-El Dorado	3,400	3,260	96

COUNTY	MARKET	HOUSEHOLDS	TV's	%
LOUISIANA—*Cont'd*				
East Feliciana	Baton Rouge	4,000	3,860	97
Evangeline	Lafayette, LA	10,900	10,580	97
Franklin	Monroe-El Dorado	7,500	7,280	97
Grant	Alexandria, LA	5,300	5,110	96
Iberia	Lafayette, LA	20,300	19,910	98
Iberville	Baton Rouge	9,000	8,800	98
Jackson	Monroe-El Dorado	5,900	5,650	96
Jefferson	New Orleans	138,900	137,490	99
Jefferson Davis	Lafayette, LA	9,700	9,500	98
Lafayette	Lafayette, LA	41,700	40,980	98
Lafourche	New Orleans	21,800	21,530	99
La Salle	Monroe-El Dorado	5,500	5,290	96
Lincoln	Monroe-El Dorado	11,600	11,350	98
Livingston	Baton Rouge	14,900	14,660	98
Madison	Monroe-El Dorado	4,700	4,500	96
Morehouse	Monroe-El Dorado	10,800	10,470	97
Natchitoches	Shreveport	11,400	10,700	94
Orleans	New Orleans	208,500	203,460	98
Ouachita	Monroe-El Dorado	46,300	45,300	98
Plaquemines	New Orleans	7,500	7,350	98
Pointe Coupee	Baton Rouge	6,500	6,230	96
Rapides	Alexandria, LA	38,800	37,780	97
Red River	Shreveport	3,000	2,880	96
Richland	Monroe-El Dorado	7,200	7,040	98
Sabine	Shreveport	6,600	6,280	95
St Bernard	New Orleans	18,600	18,450	99
St Charles	New Orleans	9,700	9,480	98
St Helena	Baton Rouge	2,800	2,690	96
St James	New Orleans	4,900	4,770	97
St John the Bapt	New Orleans	7,100	6,990	98
St Landry	Lafayette, LA	25,300	24,600	97
St Martin	Lafayette, LA	10,300	10,110	98
St Mary	Baton Rouge	18,000	17,590	98
St Tammany	New Orleans	28,600	28,040	98
Tangipahoa	New Orleans	23,500	22,580	96
Tensas	Monroe-El Dorado	2,600	2,550	98
Terrebonne	New Orleans	25,600	25,170	98
Union	Monroe-El Dorado	6,400	6,330	99
Vermilion	Lafayette, LA	15,100	14,910	99
Vernon	Alexandria, LA	10,500	9,980	95
Washington	New Orleans	14,300	13,690	96
Webster	Shreveport	14,400	14,120	98
West Baton Rouge	Baton Rouge	5,500	5,410	98
West Carroll	Monroe-El Dorado	4,600	4,490	98
West Feliciana	Baton Rouge	1,300	1,260	97
Winn	Monroe-El Dorado	5,600	5,420	97
	STATE TOTAL	1,290,400	1,261,820	98
MAINE				
Androscoggin	Portland-Poland Spring	33,600	33,150	99
Aroostook	Presque Isle	30,200	29,710	98
Cumberland	Portland-Poland Spring	72,300	71,190	98
Franklin	Portland-Poland Spring	8,300	8,150	98
Hancock	Bangor	15,200	14,980	99
Kennebec	Portland-Poland Spring	34,900	34,410	99
Knox	Bangor	12,300	12,040	98

COUNTY	MARKET	HOUSEHOLDS	TV's	%
MAINE—*Cont'd*				
Lincoln	Portland-Poland Spring	9,200	9,100	99
Oxford	Portland-Poland Spring	16,300	16,020	98
Penobscot	Bangor	45,600	44,930	99
Piscataquis	Bangor	6,100	6,010	99
Sagadahoc	Portland-Poland Spring	9,600	9,420	98
Somerset	Bangor	15,800	15,490	98
Waldo	Bangor	9,800	9,670	99
Washington	Bangor	12,700	12,480	98
York	Portland-Poland Spring	43,500	43,100	99
	STATE TOTAL	375,400	369,850	99
MARYLAND				
Allegany	Washington, DC, Hagerstown	31,000	30,300	98
Anne Arundel	Baltimore	112,900	111,820	99
Baltimore	Baltimore	523,100	514,810	98
Calvert	Washington, DC, Hagerstown	8,800	8,450	96
Caroline	Baltimore	8,500	8,340	98
Carroll	Baltimore	29,300	28,740	98
Cecil	Baltimore	16,900	16,650	99
Charles	Washington, DC, Hagerstown	19,100	18,680	98
Dorchester	Baltimore	11,000	10,820	98
Frederick	Washington, DC, Hagerstown	34,400	33,870	98
Garrett	Pittsburgh	8,600	8,210	95
Harford	Baltimore	46,200	45,650	99
Howard	Baltimore	36,400	36,150	99
Kent	Baltimore	6,300	6,200	98
Montgomery	Washington, DC, Hagerstown	200,800	198,730	99
Prince Georges	Washington, DC, Hagerstown	222,200	219,620	99
Queen Annes	Baltimore	7,800	7,630	98
St Marys	Washington, DC, Hagerstown	15,800	15,320	97
Somerset	Salisbury	7,100	6,930	98
Talbot	Baltimore	10,300	10,090	98
Washington	Washington, DC, Hagerstown	39,400	38,410	97
Wicomico	Salisbury	22,300	21,910	98
Worcester	Salisbury	9,800	9,460	97
	STATE TOTAL	1,428,000	1,406,790	99
MASSACHUSETTS				
Barnstable	Boston, Manchester, Worcestr	55,200	54,640	99
Berkshire	Albany-Schenectady-Troy	51,100	50,320	98
Bristol	Providence	169,400	167,570	99
Dukes	Providence	3,900	3,800	97
Essex	Boston, Manchester, Worcestr	221,100	218,330	99
Franklin	Springfield-Holyoke	24,700	24,170	98
Hampden	Springfield-Holyoke	161,300	159,020	99
Hampshire	Springfield-Holyoke	42,000	40,970	98
Middlesex	Boston, Manchester, Worcestr	473,100	466,690	99
Nantucket	Boston, Manchester, Worcestr	2,300	2,270	99
Norfolk	Boston, Manchester, Worcestr	205,600	204,070	99
Plymouth	Boston, Manchester, Worcestr	129,800	128,640	99
Suffolk	Boston, Manchester, Worcestr	268,300	260,290	97
Worcester	Boston, Manchester, Worcestr	221,200	218,740	99
	STATE TOTAL	2,029,000	1,999,520	99

COUNTY	MARKET	HOUSEHOLDS	TV's	%

MICHIGAN

COUNTY	MARKET	HOUSEHOLDS	TV's	%
Alcona	Flint-Saginaw-Bay City	3,700	3,610	98
Alger	Marquette	3,200	3,150	98
Allegan	Grand Rapids-Kalmzoo-B. Crk	24,100	23,730	98
Alpena	Alpena	11,000	10,820	98
Antrim	Traverse City-Cadillac	5,600	5,450	97
Arenac	Flint-Saginaw-Bay City	4,800	4,740	99
Baraga	Marquette	2,700	2,650	98
Barry	Grand Rapids-Kalmzoo-B. Crk	14,300	14,120	99
Bay	Flint-Saginaw-Bay City	39,200	38,890	99
Benzie	Traverse City-Cadillac	3,700	3,530	95
Berrien	South Bend-Elkhart	61,600	60,470	98
Branch	Grand Rapids-Kalmzoo-B. Crk	13,000	12,720	98
Calhoun	Grand Rapids-Kalmzoo-B. Crk	49,600	49,100	99
Cass	South Bend-Elkhart	16,000	15,770	99
Charlevoix	Traverse City-Cadillac	6,700	6,640	99
Cheboygan	Traverse City-Cadillac	6,800	6,680	98
Chippewa	Traverse City-Cadillac	12,800	12,570	98
Clare	Flint-Saginaw-Bay City	8,600	8,510	99
Clinton	Lansing	17,400	17,120	98
Crawford	Traverse City-Cadillac	3,200	3,130	98
Delta	Green Bay	13,900	13,750	99
Dickinson	Green Bay	9,700	9,540	98
Eaton	Lansing	27,400	27,100	99
Emmet	Traverse City-Cadillac	7,000	6,840	98
Genesee	Flint-Saginaw-Bay City	150,100	148,320	99
Gladwin	Flint-Saginaw-Bay City	6,200	6,120	99
Gogebic	Duluth-Superior	8,000	7,750	97
Grand Traverse	Traverse City-Cadillac	15,300	15,140	99
Gratiot	Flint-Saginaw-Bay City	13,000	12,750	98
Hillsdale	Lansing	14,600	14,240	98
Houghton	Marquette	13,400	12,730	95
Huron	Flint-Saginaw-Bay City	12,300	12,100	98
Ingham	Lansing	92,700	90,970	98
Ionia	Grand Rapids-Kalmzoo-B. Crk	15,600	15,460	99
Iosco	Flint-Saginaw-Bay City	9,900	9,800	99
Iron	Marquette	6,600	6,420	97
Isabella	Flint-Saginaw-Bay City	15,600	15,310	98
Jackson	Lansing	49,500	48,860	99
Kalamazoo	Grand Rapids-Kalmzoo-B. Crk	68,400	67,500	99
Kalkaska	Traverse City-Cadillac	3,700	3,640	98
Kent	Grand Rapids-Kalmzoo-B. Crk	144,600	142,320	98
Keweenaw	Marquette	1,000	990	99
Lake	Traverse City-Cadillac	2,600	2,540	98
Lapeer	Detroit	20,600	20,310	99
Leelanau	Traverse City-Cadillac	4,400	4,360	99
Lenawee	Toledo	29,800	29,450	99
Livingston	Detroit	28,700	28,390	99
Luce	Traverse City-Cadillac	2,400	2,350	98
Mackinac	Traverse City-Cadillac	4,000	3,880	97
Macomb	Detroit	211,600	210,120	99
Manistee	Traverse City-Cadillac	8,300	8,140	98
Marquette	Marquette	23,800	23,460	99
Mason	Traverse City-Cadillac	9,000	8,830	98
Mecosta	Traverse City-Cadillac	11,500	11,280	98
Menominee	Green Bay	9,300	9,230	99
Midland	Flint-Saginaw-Bay City	22,300	22,140	99
Missaukee	Traverse City-Cadillac	3,400	3,380	99
Monroe	Detroit	41,400	40,930	99

COUNTY	MARKET	HOUSEHOLDS	TV's	%
MICHIGAN—*Cont'd*				
Montcalm	Grand Rapids-Kalmzoo-B. Crk	16,300	15,960	98
Montmorency	Traverse City-Cadillac	2,800	2,720	97
Muskegon	Grand Rapids-Kalmzoo-B. Crk	52,500	51,830	99
Newaygo	Grand Rapids-Kalmzoo-B. Crk	10,400	10,210	98
Oakland	Detroit	323,000	320,590	99
Oceana	Grand Rapids-Kalmzoo-B. Crk	7,500	7,280	97
Ogemaw	Flint-Saginaw-Bay City	5,500	5,470	99
Ontonagon	Marquette	4,300	4,110	96
Osceola	Traverse City-Cadillac	6,700	6,600	99
Oscoda	Traverse City-Cadillac	2,700	2,610	97
Otsego	Traverse City-Cadillac	4,900	4,810	98
Ottawa	Grand Rapids-Kalmzoo-B. Crk	46,100	45,320	98
Presque Isle	Traverse City-Cadillac	4,700	4,560	97
Roscommon	Traverse City-Cadillac	6,300	6,230	99
Saginaw	Flint-Saginaw-Bay City	73,800	73,050	99
St Clair	Detroit	45,700	45,130	99
St Joseph	South Bend-Elkhart	19,400	18,910	97
Sanilac	Detroit	14,100	13,830	98
Schoolcraft	Green Bay	3,400	3,270	96
Shiawassee	Flint-Saginaw-Bay City	23,500	23,290	99
Tuscola	Flint-Saginaw-Bay City	17,700	17,520	99
Van Buren	Grand Rapids-Kalmzoo-B. Crk	22,200	21,890	99
Washtenaw	Detroit	84,300	82,280	98
Wayne	Detroit	855,100	840,440	98
Wexford	Traverse City-Cadillac	7,900	7,830	99
	STATE TOTAL	3,100,400	3,055,580	99
MINNESOTA				
Aitkin	Duluth-Superior	5,400	5,240	97
Anoka	Minneapolis-St. Paul	57,800	57,220	99
Becker	Fargo-Valley City	10,100	9,610	95
Beltrami	Alexandria, MN	10,500	10,070	96
Benton	Minneapolis-St. Paul	7,000	6,910	99
Big Stone	Alexandria, MN	2,900	2,850	98
Bl Erth-Ncl-S	Mankato	20,000	19,610	98
Brown	Mankato	10,400	10,210	98
Carlton	Duluth-Superior	10,200	10,080	99
Carver	Minneapolis-St. Paul	11,400	11,350	100
Cass	Alexandria, MN	7,800	7,590	97
Chippewa	Alexandria, MN	6,200	6,100	98
Chisago	Minneapolis-St. Paul	8,100	8,010	99
Clay	Fargo-Valley City	15,600	15,450	99
Clearwater	Fargo-Valley City	3,100	2,930	95
Cook	Duluth-Superior	1,500	1,450	97
Cottonwood	Mankato	5,900	5,700	97
Crow Wing	Alexandria, MN	15,200	14,800	97
Dakota	Minneapolis-St. Paul	57,800	57,460	99
Dodge	Mason City-Austin-Rochestr	4,600	4,530	98
Douglas	Alexandria, MN	9,400	9,230	98
Faribault	Mason City-Austin-Rochestr	7,600	7,510	99
Fillmore	Mason City-Austin-Rochestr	8,500	8,390	99
Freeborn	Mason City-Austin-Rochestr	13,600	13,480	99
Goodhue	Minneapolis-St. Paul	14,600	14,350	98
Grant	Alexandria, MN	2,700	2,680	99
Hennepin	Minneapolis-St. Paul	336,100	330,400	98

COUNTY	MARKET	HOUSEHOLDS	TV's	%

MINNESOTA—*Cont'd*

COUNTY	MARKET	HOUSEHOLDS	TV's	%
Houston	La Crosse-Eau Claire	5,900	5,790	98
Hubbard	Alexandria, MN	4,900	4,750	97
Isanti	Minneapolis-St. Paul	7,200	7,000	97
Itasca	Duluth-Superior	14,500	14,180	98
Jackson	Mankato	5,200	5,090	98
Kanabec	Minneapolis-St. Paul	4,600	4,490	98
Kandiyohi	Minneapolis-St. Paul	11,700	11,450	98
Kittson	Fargo-Valley City	2,600	2,530	97
Koochiching	Duluth-Superior	6,400	6,130	96
Lac Qui Parle	Alexandria, MN	3,900	3,830	98
Lake	Duluth-Superior	5,000	4,950	99
Lake of the Wood	Fargo-Valley City	1,400	1,280	91
Le Sueur	Minneapolis-St. Paul	8,000	7,840	98
Lincoln	Sioux Falls (Mitchell)	3,100	3,060	99
Lyon	Minneapolis-St. Paul	8,100	7,990	99
McLeod	Minneapolis-St. Paul	10,300	10,120	98
Mahnomen	Fargo-Valley City	2,000	1,950	98
Marshall	Fargo-Valley City	5,000	4,870	97
Martin	Mankato	9,700	9,530	98
Meeker	Minneapolis-St. Paul	7,600	7,440	98
Mille Lacs	Minneapolis-St. Paul	6,700	6,540	98
Morrison	Minneapolis-St. Paul	9,100	8,920	98
Mower	Mason City-Austin-Rochestr	14,600	14,500	99
Murray	Sioux Falls (Mitchell)	4,200	4,140	99
Nicollet-N	Minneapolis-St. Paul	4,400	4,300	98
Nobles	Sioux Falls (Mitchell)	8,100	7,990	99
Norman	Fargo-Valley City	3,700	3,600	97
Olmsted	Mason City-Austin-Rochestr	31,800	31,200	98
Otter Tail	Fargo-Valley City	18,300	17,880	98
Pennington	Fargo-Valley City	5,500	5,320	97
Pine	Minneapolis-St. Paul	7,000	6,790	97
Pipestone	Sioux Falls (Mitchell)	4,300	4,150	97
Polk	Fargo-Valley City	12,800	12,590	98
Pope	Alexandria, MN	4,300	4,270	99
Ramsey	Minneapolis-St. Paul	159,900	157,280	98
Red Lake	Fargo-Valley City	1,600	1,570	98
Redwood	Minneapolis-St. Paul	7,200	7,090	98
Renville	Minneapolis-St. Paul	7,800	7,640	98
Rice	Minneapolis-St. Paul	13,600	13,450	99
Rock	Sioux Falls (Mitchell)	4,100	4,000	98
Roseau	Fargo-Valley City	4,300	4,100	95
St Louis	Duluth-Superior	79,700	78,090	98
Scott	Minneapolis-St. Paul	12,900	12,770	99
Sherburne	Minneapolis-St. Paul	9,300	9,130	98
Sibley	Minneapolis-St. Paul	5,400	5,290	98
Stearns	Minneapolis-St. Paul	29,100	28,610	98
Steele	Minneapolis-St. Paul	10,900	10,710	98
Stevens	Alexandria, MN	3,600	3,490	97
Swift	Alexandria, MN	4,700	4,560	97
Todd	Alexandria, MN	8,800	8,600	98
Traverse	Alexandria, MN	2,200	2,160	98
Wabasha	Minneapolis-St. Paul	6,900	6,720	97
Wadena	Alexandria, MN	4,900	4,760	97
Waseca	Minneapolis-St. Paul	6,400	6,250	98
Washington	Minneapolis-St. Paul	33,000	32,700	99
Watonwan	Mankato	4,800	4,720	98
Wilkin	Fargo-Valley City	2,800	2,790	100
Winona	La Crosse-Eau Claire	15,800	15,490	98

COUNTY	MARKET	HOUSEHOLDS	TV's	%
MINNESOTA—*Cont'd*				
Wright	Minneapolis-St. Paul	16,200	15,880	98
Yellow Medicine	Minneapolis-St. Paul	5,200	5,100	98
	STATE TOTAL	1,387,000	1,362,660	98
MISSISSIPPI				
Adams	Jackson, MS	12,400	11,790	95
Alcorn	Memphis	10,600	10,120	95
Amite	Baton Rouge	4,100	3,870	94
Attala	Jackson, MS	6,700	6,450	96
Benton	Memphis	2,200	2,150	98
Bolivar	Greenwood	13,700	12,810	94
Calhoun	Columbus-Tupelo	5,400	5,180	96
Carroll	Greenwood	2,500	2,370	95
Chickasaw	Columbus-Tupelo	5,800	5,510	95
Choctaw	Columbus-Tupelo	3,100	2,880	93
Claiborne	Jackson, MS	3,500	3,220	92
Clarke	Meridian	5,400	5,220	97
Clay	Columbus-Tupelo	6,400	6,120	96
Coahoma	Memphis	11,900	11,110	93
Copiah	Jackson, MS	8,200	7,760	95
Covington	Hattiesburg-Laurel	4,700	4,560	97
De Soto	Memphis	15,300	14,870	97
Forrest	Hattiesburg-Laurel	21,500	20,940	97
Franklin	Jackson, MS	2,900	2,720	94
George	Mobile-Pensacola	4,600	4,440	97
Greene	Mobile-Pensacola	3,100	2,980	96
Grenada	Columbus-Tupelo	6,900	6,590	96
Hancock	New Orleans	6,400	6,180	97
Harrison	Biloxi-Gulfport	47,400	46,210	97
Hinds	Jackson, MS	77,100	75,480	98
Holmes	Jackson, MS	6,600	6,130	93
Humphreys	Jackson, MS	4,100	3,920	96
Issaquena	Jackson, MS	600	570	95
Itawamba	Columbus-Tupelo	6,000	5,830	97
Jackson	Mobile-Pensacola	34,400	33,770	98
Jasper	Hattiesburg-Laurel	5,200	5,020	97
Jefferson	Jackson, MS	2,400	2,260	94
Jefferson Davis	Jackson, MS	4,000	3,910	98
Jones	Hattiesburg-Laurel	20,800	20,280	98
Kemper	Meridian	3,000	2,750	92
Lafayette	Memphis	8,100	7,910	98
Lamar	Hattiesburg-Laurel	6,300	6,060	96
Lauderdale	Meridian	25,800	24,990	97
Lawrence	Jackson, MS	4,000	3,820	96
Leake	Jackson, MS	6,400	6,130	96
Lee	Columbus-Tupelo	18,800	18,410	98
Leflore	Greenwood	13,000	12,320	95
Lincoln	Jackson, MS	9,100	8,830	97
Lowndes	Columbus-Tupelo	17,000	16,560	97
Madison	Jackson, MS	9,700	9,310	96
Marion	Hattiesburg-Laurel	8,100	7,740	96
Marshall	Memphis	7,300	6,840	94
Monroe	Columbus-Tupelo	11,400	11,000	96
Montgomery	Columbus-Tupelo	4,200	3,980	95
Neshoba	Meridian	7,700	7,370	96
Newton	Meridian	6,700	6,480	97

COUNTY	MARKET	HOUSEHOLDS	TV's	%
MISSISSIPPI—*Cont'd*				
Noxubee	Columbus-Tupelo	4,000	3,630	91
Oktibbeha	Columbus-Tupelo	10,500	10,170	97
Panola	Memphis	8,300	8,010	97
Pearl River	New Orleans	9,100	8,870	97
Perry	Hattiesburg-Laurel	3,200	3,070	96
Pike	Jackson, MS	11,600	11,010	95
Pontotoc	Memphis	7,000	6,620	95
Prentiss	Columbus-Tupelo	7,500	7,280	97
Quitman	Memphis	4,000	3,730	93
Rankin	Jackson, MS	18,300	17,810	97
Scott	Jackson, MS	7,200	6,970	97
Sharkey	Jackson, MS	2,200	2,090	95
Simpson	Jackson, MS	6,900	6,670	97
Smith	Jackson, MS	4,800	4,670	97
Stone	Biloxi-Gulfport	2,500	2,370	95
Sunflower	Greenwood	9,500	9,080	96
Tallahatchie	Greenwood	5,300	4,920	93
Tate	Memphis	5,800	5,580	96
Tippah	Memphis	6,700	6,510	97
Tishomingo	Columbus-Tupelo	6,400	6,160	96
Tunica	Memphis	3,200	3,010	94
Union	Memphis	7,500	7,330	98
Walthall	New Orleans	4,200	4,020	96
Warren	Jackson, MS	16,900	16,250	96
Washington	Jackson, MS	22,000	20,810	95
Wayne	Hattiesburg-Laurel	5,600	5,340	95
Webster	Columbus-Tupelo	3,500	3,360	96
Wilkinson	Baton Rouge	3,000	2,810	94
Winston	Columbus-Tupelo	6,600	6,410	97
Yalobusha	Memphis	4,200	3,970	95
Yazoo	Jackson, MS	9,300	8,890	96
	STATE TOTAL	769,300	741,140	96
MISSOURI				
Adair	Ottumwa-Kirksville	8,900	8,640	97
Andrew	St. Joseph	5,300	5,270	99
Atchison	Omaha	3,300	3,210	97
Audrain	Columbia-Jefferson City	10,000	9,700	97
Barry	Springfield, MO	8,700	8,390	96
Barton	Joplin-Pittsburg	4,400	4,300	98
Bates	Kansas City	6,300	6,110	97
Benton	Columbia-Jefferson City	5,400	5,220	97
Bollinger	Paducah-C. Girardeau-Harrbg	3,600	3,520	98
Boone	Columbia-Jefferson City	29,900	29,150	97
Buchanan	St. Joseph	32,500	32,000	98
Butler	Paducah-C. Girardeau-Harrbg	14,300	13,850	97
Caldwell	Kansas City	3,900	3,820	98
Callaway	Columbia-Jefferson City	8,800	8,530	97
Camden	Springfield, MO	7,200	6,980	97
Cape Girardeau	Paducah-C. Girardeau-Harrbg	18,600	18,230	98
Carroll	Kansas City	4,800	4,660	97
Carter	Paducah-C. Girardeau-Harrbg	1,800	1,690	94
Cass	Kansas City	16,800	16,480	98
Cedar	Springfield, MO	4,500	4,250	94
Chariton	Columbia-Jefferson City	3,700	3,600	97
Christian	Springfield, MO	8,000	7,750	97

COUNTY	MARKET	HOUSEHOLDS	TV's	%
MISSOURI—*Cont'd*				
Clark	Quincy-Hannibal-Keokuk	3,100	3,060	99
Clay	Kansas City	45,900	45,380	99
Clinton	Kansas City	5,600	5,530	99
Cole	Columbia-Jefferson City	18,300	17,980	98
Cooper	Columbia-Jefferson City	5,800	5,610	97
Crawford	St. Louis	6,200	6,100	98
Dade	Springfield, MO	3,200	3,110	97
Dallas	Springfield, MO	4,900	4,770	97
Daviess	Kansas City	3,400	3,300	97
De Kalb	St. Joseph	3,100	3,050	98
Dent	Springfield, MO	4,400	4,200	95
Douglas	Springfield, MO	4,200	3,990	95
Dunklin	Memphis	13,700	13,310	97
Franklin	St. Louis	22,000	21,540	98
Gasconade	St. Louis	5,400	5,310	98
Gentry	St. Joseph	3,500	3,430	98
Greene	Springfield, MO	62,700	61,240	98
Grundy	Kansas City	4,500	4,430	98
Harrison	St. Joseph	4,000	3,900	98
Henry	Kansas City	7,800	7,640	98
Hickory	Springfield, MO	3,000	2,920	97
Holt	St. Joseph	3,100	3,030	98
Howard	Columbia-Jefferson City	3,800	3,740	98
Howell	Springfield, MO	11,100	10,670	96
Iron	St. Louis	3,900	3,800	97
Jackson	Kansas City	248,200	241,950	97
Jasper	Joplin-Pittsburg	32,300	31,640	98
Jefferson	St. Louis	39,300	38,730	99
Johnson	Kansas City	11,500	11,130	97
Knox	Quincy-Hannibal-Keokuk	2,100	2,020	96
Laclede	Springfield, MO	9,000	8,670	96
Lafayette	Kansas City	10,600	10,380	98
Lawrence	Springfield, MO	10,800	10,480	97
Lewis	Quincy-Hannibal-Keokuk	3,800	3,690	97
Lincoln	St. Louis	7,200	7,030	98
Linn	Kansas City	6,400	6,300	98
Livingston	Kansas City	6,000	5,860	98
McDonald	Joplin-Pittsburg	5,700	5,420	95
Macon	Quincy-Hannibal-Keokuk	6,800	6,580	97
Madison	St. Louis	3,700	3,600	97
Maries	Columbia-Jefferson City	2,600	2,490	96
Marion	Quincy-Hannibal-Keokuk	10,800	10,620	98
Mercer	Des Moines-Ames	1,900	1,850	97
Miller	Columbia-Jefferson City	6,300	6,170	98
Mississippi	Paducah-C. Girardeau-Harrbg	5,600	5,500	98
Moniteau	Columbia-Jefferson City	4,500	4,420	98
Monroe	Quincy-Hannibal-Keokuk	3,800	3,750	99
Montgomery	St. Louis	4,200	4,080	97
Morgan	Columbia-Jefferson City	4,900	4,710	96
New Madrid	Paducah-C. Girardeau-Harrbg	8,100	7,840	97
Newton	Joplin-Pittsburg	13,400	13,230	99
Nodaway	St. Joseph	7,700	7,550	98
Oregon	Springfield, MO	4,300	4,050	94
Osage	Columbia-Jefferson City	3,900	3,880	99
Ozark	Springfield, MO	3,100	2,940	95
Pemiscot	Memphis	8,300	8,020	97
Perry	St. Louis	5,500	5,390	98
Pettis	Columbia-Jefferson City	13,800	13,460	98

COUNTY	MARKET	HOUSEHOLDS	TV's	%
MISSOURI—*Cont'd*				
Phelps	Columbia-Jefferson City	10,700	10,190	95
Pike	Quincy-Hannibal-Keokuk	6,600	6,390	97
Platte	Kansas City	13,500	13,350	99
Polk	Springfield, MO	7,300	7,130	98
Pulaski	Springfield, MO	8,600	8,520	99
Putnam	Ottumwa-Kirksville	2,800	2,690	96
Ralls	Quincy-Hannibal-Keokuk	3,200	3,180	99
Randolph	Columbia-Jefferson City	9,000	8,730	97
Ray	Kansas City	7,000	6,860	98
Reynolds	Paducah-C. Girardeau-Harrbg	2,400	2,230	93
Ripley	Jonesboro	5,000	4,490	90
St Charles	St. Louis	37,000	36,550	99
St Clair	Kansas City	3,900	3,690	95
St Francois	St. Louis	14,300	14,060	98
St Louis	St. Louis	510,900	499,600	98
Ste Genevieve	St. Louis	4,500	4,430	98
Saline	Kansas City	8,300	8,100	98
Schuyler	Ottumwa-Kirksville	2,100	2,040	97
Scotland	Quincy-Hannibal-Keokuk	2,300	2,260	98
Scott	Paducah-C. Girardeau-Harrbg	12,700	12,470	98
Shannon	Springfield, MO	2,900	2,730	94
Shelby	Quincy-Hannibal-Keokuk	3,100	3,030	98
Stoddard	Paducah-C. Girardeau-Harrbg	10,700	10,540	99
Stone	Springfield, MO	5,400	5,280	98
Sullivan	Ottumwa-Kirksville	3,100	3,010	97
Taney	Springfield, MO	7,400	7,190	97
Texas	Springfield, MO	8,300	7,990	96
Vernon	Joplin-Pittsburg	7,200	7,100	99
Warren	St. Louis	4,800	4,720	98
Washington	St. Louis	5,100	4,960	97
Wayne	Paducah-C. Girardeau-Harrbg	4,100	3,990	97
Webster	Springfield, MO	7,100	6,830	96
Worth	St. Joseph	1,300	1,280	98
Wright	Springfield, MO	6,000	5,800	97
	STATE TOTAL	1,732,000	1,691,230	98
MONTANA				
Beaverhead	Butte	3,300	3,020	92
Big Horn	Billings	3,200	3,100	97
Blaine	Great Falls	2,700	2,480	92
Broadwater	Great Falls	1,300	1,260	97
Carbon	Billings	3,500	3,310	95
Carter	Rapid City	600	570	95
Cascade	Great Falls	30,100	29,550	98
Chouteau	Great Falls	2,400	2,380	99
Custer	Salt Lake City	4,900	4,660	95
Daniels	Minot-Bismarck-Dickinson	1,400	1,360	97
Dawson	Glendive	3,800	3,720	98
Deer Lodge	Butte	5,100	4,980	98
Fallon	Glendive	1,300	1,230	95
Fergus	Great Falls	4,800	4,580	95
Flathead	Missoula	16,700	16,080	96
Gallatin	Butte	14,400	13,860	96
Garfield	Billings	600	550	92
Glacier	Great Falls	3,500	3,300	94
Golden Valley	Billings	400	380	95

COUNTY	MARKET	HOUSEHOLDS	TV's	%
MONTANA—*Cont'd*				
Granite	Butte	1,000	980	98
Hill	Great Falls	6,300	5,990	95
Jefferson	Butte	2,400	2,290	95
Judith Basin	Great Falls	1,100	1,060	96
Lake	Missoula	6,600	6,440	98
Lewis and Clark	Butte	14,700	14,370	98
Liberty	Great Falls	800	790	99
Lincoln	Spokane	5,600	5,410	97
McCone	Minot-Bismarck-Dickinson	900	870	97
Madison	Butte	2,100	2,050	98
Meagher	Great Falls	800	770	96
Mineral	Missoula	1,500	1,470	98
Missoula	Missoula	23,900	22,940	96
Musselshell	Billings	1,900	1,790	94
Park	Salt Lake City	5,100	4,830	95
Petroleum	Billings	200	190	95
Phillips	Great Falls	2,200	2,010	91
Pondera	Great Falls	2,400	2,260	94
Powder River	Rapid City	900	840	93
Powell	Butte	2,800	2,670	95
Prairie	Glendive	600	560	93
Ravalli	Missoula	7,300	7,060	97
Richland	Minot-Bismarck-Dickinson	3,900	3,790	97
Roosevelt	Minot-Bismarck-Dickinson	3,400	3,220	95
Rosebud	Billings	3,700	3,430	93
Sanders	Spokane	3,500	3,430	98
Sheridan	Minot-Bismarck-Dickinson	2,300	2,230	97
Silver Bow	Butte	15,500	15,150	98
Stillwater	Billings	2,000	1,960	98
Sweet Grass	Billings	1,400	1,290	92
Teton	Great Falls	2,200	2,130	97
Toole	Great Falls	2,100	2,040	97
Treasure	Billings	400	390	98
Valley	Great Falls	5,200	5,040	97
Wheatland	Billings	800	770	96
Wibaux	Minot-Bismarck-Dickinson	400	390	98
Yellowstone	Billings	37,600	36,760	98
	STATE TOTAL	279,500	270,030	97
NEBRASKA				
Adams	Lincoln & Hstngs-Krny Plus	11,200	11,100	99
Antelope	Lincoln & Hstngs-Krny Plus	3,500	3,430	98
Arthur	North Platte	200	200	100
Banner	Cheyenne-Scottsblf-Sterlng	300	300	100
Blaine	North Platte	200	200	100
Boone	Lincoln & Hstngs-Krny Plus	2,900	2,810	97
Box Butte	Rapid City	4,000	3,940	99
Boyd	Sioux Falls (Mitchell)	1,200	1,170	98
Brown	Lincoln & Hstngs-Krny Plus	1,500	1,450	97
Buffalo	Lincoln & Hstngs-Krny Plus	11,700	11,550	99
Burt	Omaha	3,300	3,270	99
Butler	Omaha	3,400	3,350	99
Cass	Omaha	7,100	7,050	99
Cedar	Sioux City	3,600	3,560	99
Chase	Lincoln & Hstngs-Krny Plus	1,700	1,680	99
Cherry	Sioux Falls (Mitchell)	2,500	2,410	96

COUNTY	MARKET	HOUSEHOLDS	TV's	%
NEBRASKA—*Cont'd*				
Cheyenne	Rapid City	3,800	3,740	98
Clay	Lincoln & Hstngs-Krny Plus	3,100	3,080	99
Colfax	Omaha	3,800	3,670	97
Cuming	Omaha	4,000	3,940	99
Custer	Lincoln & Hstngs-Krny Plus	5,400	5,270	98
Dakota	Sioux City	5,600	5,560	99
Dawes	Rapid City	3,200	3,120	98
Dawson	Lincoln & Hstngs-Krny Plus	8,300	8,130	98
Deuel	Cheyenne-Scottsblf-Sterlng	1,000	990	99
Dixon	Sioux City	2,700	2,670	99
Dodge	Omaha	12,800	12,610	99
Douglas	Omaha	147,600	144,470	98
Dundy	Lincoln & Hstngs-Krny Plus	1,000	980	98
Fillmore	Lincoln & Hstngs-Krny Plus	3,200	3,110	97
Franklin	Lincoln & Hstngs-Krny Plus	1,800	1,780	99
Frontier	Lincoln & Hstngs-Krny Plus	1,300	1,280	98
Furnas	Lincoln & Hstngs-Krny Plus	2,500	2,440	98
Gage	Lincoln & Hstngs-Krny Plus	8,500	8,410	99
Garden	Rapid City	1,400	1,350	96
Garfield	Lincoln & Hstngs-Krny Plus	1,100	1,090	99
Gosper	Lincoln & Hstngs-Krny Plus	700	700	100
Grant	Rapid City	500	490	98
Greeley	Lincoln & Hstngs-Krny Plus	1,200	1,170	98
Hall	Lincoln & Hstngs-Krny Plus	17,100	16,870	99
Hamilton	Lincoln & Hstngs-Krny Plus	3,100	3,030	98
Harlan	Lincoln & Hstngs-Krny Plus	2,000	1,980	99
Hayes	Lincoln & Hstngs-Krny Plus	400	400	100
Hitchcock	Wichita-Hutchinson Plus	2,100	2,080	99
Holt	Lincoln & Hstngs-Krny Plus	4,600	4,510	98
Hooker	North Platte	300	290	97
Howard	Lincoln & Hstngs-Krny Plus	2,700	2,660	99
Jefferson	Lincoln & Hstngs-Krny Plus	3,900	3,840	98
Johnson	Omaha	1,900	1,870	98
Kearney	Lincoln & Hstngs-Krny Plus	2,500	2,470	99
Keith	North Platte	3,800	3,730	98
Keya Paha	Sioux Falls (Mitchell)	400	400	100
Kimball	Cheyenne-Scottsblf-Sterlng	2,100	2,090	100
Knox	Sioux City	4,100	4,010	98
Lancaster	Lincoln & Hstngs-Krny Plus	67,100	65,600	98
Lincoln	North Platte	13,200	12,950	98
Logan	North Platte	200	200	100
Loup	Lincoln & Hstngs-Krny Plus	300	300	100
McPherson	North Platte	200	200	100
Madison	Sioux City	10,800	10,590	98
Merrick	Lincoln & Hstngs-Krny Plus	3,000	2,950	98
Morrill	Cheyenne-Scottsblf-Sterlng	2,200	2,150	98
Nance	Lincoln & Hstngs-Krny Plus	1,800	1,770	98
Nemaha	Omaha	3,100	3,060	99
Nuckolls	Lincoln & Hstngs-Krny Plus	2,400	2,330	97
Otoe	Omaha	6,000	5,910	99
Pawnee	Omaha	1,300	1,270	98
Perkins	Lincoln & Hstngs-Krny Plus	1,400	1,400	100
Phelps	Lincoln & Hstngs-Krny Plus	3,900	3,860	99
Pierce	Sioux City	3,300	3,260	99
Platte	Lincoln & Hstngs-Krny Plus	9,400	9,300	99
Polk	Lincoln & Hstngs-Krny Plus	2,300	2,290	100
Red Willow	Lincoln & Hstngs-Krny Plus	5,000	4,920	98
Richardson	Omaha	4,500	4,410	98

COUNTY	MARKET	HOUSEHOLDS	TV's	%

NEBRASKA—*Cont'd*

COUNTY	MARKET	HOUSEHOLDS	TV's	%
Rock	Lincoln & Hstngs-Krny Plus	700	690	99
Saline	Lincoln & Hstngs-Krny Plus	5,400	5,330	99
Sarpy	Omaha	22,900	22,710	99
Saunders	Omaha	6,700	6,610	99
Scotts Bluff	Cheyenne-Scottsblf-Sterlng	13,400	13,190	98
Seward	Omaha	5,000	4,850	97
Sheridan	Rapid City	2,800	2,730	98
Sherman	Lincoln & Hstngs-Krny Plus	1,600	1,570	98
Sioux	Rapid City	700	690	99
Stanton	Omaha	2,600	2,550	98
Thayer	Lincoln & Hstngs-Krny Plus	3,000	2,970	99
Thomas	North Platte	400	390	98
Thurston	Sioux City	2,400	2,380	99
Valley	Lincoln & Hstngs-Krny Plus	2,100	2,040	97
Washington	Omaha	5,700	5,650	99
Wayne	Sioux City	3,000	2,970	99
Webster	Lincoln & Hstngs-Krny Plus	2,200	2,120	96
Wheeler	Lincoln & Hstngs-Krny Plus	300	300	100
York	Lincoln & Hstngs-Krny Plus	5,600	5,540	99
	STATE TOTAL	561,700	551,750	98

NEVADA

COUNTY	MARKET	HOUSEHOLDS	TV's	%
Carson City	Reno	10,700	10,320	96
Churchill	Reno	4,600	4,390	95
Clark	Las Vegas	131,800	129,050	98
Douglas	Reno	5,200	5,130	99
Elko	Salt Lake City	6,200	5,580	90
Esmeralda	Reno	500	450	90
Eureka	Salt Lake City	500	450	90
Humboldt	Reno	2,500	2,310	92
Lander	Reno	1,200	1,110	93
Lincoln	Las Vegas	1,100	1,050	95
Lyon	Reno	3,700	3,490	94
Mineral	Reno	2,500	2,320	93
Nye	Reno	2,200	2,030	92
Pershing	Reno	1,200	1,160	97
Storey	Reno	300	290	97
Washoe	Reno	62,100	59,510	96
White Pine	Salt Lake City	3,400	3,260	96
	STATE TOTAL	239,700	231,900	97

NEW HAMPSHIRE

COUNTY	MARKET	HOUSEHOLDS	TV's	%
Belknap	Portland-Poland Spring	13,800	13,580	98
Carroll	Portland-Poland Spring	9,100	8,840	97
Cheshire	Boston, Manchester, Worcestr	20,500	20,020	98
Coos	Portland-Poland Spring	12,000	11,810	98
Grafton	Portland-Poland Spring	20,900	20,320	97
Hillsborough	Boston, Manchester, Worcestr	85,900	84,940	99
Merrimack	Boston, Manchester, Worcestr	30,800	30,290	98
Rockingham	Boston, Manchester, Worcestr	57,100	56,510	99
Strafford	Boston, Manchester, Worcestr	25,900	25,570	99
Sullivan	Boston, Manchester, Worcestr	12,100	11,800	98
	STATE TOTAL	288,100	283,680	98

COUNTY	MARKET	HOUSEHOLDS	TV's	%
NEW JERSEY				
Atlantic	Philadelphia	73,900	72,590	98
Bergen	New York	301,000	298,340	99
Burlington	Philadelphia	103,500	102,660	99
Camden	Philadelphia	161,600	159,980	99
Cape May	Philadelphia	29,300	28,850	98
Cumberland	Philadelphia	46,000	45,300	98
Essex	New York	305,400	297,900	98
Gloucester	Philadelphia	62,900	62,250	99
Hudson	New York	214,800	209,990	98
Hunterdon	New York	25,600	25,190	98
Mercer	Philadelphia	110,700	109,080	99
Middlesex	New York	179,900	177,920	99
Monmouth	New York	154,400	152,850	99
Morris	New York	122,000	121,010	99
Ocean	New York	113,200	111,960	99
Passaic	New York	159,300	155,970	98
Salem	Philadelphia	22,500	22,280	99
Somerset	New York	63,800	63,040	99
Sussex	New York	32,900	32,470	99
Union	New York	176,300	173,900	99
Warren	Philadelphia	28,500	28,200	98
	STATE TOTAL	2,487,500	2,451,730	99
NEW MEXICO				
Bernalillo	Albuquerque, Farmington	137,600	134,140	97
Catron	Tucson (Nogales)	800	680	85
Chaves	Roswell	17,700	17,120	97
Colfax	Albuquerque, Farmington	5,100	4,850	95
Curry	Amarillo	14,500	14,240	98
De Baca	Lubbock	1,000	950	95
Dona Ana	El Paso	25,400	24,480	96
Eddy	Roswell	16,700	16,310	98
Grant	El Paso	8,000	7,570	95
Guadalupe	Albuquerque, Farmington	1,600	1,460	91
Harding	Albuquerque, Farmington	600	530	88
Hidalgo	Tucson (Nogales)	2,100	1,920	91
Lea-N	Roswell	17,100	16,740	98
Lea-S	Odessa-Midland-Monahans	2,400	2,390	100
Lincoln	Albuquerque, Farmington	3,900	3,510	90
Los Alamos	Albuquerque, Farmington	5,500	5,410	98
Luna	El Paso	5,500	5,170	94
McKinley	Albuquerque, Farmington	15,300	12,910	84
Mora	Albuquerque, Farmington	1,700	1,410	83
Otero	El Paso	12,900	12,660	98
Quay	Amarillo	4,200	4,050	96
Rio Arriba	Albuquerque, Farmington	8,200	7,240	88
Roosevelt	Amarillo	6,300	6,060	96
Sandoval	Albuquerque, Farmington	6,400	5,980	93
San Juan	Albuquerque, Farmington	22,900	20,760	91
San Miguel	Albuquerque, Farmington	6,800	6,250	92
Santa Fe	Albuquerque, Farmington	22,300	21,410	96
Sierra	Albuquerque, Farmington	4,300	3,740	87
Socorro	Albuquerque, Farmington	3,300	3,120	95
Taos	Albuquerque, Farmington	6,600	5,860	89
Torrance	Albuquerque, Farmington	2,600	2,430	93

COUNTY	MARKET	HOUSEHOLDS	TV's	%
NEW MEXICO—*Cont'd*				
Union	Amarillo	1,900	1,720	91
Valencia	Albuquerque, Farmington	14,900	14,260	96
	STATE TOTAL	406,100	387,330	95
NEW YORK				
Albany	Albany-Schenectady-Troy	103,700	102,080	98
Allegany	Buffalo	17,100	16,710	98
Bronx	New York	491,800	477,180	97
Broome	Binghamton	78,600	77,370	98
Cattaraugus	Buffalo	31,200	30,500	98
Cayuga	Syracuse, Elmira	27,100	26,690	98
Chautauqua	Buffalo	53,900	52,740	98
Chemung	Syracuse, Elmira	34,700	34,180	99
Chenango	Syracuse, Elmira	16,800	16,560	99
Clinton	Burlington-Plattsburgh	25,300	24,970	99
Columbia	Albany-Schenectady-Troy	20,000	19,760	99
Cortland	Syracuse, Elmira	17,200	16,990	99
Delaware	Binghamton	17,000	16,660	98
Dutchess	New York	77,600	76,410	98
Erie	Buffalo	382,100	377,340	99
Essex	Burlington-Plattsburgh	12,400	12,210	98
Franklin	Burlington-Plattsburgh	15,200	14,730	97
Fulton	Albany-Schenectady-Troy	21,900	21,650	99
Genesee	Buffalo	21,300	21,060	99
Greene	Albany-Schenectady-Troy	15,000	14,800	99
Hamilton	Albany-Schenectady-Troy	2,000	1,990	100
Herkimer	Utica	24,900	24,630	99
Jefferson	Watertown	33,300	33,030	99
Kings	New York	896,200	866,110	97
Lewis	Watertown	8,200	8,090	99
Livingston	Rochester	18,800	18,520	99
Madison	Syracuse, Elmira	21,000	20,660	98
Monroe	Rochester	253,000	249,970	99
Montgomery	Albany-Schenectady-Troy	21,800	21,520	99
Nassau	New York	444,600	441,510	99
New York	New York	704,200	655,980	93
Niagara	Buffalo	83,100	82,250	99
Onondaga	Syracuse, Elmira	164,700	162,540	99
Ontario	Rochester	30,500	30,170	99
Orange	New York	85,700	84,440	99
Orleans	Buffalo	13,600	13,370	98
Oswego	Syracuse, Elmira	36,400	36,040	99
Otsego	Utica	19,800	19,490	98
Putnam	New York	24,300	24,120	99
Queens	New York	772,700	761,940	99
Rensselaer	Albany-Schenectady-Troy	51,900	51,200	99
Richmond	New York	111,000	109,780	99
Rockland	New York	73,800	72,700	99
St Lawrence-E	Burlington-Plattsburgh	13,900	13,690	98
St Lawrence-W	Watertown	23,200	22,830	98
Saratoga	Albany-Schenectady-Troy	48,300	47,660	99
Schenectady	Albany-Schenectady-Troy	56,600	56,010	99
Schoharie	Albany-Schenectady-Troy	10,100	9,920	98
Schuyler	Syracuse, Elmira	6,700	6,580	98
Seneca	Syracuse, Elmira	11,200	11,080	99
Steuben	Syracuse, Elmira	35,900	35,130	98

COUNTY	MARKET	HOUSEHOLDS	TV's	%
NEW YORK—*Cont'd*				
Suffolk	New York	388,000	384,750	99
Sullivan	New York	22,900	22,010	96
Tioga	Binghamton	16,600	16,320	98
Tompkins	Syracuse, Elmira	30,100	28,690	95
Ulster	New York	56,400	55,060	98
Warren	Albany-Schenectady-Troy	19,400	19,110	99
Washington	Albany-Schenectady-Troy	18,700	18,480	99
Wayne	Rochester	28,500	28,210	99
Westchester	New York	293,200	289,260	99
Wyoming	Buffalo	12,500	12,370	99
Yates	Syracuse, Elmira	7,300	7,230	99
Oneida-E	Utica	55,100	54,270	98
Oneida-W	Syracuse, Elmira	35,300	34,810	99
	STATE TOTAL	6,565,300	6,414,110	98
NORTH CAROLINA				
Alamance	Greensboro-H. Point-W. Salem	35,600	35,080	99
Alexander	Charlotte	7,200	7,050	98
Alleghany	Greensboro-H. Point-W. Salem	3,600	3,550	99
Anson	Charlotte	7,900	7,750	98
Ashe	Charlotte	7,200	6,910	96
Avery	Tri-Cities; TN-VA	4,700	4,500	96
Beaufort	Greenville-N. Bern-Washngtn	13,600	13,240	97
Bertie	Greenville-N. Bern-Washngtn	6,700	6,280	94
Bladen	Wilmington	9,300	8,950	96
Brunswick	Wilmington	11,800	11,290	96
Buncombe	Greenville-Spart-Asheville	58,500	56,650	97
Burke	Charlotte	21,600	21,150	98
Cabarrus	Charlotte	28,100	27,620	98
Caldwell	Charlotte	20,300	19,880	98
Camden	Norfolk-Portsmth-Newpt Nws	1,800	1,760	98
Carteret	Greenville-N. Bern-Washngtn	13,100	12,640	96
Caswell	Greensboro-H. Point-W. Salem	6,200	6,080	98
Catawba	Charlotte	35,200	34,690	99
Chatham	Raleigh-Durham	10,400	10,180	98
Cherokee	Chattanooga	6,300	6,010	95
Chowan	Norfolk-Portsmth-Newpt Nws	4,100	4,010	98
Clay	Atlanta	1,900	1,800	95
Cleveland	Charlotte	26,800	26,360	98
Columbus	Wilmington	17,300	16,690	96
Craven	Greenville-N. Bern-Washngtn	22,200	21,760	98
Cumberland	Raleigh-Durham	70,100	68,800	98
Currituck	Norfolk-Portsmth-Newpot Nws	3,600	3,520	98
Dare	Norfolk-Portsmth-Newpot Nws	3,700	3,580	97
Davidson	Greensboro-H. Point-W. Salem	36,000	34,990	97
Davie	Greensboro-H. Point-W. Salem	7,600	7,260	96
Duplin	Greenville-N. Bern-Washngtn	13,300	12,900	97
Durham	Raleigh-Durham	52,800	51,240	97
Edgecombe-Nash-E	Greenville-N. Bern-Washngtn	33,000	32,150	97
Forsyth	Greensboro-H. Point-W. Salem	83,400	81,630	98
Franklin	Raleigh-Durham	9,000	8,730	97
Gaston	Charlotte	53,300	52,270	98
Gates	Norfolk-Portsmth-Newpt Nws	2,600	2,500	96
Graham	Knoxville	1,900	1,820	96
Granville	Raleigh-Durham	9,500	9,300	98
Greene	Greenville-N. Bern-Washngtn	4,800	4,710	98

COUNTY	MARKET	HOUSEHOLDS	TV's	%

NORTH CAROLINA—*Cont'd*

COUNTY	MARKET	HOUSEHOLDS	TV's	%
Guilford	Greensboro-H. Point-W. Salem	107,100	105,150	98
Halifax	Greenville-N. Bern-Washngtn	17,000	16,300	96
Harnett	Raleigh-Durham	18,100	17,650	98
Haywood	Greenville-Spart-Asheville	15,800	15,310	97
Henderson	Greenville-Spart-Asheville	19,600	19,000	97
Hertford	Norfolk-Portsmth-Newpt Nws	7,400	7,100	96
Hoke	Raleigh-Durham	4,800	4,660	97
Hyde	Greenville-N. Bern-Washngtn	2,000	1,880	94
Iredell	Charlotte	27,200	26,430	97
Jackson	Greenville-Spart-Asheville	7,800	7,530	97
Johnston	Raleigh-Durham	23,400	22,870	98
Jones	Greenville-N. Bern-Washngtn	3,000	2,870	96
Lee	Raleigh-Durham	11,200	10,980	98
Lenoir	Greenville-N. Bern-Washngtn	20,400	19,850	97
Lincoln	Charlotte	13,200	13,060	99
McDowell	Greenville-Spart-Asheville	11,800	11,510	98
Macon	Greenville-Spart-Asheville	6,900	6,620	96
Madison	Greenville-Spart-Asheville	5,400	5,130	95
Martin	Greenville-N. Bern-Washngtn	8,200	7,990	97
Mecklenburg	Charlotte	132,300	129,950	98
Mitchell	Greenville-Spart-Asheville	4,900	4,810	98
Montgomery	Greensboro-H. Point-W. Salem	6,600	6,380	97
Moore	Raleigh-Durham	14,500	14,140	98
Nash-W	Raleigh-Durham	7,300	7,060	97
New Hanover	Wilmington	38,400	37,500	98
Northampton	Norfolk-Portsmth-Newpt Nws	6,800	6,450	95
Onslow	Greenville-N. Bern-Washngtn	26,600	26,030	98
Orange	Raleigh-Durham	24,200	23,410	97
Pamlico	Greenville-N. Bern-Washngtn	3,600	3,490	97
Pasquotank	Norfolk-Portsmth-Newpt Nws	9,800	9,580	98
Pender	Wilmington	7,000	6,660	95
Perquimans	Norfolk-Portsmth-Newpt Nws	2,800	2,710	97
Person	Raleigh-Durham	9,000	8,710	97
Pitt	Greenville-N. Bern-Washngtn	25,700	25,000	97
Polk	Greenville-Spart-Asheville	4,400	4,310	98
Randolph	Greensboro-H. Point-W. Salem	30,000	29,140	97
Richmond	Charlotte	14,200	13,820	97
Robeson	Wilmington	28,300	27,380	97
Rockingham	Greensboro-H. Point-W. Salem	27,600	27,060	98
Rowan	Charlotte	33,200	32,570	98
Rutherford	Greenville-Spart-Asheville	18,100	17,810	98
Sampson	Raleigh-Durham	15,600	15,290	98
Scotland	Florence, SC	9,300	9,030	97
Stanly	Charlotte	16,400	16,240	99
Stokes	Greensboro-H. Point-W. Salem	10,100	9,920	98
Surry	Greensboro-H. Point-W. Salem	20,000	19,710	99
Swain	Greenville-Spart-Asheville	3,600	3,400	94
Transylvania	Greenville-Spart-Asheville	7,000	6,890	98
Tyrrell	Norfolk-Portsmth-Newpt Nws	1,400	1,340	96
Union	Charlotte	21,200	20,730	98
Vance	Raleigh-Durham	11,200	10,930	98
Wake	Raleigh-Durham	98,500	96,630	98
Warren	Raleigh-Durham	5,600	5,470	98
Washington	Greenville-N. Bern-Washngtn	4,500	4,320	96
Watauga	Charlotte	9,700	9,310	96
Wayne	Raleigh-Durham	28,800	28,150	98
Wilkes	Greensboro-H. Point-W. Salem	18,800	18,160	97
Wilson	Greenville-N. Bern-Washngtn	19,800	19,380	98

COUNTY	MARKET	HOUSEHOLDS	TV's	%

NORTH CAROLINA—*Cont'd*

Yadkin	Greensboro-H. Point-W. Salem	10,100	9,870	98
Yancey	Greenville-Spart-Asheville	5,100	4,740	93
	STATE TOTAL	1,888,300	1,842,650	98

NORTH DAKOTA

Adams	Minot-Bismarck-Dickinson	1,400	1,370	98
Barnes	Fargo-Valley City	4,900	4,820	98
Benson	Fargo-Valley City	2,800	2,730	98
Billings	Minot-Bismarck-Dickinson	300	300	100
Bottineau	Minot-Bismarck-Dickinson	2,700	2,690	100
Bowman	Minot-Bismarck-Dickinson	1,300	1,270	98
Burke	Minot-Bismarck-Dickinson	1,400	1,370	98
Burleigh	Minot-Bismarck-Dickinson	16,700	16,410	98
Cass	Fargo-Valley City	29,100	28,360	97
Cavalier	Fargo-Valley City	4,300	4,250	99
Dickey	Fargo-Valley City	2,700	2,650	98
Divide	Minot-Bismarck-Dickinson	1,500	1,460	97
Dunn	Minot-Bismarck-Dickinson	1,400	1,360	97
Eddy	Fargo-Valley City	1,300	1,280	98
Emmons	Minot-Bismarck-Dickinson	1,800	1,770	98
Foster	Fargo-Valley City	1,400	1,380	99
Golden Valley	Minot-Bismarck-Dickinson	800	790	99
Grand Forks	Fargo-Valley City	20,900	20,520	98
Grant	Minot-Bismarck-Dickinson	1,800	1,760	98
Griggs	Fargo-Valley City	1,700	1,680	99
Hettinger	Minot-Bismarck-Dickinson	1,600	1,570	98
Kidder	Minot-Bismarck-Dickinson	1,200	1,190	99
La Moure	Fargo-Valley City	2,300	2,280	99
Logan	Minot-Bismarck-Dickinson	1,300	1,270	98
McHenry	Minot-Bismarck-Dickinson	2,900	2,840	98
McIntosh	Minot-Bismarck-Dickinson	1,900	1,840	97
McKenzie	Minot-Bismarck-Dickinson	1,800	1,770	98
McLean	Minot-Bismarck-Dickinson	4,200	4,140	99
Mercer	Minot-Bismarck-Dickinson	2,400	2,330	97
Morton	Minot-Bismarck-Dickinson	8,000	7,880	99
Mountrail	Minot-Bismarck-Dickinson	2,900	2,820	97
Nelson	Fargo-Valley City	2,000	1,980	99
Oliver	Minot-Bismarck-Dickinson	800	790	99
Pembina	Fargo-Valley City	3,600	3,480	97
Pierce	Minot-Bismarck-Dickinson	2,100	2,050	98
Ramsey	Fargo-Valley City	4,900	4,780	98
Ransom	Fargo-Valley City	2,400	2,330	97
Renville	Minot-Bismarck-Dickinson	1,200	1,190	99
Richland	Fargo-Valley City	7,200	7,060	98
Rolette	Minot-Bismarck-Dickinson	3,600	3,480	97
Sargent	Fargo-Valley City	2,100	2,070	99
Sheridan	Minot-Bismarck-Dickinson	1,100	1,080	98
Sioux	Minot-Bismarck-Dickinson	800	760	95
Slope	Minot-Bismarck-Dickinson	400	390	98
Stark	Minot-Bismarck-Dickinson	6,000	5,910	99
Steele	Fargo-Valley City	1,400	1,390	99
Stutsman	Fargo-Valley City	8,100	7,980	99
Towner	Fargo-Valley City	1,300	1,270	98
Traill	Fargo-Valley City	3,500	3,440	98
Walsh	Fargo-Valley City	5,900	5,810	98
Ward	Minot-Bismarck-Dickinson	19,900	19,590	98

COUNTY	MARKET	HOUSEHOLDS	TV's	%
NORTH DAKOTA—*Cont'd*				
Wells	Minot-Bismarck-Dickinson	2,500	2,400	96
Williams	Minot-Bismarck-Dickinson	6,900	6,760	98
	STATE TOTAL	218,400	214,140	98
OHIO				
Adams	Cincinnati	8,500	8,130	96
Allen	Lima	36,300	35,780	99
Ashland	Cleveland, Akron	14,500	14,280	98
Ashtabula	Cleveland, Akron	35,000	34,450	98
Athens	Charleston-Huntington	14,200	13,780	97
Auglaize	Dayton	14,000	13,870	99
Belmont	Wheeling-Steubenville	30,400	30,020	99
Brown	Cincinnati	9,900	9,650	97
Butler	Cincinnati	82,600	81,490	99
Carroll	Wheeling-Steubenville	8,700	8,590	99
Champaign	Dayton	11,300	11,060	98
Clark	Dayton	51,000	50,380	99
Clermont	Cincinnati	35,800	35,280	99
Clinton	Cincinnati	10,900	10,750	99
Columbiana	Pittsburgh	39,700	38,810	98
Coshocton	Cleveland, Akron	12,600	12,220	97
Crawford	Cleveland, Akron	17,700	17,300	98
Cuyahoga	Cleveland, Akron	559,800	551,440	99
Darke	Dayton	18,300	17,980	98
Defiance	Toledo	11,800	11,610	98
Delaware	Columbus, OH	17,500	17,230	98
Erie	Cleveland, Akron	25,800	25,560	99
Fairfield	Columbus, OH	30,200	29,940	99
Fayette	Columbus, OH	9,300	9,130	98
Franklin	Columbus, OH	302,700	299,330	99
Fulton	Toledo	12,000	11,750	98
Gallia	Charleston-Huntington	10,400	10,180	98
Geauga	Cleveland, Akron	21,000	20,480	98
Greene	Dayton	40,100	39,650	99
Guernsey	Wheeling-Steubenville	14,200	13,910	98
Hamilton	Cincinnati	314,500	309,720	98
Hancock	Toledo	21,700	21,350	98
Hardin	Toledo	12,500	12,250	98
Harrison	Wheeling-Steubenville	6,400	6,300	98
Henry	Toledo	9,000	8,890	99
Highland	Cincinnati	11,700	11,310	97
Hocking	Columbus, OH	7,600	7,430	98
Holmes	Cleveland, Akron	7,000	5,630	80
Huron	Cleveland, Akron	16,800	16,600	99
Jackson	Charleston-Huntington	10,400	10,140	98
Jefferson	Wheeling-Steubenville	32,100	31,750	99
Knox	Columbus, OH	14,500	14,400	99
Lake	Cleveland, Akron	67,400	66,980	99
Lawrence	Charleston-Huntington	21,100	20,800	99
Licking	Columbus, OH	39,400	38,900	99
Logan	Dayton	13,600	13,400	99
Lorain	Cleveland, Akron	86,300	85,370	99
Lucas	Toledo	176,800	174,690	99
Madison	Columbus, OH	10,400	10,220	98
Mahoning	Youngstown	96,100	94,910	99
Marion	Columbus, OH	22,700	22,330	98

COUNTY	MARKET	HOUSEHOLDS	TV's	%
OHIO—*Cont'd*				
Medina	Cleveland, Akron	32,900	32,610	99
Meigs	Charleston-Huntington	7,800	7,580	97
Mercer	Dayton	11,600	11,450	99
Miami	Dayton	31,000	30,600	99
Monroe	Wheeling-Steubenville	5,200	5,070	98
Montgomery	Dayton	202,800	200,650	99
Morgan	Columbus, OH	4,500	4,450	99
Morrow	Columbus, OH	8,000	7,810	98
Muskingum	Zanesville	28,600	28,180	99
Noble	Wheeling-Steubenville	4,400	4,210	96
Ottawa	Toledo	13,400	13,290	99
Paulding	Ft. Wayne	6,300	6,160	98
Perry	Columbus, OH	10,000	9,770	98
Pickaway	Columbus, OH	14,400	14,220	99
Pike	Columbus, OH	6,900	6,690	97
Portage	Cleveland, Akron	40,100	39,540	99
Preble	Dayton	12,500	12,310	98
Putnam	Toledo	9,700	9,570	99
Richland	Cleveland, Akron	43,800	43,030	98
Ross	Columbus, OH	20,100	19,750	98
Sandusky	Toledo	20,900	20,730	99
Scioto	Charleston-Huntington	30,100	29,440	98
Seneca	Toledo	18,500	18,140	98
Shelby	Dayton	12,800	12,690	99
Stark	Cleveland, Akron	130,300	128,480	99
Summit	Cleveland, Akron	185,100	182,850	99
Trumbull	Youngstown	78,600	77,660	99
Tuscarawas	Cleveland, Akron	28,600	27,900	98
Union	Columbus, OH	9,800	9,650	98
Van Wert	Ft. Wayne	10,400	10,340	99
Vinton	Charleston-Huntington	3,400	3,210	94
Warren	Cincinnati	27,800	27,390	99
Washington	Parkersburg	20,100	19,720	98
Wayne	Cleveland, Akron	29,900	28,880	97
Williams	Toledo	12,200	12,000	98
Wood	Toledo	34,800	34,260	98
Wyandot	Toledo	7,600	7,530	99
	STATE TOTAL	3,679,100	3,625,210	99
OKLAHOMA				
Adair	Tulsa	5,900	5,500	93
Alfalfa	Oklahoma City	3,300	3,220	98
Atoka	Ada-Ardmore	3,800	3,660	96
Beaver	Wichita-Hutchinson Plus	2,500	2,440	98
Beckham	Oklahoma City	6,900	6,660	97
Blaine	Oklahoma City	4,800	4,620	96
Bryan	Ada-Ardmore	11,300	10,820	96
Caddo	Oklahoma City	12,100	11,740	97
Canadian	Oklahoma City	16,300	15,940	98
Carter	Ada-Ardmore	16,500	15,990	97
Cherokee	Tulsa	9,900	9,570	97
Choctaw	Ada-Ardmore	6,500	5,990	92
Cimarron	Amarillo	1,500	1,430	95
Cleveland	Oklahoma City	36,300	35,750	98
Coal	Ada-Ardmore	2,500	2,430	97
Comanche	Wichita Falls-Lawton	35,100	34,310	98

COUNTY	MARKET	HOUSEHOLDS	TV's	%

OKLAHOMA—*Cont'd*

COUNTY	MARKET	HOUSEHOLDS	TV's	%
Cotton	Wichita Falls-Lawton	2,600	2,560	98
Craig	Tulsa	5,300	5,130	97
Creek	Tulsa	19,200	18,590	97
Custer	Oklahoma City	8,700	8,490	98
Delaware	Tulsa	7,800	7,450	96
Dewey	Oklahoma City	2,200	2,120	96
Ellis	Oklahoma City	2,000	1,880	94
Garfield	Oklahoma City	24,100	23,710	98
Garvin	Oklahoma City	11,100	10,880	98
Grady	Oklahoma City	14,800	14,410	97
Grant	Oklahoma City	3,100	2,970	96
Greer	Wichita Falls-Lawton	3,400	3,330	98
Harmon	Oklahoma City	2,100	2,030	97
Harper	Oklahoma City	2,100	2,040	97
Haskell	Tulsa	3,900	3,740	96
Hughes	Oklahoma City	5,800	5,790	100
Jackson	Wichita Falls-Lawton	12,600	12,200	97
Jefferson	Wichita Falls-Lawton	3,800	3,700	97
Johnston	Ada-Ardmore	3,800	3,720	98
Kay	Oklahoma City	19,600	19,180	98
Kingfisher	Oklahoma City	5,200	5,060	97
Kiowa	Wichita Falls-Lawton	5,300	5,100	96
Latimer	Tulsa	3,300	3,170	96
Le Flore	Ft. Smith	13,700	12,970	95
Lincoln	Oklahoma City	8,600	8,300	97
Logan	Oklahoma City	8,800	8,650	98
Love	Dallas-Ft. Worth	2,600	2,490	96
McClain	Oklahoma City	7,800	7,630	98
McCurtain	Shreveport	13,400	12,690	95
McIntosh	Tulsa	5,400	5,280	98
Major	Oklahoma City	3,400	3,280	96
Marshall	Ada-Ardmore	3,800	3,710	98
Mayes	Tulsa	11,600	11,270	97
Murray	Oklahoma City	3,800	3,720	98
Muskogee	Tulsa	24,700	24,020	97
Noble	Oklahoma City	4,300	4,240	99
Nowata	Tulsa	4,100	3,990	97
Okfuskee	Tulsa	4,600	4,390	95
Oklahoma	Oklahoma City	206,200	202,630	98
Okmulgee	Tulsa	13,900	13,470	97
Osage	Tulsa	13,300	12,990	98
Ottawa	Joplin-Pittsburg	12,400	12,000	97
Pawnee	Tulsa	5,700	5,610	98
Payne	Oklahoma City	22,000	21,390	97
Pittsburg	Tulsa	13,700	13,240	97
Pontotoc	Ada-Ardmore	13,100	12,830	98
Pottawatomie	Oklahoma City	20,600	20,120	98
Pushmataha	Ada-Ardmore	3,900	3,480	89
Roger Mills	Amarillo	1,800	1,720	96
Rogers	Tulsa	13,000	12,720	98
Seminole	Oklahoma City	11,100	10,780	97
Sequoyah	Ft. Smith	9,400	8,950	95
Stephens	Wichita Falls-Lawton	15,800	15,460	98
Texas	Amarillo	6,700	6,460	96
Tillman	Wichita Falls-Lawton	4,500	4,390	98
Tulsa	Tulsa	160,800	157,730	98
Wagoner	Tulsa	10,600	10,290	97
Washington	Tulsa	16,400	16,210	99

COUNTY	MARKET	HOUSEHOLDS	TV's	%
OKLAHOMA—*Cont'd*				
Washita	Oklahoma City	5,500	5,350	97
Woods	Oklahoma City	4,300	4,220	98
Woodward	Oklahoma City	6,800	6,550	96
	STATE TOTAL	1,059,100	1,032,540	97
OREGON				
Baker	Boise	6,200	5,910	95
Benton	Portland, OR	22,600	21,510	95
Clackamas	Portland, OR	74,400	72,480	97
Clatsop	Portland, OR	12,200	11,440	94
Columbia	Portland, OR	12,300	11,870	97
Coos	Eugene	22,300	21,470	96
Crook	Portland, OR	4,900	4,690	96
Curry	Eureka	6,000	5,640	94
Deschutes	Portland, OR	16,600	16,080	97
Douglas	Eugene	30,100	28,860	96
Gilliam	Portland, OR	700	660	94
Grant	Boise	3,000	2,800	93
Harney	Portland, OR	2,800	2,540	91
Hood River	Portland, OR	5,800	5,480	94
Jackson	Medford-Klamath Falls	45,100	43,610	97
Jefferson	Portland, OR	3,500	3,310	95
Josephine	Medford-Klamath Falls	20,400	19,570	96
Klamath	Medford-Klamath Falls	21,000	20,270	97
Lake	Medford-Klamath Falls	2,600	2,420	93
Lane	Eugene	93,000	89,820	97
Lincoln	Portland, OR	11,700	11,080	95
Linn	Portland, OR	31,000	29,920	97
Malheur	Boise	8,700	8,460	97
Marion	Portland, OR	66,500	64,510	97
Morrow	Yakima	2,100	1,940	92
Multnomah	Portland, OR	223,100	215,890	97
Polk	Portland, OR	15,800	15,260	97
Sherman	Portland, OR	900	870	97
Tillamook	Portland, OR	7,400	7,120	96
Umatilla	Yakima	19,400	18,390	95
Union	Spokane	8,900	8,450	95
Wallowa	Spokane	2,800	2,680	96
Wasco	Portland, OR	7,700	7,270	94
Washington	Portland, OR	72,300	71,030	98
Wheeler	Portland, OR	600	570	95
Yamhill	Portland, OR	17,100	16,380	96
	STATE TOTAL	901,500	870,250	97
PENNSYLVANIA				
Adams	Harrisburg-Lncstr-Leb-York	20,700	20,170	97
Allegheny	Pittsburgh	527,700	520,500	99
Armstrong	Pittsburgh	28,100	27,710	99
Beaver	Pittsburgh	71,700	70,770	99
Bedford	Johnstown-Altoona	15,800	15,430	98
Berks	Philadelphia	116,200	114,150	98
Blair	Johnstown-Altoona	48,100	47,300	98

COUNTY	MARKET	HOUSEHOLDS	TV's	%

PENNSYLVANIA—*Cont'd*

COUNTY	MARKET	HOUSEHOLDS	TV's	%
Bradford	Binghamton	20,300	19,820	98
Bucks	Philadelphia	150,500	149,030	99
Butler	Pittsburgh	45,800	45,310	99
Cambria	Johnstown-Altoona	65,800	64,940	99
Cameron	Johnstown-Altoona	2,700	2,630	97
Carbon	Wilkes Barre-Scranton	19,100	18,820	99
Centre	Johnstown-Altoona	34,100	32,710	96
Chester	Philadelphia	96,600	95,060	98
Clarion	Pittsburgh	13,700	13,370	98
Clearfield	Johnstown-Altoona	28,700	28,080	98
Clinton	Wilkes Barre-Scranton	13,100	12,840	98
Columbia	Wilkes Barre-Scranton	21,600	21,270	98
Crawford	Erie	29,600	29,000	98
Cumberland	Harrisburg-Lncstr-Leb-York	60,800	59,940	99
Dauphin	Harrisburg-Lncstr-Leb-York	86,500	84,870	98
Delaware	Philadelphia	195,300	193,370	99
Elk	Johnstown-Altoona	12,100	11,900	98
Erie	Erie	91,900	90,810	99
Fayette	Pittsburgh	54,600	53,870	99
Forest	Johnstown-Altoona	1,900	1,850	97
Franklin	Washington, DC, Hagerstown	37,900	36,500	96
Fulton	Johnstown-Altoona	4,100	3,920	96
Greene	Pittsburgh	14,000	13,700	98
Huntingdon	Johnstown-Altoona	13,400	12,970	97
Indiana	Pittsburgh	27,900	27,330	98
Jefferson	Johnstown-Altoona	17,100	16,830	98
Juniata	Harrisburg-Lncstr-Leb-York	5,900	5,760	98
Lackawanna	Wilkes Barre-Scranton	86,300	85,490	99
Lancaster	Harrisburg-Lncstr-Leb-York	121,300	114,760	95
Lawrence	Pittsburgh	35,000	34,510	99
Lebanon	Harrisburg-Lncstr-Leb-York	35,300	34,390	97
Lehigh	Philadelphia	99,100	97,620	99
Luzerne	Wilkes Barre-Scranton	124,100	122,620	99
Lycoming	Wilkes Barre-Scranton	40,800	39,820	98
McKean	Buffalo	18,800	18,400	98
Mercer	Youngstown	43,200	42,590	99
Mifflin	Johnstown-Altoona	16,100	15,470	96
Monroe	Wilkes Barre-Scranton	21,100	20,790	99
Montgomery	Philadelphia	215,500	213,410	99
Montour	Wilkes Barre-Scranton	5,000	4,830	97
Northampton	Philadelphia	79,600	78,220	98
Northumberland	Wilkes Barre-Scranton	38,700	37,860	98
Perry	Harrisburg-Lncstr-Leb-York	12,000	11,720	98
Philadelphia	Philadelphia	661,600	646,350	98
Pike	New York	6,100	6,020	99
Potter	Buffalo	6,200	5,940	96
Schuylkill	Wilkes Barre-Scranton	59,300	58,050	98
Snyder	Harrisburg-Lncstr-Leb-York	10,100	9,770	97
Somerset	Johnstown-Altoona	28,900	28,200	98
Sullivan	Wilkes Barre-Scranton	1,900	1,840	97
Susquehanna	Binghamton	13,800	13,490	98
Tioga	Binghamton	14,000	14,530	97
Union	Wilkes Barre-Scranton	9,600	9,350	97
Venango	Pittsburgh	21,800	21,220	97
Warren	Erie	15,600	15,150	97
Washington	Pittsburgh	76,600	75,670	99
Wayne	Wilkes Barre-Scranton	12,500	12,140	97
Westmoreland	Pittsburgh	131,600	129,780	99

COUNTY	MARKET	HOUSEHOLDS	TV's	%
PENNSYLVANIA—*Cont'd*				
Wyoming	Wilkes Barre-Scranton	8,900	8,670	97
York	Harrisburg-Lncstr-Leb-York	105,600	103,560	98
	STATE TOTAL	4,169,300	4,093,760	98
RHODE ISLAND				
Bristol	Providence	15,100	14,990	99
Kent	Providence	50,000	49,670	99
Newport	Providence	26,200	25,950	99
Providence	Providence	204,500	201,890	99
Washington	Providence	26,100	25,830	99
	STATE TOTAL	321,900	318,330	99
SOUTH CAROLINA				
Abbeville	Greenville-Spart-Asheville	7,600	7,320	96
Aiken	Augusta	32,400	31,690	98
Allendale	Augusta	3,300	3,180	96
Anderson	Greenville-Spart-Asheville	42,700	41,990	98
Bamberg	Augusta	5,100	4,810	94
Barnwell	Augusta	5,800	5,570	96
Beaufort	Savannah	15,500	15,070	97
Berkeley	Charleston, SC	21,600	20,940	97
Calhoun	Columbia, SC	3,600	3,500	97
Charleston	Charleston, SC	82,800	81,090	98
Cherokee	Greenville-Spart-Asheville	14,800	14,500	98
Chester	Charlotte	10,200	9,920	97
Chesterfield	Charlotte	11,400	11,050	97
Clarendon	Columbia, SC	8,000	7,570	95
Colleton	Charleston, SC	9,500	9,130	96
Darlington	Florence, SC	18,100	17,650	98
Dillon	Florence. SC	8,700	8,440	97
Dorchester	Charleston, SC	14,700	14,390	98
Edgefield	Augusta	4,800	4,710	98
Fairfield	Columbia, SC	5,900	5,700	97
Florence	Florence, SC	32,200	31,530	98
Georgetown	Charleston, SC	11,400	11,030	97
Greenville	Greenville-Spart-Asheville	94,200	92,580	98
Greenwood	Greenville-Spart-Asheville	18,600	18,270	98
Hampton	Augusta	5,500	5,280	96
Horry	Wilmington	29,200	28,310	97
Jasper	Savannah	4,100	3,900	95
Kershaw	Columbia, SC	11,600	11,290	97
Lancaster	Charlotte	14,600	14,280	98
Laurens	Greenville-Spart-Asheville	16,400	16,110	98
Lee	Columbia, SC	5,200	4,920	95
Lexington	Columbia, SC	42,100	41,310	98
McCormick	Augusta	2,300	2,250	98
Marion	Florence, SC	10,400	10,050	97
Marlboro	Florence, SC	9,000	8,720	97
Newberry	Greenville-Spart-Asheville	11,000	10,730	98
Oconee	Greenville-Spart-Asheville	15,700	15,360	98
Orangeburg	Columbia, SC	23,800	22,940	96
Pickens	Greenville-Spart-Asheville	22,800	22,340	98
Richland	Columbia, SC	73,200	71,710	98
Saluda	Augusta	4,600	4,500	98

COUNTY	MARKET	HOUSEHOLDS	TV's	%

SOUTH CAROLINA—*Cont'd*

Spartanburg	Greenville-Spart-Asheville	67,500	66,230	98
Sumter	Columbia, SC	24,900	24,200	97
Union	Greenville-Spart-Asheville	10,900	10,680	98
Williamsburg	Charleston, SC	10,100	9,820	97
York	Charlotte	31,300	30,800	98
	STATE TOTAL	929,100	907,360	98

SOUTH DAKOTA

Aurora	Sioux Falls (Mitchell)	1,500	1,450	97
Beadle	Sioux Falls (Mitchell)	7,200	7,040	98
Bennett	Rapid City	1,000	940	94
Bon Homme	Sioux Falls (Mitchell)	3,100	3,020	97
Brookings	Sioux Falls (Mitchell)	7,400	7,170	97
Brown	Sioux Falls (Mitchell)	13,100	12,900	98
Brule	Sioux Falls (Mitchell)	1,800	1,760	98
Buffalo	Sioux Falls (Mitchell)	400	360	90
Butte	Rapid City	3,200	3,110	97
Campbell	Minot-Bismarck-Dickinson	900	850	94
Charles Mix	Sioux Falls (Mitchell)	3,500	3,400	97
Clark	Sioux Falls (Mitchell)	2,500	2,460	98
Clay	Sioux City	4,400	4,300	98
Codington	Sioux Falls (Mitchell)	7,400	7,290	99
Corson	Minot-Bismarck-Dickinson	1,400	1,320	94
Custer	Rapid City	2,200	2,140	97
Davison	Sioux Falls (Mitchell)	6,700	6,540	98
Day	Sioux Falls (Mitchell)	3,300	3,190	97
Deuel	Sioux Falls (Mitchell)	2,100	2,060	98
Dewey	Minot-Bismarck-Dickinson	1,800	1,700	94
Douglas	Sioux Falls (Mitchell)	1,300	1,260	97
Edmunds	Sioux Falls (Mitchell)	1,900	1,850	97
Fall River	Rapid City	3,300	3,170	96
Faulk	Sioux Falls (Mitchell)	1,100	1,070	97
Grant	Sioux Falls (Mitchell)	3,000	2,940	98
Gregory	Sioux Falls (Mitchell)	2,700	2,650	98
Haakon	Rapid City	1,200	1,160	97
Hamlin	Sioux Falls (Mitchell)	2,400	2,360	98
Hand	Sioux Falls (Mitchell)	1,800	1,770	98
Hanson	Sioux Falls (Mitchell)	1,200	1,180	98
Harding	Rapid City	600	570	95
Hughes	Sioux Falls (Mitchell)	4,900	4,840	99
Hutchinson	Sioux Falls (Mitchell)	3,500	3,380	97
Hyde	Sioux Falls (Mitchell)	800	790	99
Jackson	Rapid City	600	570	95
Jerauld	Sioux Falls (Mitchell)	1,000	980	98
Jones	Sioux Falls (Mitchell)	600	580	97
Kingsbury	Sioux Falls (Mitchell)	2,400	2,370	99
Lake	Sioux Falls (Mitchell)	3,900	3,820	98
Lawrence	Rapid City	6,400	6,260	98
Lincoln	Sioux Falls (Mitchell)	5,000	4,920	98
Lyman	Sioux Falls (Mitchell)	1,300	1,280	98
McCook	Sioux Falls (Mitchell)	2,300	2,270	99
McPherson	Sioux Falls (Mitchell)	1,600	1,550	97
Marshall	Sioux Falls (Mitchell)	2,200	2,130	97
Meade	Rapid City	5,500	5,340	97
Mellette	Sioux Falls (Mitchell)	700	660	94
Miner	Sioux Falls (Mitchell)	1,300	1,270	98

COUNTY	MARKET	HOUSEHOLDS	TV's	%

SOUTH DAKOTA—*Cont'd*

COUNTY	MARKET	HOUSEHOLDS	TV's	%
Minnehaha	Sioux Falls (Mitchell)	35,200	34,690	99
Moody	Sioux Falls (Mitchell)	2,500	2,490	100
Pennington	Rapid City	26,000	25,530	98
Perkins	Minot-Bismarck-Dickinson	1,800	1,730	96
Potter	Sioux Falls (Mitchell)	1,300	1,270	98
Roberts	Sioux Falls (Mitchell)	3,800	3,650	96
Sanborn	Sioux Falls (Mitchell)	1,100	1,070	97
Shannon	Rapid City	2,200	2,020	92
Spink	Sioux Falls (Mitchell)	3,400	3,350	99
Stanley	Sioux Falls (Mitchell)	800	770	96
Sully	Sioux Falls (Mitchell)	800	780	98
Todd	Sioux Falls (Mitchell)	1,900	1,780	94
Tripp	Sioux Falls (Mitchell)	2,800	2,760	99
Turner	Sioux Falls (Mitchell)	3,700	3,610	98
Union	Sioux City	4,100	3,990	97
Walworth	Minot-Bismarck-Dickinson	2,700	2,630	97
Washabaugh	Rapid City	300	280	93
Yankton	Sioux Falls (Mitchell)	5,600	5,410	97
Ziebach	Rapid City	1,000	900	90
	STATE TOTAL	240,400	234,700	98

TENNESSEE

COUNTY	MARKET	HOUSEHOLDS	TV's	%
Anderson	Knoxville	22,700	22,350	98
Bedford	Nashville, Bowling Green	9,600	9,460	99
Benton	Nashville, Bowling Green	4,600	4,470	97
Bledsoe	Chattanooga	3,000	2,780	93
Blount	Knoxville	25,900	25,430	98
Bradley	Chattanooga	21,100	20,640	98
Campbell	Knoxville	11,100	10,590	95
Cannon	Nashville, Bowling Green	3,900	3,720	95
Carroll	Nashville, Bowling Green	10,400	9,960	96
Carter	Tri-Cities; TN-VA	16,500	16,300	99
Cheatham	Nashville, Bowling Green	5,600	5,470	98
Chester	Memphis	4,100	3,990	97
Claiborne	Knoxville	8,500	8,090	95
Clay	Nashville, Bowling Green	2,500	2,410	96
Cocke	Knoxville	9,300	9,000	97
Coffee	Nashville, Bowling Green	12,100	11,780	97
Crockett	Memphis	5,200	5,110	98
Cumberland	Knoxville	8,800	8,310	94
Davidson	Nashville, Bowling Green	165,000	162,280	98
Decatur	Nashville, Bowling Green	3,700	3,520	95
De Kalb	Nashville, Bowling Green	4,900	4,760	97
Dickson	Nashville, Bowling Green	9,900	9,690	98
Dyer	Memphis	11,800	11,480	97
Fayette	Memphis	6,600	6,250	95
Fentress	Knoxville	4,600	4,300	93
Franklin	Nashville, Bowling Green	10,100	9,790	97
Gibson	Memphis	17,600	17,250	98
Giles	Nashville, Bowling Green	8,500	8,270	97
Grainger	Knoxville	5,800	5,540	96
Greene	Tri-Cities; TN-VA	17,200	16,750	97
Grundy	Chattanooga	4,400	4,230	96
Hamblen	Knoxville	15,200	14,810	97
Hamilton	Chattanooga	106,800	104,940	98
Hancock	Knoxville	2,200	2,120	96

COUNTY	MARKET	HOUSEHOLDS	TV's	%

TENNESSEE—*Cont'd*

COUNTY	MARKET	HOUSEHOLDS	TV's	%
Hardeman	Memphis	6,300	5,070	96
Hardin	Jackson, TN	7,300	6,910	95
Hawkins	Tri-Cities; TN-VA	12,700	12,260	97
Haywood	Memphis	6,700	6,410	96
Henderson	Jackson, TN	7,200	6,940	96
Henry	Nashville, Bowling Green	10,300	9,910	96
Hickman	Nashville, Bowling Green	5,100	4,940	97
Houston	Nashville, Bowling Green	2,200	2,130	97
Humphreys	Nashville, Bowling Green	5,400	5,280	98
Jackson	Nashville, Bowling Green	3,200	3,030	95
Jefferson	Knoxville	9,600	9,370	98
Johnson	Tri-Cities; TN-VA	4,600	4,430	96
Knox	Knoxville	105,900	103,810	98
Lake	Paducah-C. Girardeau-Harrbg	2,400	2,310	96
Lauderdale	Memphis	7,900	7,630	97
Lawrence	Nashville, Bowling Green	11,700	11,260	96
Lewis	Nashville, Bowling Green	3,300	3,230	98
Lincoln	Nashville, Bowling Green	8,900	8,640	97
Loudon	Knoxville	9,800	9,630	98
McMinn	Chattanooga	15,100	14,890	99
McNairy	Memphis	7,700	7,450	97
Macon	Nashville, Bowling Green	5,300	5,120	97
Madison	Jackson, TN	25,400	24,700	97
Marion	Chattanooga	7,300	7,100	97
Marshall	Nashville, Bowling Green	6,600	6,400	97
Maury	Nashville, Bowling Green	16,100	15,810	98
Meigs	Chattanooga	2,300	2,260	98
Monroe	Knoxville	8,600	8,410	98
Montgomery	Nashville, Bowling Green	23,700	23,280	98
Moore	Nashville, Bowling Green	1,400	1,360	97
Morgan	Knoxville	4,800	4,600	96
Obion	Paducah-C. Girardeau-Harrbg	12,900	12,590	98
Overton	Nashville, Bowling Green	5,800	5,510	95
Perry	Nashville, Bowling Green	2,300	2,240	97
Pickett	Nashville, Bowling Green	1,500	1,450	97
Polk	Chattanooga	4,300	4,180	97
Putnam	Nashville, Bowling Green	15,000	14,550	97
Rhea	Chattanooga	7,800	7,490	96
Roane	Knoxville	15,200	14,900	98
Robertson	Nashville, Bowling Green	11,500	11,290	98
Rutherford	Nashville, Bowling Green	23,800	23,320	98
Scott	Knoxville	5,600	5,330	95
Sequatchie	Chattanooga	2,400	2,350	98
Sevier	Knoxville	12,700	12,470	98
Shelby	Memphis	251,400	246,380	98
Smith	Nashville, Bowling Green	5,100	4,960	97
Stewart	Nashville, Bowling Green	3,200	3,130	98
Sullivan	Tri-Cities; TN-VA	47,900	47,140	98
Sumner	Nashville, Bowling Green	25,400	24,820	98
Tipton	Memphis	9,900	9,610	97
Trousdale	Nashville, Bowling Green	1,900	1,860	98
Unicoi	Tri-Cities; TN-VA	6,100	5,930	97
Union	Knoxville	3,600	3,490	97
Van Buren	Nashville, Bowling Green	1,300	1,250	96
Warren	Nashville, Bowling Green	10,900	10,560	97
Washington	Tri-Cities; TN-VA	28,700	27,970	97
Wayne	Nashville, Bowling Green	4,400	4,230	96
Weakley	Paducah-C. Girardeau-Harrbg	11,300	11,020	98

COUNTY	MARKET	HOUSEHOLDS	TV's	%
TENNESSEE—*Cont'd*				
White	Nashville, Bowling Green	6,500	6,240	96
Williamson	Nashville, Bowling Green	16,700	16,460	99
Wilson	Nashville, Bowling Green	17,600	17,280	98
	STATE TOTAL	1,506,700	1,471,410	98
TEXAS				
Anderson	Dallas-Ft. Worth	12,300	11,820	96
Andrews	Odessa-Midland-Monahans	4,100	4,080	100
Angelina	Tyler	19,100	18,460	97
Aransas	Corpus Christi	4,400	4,170	95
Archer	Wichita Falls-Lawton	2,300	2,270	99
Armstrong	Amarillo	1,000	980	98
Atascosa	San Antonio	6,300	6,020	96
Austin	Houston	6,200	5,930	96
Bailey	Lubbock	2,600	2,510	97
Bandera	San Antonio	2,400	2,330	97
Bastrop	Austin	7,900	7,500	95
Baylor	Wichita Falls-Lawton	1,900	1,850	97
Bee	Corpus Christi	7,300	7,020	96
Bell	Waco-Temple	53,900	52,730	98
Bexar	San Antonio	290,100	281,730	97
Blanco	Austin	1,700	1,630	96
Borden	Lubbock	400	390	98
Bosque	Dallas-Ft. Worth	6,000	5,830	97
Bowie	Shreveport	27,300	26,750	98
Brazoria	Houston	43,200	42,390	98
Brazos	Waco-Temple	26,000	25,020	96
Brewster	Odessa-Midland-Monahans	2,700	2,430	90
Briscoe	Amarillo	800	780	98
Brooks	Corpus Christi	2,400	2,240	93
Brown	Abilene-Sweetwater	13,400	12,840	96
Burleson	Waco-Temple	4,000	3,750	94
Burnet	Austin	6,400	6,280	98
Caldwell	San Antonio	6,400	6,180	97
Calhoun	Houston	5,100	4,940	97
Callahan	Abilene-Sweetwater	4,200	4,100	98
Cameron	Harlingen-Weslaco	56,000	52,970	95
Camp	Shreveport	2,900	2,780	96
Carson	Amarillo	2,400	2,360	98
Cass	Shreveport	9,600	9,330	97
Castro	Amarillo	2,800	2,760	99
Chambers	Houston	4,600	4,450	97
Cherokee	Tyler	12,100	11,650	96
Childress	Amarillo	3,000	2,820	94
Clay	Wichita Falls-Lawton	3,300	3,260	99
Cochran	Lubbock	1,500	1,460	97
Coke	Abilene-Sweetwater	1,200	1,170	98
Coleman	Abilene-Sweetwater	4,400	4,320	98
Collin	Dallas-Ft. Worth	37,900	37,110	98
Collingsworth	Amarillo	2,000	1,860	93
Colorado	Houston	6,300	6,020	96
Comal	San Antonio	10,500	10,280	98
Comanche	Dallas-Ft. Worth	5,100	4,970	97
Concho	San Angelo	1,000	970	97
Cooke	Dallas-Ft. Worth	9,300	9,000	97
Coryell	Waco-Temple	12,100	11,880	98

COUNTY	MARKET	HOUSEHOLDS	TV's	%

TEXAS—*Cont'd*

COUNTY	MARKET	HOUSEHOLDS	TV's	%
Cottle	Amarillo	1,100	1,050	95
Crane	Odessa-Midland-Monahans	1,500	1,480	99
Crockett	Odessa-Midland-Monahans	1,500	1,420	95
Crosby	Lubbock	2,700	2,660	99
Culberson	Odessa-Midland-Monahans	1,100	1,050	95
Dallam	Amarillo	2,100	1,990	95
Dallas	Dallas-Ft. Worth	511,200	500,720	98
Dawson	Lubbock	5,800	5,640	97
Deaf Smith	Amarillo	5,400	5,230	97
Delta	Dallas-Ft. Worth	1,800	1,710	95
Denton	Dallas-Ft. Worth	34,000	33,030	97
De Witt	San Antonio	7,300	7,050	97
Dickens	Lubbock	1,400	1,360	97
Dimmit	San Antonio	3,000	2,610	87
Donley	Amarillo	1,400	1,330	95
Duval	Corpus Christi	3,800	3,520	93
Eastland	Abilene-Sweetwater	8,000	7,740	97
Ector	Odessa-Midland-Monahans	37,100	36,370	98
Edwards	San Antonio	900	840	93
Ellis	Dallas-Ft. Worth	18,800	18,320	97
El Paso	El Paso	132,200	129,410	98
Erath	Dallas-Ft. Worth	7,600	7,330	96
Falls	Waco-Temple	6,400	6,050	95
Fannin	Dallas-Ft. Worth	9,100	8,810	97
Fayette	Austin	7,400	6,880	93
Fisher	Abilene-Sweetwater	2,500	2,480	99
Floyd	Lubbock	3,800	3,650	96
Foard	Wichita Falls-Lawton	800	780	98
Fort Bend	Houston	25,200	24,500	97
Franklin	Shreveport	2,500	2,370	95
Freestone	Dallas-Ft. Worth	4,800	4,570	95
Frio	San Antonio	3,600	3,430	95
Gaines	Lubbock	3,800	3,690	97
Galveston	Houston	69,000	67,470	98
Garza	Lubbock	2,000	1,950	98
Gillespie	San Antonio	4,800	4,560	95
Glasscock	Odessa-Midland-Monahans	300	300	100
Goliad	San Antonio	1,900	1,790	94
Gonzales	San Antonio	5,700	5,520	97
Gray	Amarillo	10,000	9,810	98
Grayson	Dallas-Ft. Worth	31,500	30,810	98
Gregg	Shreveport	30,900	30,180	98
Grimes	Houston	4,300	4,070	95
Guadalupe	San Antonio	13,500	12,920	96
Hale	Lubbock	11,900	11,720	98
Hall	Amarillo	2,200	2,130	97
Hamilton	Dallas-Ft. Worth	3,400	3,290	97
Hansford	Amarillo	2,100	2,070	99
Hardeman	Wichita Falls-Lawton	2,700	2,640	98
Hardin	Beaumont-Port Arthur	12,500	12,050	96
Harris	Houston	761,200	740,070	97
Harrison	Shreveport	15,800	15,300	97
Hartley	Amarillo	1,100	1,090	99
Haskell	Abilene-Sweetwater	3,000	2,950	98
Hays	San Antonio	10,500	10,130	96
Hemphill	Amarillo	1,800	1,740	97
Henderson	Dallas-Ft. Worth	11,300	11,000	97
Hidalgo	Harlingen-Weslaco	65,100	62,000	95

COUNTY	MARKET	HOUSEHOLDS	TV's	%
TEXAS—*Cont'd*				
Hill	Dallas-Ft. Worth	9,200	8,980	98
Hockley	Lubbock	7,000	6,880	98
Hood	Dallas-Ft. Worth	4,500	4,460	99
Hopkins	Dallas-Ft. Worth	8,600	8,300	97
Houston	Tyler	6,000	5,600	93
Howard	Odessa-Midland-Monahans	12,300	12,020	98
Hudspeth	El Paso	1,200	1,120	93
Hunt	Dallas-Ft. Worth	18,200	17,820	98
Hutchinson	Amarillo	9,900	9,800	99
Irion	San Angelo	400	380	95
Jack	Dallas-Ft. Worth	2,600	2,520	97
Jackson	Houston	4,700	4,470	95
Jasper	Beaumont-Port Arthur	8,900	8,490	95
Jeff Davis	Odessa-Midland-Monahans	500	460	92
Jefferson	Beaumont-Port Arthur	89,200	87,420	98
Jim Hogg	Corpus Christi	1,200	1,110	93
Jim Wells	Corpus Christi	10,200	9,600	94
Johnson	Dallas-Ft. Worth	22,300	21,730	97
Jones	Abilene-Sweetwater	6,800	6,660	98
Karnes	San Antonio	4,000	3,840	96
Kaufman	Dallas-Ft. Worth	12,000	11,800	98
Kendall	San Antonio	3,500	3,370	96
Kenedy	Corpus Christi	200	190	95
Kent	Lubbock	500	460	92
Kerr	San Antonio	9,100	8,720	96
Kimble	San Antonio	1,700	1,550	91
King	Wichita Falls-Lawton	200	190	95
Kinney	San Antonio	700	640	91
Kleberg	Corpus Christi	10,000	9,670	97
Knox	Wichita Falls-Lawton	2,000	1,920	96
Lamar	Dallas-Ft. Worth	15,100	14,230	94
Lamb	Lubbock	6,200	6,060	98
Lampasas	Waco-Temple	4,400	4,190	95
La Salle	San Antonio	1,600	1,480	93
Lavaca	San Antonio	7,100	6,450	91
Lee	Austin	4,000	3,790	95
Leon	Waco-Temple	3,600	3,330	93
Liberty	Houston	14,200	13,760	97
Limestone	Dallas-Ft. Worth	6,700	6,520	97
Lipscomb	Amarillo	1,500	1,410	94
Live Oak	San Antonio	2,400	2,300	96
Llano	Austin	3,600	3,530	98
Loving	Odessa-Midland-Monahans	100	100	100
Lubbock	Lubbock	72,400	71,010	98
Lynn	Lubbock	3,200	3,150	98
McCulloch	Abilene-Sweetwater	3,100	2,890	93
McLennan	Waco-Temple	57,400	56,290	98
McMullen	San Antonio	300	290	97
Madison	Waco-Temple	2,900	2,820	97
Marion	Shreveport	2,900	2,830	98
Martin	Odessa-Midland-Monahans	1,600	1,570	98
Mason	Austin	1,400	1,280	91
Matagorda	Houston	10,100	9,680	96
Maverick	San Antonio	6,000	5,360	89
Medina	San Antonio	6,800	6,600	97
Menard	Abilene-Sweetwater	1,100	990	90
Midland	Odessa-Midland-Monahans	26,400	25,940	98
Milam	Waco-Temple	7,900	7,450	94

COUNTY	MARKET	HOUSEHOLDS	TV's	%

TEXAS—*Cont'd*

COUNTY	MARKET	HOUSEHOLDS	TV's	%
Mills	Waco-Temple	1,700	1,600	94
Mitchell	Abilene-Sweetwater	3,000	2,880	96
Montague	Wichita Falls-Lawton	6,900	6,700	97
Montgomery	Houston	31,900	30,770	96
Moore	Amarillo	4,900	4,870	99
Morris	Shreveport	4,700	4,540	97
Motley	Lubbock	800	750	94
Nacogdoches	Shreveport	14,700	14,180	96
Navarro	Dallas-Ft. Worth	12,000	11,800	98
Newton	Beaumont-Port Arthur	4,200	4,080	97
Nolan	Abilene-Sweetwater	6,000	5,880	98
Nueces	Corpus Christi	80,100	77,950	97
Ochiltree	Amarillo	3,100	3,010	97
Oldham	Amarillo	600	590	98
Orange	Beaumont-Port Arthur	28,500	27,960	98
Palo Pinto	Dallas-Ft. Worth	8,900	8,630	97
Panola	Shreveport	6,500	6,200	95
Parker	Dallas-Ft. Worth	11,600	11,310	98
Parmer	Amarillo	2,600	2,530	97
Pecos	Odessa-Midland-Monahans	4,600	4,370	95
Polk	Houston	6,800	6,360	94
Potter	Amarillo	35,800	35,180	98
Presidio	Odessa-Midland-Monahans	1,500	1,350	90
Rains	Dallas-Ft. Worth	1,800	1,730	96
Randall	Amarillo	24,300	23,970	99
Reagan	Odessa-Midland-Monahans	1,200	1,190	99
Real	San Antonio	800	730	91
Red River	Shreveport	5,200	5,070	98
Reeves	Odessa-Midland-Monahans	4,700	4,530	96
Refugio	Corpus Christi	3,000	2,940	98
Roberts	Amarillo	500	500	100
Robertson	Waco-Temple	5,500	5,310	97
Rockwall	Dallas-Ft. Worth	3,700	3,650	99
Runnels	Abilene-Sweetwater	4,700	4,660	99
Rusk	Shreveport	14,300	13,940	97
Sabine	Beaumont-Port Arthur	2,700	2,500	93
San Augustine	Shreveport	2,900	2,760	95
San Jacinto	Houston	2,500	2,170	87
San Patricio	Corpus Christi	15,700	15,180	97
San Saba	Waco-Temple	2,300	2,190	95
Schleicher	San Angelo	1,000	960	96
Scurry	Lubbock	6,600	6,520	99
Shackelford	Abilene-Sweetwater	1,200	1,160	97
Shelby	Shreveport	7,500	7,200	96
Sherman	Amarillo	1,300	1,270	98
Smith	Tyler	41,500	40,480	98
Somervell	Dallas-Ft. Worth	1,800	1,750	97
Starr	Harlingen-Weslaco	5,400	4,830	89
Stephens	Dallas-Ft. Worth	3,900	3,790	97
Sterling	Abilene-Sweetwater	400	390	98
Stonewall	Abilene-Sweetwater	900	890	99
Sutton	Dallas-Ft. Worth	1,500	1,370	91
Swisher	Amarillo	3,500	3,470	99
Tarrant	Dallas-Ft. Worth	267,500	262,640	98
Taylor	Abilene-Sweetwater	39,100	38,330	98
Terrell	Odessa-Midland-Monahans	500	460	92
Terry	Lubbock	4,400	4,360	99
Throckmorton	Wichita Falls-Lawton	800	770	96

COUNTY	MARKET	HOUSEHOLDS	TV's	%
TEXAS—*Cont'd*				
Titus	Shreveport	7,200	7,010	97
Tom Green	San Angelo	29,000	28,300	98
Travis	Austin	133,200	129,500	97
Trinity	Houston	3,100	2,990	96
Tyler	Beaumont-Port Arthur	5,100	4,850	95
Upshur	Shreveport	9,000	8,690	97
Upton	Odessa-Midland-Monahans	1,800	1,740	97
Uvalde	San Antonio	6,200	5,710	92
Val Verde	San Antonio	9,800	9,290	95
Van Zandt	Dallas-Ft. Worth	10,900	10,600	97
Victoria	San Antonio	19,900	19,080	96
Walker	Houston	9,500	8,950	94
Waller	Houston	4,600	4,390	95
Ward	Odessa-Midland-Monahans	4,200	4,130	98
Washington	Houston	7,500	7,050	94
Webb	Laredo	24,800	23,800	96
Wharton	Houston	11,700	11,290	96
Wheeler	Amarillo	2,500	2,450	98
Wichita	Wichita Falls-Lawton	44,600	43,860	98
Wilbarger	Wichita Falls-Lawton	5,800	5,670	98
Willacy	Harlingen-Weslaco	4,800	4,510	94
Williamson	Austin	19,200	18,540	97
Wilson	San Antonio	4,600	4,410	96
Winkler	Odessa-Midland-Monahans	3,500	3,410	97
Wise	Dallas-Ft. Worth	8,000	7,890	99
Wood	Dallas-Ft. Worth	8,500	8,340	98
Yoakum	Lubbock	2,800	2,690	96
Young	Wichita Falls-Lawton	7,000	6,870	98
Zapata	Laredo	2,000	1,810	91
Zavala	San Antonio	3,100	2,840	92
	STATE TOTAL	4,419,400	4,296,280	97
UTAH				
Beaver	Salt Lake City	1,500	1,460	97
Box Elder	Salt Lake City	9,700	9,570	99
Cache	Salt Lake City	16,000	15,540	97
Carbon	Salt Lake City	7,200	7,020	98
Daggett	Salt Lake City	100	90	90
Davis	Salt Lake City	31,800	31,500	99
Duchesne	Salt Lake City	4,100	3,920	96
Emery	Salt Lake City	2,500	2,440	98
Garfield	Salt Lake City	1,000	940	94
Grand	Salt Lake City	2,000	1,830	92
Iron	Salt Lake City	4,900	4,760	97
Juab	Salt Lake City	1,700	1,660	98
Kane	Salt Lake City	1,000	930	93
Millard	Salt Lake City	2,800	2,750	98
Morgan	Salt Lake City	1,600	1,550	97
Piute	Salt Lake City	300	290	97
Rich	Salt Lake City	500	490	98
Salt Lake	Salt Lake City	175,100	171,280	98
San Juan	Salt Lake City	3,100	2,380	77
Sanpete	Salt Lake City	4,700	4,590	98
Sevier	Salt Lake City	4,600	4,490	98
Summit	Salt Lake City	2,400	2,350	98
Tooele	Salt Lake City	7,200	7,050	98

COUNTY	MARKET	HOUSEHOLDS	TV's	%
UTAH—*Cont'd*				
Uintah	Salt Lake City	6,000	5,950	99
Utah	Salt Lake City	50,600	48,760	96
Wasatch	Salt Lake City	2,200	2,130	97
Washington	Salt Lake City	6,300	5,790	92
Wayne	Salt Lake City	500	490	98
Weber	Salt Lake City	45,100	44,300	98
	STATE TOTAL	396,500	386,300	97
VERMONT				
Addison	Burlington-Plattsburgh	8,600	8,450	98
Bennington	Albany-Schenectady-Troy	11,700	11,430	98
Caledonia	Burlington-Plattsburgh	9,200	8,990	98
Chittenden	Burlington-Plattsburgh	36,300	36,650	98
Essex	Burlington-Plattsburgh	2,400	2,350	98
Franklin	Burlington-Plattsburgh	11,300	11,150	99
Grand Isle	Burlington-Plattsburgh	1,400	1,390	99
Lamoille	Burlington-Plattsburgh	5,200	5,110	98
Orange	Burlington-Plattsburgh	7,100	7,000	99
Orleans	Burlington-Plattsburgh	7,900	7,790	99
Rutland	Burlington-Plattsburgh	19,800	19,240	97
Washington	Burlington-Plattsburgh	17,200	16,910	98
Windham	Boston, Manchester, Worcestr	12,800	12,250	96
Windsor	Burlington-Plattsburgh	18,100	17,660	98
	STATE TOTAL	169,000	165,370	98
VIRGINIA				
Accomack	Norfolk-Portsmth-Newpt Nws	11,900	11,290	95
Albemarle	Richmond-Petrsbg, Charltsvl	32,200	30,710	95
Alleghany	Roanoke-Lynchburg	9,800	9,490	97
Amelia	Richmond-Petrsbg, Charltsvl	2,800	2,710	97
Amherst	Roanoke-Lynchburg	8,100	7,840	97
Appomattox	Roanoke-Lynchburg	3,700	3,610	98
Arlington	Washington, DC, Hagerstown	114,800	112,550	98
Augusta	Richmond-Petrsbg, Charltsvl	31,000	30,410	98
Bath	Roanoke-Lynchburg	1,900	1,840	97
Bedford	Roanoke-Lynchburg	12,800	12,490	98
Bland	Beckley-Bluefield-Oak Hill	2,200	2,120	96
Botetourt	Roanoke-Lynchburg	7,800	7,610	98
Brunswick	Richmond-Petrsbg, Charltsvl	4,800	4,650	97
Buchanan	Tri-Cities; TN-VA	10,300	9,860	96
Buckingham	Richmond-Petrsbg, Charltsvl	3,800	3,620	95
Campbell	Roanoke-Lynchburg	38,200	37,340	98
Caroline	Richmond-Petrsbg, Charltsvl	5,000	4,830	97
Carroll	Roanoke-Lynchburg	11,100	10,670	96
Charlotte	Roanoke-Lynchburg	4,100	3,930	96
Charles City	Richmond-Petrsbg, Charltsvl	1,800	1,710	95
Chesterfield	Richmond-Petrsbg, Charltsvl	43,700	43,250	99
Clarke	Washington, DC, Hagerstown	3,200	3,130	98
Craig	Roanoke-Lynchburg	1,600	1,530	96
Culpeper	Washington, DC, Hagerstown	7,200	7,010	97
Cumberland	Richmond-Petrsbg, Charltsvl	2,200	2,080	95
Dickenson	Tri-Cities; TN-VA	6,100	5,920	97
Dinwiddie	Richmond-Petrsbg, Charltsvl	22,200	21,630	97
Essex	Richmond-Petrsbg, Charltsvl	2,500	2,410	96

COUNTY	MARKET	HOUSEHOLDS	TV's	%

VIRGINIA—*Cont'd*

COUNTY	MARKET	HOUSEHOLDS	TV's	%
Fairfax	Washington, DC, Hagerstown	183,100	181,460	99
Fauquier	Washington, DC, Hagerstown	9,600	9,340	97
Floyd	Roanoke-Lynchburg	3,600	3,520	98
Fluvanna	Richmond-Petrsbg, Charltsvl	3,500	3,350	96
Franklin	Roanoke-Lynchburg	10,600	10,310	97
Frederick	Washington, DC, Hagerstown	19,200	18,970	99
Giles	Roanoke-Lynchburg	6,100	5,960	98
Goucester	Norfolk-Portsmth-Newpt Nws	6,500	6,380	98
Goochland	Richmond-Petrsbg, Charltsvl	3,400	3,240	95
Grayson	Roanoke-Lynchburg	5,600	5,310	95
Greene	Richmond-Petrsbg, Charltsvl	2,300	2,130	93
Greensville	Richmond-Petrsbg, Charltsvl	5,300	5,070	96
Halifax	Roanoke-Lynchburg	12,100	11,480	95
Hanover	Richmond-Petrsbg, Charltsvl	16,600	16,240	98
Henrico	Richmond-Petrsbg, Charltsvl	148,300	145,070	98
Henry	Roanoke-Lynchburg	24,900	24,380	98
Highland	Roanoke-Lynchburg	900	870	97
Isle of Wight	Norfolk-Portsmth-Newpt Nws	6,600	6,350	96
James City	Norfolk-Portsmth-Newpt Nws	9,500	9,230	97
King and Queen	Richmond-Petrsbg, Charltsvl	1,900	1,810	95
King George	Washington, DC, Hagerstown	3,300	3,260	99
King William	Richmond-Petrsbg, Charltsvl	2,600	2,530	97
Lancaster	Richmond-Petrsbg, Charltsvl	3,400	3,280	96
Lee	Tri-Cities; TN-VA	10,100	9,730	96
Loudoun	Washington, DC, Hagerstown	17,800	17,580	99
Louisa	Richmond-Petrsbg, Charltsvl	5,600	5,290	94
Lunenburg	Richmond-Petrsbg, Charltsvl	4,000	3,860	97
Madison	Richmond-Petrsbg, Charltsvl	3,500	3,310	95
Mathews	Norfolk-Portsmth-Newpt Nws	3,300	3,130	95
Mecklenburg	Roanoke-Lynchburg	9,800	9,470	97
Middlesex	Richmond-Petrsbg, Charltsvl	2,700	2,610	97
Montgomery	Roanoke-Lynchburg	23,600	22,920	97
Nelson	Richmond-Petrsbg, Charltsvl	3,900	3,660	94
New Kent	Richmond-Petrsbg, Charltsvl	2,300	2,230	97
Newport News	Norfolk-Portsmth-Newpt Nws	88,600	86,970	98
Norfolk	Norfolk-Portsmth-Newpt Nws	159,100	155,760	98
Northampton	Norfolk-Portsmth-Newpt Nws	5,800	5,560	96
Northumberland	Richmond-Petrsbg, Charltsvl	3,600	3,500	97
Nottoway	Richmond-Petrsbg, Charltsvl	4,400	4,280	97
Orange	Richmond-Petrsbg, Charltsvl	6,000	5,850	98
Page	Washington, DC, Hagerstown	7,000	6,790	97
Patrick	Greensboro-H. Point- W. Salem	5,800	5,610	97
Pittsylvania	Roanoke-Lynchburg	37,200	36,280	98
Powhatan	Richmond-Petrsbg, Charltsvl	3,100	3,000	97
Prince Edward	Richmond-Petrsbg, Charltsvl	5,100	4,910	96
Prince George	Richmond-Petrsbg, Charltsvl	13,300	13,150	99
Prince William	Washington, DC, Hagerstown	40,300	39,910	99
Pulaski	Roanoke-Lynchburg	10,800	10,530	98
Rappahannock	Washington, DC, Hagerstown	2,000	1,930	97
Richmond	Richmond-Petrsbg, Charltsvl	2,400	2,320	97
Roanoke	Roanoke-Lynchburg	71,700	70,630	99
Rockbridge	Roanoke-Lynchburg	9,900	9,590	97
Rockingham	Harrisonburg	24,500	23,520	96
Russell	Tri-Cities; TN-VA	8,800	8,390	95
Scott	Tri-Cities; TN-VA	8,500	8,140	96
Shenandoah	Washington, DC, Hagerstown	9,900	9,640	97
Smyth	Tri-Cities; TN-VA	10,600	10,440	98
Southampton	Norfolk-Portsmth-Newpt Nws	8,300	7,960	96

COUNTY	MARKET	HOUSEHOLDS	TV's	%
VIRGINIA—*Cont'd*				
Spotsylvania	Washington, DC, Hagerstown	14,900	14,470	97
Stafford	Washington, DC, Hagerstown	10,500	10,290	98
Suffolk City	Norfolk-Portsmth-Newpt Nws	15,400	14,860	96
Surry	Norfolk-Portsmth-Newpt Nws	1,900	1,830	96
Sussex	Richmond-Petrsbg, Charltsvl	3,400	3,320	98
Tazewell	Beckley-Bluefield-Oak Hill	16,400	16,010	98
Virginia Beach	Norfolk-Portsmth-Newpt Nws	70,100	69,370	99
Warren	Washington, DC, Hagerstown	7,300	7,170	98
Washington	Tri-Cities; TN-VA	21,800	21,080	97
Westmoreland	Washington, DC, Hagerstown	4,900	4,740	97
Wise	Tri-Cities; TN-VA	17,300	16,770	97
Wythe	Roanoke-Lynchburg	8,200	8,000	98
York	Norfolk-Portsmth-Newpt Nws	12,600	12,360	98
	STATE TOTAL	1,733,700	1,694,500	98
WASHINGTON				
Adams	Spokane	4,900	4,770	97
Asotin	Spokane	5,500	5,320	97
Benton	Yakima	30,500	29,880	98
Chelan	Spokane	16,300	15,780	97
Clallam	Seattle-Tacoma	15,500	14,830	96
Clark	Portland, OR	60,300	58,580	97
Columbia	Spokane	1,600	1,510	94
Cowlitz	Portland, OR	26,800	26,150	98
Douglas	Spokane	7,200	7,060	98
Ferry	Spokane	2,100	1,990	95
Franklin	Yakima	9,800	9,430	96
Garfield	Spokane	1,000	960	96
Grant	Spokane	16,900	16,360	97
Grays Harbor	Seattle-Tacoma	23,300	22,280	96
Island	Seattle-Tacoma	13,600	13,260	98
Jefferson	Seattle-Tacoma	4,900	4,700	96
King	Seattle-Tacoma	456,100	441,040	97
Kitsap	Seattle-Tacoma	45,300	44,210	98
Kittitas	Yakima	8,900	8,110	91
Klickitat	Portland, OR	5,200	4,920	95
Lewis	Seattle-Tacoma	19,000	18,120	95
Lincoln	Spokane	4,000	3,930	98
Mason	Seattle-Tacoma	9,300	9,030	97
Okanogan	Spokane	10,900	10,390	95
Pacific	Seattle-Tacoma	6,200	5,770	93
Pend Oreille	Spokane	2,800	2,700	96
Pierce	Seattle-Tacoma	148,400	144,460	97
San Juan	Seattle-Tacoma	2,600	2,520	97
Skagit	Seattle-Tacoma	20,600	19,930	97
Skamania	Portland, OR	2,200	2,100	95
Snohomish	Seattle-Tacoma	97,400	95,090	98
Spokane	Spokane	117,200	114,360	98
Stevens	Spokane	9,000	8,530	95
Thurston	Seattle-Tacoma	38,600	37,700	98
Wahkiakum	Portland, OR	1,300	1,250	96
Walla Walla	Yakima	15,900	15,130	95
Whatcom	Seattle-Tacoma	34,400	33,290	97
Whitman	Spokane	12,700	11,960	94
Yakima	Yakima	58,200	56,610	97
	STATE TOTAL	1,366,400	1,324,010	97

COUNTY	MARKET	HOUSEHOLDS	TV's	%
WEST VIRGINIA				
Barbour	Clarksburg-Weston	5,700	5,560	98
Berkeley	Washington, DC, Hagerstown	14,700	14,410	98
Boone	Charleston-Huntington	9,700	9,420	97
Braxton	Charleston-Huntington	4,700	4,510	96
Brooke	Wheeling-Steubenville	10,500	10,370	99
Cabell	Charleston-Huntington	39,600	38,850	98
Calhoun	Charleston-Huntington	2,700	2,560	95
Clay	Charleston-Huntington	3,400	3,220	95
Doddridge	Clarksburg-Weston	2,500	2,280	91
Fayette	Beckley-Bluefield-Oak Hill	18,900	18,540	98
Gilmer	Clarksburg-Weston	2,700	2,580	96
Grant	Harrisonburg	2,900	2,730	94
Greenbrier	Beckley-Bluefield-Oak Hill	11,900	11,500	97
Hampshire	Washington, DC, Hagerstown	4,900	4,580	93
Hancock	Wheeling-Steubenville	13,800	13,630	99
Hardy	Washington, DC, Hagerstown	3,300	3,130	95
Harrison	Clarksburg-Weston	28,900	28,530	99
Jackson	Charleston-Huntington	7,500	7,370	98
Jefferson	Washington, DC, Hagerstown	8,600	8,310	97
Kanawha	Charleston-Huntington	81,200	79,500	98
Lewis	Clarksburg-Weston	6,500	6,340	98
Lincoln	Charleston-Huntington	7,100	6,840	96
Logan	Charleston-Huntington	15,900	15,540	98
McDowell	Beckley-Bluefield-Oak Hill	16,500	15,850	96
Marion	Pittsburgh	24,400	24,000	98
Marshall	Wheeling-Steubenville	14,200	14,030	99
Mason	Charleston-Huntington	8,700	8,480	97
Mercer	Beckley-Bluefield-Oak Hill	24,300	23,630	97
Mineral	Washington, DC, Hagerstown	9,100	8,780	96
Mingo	Charleston-Huntington	11,700	11,070	95
Monongalia	Pittsburgh	23,800	23,110	97
Monroe	Beckley-Bluefield-Oak Hill	4,200	4,120	98
Morgan	Washington, DC, Hagerstown	3,300	3,150	95
Nicholas	Charleston-Huntington	8,600	8,340	97
Ohio	Wheeling-Steubenville	22,200	21,900	99
Pendleton	Harrisonburg	2,400	2,220	93
Pleasants	Wheeling-Steubenville	2,400	2,380	99
Pocahontas	Roanoke-Lynchburg	3,300	3,160	96
Preston	Pittsburgh	9,300	8,820	95
Putnam	Charleston-Huntington	10,700	10,390	97
Raleigh	Beckley-Bluefield-Oak Hill	28,900	28,210	98
Randolph	Clarksburg-Weston	9,200	8,880	97
Ritchie	Clarksburg-Weston	4,000	3,900	98
Roane	Charleston-Huntington	5,300	5,010	95
Summers	Beckley-Bluefield-Oak Hill	5,400	5,170	96
Taylor	Clarksburg-Weston	5,800	5,680	98
Tucker	Pittsburgh	2,800	2,730	98
Tyler	Wheeling-Steubenville	3,600	3,540	98
Upshur	Clarksburg-Weston	8,100	7,840	97
Wayne	Charleston-Huntington	14,000	13,560	97
Webster	Charleston-Huntington	4,000	3,880	97
Wetzel	Wheeling-Steubenville	7,200	6,980	97
Wirt	Charleston-Huntington	1,700	1,620	95
Wood	Parkersburg	31,000	30,510	98
Wyoming	Beckley-Bluefield-Oak Hill	10,500	10,260	98
	STATE TOTAL	648,200	631,500	97

COUNTY	MARKET	HOUSEHOLDS	TV's	%
WISCONSIN				
Adams	Wausau, Rhinelander	4,400	4,330	98
Ashland	Duluth-Superior	5,800	5,650	97
Barron	Minneapolis-St. Paul	13,600	13,310	98
Bayfield	Duluth-Superior	4,900	4,720	96
Brown	Green Bay	56,300	55,860	99
Buffalo	La Crosse-Eau Claire	5,000	4,920	98
Burnett	Minneapolis-St. Paul	4,600	4,440	97
Calumet	Green Bay	8,800	8,740	99
Chippewa	La Crosse-Eau Claire	15,600	15,480	99
Clark	La Crosse-Eau Claire	11,000	10,820	98
Columbia	Madison	15,200	14,900	98
Crawford	Cedar Rapids-Watrloo, Dubuq	5,600	5,500	98
Dane	Madison	111,800	109,000	97
Dodge	Milwaukee	24,600	24,300	99
Door	Green Bay	8,600	8,540	99
Douglas	Duluth-Superior	16,700	16,450	99
Dunn	Minneapolis-St. Paul	10,900	10,600	97
Eau Claire	La Crosse-Eau Claire	25,800	25,420	99
Florence	Marquette	1,200	1,190	99
Fond Du Lac	Green Bay	28,800	28,500	99
Forest	Green Bay	2,800	2,780	99
Grant	Cedar Rapids-Watrloo, Dubuq	16,100	15,840	98
Green	Madison	10,500	10,370	99
Green Lake	Green Bay	6,800	6,680	98
Iowa	Madison	6,700	6,570	98
Iron	Duluth-Superior	2,800	2,770	99
Jackson	La Crosse-Eau Claire	5,800	5,720	99
Jefferson	Milwaukee	22,400	21,990	98
Juneau	La Crosse-Eau Claire	7,200	7,080	98
Kenosha	Chicago	43,500	43,080	99
Kewaunee	Green Bay	6,700	6,650	99
La Crosse	La Crosse-Eau Claire	30,800	30,440	99
Lafayette	Madison	5,900	5,820	99
Langlade	Wausau, Rhinelander	7,300	7,110	97
Lincoln	Wausau, Rhinelander	9,200	9,110	99
Manitowoc	Green Bay	28,100	27,830	99
Marathon	Wausau, Rhinelander	35,100	34,730	99
Marinette	Green Bay	13,800	13,700	99
Marquette	Madison	4,000	3,900	98
Menominee	Green Bay	700	700	100
Milwaukee	Milwaukee	362,000	356,740	99
Monroe	La Crosse-Eau Claire	11,600	11,350	98
Oconto	Green Bay	10,200	10,060	99
Oneida	Wausau, Rhinelander	11,300	11,070	98
Outagamie	Green Bay	40,200	39,930	99
Ozaukee	Milwaukee	20,700	20,540	99
Pepin	Minneapolis-St. Paul	2,600	2,510	97
Pierce	Minneapolis-St. Paul	10,000	9,840	98
Polk	Minneapolis-St. Paul	10,900	10,670	98
Portage	Wausau, Rhinelander	16,100	15,800	98
Price	Wausau, Rhinelander	6,000	5,760	96
Racine	Milwaukee	59,700	58,930	99
Richland	Madison	5,900	5,730	97
Rock	Rockford	45,500	44,950	99
Rusk	La Crosse-Eau Claire	5,400	5,190	96
St. Croix	Minneapolis-St. Paul	13,300	13,100	98
Sauk	Madison	14,400	14,100	98
Sawyer	Duluth-Superior	4,600	4,430	96

COUNTY	MARKET	HOUSEHOLDS	TV's	%
WISCONSIN—*Cont'd*				
Shawano	Green Bay	12,600	12,390	98
Sheboygan	Milwaukee	35,200	34,820	99
Taylor	Wausau, Rhinelander	6,200	5,960	96
Trempealeau	La Crosse-Eau Claire	8,700	8,530	98
Vernon	La Crosse-Eau Claire	8,800	8,600	98
Vilas	Wausau, Rhinelander	5,700	5,620	99
Walworth	Milwaukee	22,700	22,370	99
Washburn	Duluth-Superior	5,000	4,810	96
Washington	Milwaukee	24,600	24,300	99
Waukesha	Milwaukee	81,700	81,000	99
Waupaca	Green Bay	14,900	14,640	98
Waushara	Green Bay	6,100	5,970	98
Winnebago	Green Bay	44,600	44,240	99
Wood	Wausau, Rhinelander	23,000	22,780	99
	STATE TOTAL	1,595,600	1,572,270	99
WYOMING				
Albany	Denver	10,200	9,720	95
Big Horn	Billings	4,300	4,150	97
Campbell	Rapid City	5,900	5,870	99
Carbon	Denver	6,600	6,250	95
Converse	Casper-Riverton	3,400	3,310	97
Crook	Rapid City	1,800	1,730	96
Fremont	Casper-Riverton	10,800	10,300	95
Goshen	Cheyenne-Scottsblf-Sterlng	5,000	4,930	99
Hot Springs	Salt Lake City	2,200	2,130	97
Johnson	Casper-Riverton	2,800	2,700	96
Laramie	Cheyenne-Scottsblf-Sterlng	24,000	23,650	99
Lincoln	Idaho Falls-Pocatello	4,000	3,820	96
Natrona	Casper-Riverton	21,800	21,340	98
Niobrara	Casper-Riverton	1,200	1,170	98
Park	Billings	7,700	7,550	98
Platte	Denver	3,300	3,220	98
Sheridan	Rapid City	9,300	8,960	96
Sublette	Casper-Riverton	1,600	1,540	96
Sweetwater	Salt Lake City	12,800	12,420	97
Teton	Idaho Falls-Pocatello	2,400	2,340	98
Uinta	Salt Lake City	3,400	3,320	98
Washakie	Casper-Riverton	3,000	2,910	97
Weston	Rapid City	2,500	2,420	97
	STATE TOTAL	150,000	145,750	97

ARBITRON*

COUNTY	MARKET	HOUSEHOLDS	TV's	%
ALABAMA				
Autauga	Montgomery	9,300	8,900	96
Baldwin	Mobile-Pensacola	24,500	24,000	98
Barbour	Columbus, GA	9,200	8,700	95
Bibb	Birmingham	4,500	4,300	96
Blount	Birmingham	12,400	12,100	97
Bullock	Montgomery	3,500	3,300	94
Butler	Montgomery	7,300	7,000	96
Calhoun	Anniston	38,600	37,800	98
Chambers	Columbus, GA	13,100	12,700	97
Cherokee	Atlanta	7,000	6,800	97
Chilton	Birmingham	10,500	10,100	97
Choctaw	Meridian	5,900	5,600	94
Clarke	Mobile-Pensacola	9,400	8,900	95
Clay	Birmingham	5,300	5,100	97
Cleburne	Atlanta	4,100	4,000	96
Coffee	Dothan	12,700	12,300	97
Colbert	Huntsville-Decatur-Florence	17,500	17,000	97
Conecuh	Mobile-Pensacola	5,100	4,800	95
Coosa	Birmingham	3,700	3,600	96
Covington	Montgomery	13,200	12,800	97
Crenshaw	Montgomery	5,500	5,300	96
Cullman	Birmingham	21,300	20,900	98
Dale	Dothan	13,300	13,000	98
Dallas	Selma	18,000	17,300	96
De Kalb	Chattanooga	18,200	17,700	97
Elmore	Montgomery	12,600	12,200	97
Escambia	Mobile-Pensacola	11,500	11,100	96
Etowah	Birmingham	33,900	33,300	98
Fayette	Birmingham	6,100	5,900	97
Franklin	Huntsville-Decatur-Florence	10,200	9,800	96
Geneva	Dothan	8,800	8,500	97
Greene	Meridian	3,200	3,000	92
Hale	Birmingham	4,500	4,200	94
Henry	Dothan	5,300	5,100	96
Houston	Dothan	26,200	25,700	98
Jackson	Chattanooga	17,600	17,100	97
Jefferson	Birmingham	231,100	227,500	98
Lamar	Columbus-Tupelo	6,300	6,100	96
Lauderdale	Huntsville-Decatur-Florence	26,300	25,400	97
Lawrence	Huntsville-Decatur-Florence	9,500	9,100	96
Lee	Columbus, GA	23,600	22,900	97
Limestone	Huntsville-Decatur-Florence	14,400	13,900	97
Lowndes	Montgomery	3,700	3,400	93
Macon	Montgomery	8,500	8,100	95
Madison	Huntsville-Decatur-Florence	58,100	56,600	97
Marengo	Meridian	7,900	7,500	94
Marion	Birmingham	9,800	9,500	97
Marshall	Huntsville-Decatur-Florence	21,900	21,400	98
Mobile	Mobile-Pensacola	112,500	110,700	98
Monroe	Mobile-Pensacola	6,900	6,500	94
Montgomery	Montgomery	63,200	61,700	98
Morgan	Huntsville-Decatur-Florence	30,000	29,200	97
Perry	Birmingham	3,900	3,600	93
Pickens	Columbus-Tupelo	7,100	6,700	95
Pike	Montgomery	8,700	8,300	96
Randolph	Atlanta	6,800	6,500	96

*Arbitron information © 1978 by The Arbitron Company.

COUNTY	MARKET	HOUSEHOLDS	TV's	%
ALABAMA—*Cont'd*				
Russell	Columbus, GA	14,700	14,200	97
St Clair	Birmingham	12,100	11,800	97
Shelby	Birmingham	17,500	17,100	98
Sumter	Meridian	5,400	5,100	94
Talladega	Birmingham	22,700	22,100	97
Tallapoosa	Montgomery	13,000	12,600	97
Tuscaloosa	Tuscaloosa	40,600	39,500	97
Walker	Birmingham	23,500	23,000	98
Washington	Mobile-Pensacola	5,200	5,000	96
Wilcox	Montgomery	4,400	4,100	93
Winston	Birmingham	7,600	7,400	97
	STATE TOTAL	1,259,900	1,226,500	97
ALASKA (Anchorage ADI Only)				
Anchorage	Anchorage	59,000	56,300	95
Kenai-Cook Inlet	Anchorage	5,500	3,700	67
Matanuska-Susitna	Anchorage	5,000	3,700	74
Seward	Anchorage	1,100	900	84
	STATE TOTAL	70,600	64,600	92
ARIZONA				
Apache North	Albuquerque	9,200	7,800	85
Apache South	Tucson	1,900	1,600	82
Cochise	Tucson	25,800	24,500	95
Coconino	Flagstaff	20,700	18,500	90
Gila	Phoenix	11,800	11,100	94
Graham	Tucson	6,600	6,100	92
Greenlee	Phoenix	3,900	3,700	95
Maricopa	Phoenix	455,100	442,000	97
Mohave	Phoenix	15,800	14,700	93
Navajo	Phoenix	17,000	14,900	87
Pima	Tucson	168,500	163,600	97
Pinal	Phoenix	27,600	26,300	95
Santa Cruz	Tucson	5,600	5,300	95
Yavapai	Phoenix	20,700	19,200	93
Yuma	El Centro-Yuma	24,100	22,300	92
	STATE TOTAL	814,300	781,600	96
ARKANSAS				
Arkansas	Little Rock	7,900	7,600	97
Ashley	Monroe-El Dorado	8,600	8,200	95
Baxter	Springfield, MO	9,900	9,300	94
Benton	Joplin-Pittsburg	22,800	21,700	95
Boone	Springfield, MO	9,200	8,700	95
Bradley	Little Rock	4,900	4,600	95
Calhoun	Little Rock	1,800	1,700	95
Carroll	Springfield, MO	5,900	5,600	95
Chicot	Monroe-El Dorado	5,700	5,300	92
Clark	Little Rock	8,000	7,600	96
Clay	Jonesboro	8,200	7,800	95
Cleburne	Little Rock	5,600	5,300	95
Cleveland	Little Rock	2,500	2,300	93

COUNTY	MARKET	HOUSEHOLDS	TV's	%

ARKANSAS—*Cont'd*

COUNTY	MARKET	HOUSEHOLDS	TV's	%
Columbia	Shreveport-Texarkana	8,600	8,200	95
Conway	Little Rock	8,800	8,400	96
Craighead	Jonesboro	22,800	22,200	97
Crawford	Ft. Smith	11,700	11,100	95
Crittenden	Memphis	14,500	13,700	95
Cross	Memphis	6,100	5,800	96
Dallas	Little Rock	3,300	3,100	95
Desha	Little Rock	5,700	5,400	94
Drew	Little Rock	5,700	5,300	94
Faulkner	Little Rock	12,500	12,000	96
Franklin	Ft. Smith	4,400	4,200	95
Fulton	Springfield, MO	3,300	3,000	90
Garland	Little Rock	26,700	25,600	96
Grant	Little Rock	4,300	4,100	96
Greene	Jonesboro	11,300	10,900	96
Hempstead	Shreveport-Texarkana	7,100	6,700	95
Hot Spring	Little Rock	8,800	8,400	96
Howard	Shreveport-Texarkana	5,100	4,900	96
Independence	Little Rock	9,100	8,700	95
Izard	Little Rock	4,200	3,800	91
Jackson	Little Rock	8,100	7,700	95
Jefferson	Little Rock	27,500	26,500	96
Johnson	Little Rock	6,100	5,700	94
Lafayette	Shreveport-Texarkana	3,400	3,300	96
Lawrence	Jonesboro	7,900	7,500	95
Lee	Memphis	5,600	5,200	93
Lincoln	Little Rock	3,800	3,600	94
Little River	Shreveport-Texarkana	3,700	3,500	94
Logan	Ft. Smith	6,600	6,300	95
Lonoke	Little Rock	10,900	10,600	97
Madison	Springfield, MO	3,900	3,500	91
Marion	Springfield, MO	4,300	4,100	95
Miller	Shreveport-Texarkana	12,400	12,000	96
Mississippi	Memphis	20,200	19,400	96
Monroe	Little Rock	4,700	4,400	93
Montgomery	Little Rock	2,700	2,500	94
Nevada	Shreveport-Texarkana	3,900	3,700	94
Newton	Springfield, MO	2,600	2,300	90
Ouachita	Little Rock	10,300	9,800	95
Perry	Little Rock	2,600	2,500	97
Phillips	Memphis	11,600	10,800	93
Pike	Little Rock	3,300	3,100	95
Poinsett	Memphis	9,200	8,900	96
Polk	Little Rock	6,400	6,000	94
Pope	Little Rock	13,100	12,600	96
Prairie	Little Rock	3,900	3,700	95
Pulaski	Little Rock	118,300	115,500	98
Randolph	Jonesboro	6,500	6,100	94
St Francis	Memphis	9,900	9,300	94
Saline	Little Rock	15,100	14,800	98
Scott	Ft. Smith	3,600	3,400	94
Searcy	Little Rock	3,200	3,000	93
Sebastian	Ft. Smith	33,200	32,400	97
Sevier	Shreveport-Texarkana	4,900	4,700	96
Sharp	Jonesboro	4,900	4,400	91
Stone	Little Rock	2,800	2,600	93
Union	Monroe-El Dorado	16,700	16,100	96
Van Buren	Little Rock	3,800	3,600	95

COUNTY	MARKET	HOUSEHOLDS	TV's	%
ARKANSAS—*Cont'd*				
Washington	Tulsa	32,700	31,000	95
White	Little Rock	17,800	17,100	96
Woodruff	Little Rock	3,800	3,600	94
Yell	Little Rock	6,300	6,000	95
	STATE TOTAL	767,200	734,000	96
CALIFORNIA				
Alameda	San Francisco	436,700	417,500	96
Alpine	Reno	500	400	81
Amador	Sacramento-Stockton	6,900	6,400	93
Butte	Chico-Redding	51,500	48,100	93
Calaveras	Sacramento-Stockton	6,800	6,300	93
Colusa	Chico-Redding	5,300	4,900	93
Contra Costa East	Sacramento-Stockton	5,500	5,400	97
Contra Costa West	San Francisco	216,200	209,200	97
Del Norte	Eureka	6,000	5,400	91
El Dorado East	Reno	9,300	8,800	95
El Dorado West	Sacramento-Stockton	18,000	17,100	95
Fresno	Fresno	161,500	152,800	95
Glenn	Chico-Redding	7,400	7,000	95
Humboldt	Eureka	40,100	37,700	94
Imperial	El Centro-Yuma	29,400	26,500	90
Inyo	Los Angeles	7,200	6,100	85
Kern East	Los Angeles	19,100	18,200	95
Kern West	Bakersfield	104,300	99,000	95
Kings	Fresno	23,500	21,900	93
Lake	San Francisco	13,000	11,600	89
Lassen	Reno	7,000	6,300	91
Los Angeles	Los Angeles	2,731,800	2,625,200	96
Madera	Fresno	17,500	16,400	94
Marin	San Francisco	84,800	81,000	96
Mariposa	Sacramento-Stockton	3,800	3,400	89
Mendocino	San Francisco	23,200	20,700	89
Merced	Fresno	42,400	40,100	94
Modoc	Chico-Redding	3,400	3,000	90
Mono	Sacramento-Stockton	3,000	2,400	80
Monterey	Salinas-Monterey	85,000	80,400	95
Napa	San Francisco	35,600	33,800	95
Nevada	Sacramento-Stockton	17,000	15,600	92
Orange	Los Angeles	682,100	664,800	97
Placer East	Reno	3,000	2,800	95
Placer West	Sacramento-Stockton	33,700	31,900	95
Plumas	Sacramento-Stockton	5,600	5,100	91
Riverside East	Phoenix	6,400	6,100	95
Riverside West	Los Angeles	167,000	158,000	95
Riverside Central	Palm Springs	47,800	45,200	95
Sacramento	Sacramento-Stockton	270,100	259,700	96
San Benito	Salinas-Monterey	7,500	7,000	93
San Bernardino East	Phoenix	2,400	2,300	95
San Bernardino West	Los Angeles	266,500	254,300	95
San Diego	San Diego	650,600	624,500	96
San Francisco	San Francisco	312,100	284,600	91
San Joaquin	Sacramento-Stockton	103,200	97,000	94
San Luis Obispo	Snta Brbra-Snta Maria-Sn Luis Obispo	54,100	50,700	94
San Mateo	San Francisco	224,900	218,800	97

COUNTY	MARKET	HOUSEHOLDS	TV's	%
CALIFORNIA—*Cont'd*				
Santa Barbara North	Snta Brbra-Snta Maria-Sn Luis Obispo	45,700	43,200	94
Santa Barbara South	Snta Brbra-Snta Maria-Sn Luis Obispo	60,400	57,000	94
Santa Clara East	San Francisco	12,800	12,300	96
Santa Clara West	San Francisco	427,400	411,300	96
Santa Cruz	Salinas-Monterey	71,000	66,700	94
Shasta	Chico-Redding	36,900	35,200	95
Sierra	Sacramento-Stockton	1,300	1,200	89
Siskiyou	Medford	14,400	13,000	90
Solano East	Sacramento-Stockton	36,100	34,900	97
Solano West	San Francisco	34,900	33,800	97
Sonoma	San Francisco	102,400	96,100	94
Stanislaus	Sacramento-Stockton	88,500	82,600	93
Sutter	Sacramento-Stockton	17,900	17,100	96
Tehama	Chico-Redding	12,900	12,400	96
Trinity	Chico-Redding	4,400	3,900	89
Tulare	Fresno	77,500	72,900	94
Tuolumne	Sacramento-Stockton	11,000	10,200	92
Ventura	Los Angeles	161,800	156,200	97
Yolo	Sacramento-Stockton	39,000	36,900	95
Yuba	Sacramento-Stockton	16,000	15,300	95
	STATE TOTAL	8,332,000	7,963,600	96
COLORADO				
Adams	Denver	73,100	72,300	99
Alamosa	Albuquerque	4,000	3,700	93
Arapahoe	Denver	82,900	81,600	98
Archuleta	Albuquerque	1,200	1,100	90
Baca	Colorado Springs-Pueblo	2,200	1,900	86
Bent	Colorado Springs-Pueblo	2,400	2,300	95
Boulder	Denver	64,800	62,500	96
Chaffee	Denver	4,600	4,300	94
Cheyenne	Colorado Springs-Pueblo	700	600	92
Clear Creek	Denver	1,800	1,700	95
Conejos	Albuquerque	2,100	1,900	92
Costilla	Albuquerque	1,000	900	85
Crowley	Colorado Springs-Pueblo	1,100	1,100	97
Custer	Colorado Springs-Pueblo	300	300	92
Delta	Grand Junction	8,000	7,500	94
Denver	Denver	202,900	197,000	97
Dolores	Albuquerque	600	500	85
Douglas	Denver	6,700	6,600	99
Eagle	Denver	3,400	3,100	92
Elbert	Denver	2,400	2,300	95
El Paso	Colorado Springs-Pueblo	95,100	93,100	98
Fremont	Colorado Springs-Pueblo	10,200	9,700	95
Garfield	Denver	7,900	7,400	93
Gilpin	Denver	900	900	96
Grand	Denver	2,600	2,400	91
Gunnison	Denver	3,100	2,800	91
Hinsdale	Grand Junction	600	600	98
Huerfano	Colorado Springs-Pueblo	2,600	2,400	92
Jackson	Denver	600	600	95
Jefferson	Denver	116,100	114,600	99
Kiowa	Colorado Springs-Pueblo	900	800	92

COUNTY	MARKET	HOUSEHOLDS	TV's	%
COLORADO—*Cont'd*				
Kit Carson	Wichita-Hutchinson	2,900	2,700	92
Lake	Denver	3,100	2,900	94
La Plata	Albuquerque	8,500	8,000	94
Larimer	Denver	47,200	45,800	97
Las Animas	Colorado Springs-Pueblo	6,300	5,700	91
Lincoln	Colorado Springs-Pueblo	1,900	1,800	95
Logan	Cheyenne	7,300	7,000	95
Mesa	Grand Junction	26,500	25,500	96
Mineral	Colorado Springs-Pueblo	200	200	87
Moffat	Denver	3,900	3,500	91
Montezuma	Albuquerque	5,100	4,800	94
Montrose	Grand Junction	7,600	7,200	95
Morgan	Denver	7,800	7,600	98
Otero	Colorado Springs-Pueblo	9,200	8,800	96
Ouray	Grand Junction	800	700	90
Park	Denver	1,900	1,800	94
Phillips	Cheyenne	2,000	1,900	97
Pitkin	Denver	4,000	3,500	87
Prowers	Colorado Springs-Pueblo	5,000	4,600	91
Pueblo	Colorado Springs-Pueblo	44,500	43,500	98
Rio Blanco	Denver	1,900	1,800	95
Rio Grande	Albuquerque	3,700	3,400	92
Routt	Denver	4,400	4,000	90
Saguache	Albuquerque	1,300	1,200	91
San Juan	Grand Junction	300	300	95
San Miguel	Grand Junction	1,000	900	91
Sedgwick	Cheyenne	1,300	1,200	96
Summit	Denver	2,200	2,100	94
Teller	Colorado Springs-Pueblo	2,900	2,800	97
Washington	Denver	2,200	2,100	94
Weld	Denver	37,700	36,800	98
Yuma	Wichita-Hutchinson	3,600	3,400	94
	STATE TOTAL	965,000	936,000	97
CONNECTICUT				
Fairfield	New York	283,000	276,600	98
Hartford	Hartford-New Haven	287,300	278,700	97
Litchfield	Hartford-New Haven	55,200	53,300	97
Middlesex	Hartford-New Haven	43,800	42,300	97
New Haven	Hartford-New Haven	269,000	261,900	97
New London	Providence	80,900	77,600	96
Tolland	Hartford-New Haven	35,500	34,200	96
Windham	Boston	34,900	33,600	96
	STATE TOTAL	1,089,600	1,058,200	97
DELAWARE				
Kent	Philadelphia	30,700	30,000	98
New Castle	Philadelphia	138,200	136,700	99
Sussex	Salisbury	33,200	32,100	97
	STATE TOTAL	202,100	198,800	98

COUNTY	MARKET	HOUSEHOLDS	TV's	%
DISTRICT OF COLUMBIA				
District of Columbia	Washington, DC	279,400	271,700	97
	STATE TOTAL	279,400	271,700	97
FLORIDA				
Alachua	Gainesville	45,700	43,400	95
Baker	Jacksonville	3,800	3,700	96
Bay	Panama City	33,200	32,300	97
Bradford	Jacksonville	5,300	5,100	96
Brevard	Orlando-Daytona Beach	82,200	80,200	98
Broward	Miami	369,500	363,700	98
Calhoun	Panama City	2,300	2,100	93
Charlotte	Ft. Myers	21,200	20,400	96
Citrus	Tampa-St. Petersburg	16,300	15,500	95
Clay	Jacksonville	18,400	17,800	97
Collier	Ft. Myers	27,100	25,600	94
Columbia	Jacksonville	10,400	9,900	95
Dade	Miami	560,800	584,100	98
De Soto	Tampa-St. Petersburg	6,000	5,700	96
Dixie	Gainesville	2,400	2,200	91
Duval	Jacksonville	202,600	198,300	98
Escambia	Mobile-Pensacola	77,800	76,200	98
Flagler	Orlando-Daytona Beach	2,600	2,500	95
Franklin	Panama City	2,900	2,700	93
Gadsden	Tallahassee	9,800	9,200	94
Gilchrist	Gainesville	2,100	2,000	95
Glades	West Palm Beach	1,800	1,700	93
Gulf	Panama City	3,400	3,200	95
Hamilton	Jacksonville	3,300	3,100	93
Hardee	Tampa-St. Petersburg	5,900	5,700	97
Hendry	Ft. Myers	5,700	5,300	94
Hernando	Tampa-St. Petersburg	12,900	12,400	96
Highlands	Tampa-St. Petersburg	15,900	15,200	96
Hillsborough	Tampa-St. Petersburg	219,700	214,100	97
Holmes	Dothan	5,300	4,900	92
Indian River	Miami	18,800	18,000	96
Jackson	Dothan	13,900	13,000	93
Jefferson	Tallahassee	3,200	3,000	93
Lafayette	Tallahassee	1,300	1,200	92
Lake	Orlando-Daytona Beach	36,400	35,400	97
Lee	Ft. Myers	71,600	69,500	97
Leon	Tallahassee	47,600	45,800	96
Levy	Gainesville	6,200	5,700	92
Liberty	Tallahassee	1,600	1,500	93
Madison	Tallahassee	5,000	4,600	91
Manatee	Tampa-St. Petersburg	57,400	56,000	98
Marion	Orlando-Daytona Beach	37,700	35,800	95
Martin	West Palm Beach	20,300	19,600	97
Monroe	Miami	18,200	17,100	94
Nassau	Jacksonville	11,000	10,700	97
Okaloosa	Mobile-Pensacola	33,600	32,800	98
Okeechobee	West Palm Beach	6,300	6,100	97
Orange	Orlando-Daytona Beach	155,000	151,400	98
Osceola	Orlando-Daytona Beach	16,700	16,100	97
Palm Beach	West Palm Beach	196,000	189,800	97
Pasco	Tampa-St. Petersburg	66,800	64,800	97
Pinellas	Tampa-St. Petersburg	318,100	311,100	98

COUNTY	MARKET	HOUSEHOLDS	TV's	%
FLORIDA—*Cont'd*				
Polk	Tampa-St. Petersburg	103,000	100,200	97
Putnam	Jacksonville	16,400	15,800	97
St Johns	Jacksonville	15,800	15,300	97
St Lucie	West Palm Beach	28,100	27,100	96
Santa Rosa	Mobile-Pensacola	17,100	16,700	98
Sarasota	Tampa-St. Petersburg	77,200	75,200	97
Seminole	Orlando-Daytona Beach	52,900	51,600	97
Sumter	Orlando-Daytona Beach	7,600	7,200	95
Suwannee	Jacksonville	6,700	6,200	93
Taylor	Tallahassee	4,800	4,500	93
Union	Jacksonville	2,600	2,500	95
Volusia	Orlando-Daytona Beach	90,300	87,900	97
Wakulla	Tallahassee	3,100	3,000	96
Walton	Panama City	7,000	6,600	94
Washington	Panama City	4,600	4,300	94
	STATE TOTAL	3,356,200	3,265,300	97
GEORGIA				
Appling	Savannah	4,900	4,600	93
Atkinson	Albany, GA	1,700	1,500	90
Bacon	Savannah	3,100	2,900	94
Baker	Albany, GA	1,000	900	92
Baldwin	Atlanta	7,600	7,200	95
Banks	Atlanta	2,200	2,100	95
Barrow	Atlanta	7,000	6,800	97
Bartow	Atlanta	12,100	11,800	97
Ben Hill	Albany, GA	5,200	4,900	94
Berrien	Albany, GA	4,400	4,100	93
Bibb	Macon	47,000	45,700	97
Bleckley	Macon	3,800	3,600	94
Brantley	Jacksonville	2,600	2,500	95
Brooks	Tallahassee	4,700	4,500	95
Bryan	Savannah	2,800	2,700	96
Bulloch	Savannah	10,900	10,400	96
Burke	Augusta	5,500	5,100	93
Butts	Atlanta	3,900	3,800	96
Calhoun	Albany, GA	2,100	1,900	90
Camden	Jacksonville	3,800	3,700	97
Candler	Savannah	2,300	2,200	94
Carroll	Atlanta	18,700	18,200	97
Catoosa	Chattanooga	11,900	11,700	98
Charlton	Jacksonville	2,000	1,900	95
Chatham	Savannah	62,800	61,100	97
Chattahoochee	Columbus, GA	2,100	2,100	98
Chattooga	Chattanooga	8,000	7,700	97
Cherokee	Atlanta	14,400	14,100	98
Clarke	Atlanta	23,400	22,600	96
Clay	Columbus, GA	1,200	1,100	93
Clayton	Atlanta	44,000	43,400	99
Clinch	Jacksonville	1,900	1,800	94
Cobb	Atlanta	83,900	82,900	99
Coffee	Albany, GA	7,800	7,300	94
Colquitt	Albany, GA	11,300	10,900	96
Columbia	Augusta	10,400	10,000	96
Cook	Albany, GA	4,200	4,000	95
Coweta	Atlanta	12,400	11,900	96

COUNTY	MARKET	HOUSEHOLDS	TV's	%

GEORGIA—*Cont'd*

COUNTY	MARKET	HOUSEHOLDS	TV's	%
Crawford	Macon	2,000	1,800	92
Crisp	Albany, GA	6,300	5,900	94
Dade	Chattanooga	3,900	3,800	97
Dawson	Atlanta	1,800	1,700	95
Decatur	Tallahassee	8,200	7,800	96
De Kalb	Atlanta	153,900	152,300	99
Dodge	Macon	5,800	5,500	95
Dooly	Macon	3,700	3,500	94
Dougherty	Albany, GA	29,000	28,000	97
Douglas	Atlanta	16,100	15,700	98
Early	Dothan	4,300	4,000	94
Echols	Tallahassee	500	500	92
Effingham	Savannah	4,800	4,600	96
Elbert	Greenville-Spartanburg-Asheville	6,300	6,100	97
Emanuel	Augusta	7,100	6,700	94
Evans	Savannah	3,000	2,900	96
Fannin	Chattanooga	5,200	4,900	95
Fayette	Atlanta	6,200	6,000	97
Floyd	Atlanta	27,600	26,800	97
Forsyth	Atlanta	7,600	7,400	98
Franklin	Greenville-Spartanburg-Asheville	4,900	4,800	97
Fulton	Atlanta	208,200	204,100	98
Gilmer	Atlanta	3,600	3,400	95
Glascock	Augusta	700	700	95
Glynn	Jacksonville	15,200	14,700	97
Gordon	Atlanta	9,300	9,000	97
Grady	Tallahassee	6,600	6,300	96
Greene	Atlanta	3,300	3,100	94
Gwinnett	Atlanta	42,900	42,000	98
Habersham	Atlanta	8,200	7,900	96
Hall	Atlanta	23,400	22,800	97
Hancock	Augusta	2,800	2,600	91
Haralson	Atlanta	6,500	6,300	97
Harris	Columbus, GA	3,800	3,600	95
Hart	Greenville-Spartanburg-Asheville	5,700	5,500	97
Heard	Atlanta	2,100	2,000	95
Henry	Atlanta	9,500	9,100	96
Houston	Macon	23,100	22,500	98
Irwin	Albany, GA	2,900	2,700	94
Jackson	Atlanta	8,400	8,100	96
Jasper	Atlanta	2,200	2,100	93
Jeff Davis	Savannah	3,700	3,500	94
Jefferson	Augusta	5,100	4,800	94
Jenkins	Augusta	2,800	2,700	95
Johnson	Augusta	2,300	2,200	95
Jones	Macon	5,200	4,900	95
Lamar	Atlanta	3,600	3,400	96
Lanier	Albany, GA	1,800	1,700	93
Laurens	Macon	11,800	11,100	94
Lee	Albany, GA	3,200	3,000	94
Liberty	Savannah	6,200	5,900	96
Lincoln	Augusta	1,900	1,800	95
Long	Savannah	1,000	900	94
Lowndes	Tallahassee	21,200	20,200	95
Lumpkin	Atlanta	2,700	2,600	97
McDuffie	Augusta	6,000	5,700	96
McIntosh	Savannah	2,700	2,500	94
Macon	Columbus, GA	3,600	3,400	93

COUNTY	MARKET	HOUSEHOLDS	TV's	%

GEORGIA—*Cont'd*

COUNTY	MARKET	HOUSEHOLDS	TV's	%
Madison	Greenville-Spartanburg-Asheville	5,400	5,200	96
Marion	Columbus, GA	2,200	2,000	91
Meriwether	Atlanta	6,100	5,800	95
Miller	Dothan	1,800	1,700	93
Mitchell	Albany, GA	6,000	5,700	94
Monroe	Atlanta	3,500	3,300	95
Montgomery	Savannah	1,900	1,700	91
Morgan	Atlanta	3,100	2,900	94
Murray	Chattanooga	6,000	5,700	95
Muscogee	Columbus, GA	55,100	53,800	98
Newton	Atlanta	10,700	10,400	97
Oconee	Atlanta	3,200	3,100	98
Oglethorpe	Atlanta	2,600	2,500	95
Paulding	Atlanta	8,200	8,000	98
Peach	Macon	6,300	6,000	96
Pickens	Atlanta	3,700	3,600	96
Pierce	Savannah	3,500	3,300	95
Pike	Atlanta	2,600	2,400	94
Polk	Atlanta	10,600	10,300	97
Pulaski	Macon	2,800	2,600	94
Putnam	Atlanta	2,500	2,400	95
Quitman	Columbus, GA	600	600	93
Rabun	Atlanta	3,500	3,300	95
Randolph	Columbus, GA	3,100	2,900	93
Richmond	Augusta	47,100	46,000	98
Rockdale	Atlanta	9,800	9,500	97
Schley	Columbus, GA	800	800	94
Screven	Augusta	4,100	3,800	94
Seminole	Dothan	2,800	2,700	95
Spalding	Atlanta	16,000	15,500	97
Stephens	Greenville-Spartanburg-Asheville	8,500	8,200	96
Stewart	Columbus, GA	1,600	1,500	91
Sumter	Columbus, GA	8,900	8,300	94
Talbot	Columbus, GA	1,500	1,400	93
Taliaferro	Augusta	800	700	93
Tattnall	Savannah	4,900	4,700	95
Taylor	Columbus, GA	2,400	2,300	94
Telfair	Albany, GA	3,700	3,400	92
Terrell	Columbus, GA	3,700	3,500	94
Thomas	Tallahassee	12,600	12,100	96
Tift	Albany, GA	10,300	9,800	95
Toombs	Savannah	7,300	6,800	93
Towns	Atlanta	1,500	1,400	96
Treutlen	Augusta	2,000	1,900	93
Troup	Atlanta	15,600	14,900	96
Turner	Albany, GA	3,000	2,800	95
Twiggs	Macon	2,100	2,000	94
Union	Atlanta	2,900	2,800	96
Upson	Atlanta	8,500	8,200	96
Walker	Chattanooga	19,300	18,900	98
Walton	Atlanta	9,900	9,600	97
Ware	Jacksonville	12,200	11,700	96
Warren	Augusta	1,800	1,700	93
Washington	Augusta	5,400	5,000	92
Wayne	Savannah	6,200	5,900	96
Webster	Columbus, GA	600	500	90
Wheeler	Savannah	1,800	1,700	92
White	Atlanta	3,000	2,900	95

COUNTY	MARKET	HOUSEHOLDS	TV's	%
GEORGIA—*Cont'd*				
Whitfield	Chattanooga	19,600	19,100	98
Wilcox	Albany, GA	2,500	2,400	95
Wilkes	Augusta	3,400	3,100	93
Wilkinson	Macon	3,000	2,800	95
Worth	Albany, GA	5,500	5,200	95
	STATE TOTAL	1,672,000	1,619,800	97
IDAHO				
Ada	Boise	53,400	52,000	97
Adams	Boise	1,100	1,000	94
Bannock	Idaho Falls-Pocatello	20,200	19,600	97
Bear Lake	Salt Lake City	2,300	2,200	96
Benewah	Spokane	2,900	2,800	96
Bingham	Idaho Falls-Pocatello	10,100	9,900	98
Blaine	Boise	3,300	3,100	95
Boise	Boise	800	800	96
Bonner	Spokane	7,800	7,500	96
Bonneville	Idaho Falls-Pocatello	19,600	19,300	98
Boundary	Spokane	2,500	2,300	94
Butte	Idaho Falls-Pocatello	900	900	98
Camas	Boise	200	200	99
Canyon	Boise	27,000	26,000	96
Caribou	Salt Lake City	2,500	2,400	96
Cassia	Twin Falls	6,300	6,100	98
Clark	Idaho Falls-Pocatello	500	500	94
Clearwater	Spokane	3,500	3,300	95
Custer	Idaho Falls-Pocatello	1,300	1,200	92
Elmore	Boise	6,600	6,400	97
Franklin	Salt Lake City	3,000	2,900	96
Fremont	Idaho Falls-Pocatello	3,400	3,300	98
Gem	Boise	3,900	3,800	97
Gooding	Twin Falls	4,200	4,100	97
Idaho	Spokane	4,500	4,200	93
Jefferson	Idaho Falls-Pocatello	4,600	4,500	99
Jerome	Twin Falls	5,600	5,500	98
Kootenai	Spokane	18,900	18,500	98
Latah	Spokane	9,700	9,200	95
Lemhi	Missoula-Butte	2,200	2,000	90
Lewis	Spokane	1,900	1,800	97
Lincoln	Twin Falls	1,400	1,400	96
Madison	Idaho Falls-Pocatello	4,200	4,100	98
Minidoka	Idaho Falls-Pocatello	6,400	6,200	96
Nez Perce	Spokane	12,100	11,700	97
Oneida	Salt Lake City	1,200	1,200	97
Owyhee	Boise	2,600	2,500	97
Payette	Boise	6,100	5,900	97
Power	Idaho Falls-Pocatello	2,000	1,900	95
Shoshone	Spokane	6,500	6,300	97
Teton	Idaho Falls-Pocatello	700	700	99
Twin Falls	Twin Falls	18,000	17,600	98
Valley	Boise	1,600	1,500	94
Washington	Boise	3,300	3,100	95
	STATE TOTAL	300,800	291,400	97

COUNTY	MARKET	HOUSEHOLDS	TV's	%
ILLINOIS				
Adams	Quincy-Hannibal	25,600	25,000	98
Alexander	Paducah-Cape Girardeau- Harrisburg	5,500	5,100	94
Bond	St. Louis	5,400	5,100	95
Boone	Rockford	9,600	9,300	97
Brown	Quincy-Hannibal	2,500	2,400	95
Bureau	Davenport-Rock Is-Moline (Quad City)	13,100	12,700	97
Calhoun	St. Louis	2,200	2,100	96
Carroll	Davenport-Rock Is-Moline (Quad City)	7,100	6,900	97
Cass	Quincy-Hannibal	5,600	5,400	96
Champaign	Springfield-Decatur-Champaign	56,400	54,600	97
Christian	Springfield-Decatur-Champaign	14,300	13,900	97
Clark	Terre Haute	6,400	6,100	96
Clay	Terre Haute	5,800	5,400	93
Clinton	St. Louis	9,800	9,500	97
Coles	Springfield-Decatur-Champaign	17,500	16,900	97
Cook	Chicago	1,909,100	1,863,200	98
Crawford	Terre Haute	8,300	8,000	97
Cumberland	Terre Haute	3,900	3,700	95
Dekalb	Chicago	22,900	22,300	98
De Witt	Springfield-Decatur-Champaign	6,500	6,300	97
Douglas	Springfield-Decatur-Champaign	7,300	7,100	97
Dupage	Chicago	171,700	169,700	99
Edgar	Terre Haute	8,500	8,200	97
Edwards	Evansville	3,300	3,100	94
Effingham	Terre Haute	10,400	9,800	94
Fayette	St. Louis	7,800	7,400	95
Ford	Springfield-Decatur-Champaign	5,200	5,100	97
Franklin	Paducah-Cape Girardeau- Harrisburg	18,400	17,600	96
Fulton	Peoria	17,100	16,500	97
Gallatin	Evansville	2,500	2,300	93
Greene	St. Louis	6,200	6,000	97
Grundy	Chicago	10,300	10,100	98
Hamilton	Paducah-Cape Girardeau- Harrisburg	3,400	3,100	92
Hancock	Quincy-Hannibal	8,000	7,800	97
Hardin	Paducah-Cape Girardeau- Harrisburg	2,200	2,100	96
Henderson	Davenport-Rock Is-Moline (Quad City)	3,100	3,000	96
Henry	Davenport-Rock Is-Moline (Quad City)	21,000	20,600	98
Iroquois	Chicago	12,400	12,000	97
Jackson	Paducah-Cape Girardeau- Harrisburg	18,600	17,700	95
Jasper	Terre Haute	4,100	3,900	95
Jefferson	St. Louis	13,700	13,000	95
Jersey	St. Louis	6,500	6,300	96
Jo Daviess	Cedar Rapids-Waterloo	7,700	7,300	95
Johnson	Paducah-Cape Girardeau- Harrisburg	3,400	3,200	95
Kane	Chicago	88,500	86,600	98
Kankakee	Chicago	31,500	30,700	97
Kendall	Chicago	10,600	10,400	98

COUNTY	MARKET	HOUSEHOLDS	TV's	%

ILLINOIS—*Cont'd*

COUNTY	MARKET	HOUSEHOLDS	TV's	%
Knox	Davenport-Rock Is-Moline (Quad City)	22,600	22,200	98
Lake	Chicago	120,700	119,200	99
La Salle	Chicago	38,600	37,400	97
Lawrence	Terre Haute	6,700	6,400	96
Lee	Rockford	11,200	10,900	97
Livingston	Chicago	13,800	13,200	96
Logan	Peoria	10,300	10,000	97
McDonough	Quincy-Hannibal	12,300	11,900	97
McHenry	Chicago	43,500	43,000	99
McLean	Peoria	42,400	40,900	97
Macon	Springfield-Decatur-Champaign	48,300	47,000	97
Macoupin	St. Louis	17,500	17,000	97
Madison	St. Louis	85,900	84,100	98
Marion	St. Louis	15,400	14,800	96
Marshall	Peoria	4,900	4,700	96
Mason	Peoria	7,700	7,500	97
Massac	Paducah-Cape Girardeau-Harrisburg	5,400	5,100	95
Menard	Springfield-Decatur-Champaign	4,400	4,200	96
Mercer	Davenport-Rock Is-Moline (Quad City)	6,600	6,500	98
Monroe	St. Louis	6,500	6,300	97
Montgomery	St. Louis	12,000	11,600	96
Morgan	Springfield-Decatur-Champaign	13,200	12,600	96
Moultrie	Springfield-Decatur-Champaign	4,500	4,300	95
Ogle	Rockford	14,900	14,500	97
Peoria	Peoria	75,000	73,000	97
Perry	St. Louis	8,400	8,000	96
Piatt	Springfield-Decatur-Champaign	6,000	5,900	98
Pike	Quincy-Hannibal	7,700	7,400	96
Pope	Paducah-Cape Girardeau-Harrisburg	1,700	1,600	92
Pulaski	Paducah-Cape Girardeau-Harrisburg	3,900	3,600	93
Putnam	Peoria	2,000	1,900	95
Randolph	St. Louis	11,300	10,900	97
Richland	Terre Haute	6,300	6,000	95
Rock Island	Davenport-Rock Is-Moline (Quad City)	61,400	60,500	98
St. Clair	St. Louis	96,300	93,700	97
Saline	Paducah-Cape Girardeau-Harrisburg	11,900	11,400	95
Sangamon	Springfield-Decatur-Champaign	67,900	65,500	96
Schuyler	Quincy-Hannibal	3,100	3,000	97
Scott	Quincy-Hannibal	2,500	2,400	98
Shelby	Springfield-Decatur-Champaign	8,900	8,500	95
Stark	Peoria	3,000	2,900	97
Stephenson	Rockford	17,300	16,800	97
Tazewell	Peoria	45,400	44,400	98
Union	Paducah-Cape Girardeau-Harrisburg	6,700	6,500	96
Vermilion	Springfield-Decatur-Champaign	38,000	36,900	97
Wabash	Evansville	5,500	5,200	95
Warren	Davenport-Rock Is-Moline (Quad City)	7,900	7,700	98
Washington	St. Louis	6,000	5,700	95
Wayne	Evansville	7,000	6,500	93

COUNTY	MARKET	HOUSEHOLDS	TV's	%
ILLINOIS—*Cont'd*				
White	Evansville	6,900	6,400	93
Whiteside	Davenport-Rock Is-Moline			
	(Quad City)	22,800	22,200	97
Will	Chicago	97,700	96,000	98
Williamson	Paducah-Cape Girardeau-			
	Harrisburg	20,800	20,000	96
Winnebago	Rockford	86,800	84,900	98
Woodford	Peoria	10,400	10,000	96
	STATE TOTAL	3,966,700	3,865,200	97
INDIANA				
Adams	Ft. Wayne	8,700	8,400	97
Allen	Ft. Wayne	97,500	95,300	98
Bartholomew	Indianapolis	20,600	20,100	97
Benton	Indianapolis	3,700	3,600	97
Blackford	Indianapolis	5,600	5,500	97
Boone	Indianapolis	12,000	11,800	98
Brown	Indianapolis	3,300	3,200	97
Carroll	Indianapolis	6,300	6,200	98
Cass	Indianapolis	13,700	13,200	97
Clark	Louisville	29,200	28,400	97
Clay	Terre Haute	9,100	8,900	98
Clinton	Indianapolis	11,200	11,000	98
Crawford	Louisville	3,300	3,100	93
Daviess	Terre Haute	8,900	8,500	95
Dearborn	Cincinnati	10,900	10,600	98
Decatur	Indianapolis	8,300	8,000	97
De Kalb	Ft. Wayne	10,500	10,300	98
Delaware	Indianapolis	42,400	41,500	98
Dubois	Evansville	9,800	9,300	95
Elkhart	South Bend-Elkhart	44,400	42,900	97
Fayette	Cincinnati	9,500	9,300	97
Floyd	Louisville	19,700	19,300	98
Fountain	Indianapolis	6,600	6,400	97
Franklin	Cincinnati	5,700	5,400	95
Fulton	South Bend-Elkhart	6,100	5,900	97
Gibson	Evansville	11,100	10,700	97
Grant	Indianapolis	28,700	27,800	97
Greene	Terre Haute	10,600	10,200	97
Hamilton	Indianapolis	25,000	24,500	98
Hancock	Indianapolis	14,300	14,000	98
Harrison	Louisville	8,100	7,800	97
Hendricks	Indianapolis	21,000	20,600	98
Henry	Indianapolis	18,500	18,100	98
Howard	Indianapolis	30,900	30,200	98
Huntington	Ft. Wayne	12,200	11,900	98
Jackson	Louisville	12,100	11,800	97
Jasper	Chicago	7,800	7,600	97
Jay	Indianapolis	8,600	8,300	96
Jefferson	Louisville	9,000	8,700	97
Jennings	Indianapolis	6,500	6,300	96
Johnson	Indianapolis	22,800	22,500	99
Knox	Terre Haute	15,100	14,600	97
Kosciusko	South Bend-Elkhart	18,600	18,000	97
La Grange	South Bend-Elkhart	7,200	6,700	93
Lake	Chicago	176,100	172,500	98

COUNTY	MARKET	HOUSEHOLDS	TV's	%

INDIANA—*Cont'd*

COUNTY	MARKET	HOUSEHOLDS	TV's	%
La Porte	Chicago	34,500	33,900	98
Lawrence	Indianapolis	15,000	14,600	97
Madison	Indianapolis	48,600	47,700	98
Marion	Indianapolis	273,900	268,000	98
Marshall	South Bend-Elkhart	13,100	12,700	97
Martin	Terre Haute	3,600	3,500	96
Miami	Indianapolis	13,100	12,700	97
Monroe	Indianapolis	31,500	30,100	96
Montgomery	Indianapolis	12,100	11,800	98
Morgan	Indianapolis	15,800	15,400	98
Newton	Chicago	4,900	4,800	97
Noble	Ft. Wayne	11,200	10,900	97
Ohio	Cincinnati	1,700	1,700	98
Orange	Louisville	6,500	6,200	96
Owen	Indianapolis	4,500	4,400	97
Parke	Terre Haute	5,800	5,700	98
Perry	Evansville	6,100	5,800	95
Pike	Evansville	5,100	4,800	95
Porter	Chicago	32,100	31,400	98
Posey	Evansville	7,500	7,100	95
Pulaski	South Bend-Elkhart	4,500	4,300	95
Putnam	Indianapolis	9,400	9,100	97
Randolph	Indianapolis	10,500	10,200	97
Ripley	Cincinnati	7,900	7,600	96
Rush	Indianapolis	7,000	6,900	98
St. Joseph	South Bend-Elkhart	79,600	78,000	98
Scott	Louisville	6,200	5,900	95
Shelby	Indianapolis	13,700	13,400	98
Spencer	Evansville	5,600	5,400	96
Starke	South Bend-Elkhart	7,100	6,900	97
Steuben	Ft. Wayne	8,400	8,200	98
Sullivan	Terre Haute	7,800	7,600	97
Switzerland	Cincinnati	2,500	2,400	95
Tippecanoe	Lafayette, IN	37,000	35,600	96
Tipton	Indianapolis	5,400	5,300	98
Union	Cincinnati	2,600	2,500	96
Vanderburgh	Evansville	56,900	55,100	97
Vermillion	Terre Haute	6,300	6,100	97
Vigo	Terre Haute	38,600	37,600	97
Wabash	Ft. Wayne	12,000	11,500	96
Warren	Indianapolis	2,700	2,600	96
Warrick	Evansville	12,000	11,600	96
Washington	Louisville	6,900	6,600	95
Wayne	Dayton	26,300	25,600	97
Wells	Ft. Wayne	8,500	8,200	97
White	Indianapolis	8,000	7,800	97
Whitley	Ft. Wayne	8,500	8,300	98
	STATE TOTAL	1,819,700	1,772,400	97

IOWA

COUNTY	MARKET	HOUSEHOLDS	TV's	%
Adair	Des Moines	3,700	3,600	98
Adams	Omaha	2,500	2,400	96
Allamakee	Cedar Rapids-Waterloo	5,200	5,100	97
Appanoose	Des Moines	6,300	6,100	96
Audubon	Omaha	3,200	3,100	98
Benton	Cedar Rapids-Waterloo	8,400	8,300	98

COUNTY	MARKET	HOUSEHOLDS	TV's	%
IOWA—*Cont'd*				
Black Hawk	Cedar Rapids-Waterloo	45,400	44,700	98
Boone	Des Moines	9,600	9,400	98
Bremer	Cedar Rapids-Waterloo	8,100	7,900	98
Buchanan	Cedar Rapids-Waterloo	7,200	7,000	98
Buena Vista	Sioux City	7,900	7,700	98
Butler	Cedar Rapids-Waterloo	6,400	6,200	97
Calhoun	Des Moines	5,200	5,100	98
Carroll	Des Moines	7,300	7,200	98
Cass	Omaha	6,300	6,200	98
Cedar	Cedar Rapids-Waterloo	6,400	6,300	98
Cerro Gordo	Rochester-Mason City-Austin	18,000	17,700	98
Cherokee	Sioux City	5,800	5,700	98
Chickasaw	Cedar Rapids-Waterloo	5,300	5,200	97
Clarke	Des Moines	3,300	3,200	97
Clay	Sioux City	7,200	7,000	97
Clayton	Cedar Rapids-Waterloo	7,500	7,200	96
Clinton	Davenport-Rock Is-Moline			
	(Quad City)	20,600	20,300	99
Crawford	Omaha	6,900	6,800	98
Dallas	Des Moines	9,900	9,700	98
Davis	Ottumwa-Kirksville	3,300	3,200	97
Decatur	Des Moines	3,600	3,400	95
Delaware	Cedar Rapids-Waterloo	6,200	6,100	98
Des Moines	Davenport-Rock Is-Moline			
	(Quad City)	17,100	16,700	98
Dickinson	Sioux City	5,300	5,100	96
Dubuque	Cedar Rapids-Waterloo	28,700	27,900	97
Emmet	Mankato	5,000	4,800	95
Fayette	Cedar Rapids-Waterloo	9,400	9,200	98
Floyd	Rochester-Mason City-Austin	7,600	7,400	98
Franklin	Cedar Rapids-Waterloo	5,200	5,100	98
Fremont	Omaha	3,600	3,500	98
Greene	Des Moines	4,700	4,600	98
Grundy	Cedar Rapids-Waterloo	5,200	5,100	98
Guthrie	Des Moines	5,100	5,000	98
Hamilton	Des Moines	6,700	6,600	98
Hancock	Rochester-Mason City-Austin	5,400	5,300	98
Hardin	Des Moines	8,200	8,000	98
Harrison	Omaha	6,200	6,100	98
Henry	Davenport-Rock Is-Moline			
	(Quad City)	6,400	6,100	96
Howard	Rochester-Mason City-Austin	4,000	3,800	95
Humboldt	Des Moines	4,400	4,300	97
Ida	Sioux City	3,200	3,100	98
Iowa	Cedar Rapids-Waterloo	5,300	5,200	97
Jackson	Davenport-Rock Is-Moline			
	(Quad City)	7,400	7,200	97
Jasper	Des Moines	13,300	13,100	98
Jefferson	Ottumwa-Kirksville	5,500	5,300	97
Johnson	Cedar Rapids-Waterloo	28,000	27,000	97
Jones	Cedar Rapids-Waterloo	6,800	6,700	98
Keokuk	Cedar Rapids-Waterloo	5,600	5,400	96
Kossuth	Rochester-Mason City-Austin	7,900	7,800	98
Lee	Quincy-Hannibal	15,400	15,100	98
Linn	Cedar Rapids-Waterloo	58,700	57,800	98
Louisa	Davenport-Rock Is-Moline			
	(Quad City)	4,100	4,000	97
Lucas	Des Moines	4,200	4,000	96

COUNTY	MARKET	HOUSEHOLDS	TV's	%
IOWA—*Cont'd*				
Lyon	Sioux Falls-Mitchell	4,400	4,300	97
Madison	Des Moines	5,000	4,900	98
Mahaska	Des Moines	8,200	8,000	97
Marion	Des Moines	10,000	9,800	98
Marshall	Des Moines	15,500	15,300	99
Mills	Omaha	4,800	4,700	98
Mitchell	Rochester-Mason City-Austin	4,000	3,900	98
Monona	Sioux City	4,700	4,600	97
Monroe	Des Moines	3,600	3,500	97
Montgomery	Omaha	5,400	5,300	98
Muscatine	Davenport-Rock Is-Moline			
	(Quad City)	14,400	14,100	98
O'Brien	Sioux City	6,300	6,200	98
Osceola	Sioux Falls-Mitchell	2,900	2,800	97
Page	Omaha	7,800	7,600	97
Palo Alto	Sioux City	4,700	4,500	96
Plymouth	Sioux City	8,100	8,000	98
Pocahontas	Des Moines	4,200	4,100	97
Polk	Des Moines	110,300	108,500	98
Pottawattamie	Omaha	29,600	29,000	98
Poweshiek	Des Moines	7,100	6,900	98
Ringgold	Des Moines	2,600	2,500	98
Sac	Sioux City	5,900	5,700	97
Scott	Davenport-Rock Is-Moline			
	(Quad City)	53,000	52,100	98
Shelby	Omaha	5,000	4,900	98
Sioux	Sioux City	9,600	9,200	96
Story	Des Moines	22,800	22,300	98
Tama	Cedar Rapids-Waterloo	7,500	7,300	98
Taylor	Omaha	3,200	3,100	96
Union	Des Moines	5,300	5,100	97
Van Buren	Ottumwa-Kirksville	3,300	3,200	96
Wapello	Des Moines	15,300	15,000	98
Warren	Des Moines	10,600	10,400	98
Washington	Cedar Rapids-Waterloo	6,600	6,400	96
Wayne	Des Moines	4,000	3,800	96
Webster	Des Moines	16,500	16,100	98
Winnebago	Rochester-Mason City-Austin	5,200	5,100	98
Winneshiek	Cedar Rapids-Waterloo	6,600	6,400	97
Woodbury	Sioux City	37,600	36,900	98
Worth	Rochester-Mason City-Austin	3,200	3,100	98
Wright	Des Moines	5,900	5,800	98
	STATE TOTAL	1,031,000	1,008,500	98
KANSAS				
Allen	Joplin-Pittsburg	6,000	5,700	96
Anderson	Kansas City	3,200	3,100	97
Atchison	Kansas City	6,700	6,600	98
Barber	Wichita-Hutchinson	2,500	2,400	96
Barton	Wichita-Hutchinson	11,500	11,300	98
Bourbon	Joplin-Pittsburg	7,000	6,800	97
Brown	Kansas City	5,000	4,800	97
Butler	Wichita-Hutchinson	15,400	15,000	98
Chase	Wichita-Hutchinson	1,400	1,300	95
Chautauqua	Tulsa	2,200	2,100	97
Cherokee	Joplin-Pittsburg	8,600	8,400	98

COUNTY	MARKET	HOUSEHOLDS	TV's	%
KANSAS—*Cont'd*				
Cheyenne	Wichita-Hutchinson	1,700	1,600	96
Clark	Wichita-Hutchinson	1,100	1,100	97
Clay	Topeka	3,900	3,700	94
Cloud	Lincoln-Hastings-Kearney	4,800	4,500	95
Coffey	Topeka	3,300	3,100	94
Comanche	Wichita-Hutchinson	1,100	1,000	94
Cowley	Wichita-Hutchinson	13,000	12,600	97
Crawford	Joplin-Pittsburg	15,100	14,700	97
Decatur	Wichita-Hutchinson	1,900	1,800	97
Dickinson	Wichita-Hutchinson	8,200	7,900	87
Doniphan	Kansas City	3,400	3,300	97
Douglas	Kansas City	21,900	21,100	97
Edwards	Wichita-Hutchinson	1,900	1,800	97
Elk	Wichita-Hutchinson	1,600	1,500	95
Ellis	Wichita-Hutchinson	8,600	8,400	98
Ellsworth	Wichita-Hutchinson	2,400	2,300	96
Finney	Wichita-Hutchinson	8,100	7,900	97
Ford	Wichita-Hutchinson	8,700	8,500	98
Franklin	Kansas City	8,000	7,800	97
Geary	Topeka	10,600	10,300	98
Gove	Wichita-Hutchinson	1,400	1,300	95
Graham	Wichita-Hutchinson	1,700	1,700	97
Grant	Wichita-Hutchinson	2,200	2,100	97
Gray	Wichita-Hutchinson	2,200	2,100	97
Greeley	Wichita-Hutchinson	700	700	96
Greenwood	Wichita-Hutchinson	4,300	4,100	96
Hamilton	Wichita-Hutchinson	1,300	1,200	95
Harper	Wichita-Hutchinson	3,900	3,800	97
Harvey	Wichita-Hutchinson	11,100	10,700	97
Haskell	Wichita-Hutchinson	1,600	1,600	97
Hodgeman	Wichita-Hutchinson	900	900	95
Jackson	Topeka	4,700	4,500	96
Jefferson	Topeka	4,800	4,600	97
Jewell	Lincoln-Hastings-Kearney	2,200	2,000	93
Johnson	Kansas City	80,500	79,700	99
Kearny	Wichita-Hutchinson	1,100	1,100	97
Kingman	Wichita-Hutchinson	3,800	3,700	98
Kiowa	Wichita-Hutchinson	2,000	1,900	94
Labette	Joplin-Pittsburg	10,000	9,700	97
Lane	Wichita-Hutchinson	1,100	1,100	97
Leavenworth	Kansas City	18,200	17,800	98
Lincoln	Wichita-Hutchinson	1,800	1,700	94
Linn	Kansas City	3,800	3,700	96
Logan	Wichita-Hutchinson	1,400	1,300	95
Lyon	Topeka	12,600	12,000	96
McPherson	Wichita-Hutchinson	9,700	9,200	95
Marion	Wichita-Hutchinson	5,100	4,900	95
Marshall	Topeka	5,700	5,400	96
Meade	Wichita-Hutchinson	2,000	2,000	99
Miami	Kansas City	7,600	7,500	98
Mitchell	Wichita-Hutchinson	3,100	2,900	95
Montgomery	Tulsa	16,500	15,900	96
Morris	Topeka	2,900	2,800	95
Morton	Amarillo	1,200	1,100	96
Nemaha	Topeka	3,900	3,800	97
Neosho	Joplin-Pittsburg	7,200	7,000	97
Ness	Wichita-Hutchinson	2,000	1,900	97
Norton	Wichita-Hutchinson	2,500	2,400	96

COUNTY	MARKET	HOUSEHOLDS	TV's	%
KANSAS—*Cont'd*				
Osage	Topeka	5,400	5,200	97
Osborne	Wichita-Hutchinson	2,600	2,500	94
Ottawa	Wichita-Hutchinson	2,600	2,500	94
Pawnee	Wichita-Hutchinson	2,800	2,700	97
Phillips	Lincoln-Hastings-Kearney	3,200	3,000	94
Pottawatomie	Topeka	5,100	4,900	96
Pratt	Wichita-Hutchinson	3,900	3,800	97
Rawlins	Wichita-Hutchinson	1,500	1,400	96
Reno	Wichita-Hutchinson	24,600	24,100	98
Republic	Lincoln-Hastings-Kearney	3,400	3,300	96
Rice	Wichita-Hutchinson	4,900	4,800	98
Riley	Topeka	17,800	17,100	96
Rooks	Wichita-Hutchinson	3,100	3,000	97
Rush	Wichita-Hutchinson	2,000	1,900	97
Russell	Wichita-Hutchinson	3,600	3,500	96
Saline	Wichita-Hutchinson	18,300	17,800	97
Scott	Wichita-Hutchinson	2,300	2,200	97
Sedgwick	Wichita-Hutchinson	125,400	123,100	98
Seward	Wichita-Hutchinson	6,600	6,400	97
Shawnee	Topeka	55,400	54,200	98
Sheridan	Wichita-Hutchinson	1,100	1,100	96
Sherman	Wichita-Hutchinson	3,000	2,900	97
Smith	Lincoln-Hastings-Kearney	2,400	2,300	96
Stafford	Wichita-Hutchinson	2,900	2,800	97
Stanton	Wichita-Hutchinson	800	800	95
Stevens	Wichita-Hutchinson	1,700	1,600	94
Sumner	Wichita-Hutchinson	9,300	9,100	97
Thomas	Wichita-Hutchinson	3,500	3,300	95
Trego	Wichita-Hutchinson	1,700	1,600	95
Wabaunsee	Topeka	2,500	2,400	95
Wallace	Wichita-Hutchinson	800	800	95
Washington	Lincoln-Hastings-Kearney	3,700	3,500	95
Wichita	Wichita-Hutchinson	1,000	900	95
Wilson	Joplin-Pittsburg	5,000	4,700	95
Woodson	Joplin-Pittsburg	1,700	1,600	95
Wyandotte	Kansas City	64,800	63,500	98
	STATE TOTAL	847,900	824,500	97
KENTUCKY				
Adair	Bowling Green	5,200	4,900	95
Allen	Nashville	5,000	4,900	97
Anderson	Lexington	4,100	4,000	98
Ballard	Paducah-Cape Girardeau-Harrisburg	3,500	3,400	98
Barren	Nashville	11,000	10,700	98
Bath	Lexington	3,200	3,000	95
Bell	Knoxville	11,100	10,700	96
Boone	Cincinnati	12,000	11,900	99
Bourbon	Lexington	6,700	6,500	98
Boyd	Charleston-Huntington	18,000	17,800	99
Boyle	Lexington	8,500	8,300	97
Bracken	Cincinnati	2,800	2,700	98
Breathitt	Lexington	5,000	4,600	92
Breckinridge	Louisville	5,800	5,600	97
Bullitt	Louisville	10,700	10,500	98
Butler	Nashville	3,800	3,700	97

COUNTY	MARKET	HOUSEHOLDS	TV's	%
KENTUCKY—*Cont'd*				
Caldwell	Paducah-Cape Girardeau- Harrisburg	5,000	4,800	96
Calloway	Paducah-Cape Girardeau- Harrisburg	11,200	11,000	98
Campbell	Cincinnati	27,500	27,300	99
Carlisle	Paducah-Cape Girardeau- Harrisburg	2,200	2,200	98
Carroll	Cincinnati	3,100	3,000	98
Carter	Charleston-Huntington	7,900	7,700	97
Casey	Lexington	4,700	4,400	95
Christian	Nashville	21,400	20,900	98
Clark	Lexington	9,600	9,300	97
Clay	Lexington	6,400	6,000	94
Clinton	Nashville	2,800	2,700	95
Crittenden	Paducah-Cape Girardeau- Harrisburg	3,700	3,600	97
Cumberland	Nashville	2,300	2,200	95
Daviess	Evansville	27,800	27,300	98
Edmonson	Nashville	3,300	3,100	95
Elliott	Charleston-Huntington	1,800	1,800	98
Estill	Lexington	4,600	4,300	93
Fayette	Lexington	67,000	65,800	98
Fleming	Cincinnati	4,300	4,200	97
Floyd	Charleston-Huntington	13,900	13,400	96
Franklin	Louisville	13,700	13,400	98
Fulton	Paducah-Cape Girardeau- Harrisburg	3,400	3,300	97
Gallatin	Cincinnati	1,600	1,600	98
Garrard	Lexington	3,300	3,200	97
Grant	Cincinnati	4,800	4,700	98
Graves	Paducah-Cape Girardeau- Harrisburg	12,700	12,500	98
Grayson	Louisville	7,100	6,800	96
Green	Louisville	3,700	3,600	96
Greenup	Charleston-Huntington	11,100	10,900	98
Hancock	Evansville	2,400	2,300	97
Hardin	Louisville	19,700	19,400	98
Harlan	Knoxville	14,100	13,600	96
Harrison	Cincinnati	5,400	5,300	98
Hart	Bowling Green	5,600	5,500	97
Henderson	Evansville	13,300	13,000	98
Henry	Louisville	4,200	4,100	97
Hickman	Paducah-Cape Girardeau- Harrisburg	2,200	2,200	98
Hopkins	Evansville	16,600	16,100	97
Jackson	Lexington	3,300	3,000	92
Jefferson	Louisville	238,900	236,300	99
Jessamine	Lexington	8,100	7,800	96
Johnson	Charleston-Huntington	7,800	7,500	97
Kenton	Cincinnati	45,000	44,700	99
Knott	Charleston-Huntington	5,200	4,900	93
Knox	Knoxville	9,600	9,100	95
Larue	Louisville	4,000	3,900	98
Laurel	Knoxville	10,900	10,400	95
Lawrence	Charleston-Huntington	4,500	4,400	97
Lee	Lexington	2,600	2,400	92
Leslie	Knoxville	4,000	3,700	92
Letcher	Bristol-Kingsport-Johnson City	9,300	8,800	95

COUNTY	MARKET	HOUSEHOLDS	TV's	%
KENTUCKY—*Cont'd*				
Lewis	Charleston-Huntington	4,300	4,100	96
Lincoln	Lexington	6,400	6,100	96
Livingston	Paducah-Cape Girardeau-Harrisburg	3,600	3,500	97
Logan	Nashville	7,800	7,600	98
Lyon	Paducah-Cape Girardeau-Harrisburg	2,000	1,900	97
McCracken	Paducah-Cape Girardeau-Harrisburg	22,900	22,600	98
McCreary	Knoxville	4,900	4,600	94
McLean	Evansville	4,000	3,900	98
Madison	Lexington	15,300	14,700	96
Magoffin	Charleston-Huntington	3,700	3,500	95
Marion	Louisville	4,800	4,700	98
Marshall	Paducah-Cape Girardeau-Harrisburg	8,500	8,400	98
Martin	Charleston-Huntington	3,400	3,200	95
Mason	Cincinnati	5,700	5,600	98
Meade	Louisville	5,100	5,000	99
Menifee	Lexington	1,300	1,200	95
Mercer	Lexington	6,500	6,300	97
Metcalfe	Nashville	3,200	3,100	97
Monroe	Nashville	4,400	4,300	97
Montgomery	Lexington	6,200	5,900	95
Morgan	Charleston-Huntington	3,700	3,500	95
Muhlenberg	Nashville	12,000	11,700	98
Nelson	Louisville	7,400	7,300	98
Nicholas	Lexington	2,500	2,400	96
Ohio	Evansville	7,800	7,600	97
Oldham	Louisville	6,300	6,200	99
Owen	Cincinnati	3,300	3,200	97
Owsley	Lexington	1,700	1,500	91
Pendleton	Cincinnati	3,600	3,600	99
Perry	Bristol-Kingsport-Johnson City	9,100	8,600	94
Pike	Charleston-Huntington	22,700	21,900	97
Powell	Lexington	2,700	2,500	93
Pulaski	Lexington	16,200	15,300	95
Robertson	Cincinnati	700	700	98
Rockcastle	Lexington	3,900	3,600	93
Rowan	Lexington	4,600	4,400	96
Russell	Louisville	4,300	4,100	96
Scott	Lexington	6,600	6,400	97
Shelby	Louisville	7,300	7,200	98
Simpson	Nashville	5,500	5,400	98
Spencer	Louisville	1,900	1,900	98
Taylor	Louisville	6,500	6,300	97
Todd	Nashville	4,000	3,900	97
Trigg	Nashville	3,000	2,900	98
Trimble	Louisville	1,900	1,900	98
Union	Evansville	5,000	4,900	97
Warren	Bowling Green	22,000	21,500	98
Washington	Louisville	3,300	3,200	98
Wayne	Knoxville	5,300	4,900	93
Webster	Knoxville	5,800	5,600	97
Whitley	Knoxville	10,700	10,300	96
Wolfe	Lexington	2,200	2,100	93
Woodford	Lexington	6,200	6,000	97
	STATE TOTAL	1,178,700	1,149,300	97

COUNTY	MARKET	HOUSEHOLDS	TV's	%
LOUISIANA				
Acadia	Lafayette, LA	17,300	16,700	96
Allen	Lafayette, LA	6,400	6,100	95
Ascension	Baton Rouge	13,200	12,600	95
Assumption	Baton Rouge	5,900	5,600	95
Avoyelles	Alexandria, LA	12,400	11,800	95
Beauregard	Lake Charles	9,100	8,600	94
Bienville	Shreveport-Texarkana	5,900	5,600	95
Bossier	Shreveport-Texarkana	22,900	22,300	97
Caddo	Shreveport-Texarkana	86,700	84,400	97
Calcasieu	Lake Charles	52,500	51,300	98
Caldwell	Monroe-El Dorado	3,100	2,900	95
Cameron	Lake Charles	2,900	2,800	96
Catahoula	Monroe-El Dorado	3,600	3,300	92
Claiborne	Shreveport-Texarkana	5,700	5,400	95
Concordia	Monroe-El Dorado	6,300	5,900	93
De Soto	Shreveport-Texarkana	8,000	7,500	94
East Baton Rouge	Baton Rouge	112,300	109,900	98
East Carroll	Monroe-El Dorado	3,400	3,200	93
East Feliciana	Baton Rouge	4,000	3,700	93
Evangeline	Lafayette, LA	10,800	10,100	94
Franklin	Monroe-El Dorado	7,400	7,100	95
Grant	Alexandria, LA	5,400	5,100	95
Iberia	Lafayette, LA	20,400	19,800	97
Iberville	Baton Rouge	9,000	8,600	96
Jackson	Monroe-El Dorado	5,800	5,600	96
Jefferson	New Orleans	139,000	137,000	99
Jefferson Davis	Lafayette, LA	9,800	9,400	96
Lafayette	Lafayette, LA	42,000	40,900	97
Lafourche	New Orleans	21,800	21,200	97
La Salle	Monroe-El Dorado	5,500	5,200	95
Lincoln	Monroe-El Dorado	11,600	11,300	97
Livingston	Baton Rouge	14,900	14,300	96
Madison	Monroe-El Dorado	4,700	4,400	93
Morehouse	Monroe-El Dorado	10,700	10,200	96
Natchitoches	Shreveport-Texarkana	11,400	10,500	92
Orleans	New Orleans	207,700	202,600	98
Ouachita	Monroe-El Dorado	46,600	45,400	98
Plaquemines	New Orleans	7,400	7,200	97
Pointe Coupee	Baton Rouge	6,500	6,200	95
Rapides	Alexandria, LA	38,700	37,700	97
Red River	Shreveport-Texarkana	3,000	2,800	93
Richland	Monroe-El Dorado	7,100	6,800	95
Sabine	Shreveport-Texarkana	6,600	6,100	92
St Bernard	New Orleans	18,700	18,600	99
St Charles	New Orleans	9,700	9,500	98
St Helena	Baton Rouge	2,800	2,600	93
St James	New Orleans	4,800	4,600	96
St John the Baptist	New Orleans	7,200	6,900	96
St Landry	Lafayette, LA	25,200	23,800	95
St Martin	Lafayette, LA	10,300	10,000	97
St Mary	Baton Rouge	18,000	17,500	97
St Tammany	New Orleans	28,800	28,000	97
Tangipahoa	New Orleans	23,500	22,400	96
Tensas	Monroe-El Dorado	2,600	2,400	92
Terrebonne	New Orleans	25,600	24,900	97
Union	Monroe-El Dorado	6,400	6,200	97
Vermilion	Lafayette, LA	15,100	14,700	97
Vernon	Alexandria, LA	10,400	9,800	94

COUNTY	MARKET	HOUSEHOLDS	TV's	%
LOUISIANA—*Cont'd*				
Washington	New Orleans	14,200	13,500	95
Webster	Shreveport-Texarkana	14,300	13,700	96
West Baton Rouge	Baton Rouge	5,600	5,400	96
West Carroll	Monroe-El Dorado	4,500	4,300	95
West Feliciana	Baton Rouge	1,300	1,200	94
Winn	Monroe-El Dorado	5,600	5,300	94
	STATE TOTAL	1,290,000	1,250,400	97
MAINE				
Androscoggin	Portland-Poland Spring	33,400	32,400	97
Aroostook	Presque Isle	30,200	28,700	95
Cumberland	Portland-Poland Spring	72,100	70,000	97
Franklin	Portland-Poland Spring	8,400	7,900	93
Hancock	Bangor	15,100	14,600	96
Kennebec	Portland-Poland Spring	34,900	33,500	96
Knox	Bangor	12,300	11,600	94
Lincoln	Portland-Poland Spring	9,200	8,800	96
Oxford	Portland-Poland Spring	16,300	15,800	97
Penobscot	Bangor	45,700	44,100	97
Piscataquis	Bangor	6,100	5,900	96
Sagadahoc	Portland-Poland Spring	9,500	9,100	96
Somerset	Bangor	15,900	15,200	96
Waldo	Bangor	9,800	9,300	95
Washington	Bangor	12,800	12,100	94
York	Portland-Poland Spring	43,500	42,400	97
	STATE TOTAL	375,200	361,400	96
MARYLAND				
Allegany	Washington, DC	30,900	30,200	98
Anne Arundel	Baltimore	113,400	112,000	99
Baltimore	Baltimore	521,900	515,400	99
Calvert	Washington, DC	8,800	8,500	97
Caroline	Baltimore	8,500	8,200	97
Carroll	Baltimore	29,300	28,900	99
Cecil	Baltimore	16,800	16,600	99
Charles	Washington, DC	19,200	18,700	97
Dorchester	Baltimore	11,000	10,600	97
Frederick	Washington, DC	34,400	33,800	98
Garrett	Pittsburgh	8,700	8,300	96
Harford	Baltimore	46,100	45,400	99
Howard	Baltimore	37,000	36,500	99
Kent	Baltimore	6,200	6,100	98
Montgomery	Washington, DC	200,700	198,700	99
Prince Georges	Washington, DC	221,400	219,400	99
Queen Annes	Baltimore	7,900	7,700	97
St Marys	Washington, DC	15,800	15,500	98
Somerset	Salisbury	7,100	6,800	95
Talbot	Baltimore	10,300	10,100	98
Washington	Washington, DC	39,500	38,700	98
Wicomico	Salisbury	22,300	21,700	97
Worcester	Salisbury	9,700	9,300	95
	STATE TOTAL	1,426,900	1,407,100	99

COUNTY	MARKET	HOUSEHOLDS	TV's	%
MASSACHUSETTS				
Barnstable	Boston	55,500	53,600	97
Berkshire	Albany-Schenectady-Troy	50,900	49,200	97
Bristol	Providence	169,100	165,400	98
Dukes	Providence	3,800	3,500	92
Essex	Boston	220,000	215,300	98
Franklin	Springfield, MA	24,700	23,300	94
Hampden	Springfield, MA	160,500	155,900	97
Hampshire	Springfield, MA	41,900	40,200	96
Middlesex	Boston	471,700	461,300	98
Nantucket	Boston	2,200	2,100	94
Norfolk	Boston	205,100	201,400	98
Plymouth	Boston	129,900	126,800	98
Suffolk	Boston	266,500	254,700	96
Worcester	Boston	220,800	15,000	97
	STATE TOTAL	2,022,600	1,967,700	97
MICHIGAN				
Alcona	Alpena	3,600	3,400	94
Alger	Green Bay	3,200	3,100	96
Allegan	Grand Rapids-Kalamazoo-Battle Creek	24,100	23,600	98
Alpena	Alpena	11,000	10,300	94
Antrim	Traverse City-Cadillac	5,500	5,300	97
Arenac	Flint-Saginaw-Bay City	4,800	4,600	97
Baraga	Marquette	2,700	2,600	96
Barry	Grand Rapids-Kalamazoo-Battle Creek	14,300	14,000	98
Bay	Flint-Saginaw-Bay City	39,000	38,300	98
Benzie	Traverse City-Cadillac	3,800	3,600	96
Berrien	South Bend-Elkhart	61,500	59,800	97
Branch	Grand Rapids-Kalamazoo-Battle Creek	13,000	12,700	98
Calhoun	Grand Rapids-Kalamazoo-Battle Creek	49,400	48,600	98
Cass	South Bend-Elkhart	16,000	15,600	98
Charlevoix	Traverse City-Cadillac	6,700	6,500	97
Cheboygan	Traverse City-Cadillac	6,900	6,500	95
Chippewa	Traverse City-Cadillac	12,900	12,400	96
Clare	Traverse City-Cadillac	8,700	8,400	96
Clinton	Lansing	17,400	17,100	98
Crawford	Traverse City-Cadillac	3,200	3,000	95
Delta	Green Bay	13,900	13,400	96
Dickinson	Green Bay	9,700	9,500	98
Eaton	Lansing	27,500	27,000	98
Emmet	Traverse City-Cadillac	7,000	6,700	96
Genesee	Flint-Saginaw-Bay City	149,800	147,500	98
Gladwin	Flint-Saginaw-Bay City	6,200	6,000	96
Gogebic	Duluth-Superior	8,000	7,700	96
Grand Traverse	Traverse City-Cadillac	15,400	14,900	97
Gratiot	Flint-Saginaw-Bay City	12,900	12,600	97
Hillsdale	Lansing	14,600	14,100	97
Houghton	Marquette	13,300	12,600	95
Huron	Flint-Saginaw-Bay City	12,200	11,800	97
Ingham	Lansing	92,300	90,300	98
Ionia	Grand Rapids-Kalamazoo-Battle Creek	15,700	15,600	98

COUNTY	MARKET	HOUSEHOLDS	TV's	%
MICHIGAN—*Cont'd*				
Iosco	Flint-Saginaw-Bay City	10,000	9,800	98
Iron	Marquette	6,600	6,400	97
Isabella	Flint-Saginaw-Bay City	15,700	15,200	97
Jackson	Lansing	49,300	48,400	98
Kalamazoo	Grand Rapids-Kalamazoo-Battle Creek	68,300	66,900	98
Kalkaska	Traverse City-Cadillac	3,600	3,400	96
Kent	Grand Rapids-Kalamazoo-Battle Creek	144,100	140,600	98
Keweenaw	Marquette	1,000	1,000	97
Lake	Traverse City-Cadillac	2,600	2,500	95
Lapeer	Detroit	20,700	20,300	98
Leelanau	Traverse City-Cadillac	4,400	4,200	96
Lenawee	Toledo	29,700	29,100	98
Livingston	Detroit	28,800	28,400	98
Luce	Traverse City-Cadillac	2,400	2,300	95
Mackinac	Traverse City-Cadillac	3,900	3,700	96
Macomb	Detroit	211,300	209,500	99
Manistee	Traverse City-Cadillac	8,400	8,100	97
Marquette	Marquette	23,900	23,400	98
Mason	Traverse City-Cadillac	9,000	8,500	95
Mecosta	Traverse City-Cadillac	11,600	11,200	97
Menominee	Green Bay	9,200	9,000	97
Midland	Flint-Saginaw-Bay City	22,200	21,900	99
Missaukee	Traverse City-Cadillac	3,500	3,300	95
Monroe	Detroit	41,400	40,800	98
Montcalm	Grand Rapids-Kalamazoo-Battle Creek	16,300	15,900	98
Montmorency	Traverse City-Cadillac	2,800	2,600	94
Muskegon	Grand Rapids-Kalamazoo-Battle Creek	52,300	51,200	98
Newaygo	Grand Rapids-Kalamazoo-Battle Creek	10,400	10,100	97
Oakland	Detroit	322,200	319,000	99
Oceana	Grand Rapids-Kalamazoo-Battle Creek	7,500	7,100	95
Ogemaw	Flint-Saginaw-Bay City	5,400	5,200	97
Ontonagon	Marquette	4,300	4,000	94
Osceola	Traverse City-Cadillac	6,800	6,600	97
Oscoda	Traverse City-Cadillac	2,700	2,500	92
Otsego	Traverse City-Cadillac	5,000	4,800	97
Ottawa	Grand Rapids-Kalamazoo-Battle Creek	46,100	45,100	98
Presque Isle	Traverse City-Cadillac	4,600	4,300	93
Roscommon	Traverse City-Cadillac	6,400	6,300	98
Saginaw	Flint-Saginaw-Bay City	73,600	72,300	98
St. Clair	Detroit	45,600	44,700	98
St. Joseph	South Bend-Elkhart	19,400	19,000	98
Sanilac	Detroit	14,100	13,700	97
Schoolcraft	Green Bay	3,400	3,200	95
Shiawassee	Flint-Saginaw-Bay City	23,400	22,900	98
Tuscola	Flint-Saginaw-Bay City	17,800	17,400	98
Van Buren	Grand Rapids-Kalamazoo-Battle Creek	22,100	21,700	98
Washtenaw	Detroit	84,200	81,300	97
Wayne	Detroit	847,700	833,000	98
Wexford	Traverse City-Cadillac	7,900	7,700	97
	STATE TOTAL	3,089,800	3,028,400	98

COUNTY	MARKET	HOUSEHOLDS	TV's	%
MINNESOTA				
Aitkin	Duluth-Superior	5,400	5,200	97
Anoka	Minneapolis-St. Paul	58,000	57,600	99
Becker	Fargo	10,200	9,800	96
Beltrami	Alexandria, MN	10,500	9,600	91
Benton	Minneapolis-St. Paul	7,000	6,800	97
Big Stone	Alexandria, MN	2,900	2,800	97
Blue Earth	Mankato	17,300	16,800	97
Brown	Minneapolis-St. Paul	10,400	10,000	96
Carlton	Duluth-Superior	10,200	10,000	98
Carver	Minneapolis-St. Paul	11,500	11,300	99
Cass	Alexandria, MN	7,800	7,100	92
Chippewa	Alexandria, MN	6,300	6,000	96
Chisago	Minneapolis-St. Paul	8,100	7,900	97
Clay	Fargo	15,600	15,400	99
Clearwater	Fargo	3,100	2,900	92
Cook	Duluth-Superior	1,500	1,400	95
Cottonwood	Mankato	5,800	5,400	92
Crow Wing	Alexandria, MN	15,300	14,600	96
Dakota	Minneapolis-St. Paul	58,000	57,300	99
Dodge	Rochester-Mason City-Austin	4,600	4,400	97
Douglas	Alexandria, MN	9,400	9,100	96
Faribault	Rochester-Mason City-Austin	7,500	7,300	97
Fillmore	Rochester-Mason City-Austin	8,500	8,300	97
Freeborn	Rochester-Mason City-Austin	13,600	13,300	98
Goodhue	Minneapolis-St. Paul	14,700	14,400	98
Grant	Alexandria, MN	2,700	2,600	98
Hennepin	Minneapolis-St. Paul	334,600	328,400	98
Houston	La Crosse-Eau Claire	5,800	5,600	97
Hubbard	Alexandria, MN	4,900	4,500	91
Isanti	Minneapolis-St. Paul	7,200	7,000	97
Itasca	Duluth-Superior	14,500	13,900	96
Jackson	Mankato	5,200	5,000	96
Kanabec	Minneapolis-St. Paul	4,600	4,400	96
Kandiyohi	Minneapolis-St. Paul	11,700	11,200	96
Kittson	Fargo	2,600	2,400	93
Koochiching	Duluth-Superior	6,300	5,900	93
Lac Qui Parle	Alexandria, MN	3,900	3,800	96
Lake	Duluth-Superior	4,900	4,800	98
Lake of the Woods	Fargo	1,400	1,200	86
Le Sueur	Minneapolis-St. Paul	8,000	7,800	97
Lincoln	Sioux Falls-Mitchell	3,100	3,000	96
Lyon	Minneapolis-St. Paul	8,000	7,700	96
McLeod	Minneapolis-St. Paul	10,200	10,000	98
Mahnomen	Fargo	2,000	1,900	96
Marshall	Fargo	5,000	4,800	96
Martin	Mankato	9,600	9,300	97
Meeker	Minneapolis-St. Paul	7,700	7,500	97
Mille Lacs	Minneapolis-St. Paul	6,700	6,500	97
Morrison	Minneapolis-St. Paul	9,100	8,700	95
Mower	Rochester-Mason City-Austin	14,500	14,200	98
Murray	Sioux Falls-Mitchell	4,300	4,200	97
Nicollet	Minneapolis-St. Paul	7,100	6,900	97
Nobles	Sioux Falls-Mitchell	8,000	7,900	98
Norman	Fargo	3,700	3,500	96
Olmsted	Rochester-Mason City-Austin	31,800	31,200	98
Otter Tail	Alexandria, MN	18,300	17,500	96
Pennington	Fargo	5,600	5,300	95
Pine	Minneapolis-St. Paul	7,000	6,700	96

COUNTY	MARKET	HOUSEHOLDS	TV's	%
MINNESOTA—*Cont'd*				
Pipestone	Sioux Falls-Mitchell	4,300	4,200	97
Polk	Fargo	12,800	12,400	97
Pope	Alexandria, MN	4,400	4,200	95
Ramsey	Minneapolis-St. Paul	159,000	156,300	98
Red Lake	Fargo	1,600	1,500	96
Redwood	Minneapolis-St. Paul	7,200	6,800	94
Renville	Minneapolis-St. Paul	7,700	7,400	96
Rice	Minneapolis-St. Paul	13,500	13,200	97
Rock	Sioux Falls-Mitchell	4,100	4,000	98
Roseau	Fargo	4,300	3,800	88
St Louis	Duluth-Superior	79,900	78,000	98
Scott	Minneapolis-St. Paul	13,000	12,900	99
Sherburne	Minneapolis-St. Paul	9,300	9,100	98
Sibley	Minneapolis-St. Paul	5,400	5,300	98
Stearns	Minneapolis-St. Paul	29,200	28,300	97
Steele	Minneapolis-St. Paul	10,900	10,700	98
Stevens	Alexandria, MN	3,600	3,500	97
Swift	Minneapolis-St. Paul	4,700	4,500	96
Todd	Alexandria, MN	8,800	8,300	95
Traverse	Alexandria, MN	2,200	2,100	97
Wabasha	Minneapolis-St. Paul	6,900	6,700	98
Wadena	Alexandria, MN	4,900	4,600	93
Waseca	Minneapolis-St. Paul	6,400	6,200	98
Washington	Minneapolis-St. Paul	33,200	32,800	99
Watonwan	Mankato	4,800	4,600	96
Wilkin	Fargo	2,800	2,700	98
Winona	La Crosse-Eau Claire	15,700	15,200	97
Wright	Minneapolis-St. Paul	16,100	15,700	97
Yellow Medicine	Minneapolis-St. Paul	5,200	4,800	93
	STATE TOTAL	1,385,100	1,349,800	97
MISSISSIPPI				
Adams	Monroe-El Dorado	12,300	11,800	96
Alcorn	Memphis	10,500	10,100	96
Amite	Baton Rouge	4,100	3,900	95
Attala	Jackson, MS	6,600	6,300	95
Benton	Memphis	2,200	2,100	96
Bolivar	Greenwood-Greenville	13,600	12,700	93
Calhoun	Columbus-Tupelo	5,400	5,200	96
Carroll	Greenwood-Greenville	2,500	2,300	93
Chickasaw	Columbus-Tupelo	5,700	5,400	96
Choctaw	Columbus-Tupelo	3,100	2,900	95
Claiborne	Jackson, MS	3,500	3,300	94
Clarke	Meridian	5,400	5,200	96
Clay	Columbus-Tupelo	6,400	6,100	96
Coahoma	Memphis	11,800	11,100	94
Copiah	Jackson, MS	8,200	7,900	96
Covington	Laurel-Hattiesburg	4,600	4,400	96
De Soto	Memphis	15,300	14,600	95
Forrest	Laurel-Hattiesburg	21,600	21,100	98
Franklin	Jackson, MS	2,800	2,600	94
George	Mobile-Pensacola	4,600	4,500	98
Greene	Mobile-Pensacola	3,100	2,900	95
Grenada	Memphis	6,800	6,500	95
Hancock	New Orleans	6,500	6,300	97
Harrison	Biloxi-Gulfport-Pascagoula	47,500	46,600	98
Hinds	Jackson, MS	76,900	75,400	98

COUNTY	MARKET	HOUSEHOLDS	TV's	%

MISSISSIPPI—*Cont'd*

COUNTY	MARKET	HOUSEHOLDS	TV's	%
Holmes	Jackson, MS	6,500	6,100	94
Humphreys	Jackson, MS	4,000	3,800	95
Issaquena	Jackson, MS	600	600	93
Itawamba	Columbus-Tupelo	6,000	5,800	96
Jackson	Mobile-Pensacola	34,300	33,600	98
Jasper	Laurel-Hattiesburg	5,200	5,000	97
Jefferson	Jackson, MS	2,400	2,200	92
Jefferson Davis	Jackson, MS	4,000	3,800	94
Jones	Laurel-Hattiesburg	20,700	20,200	98
Kemper	Meridian	3,000	2,800	94
Lafayette	Memphis	8,000	7,700	96
Lamar	Laurel-Hattiesburg	6,400	6,200	97
Lauderdale	Meridian	25,700	25,100	98
Lawrence	Jackson, MS	4,000	3,800	95
Leake	Jackson, MS	6,400	6,200	96
Lee	Columbus-Tupelo	18,900	18,300	97
Leflore	Greenwood-Greenville	12,900	12,200	95
Lincoln	Jackson, MS	9,000	8,700	96
Lowndes	Columbus-Tupelo	17,000	16,500	97
Madison	Jackson, MS	9,700	9,200	95
Marion	Laurel-Hattiesburg	8,100	7,700	96
Marshall	Memphis	7,200	6,900	95
Monroe	Columbus-Tupelo	11,400	11,000	97
Montgomery	Columbus-Tupelo	4,100	3,900	94
Neshoba	Meridian	7,700	7,400	97
Newton	Meridian	6,600	6,400	97
Noxubee	Columbus-Tupelo	4,000	3,700	93
Oktibbeha	Columbus-Tupelo	10,600	10,100	95
Panola	Memphis	8,400	8,100	96
Pearl River	New Orleans	9,000	8,700	97
Perry	Laurel-Hattiesburg	3,200	3,100	96
Pike	Jackson, MS	11,600	11,100	96
Pontotoc	Columbus-Tupelo	6,900	6,600	96
Prentiss	Columbus-Tupelo	7,600	7,300	97
Quitman	Memphis	4,000	3,800	95
Rankin	Jackson, MS	18,300	17,800	97
Scott	Jackson, MS	7,300	7,000	97
Sharkey	Jackson, MS	2,200	2,100	94
Simpson	Jackson, MS	6,800	6,600	97
Smith	Jackson, MS	4,900	4,700	96
Stone	Biloxi-Gulfport-Pascagoula	2,500	2,400	97
Sunflower	Greenwood-Greenville	9,400	8,800	93
Tallahatchie	Memphis	5,300	4,900	93
Tate	Memphis	5,700	5,500	96
Tippah	Memphis	6,800	6,600	97
Tishomingo	Columbus-Tupelo	6,300	6,000	95
Tunica	Memphis	3,200	3,000	95
Union	Memphis	7,400	7,200	98
Walthall	Jackson, MS	4,200	4,000	95
Warren	Jackson, MS	17,000	16,400	96
Washington	Jackson, MS	21,900	20,900	95
Wayne	Laurel-Hattiesburg	5,600	5,300	95
Webster	Columbus-Tupelo	3,500	3,300	95
Wilkinson	Baton Rouge	3,000	2,800	93
Winston	Columbus-Tupelo	6,500	6,200	95
Yalobusha	Memphis	4,200	4,000	95
Yazoo	Jackson, MS	9,300	8,900	96
	STATE TOTAL	767,400	739,200	96

COUNTY	MARKET	HOUSEHOLDS	TV's	%
MISSOURI				
Adair	Ottumwa-Kirksville	8,800	8,600	97
Andrew	Kansas City	5,300	5,200	97
Atchison	Omaha	3,300	3,200	97
Audrain	Columbia-Jefferson City	9,900	9,700	97
Barry	Springfield, MO	8,700	8,300	96
Barton	Joplin-Pittsburg	4,400	4,200	96
Bates	Kansas City	6,300	6,000	95
Benton	Springfield, MO	5,300	5,000	94
Bollinger	Paducah-Cape Girardeau-Harrisburg	3,600	3,400	94
Boone	Columbia-Jefferson City	29,900	28,900	97
Buchanan	St. Joseph	32,300	31,400	97
Butler	Paducah-Cape Girardeau-Harrisburg	14,300	13,500	94
Caldwell	Kansas City	3,800	3,700	97
Callaway	Columbia-Jefferson City	8,900	8,600	97
Camden	Springfield, MO	7,100	6,700	95
Cape Girardeau	Paducah-Cape Girardeau-Harrisburg	18,700	18,100	97
Carroll	Kansas City	4,800	4,600	96
Carter	Paducah-Cape Girardeau-Harrisburg	1,700	1,500	88
Cass	Kansas City	16,900	16,500	98
Cedar	Springfield, MO	4,600	4,400	95
Chariton	Columbia-Jefferson City	3,700	3,500	95
Christian	Springfield, MO	8,000	7,700	97
Clark	Quincy-Hannibal	3,100	3,000	96
Clay	Kansas City	45,800	45,200	99
Clinton	Kansas City	5,600	5,400	97
Cole	Columbia-Jefferson City	18,400	18,100	98
Cooper	Columbia-Jefferson City	5,700	5,500	97
Crawford	St. Louis	6,200	5,800	93
Dade	Springfield, MO	3,200	3,100	97
Dallas	Springfield, MO	4,900	4,700	96
Daviess	Kansas City	3,400	3,300	97
De Kalb	Kansas City	3,100	3,000	96
Dent	Springfield, MO	4,400	4,000	91
Douglas	Springfield, MO	4,100	3,900	95
Dunklin	Memphis	13,600	13,000	95
Franklin	St. Louis	22,100	21,600	98
Gasconade	St. Louis	5,300	5,000	95
Gentry	St. Joseph	3,500	3,300	96
Greene	Springfield, MO	62,500	61,100	98
Grundy	Kansas City	4,400	4,200	96
Harrison	St. Joseph	4,000	3,800	96
Henry	Kansas City	7,800	7,500	96
Hickory	Springfield, MO	2,900	2,800	95
Holt	St. Joseph	3,100	2,900	95
Howard	Columbia-Jefferson City	3,800	3,700	97
Howell	Springfield, MO	11,100	10,100	91
Iron	St. Louis	3,900	3,700	94
Jackson	Kansas City	246,800	240,700	98
Jasper	Joplin-Pittsburg	32,200	31,300	97
Jefferson	St. Louis	39,300	38,600	98
Johnson	Kansas City	11,500	11,200	97
Knox	Quincy-Hannibal	2,100	2,000	97
Laclede	Springfield, MO	9,000	8,600	96
Lafayette	Kansas City	10,700	10,400	97

COUNTY	MARKET	HOUSEHOLDS	TV's	%
MISSOURI—*Cont'd*				
Lawrence	Springfield, MO	10,700	10,300	96
Lewis	Quincy-Hannibal	3,800	3,700	96
Lincoln	St. Louis	7,100	6,900	97
Linn	Kansas City	6,400	6,100	96
Livingston	Kansas City	5,900	5,700	96
McDonald	Joplin-Pittsburg	5,700	5,500	96
Macon	Quincy-Hannibal	6,700	6,500	97
Madison	St. Louis	3,700	3,500	95
Maries	Columbia-Jefferson City	2,600	2,500	95
Marion	Quincy-Hannibal	10,700	10,400	98
Mercer	Des Moines	1,900	1,800	95
Miller	Columbia-Jefferson City	6,300	6,100	96
Mississippi	Paducah-Cape Girardeau- Harrisburg	5,600	5,400	96
Moniteau	Columbia-Jefferson City	4,500	4,300	97
Monroe	Quincy-Hannibal	3,700	3,600	97
Montgomery	Columbia-Jefferson City	4,200	4,000	96
Morgan	Columbia-Jefferson City	4,900	4,700	96
New Madrid	Paducah-Cape Girardeau- Harrisburg	8,000	7,600	95
Newton	Joplin-Pittsburg	13,400	13,100	97
Nodaway	St. Joseph	7,700	7,400	97
Oregon	Springfield, MO	4,200	3,700	89
Osage	Columbia-Jefferson City	3,900	3,700	94
Ozark	Springfield, MO	3,100	2,900	94
Pemiscot	Memphis	8,100	7,700	95
Perry	St. Louis	5,600	5,400	96
Pettis	Columbia-Jefferson City	13,700	13,200	96
Phelps	St. Louis	10,600	10,000	94
Pike	St. Louis	6,600	6,300	96
Platte	Kansas City	13,600	13,400	98
Polk	Springfield, MO	7,200	6,900	95
Pulaski	Springfield, MO	8,700	8,300	96
Putnam	Ottumwa-Kirksville	2,700	2,600	98
Ralls	Quincy-Hannibal	3,200	3,100	98
Randolph	Columbia-Jefferson City	9,100	8,800	97
Ray	Kansas City	6,900	6,700	97
Reynolds	St. Louis	2,400	2,200	91
Ripley	Jonesboro	5,000	4,500	89
St Charles	St. Louis	37,100	36,500	98
St Clair	Kansas City	3,900	3,700	94
St Francois	St. Louis	14,300	13,900	97
St Louis	St. Louis	508,600	497,200	98
Ste Genevieve	St. Louis	4,500	4,400	97
Saline	Kansas City	8,200	7,900	97
Schuyler	Ottumwa-Kirksville	2,100	2,000	95
Scotland	Quincy-Hannibal	2,300	2,200	97
Scott	Paducah-Cape Girardeau- Harrisburg	12,700	12,300	97
Shannon	Springfield, MO	3,000	2,700	88
Shelby	Quincy-Hannibal	3,100	3,000	96
Stoddard	Paducah-Cape Girardeau- Harrisburg	10,700	10,300	96
Stone	Springfield, MO	5,500	5,100	94
Sullivan	Ottumwa-Kirksville	3,000	2,900	96
Taney	Springfield, MO	7,500	7,200	96
Texas	Springfield, MO	8,300	7,700	93
Vernon	Joplin-Pittsburg	7,200	6,900	96

COUNTY	MARKET	HOUSEHOLDS	TV's	%
MISSOURI—*Cont'd*				
Warren	St. Louis	4,700	4,500	96
Washington	St. Louis	5,100	4,900	96
Wayne	Paducah-Cape Girardeau-Harrisburg	4,100	3,800	94
Webster	Springfield, MO	7,100	6,800	95
Worth	St. Joseph	1,300	1,300	98
Wright	Springfield, MO	6,100	5,700	94
	STATE TOTAL	1,726,300	1,674,600	97
MONTANA				
Beaverhead	Missoula-Butte	3,200	2,900	91
Big Horn	Billings	3,200	3,000	92
Blaine	Great Falls	2,700	2,400	90
Broadwater	Great Falls	1,300	1,200	93
Carbon	Billings	3,600	3,400	95
Carter	Rapid City	600	500	90
Cascade	Great Falls	29,900	29,100	97
Chouteau	Great Falls	2,400	2,300	96
Custer	Miles City-Glendive	4,900	4,500	92
Daniels	Minot-Bismarck-Dickinson	1,400	1,300	94
Dawson	Miles City-Glendive	3,800	3,600	94
Deer Lodge	Missoula-Butte	5,000	4,900	97
Fallon	Rapid City	1,300	1,200	93
Fergus	Salt Lake City	4,800	4,400	93
Flathead	Missoula-Butte	16,800	16,000	95
Gallatin	Missoula-Butte	14,400	13,700	95
Garfield	Billings	600	500	83
Glacier	Great Falls	3,400	3,100	93
Golden Valley	Billings	400	400	91
Granite	Missoula-Butte	1,000	1,000	96
Hill	Great Falls	6,300	6,000	96
Jefferson	Missoula-Butte	2,400	2,300	94
Judith Basin	Great Falls	1,000	900	93
Lake	Missoula-Butte	6,700	6,400	95
Lewis & Clark	Helena	14,700	14,000	95
Liberty	Great Falls	800	800	96
Lincoln	Spokane	5,500	5,200	94
McCone	Minot-Bismarck-Dickinson	900	800	92
Madison	Missoula-Butte	2,100	2,000	97
Meagher	Great Falls	800	700	91
Mineral	Missoula-Butte	1,500	1,400	96
Missoula	Missoula-Butte	23,800	22,700	95
Musselshell	Billings	1,900	1,800	93
Park	Billings	5,100	4,800	95
Petroleum	Billings	200	200	90
Phillips	Great Falls	2,200	2,000	90
Pondera	Great Falls	2,400	2,300	96
Powder River	Billings	900	800	87
Powell	Missoula-Butte	2,700	2,500	94
Prairie	Miles City-Glendive	600	500	88
Ravalli	Missoula-Butte	7,400	7,000	95
Richland	Minot-Bismarck-Dickinson	3,800	3,600	95
Roosevelt	Minot-Bismarck-Dickinson	3,400	3,300	96
Rosebud	Billings	3,800	3,500	91
Sanders	Spokane	3,500	3,200	91
Sheridan	Minot-Bismarck-Dickinson	2,300	2,200	96

COUNTY	MARKET	HOUSEHOLDS	TV's	%
MONTANA—*Cont'd*				
Silver Bow	Missoula-Butte	15,300	14,800	97
Stillwater	Billings	2,000	2,000	98
Sweet Grass	Billings	1,400	1,300	90
Teton	Great Falls	2,200	2,100	96
Toole	Great Falls	2,100	2,000	96
Treasure	Billings	400	400	92
Valley	Great Falls	5,100	4,700	93
Wheatland	Billings	800	700	93
Wibaux	Minot-Bismarck-Dickinson	400	400	94
Yellowstone	Billings	37,700	36,800	98
	STATE TOTAL	278,800	265,500	95
NEBRASKA				
Adams	Lincoln-Hastings-Kearney	11,200	11,000	98
Antelope	Lincoln-Hastings-Kearney	3,500	3,300	95
Arthur	North Platte	200	200	95
Banner	Cheyenne	300	300	97
Blaine	North Platte	200	200	90
Boone	Lincoln-Hastings-Kearney	2,800	2,700	97
Box Butte	Rapid City	4,000	3,900	97
Boyd	Sioux Falls-Mitchell	1,200	1,100	95
Brown	Lincoln-Hastings-Kearney	1,500	1,400	94
Buffalo	Lincoln-Hastings-Kearney	11,700	11,400	98
Burt	Omaha	3,300	3,200	98
Butler	Omaha	3,400	3,300	96
Cass	Omaha	7,100	7,000	98
Cedar	Sioux City	3,600	3,500	98
Chase	Lincoln-Hastings-Kearney	1,700	1,700	97
Cherry	Sioux Falls-Mitchell	2,500	2,400	96
Cheyenne	Denver	3,700	3,600	96
Clay	Lincoln-Hastings-Kearney	3,100	3,100	99
Colfax	Omaha	3,800	3,700	96
Cuming	Omaha	4,000	3,900	97
Custer	Lincoln-Hastings-Kearney	5,300	5,100	95
Dakota	Sioux City	5,600	5,500	99
Dawes	Rapid City	3,200	3,000	95
Dawson	Lincoln-Hastings-Kearney	8,300	8,100	97
Deuel	Cheyenne	1,000	1,000	97
Dixon	Sioux City	2,700	2,700	98
Dodge	Omaha	12,700	12,500	99
Douglas	Omaha	147,100	144,300	98
Dundy	Wichita-Hutchinson	1,000	1,000	96
Fillmore	Lincoln-Hastings-Kearney	3,200	3,100	98
Franklin	Lincoln-Hastings-Kearney	1,800	1,800	97
Frontier	Lincoln-Hastings-Kearney	1,300	1,300	97
Furnas	Lincoln-Hastings-Kearney	2,500	2,400	95
Gage	Lincoln-Hastings-Kearney	8,400	8,200	97
Garden	Rapid City	1,400	1,300	93
Garfield	Lincoln-Hastings-Kearney	1,100	1,000	95
Gosper	Lincoln-Hastings-Kearney	700	700	98
Grant	Rapid City	500	500	91
Greeley	Lincoln-Hastings-Kearney	1,200	1,100	94
Hall	Lincoln-Hastings-Kearney	17,000	16,600	98
Hamilton	Lincoln-Hastings-Kearney	3,100	3,000	98
Harlan	Lincoln-Hastings-Kearney	2,000	1,900	97
Hayes	Lincoln-Hastings-Kearney	400	400	97

COUNTY	MARKET	HOUSEHOLDS	TV's	%
NEBRASKA—*Cont'd*				
Hitchcock	Wichita-Hutchinson	2,100	2,100	98
Holt	Lincoln-Hastings-Kearney	4,500	4,200	93
Hooker	North Platte	300	300	99
Howard	Lincoln-Hastings-Kearney	2,700	2,600	97
Jefferson	Lincoln-Hastings-Kearney	3,900	3,800	97
Johnson	Omaha	1,900	1,800	97
Kearney	Lincoln-Hastings-Kearney	2,500	2,500	99
Keith	Denver	3,700	3,600	98
Keya Paha	Sioux Falls-Mitchell	400	400	96
Kimball	Denver	2,100	2,100	99
Knox	Sioux Falls-Mitchell	4,100	3,900	94
Lancaster	Lincoln-Hastings-Kearney	67,100	65,800	98
Lincoln	North Platte	13,200	12,900	97
Logan	North Platte	200	200	94
Loup	Lincoln-Hastings-Kearney	300	300	96
McPherson	North Platte	200	200	92
Madison	Sioux City	10,800	10,400	96
Merrick	Lincoln-Hastings-Kearney	3,000	2,900	97
Morrill	Cheyenne	2,200	2,100	95
Nance	Lincoln-Hastings-Kearney	1,800	1,700	96
Nemaha	Omaha	3,100	3,000	97
Nuckolls	Lincoln-Hastings-Kearney	2,400	2,300	96
Otoe	Omaha	5,900	5,800	98
Pawnee	Omaha	1,300	1,200	95
Perkins	Lincoln-Hastings-Kearney	1,400	1,400	99
Phelps	Lincoln-Hastings-Kearney	3,900	3,800	99
Pierce	Sioux City	3,200	3,100	97
Platte	Lincoln-Hastings-Kearney	9,400	9,200	98
Polk	Lincoln-Hastings-Kearney	2,300	2,300	99
Red Willow	Lincoln-Hastings-Kearney	4,900	4,800	97
Richardson	Omaha	4,500	4,400	97
Rock	Lincoln-Hastings-Kearney	700	700	95
Saline	Lincoln-Hastings-Kearney	5,400	5,300	97
Sarpy	Omaha	22,900	22,700	99
Saunders	Omaha	6,600	6,500	98
Scotts Bluff	Cheyenne	13,400	13,000	97
Seward	Lincoln-Hastings-Kearney	5,000	4,800	96
Sheridan	Rapid City	2,800	2,700	96
Sherman	Lincoln-Hastings-Kearney	1,600	1,500	96
Sioux	Rapid City	700	700	95
Stanton	Sioux City	2,500	2,400	96
Thayer	Lincoln-Hastings-Kearney	3,000	2,900	97
Thomas	North Platte	400	400	90
Thurston	Sioux City	2,400	2,300	97
Valley	Lincoln-Hastings-Kearney	2,100	2,000	95
Washington	Omaha	5,600	5,500	99
Wayne	Sioux City	3,000	3,000	99
Webster	Lincoln-Hastings-Kearney	2,200	2,200	98
Wheeler	Lincoln-Hastings-Kearney	300	300	94
York	Lincoln-Hastings-Kearney	5,600	5,400	96
	STATE TOTAL	559,800	546,800	98
NEVADA				
Churchill	Reno	4,500	4,400	97
Clark	Las Vegas	132,300	128,900	97
Douglas	Reno	5,300	5,000	94

COUNTY	MARKET	HOUSEHOLDS	TV's	%
NEVADA—*Cont'd*				
Elko	Salt Lake City	6,100	5,500	90
Esmeralda	Reno	500	400	82
Eureka	Salt Lake City	500	400	85
Humboldt	Reno	2,500	2,400	95
Lander	Reno	1,200	1,100	89
Lincoln	Las Vegas	1,100	1,000	93
Lyon	Reno	3,700	3,500	94
Mineral	Reno	2,500	2,400	95
Nye	Reno	2,100	1,900	88
Carson City	Reno	10,900	10,500	97
Pershing	Reno	1,200	1,100	95
Storey	Reno	300	300	92
Washoe	Reno	62,400	60,200	96
White Pine	Salt Lake City	3,400	3,200	95
	STATE TOTAL	240,500	232,200	97
NEW HAMPSHIRE				
Belknap	Portland-Poland Spring	13,900	13,500	97
Carroll	Portland-Poland Spring	9,100	8,800	96
Cheshire	Boston	20,500	19,400	95
Coos	Portland-Poland Spring	11,900	11,500	97
Grafton	Burlington-Plattsburgh	20,900	19,700	94
Hillsborough	Boston	85,500	83,400	98
Merrimack	Boston	30,700	29,500	96
Rockingham	Boston	57,000	55,600	97
Strafford	Boston	25,900	25,000	97
Sullivan	Portland-Poland Spring	12,000	11,300	94
	STATE TOTAL	287,400	277,700	97
NEW JERSEY				
Atlantic	Philadelphia	73,900	71,600	97
Bergen	New York	299,200	295,900	99
Burlington	Philadelphia	103,200	101,700	99
Camden	Philadelphia	161,300	158,900	99
Cape May	Philadelphia	29,500	28,700	97
Cumberland	Philadelphia	45,900	44,900	98
Essex	New York	303,100	296,200	98
Gloucester	Philadelphia	63,100	62,200	99
Hudson	New York	213,500	209,000	98
Hunterdon	New York	25,600	25,000	98
Mercer	Philadelphia	110,500	107,800	98
Middlesex	New York	179,100	176,700	99
Monmouth	New York	153,800	151,100	98
Morris	New York	121,500	120,000	99
Ocean	New York	114,500	112,700	98
Passaic	New York	158,300	155,400	98
Salem	Philadelphia	22,400	21,900	98
Somerset	New York	63,700	62,700	98
Sussex	New York	32,900	32,000	97
Union	New York	175,200	172,800	99
Warren	Philadelphia	28,500	27,800	97
	STATE TOTAL	2,478,700	2,435,000	98

COUNTY	MARKET	HOUSEHOLDS	TV's	%
NEW MEXICO				
Bernalillo	Albuquerque	137,200	134,000	98
Catron	Tucson	800	700	85
Chaves	Roswell	17,800	17,300	97
Colfax	Albuquerque	5,000	4,600	92
Curry	Amarillo	14,400	13,900	96
De Baca	Lubbock	1,000	900	95
Dona Ana	El Paso	25,400	24,200	95
Eddy	Roswell	16,700	16,200	97
Grant	Albuquerque	8,000	7,400	93
Guadalupe	Albuquerque	1,600	1,500	91
Harding	Albuquerque	500	400	87
Hidalgo	Tucson	2,100	1,900	91
Lea North	Roswell	17,100	16,500	96
Lea South	Odessa-Midland	2,600	2,500	96
Lincoln	Albuquerque	4,000	3,700	94
Los Alamos	Albuquerque	5,400	5,300	98
Luna	El Paso	5,500	5,200	95
McKinley	Albuquerque	15,400	13,800	89
Mora	Albuquerque	1,700	1,400	83
Otero	El Paso	12,800	12,400	97
Quay	Amarillo	4,100	3,800	93
Rio Arriba	Albuquerque	8,200	7,400	90
Roosevelt	Lubbock	6,200	5,900	96
Sandoval	Albuquerque	6,500	6,000	92
San Juan	Farmington	22,900	21,000	92
San Miguel	Albuquerque	6,800	6,100	90
Santa Fe	Albuquerque	22,300	21,300	96
Sierra	Albuquerque	4,400	4,000	91
Socorro	Albuquerque	3,300	3,200	96
Taos	Albuquerque	6,600	5,800	88
Torrance	Albuquerque	2,600	2,400	93
Union	Amarillo	1,900	1,700	90
Valencia	Albuquerque	14,900	14,600	98
	STATE TOTAL	405,700	387,000	95
NEW YORK				
Albany	Albany-Schenectady-Troy	102,800	100,100	97
Allegany	Buffalo	17,200	16,500	96
Bronx	New York	486,600	474,400	97
Broome	Binghamton	78,700	76,900	98
Cattaraugus	Buffalo	31,100	30,100	97
Cayuga	Syracuse	27,100	26,200	97
Chautauqua	Buffalo	53,900	52,400	97
Chemung	Elmira	34,500	33,300	97
Chenango	Binghamton	16,900	16,300	97
Clinton	Burlington-Plattsburgh	25,400	24,900	98
Columbia	Albany-Schenectady-Troy	20,000	19,400	97
Cortland	Syracuse	17,200	16,700	97
Delaware	Binghamton	17,000	16,100	95
Dutchess	New York	77,800	75,300	97
Erie	Buffalo	380,600	373,500	98
Essex	Burlington-Plattsburgh	12,400	12,000	97
Franklin	Burlington-Plattsburgh	15,200	14,600	96
Fulton	Albany-Schenectady-Troy	21,800	21,200	97
Genesee	Buffalo	21,300	20,900	98
Greene	Albany-Schenectady-Troy	15,100	14,700	97

COUNTY	MARKET	HOUSEHOLDS	TV's	%

NEW YORK—*Cont'd*

COUNTY	MARKET	HOUSEHOLDS	TV's	%
Hamilton	Albany-Schenectady-Troy	2,000	1,900	95
Herkimer	Utica	24,800	24,100	97
Jefferson	Watertown-Carthage	33,400	32,600	98
Kings	New York	889,500	864,000	97
Lewis	Watertown-Carthage	8,300	8,000	97
Livingston	Rochester, NY	18,800	18,300	97
Madison	Syracuse	21,000	20,500	97
Monroe	Rochester, NY	252,900	247,400	98
Montgomery	Albany-Schenectady-Troy	21,700	21,000	97
Nassau	New York	442,600	438,600	99
New York	New York	701,200	644,500	92
Niagara	Buffalo	83,000	81,400	98
Oneida East	Utica	60,700	59,300	98
Oneida West	Syracuse	29,600	28,900	98
Onondaga	Syracuse	164,000	160,700	98
Ontario	Rochester, NY	30,500	29,800	98
Orange	New York	85,600	83,100	97
Orleans	Buffalo	13,500	13,100	97
Oswego	Syracuse	36,300	35,500	98
Otsego	Utica	19,800	19,000	96
Putnam	New York	24,300	23,700	98
Queens	New York	770,000	757,100	98
Rensselaer	Albany-Schenectady-Troy	51,500	50,000	97
Richmond	New York	110,900	109,300	99
Rockland	New York	73,500	71,800	98
St. Lawrence	Watertown-Carthage	37,200	36,100	97
Saratoga	Albany-Schenectady-Troy	48,100	47,100	98
Schenectady	Albany-Schenectady-Troy	56,000	54,800	98
Schoharie	Albany-Schenectady-Troy	10,100	9,700	96
Schuyler	Syracuse	6,700	6,400	96
Seneca	Syracuse	11,200	11,000	98
Steuben	Elmira	36,000	34,700	96
Suffolk	New York	387,300	381,100	98
Sullivan	New York	23,000	21,900	95
Tioga	Binghamton	16,700	16,200	97
Tompkins	Syracuse	30,200	28,000	93
Ulster	New York	56,300	53,800	96
Warren	Albany-Schenectady-Troy	19,400	18,700	96
Washington	Albany-Schenectady-Troy	18,700	18,200	97
Wayne	Rochester, NY	28,500	27,700	97
Westchester	New York	290,400	284,900	98
Wyoming	Buffalo	12,600	12,400	98
Yates	Syracuse	7,200	6,900	96
	STATE TOTAL	6,537,600	6,348,700	97

NORTH CAROLINA

COUNTY	MARKET	HOUSEHOLDS	TV's	%
Alamance	Greensboro-Winston Salem-High Point	7,200	7,000	97
Alexander	Charlotte			
Alleghany	Greensboro-Winston Salem-High Point	3,600	3,400	95
Anson	Charlotte	7,800	7,400	95
Ashe	Charlotte	7,200	6,800	94
Avery	Charlotte	4,600	4,300	94
Beaufort	Greenville-New Bern-Washington	13,600	13,100	97
Bertie	Greenville-New Bern-Washington	6,700	6,300	94

COUNTY	MARKET	HOUSEHOLDS	TV's	%

NORTH CAROLINA—*Cont'd*

COUNTY	MARKET	HOUSEHOLDS	TV's	%
Bladen	Wilmington	9,300	8,700	93
Brunswick	Wilmington	11,800	11,300	96
Buncombe	Greenville-Spartanburg-Asheville	58,300	56,400	97
Burke	Charlotte	21,600	21,000	97
Cabarrus	Charlotte	27,900	27,400	98
Caldwell	Charlotte	20,200	19,700	97
Camden	Norfolk-Portsmth-Newport News-Hamptn	1,800	1,700	97
Carteret	Greenville-New Bern-Washington	13,100	12,700	97
Caswell	Greensboro-Winston Salem-High Point	6,200	5,900	96
Catawba	Charlotte	35,000	34,400	98
Chatham	Raleigh-Durham	10,300	9,900	96
Cherokee	Chattanooga	6,400	6,000	94
Chowan	Norfolk-Portsmth-Newport News-Hamptn	4,100	3,900	96
Clay	Atlanta	1,900	1,800	93
Cleveland	Charlotte	26,700	26,000	97
Columbus	Wilmington	17,300	16,400	95
Craven	Greenville-New Bern-Washington	22,300	21,800	98
Cumberland	Raleigh-Durham	70,200	68,100	97
Currituck	Norfolk-Portsmth-Newport News-Hamptn	3,700	3,500	94
Dare	Norfolk-Portsmth-Newport News-Hamptn	3,700	3,500	94
Davidson	Greensboro-Winston Salem-High Point	36,000	35,100	97
Davif	Greensboro-Winston Salem-High Point	7,600	7,300	96
Duplin	Greenville-New Bern-Washington	13,200	12,600	95
Durham	Raleigh-Durham	52,700	51,000	97
Edgecombe	Greenville-New Bern-Washington	17,600	17,000	97
Forsyth	Greensboro-Winston Salem-High Point	83,400	81,500	98
Franklin	Raleigh-Durham	9,000	8,500	95
Gaston	Charlotte	53,000	51,800	98
Gates	Norfolk-Portsmth-Newport News-Hamptn	2,600	2,400	94
Graham	Knoxville	1,900	1,800	94
Granville	Raleigh-Durham	9,400	9,000	96
Greene	Greenville-New Bern-Washington	4,800	4,600	96
Guilford	Greensboro-Winston Salem-High Point	107,000	104,900	98
Halifax	Greenville-New Bern-Washington	17,000	16,000	94
Harnett	Raleigh-Durham	18,000	17,300	96
Haywood	Greenville-Spartanburg-Asheville	15,800	15,200	96
Henderson	Greenville-Spartanburg-Asheville	19,700	19,000	96
Hertford	Norfolk-Portsmth-Newport News-Hamptn	7,300	7,000	96
Hoke	Raleigh-Durham	4,800	4,500	94
Hyde	Greenville-New Bern-Washington	2,000	1,800	92
Iredell	Charlotte	27,000	26,300	97
Jackson	Greenville-Spartanburg-Asheville	7,700	7,200	94
Johnston	Raleigh-Durham	23,400	22,500	96
Jones	Greenville-New Bern-Washington	2,900	2,800	96
Lee	Raleigh-Durham	11,300	10,900	97
Lenoir	Greenville-New Bern-Washington	20,400	19,700	97
Lincoln	Charlotte	13,200	12,900	98

COUNTY	MARKET	HOUSEHOLDS	TV's	%

NORTH CAROLINA—*Cont'd*

McDowell	Greenville-Spartanburg-Asheville	11,800	11,400	96
Macon	Greenville-Spartanburg-Asheville	6,900	6,400	92
Madison	Greenville-Spartanburg-Asheville	5,400	5,000	93
Martin	Greenville-New Bern-Washington	8,100	7,800	96
Mecklenburg	Charlotte	132,000	129,300	98
Mitchell	Greenville-Spartanburg-Asheville	4,800	4,600	95
Montgomery	Greensboro-Winston Salem-High Point	6,600	6,400	97
Moore	Raleigh-Durham	14,400	13,800	96
Nash	Raleigh-Durham	22,700	21,900	96
New Hanover	Wilmington	38,400	37,400	97
Northampton	Norfolk-Portsmth-Newport News-Hamptn	6,800	6,400	94
Onslow	Greenville-New Bern-Washington	26,400	25,900	98
Orange	Raleigh-Durham	24,200	23,100	96
Pamlico	Greenville-New Bern-Washington	3,600	3,500	97
Pasquotank	Norfolk-Portsmth-Newport News-Hamptn	9,800	9,400	96
Pender	Wilmington	7,100	6,700	94
Perquimans	Norfolk-Portsmth-Newport News-Hamptn	2,800	2,700	96
Person	Raleigh-Durham	8,900	8,600	97
Pitt	Greenville-New Bern-Washington	25,700	24,800	97
Polk	Greenville-Spartanburg-Asheville	4,400	4,200	95
Randolph	Greensboro-Winston Salem-High Point	30,000	29,200	97
Richmond	Charlotte	14,200	13,700	97
Robeson	Wilmington	28,200	26,800	95
Rockingham	Greensboro-Winston Salem-High Point	27,600	26,900	98
Rowan	Charlotte	32,800	32,000	98
Rutherford	Greenville-Spartanburg-Asheville	18,100	17,700	98
Sampson	Raleigh-Durham	15,500	14,800	96
Scotland	Florence, SC	9,200	8,800	96
Stanly	Charlotte	16,400	16,000	97
Stokes	Greensboro-Winston Salem-High Point	10,100	9,800	97
Surry	Greensboro-Winston Salem-High Point	20,000	19,300	97
Swain	Greenville-Spartanburg-Asheville	3,700	3,400	91
Transylvania	Greenville-Spartanburg-Asheville	6,900	6,600	96
Tyrrell	Greenville-New Bern-Washington	1,400	1,300	94
Union	Charlotte	21,200	20,500	97
Vance	Raleigh-Durham	11,200	10,800	96
Wake	Raleigh-Durham	98,500	95,900	97
Warren	Raleigh-Durham	5,500	5,200	94
Washington	Greenville-New Bern-Washington	4,500	4,300	96
Watauga	Charlotte	9,700	9,200	95
Wayne	Raleigh-Durham	28,700	27,700	97
Wilkes	Greensboro-Winston Salem-High Point	18,800	18,000	96
Wilson	Raleigh-Durham	19,800	19,100	96
Yadkin	Greensboro-Winston Salem-High Point	10,100	9,700	96
Yancey	Greenville-Spartanburg-Asheville	5,100	4,700	93
	STATE TOTAL	1,884,700	1,824,500	97

COUNTY	MARKET	HOUSEHOLDS	TV's	%
NORTH DAKOTA				
Adams	Minot-Bismarck-Dickinson	1,400	1,300	96
Barnes	Fargo	4,900	4,800	98
Benson	Fargo	2,800	2,700	95
Billings	Minot-Bismarck-Dickinson	300	300	97
Bottineau	Minot-Bismarck-Dickinson	2,700	2,600	97
Bowman	Minot-Bismarck-Dickinson	1,200	1,100	96
Burke	Minot-Bismarck-Dickinson	1,400	1,300	96
Burleigh	Minot-Bismarck-Dickinson	16,800	16,400	98
Cass	Fargo	29,000	28,500	98
Cavalier	Fargo	4,300	4,000	92
Dickey	Fargo	2,700	2,600	96
Divide	Minot-Bismarck-Dickinson	1,500	1,400	95
Dunn	Minot-Bismarck-Dickinson	1,300	1,200	95
Eddy	Fargo	1,300	1,300	98
Emmons	Minot-Bismarck-Dickinson	1,800	1,700	97
Foster	Fargo	1,400	1,400	97
Golden Valley	Minot-Bismarck-Dickinson	800	800	97
Grand Forks	Fargo	21,000	20,600	98
Grant	Minot-Bismarck-Dickinson	1,700	1,600	96
Griggs	Fargo	1,700	1,700	97
Hettinger	Minot-Bismarck-Dickinson	1,600	1,500	97
Kidder	Minot-Bismarck-Dickinson	1,200	1,200	98
La Moure	Fargo	2,300	2,200	97
Logan	Minot-Bismarck-Dickinson	1,300	1,200	96
McHenry	Minot-Bismarck-Dickinson	2,900	2,800	97
McIntosh	Minot-Bismarck-Dickinson	1,800	1,700	94
McKenzie	Minot-Bismarck-Dickinson	1,800	1,700	97
McLean	Minot-Bismarck-Dickinson	4,200	4,100	98
Mercer	Minot-Bismarck-Dickinson	2,400	2,300	95
Morton	Minot-Bismarck-Dickinson	8,000	7,800	97
Mountrail	Minot-Bismarck-Dickinson	2,900	2,800	96
Nelson	Fargo	2,000	2,000	98
Oliver	Minot-Bismarck-Dickinson	800	800	97
Pembina	Fargo	3,600	3,400	94
Pierce	Minot-Bismarck-Dickinson	2,100	2,000	96
Ramsey	Fargo	4,800	4,600	97
Ransom	Fargo	2,400	2,300	98
Renville	Minot-Bismarck-Dickinson	1,200	1,200	99
Richland	Fargo	7,100	6,900	97
Rolette	Minot-Bismarck-Dickinson	3,600	3,300	92
Sargent	Fargo	2,100	2,000	98
Sheridan	Minot-Bismarck-Dickinson	1,100	1,100	96
Sioux	Minot-Bismarck-Dickinson	800	700	91
Slope	Minot-Bismarck-Dickinson	400	400	97
Stark	Minot-Bismarck-Dickinson	5,900	5,700	97
Steele	Fargo	1,400	1,400	98
Stutsman	Fargo	8,100	8,000	98
Towner	Fargo	1,300	1,200	96
Traill	Fargo	3,400	3,300	98
Walsh	Fargo	6,000	5,800	97
Ward	Minot-Bismarck-Dickinson	19,900	19,400	98
Wells	Fargo	2,400	2,300	97
Williams	Minot-Bismarck-Dickinson	6,900	6,700	97
	STATE TOTAL	217,700	211,100	97
OHIO				
Adams	Cincinnati	8,500	7,900	93

COUNTY	MARKET	HOUSEHOLDS	TV's	%

OHIO—*Cont'd*

COUNTY	MARKET	HOUSEHOLDS	TV's	%
Allen	Lima	36,100	35,100	97
Ashland	Cleveland	14,400	14,100	98
Ashtabula	Cleveland	34,800	34,000	98
Athens	Charleston-Huntington	14,000	13,400	95
Auglaize	Dayton	14,000	13,600	97
Belmont	Wheeling-Steubenville	30,200	29,500	98
Brown	Cincinnati	9,800	9,400	96
Butler	Cincinnati	82,400	80,900	98
Carroll	Wheeling-Steubenville	8,800	8,600	98
Champaign	Dayton	11,200	11,000	98
Clark	Dayton	50,400	49,500	98
Clermont	Cincinnati	36,000	35,300	98
Clinton	Dayton	10,800	10,600	98
Columbiana	Youngstown	39,500	38,600	98
Coshocton	Cleveland	12,500	11,900	95
Crawford	Columbus, OH	17,700	17,200	97
Cuyahoga	Cleveland	555,300	545,400	98
Darke	Dayton	18,300	17,900	98
Defiance	Toledo	11,700	11,400	98
Delaware	Columbus, OH	17,500	17,200	98
Erie	Cleveland	25,700	25,200	98
Fairfield	Columbus, OH	30,200	29,700	98
Fayette	Columbus, OH	9,200	8,900	97
Franklin	Columbus, OH	301,600	296,200	98
Fulton	Toledo	12,100	11,700	97
Gallia	Charleston-Huntington	10,400	9,900	96
Geauga	Cleveland	21,000	20,500	98
Greene	Dayton	40,100	39,400	98
Guernsey	Wheeling-Steubenville	14,100	13,600	96
Hamilton	Cincinnati	312,400	305,300	98
Hancock	Toledo	21,600	21,200	98
Hardin	Toledo	12,500	12,100	97
Harrison	Wheeling-Steubenville	6,300	6,100	97
Henry	Toledo	9,000	8,800	98
Highland	Cincinnati	11,700	11,200	96
Hocking	Columbus, OH	7,500	7,300	97
Holmes	Cleveland	7,000	6,400	91
Huron	Cleveland	16,700	16,300	98
Jackson	Charleston-Huntington	10,400	10,000	96
Jefferson	Wheeling-Steubenville	31,900	31,300	98
Knox	Columbus, OH	14,400	14,100	98
Lake	Cleveland	67,300	66,600	99
Lawrence	Charleston-Huntington	20,900	20,300	97
Licking	Columbus, OH	39,200	38,500	98
Logan	Columbus, OH	13,500	13,200	98
Lorain	Cleveland	86,100	84,800	98
Lucas	Toledo	176,000	173,100	98
Madison	Columbus, OH	10,400	10,100	97
Mahoning	Youngstown	95,400	93,900	98
Marion	Columbus, OH	22,500	22,100	98
Medina	Cleveland	33,000	32,400	98
Meigs	Charleston-Huntington	7,800	7,500	96
Mercer	Dayton	11,500	11,200	98
Miami	Dayton	30,800	30,300	98
Monroe	Wheeling-Steubenville	5,200	5,000	95
Montgomery	Dayton	201,500	198,500	99
Morgan	Columbus, OH	4,400	4,200	95
Morrow	Columbus, OH	8,000	7,800	98

COUNTY	MARKET	HOUSEHOLDS	TV's	%
OHIO—*Cont'd*				
Muskingum	Zanesville	28,500	27,700	97
Noble	Wheeling-Steubenville	4,300	4,000	94
Ottawa	Toledo	13,300	13,100	98
Paulding	Ft. Wayne	6,300	6,100	97
Perry	Columbus, OH	10,000	9,700	97
Pickaway	Columbus, OH	14,400	14,200	98
Pike	Columbus, OH	7,000	6,700	95
Portage	Cleveland	40,000	39,400	98
Preble	Dayton	12,400	12,200	98
Putnam	Toledo	9,600	9,300	97
Richland	Cleveland	43,500	42,500	98
Ross	Columbus, OH	20,100	19,500	97
Sandusky	Toledo	20,700	20,400	98
Scioto	Charleston-Huntington	30,100	29,100	97
Seneca	Toledo	18,400	18,000	98
Shelby	Dayton	12,700	12,500	98
Stark	Cleveland	129,700	127,200	98
Summit	Cleveland	184,100	181,300	98
Trumbull	Youngstown	78,100	76,800	98
Tuscarawas	Cleveland	28,500	27,600	97
Union	Columbus, OH	9,800	9,600	97
Van Wert	Ft. Wayne	10,300	10,100	98
Vinton	Charleston-Huntington	3,400	3,300	96
Warren	Cincinnati	27,800	27,300	98
Washington	Charleston-Huntington	20,000	19,200	96
Wayne	Cleveland	29,800	28,600	96
Williams	Toledo	12,100	11,700	97
Wood	Toledo	34,700	34,100	98
Wyandot	Toledo	7,600	7,400	97
	STATE TOTAL	3,660,400	3,585,800	98
OKLAHOMA				
Adair	Tulsa	5,900	5,500	93
Alfalfa	Oklahoma City	3,300	3,200	96
Atoka	Ardmore-Ada	3,800	3,700	97
Beaver	Wichita-Hutchinson	2,500	2,400	97
Beckham	Oklahoma City	6,800	6,500	95
Blaine	Oklahoma City	4,800	4,700	97
Bryan	Ardmore-Ada	11,300	10,700	95
Caddo	Oklahoma City	12,100	11,700	97
Canadian	Oklahoma City	16,400	16,100	98
Carter	Ardmore-Ada	16,500	16,000	97
Cherokee	Tulsa	9,900	9,500	96
Choctaw	Ardmore-Ada	6,500	6,000	92
Cimarron	Amarillo	1,400	1,300	94
Cleveland	Oklahoma City	36,300	35,400	97
Coal	Ardmore-Ada	2,500	2,400	98
Comanche	Whicita Falls-Lawton	35,100	34,400	98
Cotton	Wichita Falls-Lawton	2,600	2,500	98
Craig	Tulsa	5,300	5,100	97
Creek	Tulsa	19,200	18,600	97
Custer	Oklahoma City	8,700	8,400	97
Delaware	Tulsa	7,700	7,300	94
Dewey	Oklahoma City	2,200	2,100	95
Ellis	Oklahoma City	2,000	1,900	93

COUNTY	MARKET	HOUSEHOLDS	TV's	%
OKLAHOMA—*Cont'd*				
Garfield	Oklahoma City	24,200	23,700	98
Garvin	Oklahoma City	11,100	10,900	98
Grady	Oklahoma City	14,800	14,400	97
Grant	Oklahoma City	3,100	3,000	97
Greer	Wichita Falls-Lawton	3,400	3,200	95
Harmon	Oklahoma City	2,100	2,000	96
Harper	Oklahoma City	2,000	1,900	97
Haskell	Tulsa	3,900	3,700	96
Hughes	Tulsa	5,800	5,700	98
Jackson	Wichita Falls-Lawton	12,600	12,300	98
Jefferson	Wichita Falls-Lawton	3,800	3,700	97
Johnston	Ardmore-Ada	3,800	3,600	95
Kay	Oklahoma City	19,600	19,100	97
Kingfisher	Oklahoma City	5,200	5,100	98
Kiowa	Wichita Falls-Lawton	5,200	5,000	97
Latimer	Tulsa	3,300	3,100	92
Le Flore	Ft. Smith	13,700	13,000	95
Lincoln	Oklahoma City	8,600	8,400	98
Logan	Oklahoma City	8,800	8,500	97
Love	Dallas-Ft. Worth	2,600	2,500	96
McClain	Oklahoma City	7,800	7,700	98
McCurtain	Shreveport-Texarkana	13,400	12,600	94
McIntosh	Tulsa	5,400	5,200	96
Major	Oklahoma City	3,300	3,100	94
Marshall	Ardmore-Ada	3,800	3,700	97
Mayes	Tulsa	11,600	11,200	97
Murray	Oklahoma City	3,800	3,700	98
Muskogee	Tulsa	24,600	23,800	97
Noble	Oklahoma City	4,300	4,200	98
Nowata	Tulsa	4,100	4,000	98
Okfuskee	Tulsa	4,500	4,300	95
Oklahoma	Oklahoma City	205,400	201,600	98
Okmulgee	Tulsa	13,800	13,400	97
Osage	Tulsa	13,400	13,100	98
Ottawa	Joplin-Pittsburg	12,400	12,100	98
Pawnee	Tulsa	5,700	5,500	97
Payne	Oklahoma City	22,000	21,300	97
Pittsburg	Tulsa	13,700	13,200	96
Pontotoc	Ardmore-Ada	13,100	12,900	98
Pottawatomie	Oklahoma City	20,600	20,100	97
Pushmataha	Ardmore-Ada	3,900	3,600	93
Roger Mills	Amarillo	1,800	1,700	94
Rogers	Tulsa	13,000	12,600	97
Seminole	Oklahoma City	11,000	10,700	97
Sequoyah	Ft. Smith	9,500	9,000	95
Stephens	Wichita Falls-Lawton	15,800	15,500	98
Texas	Wichita-Hutchinson	6,600	6,400	97
Tillman	Wichita Falls-Lawton	4,500	4,400	97
Tulsa	Tulsa	160,300	157,500	98
Wagoner	Tulsa	10,700	10,400	97
Washington	Tulsa	16,300	16,100	99
Washita	Oklahoma City	5,500	5,400	98
Woods	Oklahoma City	4,300	4,100	96
Woodward	Oklahoma City	6,700	6,400	95
	STATE TOTAL	1,057,000	1,028,700	97

COUNTY	MARKET	HOUSEHOLDS	TV's	%
OREGON				
Baker	Boise	6,300	5,800	92
Benton	Portland, OR	22,600	20,500	91
Clackamas	Portland, OR	74,400	70,900	95
Clatsop	Portland, OR	12,200	11,200	92
Columbia	Portland, OR	12,300	11,600	94
Coos	Eugene	22,400	20,000	89
Crook	Portland, OR	4,800	4,400	92
Curry	Eureka	6,100	5,400	89
Deschutes	Portland, OR	16,700	15,400	92
Douglas	Eugene	30,100	28,100	93
Gilliam	Portland, OR	700	600	91
Grant	Boise	3,000	2,400	82
Harney	Portland, OR	2,800	2,500	89
Hood River	Portland, OR	5,800	5,300	91
Jackson	Medford	44,900	42,700	95
Jefferson	Portland, OR	3,500	3,200	93
Josephine	Medford	20,600	18,900	92
Klamath	Medford	21,000	20,000	95
Lake	Medford	2,600	2,300	90
Lane	Eugene	93,000	88,100	95
Lincoln	Portland, OR	11,700	10,400	89
Linn	Portland, OR	31,100	29,400	94
Malheur	Boise	8,800	8,300	94
Marion	Portland, OR	66,600	62,800	94
Morrow	Yakima	2,100	1,900	89
Multnomah	Portland, OR	222,800	211,000	95
Polk	Portland, OR	15,900	15,100	95
Sherman	Portland, OR	900	900	95
Tillamook	Portland, OR	7,300	6,500	90
Umatilla	Yakima	19,600	17,900	91
Union	Spokane	8,900	8,000	90
Wallowa	Spokane	2,800	2,500	89
Wasco	Portland, OR	7,600	7,000	92
Washington	Portland, OR	72,500	70,100	97
Wheeler	Portland, OR	600	500	91
Yamhill	Portland, OR	17,200	16,000	93
	STATE TOTAL	902,200	847,600	94
PENNSYLVANIA				
Adams	Harrisburg-York-Lancaster-Lebanon	20,600	19,900	96
Allegheny	Pittsburgh	524,000	512,800	98
Armstrong	Pittsburgh	28,000	27,200	97
Beaver	Pittsburgh	71,400	70,000	98
Bedford	Johnstown-Altoona	15,700	15,000	95
Berks	Philadelphia	116,300	113,200	97
Blair	Johnstown-Altoona	47,900	46,600	97
Bradford	Binghamton	20,200	19,500	97
Bucks	Philadelphia	150,800	148,500	98
Butler	Pittsburgh	45,700	44,800	98
Cambria	Johnstown-Altoona	65,900	64,400	98
Cameron	Johnstown-Altoona	2,700	2,600	98
Carbon	Wilkes Barre-Scranton	18,900	18,400	97
Centre	Johnstown-Altoona	34,100	32,600	96
Chester	Philadelphia	96,800	94,600	98
Clarion	Pittsburgh	13,700	13,200	97
Clearfield	Johnstown-Altoona	28,700	27,900	97

COUNTY	MARKET	HOUSEHOLDS	TV's	%

PENNSYLVANIA—*Cont'd*

COUNTY	MARKET	HOUSEHOLDS	TV's	%
Clinton	Johnstown-Altoona	13,000	12,600	97
Columbia	Wilkes Barre-Scranton	21,600	20,900	97
Crawford	Erie	29,500	28,300	96
Cumberland	Harrisburg-York-Lancaster-Lebanon	60,900	59,200	97
Dauphin	Harrisburg-York-Lancaster-Lebanon	86,400	83,700	97
Delaware	Philadelphia	194,200	191,700	99
Elk	Johnstown-Altoona	12,000	11,600	97
Erie	Erie	91,500	89,600	98
Fayette	Pittsburgh	54,400	52,400	96
Forest	Johnstown-Altoona	1,800	1,800	98
Franklin	Washington, DC	38,100	36,200	95
Fulton	Washington, DC	4,100	3,800	93
Greene	Pittsburgh	14,000	13,500	96
Huntingdon	Johnstown-Altoona	13,400	12,800	96
Indiana	Pittsburgh	28,000	27,100	97
Jefferson	Johnstown-Altoona	17,000	16,500	97
Juniata	Harrisburg-York-Lancaster-Lebanon	5,900	5,500	93
Lackawanna	Wilkes Barre-Scranton	86,000	84,300	98
Lancaster	Harrisburg-York-Lancaster-Lebanon	121,400	115,000	95
Lawrence	Pittsburgh	34,700	33,800	97
Lebanon	Harrisburg-York-Lancaster-Lebanon	34,900	33,700	97
Lehigh	Philadelphia	98,900	96,600	98
Luzerne	Wilkes Barre-Scranton	123,200	120,500	98
Lycoming	Wilkes Barre-Scranton	40,600	38,600	95
McKean	Buffalo	18,800	18,100	96
Mercer	Youngstown	43,000	41,800	97
Mifflin	Johnstown-Altoona	16,000	15,200	95
Monroe	Wilkes Barre-Scranton	21,200	20,600	97
Montgomery	Philadelphia	215,000	211,400	98
Montour	Wilkes Barre-Scranton	5,000	4,800	95
Northampton	Philadelphia	79,300	77,200	97
Northumberland	Wilkes Barre-Scranton	38,700	37,000	96
Perry	Harrisburg-York-Lancaster-Lebanon	12,000	11,500	96
Philadelphia	Philadelphia	657,200	638,600	97
Pike	New York	6,200	5,900	95
Potter	Buffalo	6,100	5,800	95
Schuylkill	Wilkes Barre-Scranton	59,000	57,000	97
Snyder	Wilkes Barre-Scranton	10,100	9,400	93
Somerset	Johnstown-Altoona	28,900	27,900	96
Sullivan	Wilkes Barre-Scranton	1,900	1,800	96
Susquehanna	Wilkes Barre-Scranton	13,900	13,500	97
Tioga	Elmira	14,000	13,300	95
Union	Wilkes Barre-Scranton	9,500	8,900	93
Venango	Pittsburgh	21,800	20,800	95
Warren	Erie	15,500	14,700	95
Washington	Pittsburgh	76,400	74,500	98
Wayne	Wilkes Barre-Scranton	12,500	11,800	94
Westmoreland	Pittsburgh	131,300	128,700	98
Wyoming	Wilkes Barre-Scranton	8,900	8,600	96
York	Harrisburg-York-Lancaster-Lebanon	105,300	102,300	97
	STATE TOTAL	4,154,400	4,042,000	97

RHODE ISLAND

COUNTY	MARKET	HOUSEHOLDS	TV's	%
Bristol	Providence	15,100	14,900	98
Kent	Providence	49,900	49,100	98
Newport	Providence	26,100	25,500	98

COUNTY	MARKET	HOUSEHOLDS	TV's	%
RHODE ISLAND—_Cont'd_				
Providence	Providence	203,300	198,500	98
Washington	Providence	26,000	25,200	97
	STATE TOTAL	320,400	313,200	98
SOUTH CAROLINA				
Abbeville	Greenville-Spartanburg-Asheville	7,600	7,200	95
Aiken	Augusta	32,400	31,600	98
Allendale	Augusta	3,300	3,000	92
Anderson	Greenville-Spartanburg-Asheville	42,700	41,500	97
Bamberg	Augusta	5,000	4,700	94
Barnwell	Augusta	5,800	5,500	95
Beaufort	Savannah	15,500	14,900	96
Berkeley	Charleston, SC	21,600	20,500	95
Calhoun	Columbia, SC	3,700	3,400	93
Charleston	Charleston, SC	82,700	80,300	97
Cherokee	Greenville-Spartanburg-Asheville	14,800	14,400	97
Chester	Charlotte	10,200	9,800	96
Chesterfield	Charlotte	11,500	10,900	95
Clarendon	Columbia, SC	8,000	7,300	91
Colleton	Charleston, SC	9,500	8,900	93
Darlington	Florence, SC	18,100	17,400	96
Dillon	Florence, SC	8,700	8,300	95
Dorchester	Charleston, SC	14,800	14,200	96
Edgefield	Augusta	4,800	4,600	95
Fairfield	Columbia, SC	5,900	5,500	94
Florence	Florence, SC	32,200	31,100	97
Georgetown	Charleston, SC	11,500	10,900	94
Greenville	Greenville-Spartanburg-Asheville	93,800	91,700	98
Greenwood	Greenville-Spartanburg-Asheville	18,600	18,100	97
Hampton	Savannah	5,500	5,100	93
Horry	Wilmington	29,400	28,000	95
Jasper	Savannah	4,200	3,900	93
Kershaw	Columbia, SC	11,500	11,000	95
Lancaster	Charlotte	14,500	14,100	97
Laurens	Greenville-Spartanburg-Asheville	16,400	15,900	97
Lee	Columbia, SC	5,100	4,700	93
Lexington	Columbia, SC	42,000	40,400	96
McCormick	Augusta	2,300	2,200	94
Marion	Florence, SC	10,400	9,800	94
Marlboro	Florence, SC	9,000	8,500	95
Newberry	Greenville-Spartanburg-Asheville	11,000	10,600	96
Oconee	Greenville-Spartanburg-Asheville	15,700	15,300	97
Orangeburg	Columbia, SC	23,800	22,300	94
Pickens	Greenville-Spartanburg-Asheville	22,900	22,100	96
Richland	Columbia, SC	73,000	70,500	97
Saluda	Augusta	4,600	4,400	95
Spartanburg	Greenville-Spartanburg-Asheville	67,400	65,700	97
Sumter	Columbia, SC	24,800	23,700	96
Union	Greenville-Spartanburg-Asheville	11,000	10,700	97
Williamsburg	Charleston, SC	10,100	9,400	93
York	Charlotte	31,400	30,400	97
	STATE TOTAL	928,700	894,400	96
SOUTH DAKOTA				
Aurora	Sioux Falls-Mitchell	1,500	1,400	95

COUNTY	MARKET	HOUSEHOLDS	TV's	%
SOUTH DAKOTA—*Cont'd*				
Beadle	Sioux Falls-Mitchell	7,100	6,800	96
Bennett	Rapid City	1,000	900	93
Bon Homme	Sioux Falls-Mitchell	3,100	2,900	95
Brookings	Sioux Falls-Mitchell	7,300	7,100	97
Brown	Sioux Falls-Mitchell	13,000	12,800	98
Brule	Sioux Falls-Mitchell	1,800	1,700	97
Buffalo	Sioux Falls-Mitchell	400	400	89
Butte	Rapid City	3,200	3,100	96
Campbell	Minot-Bismarck-Dickinson	900	800	94
Charles Mix	Sioux Falls-Mitchell	3,500	3,300	94
Clark	Sioux Falls-Mitchell	2,400	2,300	97
Clay	Sioux City	4,400	4,300	98
Codington	Sioux Falls-Mitchell	7,500	7,400	98
Corson	Minot-Bismarck-Dickinson	1,300	1,200	91
Custer	Rapid City	2,200	2,100	95
Davison	Sioux Falls-Mitchell	6,700	6,400	96
Day	Sioux Falls-Mitchell	3,300	3,200	97
Deuel	Sioux Falls-Mitchell	2,000	1,900	97
Dewey	Minot-Bismarck-Dickinson	1,800	1,600	91
Douglas	Sioux Falls-Mitchell	1,300	1,200	95
Edmunds	Sioux Falls-Mitchell	1,900	1,800	95
Fall River	Rapid City	3,300	3,200	96
Faulk	Sioux Falls-Mitchell	1,100	1,100	96
Grant	Sioux Falls-Mitchell	3,000	2,900	96
Gregory	Sioux Falls-Mitchell	2,600	2,500	96
Haakon	Rapid City	1,200	1,200	96
Hamlin	Sioux Falls-Mitchell	2,400	2,300	97
Hand	Sioux Falls-Mitchell	1,800	1,700	97
Hanson	Sioux Falls-Mitchell	1,200	1,200	97
Harding	Rapid City	600	600	94
Hughes	Sioux Falls-Mitchell	5,000	4,900	98
Hutchinson	Sioux Falls-Mitchell	3,400	3,300	96
Hyde	Sioux Falls-Mitchell	800	800	98
Jackson	Rapid City	600	600	94
Jerauld	Sioux Falls-Mitchell	1,000	1,000	96
Jones	Sioux Falls-Mitchell	600	600	96
Kingsbury	Sioux Falls-Mitchell	2,400	2,300	97
Lake	Sioux Falls-Mitchell	3,900	3,800	98
Lawrence	Rapid City	6,300	6,100	96
Lincoln	Sioux Falls-Mitchell	5,100	5,000	98
Lyman	Sioux Falls-Mitchell	1,300	1,300	98
McCook	Sioux Falls-Mitchell	2,300	2,300	98
McPherson	Minot-Bismarck-Dickinson	1,500	1,400	95
Marshall	Sioux Falls-Mitchell	2,200	2,100	95
Meade	Rapid City	5,600	5,400	96
Mellette	Sioux Falls-Mitchell	700	600	93
Miner	Sioux Falls-Mitchell	1,300	1,300	97
Minnehaha	Sioux Falls-Mitchell	35,000	34,600	99
Moody	Sioux Falls-Mitchell	2,500	2,400	97
Pennington	Rapid City	26,000	25,400	98
Perkins	Minot-Bismarck-Dickinson	1,800	1,700	93
Potter	Sioux Falls-Mitchell	1,300	1,300	96
Roberts	Sioux Falls-Mitchell	3,800	3,600	96
Sanborn	Sioux Falls-Mitchell	1,100	1,000	95
Shannon	Rapid City	2,100	1,800	87
Spink	Sioux Falls-Mitchell	3,400	3,300	98
Stanley	Sioux Falls-Mitchell	800	800	95
Sully	Sioux Falls-Mitchell	800	800	98

COUNTY	MARKET	HOUSEHOLDS	TV's	%

SOUTH DAKOTA—*Cont'd*

Todd	Sioux Falls-Mitchell	1,900	1,700	89
Tripp	Sioux Falls-Mitchell	2,800	2,700	97
Turner	Sioux Falls-Mitchell	3,700	3,600	98
Union	Sioux City	4,000	4,000	99
Walworth	Minot-Bismarck-Dickinson	2,700	2,500	94
Washabaugh	Rapid City	300	300	91
Yankton	Sioux Falls-Mitchell	5,600	5,400	97
Ziebach	Rapid City	1,000	900	88
	STATE TOTAL	239,400	231,900	97

TENNESSEE

Anderson	Knoxville	22,600	22,200	98
Bedford	Nashville	9,600	9,400	98
Benton	Nashville	4,600	4,500	97
Bledsoe	Chattanooga	3,000	2,900	96
Blount	Knoxville	25,900	25,400	98
Bradley	Chattanooga	21,000	20,600	98
Campbell	Knoxville	11,200	10,800	96
Cannon	Nashville	3,800	3,700	97
Carroll	Nashville	10,500	10,100	97
Carter	Bristol-Kingsport-Johnson City	16,300	15,900	98
Cheatham	Nashville	5,600	5,500	98
Chester	Memphis	4,200	4,100	97
Claiborne	Knoxville	8,500	8,100	95
Clay	Nashville	2,500	2,400	96
Cocke	Knoxville	9,200	8,900	96
Coffee	Nashville	12,100	11,900	98
Crockett	Memphis	5,200	5,100	97
Cumberland	Knoxville	8,800	8,400	96
Davidson	Nashville	165,000	163,100	99
Decatur	Nashville	3,600	3,500	96
De Kalb	Nashville	4,900	4,700	97
Dickson	Nashville	9,900	9,700	98
Dyer	Memphis	11,800	11,500	97
Fayette	Memphis	6,600	6,300	95
Fentress	Knoxville	4,600	4,400	95
Franklin	Nashville	10,100	9,900	98
Gibson	Memphis	17,500	17,000	97
Giles	Nashville	8,400	8,100	96
Grainger	Knoxville	5,800	5,500	96
Greene	Bristol-Kingsport-Johnson City	17,000	16,600	97
Grundy	Chattanooga	4,400	4,200	96
Hamblen	Knoxville	15,100	14,700	97
Hamilton	Chattanooga	106,300	104,800	99
Hancock	Bristol-Kingsport-Johnson City	2,200	2,100	96
Hardeman	Memphis	6,300	6,100	96
Hardin	Jackson, TN	7,300	7,000	96
Hawkins	Bristol-Kingsport-Johnson City	12,600	12,200	97
Haywood	Memphis	6,800	6,500	96
Henderson	Jackson, TN	7,100	6,900	97
Henry	Nashville	10,400	10,000	97
Hickman	Nashville	5,000	4,900	97
Houston	Nashville	2,200	2,100	96
Humphreys	Nashville	5,400	5,300	98
Jackson	Nashville	3,200	3,100	96
Jefferson	Knoxville	9,600	9,400	98

COUNTY	MARKET	HOUSEHOLDS	TV's	%
TENNESSEE—*Cont'd*				
Johnson	Bristol-Kingsport-Johnson City	4,600	4,400	97
Knox	Knoxville	105,700	103,900	98
Lake	Paducah-Cape Girardeau-			
	Harrisburg	2,400	2,300	97
Lauderdale	Memphis	7,900	7,700	97
Lawrence	Nashville	11,700	11,400	97
Lewis	Nashville	3,300	3,200	97
Lincoln	Huntsville-Decatur-Florence	8,900	8,600	97
Loudon	Knoxville	9,800	9,600	98
McMinn	Chattanooga	15,200	14,900	98
McNairy	Memphis	7,600	7,300	96
Macon	Nashville	5,400	5,300	97
Madison	Jackson, TN	25,300	24,700	97
Marion	Chattanooga	7,400	7,300	98
Marshall	Nashville	6,500	6,400	98
Maury	Nashville	16,100	15,800	98
Meigs	Chattanooga	2,300	2,200	98
Monroe	Knoxville	8,500	8,200	97
Montgomery	Nashville	23,800	23,400	98
Moore	Nashville	1,400	1,400	97
Morgan	Knoxville	4,900	4,700	97
Obion	Paducah-Cape Girardeau-			
	Harrisburg	12,800	12,500	98
Overton	Nashville	5,900	5,700	96
Perry	Nashville	2,200	2,100	97
Pickett	Nashville	1,500	1,400	95
Polk	Chattanooga	4,300	4,200	97
Putnam	Nashville	15,000	14,600	97
Rhea	Chattanooga	7,800	7,600	97
Roane	Knoxville	15,200	14,900	98
Robertson	Nashville	11,500	11,300	98
Rutherford	Nashville	23,800	23,400	98
Scott	Knoxville	5,500	5,200	95
Sequatchie	Chattanooga	2,400	2,300	97
Sevier	Knoxville	12,800	12,400	97
Shelby	Memphis	251,300	247,000	98
Smith	Nashville	5,100	5,000	98
Stewart	Nashville	3,200	3,100	97
Sullivan	Bristol-Kingsport-Johnson City	47,700	47,000	98
Sumner	Nashville	25,500	25,000	98
Tipton	Memphis	9,800	9,500	97
Trousdale	Nashville	1,900	1,900	97
Unicoi	Bristol-Kingsport-Johnson City	6,000	5,800	97
Union	Knoxville	3,600	3,400	96
Van Buren	Nashville	1,300	1,200	95
Warren	Nashville	10,800	10,500	97
Washington	Bristol-Kingsport-Johnson City	28,700	28,200	98
Wayne	Nashville	4,400	4,200	95
Weakley	Paducah-Cape Girardeau-			
	Harrisburg	11,200	10,900	97
White	Nashville	6,500	6,300	97
Williamson	Nashville	16,700	16,300	98
Wilson	Nashville	17,700	17,300	98
	STATE TOTAL	1,504,500	1,472,400	98
TEXAS				
Anderson	Dallas-Ft. Worth	12,400	11,900	96

COUNTY	MARKET	HOUSEHOLDS	TV's	%

TEXAS—*Cont'd*

COUNTY	MARKET	HOUSEHOLDS	TV's	%
Andrews	Odessa-Midland	4,100	4,000	97
Angelina	Tyler	19,100	18,500	97
Aransas	Corpus Christi	4,300	4,200	98
Archer	Wichita Falls-Lawton	2,300	2,300	98
Armstrong	Amarillo	1,000	1,000	97
Atascosa	San Antonio	6,300	6,000	95
Austin	Houston	6,100	5,700	94
Bailey	Lubbock	2,600	2,500	97
Bandera	San Antonio	2,400	2,300	97
Bastrop	Austin, TX	7,900	7,500	95
Baylor	Wichita Falls-Lawton	1,900	1,900	98
Bee	Corpus Christi	7,300	6,900	95
Bell	Waco-Temple	53,800	52,600	98
Bexar	San Antonio	288,900	281,200	97
Blanco	Austin, TX	1,700	1,600	96
Borden	Lubbock	400	400	96
Bosque	Dallas-Ft. Worth	6,000	5,800	96
Bowie	Shreveport-Texarkana	27,200	26,400	97
Brazoria	Houston	43,500	42,600	98
Brazos	Waco-Temple	26,200	25,300	96
Brewster	Odessa-Midland	2,600	2,400	92
Briscoe	Amarillo	800	800	97
Brooks	Corpus Christi	2,400	2,300	95
Brown	Abilene-Sweetwater	13,500	12,800	95
Burleson	Waco-Temple	4,000	3,700	93
Burnet	Austin, TX	6,400	6,200	97
Caldwell	San Antonio	6,300	6,000	96
Calhoun	Houston	5,100	4,900	96
Callahan	Abilene-Sweetwater	4,100	4,000	97
Cameron	McAllen-Brownsville (LRGV)	56,200	54,300	97
Camp	Shreveport-Texarkana	2,900	2,700	94
Carson	Amarillo	2,400	2,400	99
Cass	Shreveport-Texarkana	9,600	9,200	96
Castro	Amarillo	2,800	2,700	96
Chambers	Houston	4,600	4,500	98
Cherokee	Tyler	12,000	11,400	95
Childress	Amarillo	3,000	2,900	96
Clay	Wichita Falls-Lawton	3,300	3,200	98
Cochran	Lubbock	1,400	1,400	97
Coke	Abilene-Sweetwater	1,200	1,200	97
Coleman	Abilene-Sweetwater	4,400	4,300	97
Collin	Dallas-Ft. Worth	38,100	37,000	97
Collingsworth	Amarillo	2,000	1,900	93
Colorado	Houston	6,300	6,000	94
Comal	San Antonio	10,500	10,200	97
Comanche	Dallas-Ft. Worth	5,100	4,800	94
Concho	San Angelo	1,000	1,000	97
Cooke	Dallas-Ft. Worth	9,200	8,900	97
Coryell	Waco-Temple	12,100	11,800	98
Cottle	Amarillo	1,100	1,000	95
Crane	Odessa-Midland	1,500	1,500	99
Crockett	Odessa-Midland	1,500	1,400	94
Crosby	Lubbock	2,700	2,600	98
Culberson	Odessa-Midland	1,000	900	94
Dallam	Amarillo	2,100	2,000	96
Dallas	Dallas-Ft. Worth	509,600	500,700	98
Dawson	Lubbock	5,700	5,500	97
Deaf Smith	Amarillo	5,400	5,300	98

COUNTY	MARKET	HOUSEHOLDS	TV's	%

TEXAS—*Cont'd*

COUNTY	MARKET	HOUSEHOLDS	TV's	%
Delta	Dallas-Ft. Worth	1,800	1,700	95
Denton	Dallas-Ft. Worth	33,900	33,200	98
De Witt	San Antonio	7,200	6,800	94
Dickens	Lubbock	1,400	1,400	97
Dimmit	San Antonio	3,000	2,700	90
Donley	Amarillo	1,400	1,300	95
Duval	Corpus Christi	3,700	3,400	93
Eastland	Abilene-Sweetwater	8,100	7,800	96
Ector	Odessa-Midland	37,000	36,300	98
Edwards	San Antonio	900	800	91
Ellis	Dallas-Ft. Worth	18,800	18,300	97
El Paso	El Paso	132,400	129,700	98
Erath	Dallas-Ft. Worth	7,600	7,400	97
Falls	Waco-Temple	6,300	6,000	96
Fannin	Dallas-Ft. Worth	9,100	8,700	95
Fayette	Austin, TX	7,400	6,600	90
Fisher	Abilene-Sweetwater	2,500	2,400	96
Floyd	Lubbock	3,800	3,700	98
Foard	Wichita Falls-Lawton	800	800	98
Fort Bend	Houston	25,300	24,400	97
Franklin	Shreveport-Texarkana	2,500	2,400	95
Freestone	Dallas-Ft. Worth	4,700	4,400	95
Frio	San Antonio	3,600	3,400	93
Gaines	Lubbock	3,800	3,700	98
Galveston	Houston	69,000	67,300	97
Garza	Lubbock	2,000	1,900	97
Gillespie	San Antonio	4,800	4,400	92
Glasscock	Odessa-Midland	300	300	99
Goliad	San Antonio	1,900	1,800	94
Gonzales	San Antonio	5,700	5,400	95
Gray	Amarillo	9,900	9,700	98
Grayson	Dallas-Ft. Worth	31,400	30,500	97
Gregg	Shreveport-Texarkana	30,800	29,900	97
Grimes	Houston	4,200	3,900	94
Guadalupe	San Antonio	13,500	12,900	96
Hale	Lubbock	11,900	11,600	97
Hall	Amarillo	2,100	2,000	94
Hamilton	Dallas-Ft. Worth	3,400	3,200	95
Hansford	Amarillo	2,100	2,100	98
Hardeman	Wichita Falls-Lawton	2,700	2,600	95
Hardin	Beaumont-Port Arthur	12,500	12,000	96
Harris	Houston	765,100	749,000	98
Harrison	Shreveport-Texarkana	15,700	15,100	96
Hartley	Amarillo	1,000	1,000	98
Haskell	Abilene-Sweetwater	3,000	2,900	96
Hays	Austin, TX	10,500	10,100	96
Hemphill	Amarillo	1,800	1,700	97
Henderson	Dallas-Ft. Worth	11,400	10,900	96
Hidalgo	McAllen-Brownsville (LRVG)	65,300	62,700	96
Hill	Dallas-Ft. Worth	9,100	8,800	96
Hockley	Lubbock	7,000	6,900	99
Hood	Dallas-Ft. Worth	4,400	4,300	97
Hopkins	Dallas-Ft. Worth	8,600	8,200	96
Houston	Tyler	5,900	5,500	93
Howard	Odessa-Midland	12,300	12,100	98
Hudspeth	El Paso	1,100	1,000	92
Hunt	Dallas-Ft. Worth	18,100	17,500	97
Hutchinson	Amarillo	9,900	9,800	99

COUNTY	MARKET	HOUSEHOLDS	TV's	%

TEXAS—*Cont'd*

COUNTY	MARKET	HOUSEHOLDS	TV's	%
Irion	San Angelo	400	400	94
Jack	Wichita Falls-Lawton	2,600	2,500	98
Jackson	Houston	4,700	4,500	95
Jasper	Beaumont-Port Arthur	8,800	8,400	96
Jeff Davis	Odessa-Midland	500	500	90
Jefferson	Beaumont-Port Arthur	89,000	87,500	98
Jim Hogg	Corpus Christi	1,200	1,100	92
Jim Wells	Corpus Christi	10,100	9,600	95
Johnson	Dallas-Ft. Worth	22,400	21,900	98
Jones	Abilene-Sweetwater	6,900	6,700	97
Karnes	San Antonio	4,000	3,800	95
Kaufman	Dallas-Ft. Worth	11,900	11,400	96
Kendall	San Antonio	3,500	3,300	94
Kenedy	Corpus Christi	200	200	97
Kent	Lubbock	500	500	98
Kerr	San Antonio	9,100	8,600	95
Kimble	San Antonio	1,700	1,500	91
King	Abilene-Sweetwater	200	200	92
Kinney	San Antonio	700	600	89
Kleberg	Corpus Christi	9,900	9,600	97
Knox	Wichita Falls-Lawton	2,000	1,900	96
Lamar	Dallas-Ft. Worth	15,100	14,000	92
Lamb	Lubbock	6,100	6,000	98
Lampasas	Waco-Temple	4,400	4,300	97
La Salle	San Antonio	1,600	1,500	92
Lavaca	San Antonio	7,000	6,400	91
Lee	Austin, TX	4,000	3,800	95
Leon	Waco-Temple	3,600	3,300	92
Liberty	Houston	14,200	13,600	96
Limestone	Dallas-Ft. Worth	6,600	6,300	95
Lipscomb	Amarillo	1,500	1,400	94
Live Oak	San Antonio	2,400	2,300	96
Llano	Austin, TX	3,600	3,400	95
Loving	Odessa-Midland	100	100	97
Lubbock	Lubbock	72,300	70,900	98
Lynn	Lubbock	3,100	3,000	97
McCulloch	Abilene-Sweetwater	3,100	2,900	92
McLennan	Waco-Temple	57,200	55,800	98
McMullen	San Antonio	300	300	95
Madison	Waco-Temple	2,900	2,700	93
Marion	Shreveport-Texarkana	2,900	2,700	94
Martin	Odessa-Midland	1,600	1,600	98
Mason	Autin, TX	1,300	1,200	91
Matagorda	Houston	10,100	9,700	96
Maverick	San Antonio	6,000	5,300	89
Medina	San Antonio	6,800	6,500	95
Menard	Abilene-Sweetwater	1,100	1,000	88
Midland	Odessa-Midland	26,300	25,800	98
Milam	Waco-Temple	7,800	7,400	95
Mills	Waco-Temple	1,700	1,600	94
Mitchell	Dallas-Ft. Worth	3,000	2,900	96
Montague	Wichita Falls-Lawton	6,800	6,600	97
Montgomery	Houston	32,100	30,700	96
Moore	Amarillo	4,900	4,800	98
Morris	Shreveport-Texarkana	4,700	4,500	97
Motley	Lubbock	700	600	92
Nacogdoches	Tyler	14,700	13,900	94
Navarro	Dallas-Ft. Worth	12,000	11,500	96

COUNTY	MARKET	HOUSEHOLDS	TV's	%

TEXAS—*Cont'd*

COUNTY	MARKET	HOUSEHOLDS	TV's	%
Newton	Beaumont-Port Arthur	4,100	3,800	93
Nolan	Abilene-Sweetwater	6,100	6,000	98
Nueces	Corpus Christi	79,900	77,700	97
Ochiltree	Amarillo	3,100	3,000	97
Oldham	Amarillo	600	600	97
Orange	Beaumont-Port Arthur	28,500	27,900	98
Palo Pinto	Dallas-Ft. Worth	8,800	8,500	96
Panola	Shreveport-Texarkana	6,500	6,200	96
Parker	Dallas-Ft. Worth	11,500	11,200	98
Parmer	Amarillo	2,600	2,500	97
Pecos	Odessa-Midland	4,500	4,300	96
Polk	Houston	6,800	6,400	94
Potter	Amarillo	35,600	35,000	98
Presidio	Odessa-Midland	1,500	1,300	90
Rains	Dallas-Ft. Worth	1,800	1,700	96
Randall	Amarillo	24,500	24,300	99
Reagan	Odessa-Midland	1,200	1,200	99
Real	San Antonio	800	700	89
Red River	Shreveport-Texarkana	5,200	4,800	93
Reeves	Odessa-Midland	4,700	4,500	96
Refugio	Corpus Christi	2,900	2,800	97
Roberts	Amarillo	500	500	99
Robertson	Waco-Temple	5,500	5,200	95
Rockwall	Dallas-Ft. Worth	3,800	3,700	96
Runnels	Abilene-Sweetwater	4,600	4,500	97
Rusk	Shreveport-Texarkana	14,300	13,800	96
Sabine	Beaumont-Port Arthur	2,700	2,500	92
San Augustine	Shreveport-Texarkana	2,900	2,700	93
San Jacinto	Houston	2,500	2,300	91
San Patricio	Corpus Christi	15,800	15,200	96
San Saba	Austin, TX	2,200	2,100	95
Schleicher	San Angelo	1,000	1,000	96
Scurry	Lubbock	6,700	6,500	97
Shackelford	Abilene-Sweetwater	1,200	1,200	96
Shelby	Shreveport-Texarkana	7,400	7,000	94
Sherman	Amarillo	1,300	1,300	97
Smith	Tyler	41,400	40,100	97
Somervell	Dallas-Ft. Worth	1,800	1,700	97
Starr	McAllen-Brownsville (LRVG)	5,400	5,000	93
Stephens	Dallas-Ft. Worth	3,800	3,600	96
Sterling	San Angelo	400	400	95
Stonewall	Abilene-Sweetwater	900	900	98
Sutton	San Angelo	1,500	1,400	91
Swisher	Amarillo	3,500	3,400	98
Tarrant	Dallas-Ft. Worth	266,700	262,000	98
Taylor	Abilene-Sweetwater	39,000	38,300	98
Terrell	Odessa-Midland	500	500	91
Terry	Lubbock	4,400	4,300	97
Throckmorton	Wichita Falls-Lawton	800	800	95
Titus	Shreveport-Texarkana	7,200	6,900	96
Tom Green	San Angelo	29,100	28,400	97
Travis	Austin, TX	133,100	129,600	97
Trinity	Houston	3,000	2,800	92
Tyler	Beaumont-Port Arthur	5,100	4,800	94
Upshur	Shreveport-Texarkana	9,000	8,700	96
Upton	Odessa-Midland	1,800	1,700	97
Uvalde	San Antonio	6,200	5,800	94
Val Verde	San Antonio	9,800	9,100	93

COUNTY	MARKET	HOUSEHOLDS	TV's	%
TEXAS—*Cont'd*				
Van Zandt	Dallas-Ft. Worth	10,800	10,300	96
Victoria	Victoria	20,000	19,100	96
Walker	Houston	9,500	8,800	93
Waller	Houston	4,600	4,400	95
Ward	Odessa-Midland	4,200	4,100	98
Washington	Houston	7,400	6,800	92
Webb	Laredo	24,800	23,700	96
Wharton	Houston	11,700	11,200	96
Wheeler	Amarillo	2,400	2,200	94
Wichita	Wichita Falls-Lawton	44,400	43,800	99
Wilbarger	Wichita Falls-Lawton	5,800	5,700	99
Willacy	McAllen-Brownsville (LRGV)	4,700	4,500	96
Williamson	Austin, TX	19,300	18,600	96
Wilson	San Antonio	4,600	4,300	94
Winkler	Odessa-Midland	3,400	3,300	97
Wise	Dallas-Ft. Worth	8,000	7,800	98
Wood	Dallas-Ft. Worth	8,400	8,100	96
Yoakum	Lubbock	2,800	2,800	98
Young	Wichita Falls-Lawton	7,100	6,900	97
Zapata	Laredo	1,900	1,700	89
Zavala	San Antonio	3,100	2,800	90
	STATE TOTAL	4,415,500	4,292,700	97
UTAH				
Beaver	Salt Lake City	1,500	1,400	96
Box Elder	Salt Lake City	9,700	9,500	98
Cache	Salt Lake City	16,000	15,400	96
Carbon	Salt Lake City	7,300	7,000	96
Daggett	Salt Lake City	100	100	89
Davis	Salt Lake City	31,900	31,500	99
Duchesne	Salt Lake City	4,100	3,900	94
Emery	Salt Lake City	2,500	2,400	97
Garfield	Salt Lake City	1,000	900	89
Grand	Salt Lake City	2,000	1,800	89
Iron	Salt Lake City	4,800	4,400	92
Juab	Salt Lake City	1,700	1,600	97
Kane	Salt Lake City	1,000	900	86
Millard	Salt Lake City	2,800	2,700	96
Morgan	Salt Lake City	1,600	1,500	96
Piute	Salt Lake City	300	300	95
Rich	Salt Lake City	500	500	94
Salt Lake	Salt Lake City	175,200	171,600	98
San Juan	Salt Lake City	3,100	2,800	89
Sanpete	Salt Lake City	4,700	4,500	96
Sevier	Salt Lake City	4,600	4,500	97
Summit	Salt Lake City	2,300	2,200	97
Tooele	Salt Lake City	7,200	7,100	98
Unitah	Salt Lake City	6,000	5,700	95
Utah	Salt Lake City	50,900	49,600	97
Wasatch	Salt Lake City	2,200	2,100	96
Washington	Salt Lake City	6,300	5,800	92
Wayne	Salt Lake City	500	500	97
Weber	Salt Lake City	45,000	44,100	98
	STATE TOTAL	396,800	386,300	97

COUNTY	MARKET	HOUSEHOLDS	TV's	%
VERMONT				
Addison	Burlington-Plattsburgh	8,500	8,100	95
Bennington	Albany-Schenectady-Troy	11,800	11,200	95
Caledonia	Burlington-Plattsburgh	9,200	8,800	96
Chittenden	Burlington-Plattsburgh	36,400	35,300	97
Essex	Portland-Poland Spring	2,400	2,300	97
Franklin	Burlington-Plattsburgh	11,200	11,000	98
Grand Isle	Burlington-Plattsburgh	1,400	1,400	98
Lamoille	Burlington-Plattsburgh	5,300	5,100	97
Orange	Burlington-Plattsburgh	7,000	6,600	95
Orleans	Burlington-Plattsburgh	8,000	7,800	97
Rutland	Burlington-Plattsburgh	19,800	18,900	95
Washington	Burlington-Plattsburgh	17,200	16,600	97
Windham	Boston	12,700	11,600	91
Windsor	Burlington-Plattsburgh	18,200	17,200	95
	STATE TOTAL	169,100	161,900	96
VIRGINIA				
Accomack	Norfolk-Portsmth-Newport News-Hamptn	11,800	11,100	94
Albemarle	Richmond	32,200	30,600	95
Alleghany	Roanoke-Lynchburg	9,700	9,400	97
Amelia	Richmond	2,800	2,600	93
Amherst	Roanoke-Lynchburg	8,100	7,700	96
Appomattox	Roanoke-Lynchburg	3,700	3,600	96
Arlington	Washington, DC	114,100	112,400	99
Augusta	Richmond	30,900	29,900	97
Bath	Roanoke-Lynchburg	1,900	1,800	96
Bedford	Roanoke-Lynchburg	12,800	12,300	96
Bland	Bluefield-Beckley-Oak Hill	2,200	2,000	92
Botetourt	Roanoke-Lynchburg	7,800	7,600	97
Brunswick	Richmond	4,700	4,400	94
Buchanan	Bristol-Kingsport-Johnson City	10,400	9,700	94
Buckingham	Richmond	3,700	3,500	94
Campbell	Roanoke-Lynchburg	38,100	37,000	97
Caroline	Richmond	5,000	4,800	95
Carroll	Roanoke-Lynchburg	11,000	10,400	95
Charles City	Richmond	1,800	1,700	93
Charlotte	Roanoke-Lynchburg	4,100	3,900	95
Chesterfield	Richmond	37,300	36,700	98
Clarke	Washington, DC	3,100	3,000	98
Craig	Roanoke-Lynchburg	1,600	1,500	95
Culpeper	Washington, DC	7,200	7,000	97
Cumberland	Richmond	2,200	2,000	93
Dickenson	Bristol-Kingsport-Johnson City	6,100	5,800	96
Dinwiddie	Richmond	28,800	27,600	96
Essex	Richmond	2,500	2,400	94
Fairfax	Washington, DC	182,500	180,700	99
Fauquier	Washington, DC	9,700	9,400	97
Floyd	Roanoke-Lynchburg	3,500	3,400	96
Fluvanna	Richmond	3,500	3,300	95
Franklin	Roanoke-Lynchburg	10,600	10,200	96
Frederick	Washington, DC	19,200	18,700	97
Giles	Roanoke-Lynchburg	6,100	5,900	97
Gloucester	Norfolk-Portsmth-Newport News-Hamptn	6,500	6,300	97
Goochland	Richmond	3,400	3,200	95

COUNTY	MARKET	HOUSEHOLDS	TV's	%

VIRGINIA—*Cont'd*

COUNTY	MARKET	HOUSEHOLDS	TV's	%
Grayson	Roanoke-Lynchburg	5,600	5,400	96
Greene	Richmond	2,200	2,000	91
Greensville	Richmond	5,300	5,000	95
Halifax	Roanoke-Lynchburg	12,000	11,400	95
Hampton-Newport News	Norfolk-Portsmth-Newport News-Hamptn	88,800	87,200	98
Hanover	Richmond	16,700	16,000	96
Henrico	Richmond	147,800	144,400	98
Henry	Roanoke-Lynchburg	24,800	24,100	97
Highland	Roanoke-Lynchburg	900	900	96
Isle of Wight	Norfolk-Portsmth-Newport News-Hamptn	6,600	6,400	97
James City	Norfolk-Portsmth-Newport News-Hamptn	9,500	9,200	97
King and Queen	Richmond	1,900	1,800	94
King George	Washington, DC	3,300	3,200	97
King William	Richmond	2,500	2,400	97
Lancaster	Richmond	3,400	3,300	96
Lee	Bristol-Kingsport-Johnson City	10,100	9,500	94
Loudoun	Washington, DC	17,900	17,300	97
Louisa	Richmond	5,700	5,400	94
Lunenburg	Richmond	4,000	3,800	96
Madison	Washington	3,500	3,300	94
Mathews	Norfolk-Portsmth-Newport News-Hamptn	3,300	3,200	96
Mecklenburg	Raleigh-Durham	9,700	9,200	95
Middlesex	Richmond	2,700	2,600	96
Montgomery	Roanoke-Lynchburg	23,600	22,900	97
Nansemond	Norfolk-Portsmth-Newport News-Hamptn	15,400	14,700	96
Nelson	Roanoke-Lynchburg	3,800	3,600	94
New Kent	Richmond	2,400	2,300	96
Norfolk	Norfolk-Portsmth-Newport News-Hamptn	157,600	154,100	98
Northampton	Norfolk-Portsmth-Newport News-Hamptn	5,800	5,500	95
Northumberland	Richmond	3,600	3,500	96
Nottoway	Richmond	4,400	4,200	96
Orange	Richmond	6,000	5,700	94
Page	Washington, DC	7,100	7,000	98
Patrick	Greensboro-Winston Salem-High Point	5,700	5,400	95
Pittsylvania	Roanoke-Lynchburg	37,100	35,800	96
Powhatan	Richmond	3,200	3,100	96
Prince Edward	Richmond	5,200	5,000	95
Prince George	Richmond	13,200	12,900	98
Prince William	Washington, DC	40,400	39,700	98
Pulaski	Roanoke-Lynchburg	10,900	10,600	97
Rappahannock	Washington, DC	2,000	1,900	95
Richmond	Richmond	2,400	2,300	96
Roanoke	Roanoke-Lynchburg	71,400	69,900	98
Rockbridge	Roanoke-Lynchburg	9,800	9,400	96
Rockingham	Harrisonburg	24,700	23,900	97
Russell	Bristol-Kingsport-Johnson City	8,900	8,400	95
Scott	Bristol-Kingsport-Johnson City	8,600	8,100	94
Shenandoah	Washington, DC	9,900	9,600	97
Smyth	Bristol-Kingsport-Johnson City	10,600	10,300	97

COUNTY	MARKET	HOUSEHOLDS	TV's	%
VIRGINIA—*Cont'd*				
Southampton	Norfolk-Portsmth-Newport News-Hamptn	8,300	7,900	95
Spotsylvania	Washington, DC	14,800	14,300	97
Stafford	Washington, DC	10,600	10,300	97
Surry	Norfolk-Portsmth-Newport News-Hamptn	1,800	1,700	95
Sussex	Richmond	3,400	3,200	93
Tazewell	Bluefield-Beckley-Oak Hill	16,500	15,900	96
Virginia Beach	Norfolk-Portsmth-Newport News-Hamptn	70,100	68,900	98
Warren	Washington, DC	7,400	7,100	96
Washington	Bristol-Kingsport-Johnson City	21,800	21,100	97
Westmoreland	Washington, DC	4,900	4,600	94
Wise	Bristol-Kingsport-Johnson City	17,400	16,600	95
Wythe	Roanoke-Lynchburg	8,200	7,800	95
York	Norfolk-Portsmth-Newport News-Hamptn	12,600	12,300	98
	STATE TOTAL	1,730,300	1,682,000	97
WASHINGTON				
Adams	Yakima	4,900	4,700	95
Asotin	Spokane	5,500	5,300	96
Benton	Yakima	30,400	29,000	95
Chelan	Spokane	6,300	15,300	94
Clallam	Seattle-Tacoma	15,600	14,600	94
Clark	Portland, OR	60,500	58,300	96
Columbia	Spokane	1,600	1,400	90
Cowlitz	Portland, OR	26,800	25,500	95
Douglas	Spokane	7,200	6,900	95
Ferry	Spokane	2,100	1,900	90
Franklin	Yakima	10,000	9,500	95
Garfield	Spokane	900	800	92
Grant	Spokane	17,100	16,100	94
Grays Harbor	Seattle-Tacoma	23,300	21,200	91
Island	Seattle-Tacoma	13,600	13,200	97
Jefferson	Seattle-Tacoma	4,900	4,600	94
King	Seattle-Tacoma	455,900	432,900	95
Kitsap	Seattle-Tacoma	45,400	43,800	96
Kittitas East	Yakima	7,200	6,600	93
Kittitas West	Seattle-Tacoma	1,600	1,500	86
Klickitat	Portland, OR	5,200	4,700	90
Lewis	Seattle-Tacoma	19,000	17,700	93
Lincoln	Spokane	4,000	3,800	96
Mason	Seattle-Tacoma	9,300	8,900	96
Okanogan	Spokane	10,900	9,900	91
Pacific	Portland, OR	6,200	5,600	91
Pend Oreille	Spokane	2,800	2,600	94
Pierce	Seattle-Tacoma	148,100	142,600	96
San Juan	Seattle-Tacoma	2,600	2,400	94
Skagit	Seattle-Tacoma	20,700	19,600	95
Skamania	Portland, OR	2,100	1,900	92
Snohomish	Seattle-Tacoma	97,500	93,600	96
Spokane	Spokane	116,900	111,500	95
Stevens	Spokane	9,100	8,400	93
Thurston	Seattle-Tacoma	39,000	37,400	96

COUNTY	MARKET	HOUSEHOLDS	TV's	%

WASHINGTON—*Cont'd*

Wahkiakum	Portland, OR	1,300	1,200	92
Walla Walla	Yakima	15,900	14,500	91
Whatcom	Bellingham	34,300	32,300	94
Whitman	Spokane	12,700	11,900	94
Yakima	Yakima	58,600	54,900	94
	STATE TOTAL	1,367,000	1,298,500	95

WEST VIRGINIA

Barbour	Clarksburg-Weston	5,800	5,500	96
Berkeley	Washington, DC	14,700	14,400	98
Boone	Charleston-Huntington	9,700	9,400	97
Braxton	Charleston-Huntington	4,700	4,400	93
Brooke	Wheeling-Steubenville	10,400	10,300	99
Cabell	Charleston-Huntington	39,500	38,800	98
Calhoun	Charleston-Huntington	2,700	2,600	95
Clay	Charleston-Huntington	3,500	3,300	95
Doddridge	Clarksburg-Weston	2,400	2,300	95
Fayette	Bluefield-Beckley-Oak Hill	18,900	18,400	97
Gilmer	Clarksburg-Weston	2,700	2,600	95
Grant	Harrisonburg	2,900	2,700	92
Greenbrier	Bluefield-Beckley-Oak Hill	11,900	11,300	95
Hampshire	Washington, DC	4,800	4,500	94
Hancock	Pittsburgh	13,700	13,600	99
Hardy	Harrisonburg	3,300	3,000	91
Harrison	Clarksburg-Weston	28,900	28,400	98
Jackson	Charleston-Huntington	7,600	7,400	98
Jefferson	Washington, DC	8,500	8,300	97
Kanawha	Charleston-Huntington	80,600	79,100	98
Lewis	Clarksburg-Weston	6,500	6,300	96
Lincoln	Charleston-Huntington	7,100	6,800	96
Logan	Charleston-Huntington	15,900	15,500	97
McDowell	Bluefield-Beckley-Oak Hill	16,500	15,700	95
Marion	Pittsburgh	24,300	23,700	98
Marshall	Wheeling-Steubenville	14,100	13,900	98
Mason	Charleston-Huntington	8,700	8,500	98
Mercer	Bluefield-Beckley-Oak Hill	24,200	23,500	97
Mineral	Washington, DC	9,100	8,800	96
Mingo	Charleston-Huntington	11,700	11,200	96
Monongalia	Pittsburgh	23,700	22,800	96
Monroe	Bluefield-Beckley-Oak Hill	4,100	3,700	91
Morgan	Washington, DC	3,300	3,200	96
Nicholas	Charleston-Huntington	8,600	8,300	96
Ohio	Wheeling-Steubenville	22,100	21,800	99
Pendleton	Harrisonburg	2,400	2,200	94
Pleasants	Wheeling-Steubenville	2,400	2,300	97
Pocahontas	Roanoke-Lynchburg	3,200	2,800	89
Preston	Pittsburgh	9,400	9,000	96
Putnam	Charleston-Huntington	10,700	10,500	98
Raleigh	Bluefield-Beckley-Oak Hill	29,100	28,100	96
Randolph	Clarksburg-Weston	9,200	8,800	95
Ritchie	Clarksburg-Weston	4,000	3,800	95
Roane	Charleston-Huntington	5,300	5,100	95
Summers	Bluefield-Beckley-Oak Hill	5,300	4,900	93
Taylor	Clarksburg-Weston	5,800	5,600	96
Tucker	Pittsburgh	2,800	2,700	95
Tyler	Wheeling-Steubenville	3,500	3,400	96

COUNTY	MARKET	HOUSEHOLDS	TV's	%
WEST VIRGINIA—*Cont'd*				
Upshur	Clarksburg-Weston	8,200	7,900	96
Wayne	Charleston-Huntington	14,000	13,600	97
Webster	Clarksburg-Weston	3,900	3,700	94
Wetzel	Wheeling-Steubenville	7,200	7,000	97
Wirt	Charleston-Huntington	1,700	1,600	96
Wood	Parkersburg	30,900	30,100	97
Wyoming	Bluefield-Beckley-Oak Hill	10,500	10,000	95
	STATE TOTAL	646,600	627,100	97
WISCONSIN				
Adams	Wausau-Rhinelander	4,300	4,100	95
Ashland	Duluth-Superior	5,800	5,600	97
Barron	Minneapolis-St. Paul	13,600	13,000	96
Bayfield	Duluth-Superior	5,000	4,900	97
Brown	Green Bay	56,100	55,400	99
Buffalo	La Crosse-Eau Claire	4,900	4,700	96
Burnett	Minneapolis-St. Paul	4,600	4,400	95
Calumet	Green Bay	8,700	8,500	98
Chippewa	La Crosse-Eau Claire	15,500	15,100	98
Clark	Wausau-Rhinelander	11,000	10,500	95
Columbia	Madison	15,100	14,600	97
Crawford	La Crosse-Eau Claire	5,600	5,400	97
Dane	Madison	111,800	108,100	97
Dodge	Milwaukee	24,500	23,800	97
Door	Green Bay	8,700	8,500	98
Douglas	Duluth-Superior	16,600	16,200	98
Dunn	Minneapolis-St. Paul	10,900	10,500	96
Eau Claire	La Crosse-Eau Claire	25,900	25,200	97
Florence	Marquette	1,200	1,200	96
Fond Du Lac	Green Bay	28,700	28,000	97
Forest	Wausau-Rhinelander	2,800	2,600	94
Grant	Cedar Rapids-Waterloo	16,000	15,200	95
Green	Madison	10,600	10,300	97
Green Lake	Green Bay	6,700	6,500	97
Iowa	Madison	6,800	6,500	96
Iron	Duluth-Superior	2,800	2,700	97
Jackson	La Crosse-Eau Claire	5,800	5,600	96
Jefferson	Milwaukee	22,500	22,000	98
Juneau	Madison	7,100	6,700	94
Kenosha	Chicago	43,400	42,600	98
Kewaunee	Green Bay	6,600	6,500	98
La Crosse	La Crosse-Eau Claire	30,800	30,200	98
Lafayette	Madison	6,000	5,800	97
Langlade	Wausau-Rhinelander	7,300	7,100	97
Lincoln	Wausau-Rhinelander	9,300	9,100	98
Manitowoc	Green Bay	28,000	27,600	99
Marathon	Wausau-Rhinelander	35,000	34,400	98
Marinette	Green Bay	13,800	13,600	98
Marquette	Madison	4,100	3,900	95
Menominee	Green Bay	700	600	91
Milwaukee	Milwaukee	359,000	352,200	98
Monroe	La Crosse-Eau Claire	11,600	11,200	96
Oconto	Green Bay	10,200	9,900	97
Oneida	Wausau-Rhinelander	11,500	11,000	96
Outagamie	Green Bay	40,200	39,800	99
Ozaukee	Milwaukee	20,700	20,300	98

COUNTY	MARKET	HOUSEHOLDS	TV's	%

WISCONSIN—*Cont'd*

Pepin	Minneapolis-St. Paul	2,600	2,500	96
Pierce	Minneapolis-St. Paul	10,000	9,700	97
Polk	Minneapolis-St. Paul	11,000	10,700	98
Portage	Wausau-Rhinelander	16,000	15,600	97
Price	Wausau-Rhinelander	6,000	5,700	94
Racine	Milwaukee	59,700	58,900	99
Richland	Madison	5,800	5,600	96
Rock	Rockford	45,400	44,500	98
Rusk	La Crosse-Eau Claire	5,400	5,200	96
St Croix	Minneapolis-St. Paul	13,400	13,200	98
Sauk	Madison	14,300	13,700	96
Sawyer	Duluth-Superior	4,500	4,300	94
Shawano	Green Bay	12,700	12,400	98
Sheboygan	Milwaukee	35,000	34,400	98
Taylor	Wausau-Rhinelander	6,200	6,000	96
Trempealeau	La Crosse-Eau Claire	8,600	8,200	95
Vernon	La Crosse-Eau Claire	8,700	8,400	96
Vilas	Wausau-Rhinelander	5,800	5,600	96
Walworth	Milwaukee	22,700	22,200	98
Washburn	Duluth-Superior	5,000	4,800	97
Washington	Milwaukee	24,700	24,300	98
Waukesha	Milwaukee	81,800	80,600	98
Waupaca	Green Bay	14,900	14,600	98
Waushara	Green Bay	6,200	6,000	96
Winnebago	Green Bay	44,500	43,900	99
Wood	Wausau-Rhinelander	22,900	22,400	98
	STATE TOTAL	**1,591,600**	**1,555,000**	**98**

WYOMING

Albany	Denver	10,200	9,500	94
Big Horn	Billings	4,400	4,100	94
Campbell	Rapid City	6,000	5,500	92
Carbon	Casper-Riverton	6,600	6,200	93
Converse	Casper-Riverton	3,500	3,300	94
Crook	Rapid City	1,800	1,600	91
Fremont	Casper-Riverton	10,800	10,400	96
Goshen	Cheyenne	5,100	4,900	96
Hot Springs	Casper-Riverton	2,200	2,000	93
Johnson	Casper-Riverton	2,700	2,500	92
Laramie	Cheyenne	24,200	23,600	97
Lincoln	Idaho Falls-Pocatello	4,000	3,700	93
Natrona	Casper-Riverton	22,000	21,300	97
Niobrara	Casper-Riverton	1,200	1,100	94
Park	Billings	7,500	7,000	94
Platte	Denver	3,400	3,200	93
Sheridan	Billings	9,400	8,700	93
Sublette	Casper-Riverton	1,600	1,500	92
Sweetwater	Salt Lake City	12,900	12,200	94
Teton	Idaho Falls-Pocatello	2,500	2,400	94
Uinta	Salt Lake City	3,400	3,200	95
Washakie	Casper-Riverton	3,000	2,900	95
Weston	Rapid City	2,400	2,200	93
Yellowstone National Park	Billings	200	200	95
	STATE TOTAL	**151,000**	**143,200**	**95**
	TOTAL U.S.	**76,162,200**	**73,901,100**	**97**

Cable Television

This section contains information on cable and subscription, or pay-cable, television. Cable is an overall service that improves reception when hooked up to the television, and offers programming such as news, weather, and shopping guides not available on network television. Pay-cable is an additional service with special features not provided to regular cable customers. These features are shown on separate cable channels, and include first-run movies, documentaries, sports, and special features.

CABLE TELEVISION STATISTICS

Size of Industry

Number of cable TV systems	approx. 4,100
Number of communities served	approx. 9,600
Subscribers (homes served)	14.5 million
Penetration:	
Homes served as percent of homes passed by cable	55%
Homes served as percent of U.S. TV households	20%
Homes passed by cable	approx. 26.4 million

Employment

	32,000
Miles of plant in place	290,000
Industry revenues for 1977	$1.2 billion
Pay-cable revenues for 1977	$85.8 million

Construction costs:*
   Average cost of aerial plant is $6,300/mile
   Average cost of underground plant is $12,000/mile
   Cost of underground plant in dense urban areas runs as
      high as $80,000 per mile

Subscriber Fees

Typical one-time installation fee:	$15.00
Average monthly fee:	$7.00
Range of monthly fees in typical larger market systems (built since 1972):	$8.00–10.00

Services

Retransmission of local broadcast signals
Importation of independent TV stations from nearby cities
   (subject to FCC regulations)
Origination of local (community-oriented) programs
News ticker, stock reports, weather reports
Public access, educational programming, local government
   access, leased channels

Location

Cable systems are located in all 50 states plus the
   Virgin Islands, Puerto Rico, and Guam

Pennsylvania has the most systems: 328 systems serve more than 1,210,250 subscribers in 1,550 communities

California has the most subscribers: 1,681,030 households in 786 communities, served by 290 systems

---

Cablevision magazine.

STATE STATISTICS*	NUMBER OF CATV SYSTEMS	NUMBER OF COMMUNITIES SERVED BY CATV	TOTAL CATV SUBSCRIBERS
Alabama	88	129	224,735
Alaska	13	19	13,480
Arizona	43	75	74,133
Arkansas	100	133	148,647
California	290	786	1,681,030
Colorado	42	91	93,269
Connecticut	16	54	154,108
Delaware	9	31	71,350
Florida	122	353	528,432
Georgia	86	167	298,707
Hawaii	10	64	77,228
Idaho	49	83	62,517
Illinois	96	216	379,486
Indiana	84	138	252,442
Iowa	50	62	98,711
Kansas	122	144	185,180
Kentucky	123	284	187,699
Louisiana	44	82	156,651
Maine	34	68	86,004
Maryland	30	85	101,613
Massachusetts	34	74	189,698
Michigan	91	282	324,024
Minnesota	95	140	144,274
Mississippi	69	110	182,099
Missouri	87	121	155,412
Montana	35	57	90,222
Nebraska	48	55	81,794
Nevada	10	30	32,306
New Hampshire	38	75	85,381
New Jersey	36	189	303,240
New Mexico	33	69	100,189
New York	183	729	987,756
North Carolina	59	114	210,199
North Dakota	31	37	97,825
Ohio	177	468	644,217
Oklahoma	99	111	192,385
Oregon	101	205	192,459
Pennsylvania	328	1,550	1,210,250
Rhode Island	1	1	3,062
South Carolina	40	77	106,380
South Dakota	18	25	46,731
Tennessee	78	117	145,403
Texas	255	369	740,267
Utah	6	13	15,549
Vermont	39	100	71,502
Virginia	77	166	176,546
Washington	102	242	302,495
West Virginia	181	506	294,306
Wisconsin	78	146	166,119
Wyoming	27	48	74,340
Guam	1	1	12,800
Marianas	1	1	1,100
Puerto Rico	1	5	13,125
Virgin Islands	1	1	1,200

*1978 *Television Factbook,* Services Volume.

Information for this section provided by the National Cable Television Association and reproduced with their permission.

Pay-Cable Television

Subscription television (STV), or pay TV, involves transmitting television programs over the air to viewers who pay a fee for the service. The transmissions are "scrambled," so they may be received only by a receiver equipped with a decoder. A subscriber who tunes in to the channel on which the station operates will see a scrambled picture and hear garbled sound. To receive the program in unscrambled form, he activates the decoder.

The FCC has approved several systems, among them one by which the subscriber pays a monthly fee for the decoder and can receive unlimited STV programming. Under another method, the decoder records on tape that a particular program has been viewed; at the end of the month, the subscriber pays for programs the tape reports were viewed.

HOW PAY TV DEVELOPED

Section 303(g) of the Communications Act requires the commission to "study new uses of radio, provide for experimental uses of frequencies, and generally encourage the larger and more effective use of radio in the public interest."

The FCC authorized preliminary over-the-air toll-TV experimentation as early as 1950. In that year, the Skiatron system was tested over WOR-TV, New York City. In 1951, the Telemeter system was tested over KTLA(TV), Los Angeles, and Zenith tested its system over its own experimental station in Chicago. These tests were made without general public participation, using a limited number of special receivers.

On February 10, 1955, the commission instituted proceedings to determine whether it should authorize TV stations to transmit programs paid for on a subscription basis (Docket 11279). Resulting comments on the many legal, technical, and policy questions involved in this and subsequent steps of the proceedings produced 92 docket volumes reflecting the views of more than 25,000 persons.

Two of the legal points on which comments were invited were whether the commission had authority under the Communications Act to authorize and regulate subscription-TV operations, and whether such operations constituted "broadcasting" within the meaning of the act.

On May 23, 1957, the commission concluded that it had authority to authorize the use of TV broadcast frequencies for subscription operations if it found it would be in the public interest to do so. It left for future determination whether this service was to be construed as broadcasting or should be classified as some other service. The commission also said it believed trial demonstrations of toll TV were essential to a proper evaluation of the complex and difficult problems involved in it, and invited comments on the conditions under which trial operations might be authorized. At that time, only three systems for encoding and decoding TV signals

had been presented to the FCC. The systems differed mainly in the way the transmissions were scrambled and unscrambled, and whether coin boxes, punch cards, or tape were used to bill subscribers.

The First Report

On October 17, 1957, the FCC adopted its first report on the proceedings. It indicated it was prepared to consider applications to conduct trial pay-TV operations over TV stations if prescribed conditions were met. The Commission held that a test was necessary to (1) enable the public to register its own judgment on such a service, (2) obtain information to help the FCC determine the competitive effect of pay service on the free system, (3) obtain operating information about any need to standardize technical equipment and methods, and (4) determine on the basis of experience whether toll-TV service required additional controls, including possible amendments to the Communications Act.

The Second Report

In a second report, released February 27, 1958, the commission deferred action on applications for trial pay-TV operations until after the close of the 85th Congress, to afford Congress an opportunity to consider pending legislation on the issue. This was in accord with resolutions adopted February 6 and 19 by the Interstate and Foreign Commerce Committee of the House and the Commerce Committee of the Senate. The commission on July 23, 1958, again deferred action, so that the first session of the 86th Congress could resume consideration of the subject. No national laws in respect of pay TV have yet been adopted.

Public Pay-TV Tests

Upon further review, the FCC on March 24, 1959, issued a third report announcing it was prepared to consider any pay-TV application by a commercial TV station conforming with revised requirements set out in the report. Among other things, these conditions limited three-year trial authorizations to markets in which there were at least four commercial TV stations (including the pay-TV operator's), to the trial of any system in only one market, to one trial system per market, and to subscriptions being broadcast over only one local TV station at a time. The commission also decided that, to get the trial pay-TV programs, the public should not be called upon to purchase any special equipment, and that stations engaging in pay-TV operations must broadcast at least the prescribed minimum number of hours of free programs.

The Hartford Test

On June 22, 1960, Hartford Phonevision Co. (later RKO General Phonevision Co.), a licensee of WHCT, Channel 18, Hartford, Connecticut, applied for authorization to conduct a three-year trial subscription-TV operation over that station. Objections were received and a hearing was held the following October (Docket 13814). The commission, on February 23, 1961, granted the application.

On March 8, 1962, the U.S. Circuit Court of Appeals upheld the commission's power to authorize the Hartford test, and on October 8, the U.S. Supreme Court declined to review that decision. The station began toll-TV operations June 29, 1962, and concluded them in January 1969.

Participating in the Hartford test were RKO General, Inc. (of which RKO General Phonevision Co. was a wholly owned subsidiary), the holder of the local franchise for the Phonevision subscription system used in the trial; the Zenith Radio Corporation, the developer and patent holder of that system; and Television Entertainment Co., Inc. (Teco), Zenith's patent licensee. RKO assumed the expenses of the test. (In 1962, the commission authorized a public pay-TV test by KTCO, Channel 2, Denver, but the project, never started, was abandoned in 1964.)

The Test Results

The Hartford experience and other information in the record (Docket 11279) suggested that about 85 percent of pay-TV programming would be feature films. Other programming would consist of sports events not available on conventional TV, plus the required 10 percent of programs other than sports and feature films.

In addition to normal rental and installation charges, the average per-program cost of feature films to a Hartford subscriber was slightly more than $1 per showing, regardless of the number of viewers for each set.

While no heavyweight title fights were shown on conventional TV during the Hartford test, they were shown in theaters and auditoriums on closed-circuit TV. A Sonny Liston–Cassius Clay fight was shown in theaters in Hartford at $5 per person and over Hartford pay TV for $3 per subscriber. A survey conducted after the fight showed that an average of nine persons watched each set tuned to the pay-TV station.

Further Proceedings

On March 10, 1965, Zenith and Teco filed a joint petition for further rulemaking in Docket 11279 to authorize nationwide over-the-air subscription television. In a further notice of proposed rulemaking and a notice of inquiry adopted March 21, 1966, the FCC expanded the proceedings to include not only over-the-air pay TV but also the question of what the appropriate role, if any, of the federal government should be with regard to wire or cable subscription television operations. On July 3, 1967, the FCC's Subscription Television Committee submitted to the commission a proposed fourth report and order. This proposed an over-the-air subscription television service. The rules were designed to integrate subscription television into the total TV system so that good programming would continue to be available over conventional TV stations.

Pay TV Established

To aid in resolving the issue, on October 2 and 3, 1967, the commission heard arguments primarily on the fourth report and order. It was from these proceedings that, on December 12, 1968, the commission formally established over-the-air subscription television as a regular broadcast service. Operators of the new service were required to have the usual license needed for a television broadcasting station plus separate authorization to use the station for pay TV. Technical standards for the new service were established September 4, 1969. They authorized those engaged in pay TV to use any technical system certified by the commission.

The Final Court Test

Because pay-TV programming was expected to rely heavily on current feature films, motion-picture theater owners were concerned about the effect the new service would have on their business. The National Association of Theater Owners and the Joint Committee Against Toll TV appealed to the U.S. Circuit Court of Appeals for the District of Columbia. On September 30, 1969, the court affirmed the FCC's action. The U.S. Supreme Court denied a petition for review, thus ending the litigation and leaving the circuit court's decision in effect.

FCC REGULATION

The rules governing pay TV are designed so the service will supplement conventional television, not replace it. To make sure that conventional TV remains a viable service and that the viewing public's investment in television sets purchased in the expectation of receiving programs from conventional stations is protected, the commission adopted a number of rules that limit the number and scope of pay-TV operations and provide protection against the removal of program material from free TV for use on pay systems.

For example, only one station in a community may be authorized to engage in pay-TV operations (it may be a new station or one already in operation), and such authorization may be granted only in communities that also receive conventional commercial TV from at least four stations, in addition to the pay-TV system. Educational TV stations and CATV systems do not count in calculating the number of stations. Moreover, the FCC does not require that the four stations be licensed to the community in which pay TV is authorized, but it does require that viewers in the community receive at least four commercial stations off the air, and at least 10 percent of pay-TV programming must consist of telecasts other than feature films and sports events.

The rules were not designed to give 100 percent protection to conventional TV, for the commission felt that some degree of competition between free and pay TV could result in benefit to the viewing public.

Feature Films

The rules permit feature films to be broadcast on pay TV under these conditions only:

1. If the film has been in general release in U.S. theaters for three years or less prior to its proposed broadcast, or
2. If a conventional TV station in the subscription television station market holds a right to exhibit the film, or
3. If the film has been in general release to theaters in the U.S. for more than ten years prior to its proposed pay-TV broadcast and has not been shown over conventional TV in the subscription station's market for three years, or
4. If the film is in a foreign language.

Feature films excluded by the rules may be broadcast if it can be shown that they are not desired for exhibition over conventional television in the market, or that the owners of the broadcast rights to the film, even without the existence of subscription TV, would not make the film available to conventional television.

Sports Events

Sports events may not be broadcast live except where an event has not been carried live on conventional television in the market of the pay-TV station in any one of the five seasons preceding the proposed subscription broadcast. Regularly recurring events, such as the Olympic Games, may not be shown on a subscription basis if they have been carried live on conventional TV in the subscription market during any one of the ten years preceding the proposed pay-TV broadcast. New sports events resulting from the restructuring of existing sports may not be broadcast on a subscription basis until five seasons after their first occurrence.

HOW TO APPLY FOR STV

Subscription-TV authorizations will be granted only to licensees or permittees of commercial television broadcast stations. Such an authorization will be issued only for a station whose principal community is located entirely within the Grade A signal contours of five or more commercial TV stations (including that of the applicant), whether the principal community each station is authorized to serve is the same as that of the applicant or is a nearby community.

Criteria for STV applications are detailed in the commission's fifth report and order, adopted September 4, 1969. The application, among other things, must spell out the methods for disseminating coding information and for billing and collecting charges, the terms of subscriber contracts, and the approximate number of subscribers to be served.

Applications must contain information sufficient to enable the FCC to determine that the applicant and franchise holder have the financial capacity to continue operations for one year after construction of the STV facilities.

PAY-CABLE TELEVISION

Pay-cable television is a premium programming service offered to CATV subscribers by a growing number of CATV operators. For an extra monthly fee, pay-cable subscribers receive a separate channel of high-quality programming beyond the basic CATV service. This pay-cable programming, which usually includes current movies, sports not available on commercial TV, drama, cultural and children's programs, and entertainment specials, is presented in unedited form and without commercial interruptions.

Pay-cable programming is usually presented daily on pay-cable channels and is often repeated during the week or month for viewers' convenience. The special programming can be delivered to the cable system in several ways. It can be originated at the cable system, or it can be fed to the cable system via terrestrial microwave or domestic communications satellite.

Pay-Cable Statistics*

Pay-cable subscribers	3.6 million
Cable subscribers	14.5 million
Cable systems offering pay-cable service	1,232
Total cable systems	4,100
Number of basic cable subscribers of systems offering pay cable	10 million
Number of states where pay cable is in operation	50
Typical pay-cable rate (per month)	$8.00
Number of domestic satellite ground stations utilized for pay-cable service	785

*1978 *Television Factbook,* Services Volume.

Pay-Cable Suppliers

Associated Press
50 Rockefeller Plaza
New York, NY 10020
(212) 262-4000
Contact: Henry Heilbrunn

Bestvision, Inc.
5540 W. Glendale
Suite C-160
Glendale, AZ 85301
(602) 931-9157
Contact: Bob Brown

BroadBand
295 Madison Ave.
New York, NY 10011
(212) 685-5320
Contact: Charles Lenz

Cinemerica, Inc.
9477 Brighton Way
Beverly Hills, CA 90210
(213) 550-8355
Contact: Ken Silverman

Hollywood Home Theatre
1345 Ave. of the Americas
New York, NY 10019
(212) 246-8400
Contact: John Berentson

Home Box Office
Time/Life Bldg.
Rockefeller Center
New York, NY 10020
(212) 556-2433
Contact: John Barrington

Pay TV Services
3718 Woodsong Ct.
Dunwoody, GA 30338
(404) 394-3467
Contact: Gerry Burge

Reuters
1700 Broadway
New York, NY 10019
(212) 582-4030
Contact: Michael Blair

Satori Productions
250 W. 57th St.
Suite 2105
New York, NY 10019
(212) 581-8450
Contact: Gary Connor

Showtime
Viacom International, Inc.
1211 Ave. of the Americas
New York, NY 10022
(212) 575-5175
Contact: Jeff Reiss

United Press International
220 E. 42nd St.
New York, NY 10019
(212) 682-0400
Contact: Frank Jaksic

Careers in Television

The glamour and excitement of television make a broadcasting career attractive to many young people. Television is America's greatest entertainment medium. It also has immense power to inform and educate. It is a vigorous, growing industry that offers young people a scope of work and a challenge few other businesses can match.

The progress of television depends on the quality of the young men and women who choose it as a career. Television calls for active young people with the ingenuity, vision, and boldness necessary to push television further ahead and keep it an ever-expanding service.

FINDING A JOB

Television holds many rewards, and competition for jobs is keen when you are after them, and keener when you get them. Security depends on ability, not seniority.

Most beginners start out in small stations, where experience requirements, and salaries are moderate. Such stations offer opportunities to be involved in all aspects of broadcasting, because their small staffs must handle a good number of jobs; for example, a traffic manager may write ad copy. The experience that is acquired there often leads to a job in a larger station in a larger city. Of course, many people remain at small or medium-sized stations and establish satisfying careers. Salaries vary widely, depending upon the size and location of the station. They tend to be higher at stations in larger cities.

Many now in television started out in radio: the two types of broadcasting are similar. Most television executives, especially at the station level, feel that radio is a good background for television.

If you have an interest in television and feel that you have skills that will interest management, write to the station or network for which you would like to work. You should include a resume that lists your educational qualifications and work experience and highlights any work experience that relates to broadcasting. If you have an audition tape, you should include that too. A visit, arranged in advance, to the station or network can, of course, be helpful.

The call letters of stations and networks, their addresses, and the names of their executives and officers are available from several industry directories. Two useful ones, which may be purchased or consulted in public libraries, are these:

Broadcasting Yearbook
Broadcasting Publications, Inc.
1735 DeSales St., NW
Washington, D.C. 20036

Television Factbook
1836 Jefferson Pl. NW
Washington, D.C. 20006

In an effort to increase ethnic-minority employment in the broadcast industry, the National Association of Broadcasting (NAB) in 1973 established an Employment Clearinghouse. The purposes of the clearinghouse are, among others, to disseminate information about minorities in the industry and to encourage minority involvement in all facets of broadcasting. The clearinghouse is operated by NAB's Office of Community Affairs and is partially financed by broadcast networks and broadcast groups. For more information concerning clearinghouse services write to: The Coordinator of Employment Clearinghouse, NAB, 1771 N Street, NW, Washington, D.C. 20036.

There are job opportunities in fields allied to commercial television that may lead to jobs in television or provide satisfying careers in themselves. Such opportunities are to be found in program-production companies, advertising agencies, station-representative work, industry trade associations, broadcasting trade publications, universities and schools that offer radio and television training, educational radio and television stations, and various branches of the state and federal governments. The two publications just listed contain information on many of these fields.

A WORD ABOUT EDUCATION

For most entry-level jobs in broadcasting the minimum educational requirement is a high-school diploma, although for many jobs some college training is preferred. A high-school graduate may be able to get a job in sales, for example, and may be talented enough to progress to management ranks without a college degree, but opportunities are much greater with one.

This is also true for technicians. Some technical training in electronics is required for entry jobs in engineering departments. And in accordance with Federal Communications Commission (FCC) regulations, anyone who operates or adjusts a broadcast transmitter must have an FCC Radiotelephone First Class Operator's License. To obtain this license, an applicant must pass a series of technical examinations given by the FCC. A course in electronics at an accredited technical institute is probably the best way to prepare for the FCC tests.

In the programming area, a basic proficiency in announcing is often enough to get an announcer's job, but a program manager needs a broader background as well as administrative and supervisory skills. A course at a university provides a good base for advancement.

Thus, those who want to make a career in television and want to give themselves the best chance to progress to the top ranks in it should carefully consider the value of college: it will give them a broad vision, a depth of understanding, and a skill for learning new concepts rapidly.

For those who want to major in broadcasting, the Broadcast Education Association (BEA), an organization of broadcasters and more than 200 schools and colleges offering course work in radio and television, will supply information about its member schools. Inquiries should be addressed to: The Executive Secretary, BEA, National Association of Broadcasters, 1771 N Street, NW, Washington, D.C. 20036.

The student who is unable or does not wish to attend a four-year college or university can pursue a two-year course in broadcasting at the junior-college or community-college level and will find that such a course provides ample training for an entry job in broadcasting. Later, if the student desires more schooling or wishes to earn a bachelor's degree, credits earned in a two-year program can be transferred to a four-year program. Details on schools offering two-year programs in broadcasting may be secured from BEA or NAB at the address given.

Numerous scholarships are awarded each year by NAB and other associations, by stations, and by individual broadcasters to young people interested in television. A listing of these is available without charge from NAB.

THE TYPICAL STATION AND ITS JOBS

Almost all stations, large or small, have four divisions—programming, engineering, sales, and administration. Under this conventional set up, news personnel are within the programming department, but an increasing number of stations have elevated news to equal status with the other four divisions. Most stations have similar jobs within the four divisions, although there are substantial differences in job requirements, approach, and compensation between large and small stations.

A television station in a small city may employ only 30 people, whereas a station in a metropolitan area may employ up to 250. This means, of course, that in a small station a job often consists of a combination of several jobs, which would be kept separate at a large station.

PROGRAMMING

The efforts of all who work in a television station—sales people, engineers, continuity writers, promotion managers, administrators—are directed toward the ultimate product of the station: its program service. But the planning and execution of this service is the responsibility of the programming department.

Local programs are conceived and produced by the programming staff of the station. All stations produce a variety of local shows, such as religious, talk, and children's programs, as well as cover sports and public events. News and public affairs programming form an important part of the television station's local programming. Most large stations and many smaller outlets have reporters covering news events that take place in the station's broadcast area.

One of the great continuing developments in the history of television is that of electronic journalism. Recent studies show the American public relying on television for the largest share of its news—local, regional, national, and international.

A second source of programming consists of material supplied by independent program producers and syndication companies. These programs may be feature-length or shorter films; they include dramas, comedies, documentaries, etc. The material offered by outside production companies must be screened so that management decisions on its purchase and use can be made.

Most television stations are affiliated with one of the three national television networks; the remaining stations are "independent." Each network owns five stations; the others carrying network programs are affiliates. An affiliate station has a contractual arrangement by which it agrees to carry programs supplied by the network during part of the broadcast day. These stations buy or produce their own programs for the remainder of the broadcast day. Independent stations buy or produce all of their programs. The networks provide programs that would be too expensive and elaborate for an individual station to produce. The network buys and shows the programs on its stations and affiliates and shares sales revenues with the stations that carry them.

The *Program-Director* is responsible for everything that is broadcast over the air. In collaboration with the general manager and the sales manager, the program director determines and administers the station's programming policies, and plans the most effective programming schedule for the station. On a daily basis, he or she supervises the activities of the department's staff and attends to such matters as work assignments and schedules, budgets, and production problems. Most program directors have worked their way up through the programming department, and quite a few are former directors or announcers who have acquired experience and have demonstrated ability in supervision and administration.

The *Production Manager* reports to the program director and handles many of the details involved in producing the station's programs. The person in this position determines staff, space, and equipment requirements, supervises studio activities, secures stage properties, and performs dozens of other tasks associated with production.

The *Producer-Director* plans and supervises the production of a show or series of shows (and sometimes commercial announcements) both in rehearsal and during on-the-air presentation. The work includes the selection of material and performers, the planning of the sets, lights, and properties, and the determination of the sequence and angles of camera shots. This person directs the performers, studio technicians, and production workers for a show, and coordinates the various elements of the program, including the selection of film, scripts, and music, and also maintains budgetary controls.

The job of producer-director is one of the most demanding in television. The producer-director is at the hub of the production effort and must be, simultaneously, a supervisor, an administrator, and an artist.

One of the basic jobs in the program department is that of *Staff Announcer*. A typical staff announcer reads commercial copy, introduces live and recorded programs, gives station identification and time signals, and makes promotional and public-service announcements.

Certain aptitudes are necessary for staff announcers. The first, of course, is a voice that conveys warmth, sincerity, and integrity. Most television stations emphasize informality, but will not tolerate a sloppy or careless delivery, so good diction and grammar are important. As for appearance, stations generally prefer a natural but groomed look, rather than artificial glamor. Some acting talent and an ability to memorize are also important. Although many stations do not require a college degree for this position, quite a few do, and the number is growing. A knowledge of history, public affairs, government, and the arts is helpful to any announcer and very important to those who want to progress to news, public affairs, and editorializing.

When an announcer has acquired sufficient experience he or she may be given the opportunity to become a *Special Program Performer,* which usually offers a higher salary. The special program performer is important in television. Personality contributes strongly to the image viewers have of a station and a special program performer must have a good personality. The work requires a combination of talent, showmanship, technical knowledge, and creative flair.

The usual areas of specialty are sports, news, farm affairs, consumer affairs, and the arts. A specialist in any of these areas must stay informed of developments in it. He or she must stay in touch with interested groups and often participate in their activities by giving speeches, attending meetings, etc. The duties may also involve working as a liaison with sponsors whose products lend themselves to the particular program.

The special program performers often deal with production matters peculiar to their shows. For example, a sportscaster may secure the guests to be interviewed and collect information, ancedotes, and other items with which to ad lib. If portions of a show are based on a script, often the sportscaster will prepare that script. The farm editor or the consumer-affairs editor has similar responsibilities.

All television stations have a *News Director* who is responsible for the gathering and dissemination of news. He or she determines the over-all news policy of the station, supervises news people, and also may serve as a reporter. The *Newscaster* serves as a reporter, collecting local news and selecting stories from the wire services, editing and rewriting them for the local audience. Investigative-reporting skills are a must. With microphone and film or video-tape camera, the newscaster-reporter covers fires, meetings, elections, and other newsworthy events. The newscaster is not only a reporter but also a performer who delivers the news on the air. So an ability to write good copy is an essential skill. A news sense—that is, a knowledge of what is important and interesting and where to find it—and a liking for news is vital to a good newscaster. Most stations seek news reporters with college degrees in broadcasting or journalism. The power to inform immediately makes television news an exciting, rewarding career for the trained broadcast journalist.

More and more television stations are editorializing on local and national issues, and the news staff play an important role in this activity. Some stations have an editorial board that sets editorial policies. Others rely on one person to research, write, and deliver editorials. In either case, the editorial work is normally handled by news people.

About 50 percent of all commercial television programming is on film, about 15 percent is live, and about 35 percent is recorded on video tape. Many stations employ a special staff to handle the responsibilities of filmed programs.

The *Film Director* handles the screening and preparation of all film used on the station, and often participates in purchase decisions. *Film Editors* cut, splice, and clean film under the director's supervision. Many stations hire both *Film Photographers* and *Video-Tape Photographers* to cover the news. The video-tape photographer makes recordings on electronic equipment that permits instantaneous playback. Video tape is used to record live shows and to prerecord programs for future broadcasts.

There are a number of other production jobs in the typical television station. Though none of these requires a college education, a college education is probably necessary for those who want to progress to supervisory jobs.

The *Floor Manager* directs the performers on the studio floor in accordance with the director's instructions, relaying stage directions and cues. The *Program Assistant* coordinates the various parts of the show by assisting the producer-director, and also attends to props and makeup service, prepares cue cards and scripts, and usually times the rehearsals and the telecast.

Stage Directors work on the studio floor arranging sets, backdrops, and lighting and handling the various movable properties. Most stations employ *Graphic Artists* or *Scenic Designers* who plan set designs, construct scenery, paint backdrops, and handle lettering and art work. Some larger stations have *Makeup Artists* and *Costumers,* and other such specialists.

Dramatic Actors or *Actresses* are occasionally used at the local-station level for a single program or series of programs, but the majority of dramatic programs are provided either by the network or by independent producers.

Most stations have promotion departments headed by a *Promotion Manager.* The basic duty of this department is to secure publicity for the station, its programs, and its talent. The work typically involves the planning and layout of advertising campaigns and promotional activities aimed at the station's audience. The promotion department may also handle sales promotions, which include the planning and layout of advertising for trade journals and the production of sales brochures and other material used by the sales department.

The basic jobs of a *Continuity Writer* are to write commercial announcements, write public-service announcements, and occasionally create program material. The first requirement for this position is an ability to write persuasive copy. A creative imagination is the difference between a fair and an excellent copywriter. A continuity writer must be able to produce material quickly and under pressure—careful rewriting is not always possible.

ENGINEERING

In the technical nerve center of a television station, surrounded by banks of electronic equipment, the *Broadcast Technician* performs his part in bringing television to the audience, switching from the network program originating in New York to a projector for a film commercial and then to a camera in the studio for a live show. At the transmitter, other technicians monitor the equipment and adjust it for the best possible picture, while yet others may be standing by outside the studios ready to relay news or sports events.

The engineering department is the vital link between the television station and the public. All of the work of the program and sales departments, as well as all of the other employees of the station, depends on the strength, clarity, and reliability of the signal sent out from the station's transmitter. The transmitter must be periodically inspected and adjusted to assure proper operation, and studio equipment must be maintained at peak performance.

The *Chief Engineer* is the head of the engineering department, supervising from half-a-dozen to forty technicians. The work involves planning and coordinating the engineering work for shows, including the assignments and schedules of technicians. This person is responsible for the maintenance of equipment, makes recommendations regarding the purchase of new equipment, and may often modify equipment for the station's special needs.

The "chief" is usually someone with considerable experience who has spent a number of years as a working technician. This position requires a fully qualified engineer with an FCC First Class Radiotelephone Operator's License.

The *Broadcast Technician* is concerned with the operation and maintenance of complex electronic equipment, and often operates projection equipment and sound booms and handles lighting. Those who are interested in the operation and maintenance of advanced technical gear need a thorough grounding in electronics. However, the operation of some of the equipment, such as cameras, microphone booms, and the control board, does not require a high degree of training in electronics.

In some stations, those termed "technicians" do all this work. Other stations divide the work into specialized responsibilities, such as those of the camera operator, the audio-control operator, and the switcher. Those who can handle the full range of tasks are the best paid, and many become chief engineers. Some people come into broadcasting in these less-skilled jobs and pursue courses in electronics that will enable them to handle the more complex assignments and equipment.

To progress to the top technical ranks in broadcasting, a First Class Radiotelephone Operator's License is essential. In order to get such a license, the prospective technician must pass a series of written examinations covering the theory, construction, and operation of transmission and receiving equipment, the characteristics of electromagnetic waves, and U.S. government and international regulations governing broadcasting. Information about these examinations can be secured from the Federal Communications Commission, Washington, D.C. 20554.

The education normally required is at least a high-school diploma plus technical and trade-school courses. The aptitudes needed are an interest in and knowledge of electronics, plus some manual dexterity and quick responsiveness to directions. Some smaller-market stations will hire applicants with a trade-school diploma and no experience, but most stations require some radio and television or other technical experience.

In the last few years, reliable and accurate automatic equipment has been developed for both studio and transmitter use. Such technological advances as remotely controlled transmitters and automatic programming equipment have tended to reduce the number of technical jobs in stations. This has resulted in a decrease in the size of the typical engineering department and a shift in emphasis from operations to maintenance work, which requires a relatively high degree of technical background.

SALES

Unlike magazines and newspapers, commercial television relies on a single source of revenue—the advertiser, who buys time to sell a product or service. Stations receive three types of revenue: network, national–regional, and local. If a station is a network affiliate it usually receives compensation from the network for carrying the programs that have been sold by the network to commercial sponsors.

Some advertisers do not need the national coverage for their advertising that a network provides. They prefer, often because their product is not nationally distributed or because they need to strengthen sales in a particular area, to "spot" their advertising in certain markets. For the purpose of reaching these advertisers or their advertising agencies, which are generally located in large, distant cities, many stations employ a *National Sales Representative* on a commission basis. The "sales rep" functions as an out-of-town sales force for the station.

Sales to local merchants in the station's coverage area handled by its own staff. In theory, the sales staff of a station is selling segments of time, but actually it is selling programs and the audience for them.

The *Sales Manager's* job in television normally combines selling with management. The typical sales manager may do a certain amount of selling, but is mainly responsible for setting the sales policy of the station and for supervising the day-to-day work of the sales staff. He or she develops sales plans and packages to appeal to sponsors, and plans sales campaigns in keeping with the season, the special programs of the station, etc. He or she often works with the program director in developing salable programs.

Almost all sales managers in broadcasting have had successful careers as salesmen, and more general managers come from the ranks of sales managers than from any other broadcasting job.

The *Salesperson* sells television time in the form of programs, portions of programs, or commercial announcements to advertisers or their agencies. He or she must be familiar with the station's program schedule and with its available time spots. This person proposes a commercial schedule to the sponsor and closes the sale when a contract is signed, and then may write commercial copy tailored to the particular sponsor's needs. The salesperson maintains contact with sponsors and administers their accounts by handling changes in schedules, rotation of copy, special sales campaigns, etc.

Most television-time salespeople are high-school graduates, and many are college graduates. College is not mandatory, but with schooling in advertising, broadcasting, or marketing, a salesperson is better equipped to understand and solve his client's problems. Radio, newspaper, or magazine sales experience, or advertising-agency experience, is also valuable. Sales experience in a particular market, especially with prospective advertisers, is generally regarded as a valuable asset.

The most important aptitude in a salesperson, of course, is the ability to sell. Salesmanship is usually a combination of verbal ease, hard work, competitiveness, and personality. The really good salesperson is imaginative: he or she understands a client's business and can envision advertising approaches that will appeal to the client.

The job of *Traffic Manager* is largely paperwork. It involves the preparation of the daily logs of the station's program activity, using information collected from the sales, programming, engineering, and other departments, as well as from the station's national sales representatives and its network, if the station is a network affiliate. Nearly all information relating to the programs and commercials to be telecast comes in to the traffic manager, who collates the information and distributes it. Often two or three *Traffic Clerks* report to the traffic manager.

Many traffic managers also prepare (for the sales department) availability sheets showing unsold time periods. In some stations a *Sales Service Clerk* handles availability sheets and contract material.

A high-school diploma is desirable. Business-school training is an asset. This job involves the handling of a substantial amount of detailed work and the necessity of meeting daily deadlines. Thus, an accurate and systematic person who can take the pressure of deadlines is normally the most successful traffic manager. Since the work involves dealing with almost all of the departments of the station, an ability to work well with others is essential.

GENERAL ADMINISTRATION

In this area of a television station's activities, under the direction of the general manager, are concentrated the business management and administrative work involved in running the station. The job of *General Manager* requires a combination of business ability and creativity. The general manager has usually had successful experience in sales, programming, or engineering. The responsibilities include the handling of the day-to-day matters of station operations in consultation with the program manager, the sales manager, and the chief engineer. The general manager determines the general policies of the station and supervises the implementation of these policies. Normally he or she handles the station's relations with the FCC and other government bodies and participates in many community activities on behalf of the station.

Under the general manager is the financial department, which is headed by a *Controller* or *Business Manager* who oversees the station's financial transactions and prepares reports on them. Often, the controller is also involved in personnel and labor-relations matters.

There are many organizations in broadcasting that own several stations. Frequently, these group owners have a headquarters staff which generally oversees the activities of the stations in the group. These headquarters jobs are usually specialized and involve finance, law, labor relations, and personnel work.

NETWORK TELEVISION JOBS

Basically, a television network is involved in the same activities as any individual station—producing and distributing programs and selling time to advertisers. Thus, television networks have all of the basic jobs found at the station level and some others that are unique to network operations because of the network's size, the complexity of its programming, and its far-flung operations. Normally, network jobs are filled by people with considerable experience—which they have often acquired at local stations.

Top network people plan the network's regularly scheduled programming, which is divided into entertainment and news. The production nucleus of entertainment includes producers, directors, writers, musical directors, announcers, costumers, scenic designers, and production assistants. Performers, such as actors, singers, dancers, and comedians, are usually hired on a free-lance basis for a particular show or series of shows. The technical and stage crews, make-up artists, and production coordinators are also part of the production unit.

Network news and public-affairs departments provide extensive coverage of national and international news and special events for their affiliates. Many of the same production jobs are available in news and public affairs as exist for entertainment programs. In addition, the news and public-affairs departments employs news directors, researchers, and commentators, as well as foreign and domestic correspondents.

Network selling involves contact with large companies and their advertising agencies to plan and execute nationwide sales campaigns. The sales department is supported by advertising and promotion personnel, as well as by the publicity and research departments.

Engineering at the network level requires highly skilled people competent in the operation and maintenance of advanced equipment. A substantial number of network engineers are engaged in experimental and developmental work.

A key part of a network is its affiliate stations, for these carry some programming produced at the network level. Networks have departments to handle their affiliate relations in such matters as agreements to carry programs, clearances for programs, and technical arrangements. All networks own and operate a number of television and radio stations as divisions of network activity. Other network departments are involved in research, publicity and promotion, law, program standards, and finance.

College and University Programs
in Broadcasting and Communications

The following list of colleges and universities offering programs in broadcasting and communications is based on one compiled by Dr. Harold Niven at the National Association of Broadcasters. We are very grateful for permission to include it in the book.

In the interest of space, the information within the entries has been abbreviated. A sample entry with explanation is provided for the reader's convenience.

Sample entry
University
City, State, Zip Code
Telephone number
1. *Speech,* 39 hrs., 13 courses (sem.), 22 grad. hrs., 6 courses; Journalism, 6 hrs., 2 courses
2. *Degrees:* BA, 35 majors, MA, 12 majors, PhD., 2 majors
3. *Facilities:* 2 radio C/L, TV C/L, FM station (WXYZ), CCTV, VTR
4. *Undergraduate scholarships:* 4—average amount $1000
   Graduate assistantships: 4—average amount 3500
   Tuition remitted: 100%
   Av. no. hrs./week required: 20

5. *Highest faculty degrees:* PhD
6. *Contact:* Thomas Henry, chairman

Explanation
1. Departments of the school offering radio–TV courses. Number of hours and number of courses on a semester or quarterly basis (undergraduate and graduate) offered by each department.
2. Degrees offered by the school, and number of radio-TV majors.
3. Broadcasting facilities used for instructional purposes. *Code:*
   - c/l = classroom lab
   - cctv = closed circuit television
   - vtr = video tape recorder
   - etv = educational television
   - catv = cable television
4. Number of undergraduate scholarships and graduate assistantships offered by the school, along with the dollar amount. Also the percent of tuition remitted for graduate assistantships and the average number of course hours per week required for the assistantship.
5. Highest degree held by any member of the faculty teaching radio and TV courses.
6. The person in charge of broadcasting and communications education.

Four-Year Colleges And Universities
Offering Degrees In Broadcasting

ALABAMA

Auburn University
Auburn, AL 36830
Tel. (205) 826-4682
Speech, 102 hrs., 21 courses (qr.), 61 grad. hrs., 12 courses
Degrees: BA, 50 majors, MA, 7 majors
Facilities: radio C/L, TV C/L, FM station (WEGL), ETV (WAIQ-TV), CCTV, VTR, film studio
Highest faculty degree: PhD
Contact: Bert E. Bradley, chairman

University of Alabama
University, AL 35486
Tel. (205) 348-6350
Broadcast & film communications, 79 hrs., 26 courses (sem.); mass communications, 45 hrs., 15 courses, 90 grad. hrs., 28 courses
Degrees: BA, 110 majors, MA, 17 majors
Facilities: 4 radio C/L, TV C/L, carrier current (WABP), FM station (WVAL), CCTV, VTR, ETV station (WBIQ), film studio, CATV
Undergraduate scholarships: 2—average amount $500
Graduate assistantships: 4—average amount $2450
Tuition remitted: 66%
Av. no. hrs./wk. required: 20
Highest faculty degree: MA
Contact: W. Knox Hagood, chairman

ALASKA

University of Alaska
Fairbanks, AK 99701
Tel. (907) 479-7761
Journalism & broadcasting, 27 hrs., 9 courses (sem.)
Degrees: BA, 10 majors
Facilities: radio C/L, TV C/L, FM station (KUAC), ETV (KUAC-TV), VTR
Highest faculty degree: MA
Contact: Donald Upham, chairman

205

ARIZONA

Arizona State University
Tempe, AZ 85281
Tel. (602) 965-5013
Mass communications, 54 hrs., 30 courses (sem.);
educational technology, 11 hrs., 5 courses
Degrees: BA, BS, 418 majors
Facilities: TV station (KAET), CCTV, VTR
Undergraduate scholarships: 4—average amount
$250
Highest faculty degree: EdD
Contact: Joe W. Milner, chairman

Northern Arizona University
Flagstaff, AZ 86001
Tel. (602) 523-9011
Speech, 33 hrs., 11 courses (sem.); journalism, 12
hrs., 4 courses, 3 grad. hrs., 1 course
Degrees: BA, 50 majors
Facilities: 2 radio C/L, TV C/L, FM station (KAXR),
carrier current (KNAU), CCTV, VTR
Highest faculty degree: PhD
Contact: Ron L. McIntyre, chairman

University of Arizona
Tucson, AZ 85721
Tel. (602) 884-1434
Radio–television, 57 hrs., 23 courses (sem.); speech,
8 hrs., 3 courses; journalism, 12 hrs., 4 courses;
marketing, 12 hrs., 4 courses; drama, 10 hrs., 4
courses
Degrees: BA, 82 majors
Facilities: 2 radio C/L, 2 TV C/L, AM station
(KUAT), FM station (KUAT-FM), TV station
(KUAT-TV), PTV, CCTV, VTR, film studios
Undergraduate scholarships: 3—average amount
$500
Highest faculty degree: MA
Contact: Frank Barreca, chairman

ARKANSAS

Arkansas State University
State University, AR 72476
Tel. (501) 972-3070
Radio–TV, 61 hrs., 21 courses (sem.)
Degrees: BS, 207 majors, MS, 9 majors
Facilities: 4 radio C/L, 4 TV C/L, FM station
(KASU), full-color TV studios, CATV
Undergraduate scholarships: 2—average amount
$400
Highest faculty degree: MA
Contact: Charles L. Rasberry, chairman

John Brown University
Siloam Springs, AR 72761
Tel. (501) 524-3131
Broadcasting, 35 hrs., 12 courses (sem.)
Degrees: BS, 35 majors
Facilities: radio C/L, AM station (KUOA), FM sta-
tion (KCMK), carrier current (KJBU), TV
classroom–studio with color camera
Highest faculty degree: PhD
Contact: Ralph C. Kennedy, chairman

CALIFORNIA

California Institute of the Arts
Valencia, CA 91355
Tel. (805) 255-1050
Film–video, 16 hrs., 2 courses (qr.), 8 grad. hrs., 1
course
Degrees: BA, 8 majors, MA, 2 majors
Facilities: 2 TV C/L, VTR, film studio
Undergraduate scholarships: 23—average amount
$1460
Graduate fellowships/grants: 5—average amount
$2374
Highest faculty degree: PhD
Contact: Alexander Mackendrick, chairman

California Polytechnic State University
San Luis Obispo, CA 93407
Tel. (805) 546-2495
Journalism, 20 hrs., 6 courses (qr.); speech, 7 hrs., 2
courses
Degrees: BA, 235 majors
Facilities: 2 radio C/L, 2 TV C/L, FM station
(KCPR), CCTV, 2 VTR
Highest faculty degree: MA
Contact: *Edward J. Zuchelli, chairman*

California State University at Chico
Chico, CA 95926
Tel. (916) 895-6877
Center for Information and Communications Studies,
60 hrs., 20 courses (sem.), 12 grad. hrs., 4 courses
Degrees: BA, 190 majors
Facilities: 3 radio C/L, 2 TV C/L, FM station
(KCHO), carrier current (KCSC), ETC, CCTV,
VTR
Highest faculty degree: PhD
Contact: George Rogers, chairman

California State University at Fresno
Fresno, CA 93740
Tel. (209) 487-2327
Radio–TV, 90 hrs., 32 courses (sem.); journalism,
15 hrs., 5 courses; drama, 9 hrs., 3 courses, 60
grad. hrs., 22 courses
Degrees: BA, 100 majors, MA, 15 majors
Facilities: 3 radio C/L, TV C/L, carrier current
(KRSR), CCTV, VTR
Graduate assistantships: 2—average amount $2500
Av. no. hrs./wk. required: 20
Highest faculty degree: PhD
Contact: John P. Highlander, chairman

California State University at Fullerton
Fullerton, CA 92631
Tel. (213) 870-3517
Communications, 50 hrs., 17 courses (sem.); theatre,
15 hrs., 5 courses, 18 grad. hrs., 6 courses
Degrees: BA, 100 majors, MA, 35 majors
Facilities: radio C/L, TV C/L, CCTV, VTR, film
studio
Graduate assistantships: 3–5—average amount
$2400
Av. no. hrs./wk. required: 20
Highest faculty degree: PhD
Contact: George A. Mastroianni, chairman

California State University at Long Beach
Long Beach, CA 90840
Tel. (213) 498-5404
Radio–TV–film, 80 hrs., 30 courses (sem.)
Degrees: BA, 350 majors
Facilities: FM station (KSUL), 2 CCTV, film studio
Highest faculty degree: PhD
Contact: Robert G. Finney, chairman

California State University at Los Angeles
Los Angeles, CA 90032
Tel. (213) 224-3396
Speech, communications, and drama, 40 hrs., 10 courses (qr.); journalism, 8 hrs., 2 courses, 24 grad. hrs., 6 courses; other depts., 8 grad. hrs., 2 courses
Degrees: BA, 95 majors
Facilities: radio C/L, 2 TV C/L, CCTV, VTR
Highest faculty degree: PhD
Contact: Anthony Adams, chairman

California State University at Northridge
Northridge, CA 91324
Tel. (213) 885-3192
Radio–TV–film, 124 hrs., 44 courses (sem.), 91 grad. hrs., 30 courses
Degrees: BA, 450 majors, MA, 35 majors
Facilities: 2 radio C/L, TV C/L, FM station (KCSN), CCTV, VTR, film studio
Highest faculty degree: PhD
Contact: Bertram Barer, chairman

California State University at Sacramento
Sacramento, CA 95819
Tel. (916) 454-6285
Communications studies, 40 hrs., 14 courses (sem.), 6 grad. hrs., 2 courses
Degrees: BA, 75 majors
Facilities: 2 radio C/L, TV C/L, FM station (KERS), carrier current, CCTV, VTR
Highest faculty degree: MA
Contact: Roger L. Walters, chairman

San Diego State University
San Diego, CA 92115
Tel. (714) 286-6575
Telecommunications and film, 164 hrs., 53 courses (sem.), 45 grad. hrs., 15 courses
Degrees: BA, 244 majors, BS, 195 majors, MA, 41 majors
Facilities: 4 radio C/L, 3 TV C/L, FM station (KPBS), carrier current (KCR-AM), TV station (KPBS-TV), ETV, CCTV, VTR, film studios
Undergraduate scholarships: 3—average amount $500
Graduate fellowships/grants: 1—average amount $2500
Graduate assistantships: vary in numbers and amount
Av. no. hrs./wk. required: 8–12
Highest faculty degree: MA
Contact: Kenneth K. Jones, chairman

San Francisco State University
San Francisco, CA 94132
Tel. (415) 469-1787

Broadcast communication arts, 158 hrs., 57 courses (sem.), 52 grad. hrs., 14 courses
Degrees: BA, 400 majors, MA, 120 majors
Facilities: 6 radio C/L, 3 TV C/L, carrier current (KSFS), CCTV, VTR
Graduate assistantships: 3—average amount $1200 per sem.
Av. no. hrs./wk. required: 10
Highest faculty degree: PhD
Contact: Stuart Hyde, chairman

San Jose State University
San Jose, CA 95192
Tel. (408) 277-2763
Theatre arts, 57 hrs., 18 courses (sem.); journalism, 15 hrs., 5 courses, 44 grad. hrs., 14 courses; other depts., 15 grad. hrs., 5 courses
Degrees: BA, 200 majors, MA, 10 majors
Facilities: 2 radio C/L, 2 TV C/L, FM station (KSJS), CCTV, VTR, film studios
Highest faculty degree: PhD
Contact: Clarence E. Flick

Stanford University
Stanford, CA 94305
Tel. (415) 497-4904
Communications, 33 hrs., 13 courses (qr.), 29 grad. hrs., 12 courses
Degrees: BA, 70 majors, MA, 3 majors
Facilities: TV C/L, FM station (KZSU), CCTV, VTR, use commercial station (KPIX-TV), film studio
Graduate fellowships/grants: 5—average amount $3000
Graduate assistantships: 4—average amount $2700
Tuition remitted: 50% for half-time, 25% for quarter-time students
Av. no. hrs./wk. required: 20 hrs. for half-time, 10 hrs. for quarter-time students
Highest faculty degree: PhD
Contact: Henry Breitrose, chairman

University of California
Los Angeles, CA 90014
Tel. (213) 825-5761
Theatre arts, 112 hrs., 20 courses (qr.), 45 grad. hrs., 15 courses
Degrees: BA, 470 majors, MA, 350 majors, PhD, 50 majors
Facilities: radio C/L, 3 TV C/L, carrier current CCTV, VTR, film studios
Highest faculty degree: PhD
Contact: John W. Young, chairman

University of Southern California
Los Angeles, CA 90007
Tel. (213) 741-2311
Broadcasting, two degree options within the school of journalism: (a) broadcast journalism and broadcast general (management–advertising), BA-degree sequence; (b) broadcast journalism, MA-degree sequence. BA includes 32 units of broadcasting/journalism and 100 units of liberal-arts courses. MA includes 32 units of broadcasting with a core of 16 basic mass-

communications courses. Thesis or examination option. A pregraduate broadcasting–journalism program of 12 units is required before entry into graduate status.

Degrees: BA, 53 majors, MA, 7 majors

Facilities: TV studio, portapacks, radio studio and station (KSCR), RTV, editing terminals, CTV remote setup

Undergraduate scholarships: write or phone for information

Highest faculty degree: MS

Contact: Joseph Saltzman, chairman

COLORADO

Colorado State University
Fort Collins, CO 80523
Tel. (303) 491-6140

Speech & theatre arts, 42 hrs., 34 courses (sem.), plus internship; individual study and thesis, technical journalism, 27 hrs., 22 courses, 3 grad. hrs., 3 courses

Degrees: BA, 62 majors, MA, 11 majors

Facilities: 2 radio C/L, 2 TV C/L, FM station (KCSU), CCTV, VTR, use Denver radio & TV, film studio

Undergraduate scholarships: 5—average amount $200

Graduate assistantships: 17—average amount $2790, 1st year $2970, 2nd year

Tuition remitted: 100%; fees only paid by student

Highest faculty degree: PhD

Contact: Robert K. MacLauchlin, chairman

University of Colorado
Boulder, CO 80309
Tel. (303) 492-7306

Communications, 42 hrs., 14 courses (sem.), 27 grad. hrs., 9 courses; journalism, 6 hrs., 2 courses, 3 grad. hrs., 1 course

Degrees: BA, 150 majors, MA, 15 majors, PhD, 50 majors

Facilities: 2 radio C/L, 2 TV C/L, CCTV, VTR, film studio

Undergraduate scholarships: 1—average amount full tuition

Graduate assistantships: 2—average amount $3800

Tuition remitted: 100%

Av. no. hrs./wk. required: 20

Highest faculty degree: MS

Contact: Harold E. Hill, chairman

University of Denver
Denver, CO 80210
Tel. (303) 753-2166

Mass communications, 190 hrs., 114 courses (qr.), 126 grad. hrs., 48 courses

Degrees: BA, 250 majors, MA, 50 majors

Facilities: radio C/L, TV C/L, VTR

Undergraduate scholarships: 1—average amount $1000

Graduate assistantships: 6—average amount $800 per qr.

Tuition remitted: 10 hrs./qr.

Av. no. hrs./wk. required: 10

Highest faculty degree: PhD

Contact: Harold Mendelsohn, chairman

University of Southern Colorado
Pueblo, CO 81001
Tel. (303) 549-2818

Mass communications, 38 hrs., 14 courses (qr.)

Degrees: BA, BS, 200 majors

Facilities: radio C/L, TV C/L, FM station (KTSC), ETV station (KTSC-TV), CCTV

Contact: Donald Wayne

CONNECTICUT

University of Bridgeport
Bridgeport, CT 06602
Tel. (203) 576-4128

Journalism–communications, 28 hrs., 8 courses (sem.), 6 grad. hrs., 2 courses; other depts., 3 grad. hrs., 1 course

Degrees: BA, 15 majors, MA, 5 majors

Facilities: radio C/L, TV C/L, FM station (WPKN), carrier current, CCTV, VTR

Undergraduate scholarships: 5—average amount $750

Highest faculty degree: BA

Contact: Ted White, chairman

DELAWARE

University of Delaware
Newark, DE 19711
Tel. (302) 738-2777

Speech–communications, 24 hrs., 8 courses (sem.), 15 grad. hrs., 5 courses; English, 6 hrs., 2 courses; art, 6 hrs., 2 courses; education, 6 hrs., 2 courses; other depts., 6 grad. hrs., 2 courses

Degrees: BA, 40 majors, MA, 5 majors

Facilities: radio C/L, 2 TV C/L, carrier current (WDRB), CCTV, VTR

Graduate fellowships/grants: 2—average amount $3000

Graduate assistantships: 3—average amount $2800

Tuition remitted: 100%

Av. no. hrs./wk. required: 15

Highest faculty degree: PhD

Contact: Malthon M. Anapol, chairman

DISTRICT OF COLUMBIA

The American University
Washington, DC 20016
Tel. (202) 686-2055

Communications, 64 hrs., 21 courses (sem.), 48 grad. hrs., 16 courses

Degrees: BA, 98 majors, MA, 20 majors

Facilities: radio C/L, TV C/L, AM station (WAMU), FM station (WAMU), CCTV, VTR

Graduate assistantships: 3—average amount $2500

Teaching associates: average amount $4000 per year

Tuition remitted: 100%

Av. no. hrs./wk. required: 20

Highest faculty degree: PhD

Contact: Lincoln Furber, chairman

Howard University
Washington, DC 20059
Tel. (202) 636-7927

Broadcast productions, broadcast management, and film directing, 36 hrs., 12 courses (sem.)

Degrees: BA, 400 majors
Facilities: 2 TV C/L, carrier current (WHBC-AM), commercial FM station (WHUR), TV station (WHMM), film studio

FLORIDA

Florida State University
Tallahassee, FL 32306
Tel. (904) 644-5034
Mass communications, 90 hrs., 2 courses (qr.), 60 grad. hrs., 16 courses
Degrees: BS, 285 majors, MA, 17 majors, PhD, 25 majors
Facilities: 1 radio C/L, 1 TV C/L, FM station (WFSU), TV station (WFSU), CCTV, VTR
Undergraduate scholarships: 2—average amount $3000
Graduate fellowships: 1—average amount $5000
Graduate assistantships: 5—average amount $4265
Tuition remitted: varies
Av. no. hrs./wk. required: 20
Highest faculty degree: PhD
Contact: Tom W. Hoffer

Florida Technological University
Orlando, FL 32816
Tel. (305) 275-2681
Communications, 102 hrs., 28 courses (qr.), 36 grad. hrs., 9 courses; other depts., 12 grad. hrs., 4 courses
Degrees: BA, 125 majors, MA, 6 majors
Facilities: 5 radio C/L, 3 TV C/L, carrier current (WFTU), CCTV, VTR, 2 film studios
Graduate assistantships: 10—average amount $2400
Av. no. hrs./wk. required: 20
Highest faculty degree: PhD
Contact: Robert L. Arnold, chairman

University of Florida
Gainesville, FL 32611
Tel. (904) 392-0463
Broadcasting & film production, 45 hrs., 12 courses (qr.), 36 grad. hrs., 10 courses
Degrees: BA, 227 majors, MA, 9 majors
Facilities: 2 radio C/L, 2 TV C/L, AM station (WRUF), FM station (WRUF), TV station (WUFT), ETV, CCTV, VTR
Graduate assistantships: 3—average amount $2600
Av. no. hrs./wk. required: 10–15
Highest faculty degree: EdD
Contact: Kenneth A. Christiansen, chairman

University of Miami
Coral Gables, FL 33124
Tel. (305) 284-2265
Communications, 166 hrs., 30 courses (sem.)
Degrees: BA, BFA, 450 majors
Facilities: 2 radio C/L, 2 TV C/L, FM station (WVUM), CCTV, VTR, film studio
Highest faculty degree: PhD
Contact: Josephine A. Johnson, chairman

University of South Florida
Tampa, FL 33620
Tel. (813) 974-2591
Mass communications, 48 hrs., 12 courses (qr.)
Degrees: BA, 144 majors
Facilities: 2 radio C/L, TV C/L, TV station (WUSF-TV), ETV, CCTV, VTR, film studio
Highest faculty degree: PhD
Contact: Manny Lucoff, chairman

University of West Florida
Pensacola, FL 32504
Tel. (904) 476-9500
Communication arts, 75 hrs., 15 courses (qr.)
Degrees: BA, 160 majors, MA, 30 majors
Facilities: 2 radio C/L, 2 TV C/L, CCTV, kinescope, VTR
Highest faculty degree: PhD
Contact: Churchill L. Roberts, chairman

GEORGIA

Clark College
Atlanta, GA 30314
Tel. (404) 681-3080
Mass communications, 88 hrs., 20 courses (sem.)
Degrees: BA, 485 majors total from the Atlanta University Center undergraduate schools
Facilities: radio C/L, TV C/L, FM station (WCLK), VTR
Undergraduate scholarships: 10—average amount $500
Highest faculty degree: PhD
Contact: Gloria P. Walker, director

University of Georgia
Athens, GA 30602
Tel. (404) 542-3785
Radio–TV–film, 90 hrs., 18 courses (qr.), 50 grad. hrs., 10 courses; journalism, 10 hrs., 2 courses
Degrees: BA, 237 majors, MA, 25 majors
Facilities: 5 radio C/L, 3 TV C/L, FM station (WUOG), TV station (WGTV), CCTV, film studio, portable TV equipment
Graduate assistantships: 8—average amount $2000
Av. no. hrs./wk. required: 15
Highest faculty degree: PhD
Contact: Worth McDoughald, chairman

HAWAII

University of Hawaii
Honolulu, HI 96822
Tel. (808) 955-7878
Communications, 33 hrs., 11 courses (sem.); education communications, 6 hrs., courses; other depts., 6 grad. hrs., 2 courses
Degrees: BA, 31 majors
Facilities: radio C/L, TV C/L, FM station (KTUH), TV station (KHET), ETV, CCTV, VTR
Graduate fellowships/grants: 15—average amount $4000
Graduate assistantships: 6—average amount $3708
Tuition remitted: 100%
Av. no. hrs./wk. required: 20
Highest faculty degree: PhD
Contact: R. L. Rider, chairman

IDAHO

Idaho State University
Pocatello, ID 83201
Tel. (208) 236-2857
Journalism, 8 hrs., 3 courses (sem.)
Degrees: BA, 12 majors
Facilities: radio C/L, TV C/L, FM station (KBGL), carrier current, TV station (KBGL), ETV, CCTV, VTR, film studios
Undergraduate scholarships: 2—average amount $250
Highest faculty degree: MA
Contact: William J. Ryan, chairman

University of Idaho
Moscow, ID 83843
Tel. (208) 885-6458
Radio–TV, 56 hrs., 25 courses (sem.)
Degrees: BA, BS, 60 majors
Facilities: 2 radio C/L, TV C/L, FM station (KUID), TV station (KUID), ETV, CCTV, 4 VTR
Undergraduate scholarships: 3—average amount $50
Highest faculty degree: MA
Contact: Peter Haggart, chairman

ILLINOIS

Eastern Illinois University
Charleston, IL 61920
Tel. (217) 581-2016
Speech–communications, 27 hrs., 9 courses (sem.); journalism, 3 hrs., 1 course; instructional media, 12 hrs., 4 courses, 3 grad. hrs., 1 course; other depts., 6 grad. hrs., 2 courses
Degrees: BA, 50 majors
Facilities: 2 radio C/L, 3 TV C/L, carrier current (WELH), VTR, film studios
Graduate assistantships: 1—average amount $2400
Tuition remitted: yes
Av. no. hrs./wk. required: 12
Highest faculty degree: PhD
Contact: Jack C. Rang, director

Illinois State University
Normal, IL 61761
Tel. (309) 438-3671
Information sciences, 68 hrs., 23 courses (sem.), 27 grad. hrs., 9 courses
Degrees: BS, BA, 214 majors
Facilities: radio C/L, 2 TV C/L, FM station (WGLT), carrier current (WILN), CCTV, VTR
Graduate assistantships: 4—average amount $280 per mo.
Tuition remitted: 100%
Av. no. hrs./wk. required: 15
Highest faculty degree: PhD
Contact: Suraj Kapoor, chairman

Northern Illinois University
DeKalb, IL 60115
Tel. (815) 753-1563
Speech–communications, 69 hrs., 23 courses (sem.), 40 grad. hrs., 14 courses
Degrees: BA, 150 majors, MA, 25 majors
Facilities: 3 radio C/L, 3 TV C/L, FM station (WNIU), carrier current, CCTV, VTR, film studios
Undergraduate scholarships: 5
Av. no. hrs./wk. required: 10
Graduate assistantships: 6
Monthly stipend plus tuition remitted: 100%
Av. no. hrs./wk. required: 20
Highest faculty degree: PhD
Contact: Jon T. Powell, chairman

Northwestern University
Evanston, IL 60201
Tel. (312) 492-7315 (radio–TV–film)
             492-3741 (journalism)
Radio–TV–film, 36 units, 32 courses (qr.), 25 grad. units, 25 courses; journalism (news–editorial), 15 units, 5 courses (qr.), 9 grad. units, 3 courses
Degrees: BA, 215 majors, MA, 28 majors, PhD, 16 majors
Degrees: BA, 40 majors, MA, 30 majors
Facilities: 5 radio C/L, 3 TV C/L, FM station (WNUR), CCTV, VTR, film studio
Graduate fellowships: 2—average amount $2400 (radio –TV–film)
Graduate assistantships: 7—average amount $2400 (radio–TV–film)
Tuition remitted: 100%
Av. no. hrs./wk. required: 12
Graduate assistantships: 12—average amount $1700 (journalism)
Tuition remitted: 100%
Av. no. hrs./wk. required: 5
Highest faculty degree: PhD
Contact: Dr. Elizabeth Yamashita, chairman

Southern Illinois University at Carbondale
Carbondale, IL 62901
Tel. (618) 453-4343
Radio–TV, 160 hrs., 49 courses (sem.), 59 grad. hrs., 26 courses
Degrees: BS, 650 majors, MA, 23 majors
Facilities: 4 radio C/L, 2 TV C/L, FM station (WSIU), carrier current (WIDB), TV station (WSIU-TV), ETV, CCTV, film studio
Graduate assistantships: 12—average amount $3150
Tuition remitted: yes
Av. no. hrs./wk. required: 20
Highest faculty degree: PhD
Contact: Charles T. Lynch, chairman

Southern Illinois University at Edwardsville
Edwardsville, IL 62025
Tel. (618) 692-2230
Mass communications, 112 hrs., 26 courses (qr.), 82 grad. hrs., 16 courses
Degrees: BA, 204 majors, MA, 25 majors
Facilities: 2 radio C/L, TV C/L, FM station (WSIE), CCTV, VTR
Highest faculty degree: PhD
Contact: John A. Regnell, chairman

University of Illinois at Chicago Circle
Chicago, IL 60608
Tel. (312) 966-3187

Speech & theatre, 53 hrs., 12 courses (qr.), 24 grad. hrs., 7 courses
Degrees: BA, 175 majors, MA, 16 majors
Facilities: radio C/L, TV C/L, FM station (WCIU), CCTV, VTR
Graduate assistantships: 2—average amount $2000
Tuition remitted: 100%
Av. no. hrs./wk. required: 20
Highest faculty degree: PhD
Contact: R. V. Harnack, chairman

University of Illinois at Urbana
Urbana, IL 61801
Tel. (217) 333-2350
The department has suspended admission to its radio–TV curriculums until it has completed long-range plans for future broadcasting instruction. Meanwhile, however, it offers courses for non-majors.
Facilities: radio C/L, 2 TV C/L, TV station (WILL-TV), ETV, VTR, film facilities
Highest faculty degree: PhD
Contact: Theodore Peterson, dean

Western Illinois University
Macomb, IL 61455
Tel. (309) 298-1507
Communication arts & sciences, 84 hrs., 21 courses (qr.); learning resources, 20 hrs., 6 courses, 40 grad. hrs., 10 courses
Degrees: BA, 200 majors, MA, 3 majors
Facilities: 2 radio C/L, TV C/L, FM station (WIUM), CCTV, VTR, CATV
Undergraduate scholarships: 1—average amount $100
Graduate assistantships: 2—average amount $2610
Tuition remitted: 100%
Av. no. hrs./wk. required: 14
Highest faculty degree: PhD
Contact: William L. Cathcart, chairman

Wheaton College
Wheaton, IL 60187
Tel. (312) 682-5093
Speech communications, 20 hrs., 5 courses (qr.)
Degrees: BA, 39 majors
Facilities: 2 radio C/L, TV C/L, FM station (WETN), CCTV, VTR
Undergraduate scholarships: average amount $300 per qr.
Highest faculty degree: MA
Contact: Stuart Johnson, chairman

INDIANA

Ball State University
Muncie, IN 47306
Tel. (317) 285-4771
Radio & TV, 164 hrs., 43 courses (qr.)
Degrees: BA, MA
Facilities: 4 radio C/L, 2 TV C/L, FM station (WBST), TV station (WIPB), CCTV, VTR, film studio
Undergraduate scholarships: 1—average amount $3000
Graduate assistantships: 1—average amount $2700

Tuition remitted: yes
Av. no. hrs./wk. required: ½ time
Highest faculty degree: PhD
Contact: William H. Tomlinson, chairman

Butler University
Indianapolis, IN 46208
Tel. (317) 283-9241
Radio & TV, 85 hrs., 30 courses (sem.), 36 grad. hrs., 13 courses
Degrees: BA, 45 majors, MA, 20 majors
Facilities: 2 radio C/L, TV C/L, FM station (WAJC), VTR
Undergraduate scholarships: 2—average amount $1850
Highest faculty degree: MA
Contact: James R. Phillippe, chairman

Indiana State University
Terre Haute, IN 47809
Tel. (812) 232-6311
Speech, 78 hrs., 26 courses (sem.), 33 grad. hrs., 11 courses
Degrees: BA, 120 majors, MA, 12 majors
Facilities: 6 radio C/L, 2 TV C/L, FM station (WISU), VTR, 3 film studios
Undergraduate scholarships: 10—average amount $350 per year
Graduate assistantships: 3—average amount $2000 per year
Tuition remitted: yes
Av. no. hrs./wk. required: 20
Highest faculty degree: PhD
Contact: Joe T. Duncan, chairman

Indiana University
Bloomington, IN 47401
Tel. (812) 337-6895
Telecommunications, 105 hrs., 34 courses (sem.), 60 grad. hrs., 19 courses; journalism, 18 hrs., 6 courses; business, 3 hrs., 1 course, education, 15 hrs., 5 courses, 21 grad. hrs., 7 courses
Degrees: BA, 214 majors, MA, 36 majors, PhD, 14 majors
Facilities: 3 radio C/L, 2 TV C/L, FM station (WFIU), carrier current (WIUS), ETV station (WTIU), CCTV, VTR
Undergraduate scholarships: 3—average amount $250
Graduate fellowships: 1—average amount $2500
Graduate assistantships: 10—average amount $2700
Tuition remitted: amount varies
Av. no. hrs./wk. required: 7–20
Highest faculty degree: PhD
Contact: Charles Sherman, chairman

Purdue University
W. Lafayette, IN 47907
Tel. (317) 745-6292
Communication, 54 hrs., 18 courses (sem.), 24 grad. hrs., 8 courses
Degrees: BA, 110 majors, MA, 15 majors
Facilities: radio C/L, TV C/L, AM station (WBAA), CCTV, VTR, film studios

Graduate assistantships: 5—average amount $3000
Tuition remitted: yes
Av. no. hrs./wk. required: 20
Highest faculty degree: PhD
Contact: W. K. Schwienher, chairman

University of Evansville
Evansville, IN 47702
Tel. (812) 479-2165
Communications, 50 hrs., 13 courses (qr.)
Degrees: BA, 80 majors
Facilities: radio C/L, 2 TV C/L, FM station (WEVC), TV station (WNIN), ETV, VTR, film studio
Highest faculty degree: MFA
Contact: Robert Field, chairman

IOWA

Drake University
Des Moines, IA 50311
Tel. (515) 271-3123
Radio–TV, 24 hrs., 9 courses (sem.); broadcast news, 24 hrs., 9 courses (sem.), journalism, 8 hrs., 3 courses
Degrees: BA, 132 majors
Facilities: radio C/L, TV C/L, CCTV, VTR, 3 radio studios being built, use KCCI-TV
Highest faculty degree: MS
Contact: James S. Duncan, chairman

Iowa State University of Science & Technology
Ames, IA 50010
Tel. (515) 294-5000
Telecommunicative arts, 77 hrs., 22 courses (qr.); journalism & mass communications, 30 hrs., 9 courses; English, 3 hrs., 1 course; education, 9 hrs., 3 courses; engineering, 3 hrs., 1 course; psychology, 3 hrs., 1 course, 24 grad. hrs., 6 courses; other depts., 18 grad. hrs., 6 courses
Degrees: BA, 80 majors, MA, 6 majors
Facilities: 2 radio C/L, TV C/L, AM station (WOI), FM station (WOI-FM), carrier current (KPGY), TV station (WOI), CCTV, VTR, film studios
Highest faculty degree: PhD
Contact: George P. Wilson, Jr., chairman

University of Iowa
Iowa City, IA 52242
Tel. (319) 353-5667
Div. of broadcasting & film, 138 hrs., 45 courses (sem.), 132 grad. hrs., 43 courses; journalism, 26 hrs., 8 courses, 26 grad. hrs., 8 courses
Degrees: BA, 140 majors, MA, 30 majors, PhD, 13 majors
Facilities: 2 radio C/L, 1 TV C/L, AM station (WSUI), FM station (KSUI-FM), carrier current (KICR), VTR, film studio
Graduate assistantships: 20—average amount $5100
Tuition remitted: out-of-state residents pay tuition
Av. no. hrs./wk. required: 20
Highest faculty degree: PhD
Contact: Robert Pepper, chairman

University of Northern Iowa
Cedar Falls, IA 50613

Tel. (319) 273-6209
Speech–radio–TV, 31 hrs., 10 courses (sem.); speech, 10 courses; journalism, 2 courses
Degrees: BA, 45 majors
Facilities: radio C/L, 3 TV C/L, carrier current (KCRS), CCTV, VTR
Highest faculty degree: MA
Contact: Charles B. Scholz, chairman

KANSAS

Fort Hays State University
Hays, KS 67601
Tel. (913) 628-5373
Radio–TV, 51 hrs., 10 courses (sem.); speech, 10 hrs., 3 courses, 32 grad. hrs., 9 courses
Degrees: BA, 35 majors
Facilities: 3 radio C/L, 4 TV C/L, carrier current (KFHS), CCTV, VTR, use commercial facilities
Highest faculty degree: MA
Contact: Jack R. Heather, chairman

Kansas State University
Manhattan, KS 66506
Tel. (913) 532-6890
Journalism & mass communications, 95 hrs., 34 courses (sem.), 66 grad. hrs., 22 courses
Degrees: BA, 71 majors, MA, 5 majors
Facilities: radio C/L, TV C/L, FM station (KSDB), CCTV, VTR
Undergraduate scholarships: 3—average amount $500
Graduate assistantships: 1—average amount $3200
Tuition remitted: out-of-state portion
Av. no. hrs./wk. required: 20
Highest faculty degree: PhD
Contact: Walter Bunge, chairman

University of Kansas
Lawrence, KS 66045
Tel. (913) 864-3991
Radio–TV–film, 128 hrs., 51 courses (sem.), 91 grad. hrs., 16 courses
Degrees: BA, 220 majors, MA, 26 majors
Facilities: 3 radio C/L, 2 TV C/L, AM station (KFKU), FM stations (KANU, KJHK), CCTV, VTR, film studio
Graduate assistantships: 6—average amount $3200
Tuition remitted: fees for out-of-state students
Av. no. hrs./wk. required: 20
Highest faculty degree: PhD
Contact: Bruce A. Linton, chairman

Washburn University
Topeka, KS 66621
Tel. (913) 239-6500
Communication arts, 54 hrs. (sem.); business, 6 hrs., 12 grad. hrs., 4 courses
Degrees: BA, 70 majors
Facilities: radio C/L, 2 TV C/L, TV station (KTWU), ETV, CCTV, VTR
Undergraduate scholarships: 2—average amount $150
Highest faculty degree: EdD
Contact: Dale N. Anderson, chairman

Wichita State University
Wichita, KS 67208
Tel. (316) 689-3390
Speech, 55 hrs., 19 courses (sem.); journalism, 6 hrs.,
2 courses, 21 grad. hrs., 7 courses
Degrees: BA, 75 majors, MA, 25 majors
Undergraduate scholarships: 2—average amount
$250
Highest faculty degree: PhD
Contact: Frank L. Kelly, chairman

KENTUCKY

Eastern Kentucky University
Richmond, KY 40475
Tel. (606) 622-3435
Mass communications, 64 hrs., 23 courses (sem.), 3
grad. hrs., 11 courses
Degrees: BA broadcasting, 163 majors, BA jour-
nalism, and BA public relations
Facilities: 3 radio C/L, 2 TV C/L, 1 F C/L, FM station
(WEKU), CCTV, VTR
Highest faculty degree: MA
Contact: James S. Harris, chairman

Murray State University
Murray, KY 42071
Tel. (502) 762-6191
Communications, 51 hrs., 17 courses (sem.), 33 grad.
hrs., 11 courses
Degrees: BA, 107 majors, MA, 4 majors
Facilities: 4 radio C/L, 3 TV C/L, FM station
(WKMS), TV station (WKMU), ETV, CCTV,
VTR, CATV, film studios
Undergraduate scholarships: 8—average amount
$800
Graduate assistantships: 2—average amount $1800
Tuition remitted: out-of-state portion
Av. no. hrs./wk. required: 10–20
Highest faculty degree: PhD
Contact: Robert McGaughey, chairman

University of Kentucky
Lexington, KY 40506
Tel. (606) 257-2911
Telecommunications, 45 hrs., 18 courses (sem.)
Degrees: BA, 80 majors, MA, 5 majors
Facilities: radio C/L, 3 TV C/L, FM station
(WBKY), CCTV, VTR, film studio
Graduate fellowships: 2—average amount $3000
Graduate assistantships: 3—average amount $2500
Av. no. hrs./wk. required: 20
Highest faculty degree: PhD
Contact: G. Norman VanTubergen, chairman

Western Kentucky University
Bowling Green, KY 42101
Tel. (502) 745-4143
Mass communications, 57 hrs., 19 courses (sem.)
Degrees: BA, 100 majors
Broadcasting, 60 hrs., 20 courses (sem.)
Degrees: BA, 400 majors
Film, 30 hrs., 10 courses (minor)
Facilities: 2 radio C/L, TV C/L, CCTV, VTR, use
educational and commercial radio, film studios

Undergraduate scholarships: 4—average amount
$100
Highest faculty degree: EdD
Contact: Randall Capps, chairman

LOUISIANA

Grambling State University
Grambling, LA 71245
Tel. (318) 247-6941
Speech & drama, 9 hrs., 3 courses (sem.); audio-
visual, 6 hrs.
Degrees: BA, 6 majors
Facilities: 2 radio C/L, TV C/L, FM station
(KGRM), CCTV, VTR, film studio
Highest faculty degree: MA
Contact: Allen Williams, chairman

Louisiana State University
Baton Rouge, LA 70803
Tel. (504) 388-4172
Speech, 24 hrs., 8 courses (sem.), 18 grad. hrs., 6
courses; journalism, 6 hrs., 2 courses, 6 grad.
hrs., 2 courses
Degrees: BA, 15 majors, MA, 1 major, PhD, 1 major
Facilities: radio C/L, TV C/L, carrier current
(WLSU), CCTV, VTR
Highest faculty degree: PhD
Contact: John H. Pennybacker, chairman

Loyola University
New Orleans, LA 70118
Tel. (504) 865-3430
Communications (broadcasting, film, & journalism),
35 hrs. (sem.)
Degrees: BA, 325 majors
Facilities: 2 radio-production rooms, 5 audio
recording booths, 2 TV studios, projection
facilities, engineering shop, owns and operates
TV station WWL-AM/FM
Highest faculty degree: PhD
Contact: William M. Hammel, chairman

Northeast Louisiana University
Monroe, LA 71201
Tel. (318) 342-4007
Speech, 42 hrs., 14 courses (sem.); journalism, 18
hrs., 6 courses; management, 12 hrs., 4 courses;
marketing, 12 hrs., 4 courses; 9 grad. hrs., 3
courses; other depts., 9 hrs., 3 courses
Degrees: BA, 22 majors
Facilities: 2 radio C/L, 2 TV C/L, FM station
(KNLU), TV station, ETV, CCTV, VTR, film
studios
Undergraduate scholarships: 5—average amount
$400
Graduate fellowships/grants: 7—average amount
$2400
Tuition remitted: yes
Av. no. hrs./wk. required: 15
Highest faculty degree: PhD
Contact: V. Jackson Smith, chairman

University of Southwestern Louisiana
Lafayette, LA 70501
Tel. (318) 233-3850

Speech, 59 hrs., 21 courses (sem.), 19 grad. hrs., 7 courses
Degrees: BA, 50 majors, MA, 6 majors
Facilities: 2 radio C/L, TV C/L, FM station (KRVS), TV station (WBJ), ETV, CCTV, VTR
Graduate assistantships: 4—average amount $2000
Tuition required: 100%
Av. no. hrs./wk. required: 20
Highest faculty degree: MA
Contact: Bernard C. Crocker

MAINE

University of Maine at Orono
Orono, ME 04473
Tel. (207) 581-7624
Performing arts, broadcasting, film, 45 hrs., 14 courses (sem.); journalism, 9 hrs., 3 courses, 30 grad. hrs., 10 courses
Degrees: BA, 60 majors
Facilities: 3 radio C/L, TV C/L, FM station (WMEB), TV station (WMEB-TV), ETV, CCTV, VTR, film studios
Highest faculty degree: PhD
Contact: Saul N. Scher, chairman

MARYLAND

Towson State College
Baltimore, MD 21204
Tel. (301) 823-7500
Communication arts & sciences, 21 hrs., 5 courses (sem.), 15 grad. hrs., 3 courses; other depts., 15 grad. hrs., 3 courses
Degrees: BA, 150 majors
Facilities: 2 radio C/L, TV C/L, FM station (WCVT), carrier current (WCVT), CCTV, VTR
Highest faculty degree: MA
Contact: John MacKerron, chairman

University of Maryland
College Park, MD 20742
Tel. (301) 454-2541
Speech & dramatic art, 108 hrs., 36 courses (sem.); journalism, 18 hrs., 6 courses; educational technology, 9 courses, 66 grad. hrs., 22 courses; other depts., 9 grad. hrs., 3 courses
Degrees: 263 majors, MA, 30 majors
Facilities: 2 F/SL, 2 TV C/L, AM station (WMUC), carrier current, CCTV, VTR, film studios
Undergraduate scholarships: 15—average amount $3000
Tuition remitted: 100%
Av. no. hrs./wk. required: 20
Highest faculty degree: PhD
Contact: Donald H. Kirkley, director of graduate studies

MASSACHUSETTS

Boston University
Boston, MA 02215
Tel. (617) 353-3483
Broadcasting & film, 64 hrs., 16 courses (sem.); journalism, 12 hrs., 3 courses; research, 4 hrs., 1 course, 40 grad. hrs., 10 courses

Degrees: BA, 224 majors, MA, 50 majors
Facilities: 2 radio C/L, 2 TV C/L, FM station (WBUR), carrier current (WTBU), CCTV, VTR, 2 film studios
Graduate fellowships/grants: 2—average amount $1000
Graduate assistantships: 10—average amount $500
Tuition remitted: varies
Av. no. hrs./wk. required: 10
Highest faculty degree: PhD
Contact: Robert R. Smith, chairman

Emerson College
Boston, MA 02116
Tel. (617) 262-2010
Mass communications, 90 hrs., 30 courses (sem.), 48 grad. hrs., 16 courses
Degrees: BA, 116 majors, MA, 32 majors
Facilities: 7 radio C/L, 10 TV C/L, FM station (WERS), carrier current (WECB), CCTV, VTR, 3 film studios
Highest faculty degree: MEd
Contact: Charles Phillips, chairman

University of Massachusetts
Amherst, MA 01002
Tel. (413) 545-2260
Communications studies, 54 hrs., 18 courses (sem.), 16 grad. courses; education, 14 hrs., 6 courses; business, 9 hrs., 3 courses; journalism, 24 hrs., 6 courses
Degrees: BA, 250 majors, MA, 20 majors, PhD, 10 majors
Facilities: radio C/L, TV C/L, FM stations (KMUA, WFCR), CCTV, VTR, film studio
Graduate assistantships: 15—average amount $3800
Tuition remitted: non-resident fees
Av. no. hrs./wk. required: 20
Highest faculty degree: PhD
Contact: Kenneth L. Brown, chairman

MICHIGAN

Central Michigan University
Mt. Pleasant, MI 48859
Tel. (517) 774-3852
Broadcast & cinematic arts, 108 hrs., 28 courses (sem.); journalism, 3 hrs., 1 course; physics, 7 hrs., 2 courses, 66 grad. hrs., 17 courses; other depts., 4 grad. hrs., 1 course
Degrees: BA, 380 majors, MA, 14 majors
Facilities: 2 radio C/L, TV C/L, FM station (WMHW), TV station (WCMU-TV), ETV, CCTV, VTR, film studio
Undergraduate scholarships: 20—average amount $300
Graduate assistantships: 1–2—average amount $3250
Tuition remitted: out-of-state
Av. no. hrs./wk. required: 12
Highest faculty degree: PhD
Contact: Peter B. Orlik, chairman

Eastern Michigan University
Ypsilanti, MI 48197
Tel. (313) 487-3030
Speech & dramatic arts, 60 hrs., 28 courses (sem.);
education, 8 hrs., 4 courses, 41 grad. hrs., 16
courses; other depts., 8 grad. hrs., 4 courses
Degrees: BA, 140 majors
Facilities: 2 radio C/L, 2 TV C/L, FM station
(WEMU), carrier current (WQBR), CCTV, VTR
Undergraduate scholarships: 11—average amount
$250 per sem.
Highest faculty degree: MA
Contact: William V. Swisher, chairman

Michigan State University
East Lansing, MI 48824
Tel. (517) 355-8372
Telecommunications, 126 hrs., 32 courses (qr.), 76
grad. hrs., 19 courses; journalism, 8 hrs., 2
courses; theatre, 8 hrs., 2 courses; advertising, 7
hrs., 2 courses; communications, 8 hrs., 2
courses, 20 grad. hrs., 5 courses
Degrees: BA, 257 majors, MA 27 majors, PhD, 16
majors
Facilities: 3 radio C/L, 2 TV C/L, AM station
(WKAR), FM station (WKAR-FM), carrier cur-
rent ETV station (WKAR-TV), CCTV, VTR,
film studios
Graduate fellowships: 2—average amount $500
Graduate assistantships: 8—average amount $4200
Av. no. hrs./wk. required: 20
Highest faculty degree: PhD
Contact: Robert Schlater, chairman

Northern Michigan University
Marquette, MI 49855
Tel. (906) 227-2180
Speech, 25 hrs., 6 courses (sem.); English, 8 hrs., 2
courses, 8 grad. hrs., 2 courses
Degrees: BA, 20 majors
Facilities: radio C/L, 2 TV C/L, FM station
(WNMU-FM), carrier current (WBKX), TV sta-
tion (WNPU), ETV, CCTV, VTR
Highest faculty degree: PhD
Contact: William Buccalo, chairman

University of Detroit
Detroit, MI 48221
Tel. (313) 927-1173
*Communication studies (includes broadcast media,
journalism, public relations, speech communications,
and advertising),* 116 hrs., 36 courses, (sem.)
Degrees: BA, 200 majors
Facilities: radio C/L, 2 TV C/L, carrier current,
CCTV, VTR
Undergraduate scholarships: available through uni-
versity and department programs. Amount varies
with program.
Highest faculty degree: PhD
Contact: Charles Dause, chairman

University of Michigan
Ann Arbor, MI 48109
Tel. (313) 764-5350
Speech, communications, theatre, 71 hrs., 26 courses

(sem.), 66 grad. hrs., 24 courses; journalism, 46
hrs., 14 courses, 46 grad. hrs., 14 courses
Degrees: BA, 100 majors, MA, 40 majors, PhD, 21
majors, EdD, 1 major
Facilities: 2 radio C/L, 2 TV C/L, FM station
(WUOM), carrier current (WCBN), CCTV,
VTR, film studios
Undergraduate scholarships: 6—average amount
$400
Graduate fellowships: 6—average amount $3000
Graduate assistantships: 15—average amount
$2000
Tuition remitted: out-of-state fees
Highest faculty degree: MA
Contact: Garnet Garrison, chairman

Wayne State University
Detroit, MI 48202
Tel. (313) 577-4163
Radio, TV, & film, 132 hrs., 37 courses (qr.), 87
grad. hrs., 26 courses; journalism, 8 hrs., 2
courses; art, 4 hrs., 1 course, 4 grad. hrs., 1 course
Degrees: BA, 150 majors, MA, 45 majors, PhD, 10
Facilities: radio C/L, 2 TV C/L, FM station (WDET),
carrier-current station (WAYN), CCTV, VTR
Undergraduate scholarships: 1—average amount
$500
Graduate fellowships: 2—average amount $3200
Graduate assistantships: 6—average amount $3500
Tuition remitted: 50%
Av. no. hrs./wk. required: 20
Highest faculty degree: PhD
Contact: John Spalding, chairman

Western Michigan University
Kalamazoo, MI 49008
Tel. (616) 383-4071
Communication arts & sciences, 59 hrs., 22 courses
(sem.), 30 grad. hrs., 10 courses
Degrees: BA, 375 majors
Facilities: 2 radio C/L, 2 TV C/L, FM station
(WMUK), carrier current (WIDR), CCTV,
VTR, film studios
Highest faculty degree: MS
Contact: Jules Rossman, chairman

MINNESOTA

Bemidji State College
Bemidji, MN 55601
Tel. (218) 755-2985
Communications, 48 hrs., 16 courses
Degrees: BA, 20 majors
Facilities: 2 radio C/L, TV C/L, FM station (KBSB),
carrier current, VTR, film studio
Highest faculty degree: MS
Contact: Robert K. Smith, chairman

University of Minnesota
Duluth, MN 55812
Tel. (218) 726-8229
Speech–communications, 38 hrs., 11 courses (qr.)
Degrees: BA, 29 majors

Facilities: 2 radio C/L, 2 TV C/L, FM station (WDTH), CCTV, VTR, film studios
Highest faculty degree: PhD
Contact: Jerry K. Frye, chairman

University of Minnesota
Minneapolis, MN 55455
Tel. (615) 373-2617
Speech–communications, 86 hrs., 22 courses (qr.), 56 grad. hrs., 15 courses
Degrees: BA, 70 majors, MA, 18 majors, PhD, 4 majors
Journalism–mass communications, 40 hrs., 9 courses, 22 grad. hrs., 5 courses
Degrees: BA, 60 majors, MA, 15 majors
Facilities: 6 radio C/L, 4 TV C/L, FM station (KUOM), carrier current (WMMR), CCTV, VTR, film studios
Undergraduate scholarships: 3—average amount $800 (speech–communications)
Graduate fellowships: 1—average amount $1800 (speech–communications)
Graduate assistantships: 4—average amount $5250 (speech–communications)
Tuition remitted: out-of-state tuition
Graduate assistantships: 5—average amount $3500 (journalism)
Tuition remitted: out-of-state tuition
Av. no. hrs./wk. required: 20
Highest faculty degree: PhD
Contact: Leonard Bart, chairman

MISSISSIPPI

Mississippi State University
Mississippi State, MS 39762
Tel. (601) 325-4908
Communications, 51 hrs., 21 courses (sem.), 18 grad. hrs., 6 courses
Degrees: BA, 180 majors
Facilities: radio C/L, TV C/L, FM station (WMSB), VTR, local cable outlet with color studio
Undergraduate scholarships: 1—average amount $200
Highest faculty degree: PhD
Contact: Robert G. Anderson, chairman

University of Mississippi
University, MS 38667
Tel. (601) 232-7305
Speech–theatre (R/TV div.), 69 hrs., 31 courses (sem.), 51 grad. hrs., 17 courses
Degrees: BA, 200 majors, MA, 20 majors, PhD, 6 majors
Facilities: 2 radio C/L, 3 TV C/L, carrier-current FM and AM cable station (WCBH), VTR, CCTV
Highest faculty degree: PhD
Contact: Richard B. Hayes, chairman

University of Southern Mississippi
Hattiesburg, MS 39401
Tel. (601) 266-7198
Communications, 64 hrs., 16 courses (qr.), 16 grad. hrs., 4 courses; journalism, 16 hrs., 4 courses, 6 grad. hrs.
Degrees: BA, 97 majors, MA, 5 majors, PhD, 19 majors

Facilities: 2 radio C/L, TV C/L, carrier current (WMSU), VTR, film studio
Contact: James Hall, chairman

MISSOURI

Central Missouri State University
Warrensburg, MO 64093
Tel. (816) 429-4841
Mass communications, 73 hrs., 28 courses (sem.), 15 grad. hrs., 5 courses
Degrees: BA, 150 majors, MA, 20 majors
Facilities: 4 radio C/L, 2 TV C/L, FM station (KCMW), TV station (KMDS-TV), CCTV, VTR, film studios
Graduate assistantships: 4—average amount $2100 per 9 mos.
Av. no. hrs./wk. required: 12
Highest faculty degree: PhD
Contact: David Eshelman, chairman

The Lindenwood Colleges
St. Charles, MO 63301
Tel. (314) 723-7152
Communication arts, 70 hrs., 17 courses (sem.)
Degrees: BA, 58 majors
Facilities: 2 radio C/L, TV C/L, AM station & FM station (KCLC), carrier current (KCLC), CCTV, VTR, film studio
Undergraduate scholarships: 20—average amount $750
Highest faculty degree: MA
Contact: Eugene Uram, chairman

Park College
Suburban Kansas City, MO 64152
Tel. (816) 741-2000
Communication arts, 69 hrs., 19 courses (sem.); physics, 6 hrs., 3 courses
Degrees: BA, 50 majors
Facilities: 2 radio C/L, FM station (KGSP), CCTV, VTR
Undergraduate assistantships: available
Highest faculty degree: MA
Contact: Lowell A. Connor, chairman

St. Louis University
St. Louis, MO 63101
Tel. (314) 535-3300
Communications & theatre, 30 hrs., 9 courses (sem.), 21 grad. hrs., 7 courses,
Degrees: BA, 15 majors, MA, 1 major
Facilities: radio C/L, TV C/L, VTR
Highest faculty degree: MA
Contact: Charles Paterson, chairman

Stephens College
Columbia, MO 65201
Tel. (314) 442-2211
TV–radio–film, 90 hrs., 30 courses
Degrees: BA, 45 majors
Facilities: 2 radio C/L, 2 TV C/L, FM station (KWWC), TV station (KWWC-TV), CCTV, kinescope VTR, film studio
Undergraduate assistantships: 6—average amount $500

Undergraduate scholarships: 2
Highest faculty degree: MEd
Contact: Sara Ann Fay, chairman

University of Missouri
Columbia, MO 65201
Tel. (314) 882-3046 (speech)
            882-4865 (journalism)
Speech & dramatic arts, 54 hrs., 17 courses (sem.), 47 grad. hrs., 14 courses
Degrees: BA, 100 majors, MA, 12 majors, PhD, 4 majors
Broadcast journalism, 27 hrs., 10 courses, 23 grad. hrs., 8 courses
Degrees: BA, 149 majors, MA, 21 majors, PhD, 1 major
Facilities: 3 radio C/L, 3 TV C/L, FM station (KBIA), carrier current (KCCS), commercial TV station (KOMU-TV), CCTV, VTR, film studio
Graduate assistantships: 2—average amount $3200 (speech)
Tuition remitted: 100%
Graduate assistantships: 1—average amount $2800 (journalism)
Tuition remitted: 100%
Av. no. hrs./wk. required: 20
Highest faculty degree: PhD
Contact: Joseph G. Wolfe, chairman

University of Missouri
Kansas City, MO 64110
Tel. (816) 276-1185
Communication studies, 90 hrs., 30 courses (sem.); English (journalism), 18 hrs., 6 courses; history, 3 hrs., 1 course; art, 3 hrs., 1 course
Degrees: BA, 150 majors, MA, 25 majors
Facilities: 2 radio C/L, TV C/L, FM station (KCUR), VTR, TV remote van, film studios
Graduate assistantships: 2—average amount $3200
Av. no. hrs./wk. required: 20
Highest faculty degree: MA
Contact: Sam Scott, chairman

MONTANA

Montana State University
Bozeman, MT 59715
Tel. (406) 994-3437
Film–TV, 50 hrs., 16 courses (qr.), 12 grad. hrs., 4 courses
Degrees: BS, TV production, 90 majors, BS, motion-picture production, 85 majors, BS, photography, 80 majors
Facilities: TV C/L, CCTV, VTR, CTS satellite, film studio, photography studios
Highest faculty degree: MA
Contact: Fred L. Gerber, chairman

University of Montana
Missoula, MT 59801
Tel. (406) 243-4931
Radio–TV, 45 hrs., 16 courses (qr.); drama, 10 hrs., 3 courses; journalism, 15 hrs., 5 courses, 21 grad. hrs., 7 courses; other depts., 18 grad. hrs., 6 courses
Degrees: BA, 52 majors, MA, 2 majors

Facilities: 3 radio C/L, TV C/L, FM station (KURM), CCTV, VTR, use commercial facilities (KGVO-TV)
Undergraduate scholarships: 5—average amount $400
Graduate assistantships: 1—average amount $2000
Tuition remitted: 100%
Av. no. hrs./wk. required: 15
Highest faculty degree: MA
Contact: Philip J. Hess, chairman

NEBRASKA

Creighton University
Omaha, NB 68178
Tel. (402) 536-2825
Journalism, 25 hrs., 10 courses (sem.)
Degrees: BA, 10 majors
Facilities: radio C/L, TV C/L, carrier current (KOCU), CCTV, VTR, film studios
Undergraduate scholarships: 2—average amount $750
Highest faculty degree: MA
Contact: Bruce Hough, chairman

University of Nebraska
Lincoln, NB 68508
Tel. (402) 472-3054
Journalism, 45 hrs., 15 courses (sem.), 33 grad. hrs., 9 courses
Degrees: BA, 220 majors, MA, 12 majors
Facilities: 6 radio C/L, 5 TV C/L, FM station (KRNU), TV station (KUON-TV), AP, UPI weather teletype services, film studios
Undergraduate scholarships: 8—average amount $200
Graduate assistantships/fellowships: number varies
Highest faculty degree: PhD
Contact: Larry Walklin, chairman

University of Nebraska at Omaha
Omaha, NB 68101
Tel. (402) 554-2600
Communications, 31 hrs. in broadcast journalism, 30 hrs. in broadcast production, 12 courses (sem.), 13 grad. hrs., 4 courses
Degrees: BA, BS, 27 majors, MA, 25 majors
Facilities: radio C/L, TV C/L, FM station (KVNO), TV station (KYNE-TV), ETV, CCTV, VTR
Highest faculty degree: PhD
Contact: Hugh P. Cowdin, chairman

NEVADA

University of Nevada
Reno, NV 89507
Tel. (702) 784-6531
Journalism, 29 hrs., 10 courses (sem.), 6 grad. hrs., 2 courses
Degrees: BA, 23 majors
Facilities: 2 radio C/L, 2 TV C/L, FM station (KUNR), CCTV, VTR
Undergraduate scholarships: 10—average amount $200
Graduate assistantships: 2—average amount $2850
Tuition remitted: 100%
Av. no. hrs./wk. required: 20
Contact: Wendell H. Dobbs, chairman

NEW JERSEY

Seton Hall University
South Orange, NJ 07079
Tel. (201) 762-9000
Communications, 60 hrs., 16 courses (sem.), 6 grad.
    hrs., 1 course
Degrees: BA, 210 majors
Facilities: radio C/L, 2 TV C/L, FM station (WSOU),
    CCTV, VTR, film studio
Undergraduate scholarships: 1—average amount
    $500 per sem.
Highest faculty degree: PhD
Contact: Al Paul Klose, chairman

Trenton State College
Trenton, NJ 08619
Tel. (609) 771-2106
Speech–theatre, 9 hrs., 4 courses (sem.); media, 15
    hrs., 5 courses; education, 9 hrs., 3 courses
Degrees: BA, 20 majors
Facilities: 3 radio C/L, 2 TV C/L, FM station
    (WTSR), ETV, CCTV, VTR
Highest faculty degree: EdD
Contact: Richard Whewer, associate professor

The William Paterson College
Wayne, NJ 07470
Tel. (201) 595-2167
Communications, 36 hrs., 12 courses (sem.), 30 grad.
    hrs., 10 courses
Degrees: BA, 82 majors, MA, 70 majors
Facilities: radio C/L, 2 TV C/L, carrier current
    (WPSC), VTR, CCTV, film studio
Highest faculty degree: PhD
Contact: Anthony Maltese, chairman

NEW MEXICO

New Mexico State University
Las Cruces, NM 88003
Tel. (505) 646-2212
Journalism & mass communications, 51 hrs., 18
    courses (sem.); other depts., 12 grad. hrs., 4
    courses
Degrees: BA, 130 majors
Facilities: 3 radio C/L, 2 TV C/L, FM station
    (KRWG), carrier current (KNMS), TV station
    (KRWG-TV), ETV, CCTV, kinescope, VTR,
    film studio
Undergraduate stipends: 25—average amount
    $200/mo.
Highest faculty degree: PhD
Contact: Frank F. Hash, chairman

NEW YORK

Brooklyn College
Brooklyn, NY 11210
Tel. (212) 780-5555
TV & radio, 75 hrs., 25 courses (sem.), 57 grad. hrs.,
    20 courses
Degrees: BA, 295 majors, MA, 75 majors
Facilities: 3 TV C/L, carrier current (WBCR),
    CCTV, kinescope, VTR
Graduate assistantships: 24—average amount
    $2500

Av. no. hrs./wk. required: 20
Highest faculty degree: PhD
Contact: Robert C. Williams, chairman

College of New Rochelle
New Rochelle, NY 10801
Tel. (914) 632-5300
Communication arts, 27 hrs., 9 courses (sem.), 9
    grad. hrs., 3 courses
Degrees: BA, 80 majors
Facilities: TV C/L, CCTV, VTR, film studio
Highest faculty degree: PhD
Contact: James O'Brien, chairman

Columbia University
New York, NY 10027
Tel. (212) 280-3828
Graduate school of journalism, 9 courses (sem.)
Degrees: MA, 156 majors
Facilities: radio C/L, TV C/L, film studio
Highest faculty degree: PhD
Contact: Fred W. Friendly, chairman

Cornell University
Ithaca, NY 14850
Tel. (607) 256-2111
Communication arts, 9 hrs., 3 courses (sem.), 9 grad.
    hrs., 3 courses
Degrees: BS, 35 majors
Facilities: radio C/L, TV C/L, CCTV, VTR
Contact: Chester H. Freeman, chairman

Fordham University
Bronx, NY 10458
Tel. (212) 933-2233
Communications, 45 hrs., 15 courses (sem.)
Degrees: BA, 325 majors, MA, 50 majors
Facilities: 2 radio C/L, FM station (WFUV)
Highest faculty degree: PhD
Contact: Ralph Dengler, chairman

Herbert H. Lehman College
Bronx, NY 10458
Tel. (212) 960-8136
Speech & theatre, 45 hrs., 15 courses (sem.)
Degrees: BA, 150 majors
Facilities: radio C/L, TV C/L, carrier current,
    CCTV, VTR, film studio
Highest faculty degree: PhD
Contact: Frank Kahn, chairman

Hofstra University
Hempstead, NY 11550
Tel. (516) 560-3676
Communications, 45 hrs., 12 courses (sem.)
Degrees: BA, 300 majors
Facilities: radio C/L, 2 TV C/L, FM station
    (WVHC), CCTV, VTR
Undergraduate scholarships: 8—average amount
    $1125
Highest faculty degree: MA
Contact: William Renn, chairman

Ithaca College
Ithaca, NY 14850
Tel. (607) 274-3214
TV–radio, 72 hrs., 24 courses (sem.); cinema, 51

hrs., 17 courses; educational communications, 30 hrs., 10 courses
Degrees: BA, 150 majors
Facilities: 4 radio C/L, 2 TV C/L, FM station (WIBC), carrier current, ETV, VTR, film studios
Highest faculty degree: PhD
Contact: Dana Ulluth, assistant professor

New York University
New York, NY 10003
Tel. (212) 598-3702
Undergraduate film & TV, 116 hrs., 26 courses (sem.); journalism, 12 hrs., 3 courses; 82 grad. hrs., 19 courses
Degrees: BA, 200 majors
Facilities: 2 radio C/L, 2 TV C/L, FM station (WNYU), VTR, film studio
Undergraduate assistantships: 6—average amount $1000 per 9 mos.
Highest faculty degree: PhD
Contact: Richard J. Goggin, chairman

Queens College
Flushing, NY 11367
Tel. (212) 520-7353
Communication arts & sciences, 54 hrs., 18 courses (sem.)
Degrees: BA, 100 majors
Facilities: TV C/L, CCTV, VTR, film studios
Highest faculty degree: PhD
Contact: Gary Gumpert, chairman

State University at Brockport
Brockport, NY 14420
Tel. (716) 395-2511
Speech–communications, 30 hrs., 10 courses (sem.), 6 grad. hrs., 2 courses
Degrees: BS/BA, 80 majors
Facilities: carrier current (WBSU), CCTV, VTR
Highest faculty degree: MS
Contact: Helen McLaughlin, associate professor

State University of New York at Geneseo
Geneseo, NY 14454
Tel. (716) 245-5228
Speech–communications, 66 hrs., 22 courses (sem.), 16 grad. hrs.
Degrees: BA, 200 majors
Facilities: 3 radio C/L, 2 TV C/L, FM station (WGSU), carrier current (WGBC), CCTV, VTR, (GSTV)
Contact: Dr. R. S. Rutherford

State University of New York at Oswego
Oswego, NY 13126
Tel. (315) 341-2147
Communications studies, 81 hrs., 22 courses (sem.)
Degrees: BA, 150 majors
Facilities: 2 radio C/L, 2 TV C/L, FM station (WRVO), carrier current (WOCR), CCTV, VTR
Highest faculty degree: PhD
Contact: Lewis B. O'Donnell, chairman

State University of New York at Plattsburgh
Plattsburgh, NY 12901

Tel. (518) 564-2114
Communications & theatre arts, 36 hrs., 12 courses (sem.), 6 grad. hrs., 2 courses
Degrees: BA, 56 majors
Facilities: 2 radio C/L, TV C/L, carrier current (WKGO), TV station (WCFE)
Highest faculty degree: PhD
Contact: Phillip Reines, chairman

Syracuse University
Syracuse, NY 13210
Tel. (315) 423-4004
TV–radio, 96 hrs., 32 courses (sem.), 75 grad. hrs., 25 courses; film, 30 hrs., 10 courses; art–drama–film, 30 hrs., 10 courses, 30 grad. hrs., 10 courses
Degrees: BA, 400 majors, MA, 65 majors, PhD, 5 majors
Facilities: 7 radio C/L, 2 TV C/L, FM station (WAER), CCTV, VTR, film studios
Graduate assistantships: 14—average amount $3000
Tuition remitted: 24 sem. hrs.
Av. no. hrs./wk. required: 20
Highest faculty degree: PhD
Contact: Lawrence Myers, Jr., chairman

NORTH CAROLINA

Shaw University
Raleigh, NC 27602
Tel. (919) 755-4890
Radio–TV–film, 54 hrs., 18 courses (sem.)
Degrees: BA, 12 majors
Facilities: radio C/L, TV C/L, FM station (WSHA), carrier current (WSHA), VTR, film-production facility
Undergraduate scholarships: 20
Highest faculty degree: MA
Contact: Paul F. Vandergrift

University of North Carolina at Chapel Hill
Chapel Hill, NC 27514
Tel. (919) 933-2311
Radio–TV/motion pictures, 91 hrs., 30 courses (sem.); journalism, 9 hrs., 3 courses; English, 3 hrs., 1 course; education, 3 hrs., 1 course, 63 grad. hrs., 21 courses; other depts., 12 grad. hrs., 4 courses
Degrees: BA, 80 majors, MA, 20 majors
Facilities: 2 radio C/L, 2 TV C/L, FM station (WUNC), TV station (WUNC-TV), ETV, VTR, film studios
Undergraduate scholarships: 9—average amount $900
Graduate fellowships/grants: 4—average amount $2500
Graduate assistantships: 10—average amount $1000
Av. no. hrs./wk. required: 10
Highest faculty degree: PhD
Contact: A. Richard Elam, chairman

Wake Forest University
Winston-Salem, NC 27109
Tel. (919) 725-9711

Speech–communications & theatre arts, 34 credits, 9
courses (sem.); journalism, 12 hrs., 4 courses, 15
grad. hrs., 5 courses
Degrees: BA, 11 majors
Facilities: FM station (WFDD), CCTV, VTR, use
commercial facilities, film equipment
Graduate fellowships/grants: varies—average
amount $3500
Graduate assistantships: 1—average amount $6250
Av. no. hrs./wk. required: 12–15
Highest faculty degree: PhD
Contact: Julian C. Burroughs, Jr., chairman

NORTH DAKOTA

University of North Dakota
Grand Forks, ND 58201
Tel. (701) 777-2577
Speech–radio–TV, 36 hrs., 13 courses (sem.); jour-
nalism, 8 hrs., 3 courses, 30 grad. hrs., 11
courses; other depts., 3 grad. hrs., 1 course
Degrees: 40 majors, MA, 4 majors
Facilities: 6 radio C/L, TV C/L, AM station (KFJM),
FM station (KFJM), TV station (KGFE), ETV,
VTR
Undergraduate scholarships: 10–15—average
amount varies
Graduate assistantships: 2—average amount $2500
Av. no. hrs./wk. required: 12
Highest faculty degree: MS
Contact: David Beach, chairman

OHIO

Ashland College
Ashland, OH 44805
Tel. (419) 289-5000
Speech, radio–TV, 48 hrs., 11 courses (sem.)
Degrees: BA, 135 majors
Facilities: 12 radio C/L, FM station (WRDL),
CCTV, 5 VTR
Undergraduate scholarships: 4—average amount
$400
Av. no. hrs./wk. required: 5–7
Highest faculty degree: BA
Contact: Richard Leidy, chairman

Bowling Green State University
Bowling Green, OH 43402
Tel. (419) 372-2214
Speech–communications, 140 hrs., 35 courses (qr.),
96 grad. hrs., 24 courses
Degrees: BA or BAC, 300 majors, MA, 25 majors,
PhD, 15 majors
Facilities: 4 radio C/L, TV C/L, FM station
(WBGU), carrier current (WFAL), ETV station
(WBGU-TV), CCTV, VTR, film studios
Undergraduate scholarships: 1—average amount tui-
tion
Graduate fellowships: 8—average amount $3300 &
tuition
Graduate assistantships: 9—average amount $2500
Tuition remitted: 100%
Av. no. hrs./wk. required: 18

Highest faculty degree: PhD
Contact: Robert K. Clark, associate professor

The College of Wooster
Wooster, OH 44691
Tel. (216) 264-1234
Speech, 4 courses, plus independent study
Degrees: BA, 20 majors
Facilities: radio C/L, TV C/L, FM station (WCWS),
VTR
Highest faculty degree: PhD
Contact: Winford B. Logan, chairman

Kent State University
Kent, OH 44242
Tel. (216) 672-2468
Telecommunications, 107 hrs., 29 courses, (qr.), 75
grad. hrs., 21 courses
Degrees: BS, BA, 60 majors, MA, 277 majors
Journalism, 5 hrs., 2 courses
Facilities: 4 radio C/L, 2 TV C/L, FM public radio
station (WKSU), carrier current (WKSR),
CCTV, VTR
Highest faculty degree: PhD
Contact: John C. Weiser, chairman

Marietta College
Marietta, OH 45750
Tel. (614), 373-0200
Speech, radio–TV, 39 hrs., 13 courses (sem.)
Degrees: BA, 25 majors
Facilities: 2 radio C/L, TV C/L, FM station (WCMO)
Undergraduate scholarships: 1—average amount
$500
Highest faculty degree: PhD
Contact: Bernard A. Russi, Jr., chairman

Miami University
Oxford, OH 45056
Tel. (513) 529-3521
*Communications & theatre, mass-communications
tracks:* production, broadcast journalism, mass-
communications research
Degrees: MA, 30 majors, MS in mass com-
munications, 25 majors
Facilities: 4 radio C/L, 2 TV C/L, FM station
(WMUB), ETV, film facilities
Graduate assistantships: 4—average amount $3100
Av. no. hrs./wk. required: 20
Highest faculty degree: PhD
Contact: Ernest E. Phelps, chairman

Ohio State University
Columbus, OH 43210
Tel. (614) 422-3400
Communications, 54 hrs., 17 courses (qr.), 33 grad.
hrs., 11 courses
Degrees: BA, 150 majors, MA, 30 majors, PhD, 3
majors
Journalism, 19 hrs., 3 courses; media communications, 16 hrs., 2 courses; education, 6 hrs., 2
courses; photography & cinema, 24 hrs., 6
courses

Facilities: radio C/L, 2 TV C/L, AM station (WOSU), FM station (WOSU), carrier current (WOSR), ETV station (WOSU-TV), CCTV, VTR, film studios.
Graduate fellowships: varies—average amount $3600
Graduate assistantships: varies—average amount $3600
Tuition remitted: 100%
Av. no. hrs./wk. required: 20
Highest faculty degree: PhD
Contact: Joseph Foley, chairman

Ohio University
Athens, OH 45701
Tel. (614) 594-5503
Radio–TV, 168 hrs., 39 courses (qr.), 105 grad. hrs., 26 courses
Degrees: BA, 650 majors, MA, 20 majors, PhD, 10 majors
Facilities: 10 radio C/L, 3 TV C/L, AM station (WOUB), FM station (WOUB), ETV station (WOUB-TV, WOUC-TV), CCTV, VTR
Undergraduate scholarships: 20—average amount $450
Graduate fellowships: 3—average amount tuition
Graduate assistantships: 11—average amount $2750
Tuition remitted: 100%
Av. no. hrs./wk. required: 15
Highest faculty degree: PhD
Contact: Drewrey McDaniel, chairman

Otterbein College
Westerville, OH 43081
Tel. (614) 890-3000, ext. 357
Speech & theatre, 27 hrs., 5 courses (qr.)
Degrees: BA, 40 majors
Facilities: radio C/L, FM station (WOBN), VTR
Undergraduate scholarships: 5—average amount $500
Highest faculty degree: PhD
Contact: James Grissinger, chairman

University of Akron
Akron, OH 44325
Tel. (216) 678-1656
Speech & theatre arts, 35 hrs., 7 courses (qr.), 25 grad. hrs., 6 courses
Degrees: BA, 85 majors, MA, 15 majors
Facilities: radio C/L, TV C/L, FM station (WAUP), carrier current (WRHA), TV station (WNEO), ETV, CCTV, VTR, film studio
Graduate assistantships: 5—average amount $2700
Tuition remitted: 100%
Av. no. hrs./wk. required: 20
Highest faculty degree: PhD
Contact: Ruth B. Lewis, chairman

The University of Cincinnati
Cincinnati, OH 45221
Tel. (513) 475-4394

Div. of broadcasting, 126 hrs., 42 courses (qr.), 75 grad. hrs.; English., 12 hrs., 4 courses; speech, 18 hrs., 6 courses
Degrees: BFA, 185 majors, MA, 10 majors
Facilities: 2 radio C/L, 2 TV C/L, FM station (WGUC), carrier current (WFIB), TV station (WCET), ETV, VTR, film studios
Graduate scholarships: 3—full tuition
Av. no. hrs./wk. required: 8
Graduate teaching assistantships: 1—average amount $2700
Tuition remitted: 100%
Av. no. hrs/wk. required: 20
Highest faculty degree: PhD
Contact: Morleen Getz-Rouse, chairman

University of Dayton
Dayton, OH 45409
Tel. (513) 229-2340
Communication arts, 12 hrs., 4 courses (sem.)
Degrees: BA, 64 majors
Facilities: 2 radio C/L, 2 TV C/L, FM station (WVUD), CCTV, VTR
Highest faculty degree: MA
Contact: George C. Biersack, chairman

Xavier University
Cincinnati, OH 45207
Tel. (513) 745-3736
Communication arts, 42 hrs., 23 courses (sem.), 41 grad. hrs., 20 courses
Degrees: BA, 75 majors, MA, 20 majors
Facilities: 4 radio C/L, TV C/L, FM station (WVXU), CCTV, VTR
Highest faculty degree: PhD
Contact: Lawrence J. Flynn, chairman

OKLAHOMA

Central State University
Edmond, OK 73034
Tel. (405) 341-2980
Oral communications (broadcasting), 33 hrs., 11 courses (sem.), 18 grad. hrs., 6 courses; other depts., 9 hrs., 3 courses
Degrees: BA, 85 majors, MA, 1 major, MS, 2 majors
Facilities: 4 radio C/L, 2 TV C/L, FM station (KCSC)
Undergraduate scholarships: 4—average amount $400
Highest faculty degree: PhD
Contact: Jack Deskin, chairman

Oklahoma City University
Oklahoma City, OK 73106
Tel. (405) 525-5411
Speech & theatre, 18 hrs., 6 courses (sem.)
Degrees: BA, 50 majors
Facilities: radio C/L
Highest faculty degree: PhD
Contact: Robert J. Varga, chairman

Oklahoma State University
Stillwater, OK 74074
Tel. (405) 624-6354

Radio, TV, film, 49 hrs., 18 courses (sem.), 42 grad. hrs., 14 courses; theatre, 6 hrs., 2 courses; advertising, 3 hrs., 1 course, 9 grad. hrs., 3 courses
Degrees: BS & BA, 210 majors, MA, 10 majors, EdD, 2 majors
Facilities: 5 radio C/L, 2 TV C/L, commercial FM station (KVRO), educational FM station (KOSU), CCTV, VTR, film studio
Undergraduate scholarships: 6—average amount $200
Graduate assistantships: 6—average amount $2150
Tuition remitted: out-of-state
Av. no. hrs./wk. required: 15
Highest faculty degree: MA
Contact: Philip E. Paulin, chairman

University of Oklahoma
Norman, OK 73069
Tel. (405) 325-3111
Speech–communications, 40 hrs., 14 courses (sem.), 10 grad. hrs., 4 courses; journalism, 15 hrs., 6 courses; drama, 12 hrs., 3 courses
Degrees: BA, 30 majors, MA, 8 majors
Facilities: radio C/L, TV C/L, AM station (WNAD), FM station (KGOU), ETV station (KTTV)
Highest faculty degree: PhD
Contact: Lowell Conner, chairman

University of Tulsa
Tulsa, OK 74104
Tel. (918) 939-6351
Communications, 47 hrs., 16 courses (sem.)
Degrees: BA, 110 majors
Facilities: 4 radio C/L, TV C/L, FM station (KWGS), VTR, film studio
Undergraduate scholarships: 20—average amount $300
Highest faculty degree: PhD
Contact: Thomas W. Bohn, chairman

OREGON

Oregon State University
Corvallis, OR 97331
Tel. (503) 754-3066
Broadcast media communications, 87 hrs., 27 courses (qr.), plus internship, 15 hrs.; journalism, 6 hrs., 2 courses, 15 grad. hrs., 5 courses
Degrees: BA, 125 majors, MAIS (MA, Interdisciplinary Studies), 15 majors
Facilities: 2 radio C/L, 3 TV C/L, FM station (KBUR), TV stations (KBUR-TV, KOAC-TV), ETV, VTR
Undergraduate scholarships: 2—average amount $700
Highest faculty degree: PhD
Contact: Richard Weinman, chairman

Pacific University
Forest Grove, OR 97116
Tel. (503) 352-6151
Speech & communications, 33 hrs., 13 courses (sem.); business, 6 hrs., 2 courses; fine arts, 9 hrs., 3 courses

Degrees: BA, 11 majors
Facilities: 3 radio C/L, 2 TV C/L, carrier current (KPUR), CCTV, VTR, film studio
Highest faculty degree: PhD
Contact: Fred Scheller, chairman

Southern Oregon State College
Ashland, OR 97520
Tel. (503) 482-6423
Speech communications, 23 hrs., 10 courses (qr.); journalism, 17 hrs., 6 courses
Degrees: BA, 40 majors
Facilities: 3 radio C/L, FM station (KSOR)
Undergraduate scholarships: 1—average amount $200
Highest faculty degree: MA
Contact: Ronald Kramer, chairman

University of Oregon
Eugene, OR 97403
Tel. (503) 686-4171 (telecommunications)
　　(503) 686-3900 (journalism)
Telecommunications, 121 hrs., 40 courses (qr.), 64 grad. hrs., 21 courses
Degrees: BA, 109 majors, MA, 12 majors, PhD, 6 majors
Journalism, 21 hrs., 7 courses, 18 grad. hrs., 6 courses
Degrees: BA, 60 majors, MA, 5 majors
Facilities: 3 radio C/L, 2 TV C/L, FM station (WKAX), CCTV, 1 CATV, VTR
Highest faculty degree: PhD
Contact: Ronald E. Sheriffs, chairman

PENNSYLVANIA

Clarion State College
Clarion, PA 16214
Tel. (814) 226-6000
Communications, 35 hrs., 18 courses (sem.), 35 grad. hrs., 18 courses
Degrees: BA, 150 majors, MA, 45 majors
Facilities: radio C/L, 2 TV C/L, public radio station (WCUC-FM), carrier current (WCCB), CCTV, VTR, film studios
Graduate assistantships: 11—average amount $1200
Tuition remitted: 100%
Av. no. hrs./wk. required: 10
Highest faculty degree: EdD
Contact: James Cole, chairman

Duquesne University
Pittsburgh, PA 15219
Tel. (412) 434-6446
Journalism, 12 hrs., 3–6 courses (sem.)
Degrees: BA, 51 majors
Facilities: FM station (WDUQ), ETV, VTR, film studios
Highest faculty degree: PhD
Contact: Nancy C. Jones, chairman

Kutztown State College
Kutztown, PA 19530
Tel. (215) 683-4492

Television production, 32 hrs., 4 courses (sem.), 3 grad. hrs., 1 course
Degrees: BA, 12 majors
Facilities: 3 studios, mobile TV van, CCTV, microwave & cable 2-way TV
Highest faculty degree: PhD
Contact: Robert P. Fina, chairman

Pennsylvania State University
University Park, PA 16802
Tel. (814) 865-3261
Speech communication, 27 hrs., 9 courses (qr.), 21 grad. hrs., 9 courses
Degrees: BA, 155 majors, MA, 10 majors, PhD, 8 majors
Facilities: radio C/L, TV C/L, FM station (WDFM), ETV station (WPBX-TV), CCTV, VTR, film studio
Graduate assistantships: 3—average amount $2700
Tuition remitted: 100%
Av. no. hrs./wk. required: 18–20
Highest faculty degree: PhD
Contact: Harold Nelson, chairman

Point Park College
Pittsburgh, PA 15222
Tel. (412) 391-4100
Journalism & communications, 19 hrs., 7 courses (sem.)
Degrees: BA, 20 majors
Facilities: radio C/L, TV C/L, carrier current (WPPJ), CCTV, VTR
Undergraduate scholarships: 2—average amount $9500 for 4 years
Highest faculty degree: MFA
Contact: William A. Jewett, Jr., chairman

Temple University
Philadelphia, PA 19122
Tel. (215) 787-8423
Radio, TV, film, 382 hrs., 96 courses (sem.), 268 grad. hrs., 67 courses; journalism, 36 hrs., 9 courses; educational media, 9 hrs., 12 courses, 45 grad. hrs., 12 courses
Degrees: BA, 1100 majors, MA, 120 majors, MFA, 20 majors, PhD, 15 majors
Facilities: 7 radio C/L, 6 TV C/L, FM station (WRTI), CCTV, VTR, film studios
Undergraduate scholarships: 2—average amount $500
Graduate fellowships: 6—average amount $3000
Graduate assistantships: 22—average amount $3100
Tuition remitted: 100%
Av. no. hrs./wk. required: 20
Highest faculty degree: PhD
Contact: Timothy Lyons, associate professor

Westminister College
New Wilmington, PA 16142
Tel. (412) 946-6710
Speech & drama, 24 hrs., 6 courses
Degrees: BA, 22 majors
Facilities: 3 radio C/L, FM stations (WKPS)

Undergraduate scholarships: 4—average amount $300
Highest faculty degree: MA
Contact: Mark C. Klinger, III, chairman

SOUTH CAROLINA

University of South Carolina
Columbia, SC 29208
Tel. (803) 777-4102
Broadcasting sequence, 41 hrs., 14 courses (sem.); art, 6 hrs., 2 courses; English, 3 hrs., 1 course; music, 9 hrs., 3 courses; education, 6 hrs., 2 courses, 15 grad. hrs., 5 courses; other depts., 6 grad. hrs., 2 courses
Degrees: BA, 140 majors, MA, 20 majors
Facilities: 6 radio C/L, TV C/L, FM station (WUSC), VTR
Undergraduate scholarships: 4—average amount $200
Graduate assistantships: 3—average amount $2000
Tuition remitted: 100%
Av. no. hrs./wk. required: 15
Highest faculty degree: PhD
Contact: Richard M. Uray, chairman

SOUTH DAKOTA

South Dakota State University
Brookings, SD 57007
Tel. (605) 688-4171
Journalism & mass communications, 21 hrs., 8 courses (sem.), 3 grad. hrs., 1 course
Degrees: BA and BS, 22 majors
Facilities: 3 radio C/L, 2 TV C/L, FM station (KESD), TV station (KESD-TV), ETV, CCTV, VTR, film studio
Undergraduate scholarships: 8—average amount $250
Highest faculty degree: MA
Contact: Kenneth Eich, assistant professor

The University of South Dakota
Vermillion, SD 57069
Tel. (605) 677-5474
Mass communications, 90 hrs., 30 courses, plus 12 hrs. internship (sem.), 57 grad. hrs., 19 courses
Degrees: BA, 200 majors, MA, 10 majors
Facilities: 2 radio C/L, TV C/L, AM station (KUSD), FM station (KUSD), TV stations (KUSD-TV, KZSD-TV), ETV, CCTV, VTR, film studio, mass-media center
Undergraduate scholarships: 10—average amount $500
Graduate assistantships: 4—average amount $300–$2500
Tuition remitted: 2/3%
Av. no. hrs./wk. required: 20
Highest faculty degree: PhD
Contact: Clayland H. Waite, chairman

TENNESSEE

Memphis State University
Memphis, TN 38111
Tel. (901) 454-2001
Speech & drama, 126 hrs., 26 courses (sem.); journalism, 21 hrs., 7 courses; marketing, 9 hrs., 3 courses, 72 grad. hrs., 22 courses
Degrees: BA, 225 majors, MA, 35 majors
Facilities: 3 radio C/L, TV C/L, TV station (WKNO), ETV, CCTV, VTR, use commercial stations (WHBQ-TV, WMC-TV)
Undergraduate scholarships: 2—average amount $300
Graduate fellowships/grants: 1—average amount $1000
Graduate assistantships: 3–4—average amount $2600
Tuition remitted: 100% out-of-state
Av. no. hrs./wk. required: 20
Highest faculty degree: PhD
Contact: Marvin R. Bensman, chairman

Southern Missionary College
Collegedale, TN 37315
Tel. (615) 396-4216
Communications, 30 hrs., 12 courses (sem.)
Degree: BA, 10 majors
Facilities: 1 radio C/L, 1 TV C/L, FM station (WSMC-FM), VTR
Highest faculty degree: PhD
Contact: Don Dick, chairman

The University of Tennessee
Knoxville, TN 37916
Tel. (615) 974-5281
Broadcasting, 60 hrs., 20 courses (qr.); advertising, 10 hrs., 2 courses; communications, 9 hrs., 3 courses; journalism, 15 hrs., 3 courses, 42 grad. hrs., 14 courses; other depts., 20 grad. hrs., 5 courses
Degrees: BA, 75 majors, MA, 17 majors, PhD, 2 majors
Facilities: 2 radio C/L, TV C/L, FM station (WUOT), TV station (WSJK), ETV, CCTV, VTR
Undergraduate scholarships: 2—average amount $300
Graduate assistantships: 2—average amount $1800
Tuition remitted: 100%
Av. no. hrs./wk. required: 12
Highest faculty degree: PhD
Contact: Darrel W. Holt, chairman

TEXAS

Baylor University
Waco, TX 76703
Tel. (817) 755-1511
Oral communication, 47 hrs., 16 courses (sem.)
Degree: BA, 110 majors
Facilities: TV C/L, FM station (KWBU), CCTV, VTR
Highest faculty degree: PhD
Contact: Peter K. Pringle, chairman

East Texas State University
Commerce, TX 75428
Tel. (214) 468-6103
Radio–TV (major), 10 courses (3 sem. hrs.), plus 1 hr. lab practicum each sem. (BS/BA degree), additional: 2 credits journalism, 2 courses marketing/management; radio—TV (minor), 6 courses (2 sem. hrs.), plus 1 hr. practicum each sem.; film, 6 courses (3 sem. hrs.)
Facilities: KETR-FM stereo, UPI affiliate, 2 studios, news-production studio, cable radio (KKOM), 1 studio, 1 TV studio, mini-cam with VTR, 3 film/photo studios
Highest faculty degree: PhD
Contact: Robert B. Sanders, director

Lamar University
Beaumont, TX 77710
Tel. (713) 838-7122
Communications, 26 hrs., 14 courses (sem.)
Degree: BA, 60 majors
Facilities: 3 radio C/L, 2 TV C/L, FM station (KVLU, CPB–NPR), VTR, film studio
Undergraduate scholarships: 5—average amount $100 per sem.
Highest faculty degree: MA
Contact: Jerry Hudson, assistant professor

North Texas State University
Denton, TX 76203
Tel. (817) 788-2537
Radio, TV, film, 60 hrs., 20 courses (sem.), 27 grad. hrs., 9 courses; journalism, 21 hrs., 7 courses; public address, 6 hrs., 2 courses, 15 grad. hrs., 5 courses
Degrees: BA, 255 majors, MA, 10 majors, PhD, 2 majors
Facilities: 2 radio C/L, TV C/L, FM station (KNTU), CCTV, VTR
Graduate assistantships: 3—average amount $2000
Tuition remitted: out-of-state
Av. no. hrs./wk. required: 20
Highest faculty degree: PhD
Contact: Edwin L. Glick, chairman

Sam Houston State University
Huntsville, TX 77341
Tel. (713) 295-6211
Radio–TV–film, 69 hrs., 23 courses, plus 1 hr. lab credit (sem.); photography, 12 hrs., 4 courses; journalism, 3 hrs., 1 course; art, 3 hrs., 1 course
Degrees: BA, 125 majors
Undergraduate assistantships: 5
Av. no. hrs./wk. required: 15
Highest faculty degree: PhD
Contact: Robert Eubanks, chairman

Southern Methodist University
Dallas, TX 75275
Tel. (214) 692-3090
Broadcast–film arts, 147 hrs., 50 courses (sem.), 79 grad. hrs., 25 courses
Degrees: BA, 98 majors, MA, 12 majors

Facilities: 2 radio C/L, TV C/L, carrier current, VTR, use facilities KTVT-TV
Undergraduate/graduate scholarships: 8—average amount $450 per sem.
Highest faculty degree: PhD
Contact: James B. McGrath, chairman

Texas Christian University
Forth Worth, TX 76129
Tel. (817) 926-2461
Radio–TV–film, 60 hrs., 19 courses (sem.), 30 grad. hrs., 10 courses
Degrees: BA, 118 majors, MA, 8 majors
Facilities: 2 radio C/L, 3 TV C/L, FM station (KTCU), CCTV, VTR, film studio
Highest faculty degree: PhD
Contact: R. C. Norris, chairman

Texas Technical University
Lubbock, TX 79409
Tel. (806) 742-2282
Mass communications, 51 hrs., 17 courses (sem.), 12 grad. hrs., 4 courses
Degrees: BA, 205 majors, MA, 6 majors
Facilities: FM station (KTXT), TV station (KTXT), ETV, CCTV, VTR, CATV
Graduate assistantships: 1—average amount $3200
Av. no. hrs./wk. required: 20
Highest faculty degree: EdD
Contact: Dennis A. Harp, chairman

Texas Woman's University
Denton, TX 76204
Tel. (806) 742-3382
Speech, 38 hrs., 10 courses (sem.), 12 grad. hrs., 4 courses
Degrees: BA, 12 majors
Facilities: 3 radio C/L, 3 TV C/L, CCTV, VTR
Undergraduate scholarships: average amount $400
Highest faculty degree: PhD
Contact: Thornton A. Klos, chairman

University of Houston
Houston, TX 77004
Tel. (713) 749-1745
Communications, 60 hrs., 20 courses (sem.)
Degrees: BA, 175 majors
Facilities: radio C/L, TV C/L, FM station (KUHR), TV station (KUHT), ETV, VTR, use commercial station (KHTV), film studios
Undergraduate scholarships: 8—average amount $800–900 per year
Highest faculty degree: PhD
Contact: William Hawes, chairman

University of Texas at Arlington
Arlington, TX 76019
Tel. (817) 273-2163
Radio–television, 45 hrs., 15 courses (sem.)
Degrees: 150 majors
Facilities: 3 radio C/L, 2 TV C/L, 5 VTR
Highest faculty degree: PhD
Contact: Chapin Ross, chairman

University of Texas at Austin
Austin, TX 78712
Tel. (512) 471-2791
Radio, TV, film, 121 hrs., 43 courses (sem.), 51 grad. hrs., 17 courses
Degrees: BA, 550 majors, MA, 73 majors, PhD, 16 majors
Facilities: 3 radio C/L, 3 TV C/L, VTR, film studios
Highest faculty degree: PhD
Contact: Robert E. Davis, chairman

University of Texas at El Paso
El Paso, TX 79968
Tel. (915) 747-5129
Radio–TV, 62 hrs., 26 courses (sem.)
Degrees: BA, 250 majors
Facilities: 6 radio C/L, 3 TV C/L, FM station (KTEP), carrier current (KVOF), CCTV, VTR
Undergraduate scholarships: 12—average amount $150 per sem.
Highest faculty degree: PhD
Contact: Francisco J. Lewels, associate professor

West Texas State University
Canyon, TX 79016
Tel. (806) 656-3248
Speech, 24 hrs., 8 courses (sem.), 12 grad. hrs., 4 courses
Degrees: BA, 55 majors
Facilities: radio C/L, TV C/L, CCTV, VTR

UTAH

Brigham Young University
Provo, UT 84601
Tel. (801) 375-1211
Communications, 40 hrs., 30 courses (sem.), 30 grad. hrs., 13 courses
Degrees: BA, 30 majors, MA, 15 majors
Facilities: 3 radio C/L, 2 TV C/L, FM station (KBYO), ETV station (KBYU-TV), CCTV, VTR
Highest faculty degree: EdD
Contact: Owen S. Rich, professor

University of Utah
Salt Lake City, UT 84112
Tel. (801) 581-6302
Communications, 95 hrs., 21 courses (qr.), 47 grad. hrs., 12 courses
Degrees: BA, 60 majors, MA, 20 majors, PhD, 8 majors
Facilities: 2 radio C/L, 3 TV C/L, FM station (KUER), ETV station (KUED), CCTV, kinescope, VTR
Undergraduate scholarships: 10—average amount $350
Graduate assistantships: 10—average amount $3600
Tuition remitted: 100%
Av. no. hrs./wk. required: 20
Highest faculty degree: PhD
Contact: Robert Tiemens, chairman

Utah State University
Logan, UT 84322
Tel. (801) 752-4100
Communications, 41–51 hrs. (qr.) required for undergraduate major, 45 grad. hrs. for MS
Degrees: BS, 35 majors, MS, 4 majors
Facilities: 1 radio C/L, 2 TV C/L, FM station (KUSU), ETV, CCTV, VTR
Graduate assistantships: 1—average amount $2500
Av. no. hrs./wk. required: 10
Highest faculty degree: PhD
Contact: Burrell Hansen, professor

Weber State College
Ogden, UT 84403
Tel. (801) 399-5941
Communications, 35 hrs., 12 courses (qr.)
Degrees: BA, 35 majors
Facilities: radio C/L, TV C/L, FM station (KWCR), CCTV
Undergraduate scholarships: 4—average amount tuition
Av. no. hrs./wk. required: 20
Highest faculty degree: MS, MA
Contact: R. Kumar, chairman

VERMONT

University of Vermont
Burlington, VT 05401
Tel. (802) 656-3214
Communications & theatre, 36 hrs., 12 courses (sem.), 24 grad. hrs., 8 courses
Degrees: BA, 75 majors, MA, 8 majors
Facilities: radio C/L, TV C/L, FM station (WRUV), carrier current (WRUV), TV station (WETK), ETV, CCTV, VTR
Graduate assistantships: 1—average amount $2700
Tuition remitted: yes
Av. no. hrs./wk. requirred: 12
Highest faculty degree: PhD
Contact: William J. Lewis, chairman

VIRGINIA

Hampton Institute
Hampton, VA 23668
Tel. (804) 727-5400
Mass-media arts: in major, 72 hrs.; outside major, 49 hrs.
Degrees: BA, 222 majors
Facilities: 3 radio C/L, TV C/L, FM station (WHOV), ETV, CCTV, VTR
Highest faculty degree: PhD
Contact: William Kearney, chairman

James Madison University
Harrisonburg, VA 22801
Tel. (703) 433-6228
Communications, 50 hrs., 19 courses (sem.), 9 grad. hrs., 3 courses
Degrees: BA, 30 majors

Facilities: 2 radio C/L, 2 TV C/L, FM station (WMRA), TV station (WVPT), ETV, CCTV, VTR, use commercial facilities (WSVA-AM/TV, WBTX)
Highest faculty degree: PhD
Contact: Donald L. McConkey, chairman

Norfolk State College
Norfolk, VA 23504
Tel. (804) 623-8460
Mass communications, 60 hrs., 16 courses (sem.), 15 grad. hrs., 6 courses
Degrees: BA, 250 majors
Facilities: radio C/L, 2 TV C/L, carrier current (WNSC), FM station, CCTV, VTR
Highest faculty degree: EdD
Contact: Wilbert D. Edgerton, chairman

Washington and Lee University
Lexington, VA 24450
Tel. (703) 463-9111
Journalism & communications, 15 hrs., 5 courses (sem.)
Degrees: BA, 40 majors
Facilities: 2 radio C/L, TV C/L, FM station (WLUR), CCTV, film studio
Highest faculty degree: PhD
Contact: R. H. MacDonald, chairman

WASHINGTON

Eastern Washington State College
Cheney, WA 99004
Tel. (509) 359-2220
Radio–TV, 115 hrs., 28 courses (qr.)
Degrees: BA, 140 majors
Facilities: 2 radio C/L, 2 TV C/L, FM station (KEWC), carrier current (KEWC), CCTV, 3 VTR, film studio, multi-track audio recording use CATV
Highest faculty degree: PhD
Contact: Howard E. Hopf, chairman

University of Washington
Seattle, WA 98195
Tel. (206) 543-1764
Communications, 68 hrs., 21 courses (qr.), 15 grad. hrs., 6 courses
Degrees: BA, 60 majors, MA, 5 majors
Facilities: 3 radio C/L, 2 TV C/L, FM station (KUOW), ETV station (KCTS), CCTV, VTR
Undergraduate scholarships: 1—average amount $400
Graduate assistantships: 2—average amount $2700
Tuition remitted: 100% resident
Av. no. hrs./wk. required: 10
Highest faulty degree: MA
Contact: Pat Cranston, chairman

Washington State University
Pullman, WA 99164
Tel. (509) 335-1556
Communications, 53 hrs, 14 courses (sem.); education, 9 hrs., 3 courses, 15 grad. hrs., 5 courses

Degrees: BA, 97 majors
Facilities: 5 radio C/L, 2 TV C/L, AM station (KWSU), carrier current (KUGR), TV station (KWSU-TV), CCTV, VTR, film studios
Undergraduate scholarships: 5—average amount $265
Highest faculty degree: MA
Contact: Hugh Rundell, chairman

Western Washington University
Bellingham, WA 98225
Tel. (206) 676-3000
Speech, 54 hrs., 14 courses (qr.); journalism, 6 hrs., 3 courses, 30 grad. hrs., 7 courses
Degrees: BA, 40 majors, MA, 2 majors
Facilities: 4 radio C/L, 3 TV C/L, FM station (KUGS), carrier current, CCTV, VTR
Highest faculty degree: PhD
Contact: Alden C. Smith, chairman

WEST VIRGINIA

Fairmount State College
Fairmont, WV 26554
Tel. (304) 367-4000
Speech, 17 hrs., 5 courses (sem.)
Degrees: BA, 6 majors
Facilities: 2 radio C/L, 2 TV C/L, CCTV, 12 VTR
Highest faculty degree: MA
Contact: Charles G. Manly, chairman

Marshall University
Huntington, WV 25701
Tel. (304) 696-6786
Speech, 60 hrs., 20 courses (sem.); journalism, 10 hrs., 3 courses, 36 grad. hrs., 12 courses
Degrees: BA, 75 majors, MA, 10 majors
Facilities: 2 radio C/L, TV C/L, FM station (WMUL), TV station (WMUL), ETV, CCTV, VTR
Undergraduate scholarships: 5—average amount $200
Graduate assistantships: 4—average amount $1800
Tuition remitted: 100%
Av. no. hrs./wk. required: 20
Highest faculty degree: PhD
Contact: Dorothy R. Johnson, chairman

West Virginia University
Morgantown, WV 26506
Tel. (304) 293-3505
Journalism, 30 hrs., 7 courses (sem.), 12 grad. hrs., 3 courses
Degrees: BSJ, 50 majors
Facilities: radio C/L, TV C/L, TV station (WWVU), ETV, VTR
Undergraduate scholarships: 1—average amount $500
Graduate assistantships: 1—average amount $2600
Tuition remitted: 100%
Av. no. hrs./wk. required: 17
Highest faculty degree: PhD
Contact: Charles F. Cremer, chairman

WISCONSIN

Marquette University
Milwaukee, WI 53233
Tel. (414) 224-7074
Broadcast communication, 90 hrs., 30 courses (sem.); journalism, 30 hrs., 10 courses, 48 grad. hrs., 16 courses
Degrees: BA, 165 majors, MA, 6 majors
Facilities: 4 radio C/L, 2 TV C/L, carrier current, CCTV, VTR, film studio
Undergraduate scholarships: 3—average amount $300
Graduate assistantships: 6—average amount $2600
Tuition remitted: 100%
Av. no. hrs./wk. required: 20
Highest faculty degree: PhD
Contact: James T. Tiedge, chairman

University of Wisconsin at LaCrosse
LaCrosse, WI 54601
Tel. (608) 784-6050
Mass communications, 30 hrs., 11 courses (sem.); speech, 3 hrs., 1 course, 8 grad. hrs., 3 courses
Degrees: BA, 50 majors
Facilities: 2 radio C/L, 2 TV C/L, FM station (WLSU), CCTV, VTR
Highest faculty degree: MA
Contact: Joseph Zobin, chairman

University of Wisconsin at Madison
Madison, WI 53706
Tel. (608) 262-2543
Communication arts, 126 hrs., 42 courses (sem.), 111 grad. hrs., 37 courses; journalism, 14 hrs., 4 courses, 3 grad. hrs., 1 course
Degrees: BA, 320 majors, MA, 48 majors, PhD, 38 majors
Facilities: 3 radio C/L, 2 TV C/L, AM station (WHA), FM station (WERN), carrier current (WHLA, WWSR), ETV station (WHA), CCTV, kinescope, VTR, film studio
Undergraduate scholarships: 2—average amount $1000
Graduate fellowships: 4—average amount $4500
Graduate assistantships: 20—average amount $3627–$5990
Highest faculty degree: PhD
Contact: Ordean G. Ness, chairman

University of Wisconsin at Milwaukee
Milwaukee, WI 53201
Tel. (414) 963-4664
Mass communications, 51 hrs., 17 courses (sem.), 15 grad. hrs., 4 courses
Degrees: BA, 76 majors, MA, 4 majors
Facilities: 2 radio C/L, TV C/L, FM station (WUWM), CCTV, VTR, film studios
Highest faculty degree: PhD
Contact: Ruane Hill, chairman

University of Wisconsin at Oshkosh
Oshkosh, WI 54901
Tel. (414) 424-3131

Speech, 102 hrs., 31 courses (sem.), 5 grad. hrs., 5 courses
Degrees: BA, 125 majors
Facilities: 6 radio C/L, 7 TV C/L, FM station (WRST), CCTV, VTR, film studios
Undergraduate scholarships: 2—amount $50
Highest faculty degree: PhD
Contact: Robert L. Snyder, chairman

University of Wisconsin at Platteville
Platteville, WI 53818
Tel. (608) 342-1627
Communications, 58 hrs., 21 courses
Degrees: BA/BS, 179 majors
Facilities: 3 radio C/L, TV C/L, FM station (WSUP), carrier current (WSUP), CCTV, VTR, film studio
Highest faculty degree: PhD
Contact: Thomas J. Jonas, chairman

University of Wisconsin at Stevens Point
Stevens Point, WI 54481
Tel. (715) 346-2696
Communications, 28 hrs., 10 courses (qr.)
Degrees: BA, 15 majors, BS, 200 majors
Facilities: radio C/L, 2 TV C/L, FM station (WSUS), VTR, film studio
Highest faculty degree: MA
Contact: Robert J. Burull, chairman

University of Wisconsin at Superior
Superior, WI 54880
Tel. (715) 392-8101

Speech, 51 hrs., 15 courses (sem.), 33 grad. hrs., 11 courses
Facilities: 2 radio C/L, 2 TV C/L, FM station (WSSU), CCTV, VTR

University of Wisconsin at Whitewater
Whitewater, WI 53190
Tel. (414) 472-1034
Speech–communications, 27 hrs., 10 courses (sem.); journalism, 8 hrs., 2 courses
Degrees: BA, 15 majors
Facilities: 2 radio C/L, TV C/L, FM station (WSUW), CCTV, VTR
Highest faculty degree: MA
Contact: Raymond L. Carroll, instructor

WYOMING

University of Wyoming
Laramie, WY 82071
Tel. (307) 766-6277
Communications & broadcasting, 58 hrs., 20 courses (sem.); journalism, 6 hrs., 2 courses, 42 grad. hrs., 14 courses
Degrees: BA, BS, 80 majors
Facilities: 2 radio C/L, 4 radio production rms., TV C/L, Stereo FM station (KUWR), CCTV, VTR, film studios
Undergraduate scholarships: 3—average amount $1000
Highest faculty degree: PhD
Contact: James W. Welke, chairman

Colleges and Universities Offering Courses in Broadcasting

CALIFORNIA

Humboldt State University
Arcata, CA 98521
Tel. (707) 826-3261
Speech communication, 12 hrs., 3 courses (qr.)
Facilities: 2 radio C/L, FM station (KHSU), carrier current
Highest faculty degree: EdD
Contact: Don Korshner, chairman

CONNECTICUT

Western Connecticut State College
Danbury, CT 06810
Tel. (203) 792-1400
Audiovisual–TV center, 6 hrs., 2 courses (sem.); speech, 3 hrs., 1 course, 6 grad. hrs., 2 courses
Facilities: radio C/L, TV C/L, FM station (WXCI), CCTV, VTR, film studio
Contact: George J. Theisen, chairman

DISTRICT OF COLUMBIA

George Washington University
Washington, DC 20006
Tel. (202) 676-6225

Journalism, 3 hrs., 1 course (sem.); speech, 12 hrs.
Facilities: TV C/L, carrier current (WRGW)
Highest faculty degree: MA
Contact: George Cheely, chairman

GEORGIA

Georgia State University
Atlanta, GA 30303
Tel. (404) 658-3200
Journalism, 25 hrs., 5 courses (qr.), 10 grad. hrs., 2 courses
Facilities: TV C/L, CCTV, VTR
Highest faculty degree: MA
Contact: Edward G. Luck, chairman

MARYLAND

Morgan State College
Baltimore, MD 21239
Tel. (301) 893-3333
Speech communication & theatre arts, 9 hrs., 3 courses (sem.)
Highest faculty degree: PhD
Contact: Lucia S. Hawthorne, chairman

MONTANA

Eastern Montana College
Billings, MT 59103

Tel. (406) 657-2259
Communication arts dept., 21 hrs., plus 8 hrs. (optional credits), practicums
Facilities: FM station (KEMC)
Highest faculty degree: PhD
Contact: Anneke-Jan Boden

NEW HAMPSHIRE

University of New Hampshire
Durham, NH 03824
Tel. (603) 862-1047
Speech & drama, 8 hrs., 2 courses (sem.)
Facilities: FM station (WUNH), TV station (WUNH-TV), ETV, VTR
Highest faculty degree: PhD
Contact: David J. Magidson, chairman

NEW YORK

Fredonia State University College
Fredonia, NY 14063
Tel. (716) 673-3405
Special studies: communications media concentration
Facilities: radio C/L, TV C/L, carrier current (WCVF), CCTV, VTR
Highest faculty degree: PhD
Contact: William Jungels, assistant professor

Rochester Institute of Technology
Rochester, NY 14623
Tel. (716) 475-2716
Photographic arts & sciences, 12 hrs., 4 courses (qr.), 9 grad. hrs., 1 course
Facilities: TV studio, 2 TV C/L, TV remote systems, portable TV camera, CCTV, sound gear
Highest faculty degree: MA
Contact: Richard Floberg, chairman

St. John's University
Jamaica, NY 11439
Tel. (212) 969-8000
Communication arts, 30 hrs., 10 courses (sem.)
Facilities: radio C/L, 2 TV C/L, AM station (WSJU), CCTV, VTR
Highest faculty degree: MA
Contact: Marguerite Donnelly, associate professor

St. Lawrence University
Canton, NY 13617
Tel. (315) 379-6302
Radio & television, 16 hrs., 4 courses (sem.)
Facilities: 2 radio C/L, TV C/L, FM station (WSLU), carrier current (KSLU), CCTV, VTR, film studio
Highest faculty degree: BS
Contact: Richard D. Hutto, chairman

NORTH CAROLINA

North Carolina State University
Raleigh, NC 27607
Tel. (919) 737-2450
Speech–communications, 12 hrs., 4 courses (sem.); sociology, 3 hrs., 1 course; education, 3 hrs., 1 course; English, 3 hrs., 1 course

Facilities: radio C/L, 4 TV C/L, FM station (WKNC), carrier current (KPAK), TV station (WUNC), ETV, CCTV, VTR, use commercial facilities (WRAL-TV), film studios
Highest faculty degree: MA
Contact: Edward T. Funkhouser, instructor

OHIO

Capital University
Columbus, OH 43209
Tel. (614) 236-6201
Speech, 18 hrs., 5 courses (sem.)
Facilities: 2 radio C/L, 2 TV C/L, VTR
Highest faculty degree: PhD
Contact: Armin Langholz, chairman

University of Toledo
Toledo, OH 43606
Tel. (419) 537-2005
Communication, 44 hrs., 11 courses (qr.); journalism, 4 hrs., 1 course
Facilities: radio C/L, TV C/L, carrier current (WERC), CCTV, VTR
Highest faculty degree: MA
Contact: Richard J. Knecht, chairman

OREGON

Linfield College
McMinnville, OR 97128
Tel. (503) 472-4121
Communication, 7 hrs., 2 courses (sem.)
Facilities: 3 radio C/L, TV C/L, FM station (KSLC), CCTV, VTR
Highest faculty degree: PhD
Contact: Craig Singletary, chairman

PENNSYLVANIA

Geneva College
Beaver Falls, PA 15010
Tel. (412) 846-5100
Speech–communications, 16 hrs., 4 courses (sem.)
Facilities: radio C/L, FM station (WGEV), film studio
Highest faculty degree: MS
Contact: C. Benjamin Hale, Jr., chairman

Villanova University
Villanova, PA 19085
Tel. (215) 527-2100
Speech–communications, 3 hrs., 1 course (sem.)
Facilities: radio C/L, TV C/L, carrier current, CCTV, VTR
Highest faculty degree: MS
Contact: R. G. Wilke, chairman

WASHINGTON

Central Washington State College
Ellensburg, WA 98926
Tel. (509) 963-3342
Mass media, 19 hrs., 10 courses (qr.)

Facilities: radio C/L, TV C/L, AM station (KCWS), carrier current, TV station (KCWS), CCTV, VTR
Undergraduate scholarships: 1—average amount $75
Highest faculty degree: MA
Contact: Roger R. Reynolds, chairman

Walla Walla College
College Place, WA 99324
Tel. (509) 527-2454
Communications, 8 hrs., 3 courses (qr.)
Facilities: FM station (KGTS)
Highest faculty degree: PhD
Contact: Loren Dickinson, chairman

WISCONSIN

Beloit College
Beloit, WI 53511
Tel. (608) 365-3391
Theatre arts, 4 hrs., 1 course
Facilities: 3 radio C/L, TV C/L, FM station (WBCR), VTR

Highest faculty degree: MS
Contact: Carl G. Balson, chairman

St. Norbert College
DePere, WI 54115
Tel. (414) 336-3181
Communication arts, 8 hrs., 2 courses (sem.)
Facilities: TV station (WFRV), VTR
Undergraduate scholarships: 1—average amount $100
Highest faculty degree: MA
Contact: John D. Giovannini, chairman

University of Wisconsin at Eau Claire
Eau Claire, WI 54701
Tel. (715) 836-2300
Speech, 36 hrs., 11 courses (sem.); journalism, 6 hrs., 2 courses, 3 grad. hrs., 1 course
Facilities: 3 radio C/L, 2 TV C/L, FM station (WUEC), VTR
Highest faculty degree: PhD
Contact: Robert L Bailey, chairman

Two-Year Colleges Offering Programs in Broadcasting

*In this section the number of technical (eg, electronics) course offered by the school is also listed.

ALABAMA

Gadsden State Junior College
Gadsden, AL 35903
Tel. (205) 564-0484
Broadcasting, 55 hrs., 11 courses (qr.); technical courses, 5 hrs., 1 course
1st-year students: 25
2nd-year students: 20
Facilities: 2 radio C/L, 2 TV C/L, FM station (WEXP), CCTV
Highest faculty degree: MA
Contact: Donald R. Smith, chairman

ARIZONA

Phoenix College
Phoenix, AZ 85013
Tel. (602) 253-6108
Mass communications, 25 hrs., 9 courses (sem.); technical courses, 6 hrs., 2 courses
1st-year students: 53
2nd-year students: 20
Facilities: 2 radio C/L, FM station (KMCR)
Highest faculty degree: MA
Contact: Donald J. Richardson, chairman

CALIFORNIA

Butte College
Oroville, CA 95926
Tel. (916) 895-2451
Mass communications, 16 hrs., 4 courses (qr.); technical courses—electronics, 12 hrs., 3 courses
1st-year students: 25

2nd-year students: 15
Facilities: use commercial station (KFMF-FM)
Highest faculty degree: MA
Contact: Mark Hall, chairman

City College of San Francisco
San Francisco, CA 94112
Tel. (415) 209-3525
Broadcasting, 50 hrs., 14 courses (sem.); technical courses—electronic engineering, 15 hrs., 5 courses
1st-year students: 125
2nd-year students: 75
Facilities: 6 radio C/L, 3 TV C/L, FM station (CABLE 909), carrier current (KCSF), 3 electronic labs, CCTV, VTR
Scholarships: 5—average amount $50
2—average amount $200
Highest faculty degree: MA
Contact: Henry Leff, chairman

College of San Mateo
San Mateo, CA 94402
Tel. (415) 574-6586
Telecommunications, 42 hrs., 14 courses (sem.); technical courses, 16 hrs., 6 courses
1st-year students: 175
2nd year students: 100
Facilities: 3 radio C/L, 2 TV C/L, FM station (KCSM), TV station (KCSM-TV), ETV, CCTV, VTR, use commercial stations (KRON-TV, KGO-TV)
Highest faculty degree: MA
Contact: Doug Montgomery, chairman

College of the Desert
Palm Desert, CA 92260
Tel. (714) 346-8041

Radio–television, 121 hrs., 17 courses (sem.); technical courses—engineering technology, 131 hrs., 29 courses
1st-year students: 10
2nd-year students: 5
Facilities: 2 radio C/L, 1 TV C/L, electronic lab, CCTV, VTR, portable color camera
Assistantships: 3—average amount $2.50 per hr.
Av. no. hrs./wk. required: 15 max.
Highest faculty degree: MA
Contact: Wendell Ford, chairman

Consumnes River College
Sacramento, CA 95823
Tel. (916) 421-1000
Communications, 49 units, 15 courses (sem.)
1st-year students: 90
2nd-year students: 40
Facilities: radio C/L, TV C/L, carrier current (KCOS), CCTV, VTR
Scholarships: 3—average amount $200
Highest faculty degree: MA
Contact: Doree Steinmann, chairman

Fullerton College
Fullerton, CA 92634
Tel. (714) 871-8000
Theatre arts, 76 hrs., 8 courses (sem.); technical courses, 14 hrs., 3 courses
1st-year students: 70
2nd-year students: 55
Facilities: 9 radio C/L, 4 TV C/L, FM station (KBPK), 2 electronic labs, CCTV, VTR
Scholarships: 1—average amount $50–$100
Assistantships: 1–3—average amount $50–$100
Av. no. hrs./wk. required: 4–6
Highest faculty degree: MA
Contact: Richard W. Thompson, chairman

Grossmont College
El Cajon, CA 92020
Tel. (714) 465-1700
Communication arts/telecommunications, 43 hrs., 14 courses (sem.)
1st-year students: 60
2nd-year students: 30
Facilities: 2 radio C/L, 2 TV C/L, carrier current (KGR), CCTV, VTR
Scholarships: 2—average amount $100
Assistantships: 4—average amount $300
Av. no. hrs./wk. required: 10
Highest faculty degree: MA
Contact: J. D. Scouller, chairman

Long Beach City College
Long Beach, CA 90808
Tel. (213) 420-4308
Speech–theatre arts, 30 hrs., 11 courses (sem.); technical courses—electronics, 45 hrs., 15 courses
1st-year students: 75
2nd-year students: 50
Facilities: 2 radio C/L, TV C/L, carrier current, CCTV, VTR
Assistantships: 2—average amount $3.00 per day
Highest faculty degree: PhD
Contact: Lynne S. Gross, chairman

Merced College
Merced, CA 95340
Tel. (219) 723-4321
Mass communications, 25 hrs., 12 courses (sem.); technical courses—electronics, 30 hrs., 10 courses
1st-year students: 20
2nd-year students: 30
Facilities: 3 radio C/L, TV C/L, FM station (KBDR), CCTV, VTR
Assistantships: 2—average amount $1200 per yr.
Av. no. hrs./wk. required: 15 (must meet federal work-study requirements)
Highest faculty degree: MA
Contact: Ralph R. Donald, chairman

Moorpark College
Moorpark, CA 93021
Tel. (805) 529-2321
Telecommunications, 51 hrs., 17 courses (sem.), technical courses—electronics technology, 30 hrs., 10 courses
1st-year students: 60
2nd-year students: 40
Facilities: radio C/L, TV C/L, electronic lab, CCTV, VTR, use commercial stations (KVEN/KHAV-FM, KNJP-FM)
Assistantships: 2—average amount $1280
Av. no. hrs./wk. required: 20
Highest faculty degree: MS
Contact: Alfred James Miller, chairman

Orange Coast College
Costa Mesa, CA 92626
Tel. (714) 556-5651
Broadcast arts, 30 hrs., 15 courses (sem.)
1st-year students: 100
2nd-year students: 40
Facilities: radio C/L, TV C/L, carrier current (KOCR), CCTV, VTR
Highest faculty degree: BA
Contact: Peter J. Scarpello, chairman

Pasadena City College
Pasadena, CA 91106
Tel. (213) 578-7216
Telecommunications, 53 hrs., 12 courses (sem.), technical courses, 40 hrs., 11 courses
1st-year students: 124
2nd-year students: 75
Facilities: 8 radio C/L, 4 TV C/L, FM station (KPCS), 3 electronic labs, CCTV, VTR
Highest faculty degree: PhD
Contact: Harold E. Salisbury, chairman

Rio Hondo College
Whittier, CA 90608
Tel. (213) 692-0921
Communications, 32 hrs., 8 courses (sem.); social sciences, 3 hrs., 1 course; technical courses, 12 hrs., 4 courses
1st-year students: 72
2nd-year students: 50

Facilities: 4 radio C/L, 2 TV C/L, carrier current (KRCH), 2 electronic labs, CCTV, VTR
Highest faculty degree: MA
Contact: Jay R. Loughrin, chairman

San Bernardino Valley College
San Bernardino, CA 92403
Tel. (714) 885-0231
Telecommunications, 36 hrs., 19 courses (sem.)
1st-year students: 70
2nd-year students: 40
Facilities: 3 radio C/L, 2 TV C/L, FM station (KVCR), TV station (KVCR), ETV, CCTV, VTR, film studio
Assistantships: 2—average amount $750 per sem.
Av. no. hrs./wk. required: 20
Highest faculty degree: MA
Contact: John Kirkwood, chairman

San Diego City College
San Diego, CA 92101
Tel. (714) 234-1062
Telecommunications, 86 hrs., 16 courses (sem.); speech, 3 hrs., 1 course
1st-year students: 180
2nd-year students: 120
Facilities: 5 radio C/L, 2 TV C/L, FM station (KSDS), CCTV, VTR

Santa Rosa Junior College
Santa Rosa, CA 95401
Tel. (707) 527-4398
Speech, 16 hrs., 4 courses (sem.)
1st-year students: 68
2nd-year students: 40
Facilities: TV C/L, carrier current (KVRE), CCTV, kinescope, VTR, film studio
Highest faculty degree: PhD
Contact: John Bigby, chairman

Shatsa College
Redding, CA 96001
Tel. (916) 241-3523
Speech–drama, 18 hrs., 6 courses (sem.); technical courses—electronics, 20 hrs., 5 courses
1st-year students: 16
2nd-year students: 7
Facilities: radio C/L, TV C/L, electronic lab, CCTV, VTR
Highest faculty degree: MA
Contact: J. L. Carpenter, chairman

FLORIDA

Pensacola Junior College
Pensacola, FL 32504
Tel. (904) 476-5410
Broadcasting, 18 hrs., 6 courses (sem.)
1st- and 2nd-year students: 160
Facilities: 2 TV C/L, TV station (WSRE), ETV, CCTV, VTR
Highest faculty degree: MA
Contact: Mike Piscitelli, chairman

IDAHO

Ricks College
Rexburg, ID 83440
Tel. (208) 356-2204
Communications, 17 hrs., 6 courses (sem.); business, 5 hrs., 2 courses; technical courses—electronics, 17 hrs., 5 courses
1st-year students: 15
2nd-year students: 8
Facilities: 2 radio C/L, TV C/L, FM station (KRIC), carrier current (KVIK), 2 electronic labs, CCTV, VTR
Scholarships: 2—average amount $400
Assistantships: 1
Highest faculty degree: PhD
Contact: Kay Wilkins, chairman

ILLINOIS

Black Hawk College
Moline, IL 61265
Tel. (309) 796-1311
Television & radio, 43 hrs., 13 courses (sem.); technical courses, 36 hrs., 8 courses
1st-year students: 30
2nd-year students: 21
Facilities: 2 radio C/L, 2 TV C/L, carrier current (WCHO), 2 electronic labs, 3 CCTV, VTR, use commercial station (WQAD), cable TV UHF
Highest faculty degree: EdD
Contact: Robert White, professor

College of DuPage
Glen Ellyn, IL 60137
Tel. (312) 858-2800
Media, 45 hrs., 14 courses (qr.); technical courses, 5 hrs., 1 course
1st- and 2nd-year students: 200
Facilities: 2 TV C/L, CCTV
Highest faculty degree: MA
Contact: Gary C. Bergland, chairman

Illinois Eastern Community Colleges—Campus of Wabash Valley College
Mt. Carmel, IL 62863
Tel. (618) 262-8641
Radio/TV broadcasting, 83 hrs., 19 courses (qr.), technical courses—electronic engineering, 40 hrs., 10 courses
1st-year students: 8
2nd-year students: 6
Facilities: 4 radio C/L, TV C/L, FM station (WVJC), carrier current (WWVC-AM), electronic lab., ETV, VTR
Contact: Richard T. Ammon, instructor

Lake Land College
Mattoon, IL 61938
Tel. (217) 235-3131
Radio, 52 hrs., 13 courses (qr.); TV, 8 hrs., 2 courses; technical courses, 4 hrs., 1 course
1st-year students: 20
2nd-year students: 15

Facilities: radio C/L, TV C/L, FM station (WLKL), 2 electronic labs, CCTV, local cable systems
Highest faculty degree: BS
Contact: Kenneth S. Beno, chairman

Parkland College
Champaign, IL 61820
Tel. (217) 351-2450
Communications, 52 hrs., 17 courses (sem.); technical courses—electronics, 80 hrs., 21 courses
1st-year students: 35
2nd-year students: 51
Facilities: radio C/L, 2 electronic labs, FM station (WPCD-college station), use commercial stations (WCIA-TV, WLRW-FM)
Highest faculty degree: MA
Contact: Edward G. Kelly, chairman

INDIANA

Vincennes University
Vincennes, IN 47591
Tel. (812) 882-2237
Broadcast-production technology, 36 hrs., 8 courses (sem.)
1st-year students: 53
2nd-year students: 33
Facilities: 3 radio C/L, 2 TV C/L, FM station (WVUB), TV station (WVUT), CCTV, VTR, mobile studio
Scholarships: 3—average amount $500
Highest faculty degree: MS
Contact: Mark R. Lange, chairman

IOWA

Iowa Central Community College
Port Dodge, IA 50501
Tel. (515) 576-6049
Broadcast services–education, 30 hrs., 10 courses (sem.); technical courses, 19 hrs., 5 courses
1st-year students: 32
2nd-year students: 19
Facilities: radio C/L, FM station (KICB), carrier current (KICB)
Scholarships: 1—average amount $100
Highest faculty degree: MA
Contact: Ben. J. Jarman, chairman

KANSAS

Barton County Community Junior College
Great Bend, KS 67530
Tel. (316) 792-2701
Broadcasting, 15 hrs., 6 courses; technical courses—electronics, 30 hrs., 12 courses
1st-year students: 8
2nd-year students: 12
Facilities: 2 radio C/L, TV C/L, FM station (KBJC), 2 electronic labs, CCTV, VTR
Scholarships: 1—average amount $350
Highest faculty degree: MA
Contact: Ken Kempner, chairman

Garden City Community College
Garden City, KS 67846
Tel. (316) 276-7611
Speech & drama, 3 hrs., 1 course (sem.)
1st-year students: 15
2nd-year students: 7
Facilities: VTR
Highest faculty degree: MS
Contact: Kirk Ashton, chairman

KENTUCKY

Ashland Community College
Ashland, KY 41101
Tel. (606) 325-8586
English, 16 hrs., 6 courses (sem.); technical courses, 10 hrs., 2 courses
1st-year students: 20
2nd-year students: 5
Facilities: radio C/L, TV C/L, carrier current, electronic lab, CCTV, VTR
Highest faculty degree: MA
Contact: William Sadler, chairman

Somerset Community College
Somerset, KY 42501
Tel. (606) 678-8174
Communications, 10 hrs., 4 courses (sem.)
1st-year students: 14
2nd-year students: 4
Facilities: radio C/L, TV C/L, FM station (WSCC), electronic lab, CCTV, VTR, use commercial station (WSFC)
Highest faculty degree: MA
Contact: Don Orwin, chairman

MARYLAND

Community College of Baltimore
Baltimore, MD 21215
Tel. (301) 462-5800
Speech, drama, radio & TV, 24 hrs., 8 courses (sem.); technical courses—electronics, 24 hrs., 8 courses
1st-year students: 64
2nd-year students: 5
Facilities: radio C/L, TV C/L, FM station (WBJC), electronic lab, CCTV, VTR, use commercial station (WJZ-TV)
Assistantships: 1—average amount minimum wage
Av. no. hrs./wk. required: 12
Highest faculty degree: MA
Contact: A. Frank Holston, chairman

Harford Community College
Bel Air, MD 21014
Tel. (301) 838-1000
Mathematics & engineering, 6 hrs., 3 courses (sem.); humanities, 9 hrs., 3 courses; technical courses, 6 hrs., 2 courses; electronics, 14 hrs., 4 courses
1st-year students: 5
2nd-year students: 3
Facilities: radio C/L, FM station (WHFC)
Highest faculty degree: PhD
Contact: Paul G. Yorkis, chairman

MASSACHUSETTS

Mt. Wachusett Community College
Gardner, MA 01440
Tel. (617) 632-6600
Public communications, 51 hrs., 17 courses (sem.);
business, 18 hrs., 6 courses; technical courses—
science & technology, 18 hrs., 6 courses
1st-year students: 50
2nd-year students: 40
Facilities: 4 radio C/L, 2 TV C/L, 2 electronic labs,
cable TV channel, ETV, CCTV, VTR, use commercial stations (WGAW, WEIM), closed-circuit
radio station, remote color-TV van
Highest faculty degree: MS
Contact: Vincent S. Islenti, chairman

MICHIGAN

Delta College
University Center, MI 48710
Tel. (517) 686-0400
TV, 45 hrs., 13 courses (sem.)
1st-year students: 40
2nd-year students: 20
Facilities: radio C/L, TV C/L, TV station (WUCM),
ETV, CCTV, VTR, film studio
Highest faculty degree: MA
Contact: William J. Ballard, chairman

St. Clair County Community College
Port Huron, MI 48060
Tel. (313) 984-3881
*Communications media, transfer and occupational
associate-degree programs,* 27 hrs., 14 courses
1st- and 2nd-year students: 74
Facilities: radio C/L, TV C/L, FM station (WSGR), 2
electronic labs, CCTV, VTR
Scholarships: 3—average amount full tuition
Highest faculty degree: MS
Contact: Donna R. Williams, chairman

MINNESOTA

Duluth Area Vocational Technical Institute
Duluth, MN 55811
Tel. (218) 728-2801
Broadcasting, 540 hrs., 108 courses; technical
courses, 540 hrs., 108 courses
1st-year students: 18
2nd-year students: 18
Facilities: 3 radio C/L, carrier current (KBCT), 2
electronic labs, VTR, use commercial stations
(WDIO-TV, KDAL Radio-TV)
Highest faculty degree: MA
Contact: Doyle Cossin, chairman

Rochester Community College
Rochester, MN 55901
Tel. (507) 288-6101
Journalism, 18 hrs., 5 courses (qr.); business, 3 hrs.,
1 course
1st-year students: 12
2nd-year students: 6

Facilities: 2 radio C/L, TV C/L, CCTV, VTR
Highest faculty degree: MS
Contact: Jim Kehoe, chairman

MISSISSIPPI

**Mississippi Gulf Coast Junior College (Jefferson
Davis Campus)**
Gulfport, MS 39501
Tel. (601) 896-3355
Broadcasting, 30 hrs., 10 courses (sem.)
1st-year students: 16
2nd-year students: 8
Facilities: 2 radio C/L, carrier current (WJDC)
Highest faculty degree: BS
Contact: Douglas Hendon, chairman

NEBRASKA

**Northeast Nebraska Technical Community Col-
lege**
Norfolk, NB 68701
Tel. (402) 371-2020
Creative arts, 14 hrs., 10 courses (sem.); technical
courses—electronics, 12 hrs., 4 courses
1st-year students: 5
2nd-year students: 8
Facilities: 4 radio C/L, 5 TV C/L, CCTV, VTR, use
commercial stations (WJAG AM-FM, WHQL-
TV)
Highest faculty degree: MA
Contact: Thomas L. DeBusk, chairman

NEW YORK

Alfred State College
Alfred, NY 14902
Tel. (607) 871-6149
Communications media, 24 hrs., 24 courses (sem.);
technical courses—electrical, 50 hrs., 13 courses
1st-year students: 50
2nd-year students: 50
Facilities: radio C/L, TV C/L, FM station (WETD),
carrier current (WVAT), electronic labs, CCTV,
VTR, studio & remote color equipment, elec-
tronic editing, CATV channel 24-hours-a-day,
satellite-receiving site
Highest faculty degree: PhD
Contact: Jerry A. Gordon, chairman

Nassau Community College
Garden City, NY 11530
Tel. (516) 742-0600
Communications, 15 hrs., 3 courses (sem.)
1st-year students: 20
2nd-year students: 15
Facilities: radio C/L, TV C/L, FM station (WHPC),
TV station (WHLI), ETV, CCTV, VTR
Highest faculty degree: EdD
Contact: Edward DeRoo, chairman

Onondaga Community College
Syracuse, NY 13215
Tel. (315) 469-7741

Radio–TV, 9 hrs., 3 courses (sem.); technical courses, 18 hrs., 5 courses
1st-year students: 80
2nd-year students: 40
Facilities: radio C/L, TV C/L, carrier current (WOCC), CCTV, VTR
Highest faculty degree: MS
Contact: Catherine Stampalia, chairman

Suffolk County Community College
Selden, NY 11784
Tel. (516) 233-5257
Speech–theatre, 24 hrs., 8 courses (sem.)
1st-year students: 40
2nd-year students: 20
Facilities: 3 radio C/L, TV C/L, carrier current (WSCC), VTR, film studio
Scholarships: 1—average amount $150
Assistantships: 5
Highest faculty degree: MA
Contact: Howard L. Stevens, chairman

NORTH CAROLINA

Lenoir Community College
Kingston, NC 28501
Tel. (919) 527-6223
Broadcasting technology, 51 hrs., 17 courses (qr.)
1st-year students: 19
2nd-year students: 11
Facilities: 2 radio C/L, TV C/L, carrier current (WLCC), VTR, use commercial stations (WITN-TV, WCTI-TV)
Highest faculty degree: BS
Contact: A. W. Carruth, Jr., chairman

OHIO

Ohio University
Zanesville, OH 43701
Tel. (614) 453-0762
Communications, 50 hrs., 16 courses (qr.); technical courses, 22 hrs., 5 courses
1st-year students: 21
2nd-year students: 22
Facilities: radio C/L, TV C/L, VTR, use commercial station (WHIZ-TV)
Highest faculty degree: MA
Contact: Reed Smith, chairman

OREGON

Blue Mountain Community College
Pendleton, OR 97801
Tel. (503) 276-1260
Broadcasting, 40 hrs., 8 courses (qr.); study skills, 6 hrs., 2 courses; technical courses, 6 hrs., 1 course; electronics, 67 hrs., 18 courses
1st-year students: 15
2nd-year students: 10
Facilities: 5 radio C/L, 3 TV C/L, FM station (KRBM), 3 electronic labs, CCTV, VTR
Scholarships: Oregon Association of Broadcasters—competitive
Contact: Blaine T. Hanks, chairman

Portland Community College
Portland, OR 97219
Tel. (503) 244-6111
Radio/TV broadcasting, 25 hrs., 5 courses (qr.)
1st-year students: 50
2nd-year students: 40
Facilities: 4 radio C/L, TV C/L, carrier current (KPCC), CCTV, VTR, use commercial stations (KEX, KGW, KPTV, KILO, KVAN, KJIB, KRDR)
Scholarships: 1—average amount $600
Student help: 3—average amount tuition
Av. no. hrs./wk. required: 15
Highest faculty degree: PhD
Contact: Keith Allen Glutsch

PENNSYLVANIA

Pennsylvania State University (Wilkes-Barre Campus)
Wilkes-Barre, PA 18708
Tel. (717) 675-2171
Mass communications–broadcasting, 12 hrs., 4 courses (sem.)
1st-year students: 26
2nd-year students: 17
Facilities: radio C/L, TV C/L, FM station (WPSI), CCTV, VTR, ETV
College work–study program: 3—average amount $30 per wk.
Av. no. hrs./wk. required: 15
Highest faculty degree: MA
Contact: Ralph E. Carmode, chairman

SOUTH CAROLINA

Tri County Technical College
Pendleton, SC 29670
Tel. (803) 646-3227
Radio & TV broadcasting, 45 hrs., 15 courses (qr.)
1st-year students: 20
2nd-year students: 14
Facilities: 2 radio C/L, TV C/L, VTR
Scholarships: 2
Av. no. hrs./wk. required: college work–study program
Highest faculty degree: BA
Contact: Charles H. Jordan, chairman

SOUTH DAKOTA

Black Hills State College
Spearfish, SD 57783
Tel. (605) 642-6737
Communications, 25 hrs., 8 courses (sem.); industrial arts, 23 hrs., 8 courses
1st-year students: 6
2nd-year students: 6
Facilities: radio C/L, 2 TV C/L, FM station (KBHU), carrier current, CCTV, VTR
Highest faculty degree: MA
Contact: Richard Boyd, chairman

TENNESSEE

Jackson State Community College
Jackson, TN 38301
Tel. (901) 424-3520
Instructional-media center, 15 hrs., 7 courses (qr.)
1st-year students: 9
2nd-year students: 5
Facilities: TV C/L, CCTV, VTR
Highest faculty degree: MEd
Contact: Charles J. Cooper, chairman

TEXAS

Central Texas College
Killeen, TX 76541
Tel. (812) 526-1176
Telecommunications, 18 hrs., 6 courses (sem.); jour-
   nalism, 8 hrs., 2 courses; technical courses, 21
   hrs., 7 courses
1st-year students: 40
2nd-year students: 40
Facilities: 3 radio C/L, 2 TV C/L, FM station
   (KNCT), TV station (KNCT), ETV, VTR, film
   studio
Scholarships: 1—average amount $1000
Assistantships: 10—average amount $4000
Av. no. hrs./wk. required: 40
Highest faculty degree: MA
Contact: P. Anthony Zeiss, chairman

Odessa College
Odessa, TX 79760
Tel. (915) 337-5381
Communications & theatre, 19 hrs., 6 courses (sem.);
   technical courses—electricity/electronics, 31
   hrs., 10 courses
1st-year students: 20
2nd-year students: 10
Facilities: 3 radio C/L, 2 TV C/L, FM station
   (KOCV), cable TV, VTR
Scholarships: 10—average amount $150 each
Highest faculty degree: MA
Contact: Wallace R. Jackson, chairman

San Antonio College
San Antonio, TX 78284
Tel. (512) 734-7311
Radio–television–film, 32 hrs., 11 courses (sem.);
   journalism, 3 hrs., 1 course
1st-year students: 150
2nd-year students: 100
Facilities: 6 radio C/L, 2 TV C/L, FM station
   (KSYM), carrier current (WSAC), 1 film-editing
   lab, 1 film studio
Scholarships: 3—average amount $100
Assistantships: 4—average amount $115 per mo.
Highest faculty degree: MFA
Contact: Jean M. Longwith, chairman

VIRGINIA

Virginia Western Community College
Roanoke, VA 24015
Tel. (703) 982-7269
Radio/TV production technology, 45 hrs. (qr.); art/
   speech, 5 hrs., 2 courses; technical courses—
   engineering, 6 hrs., 2 courses
1st-year students: 45
2nd-year students: 20
Facilities: 2 radio C/L, color TV C/L, FM station
   (WVWR), carrier current (WCTR), electronic
   lab., CCTV, VTR
Assistantships: 2 class credits
Av. no. hrs./wk. required: 15
Highest faculty degree: MS
Contact: Gary M. Kazanjian, chairman

WASHINGTON

Lower Columbia College
Longview, WA 98632
Tel. (206) 425-6500
Communications, 19 hrs., 7 courses (qr.); technical
   courses—electronics, 60 hrs., 18 courses
1st-year students: 7
2nd-year students: 1
Facilities: FM station (KLVR), VTR
Highest faculty degree: MS
Contact: John Diehnel, chairman

WISCONSIN

Milwaukee Area Technical College
Milwaukee, WI 43203
Tel. (414) 271-1036
Telecasting, 35 hrs., 11 courses (sem.); technical
   courses, 35 hrs., 10 courses
1st-year students: 31
2nd-year students: 19
Facilities: 4 TV C/L, electronic lab, TV stations
   (WMVS, WMVT), ETV, CCTV, VTR, film
   studios
Highest faculty degree: PhD
Contact: Otto Schlaak, chairman

WYOMING

Central Wyoming College
Riverton, WY 82501
Tel. (307) 856-9291
Radio–TV, 30 hrs., 14 courses (sem.); technical
   courses, 2 hrs., 1 course
1st-year students: 5
2nd-year students: 6
Facilities: 2 radio C/L, 2 TV C/L, FM station
   (KCWC), electronic lab, CCTV, VTR, use com-
   mercial stations (KVOW, KOVE, KWRB-TV)
Scholarships: 2—average amount tuition
Assistantships: 1—average amount $1000
Av. no. hrs./wk. required: 12
Highest faculty degree: MA
Contact: Clive Thirkill, chairman

College Television Stations

ALABAMA

WAIQ-TV Channel 26
Auburn University
Auburn, AL 36830
(205) 826-4110
Contact: Ed Wegener

ALASKA

KUAC-TV Channel 9
University of Alaska
Fairbanks, AK 99701
(907) 479-7491
Contact: Donald B. Upham

ARIZONA

KAET-TV Channel 8
Arizona State University
Tempe, AZ 85281
(602) 965-3506
Contact: Robert H. Ellis

KUAT-TV Channel 6
University of Arizona
Tucson, AZ 85721
(602) 884-1434
Contact: Frank Barreca

CALIFORNIA

KOCE-TV Channel 50
Coast Community College
Huntington Beach, CA 92647
(714) 897-0302
Contact: William Furniss

KVCR-TV Channel 24
San Bernadino Community College
San Bernadino, CA 92403
(714) 885-0231
Contact: Fred R. Burgess

KPBS-TV Channel 15
San Diego State University
San Diego, CA 92115
(714) 286-6415
Contact: Paul J. Steen

KCSM-TV Channel 14
San Mateo Community College
San Mateo, CA 94402
(415) 574-6586
Contact: Douglas B. Montgomery

COLORADO

KTSC-TV Channel 8
University of Southern Colorado
Pueblo, CO 81104
(303) 549-3220
Contact: John C. Crabbe

FLORIDA

WUFT-TV Channel 5
University of Florida
Gainesville, FL 32611
(904) 392-0471
Contact: David T. Brugger

WSRE-TV Channel 23
Pensacola Junior College
Pensacola, FL 32504
(904) 476-5418
Contact: Eric C. Smith, Jr.

WFSU-TV Channel 11
Florida State University
Tallahassee, FL 32306
(904) 644-1731
Contact: Edward L. Herp

WUSF-TV Channel 16
University of Southern Florida
Tampa, FL 33620
(813) 974-4000
Contact: Dr. William Mitchell

GEORGIA

WGTV-TV Channel 8
University of Georgia
Athens, GA 30602
(404) 542-3554
Contact: Dr. William H. Hale, Jr.

HAWAII

WHET-TV Channel 11
University of Hawaii
Honolulu, HI 96822
(808) 955-7878
Contact: Mary G. F. Bitterman

KMEB-TV Channel 10
University of Hawaii
Wailuku, HI 96743
(808) 955-7878
Contact: Mary G. F. Bitterman

237

IDAHO

KAID-TV Channel 4
Boise State University
Boise, ID 83725
(208) 385-3344
Contact: Jack A. Schlaefle

KUID-TV Channel 12
University of Idaho
Moscow, ID 83843
(208) 885-6723
Contact: Arthur Hook

KBGL-TV Channel 10
Idaho State University
Pocatello, ID 83201
(208) 236-2857
Contact: Herbert Everitt

ILLINOIS

WUSI-TV Channel 8
Southern Illinois University
Carbondale, IL 62901
(618) 453-4343
Contact: David B. Rochelle

WUSI-TV Channel 16
Southern Illinois University
Olney, IL 62450
(618) 453-4343
Contact: David B. Rochelle

WILL-TV Channel 12
University of Illinois
Urbana, IL 61801
(217) 333-1070
Contact: Donald P. Mullally

INDIANA

WTIU-TV Channel 30
Indiana University
Bloomington, IN 47401
(812) 337-5900
Contact: Donley F. Fedderson

WIPB-TV Channel 49
Ball State University
Muncie, IN 47303
(317) 285-4771
Contact: James R. Needham

WVUT-TV Channel 22
Vincennes University
Vincennes, IN 47591
(812) 882-2237
Contact: James L. Jernigan

IOWA

WOI-TV Channel 5
Iowa State University of Science and Technology
Ames, IA 50010
(515) 294-5555
Contact: Robert C. Mulhall

KANSAS

KTWU-TV Channel 11
Washburn University
Topeka, KS 66621
(913) 272-8181
Contact: Dr. Dale Anderson

LOUISIANA

WWL-TV Channel 4
Loyola State University
New Orleans, LA 70118
(504) 529-4444
Contact: Michael Early

MAINE

WCBB-TV Channel 10
Colby College
Bates College
Bowdoin College
Augusta, ME 04204
(207) 783-9101
Contact: H. Odell Skinner

WMEG-TV Channel 26
University of Maine
Biddeford, ME 04005
(207) 866-4493
Contact: Thomas Strauss

WMED-TV Channel 13
University of Maine
Calais, ME 04619
(207) 866-4493
Contact: Thomas Strauss

WMEB-TV Channel 12
University of Maine
Orono, ME 04473
(207) 866-4493
Contact: Thomas Strauss

WMEM-TV Channel 10
University of Maine
Presque Isle, ME 04769
(207) 866-4493
Contact: Thomas Strauss

MICHIGAN

WGVC-TV Channel 35
Grand Valley State College
Allendale, MI 49401
(616) 895-6691
Contact: Gordon Lawrence

WCMU-TV Channel 14
Central Michigan University
Mt. Pleasant, MI 48859
(517) 774-3105
Contact: William J. Grigaliunas

WCML-TV Channel 6
Central Michigan University
Alpena, MI 49707
(517) 774-3105
Contact: William J. Grigaliunas

WKAR-TV Channel 23
Michigan State University
East Lansing, MI 48824
(517) 355-2300
Contact: Robert D. Page

WNMU-TV Channel 13
Northern Michigan University
Marquette, MI 49855
(906) 227-1300
Contact: Bruce Tusner

WUCM-TV Channel 19
Delta College
University Center, MI 48710
(517) 686-0400
Contact: William J. Ballard

MISSOURI

KOMU-TV Channel 8
University of Missouri
Columbia, MO 65201
(314) 442-1122
Contact: Thomas R. Gray

NEBRASKA

KUON-TV Channel 12
University of Nebraska
Lincoln, NB 68508
(402) 472-3611
Contact: Jack G. McBride

NEW HAMPSHIRE

WEDB-TV Channel 40
University of New Hampshire
Berlin, NH 03570
(603) 862-1047
Contact: Keith J. Nighbert

WENH-TV Channel 11
University of New Hampshire
Durham, NH 03824
(603) 862-1047
Contact: Keith J. Nighbert

WHED-TV Channel 15
University of New Hampshire
Hanover, NH 03755
(603) 862-1047
Contact: Keith J. Nighbert

WEKU-TV Channel 52
University of New Hampshire
Keene, NH 03431
(603) 862-1047
Contact: Keith J. Nighbert

WLED-TV Channel 49
University of New Hampshire
Littleton, NH 03561
(603) 862-1047
Contact: Keith J. Nighbert

NEW MEXICO

KNME-TV Channel 5
University of New Mexico
Albuquerque, NM 87106
(505) 277-2121
Contact: Robert M. Gordon

KOAT-TV Channel 7
University of New Mexico
Albuquerque, NM 87131
(505) 247-0101
Contact: Max Sklower

KRWG-TV Channel 22
New Mexico State University
Las Cruces, NM 88001
(505) 646-4525
Contact: James A. Dryden

KENW-TV Channel 3
Eastern New Mexico University
Portales, NM 88130
(505) 562-3112
Contact: Duane W. Ryan

NEW YORK

WCFE-TV Channel 57
State University College
Plattsburgh, NY 12901
(518) 564-2114
Contact: Paul C. Hassenplug

NORTH CAROLINA

WUNF-TV Channel 33
University of North Carolina
Asheville, NC 28801
(919) 933-8191
Contact: George E. Bair

QUNC-TV Channel 4
University of North Carolina
Chapel Hill, NC 27514
(919) 933-8191
Contact: George E. Bair

WUND-TV Channel 2
University of North Carolina
Columbia, NC 27925
(919) 933-8191
Contact: George E. Bair

WUNG-TV Channel 58
University of North Carolina
Concord, NC 28025
(919) 933-8191
Contact: George E. Bair

WUNK-TV Channel 25
University of North Carolina
Greenville, NC 27823
(919) 933-8191
Contact: George E. Bair

WUNE-TV Channel 17
University of North Carolina
Linville, NC 28646
(919) 933-8191
Contact: George E. Bair

WUNJ-TV Channel 39
University of North Carolina
Wilmington, NC 28401
(919) 933-8191
Contact: George E. Bair

WUNL-TV Channel 26
University of North Carolina
Winston-Salem, NC 27514
(919) 933-8191
Contact: George E. Bair

OHIO

WNEO-TV Channel 49
University of Akron
Akron, OH 44304
(216) 678-1656
Contact: Phillip C. English

WOUB-TV Channel 20
Ohio University
Athens, OH 45701
(614) 594-5409
Contact: N. Joseph Welling

WOUC-TV Channel 44
Ohio University
Athens, OH 45701
(614) 594-5409
Contact: N. Joseph Welling

WBGU-TV Channel 57
Bowling Green State University
Bowling Green, OH 43402
(419) 372-0121
Contact: Duane E. Tucker

WPBO-TV Channel 42
Ohio State University
Columbus, OH 43210
(614) 421-2540
Contact: Elizabeth A. Young

WOSU-TV Channel 34
Ohio State University
Columbus, OH 43210
(614) 421-2540
Contact: Elizabeth A. Young

OREGON

KOAC-TV Channel 7
Oregon State University
Corvallis, OR 97331
(503) 229-4892
Contact: Donald Bryant

PENNSYLVANIA

WPSX-TV Channel 3
Pennsylvania State University
University Park, PA 16802
(814) 865-9531
Contact: David L. Phillips

SOUTH DAKOTA

KESD-TV Channel 8
South Dakota State University
Brookings, SD 57006
(615) 699-4191
Contact: Eric F. Brown

KUSD-TV Channel 2
University of South Dakota
Vermillion, SD 57069
(605) 677-5277
Contact: Martin P. Busch

KZSD-TV Channel 8
University of South Dakota
Vermillion, SD 57068
(605) 624-4497
Contact: Martin P. Busch

TENNESSEE

WSJK-TV Channel 2
University of Tennessee
Knoxville, TN 37916
(615) 974-5281
Contact: Ernest A. Curtis, Jr.

TEXAS

KAMU-TV Channel 15
Texas A & M University
College Station, TX 77843
(713) 854-5611
Contact: Dr. Mel Chastain

KUHT-TV Channel 18
University of Houston
Houston, TX 77004
(713) 748-6814
Contact: James L. Bauer

KNCT-TV Channel 46
Central Texas College
Killeen, TX 76541
(817) 526-1182
Contact: P. Anthony Zeiss

KTXT-TV Channel 5
Texas Technical University
Lubbock, TX 79409
(806) 742-2209
Contact: Mike Mezack

UTAH

KBYU-TV Channel 11
Brigham Young University
Provo, UT 84601
(801) 374-1211
Contact: Bruce L. Christensen

KUED-TV Channel 7
University of Utah
Salt Lake City, UT 84112
(801) 581-7777
Contact: Robert Reed

VERMONT

WETK-TV Channel 33
University of Vermont
Burlington, VT 05401
(802) 656-3311
Contact: John W. Dunlop

WVER-TV Channel 28
University of Vermont
Rutland, VT 05701
(802) 656-3311
Contact: John W. Dunlop

WVTB-TV Channel 20
University of Vermont
St. Johnsbury, VT 05819
(802) 656-3311
Contact: John W. Dunlop

WVTA-TV Channel 41
University of Vermont
Windsor, VT 05089
(802) 656-3311
Contact: John W. Dunlop

WASHINGTON

KWSU-TV Channel 10
Washington State University
Pullman, WA 99163
(509) 335-2681
Contact: Lyle Mettler

KCTS-TV Channel 9
University of Washington
Seattle, WA 98105
(206) 543-2000
Contact: Dr. Richard Meyer

WISCONSIN

WHA-TV Channel 21
University of Wisconsin
Madison, WI 53706
(608) 263-2121
Contact: Ronald C. Bornstein

Commercial Television Stations

ALABAMA

Anniston
WHMA-TV Channel 40 (CBS)
1330 Noble St.
Anniston, AL 36202
(205) 237-8651
Contact: Harry E. Mabry

Birmingham
WAPI-TV Channel 13 (NBC)
Box 10502
Birmingham, AL 35202
(205) 933-2720
Contact: Donald D. Wear

WBMG-TV Channel 42 (CBS)
2075 Golden Crest Dr.
Birmingham, AL 35209
(205) 252-9821
Contact: Hugh M. Smith

WBRC-TV Channel 6 (ABC)
Box 6
Birmingham, AL 35201
(205) 322-4701
Contact: Nick Bolton

Dothan
WDHN-TV Channel 18 (ABC)
Box 2228
Dothan, AL 36301
(205) 794-2651
Contact: Emery McCullough

WTVY-TV Channel 4 (CBS)
Box 1089
Dothan, AL 36301
(205) 792-3195
Contact: Eldon Klapel

Florence
WOWL-TV Channel 15 (NBC)
840 Cypress Mill Rd.
Florence, AL 35630
(205) 764-7711
Contact: Jack A. Worley

Huntsville
WAAY-TV Channel 31 (NBC)
1000 Monte Sano Blvd.
Huntsville, AL 35801
(205) 539-1783
Contact: Cecil Ruffin

WHNT-TV Channel 19 (CBS)
960 Monte Sano Blvd.
Huntsville, AL 35801
(205) 539-5743
Contact: Tom M. Percer

WYUR-TV Channel 48 (ABC)
4848 Governors Dr.
Huntsville, AL 35801
(205) 533-4848
Contact: William G. Evans

Mobile
WALA-TV Channel 10 (NBC)
210 Government St.
Mobile, AL 36601
(205) 433-3754
Contact: H. Ray McGuire

WKRG-TV Channel 5 (CBS)
162 St.Louis St.
Mobile, AL 36601
(205) 432-5501
Contact: C. P. Persons, Jr.

Montgomery
WCOV-TV Channel 20 (CBS)
1369 Adrian La.
Montgomery, AL 36105
(205) 288-7020
Contact: Karl Richards

WKAB-TV Channel 32 (ABC)
3251 Harrison Rd.
Montgomery, AL 36109
(205) 272-5331
Contact: Ken Lucas

WSFA-TV Channel 12 (NBC)
10 E. Delano St.
Montgomery, AL 36105
(205) 281-2900
Contact: Thomas J. Josephson

WSLA-TV Channel 8 (CBS)
Box 1888
Landline Rd.
Selma, AL 36701
(205) 875-2240
Contact: Thomas Bond

Tuscaloosa
WCFT-TV Channel 33 (CBS)
41st Ave. at 35th St.
Tuscaloosa, AL 35401
(205) 533-1333
Contact: Stan Siegal

ALASKA

Anchorage
KENI-TV Channel 2 (NBC)
4th Ave.
Anchorage, AK 99501
(907) 272-7461
Contact: Alvin O. Bramstedt

KIMO-TV Channel 13 (ABC)
3910 Seward Hwy.
Anchorage, AK 99502
(907) 279-9437
Contact: Duane L. Triplett

KTVA Channel 11 (CBS)
Box 2200
Anchorage, AK 99510
(907) 272-3456
Contact: Ron Moore

Fairbanks
KTVF Channel 11 (ABC, CBS)
Box 950
Fairbanks, AK 99701
(907) 452-5721
Contact: Henry H. Hove

WFAR-TV Channel 2 (ABC, NBC)
516 2nd Ave.
Fairbanks, AK 99701
(907) 452-2125
Contact: Bill Walley

Juneau
KINY-TV Channel 8 (NBC)
231 S. Franklin St.
Juneau, AK 99801
(907) 586-1800
Contact: Ken Wiley

Sitka
KIFW-TV Channel 13 (CBS)
Box 299
Sitka, AK 99835
(907) 747-3244
Contact: Steven L. Rhyner

ARIZONA

Flagstaff
KOAI-TV Channel 2 (NBC)
Box 1843
Flagstaff, AZ 86002
(602) 774-1818
Contact: Wendell Elliott, Jr.

Phoenix
KOOL-TV Channel 10 (CBS)
511 W. Adams St.
Phoenix, AZ 85003
(602) 257-1234
Contact: Bob Davies

KPAZ-TV Channel 21
3551 E. McDowell Rd.
Phoenix, AZ 85008
(602) 273-1477
Contact: C. E. Scopvold

KPHO-TV Channel 5
4016 N. Black Canyon
Phoenix, AZ 85017
(602) 248-7474
Contact: William C. McReynolds

KTAR-TV Channel 13 (NBC)
1101 N. Central Ave.
Phoenix, AZ 85001
(602) 258-7333
Contact: Robert Allingham

KTVK-TV Channel 3 (ABC)
3435 N. 16th St.
Phoenix, AZ 85016
(602) 266-5691
Contact: Burton B. LaDow

Tucson
KGUN-TV Channel 9 (ABC)
2175 N. 6th Ave.
Tucson, AZ 85703
(602) 792-9933
Contact: George Wallace

KOLD-TV Channel 13 (CBS)
115 W. Drachman St.
Tucson, AZ 85705
(602) 624-2511
Contact: Jim Pratt

KVOA-TV Channel 4 (NBC)
209 W. Elm St.
Tucson, AZ 85705
(602) 795-0311
Contact: John Ruby

KZAZ-TV Channel 11
2445 N. Tucson Blvd.
Tucson, AZ 85716
(602) 795-0311
Contact: Gene Adelstein

Yuma
KYEL-TV Channel 13 (NBC)
1301 S. 3rd Ave.
Yuma, AZ 85364
(602) 782-3881
Contact: Cliff Brown

ARKANSAS

El Dorado
KTVE-TV Channel 10 (ABC)
400 W. Main St.
El Dorado, AR 71730
(501) 862-6651
Contact: James S. Tighe

Fort Smith
KFPW-TV Channel 40 (ABC, CBS)
2415 N. Albert Pike
Fort Smith, AR 72901
(501) 783-4105
Contact: Robert Hernreich

KFSM-TV Channel 5 (ABC, NBC)
318 N. 13th St.
Fort Smith, AR 72901
(501) 783-3131
Contact: Robert Browning

Jonesboro
KAIT-TV Channel 8 (ABC)
Box 790
Jonesboro, AR 72401
(501) 932-4288
Contact: Darrel Cunningham

Little Rock
KARK-TV Channel 4 (NBC)
3rd & Louisiana Sts.
Little Rock, AR 72203
(501) 376-2481
Contact: David J. Jones

KATV Channel 7 (ABC)
401 Main St.
Little Rock, AR 72201
(501) 372-7777
Contact: Dale Nicholson

KTHV Channel 11 (CBS)
8th & Izard Sts.
Little Rock, AR 72203
(501) 374-3764
Contact: Robert L. Brown

CALIFORNIA

Anaheim
KBSA-TV Channel 46
1404 E. Ball Rd.
Anaheim, CA 92805
(714) 636-4455
Contact: W. Kenneth Connolly

Bakersfield
KBAK-TV Channel 29 (ABC)
2210 Chester Ave.
Bakersfield, CA 93301
(805) 327-7955
Contact: Robert Curry

KERO-TV Channel 23 (NBC)
Box 2367
Bakersfield, CA 93303
(805) 327-1441
Contact: Ray Watson

KJTV Channel 17 (CBS)
Box 226
Bakersfield, CA 93302
(805) 327-7511
Contact: Joe Niccoli

Burbank
KNBC Channel 4 (NBC)
3000 W. Alameda Ave.
Burbank, CA 91523
(213) 845-7000 or 849-3911
Contact: John Rohrbeck

Chico
KHSL-TV Channel 12 (CBS)
180 E. 4th St.
Chico, CA 95926
(916) 342-0141
Contact: C. H. Kinsley

El Centro
KECC-TV Channel 9 (CBS)
778 State St.
El Centro, CA 92243
(714) 352-9670
Contact: Randy Campbell

Eureka
KIEM-TV Channel 3 (CBS, NBC)
5650 S. Broadway
Eureka, CA 95501
(707) 443-3123
Contact: Harvey Ingham

KVIQ-TV Channel 6 (ABC)
1800 Broadway
Eureka, CA 95501
(707) 443-3061
Contact: Allen Jones

Fresno
KAIL-TV Channel 53
Box 5160
Fresno, CA 93755
(209) 299-2104
Contact: John Lockhart

KFSN-TV Channel 30 (CBS)
1777 G St.
Fresno, CA 93706
(209) 442-1170
Contact: Walter C. Liss

KJEO-TV Channel 47 (ABC)
4880 N. 1st St.
Fresno, CA 93755
(209) 222-2411
Contact: William Sawyers

KMJ-TV Channel 24 (NBC)
1544 Van Ness Ave.
Fresno, CA 93721
(209) 268-6666
Contact: Jim Thompson

Glendale
KHOF-TV Channel 30
Faith Center
1615 S. Glendale Ave.
Glendale, CA 91205
(213) 245-7575
Contact: Dave Footill

Hanford
KFTV Channel 47 (SIN)
8515 E. Lacey Blvd.
Hanford, CA 93230
(209) 584-3362
Contact: Ernesto Ballesté

Hollywood
KCOP-TV Channel 13
915 N. La Brea Ave.
Hollywood, CA 90038
(213) 851-1000
Contact: Evan Thompson

KHJ-TV Channel 9
5515 Melrose Ave.
Hollywood, CA 90038
(213) 462-2133
Contact: Lionel Schaen

KMEX-TV Channel 34
721 N. Bronson Ave.
Hollywood, CA 90038
(213) 466-8131
Contact: Sandra Gibson

Los Angeles
KABC-TV Channel 7 (ABC)
4151 Prospect Ave.
Los Angeles, CA 90027
(213) 663-3311
Contact: John Severino

KBSC-TV Channel 52
5752 Sunset Blvd.
Los Angeles, CA 90028
(213) 461-3611
Contact: J. Bruce Johansen

KNXT Channel 2 (CBS)
6121 Sunset Blvd.
Los Angeles, CA 90028
(213) 469-1212
Contact: Van Gordon Sauter

KTLA Channel 5
5800 Sunset Blvd.
Los Angeles, CA 90028
(213) 469-3181
Contact: Anthony Cassara

KTTV Channel 11
5746 Sunset Blvd.
Los Angeles, CA 90028
(213) 462-7111
Contact: Charles Young

KWHY-TV Channel 22
5545 Sunset Blvd.
Los Angeles, CA 90028
(213) 466-5441
Contact: Robert W. Bunn

Modesto
KLOC-TV Channel 19
2842 Iowa Ave.
Modesto, CA 95352
(209) 529-2024
Contact: Chester Smith

Monterey
KMST Channel 46 (CBS)
46 Garden Ct.
Monterey, CA 93940
(408) 649-0460
Contact: Chuck Muntean

Oakland
KTVU Channel 2
1 Jack London Sq.
Oakland, CA 94607
(415) 834-2000
Contact: Robert Most

Palm Springs
KMIR-TV Channel 36 (NBC)
1151 N. Indian Ave.
Palm Springs, CA 92262
(714) 325-7021
Contact: John Conte

KPLM-TV Channel 42 (ABC)
36-270 Plaza Dr.
Palm Springs, CA 92262
(714) 328-8881
Contact: Jack Latham

Redding
KRCR-TV Channel 7 (ABC)
Box 7R
2270 Pioneer Dr.
Redding, CA 96001
(916) 243-7777
Contact: Richard Green

Sacramento
KCRA-TV Channel 3 (NBC)
310 10th St.
Sacramento, CA 95814
(916) 444-7300
Contact: Don Saraceno

KMUV-TV Channel 31
500 Media Pl.
Sacramento, CA 95813
(916) 929-0300
Contact: Mike J. Pappas

KTXL Channel 40 (CBS)
4655 Fruitridge Rd.
Sacramento, CA 95820
(916) 452-8221
Contact: Jack Matranga

KXTV Channel 10 (CBS)
Box 10
Sacramento, CA 95801
(916) 441-2345
Contact: Joseph Lake

Salinas
KSBW-TV Channel 8 (NBC)
238 John St.
Salinas, CA 93901
(408) 422-6422
Contact: Keith H. Moon

KSBY-TV Channel 6 (NBC)
Box 1651
238 John St.
Salinas, CA 93901
(408) 422-6422
Contact: Larry Fischer

San Bernardino
KSCI-TV Channel 18
280 S. I St.
San Bernardino, CA 92410
(213) 479-8081
Contact: Walter Koch

San Diego
KCST-TV Channel 39 (NBC)
8330 Engineer Rd.
San Diego, CA 92111
(714) 279-3939
Contact: Bill Fox

KFMB-TV Channel 8 (CBS)
7677 Engineer Rd.
San Diego, CA 92111
(714) 292-5363
Contact: William Moyland

KGTV Channel 10 (ABC)
Box 81047
San Diego, CA 92138
(714) 262-2421
Contact: Clayton Brace

Mission Cable TV Channel 2
Box 19700
San Diego, CA 92119
(714) 562-1180
Contact: Donald O. Williams

XETV Channel 6 (ABC, CBS, NBC)
8253 Ronson Rd.
San Diego, CA 92111
(714) 279-6666
Contact: Martin Colby

San Francisco
KBHK-TV Channel 44
420 Taylor St.
San Francisco, CA 94102
(415) 885-3750
Contact: L. William White

KDTV Channel 60
2200 Palon Ave.
San Francisco, CA 94124
(415) 826-6990
Contact: Robert Munoz

KEMO-TV Channel 20
2500 Marin St.
San Francisco, CA 94124
(415) 285-6420
Contact: Rene de la Rosa

KGO-TV Channel 7 (ABC)
277 Golden Gate Ave.
San Francisco, CA 94102
(415) 863-0077
Contact: Russ Coughlan

KPIX Channel 5 (CBS)
2655 Van Ness Ave.
San Francisco, CA 94109
(415) 776-5100
Contact: George Resing

KRON-TV Channel 4 (NBC)
1001 Van Ness Ave.
San Francisco, CA 94119
(415) 441-4444
Contact: F. A. Martin, III

KTSF-TV Channel 26
285 Berry St.
San Francisco, CA 94107
(415) 495-4995
Contact: Richard O'Hearn

KVOF Channel 38
601 Taraval St.
San Francisco, CA 94116
(415) 665-5410
Contact: Eugene Scott

San Jose
KGSC-TV Channel 36
1536 Kerley Dr.
San Jose, CA 95112
(408) 298-6676
Contact: Sid Connolly

KNTV Channel 11 (ABC)
645 Park Ave.
San Jose, CA 95110
(408) 286-1111
Contact: Robert Hosfeldt

San Luis Obispo
KSBY-TV Channel 6 (NBC)
Hill & Mountain View
San Luis Obispo, CA 93401
(408) 422-6422
Contact: Larry Fischer

San Ysidro
XEWT-TV Channel 12
Box 44-K
San Ysidro, CA 92073
(903) 385-9201
Contact: Jose Marquez

Santa Ana
KLXA-TV Channel 40
2442 Michelle Rd.
Santa Ana, CA 92711
(714) 832-2950
Contact: Paul Crouch

Santa Barbara
KEYT Channel 3 (ABC)
730 Miramonte Dr.
Santa Barbara, CA 93109
(805) 965-8533
Contact: Hal O'Donnell

Santa Maria
KCOY-TV Channel 12 (CBS)
1503 N. McClelland St.
Santa Maria, CA 93454
(805) 922-1943
Contact: Robert Burris

Stockton
KOVR Channel 13 (ABC)
225 E. Miner Ave.
Stockton, CA 95201
(209) 466-6981
Contact: Ramsey Elliott

Visalia
KMPH-TV Channel 26
2600 S. Mooney Blvd.
Visalia, CA 93277
(209) 733-2600
Contact: Harry Pappas

COLORADO

Colorado Springs
KKTV Channel 11 (CBS)
3100 N. Nevada Ave.
Colorado Springs, CO 80901
(303) 634-2844
Contact: George W. Jeffrey

KRDO-TV Channel 13 (ABC)
399 S. 8th St.
Colorado Springs, CO 80901
(303) 632-1515
Contact: Don Long

Denver
KBTV Channel 9 (ABC)
1089 Bannock St.
Denver, CO 80217
(303) 825-5288
Contact: Charles T. Leasure

KMGH-TV Channel 7 (CBS)
123 Speer Blvd.
Denver, CO 80217
(303) 832-7777
Contact: Bob Hart

KOA-TV Channel 4 (NBC)
1044 Lincoln St.
Denver, CO 80217
(303) 861-8111
Contact: Mick Schafbuch

KWGN Channel 2
550 Lincoln St.
Denver, CO 80203
(303) 832-2222
Contact: Robert A. Innes

Durango
KREZ-TV Channel 6
West Bldg.
Durango, CO
(303) 247-0820
*Contact:*Rick Bergethon

Grand Junction
KREX-TV Channel 5 (ABC, CBS, NBC)
Hillcrest Manor
Grand Junction, CO 81501
(303) 242-5000
Contact: Carl Q. Anderson

Montrose
KREY-TV Channel 10
610 N. 1st St.
Montrose, CO 81401
(303) 249-9601
Contact: Frank Bell

Pueblo
KOAA-TV Channel 5 (NBC)
2200 7th Ave.
Pueblo, CO 81002
(303) 544-5782
Contact: John O. Gilbert

Sterling
KTVS Channel 3
204½ Main St.
Sterling, CO
(303) 522-5743
Contact: Gene Huston

CONNECTICUT

Hartford
WFSB-TV Channel 3 (CBS)
3 Constitution Plaza
Hartford, CT 06115
(203) 525-0801
Contact: Daniel Gold

WHCT Channel 18
555 Asylum St.
Hartford, CT 06105
(203) 525-2611
Contact: Ken Boudreau

New Haven
WTNH-TV Channel 8 (ABC)
135 College St.
New Haven, CT 06510
(209) 777-3611
Contact: Kenneth Boridreau

Waterbury
WATR-TV Channel 20 (NBC)
79 Baldwin Ave.
Waterbury, CT 06706
(203) 755-1121
Contact: Bob Holczer

West Hartford
WHNB-TV Channel 30 (NBC)
1422 New Britain Ave.
West Hartford, CT 06110
(203) 521-3030
Contact: Robert W. Bray

DISTRICT OF COLUMBIA

WDCA-TV Channel 20
5202 River Rd.
Washington, DC 20016
(301) 654-2600
Contact: Milton Grant

WJLA-TV Channel 7 (ABC)
4461 Connecticut Ave., NW
Washington, DC 20008
(202) 686-3000
Contact: Thomas B. Cookerly

WRC-TV Channel 4 (NBC)
40001 Nebraska Ave., NW
Washington, DC 20016
(202) 686-4000
Contact: Monte Newman

WTOP-TV Channel 9 (CBS)
40th & Brandywine Sts., NW
Washington, DC 20016
(202) 686-6000
Contact: James T. Lynagh

WTTG Channel 5
5151 Wisconsin Ave., NW
Washington, DC 20016
(202) 244-5151
Contact: William Carpenter

FLORIDA

Bonita Springs
WEVU-TV Channel 26 (ABC)
Box N
Hwy. 41
Bonita Springs, FL 33923
Contact: Joseph Buerry

Daytona Beach
WESH-TV Channel 2 (NBC)
Box 1551
Daytona Beach, FL 32015
(904) 252-2222
Contact: Walter Strouse

Fort Myers
WBBH-TV Channel 20 (NBC)
3719 Central Ave.
Fort Myers, FL 33901
(813) 936-0195
Contact: Howard L. Hoffman

WINK-TV Channel 11 (CBS)
2824 Palm Beach Blvd.
Fort Myers, FL 33902
(813) 334-1131, 334-1132
Contact: Robert Doty

Fort Pierce
WTVX Channel 34 (CBS)
Box 313
Fort Pierce, FL 33450
(305) 464-5220
Contact: Jim Holmes

Gainesville
WCJB Channel 20 (ABC)
20 N. Millhopper Rd.
Gainesville, FL 32604
(904) 372-3543
Contact: John S. Lotz

Hallandale
WKID Channel 51
3130 S.W. 19th St.
Hallandale, FL 33009
(305) 963-1400
Contact: Don Sundquist

Hollywood
WHFT-TV Channel 45
2843 Pembroke Rd.
Hollywood, FL 33021
(305) 962-1700
Contact: G. Kent Smith

Jacksonville
WJKS-TV Channel 17 (ABC)
Hogan Rd. at Newton
Jacksonville, FL 32216
(904) 641-1700
Contact: Gary Adler

WJXT Channel 4 (CBS)
1851 Southampton Rd.
Jacksonville, FL 32207
(904) 399-4000
Contact: Alan E. Perris

WTLV Channel 12 (NBC)
1070 E. Adams St.
Jacksonville, FL 32201
(904) 354-1212
Contact: Gert Schmidt

Miami
WCIX-TV Channel 6
1111 Brickell Ave.
Miami, FL 33131
(305) 377-0811
Contact: E. Q. Adams

WCKT Channel 7 (NBC)
1401 79th St., Causeway
Miami, FL 33141
(305) 751-6692
Contact: Allen Sternberg

WLTV Channel 23 (SIN)
695 N.W. 199th St.
N. Miami, FL 33169
(305) 652-4000
Contact: Vivian Quevedo

WPLG Channel 10 (ABC)
3900 Biscayne Blvd.
Miami, FL 33137
(305) 573-7111
Contact: G. William Ryan

WTVJ Channel 4 (CBS)
316-18 N. Miami Ave.
Miami, FL 33128
(305) 377-8241
Contact: Bill Brazzil

Orlando
WDBO-TV Channel 6 (CBS)
750 N. Texas Ave.
Orlando, FL 32804
(305) 843-0006
Contact: Arnold Schoen

WFTV Channel 9 (ABC)
639 W. Central Blvd.
Orlando, FL 32802
(305) 841-9000
Contact: Walter Windsor

WSWB-TV Channel 35
11510 E. Colonial Dr.
Orlando, FL 32807
(305) 273-2300
Contact: Ray Balsom

Panama City
WJHG-TV Channel 7 (ABC)
8195 W. Hwy. 98
Panama City, FL 32401
(904) 234-2125
Contact: Ray Holloway

WMBB-TV Channel 13 (NBC)
232 Harrison Ave.
Panama City, FL 32401
(904) 769-2313
Contact: Doug Grimm

Pembrook Park
WKID-TV Channel 51
2090 Southwest 30th Ave.
Pembrook Park, FL 33009
(305) 454-5100
Contact: John Koenig

Pensacola
WEAR-TV Channel 3 (ABC)
U.S. Hwy. 90, W
Pensacola, FL 32581
(904) 455-7311
Contact: Milt de Reyna

St. Petersburg
WLCY-TV Channel 10 (ABC)
11450 Gandy Blvd.
St. Petersburg, FL 33733
(813) 577-1111
Contact: Todd Spoeri

WTOG-TV Channel 44
365 105th Terr., NE
St. Petersburg, FL 33702
(813) 576-4444
Contact: Gary Simcox

Sarasota
WXLT-TV Channel 40 (ABC)
5725 Lawton Dr.
Sarasota, FL 33578
(813) 922-0777
Contact: Robert Nelson

Tallahassee
WCTV Channel 6 (CBS)
Rte. 12
Tallahassee, FL 32303
(904) 386-4141
Contact: Joseph Hosford

WECA-TV Channel 27 (ABC)
U.S. Rte. 319
Tallahassee, FL 32302
(904) 386-3127
Contact: Thomas Scanlan

Tampa
WFLA-TV Channel 8 (NBC)
905 Jackson St.
Tampa, FL 33601
(813) 229-7781
Contact: C. Wesley Quinn

WTVT Channel 13 (CBS)
3213 John F. Kennedy Blvd.
Tampa, FL 33622
(813) 876-1313
Contact: Crawford P. Rice

West Palm Beach
WPEC Channel 12 (ABC)
WPEC, Fairfield Dr.
West Palm Beach, FL 33407
(305) 848-7211
Contact: Alex Dreyfoos

WPTV Channel 5 (NBC)
622 N. Flagler Dr.
West Palm Beach, FL 33401
(305) 655-5455
Contact: Ronald Regalbuto

GEORGIA

Albany
WALB-TV Channel 10 (NBC)
Stuart Ave.
Albany, GA 31706
(912) 435-8386
Contact: Raymond Carow

Atlanta
WAGA-TV Channel 5 (CBS)
1551 Briarcliff Rd., NE
Atlanta, GA 30302
(404) 875-5551
Contact: Shelly Schwab

WANX-TV Channel 46
1810 Briarcliff Rd., NE
Atlanta, GA 30359
(404) 325-3103
Contact: Everett Martin

WATL-TV Channel 36
1800 Peachtree St., NW
Atlanta, GA 30309
(404) 355-0036
Contact: Don Kennedy

WSB-TV Channel 2 (NBC)
1601 W. Peachtree St.
N.E. Atlanta, GA 30309
(404) 897-7000
Contact: Don Heald

WTCG Channel 17 (NBC)
1018 W. Peachtree St., NW
Atlanta, GA 30309
(404) 875-7317
Contact: Sid Pike

WXIA-TV Channel 11 (ABC)
1611 W. Peachtree St., NE
Atlanta, GA 30309
(404) 892-1611
Contact: Jeff Davidson

Augusta
WATU-TV Channel 26 (NBC)
Pinelog Rd.
Augusta, GA 29811
(803) 824-5527
Contact: Lee Sheridan

WJBF Channel 6 (ABC)
Box 1404
Augusta, GA 30903
(404) 722-6664
Contact: John Radeck

WRDW-TV Channel 12 (CBS)
Drawer 1212
Augusta, GA 30903
(803) 278-1212
Contact: James Armstead

Columbus
WRBL-TV Channel 3 (CBS)
1350 13th Ave.
Columbus, GA 31902
(404) 322-0601
Contact: Bob Walton

WTVM Channel 9 (ABC)
1909 Wynnton Rd.
Columbus, GA 31902
(404) 324-6471
Contact: Lynn Avery

WYEA-TV Channel 38 (NBC)
6140 Buena Vista Rd.
Columbus, GA 31907
(404) 561-3838
Contact: Walter McCroba

Macon
WCWB-TV Channel 41 (NBC)
6525 Ocmulgee E. Blvd.
Macon, GA 31208
(912) 746-1455
Contact: Loren NeSmith

WMAZ-TV Channel 13 (CBS)
1314 Gray Hwy.
Macon, GA 31211
(912) 746-7311
Contact: Albert Sanders

Rossville
WRIP-TV Channel 61
Ellis Rd.
Rossville, GA 30741
(404) 866-3855
Contact: Jay Sadow

Savannah
WJCL Channel 22 (ABC)
10001 Abercorn Expwy.
Savannah, GA 31406
(912) 352-2022
Contact: Jay Pierce

WSAV-TV Channel 3 (NBC)
Broadcasting Center
1430 E. Victory Dr.
Savannah, GA 31402
(912) 236-0303
Contact: Tom Matthews

WTOC-TV Channel 11 (CBS)
Box 8086
Savannah, GA 31402
(912) 232-0127
Contact: F. S. Knight

HAWAII

Honolulu
KAII-TV Channel 7 (NBC) - Satellite
1170 Auahi St.
Honolulu, HI 96814
(808) 531-8585
Contact: George B. Hagar

KGMB-TV Channel 9 (CBS)
Box 581
Honolulu, HI 96809
(808) 941-3011
Contact: Richard Weiner

KGMD-TV Channel 9 (CBS) - Satellite
Box 581
Honolulu, HI 96809
(808) 941-3011
Contact: Richard Weiner

KGMV-TV Channel 3 (CBS) - Satellite
Box 581
Honolulu, HI 96809
(808) 941-3011
Contact: Lloyd Loers

KHAW-TV Channel 11 (NBC) - Satellite
1170 Auahi St.
Honolulu, HI 96814
(808) 531-8585
Contact: George B. Hagar

KHON-TV Channel 2 (NBC)
1170 Auahi St.
Honolulu, HI 96814
(808) 531-8585
Contact: George B. Hagar

KHVO-TV Channel 13 (ABC) - Satellite
1290 Ala Moana Blvd.
Honolulu, HI 96814
(808) 537-3991
Contact: Richard T. Grimm

KIKU-TV Channel 13
150-B Puuhale Rd.
Honolulu, HI 96819
(808) 847-1178
Contact: Joanne Ninomiya

KITV-TV Channel 4 (ABC)
1290 Ala Moana Blvd.
Honolulu, HI 96814
(808) 537-3991
Contact: Richard T. Grimm

KMVI-TV Channel 12 (ABC) - Satellite
1290 Ala Moana Blvd.
Honolulu, HI 96814
(808) 537-3991
Contact: Richard T. Grimm

IDAHO

Boise
KBCI-TV Channel 2 (CBS)
Box 2
Boise, ID 83701
(208) 336-5222
Contact: James A. Johntz, Jr.

KTVB Channel 7 (NBC)
Box 7778
Boise, ID 83707
(208) 375-7277
Contact: Robert E. Krueger

Idaho Falls
KID-TV Channel 3 (CBS)
1255 E. 17th St.
Idaho Falls, ID 83401
(208) 522-5100
Contact: Dwain Silvester

KIFI-TV Channel 8 (NBC)
1915 N. Yellowstone Hwy.
Idaho Falls, ID 83401
(208) 523-1171
Contact: Jim Brady

Lewiston
KLEW-TV Channel 3
1115 Idaho St.
Lewiston, ID 83501
(208) 746-2636
Contact: Gerald Cornwell

Nampa
KIVI Channel 6 (ABC)
1866 E. Chisholm Dr.
Nampa, ID 83651
(208) 336-0500
Contact: David Eaton

Pocatello
KPVI Channel 6 (ABC)
Box 667
Pocatello, ID 83201
(208) 233-6667
Contact: Michael Gee

Twin Falls
KMVT Channel 11 (ABC, CBS, NBC)
Elizabeth St.
Twin Falls, ID 83301
(208) 733-1280
Contact: Harold Hirte

ILLINOIS

Champaign
WCIA Channel 3 (CBS)
509 S. Neil St.
Champaign, IL 61820
(217) 356-8333
Contact: Guy Main

WICD Channel 15 (NBC)
17-19 E. University Ave.
Champaign, IL 61820
(217) 352-7673
Contact: Vance Daube

Chicago
WBBM-TV/Chicago Channel 2 (CBS)
630 N. McClurg Ct.
Chicago, IL 60611
(312) 944-6000
Contact: David Nelson

WCFC Channel 38
20 N. Wacker Dr.
Chicago, IL 60606
(312) 782-3839
Contact: Jerry Rose

WCIU-TV Channel 26
141 W. Jackson St.
Chicago, IL 60604
(312) 663-0260
Contact: Herman Sitrick

WFLD-TV Channel 32
300 N. State St.
Chicago, IL 60610
(312) 663-0260
Contact: James Warner

WGN-TV Channel 9
2501 Bradley Pl.
Chicago, IL 60618
(312) 528-2311
Contact: Sheldon Cooper

WLS-TV Channel 7 (ABC)
190 N. State St.
Chicago, IL 60601
(312) 263-0800
Contact: Philip Boyer

WMAQ-TV Channel 5 (NBC)
Merchandise Mart Plaza
Chicago, IL 60654
(312) 861-5555
Contact: Albert Jerome

WSNS-TV Channel 44
430 W. Grant Pl.
Chicago, IL 60614
(312) 929-1200
Contact: Edward Morris

WTTW-TV Channel 11
5400 N. St. Louis Ave.
Chicago, IL 60625
(312) 583-5000
Contact: William McCarter

Creve Coeur
WRAU-TV Channel 19 (ABC)
500 N. Stewart St.
Creve Coeur, IL 61611
(309) 694-4351
Contact: Robert Rice

Decatur
WAND Channel 17
Southside Dr.
Decatur, IL 62525
(217) 428-4304
Contact: Barrett Geoghegan

East Peoria
WEEK-TV Channel 25 (NBC)
2907 Springfield Rd.
East Peoria, IL 61611
(309) 699-3961
Contact: Philip Mergener

Harrisburg
WSIL-TV Channel 3 (ABC)
21 W. Poplar St.
Harrisburg, IL 62946
(618) 253-7837
Contact: O. L. Turner

Moline
WQAD-TV Channel 8 (ABC)
3003 Park 16th St.
Moline, IL 61265
(309) 764-9694
Contact: Richard Gilbert

Peoria
WMBD-TV Channel 31 (CBS)
3131 N. University Ave.
Peoria, IL 61604
(309) 688-1313
Contact: Gene Robinson

Quincy
KHQA-TV Channel 7 (CBS)
510 Maine St
Quincy, IL 62301
(217) 222-6200/6215
Contact: John Phillips

WGEM-TV Channel 10 (NBC)
Hotel Quincy
Quincy, IL 62301
(217) 222-6840
Contact: Dave Oakley

Rock Island
WHBF-TV Channel 4 (CBS)
Rock Island Broadcasting Co.
Telco Bldg.
Rock Island, IL 61201
(309) 786-5441
Contact: Robert Sinnett

Rockford
WIFR-TV Channel 23 (CBS)
2523 N. Meridian Rd.
Rockford, IL 61105
(815) 965-0523
Contact: Eugene Angle

WREX-TV Channel 13 (ABC)
West Auburn & Winnebago Rds.
Rockford, IL 61105
(815) 968-1813
Contact: Jack McWeeny

WTVO Channel 17 (NBC)
Meridian Rd.
Rockford, IL 61105
(815) 963-5413
Contact: Harold Froelich

Springfield
WICS-TV Channel 20 (NBC)
2680 E. Cook St.
Springfield, IL 62708
(217) 753-5620
Contact: Milton Friedland

INDIANA

Elkhart
WSJV-TV Channel 28 (ABC)
58096 County Rd. 7
Elkhart, IN 46514
(219) 233-9353
Contact: Don Fuller

Evansville
WEHT-TV Channel 25 (CBS)
Box 395
Evansville, IN 47703
(812) 424-9215
Contact: Ernest Maddin

WFIE-TV Channel 14 (NBC)
1115 Mt. Auburn Rd.
Evansville, IN 47712
(312) 426-1414
Contact: Kelly Atherton

WTVW Channel 7 (ABC)
477 Carpenter St.
Evansville, IN 47736
(812) 422-1121
Contact: Berry Smith

Farmersburg
WTWO Channel 2 (NBC)
Illiana Telecasting Corp.
U.S. Hwy. 41 S
Farmersburg, IN 47850
(312) 232-9504
Contact: J. T. Gelder

Fort Wayne
WANE-TV Channel 15 (CBS)
Box 1515
Fort Wayne, IN 46801
(219) 424-1515
Contact: Reid Chapman

WKJG-TV Channel 33 (NBC)
2633 W. State Blvd.
Fort Wayne, IN 46808
(219) 422-7474
Contact: Hillard Gates

WPTA Channel 21 (ABC)
3401 Butler Rd.
Fort Wayne, IN 46808
(219) 483-0584
Contact: Edward Metcalfe

Indianapolis
WHMB-TV Channel 40
Box 50250
Indianapolis, IN 46250
(317) 773-5050
Contact: Neal Hail

WISH-TV Channel 8 (CBS)
1950 N. Meridian St.
Indianapolis, IN 46202
(317) 924-4381
Contact: Duane Harm

WRTV Channel 6 (NBC)
1330 N. Meridian St.
Indianapolis, IN 46206
(317) 635-9788
Contact: Jerry Chapman

WTHR Channel 13 (ABC)
1401 N. Meridian St.
Indianapolis, IN 46202
(317) 639-2311
Contact: Christopher Duffy

WTTV Channel 4
3490 Bluff Rd.
Indianapolis, IN 46217
(317) 787-2211
Contact: Jim Hair

Lafayette
WLFI-TV Channel 18 (CBS)
Box 18
Lafayette, IN 47902
(317) 463-3516
Contact: Harold Shively

Noblesville
WHMB-TV Channel 40
10511 Greenfield Ave.
Noblesville, IN 46060
(317) 773-5050
Contact: Neal Hail

South Bend
WNDU-TV Channel 16 (NBC)
Michiana Telecasting Corp.
Box 1616
South Bend, IN 46634
(219) 233-7111
Contact: Bazil O'Hagan

WSBT-TV Channel 22 (CBS)
300 W. Jefferson Blvd.
South Bend. IN 46601
(219) 233-3141
Contact: Jack Douglas

Terre Haute
WBAK-TV Channel 38 (ABC)
2nd at Poplar
Terre Haute, IN 47808
(812) 238-1515
Contact: Milton Dempsey

WIIL-TV Channel 38 (ABC)
2nd at Poplar
Terre Haute, IN 47808
(812) 238-1515
Contact: William White

WTHI-TV Channel 10 (CBS)
918 Ohio St.
Terre Haute, IN 47808
(812) 232-9481
Contact: Robert K. Larr

WTWO-TV Channel 2 (NBC)
Box 299
Terre Haute, IN 47808
(812) 232-9504
Contact: James Underwood

IOWA

Ames
WOI-TV Channel 5 (ABC)
WOI Bldg.
Ames, IA 50010
(515) 294-5555
Contact: Robert C. Mulhall

Cedar Rapids
KCRG-TV Channel 9 (ABC)
2nd Ave. at 5th St., SE
Cedar Rapids, IA 52401
(319) 398-8422
Contact: Ed Lasko

WMT-TV Channel 2 (CBS)
Box 2147
Cedar Rapids, IA 52406
(319) 395-6000
Contact: Lew Van Nostrand

Davenport
WOC-TV Channel 6 (NBC)
805 Brady St.
Davenport, IA 52805
(319) 324-1661
Contact: Lee Marts

Des Moines
KCCI-TV Channel 8 (CBS)
9th & Pleasant Sts.
Des Moines, IA 50308
(515) 243-4141
Contact: Bill Hippee

WHO-TV Channel 13 (NBC)
1100 Walnut St.
Des Moines, IA 50308
(515) 288-6511
Contact: George C. Carpenter

Dubuque
KDUB-TV Channel 40 (ABC)
1 Dubuque Plaza
Dubuque, IA 52001
(291) 556-4040
Contact: Chuck Cyberski

Fort Dodge
KUFD-TV (NBC)
Television Sq.
Fort Dodge, IA 50501
(515) 576-7606
Contact: Larry Steinbruch

Mason City
KGLO-TV Channel 3 (CBS)
2nd & Pennsylvania Sts.
Mason City, IA 50401
(515) 423-2540
Contact: Lloyd Loers

Ottumwa
KTVO Channel 3 (ABC, CBS)
211 E. 2nd St.
Ottumwa, IA 52501
(515) 682-4535
Contact: Jack Parris

Sioux City
KCAU-TV Channel 9 (ABC)
7th & Douglas Sts.
Sioux City, IA 51101
(712) 277-2345
Contact: Jack Gilbert

KMEG-TV Channel 14 (CBS)
7th & Floyd Blvd.
Sioux City, IA 51102
(712) 277-3554
Contact: Jack Parris

KTIV Channel 4 (NBC)
10th & Grandview
Sioux City, IA 51103
(712) 258-0545
Contact: Lyn P. Stoyer

Waterloo
KWWL-TV Channel 7 (NBC)
KWWL Bldg., E. 4th & Franklin
Waterloo, IA 50703
(319) 291-1200
Contact: James Bradley

KANSAS

Copeland
KUPK Channel 13 (ABC)
Box 216
Copeland, KS 67837
(316) 668-2960
Contact: Bob Surber

Dodge City
KTVC-TV Channel 6 (CBS)
Box 157
Dodge City, KS 67801
(316) 227-3121
Contact: William Bailey

Ensign
KTVC Channel 6 (CBS)
Southwest Kansas Television Co., Inc.
Hwy. 23
Ensign, KS 67841
(316) 865-4961
Contact: William Bailey

Fairway
KCMO-TV Channel 5 (CBS)
4500 Johnson Dr.
Fairway, KS 66205
(913) 677-7230
Contact: Charles McAbee

Hays
KAYS-TV Channel 7 (CBS)
2300 Hall St.
Hays, KS 67601
(913) 625-2578
Contact: Bernie Brown

Oberlin
KOMC Channel 8 (NBC)
U.S. Hwy. 36
Oberlin, KS
(913) 475-2248
Contact: Robert Berkheimer

Pittsburg
KOAM-TV Channel 7 (NBC)
Box 659
Pittsburg, KS 66762
(316) 231-0400
Contact: Bill Bengtson

Topeka
KTSB Channel 27 (NBC)
Box 2700
Topeka, KS 66601
(913) 582-4000
Contact: William R. Hirshey

WIBW-TV Channel 13 (CBS)
Box 119
Topeka, KS 66601
(913) 272-3456
Contact: Paul Winders

Wichita
KAKE-TV Channel 10 (ABC)
1500 N. West St.
Wichita, KS 67201
(316) 943-4221
Contact: Martin Umansky

KARD-TV Channel 3 (NBC)
833 N. Main St.
Wichita, KS 67201
(316) 265-5631
Contact: Frank Chappell

KCKT Channel 2 (NBC)
c/o KARD-TV
833 N. Main St.
Wichita, KS 67201
(316) 265-5631
Contact: Bill Ranker

KGLD Channel 11 (NBC)
c/o KARD-TV
833 N. Main St.
Wichita, KS 67201
(316) 265-5631
Contact: Jim Austin

KTVH Channel 12 (CBS)
2815 E. 37th St.
Wichita, KS 67201
(316) 838-1411
Contact: M. Dale Larsen

KENTUCKY

Bowling Green
WBKO Channel 13 (ABC)
537 E. 10th St.
Bowling Green, KY 42101
(502) 781-1313
Contact: Randy Odil

Hazard
WKYH-TV Channel 57 (NBC)
Box 929
Hazard, KY 41701
(606) 436-4444
Contact: William D. Gorman, Jr.

Henderson
WEHT-TV Channel 25 (CBS)
800 Marywood Dr.
Henderson, KY 42420
(502) 826-9566
Contact: Ernest D. Madden

Lexington
WKYT-TV Channel 27 (CBS)
Box 5037
Lexington, KY 40505
(606) 299-0411
Contact: Al Taylor

WLEX-TV Channel 18 (NBC)
Russell Cave Pike
Lexington, KY 40501
(606) 255-4404
Contact: Robert Jones

WTVQ-TV Channel 62 (ABC)
Box 5590
Lexington, KY 40505
(606) 299-6262
Contact: Mike McMellon

Louisville
WAVE-TV Channel 3 (NBC)
Box 32970
Louisville, KY 40232
(502) 585-2201
Contact: H. Lee Browning

WDRB-TV Channel 41
1051 E. Main St.
Louisville, KY 40206
(502) 584-9701
Contact: Elmer F. Jaspan

WHAS-TV Channel 11 (CBS)
520 W. Chestnut St.
Louisville, KY 40202
(502) 582-7310
Contact: Robert Taylor

WLKY-TV Channel 32 (ABC)
1918 Mellwood Ave.
Louisville, KY 40206
(502) 893-3671
Contact: Paul Blue

Paducah
WPSD-TV Channel 6 (NBC)
Box 1197
Paducah, KY 42001
(502) 442-8214
Contact: Sam Livingston

LOUISIANA

Alexandria
KALB-TV Channel 5 (NBC)
605-11 Washington St.
Alexandria, LA 71301
(318) 445-2456
Contact: Robert E. Miller

Baton Rouge
WAFB-TV Channel 9 (CBS)
844 Government St.
Baton Rouge, LA 70822
(504) 383-9999
Contact: Tom E. Gibbens

WBRZ Channel 2 (ABC)
1650 Highland Rd.
Baton Rouge, LA 70821
(504) 387-2222
Contact: Douglas L. Manship

WRBT Channel 33 (NBC)
5320 Essen La.
Baton Rouge, LA 70808
(504) 766-3233
Contact: Cyril E. Vetter

Lafayette
KATC Channel 3 (ABC)
1103 Eraste Landry Rd.
Lafayette, LA 70501
(318) 232-6111
Contact: William A. Patton

KLFY-TV Channel 10 (CBS)
2101 Jefferson St.
Lafayette, LA 70502
(318) 233-2152
Contact: M. N. Bostick

Lake Charles
KPLC-TV Channel 7 (NBC)
320 Division St.
Lake Charles, LA 70601
(318) 439-9071
Contact: Albert H. Smith

Monroe
KNOE-TV Channel 8 (CBS)
KNOE Rd.
Monroe, LA 71201
(318) 322-8155
Contact: Paul H. Goldman

New Orleans
WDSU-TV Channel 6 (NBC)
520 Royal St.
New Orleans, LA 70130
(504) 588-9378
Contact: K. James Yager

WGNO-TV Channel 26 (ABC,
2 Canal St.
New Orleans, LA 70130
(504) 522-6211
Contact: Seymour Smith

WVUE Channel 8 (ABC)
1025 S. Jefferson Pkwy.
New Orleans, LA 70185
(504) 486-6161
Contact: Douglas J. Elleson

WWL-TV Channel 4 (CBS)
1024 N. Rampart St.
New Orleans, LA 70116
(504) 529-4444
Contact: J. Michael Early

Shreveport
KSLA-TV Channel 12 (CBS)
Box 4812
Shreveport, LA 71104
(318) 424-8101
Contact: Winston B. Linam

KTAL-TV Channel 6 (NBC)
3150 N. Market St.
Shreveport, LA 71107
(318) 425-2422
Contact: H. Lee Bryant

KTBS-TV Channel 3 (ABC)
312 E. Kings Hwy.
Shreveport, LA 71104
(318) 868-3644
Contact: E. Newton Wray

West Monroe
KLAA Channel 14 (NBC)
701 Parkwood Dr.
West Monroe, LA 71291
(318) 388-0114
Contact: David Padburg

MAINE

Bangor
WABI-TV Channel 5 (CBS)
35 Hildreth St.
Bangor, ME 04401
(207) 947-8321
Contact: George Gonyar

WLBZ-TV Channel 2 (NBC)
329 Mt. Hope Ave.
Bangor, ME 04401
(207) 942-4822
Contact: Margo Cobb

WVII Channel 7 (ABC)
41 Farm Rd.
Bangor, ME 04401
(207) 945-6457
Contact: James DeBold

Portland
WCSH-TV Channel 6 (NBC)
1 Congress Sq.
Portland, ME 04101
(207) 772-0181
Contact: Bruce McGorrell

WGAN-TV Channel 13 (CBS)
Broadcast Center Northport Plaza
Portland, ME 04104
(207) 797-9330
Contact: Dave King

WMTW-TV Channel 8 (ABC)
638 Lafayette Town House
Portland, ME 04101
(207) 773-5664
Contact: Bob Joyce

Presque Isle
WAGM-TV Channel 8 (CBS)
Mayesville Rd.
Presque Isle, ME 04769
(207) 764-4461
Contact: Keith Fowles

MARYLAND

Baltimore
WBAL-TV Channel 11 (NBC)
3800 Hooper Ave.
Baltimore, MD 21211
(301) 467-3000
Contact: Lawrence M. Carino

WBFF-TV Channel 45
Television Hill
Baltimore, MD 21211
(301) 462-4500
Contact: Frederick Himes

WJZ-TV Channel 13 (ABC)
Television Hill
Baltimore, MD 21211
(301) 466-0013
Contact: Bill Baker

WMAR-TV Channel 2 (CBS)
6400 York Rd.
Baltimore, MD 21212
(301) 377-2222
Contact: Dale B. Wright

Hagerstown
WHAG-TV Channel 25 (NBC)
Alexander Motor Inn
Hagerstown, MD 21740
(301) 797-4400
Contact: Arch H. McDonald

Salisbury
WBOC-TV Channel 16 (ABC, CBS, NBC)
Radio-TV Park
Salisbury, MD 21801
(301) 749-1111
Contact: Samuel S. Carey

MASSACHUSETTS

Boston
WBZ-TV Channel 4 (NBC)
1170 Soldiers Field Rd.
Boston, MA 02134
(617) 787-7000
Contact: Seymour Yanoff

WLVI-TV Channel 56
75 Morrissey Blvd.
Boston, MA 02125
(617) 288-3200
Contact: Steven A. Bell

WNAC-TV Channel 7 (CBS)
RKO General Bldg.
Government Center
Boston, MA 02114
(617) 725-2700
Contact: John Sawkill

WSBK-TV Channel 38 (NBC)
83 Birmingham Pkwy.
Boston, MA 02135
(617) 783-3838
Contact: Daniel Berkery

Needham
WCVB-TV Channel 5 (ABC)
5 TV Pl.
Needham, MA 02192
(617) 449-0400
Contact: Robert M. Bennett

New Bedford
WTEV Channel 6 (ABC)
Television Center
New Bedford, MA 02740
(617) 993-2651
Contact: Vance Eckersley

Springfield
WHYN-TV Channel 40 (ABC)
1300 Liberty St.
Springfield, MA 01101
(413) 785-1911
Contact: Gilbert Lefkovich

WRLP Channel 32 (NBC)
Springfield Television Broadcasting Corp.
Box 2210
Springfield, MA 01101
(413) 774-3142
Contact: William M. Pepin

WWLP Channel 22 (NBC)
Box 2210
Springfield, MA 01101
(413) 786-2200
Contact: Wallace Sawyer

Worcester
WSMW-TV Channel 27
127 Beverly Rd.
Worcester, MA 01605
(617) 852-0027
Contact: Brian A. Higgins

MICHIGAN

Allendale
WGVC-TV Channel 35 (NBC)
301 Manitou
Allendale, MI 49401
(616) 895-6691
Contact: Gordon Lawrence

Alpena
WBKB-TV Channel 11 (CBS)
1390 Bagley St.
Alpena, MI 49707
(517) 356-3434
Contact: Thomas Desinger

Battle Creek
WUHQ-TV Channel 41, Inc. (ABC)
Box 1616
Battle Creek, MI 49016
(616) 968-9341
Contact: Lee G. Stevens

Birmingham
WXON-TV Channel 20
30100 Telegraph Rd.
Suite 160
Birmingham, MI 48010
(313) 646-4555
Contact: Aben E. Johnson

Cadillac
WWTV Channel 9 (CBS)
Box 627
Cadillac, MI 49601
(616) 775-3478
Contact: Gene Ellerman

WWUP-TV Channel 10 (ABC, CBS)
Box 627
Cadillac, MI
(616) 775-3478
Contact: Gene Ellerman

Clio
WEYI-TV Channel 25 (CBS)
2225 W. Willard Rd.
Clio, MI 48420
(313) 687-1000
Contact: Bruce Fleming

Detroit
CBET Channel 9 (CBC)
Box 9
Detroit, MI 48226
(313) 961-7200
Contact: Harry L. Hackney

WGPR-TV Channel 62
3140 E. Jefferson Ave.
Detroit, MI 48207
(313) 259-8862
Contact: Dr. William V. Banks

WTUS-TV Channel 10 (CBS)
7441 Second Ave.
Detroit, MI 48202
(313) 873-7200
Contact: Jim Christianson

WTVS-TV Channel 56
7441 Second Ave.
Detroit, MI 48202
(313) 873-7200
Contact: Jim Christianson

WWJ-TV Channel 4 (NBC)
622 Lafayette Blvd.
Detroit, MI 48231
(313) 222-2000
Contact: Jack B. Allen

Flint
WJRT-TV Channel 12 (ABC)
2302 Lapeer Rd.
Flint, MI 48503
(313) 239-6611
Contact: William E. Wuerch

Grand Rapids
WOTV Channel 3 (NBC)
120 College St., SE
Grand Rapids, MI 49501
(616) 459-4125
Contact: Marv Chauvin

WZZM-TV Channel 13 (ABC)
Box Z
Grand Rapids, MI 49501
(616) 364-9551
Contact: George U. Lyons

Kalamazoo
WKZO-TV Channel 3 (CBS)
590 W. Maple St.
Kalamazoo, MI 49008
(616) 345-2101
Contact: Carl E. Lee

Lansing
WILX-TV Channel 10 (NBC)
100 N. Pennsylvania Ave.
Lansing, MI 48909
(517) 783-2621
Contact: William J. Hart

WJIM-TV Channel 6 (CBS)
2820 E. Saginaw St.
Lansing, MI 48901
(517) 372-8282
Contact: James H. Gross

Marquette
WLUC-TV Channel 6 (ABC, CBS)
Box 460
Marquette, MI 49855
(906) 475-4161
Contact: Thomas Gagnon

Saginaw
WNEM-TV Channel 5 (NBC)
5700 Becker Rd.
Saginaw, MI 48606
(517) 755-8191
Contact: Bruce Fleming

Southfield
WJBK-TV Channel 2 (CBS)
No. 2 Storer Pl.
Southfield, MI 48075
(313) 557-9000
Contact: Don Hamlin

WKBD-TV Channel 50
26955 W. Eleven Mile Rd.
Southfield, MI 48034
(313) 444-8500
Contact: George H. Williams

WXYZ-TV Channel 7 (ABC)
20777 W. Ten Mile Rd.
Southfield, MI 48075
(313) 444-1111
Contact: Jim Osborn

Traverse City
WGTQ-TV Channel 8 (ABC)
(Satellite to WGTU-TV)
Traverse City, MI 49684
(616) 947-7675
Contact: James J. Matthews

WGTU-TV Channel 29 (ABC)
201 E. Front St.
Traverse City, MI 49684
(616) 946-2900
Contact: James J. Matthews

WPBN-TV Channel 7 (NBC)
314 E. Front St.
Traverse City, MI 49684
(616) 947-7675
Contact: Harry Lipson

WTOM-TV Channel 4 (NBC)
Paul Bunyan Bldg.
Traverse City, MI 49684
(616) 947-7675
Contact: Harry R. Lipson

MINNESOTA

Alexandria
KCMT Channel 7 (ABC, NBC)
720 Hawthorne
Alexandria, MN 56308
(612) 763-5166
Contact: Ken Bechtell

Austin
KAAL Channel 6 (ABC)
1701 10th Pl., NE
Austin, MN 55913
(507) 433-8836
Contact: John MacGregor

Duluth
KBJR-TV Channel 6 (NBC)
230 E. Superior St.
Duluth, MN 55802
(218) 727-8484
Contact: Rick Pearson

KDAL-TV Channel 3 (CBS)
425 W. Superior St.
Duluth, MN 55802
(218) 727-8911
Contact: John LaForge

WDIO-TV Channel 10 (ABC)
10 Observation Rd.
Duluth, MN 55811
(218) 727-6864
Contact: Frank Befera

WIRT Channel 13
10 Observation Rd.
Duluth, MN 55810
(218) 727-6864
Contact: Frank Befera

Hackensack
KNMT-TV Channel 12
Rte. 1
Hackensack, MN 56452
(218) 675-6115
Contact: Kenneth Bechtel

Mankato
KEYC-TV Channel 12 (CBS)
Box 128
Mankato, MN 56001
(507) 387-7905
Contact: Hap Halligan

Minneapolis
KMSP-TV Channel 9 (ABC)
6975 York Ave., S
Minneapolis, MN 55435
(612) 925-3300
Contact: Roland King

KSTP-TV Channel 5 (NBC)
3415 University Ave.
Minneapolis, MN 55414
(612) 645-2724
Contact: S. Hubbard

WCCO-TV Channel 4 (CBS)
50 S. 9th St.
Minneapolis, MN 55402
(612) 338-0552
Contact: Jim Rupp

WTCN-TV Channel 11
441 Boone Ave., N
Minneapolis, MN 55427
(612) 546-1111
Contact: Robert Fransen

Rochester
KTTC Channel 10 (NBC)
601 1st Ave., SW
Rochester, MN 55901
(507) 288-4444
Contact: Edward Hutchings

MISSISSIPPI

Biloxi
WLOX-TV Channel 13 (ABC)
W. Biloxi St.
Biloxi, MS 39533
(601) 896-1313
Contact: Thomas B. Maguire

Columbus
WCBI-TV Channel 4 (CBS)
Hwy. 12, N
Columbus, MS 39701
(601) 328-5631
Contact: Don McGouirk

Greenwood
WABG-TV Channel 6 (ABC)
2001 Garrard Ave.
Greenwood, MS
(601) 453-4001
Contact: Henry W. Hughes

Hattiesburg
WDAM-TV Channel 7 (NBC)
Hwy. 11, N
Hattiesburg, MS 39401
(601) 544-4730
Contact: Marvin Reuben

Jackson
WAPT-TV Channel 16 (ABC)
Box 10297
Jackson, MS 39209
(601) 922-1607
Contact: Lewis Hopper

WJTV-12 Channel 12 (CBS)
Robinson Rd., Ext. & TV Rd.
Jackson, MS 39204
(601) 372-6311
Contact: Owens Alexander

WLBT Channel 3 (NBC)
715 S. Jefferson St.
Jackson, MS 39205
(601) 948-3333
Contact: William Dilday

Meridian
WHTV Channel 24 (ABC, NBC)
Boseman Way
Meridian, MS 39301
(601) 693-2933
Contact: Ronald E. Hale

WTOK-TV Channel 11 (CBS)
9th St. & 23rd Ave.
Meridian, MS 39301
(601) 693-1441
Contact: Robert F. Wright

Tupelo
WTWV Channel 9 (ABC, NBC)
Box 350
Beech Springs Rd.
Tueplo, MS 38801
(601) 842-7620
Contact: Charlie H. Hicks

MISSOURI

Cape Girardeau
KFVS-TV Channel 12 (CBS)
324 Broadway
Cape Girardeau, MO 63701
(314) 335-5511
Contact: Robert C. Hirsch

Columbia
KCBJ-TV Channel 17 (ABC)
14 S. 7th St.
Columbia, MO 65201
(314) 449-0917
Contact: Richard Koenig

KOMU-TV Channel 8 (NBC)
Hwy. 63, S
Columbia, MO 65201
(314) 442-1122
Contact: Thomas R. Gray

Hannibal
KHQA-TV Channel 7 (CBS)
Lee Enterprises, Inc.
2333 Palmyra Rd.
Hannibal, MO 62301
(217) 222-6200
Contact: Lloyd Loers

Jefferson City
KRCG-TV Channel 13 (CBS)
Hwy. 54, N
Jefferson City, MO 65101
(314) 636-6188
Contact: Edward Schuelein

Joplin
KODE-TV Channel 12 (ABC)
1928 W. 13th St.
Joplin, MO 64801
(417) 623-7260
Contact: John S. Markward

KTVS Channel 16 (CBS)
1502 Cleveland
Joplin, MO 64801
(417) 781-2345
Contact: Bill Clarke

Kansas City
KBMA-TV Channel 41
1 Penn Valley Park
Kansas City, MO 64108
(816) 756-1441
Contact: Bob Wormington

KCMO-TV Channel 5 (CBS)
125 E. 31st St.
Kansas City, MO 64108
(816) 531-6789
Contact: Charles M. McAbee, Jr.

KMBC-TV Channel 9 (ABC)
11th & Central
Kansas City, MO 64105
(816) 421-2650
Contact: R. Kent Replogle

KMOS-TV Channel 6
114 W. 11th St.
Kansas City, MO 64105
(816) 826-1651
Contact: Edward J. Schuelein

WDAF-TV Channel 4 (NBC)
Signal Hill
Kansas City, MO 64108
(816) 753-4567
Contact: Ro Grignon

Kirksville
KTVO-TV Channel 3 (ABC)
Television Park
Hy. 63, N.
Kirksville, MO 63501
(816) 665-7781
Contact: Jack Paris

St. Joseph
KQTV Channel 2 (ABC)
40th & Faraon Sts.
St. Joseph, MO 64506
(816) 364-2371
Contact: Wes Ferns

St. Louis
KDNL-TV Channel 30
1215 Cole St.
St. Louis, MO 63106
(314) 436-3030
Contact: Jack Petrik

KMOX-TV Channel 4 (CBS)
1 Memorial Dr.
St. Louis, MO 63102
(314) 621-2345
Contact: John McKay

KPLR-TV Channel 11
4935 Lindell Blvd.
St. Louis, MO 63108
(314) 367-7211
Contact: Harold E. Protter

KSD-TV Channel 5 (NBC)
1111 Olive St.
St. Louis, MO 63101
(314) 421-5055
Contact: Ray Karpowicz

KTVI Channel 2 (ABC)
5915 Berthold Ave.
St. Louis, MO 63110
(314) 647-7777
Contact: Ralph Hansen

Springfield
KMTC Channel 27 (ABC)
3000 E. Cherry St.
Springfield, MO 65804
(417) 862-2727
Contact: E. Meyer

KOLR-TV Channel 10 (CBS)
2650 E. Division St.
Springfield, MO 65805
(417) 862-7474
Contact: Kevin McAndrews

KYTV Channel 3 (NBC)
999 W. Sunshine
Springfield, MO 65804
(417) 866-2766
Contact: Donald S. Moeller

MONTANA

Billings
KTVQ Channel 2 (NBC)
The Montana Network
3203 3rd Ave.
Billings, MT 59103
(406) 252-5611
Contact: Victor Miller

KULR-TV Channel 8 (ABC, NBC)
Box 2512
Indian Caves Rd.
Billings, MT 59103
(406) 252-4676
Contact: Bob Merrill

Butte
KPAX-TV Channel 8
Box 3500
1003 S. Montana St.
Butte, MT 59701
(406) 792-0444
Contact: Paul Simitzes

KXLF-TV Channel 4 (ABC, CBS)
1003 S. Montana St.
Butte, MT 59701
(406) 792-0444
Contact: Paul Simitzes

Glendive
KXGN-TV Channel 5 (CBS, NBC)
210 S. Douglas
Glendive, MT 59330
(406) 365-3377
Contact: Dan Frenzel

Great Falls
KFBB-TV Channel 5 (ABC)
Box 1139
Great Falls, MT 59403
(406) 453-4377
Contact: Scott Marriner

KRTV Channel 3 (CBS, NBC)
Box 1331
Havre Hwy.
Great Falls, MT 59403
(406) 453-2433
Contact: Clifford E. Ewing

Helena
KTCM Channel 12 (NBC)
2433 N. Montana Ave.
Helena, MT 59601
(406) 443-5050
Contact: Gary Tyree

Missoula
KCFW-TV Channel 9 (NBC)
Box 1503
Missoula, MT 59801
(406) 755-5239
Contact: Mike Stocklin

KGVO-TV Channel 13 (NBC)
340 W. Main St.
Missoula, MT 59806
(406) 543-8313
Contact: Doug G. Moore

KTVM Channel 6
340 W. Main St.
Missoula, MT 59801
(406) 543-8313
Contact: Dale G. Moore

Miles City
KYUS-TV Channel 3 (NBC)
Yellowstone Hill
Miles City, MT 59301
(406) 232-3540
Contact: David G. Rivenes

NEBRASKA

Grand Island
KGIN-TV Channel 11
231 S. Locust St.
Grand Island, NB 68801
(308) 382-6100
Contact: Bob Schnuelle

Hastings
KHAS-TV Channel 5 (NBC)
Box 578
Hastings, NB 68901
(402) 463-1321
Contact: Duane L. Watts

Hays Springs
KDUH-TV
Hwy. 87
Hays Springs, NB 69347
(605) 638-2741
Contact: Dan Lesmeister

Kearney
KCNA-TV Channel 8
c/o KHGI-TV
Kearney, NB 68847
(308) 743-2494
Contact: James Johnson

KHGI-TV Channel 13 (ABC)
Kearney, NB 68847
(308) 743-2494
Contact: James Johnson

KSNB-TV Channel 4
Box 220
Kearney, NB 68847
(308) 743-2494
Contact: James Johnson

KWNB-TV Channel 5
Box 220
Kearney, NB 68847
(308) 743-2494
Contact: James Johnson

Lincoln
KOLN-TV Channel 10 (CBS)
40th & West Sts.
Lincoln, NB 68503
(402) 467-4321
Contact: Paul Jensen

North Platte
KNOP-TV Channel 2 (NBC)
Box 749
North Platte, NB 69101
(308) 532-2222
Contact: Ulysses Carlini

Omaha
KETV Channel 7 (ABC)
27th & Douglas Sts.
Omaha, NB 68131
(402) 345-7777
Contact: Ken Elkins

KMTV Channel 3 (NBC)
2615 Farnam St.
Omaha, NB 68131
(402) 345-3333
Contact: Owen Saddler

WOWT Channel 6 (CBS)
3501 Farnam St.
Omaha, NB 68131
(402) 346-6666
Contact: James Smith

Scotts Bluff
KSTF Channel 10
1402 1st Ave.
Scotts Bluff, NB 69361
(308) 634-7755
Contact: Bill Brennan

NEVADA

Las Vegas
KLAS-TV Channel 8 (CBS)
3228 Channel 8 Dr.
Las Vegas, NV 89109
(702) 733-8850
Contact: Mark Smith

KORK-TV Channel 3 (NBC)
4100 Boulder Hwy.
Las Vegas, NV 89101
(702) 451-7600
Contact: Gene Spry

KSHO-TV Channel 13 (ABC)
3355 Valley View Blvd.
Las Vegas, NV 89102
(702) 876-1313
Contact: Arthur P. Williams

KVVU-TV Channel 5
1555 E. Flamingo Rd.
Las Vegas, NV 89109
(702) 735-3191
Contact: S. Rusty Durante

Reno
KCRL-TV Channel 4 (NBC)
1790 Vassar St.
Reno, NV 89510
(702) 322-9145
Contact: Jim Elliott

KOLO-TV Channel 8 (ABC)
770 E. 5th St.
Reno, NV 89505
(702) 786-8880
Contact: James C. Herzig

KTVN-TV Channel 2 (CBS)
4925 Energy Way
Reno, NV 89510
(702) 786-2212
Contact: Lee Hirshland

NEW HAMPSHIRE

Manchester
WMUR-TV Channel 9 (ABC)
1819 Elm St.
Manchester, NH 03104
(603) 623-8061
Contact: Sam Phillips

NEW JERSEY

Newark
WNJU-TV Channel 47
1020 Broad St.
Newark, NJ 07102
(201) 643-9100
Contact: Carlos Barba

Paterson
WXTV-TV Channel 41
641 Main St.
Paterson, NJ 07503
(201) 345-0041
Contact: Ivan Egas

West Orange
WTVG-TV Channel 68
416 Eagle Rock Ave.
West Orange, NJ 07052
(201) 731-9024
Contact: Ken Taishoft

Wildwood
WCMC-TV Channel 40 (NBC)
3010 New Jersey Ave.
Wildwood, NJ 08260
(609) 522-1416
Contact: William Wotring

NEW MEXICO

Albuquerque
KGGM-TV Channel 13 (CBS)
1414 Coal Ave., SW
Albuquerque, NM 87103
(505) 243-2285
Contact: Bruce Hebenstreit

KMXN-TV Channel 23
505 Marquette, NW
Albuquerque, NM 87102
(505) 843-7023
Contact: Manny Canta

KOAT-TV Channel 7 (ABC)
1377 University Ave., NE
Albuquerque, NM 87106
(505) 247-0101
Contact: Max Sklower

KOB-TV Channel 4 (NBC)
4 Broadcast Plaza, SW
Albuquerque, NM 87103
(505) 243-4411
Contact: Jerry Danziger

Carlsbad
KAVE-TV Channel 6 (ABC)
Box 219
Carlsbad, NM 88220
(505) 885-3931
Contact: Edwin Booth

Farmington
KIVA-TV Channel 12 (NBC)
Box 1620
Farmington, NM 87401
(505) 327-9881
Contact: John R. Catsis

Portales
KFWD-TV Channel 12 (CBS)
Box 865
Portales, NM 88130
(505) 276-8444
Contact: Mike Lee

Roswell
KBIM-TV Channel 10 (CBS)
308 N. Main St.
Roswell, NM 88201
(505) 622-2121
Contact: Joe Carriere

NEW YORK

Albany
WAST Channel 13 (ABC)
Box 4035
Albany, NY 12204
(518) 436-4791
Contact: Michael Corken

WCDC Channel 19
341 Northern Blvd.
Albany, NY 12204
(518) 436-4822
Contact: Terrence McGuirk

WTEN Channel 10 (ABC)
341 Northern Blvd.
Albany, NY 12204
(518) 436-4822
Contact: Terrence McGuirk

Binghamton
WBJA-TV Channel 34 (ABC)
Box 813
Binghamton, NY 13902
(607) 798-7111
Contact: Ralph Fabrizio

WBNG-TV Channel 12 (CBS)
50 Front St.
Binghamton, NY 13902
(607) 723-7311
Contact: Donald Snyder

WICZ-TV Channel 40 (NBC)
Vestal Pkwy., E
Binghamton, NY 13902
(607) 798-7873
Contact: Jesse Pevear

Buffalo
WIVB-TV Channel 4 (CBS)
2077 Elmwood Ave.
Buffalo, NY 14207
(716) 876-0930
Contact: George Lilly

WGR-TV Channel 2 (NBC)
259 Delaware Ave.
Buffalo, NY 14202
(716) 856-1414
Contact: Philip Jones

WKBW-TV Channel 7 (ABC)
1420 Main St.
Buffalo, NY 14209
(716) 883-0770
Contact: Phillip Beuth

Central Islip
WSNL-TV Channel 67
Long Island Expwy. South Service Rd.
Central Islip, NY 11722
(212) 895-6700
Contact: Herbert Lefkowitz

Elmira
WENY-TV Channel 36 (ABC)
Box 208
Elmira, NY 14902
(607) 739-3636
Contact: C. Robert Edwards

Grand Island
WUTV Channel 29
951 Whitehaven Rd.
Grand Island, NY 14072
(716) 773-7531
Contact: Herman Pease

New York City
WABC-TV Channel 7 (ABC)
1330 Ave. of the Americas
New York, NY 10019
(212) 581-7777
Contact: Kenneth H. MacQueen

WCBS-TV Channel 2 (CBS)
51 W. 52nd St.
New York, NY 10019
(212) 975-4321
Contact: Thomas Leahy

WNBC-TV Channel 4 (NBC)
30 Rockefeller Plaza
New York, NY 10020
(202) 664-4444
Contact: Ann Berk

WNEW-TV Channel 5
205 E. 67th St.
New York, NY 10021
(212) 535-1000
Contact: S. James Coppersmith

WOR-TV Channel 9
1440 Broadway
New York, NY 10018
(212) 764-7000
Contact: Robert Williamson

WPIX Channel 11
11 WPIX Plaza
New York, NY 10017
(212) 949-1100
Contact: Richard Hughes

WXTV Channel 41
250 Park Ave.
New York, NY 10017
(212) 697-0585
Contact: Ivan Egas

Plattsburgh
WPTZ Channel 5 (NBC)
Box 249
Plattsburgh, NY 12901
(518) 561-5555
Contact: Robert Paxson

Rochester
WHEC-TV Channel 10 (CBS)
191 East Ave.
Rochester, NY 14604
(716) 546-5670
Contact: Jack Decker

WOKR Channel 13 (ABC)
4225 W. Henrietta Rd.
Rochester, NY 14623
(716) 334-8700
Contact: Francis Diprosa

WROC-TV Channel 8 (NBC)
201 Humboldt St.
Rochester, NY 14610
(716) 288-8400
Contact: Allan Fever

Schenectady
WMHT-TV Channel 17
17 Fern Ave.
Schenectady, NY 12306
(518) 356-1700
Contact: Donald Schein

WRGB-TV Channel 6 (NBC)
1400 Balltown Rd.
Schenectady, NY 12309
(518) 385-1385
Contact: James Delmonico

Shoppingtown
WNYS-TV Channel 9 (ABC)
Box 9
Shoppingtown, NY 13214
(315) 446-4780
Contact: Charles Kennedy

Syracuse
WSYE-TV Channel 18
1030 James St.
Syracuse, NY 13203
(607) 733-5536
Contact: Don Buies

WSYR-TV Channel 3 (NBC)
1030 James St.
Syracuse, NY 13203
(315) 474-3911
Contact: David Shurtleff

WTVH Channel 5 (CBS)
980 James St.
Syracuse, NY 13203
(315) 474-8511
Contact: Larry Rhodes

Utica
WKTV Channel 2 (NBC)
Smith Hill Rd.
Utica, NY 13503
(315) 733-0404, 797-7440
Contact: Sheldon Storrier

WUTR-TV Channel 20 (ABC)
Box 20
Smith Hill
Utica, NY 13503
(315) 797-5220
Contact: Edward Bizzell

Watertown
WWNY-TV Channel 7 (ABC, CBS)
120 Arcade St.
Watertown, NY 13601
(315) 788-3800
Contact: Tony Malara

NORTH CAROLINA

Asheville
WANC-TV Channel 21
75 Scenic Hwy.
Asheville, NC 28804
(704) 254-4663
Contact: Meredith S. Thoms

WLOS-TV Channel 13 (ABC)
Box 2150
Asheville, NC 28802
(704) 255-0013
Contact: Morton S. Cohn

Charlotte
WBTV Channel 3 (CBS)
1 Julian Price Pl.
Charlotte, NC 28208
(704) 374-3500
Contact: James G. Babb, Jr.

WCCB-TV Channel 18 (ABC)
1 Television Pl.
Charlotte, NC 28205
(704) 372-1800
Contact: Kent Lillie

WRET-TV Channel 36
Box 12665
Charlotte, NC 28205
(704) 536-3636
Contact: James Thrash

WSOC-TV Channel 9 (NBC)
Box 2536
Charlotte, NC 28243
(704) 372-0930
Contact: Jack Callaghan

Durham
WRDU-TV Channel 28 (NBC)
Box 8706
Hwy. 54
Durham, NC 27707
(919) 544-1786
Contact: Doug McLarty

WTVD Channel 11 (CBS)
Capital Cities Broadcasting Corp.
Box 2009
2410 Broad St.
Durham, NC 27702
(919) 477-2131
Contact: Mike Thompson

Greensboro
WFMY-TV Channel 2 (CBS)
Phillips Ave. & White St.
Greensboro, NC 27420
(919) 274-0114
Contact: Charles Whitehurst

Greenville
WNCT-TV Channel 9 (CBS)
Box 898
Greenville, NC 27834
(919) 756-3180
Contact: Black Lewis

Hickory
WHKY-TV Channel 14
526 Main Ave., SE
Hickory, NC 28601
(704) 322-5726
Contact: Thomas S. Long

High Point
WGHP-TV Channel 8 (ABC)
400 N. Main St.
High Point, NC 27260
(919) 883-7131
Contact: Eugene Bohi

New Bern
WCTI-TV Channel 12 (ABC)
Box 2325
Park Ave.
New Bern, NC 28560
(919) 637-2111
Contact: Bill Jenkins

Raleigh
WRAL-TV Channel 5 (ABC)
2619 Western Blvd.
Raleigh, NC 27606
(919) 828-2511
Contact: James Goodman

Washington
WITN-TV Channel 7 (NBC)
Hwy. 17, S
Washington, NC 27889
(919) 946-3131
Contact: Dick Paul

Wilmington
WECT Channel 6 (NBC)
322 Shipyard Blvd.
Wilmington, NC 28401
(919) 791-8070
Contact: Paul A. Brissette, Jr.

WWAY Channel 3 (ABC)
615 N. Front St.
Wilmington, NC 28401
(919) 762-8581
Contact: Mitchell Saieed

Winston-Salem
WXII-TV Channel 12 (NBC)
700 Coliseum Dr.
Winston-Salem, NC 27106
(919) 723-9241
Contact: Jim Tandy

NORTH DAKOTA

Bismarck
KFYR-TV Channel 5 (ABC, NBC)
4th & Broadway
Bismarck, ND 58501
(701) 223-0900
Contact: Claire Holmberg

KMOT Channel 10
Broadway at 5th
Bismarck, ND 58501
(701) 223-0900
Contact: Stan Wilson

KUMV-TV Channel 8
Broadway at 4th
Bismarck, ND 58501
(701) 223-0900
Contact: Roger Rien

KXMB-TV Channel 12
Box 1617
Bismarck, ND 58501
(701) 223-9197
Contact: John Von Rueden

Dickinson
KDIX-TV Channel 2
119 2nd Ave., W
Dickinson, ND 58601
(701) 225-5133
Contact: Warren Vranna

Fargo
KTHI-TV Channel 11 (ABC)
1350 21st Ave., S
Fargo, ND 58102
(701) 237-5211
Contact: Paul Wickre

KXJB Channel 4 (CBS)
4000 W. Main St.
Fargo, ND 58102
(701) 282-0444
Contact: John W. Boler

WDAY-TV Channel 6 (NBC)
207 5th St., N
Fargo, ND 58102
(701) 237-6500
Contact: Lee Stewart

WDAZ-TV Channel 8
207 5th St., N
Fargo, ND 58102
(701) 237-6500
Contact: Curt Sorbo

Minot
KXMC-TV Channel 13
Box 1686
Minot, ND 58702
(701) 852-2104
Contact: Rod Romine

KXMD-TV Channel 11
Box 1686
Minot, ND 58702
(701) 852-2104
Contact: John Blake

OHIO

Akron
WAKR-TV Channel 23 (ABC)
853 Copley Rd.
Akron, OH 44320
(216) 535-7831
Contact: R. I. Bostian

Canton
WJAN-TV Channel 17
Box 8080
Canton, OH 44711
(216) 875-5542
Contact: Robert Carano

Cincinnati
WCPO-TV Channel 9 (CBS)
500 Central Ave.
Cincinnati, OH 45202
(513) 721-9900
Contact: Robert D. Gordon

WKRC-TV Channel 12 (ABC)
1906 Highland Ave.
Cincinnati, OH 45219
(513) 651-1200
Contact: Robert C. Wiegand

WLWT Channel 5 (NBC)
140 W. 9th St.
Cincinnati, OH 45202
(513) 352-5000
Contact: Walter E. Bartlett

WXIX-TV Channel 19
10490 Taconic Terr.
Cincinnati, OH 45215
(513) 772-1919
Contact: Allan W. Ginsberg

Cleveland
WEWS Channel 5 (ABC)
Euclid at 30th
Cleveland, OH 44115
(216) 432-1500
Contact: Ernest Sindelar

WJKW-TV Channel 8 (CBS)
5800 S. Marginal Rd.
Cleveland, OH 44103
(216) 431-8888
Contact: Francis Brady

WKYC-TV Channel 3 (NBC)
1403 E. 6th St.
Cleveland, OH 44114
(216) 696-1100
Contact: Charles Gerber

Columbus
WBNS-TV Channel 10 (CBS)
770 Twin Rivers Dr.
Columbus, OH 43215
(614) 460-3700
Contact: Gene D'Angelo

WCMH-TV Channel 4 (NBC)
3165 Olentangy River Rd.
Columbus, OH 43216
(614) 263-5441
Contact: Benjamin D. McKeel

WTVN-TV Channel 4 (NBC)
Taft Broadcasting Co.
Box 718
753 Harmon Ave.
Columbus, OH 43216
(614) 228-5801
Contact: Fred von Stade

Dayton
WDTN Channel 2 (NBC)
4595 S. Dixie Ave.
Dayton, OH 45401
(513) 293-2101
Contact: Ray W. Colie

WHIO-TV Channel 7 (CBS)
1414 Wilmington Ave.
Dayton, OH 45401
(513) 254-5311
Contact: Jack P. McCarthy

WKEF Channel 22 (ABC)
1731 Soldiers Home & West Carrollton Rd.
Dayton, OH 45418
(513) 263-2662
Contact: James Graham

Lima
WLIO Channel 35 (ABC, NBC)
1424 Rice Ave.
Lima, OH 45805
Contact: James C. Dages

Louisville
WJAN-TV Channel 17
6600 Atlantic Blvd.
Louisville, OH 44641
(216) 875-5542
Contact: David Kelton

Parma
WUAB-TV Channel 43
8443 Day Dr.
Parma, OH 44129
(216) 845-6043
Contact: Jack Moffitt

Steubenville
WSTV-TV Channel 9 (ABC, CBS)
320 Market St.
Steubenville, OH 43952
(614) 282-0911
Contact: Ray J. Chumley

Toledo
WDHO-TV Channel 24 (ABC)
300 S. Byrne Rd.
Toledo, OH 43615
(419) 535-0024
Contact: Arthur M. Dorfner

WSPD-TV Channel 13 (NBC)
136 Huron St.
Toledo, OH 43604
(419) 255-1313
Contact: H. W. Ray

WTOL-TV Channel 11 (CBS)
604 Jackson St.
Toledo, OH 43601
(419) 244-7411
Contact: Law Epps

Youngstown
WFMJ-TV Channel 21 (NBC)
101 W. Boardman St.
Youngstown, OH 44503
(216) 744-8611
Contact: Mitchell Stanley

WKBN-TV Channel 27 (CBS)
3930 Sunset Blvd.
Youngstown, OH 44501
(216) 782-1144
Contact: W. P. Williamson, III

WYTV Channel 33 (ABC)
3800 Shady Run Rd.
Youngstown, OH 44502
(216) 783-2930
Contact: Geoffrey Pearce

Zanesville
WHIZ-TV Channel 18 (NBC)
N. 5th St.
Zanesville, OH 43701
(614) 452-5431
Contact: Robert Hodous

OKLAHOMA

Ada
KTEN Channel 10 (ABC)
Box 10
1600 Arlington
Ada, OK 74820
(405) 332-3311
Contact: Bill Hoover

Ardmore
KXII-TV Channel 12 (CBS)
Hwy. 75, Lincoln Center
Ardmore, OK 73401
(405) 223-0946
Contact: C. H. Balding

Lawton
KSWO-TV Channel 7 (ABC)
Box 708
Lawton, OK 73502
(405) 355-7000
Contact: Larry Patton

Oklahoma City
KOCO-TV Channel 5 (ABC)
3705 N.W. 63rd
Oklahoma City, OK 73132
(405) 848-3311
Contact: Mike Palmer

KTVY Channel 4 (NBC)
Box 14068
Oklahoma City, OK 73114
(405) 478-1212
Contact: Tom Parrington

KWTV Channel 9 (CBS)
7401 N. Kelley St.
Oklahoma City, OK 73114
(405) 843-6641
Contact: Jacques DeLier

Tulsa
KOTV Channel 6 (CBS)
302 S. Frankfort St.
Tulsa, OK 74120
(918) 582-9233
Contact: Duane Harm

KTEW Channel 2 (NBC)
3701 S. Peoria St.
Tulsa, OK 74101
(918) 742-5561
Contact: William S. Ritchie

KTUL-TV Channel 8 (ABC)
Lookout Mountain
Tulsa, OK 74101
(918) 446-3351
Contact: Tom Goodgame

OREGON

Coos Bay
KCBY-TV Channel 11
Box 1156
Coos Bay, OR 97420
(503) 269-1111
Contact: Mary Miller

Eugene
KEZI-TV Channel 9 (ABC)
2225 Coburg Rd.
Eugene, OR 97401
(503) 343-3301
Contact: Jim Putney

KVAL-TV Channel 13 (NBC)
Box 1313
Eugene, OR 97401
(503) 342-4961
Contact: Glenn Nickell

Klamath Falls
KOTI-TV Channel 3 (ABC, CBS)
239 Main St.
Klamath Falls, OR 97601
(503) 884-8131
Contact: Dan Markham

Medford
KOBI-TV Channel 5 (ABC, CBS)
2000 Crater Lake Hwy.
Medford, OR 97501
(503) 779-5555
Contact: Jerold R. Poolos

KTUL-TV Channel 10 (ABC, NBC)
Rossanley Dr.
Medford, OR 97501
(503) 773-7373
Contact: Lawrence Pavelionis

Portland
KATU Channel 2 (ABC)
2153 N.E. Sandy Blvd.
Portland, OR 97232
(503) 233-2422
Contact: Thomas R. Dargan

KGW-TV Channel 8 (NBC)
1501 S.W. Jefferson St.
Portland, OR 97201
(503) 226-5134
Contact: Forest W. Amsden

KOIN-TV Channel 6 (CBS)
140 S.W. Columbia St.
Portland, OR 97201
(503) 243-6666
Contact: Richard J. Butterfield

KPTV Channel 12
Box 3401
Portland, OR 97208
(503) 222-9921
Contact: John Hanson

Roseburg
KPIC-TV Channel 4
1850 N.E. Stephens St.
Roseburg, OR 97470
(503) 675-0213
Contact: Aaron Bol

PENNSYLVANIA

Allentown
WFMZ-TV Channel 69
East Rock Rd.
Allentown, PA 18103
(215) 797-4530
Contact: Richard C. Dean

Altoona
WOPC Channel 38 (ABC)
Box 609
Wopsononock Lookout
Altoona, PA 16603
(814) 943-2607
Contact: John R. Powley

WTAJ-TV Channel 10 (CBS)
5000 6th Ave.
Altoona, PA 16602
(814) 944-2031
Contact: Ian Harrower

Erie
WICU-TV Channel 12 (NBC)
3514 State St.
Erie, PA 16512
(814) 454-5201
Contact: Robert Lunquist

WJET-TV Channel 24 (ABC)
8455 Peach St.
Erie, PA 16509
(814) 864-4902
Contact: Pete Coticchia

WSEE Channel 35 (CBS)
1220 Peach St.
Erie, PA 16501
(814) 455-7575
Contact: Edward Zellefrow

Harrisburg
WHP-TV Channel 21 (CBS)
3300 N. 6th St.
Harrisburg, PA 17110
(717) 238-2100
Contact: Joseph Higgins

WTPA Channel 27 (ABC)
3235 Hoffman St.
Harrisburg, PA 17105
(717) 238-7171
Contact: Paul S. Abbott

Johnstown
WJAC-TV Channel 6 (NBC)
Box 38
Johnstown, PA 15907
(814) 255-5831
Contact: Alvin Schrott

WJNL-TV Channel 19 (ABC, CBS)
Cover Hill
Johnstown, PA 15902
(814) 535-8554
Contact: John Cunningham

Lancaster
WGAL-TV Channel 8 (NBC)
Lincoln Hwy., W
Lancaster, PA 17604
(717) 393-5851
Contact: Harold Miller

Lebanon
WLYH-TV Channel 15 (CBS)
R.D. No. 5
Lebanon, PA 17042
(717) 273-4551
Contact: David Dodds

Philadelphia
KYW-TV Channel (NBC)
Independence Mall, E
Philadelphia, PA 19106
(215) 238-4700
Contact: Alan J. Bell

WCAU-TV Channel 10 (CBS)
City & Monument Aves.
Philadelphia, PA 19131
(215) 839-7000
Contact: Robert Hosking

WKBS-TV Channel 48
3201 S. 26th St.
Philadelphia, PA 19145
(215) 336-6400
Contact: Kenneth MacDonald

WPHL-TV Channel 17 (NBC)
5001 Wynnefield Ave.
Philadelphia, PA 19131
(215) 878-1700
Contact: Ted Baze

WPVI-TV Channel 6 (ABC)
4100 City Line Ave.
Philadelphia, PA 19131
(215) 878-9700
Contact: Lawrence Pollock

WTAF-TV Channel 29
4th & Market Sts.
Philadelphia, PA 19106
(215) 925-2929
Contact: Carlo Anneke

Pittsburgh
KDKA-TV Channel 2 (CBS)
1 Gateway Center
Pittsburgh, PA 15222
(412) 391-3000
Contact: Jonathan S. Hayes

WIIC-TV Channel 11 (NBC)
341 Rising Main Ave.
Pittsburgh, PA 15214
(412) 237-1100
Contact: Leonard Swanson

WPGH-TV Channel 53
750 Ivory Ave.
Pittsburgh, PA 15214
(412) 931-8600
Contact: Albert Holtz

WTAE-TV Channel 4 (ABC)
400 Ardmore Blvd.
Pittsburgh, PA 15230
(412) 242-4300
Contact: John Conomikes

Scranton
WDAU-TV Channel 22 (CBS)
1000 Wyoming Ave.
Scranton, PA 18509
(717) 342-7634
Contact: Madge Holcomb

Wilkes-Barre
WBRE-TV Channel 28 (NBC)
62 S. Franklin St.
Wilkes-Barre, PA 18703
(717) 823-3101
Contact: David Baltimore

WNEP-TV Channel 61 (ABC)
Wilkes-Barre–Scranton Airport, PA 18614
(717) 826-1616
Contact: Thomas Shelburne

York
WSBA-TV Channel 43 (CBS)
Box 1868
York, PA 17405
Contact: Robert Stough

PUERTO RICO

Aguadilla
WVEO-TV Channel 44
P.O. Box W
Aguadilla, PR 00603
(809) 832-4560
Contact: Dr. Pablo Guardiola

Hato Rey
WKAQ-TV Channel 2
Telemundo, Inc.
383 Roosevelt Ave.
Hato Rey, PR 00917
(809) 764-0202
Contact: Rafael Ruiz

Mayaguez
WOLE-TV Channel 12
Box 1194
Mayaguez, PR 00708
(809) 832-4160
Contact: Amadeo Nazario

WORA-TV Channel 5
Box 43
Mayaguez, PR 00708
(809) 832-1150
Contact: Maureen Justiniano

Old San Juan Station
WRIK-TV Channel 7
Box A
Old San Juan Station, PR 00902
(809) 724-7575
Contact: Peter L. Moreno

Ponce
WSUR-TV Channel 9
Box 471
La Rambla
Ponce, PR 00905
(809) 842-4178
Contact: Ralph Perez Perry

San Juan
WAPA-TV Channel 4 (NBC)
Box 2050
San Juan, PR 00936
(809) 783-4440
Contact: Rafael Duany

WKAQ-TV Channel 2
383 Franklin D. Roosevelt Ave.
San Juan, PR 00936
(809) 764-0202
Contact: Rafael Ruiz

WKBM-TV Channel 11
657 Condado St.
San Juan, PR 00905
(809) 723-8040
Contact: Ralph Perez Perry

RHODE ISLAND

East Providence
WPRI-TV Channel 12 (ABC)
25 Catamore Blvd.
E. Providence, RI 02914
(401) 438-7200
Contact: Edwin W. Pfeiffer

Providence
WJAR-TV Channel 10 (NBC)
176 Weybosset St.
Providence, RI 02903
(401) 751-5700
Contact: Leonard S. Davey, Jr.

SOUTH CAROLINA

Anderson
WAIM-TV Channel 40 (ABC, CBS)
Box 4047
Station B
Anderson, SC 29621
(803) 226-1511
Contact: Betty K. Black

Beech Island
WATU-TV Channel 26
Pine Log Rd.
Beech Island, SC 29841
(803) 824-5527
Contact: Terry L. Brown

Charleston
WCBD-TV Channel 2 (ABC)
Box 879
Charleston, SC 29402
(803) 884-4141
Contact: Virgil Evans

WCIC-TV Channel 4 (NBC)
Box 10866
Charleston, SC 29411
(803) 884-8513
Contact: Celia Shaw

WCSC-TV Channel 5 (CBS)
485 East Bay St.
Charleston, SC 29402
(803) 723-8371
Contact: Gus Bailey

Columbia
WIS-TV Channel 10 (NBC)
1111 Bull St.
Columbia, SC 29201
(803) 799-1010
Contact: Dick Coulter

WNOK-TV Channel 19 (CBS)
6027 Devine St.
Columbia, SC 20250
(803) 776-3600
Contact: Richard Laughridge

WOLO-TV Channel 25 (ABC)
5807 Shakespeare Rd.
Columbia, SC 29204
(803) 754-7525
Contact: Don Krauss

Florence
WBTW Channel 13 (CBS)
3430 TV Rd.
Florence, SC 29501
(803) 662-1565
Contact: Joseph B. Foster

Greenville
WFBC-TV Channel 4 (NBC)
WFBC-TV Bldg.
Greenville, SC 29602
(802) 233-4601
Contact: Douglas A. Smith

WGGS-TV Channel 13 (ABC)
Box 4157
Greenville, SC 29308
(803) 242-1616
Contact: Jim McManus

Mt. Pleasant
WCIV Channel 4 (NBC)
Hwy. 703
Mt. Pleasant, SC 29464
(803) 884-8513
Contact: Celia Shaw

Spartanburg
WSPA-TV Channel 7 (CBS)
123 N. Converse St.
Spartanburg, SC 29301
(803) 585-7777
Contact: David Hardy

Sumter
WRJA-TV Channel 27
18 N. Harvin St.
Sumter, SC 29150
(803) 773-5546
Contact: James Bernard

SOUTH DAKOTA

Aberdeen
KABY-TV Channel 9
Country Club Rd.
Aberdeen, SD 57401
(605) 225-4350
Contact: Robert Kerr

Garden City
KDLO-TV Channel 3 (CBS)
Garden City, SD 57236
(605) 336-1100
Contact: Roy Thorson

Mitchell
KXON-TV Channel 5 (ABC)
Box 1049
Mitchell, SD 57301
(605) 996-7501
Contact: Errol Kapellusch

Rapid City
KEVN-TV Channel 7 (ABC)
Box 677
Rapid City, SD 57701
(605) 394-7777
Contact: Jerry Condra

KHSD-TV Channel 11
Box 1760
Rapid City, SD 57701
(605) 342-2000
Contact: Dan Lesmeister

KIVV Channel 5
Box 677
Rapid City, SD 57701
(605) 394-7777
Contact: Jerry Condra

KOTA-TV Channel 3 (ABC, NBC)
518½ St.Joseph St.
Rapid City, SD 57701
(605) 342-2000
Contact: William F. Duhamel

KSGW-TV Channel 12 (CBS)
518½ St.Joseph St.
Rapid City, SD 57701
Contact: Dan Lesmeister

Sioux Falls
KDLO-TV Channel 3
Phillips Ave. & 13th St.
Sioux Falls, SD 57236
(605) 336-1100
Contact: Evans A. Nord

KELO-TV Channel 11 (CBS)
Phillips Ave. & 13th St.
Sioux Falls, SD 57102
(605) 336-1100
Contact: Evans A. Nord

KPLO-TV Channel 6
Phillips Ave. & 13th St.
Sioux Falls, SD 57102
(605) 336-1100
Contact: Evans A. Nord

KPRY-TV Channel 4
6th & Dakota Ave.
Sioux Falls, SD 57102
(605) 336-1300
Contact: Scott Park

TENNESSEE

Bristol
WCYB-TV Channel 5 (NBC)
Box 397
Bristol, TN 37620
(703) 669-4161
Contact: Robert H. Smith

Chattanooga
WDEF-TV Channel 12 (CBS)
3300 Broad St.
Chattanooga, TN 37402
(615) 267-3392
Contact: William M. Dunaway

WRCB-TV Channel 3 (NBC)
900 Whitehall Rd.
Executive Park
Chattanooga, TN 37405
(615) 267-5412
Contact: George Stevens

WTVC Channel 9 (ABC)
410 W. 6th St.
Chattanooga, TN 37401
(615) 756-5500
Contact: Jane C. Dowden

Crossville
WCPT-TV Channel 55
313 S. Main St.
Crossville, TN 38555
(615) 484-8424
Contact: Edward M. Johnson

Jackson
WBBJ-TV Channel 7 (ABC, CBS)
Box 2387
Jackson, TN 38301
(901) 424-4515
Contact: Gerry Quick

Johnson City
WJHL-TV Channel 11 (CBS)
338 E. Main St.
Johnson City, TN 37602
(615) 926-2151
Contact: W. Hanes Lancaster, Jr.

Kingsport
WKPT-TV Channel 19 (ABC)
222 Commerce St.
Kingsport, TN 37660
(615) 245-4161
Contact: George DeVault

Knoxville
WATE-TV Channel 6 (NBC)
1306 Broadway, NE
Knoxville, TN 37901
(615) 637-9666
Contact: John McCloud

WBIR-TV Channel 10 (CBS)
1513 Hutchinson Ave.
Knoxville, TN 37917
(615) 637-1010
Contact: Neal Branch

WTVK Channel 26 (CBS)
Box 1388
Sharp's Ridge Park
Knoxville, TN 37901
(615) 687-2312
Contact: Bill Eckstein

Memphis
WHBQ-TV Channel 13 (ABC)
485 S. Highland
Memphis, TN 38111
(901) 323-7661
Contact: D. A. Noel

WMC-TV Channel 5 (NBC)
1960 Union Ave.
Memphis, TN 38104
(901) 726-0555
Contact: M. E. Greiner, Jr.

WREG-TV Channel 3 (CBS)
803 Channel 3 Dr.
Memphis, TN 38103
(901) 525-3333
Contact: Charles B. Brakefield

Nashville
WNGE Channel 2 (ABC)
441 Murfreesboro Rd.
Nashville, TN 37210
(615) 259-2200
Contact: Brian Cobb

WSM-TV Channel 4 (NBC)
5700 Knob Rd.
Nashville, TN 37209
(615) 749-2244
Contact: Tom Griscom, Jr.

WTVF Channel 5 (CBS)
474 James Robertson Pkwy.
Nashville, TN 37219
(615) 244-5000
Contact: Thomas Erwin

WZTV Channel 17
410 38th Ave., N
Nashville, TN 37209
(615) 385-1717
Contact: Ian N. Wheeler

TEXAS

Abilene
KACB-TV Channel 3
4510 S. 14th St.
Abilene, TX 79605
(915) 692-4242
Contact: William Terry

KRBC-TV Channel 9 (NBC)
4510 S. 14th St.
Abilene, TX 79604
(915) 692-4242
Contact: Dale Ackers

KTXS-TV Channel 12
U.S. Hwy. 83
Anson Bypass
Abilene, TX 79604
(915) 677-2281
Contact: Robert Jackson

Amarillo
KAMR-TV Channel 4 (NBC)
2000 N. Polk St.
Amarillo, TX 79105
(806) 383-3321
Contact: Ray Poindexter

KFDA-TV Channel 10 (CBS)
Cherry Ave. at Broadway
Amarillo, TX 79105
(806) 383-2226
Contact: Harry Neuhardt

KVII-TV Channel 7 (ABC)
4th & Polk Sts.
Amarillo, TX 79101
(806) 373-1787
Contact: James McCormick

KVIJ-TV Channel 8
4th & Polk Sts.
Amarillo, TX 79101
(806) 373-1787
Contact: James McCormick

Austin
KTBC-TV Channel 7 (CBS)
10th & Brazos
Austin, TX 78768
(512) 476-7777
Contact: Rush Evans, Jr.

KTVV-TV Channel 36 (NBC)
908 W. M. L. K. Blvd.
Austin, TX 78767
(512) 476-3636
Contact: Al Howard

KVUE-TV Channel 24 (ABC)
3201 Steck Ave.
Austin, TX 78757
(512) 459-6521
Contact: Jerry Condra

Beaumont
KBMT-TV Channel 12 (ABC)
525 Interstate 10, S
Beaumont, TX 77704
(713) 833-7512
Contact: William Moore

KFDM-TV Channel 6 (CBS)
2955 Interstate 10, E
Beaumont, TX 77706
(713) 892-6622
Contact: Terrance Ford

Big Springs
KMOM-TV Channel 9 (ABC)
2500 Kentucky Way
Big Springs, TX 79720
(915) 943-3231
Contact: Pat Hales

Bryan
KBTX-TV Channel 3
Box 3730
Bryan, TX 77801
(713) 846-7777
Contact: Harry Gillam

Corpus Christi
KIII Channel 3 (ABC)
4750 S. Padre Island Dr.
Corpus Christi, TX 78411
(512) 854-4733
Contact: Bob White

KORO-TV Channel 28
600 Bldg.
Suite 102
Corpus Christi, TX 78401
(512) 883-2823
Contact: Eva Wardlow

KRIS-TV Channel 6 (NBC)
409 S. Staples
Corpus Christi, TX 78403
(512) 883-6511
Contact: Frank Smith, Jr.

KZTV Channel 10 (CBS)
Show Room Bldg.
Corpus Christi, TX 78401
(512) 883-5415
Contact: Vann Kennedy

Dallas
KDFW-TV Channel 4 (CBS)
400 N. Griffin St.
Dallas, TX 75202
(214) 744-4000
Contact: John McCrory

KXTX-TV Channel 39
3900 Harry Hines Blvd.
Dallas, TX 75219
(214) 521-3900
Contact: Roger Baerwolf

WFAA-TV Channel 8 (ABC)
Communications Center
Dallas, TX 75202
(214) 748-9631
Contact: Dane Lane

El Paso
KDBC-TV Channel 4 (CBS)
Wyoming at Walnut St.
El Paso, TX 79999
(915) 532-6551
Contact: Ed Sleighel

KTSM-TV Channel 9 (NBC)
801 N. Oregon St.
El Paso, TX 79902
(915) 532-5421
Contact: Karl Wyler, Jr.

KVIA-TV Channel 13 (ABC)
No. 5 Executive Center
El Paso, TX 79912
(915) 532-1431
Contact: Wayne Roy

XEJ-TV Channel 5
Box 9555
El Paso, TX 79985
(915) 582-0248
Contact: P. Meneses Hoyos

XEPM-TV Channel 2
Box 9554
El Paso, TX 79985
(915) 582-2222
Contact: M. D. Heredia

Fort Worth
KTVT Channel 11
4801 W. Freeway
Fort Worth, TX 76101
(817) 738-1951
Contact: Jack Berning

KXAS-TV Channel 5 (NBC)
3900 Barnett St.
Fort Worth, TX 76101
(817) 429-1550
Contact: Blake Byrne

Harlingen
KGBT-TV Channel 4 (CBS)
1519 W. Harrison St.
Harlingen, TX 78550
(512) 423-3910
Contact: William Heyman

Houston
KDOG-TV Channel 26
3935 Westheimer Rd.
Houston, TX 77027
(713) 626-2610
Contact: Leroy Gloger

KHOU-TV Channel 11 (CBS)
1945 Allen Pkwy.
Houston, TX 77001
(713) 526-1111
Contact: James King

KHTV Channel 39
7700 Westpark Dr.
Houston, TX 77001
(713) 781-3930
Contact: Gene Jacobsen

KPRC-TV Channel 2 (NBC)
8181 Southwest Freeway
Houston, TX 77001
(713) 771-4631
Contact: Jack McGrew

KTRK-TV Channel 13 (ABC)
3310 Bissonnet
Houston, TX 77005
(713) 666-0713
Contact: Kenneth Johnson

KUHT-TV Channel 8
4513 Cullen Blvd.
Houston, TX 77004
(713) 749-2304
Contact: James Bauer

Laredo
KGNS-TV Channel 8 (ABC, NBC)
102 W. Delmar Blvd.
Laredo, TX 78041
(512) 723-7457
Contact: Hal Atkins, Jr.

KVTV Channel 13 (CBS)
2600 Shea St.
Laredo, TX 78041
(512) 723-2393
Contact: Neil Gilligan

XEFE-TV Channel 2
Box 1484
Laredo, TX 78040
(512) 724-4531
Contact: Ramoncita Esparza

Lubbock
KCBD-TV Channel 11 (NBC)
5600 Avenue A
Lubbock, TX 79408
(806) 744-1414
Contact: Robert McKinsey

KLBK-TV Channel 13 (CBS)
7400 University Ave.
Lubbock, TX 79408
(806) 745-2345
Contact: W. F. deTourmillon

KMCC-TV Channel 28 (ABC)
84th & Avenue L
Lubbock, TX 79408
(806) 745-2828
Contact: William McAlister

KSWS-TV Channel 8 (NBC)
Box 2190
Lubbock, TX 79408
(806) 744-1414
Contact: Robert McKinsey

Lufkin
KTRE-TV Channel 9
Box 729
Lufkin, TX 75901
(713) 634-7771
Contact: Errol Kapellusch

Midland
KMID-TV Channel 2 (NBC)
Drawer B
Midland, TX 79701
(915) 563-2222
Contact: Ray Herndon

Monahans
KMOM-TV Channel 9 (ABC, CBS)
Drawer N
Monahans, TX 79756
(915) 943-3231
Contact: Pat Hales

Odessa
KOSA-TV Channel 7 (CBS)
1211 N. Whitaker
Odessa, TX 79760
(915) 337-8301
Contact: Tom Hughes

Port Arthur
KJAC-TV
17th at Woodworth St.
Port Arthur, TX 77640
(713) 985-5557
Contact: Roy Shotts

San Angelo
KCTV Channel 8 (CBS)
1011 E. 28th St.
San Angelo, TX 76901
(915) 655-7383
Contact: Harry Mooradian

San Antonio
KENS-TV Channel 5 (CBS)
Avenue E & 4th St.
San Antonio, TX 78205
(512) 225-5211
Contact: William Moll

KMOL-TV Channel 4 (NBC)
1031 Navarro St.
San Antonio, TX 78205
(512) 226-4251
Contact: Edward Cheviot

KSAT-TV Channel 12 (ABC)
1408 N. St. Mary's
San Antonio, TX 78298
(512) 226-7611
Contact: James Schiavone

KWEX-TV Channel 41
411 E. Durango
San Antonio, TX 78204
(512) 227-4141
Contact: James Meek

Sherman
KXII Channel 12 (CBS, NBC)
Box 1175
Sherman, TX 75090
(214) 892-8123
Contact: Chuck Balding

Temple
KCEN-TV Channel 6 (ABC, NBC)
17 S. 3rd St.
Temple, TX 76501
(817) 773-1633
Contact: Jack Hauser

Tyler
KLTV Channel 9
Kilgore Hwy.
Tyler, TX 75701
(214) 592-3873
Contact: Frank Melton

Victoria
KXIX-TV Channel 10
Victoria Communications Corp.
Loop 175 & Port Lavaca Hwy.
Victoria, TX 77901
(512) 578-3519
Contact: Dewey Acker

Waco
KWTX-TV Channel 10 (CBS)
4520 Bosque Blvd.
Waco, TX 76710
(817) 776-1330
Contact: M. N. Bostick

Weslaco
KRGV-TV Channel 5 (ABC)
900 E. Expwy.
Weslaco, TX 78596
(512) 968-3131
Contact: John Sehill

Wichita Falls
KAUZ-TV Channel 6 (CBS)
Seymour Rd.
Wichita Falls, TX 76307
(817) 322-6957
Contact: William Hobbs

KFDX-TV Channel 3 (NBC)
4500 Seymour Hwy.
Wichita Falls, TX 76308
(817) 692-4530
Contact: Warren Silver

UTAH

Salt Lake City
KSL-TV Channel 5 (CBS)
Broadcast House
Salt Lake City, UT 84111
(801) 524-2500
Contact: Jay Lloyd

KTVX Channel 4 (ABC)
1760 Fremont Dr.
Salt Lake City, UT 84104
(801) 972-1776
Contact: Harold Woolley

KUTV Channel 2 (NBC)
179 Social Hall Ave.
Salt Lake City, UT 84111
(801) 532-2222
Contact: Robert H. Temple

VERMONT

Burlington
WCAX-TV Channel 3 (CBS)
Joy Dr., S
Burlington, VT 05401
(802) 862-5761
Contact: Stuart T. Martin

Winooski
WEZF-TV Channel 22 (ABC)
1500 Hegeman Ave.
Winooski, VT 05404
(802) 655-3663
Contact: George Roussen

VIRGINIA

Annandale
WNVT-TV Channel 53
8325 Little River Turnpike
Annandale, VA 22003
(703) 323-7000
Contact: Daniel Ward

Bristol
WCYB-TV Channel 5 (NBC)
Box 1009
Bristol, VA 24201
(703) 669-4161
Contact: Robert H. Smith

Charlottesville
WVIR-TV Channel 29 (NBC)
221 E. Main St.
Charlottesville, VA 22902
(804) 977-7082
Contact: Harold Wright, Jr.

Hampton
WVEC-TV Channel 13 (ABC)
1930 E. Pembroke Ave.
Hampton, VA 23663
(804) 722-6331
Contact: Thomas P. Chisman

Harrisonburg
WHSV-TV Channel 3 (ABC, NBC)
Rawley Pike
Harrisonburg, VA 22801
(703) 433-9191
Contact: Sammy Bland

Lynchburg
WLVA-TV Channel 13 (ABC)
Langhorne Rd.
Lynchburg, VA 24505
(804) 528-1313
Contact: Roger Divens

Norfolk
WHRO-TV Channel 15
5200 Hampton Blvd.
Norfolk, VA 23508
(804) 489-9476
Contact: John Morison

WTAR-TV Channel 3 (CBS)
720 Boush St.
Norfolk, VA 23510
(804) 446-2600
Contact: Joseph Perkins

WVEC-TV Channel 13 (ABC)
110 3rd St.
Norfolk, VA 23510
(804) 625-3636
Contact: Thomas Chisman

Portsmouth
WAVY-TV Channel 10 (NBC)
801 Wavy St.
Portsmouth, VA 23704
(804) 397-3441
Contact: Ed J. Frech

WYAH-TV Channel 27
1318 Spratley St.
Portsmouth, VA 23705
(804) 393-2505
Contact: Robert Johnson

Richmond
WTVR-TV Channel 6 (CBS)
3301 W. Broad St.
Richmond, VA 23230
(804) 355-8611
Contact: John R. Mahoney

WWBT Channel 12 (NBC)
5710 Midlothian Pike
Richmond, VA 23201
(804) 233-5461
Contact: Robert L. McRaney, Jr.

WXEX-TV Channel 8 (ABC)
Box 888
Richmond, VA 23207
(804) 643-0166
Contact: Ellis Shook

Roanoke
WDBJ-TV Channel 7 (CBS)
Box 7
Roanoke, VA 24022
Studio:
2001 Colonial Ave., SW
Roanoke, VA 24015
(703) 343-8031
Contact: John Karkrader

WSLS-TV Channel 10 (NBC)
Church Ave. & 3rd St., SW
Roanoke, VA 24011
(703) 344-9226
Contact: Robert H. Teter

WASHINGTON

Bellingham
KVOS-TV Channel 12 (CBS)
1151 Ellis St.
Bellingham, WA 98225
(206) 734-4101
Contact: Frank Jank

Kennewick
KNDU-TV Channel 25 (NBC)
3312 Kennewick Ave.
Kennewick, WA 99302
(509) 783-6151
Contact: Scott Hayne

Pasco
KEPR-TV Channel 19
2807 W. Zervis
Pasco, WA 99301
(509) 452-9111
Contact: Dale Hall

KVEW-TV Channel 42
West 1833 Court Ave.
Pasco, WA 99301
(509) 453-0351
Contact: R. Gary Pierone

Seattle
KCTS-TV Channel 9
4045 Brooklyn, NE
Seattle, WA 98105
(206) 543-2000
Contact: Richard Meyer

KING-TV Channel 5 (NBC)
320 Aurora Ave., N
Seattle, WA 98109
(206) 223-5000
Contact: Eric Bremner

KIRO-TV Channel 7 (CBS)
3rd & Broad Sts.
Seattle, WA 98121
(206) 624-7077
Contact: Leigh Stowell

KOMO-TV Channel 4 (ABC)
100 4th Ave., N.
Seattle, WA 98109
(206) 223-4000
Contact: John Behnke

Spokane
KHQ-TV Channel 6 (NBC)
4202 S. Regal Ave.
Spokane, WA 99203
(509) 448-4666
Contact: J. Birney Blair

KREM-TV Channel 2 (CBS)
Box 8037
Spokane, WA 99203
(509) 448-2000
Contact: Dean Woodring

KXLY-TV Channel 4 (ABC)
500 W. Boone Ave.
Spokane, WA 99201
(509) 328-9084
Contact: Wayne McNulty

Tacoma
KSTW-TV Channel 11
19th & Trafton Sts.
Tacoma, WA 98405
(205) 572-5789
Contact: Charles Edwards

Yakima
KAPP-TV Channel 35 (ABC)
Broadcast Center, 35 S. 1st St.
Yakima, WA 98901
(509) 453-0351
Contact: Gary Pierone

KIMA-TV Channel 29 (CBS)
2801 Terrace Hights Rd.
Yakima, WA 98901
(509) 575-0029
Contact: Dale Hazen

KNDO-TV Channel 23 (NBC)
1608 S. 24th Ave.
Yakima, WA 98901
(509) 248-2300
Contact: Hugh Davis

WEST VIRGINIA

Bluefield
WHIS-TV Channel 6 (NBC)
Cumberland Rd.
Bluefield, WV 24701
(304) 327-7114
Contact: John Shott

Bridgeport
WDTV
Box 480
Bridgeport, WV 26330
(304) 842-3558
Contact: John Peters

Charleston
WCHS-TV Channel 8 (CBS)
1111 Virginia St., E
Charleston, WV 25324
(304) 346-5358
Contact: W. P. Eaton

Clarksburg
WBOY-TV Channel 12 (ABC)
912 W. Pike St.
Clarksburg, WV 26301
(304) 624-7573
Contact: Skip Simms

Huntington
WOWK-TV Channel 13 (ABC)
625 4th Ave.
Huntington, WV 25701
(304) 525-7661
Contact: Leo M. MacCourtney

WSAZ-TV Channel 3 (NBC)
645 5th Ave.
Huntington, WV 25721
(304) 697-4781
Contact: George Andrich

Oak Hill
WOAY-TV Channel 4 (ABC)
Box 251
Oak Hill, WV 25901
(304) 469-3361
Contact: R. R. Brown

Parkersburg
CTV9 Channel 9
1737 E. 7th St.
Parkersburg, WV 26101
(304) 422-6468
Contact: Albert A. Martine

WTAP-TV Channel 15 (NBC)
121 W. 7th St.
Parkersburg, WV 26101
(304) 485-4588
Contact: Sherman Grimm

Wheeling
WTRF-TV Channel 7 (NBC)
96 16th St.
Wheeling, WV 26003
(304) 232-7777
Contact: Robert W. Ferguson

WISCONSIN

Eau Claire
WEAU-TV Channel 13 (NBC)
1907 S. Hastings Way
Eau Claire, WI 54701
(715) 832-3474
Contact: Larry Busse

Green Bay
WBAY-TV Channel 2 (CBS)
115 S. Jefferson
Green Bay, WI 54301
(414) 432-3333
Contact: William Dunaway

WFRV-TV Channel 5 (NBC)
1181 E. Mason St.
Green Bay, WI 54301
(414) 437-5411
Contact: Robert O. Southard

WJMN Channel 3 (NBC)
(Satellite to WFRV-TV)
Green Bay, WI 54301
(414) 437-5411
Contact: Robert O. Southard

WLUK-TV Channel 11 (ABC)
787 Lombardi Ave.
Green Bay, WI 54303
(414) 494-8711
Contact: Lowell Johnson

La Crosse
WKBT Channel 8 (CBS)
141 S. 6th St.
La Crosse, WI 54601
(608) 782-4678; 784-7430
Contact: Peter S. Good

WXOW-TV Channel 19 (ABC)
401 Main St.
La Crosse, WI 54601
(608) 785-0030
Contact: Terry K. Shockley

Madison
WAOW-TV Channel 9 (ABC)
5727 Tokay Blvd.
Madison, WI 53701
(608) 274-1234
Contact: Terry K. Shockley

WISC-TV Channel 3 (CBS)
4801 W. Beltline Hwy.
Madison, WI 53711
(608) 271-4321
Contact: Steve Herling

WKOW-TV Channel 27 (ABC)
5727 Tokay Blvd.
Madison, WI 53701
(608) 274-1234
Contact: Robert Wickhem

WMTV Channel 15 (NBC)
615 Forward Dr.
Madison, WI 53711
(608) 274-1515
Contact: Thomas E. Bolger

Milwaukee
WISN-TV Channel 12 (ABC)
759 N. 19th St.
Milwaukee, WI 53233
(414) 342-8812
Contact: Mickey L. Hooten

WITI-TV Channel 6 (CBS)
5445 N. 27th St.
Milwaukee, WI 53209
(414) 462-6666
Contact: Henry J. Davis

WTMJ-TV Channel 4 (NBC)
720 E. Capital Dr.
Milwaukee, WI 53201
(414) 332-9611
Contact: Richard Herbst

WVTV Channel 18
Box 1818
Milwaukee, WI 53201
(414) 442-7050
Contact: Joseph T. Loughlin

Rhinelander
WAEO-TV Channel 12 (NBC)
Box 858
Rhinelander, WI 54501
(715) 369-4700
Contact: Alvin E. O'Konski

Wausau
WAOW-TV Channel 9 (ABC)
1908 Grand Ave.
Wausau, WI 54402
(715) 842-2251
Contact: Bruce Liljegres

WSAU-TV Channel 7 (CBS)
1114 Grand Ave.
Wausau, WI 54401
(715) 345-4211
Contact: Bart Kellnhauser

WYOMING

Casper
KTWO-TV Channel 2 (ABC, CBS, NBC)
4200 E. 2nd St.
Casper, WY 82601
(307) 237-3711
Contact: Bob Dallas Price

Cheyenne
KYCU-TV Channel 5 (ABC, CBS)
2923 E. Lincolnway
Cheyenne, WY 82001
(307) 634-7755
Contact: Carl J. Occhipinti

Thermopolis
KWRB-TV Channel 10 (ABC, CBS, NBC)
500 Arapahoe
Thermopolis, WY 82443
(307) 864-2351
Contact: Mildred V. Ernst

Emmy Awards

The following list of Emmy Awards was provided by the National Academy of Television Arts & Sciences, 110 West 57th Street, New York, NY 10019 and used with their permission.

1948
Presented January 25, 1949

Most Outstanding Television Personality
Shirley Dinsdale and her puppet Judy Splinters (KTLA)

Most Popular Television Program
Pantomime Quiz Time (Mike Stokey) (KTLA)

Best Film Made For Television
"The Necklace," Marshall Grant-Realm Productions (*Your Show Time*)

Station Award
KTLA, for outstanding overall achievement in 1948

Technical Award
Charles Mesak, Don Lee Television, for "Phasefader," in recognition of an outstanding advancement in the video field.

Special Award
Louis McManus, for his original design of the Emmy

1949
Presented January 27, 1950

Best Live Show
Ed Wynn (KTTV)

Best Kinescope Show
Texaco Star Theatre (KNBH, NBC)

Best Children's Show
Time for Beany (KTLA)

Most Outstanding Live Personality
Ed Wynn (KTTV)

Best Film Made For and Viewed on Television in 1949
Life of Riley (KNBH)

Most Outstanding Kinescoped Personality
Milton Berle (KNBH, NBC)

Best Public Service, Cultural or Educational Program
Crusade in Europe (KECA-TV, KTTV)

Best Sports Coverage
Wrestling (KTLA)

Station Achievement
KTLA, for outstanding overall achievement in 1949; Honorable mention to KECA-TV

Best Commercial Made for Television
Lucky Strike, N. W. Ayer & Son, Inc., for the American Tobacco Company

Technical Award
Harold W. Jury of KTSL, Los Angeles, for the synchronizing coordinator that allows superimposition from more than one location.

1950
Presented January 23, 1951

Best Actor
Alan Young (KTTV, CBS)

Best Actress
Gertrude Berg (KTTV, CBS)

Most Outstanding Personality
Groucho Marx (KNBH, NBC)

Best Public Service
City at Night (KTLA)

Best Cultural Show
Campus Chorus and Orchestra (KTSL)

Special Events
Departure of Marines for Korea (KFMB-TV San Diego, KTLA)

Best Sports Program
Rams Football (KNBH)

Best Variety Show
The Alan Young Show (KTTV, CBS)

Best Educational Show
KFI-TV University (KFI-TV)

Best Children's Show
Time for Beany (KTLA)

Best Dramatic Show
Pulitzer Prize Playhouse (KECA-TV)

Best News Program
KTLA Newsreel

Best Games and Audience Participation Show
Truth or Consequences (KTTV, CBS)

Station Achievement
KTLA

Technical Achievement
Orthogram TV amplifier by KNBH-NBC

1951
Presented February 18, 1952

Best Dramatic Show
Studio One (CBS)

Best Comedy Show
Red Skelton Show (NBC)

Best Variety Show
Your Show of Shows (NBC)

Best Actor
Sid Caesar

Best Actress
Imogene Coca

Best Comedian or Comedienne
Red Skelton (NBC)

Special Achievement Awards
U. S. Senator Estes Kefauver, for outstanding public service on television

1952
Presented February 5, 1953

Best Dramatic Program
Robert Montgomery Presents (NBC)

Best Variety Program
Your Show of Shows (NBC)

Best Public Affairs Program
See It Now (CBS)

Best Mystery, Action, or Adventure Program
Dragnet (NBC)

Best Situation Comedy
I Love Lucy (CBS)

Best Audience Participation, Quiz, or Panel Program
What's My Line? (CBS)

Best Children's Program
Time for Beany (KTLA)

Best Actor
Thomas Mitchell

Best Actress
Helen Hayes

Best Comedian
Jimmy Durante (NBC)

Best Comedienne
Lucille Ball (CBS)

Most Outstanding Personality
Bishop Fulton J. Sheen (Dumont)

1953
Presented February 11, 1954

Best Dramatic Program
U. S. Steel Hour (ABC)

Best Situation Comedy
I Love Lucy (CBS)

Best Variety Program
Omnibus (CBS)

Best Program of News or Sports
See It Now (CBS)

Best Public Affairs Program
Victory at Sea (NBC)

Best Children's Program
Kukla, Fran and Ollie (NBC)

Best New Program (Tie)
Make Room for Daddy (ABC)
U.S. Steel Hour (ABC)

Best Male Star of Regular Series
Donald O'Connor (*Colgate Comedy Hour*) (NBC)

Best Female Star of Regular Series
Eve Arden (*Our Miss Brooks*) (CBS)

Best Series Supporting Actor
Art Carney (*Jackie Gleason Show*) (CBS)

Best Series Supporting Actress
Vivian Vance (*I Love Lucy*) (CBS)

Best Mystery, Action, or Adventure Program
Dragnet (NBC)

Best Audience Participation, Quiz, or Panel Program (Tie)
This Is Your Life (NBC)
What's My Line? (CBS)

Most Outstanding Personality
Edward R. Murrow (CBS)

1954
Presented March 7, 1955

Most Outstanding New Personality
George Gobel (NBC)

Best Cultural, Religious, or Educational Program
Omnibus (CBS)

Best Sports Program
Gillette Cavalcade of Sports (NBC)

Best Children's Program
Lassie (CBS)

Best Daytime Program
Art Linkletter's House Party (CBS)

Best Western or Adventure Series
Stories of the Century (Syndicated)

Best News Reporter or Commentator
John Daly (ABC)

Best Audience, Guest Participation, or Panel Program
This Is Your Life (NBC)

Best Actor in a Single Performance
Robert Cummings, "Twelve Angry Men" (*Studio One*) (CBS)

Best Actress in a Single Performance
Judith Anderson, "Macbeth" (*Hallmark Hall of Fame*) (NBC)

Best Male Singer
Perry Como (CBS)

Best Female Singer
Dinah Shore (NBC)

Best Supporting Actor in a Regular Series
Art Carney (*Jackie Gleason Show*) (CBS)

Best Supporting Actress in a Regular Series
Audrey Meadows (*Jackie Gleason Show*) (CBS)

Best Actor Starring in a Regular Series
Danny Thomas (*Make Room for Daddy*) (ABC)

Best Actress Starring in a Regular Series
Loretta Young (*Loretta Young Show*) (NBC)

Best Mystery or Intrigue Series
Dragnet (NBC)

Best Variety Series Including Musical Varieties
Disneyland (ABC)

Best Situation Comedy Series
Make Room for Daddy (ABC)

Best Dramatic Series
United States Steel Hour (ABC)

Best Individual Program of the Year
"Operation Undersea" (*Disneyland*) (ABC)

Best Art Direction of a Live Show
Bob Markell, "Mallory's Tragedy on Mt. Everest" (*You Are There*) (CBS)

Best Art Direction of a Filmed Show
Ralph Berger and Albert Pyke, "A Christmas Carol" (*Shower of Stars*) (CBS)

Best Direction of Photography
Lester Shorr, "I Climb the Stairs" (*Medic*) (NBC)

Best Written Dramatic Material
Reginald Rose, "Twelve Angry Men" (*Studio One*) (CBS)

Best Written Comedy Material
James Allardice, Jack Douglas, Hal Kanter, and Harry Winkler (*George Gobel Show*) (NBC)

Best Technical Achievement
NBC, color TV policy and Burbank color—John West

Best Engineering Effects
Four-quadrant screen—NBC—1954 national-election coverage—Robert Shelby

Best Television Sound Editing
George Nicholson (*Dragnet*) (NBC)

Best Television Film Editing
Grant Smith and Lynn Harrison, "Operation Undersea" (*Disneyland*) (ABC)

1955
Presented March 17, 1956

Best Children's Series
Lassie (CBS)

Best Contribution to Daytime Programming
Matinee Theatre (NBC)

Best Special Event or News Program
A-bomb coverage (CBS)

Best Documentary Program (religious, informational, educational, or interview)
Omnibus (CBS)

Best Audience Participation Series (quiz, panel, etc.)
$64,000 Question (CBS)

Best Action or Adventure Series
Disneyland ("Davy Crockett" series, etc.) (ABC)

Best Comedy Series
Phil Silvers Show: You'll Never Get Rich (CBS)

Best Variety Series
Ed Sullivan Show (CBS)

Best Music Series
Your Hit Parade (NBC)

Best Dramatic Series
Producers' Showcase (NBC)

Best Single Program of the Year
"Peter Pan" (*Producers' Showcase*) (NBC)

Best Actor—Single Performance
Lloyd Nolan, as Capt. Queeg, "Caine Mutiny Court Martial" (*Ford Star Jubilee*) (CBS)

Best Actress—Single Performance
Mary Martin, as Peter, "Peter Pan" (*Producers' Showcase*) (NBC)

Best Actor—Continuing Performance
Phil Silvers, as Sergeant Bilko (*Phil Silvers Show: You'll Never Get Rich*) (CBS)

Best Actress—Continuing Performance
Lucille Ball, as Lucy Ricardo (*I Love Lucy*) (CBS)

Best Actor in a Supporting Role
Art Carney, as Ed Norton (*Honeymooners*) (CBS)

Best Actress in a Supporting Role
Nanette Fabray (*Caesar's Hour*) (NBC)

Best Comedian
Phil Silvers (CBS)

Best Comedienne
Nanette Fabray (NBC)

Best Male Singer
Perry Como (NBC)

Best Female Singer
Dinah Shore (NBC)

Best M.C. or Program Host—Male or Female
Perry Como (NBC)

Best News Commentator or Reporter
Edward R. Murrow (CBS)

Best Specialty Act—Single or Group
Marcel Marceau (NBC)

Best Original Teleplay Writing
Rod Serling, "Patterns" (*Kraft TV Theatre*) (NBC)

Best Comedy Writing
Nat Hiken, Barry Blitser, Arnold Auerbach, Harvey Orkin, Vincent Bogert, Arnold Rosen, Coleman Jacoby, Tony Webster, and Terry Ryan (*Phil Silvers Show: You'll Never Get Rich*) (CBS)

Best Television Adaptation
Paul Gregory and Franklin Schaffner, "Caine Mutiny Court Martial," by Herman Wouk (*Ford Star Jubilee*) (CBS)

Best Musical Contribution
"Love and Marriage" by Sammy Cahn and James Van Heusen, from "Our Town" (*Producers' Showcase*) (NBC)

Best Producer—Live Series
Fred Coe (*Producers' Showcase*) (NBC)

Best Producer—Film Series
Walt Disney (*Disneyland*) (ABC)

Best Director—Live Series
Franklin Schaffner, "Caine Mutiny Court Martial" (*Ford Star Jubilee*) (CBS)

Best Director—Film Series
Nat Hiken (*Phil Silvers Show: You'll Never Get Rich*) (CBS)

Best Art Direction—Live Series
Otis Riggs (*Playwrights '56* and *Producers' Showcase*) (NBC)

Best Art Direction—Film Series
William Ferrari (*You Are There*) (CBS)

Best Cinematography for Television
William Scikner, "Black Friday" (*Medic*) (NBC)

Best Camera Work—Live Show
T. Miller (*Studio One*) (CBS)

Best Editing of a Television Film
Edward W. Williams, "Breakdown" (*Alfred Hitchcock Presents*) (CBS)

Best Choreographer
Tony Charmoli, "Show Biz" (*Your Hit Parade*) (NBC)

Best Engineering Technical Achievement
RCA tricolor picture tube, which made the commercial color receiver practicable

Best Commercial Campaign
Ford

Governor's Award (the first Presidential-sized Emmy to be awarded)
President Dwight D. Eisenhower, for his use and encouragement of television

1956
Presented March 16, 1957

Best Single Program of the Year
"Requiem for a Heavyweight" (*Playhouse 90*) (CBS)

Best New Program Series
Playhouse 90 (CBS)

Best Series—Half Hour or Less
Phil Silvers Show (CBS)

Best Series—One Hour or More
Caesar's Hour (NBC)

Best Public Service Series
See It Now (CBS)

Best Coverage of a Newsworthy Event
"Years of Crisis—Year-end Report," Edward R.
  Murrow and correspondents (CBS)

**Best Continuing Performance by an Actor in a
  Dramatic Series**
Robert Young (*Father Knows Best*) (NBC)

**Best Continuing Performance by an Actress in a
  Dramatic Series**
Loretta Young (*Loretta Young Show*) (NBC)

**Best Continuing Performance by a Comedian in
  a Series**
Sid Caesar (*Caesar's Hour*) (NBC)

**Best Continuing Performance by a Comedienne
  in a Series**
Nanette Fabray (*Caesar's Hour*) (NBC)

Best Single Performance by an Actor
Jack Palance, as a prizefighter, "Requiem for a
  Heavyweight" (*Playhouse 90*) (CBS)

Best Single Performance by an Actress
Claire Trevor, as Mrs. Dodsworth, "Dodsworth"
  (*Producers' Showcase*) (NBC)

Best Supporting Performance by an Actor
Carl Reiner (*Caesar's Hour*) (NBC)

Best Supporting Performance by an Actress
Pat Carroll (*Caesar's Hour*) (NBC)

**Best Male Personality—Continuing Perfor-
  mance**
Perry Como (NBC)

**Best Female Personality—Continuing Perfor-
  mance**
Dinah Shore (NBC)

Best News Commentator
Edward R. Murrow (CBS)

Best Teleplay Writing—Half-Hour or Less
James P. Cavanagh, "Fog Closing In" (*Alfred Hitchcock Presents*) (CBS)

Best Teleplay Writing—One Hour or More
Rod Serling, "Requiem for a Heavyweight"
  (*Playhouse 90*) (CBS)

**Best Comedy Writing—Variety or Situation
  Comedy**
Nat Hiken, Billy Friedberg, Tony Webster,
  Leonard Stern, Arnold Rosen, and Coleman
  Jacoby (*Phil Silvers Show*) (CBS)

Best Direction—Half Hour or Less
Sheldon Leonard, "Danny's Comeback" (*Danny
  Thomas Show*) (ABC)

Best Direction—One Hour or More
Ralph Nelson, "Requiem for a Heavyweight"
  (*Playhouse 90*) (CBS)

Best Art Direction—Half Hour or Less
Paul Barnes (*Your Hit Parade*) (NBC)

Best Art Direction—One Hour or More
Albert Heschong, "Requiem for a Heavyweight"
  (*Playhouse 90*) (CBS)

Best Cinematography for Television
Norbert Brodine, "The Pearl" (*Loretta Young Show*)
  (NBC)

Best Editing of a Film for Television
Frank Keller, "Our Mr. Sun" (*A. T. & T. Science
  Series*) (CBS)

Best Musical Contribution for Television
Leonard Bernstein, composing–conducting (*Omnibus*) (CBS)

Best Live Camera Work
"A Night to Remember" (*Kraft Television Theatre*)
  (NBC)

Best Engineering or Technical Achievement
Development of video tape by Ampex and further
  development and practical applications by
  CBS—dual entry

1957
Presented April 15, 1958

Best Single Program of the Year
"The Comedian" (*Playhouse 90*) (CBS)

Best New Program Series of the Year
Seven Lively Arts (CBS)

Best Dramatic Anthology Series
Playhouse 90 (CBS)

**Best Dramatic Series with Continuing Charac-
  ters**
Gunsmoke (CBS)

Best Comedy Series
Phil Silvers Show (CBS)

**Best Musical, Variety, Audience Participation,
  or Quiz Series**
Dinah Shore Chevy Show (NBC)

Best Public Service Program or Series
Omnibus (ABC, NBC)

Best Coverage of an Unscheduled Newsworthy Event
The coverage of the Rikers Island, New York, plane crash (*World News Roundup*) February 3, 1957 (CBS)

Best Continuing Performance by an Actor in a Leading Role in a Dramatic or Comedy Series
Robert Young, as Jim Anderson (*Father Knows Best*) (NBC)

Best Continuing Performance by an Actress in a Leading Role in a Dramatic or Comedy Series
Jane Wyatt, as Margaret Anderson (*Father Knows Best*) (NBC)

Best Continuing Performance (Male) in a Series by a Comedian, Singer, Host, Dancer, M.C., Announcer, Narrator, Panelist, or Any Person Who Essentially Plays Himself
Jack Benny (*Jack Benny Show*) (CBS)

Best Continuing Performance (Female) in a Series by a Comedienne, Singer, Hostess, Dancer, M.C., Announcer, Narrator, Panelist, or any Person Who Essentially Plays Herself
Dinah Shore (*Dinah Shore Chevy Show*) (NBC)

Actor—Best Single Performance, Lead or Support
Peter Ustinov, as Samuel Johnson, "The Life of Samuel Johnson" (*Omnibus*) (NBC)

Actress—Best Single Performance, Lead or Support
Polly Bergen, as Helen Morgan, "The Helen Morgan Story" (*Playhouse 90*) (CBS)

Best Continuing Supporting Performance by an Actor in a Dramatic or Comedy Series
Carl Reiner (*Caesar's Hour*) (NBC)

Best Continuing Supporting Performance by an Actress in a Dramatic or Comedy Series
Ann B. Davis, as Schultzy (*Bob Cummings Show*) (CBS, NBC)

Best News Commentary
Edward R. Murrow (*See It Now*) (CBS)

Best Teleplay Writing—Half Hour or Less
Paul Monash, "The Lonely Wizard" (*Schlitz Playhouse of Stars*) (CBS)

Best Teleplay Writing—One Hour or More
Rod Serling, "The Comedian" (*Playhouse 90*) (CBS)

Best Comedy Writing
Nat Hiken, Billy Friedberg, Phil Sharp, Terry Ryan, Coleman Jacoby, Arnold Rosen, Sidney Zelinka, A. J. Russell, and Tony Webster (*Phil Silvers Show*) (CBS)

Best Direction—Half Hour or Less
Robert Stevens, "The Glass Eye" (*Alfred Hitchcock Presents*) (CBS)

Best Direction—One Hour or More
Bob Banner, *Dinah Shore Chevy Show* (NBC)

Best Art Direction
Rouben Ter-Arutunian, "Twelfth Night" (*Hallmark Hall of Fame*) (NBC)

Best Cinematography for Television
Harold E. Wellman, "Hemo the Magnificent" (*Bell Telephone Science Series*) (CBS)

Best Live Camera Work
Playhouse 90 (CBS)

Best Editing of a Film for Television
Mike Pozen, "How to Kill a Woman" (*Gunsmoke*) (CBS)

Best Musical Contribution for Television
Leonard Bernstein, conducting and analyzing music by Johann Sebastian Bach (*Omnibus*) (ABC)

Best Engineering or Technical Achievement
Engineering and camera techniques on *Wide, Wide World* (NBC)

1958–1959
Presented May 6, 1959

Most Outstanding Single Program of the Year
"An Evening with Fred Astaire" (NBC)

Best Dramatic Series—One Hour or Longer
Playhouse 90 (CBS)

Best Dramatic Series—Less Than One Hour
Alcoa-Goodyear Theatre (NBC)

Best Comedy Series
Jack Benny Show (CBS)

Best Musical or Variety Series
Dinah Shore Chevy Show (NBC)

Best Western Series
Maverick (ABC)

Best Public Service Program or Series
Omnibus (NBC)

Best News Reporting Series
Huntley-Brinkley Report (NBC)

Best Panel, Quiz, or Audience Participation Series
What's My Line? (CBS)

Best Special Dramatic Program—One Hour or Longer
"Little Moon of Alban" (*Hallmark Hall of Fame*) (NBC)

Best Special Musical or Variety Program—One Hour or Longer
"An Evening with Fred Astaire" (NBC)

Best Special News Program
"Face of Red China," December 28, 1958 (CBS)

Best Actor in a Leading Role (Continuing Character) in a Dramatic Series
Raymond Burr, as Perry Mason (*Perry Mason*) (CBS)

Best Actress in a Leading Role (Continuing Character) in a Dramatic Series
Loretta Young (*Loretta Young Show*) (NBC)

Best Actor in a Leading Role (Continuing Character) in a Comedy Series
Jack Benny (*Jack Benny Show*) (CBS)

Best Actress in a Leading Role (Continuing Character) in a Comedy Series
Jane Wyatt, as Margaret Anderson (*Father Knows Best*) (CBS, NBC)

Best Supporting Actor (Continuing Character) in a Dramatic Series
Dennis Weaver, as Chester (*Gunsmoke*) (CBS)

Best Supporting Actress (Continuing Character) in a Dramatic Series
Barbara Hale, as Della Street (*Perry Mason*) (CBS)

Best Supporting Actor (Continuing Character) in a Comedy Series
Tom Poston, as the "Man on the Street" (*Steve Allen Show*) (NBC)

Best Supporting Actress (Continuing Character) in a Comedy Series
Ann B. Davis, as Schultzy (*Bob Cummings Show*) (NBC)

Best Performance by an Actor (Continuing Character) in a Musical or Variety Series
Perry Como (*Perry Como Show*) (NBC)

Best Performance by an Actress (Continuing Character) in a Musical or Variety Series
Dinah Shore (*Dinah Shore Chevy Show*) (NBC)

Best Single Performance by an Actor
Fred Astaire,"An Evening with Fred Astaire" (NBC)

Best Single Performance by an Actress
Julie Harris, as Brigid Mary, "Little Moon of Alban" (*Hallmark Hall of Fame*) (NBC)

Best News Commentator or Analyst
Edward R. Murrow (CBS)

Best Direction of a Single Program of a Dramatic Series—Less Than One Hour
Jack Smight, "Eddie" (*Alcoa-Goodyear Theatre*) (NBC)

Best Direction of a Single Dramatic Program—One Hour or Longer
George Schaefer, "Little Moon of Alban" (*Hallmark Hall of Fame*) (NBC)

Best Direction of a Single Program of a Comedy Series
Peter Tewksbury, "Medal for Margaret" (*Father Knows Best*) (CBS)

Best Direction of a Single Musical or Variety Program
Bud Yorkin,"An Evening with Fred Astaire" (NBC)

Best Writing of a Single Program of a Dramatic Series, Less Than One Hour
Alfred Brenner and Ken Hughes, "Eddie" (*Alcoa-Goodyear Theatre*) (NBC)

Best Writing of a Single Dramatic Program—One Hour or Longer
James Costigan, "Little Moon of Alban" (*Hallmark Hall of Fame*) (NBC)

Best Writing of a Single Program of a Comedy Series
Sam Perrin, George Balzer, Hal Goldman, and Al Gordon, "Jack Benny Show with Ernie Kovacs" (*Jack Benny Show*) (CBS)

Best Writing of a Single Musical or Variety Program
Bud Yorkin and Herbert Baker, "An Evening with Fred Astaire" (NBC)

Best Cinematography for Television
Ellis W. Carter, "Alphabet Conspiracy" (Bell Telephone special) (NBC)

Best Live Camera Work
"An Evening with Fred Astaire" (NBC)

Best Art Direction in a Television Film
Claudio Guzman, "Bernadette" (*Westinghouse Desilu Playhouse*) (CBS)

Best Art Direction in a Live Television Program
Edward Stephenson, "An Evening with Fred Astaire" (NBC)

Best Editing of a Film for Television
Silvio D'Alisera, "Meet Mr. Lincoln" (*Project 20*) (NBC)

Best Musical Contribution to a Television Program
David Rose, musical direction, "An Evening with Fred Astaire" (NBC)

Best Choreography for Television
Hermes Pan, "An Evening with Fred Astaire" (NBC)

Best Engineering or Technical Achievement
Industry-wide improvement of editing of video tape as exemplified by ABC, CBS, and NBC

1959–1960
Presented June 20, 1960

Outstanding Program Achievement in the Field of Humor
"Art Carney Special," December 4, 1959 (NBC)

Outstanding Program Achievement in the Field of Drama
Playhouse 90 (CBS)

Outstanding Program Achievement in the Field of Variety
"Fabulous Fifties," January 31, 1960 (CBS)

Outstanding Program Achievement in the Field of News
Huntley-Brinkley Report (NBC)

Outstanding Program Achievement in the Field of Public Affairs and Education
Twentieth Century (CBS)

Outstanding Achievement in the Field of Children's Programming
Huckleberry Hound (Syndicated)

Outstanding Achievement in the Field of Music
"Leonard Bernstein and the New York Philharmonic" (CBS)

Outstanding Single Performance by an Actor, Lead or Support
Laurence Olivier, "The Moon and Sixpence," October 30, 1959 (NBC)

Outstanding Single Performance by an Actress, Lead or Support
Ingrid Bergman, "The Turn of the Screw" (*Ford Startime*) October 20, 1959 (NBC)

Outstanding Performance by an Actor in a Series, Lead or Support
Robert Stack (*The Untouchables*) (ABC)

Outstanding Performance by an Actress in a Series, Lead or Support
Jane Wyatt (*Father Knows Best*) (CBS)

Outstanding Performance in a Variety or Musical Program or Series
Harry Belafonte, "Tonight with Belafonte" (*The Revlon Revue*) December 10, 1959 (CBS)

Outstanding Writing Achievement in Drama
Rod Serling (*Twilight Zone*) (CBS)

Outstanding Writing Achievement in Comedy
Sam Perrin, George Balzer, Al Gordon, and Hal Goldman (*Jack Benny Show*) (CBS)

Outstanding Writing Achievement in the Documentary Field
Howard K. Smith and Av Westin, "The Population Explosion," November 11, 1959 (CBS)

Outstanding Directorial Achievement in Drama
Robert Mulligan, "The Moon and Sixpence," October 30, 1959 (NBC)

Outstanding Directorial Achievement in Comedy
Ralph Levy and Bud Yorkin (*Jack Benny Hour* specials) (CBS)

Outstanding Achievement in Art Direction and Scenic Design
Ralph Berger and Frank Smith, "The Untouchables," April 20 and 27, 1959 (*Westinghouse-Desilu Playhouse*) (CBS)

Outstanding Achievement in Cinematography for Television
Charles Straumer, "The Untouchables," April 20 and 27, 1959 (*Westinghouse-Desilu Playhouse*) (CBS)

Outstanding Achievement in Electronic Camera Work
Winter Olympics (CBS)

Best Engineering or Technical Achievement
A new General Electric supersensitive camera tube, permitting colorcasting in no more light than is needed for black and white.

Outstanding Achievement in Film Editing for Television
Ben H. Ray and Robert L. Swanson (*The Untouchables*) (ABC)

1960–1961
Presented May 16, 1961

Outstanding Program Achievement in the Field of Humor
Jack Benny Show (CBS)

Outstanding Program Achievement in the Field of Drama
"Macbeth" (*Hallmark Hall of Fame*) November 20, 1960 (NBC)

Outstanding Program Achievement in the Field of Variety
"Astaire Time," September 28, 1960 (NBC)

Outstanding Program Achievement in the Field of News
Huntley-Brinkley Report (NBC)

Outstanding Program Achievement in the Field of Public Affairs and Education
The Twentieth Century (CBS)

Outstanding Achievement in the Field of Children's Programming
"Young People's Concert—Aaron Copland's Birthday Party," February 12, 1961 (CBS)

Outstanding Single Performance by an Actor in a Leading Role
Maurice Evans, "Macbeth" (*Hallmark Hall of Fame*) November 20, 1960 (NBC)

Outstanding Single Performance by an Actress in a Leading Role
Judith Anderson, "Macbeth" (*Hallmark Hall of Fame*) November 20, 1960 (NBC)

Outstanding Performance by an Actor in a Series, Lead
Raymond Burr (*Perry Mason*) (CBS)

Outstanding Performance by an Actress in a Series, Lead
Barbara Stanwyck (*Barbara Stanwyck Show*) (NBC)

Outstanding Performance in a Supporting Role by an Actor or Actress in a Single Program
Roddy McDowall, "Not Without Honor" (*Equitable's American Heritage*) October 21, 1960 (NBC)

Outstanding Performance in a Supporting Role by an Actor or Actress in a Series
Don Knotts, as deputy sheriff (*Andy Griffith Show*) (CBS)

Outstanding Performance in a Variety or Musical Program or Series
Fred Astaire, "Astaire Time," September 28, 1960 (NBC)

The Program of the Year
"Macbeth" (*Hallmark Hall of Fame*) November 20, 1960 (NBC)

Outstanding Achievement in the Field of Music for Television
Leonard Bernstein, "Leonard Bernstein and the New York Philharmonic" (CBS)

Outstanding Writing Achievement in Drama
Rod Serling (*The Twilight Zone*) (CBS)

Outstanding Writing Achievement in Comedy
Sherwood Schwartz, Dave O'Brien, Al Schwartz, Martin Ragaway, and Red Skelton (*Red Skelton Show*) (CBS)

Outstanding Writing Achievement in the Documentary Field
Victor Wolfson (*Winston Churchill: The Valiant Years*) (ABC)

Outstanding Directorial Achievement in Drama
George Schaefer, "Macbeth" (*Hallmark Hall of Fame*) November 20, 1960 (NBC)

Outstanding Directorial Achievement in Comedy
Sheldon Leonard (*The Danny Thomas Show*) (CBS)

Outstanding Achievement in Art Direction and Scenic Design
John J. Lloyd (*Checkmate*) (CBS)

Outstanding Achievement in Cinematography for Television
George Clemens (*Twilight Zone*) (CBS)

Outstanding Achievement in Electronic Camera Work
"Sounds of America" (*Bell Telephone Hour*) February 17, 1961 (red-eo-tape mobile unit for NBC)

Outstanding Achievement in Film Editing for Television
Harry Coswick, Aaron Nibley, and Milton Shifman (*Naked City*) (ABC)

Outstanding Engineering or Technical Achievement
Radio Corporation of America and Marconi's Wireless Telegraph Company, Ltd.—English Electric Valve Company, Ltd., for the independent development of the 4½-inch image orthicon tube and cameras.

1961–1962
Presented May 22, 1962

Outstanding Program Achievement in the Field of Humor
Bob Newhart Show (NBC)

Outstanding Program Achievement in the Field of Drama
The Defenders (CBS)

Outstanding Program Achievement in the Field of Variety
Garry Moore Show (CBS)

Outstanding Program Achievement in the Field of Music
"Leonard Bernstein and the New York Philharmonic in Japan," February 6, 1962 (CBS)

Outstanding Program Achievement in the Field of News
Huntley-Brinkley Report (NBC)

Outstanding Program Achievement in the Field of Educational and Public Affairs Programming
David Brinkley's Journal (NBC)

Outstanding Program Achievement in the Field of Children's Programming
New York Philharmonic Young People's Concerts with Leonard Bernstein (CBS)

Outstanding Single Performance by an Actor in a Leading Role
Peter Falk, as a truck driver, "The Price of Tomatoes" (*Dick Powell Show*) January 16, 1962 (NBC)

Outstanding Single Performance by an Actress in a Leading Role
Julie Harris, as Victoria, "Victoria Regina" (*Hallmark Hall of Fame*) November 30, 1961 (NBC)

Outstanding Continued Performance by an Actor in a Series, Lead
E. G. Marshall, as Lawrence Preston (*The Defenders*) (CBS)

Outstanding Continued Performance by an Actress in a Series, Lead
Shirley Booth, as Hazel (*Hazel*) (NBC)

Outstanding Performance in a Supporting Role by an Actor
Don Knotts, as Deputy Barney Fife (*Andy Griffith Show*) (CBS)

Outstanding Performance in a Supporting Role by an Actress
Pamela Brown, as Duchess of Kent, "Victoria Regina" (*Hallmark Hall of Fame*) November 30, 1961 (NBC)

Outstanding Performance in a Variety or Musical Program or Series
Carol Burnett (*Garry Moore Show*) (CBS)

Outstanding Daytime Program (Program Specifically Created for Daytime Television)
Purex Specials for Women (NBC)

The Program of the Year
"Victoria Regina" (*Hallmark Hall of Fame*) November 30, 1961 (NBC)

Outstanding Achievement in Original Music Composed for Television
Richard Rodgers (*Winston Churchill: The Valiant Years*) (ABC)

Outstanding Writing Achievement in Drama
Reginald Rose (*The Defenders*) (CBS)

Outstanding Writing Achievement in Comedy
Carl Reiner (*Dick Van Dyke Show*) (CBS)

Outstanding Writing Achievement in the Documentary Field
Lou Hazam, "Vincent Van Gogh: A Self Portrait," November 17, 1961 (NBC)

Outstanding Directorial Achievement in Drama
Franklin Schaffner (*The Defenders*) (CBS)

Outstanding Directorial Achievement in Comedy
Nat Hiken (*Car 54, Where Are You?*) (NBC)

Outstanding Achievement in Art Direction and Scenic Design
Gary Smith (*Perry Como's Kraft Music Hall*) (NBC)

Outstanding Achievement in Cinematography for Television
John S. Priestley (*Naked City*) (ABC)

Outstanding Achievement in Electronic Camera Work
Ernie Kovacs (*Ernie Kovacs Show*) (ABC)

Outstanding Achievement in Film Editing for Television
Hugh Chaloupka, Aaron Nibley, and Charles L. Freeman (*Naked City*) (ABC)

Outstanding Engineering or Technical Achievement
ABC video-tape expander, or VTX—slow motion tape developed by ABC—Mr. Albert Malang, chief engineer, video facilities, ABC

1962–1963
Presented May 26, 1963

The Program of the Year
"The Tunnel," December 10, 1962 (NBC)

Outstanding Program Achievement in the Field of Humor
The Dick Van Dyke Show (CBS)

Outstanding Program Achievement in the Field of Drama
The Defenders (CBS)

Outstanding Program Achievement in the Field of Music
"Julie and Carol at Carnegie Hall," June 11, 1962 (CBS)

Outstanding Program Achievement in the Field of Variety
The Andy Williams Show (NBC)

Outstanding Program Achievement in the Field of Panel, Quiz, or Audience Participation
G.E. College Bowl (CBS)

Outstanding Program Achievement in the Field of Children's Programming
Walt Disney's Wonderful World of Color (NBC)

Outstanding Achievement in the Field of Documentary Programs
"The Tunnel," Reuven Frank, producer, December 10, 1962 (NBC)

Outstanding Program Achievement in the Field of News
Huntley-Brinkley Report (NBC)

Outstanding Program Achievement in the Field of News Commentary or Public Affairs
David Brinkley's Journal (NBC)

Outstanding Achievement in International Reporting or Commentary
Piers Anderton, Berlin correspondent, NBC, "The Tunnel," December 10, 1962 (NBC)

Outstanding Single Performance by an Actor in a Leading Role
Trevor Howard, as Disraeli, "The Invincible Mr. Disraeli" (*Hallmark Hall of Fame*) April 4, 1963 (NBC)

Outstanding Single Performance by an Actress in a Leading Role
Kim Stanley, as Faith Parsons, "A Cardinal Act of Mercy" (*Ben Casey*) January 14 and 21, 1963 (ABC)

Outstanding Continued Performance by an Actor in a Series, Lead
E. G. Marshall, as Lawrence Preston (*The Defenders*) (CBS)

Outstanding Continued Performance by an Actress in a Series, Lead
Shirley Booth, as Hazel (*Hazel*) (NBC)

Outstanding Performance in a Supporting Role by an Actor
Don Knotts, as Deputy Barney Fife (*The Andy Griffith Show*) (CBS)

Outstanding Performance in a Supporting Role by an Actress
Glenda Farrell, as Martha Morrison, "A Cardinal Act of Mercy" (*Ben Casey*) January 14 and 21, 1963 (ABC)

Outstanding Performance in a Variety or Musical Program or Series
Carol Burnett, "Julie and Carol at Carnegie Hall," June 11, 1962 (CBS) and "Carol and Company," February 24, 1963 (CBS)

Outstanding Achievement in Composing Original Music for Television
Robert Russell Bennett, "He Is Risen" (*Project 20*) April 15, 1962 (NBC)

Outstanding Achievement in Art Direction and Scenic Design
Carroll Clark and Marvin Aubrey Davis (*Walt Disney's Wonderful World of Color*) (NBC)

Outstanding Writing Achievement in Drama
Robert Thom and Reginald Rose, "The Madman" (*The Defenders*) October 20 and 27, 1962 (CBS)

Outstanding Writing Achievement in Comedy
Carl Reiner (*The Dick Van Dyke Show*) (CBS)

Outstanding Directorial Achievement in Drama
Stuart Rosenberg, "The Madman" (*The Defenders*) October 20 and 27, 1962 (CBS)

Outstanding Directorial Achievement in Comedy
John Rich (*The Dick Van Dyke Show*) (CBS)

Outstanding Achievement in Cinematography for Television
John S. Priestley (*Naked City*) (ABC)

Outstanding Achievement in Electronic Camera Work
"The Invincible Mr. Disraeli" (*Hallmark Hall of Fame*) April 4, 1963 (NBC)

Outstanding Achievement in Film Editing for Television
Sid Katz (*The Defenders*) (CBS)

Outstanding Electronic Engineering Achievement
No nominations

The International Award
"War and Peace" (Granada TV Network, Ltd., of England)

The Station Award
"Superfluous People" (WCBS-TV, New York)

1963–1964
Presented May 25, 1964

The Program of the Year
"The Making of the President 1960," December 29, 1963 (ABC)

Outstanding Program Achievement in the Field of Comedy
The Dick Van Dyke Show (CBS)

Outstanding Program Achievement in the Field of Drama
The Defenders (CBS)

Outstanding Program Achievement in the Field of Music
Bell Telephone Hour (NBC)

Outstanding Program Achievement in the Field of Variety
The Danny Kaye Show (CBS)

Outstanding Program Achievement in the Field of Children's Programming
Discovery '63–'64 (ABC)

Outstanding Achievement in the Field of Documentary Programs
"The Making of the President 1960," David L. Wolper and Mel Stuart, producers; Theodore H. White, writer, December 29, 1963 (ABC)

Outstanding Program Achievement in the Field of News Reports
Huntley-Brinkley Report (NBC)

Outstanding Program Achievement in the Field of News Commentary or Public Affairs
"Cuba: Parts I and II—the Bay of Pigs and the Missile Crisis" (*NBC White Paper*) February 4 and 9, 1964 (NBC)

Outstanding Single Performance by an Actor in a Leading Role
Jack Klugman, as Joe Larch, "Blacklist" (*The Defenders*) January 18, 1964 (CBS)

Outstanding Single Performance by an Actress in a Leading Role
Shelley Winters, as Jenny Dworak, "Two Is the Number" (*Bob Hope Presents the Chrysler Theatre*) January 31, 1964 (NBC)

Outstanding Continued Performance by an Actor in a Series, Lead
Dick Van Dyke, as Rob Petrie (*The Dick Van Dyke Show*) (CBS)

Outstanding Continued Performance by an Actress in a Series, Lead
Mary Tyler Moore, as Laura Petrie (*The Dick Van Dyke Show*) (CBS)

Outstanding Performance in a Supporting Role by an Actor
Albert Paulsen, as Lieutenant Volkovoi, "One Day in the Life of Ivan Denisovich" (*Bob Hope Presents the Chrysler Theatre*) November 8, 1963 (NBC)

Outstanding Performance in a Supporting Role by an Actress
Ruth White, as Mrs. Mangan, "Little Moon of Alban" (*Hallmark Hall of Fame*) March 18, 1964 (NBC)

Outstanding Performance in a Variety or Musical Program or Series
Danny Kaye (*The Danny Kaye Show*) (CBS)

Outstanding Achievement in Composing Original Music for Television
Elmer Bernstein, "The Making of the President 1960," December 29, 1963 (ABC)

Outstanding Achievement in Art Direction and Scenic Design
Warren Clymer (*Hallmark Hall of Fame*) (NBC)

Outstanding Writing Achievement in Drama —Original
Ernest Kinoy, "Blacklist" (*The Defenders*) January 18, 1964 (CBS)

Outstanding Writing Achievement in Drama —Adaptation
Rod Serling, "It's Mental Work" (*Bob Hope Presents the Chrysler Theatre*) December 20, 1963, from a story by John O'Hara (NBC)

Outstanding Writing Achievement in Comedy or Variety
Carl Reiner, Sam Denoff, and Bill Persky (*The Dick Van Dyke Show*) (CBS)

Outstanding Directorial Achievement in Drama
Tom Gries, "Who Do You Kill?" (*East Side/West Side*) November 4, 1963 (CBS)

Outstanding Directorial Achievement in Comedy
Jerry Paris (*The Dick Van Dyke Show*) (CBS)

Outstanding Directorial Achievement in Variety or Music
Robert Scheerer (*The Danny Kaye Show*) (CBS)

Outstanding Achievement in Cinematography for Television
J. Baxter Peters, "The Kremlin," May 21, 1963 (NBC)

Outstanding Achievement in Electronic Photography
The Danny Kaye Show (CBS)

Outstanding Achievement in Film Editing for Television
William T. Cartwright, "The Making of the President 1960," December 29, 1963 (ABC)

The International Award
Les Raisins Verts (Radiodiffusion Television Francais)

The Station Award
"Operation Challenge—a Study in Hope" (KSD–TV, St. Louis)

1964–1965
Presented September 12, 1965

Outstanding Program Achievements in Entertainment
The Dick Van Dyke Show, Carl Reiner, producer (CBS)
"The Magnificent Yankee" (*Hallmark Hall of Fame*), January 28, 1965, George Schaefer, producer (NBC)
"My Name is Barbra," April 28, 1965, Richard Lewine, producer (CBS)
"What Is Sonata Form?" (*New York Philharmonic Young People's Concerts with Leonard Bernstein*) November 6, 1964, Roger Englander, producer (CBS)

Outstanding Individual Achievements in Entertainment

A. Actors and Performers

Leonard Bernstein (*New York Philharmonic Young People's Concerts with Leonard Bernstein*) (CBS)

Lynn Fontanne, as Fanny Dixwell Holmes, "The Magnificent Yankee" (*Hallmark Hall of Fame*) January 28, 1965 (NBC)

Alfred Lunt, as Oliver Wendell Holmes, "The Magnificent Yankee" (*Hallmark Hall of Fame*) January 28, 1965 (NBC)

Barbra Streisand, "My Name Is Barbra," April 28, 1965 (CBS)

Dick Van Dyke, as Rob Petrie (*The Dick Van Dyke Show*) (CBS)

B. Writers

David Karp, "The 700-year-old Gang" (*The Defenders*) September 24 and October 1, 1964 (CBS)

C. Directors

Paul Bogart, "The 700-year-old Gang" (*The Defenders*) September 24 and October 1, 1964 (CBS)

D. Conception, Choreography and Staging

Joe Layton, "My Name Is Barbra," April 28, 1965 (CBS)

E. Art Directors and Set Decorators

Warren Clymer, "The Holy Terror" (*Hallmark Hall of Fame*) April 7, 1965 (NBC)

Tom John, art director, "My Name Is Barbra," April 28, 1965 (CBS)

Bill Harp, set decorator, "My Name Is Barbra," April 28, 1965 (CBS)

F. Costume Designer

No winner

G. Makeup Artist

Robert O'Bradovich, "The Magnificent Yankee" (*Hallmark Hall of Fame*) January 28, 1965 (NBC)

H. Musicians

Peter Matz, music director, "My Name Is Barbra," April 28, 1965 (CBS)

I. Cinematographers

William Spencer (*Twelve O'Clock High*) (ABC)

J. Film Editors

No winner

K. Lighting Director

Phil Hymes, "The Magnificent Yankee" (*Hallmark Hall of Fame*) January 28, 1965 (NBC)

L. Special Photographic Effects

L. B. Abbott (*Voyage to the Bottom of the Sea*) (ABC)

M. Use of Special Effects

Production-team effort (*The Man from U.N.C.L.E.*) (NBC)

N. Color Consultant

Edward Ancona (*Bonanza*) (NBC)

O. Technical Director

Clair McCoy, "The Wonderful World of Burlesque," March 14, 1965 (NBC)

Outstanding Program Achievements in News, Documentaries, Information and Sports

"I, Leonardo Da Vinci" (*Saga of Western Man*), February 23, 1965, John H. Secondari and Helen Jean Rogers, producers (ABC)

"The Louvre," November 17, 1964, Lucy Jarvis, producer; John J. Sughrue, co-producer (NBC)

Outstanding Individual Achievements in News, Documentaries, Information and Sports

A. Narrators

No winner

B. Directors

John J. Sughrue, "The Louvre," November 17, 1964 (NBC)

C. Writers

Sidney Carroll, "The Louvre," November 17, 1964 (NBC)

D. Film Editors

Aram Boyajian, "The Louvre," November 17, 1964 (NBC)

E. Cinematographers

Tom Priestley, "The Louvre," November 17, 1964 (NBC)

F. Musicians

Norman dello Joio, composer–conductor, "The Louvre," November 17, 1964 (NBC)

The International Award

"Le Barbier de Seville" (Canadian Broadcasting Corporation, Canada)

The Station Award

"Ku Klux Klan" (WDSU-TV, New Orleans, LA)

1965–1966
Presented May 22, 1966

Outstanding Comedy Series

The Dick Van Dyke Show, Carl Reiner, producer (CBS)

Outstanding Variety Series

The Andy Williams Show, Bob Finkel, producer (NBC)

Outstanding Variety Special

"Chrysler Presents the Bob Hope Christmas Special," January 19, 1966, Bob Hope, executive producer (NBC)

Outstanding Dramatic Series
The Fugitive, Alan Armer, producer (ABC)

Outstanding Dramatic Program
"Ages of Man," January 23 and 30, 1966, David Susskind and Daniel Melnick, producers (CBS)

Outstanding Musical Program
"Frank Sinatra: A Man and His Music," November 24, 1965, Dwight Hemion, producer (NBC)

Outstanding Children's Program
"A Charlie Brown Christmas," December 9, 1965, Lee Mendelson and Bill Melendez, producers (CBS)

Outstanding Single Performance by an Actor in a Leading Role in a Drama
Cliff Robertson, as Quincey Parker, "The Game" (*Bob Hope Presents the Chrysler Theatre*) September 15, 1965 (NBC)

Outstanding Single Performance by an Actress in a Leading Role in a Drama
Simone Signoret, as Sara Lescaut, "A Small Rebellion" (*Bob Hope Presents the Chrysler Theatre*) February 9, 1966 (NBC)

Outstanding Continued Performance by an Actor in a Leading Role in a Dramatic Series
Bill Cosby, as Alexander Scott (*I Spy*) (NBC)

Outstanding Continued Performance by an Actress in a Leading Role in a Dramatic Series
Barbara Stanwyck, as Victoria Barkley (*The Big Valley*) (ABC)

Outstanding Continued Performance by an Actor in a Leading Role in a Comedy Series
Dick Van Dyke, as Rob Petrie (*The Dick Van Dyke Show*) (CBS)

Outstanding Continued Performance by an Actress in a Leading Role in a Comedy Series
Mary Tyler Moore, as Laura Petrie (*The Dick Van Dyke Show*) (CBS)

Outstanding Performance by an Actor in a Supporting Role in a Drama
James Daly, as Dr. O'Meara, "Eagle in a Cage" (*Hallmark Hall of Fame*) October 20, 1965 (NBC)

Outstanding Performance by an Actress in a Supporting Role in a Drama
Lee Grant, as Stella Chernak (*Peyton Place*) (ABC)

Outstanding Performance by an Actor in a Suppprting Role in a Comedy
Don Knotts, as Barney Fife, "The Return of Barney Fife" (*The Andy Griffith Show*) January 10, 1966 (CBS)

Outstanding Performance by an Actress in a Supporting Role in a Comedy
Alice Pearce, as Gladys Kravitz (*Bewitched*) (ABC)

Outstanding Writing Achievement in Drama
Millard Lampell, "Eagle in a Cage" (*Hallmark Hall of Fame*) October 20, 1965 (NBC)

Outstanding Writing Achievement in Comedy
Bill Persky and Sam Denoff, "Coast to Coast Big Mouth" (*The Dick Van Dyke Show*) September 15, 1965 (CBS)

Outstanding Writing Achievement in Variety
Al Gordon, Hal Goldman, and Sheldon Keller, "An Evening with Carol Channing," February 18, 1966 (CBS)

Outstanding Directorial Achievement in Drama
Sidney Pollack, "The Game" (*Bob Hope Presents the Chrysler Theatre*) September 15, 1965 (NBC)

Outstanding Directorial Achievement in Comedy
William Asher (*Bewitched*) (ABC)

Outstanding Directorial Achievement in Variety or Music
Alan Handley, "The Julie Andrews Show," November 28, 1965 (NBC)

Achievements in News and Documentaries
A. Programs
"American White Paper: United States Foreign Policy," September 7, 1965, Fred Freed, producer (NBC)
"KKK—the Invisible Empire" (*CBS Reports*), September 21, 1965, David Lowe, producer (CBS)
"Senate Hearings on Vietnam," February 1966, Chet Hagan, producer (NBC)

B. Individuals
No winner

Achievements in Daytime Programming
A. Programs
Camera Three, Dan Gallagher, producer (CBS)
Mutual of Omaha's Wild Kingdom, Don Meler, producer (NBC)

Achievements in Sports
A. Programs
ABC's Wide World of Sports, Roone Arledge, executive producer (ABC)
CBS Golf Classic, Frank Chirkinian, producer (CBS)
Shell's Wonderful World of Golf, Fred Raphael, producer (NBC)

B. Individual
No winner

Achievements in Educational Television
A. Programs
No winner

B. Individuals
Julia Child, *The French Chef* (NET)

Individual Achievements in Music
A. Composition
Laurence Rosenthal, "Michelangelo: The Last Giant," December 22, 1965, and February 23, 1966 (NBC)

B. Conducting
No winner

C. Arranging
No winner

D. Special
No winner

Individual Achievements in Art Direction and Allied Crafts
A. Art Direction
James Trittipo (*The Hollywood Palace*) (ABC)

B. Set Decoration
No winner

C. Costume Design
No winner

D. Wardrobe
No winner

E. Make-up
No winner

F. Special
No winner

Individual Achievements in Cinematography
A. Cinematography
Winton C. Hoch (*Voyage to the Bottom of the Sea*) (ABC)

B. Special
L. B. Abbott and Howard Lydecker, for photographic effects on *Voyage to the Bottom of the Sea* (ABC)

Individual Achievements in Film Editing
David Blewitt and William T. Cartwright, "The Making of the President 1964," October 19, 1965 (CBS)
Marvin Coil, Everett Douglas, and Ellsworth Hoagland (*Bonanza*) (NBC)

Individual Achievements in Sound Editing
No winner

Individual Achievements in Electronic Production
A. Audio Engineering
Laurence Schneider, "Seventh Annual Young Performers Program" (*New York Philharmonic Young People's Concerts with Leonard Bernstein*) February 22, 1966 (CBS)

B. Video Tape Editing
Craig Curtis and Art Schneider, "The Julie Andrews Show," November 28, 1965 (NBC)

C. Video Control
No winner

D. Lighting
Lon Stucky, "Frank Sinatra: A Man and His Music," November 24, 1965 (NBC)

E. Technical Directors
O. Tamburri, "Inherit the Wind" (*Hallmark Hall of Fame*) November 18, 1965 (NBC)

F. Electronic Cameramen
No winner

G. Special Electronic Effects
No winner

Individual Achievements in Engineering Development
Stop-action playback, MVR Corporation and CBS
Early Bird satellite, Hughes Aircraft Company and Communications Satellite Corporation

Special Classifications of Individual Achievements
Burr Tillstrom, for his "Berlin Wall" hand ballet on *That Was the Week That Was*, May 4, 1965 (NBC)

The International Award
A. Non-Fiction
Wyvern at War—No. 2: "Breakout" (Westward Television Limited, Plymouth, England)

B. Fiction
No winner

The Station Award
"I See Chicago" (WBBM-TV, Chicago, IL)

1966–1967
Presented June 4, 1967

Outstanding Comedy Series
The Monkees, Bert Schneider and Bob Rafelson, producers (NBC)

Outstanding Variety Series—awards to producer and star
The Andy Williams Show, Edward Stephenson and Bob Finkel, producers (NBC)

Outstanding Variety Special
"The Sid Caesar, Imogene Coca, Carl Reiner, Howard Morris Special," April 5, 1967, Jack Arnold, producer (CBS)

Outstanding Dramatic Series
Mission: Impossible, Joseph Gantman and Bruce Geller, producers (CBS)

Outstanding Dramatic Program
"Death of a Salesman," May 8, 1966, David Susskind and Daniel Melnick, producers (CBS)

Outstanding Musical Program
"Brigadoon," October 15, 1966, Fielder Cook, producer (ABC)

Outstanding Children's Program
"Jack and the Beanstalk," February 26, 1967, Gene Kelly, producer (NBC)

Outstanding Single Performance by an Actor in a Leading Role in a Drama
Peter Ustinov, as Socrates, "Barefoot in Athens" (*Hallmark Hall of Fame*) November 11, 1966 (NBC)

Outstanding Single Performance by an Actress in a Leading Role in a Drama
Geraldine Page, as Sookie, "A Christmas Memory" (*ABC Stage 67*) December 21, 1966 (ABC)

Outstanding Continued Performance by an Actor in a Leading Role in a Dramatic Series
Bill Cosby, as Alexander Scott (*I Spy*) (NBC)

Outstanding Continued Performance by an Actress in a Leading Role in a Dramatic Series
Barbara Bain, as Cinnamon Carter (*Mission: Impossible*) (CBS)

Outstanding Continued Performance by an Actor in a Leading Role in a Comedy Series
Don Adams, as Maxwell Smart (*Get Smart*) (NBC)

Outstanding Continued Performance by an Actress in a Leading Role in a Comedy Series
Lucille Ball, as Lucy Carmichael (*The Lucy Show*) (CBS)

Outstanding Performance by an Actor in a Supporting Role in a Drama
Eli Wallach, as Locarno, "The Poppy Is Also a Flower" (Xerox special) April 22, 1966 (ABC)

Outstanding Performance by an Actress in a Supporting Role in a Drama
Agnes Moorehead, as Emma Valentine, "Night of the Vicious Valentine" (*Wild, Wild West*) February 10, 1967 (CBS)

Outstanding Performance by an Actor in a Supporting Role in a Comedy
Don Knotts, as Barney Fife, "Barney Comes to Mayberry" (*The Andy Griffith Show*) January 23, 1967 (CBS)

Outstanding Performance by an Actress in a Supporting Role in a Comedy
Frances Bavier, as Aunt Bee (*The Andy Griffith Show*) (CBS)

Outstanding Writing Achievement in Drama
Bruce Geller (*Mission: Impossible*) September 17, 1966 (CBS)

Outstanding Writing Achievement in Comedy
Buck Henry and Leonard Stern, "Ship of Spies" (2 parts) (*Get Smart*) April 2-9, 1966 (NBC)

Outstanding Writing Achievement in Variety
Mel Brooks, Sam Denoff, Bill Persky, Carl Reiner, and Mel Tolkin, "The Sid Caesar, Imogene Coca, Carl Reiner, Howard Morris Special," April 5, 1967 (CBS)

Outstanding Directorial Achievement in Drama
Alex Segal, "Death of a Salesman," May 8, 1966 (CBS)

Outstanding Directorial Achievement in Comedy
James Frawley, "Royal Flush" (*The Monkees*) September 12, 1966 (NBC)

Outstanding Directorial Achievement in Variety or Music
Fielder Cook, "Brigadoon," October 15, 1966 (ABC)

Program and Individual Achievements in News and Documentaries
A. Programs
"China: The Roots of Madness," Mel Stuart, producer (Syndicated)
"Hall of Kings," February 14, 1967, Harry Raskey, producer (ABC)
"The Italians," January 17, 1967, Bernard Birnbaum, producer (CBS)

B. Individuals
Theodore H. White, writer, "China: The Roots of Madness" (Syndicated)

Individual Achievements in Art Direction and Allied Crafts
A. Art Direction
No winner

B. Costume Design
Ray Aghayan and Bob Mackie, "Alice Through the Looking Glass," November 6, 1966 (NBC)

C. Makeup
Dick Smith, "Mark Twain Tonight!" March 6, 1967 (CBS)

D. Mechanical Special Effects
No winner

Individual Achievements in Cinematography
A. Cinematography
No winner

B. Photographic Special Effects
L. B. Abbott (*The Time Tunnel*) (ABC)

Individual Achievements in Film and Sound Editing
Paul Krasny and Robert Watts, for film editing on *Mission: Impossible* (CBS)
Don Hall, Dick Legrand, Daniel Mandell, and John Mills, for sound editing on *Voyage to the Bottom of the Sea* (ABC)

Individual Achievements in Electronic Production
A. Technical Directors
A. J. Cunningham, "Brigadoon," October 15, 1966 (ABC)

B. Lighting Directors
Leard Davis, "Brigadoon," October 15, 1966 (ABC)

C. Video Tape Editing
No winner

D. Audio Engineering
Bill Cole, "Frank Sinatra: A Man and His Music, Part II," December 7, 1966 (CBS)

E. Sound Recording
No winner

F. Electronic Cameramen
Robert Dunn, Gorm Erickson, Ben Wolf, and Nick Demos, "Brigadoon," October 15, 1966 (ABC)

Individual Achievements in Engineering Development
Plumbicon Tube, N. V. Philips Gloeilampenfabrieken
High-band video tape recorder, Ampex Company

Special Classifications of Individual Achievements
Art Carney (*The Jackie Gleason Show*) (CBS)
Truman Capote and Eleanor Perry, for the adaptation of "A Christmas Memory" (*ABC Stage 67*) December 21, 1966 (ABC)
Arthur Miller, for the adaptation of "Death of a Salesman," May 8, 1966 (CBS)

Program and Individual Achievements in Daytime Programming
A. Programs
Mutual of Omaha's Wild Kingdom, Don Meier, producer (NBC)

B. Individuals
Mike Douglas, master of ceremonies, *The Mike Douglas Show* (Syndicated)

Program and Individual Achievements in Sports
A. Programs
ABC's Wide World of Sports, Roone Arledge, executive producer (ABC)

B. Individual
No winner

Individual Achievements in Music
A. Composition
No winner

B. Conductors
No winner

C. Arrangers
No winner

D. Musical Routines and Choral Direction
No winner

SPECIAL AWARDS

The International Award
A. Documentary
"Big Deal at Gothenburg" (Tyne Tees Television Limited, Newcastle-upon-Tyne, England)

B. Entertainment
"The Caretaker" (Rediffusion Television Limited, London, England)

The Station Award
"The Road to Nowhere" (KLZ-TV, Denver, CO)

1967–1968
Presented May 19, 1968

Outstanding Achievement Within Regularly Scheduled News Programs
A. Programs
"Crisis in the Cities" (*Public Broadcast Laboratory*) March 3, 1968, Av Westin, executive producer (NET)

B. Individuals
John Laurence and Keith Kay, CBS news correspondent and CBS news cameraman, "1st Cavalry" and "Con Thien" (*CBS Evening News with Walter Cronkite*) September 28 and October 26, 1967 (CBS)

Outstanding Achievement in Coverage of Special Events
A. Programs
No winner

B. Individuals
Frank McGee, for his commentary on satellite coverage of Adenauer's funeral, April 25, 1967 (NBC)

Outstanding Achievement in News Documentaries
A. Programs
"Africa," September 10, 1967, James Fleming, executive producer (ABC)
"Summer '67: What We Learned," September 15, 1967, Fred Freed, producer (NBC)

B. Individuals

Harry Reasoner, writer, "CBS Reports: What About Ronald Reagan?" December 12, 1967 (CBS)

Vo Huynh, cameraman, "Same Mud, Same Blood," December 1, 1967 (NBC)

Outstanding Achievement in Cultural Documentaries

A. Programs

CBS News Special, "Eric Hoffer: The Passionate State of Mind" (*CBS News Hour*) September 19, 1967, Harry Morgan, producer (CBS)

CBS News Special, "Gauguin in Tahiti: The Search for Paradise" (*CBS News Hour*) November 21, 1967, Martin Carr, producer (CBS)

"John Steinbeck's 'America and Americans,' " December 3, 1967, Lee Mendelson, producer (NBC)

"Dylan Thomas: The World I Breathe" (*NET Festival*) January 17, 1968, Perry Miller Adato, producer (NET)

B. Individuals

Nathaniel Dorsky, for his art photography for CBS News Special "Gauguin in Tahiti: the Search for Paradise" (*CBS News Hour*) November 21, 1967 (CBS)

Harry Morgan, writer, "The Wyeth Phenomenon," on *Who, What, When, Where, Why with Harry Reasoner* (*CBS News Hour*) October 3, 1967 (CBS)

Thomas A. Priestley and Robert Loweree, director of photography and film editor, "John Steinbeck's 'America and Americans,' " December 3, 1967 (NBC)

Other News and Documentary Achievements

A. Programs

The 21st Century, Isaac Kleinerman, producer (CBS)

"Science and Religion: Who Will Play God?" (*CBS News Special*) January 21, 1968, Ben Flynn, producer (CBS)

B. Individual

Georges Delerue, composer, "Our World" (*Global telecast*) June 25, 1967 (NET)

Outstanding Comedy Series

Get Smart, Burt Nodella, producer (NBC)

Outstanding Dramatic Series

Mission: Impossible, Joseph E. Gantman, producer (CBS)

Outstanding Dramatic Program

"Elizabeth the Queen" (*Hallmark Hall of Fame*) January 31, 1968, George Schaefer, producer (NBC)

Outstanding Musical or Variety Series

Rowan and Martin's Laugh-In, George Schlatter, producer (NBC)

Outstanding Musical or Variety Program

"Rowan and Martin's Laugh-In Special," September 9, 1967, George Schlatter, producer (NBC)

Outstanding Single Performance by an Actor in a Leading Role in a Drama

Melvyn Douglas, as Peter Schermann, "Do Not Go Gentle into That Good Night" (*CBS Playhouse*) October 17, 1967 (CBS)

Outstanding Single Performance by an Actress in a Leading Role in a Drama

Maureen Stapleton, as Mary O'Meaghan, "Among the Paths to Eden" (Xerox special) December 17, 1967 (ABC)

Outstanding Continued Performance by an Actor in a Leading Role in a Dramatic Series

Bill Cosby, as Alexander Scott (*I Spy*) (NBC)

Outstanding Continued Performance by an Actress in a Leading Role in a Dramatic Series

Barbara Bain, as Cinnamon Carter (*Mission: Impossible*) (CBS)

Outstanding Continued Performance by an Actor in a Leading Role in a Comedy Series

Don Adams, as Maxwell Smart (*Get Smart*) (NBC)

Outstanding Continued Performance by an Actress in a Leading Role in a Comedy Series

Lucille Ball, as Lucy (*The Lucy Show*) (CBS)

Outstanding Performance by an Actor in a Supporting Role in a Drama

Milburn Stone, as Doc (*Gunsmoke*) (CBS)

Outstanding Performance by an Actress in a Supporting Role in a Drama

Barbara Anderson, as Officer Eve Whitfield (*Ironside*) (NBC)

Outstanding Performance by an Actor in a Supporting Role in a Comedy

Werner Klemperer, as Col. Wilhelm Klink (*Hogan's Heroes*) (CBS)

Outstanding Performance by an Actress in a Supporting Role in a Comedy

Marion Lorne, as Aunt Clara (*Bewitched*) (ABC)

Outstanding Writing Achievement in Drama

Loring Mandel, "Do Not Go Gentle into That Good Night" (*CBS Playhouse*) October 17, 1967 (CBS)

Outstanding Writing Achievement in Comedy

Allan Burns and Chris Hayward, "The Coming Out Party" (*He and She*) November 15, 1967 (CBS)

Outstanding Writing Achievement in Music or Variety
Chris Beard, Phil Hahn, Jack Hanrahan, Coslough Johnson, Paul Keyes, Marc London, Allan Manings, David Panich, Hugh Wedlock, and Digby Wolfe, *Rowan and Martin's Laugh-In,* January 22, 1968 (NBC)

Outstanding Directorial Achievement in Drama
Paul Bogart, "Dear Friends" (*CBS Playhouse*) December 6, 1967 (CBS)

Outstanding Directorial Achievement in Comedy
Bruce Bilson, "Maxwell Smart, Private Eye" (*Get Smart*) October 21, 1967 (NBC)

Outstanding Directorial Achievement in Music or Variety
Jack Haley, Jr., "Movin' with Nancy," December 11, 1967 (NBC)

Outstanding Achievement in Musical Composition
Earle Hagen, "Laya" (*I Spy*) September 25, 1967 (NBC)

Outstanding Achievement in Art Direction and Scenic Design
James W. Trittipo, art director, "The Fred Astaire Show," February 7, 1968 (NBC)

Outstanding Achievement in Cinematography
Ralph Woolsey, "A Thief Is a Thief Is a Thief" (*It Takes a Thief*) January 9, 1968 (ABC)

Outstanding Achievement in Electronic Camerawork
A. J. Cunningham, technical director; Edward Chaney, Robert Fonorow, Harry Tatarian and Ben Wolfe, cameramen, "Do Not Go Gentle into That Good Night" (*CBS Playhouse*) October 17, 1967 (CBS)

Outstanding Achievement in Film Editing
Peter Johnson, "The Sounds and Sights of Chicago" (*Bell Telephone Hour*) February 16, 1968 (NBC)

Outstanding Achievement in Children's Programming
A. Programs
No winner

B. Individual
No winner

Outstanding Achievement in Daytime Programming
A. Programs
Today, Al Morgan, producer (NBC)

B. Individuals
No winner

Outstanding Achievement in Sports Programming
A. Programs
ABC's Wide World of Sports, Roone P. Arledge, executive producer (ABC)

B. Individuals
Jim McKay, sports commentator, *ABC's Wide World of Sports* (ABC)

Special Classification of Individual Achievements
Art Carney, *The Jackie Gleason Show* (CBS)
Pat Paulsen, *The Smothers Brothers Comedy Hour* (CBS)

Outstanding Individual Achievement in Music (Other than composer)
No winner

Outstanding Individual Achievement in the Visual Arts
No winner

Outstanding Individual Achievement in Electronic Production
Arthur Schneider, tape editor, "Rowan and Martin's Laugh-In Special," September 9, 1967 (NBC)

SPECIAL AWARDS

The Station Award
"Now Is the Time" (WCAU-TV, Philadelphia, PA)

Special Citation
"The Other Side of the Shadow" (WWL-TV, New Orleans, LA)
"The Other Washington" (WRC-TV, Washington, DC)

The International Award
A. Documentary
"La Section Anderson" (Office de Radiodiffusion Télévision Française, O.R.T.F., Paris, France)

B. Entertainment
"Call Me Daddy" (*Armchair Theatre*) (ABC Television, Limited, Middlesex, England)

1968 –1969
Presented June 8, 1969

Outstanding Achievement Within Regularly Scheduled News Programs
A. Programs
"Coverage of Hunger in the United States" (*The Huntley-Brinkley Report*) December 23, 1968; February 17, 18, 21; March 3, 10, 11, 1969, Wallace Westfeldt, executive producer (NBC)

B. Individuals

Charles Kuralt, James Wilson, and Robert Funk, correspondent, cameraman and soundman, respectively, for "On the Road" (*CBS Evening News with Walter Cronkite*) (CBS)

John Laurence, correspondent, "Police After Chicago" (*CBS Evening News with Walter Cronkite*) (CBS)

Outstanding Achievement in Coverage of Special Events
A. Programs

"Coverage of Martin Luther King Assassination and Aftermath" (*CBS News Special Reports*) April 4–9, 1968, Robert Wussler, Ernest Leiser, Burton Benjamin and Don Hewitt, executive producers (CBS)

B. Individuals
No winner

Outstanding News Documentary Program Achievement
A. Programs

"CBS Reports: Hunger in America" (*CBS News Hour*) May 21, 1968, Martin Carr, producer (CBS)

"Law and Order" (*Public Broadcast Laboratory*) March 2, 1969, Frederick Wiseman, producer (NET)

B. Individuals

Perry Wolff and Andy Rooney, writers, "Black History: Lost, Stolen, or Strayed—of Black America" (*CBS News Hour*) July 2, 1968 (CBS)

Outstanding Cultural Documentary and Magazine-Type Program or Series Achievement
A. Programs

"Don't Count the Candles" (*CBS News Hour*) March 26, 1968, William K. McClure, producer (CBS)

"Justice Black and the Bill of Rights" (*CBS News Hour*) December 3, 1968, Burton Benjamin, producer (CBS)

"Man Who Dances: Edward Villella" (*Bell Telephone Hour*) March 8, 1968 (Drew Associates, Inc.) Robert Drew and Mike Jackson, producers (NBC)

"The Great American Novel" (*CBS News Hour*) April 9, 1968, Arthur Barron, producer (CBS)

B. Individuals

Walter Dombrow and Jerry Sims, cinematographers, "The Great American Novel" (*CBS News Hour*) April 9, 1968 (CBS)

Tom Pettit, producer, "CBW: The Secrets of Secrecy" (*First Tuesday*) February 4, 1969 (NBC)

Lord Snowdon, cinematographer, "Don't Count the Candles" (*CBS News Hour*) March 26, 1968 (CBS)

Outstanding Comedy Series
Get Smart, Burt Nodella, producer (NBC)

Outstanding Dramatic Series
NET Playhouse, Curtis Davis, executive producer (NET)

Outstanding Dramatic Program
"Teacher, Teacher" (*Hallmark Hall of Fame*) February 5, 1969, George Lefferts, producer (NBC)

Outstanding Variety or Musical Series
Rowan and Martin's Laugh-In, Paul W. Keyes and Carolyn Raskin, producers; Dan Rowan and Dick Martin, stars (NBC)

Outstanding Variety or Musical Program
"The Bill Cosby Special," March 18, 1968, Roy Silver, executive producer; Bill Cosby, star (NBC)

Outstanding Single Performance by an Actor in a Leading Role
Paul Scofield, "Male of the Species" (*Prudential's On Stage*) January 3, 1969 (NBC)

Outstanding Single Performance by an Actress in a Leading Role
Geraldine Page, "The Thanksgiving Visitor," November 28, 1968 (ABC)

Outstanding Continued Performance by an Actor in a Leading Role in a Dramatic Series
Carl Betz (*Judd, for the Defense*) (ABC)

Outstanding Continued Performance by an Actress in a Leading Role in a Dramatic Series
Barbara Bain (*Mission: Impossible*) (CBS)

Outstanding Continued Performance by an Actor in a Leading Role in a Comedy Series
Don Adams (*Get Smart*) (NBC)

Outstanding Continued Performance by an Actress in a Leading Role in a Comedy Series
Hope Lange (*The Ghost and Mrs. Muir*) (NBC)

Outstanding Single Performance by an Actor in a Supporting Role
No winner

Outstanding Single Performance by an Actress in a Supporting Role
Anna Calder-Marshall, "Male of the Species" (*Prudential's On Stage*) January 3, 1969 (NBC)

Outstanding Continued Performance by an Actor in a Supporting Role in a Series
Werner Klemperer (*Hogan's Heroes*) (CBS)

Outstanding Continued Performance by an Actress in a Supporting Role in a Series
Susan Saint James (*The Name of the Game*) (NBC)

Outstanding Writing Achievement in Drama
J. P. Miller, "The People Next Door" (*CBS Playhouse*) October 15, 1968 (CBS)

Outstanding Writing Achievement in Comedy, Variety, or Music
Allan Blye, Bob Einstein, Murray Roman, Carl Gottlieb, Jerry Music, Steve Martin, Cecil Tuck, Paul Wayne, Cy Howard and Mason Williams (*The Smothers Brothers Comedy Hour*) February 16, 1969 (CBS)

Outstanding Directorial Achievement in Drama
David Green, "The People Next Door" (*CBS Playhouse*) October 15, 1968 (CBS)

Outstanding Directorial Achievement in Comedy, Variety, or Music
No winner

Outstanding Achievement in Musical Composition
John T. Williams, "Heidi," November 17, 1968 (NBC)

Outstanding Achievement in Art Direction and Scenic Design
William P. Ross and Lou Hafley, art director and set decorator, "The Bunker" (Parts I and II), (*Mission: Impossible*) March 2 and 9, 1969 (CBS)

Outstanding Achievement in Cinematography
George Folsey, "Here's Peggy Fleming," November 24, 1968 (NBC)

Outstanding Achievement in Electronic Camerawork
A. J. Cunningham, technical director; Nick DeMos, Bob Fonarow, Fred Gough, Jack Jennings, Dick Nelson, Rick Tanzi and Ben Wolf, cameramen, "The People Next Door" (*CBS Playhouse*) October 15, 1968 (CBS)

Outstanding Achievement in Film Editing
Bill Mosher, "An Elephant in a Cigar Box" (*Judd, for the Defense*) February 28, 1969 (ABC)

Outstanding Achievement in Children's Programming
A. Programs
No winner

B. Individuals
No winner

Outstanding Achievement in Daytime Programming
A. Programs
The Dick Cavett Show, Don Silverman, producer (ABC)

B. Individuals
No winner

Outstanding Achievement in Sports Programming
A. Programs
19th Summer Olympics Games, October 12–27, 1968, Roone P. Arledge, executive producer (ABC)

B. Individuals
Bill Bennington, Mike Freedman, Mac Memion, Robert Riger, Marv Schlenker, Andy Sidaris, Lou Volpicelli, and Doug Wilson, directors, *19th Summer Olympic Games,* October 12–27, 1968 (ABC)

Special Classification Achievements
A. Programs
Firing Line with William F. Buckley, Jr., Warren Steibel, producer (Syndicated)
Mutual of Omaha's Wild Kingdom Don Meier, producer (NBC)

B. Individuals—Variety Performances
Arte Johnson (*Rowan and Martin's Laugh-In*) (NBC)
Harvey Korman (*The Carol Burnett Show*) (CBS)

C. Individuals—Special Photographic Effects
No winner

Outstanding Individual Achievement in Music
Mort Lindsey, musical director, "Barbra Streisand: A Happening in Central Park," September 15, 1968 (CBS)

Outstanding Individual Achievement in the Visual Arts
No winner

Outstanding Individual Achievement in Electronic Production
No winner

SPECIAL AWARDS

The Station Award
"Pretty Soon Runs Out" (WHA-TV, Madison, WI)

Special Citation
"Assignment: The Young Greats" (WFIL-TV, Philadelphia, PA)

The International Award
A. Documentary
"The Last Campaign of Robert Kennedy" (Swiss Broadcasting and Television, Zurich, Switzerland)

B. Entertainment
"A Scent of Flowers" (Canadian Broadcasting Corporation, Ontario, Canada)

1969–1970
Presented June 7, 1970

Outstanding Achievement within Regularly Scheduled News Programs
A. Programs
"An Investigation of Teenage Drug Addiction—Odyssey House" (*The Huntley-Brinkley Report*) December 25 and 29, 1969, Wallace Westfeldt, executive producer; Les Crystal, producer (NBC)
"Can the World Be Saved?" (*CBS Evening News with Walter Cronkite*) Ronald Bonn, producer (CBS)

B. Individuals
No winner

Outstanding Achievement in Coverage of Special Events
A. Programs
"Apollo: A Journey to the Moon (Apollo X, XI, XII)" May 18–26, 1969; July 14–August 13, 1969; November 14–27, 1969, James W. Kitchell, executive producer (NBC)
"Solar Eclipse: A Darkness at Noon," March 7, 1970, Robert Northshield, executive producer; Walter Kravetz, producer (NBC)

B. Individuals
Walter Cronkite, reporter, "Man on the Moon: The Epic Journey of Apollo XI," July 14–August 17, 1969 (CBS)

Outstanding Achievement in News Documentary Programming
A. Programs
"Hospital" (*NET Journal*) February 2, 1970, Frederick Wiseman, producer (NET)
"The Making of the President, 1968," September 9, 1969 (Metromedia Producers Corporation) M. J. Rifkin, executive producer; Mel Stuart, producer (CBS)

A. Individuals
Frederick Wiseman, director, "Hospital" (*NET Journal*) February 2, 1970 (NET)

Outstanding Achievement in Magazine-Type Programming
A. Programs
Black Journal, William Greaves, executive producer (NET)

B. Individuals
Tom Pettit, reporter–writer, "Some Footnotes to 25 Nuclear Years" (*First Tuesday*) January 6, 1970 (NBC)

Outstanding Achievement in Cultural Documentary Programming
A. Programs
"Arthur Rubinstein," September 5, 1969, George A. Vicas, producer (NBC)
"Fathers and Sons" (*CBS News Hour*) August 12, 1969, Ernest Leiser, executive producer; Harry Morgan, producer (CBS)
"The Japanese" (*CBS News Hour*) April 23, 1969, Perry Wolff, executive producer; Igor Oganesoff, producer (CBS)

B. Individuals
Edwin O. Reischauer, commentator, "The Japanese" (*CBS News Hour*) April 23, 1969 (CBS)
Arthur Rubinstein, commentator, "Arthur Rubinstein," September 5, 1969 (NBC)

Outstanding Comedy Series
My World and Welcome to It, Sheldon Leonard, executive producer; Danny Arnold, producer (NBC)

Outstanding Dramatic Series
Marcus Welby, M.D., David Victor, executive producer; David J. O'Connell, producer (ABC)

Outstanding Dramatic Program
"A Storm in Summer" (*Hallmark Hall of Fame*) February 6, 1970, M. J. Rifkin, executive producer; Alan Landsburg, producer (NBC)

Outstanding Variety or Musical Series
The David Frost Show, Peter Baker, producer; David Frost, star (Syndicated)

Outstanding Variety or Musical Program
A. Variety and Popular Music
"Annie, the Women in the Life of a Man," February 18, 1970, Joseph Cates, executive producer; Martin Charnin, producer; Anne Bancroft, star (CBS)

B. Classical Music
"Cinderella" (National Ballet of Canada) (*NET Festival*) February 10, 1970, John Barnes and Curtis Davis, executive producers; Norman Campbell, producer (NET)

Outstanding News Series
Room 222, Gene Reynolds, producer (ABC)

Outstanding Single Performance by an Actor in a Leading Role
Peter Ustinov, "A Storm in Summer" (*Hallmark Hall of Fame*) February 6, 1970 (NBC)

Outstanding Single Performance by an Actress in a Leading Role
Patty Duke, "My Sweet Charlie" (*World Premiere*) January 20, 1970 (NBC)

Outstanding Continued Performance by an Actor in a Leading Role in a Dramatic Series
Robert Young (*Marcus Welby, M.D.*) (ABC)

Outstanding Continued Performance by an Actress in a Leading Role in a Dramatic Series
Susan Hampshire (*The Forsyte Saga*) (NET)

Outstanding Continued Performance by an Actor in a Leading Role in a Comedy Series
William Windom (*My World and Welcome to It*) (NBC)

Outstanding Continued Performance by an Actress in a Leading Role in a Comedy Series
Hope Lange (*The Ghost and Mrs. Muir*) (ABC)

Outstanding Performance by an Actor in a Supporting Role in Drama
James Brolin (*Marcus Welby, M.D.*) (ABC)

Outstanding Performance by an Actress in a Supporting Role in Drama
Gail Fisher (*Mannix*) (CBS)

Outstanding Performance by an Actor in a Supporting Role in Comedy
Michael Constantine (*Room 222*) (ABC)

Outstanding Performance by an Actress in a Supporting Role in Comedy
Karen Valentine (*Room 222*) (ABC)

Outstanding Writing Achievement in Drama
Richard Levinson and William Link, "My Sweet Charlie" (*World Premiere*) January 20, 1970 (NBC)

Outstanding Writing Achievement in Comedy, Variety, or Music
Gary Belkin, Peter Bellwood, Herb Sargent, Thomas Meehan and Judith Viorst, "Annie, the Women in the Life of a Man," February 18, 1970 (CBS)

Outstanding Directorial Achievement in Drama
Paul Bogart, "Shadow Game" (*CBS Playhouse*) May 7, 1969 (CBS)

Outstanding Directorial Achievement in Comedy, Variety or Music
Dwight A. Hemion, "The Sound of Burt Bacharach" (*Kraft Music Hall*) November 19, 1969 (NBC)

Outstanding Achievement in Choreography
Norman Maen, "This Is Tom Jones," October 23, 1969 (ABC)

Outstanding Achievement in Music Composition
A. For a series or a single program of a series (in its first year only, in the first year of original music's use only)
Morton Stevens, "A Thousand Pardons, You're Dead" (*Hawaii Five-O*) September 24, 1969 (CBS)

B. For a special program
Pete Rugolo, "The Challengers" (*CBS Friday Night Movie*) February 20, 1970 (CBS)

Outstanding Achievement in Music Direction of a Variety, Musical, or Dramatic Program
Peter Matz, "The Sound of Burt Bacharach" (*Kraft Music Hall*) November 19, 1969 (NBC)

Outstanding Achievement in Music, Lyrics, and Special Material
Arnold Margolin and Charles Fox (*Love, American Style*) (ABC)

Outstanding Achievement in Art Direction or Scenic Design
A. For a dramatic program or feature length film made for television; for a series, a single program of a series, or a special program
Jan Scott and Earl Carlson, art director and set decorator, "Shadow Game" (*CBS Playhouse*) May 7, 1969 (CBS)

B. For a Musical or Variety single program of a series or a special program
E. Jay Krause, art director, "Mitzi's 2nd Special," October 13, 1969 (NBC)

Outstanding Achievement in Lighting Direction
Leard Davis and Ed Hill (video: Richard Scovel and Clive Bassett) "Appalachian Autumn" (*CBS Playhouse*) October 7, 1969 (CBS)

Outstanding Achievement in Costume Design
Bob Mackie, "Diana Ross and The Supremes and The Temptations on Broadway," November 12, 1969 (NBC)

Outstanding Achievement in Makeup
Ray Sebastian and Louis A. Phillippi, "The Don Adams Special: Hooray for Hollywood," February 26, 1970 (CBS)

Outstanding Achievement in Cinematography for Entertainment Programming
A. For a series or a single program of a series
Walter Strenge, "Hello, Goodbye, Hello" (*Marcus Welby, M.D.*) September 23, 1969 (ABC)

B. For a special or feature length program made for television
Lionel Lindon, "Ritual of Evil" (*NBC Monday Night at the Movies*) February 23, 1970 (NBC)

Outstanding Achievement in Cinematography for News and Documentary Programming
A. Regularly scheduled News programs and coverage of Special Events
Edward Winkle "Model Hippie" (*The Huntley-Brinkley Report*) December 31, 1969 (NBC)

B. Documentary, Magazine-type or Mini-documentary programs
Thomas A. Priestly, "Sahara: La Caravane du Sel," December 19, 1969 (NBC)

Outstanding Achievement in Film Editing for Entertainment Programming
A. For a series or a single program of a series
Bill Mosher, "Sweet Smell of Failure" (*Bracken's World*) October 31, 1969 (NBC)

B. For a special or feature length program made for television
Edward M. Abroms, "My Sweet Charlie" (*World Premiere*) January 20, 1970 (NBC)

Outstanding Achievement in Film Editing for News and Documentary Programming
A. Regularly scheduled News programs and coverage of Special Events
Michael C. Shugrue, "The High School Profile" (*The Huntley-Brinkley Report*) March 13, 1970 (NBC)

B. Documentary, Magazine-type or Mini-documentary Programs
John Soh, "The Desert Whales" (*The Undersea World of Jacques Cousteau*) December 4, 1969 (ABC)

Outstanding Achievement in Film Sound Editing
Douglas H. Grindstaff, Alex Bamattre, Michael Colgan, Bill Lee, Joe Kavigan, and Josef E. Von Stroheim, "The Immortal" (*Movie of the Week*) September 30, 1969 (ABC)
Richard E. Raderman and Norman Karlin, "Charlie Noon" (*Gunsmoke*) November 3, 1969 (CBS)

Outstanding Achievement in Film Sound Mixing
Gordon L. Day and Dominick Gaffey, "The Submarine" (*Mission: Impossible*) November 16, 1969 (CBS)

Outstanding Achievement in Live or Tape Sound Mixing
Bill Cole and Dave Williams, "The Switched-on Symphony," March 14, 1970 (NBC)

Outstanding Achievement in Video Tape Editing
John Shultis, "The Sound of Burt Bacharach" ('Pas-de-deux' and 'Promises, Promises') (*Kraft Music Hall*) November 19, 1969 (NBC)

Outstanding Achievement in Technical Direction and Electronic Camerawork
Heino Ripp, technical director; Al Camoin, Gene Martin, Donald Mulvaney, and Cal Shadwell, cameramen, "The Sound of Burt Bacharach" (*Kraft Music Hall*) November 19, 1969 (NBC)

Outstanding Achievement in Children's Programming
A. Programs
Sesame Street, David D. Connell, executive producer; Sam Gibbon, Jon Stone, Lutrelle Horne, producers (NET)
The Wonderful World of Disney, Ron Miller, executive producer (NBC)

B. Individuals
Joe Raposo and Jeffrey Moss, music and lyrics for "This Way to Sesame Street," November 8, 1969 (NBC)
Jon Stone, Jeffrey Moss, Ray Sipherd, Jerry Juhl, Dan Wilcox, Dave Connell, Bruce Hart, Carole Hart and Virginia Schone, writers, "Sally Sees Sesame Street" (*Sesame Street*) November 10, 1969 (NET)

Outstanding Achievement in Daytime Programming
A. Programs
Today, Stuart Schulberg, producer (NBC)

B. Individuals
No winner

Outstanding Achievement in Sports Programming
A. Programs
The NFL games, September 20–December 21, 1969, William Fitts, executive producer (CBS)
ABC's Wide World of Sports, Roone Arledge, executive producer (ABC)

B. Individuals
Robert R. Forte, film editing for "Pre-Game Program" (Pro-Bowl game) January 18, 1970 (CBS)

Special Classification of Outstanding Program and Individual Achievement
A. Programs
Mutual of Omaha's Wild Kingdom, Don Meier, producer (NBC)

B. Individuals
Goldie Hawn (*Rowan and Martin's Laugh-In*) (NBC)

Outstanding Achievement in Any Area of Creative Technical Crafts
Jonnie Burke, special visual effects for "Time Bomb" (*Mission: Impossible*) December 14, 1969 (CBS)

SPECIAL AWARDS

Outstanding Achievement in Engineering Development

Apollo color television from space: for the conceptual aspects, an Emmy was presented to the Video Communications Division of NASA, and for development of the camera, an Emmy was presented to the Westinghouse Electric Corporation.

Citation

Ampex Corporation, for the development of the HS-200 color-television production system.

The Station Award

"The Slow Guillotine" (KNBC-TV, Los Angeles, CA)

Special Citation

"The Other Americans" (WJZ-TV, Baltimore, MD)

1970–1971
Presented May 9, 1971

Outstanding Achievement within Regularly Scheduled News Programs

A. Programs

Five-part investigation of welfare (*NBC Nightly News*) February 22–26, 1971, Wallace Westfeldt, executive producer; David Teitelbaum, producer (NBC)

B. Individuals

Bruce Morton, correspondent, "Reports from the Lt. Calley Trial" (*CBS Evening News with Walter Cronkite*) November 1970–March 1971 (CBS)

Outstanding Achievement in Coverage of Special Events

A. Programs

CBS News Space Coverage for 1970–71—"Aquarius on the Moon: The Flight of Apollo 13" and "Ten Years Later: The Flight of Apollo 14," April 11, 1970; January 31–February 9, 1971, Robert Wussler, executive producer; Joan Richman, producer (CBS)

B. Individuals

Walter Cronkite, correspondent, "CBS News Space Coverage for 1970–71—Aquarius on the Moon: The Flight of Apollo 13" and "Ten Years Later: The Flight of Apollo 14," April 11, 1970; January 31–February 9, 1971 (CBS)

Outstanding Achievement in News Documentary Programming

A. Programs

"The Selling of the Pentagon" (*CBS News*) February 23, 1971, Perry Wolff, executive producer; Peter Davis, producer (CBS)

"The World of Charlie Company" (*CBS News*) July 14, 1970, Ernest Leiser, executive producer; Russ Bensley, producer (CBS)

"NBC White Paper: Pollution is a Matter of Choice" (*NBC News*) April 7, 1970, Fred Freed, producer (NBC)

B. Individuals

John Laurence, correspondent, "The World of Charlie Company" (*CBS News*) July 14, 1970 (CBS)

Fred Freed, writer, "NBC White Paper: Pollution Is a Matter of Choice" (*NBC News*) April 7, 1970 (NBC)

Outstanding Achievement in Magazine-Type Programming

A. Programs

"Gulf of Tonkin" (*60 Minutes*) March 16, 1971, Joseph Wershba, producer (CBS)

The Great American Dream Machine, A. H. Perlmutter, Jack Willis, executive producers (PBS)

B. Individuals

Mike Wallace, correspondent, *60 Minutes* (CBS)

Outstanding Achievement in Cultural Documentary Programming

A. Programs

"The Everglades" (*NBC News*) February 16, 1971, Craig Fisher, producer (NBC)

"The Making of *Butch Cassidy and the Sundance Kid,*" November 29, 1970 (Penthouse Productions, Inc.) Ronald Preissman, producer (NBC)

"Arthur Penn, 1922– : Themes and Variants," May 26, 1970 (Robert Hughes Productions) Robert Hughes, producer (PBS)

B. Individuals

Nana Mahomo, narrator, "A Black View of South Africa" (*CBS News*) December 15, 1970 (CBS)

Robert Guenette and Theodore H. Strauss, writers, "They've Killed President Lincoln!", February 12, 1971 (Wolper Productions, Inc.) (NBC)

Robert Young, director, "The Eskimo: Fight for Life," March 24, 1970 (Education Development Center) (CBS)

Outstanding Series—Comedy

All in the Family, Norman Lear, producer (CBS)

Outstanding Series—Drama

The Bold Ones—The Senator, David Levinson, producer (NBC)

Outstanding Single Program—Drama or Comedy
"The Andersonville Trial" (*Hollywood Television Theatre*) May 17, 1970, Lewis Freedman, producer (PBS)

Outstanding Variety Series—Musical
The Flip Wilson Show, Monte Kay, executive producer; Bob Henry, producer; Flip Wilson, star (NBC)

Outstanding Variety Series—Talk
The David Frost Show, Peter Baker, producer; David Frost, star (Syndicated)

Outstanding Single Program—Variety or Musical
A. Variety and Popular Music
"Singer Presents Burt Bacharach," March 14, 1971, Gary Smith, Dwight Hemion, producers; Burt Bacharach, star (CBS)

B. Classical Music
"Leopold Stokowski" (*NET Festival*) April 28, 1970, Curtis W. Davis, executive producer; Thomas Slevin, producer; Leopold Stokowski, star (PBS)

Outstanding New Series
All in the Family, Norman Lear, producer (CBS)

Outstanding Single Performance by an Actor in a Leading Role
George C. Scott, "The Price" (*Hallmark Hall of Fame*) February 3, 1971 (NBC)

Outstanding Single Performance by an Actress in a Leading Role
Lee Grant, "The Neon Ceiling" (*World Premiere NBC Monday Night at the Movies*) February 8, 1971 (NBC)

Outstanding Continued Performance by an Actor in a Leading Role in a Dramatic Series
Hal Holbrook (*The Bold Ones—The Senator*) (NBC)

Outstanding Continued Performance by an Actress in a Leading Role in a Dramatic Series
Susan Hampshire (*Masterpiece Theatre—The First Churchills*) (PBS)

Outstanding Continued Performance by an Actor in a Leading Role in a Comedy Series
Jack Klugman (*The Odd Couple*) (ABC)

Outstanding Continued Performance by an Actress in a Leading Role in a Comedy Series
Jean Stapleton (*All in the Family*) (CBS)

Outstanding Performance by an Actor in a Supporting Role in Drama
David Burns, "The Price" (*Hallmark Hall of Fame*) February 3, 1971 (NBC)

Outstanding Performance by an Actress in a Supporting Role in Drama
Margaret Leighton, "Hamlet" (*Hallmark Hall of Fame*) November 17, 1970 (NBC)

Outstanding Performance by an Actor in a Supporting Role in Comedy
Edward Asner (*The Mary Tyler Moore Show*) (CBS)

Outstanding Performance by an Actress in a Supporting Role in Comedy
Valerie Harper (*The Mary Tyler Moore Show*) (CBS)

Outstanding Directorial Achievement in Drama
Daryl Duke, "The Day the Lion Died" (*The Bold Ones—The Senator*) October 4, 1970 (NBC)

Outstanding Directorial Achievement in Drama
Fielder Cook, "The Price" (*Hallmark Hall of Fame*) February 3, 1971 (NBC)

Outstanding Directorial Achievement in Comedy
Jay Sandrich, "Toulouse Lautrec Is One of My Favorite Artists" (*The Mary Tyler Moore Show*) October 31, 1970 (CBS)

Outstanding Directorial Achievement in Variety or Music
Mark Warren, *Rowan and Martin's Laugh-In,* October 26, 1970 (NBC)

Outstanding Directorial Achievement in Comedy, Variety or Music
Sterling Johnson, "Timex Presents Peggy Fleming at Sun Valley," January 24, 1971 (NBC)

Outstanding Achievement in Choreography
Ernest O. Flatt, *The Carol Burnett Show,* October 12, 1970 (CBS)

Outstanding Writing Achievement in Drama
Joel Oliansky, "To Taste of Death but Once" (*The Bold Ones—The Senator*) September 13, 1970 (NBC)

Outstanding Writing Achievement in Drama, Original Teleplay
Tracy Keenan Wynn and Marvin Schwartz, "Tribes" (*Movie of the Week on ABC*) November 10, 1970 (ABC)

Outstanding Writing Achievement in Drama, Adaptation
Saul Levitt, "The Andersonville Trial" (*Hollywood Television Theatre*) May 17, 1970 (PBS)

Outstanding Writing Achievement in Comedy
James L. Brooks and Allan Burns, "Support Your Local Mother" (*The Mary Tyler Moore Show*) October 24, 1970 (CBS)

Outstanding Writing Achievement in Variety or Music
Herbert Baker, Hal Goodman, Larry Klein, Bob Weiskopf, Bob Schiller, Norman Steinberg, and Flip Wilson, *The Flip Wilson Show,* December 10, 1970 (NBC)

Outstanding Writing Achievement in Comedy, Variety, or Music
Bob Ellison and Marty Farrell, "Singer Presents Burt Bacharach," March 14, 1971 (CBS)

Outstanding Achievement in Music Composition
A. For a series or a single program of a series (In the first year of music's use only)
David Rose, "The Love Child" (*Bonanza*) November 8, 1970 (NBC)

B. For a special program
Walter Scharf, "The Tragedy of the Red Salmon" (*The Undersea World of Jacques Cousteau*) November 24, 1970 (ABC)

Outstanding Achievement in Music Direction of a Variety, Musical, or Dramatic Program
Dominic Frontiere, "Swing Out, Sweet Land," November 29, 1970 (NBC)

Outstanding Achievement in Music, Lyrics, and Special Material
Ray Charles, "The First Nine Months Are the Hardest," February 24, 1971 (NBC)

Outstanding Achievement in Cinematography for Entertainment Programming
A. For a series or a single program of a series
Jack Marta, "Cynthia Is Alive and Living in Avalon" (*The Name of the Game*), October 2, 1970 (NBC)

B. For a special or feature length program made for television
Lionel Lindon, A.S.C. "Vanished," Parts I and II (*World Premiere NBC Monday* and *Tuesday Night at the Movies*) March 8 and 9, 1971 (NBC)
Bob Collins, "Timex Presents Peggy Fleming at Sun Valley" January 24, 1971 (NBC)

Outstanding Achievement in Cinematography for News and Documentary Programming
A. Regularly scheduled News programs and coverage of Special Events
Larry Travis, "Los Angeles—Earthquake" (*CBS Evening News with Walter Cronkite*) February 9, 1971 (CBS)

B. Documentary, Magazine-type or Mini-documentary programs
Jacques Renoir, "The Tragedy of the Red Salmon" (*The Undersea World of Jacques Cousteau*) November 24, 1970 (ABC)

Outstanding Achievement in Art Direction or Scenic Design
A. For a dramatic program or feature length film; a single program of a series or a special program
Peter Roden, "Hamlet" (*Hallmark Hall of Fame*) November 17, 1970 (NBC)

B. For a musical or variety single program of a series, or a special program
James W. Trittipo and George Gaines, art director and set decorator, "Robert Young and the Family," March 10, 1971 (CBS)

Outstanding Achievement in Costume Design
Martin Baugh and David Walker, "Hamlet" (*Hallmark Hall of Fame*) November 17, 1970 (NBC)

Outstanding Achievement in Makeup
Robert Dawn, "Catafalque" (*Mission: Impossible*) February 6, 1971 (CBS)

Outstanding Achievement in Film Editing for Entertainment Programming
A. For a series or a single program of a series
Michael Economou, "A Continual Roar of Musketry," Parts I and II (*The Bold Ones—The Senator*) November 22 and 29, 1970 (NBC)

B. For a special or feature length program made for television
George J. Nicholson, "Longstreet" (*Movie of the Week on ABC*) February 23, 1971 (ABC)

Outstanding Achievement in Film Editing for News and Documentary Programming
A. Regularly scheduled news programs and coverage of special events
George L. Johnson, "Prisons," Parts I–IV (*NBC Nightly News*) November 23–28, 1970 (NBC)

B. Documentary, Magazine-type or Mini-documentary programs
Robert B. Loweree and Henry J. Grennon, "Cry Help!: An NBC White Paper on Mentally Disturbed Youth," April 25, 1970 (NBC)

Outstanding Achievement in Film Sound Editing
Don Hall, Jr., Jack Jackson, Bob Weatherford, and Dick Jensen, "Tribes" (*Movie of the Week on ABC*) November 10, 1970 (ABC)

Outstanding Achievement in Film Sound Mixing
Theodore Soderberg, "Tribes" (*Movie of the Week on ABC*) November 10, 1970 (ABC)

Outstanding Achievement in Lighting Direction
John Rook, "Hamlet" (*Hallmark Hall of Fame*) November 17, 1970 (NBC)

Outstanding Achievement in Live or Tape Sound Mixing
Henry Bird, "Hamlet" (*Hallmark Hall of Fame*) November 17, 1970 (NBC)

Outstanding Achievement in Video Tape Editing
Marco Zappia, *Hee-Haw,* January 12, 1971 (CBS)

Outstanding Achievement in Technical Direction and Electronic Camerawork
Gordon Baird; Tom Ancell, Rick Bennewitz, Larry Bentley, and Jack Reader; technical director and cameramen, "The Andersonville Trial" (*Hollywood Television Theatre*) May 17, 1970 (PBS)

Outstanding Achievement in Children's Programming
A. Programs
Sesame Street, David D. Connell, executive producer; Jon Stone and Lutrelle Horne, producers (PBS)

B. Individuals
Burr Tillstrom, performer, *Kukla, Fran and Ollie* (PBS)

Outstanding Achievement in Daytime Programming
A. Programs
Today, Stuart Schulberg, producer (NBC)

B. Individuals
No winner

Outstanding Achievement in Sports Programming
A. Programs
ABC's Wide World of Sports, Roone Arledge, executive producer (ABC)

B. Individuals
Jim McKay, commentator, *ABC's Wide World of Sports* (ABC)
Don Meredith, commentator, *NFL Monday Night Football* (ABC)

Special Classification of Outstanding Program and Individual Achievement
A. Programs
No winner

B. Individuals
Harvey Korman, performer, *The Carol Burnett Show* (CBS)

Outstanding Achievement in any Area of Creative Technical Crafts
Lenwood B. Abbott and John C. Caldwell, special photographic effects for "City Beneath the Sea" (*World Premiere NBC Monday Night at the Movies*) January 25, 1971 (NBC)
Gene Widhoff, graphic-art: court room sketches of the Manson trial (*The Huntley-Brinkley Report—NBC Nightly News*) March, 1970–February, 1971 (NBC)

SPECIAL AWARDS

Outstanding Achievement in Engineering Development
The Columbia Broadcasting System, for the development of the Color Corrector, which can provide color unformity between television picture segments and scenes shot and recorded under different conditions at different times and locations.
The American Broadcasting Company, for the development of an "open-loop" synchronizing system, which enables the simultaneous synchronization of any number of color programs from remote locations.

Citations
General Electric, for the development of the portable Earth-station transmitter, which has provided the only means of getting color television pictures of Apollo splashdowns and recoveries via satellite to the mainland for worldwide distribution to the viewing public.

The Station Award
"If You Turn On" (KNXT, Los Angeles, CA)

1971–1972
Presented May 6, 1972

Outstanding Achievement Within Regularly Scheduled News Programs
A. Programs
"Defeat of Dacca" (*NBC Nightly News*) December 18, 1971, Wallace Westfeldt, executive producer; Robert Mulholland and David Teitelbaum, producers (NBC)

B. Individuals
Phil Brady, reporter, "Defeat of Dacca" (*NBC Nightly News*) December 18, 1971 (NBC)
Bob Schieffer, Phil Jones, Don Webster, and Bill Plante, correspondents, "The Air War" (*CBS Evening News with Walter Cronkite*) December 20–24, 1971 (CBS)

Outstanding Achievement for Regularly Scheduled Magazine-Type Programs
A. Programs
Chronolog, Eliot Frankel, executive producer (NBC)
The Great American Dream Machine, A. H. Perlmutter, executive producer (PBS)

B. Individuals
Mike Wallace, correspondent, *60 Minutes* (CBS)

Outstanding Achievement in Coverage of Special Events

A. Programs

"The China Trip," February 17–29, 1972, Av Westin and Wally Pfister, executive producers; Bill Lord, producer, (ABC)

"June 30, 1971, A Day for History: The Supreme Court and the Pentagon Papers," June 30, 1971, Lawrence E. Spivak, executive producer, (NBC)

"A Ride on the Moon: The Flight of Apollo 15," August 7, 1971, Robert Wussler, executive producer; Joan Richman, producer (CBS)

B. Individuals

No winner

Outstanding Documentary Program Achievement

A. Programs—Current Significance

"A Night in Jail, a Day in Court," (*CBS Reports*), January 27, 1972, Burton Benjamin, executive producer; John Sharnik, producer (CBS)

"This Child is Rated X: An NBC News White Paper on Juvenile Justice," May 2, 1971, Martin Carr, producer (NBC)

B. Programs—Cultural

"Hollywood: The Dream Factory" (*The Monday Night Special*) January 10, 1972, Nicolas Noxon, executive producer; Irwin Rosten and Bud Friedgen, producers (ABC)

"A Sound of Dolphins" (*The Undersea World of Jacques Cousteau*) February 25, 1972, Jacques Cousteau and Marshall Flaum, executive producers; Andy White, producer (ABC)

"The Unsinkable Sea Otter" (*The Undersea World of Jacques Cousteau*) September 26, 1971, Jacques Cousteau and Marshall Flaum, executive producers; Andy White, producer (ABC)

C. Individuals

Louis J. Hazam, writer, "Venice Be Damned!" May 21, 1971 (NBC)

Robert Northshield, writer, "Suffer the Little Children: An NBC News White Paper on Northern Ireland," January 11, 1972 (NBC)

Outstanding Series—Comedy

All in the Family, Norman Lear, producer (CBS)

Outstanding Series—Drama

Masterpiece Theatre—Elizabeth R, Christopher Sarson, executive producer; Roderick Graham, producer (PBS)

Outstanding Single Program—Drama or Comedy

"Brian's Song" (*Movie of the Week*) November 30, 1971, Paul Junger Witt, producer (ABC)

Outstanding Variety Series—Musical

The Carol Burnett Show, Joe Hamilton, executive producer; Arnie Rosen, producer; Carol Burnett, star (CBS)

Outstanding Variety Series—Talk

The Dick Cavett Show, John Gilroy, producer, Dick Cavett, star (ABC)

Outstanding Single Program—Variety or Musical

A. Variety and Popular Music

"Jack Lemmon in 'S Wonderful, 'S Marvelous, 'S Gershwin" (*Bell System Family Theatre*), January 17, 1972, Joseph Cates, executive producer; Martin Charnin, producer; Jack Lemmon, star (NBC)

B. Classical Music

"Beethoven's Birthday: A Celebration in Vienna with Leonard Bernstein," December 24, 1971, James Krayer, executive producer; Humphrey Burton, producer; Leonard Bernstein, star (CBS)

Outstanding New Series

Masterpiece Theatre—Elizabeth R, Christopher Sarson, executive producer; Roderick Graham, producer (PBS)

Outstanding Single Performance by an Actor in a Leading Role

Keith Michell, "Catherine Howard" (*The Six Wives of Henry VIII*) August 29, 1971 (CBS)

Outstanding Single Performance by an Actress in a Leading Role

Glenda Jackson, "Shadow in the Sun," (*Masterpiece Theatre—Elizabeth R*) February 27, 1972 (PBS)

Outstanding Continued Performance by an Actor in a Leading Role in a Dramatic Series

Peter Falk (*NBC Mystery Movie—Columbo*) (NBC)

Outstanding Continued Performance by an Actress in a Leading Role in a Dramatic Series

Glenda Jackson (*Masterpiece Theatre—Elizabeth R*) (PBS)

Outstanding Continued Performance by an Actor in a Leading Role in a Comedy Series

Carroll O'Connor (*All in the Family*) (CBS)

Outstanding Continued Performance by an Actress in a Leading Role in a Comedy Series

Jean Stapleton (*All in the Family*) (CBS)

Outstanding Performance by an Actor in a Supporting Role in Drama

Jack Warden, "Brian's Song" (*Movie of the Week*) November 30, 1971 (ABC)

Outstanding Performance by an Actress in a Supporting Role in Drama

Jenny Agutter, "The Snow Goose" (*Hallmark Hall of Fame*) November 15, 1971 (NBC)

Outstanding Performance by an Actor in a Supporting Role in Comedy

Edward Asner (*The Mary Tyler Moore Show*) (CBS)

Outstanding Performance by an Actress in a Supporting Role in Comedy (Tie)
Valerie Harper (*The Mary Tyler Moore Show*) (CBS)
Sally Struthers (*All in the Family*) (CBS)

Outstanding Achievement by a Performer in Music or Variety
Harvey Korman (*The Carol Burnett Show*) (CBS)

Outstanding Directorial Achievement in Drama
Alexander Singer, "The Invasion of Kevin Ireland" (*The Bold Ones—The Lawyers*) September 26, 1971 (NBC)

Outstanding Directorial Achievement in Drama
Tom Gries, "The Glass House" (*The New CBS Friday Night Movies*) February 4, 1972 (CBS)

Outstanding Directorial Achievement in Comedy
John Rich, "Sammy's Visit" (*All in the Family*) February 19, 1972 (CBS)

Outstanding Directorial Achievement in Variety or Music
Art Fisher, *The Sonny and Cher Comedy Hour,* January 31, 1972 (CBS)

Outstanding Directorial Achievement in Comedy, Variety, or Music
Walter C. Miller and Martin Charnin, "Jack Lemmon in 'S Wonderful, 'S Marvelous, 'S Gershwin" (*Bell System Family Theatre*) January 17, 1972 (NBC)

Outstanding Achievement in Choreography
Alan Johnson, "Jack Lemmon in 'S Wonderful, 'S Marvelous, 'S Gershwin" (*Bell System Family Theatre*) January 17, 1972 (NBC)

Outstanding Writing Achievement in Drama
Richard L. Levinson and William Link, "Death Lends a Hand" (*NBC Mystery Movie—Columbo*) October 6, 1971 (NBC)

Outstanding Writing Achievement in Drama—Original Teleplay
Allan Sloane, "To All My Friends on Shore," February 25, 1972 (CBS)

Outstanding Writing Achievement in Drama, Adaptation
William Blinn, "Brian's Song" (*Movie of the Week*) November 30, 1971 (ABC)

Outstanding Writing Achievement in Comedy
Burt Styler, "Edith's Problem" (*All in the Family*) January 8, 1972 (CBS)

Outstanding Writing Achievement in Variety or Music
Don Hinkley, Stan Hart, Larry Siegel, Woody Kling, Roger Beatty, Art Baer, Ben Joelson, Stan Burns, Mike Marmer, and Arnie Rosen (*The Carol Burnett Show*) January 26, 1972 (CBS)

Outstanding Writing Achievement in Comedy, Variety or Music
Anne Howard Bailey, "The Trial of Mary Lincoln" (*NET Opera Theatre*) February 14, 1972 (PBS)

Outstanding Achievement in Music Composition
A. For a series or a single program of a series
Pete Rugolo, "In Defense of Ellen McKay" (*The Bold Ones—The Lawyers*) November 14, 1971 (NBC)

B. For a special program
John T. Williams, "Jane Eyre" (*Bell System Family Theatre*) March 24, 1971 (NBC)

Outstanding Achievement in Music Direction of a Variety, Musical, or Dramatic Program
Elliot Lawrence, "Jack Lemmon in 'S Wonderful, 'S Marvelous, 'S Gershwin" (*Bell System Family Theatre*) January 17, 1972 (NBC)

Outstanding Achievement in Music, Lyrics, and Special Material
Ray Charles, "The Funny Side of Marriage" (*The Funny Side*) September 12, 1971 (NBC)

Outstanding Achievement in Art Direction or Scenic Design
A. For a dramatic program or feature length film made for television; a single program of a series or a special program
Jan Scott, "The Scarecrow" (*Hollywood Television Theatre*) January 10, 1972 (PBS)

B. For a Musical or Variety single program of a series or a special program
E. Jay Krause, "Diana!" April 18, 1971 (ABC)

Outstanding Achievement in Costume Design
Elizabeth Waller, "The Lion's Cub" (*Masterpiece Theatre—Elizabeth R*) February 13, 1972 (PBS)

Outstanding Achievement in Makeup
Frank Westmore, "Kung Fu" (*Movie of the Week*) February 22, 1972 (ABC)

Outstanding Achievement in Cinematography for Entertainment Programming
A. For a series or a single program of a series
Lloyd Ahern, A.S.C., "Blue Print for Murder" (*NBC Mystery Movie—Columbo*) February 9, 1972 (NBC)

B. For a special or feature length program made for television
Joseph Biroc, "Brian's Song" (*Movie of the Week*) November 30, 1971 (ABC)

Outstanding Achievement in Cinematography for News and Documentary Programming
A. **Regularly scheduled News programs and coverage of Special Events**
Peter McIntyre and Lim Youn Choul, "Dacca" (*NBC Nightly News*) December 18, 1971 (NBC)

B. **Documentary, Magazine-type or Mini-documentary programs**
Thomas Priestley, "Venice Be Damned!" May 21, 1971 (NBC)

Outstanding Achievement in Film Editing for Entertainment Programming
A. **For a series or a single program of a series**
Edward M. Abroms, "Death Lends a Hand," (*NBC Mystery Movie—Columbo*) October 6, 1971 (NBC)

B. **For a special or feature length program made for television**
Bud S. Isaacs, "Brian's Song" (*Movie of the Week*) November 30, 1971 (ABC)

Outstanding Achievement in Film Editing for News and Documentary Programming
A. **Regularly scheduled News programs and coverage of Special Events**
Darold Murray, "War Song" (*NBC Nightly News*) April 26, 1971 (NBC)

B. **Documentary, Magazine-type or Mini-documentary programs**
Spencer David Saxon, "Monkeys, Apes, and Man" (National Geographic Society Special) October 12, 1971 (CBS)

Outstanding Achievement in Film Sound Editing
Jerry Christian, James Troutman, Ronald LaVine, Sidney Lubow, Richard Raderman, Dale Johnston, Sam Caylor, John Stacy, and Jack Kirschner, "Duel" (*Movie of the Weekend*) November 13, 1971 (ABC)

Outstanding Achievement in Film Sound Mixing
Theodore Soderberg and Richrd Overton, "Fireball Forward" (*The ABC Sunday Night Movie*) March 5, 1972 (ABC)

Outstanding Achievement in Technical Direction and Electronic Camerawork
Heino Ripp, technical director; Albert Camoin, Frank Gaeta, Gene Martin and Donald Mulvaney, cameramen, "Jack Lemmon in 'S Wonderful, 'S Marvelous, 'S Gershwin" (*Bell System Family Theatre*) January 17, 1972 (NBC)

Outstanding Achievement in Lighting Direction
John Freschi, "Gideon" (*Hallmark Hall of Fame*) March 26, 1971 (NBC)

Outstanding Achievement in Video Tape Editing
Pat McKenna, "Hogans Goat" (*Special of the Week*) October 11, 1971 (PBS)

Outstanding Achievement in Live or Tape Sound Mixing
Norman H. Dewes, "The Elevator Story" (*All in the Family*) January 1, 1972 (CBS)

Special Classification of Outstanding Program and Individual Achievement
A. **General Programming**
"The Pentagon Papers," June 21, 1971, David Prowitt, executive producer; Martin Clancy, producer (PBS)

B. **Docu-Drama**
"The Search for the Nile"—Parts I–VI, January 25, February 1, 15, 22 and 29, 1972, Christopher Ralling, producer (NBC)

C. **Individuals**
Michael Hastings and Derek Marlow, writers, "The Search for the Nile"—Parts I–VI, January 25, February 1, 15, 22 and 29, 1972 (NBC)

Outstanding Achievement in Sports Programming
A. **Programs**
ABC's Wide World of Sports, Roone Arledge, executive producer (ABC)

B. **Individuals**
William P. Kelley, technical director; Jim Culley, Jack Bennett, Buddy Joseph, Mario Ciarlo, Frank Manfredi, Corey Leible, Gene Martin, Cal Shadwell, Billy Barnes, and Ron Charbonneau, cameramen, "AFC Championship Game," January 2, 1972 (NBC)

Outstanding Achievement in Children's Programming
A. **Programs**
Sesame Street, David D. Connell, executive producer; Jon Stone, producer (PBS)

B. **Individuals**
No winner

Outstanding Achievement in Daytime Drama
A. **Programs**
The Doctors, Allen Potter, producer (NBC)

B. **Individuals**
No winner

Outstanding Achievement in Daytime Programming
A. **Programs**
No winner

B. **Individuals**
No winner

Outstanding Achievement in Religious Programming
A. Programs
No winner

B. Individuals
Alfredo Antonini, music director, "And David Wept," April 11, 1971 (CBS)
Lon Stucky, lighting director, "A City of the King" (*Contact*) (Syndicated)

Outstanding Achievement in any Area of Creative Technical Crafts
Pierre Goupil, Michel Deloire, and Yves Omer, underwater cameraman, "Secrets of the Sunken Caves" (*The Undersea World of Jacques Cousteau*) March 19, 1971 (ABC)

SPECIAL AWARDS

Outstanding Achievement in Engineering Development
Lee Harrison, III, for the development of Scanimate, a unique electronic means of generating picture animation.

The Station Award
"Sickle Cell Disease: Paradox of Neglect" (WZZM-TV), Grand Rapids, MI)

1972–1973
Presented May 20, 1973

Outstanding Comedy Series
All in the Family, Norman Lear, executive producer; John Rich, producer (CBS)

Outstanding Drama Series—Continuing
The Waltons, Lee Rich, executive producer; Robert L. Jacks, producer (CBS)

Outstanding Drama/Comedy—Limited Episodes
Masterpiece Theatre—Tom Brown's Schooldays Parts I–V; John D. McRae, producer (PBS)

Outstanding Variety Musical Series
The Julie Andrews Hour, Nick Vanoff and William O. Harbach, producers; Julie Andrews, star (ABC)

Outstanding Single Program—Drama or Comedy
"A War of Children" (*The New CBS Tuesday Night Movies*) December 5, 1972, Roger Gimbel, executive producer; George Schaefer, producer (CBS)

Outstanding Single Program—Variety and Popular Music
"Singer Presents Liza with a 'Z'," September 10, 1972, Bob Fosse and Fred Ebb, producers; Liza Minnelli, star (NBC)

Outstanding Single Program—Classical Music
"The Sleeping Beauty," December 17, 1972, J. W. Barnes and Robert Kotlowitz, executive producers; Norman Campbell, producer (PBS)

Outstanding New Series
America, Michael Gill, producer (NBC)

Outstanding Program Achievement in Daytime Drama
The Edge of Night, Erwin Nicholson, producer (CBS)

Outstanding Program Achievement in Daytime
Dinah's Place, Henry Jaffe, executive producer; Fred Tatashore, producer; Dinah Shore, star (NBC)

Outstanding Single Performance by an Actor in a Leading Role
Laurence Olivier, "Long Day's Journey into Night," March 10, 1973 (ABC)

Outstanding Single Performance by an Actress in a Leading Role
Cloris Leachman, "A Brand New Life" (*Tuesday Movie Of The Week*) February 20, 1973 (ABC)

Outstanding Continued Performance by an Actor in a Leading Role
A. Drama Series—Continuing
Richard Thomas (*The Waltons*) (CBS)

B. Drama/Comedy—Limited Episodes
Anthony Murphy (*Masterpiece Theatre—Tom Brown's Schooldays*) Parts I–V (PBS)

Outstanding Continued Performance by an Actress in a Leading Role
A. Drama Series—Continuing
Michael Learned (*The Waltons*) (CBS)

B. Drama/Comedy—Limited Episodes
Susan Hampshire (*Masterpiece Theatre—Vanity Fair*) Parts I–V (PBS)

Outstanding Continued Performance by an Actor in a Leading Role in a Comedy Series
Jack Klugman (*The Odd Couple*) (ABC)

Outstanding Continued Performance by an Actress in a Leading Role in a Comedy Series
Mary Tyler Moore (*The Mary Tyler Moore Show*) (CBS)

Outstanding Performance by an Actor in a Supporting Role in Drama
Scott Jacoby, "That Certain Summer" (*Wednesday Movie of the Week*) November 1, 1972 (ABC)

Outstanding Performance by an Actress in a Supporting Role in Drama
Ellen Corby (*The Waltons*) (CBS)

Outstanding Performance by an Actor in a Supporting Role in Comedy
Ted Knight (*The Mary Tyler Moore Show*) (CBS)

Outstanding Performance by an Actress in a Supporting Role in Comedy
Valerie Harper (*The Mary Tyler Moore Show*) (CBS)

Outstanding Achievement by a Supporting Performer in Music or Variety
Tim Conway (*The Carol Burnett Show*) February 17, 1973 (CBS)

Outstanding Directorial Achievement in Drama
Jerry Thorpe, "An Eye for an Eye" (*Kung Fu*) January 25, 1973 (ABC)

Outstanding Directorial Achievement in Drama
Joseph Sargent, "The Marcus–Nelson Murders" (*The CBS Thursday Night Movies*) March 8, 1973 (CBS)

Outstanding Directorial Achievement in Comedy
Jay Sandrich, "It's Whether You Win or Lose" (*The Mary Tyler Moore Show*) October 14, 1972 (CBS)

Outstanding Directorial Achievement in Variety or Music
Bill Davis, *The Julie Andrews Hour,* September 13, 1972 (ABC)

Outstanding Directorial Achievement in Comedy, Variety, or Music
Bob Fosse, "Singer Presents Liza with a 'Z'," September 10, 1972 (NBC)

Outstanding Writing Achievement in Drama
John McGreevey, "The Scholar" (*The Waltons*) February 22, 1973 (CBS)

Outstanding Writing Achievement in Drama, Original Teleplay
Abby Mann, "The Marcus–Nelson Murders" (*The CBS Thursday Night Movies*) March 8, 1973 (CBS)

Outstanding Writing Achievement in Drama, Adaptation
Eleanor Perry, "The House Without a Christmas Tree," December 3, 1972 (CBS)

Outstanding Writing Achievement in Comedy
Michael Ross, Bernie West, and Lee Kalcheim, "The Bunkers and The Swingers" (*All in the Family*) October 28, 1972 (CBS)

Outstanding Writing Achievement in Variety or Music
Stan Hart, Larry Siegel, Gail Parent, Woody Kling, Roger Beatty, Tom Patchett, Jay Tarses, Robert Hilliard, Arnie Kogen, Bill Angelos, and Buz Kohan, *The Carol Burnett Show,* November 8, 1972 (CBS)

Outstanding Writing Achievement in Comedy, Variety or Music
Renée Taylor and Joseph Bologna, "Acts of Love—and Other Comedies," March 16, 1973 (ABC)

Outstanding Achievement in Choreography
Bob Fosse, "Singer Presents Liza with a 'Z'," September 10, 1972 (NBC)

Outstanding Achievement in Music Composition
A. For a series or a single program of a series (in the first year of music's use only)
Charles Fox, *Love, American Style* (ABC)

B. For a special program
Jerry Goldsmith, "The Red Pony" (*Bell System Family Theatre*) March 18, 1973 (NBC)

Outstanding Achievement in Music Direction of a Variety, Musical, or Dramatic Program
Peter Matz, *The Carol Burnett Show,* December 16, 1972 (CBS)

Outstanding Achievement in Music, Lyrics and Special Material
Fred Ebb and John Kander, "Singer Presents Liza with a 'Z'," September 10, 1972 (NBC)

Outstanding Achievement in Art Direction or Scenic Design
A. For a dramatic program or feature length film made for television; for a series, a single program of a series or a special program
Tom John, "Much Ado About Nothing," February 2, 1973 (CBS)

B. For a Musical or Variety single program of a series or a special program
Brian Bartholomew and Keaton S. Walker, *The Julie Andrews Hour,* September 13, 1972 (ABC)

Outstanding Achievement in Lighting Direction
John Freschi and John Casagrande, "44th Annual Oscar Awards," April 10, 1972 (NBC)
Truck Krone, "Christmas Show" (*The Julie Andrews Hour*) December 20, 1972 (ABC)

Outstanding Achievement in Costume Design
Jack Bear, *The Julie Andrews Hour,* September 27, 1972 (ABC)

Outstanding Achievement in Makeup
Del Armstrong, Ellis Burman, and Stan Winston, "Gargoyles" (*The New CBS Tuesday Night Movies*) November 21, 1972 (CBS)

Outstanding Achievement in Cinematography for Entertainment Programming
A. For a series or a single program of a series
Jack Woolf, "Eye for an Eye" (*Kung Fu*) January 25, 1973 (ABC)

B. For a special or feature length program made for television
Howard Schwartz, A.S.C., "Night of Terror" (*Tuesday Movie of the Week*) October 10, 1972 (ABC)

Outstanding Achievement in Film Editing for Entertainment Programming
A. For a series or a single program of a series
Gene Fowler, Jr., Marjorie Fowler, and Anthony Wollner, "The Literary Man" (*The Waltons*) November 30, 1972 (CBS)

B. For a special or feature length program made for television
Peter C. Johnson and Ed Spiegel, "Surrender at Appomattox—Appointment with Destiny," April 24, 1972 (CBS)

Outstanding Achievement in Film Sound Editing
Ross Taylor, Fred Brown, and David Marshall, "The Red Pony" (*Bell System Family Theatre*) March 18, 1973 (NBC)

Outstanding Achievement in Film Sound Mixing
Richard J. Wagner, George E. Porter, Eddie J. Nelson and Fred Leroy Granville, "Surrender at Appomattox—Appointment with Destiny," April 24, 1972 (CBS)

Outstanding Achievement in Live or Tape Sound Mixing
Al Gramaglia and Mahlon Fox, "Much Ado About Nothing," February 2, 1973 (CBS)

Outstanding Achievement in Video Tape Editing
Nick Giordano and Arthur Schneider, *The Julie Andrews Hour,* September 13, 1972 (ABC)

Outstanding Achievement in Technical Direction and Electronic Camerawork
Ernie Buttelman, technical director; Robert A. Kemp, James Angel, James Balden, and Dave Hilmer, cameramen, *The Julie Andrews Hour,* September 13, 1972 (ABC)

Outstanding Achievement by Individuals in Daytime Drama
Mary Fickett, performer (*All My Children*) (ABC)

Outstanding Achievement by Individuals in Daytime Programming
No winner

Outstanding Achievement in Children's Programming
A. Entertainment/Fictional
Sesame Street, Jon Stone, executive producer; Bob Cunniff, producer (PBS)
Zoom, Christopher Sarson, producer (PBS)
Tom Whedon, John Boni, Sara Compton, Tom Dunsmuir, Thad Mumford, Jeremy Stevens, and Jim Thurman, writers, *The Electric Company,* October 23, 1972 (PBS)

B. Informational/Factual
"Last of the Curlews" (*The ABC Afterschool Special*) William Hanna and Joseph Barbera, producers, October 4, 1972 (ABC)
Shari Lewis, performer, "A Picture of Us" (*NBC Children's Theatre*) March 17, 1973 (NBC)

Outstanding Achievement in Sports Programming
ABC's Wide World of Sports, Roone Arledge, executive producer (ABC)
1972 Summer Olympic Games, Roone Arledge, executive producer; August 25–September 11, 1972 (ABC)
John Croak, Charles Gardner, Jakob Hierl, Conrad Kraus, Edward McCarthy, Nick Mazur, Alex Moskovic, James Parker, Louis Rende, Ross Skipper, Robert Steinback, John DeLisa, George Boettcher, Merrit Roesser, Leo Scharf, Randy Cohen, Vito Gerardi, Harold Byers, Winfield Gross, Paul Scoskie, Peter Fritz, Leo Stephan, Gerber McBeath, Louis Torino, Michael Wenig, Tom Wight, and James Kelley, video-tape editors, *1972 Summer Olympic Games,* August 25–September 11, 1972 (ABC)

SPECIAL AWARDS

Outstanding Achievement in Engineering Development
Award to Sony for the development of the Trinitron, a picture tube providing good picture quality in color television receivers.
Award to CMX Systems, a CBS/Memorex company, for the development of a video-tape-editing system, utilizing a computer to aid the decision-making process, store the editing decisions, and implement them in the final assembly of takes.

The National Award for Community Service
"Take Des Moines . . . Please," KDIN-TV (educational station), Des Moines, IA

NEWS AND DOCUMENTARY PROGRAM AND INDIVIDUAL ACHIEVMENTS
Presented May 22, 1973

Outstanding Achievement within Regularly Scheduled News Programs
A. An Award for program segments, i.e. the presentation of individual stories (in single or multi-part) or elements within the program
"The U.S. Soviet Wheat Deal: Is There a Scandal?" (*CBS Evening News with Walter Cronkite*) September 27–October 6, 1972, Paul Greenberg and Russ Bensley, executive producers; Stanhope Gould and Linda Mason, producers (CBS)

B. **An Award for individuals contributing to the program segments**

Walter Cronkite, Dan Rather, Daniel Schorr, and Joel Blocker, correspondents, "The Watergate Affair" (*CBS Evening News with Walter Cronkite*) October 27 and 31, 1972 (CBS)

David Dick, Dan Rather, Roger Mudd, and Walter Cronkite, correspondents; "Coverage of the Shooting of Governor Wallace" (*CBS Evening News with Walter Cronkite*) May 15, 1972 (CBS)

Eric Sevareid, correspondent, "LBJ—the Man and the President," (*CBS Evening News with Walter Cronkite*) January 22, 1973 (CBS)

Outstanding Achievement for Regularly Scheduled Magazine-Type Programs

A. **An Award for programs, program segments, or series**

"The Poppy Fields of Turkey—the Heroin Labs of Marseilles—the N.Y. Connection" (*60 Minutes*) December 10, 1972, Don Hewitt, executive producer; William McClure, John Tiffin, Philip Scheffler, producers (CBS)

"The Selling of Colonel Herbert" (*60 Minutes*) February 4, 1973, Don Hewitt, executive producer; Barry Lando, producer (CBS)

60 Minutes, Don Hewitt, executive producer (CBS)

B. **An Award for individuals contributing to the program, program segments, or series achievements**

Mike Wallace, correspondent, "The Selling of Colonel Herbert" (*60 Minutes*) February 4, 1973 (CBS)

Mike Wallace, correspondent (*60 Minutes*) (CBS)

Outstanding Achievement in Coverage of Special Events

A. **An Award for program achievements**

"Coverage of the Munich Olympic Tragedy" (*ABC Special*) September 5, 1972, Roone Arledge, executive producer (ABC)

B. **An Award for individuals contributing to the program achievement**

Jim McKay, commentator, "Coverage of the Munich Olympic Tragedy" (*ABC Special*) September 5, 1972 (ABC)

Outstanding Documentary Program Achievement

A. **An Award for documentary programs dealing with events or matters of current significance**

"The Blue Collar Trap" (*NBC News White Paper*) June 27, 1972, Fred Freed, producer (NBC)

"The Mexican Connection" (*CBS Reports*) June 25, 1972, Burton Benjamin, executive producer; Jay McMullen, producer (CBS)

"One Billion Dollar Weapon: And Now the War Is Over—the American Military in the 70's" (*NBC Reports*) February 20, 1973, Fred Freed, executive producer; Craig Leake, producer (NBC)

B. **An Award for documentary programs dealing with artistic, historical, or cultural subjects**

America, Michael Gill, executive producer (NBC)

"Jane Goodall and the World of Animal Behavior: the Wild Dogs of Africa," January 22, 1973, Marshall Flaum, executive producer; Hugo Van Lawick, Bill Travers, and James Hill, producers (ABC)

C. **An Award for Individuals contributing to Documentary Programs**

Alistair Cooke, narrator, *America* (NBC)

Alistair Cooke, writer, "A Firebell in the Night" (*America*) January 23, 1973 (NBC)

Hugo Van Lawick, director, "Jane Goodall and the World of Animal Behavior: The Wild Dogs of Africa," January 22, 1973 (ABC)

Special Classification of Outstanding Program and Individual Achievement

The Advocates, Greg Harney, executive producer; Tom Burrows, Russ Morash and Peter McGhee, producers (PBS)

"VD Blues" (*Special of the Week*) October 9, 1972, Don Fouser, producer (PBS)

Outstanding Achievement in Religious Programming

"Duty Bound," March 11, 1973, Doris Ann, executive producer; Martin Hoade, producer (NBC)

Outstanding Achievement in any Area of Creative Technical Crafts

Donald Feldstein, Robert Fontana, and Joe Zuckerman, animation layout of Da Vinci's art, "Leonardo: To Know How to See," June 20, 1972 (NBC)

Outstanding Achievement in Cinematography for News and Documentary Programming

A. **Regularly scheduled News programs and coverage of Special Events**

Laurens Pierce, "Coverage of the shooting of Governor Wallace" (*CBS Evening News with Walter Cronkite*) May 15, 1972 (CBS)

B. **Documentary, Magazine-type, or Minidocumentary programs**

Des and Jen Bartlett, "The Incredible Flight of the Snow Geese," January 23, 1973 (NBC)

Outstanding Achievement in Film Editing for News and Documentary Programming

A. **Regularly scheduled News programs and coverage of Special Events**

Patrick Minerva, Martin Sheppard, George Johnson, William J. Freeda, Miguel E. Portillo, Albert J. Helias, Irwin Graf, Jean Venable, Rick Hessel, Loren Berry, Nick Wilkins, Gerry Breese, Michael Shugrue, K. Su, Edwin Einarsen, Thomas Dunphy, Russel Moore, and Robert Mole (*NBC Nightly News*) (NBC)

B. Documentary, Magazine-type or Mini-documentary programs
Les Parry, "The Incredible Flight of the Snow Geese," January 23, 1973 (NBC)

1973–1974
Presented May 28, 1974

Outstanding Comedy Series
M*A*S*H, Gene Reynolds and Larry Gelbart, producers (CBS)

Outstanding Drama Series
Masterpiece Theatre—Upstairs, Downstairs, Rex Firkin, executive producer; John Hawkesworth, producer (PBS)

Outstanding Music-Variety Series
The Carol Burnett Show, Joe Hamilton, executive producer; Ed Simmons, producer; Carol Burnett, star (CBS)

Outstanding Limited Series
NBC Sunday Mystery Movie—Columbo, Dean Hargrove and Roland Kibbee, executive producers; Douglas Benton, Robert F. O'Neill, and Edward K. Dodds, producers (NBC)

Outstanding Special—Comedy or Drama
"The Autobiography of Miss Jane Pittman," January 31, 1974, Robert Christiansen and Rick Rosenberg, producers (CBS)

Outstanding Comedy–Variety, Variety, or Music Special
"Lily," November 2, 1973, Irene Pinn, executive producer; Herb Sargent and Jerry McPhie, producers; Lily Tomlin, star (CBS)

Outstanding Children's Special
"Marlo Thomas and Friends in Free to Be . . . You and Me," March 11, 1974, Marlo Thomas and Carole Hart, producers; Marlo Thomas, star (ABC)

Best Lead Actor in a Comedy Series
Alan Alda (*M*A*S*H*) (CBS)

Best Lead Actor in a Drama Series
Telly Savalas (*Kojak*) (CBS)

Best Lead Actor in a Limited Series
William Holden (*The Blue Knight*) (NBC)

Best Lead Actor in a Drama
Hal Holbrook, "Pueblo" (*ABC Theatre*) March 29, 1973 (ABC)

Actor of the Year—Series
Alan Alda (*M*A*S*H*) (CBS)

Actor of the Year—Special
Hal Holbrook, "Pueblo" (*ABC Theatre*) March 29, 1973 (ABC)

Best Lead Actress in a Comedy Series
Mary Tyler Moore (*The Mary Tyler Moore Show*) (CBS)

Best Lead Actress in a Drama Series
Michael Learned (*The Waltons*) (CBS)

Best Lead Actress in a Limited Series
Mildred Natwick (*NBC Tuesday Mystery Movie— The Snoop Sisters*) (NBC)

Best Lead Actress in a Drama
Cicely Tyson, "The Autobiography of Miss Jane Pittman," January 31, 1974 (CBS)

Actress of the Year—Series
Mary Tyler Moore (*The Mary Tyler Moore Show*) (CBS)

Actress of the Year—Special
Cicely Tyson, "The Autobiography of Miss Jane Pittman," January 31, 1974 (CBS)

Best Supporting Actor in Comedy
Rob Reiner (*All in the Family*) (CBS)

Best Supporting Actor in Drama
Michael Moriarty, "The Glass Menagerie," December 16, 1973 (ABC)

Best Supporting Actor in Comedy-Variety, Variety, or Music
Harvey Korman (*The Carol Burnett Show*) (CBS)

Supporting Actor of the Year
Michael Moriarty, "The Glass Menagerie," December 16, 1973 (ABC)

Best Supporting Actress in Comedy
Cloris Leachman, "The Lars Affair" (*The Mary Tyler Moore Show*) September 15, 1973 (CBS)

Best Supporting Actress in Drama
Joanna Miles, "The Glass Menagerie," December 16, 1973 (ABC)

Best Supporting Actress in Comedy-Variety, Variety, or Music
Brenda Vaccaro, "The Shape of Things," October 19, 1973 (CBS)

Supporting Actress of the Year
Joanna Miles, "The Glass Menagerie," December 16, 1973 (ABC)

Best Directing in Drama
Robert Butler (*The Blue Knight*) November 15, 1973 (NBC)

Best Directing in Drama
John Korty, "The Autobiography of Miss Jane Pittman," January 31, 1974 (CBS)

Best Directing in Comedy
Jackie Cooper, "Carry On, Hawkeye" (*M*A*S*H*) November 24, 1973 (CBS)

Best Directing in Variety or Music
Dave Powers, "The Australia Show" (*The Carol Burnett Show*) December 8, 1973 (CBS)

Best Directing in Comedy-Variety, Variety or Music
Dwight Hemion, "Barbra Streisand . . . and Other Musical Instruments," November 2, 1973 (CBS)

Director of the Year—Series
Robert Butler (*The Blue Knight*) November 15, 1973 (NBC)

Director of the Year—Special
Dwight Hemion, "Barbra Streisand . . . and Other Musical Instruments," November 2, 1973 (CBS)

Best Writing in Drama
Joanna Lee, "The Thanksgiving Story" (*The Waltons*) November 15, 1973 (CBS)

Best Writing in Drama, Original Teleplay
Fay Kanin, "Tell Me Where It Hurts" (*GE Theater*) March 12, 1974 (CBS)

Best Writing in Drama, Adaptation
Tracy Keenan Wynn, "The Autobiography of Miss Jane Pittman," January 31, 1974 (CBS)

Best Writing in Comedy
Treva Silverman, "The Lou and Edie Story" (*The Mary Tyler Moore Show*) October 6, 1973 (CBS)

Best Writing in Variety or Music
Ed Simmons, Gary Belkin, Roger Beatty, Arnie Kogen, Bill Richmond, Gene Perret, Rudy De Luca, Barry Levinson, Dick Clair, Jenna McMahon, and Barry Harman (*The Carol Burnett Show*) February 16, 1974 (CBS)

Best Writing in Comedy-Variety, Variety or Music
Herb Sargent, Rosalyn Drexler, Lorne Michaels, Richard Pryor, Jim Rusk, James R. Stein, Robert Illes, Lily Tomlin, George Yanok, Jane Wagner, Rod Warren, Ann Elder, and Karyl Geld, "Lily," November 2, 1973 (CBS)

Writer of the Year—Series
Treva Silverman, "The Lou and Edie Story" (*The Mary Tyler Moore Show*) October 6, 1973 (CBS)

Writer of the Year—Special
Fay Kanin, "Tell Me Where It Hurts" (*GE Theater*) March 12, 1974 (CBS)

Outstanding Achievement in Choreography
Tony Charmoli, "Mitzi . . . A Tribute to the American Housewife," February 4, 1974 (CBS)

Best Music Composition
A. For a series or a single program of a series (in the first year of music's use only)
Morton Stevens, "Hookman" (*Hawaii Five-O*) September 11, 1973 (CBS)

B. For a special program
Fred Karlin, "The Autobiography of Miss Jane Pittman," January 31, 1974 (CBS)

Best Song or Theme
Marty Paich and David Paich, "Light the Way," from "Once More For Joey" (*Ironside*) January 17, 1974 (NBC)

Best Music Direction of a Variety, Musical, or Dramatic Program
Jack Parnell, Ken Welch, and Mitzie Welch, "Barbra Streisand . . . and Other Musical Instruments," November 2, 1973 (CBS)

Musician of the Year
Jack Parnell, Ken Welch, and Mitzie Welch, "Barbra Streisand . . . and Other Musical Instruments," November 2, 1973 (CBS)

Best Art Direction or Scenic Design
A. For a dramatic program or feature length film made for television; for a series, a single program of a series, or a special program
Jan Scott, art director; Charles Kreiner, set decorator, "The Lie" (*CBS Playhouse 90*) April 24, 1973 (CBS)

B. For a Musical or Variety single program of a series or a special program
Brian C. Bartholomew, "Barbra Streisand . . . and Other Musical Instruments," November 2, 1973 (CBS)

Art Director and Set Decorator of the Year
Jan Scott, art director; Charles Kreiner, set decorator, "The Lie" (*CBS Playhouse 90*) April 24, 1973 (CBS)

Outstanding Achievement in Costume Design
Bruce Walkup and Sandy Stewart, "The Autobiography of Miss Jane Pittman," January 31, 1974 (CBS)

Outstanding Achievement in Makeup
Stan Winston and Rick Baker, "The Autobiography of Miss Jane Pittman," January 31, 1974 (CBS)

Best Cinematography for Entertainment Programming
A. For a series or a single program of a series
Harry Wolf, A.S.C., "Any Old Port in a Storm" (*NBC Sunday Mystery Movie—Columbo*) October 7, 1973 (NBC)

B. For a special or feature length program made for television
Ted Voigtlander, A.S.C., "It's Good to Be Alive," (*GE Theater*) February 22, 1974 (CBS)

Cinematographer of the Year
Ted Voigtlander, A.S.C., "It's Good To Be Alive" (*GE Theater*) February 22, 1974 (CBS)

Best Film Editing for Entertainment Programming

A. For a series or a single program of a series

Gene Fowler, Jr., Marjorie Fowler, and Samuel E. Beetley, *The Blue Knight* (NBC)

B. For a special or feature length program made for television

Frank Morriss, "The Execution of Private Slovik" (*NBC Wednesday Night at the Movies*) March 13, 1974 (NBC)

Film Editor of the Year

Frank Morriss, "The Execution of Private Slovik" (*NBC Wednesday Night at the Movies*) March 13, 1974 (NBC)

Outstanding Achievement in Film Sound Editing

Bud Nolan, "Pueblo" (*ABC Theatre*) March 29, 1973 (ABC)

Outstanding Achievement in Film or Tape Sound Mixing

Albert A. Gramaglia and Michael Shindler, "Pueblo" (*ABC Theatre*) March 29, 1973 (ABC)

Outstanding Achievement in Video Tape Editing

Alfred Muller, "Pueblo" (*ABC Theatre*) March 29, 1973 (ABC)

Outstanding Achievement in Technical Direction and Electronic Camerawork

Gerry Bucci, technical director; Kenneth Tamburri, Dave Hilmer, Dave Smith, Jim Balden, and Ron Brooks, cameramen, "In Concert—Cat Stevens" (*ABC Wide World of Entertainment*) November 9, 1973 (ABC)

Outstanding Achievement in Lighting Direction

William M. Klages, "The Lie" (*CBS Playhouse 90*) April 24, 1973 (CBS)

Outstanding Individual Achievement in Children's Programming

Charles M. Schulz, writer, "A Charlie Brown Thanksgiving," November 20, 1973 (CBS)

William Zaharuk, art director; Peter Razmofski, set decorator; "The Borrowers," (*Hallmark Hall of Fame*) December 14, 1973 (NBC)

Special Classification of Outstanding Program and Individual Achievement

The Dick Cavett Show, John Gilroy, producer; Dick Cavett, star (ABC)

Tom Snyder, host, *Tomorrow* (NBC)

Outstanding Achievement in Sports Programming

ABC's Wide World of Sports, Roone Arledge, executive producer; Dennis Lewin, producer (ABC)

Jim McKay, host, *ABC's Wide World of Sports* (ABC)

Outstanding Achievement in any Area of Creative Technical Crafts

Lynda Gurasich, hair stylist, "The Autobiography of Miss Jane Pittman," January 31, 1974 (CBS)

SPECIAL AWARDS

Outstanding Achievement in Engineering Development awarded May 28, 1974:

Consolidated Video Systems, Inc. for the application of digital video technique to the Time Base Corrector, permitting use of smaller, lighter weight, more portable video tape equipment on news and other outside events in television broadcasting.

RCA for its leading role in the development of the quadraplex video tape cartridge equipment, providing improved production reliability and efficiency in broadcasting video taped program segments, promos, and commercials.

Awarded September 4, 1974:

The Telecopter

To John D. Silva, for the conception and expertise, and

To Golden West Broadcasters for its realization

DAYTIME PROGRAM AND INDIVIDUAL ACHIEVEMENTS

Outstanding Drama Series

The Doctors, Joseph Stuart, producer (NBC)

Outstanding Drama Special

"The Other Woman," (*ABC Matinee Today*) December 4, 1973, John Conboy, producer (ABC)

Outstanding Game Show

Password, Frank Wayne, executive producer; Howard Felsher, producer (ABC)

Outstanding Talk, Service or Variety Series

The Merv Griffin Show, Bob Murphy, producer (Syndicated)

Outstanding Entertainment Children's Series

Zoom, Jim Crum and Christopher Sarson, producers (PBS)

Outstanding Entertainment Children's Special

"Rookie of the Year" (*The ABC Afterschool Special*) October 3, 1973, Dan Wilson, producer (ABC)

Best Actor in Daytime Drama

A. For a Series

MacDonald Carey (*Days of Our Lives*) (NBC)

B. For a Special Program

Pat O'Brien, "The Other Woman" (*ABC Matinee Today*) December 4, 1973 (ABC)

Daytime Actor of the Year

Pat O'Brien, "The Other Woman," (*ABC Matinee Today*) December 4, 1973 (ABC)

Best Actress in Daytime Drama
A. For a Series
Elizabeth Hubbard (*The Doctors*) (NBC)

B. For a Special Program
Cathleen Nesbitt, "The Mask of Love" (*ABC Matinee Today*) December 7, 1973 (ABC)

Daytime Actress of the Year
Cathleen Nesbitt, "The Mask of Love" (*ABC Matinee Today*) December 7, 1973 (ABC)

Best Host or Hostess in a Game Show
Peter Marshall (*The Hollywood Squares*) (NBC)

Best Host or Hostess in a Talk, Service or Variety Series
Dinah Shore (*Dinah's Place*) (NBC)

Daytime Host of the Year
Peter Marshall (*The Hollywood Squares*) (NBC)

Best Individual Director for a Drama Series
H. Wesley Kenney (*Days of Our Lives*) (NBC)

Best Individual Director for a Special Program
H. Wesley Kenney, "Miss Kline, We Love You" (*ABC Afternoon Playbreak*) February 27, 1974 (ABC)

Best Individual Director for a Game Show
Mike Gargiulo (*Jackpot!*) (NBC)

Best Individual Director for a Talk, Service, or Variety Program
Dick Carson (*The Merv Griffin Show*—with Rosemary Clooney, Helen O'Connell, Fran Warren and Kay Starr) (Syndicated)

Daytime Director of the Year
H. Wesley Kenney, "Miss Kline, We Love You" (*ABC Afternoon Playbreak*) February 27, 1974 (ABC)

Best Writing for a Drama Series
Henry Slesar (*The Edge of Night*) (CBS)

Best Writing for a Special Program
Lila Garrett and Sandy Krinski, "Mother of the Bride" (*ABC Afternoon Playbreak*) January 9, 1974 (ABC)

Best Writing for a Game Show
Jay Redack, Harry Friedman, Harold Schneider, Gary Johnson, Steve Levitch, Rick Kellard, and Rowby Goren (*The Hollywood Squares*) (NBC)

Best Writing for a Talk, Service or Variety Program
Tony Garafalo, Bob Murphy, and Merv Griffin (*The Merv Griffin Show*—with Billie Jean King, Mark Spitz, Hank Aaron, and Johnny Unitas) (Syndicated)

Daytime Writer of the Year
Lila Garrett and Sandy Krinski, "Mother of the Bride" (*ABC Afternoon Playbreak*) January 9, 1974 (ABC)

Outstanding Musical Direction
Richard Clements, "A Special Act of Love" (*ABC Afternoon Playbreak*) November 14, 1973 (ABC)

Outstanding Art Direction or Scenic Design
Tom Trimble, art director; Brock Broughton, set decorator, *The Young and the Restless,* October 19, 1973 (CBS)

Otis Riggs, Jr., *Another World,* April 2, 1973 (NBC)

Outstanding Costume Design
Bill Jobe, "The Mask of Love" (*ABC Matinee Today*) December 7, 1973 (ABC)

Outstanding Makeup
Douglas D. Kelly, "The Mask of Love" (*ABC Matinee Today*) December 7, 1973 (ABC)

Outstanding Technical Direction and Electronic Camerawork
Lou Marchand, technical director; Gerald M. Dowd, Frank Melchiorre, and John Morris, cameramen, *One Life to Live,* July 2, 1973 (ABC)

Outstanding Lighting Direction
Richard Holbrook, *The Young and the Restless,* January 11, 1974 (CBS)

Outstanding Sound Mixing
Ernest Dellutri, *Days Of Our Lives,* July 20, 1973 (NBC)

Outstanding Editing
Gary Anderson, "Miss Kline, We Love You" (*ABC Afternoon Playbreak*) February 27, 1974 (ABC)

NEWS AND DOCUMENTARY PROGRAM AND INDIVIDUAL ACHIEVEMENTS
Presented September 4, 1974

Outstanding Achievement within Regularly Scheduled News Programs
"Coverage of the October War from Israel's Northern Front (*CBS Evening News with Walter Cronkite*) John Laurence, correspondent, October, 1973 (CBS)

"The Agnew Resignation" (*CBS Evening News with Walter Cronkite*) Paul Greenberg, executive producer; Ron Bonn, Ed Fouhy, John Lane, Don Bowers, John Armstrong, and Robert Mean, producers; Walter Cronkite, Robert Schakne, Fred Graham, Robert Pierpoint, Roger Mudd, Dan Rather, John Hart, and Eric Sevareid, correspondents, October 10, 1973 (CBS)

"The Key Biscayne Bank Charter Struggle" (*CBS Evening News with Walter Cronkite*) Ed Fouhy, producer; Robert Pierpoint, correspondent, October 15, 16, and 18, 1973 (CBS)

"Reports on World Hunger," (*NBC Nightly News*) Lester M. Crystal, executive producer; Richard Fischer and Joseph Angotti, producers; Tom Streithorst, Phil Brady, John Palmer, and Liz Trotta, correspondents, March 1974–June 1974 (NBC)

Outstanding Achievement for Regularly Scheduled Magazine-Type Programs

"America's Nerve Gas Arsenal" (*First Tuesday*) Eliot Frankel, executive producer; William B. Hill and Anthony Potter, producers; Tom Pettit, correspondent, June 5, 1973 (NBC)

"The Adversaries," (*Behind the Lines*) Carey Winfrey, executive producer; Peter Forbath, producer/reporter; Brendan Gill, host/moderator, March 28, 1974 (PBS)

"A Question of Impeachment" (*Bill Moyers' Journal*) Jerome Toobin, executive producer; Martin Clancy, producer; Bill Moyers, broadcaster, January 22, 1974 (PBS)

Outstanding Achievement in Coverage of Special Events

"Watergate: The White House Transcripts," Russ Bensley, executive producer; Sylvia Westerman, Barry Jagoda, Mark Harrington, and Jack Kelly, producers; Walter Cronkite, Dan Rather, Barry Serafin, Bob Schieffer, Daniel Schorr, Nelson Benton, Bruce Morton, Roger Mudd, and Fred Graham, correspondents, May 1, 1974 (CBS)

"Watergate Coverage," Martin Clancy, executive producer; the NPACT Staff, producers; Jim Lehrer, Peter Kaye, and Robert MacNeil, reporters; May 17–November 15, 1973 (PBS)

Outstanding Documentary Program Achievements
A. For documentary programs dealing with events or matters of current significance

"Fire!" (*ABC News Close Up*) Pamela Hill, producer; Jules Bergman, correspondent/narrator, November 26, 1973 (ABC)

"CBS News Special Report: The Senate and the Watergate Affair," Leslie Midgley, executive producer; Hal Haley, Bernard Birnbaum, and David Browning, producers; Dan Rather, Roger Mudd, Daniel Schorr, and Fred Graham, correspondents, May 13, 1973 (CBS)

Outstanding Documentary Program Achievements
B. For documentary programs dealing with artistic, historical, or cultural subjects

"Journey to the Outer Limits" (*National Geographic Society Special*) Nicholas Clapp and Dennis Kane, executive producers; Alex Grasshoff, producer; January 10, 1974 (ABC)

The World at War, Jeremy Isaacs, producer (Syndicated)

"CBS Reports: The Rockefellers," Burton Benjamin, executive producer; Howard Stringer, producer; Walter Cronkite, correspondent, December 28, 1973 (CBS)

Outstanding Interview Program

"Solzhenitsyn," (*CBS News Special*) Burton Benjamin, producer; Walter Cronkite, correspondent, June 24, 1974 (CBS)

"Henry Steele Commager" (*Bill Moyers' Journal*) Jerome Toobin, executive producer; Martin Clancy, producer; Bill Moyers, broadcaster, March 26, 1974 (PBS)

Outstanding Television News Broadcaster

Harry Reasoner (*ABC News*) March 19, 1973–June 30, 1974 (ABC)

Bill Moyers, "Essay on Watergate" (*Bill Moyers' Journal*) October 31, 1973 (PBS)

Outstanding Individual Achievement in Chilren's Programming

Ronald Baldwin, art director; Nat Mongioi, set decorator, *The Electric Company,* February 19, 1974 (PBS)

The Muppets (Jim Henson, Frank Oz, Carroll Spinney, Jerry Nelson, Richard Hunt and Fran Brill), performers, *Sesame Street* (PBS)

Jon Stone, Joseph A. Bailey, Jerry Juhl, Emily Perl Kingsley, Jeffrey Moss, Ray Sipherd, and Norman Stiles, writers, *Sesame Street,* November 19, 1973 (PBS)

Outstanding Achievement in Religious Programming

Ken Lamkin, technical director; Sam Drummy, Gary Stanton, and Robert Hatfield, cameramen, "Gift of Tears" (*This Is the Life*) (Syndicated)

Outstanding Achievement in News and Documentary Directing

Pamela Hill, "Fire!" (*ABC News Close-up*) November 26, 1973 (ABC)

Outstanding Achievement in News and Documentary Writing

No winner

Outstanding Achievement in any Area of Creative Technical Crafts

Philippe Cousteau, under-ice photography, "Beneath the Frozen World" (*The Undersea World of Jacques Cousteau*) March 3, 1974 (ABC)

John Chambers and Tom Burman, makeup, "Struggle for Survival" (*Primal Man*) June 21, 1974 (ABC)

Aggie Whelan, courtroom drawings, "The Mitchell–Stans Trial" (*CBS Evening News with Walter Cronkite*) February 19–April 29, 1974 (CBS)

Outstanding Informational Children's Series

Make a Wish, Lester Cooper, executive producer; Tom Bywaters, producer (ABC)

Outstanding Informational Children's Special

"The Runaways," March 27, 1974, Joseph Barbera and William Hanna, executive producers; Bill Schwartz, producer (ABC)

Outstanding Instructional Children's Programming
Inside/out, Larry Walcoff, executive producer (Syndicated)

Best Cinematography for News and Documentary Programming
A. Regularly scheduled News Programs and coverage of Special Events
Delos Hall, "Clanking Savannah Blacksmith: On the Road with Charles Kuralt" (*CBS Evening News with Walter Cronkite*) March 25, 1974 (CBS)

B. Documentary, Magazine-type, or Mini-documentary programs
Walter Dombrow, "Ballerina" (*60 Minutes*) February 10, 1974 (CBS)

Best Music Composition
Walter Scharf, "Beneath the Frozen World" (*The Undersea World of Jacques Cousteau*) March 3, 1974 (ABC)

Best Art Direction or Scenic Design
William Sunshine (*60 Minutes*) (CBS)

Best Film Editing for News and Documentary Programming
A. Regularly scheduled News programs and coverage of Special Events
William J. Freeda, "Profile of Poverty in Appalachia" (*NBC Nightly News*) April 29, 1973 (NBC)

B. Documentary, Magazine-type, or Mini-documentary programs
Ann Chegwidden, "The Baboons of Gombe—Jane Goodall and the World of Animal Behavior," February 1, 1974 (ABC)

Best Film or Tape Sound Mixing
Peter Pilafian, George E. Porter, Eddie J. Nelson, and Robert L. Harman, "Journey to the Outer Limits" (*National Geographic Society Special*) January 10, 1974 (ABC)

Best Film Sound Editing
Charles L. Campbell, Robert Cornett, Larry Carow, Larry Kaufman, Colin Mouat, Don Warner, and Frank R. White, "The Baboons of Gombe—Jane Goodall and the World of Animal Behavior," February 1, 1974 (ABC)

Best Video Tape Editing
Gary Anderson, "Paramount Presents . . . ABC Wide World of Entertainment," March 27, 1974 (ABC)

Best Technical Direction and Electronic Camerawork
Carl Schutzman, technical director; Joseph Schwartz and William Bell, cameramen, *60 Minutes* (CBS)

1974–1975
Presented May 19, 1975

Outstanding Comedy Series
The Mary Tyler Moore Show, James L. Brooks and Allan Burns, executive producers; Ed Weinberger and Stan Daniels, producers (CBS)

Outstanding Drama Series
Masterpiece Theatre—Upstairs, Downstairs, Rex Firkin, executive producer; John Hawkesworth, producer (PBS)

Outstanding Comedy-Variety or Music Series
The Carol Burnett Show, Joe Hamilton, executive producer; Ed Simmons, producer; Carol Burnett, star (CBS)

Outstanding Limited Series
Benjamin Franklin, Lewis Freedman, executive producer; George Lefferts and Glenn Jordan, producers (CBS)

Outstanding Special—Drama or Comedy
"The Law" (*NBC World Premiere Movie*) October 22, 1974, William Sackheim, producer (NBC)

Outstanding Special—Comedy-Variety or Music
"An Evening with John Denver," March 10, 1975, Jerry Weintraub, executive producer; Al Rogers and Rich Eustis, producers; John Denver, star (ABC)

Outstanding Classical Music Program
"Profile in Music: Beverly Sills" (*Festival '75*) March 10, 1975, Patricia Foy, producer; Beverly Sills, star (PBS)

Outstanding Lead Actor in a Comedy Series
Tony Randall (*The Odd Couple*) (ABC)

Outstanding Lead Actor in a Drama Series
Robert Blake (*Baretta*) (ABC)

Outstanding Lead Actor in a Limited Series
Peter Falk (*NBC Sunday Mystery Movie—Columbo*) (NBC)

Outstanding Lead Actor in a Special Program—Drama or Comedy
Laurence Olivier, "Love Among the Ruins" (*ABC Theatre*) March 6, 1975 (ABC)

Outstanding Lead Actress in a Comedy Series
Valerie Harper (*Rhoda*) (CBS)

Outstanding Lead Actress in a Drama Series
Jean Marsh (*Masterpiece Theatre—Upstairs, Downstairs*) (PBS)

Outstanding Lead Actress in a Limited Series
Jessica Walter (*NBC Sunday Mystery Movie—Amy Prentiss*) (NBC)

Outstanding Lead Actress in a Special Program—Drama or Comedy
Katharine Hepburn, "Love Among the Ruins" (*ABC Theatre*) March 6, 1975 (ABC)

Outstanding Continuing Performance by a Supporting Actor in a Comedy Series
Ed Asner (*The Mary Tyler Moore Show*) (CBS)

Outstanding Continuing Performance by a Supporting Actor in a Drama Series
Will Geer (*The Waltons*) (CBS)

Outstanding Continuing or Single Performance by a Supporting Actor in Variety or Music
Jack Albertson (*Cher*) March 2, 1975 (CBS)

Outstanding Single Performance by a Supporting Actor in a Comedy or Drama Special
Anthony Quale, "QB VII," Parts 1 and 2 (*ABC Movie Special*) April 29 and 30, 1974 (ABC)

Outstanding Single Performance by a Supporting Actor in a Comedy or Drama Series
Patrick McGoohan, "By Dawn's Early Light" (*NBC Sunday Mystery Movie—Columbo*) October 27, 1974 (NBC)

Outstanding Continuing Performance by a Supporting Actress in a Comedy Series
Betty White (*The Mary Tyler Moore Show*) (CBS)

Outstanding Continuing Performance by a Supporting Actress in a Drama Series
Ellen Corby (*The Waltons*) (CBS)

Outstanding Continuing or Single Performance by a Supporting Actress in Variety or Music
Cloris Leachman (*Cher*) March 2, 1975 (CBS)

Outstanding Single Performance by a Supporting Actress in a Comedy or Drama Special
Juliet Mills, "QB VII," Parts 1 and 2 (*ABC Movie Special*) April 29 and 30, 1974 (ABC)

Outstanding Single Performance by a Supporting Actress in a Comedy or Drama Series
Cloris Leachman, "Phyllis Whips Inflation" (*The Mary Tyler Moore Show*) January 18, 1975 (CBS)
Zohra Lampert, "Queen of the Gypsies" (*Kojak*) January 19, 1975 (CBS)

Outstanding Directing in a Drama Series
Bill Bain, "A Sudden Storm," (*Masterpiece Theatre—Upstairs, Downstairs*) December 22, 1974 (PBS)

Outstanding Directing in a Comedy Series
Gene Reynolds, "O.R." (*M*A*S*H*) October 8, 1974 (CBS)

Outstanding Directing in a Comedy-Variety or Music Series
Dave Powers (*The Carol Burnett Show*) December 21, 1974 (CBS)

Outstanding Directing in a Comedy-Variety or Music Special
Bill Davis, "An Evening with John Denver," March 10, 1975 (ABC)

Outstanding Directing in a Special Program—Drama or Comedy
George Cukor, "Love Among the Ruins" (*ABC Theatre*) March 6, 1975 (ABC)

Outstanding Writing in a Drama Series
Howard Fast, "The Ambassador" (*Benjamin Franklin*) November 21, 1974 (CBS)

Outstanding Writing in a Comedy Series
Ed Weinberger and Stan Daniels, "Mary Richards Goes to Jail" (*The Mary Tyler Moore Show*) September 14, 1974 (CBS)

Outstanding Writing in a Comedy-Variety or Music Series
Ed Simmons, Gary Belkin, Roger Beatty, Arnie Kogen, Bill Richmond, Gene Perret, Rudy De-Luca, Barry Levinson, Dick Clair, and Jenna McMahon, *The Carol Burnett Show,* December 21, 1974 (CBS)

Outstanding Writing in a Comedy-Variety or Music Special
Bob Wells, John Bradford, and Cy Coleman, "Shirley MacLaine: If They Could See Me Now," November 28, 1974 (CBS)

Outstanding Writing in a Special Program—Drama or Comedy—Original Teleplay
James Costigan, "Love Among the Ruins" (*ABC Theatre*) March 6, 1975 (ABC)

Outstanding Writing in a Special Program—Drama or Comedy—Adaptation
David W. Rintels, "IBM Presents Clarence Darrow," September 4, 1974 (NBC)

Outstanding Achievement in Choreography
Marge Champion, "Queen of the Stardust Ballroom," February 13, 1975

Outstanding Achievement in Music Composition for a Series
Billy Goldenberg, "The Rebel" (*Benjamin Franklin*) January 9, 1975 (CBS)

Outstanding Achievement in Music Composition for a Special
Jerry Goldsmith, "QB VII," Parts 1 and 2 (*ABC Movie Special*) April 29 and 30, 1974 (ABC)

Outstanding Achievement in Art Direction or Scenic Design
Charles Lisanby, art director; Robert Checchi, set decorator, "The Ambassador" (*Benjamin Franklin*) November 21, 1974 (CBS)

Outstanding Achievement in Art Direction or Scenic Design
Robert Kelly, art director; Robert Checchi, set decorator, *Cher,* February 12, 1975 (CBS)

Outstanding Achievement in Art Direction or Scenic Design
Carmen Dillon, art director; Tessa Davies, set decorator, "Love Among the Ruins" (*ABC Theatre*) March 6, 1975 (ABC)

Outstanding Achievement in Graphic Design and Title Sequences
Phill Norman, "QB VII," Parts 1 and 2 (*ABC Movie Special*) April 29 and 30, 1974 (ABC)

Outstanding Achievement in Cinematography for Entertainment Programming for a Series
Richard C. Glouner, A.S.C., "Playback" (*NBC Sunday Mystery Movie—Columbo*) March 2, 1975 (NBC)

Outstanding Achievement in Cinematography for Entertainment Programming for a Special
David M. Walsh, "Queen of the Stardust Ballroom," February 13, 1975 (CBS)

Outstanding Film Editing for Entertainment Programming for a Series
Douglas Hines, "An Affair to Forget" (*The Mary Tyler Moore Show*) December 21, 1974 (CBS)

Outstanding Film Editing for Entertainment Programming for a Series
Donald R. Rode, "Mirror, Mirror on the Wall" (*Petrocelli*) November 6, 1974 (NBC)

Outstanding Film Editing for Entertainment Programming for a Special
John A. Martinelli, A.C.E., "The Legend of Lizzie Borden" (*ABC Monday Night Movie*) February 10, 1975 (ABC)
Byron "Buzz" Brandt and Irving C. Rosenblum, "QB VII," Parts 1 and 2 (*ABC Movie Special*) April 29 and 30, 1974 (ABC)

Outstanding Achievement in Film Sound Editing
Marvin I. Kosberg, Richard Burrow, Milton C. Burrow, Jack Milner, Ronald Ashcroft, James Ballas, Josef Von Stroheim, Jerry Rosenthal, William Andrews, Edward Sandlin, David Horton, Alvin Kajita, Tony Garber, and Jeremy Hoenack, "QB VII," Parts 1 and 2 (*ABC Movie Special*) April 29 and 30, 1974 (ABC)

Outstanding Achievement in Film or Tape Sound Mixing
Marshall King, "The American Film Institute Salute to James Cagney," March 18, 1974 (CBS)

Outstanding Achievement in Video Tape Editing
Gary Anderson and Jim McElroy, "Judgment: The Court-Martial of Lt. William Calley," (*ABC Theatre*) January 12, 1975 (ABC)

Outstanding Achievement in Technical Direction and Electronic Camerawork
Ernie Buttelman, technical director; Jim Angel, Jim Balden, Ron Brooks, and Art LaCombe, cameramen, "The Missiles of October" (*ABC Theatre*) December 18, 1974 (ABC)

Outstanding Achievement in Lighting Direction
John Freschi, "The Perry Como Christmas Show," December 17, 1974 (CBS)

Outstanding Children's Special
"Yes, Virginia, There is a Santa Claus," December 6, 1974, Burt Rosen, executive producer; Bill Melendez and Mort Green, producers (ABC)

Outstanding Sports Event
"Jimmy Connors vs. Rod Laver Tennis Challenge," February 2, 1975, Frank Chirkinian, executive producer (CBS)

Outstanding Sports Program
Wide World of Sports, April 14, 1974, Roone Arledge, executive producer; Doug Wilson, Ned Steckel, Dennis Lewin, John Martin, and Chet Forte, producers (ABC)

Outstanding Sports Broadcaster
Jim McKay (*Wide World of Sports*) April 14, 1974 (ABC)

Special Classification of Outstanding Program and Individual Achievement
"The American Film Institute Salute to James Cagney," March 18, 1974, George Stevens, Jr., executive producer; Paul W. Keyes, producer (CBS)
Alistair Cooke, host, *Masterpiece Theatre* (PBS)

Outstanding Achievement in Special Musical Material
No winner

Outstanding Achievement in Costume Design
Guy Verhille, "The Legend Of Lizzie Borden" (*Special World Premiere—ABC Monday Night Movie*) February 10, 1975 (ABC)
Margaret Furse, "Love Among the Ruins," (*ABC Theatre*) March 6, 1975 (ABC)

Outstanding Achievement in Makeup
No winner

Outstanding Achievement in any Area of Creative Technical Crafts

Edie Panda, hairstyist, "The Ambassador" (*Benjamin Franklin*) November 21, 1974 (CBS)

Doug Nelson and Norm Schwartz, *Wide World In Concert,* double-system sound editing and synchronization for stereophonic broadcasting of television programs; series (ABC)

Outstanding Individual Achievement in Sports Programming

Gene Schwarz, technical director, 1974 World Series, October 12–17, 1974 (NBC)

Herb Altman, film editor, "The Baseball World of Joe Garagiola," May 27, 1974 (NBC)

Corey Leible, Len Basile, Jack Bennett, Lou Gerard, and Ray Figelski, electronic cameramen, 1974 Stanley Cup Playoffs, April 9–May 19, 1974 (NBC)

John Pumo, Charles D'Onofrio, Frank Florio, technical directors; George Klimcsak, Robert Kania, Harold Hoffmann, Herman Lang, George Drago, Walt Deniear, Stan Gould, Al Diamond, Charles Armstrong, Al Brantley, Sig Meyers, Frank McSpedon, George F. Naeder, James Murphy, James McCarthy, Vern Surphlis, Al Loreto, Gordon Sweeney, Jo Sidlo, William Hathaway, Gene Pescalek, and Curly Fonorow, cameramen; Masters Tournament, April 13 and 14, 1974 (CBS)

SPECIAL AWARDS

Outstanding Achievement in Engineering Development

Columbia Broadcasting System, for spearheading the development and realization of the electronic news-gathering system

Nippon Electric Company, for development of digital television frame synchronizers

DAYTIME PROGRAM AND INDIVIDUAL ACHIEVEMENTS
Presented May 15, 1975

Outstanding Daytime Drama Series

The Young and the Restless, John J. Conboy, producer; William J. Bell and Lee Phillip Bell, creators (CBS)

Outstanding Daytime Drama Special

"The Girl Who Couldn't Lose," (*ABC Afternoon Playbreak*) February 13, 1975, Ira Barmak, executive producer; Lila Garrett, producer (ABC)

Outstanding Game or Audience Participation Show

Hollywood Squares, Merrill Heatter and Bob Quigley, executive producers; Jay Redack, producer (NBC)

Outstanding Talk, Service, or Variety Series

Dinah!, Henry Jaffe and Carolyn Raskin, executive producers; Fred Tatashore, producer (Syndicated)

Outstanding Entertainment Children's Special

"Harlequin" (*The CBS Festival of Lively Arts for Young People*) April 10, 1974, Edward Villella, executive producer; Gardner Compton, producer (CBS)

Outstanding Entertainment Children's Series

Star Trek, Lou Scheimer and Norm Prescott, producers (NBC)

Outstanding Actor in a Daytime Drama Series
MacDonald Carey (*Days of Our Lives*) (NBC)

Outstanding Actor in a Daytime Drama Special
Bradford Dillman, "The Last Bride of Salem" (*ABC Afternoon Playbreak*) May 8, 1974 (ABC)

Outstanding Actress in a Daytime Drama Series
Susan Flannery (*Days of Our Lives*) (NBC)

Outstanding Actress in a Daytime Drama Special
Kay Lenz, "Heart in Hiding" (*ABC Afternoon Playbreak*) November 14, 1974 (ABC)

Outstanding Host in a Game or Audience Participation Show
Peter Marshall (*The Hollywood Squares*) (NBC)

Outstanding Host or Hostess in a Talk, Service, or Variety Series
Barbara Walters (*Today*) (NBC)

Outstanding Individual Director for a Daytime Drama Series
Richard Dunlap (*The Young and The Restless*) November 25, 1974 (CBS)

Outstanding Individual Director for a Daytime Special Program
Mort Lachman, "The Girl Who Couldn't Lose" (*ABC Afternoon Playbreak*) February 13, 1975 (ABC)

Outstanding Individual Director for a Game or Audience Participation Show
Jerome Shaw (*The Hollywood Squares*) October 28, 1974 (NBC)

Outstanding Individual Director for a Daytime Variety Program
Glen Swanson, "Dinah Salutes Broadway" (*Dinah!*) (Syndicated)

Outstanding Writing for a Daytime Drama Series
Harding LeMay, Tom King, Charles Kozloff, Jan Merlin, and Douglas Marland, *Another World* (NBC)

Outstanding Writing for a Daytime Special Program
Audrey Davis Levin, "Heart in Hiding" (*ABC Afternoon Playbreak*) November 14, 1974 (ABC)

Outstanding Individual Achievement in Daytime Programming
No winner

Outstanding Individual Achievement in Children's Programming
Elinor Bunin, graphic design and title sequences, "Funshine Saturday and Sunday," umbrella title animations for Saturday and Sunday morning children's programming, January 24 and 25, 1975 (ABC)

1975–1976
Presented May 17, 1976

Outstanding Comedy Series
The Mary Tyler Moore Show, James L. Brooks and Allan Burns, executive producers; Ed Weinberger and Stan Daniels, producers (CBS)

Outstanding Drama Series
Police Story, David Gerber and Stanley Kallis, executive producers; Liam O'Brien and Carl Pingitore, producers (NBC)

Outstanding Comedy-Variety or Music Series
NBC's Saturday Night; Lorne Michaels, producer (NBC)

Outstanding Limited Series
Masterpiece Theatre—Upstairs, Downstairs, Rex Firkin, executive producer; John Hawkesworth, producer (PBS)

Outstanding Special—Drama or Comedy
"Eleanor and Franklin" (*ABC Theatre*) January 11 and 12, 1976, David Susskind, executive producer; Harry Sherman and Audrey Mass, producers (ABC)

Outstanding Special—Comedy-Variety or Music
"Gypsy in My Soul," January 20, 1976, William O. Harbach, executive producer; Cy Coleman and Fred Ebb, producers; Shirley MacLaine, star (CBS)

Outstanding Classical Music Program
"Bernstein and the New York Philharmonic" (*Great Performances*) November 26, 1975, Klaus Hallig and Harry Kraut, executive producers; David Griffiths, producer; Leonard Bernstein, star (PBS)

Outstanding Lead Actor in a Comedy Series
Jack Albertson (*Chico and the Man*) (NBC)

Outstanding Lead Actor in a Drama Series
Peter Falk (*NBC Sunday Mystery Movie—Columbo*) (NBC)

Outstanding Lead Actor in a Limited Series
Hal Holbrook (*Sandburg's Lincoln*) (NBC)

Outstanding Lead Ator in a Drama or Comedy Special
Anthony Hopkins, "The Lindbergh Kidnapping Case" (*NBC World Premiere Movie*) February 26, 1976 (NBC)

Outstanding Lead Actor for a Single Appearance in a Drama or Comedy Series
Edward Asner (*Rich Man, Poor Man*) February 1, 1976 (ABC)

Outstanding Lead Actress in a Comedy Series
Mary Tyler Moore (*The Mary Tyler Moore Show*) (CBS)

Outstanding Lead Actress in a Drama Series
Michael Learned (*The Waltons*) (CBS)

Outstanding Lead Actress in a Limited Series
Rosemary Harris (*Masterpiece Theatre—Notorious Woman*) (PBS)

Outstanding Lead Actress in a Drama or Comedy Special
Susan Clark, "Babe," October 23, 1975 (CBS)

Outstanding Lead Actress for a Single Appearance in a Drama or Comedy Series
Kathryn Walker, "John Adams, Lawyer" (*The Adams Chronicles*) January 20, 1976 (PBS)

Outstanding Continuing Performance by a Supporting Actor in a Comedy Series
Ted Knight (*The Mary Tyler Moore Show*) (CBS)

Outstanding Continuing Performance by a Supporting Actor in a Drama Series
Anthony Zerbe (*Harry O*) (ABC)

Outstanding Continuing or Single Performance by a Supporting Actor in Variety or Music
Chevy Chase (*NBC's Saturday Night*) January 17, 1976 (NBC)

Outstanding Single Performance by a Supporting Actor in a Comedy or Drama Special
Ed Flanders, "A Moon for the Misbegotten" (*ABC Theatre*) May 27, 1975 (ABC)

Outstanding Single Performance by a Supporting Actor in a Comedy or Drama Series
Gordon Jackson, "The Beastly Hun" (*Masterpiece Theatre—Upstairs, Downstairs*) January 18, 1976 (PBS)

Outstanding Continuing Performance by a Supporting Actress in a Comedy Series
Betty White (*The Mary Tyler Moore Show*) (CBS)

Outstanding Continuing Performance by a Supporting Actress in a Drama Series
Ellen Corby (*The Waltons*) (CBS)

Outstanding Continuing or Single Performance by a Supporting Actress in a Variety or Music
Vicki Lawrence (*The Carol Burnett Show*) February 7, 1976 (CBS)

Outstanding Single Performance by a Supporting Actress in a Comedy or Drama Special
Rosemary Murphy, "Eleanor and Franklin" (*ABC Theatre*) January 11 and 12, 1976 (ABC)

Outstanding Single Performance by a Supporting Actress in a Comedy or Drama Series
Fionnuala Flanagan (*Rich Man, Poor Man*) February 2, 1976 (ABC)

Outstanding Directing in a Drama Series
David Greene (*Rich Man, Poor Man*) March 15, 1976 (ABC)

Outstanding Directing in a Comedy Series
Gene Reynolds, "Welcome to Korea" (*M*A*S*H*) September 12, 1975 (CBS)

Outstanding Directing in a Comedy-Variety or Music Series
·Dave Wilson (*NBC's Saturday Night*) October 18, 1975 (NBC)

Outstanding Directing in a Comedy-Variety or Music Special
Dwight Hemion, "Steve and Eydie: 'Our Love Is Here to Stay'," November 27, 1975 (CBS)

Outstanding Directing in a Special Program—Drama or Comedy
Daniel Petrie, "Eleanor and Franklin" (*ABC Theatre*) January 11 and 12, 1976 (ABC)

Outstanding Writing in a Drama Series
Sherman Yellen, "John Adams, Lawyer" (*The Adams Chronicles*) January 20, 1976 (PBS)

Outstanding Writing in a Comedy Series
David Lloyd, "Chuckles Bites the Dust" (*The Mary Tyler Moore Show*) October 25, 1975 (CBS)

Outstanding Writing in a Comedy-Variety or Music Series
Anne Beatts, Chevy Chase, Al Franken, Tom Davis, Lorne Michaels, Marilyn Suzanne Miller, Michael O'Donoghue, Herb Sargent, Tom Schiller, Rosie Schuster, and Alan Zweibel, *NBC's Saturday Night*, January 10, 1976 (NBC)

Outstanding Writing in a Comedy-Variety or Music Special
Jane Wagner, Lorne Michaels, Ann Elder, Christopher Guest, Earl Pomerantz, Jim Rusk, Lily Tomlin, Rod Warren, and George Yanok, "Lily Tomlin," July 25, 1975 (ABC)

Outstanding Writing in a Special Program—Drama or Comedy—Original Teleplay
James Costigan, "Eleanor and Franklin" (*ABC Theatre*) January 11 and 12, 1976 (ABC)

Outstanding Writing in a Special Program—Drama or Comedy—Adaptation
David W. Rintels, "Fear on Trial," October 2, 1975 (CBS)

Outstanding Children's Special (Tie)
"You're a Good Sport, Charlie Brown," October 28, 1975, Lee Mendelson, executive producer; Bill Melendez, producer (CBS)

Outstanding Live Sports Special
1975 World Series, October 11–22, 1975, Scotty Connal, executive producer; Roy Hammerman, producer (NBC)

Outstanding Live Sports Series
NFL Monday Night Football, Roone Arledge, executive producer; Don Ohlmeyer, producer (ABC)

Outstanding Edited Sports Special (Tie)
"XII Winter Olympic Games," February 4–15, 1976, Roone Arledge, executive producer; Chuck Howard, Don Ohlmeyer, Geoff Mason, Chet Forte, Bob Goodrich, Ellie Riger, Brice Weisman, Doug Wilson, and John Wilcox, producers (ABC)

Outstanding Edited Sports Series
ABC's Wide World of Sports, Roone Arledge, executive producer; Doug Wilson, Chet Forte, Ned Steckel, Brice Weisman, Terry Jastrow, Bob Goodrich, John Martin, Dennis Lewin, Chuck Howard, and Don Ohlmeyer, producers (ABC)

Outstanding Sports Personality
Jim McKay, "ABC's XII Winter Olympics" (*ABC's Wide World of Sports*) (ABC)

The National Award for Community Service
"Forgotten Children," WBBM-TV, Chicago, IL

Special Classification of Outstanding Program and Individual Achievement
Bicentennial Minute , Bob Markell, executive producer; Gareth Davies and Paul Waigner, producers (CBS)
The Tonight Show Starring Johnny Carson, Fred De Cordova, producer; Johnny Carson, star (NBC)
Ann Marcus, Jerry Adelman, and Daniel Gregory Browne, writers (*Mary Hartman, Mary Hartman*) (Syndicated)

Outstanding Individual Achievement in Sports Programming
Andy Sidaris, Don Ohlmeyer, Roger Goodman, Larry Kamm, Ronnie Hawkins, and Ralph Mellanby, directors, "XII Winter Olympic Games," February 4–15, 1976 (ABC)

THE CREATIVE ARTS AWARDS
Presented May 15, 1976

Outstanding Achievement in Choreography
Tony Charmoli, "Gypsy in My Soul," January 20, 1976 (CBS)

Outstanding Achievement in Music Composition for a Series
Alex North, *Rich Man, Poor Man,* March 15, 1976 (ABC)

Outstanding Achievement in Music Composition for a Special
Jerry Goldsmith, "Babe," October 23, 1975 (CBS)

Outstanding Achievement in Music Direction
Seiji Ozawa, "Central Park in the Dark/A Hero's Life" (*Evening at Symphony*) October 5, 1975 (PBS)

Outstanding Achievement in Art Direction or Scenic Design
Tom John, art director; John Wendell and Wes Laws, set decorators, *Beacon Hill* (Pilot), August 25, 1975 (CBS)

Outstanding Achievement in Art Direction or Scenic Design
Raymond Klausen, art director; Robert Checchi, set decorator, *Cher,* October 12, 1975 (CBS)

Outstanding Achievement in Art Direction or Scenic Design
Jan Scott, art director; Antony Mondello, set decorator, "Eleanor and Franklin" (*ABC Theatre*) January 11 and 12, 1976 (ABC)

Outstanding Achievement in Graphic Design and Title Sequences
Norman Sunshine, "Addie and the King of Hearts," January 25, 1976 (CBS)

Outstanding Achievement in Costume Design for a Drama Special
Joe I. Tompkins, "Eleanor and Franklin" (*ABC Theatre*) January 11 and 12, 1976 (ABC)

Outstanding Achievement in Costume Design for Music-Variety
Bob Mackie, "Mitzi . . . Roarin' in the 20's," March 14, 1976 (CBS)

Outstanding Achievement in Costume Design for a Drama or Comedy Series
Jane Robinson and Jill Silverside, "Recovery," (*Great Performances—Jennie: Lady Randolph Churchill*) October 22, 1975 (PBS)

Outstanding Achievement in Makeup
Del Armstrong and Mike Westmore, "Eleanor and Franklin" (*ABC Theatre*) January 11 and 12, 1976 (ABC)

Outstanding Achievement in Cinematography for Entertainment Programming for a Series
Harry L. Wolf, A.S.C., "Keep Your Eye on the Sparrow" (*Baretta*) April 9, 1975 (ABC)

Outstanding Achievement in Cinematography for Entertainment Programming for a Special
Paul Lohmann and Edward R. Brown, Sr., "Eleanor and Franklin" (*ABC Theatre*) January 11 and 12, 1976 (ABC)

Outstanding Film Editing for Entertainment Programming for a Series
Stanford Tischler and Fred W. Berger, "Welcome to Korea" (*M*A*S*H*) September 12, 1975 (CBS)

Outstanding Film Editing for Entertainment Programming for a Series
Samuel E. Beetley, A.C.E. and Ken Zemke, "The Quality of Mercy" (*Medical Story*) January 8, 1976 (NBC)

Outstanding Film Editing for Entertainment Programming for a Special
Michael Kahn, "Eleanor and Franklin" (*ABC Theatre*) January 11 and 12, 1976 (ABC)

Outstanding Achievement in Film Sound Editing
Douglas H. Grindstaff, Al Kajita, Marvin I. Kosberg, Hans Newman, Leon Selditz, Dick Friedman, Stan Gilbert, Hank Salerno, Larry Singer, and William Andrews, "The Quality of Mercy" (*Medical Story*) January 8, 1976 (NBC)

Outstanding Achievement in Film Sound Editing
Charles L. Campbell, Larry Neiman, Colin Mouat, Larry Carow, Don Warner, John Singleton, Tom McMullen, Joseph Divitale, Carl Kress, John Kline, and John Hanley, "The Night That Panicked America" (*The ABC Friday Night Movie*) October 31, 1975 (ABC)

Outstanding Achievement in Film Sound Mixing
Don Bassman and Don Johnson, "Eleanor and Franklin" (*ABC Theatre*) January 11 and 12, 1976 (ABC)

Outstanding Achievement in Tape Sound Mixing
Dave Williams, "Anniversary Show" (*The Tonight Show Starring Johnny Carson*) October 1, 1975 (NBC)

Outstanding Achievement in Video Tape Editing for a Series
Girish Bhargava and Manford Schorn, *The Adams Chronicles,* February 3, 1976 (PBS)

Outstanding Achievement in Video Tape Editing for a Special
Nick V. Giordano, "Alice Cooper—The Nightmare" (*Wide World: In Concert*) April 25, 1975 (ABC)

Outstanding Achievement in Technical Direction and Electronic Camerawork
Leonard Chumbley, technical director; Walter Edel, John Feher, Steve Zink, cameramen, *The Adams Chronicles,* February 3, 1976 (PBS)

Outstanding Achievement in Lighting Direction (Tie)
William Klages and Lon Stucky, "Mitzi and a Hundred Guys," March 24, 1975 (CBS)
John Freschi, "Mitzi . . . Roarin' in the 20's," March 14, 1976 (CBS)

Outstanding Achievement in Special Musical Material
Ken Welch, Mitzie Welch, and Artie Malvin, "Cinderella Gets It On" (*The Carol Burnett Show*) November 29, 1975 (CBS)

Outstanding Achievement in Any Area of Creative Technical Crafts
Jean Burt Reilly and Billie Laughridge, hairstylists, "Eleanor and Franklin" (*ABC Theatre*) January 11 and 12, 1976 (ABC)
Donald Sahlin, Kermit Love, Caroly Wilcox, John Lovelady and Rollie Krewson, costumes and props for the Muppets, *Sesame Street,* April 25, 1975 (PBS)

Outstanding Individual Achievement in Daytime Programming
Rene Lagler, art director; Richard Harvey, set decorator, *Dinah!* (Syndicated)

Outstanding Individual Achievement in Sports Programming
Jeff Cohan, Joe Aceti, John Delisa, Lou Frederick, Jack Gallivan, Jim Jennett, Carol Lehti, Howard Shapiro, Katsumi Aseada, John Fernandez, Peter Fritz, Eddie C. Joseph, Ken Klingbeil, Leo Stephan, Ted Summers, Michael Wenig, Ron Ackerman, Michael Bonifazio, Barbara Bowman, Charlie Burnham, John Croak, Charles Gardner, Marvin Gench, Victor Gonzales, Jakob Hierl, Nick Mazur, Ed McCarthy, Alex Moskovic, Arthur Nace, Lou Rende, Erskin Roberts, Merritt Roesser, Arthur Volk, Roger Haenelt, Curt Brand, Phil Mollica, George Boettcher, and Herb Ohlandt, video tape editors, "XII Winter Olympic Games," February 4–15, 1976 (ABC)
Dick Roes, Jack Kelly, Bill Sandreuter, Frank Bailey, and Jack Kestenbaum, tape sound mixers, "XII Winter Olympic Games," February 4–15, 1976 (ABC)

Outstanding Achievement in Religious Programming
Joseph J. H. Vadala, cinematographer, "A Determining Force," November 30, 1975 (NBC)

Outstanding Individual Achievement in Children's Programming
Bud Nolan and Jim Cookman, film-sound editors, "Bound for Freedom," March 7, 1976 (NBC)

SPECIAL AWARDS

Outstanding Achievement in Engineering Development
Sony Corporation for the U-matic video-cassette concept
Eastman Kodak for the development of Eastman Ektachrome video-news film

DAYTIME PROGRAM AND INDIVIDUAL ACHIEVEMENTS

Presented May 11, 1976

Outstanding Daytime Drama Series
Another World, Paul Rauch, executive producer; Joe Rothenberger and Mary S. Bonner, producers (NBC)

Outstanding Daytime Drama Special
"First Ladies' Diaries: Edith Wilson," January 20, 1976, Jeff Young, producer (NBC)

Outstanding Daytime Game or Audience Participation Show
The $20,000 Pyramid, Bob Stewart, executive producer; Anne Marie Schmitt, producer (ABC)

Outstanding Daytime Talk, Service or Variety Series
Dinah!, Henry Jaffe and Carolyn Raskin, executive producers; Fred Tatashore, producer (Syndicated)

Outstanding Entertainment Children's Series
Big Blue Marble, Henry Fownes, producer (Syndicated)

Outstanding Entertainment Children's Special
"Danny Kaye's Look-in at the Metropolitan Opera" (*The CBS Festival of Lively Arts for Young People*) April 27, 1975, Sylvia Fine, executive producer; Bernard Rothman, Jack Wohl, and Herbert Bonis, producers (CBS)

Outstanding Informational Children's Series
Go, George A. Heinemann, executive producer; Rift Fournier, J. Philip Miller, William W. Lewis, and Joan Bender, producers (NBC)

Outstanding Informational Children's Special
"Happy Anniversary, Charlie Brown," January 9, 1976, Lee Mendelson and Warren Lockhart, producers (CBS)

Outstanding Instructional Children's Programming—Series and Specials
Grammar Rock, Thomas G. Yohe, executive producer; Radford Stone, producer (ABC)

Outstanding Actor in a Daytime Drama Series
Larry Haines (*Search for Tomorrow*) (CBS)

Outstanding Actor in a Daytime Drama Special
Gerald Gordon, "First Ladies' Diaries: Rachel Jackson," April 18, 1975 (NBC)
James Luisi, "First Ladies' Diaries: Martha Washington," October 23, 1975 (NBC)

Outstanding Actress in a Daytime Drama Series
Helen Gallagher (*Ryan's Hope*) (ABC)

Outstanding Actress in a Daytime Drama Special
Elizabeth Hubbard, "First Ladies' Diaries: Edith Wilson," January 20, 1976 (NBC)

Outstanding Host or Hostess in a Game or Audience Participation Show
Allen Ludden (*Password*) (ABC)

Outstanding Host or Hostess in a Talk, Service or Variety Series
Dinah Shore (*Dinah!*) (Syndicated)

Outstanding Individual Director for a Daytime Drama Series
David Pressman, *One Life to Live,* January 26, 1976 (ABC)

Outstanding Individual Director for a Daytime Special Program
Nicholas Havinga, "First Ladies' Diaries: Edith Wilson," January 20, 1976 (NBC)

Outstanding Individual Director for a Game or Audience Participation Show
Mike Gargiulo, *The $20,000 Pyramid,* February 18, 1976 (ABC)

Outstanding Individual Director for a Daytime Variety Program
Glen Swanson, "Dinah Salutes Tony Orlando and Dawn on Their 5th Anniversary" (*Dinah!*) (Syndicated)

Outstanding Writing for a Daytime Drama Series
William J. Bell, Kay Lenard, Pat Falken Smith, Bill Rega, Margaret Stewart, Sheri Anderson, and Wanda Coleman, *Days of Our Lives* (NBC)

Outstanding Writing for a Daytime Special Program
Audrey Davis Levin, "First Ladies' Diaries: Edith Wilson," January 20, 1976 (NBC)

Outstanding Individual Achievement in Daytime Programming
No winner

Outstanding Individual Achievement in Children's Programming
The Muppets; Jim Henson, Frank Oz, Jerry Nelson, Carroll Spinney, and Richard Hunt, performers, *Sesame Street,* April 25, 1975 (PBS)

1976–1977
Presented September 11, 1977

Outstanding Continuing Performance by a Supporting Actor in a Comedy Series
Gary Burghoff (*M*A*S*H*) (CBS)

Outstanding Continuing Performance by a Supporting Actress in a Comedy Series
Mary Kay Place (*Mary Hartman, Mary Hartman*) (Syndicated)

Outstanding Continuing Performance by a Supporting Actor in a Drama Series
Gary Frank (*Family*) (ABC)

Outstanding Continuing Performance by a Supporting Actress in a Drama Series
Kristy McNichol (*Family*) (ABC)

Outstanding Children's Special
"Ballet Shoes," Parts 1 and 2 (*Piccadilly Circus*) December 27 and 28, 1976, John McRae and Joan Sullivan, producers (PBS)

Outstanding Writing in a Comedy Series
Allan Burns, James L. Brooks, Ed Weinberger, Stan Daniels, David Lloyd, Bob Ellison, "The Final Show" (*The Mary Tyler Moore Show*) March 19, 1977, (CBS)

Outstanding Directing in a Comedy Series
Alan Alda, "Dear Sigmund" (*M*A*S*H*) November 9, 1976 (CBS)

Outstanding Lead Actor for a Single Appearance in a Drama or Comedy Series
Louis Gossett, Jr., *Roots*—Part 2, January 24, 1977 (ABC)

Outstanding Lead Actress for a Single Appearance in a Drama or Comedy Series
Beulah Bondi, "The Pony Cart" (*The Waltons*) December 2, 1976 (CBS)

Outstanding Writing in a Comedy-Variety or Music Series
Anne Beatts, Dan Aykroyd, Al Franken, Tom Davis, James Downey, Lorne Michaels, Marilyn Suzanne Miller, Michael O'Donoghue, Herb Sargent, Tom Schiller, Rosie Shuster, Alan Zweibel, John Belushi, and Bill Murray, *NBC's Saturday Night,* March 12, 1977 (NBC)

Outstanding Continuing or Single Performance by a Supporting Actor in Variety or Music
Tim Conway (*The Carol Burnett Show*) (CBS)

Outstanding Continuing or Single Performance by a Supporting Actress in Variety or Music
Rita Moreno (*The Muppet Show*) (Syndicated)

Outstanding Classical Program in the Performing Arts
American Ballet Theatre, "Swan Lake" (*Great Performances—Live from Lincoln Center*) June 30, 1976, John Goberman, producer (PBS)

Outstanding Performance by a Supporting Actor in a Comedy or Drama Special
Burgess Meredith, "Tail Gunner Joe" (*The Big Event*) February 6, 1977 (NBC)

Outstanding Performance by a Supporting Actress in a Comedy or Drama Special
Diana Hyland, "The Boy in the Plastic Bubble" (*The ABC Friday Night Movie*) November 12, 1976 (ABC)

Outstanding Directing in a Special Program—Drama or Comedy
Daniel Petrie, "Eleanor and Franklin: The White House Years" (*ABC Theatre*) March 13, 1977 (ABC)

Outstanding Writing in a Special Program—Drama or Comedy—Adaptation
Stewart Stern, "Sybil" (*The Big Event*) November 14 and 15, 1976 (NBC)

Outstanding Writing in a Special Program—Drama or Comedy—Original Teleplay
Lane Slate, "Tail Gunner Joe" (*The Big Event*) February 6, 1977 (NBC)

Outstanding Lead Actor in a Drama or Comedy Special
Ed Flanders, as Harry S Truman, "Plain Speaking," October 6, 1976 (PBS)

Outstanding Lead Actress in a Drama or Comedy Special
Sally Field, "Sybil" (*The Big Event*) November 14 and 15, 1976 (NBC)

Outstanding Writing in a Drama Series
Ernest Kinoy and William Blinn, *Roots*—Part 2, January 24, 1977 (ABC)

Outstanding Directing in a Drama Series
David Green, *Roots*—Part 1, January 23, 1977 (ABC)

Outstanding Single Performance by a Supporting Actor in a Comedy or Drama Series
Edward Asner, *Roots*—Part 1, January 23, 1977 (ABC)

Outstanding Single Performance by a Supporting Actress in a Comedy or Drama Series
Olivia Cole, *Roots*—Part 8, January 30, 1977 (ABC)

Special Classification of Outstanding Program Achievement
The Tonight Show Starring Johnny Carson, Fred De Cordova, producer; Johnny Carson, star (NBC)

Outstanding Achievement in Coverage of Special Events—Individual
John C. Moffitt, director, "The 28th Annual Emmy Awards," May 17, 1976 (ABC)

Outstanding Lead Actor in a Comedy Series
Carroll O'Connor (*All in the Family*) (CBS)

Outstanding Lead Actress in a Comedy Series
Beatrice Arthur (*Maude*) (CBS)

Outstanding Comedy Series
The Mary Tyler Moore Show, Allan Burns, and James L. Brooks, executive producers; Ed Weinberger, Stan Daniels, producers (CBS)

Outstanding Writing in a Comedy-Variety or Music Special
Alan Buz Kohan and Ted Strauss, "America Salutes Richard Rodgers: The Sound of His Music," December 9, 1976 (CBS)

Outstanding Directing in a Comedy-Variety or Music Special
Dwight Hemion, "America Salutes Richard Rodgers: The Sound of His Music" December 9, 1976 (CBS)

Outstanding Special—Comedy-Variety or Music
"The Barry Manilow Special," March 2, 1977, Miles Lourie, executive producer; Steve Binder, producer; Barry Manilow, star (ABC)

Outstanding Directing in a Comedy-Variety or Music Series
Dave Powers, *The Carol Burnett Show*, February 12, 1977 (CBS)

Outstanding Comedy-Variety or Music Series
Van Dyke and Company, Byron Paul, executive producer; Allan Blye, and Bob Einstein, producers; Dick Van Dyke, star (NBC)

Outstanding Lead Actor in a Limited Series
Christopher Plummer, "The Moneychangers" (*NBC World Premiere: The Big Event*) (NBC)

Outstanding Lead Actress in a Limited Series
Patty Duke Astin (*NBC's Best Seller—Captains and the Kings*) (NBC)

Outstanding Limited Series
"Roots" (*ABC Novel for Television*) David L. Wolper, executive producer; Stan Margulies, producer (ABC)

Outstanding Lead Actor in a Drama Series
James Garner (*The Rockford Files*) (NBC)

Outstanding Lead Actress in a Drama Series
Lindsay Wagner (*The Bionic Woman*) (ABC)

Outstanding Drama Series
Masterpiece Theatre—Upstairs, Downstairs, John Hawkesworth and Joan Sullivan, producers (PBS)

Outstanding Special—Drama or Comedy (Tie)
"Eleanor and Franklin: The White House Years" (*ABC Theatre*) March 13, 1977, David Susskind, executive producer; Harry R. Sherman, producer (ABC)

"Sybil" (*NBC World Premiere Movie—The Big Event*) November 14 and 15, 1976, Peter Dunne, and Philip Capice, executive producers; Jacqueline Babbin, producer (NBC)

THE CREATIVE ARTS AWARDS

Outstanding Achievement in Music Composition for a Series (Dramatic Underscore)
Quincy Jones and Gerald Fried, *Roots*—Part 1, January 23, 1977 (ABC)

Outstanding Achievement in Music Composition for a Special (Dramatic Underscore)
Leonard Rosenman, Alan Bergman, and Marilyn Bergman, "Sybil" (*The Big Event*) November 14 and 15, 1976 (NBC)

Outstanding Achievement in Music Direction
Ian Fraser, "America Salutes Richard Rodgers: The Sound of His Music," December 9, 1976 (CBS)

Outstanding Cinematography in Entertainment Programming for a Series
Ric Waite, *NBC's Best Seller—Captains and the Kings*—Chapter 1, September 30, 1976 (NBC)

Outstanding Cinematography in Entertainment Programming for a Special
William Butler, "Raid on Entebbe" (*The Big Event*) January 9, 1977 (NBC)

Outstanding Film Editing in a Comedy Series
Douglas Hines, A.C.E., "Murray Can't Lose" (*The Mary Tyler Moore Show*) November 27, 1976 (CBS)

Outstanding Film Editing in a Drama Series
Neil Travis, *Roots*—Part 1, January 23, 1977 (ABC)

Outstanding Film Editing for a Special
Rita Roland, A.C.E. and Michael S. McLean, A.C.E., "Eleanor and Franklin: The White House Years" (*ABC Theatre*) March 13, 1977 (ABC)

Outstanding Achievement in Film Sound Editing for a Series
Larry Carow, Larry Neiman, Don Warner, Colin Mouat, George Fredrick, Dave Pettijohn, and Paul Bruce Richardson, *Roots*—Part 2, January 24, 1977 (ABC)

Outstanding Achievement in Film Sound Editing for a Special
Bernard F. Pincus, Milton C. Burrow, Gene Eliot, Don Ernst, Tony Garber, Don V. Isaacs, Larry Kaufman, William L. Manger, A. David Marshall, Richard Oswald, Edward L. Sandlin, and Russ Tinsley, "Raid on Entebbe" (*The Big Event*) January 9, 1977 (NBC)

Outstanding Achievement in Film Sound Mixing
Alan Bernard, George E. Porter, Eddie J. Nelson, and Robert L. Harman, "The Savage Bees" (*NBC Monday Night at the Movies*) November 22, 1976 (NBC)

Outstanding Art Direction or Scenic Design for a Comedy Series
Thomas E. Azzari, art director, "The Really Longest Day" (*Fish*) February 5, 1977 (ABC)

Outstanding Art Direction or Scenic Design for a Drama Series
Tim Harvey, scenic designer, *The Pallisers*—Episode 1, January 24, 1977 (PBS)

Outstanding Art Direction or Scenic Design for a Comedy-Variety or Music Series
Romain Johnston, art director, *The Mac Davis Show,* May 17, 1976 (NBC)

Outstanding Art Direction or Scenic Design for a Dramatic Special
Jan Scott, art director; Anne D. McCulley, set decorator, "Eleanor and Franklin: The White House Years" (*ABC Theatre*) March 13, 1977 (ABC)

Outstanding Art Direction or Scenic Design for a Comedy-Variety or Music Special
Robert Kelly, art director, "America Salutes Richard Rodgers: The Sound of His Music," December 9, 1976 (CBS)

Outstanding Achievement in Graphic Design and Title Sequences
Eytan Keller and Stu Bernstein, "Bell Telephone Jubilee," March 26, 1976 (NBC)

Outstanding Achievement in Costume Design for a Drama Special
Joe I. Tompkins, "Eleanor and Franklin: The White House Years" (*ABC Theatre*) March 13, 1977 (ABC)

Outstanding Achievement in Costume Design for Music-Variety
Jan Skalicky, "The Barber of Seville"—*Live from Lincoln Center Great Performances,* November 3, 1976 (PBS)

Outstanding Achievement in Costume Design for a Drama or Comedy Series
Raymond Hughes, *The Pallisers*—Episode 1, January 24, 1977 (PBS)

Outstanding Achievement in Makeup
Ken Chase, makeup design; Joe DiBella, makeup artist, "Eleanor and Franklin: The White House Years" (*ABC Theatre*) March 13, 1977 (ABC)

Outstanding Achievement in Choreography
Ron Field, "America Salutes Richard Rodgers: The Sound of His Music," December 9, 1976 (CBS)

Outstanding Achievement in Lighting Direction
William M. Klages and Peter Edwards, "The Dorothy Hamill Special," November 17, 1976 (ABC)

Outstanding Achievement in Tape Sound Mixing
Doug Nelson, "John Denver and Friend," March 29, 1976 (ABC)

Outstanding Achievement in Video Tape Editing for a Series
Roy Stewart, "The War Widow" (*Visions*) October 28, 1976 (PBS)

Outstanding Achievement in Video Tape Editing for a Special
Gary H. Anderson, "American Bandstand's 25th Anniversary," February 4, 1977 (ABC)

Outstanding Achievement in Technical Direction and Electronic Camerawork
Karl Messerschmidt, technical director; Jon Olson, Bruce Gray, John Gutierrez, Jim Dodge, and Wayne McDonald, cameramen, "Doug Henning's World of Magic," December 23, 1976 (NBC)

Outstanding Individual Achievement in Children's Programming
Jean De Joux and Elizabeth Savel, videoanimation, "Peter Pan" (*Hallmark Hall of Fame—The Big Event*) December 12, 1976 (NBC)

Outstanding Individual Achievement in Any Area of Creative Technical Crafts
Emma Di Vittorio and Vivienne Walker, hairstylists, "Eleanor and Franklin: The White House Years" (*ABC Theatre*) March 13, 1977 (ABC)

Special Classification of Outstanding Individual Achievement
Allen Brewster, Bob Roethle, William Lorenz, Manuel Martinez, Ron Fleury, Mike Welch, Jerry Burling, Walter Balderson, Chuck Droege, video-tape editing, "The First Fifty Years" (*The Big Event*) November 21, 1976 (NBC)

Outstanding Achievement in Coverage of Special Events—Individuals
Brian C. Bartholomew and Keaton S. Walker, art directors, "The 28th Annual Emmy Awards," May 17, 1976 (ABC)

1977–1978
Presented September 17, 1978

Outstanding Comedy Series
All in the Family, Mort Lachman, executive producer; Milt Josefsberg, producer (CBS)

Outstanding Writing in a Comedy Series
Bob Weiskopf and Bob Schiller, teleplay; Barry Harman and Harve Brosten, story, "Cousin Liz" (*All in the Family*) October 9, 1977 (CBS)

Outstanding Directing in a Comedy Series
Paul Bogart, "Edith's 50th Birthday" (*All in the Family*) October 16, 1977 (CBS)

Outstanding Continuing Performance by a Supporting Actor in a Comedy Series
Rob Reiner (*All in the Family*) (CBS)

Outstanding Continuing Performance by a Supporting Actress in a Comedy Series
Julie Kavner (*Rhoda*) (CBS)

Outstanding Lead Actress in a Comedy Series
Jean Stapleton (*All in the Family*) (CBS)

Outstanding Lead Actor in a Comedy Series
Carroll O'Connor (*All in the Family*) (CBS)

Outstanding Drama Series
The Rockford Files, Meta Rosenberg, executive producer; Stephen J. Cannell, supervising producer; David Chase and Charles F. Johnson, producers (NBC)

Outstanding Writing in a Drama Series
Gerald Green, *Holocaust,* April 16–19, 1978 (NBC)

Outstanding Directing in a Drama Series
Marvin J. Chomsky, *Holocaust,* April 16–19, 1978 (NBC)

Outstanding Continuing Performance by a Supporting Actor in a Drama Series
Robert Vaughn, *Washington: Behind Closed Doors* (ABC)

Outstanding Continuing Performance by a Supporting Actress in a Drama Series
Nancy Marchand (*Lou Grant*) (CBS)

Outstanding Lead Actress in a Drama Series
Sada Thompson (*Family*) (ABC)

Outstanding Lead Actor in a Drama Series
Edward Asner (*Lou Grant*) (CBS)

Outstanding Children's Special
"Halloween is Grinch Night," October 29, 1977, David H. DePatie, Friz Freleng, executive producers; Ted Geisel, producer (ABC)

Special Classification of Outstanding Program Achievement
The Tonight Show Starring Johnny Carson, Fred De Cordova, producer; Johnny Carson, star (NBC)

Outstanding Lead Actress in a Limited Series
Meryl Streep (*Holocaust*) (NBC)

Outstanding Lead Actor in a Limited Series
Michael Moriarty (*Holocaust*) (NBC)

Outstanding Limited Series
Holocaust, Herbert Brodkin, executive producer; Robert Berger, producer (NBC)

Outstanding Informational Series
The Body Human, Thomas W. Moore, executive producer; Alfred R. Kelman, producer (CBS)

Outstanding Continuing or Single Performance by a Supporting Actor in Variety or Music
Tim Conway (*The Carol Burnett Show*) (CBS)

Outstanding Continuing or Single Performance by a Supporting Actress in Variety or Music
Gilda Radner (*NBC's Saturday Night Live*) (NBC)

Outstanding Writing in a Comedy-Variety or Music Series
Ed Simmons, Roger Beatty, Rick Hawkins, Liz Sage, Robert Illes, James Stein, Franelle Silver, Larry Siegel, Tim Conway, Bill Richmond, Gene Perret, Dick Clair, and Jenna McMahon, *The Carol Burnett Show,* March 5, 1978 (CBS)

Outstanding Directing in a Comedy-Variety or Music Series
Dave Powers, *The Carol Burnett Show,* March 5, 1978 (CBS)

Outstanding Comedy-Variety or Music Series
The Muppet Show, David Lazer, executive producer; Jim Henson, producer; The Muppets—Frank Oz, Jerry Nelson, Richard Hunt, Dave Goelz; and Jim Henson—stars (Syndicated)

Outstanding Classical Program in the Performing Arts
"American Ballet Theatre's 'Giselle' " (*Great Performances—Live from Lincoln Center*) June 2, 1977, John Goberman, producer (PBS)

Outstanding Single Performance by a Supporting Actress in a Comedy or Drama Series
Blanche Baker, *Holocaust*—Part I, April 16, 1978 (NBC)

Outstanding Single Performance by a Supporting Actor in a Comedy or Drama Series
Ricardo Montalban, *How the West Was Won*—Part II, February 19, 1978 (ABC)

Outstanding Lead Actress for a Single Appearance in a Drama or Comedy Series
Rita Moreno, "The Paper Palace" (*The Rockford Files*) January 20, 1978 (NBC)

Outstanding Lead Actor for a Single Appearance in a Drama or Comedy Series
Barnard Hughes, "Judge" (*Lou Grant*) November 15, 1977 (CBS)

First Annual ATAS Governors' Award
William S. Paley, chairman of the board, CBS

Outstanding Informational Special
"The Great Whales" (*National Geographic*) February 16, 1978, Thomas Skinner, and Dennis B. Kane, executive producers; Nicolas Noxon, producer (PBS)

Outstanding Writing in a Comedy-Variety or Music Special
Lorne Michaels, Paul Simon, Chevy Chase, Tom Davis, Al Franken, Charles Grodin, Lily Tomlin, and Alan Zweibel, "The Paul Simon Special," December 8, 1977 (NBC)

Outstanding Directing in a Comedy-Variety or Music Special
Dwight Hemion, "The Sentry Collection Presents Ben Vereen—His Roots," March 2, 1978 (ABC)

Outstanding Special—Comedy-Variety or Music
"Bette Midler—Ol' Red Hair Is Back," December 7, 1977, Aaron Russo, executive producer; Gary Smith and Dwight Hemion, producers; Bette Midler, star (NBC)

Outstanding Writing in a Special Program—Drama or Comedy—Adaptation
Caryl Ledner, "Mary White," November 18, 1978 (ABC)

Outstanding Writing in a Special Program—Drama or Comedy—Original Teleplay
George Rubino, "The Last Tenant," June 25, 1978 (ABC)

Outstanding Directing in a Special Program—Drama or Comedy
David Lowell Rich, "The Defection of Simas Kudirka," January 23, 1978 (CBS)

Outstanding Performance by a Supporting Actress in a Drama or Comedy Special
Eva La Gallienne, "The Royal Family," November 9, 1977 (PBS)

Outstanding Performance by a Supporting Actor in a Comedy or Drama Special
Howard Da Silva, "Verna: USO Girl" (*Great Performances*) January 25, 1978 (PBS)

Outstanding Lead Actor in a Drama or Comedy Special
Fred Astaire, "A Family Upside Down," April 9, 1978 (NBC)

Outstanding Lead Actress in a Drama or Comedy Special

Joanne Woodward, "See How She Runs" (*GE Theater*) February 1, 1978 (CBS)

Outstanding Special—Drama or Comedy

"The Gathering," December 4, 1977, Joseph Barbera, executive producer; Harry R. Sherman, producer (ABC)

Becoming a Contestant on Game Shows

To become a contestant on a game show you need good timing, luck, and a vibrant personality. If you fall short in any one of these three, you probably won't make it as a contestant on a show, but you certainly will have a lot of fun trying.

Good Timing

Game show producers are partial to out-of-towners. They feel that people from Little Rock, Pittsburgh, or Durham provide a more interesting mix of styles of dress, mannerisms, and speech. This kind of variety looks better, and sounds better, too. Consequently, out-of-towners have a better chance of getting on game shows than do local people.

Good timing has to do with your travel plans. If you know when you are going to be in Los Angeles or New York, select the show you want to try for and then contact them at least two months in advance.

This much lead time will allow you to adjust your schedule to meet the show's taping schedule. It is important to remember that all shows tape at different times during the week if they tape at all—not only between 9 and 5, Monday through Friday, as you might imagine. Some tape on weekends, others every other week; it depends on how the show is set up. However, you really don't have to worry about taping sessions if you give them enough notice to work you into their schedule.

Luck

Luck, as it applies to game shows, involves the season you pick for your vacation and the number of people competing with you for a contestant spot. If you plan on visiting Los Angeles or New York in the summer time, especially in late August, or on major holidays, you may find that the shows aren't taping at all.

If you really want to be on a game show, plan everything around your interview date. Your vacation will go better for you, and you will be less harried. Expect competition. Many people will have the same idea as you; so be ready to be up against dozens of folks from all parts of the country.

Vibrant Personality

Most game shows test you by having you play the game as if you were a real contestant. During your period of play, the game-show people watch for a vibrant personality. Do you look like you're having

fun playing the game? It's not a good idea to fake exuberance, because it looks fake. If you are naturally enthusiastic and spirited at games, you will probably do just fine.

Moreover, on such game shows as the *$20,000 Pyramid,* it is important to have a command of English and a broad base of knowledge. Don't try out for a game show that tests skills and knowledge you are weak in. There are plenty of shows around, so choose one for which you're qualified. You will make a better showing both for the producer and for yourself when you know you are right for the game.

About Game Show People

You will find game show people friendly and most cooperative. If they could get everyone on the show, they would. The person you will deal with first is the contestant coordinator. He will explain how the interview will run—either a test or game playing, or both—and will help you do your best, with hints and encouragement. And don't be afraid to ask the contestant coordinator questions if something is unclear. It's a new experience and you are bound to be a little nervous and confused.

Other Important Points

The Federal Government strictly regulates game shows so you can be sure everything is legal.

Prospective contestants must be at least 18 years old and not a member of any professional performing union.

When it comes to expenses, travel and otherwise, game shows do not reimburse prospective contestants or contestants. So if you are thinking that trying out for a game show will be a great way to pay for your vacation, you are wrong. It's all for the fun of it—but you *could* be selected as a contestant and you could win.

Also, most game shows have rules governing the number of shows a person can be a contestant on. For instance, Ralph Edwards Productions allows a person to be a contestant on two shows in a lifetime and those two shows must be aired at least one year apart.

When writing for an appointment, use the title of the show you wish to try out for in the address. For example:

> Dating Game
> Chuck Barris Productions
> 6430 Sunset Blvd.
> Hollywood, CA 90028

About the Shows Listed Here

Only those game shows now in production are shown. Those you see on TV that do not appear on the following list are, in all probability, reruns.

CHUCK BARRIS PRODUCTIONS
6430 Sunset Blvd.
Hollywood, CA 90028
(213) 469-9080

Dating Game (Syndicated)
Prospective contestants either call or write for an appointment. Out-of-towners who qualify will be given a taping date, if available, during their stay in Los Angeles.

$1.98 Beauty Show (Syndicated)
Prospective contestants may call or write for an appointment. Out-of-towners who qualify will be given a taping date, if available, during their stay in Los Angeles.

The Gong Show (NBC)
(213) 466-9153
Prospective contestants either call or write for an audition date. Out-of-towners who pass the audition will be given a taping date, if available, during their stay in Los Angeles.

The Newlywed Game (Syndicated)
Prospective contestants either call or write for an appointment. The producers are looking for couples who relate well and often engage in spirited conversations. Out-of-towners who qualify will be given a taping date, if available, during their stay in Los Angeles.

BARRY & ENRIGHT PRODUCTIONS
1888 Century Park East
Los Angeles, CA 90067
(213) 277-3414

The Joker's Wild (Syndicated)
P.O. Box 9163
Los Angeles, CA 90048
(213) 277-9163
Prospective contestants may write or phone for an appointment. A general-knowledge test is given during the interview. Out-of-towners who qualify will be given a taping date, if available, during their stay in Los Angeles.

Tic Tac Dough (Syndicated)
(Same as *The Joker's Wild*)
Prospective contestants follow the same procedure as used for *The Joker's Wild*.

RALPH EDWARDS PRODUCTIONS
1717 N. Highland Ave.
Hollywood, CA 90028
(213) 462-2212

The Cross-wits (Syndicated)
Prospective contestants may call or write for an appointment. The interview consists of a written test based on the skills required in a particular game. Those who pass the test are called back for a run-through of the game under actual playing conditions. Qualifying out-of-towners will be given a taping date, if available, during their stay in the area.

Knockout (NBC)
(Same as *The Cross-wits*)

Name That Tune (Syndicated)
(Same as *The Cross-wits*)

The New Truth or Consequences (Syndicated)
(Same as *The Cross-wits*)

GOODSON-TODMAN PRODUCTIONS
6430 Sunset Blvd.
Los Angeles, CA 90028
(213) 464-4300

Card Sharks (NBC)
Prospective contestants may write or call for an appointment. Out-of-towners who qualify will be given a taping date, if available, during their stay in Los Angeles. Local residents will be notified at a later date if they qualify, and will be placed on a waiting list.

Family Feud (ABC)
Prospective contestants may write or phone for an appointment. When an appointment is granted, five members of a family (related by blood or marriage) are interviewed. During the interview a game is played. Local families will be notified approximately two weeks after the interview, if they qualify. Out-of-towners who qualify will be given a taping date, if available, during their stay in Los Angeles.

Match Game (CBS)
Prospective contestants from the Los Angeles area may call or write for an appointment. If accepted, they will be placed on a 14-month waiting list. Out-of-towners may call or write for an appointment two weeks prior to their arrival in Los Angeles. Those who qualify will be given a taping date, if available, during their stay in Los Angeles.

The Price Is Right (CBS)
CBS Television City
7800 Beverly Blvd.
Los Angeles, CA 90036
(213) 651-2345
Prospective contestants should write or call CBS in Los Angeles for tickets to *The Price Is Right*. Contestants are selected out of the audience the day of the taping.

HEATTER-QUIGLEY, INC.
Suite 103
9255 Sunset Blvd.
Los Angeles, CA 90069
(213) 278-8870

High Rollers (NBC)
Prospective contestants may call or write for an appointment. Out-of-towners should make an appointment at least two weeks prior to their arrival in Los Angeles. Those who qualify will be given a taping date, if available, during their stay in the area. Contestants are also selected from the studio audience and scheduled for testing. For tickets to the show, write:

> High Rollers
> NBC Ticket Information
> 3000 W. Alameda Ave.
> Burbank, CA 91523

Hollywood Squares (NBC)
(Same as *High Rollers*) When writing for tickets, be sure to use *Hollywood Squares* in the address.

MERV GRIFFIN PRODUCTIONS
1541 N. Vine St.
Hollywood, CA 90028
(213) 466-9751

Wheel of Fortune (NBC)
Prospective contestants may write or call for an appointment. The interview consists of a test of skills similar to those required to play the game.

Out-of-towners should make an appointment at least two weeks prior to their arrival in Los Angeles. Those who qualify will be given a taping date, if available, during their stay in the area.

BOB STEWART PRODUCTIONS
250 W. 57th St. #1730
New York, NY 10019
(212) 730-4515

$20,000 Pyramid (ABC)
Prospective contestants may write to ABC for tickets to attend a taping of the show. Contestants are chosen from the studio audience and given an appointment for testing. Those who live out of town may request an interview. The selection procedure normally requires up to six months and involves two interviews. Contestants are chosen on the basis of playing ability, enthusiasm, and presentability. For tickets write to:

> Pyramid Tickets
> ABC Guest Relations
> 1310 Ave. of the Americas
> New York, NY 10019

Pass the Buck (CBS)
(Same as daytime *$20,000 Pyramid*)
For tickets write to:

> Pass the Buck Tickets
> CBS Audience Control Center
> 524 W. 57th St.
> New York, NY 10019

Government Agencies and Regulations

Government Communication Agencies

The Board for International Broadcasting
1030 15th St. NW
Washington, DC 20005
(202) 254-8040
Chairman: Dr. John Gronouski

The Board for International Broadcasting was established by the Board for International Broadcasting Act of 1973 (87 Stat. 456), approved October 19, 1973.

An independent federal agency responsible to the President and the Congress, the Board for International Broadcasting consists of five members appointed for a term of three years by the President, with the advice and consent of the Senate. Members are selected from among Americans distinguished in the fields of foreign policy or mass communications; no more than three members may be of the same political party.

The Board is served by an executive staff recruited in accordance with appropriate Civil Service regulations.

Its function is to oversee the operations of Radio Liberty, which broadcasts to the Union of Soviet Socialist Republics, and Radio Free Europe, which broadcasts to Poland, Romania, Czechoslovakia, Hungary, and Bulgaria. The chief executive officer of Radio Liberty and Radio Free Europe, which have been under consolidated management since July 1, 1975, is an ex-officio member of the Board for International Broadcasting, participating in its activities but not voting in its determinations.

In making federal grants to Radio Liberty and Radio Free Europe, which were originally organized as nonprofit corporations, the Board is authorized to review their mission and operations and assess the quality, effectiveness, and integrity of their broadcasting within the United States; encourage the most efficient use of resources and undertake such studies as may be necessary to identify areas in which their operations may be made more efficient and economical; apply such financial procedures as it deems necessary to assure that grants are applied in accordance with the purposes for which such grants are made; develop evaluative procedures so as to assure that grants are applied in a manner not inconsistent with the broad foreign-policy objectives of the United States Government; have access to all books, documents, papers, and records of Radio Liberty and Radio Free Europe related or pertinent to federal assistance; procure specialized electronic equipment; receive donations, bequests, devises, gifts, and other forms of contributions of cash, services, and other property

from persons, corporations, foundations, and all other groups and entities both within the United States and abroad; use, sell, or otherwise dispose of such property for the carrying out of its functions; prescribe such regulations as the Board deems necessary to govern the manner in which its functions shall be carried out; report annually to the President and the Congress, summarizing its own activities and evaluating the operation of Radio Liberty and Radio Free Europe during the preceding fiscal year.

The publications of the Board for International Broadcasting include *The Board for International Broadcasting, Third Annual Report 1977* and *Second Annual Report 1975,* which are available from the Board; and *The Right to Know—Report of the Presidential Study Commission on International Radio Broadcasting,* which is available from the Superintendent of Documents, Government Printing Office, Washington, DC 20402.

For further information, write to the Program Officer.

The Defense Communications Agency
Washington, DC 20305
(202) 692-0018
Director: Lt. Gen. Lee M. Paschall, USAF

The Defense Communications Agency (DCA) was established on May 12, 1960, as an agency of the Department of Defense, under the direction, authority, and control of the Secretary of Defense. Its Director is responsible to the Secretary of Defense, through the Joint Chiefs of Staff.

DCA is organized into a headquarters with field activities, acting for the director in assigned geographical areas of responsibility. The field organization includes the White House Communications Agency, the Defense Commercial Communications Office, the Defense Communications Engineering Center, the National Communications System, the Defense Communications System Operations Center, and the Command and Control Technical Center.

The mission of the DCA is to perform system engineering for the Defense Communications System (DCS) and ensure that the DCS is planned, improved, operated, maintained, and managed effectively, efficiently, and economically to meet the long haul, point-to-point, and switched-network telecommunications requirements of the National Command Authorities (NCA), the Department of Defense, and, as authorized and directed, other governmental agencies; provide system engineering and technical support to the National Military Command System (NMCS) and the Minimum Essential Emergency Communications Network (MEECN); provide other engineering and technical support to the Worldwide Military Command and Control System (WWMCCS), as assigned; perform system architect functions for current and future Military Satellite Communications (MILSATCOM) Systems; provide analytical and automated data processing (ADP) support to the Joint Chiefs of Staff, the Secretary of Defense, and other Department of Defense components as directed and authorized; procure leased communications circuits, services, facilities, and equipment for the Department of Defense where authorized, and for other government agencies as directed by the Secretary of Defense, and initiate or process actions relating to regulatory and tariff matters, including rates for communications facilities leased by the Department of Defense.

For further information, write to the Director.

The Federal Communications Commission
1919 M St. NW
Washington, DC 20554
(202) 632-6336
Chairman: Charles Ferris

The Federal Communications Commission (FCC) regulates interstate and foreign communications by radio, television, wire, and cable. It is responsible for the orderly development and operation of broadcast services and the provision of rapid, efficient nationwide and worldwide telephone and telegraph services at reasonable rates. This also includes the promotion of safety of life and property through radio and the use of radio and television facilities to strengthen the national defense.

The Federal Communications Commission was created by the Communications Act of 1934 (48 Stat. 1064; 15 U.S.C. 21; 47 U.S.C. 35, 151-609) to regulate interstate and foreign communications by wire and radio in the public interest. It was assigned additional regulatory jurisdiction under the provisions of the Communications Satellite Act of 1962 (76 Stat. 419; 47 U.S.C. 701-744). The scope of the regulation includes radio and television broadcasting; telephone, telegraph, and cable television operation; two-way radio and radio operators; and satellite communication.

In administering the programs necessary to carry out its regulatory responsibility the commission is assisted by a general counsel, who in addition to his typical duties exercises exclusive control of court appeals involving broadcast matters, an executive director, a chief engineer, a chief of plans and policy, and the chiefs of five bureaus, to whom has been delegated certain licensing and grant authority.

To assist the commission in exercising its responsibility in the adjudicatory process, there is a review board to review initial decisions and write decisions and an Office of Opinions and Review to assist the commission and individual commissioners in the disposition of matters arising in cases of adjudication (as defined in the Administrative Procedure Act) which have been designated for hearing. Also, there is a corps of administrative law Judges, qualified and appointed pursuant to the requirements of the Administrative Procedure Act, who conduct evidentiary adjudicatory hearings and write initial decisions.

The FCC maintains separate bureaus to oversee the regulatory program for the following activities:

Broadcast

The Broadcast Bureau administers the regulatory program for the following broadcast services: standard (AM), frequency modulation (FM), television (TV), instructional TV fixed (ITFS), experimental, international shortwave, and related auxiliary services. It issues construction permits, operating licenses, and renewals or transfers of licenses. It oversees compliance by broadcasters with statutes and commission policies.

Cable Television

Cable-television-system operators must obtain a certificate of compliance from the commission before commencing operation or adding additional television broadcast signals to existing operations. The Cable Television Bureau administers the program for cable television and the cable television relay services (CARS), including the issuance of certificates of compliance and CAR authorizations, and maintaining regulatory relationships with state and local jurisdictions that also have responsibility and authority concerning cable-television systems.

Common Carrier Communications

In interstate and international common-carrier communications by telephone, telegraph, radio, and satellite, the Common Carrier Bureau administers the regulatory program. Common carriers include companies, organizations, or individuals providing communications services to the public for hire, who must serve all who wish to use them at established rates. In providing interstate and foreign communications services, common carriers may employ landline wire or cable facilities, point-to-point microwave radio (signals relayed by stations spaced at given intervals), land mobile radio (two-way telephone or one-way signaling communications between base and mobile units), or satellite systems. Communications services between the United States and overseas points by common carriers are provided by ocean cable, high-frequency radio, and satellite communications.

Radio Operators

The commercial-radio-operator program is administered by the Field Operations Bureau. The Safety and Special Radio Services Bureau administers the amateur operator program.

Inquiries for information on the special subjects listed in the following paragraphs and those concerning licensing/grant requirements in the various services may be directed to the person or office specified or to the chief of the bureau or office listed below as having responsibility for the service, Federal Communications Commission, 1919 M St. NW, Washington, DC 20554.

Ex-Parte

Information concerning ex-parte presentations (partisan presentations) should be directed to the Commission's executive director.

Contracts and Procurement

Direct inquiries to the Chief, Procurement Division (tel. 202-632-6407).

Equal Employment Practices by Industry

Direct inquiries to the Chief, EEO unit (tel. 202-254-6530).

Committee Management

Direct inquiries to the Chief, Management Systems Division (tel. 202-632-7513).

Employment and Recruitment

The commission's programs require attorneys, electronic engineers, economists, accountants, administrative–management and computer specialists, and clerical personnel. Requests for employment information should be directed to the Chief, Employment Branch, Personnel Division (tel. 202-632-7106). Schools interested in participating in the college-recruitment programs of the commission should direct their inquiries to the Chief, Personnel Division.

Consumer Assistance

Inquiries concerning general information on how the commission works, what FCC rules and policies mean, and how the public can participate in the decision-making process should be addressed to the Consumer Assistance Office, Room 258, 1919 M St. NW, Washington, DC (tel. 202-632-7000).

Publications

Bulletin No. 1, *Information Services and Publications,* is available on request from the Public Information Office.

Information Available for Public Inspection

At the commission's headquarters office in Washington, DC, public reference rooms maintain dockets concerning rulemaking and adjudicatory matters, copies of applications for licenses and grants, and reports required to be filed by licensees and cable-system operators (some reports are by law held confidential). In addition to the information available at the commission, each broadcasting station makes available for public reference certain information pertaining to the operation of the station, a current copy of the application filed for license, and nonconfidential reports filed with the commission. Special requests for inspection of records in the commission should be directed to the executive director; the library (commission rules and regulations); or the Public Information Office (publications, public notices, press releases).

For further information, phone or write to the Consumer Assistance Office, Federal Communications Commission, Room 258, 1919 M St. NW, Washington, DC 20554 (tel. 202-632-7000).

The International Communication Agency
1750 Pennsylvania Ave. NW
Washington, DC 20547
(202) 655-4000
Director: John E. Reihardt

The agency's four media services—broadcasting (the Voice of America), the Information Center Service, the Motion Picture and Television Service, and the Press and Publications Service—provide materials to USIS posts abroad. Other media products are acquired or produced locally by the posts.

The broadcasting service (VOA) produces and broadcasts radio programs in English and foreign languages, and operates broadcasting and relay facilities to transmit these programs. Programming includes news, reports from correspondents, commentaries, feature programs, and music.

The Information Center Service provides program support and professional guidance and materials to overseas information centers and binational centers. It promotes the distribution of American books in English and in translation, and the presentation of American music, art, drama, and other cultural activities overseas; it operates a worldwide exhibits program and donated-books program; and it supports English-teaching activities at USIS posts.

The Motion Picture and Television Service produces or acquires foreign-language motion pictures that support U.S. policies and objectives. These are shown by USIS posts and in commercial theaters overseas. It also produces or acquires news shows, TV programs, and satellite telecasts for foreign networks, and assists foreign TV teams.

The Press and Publications Service provides USIS posts overseas with a wide variety of editorial materials aimed at selected audiences. It produces a wireless file; publishes seven magazines; provides posts with pamphlets, reprints, photographs, and picture stories; and operates printing plants at three overseas locations.

The International Telecommunication Union
Place des Nations
Geneva, Switzerland
Secretary General: Mohamed Mili.

The International Telecommunication Union (ITU), a specialized agency of the United Nations, with 152 members, originated from the International Telegraph Union established in 1906. The present International Telecommunication Union resulted from a merger, in 1932, that settled upon a convention of provisions pertaining to radio, telegraph, and telephone.

The purpose of the ITU is to maintain and extend international cooperation for efficiency and economy in telecommunications by means of regulations governing telegraph, telephone, and radio services, and through technical and scientific studies to improve communications.

The Office of Telecommunications
The Department of Commerce
1800 G St. NW
Washington, DC 20504

The Office of Telecommunications (OT) was established by the Secretary of Commerce on September 20, 1970, and operates under Department Organization Order 30-5A.

The major purpose of the office is to reduce uncertainty with regard to the development of new, high-technology telecommunication systems and services, either by government or by the private sector. This is accomplished by providing telecommunications planners and users with techniques for evaluating system performance; improved ways of estimating transmission characteristics; methods that will allow a number of users to use simultaneously the same area in the electromagnetic spectrum; and information on the application of telecommunications to public services.

The office engages in research and development in four areas: the engineering and evaluation of systems; electromagnetic wave transmission and services; the efficient use of the broadcast spectrum; and telecommunications applications. It conducts research and analysis in the general field of telecommunications in behalf of other federal agencies and state and local governments. It also provides technical help to the Office of Telecommunications Policy and the Office of the President and advice for policy development.

In addition to its headquarters, the office maintains the Institute for Telecommunication Sciences and a Policy Research Division, at Boulder, Colorado; spectrum-management services in Annapolis, Maryland; and the Secretariat for the Interdepartment Radio Advisory Committee, in Washington, DC.

For further information, phone or write the Public Information Officer, the National Telecommunication and Information Administration, the Department of Commerce, 1800 G St. NW, Washington, DC 20504 (tel. 202-395-5800).

The Office of Telecommunications Policy
1800 G St. NW
Washington, DC 20504
(202) 395-5800
Director: William J. Thaler

The Office of Telecommunications Policy was created as an agency in the Executive Office of the President by Reorganization Plan 1 of 1970, effective April 20, 1970. Its responsibilities are specified in Executive Order 11556 of September 4, 1970.

The Office of Telecommunications Policy is the executive agency responsible for overall supervision of national communications matters. Its function may generally be divided into four areas: It establishes the executive branch's policies and programs pertaining to communications matters and seeks to implement them through various means, including the proposal of legislation. This area of activity includes such matters as the structure of the communications industry, the communications goals to be sought in international negotiations, desirable regulatory policies for established broadcasting and common-carrier services, and a regulatory approach to new technologies and interconnected computer systems. It coordinates the planning and evaluates the operation of the communications activities of the executive branch. This includes the establishment of policies and the setting of standards for federal communications systems, and overall guidance of federal research and development efforts.

It is responsible for the allocation and management of that portion of the radio spectrum (approximately one-half) used by the federal government.

It develops mobilization plans for the Nation's communications resources, and is responsible for administering those resources in an emergency. This includes responsibility for exercise of the President's war powers in the communications field.

The director of the office is appointed by the President with the advice and consent of the Senate. He is the President's principal adviser and executive-branch spokesman on communications matters. The deputy director is likewise appointed by the President with the advice and consent of the Senate. Those functions of the office that pertain to frequency management for federal users are under the immediate supervision of the assistant director, frequency management. Responsibility for other functions is divided among other assistant directors and the chief scientist. Technical support is provided by the Department of Commerce.

Advisory bodies which assist the director in the performance of his functions are the Electromagnetic Radiation Management Advisory Council, composed of experts in radiation and health; the Frequency Management Advisory Council, composed of communications experts from the private sector; and the Interdepartment Radio Advisory Committee, composed of representatives of federal agencies that make use of the radio spectrum. The director is also advised by the Council for Government Communications Policy and Planning, composed of representatives from federal agencies with significant communications responsibilities.

For further information, phone or write the Office of Telecommunications Policy.

The United Nations Educational, Scientific and Cultural Organization

Place de Fontenoy
Paris 75700, France
U.N. Liaison Office
2201 U.N. Bldg.
New York, NY 10017
Director General: Amadou Mahtar M'Bow
The United Nations Educational, Scientific and
Cultural Organization (UNESCO) is one of the
specialized agencies of the United Nations. Its con-
stitution was adopted November 16, 1945. As of
March 1976, there were 146 member states.
UNESCO promotes international cooperation in
the fields of education, science, mass communica-
tions, and culture. The United States is a charter
member of UNESCO.

Additional information may be obtained from
the Secretariat: US National Commission for
UNESCO, Department of State, Washington, DC
20520.

The Most Frequently Asked Questions and the FCC's Answers

The FCC and Broadcasting

1. What does the Commission do? Congress created
the Federal Communications Commission in 1934
for the purpose (among other things) of "regulating
interstate and foreign commerce in communication
by wire and radio so as to make available, as far as
possible, to all the people of the United States a
rapid, efficient, nation-wide, and world-wide wire
and radio communications service. . . ." Thus, the
commission regulates not only all broadcasting stations in this country but also all interstate and
foreign telephone, telegraph, and cable services;
satellite communications; and other elements of
communications, affecting the individual and the
general public, industry and transportation. The
commission regulates certain aspects of cable television (CATV) systems, although the franchising or
licensing of such systems is in the first instance a
matter for determination by municipalities according to local law. At present, more than 9,150 radio
and television broadcasting stations are on the air,
and several hundred more have been authorized.
Most of these are licensed for commercial operation, and are supported by advertising revenue.
However, there are approximately 860 noncommercial FM stations, 25 noncommercial educational
AM stations, and about 255 noncommercial television stations operating.

The commission does not regulate closed-circuit
television operations, and, accordingly, does not
control what events may be carried by closed circuit
or the prices that may be charged. Furthermore, the
FCC has no regulatory authority over the pro-
moters of prize fights or other sporting events,
bullfights, rodeos or other exhibitions, and cannot
direct them to offer or refrain from offering such
events to any person or persons for exhibition,
including networks or broadcast stations. Arrangements for exhibitions of this kind are the subject of private contractual agreements between the
owners of the rights and other parties. The commission does not license Canadian, Mexican, or other
foreign stations, nor does it regulate any aspect of
the operation of such stations (the names and addresses of the government agencies of Canada and
Mexico that regulate broadcasting in these countries are listed at the end of this section). Such
monitoring of broadcast stations as the commission
is empowered to engage in is directed principally to
the detection of technical violations, such as operation without authorization or on a frequency
other than the one assigned. A frequently misun-
derstood matter centers on the fact that standard
transmissions cover greater distances at night, and
therefore many stations in the standard (AM)
broadcast band must limit their operating power at
night or cease operating altogether to avoid interference with other stations on the same or adjacent
frequencies. Licenses for daytime operation were
originally sought by the applicants with the knowledge that requests for operation of full-time
facilities could not always be granted, because of
serious electrical interference with established
nighttime stations. FM-radio and TV stations are
authorized to operate unlimited hours. The Communications Act provides that the commission
"may grant construction permits and station
licenses, or modifications or renewals thereof, only
upon written application therefor received by it."
2. Does the FCC license educational stations? Under
the Communications Act, the commission licenses
educational radio and television stations to provide
nonprofit, noncommercial broadcast services, although under a special rule FM educational stations
may charge for authorized educational material
transmitted by subcarriers simultaneously with
main channel programming (multiplexing), provided funds retained by the station licensees do not
exceed actual costs incurred by the stations in the
presentation of the program material. Educational
stations may transmit educational, cultural, and entertainment programs and programs designed for
use by schools and school systems, but may not
engage in editorializing, or support or oppose any
candidates for political office. Section 326 of the act
prohibits commission censorship of broadcast matter, and the Commission does not attempt to direct
either its commercial or noncommercial broadcast
licensees to present or refrain from presenting specific programs.
*3. Are special funds available for Educational Sta-
tions?* The construction of noncommercial educational broadcasting facilities is assisted by matching
grants of federal funds under the administration of
the Department of Health, Education and Welfare,
as provided in the Communications Act.
4. What is the Corporation for Public Broadcasting?

In 1967, by amendment to the Act, the Congress established the Corporation for Public Broadcasting declaring "that a private corporation should be created to facilitate the development of educational radio and television broadcasting and to afford maximum protection to such broadcasting from extraneous interference and control." The CPB is a nonprofit corporation and is not an agency or establishment of the United States Government. The FCC believes it was the intent of the Congress to keep the Corporation free from government control (Communications Act, Sec. 398) and the Commission holds that it would not be warranted in attempting to oversee the Corporation's execution of its duties. CPB contributes to the growth and development of educational broadcasting by, among other things, assisting in financing programs for such broadcasting from its funds, which come from congressional appropriations and private sources. Under an amendment to the Communications Act, each licensee receiving assistance from CPB is required to retain for 60 days a recording of the sound portion of its broadcast of any program in which any issue of public importance is discussed, and during the period make a copy of such recording available to the FCC upon request and to any other person upon payment to the licensee or its designated entity the reasonable cost of making such copy (the address of CPB and the names and addresses of other organizations concerned with educational broadcasting are listed at the end of this section).

The Broadcaster and Programming

5. *Can the FCC censor programs?* The commission is prohibited by law from censoring broadcast matter, does not attempt to direct broadcasters in the selection or presentation of specific programming, and is not an arbiter of taste. However, no application for the construction of a broadcast station (or for the licensing or license renewal of one) will be granted unless the commission finds that the public interest, convenience, and necessity will be served by such a grant. Applicants are expected to show what they have done to ascertain the problems and needs of the people in the communities to which they seek to broadcast and what broadcast matter is proposed to meet those problems and needs.

Commercial television station licensees are also required to file with the commission an annual programming report showing the amount of time, and the percentage of total operating time, devoted to various types of programs other than entertainment and sports. The FCC encourages people to express their views on programming, preferably in writing, directly to stations and networks.

6. *Must a station maintain a public file of its application and other related material?* Each broadcasting station is required to maintain for public inspection during regular business hours in the community for which it is licensed, a public file with copies of applications filed with the commission, reports of station ownership, the FCC pamphlet "The Public

and Broadcasting—A Procedure Manual," and certain other materials. Moreover, commercial radio and television stations are required to retain in the file for three years letters and other written comments from the public regarding station operation and programming efforts. Additionally, commercial television station public files must contain copies of their annual programming reports, and the public files of commercial radio and television stations must contain an annual listing of no more than ten problems and needs of the area served, with an indication of how programming has been responsive to them in the preceding 12 months. Members of the public need not make appointments to inspect the public file of a station, nor are they required to examine its contents only at times most convenient to the licensee. Copies of all applications, as well as various other documents, also are available for public inspection in the commission's headquarters in Washington. Regulations governing availability for public inspection and reproduction of television-program logs will be found in paragraphs 61–64 of the procedure manual.

7. *What is the duration of a broadcast license?* Broadcast licenses are normally granted for a three-year period; the licenses of all stations in a given state expire at the same time. Applications for license renewal—which must contain information regarding station programming and commercial practices, both past and proposed—must be filed four months before a license's date of expiration. Six months prior to the expiration date all broadcast stations begin to present information regarding the expiration of their licenses, the availability for inspection of their applications, and the dates by which the public should file comments with the FCC regarding station operations or the availability of further information, whether from the station or from the FCC. "The Public and Broadcasting—a Procedure Manual" is available from both stations and the commission. It contains information helpful to those wishing to comment on a station's performance.

8. *Does the FCC have rules covering nondiscrimination in broadcast employment?* The commission has adopted rules that provide that "equal opportunity in employment shall be afforded by all licensees or permittees of . . . standard, FM, television, or international broadcast stations . . . to all qualified persons, and no person shall be discriminated against in employment because of race, color, religion, national origin, or sex." Moreover, commission rules require that broadcast licensees employing five or more persons file annual reports indicating employment in certain job categories of persons belonging to national minorities, and subdivided as to sex. Also, licensees employing ten or more persons must file information regarding affirmative equal-employment programs for minorities and women. This information and the annual reports are among the documents required to be made available for public inspection. (A publication explaining in detail procedures available to individuals who feel they themselves have been discriminated against is

available upon request.) The commission does not attempt to direct a licensee in its selection of an individual employee or performer for a particular program or announcement.

Complaints alleging unequal pay for equal work, or discrimination in employment because of age against persons between 40 and 65 years of age, should be filed with the nearest local wage-and-hour office, listed in telephone directories under "U.S. Department of Labor, Employment Standards Administration, Wage and Hour Division," with the request that the Broadcast Bureau of the Federal Communications Commission be advised of the wage-and-hour office's findings in the matter.

9. *Does the FCC regulate program schedules?* The commission is prohibited by Section 326 of the Communications Act from censoring broadcast matter and from taking any action which would interfere with the right of free speech in broadcasting.

10. *Can anyone force a station to accept a program or program idea?* Section 3(h) of the Communications Act states that a broadcaster shall not be deemed a common carrier. He therefore is not required to accept all matter that may be offered to him for broadcast. There is no provision of the Constitution or of any statute or regulation guaranteeing to any particular person the use of a microphone or TV camera for the presentation of broadcast material. Therefore, except under special circumstances, the broadcast licensee is under no obligation to have any particular persons as his guest or to present that person's remarks. Stations will not be licensed by the FCC if they have agreements with networks not to reject certain programs. It is not the commission's policy to review material prior to its broadcast. Persons wishing to market program ideas or scripts, or to have their recordings or other material broadcast, should deal directly with producers, stations, or networks, for the FCC cannot serve as a clearing house for talent or programs. The FCC cannot direct any person or firm in procedures for disposition of material submitted to them and will not interfere in the private disputes that may arise in this regard.

11. *Are there fixed advertising rates for broadcast stations?* While the commission would be concerned if any practice of a licensee might be in restraint of trade, result in unfair competition, or otherwise not be in accord with law, the broadcaster, as was noted before, is not a common carrier and the FCC neither requires that his advertising rates be submitted for approval nor attempts to fix his profit levels. The rates a licensee may charge a given sponsor are a matter for negotiation between the sponsor and the station. Licensees authorized to operate commercially are not required to charge or refrain from making a charge for broadcast time. Federal law and FCC rules, policies, and complaint procedures governing political broadcasting, including rates charged candidates for public office, are set forth and explained in the several publications that make up the *Political Broadcasting Primer.*

12. *Must a station present both sides of a disputed issue?* The commission does not attempt to substitute its judgment for that of the broadcast licensee regarding "open mike" or other programs in which the editorial views of the licensee himself or the opinions of other persons are set forth. However, the commission believes that licensees are obligated to give the public more than one viewpoint on a controversial issue of public importance. The constitutionality of this policy, known as the fairness doctrine, has been upheld by the Supreme Court. The policy requires a licensee who presents one side of a controversial issue of public importance to afford reasonable opportunity for presentation of opposing viewpoints on that issue. The fairness doctrine does not require exact equality of time for opposing viewpoints, and should not be confused with the law governing the use of broadcasting stations by candidates for public office. What the fairness doctrine requires is that a broadcast licensee, having presented one side of a controversial issue of public importance, make reasonable efforts to present opposing sides of the issue in his overall programming. Opposing views need not be presented on the same program, or even in the same series of programs, so long as an effort is made in good faith to present contrasting views in the station's overall programming. With the exception of certain circumstances involving political editorials of licensees, personal attacks as defined by the commission's rules, and a legal provision affecting noncommercial educational stations, licensees are not required to make, maintain, or provide to the general public scripts, tapes, or summaries of broadcast program material.

13. *Does the public have a right to reply to editorial comments by broadcasters?* Editorializing is the expression of the opinions of station licensees ("comment" generally refers to the expression of views by station guests or employees), and commercial licensees are encouraged to engage in it under the commission's policies, subject to the requirements of the fairness doctrine. (Editorializing by noncommercial educational licensees is prohibited by law.) There is no law or rule requiring that editorials or news comment—or, indeed, any kind of broadcast material—be labeled or announced as such, or requiring that it be separated or distinguished in any way from other program matter. It should be stressed that the purpose of the fairness doctrine is to protect the right of the public to be informed, not to provide broadcast time to any particular person or group. Having broadcast one side of a controversial issue of public importance, the broadcast licensee has an obligation to attempt to present contrasting viewpoints, but it lies within his discretion to select the particular format to be used in such presentations as well as the particular individual to express the various viewpoints—provided, of course, that the licensee appears to be acting reasonably and in good faith.

Several commission publications constitute the *Political Broadcasting Primer.* These set forth and explain the so-called equal-time law, as well as other federal laws, together with FCC rules, policies, and complaint procedures applicable to political-campaign broadcasting. The primer may be obtained upon request from the commission.

14. Does the FCC have rules governing the use of obscene, indecent, or profane language or material? Complaints are received objecting to on-the-air discussion of certain subjects, or to language, costuming, or actions, as offensive, and also objecting to programs whose content or scheduling is deemed unsuitable for children. The broadcast of material considered by many to be obscene or indecent is one of the most difficult problems facing the commission and the courts. There is no way to summarize briefly the subject. The material that follows is an attempt to explain the present status of this complex area of law and to chronicle the actions of the courts and the FCC.

The commission's authority in this area is governed by federal statutes and by decisions of the courts in interpreting them. On the one hand, Section 326 of the Communications Act specifically prohibits FCC censorship of broadcast material or interference with freedom of expression in broadcasting. There is no law or regulation that bars the broadcast discussion of a given subject. On the other hand, Section 1464 of the United States Criminal Code provides criminal penalties for uttering "any obscene, indecent or profane language by means of radio communication." ("Radio" is defined in the Communications Act so as to include television.) While criminal prosecution under this section is solely within the jurisdiction of the Department of Justice, the commission is authorized under provisions of the Communications Act to revoke a broadcasting license or impose a fine upon the licensee for violation of Section 1464, regardless of whether criminal prosecution has been initiated.

The courts have held in many cases that material that may be offensive to some people is not necessarily obscene as a matter of law. The United States Supreme Court adopted the present standard for determining whether a particular printed work is obscene in the case of *Miller* v. *California* (June 21, 1973). That standard is based on three considerations: "(a) whether the average person, applying contemporary community standards, would find that the work, taken as a whole, appeals to the prurient interest; (b) whether the work depicts or describes in a patently offensive way, sexual conduct specifically defined by the applicable state law, and (c) whether the work, taken as a whole, lacks serious literary, artistic, political or scientific value." The Court has applied the same standard to motion pictures and to violations of federal laws other than Section 1464. The Court has not specifically ruled on whether a particular work may be regulated because it is "indecent" in contrast to "obscene" for constitutional purposes. However, the Court has never specifically interpreted Section 1464 or any other statute with specific reference to the broadcast of questionable material, in contrast to its presentation in print or in motion pictures. It has ruled that nudity alone is not enough to make

material legally obscene under the standard established in the case of *Miller* v. *California*. A number of cases involving questions of obscenity and indecency have been before the courts.

In April of 1970 and April of 1973, "notices of apparent liability" were issued to the licensees of Stations WUHY-FM (Philadelphia, Pennsylvania) and WGLD-FM (Oak Park, Illinois) proposing to fine the stations for the broadcast of obscene and/or indecent language, but stating that the commission would welcome court review of its actions. In each case the licensees elected to pay the fines.

In July of 1973 the commission denied an application by the Illinois Citizens Committee for Broadcasting and the Illinois Division of the American Civil Liberties Union for remission of the $2,000 fine against the licensee of Station WGLD-FM. The two groups appealed the commission's decision to the United States Court of Appeals for the District of Columbia Circuit. They argued that the commission had erred in assessing the fine. On November 20, 1974, the court ruled, in effect, that the FCC does not act unconstitutionally when it determines that discussions, in a titillating context, on daytime radio call-in programs of sex acts are obscene; but in this case the court established no standards applicable to broadcast matter different from those presently applied to printed material or to motion pictures. Moreover, because the court found the material broadcast by WGLD-FM to be "obscene," it did not broach the question of the constitutionality of the commission's interpretation and application of the term *indecent*.

After inquiry into a complaint regarding certain language aired by Station WBAI-FM, New York City, the commission on February 12, 1975, issued a declaratory order concerning the use of indecent language on the public airwaves. The commission defined indecent language as "language that describes in terms patently offensive as measured by contemporary community standards for the broadcast medium, sexual or excretory activities and organs." This definition differs from the definition of obscenity in that the latter requires a demonstration that allegedly obscene material appeals to prurient interests. The commission further stated that at hours when it is likely that children will be in the audience, indecent language "cannot be redeemed by a claim that it has literary, artistic, political or scientific value." However, when the number of children composing an audience can be expected to be at a minimum, such as late-night hours, the commission "would also consider whether the material has serious literary, artistic, political or scientific value," as the (WBAI) licensee claimed. The commission's position has been challenged by the licensee of Station WBAI, and the matter is now before the courts.

The commission has stated its belief that it would be inequitable to hold a licensee responsible for indecent language where live coverage of public events was involved, and that under such circumstances it trusted that a licensee would exercise judgment and responsibility, and sensitivity to the community's needs, interests, and tastes.

On February 19, 1975, the commission submitted to Congress a *Report on the Broadcast of Violent, Indecent and Obscene Material.* The report summarized discussions with representatives of the three major commercial television networks with respect to reducing the level and intensity of violent and sexually oriented programming. (The response of the networks to the problem of violence and sex on the air was the establishment of a "family-viewing" period during the early evening hours of network-television programming). In its report the commission sought from the Congress clarification of the statutory language that prohibits the broadcast of obscene and indecent language, to assure the applicability of the statute to cable and non-cable television. In the spring of 1976 the FCC forwarded to the Congress its recommendations for specific language to achieve the clarification.

In regard to profanity, the intention of the speaker has governed in key court cases involving language commonly regarded as profane (*Hell, Damn, God damn it*), the primary consideration being whether there were uttered "words importing an imprecation of divine vengeance or implying divine condemnation, so used as to constitute a public nuisance." Complaints about such language unaccompanied by evidence of the specified import do not normally furnish a basis for commission action. Persons using expressions such as here quoted seldom intend to be taken literally.

The FCC has consistently urged concerned persons to express their views in writing to the stations and networks involved in the broadcast of programming that they consider objectionable.

15. To what extent is broadcast criticism of the government and institutions of the United States restricted? The courts have held that the First Amendment to the United States Constitution guarantees free speech, with certain very limited exceptions. Likewise, in a license-renewal case in which charges of defamation had been made, the FCC stated, in part, the following:

> It is the judgment of the Commission, as it has been the judgment of those who drafted our Constitution and of the overwhelming majority of our legislators and judges over the years, that the public interest is best served by permitting the expression of any views that do not involve (quoting from Supreme Court decisions) "a clear and present danger of serious substantive evil that rises far above public inconvenience, annoyance or unrest." . . .This principle insures that the most diverse and opposing opinions will be expressed, many of which may be even highly offensive to those officials who thus protect the rights of others to free speech. If there is to be free speech, it must be free for speech that we abhor and hate as well as for speech that we find tolerable or congenial.

Thus, broadcasts of views opposing existing laws or criticizing social conditions, government activities, or public officials, including the President, are protected by the constitutional guarantees of free speech.

16. To what extent is criticism of a race, religion, nationality, or sex restricted on radio and TV? Programs containing criticism, ridicule, or humor concerning the religion, race, nationality, sex, or other characteristics of individuals or groups are sometimes the subject of complaints received by the commission. Such broadcast material, however offensive it may sometimes be, also enjoys the protection of the First Amendment.

17. Can anything be done about distorted news stories? The commission sometimes receives allegations that a network, station, or newscaster has distorted or suppressed news, or unduly emphasized certain aspects of the news, or has staged, instigated, or fabricated news occurrences. The commission does not attempt to substitute its judgments of news values for those of a licensee, but the deliberate distortion, slanting, or "staging" of news by broadcast stations would be patently inconsistent with the public interest and would call for remedial action by the FCC. However, the commission, in order to appropriately commence action in this sensitive area, must receive significant extrinsic evidence that the news was deliberately distorted or fabricated. Were it to proceed upon the basis simply of what was said over the air, it would be in the position of determining the "truth" of each factual situation, evaluating the degree to which the matter complained of departed from the "truth," and, finally, calling upon the licensee to explain the deviation. The commission believes that such activities on its part would be inappropriate to a government licensing agency.

18. What can the FCC do about the violence and criminality presented on TV? The commission cooperates in every feasible way with the work of governmental and other organizations studying the possible influence upon human behavior of the depiction of crime or violence in broadcast programs.

To touch upon a related matter, the commission receives complaints alleging that some broadcast material, and particularly certain songs, encourage or glorify the use of narcotics or dangerous drugs. On March 5, 1972, the commission issued a public notice reminding licensees of their responsibility to acquaint themselves with the nature of their programming, including lyrics of songs. Four years earlier the commission had issued a similar reminder with reference to foreign-language programs. In its "Notice" of March 5, 1971, the commission did not state that a licensee should not broadcast a particular type of record, and made clear the fact that selection of records was a matter for the licensee's judgment. Because the public notice was widely misconstrued as a directive not to play certain kinds of records and because a number of petitions for reconsideration of the notice were received, the commission issued, on April 16, 1971, a "Memorandum Opinion and Order" treating the matter in greater detail and constituting the commission's definitive statement on the subject. It should be noted that a number of government agencies, including the Department of Justice and the Department of Health, Education and Welfare, are cooperating with the National Association of Broadcasters and with individual broadcasters in presenting material designed to acquaint young people with the dangers of narcotics.

19. *Can tobacco products be advertised on radio and TV?* Section 6 of the Federal Cigarette Labeling and Advertising Act of 1965 (Title 15 of the United States Code, Sections 1331–1340), as amended by the Public Health Cigarette Smoking Act of 1969 and further amended by the Little Cigar Act of 1973, states this: "After January 1, 1971, it shall be unlawful to advertise cigarettes and little cigars on any medium of electronic communication subject to the jurisdiction of the Federal Communications Commission." Cigarettes are defined in the Act of 1969 and little cigars in that of 1973. The law does not prohibit the broadcast advertising of such tobacco products as pipe tobacco or cigars not defined as "little cigars" in the legislation referred to here; nor does it prohibit the incidental use of any tobacco product in television programs by actors, announcers, or others.

20. *Can alcoholic beverages be advertised on radio and TV?* The FCC has consistently taken the position that prohibition of broadcast advertising of alcoholic beverages is a matter for legislative determination by the Congress. The Congress has enacted no law in this regard. The commission is prohibited by the Communications Act from censoring any broadcast matter and does not direct licensees to accept or reject such advertising or to refrain from the depiction of the use of alcoholic beverages in dramatic or other types of program matter. The National Association of Broadcasters' codes, which are aspects of self-regulatory activities among broadcasters, forbid the advertising of hard liquor and establish guidelines for advertising wine and beer as well as for the depiction of the use of alcoholic beverages in television programs. Membership in the NAB and subscription to its codes are entirely voluntary on the part of broadcast licensees.

21. *How much advertising can a station carry per hour?* No law or rule limits the amount of commercial matter that may be aired in a given period of time. Commercial time is measured in total minutes per clock hour and not all program interruptions are necessarily commercial; public service announcements, for example, are not, nor are unsponsored time signals, routine weather announcements or, generally, program-promotion announcements. Applicants for licenses or renewals are required to state the maximum amount of commercial matter proposed normally to be allowed in any clock hour and under what circumstances the proposed limits might be exceeded at times and what the limits then would be. The FCC carefully considers these proposals to determine whether they serve the public interest. Renewal applicants, in addition, are required to inform the commission of the amount of

commercial matter per hour actually broadcast during past license periods. Under certain circumstances, applications proposing more than 18 minutes of commercial time per hour for radio stations or 16 minutes of such time for television stations are considered initially by the commission to determine whether grants of applications containing such proposals would be in the public interest. In a policy statement adopted in April, 1976, the FCC stated that no question would be raised regarding excess of political spot announcements by radio stations over their normal commercial limits if occurring within the limitations specified in the policy.

22. *What can the FCC do about offensive advertising?* The FCC often receives complaints regarding the nature of certain products advertised on the air or objecting to the airing of announcements for certain products when members of the audience are at their meals. Some people are offended by advertising they believe to have been handled indecently or in poor taste. Still others complain of commercials they believe have been ineptly produced or contain grammatical errors. Under the prohibition against censorship in the Communications Act, the commission does not attempt to direct stations to present or refrain from presenting any particular program or announcement or to direct the scheduling of such material.

23. *What can be done about false or misleading advertising?* The Federal Trade Commission (Pennsylvania Ave. and 6th St. NW, Washington, DC 20580) has the primary responsibility for determining whether advertising is false or deceptive and for taking appropriate action against the sponsors of such material. The FCC, however, holds broadcast licensees responsible for exercising reasonable diligence to prevent the use of their facilities for false, deceptive, or misleading advertising, and takes cognizance of FTC findings in this regard. The two commissions have established liaison procedures under which they exchange information and maintain regular staff contacts on matters of common concern. The FTC has been studying the role in our national life, as well as the advertising, of such products as non-prescription stimulants, calmatives, and sleeping aids, and the National Association of Broadcasters has adopted guidelines for the advertising of these three classes of drug products. Complaints and inquiries regarding food or drug products believed to be dangerous should be addressed to the Food and Drug Administration, the Department of Health, Education and Welfare, 5600 Fishers La., Rockville, MD 20852.

24. *Can the sound volume of commercials be regulated?* The commission receives complaints that certain broadcast advertising is objectionably loud. The commission has made extensive inquiries into this problem and has concluded that although no method has been developed by which to measure objectively the degree of "loudness" that is acceptable, many factors pertaining to loudness can—and should—be controlled by broadcasters. Accordingly, the commission has issued a policy statement setting forth various methods by which loudness can be controlled, and has requested broadcast licensees to take appropriate measures to adhere to the policy. The commission looks into each such complaint it receives if the complainant states the call letters of the station that broadcast the offending commercials, describes the announcements or lists their sponsors, and specifies the date and approximate time of the broadcasts.

25. *Is subliminal advertising allowed on TV?* The commission receives complaints regarding the alleged use of subliminal techniques in television advertising. Such complaints usually concern words and pictures flashed briefly on the screen and of which the viewer is consciously aware. However, true subliminal advertising is designed to operate only on a subconscious level. The FCC has held that the use of subliminal techniques is inconsistent with the obligations of a licensee and has made it clear that broadcasts employing such techniques are contrary to the public interest, adding that, whether effective or not, the broadcasts are clearly intended to be deceptive.

26. *Can the FCC help settle claims against stations?* The commission does not attempt to resolve private controversies involving broadcasting stations, and generally leaves the enforcement of individual claims to the parties involved. It cannot, for example, collect contest prizes for participants or secure delivery of merchandise ordered through broadcast stations or enforce claims against stations for payment of wages or other debts. However, it is the commission's duty to consider practices that might reflect upon either the character or financial qualifications of a broadcast licensee or that could adversely affect the ability of the broadcast industry to serve the public interest. The commission will consider comments, inquiries, and complaints that may raise questions regarding the qualifications of licensees, with a view to taking such action as may be deemed appropriate.

27. *Can the fixing of broadcast contests be controlled?* It is a violation of law to prearrange or predetermine the outcome of any purportedly bona fide contest of intellectual knowledge, intellectual skill, or chance, with the intention of deceiving the broadcast audience regarding such a contest (Section 509 of the Communications Act). The FCC will give careful consideration to complaints that its licensees have engaged in any of the following prac-

tices in the conduct of contests: the dissemination of misleading or deceptive information regarding the nature of a contest, the prizes to be awarded, or the qualifications for participation by members of the public; a failure to broadcast or publish complete and clear information regarding the rules for a contest; and failure to provide the public with full and timely information concerning a change in a contest, its premature termination, or a decision not to award announced prizes.

The commission is also concerned that licensees refrain from broadcasting contests, promotions, or hoaxes that may result in alarm to the public owing to imaginary dangers, the infringement of public or private property rights or the right of privacy, annoyance or embarrassment to innocent parties, hazards to life and health, and traffic congestion or other public disorders requiring diversion of the police from other duties.

28. *Can stations run lotteries?* A lottery is a game, contest, or promotion that combines three elements: (1) a prize, (2) dependence in whole or in part upon chance in determining winners, and (3) the requirement that contestants purchase something or contribute something of value in order to compete. If any of these elements is absent, there is no lottery. Generally, Section 1304, Title 18, United States Code, prohibits the broadcast of advertisements for or information concerning lotteries (raffles, bingo, etc.). However, the restrictions of Title 18 do not apply to an advertisement, a list of prizes, or other information concerning a lottery conducted by a state when such information is broadcast by a station licensed for a location in that state or by a station licensed in an adjacent state that also conducts a lottery.

29. *Can stations solicit funds?* There is no law or regulation that prohibits the broadcast solicitation of funds for lawful purposes (including appeals by broadcast licensees for contributions to defray station operating expenses) if the monies or other items of value contributed are put to the announced purposes. When the mail is involved in solicitations, the enforcement of relevant laws is the responsibility of the United States Postal Service. Whether to permit solicitation over his facilities, is a matter within the discretion of a licensee. Section 1343 of Title 18, United States Code, provides criminal penalties for fraud by wire, radio, or television.

FCC Broadcast Regulations

One of the FCC's major activities is the regulation of broadcasting. It does this in three phases.

1. It allocates space in the radio-frequency spectrum to broadcast services, and to many non-broadcast services that also must be accommodated. The tremendous increase in the use of radio technology in recent decades has made competing demands for frequencies one of the commission's most pressing problems. Fortunately, as technology

has advanced, frequencies higher and higher in the spectrum have become usable. Apart from the frequencies used for broadcasting, frequencies in other portions of the spectrum are allocated for "broadcast auxiliary" use by remote pickup and other transmitters auxiliary to main broadcast stations.

2. It assigns stations in each service within the allocated frequency bands, with specific location,

frequency, and power. The chief consideration, though by no means the only one, is to avoid interference with other stations on the same channel (frequency) or channels adjacent in the spectrum. When an application is granted for a new station or for changed facilities the applicant receives a construction permit. Later, when the station is built and is capable of operating as proposed, a license to operate is issued.

3. It regulates existing stations—inspecting to see that stations are operating in accordance with FCC rules and the technical provisions of their authorizations, modifying authorizations when necessary, assigning station call letters, licensing transmitter operators, processing requests to assign station licenses to other parties or transfer control of the licensee corporation, and processing applications for renewal of licenses. At renewal time, the commission reviews the station's record to see if it is operating in the public interest.

Subpart E of the Federal Communications Commission Regulations

Television Broadcast Stations—General

73.601 Subpart E

What follows is a reprint of Subpart E of The Federal Communications Commission Regulations, which contains the rules and regulations (including engineering standards) governing television broadcast stations, including noncommercial educational television broadcast stations, in the United States and its territories and possessions. Television broadcast stations are assigned channels 6 megahertz (MHz) wide, designated as set forth in 73.603(a).

The complete FCC regulations are available from the FCC office in Washington, DC.

73.603 Numerical designation of television channels.

(a)

Channel No.	Frequency band (MHz)
2	54–60
3	60–66
4	66–72
5	76–82
6	82–88
7	174–180
8	180–186
9	186–192
10	192–198
11	198–204
12	204–210
13	210–216
14	470–476
15	476–482
16	482–488
17	488–494
18	494–500
19	500–506
20	506–512

Channel No.	Frequency band (MHz)
21	512–518
22	518–524
23	524–530
24	530–536
25	536–542
26	542–548
27	548–554
28	554–560
29	560–566
30	566–572
31	572–578
32	578–584
33	584–590
34	590–596
35	596–602
36	602–608
37	608–614
38	614–620
39	620–626
40	626–632
41	632–638
42	638–644
43	644–650
44	650–656
45	656–662
46	662–668
47	668–674
48	674–680
49	680–686
50	686–692
51	692–698
52	698–704
53	704–710
54	710–716
55	716–722
56	722–728
57	728–734
58	734–740
59	740–746
60	746–752
61	752–758
62	758–764
63	764–770
64	770–776
65	776–782
66	782–788
67	788–794
68	794–800
69	800–806
70	806–812
71	812–818
72	818–824
73	824–830
74	830–836
75	836–842
76	842–848
77	848–854
78	854–860
79	860–866
80	866–872

Channel No.	Frequency band (MHz)
81	872–878
82	878–884
83	884–890

(b) In Alaska and Hawaii, the frequency bands 76–82 MHz and 82–88 MHz are allocated for nonbroadcast use. These frequency bands (Channels 5 and 6) will not be assigned in Alaska or Hawaii for use by television broadcast stations.

(c) Channel 37, 608–614 MHz, is reserved exclusively for the radio astronomy service until the first Administrative Radio Conference after January 1, 1974, which is competent to review this provision.

Channel Utilization

73.606. *Table of assignments*

(a) General. The following table of assignments contains the channels assigned to the listed communities in the United States and its territories and possessions. Channels designated with an asterisk are assigned for use by noncommercial educational broadcast stations only. A station on a channel identified by a plus or minus mark is required to operate with its carrier frequencies offset 10 kHz above or below the normal carrier frequencies.

(b) Table of Assignments   Channel No.

Alabama:

Andalusia	*2−
Anniston	40−
Birmingham	6−, *10−, 13−, 21, 42+, *62+, 68+
Decatur	23−
Demopolis	*41
Dothan	4, 18, *39+, 60−
Florence	15, 26, *36−
Gadsden	44+, 60
Huntsville	19, *25+, 31+, 48−
Louisville	*43+
Mobile	5+, 10+, 15+, 21+, *31, *42
Montgomery	12, 20, *26+, 32, 45−
Munford	*7−, *16−
Selma	8−, 29−
Tuscaloosa	17, 33, *39−
Tuscumbia	47−

Alaska:

Anchorage	2−, *7−, 11, 13−
Bethel	*4
Fairbanks	2+, 4+, 7+, *9+, 11+, 13+
Juneau	*3, 8, 10
Ketchikan	2, 4, *9
Seward	4−, 9−
Sitka	13

Arizona:

Ajo	*23−
Coolidge	*43
Douglas	3, *28
Flagstaff	2, 13, *16
Globe	*14+
Holbrook	*18+
Kingman	6−, *14−
McNary	*22+
Mesa	12−
Nogales	*16+
Page	*17
Parker	*17−
Phoenix	3+, 5−, *8+, 10−, 15−, 21, 33, *39
Prescott	7, *19
Safford	*23+
Tucson	4−, *6+, 9−, 13−, 18−, *27−, 40
Tucson-Nogales	11 [2]
Yuma	11−, 13+, *16−

Arkansas:

Arkadelphia	*9+
Batesville	*17
El Dorado	10−, 18−, *30+
Fayetteville	*13−, 36
Fort Smith	5−, 24+, 40−
Harrison	*14
Hot Springs	*20, 26
Jonesboro	8−, *19−
Little Rock	*2−, 4, 7−, 11+, 16−, *29−
Mountain View	*6−
Pine Bluff	25−, 38−
Russellville	*28+

California:

Alturas	13+
Anaheim	56−
Bakersfield	17, 23−, 29, *39−
Barstow	*35+
Bishop	*14−
Blythe	*22−
Brawley	*26
Chico	12−, *18[1], 24+, *30−
Coalinga	*27−
Concord	42
Corona	52
Cotati	*22−
El Centro	7+, 9+
Eureka	3−, 6−, *13−
Fort Bragg	*17+[1]
Fresno	*18+, 24, 30+, 47, 53
Hanford	21
Indio	*19+ [1]
Los Angeles	2, 4, 5, 7, 9, 11, 13, 22, *28, 34, *58−, *68−
Modesto	19−, *23+
Oxnard	63+
Palm Springs	36−, 42
Redding	7, *9, 16 [1]
Ridgecrest	*25
Riverside	40, 46
Sacramento	3, *6, 10, 15, 31−[3], 40−
Salinas-Monterey	8+, 35−, 46−, *56, 67−
San Bernardino	18−, *24−, 30
San Diego	8, 10, *15, 39, 51
San Francisco	2+, 4−, 5+, 7−, *9+, 20−, 26−, *32+, 38, 44−, 60

San Jose	11+, 36, 48−, *54
San Luis Obispo	6+, *15+
San Mateo	*14+
Santa Ana	*50−
Santa Barbara	3−, 14, *20[1], *32[1]
Santa Cruz	*16−[1]
Santa Maria	12+
Santa Rosa	50−, *62
Stockton	13+, 58, 64
Susanville	*14
Tulare	26+
Vallejo–Fairfield	66
Ventura	16+
Visalia	43
Watsonville	*25+
Yreka City	*20+

Colorado:

Alamosa	3−, *16
Boulder	*12, 14
Colorado Springs	11, 13, 21
Craig	*16+
Denver	2, 4−, *6−, 7, 9−, 20, 31, *41
Durango	6+, *20−
Fort Collins	22−
Glenwood Springs	*19+
Grand Junction	5−, 8−, *18+
Gunnison	*17−
La Junta	*22+
Lamar	12−, *14−
Leadville	*15−
Montrose	10+, *22
Pueblo	5, *8, 26+, 32−
Salida	*23+
Sterling	3, *18+
Trinidad	*24

Connecticut:

Bridgeport	43−, *49−
Hartford	3+, 18−, *24, 61+
New Britain	30+
New Haven	8+, 59+, *65
New London	26+
Norwich	*53
Waterbury	20

Delaware:

Dover	*34
Seaford	*38
Wilmington	*12, 61

District of Columbia: 4−, 5−, 7+, 9, 14−, 20+, *26−, *32+, 50

Florida:

Boca Raton	*14 [1], *62+
Bradenton	*19
Clearwater	22
Cocoa	*18−, 52
Daytona Beach	2−, 26
Fort Lauderdale	51
Fort Myers	11+, 20+, *30
Fort Pierce	*21−, 34
Gainesville	*5−, 20
Jacksonville	4+, *7, 12+, 17, 30+, 47−, *59

Key West	16+, 22+
Lake City	*41
Lakeland	32
Leesburg	*45−, 55
Madison	*36−
Marianna	*16+
Melbourne	43+, 56
Miami	*2, 4, 6, 7−, 10+, *17−, 23−, 33, 39, 45+
Naples	26−
New Smyrna Beach	*15+
Ocala	*29, 51−
Orlando	6−, 9, *24−, 35+
Palatka	*42
Panama City	7+, 13, *22+, 28−
Pensacola	3−, *23, 33+, 44
St. Petersburg	10−, 38, 44+
Sarasota	40
Sebring	*27
Tallahassee	*11−, 27+, 40+
Tampa	*3, 8−, 13−, *16, 28
West Palm Beach	5, 12, 25+, *42+, 53

Georgia:

Albany	10, 19−, 31−
Ashburn	*23+
Athens	*8, 34
Atlanta	2, 5−, 11+, 17−, *30, 36, 46−, *57+, 69
Augusta	6+, 12−, 26, 54−
Carnesville	*52
Carrollton	*49−
Cedartown	*65−
Chatsworth	*18−
Cochran	*15
Columbus	3, 9+, *28, 38+, *48, 54+
Dawson	*25
Draketown	*27−
Elberton	*60+
Flintstone	*51−
Lafayette	*35
Macon	13+, 24+, 41+, *47+
Pelham	*14−
Rome	14+
Savannah	3+, *9−, 11, 22
Thomasville	6
Toccoa	32−, *68−
Valdosta	*33, 44−
Vidalia	*18+
Warm Springs	*22−
Waycross	*8+
Wrens	*20−
Young Harris	*50+

Hawaii:

Hilo (Hawaii)	2, *4, 9, 11, 13, 14+, 20+, 26+, *32+, *38+
Honolulu (Oahu)	2+, 4−, 9−, *11+, 13−, 14, 20, 26, 32, *38, *44
Lihue (Kauai)	3+, *8−, 10+, 12−, 15−, *21−, *27−
Wailuku (Maui)	3, 7, *10, 12, 15, 21, *27, *33

Idaho:

Boise	2, *4+, 7, 14

Louisiana:

Alexandria	5, 25+, 31+, *41+
Baton Rouge	2, 9−, *27+, 33−
De Ridder	*23
Houma	11
Lafayette	3+, 10, 15, *24
Lake Charles	7−, *18, 29−
Monroe	8+, *13, 14−, 39+
Morgan City	*14+
Natchitoches	*28−
New Iberia	36−
New Orleans	4+, 6, 8, *12, 20−, 26, *32+, 38+
Shreveport	3−, 12, *24−, 33
Tallulah	*19

Maine:

Augusta	*10−
Bangor	2−, 5+, 7−
Calais	*13−
Fort Kent	*46+
Fryeburg	*18+
Houlton	*25+
Kittery	*34
Lewiston	8−, 35−
Millinocket	*44−
Orono	*12−
Portland	6−, 13+, *26−, 51
Presque Island	8, *10+
Rumford	*43+

Maryland:

Annapolis	*22+
Baltimore	2+, 11−, 13+, 24+, 45, 54, *67−
Cumberland	52+, 65
Frederick	*62
Hagerstown	25−, *31
Oakland	*36+
Salisbury	16+, *28−
Waldorf	*56−

Massachusetts:

Boston	*2+, 4−, 5−, 7+, 25+, 38, *44+, 56, 68+
Greenfield	32+
New Bedford	6+, 28−, *47−
North Adams	19, *35
Pittsfield	51+
Springfield	22, 40, *57+
Worcester	14, 27[1], *48+, 66

Michigan:

Alpena	*6, 11
Ann Arbor	31+, *58+
Bad Axe	*15−[1]
Battle Creek	41+
Bay City	5−, *19, 61+
Cadillac	9, *27
Calumet	5−, *22−
Cheboygan	4+
Detroit	2+, 4, 7−, 20+, 50−, *56, 62
East Lansing	*23−, *69−
Escanaba	3+

Flint	12−, *28−, 66−
Grand Rapids	8+, 13+, 17, *35+
Iron Mountain	8−, *14−
Ironwood	*15−, 24+
Jackson	18+
Kalamazoo	3−, *52+
Lansing	6−, 36+, 53−
Manistee	*21
Manistique	*15+
Marquette	6−, *13, 19
Mount Clemens	38+
Mount Pleasant	*14
Muskegon	54+
Parma	10−
Petoskey	*23+
Port Huron	46+
Saginaw	25−, 45+
Sault Ste. Marie	8, 10+, *32−
Traverse City	7+, 29−
West Branch	*24

Minnesota:

Alexandria	7, *24
Appleton	*10−
Austin	6−, *15−
Bemidji	*9, 26+
Brainerd	*22
Crookston	*33
Duluth	3, *8, 10+, 21+, 27−
Ely	*17−
Fairmont	*16+
Hibbing	13−, *18−
International Falls	11, *35+
Mankato	12, *26−
Marshall	*30−
Minneapolis–St. Paul	*2−, 4, 5−, 9+, 11−, *17, 23+, 29+
Rochester	10, 47−
St. Cloud	19, *25−, 41
St. James	38
Thief River Falls	10
Wadena	*20−
Walker	12−
Wilmar	*14−
Winona	*35+, 44+
Worthington	*20

Mississippi:

Biloxi	13+, *19+, 25−
Booneville	*12−
Bude	*17+
Clarksdale	*22−
Cleveland	*31−
Columbia	*45
Columbus	4−, 27, *43
Greenville	15−, 21−
Greenwood	6+, 23+
Hattiesburg	22, *47
Houston	45+
Jackson	3, 12+, 16, *29+, 40+
Laurel	7, 18+
Meridian	11−, *14, 24−, 30−
Mississippi State	*2+
Natchez	*42+

Oxford	*18
Senatobia	*34−
Tupelo	9−
Vicksburg	35−
Yazoo City	*32−

Missouri:

Birchtree	*20−
Bowling Green	*35+
Cape Girardeau	12, 23, *39−
Carrollton	*18
Columbia	8+, 17−
Flat River	*22
Hannibal	7−
Jefferson City	13, 25, *36−
Joplin	12+, 16, *22−
Kansas City	4, 5+, 9+, *19+, 41−, 50−, 62+, *68−
King City	*28−
Kirksville	3−
LaPlata	*21+
Lowry City	*15−
Poplar Bluff	15+, *26−
Rolla	*28
St. Joseph	2−, 16−, 22
St. Louis	2, 4−, 5−, *9, 11−, 24+, 30+, *40−
Sedalia	6
Springfield	3+, 10, *21−, 27−

Montana:

Anaconda	2+
Billings	2, 8, *11, 14, 20+
Bozeman	*9
Butte	4, 6+, *7−, 18, 24
Cut Bank	*14−
Dillon	*14+
Glendive	5+, 9+, *16−
Great Falls	3+, 5+, 16, 26, *32
Hardin	4+
Havre	9+, 11+, *18−
Helena	10+, 12, *15+
Kalispell	9−, *29−
Lewiston	13
Miles City	3−, *6, 10
Missoula	8−, *11−, 13−, 17−, 23−
Wolf Point	*17+

Nebraska:

Albion	8+, *21+
Alliance	*13−
Bassett	*7−
Beatrice	*23+
Falls City	*24
Grand Island	11−, 17−
Hastings	5−, *29+
Hayes Center	6
Hay Springs	4+
Kearney	13
Lexington	*3+
Lincoln	10+, *12−, 45, 51
McCook	8−
Merriman	*12
Norfolk	*19+

North Platte	2−, *9+
Omaha	3, 6+, 7, 15, *26, 42+, *48−
Pawnee City	*33+
Scottsbluff	10−
Superior	4+

Nevada:

Boulder City	5+
Elko	10−, *14+
Ely	3−, 6+
Fallon	*25
Goldfield	2−
Las Vegas	3, 8−, *10+, 13−, 21+
McGill	*13
Reno	2, 4, *5, 8, 21+, 27+
Tonopah	9−, *17+
Winnemucca	7+, *15−
Yerington	*16+

New Hampshire:

Berlin	*40−
Concord	21+
Durham	*11
Hanover	*15+, 31
Keene	*52+
Littleton	*49+
Manchester	9−, 50−, 60+
Portsmouth	17−[1]

New Jersey:

Asbury Park	58[5]
Atlantic City	*18[1], *36, 53+
Burlington	48−
Camden	*23+
Little Falls	*50+
Newark	13−, 68
New Brunswick	*19−[1], 47+, *58
Paterson	41−
Trenton	*52−
Vineland	65−
Wildwood	40

New Mexico:

Alamogordo	*18−
Albuquerque	4+, *5+, 7+, 13+, 14−, 23−, *32+
Carlsbad	6−, *15+, 25−
Clayton	*17
Clovis	12−
Deming	*16
Farmington	12+, *15+
Gallup	3, *8−, 10
Hatch	*12
Hobbs	29+
Las Cruces	*22−, 48+
Lovington	*19
Portales	*3+
Raton	*18−
Roswell	8, 10−, 21−, 27−, *33+
Santa Fe	2+, *9+, 11−, 19−
Silver City	6, *10+
Socorro	*15−
Tucumcari	*15

New York:

Albany–Schenectady	6, 10−, 13,
	*17+, 23−, *29+, 45
Amsterdam	*39+, 55
Binghamton	12−, 34, 40−, *46+
Buffalo	2, 4−, 7+, 17, *23, 29−, 49−
Carthage	7−
Corning	*30
Elmira	18+, 36−
Glens Falls	*58−
Ithaca	52, *65+
Jamestown	26+, *46
Kingston	63
Lake Placid	5, *34+
Levittown	*21−
Massena	*18
New York	2, 4, 5+, 7, 9+, 11+, *25, 31−
Oneonta	15[1], *42
Patchogue	67
Plattsburg	*57
Poughkeepsie	54+
Riverhead	55+
Rochester	8, 10+, 13−, *21, 31+, *61+
Syracuse	3−, 5−, 9−, *24+, 43+, 62+
Utica	2−, 20+, 33, *59
Watertown	*16, 50+

North Carolina:

Andrews	*59
Asheville	13−, 21+, *33, 62+
Bryson City	*67
Burlington	16
Canton	*27
Chapel Hill	*4+
Charlotte	3, 9+, 18, 36, *42+
Columbia	*2
Concord	*58
Durham	11+, 28+
Fayetteville	40+, 62
Franklin	*56+
Goldsboro	17−
Greensboro	2−, 48−, 61
Greenville	9−, 14, *25
Hickory	14−
High Point	8−, *32+
Jacksonville	19
Kannapolis	64−
Lexington	20
Linville	*17
Morganton	23−
New Bern	12+
Raleigh	5, 22, *34−
Rocky Mount	47−
Washington	7
Waynesville	59
Wilmington	3−, 6, 29+, *39−
Wilson	30−
Winston–Salem	12, *26+, 45

North Dakota:

Bismarck	*3, 5, 12−, 17−, 26+
Devils Lake	8+, *22+
Dickinson	2+, *4−, 7
Ellendale	*19−
Fargo	6, 11+, *13, 15−
Grand Forks	*2, 14+, 27+
Jamestown	7−, *23
Minot	*6+, 10−, 13−, 14−, 24
Pembina	12
Valley City	4−
Williston	8−, 11−, *15−

Ohio:

Akron	23+, *49+, 55−
Alliance	*45+
Ashtabula	15[1]
Athens	*20
Bowling Green	*27+
Cambridge	*44−
Canton	17−, 67
Chillicothe	53
Cincinnati	5−, 9, 12, 19+, *48−, 64−
Cleveland	3, 5+, 8, 19, *25+, 61
Columbus	4−, 6+, 10+, 28−, *34, *56−
Dayton	2, 7+, 16+, 22+, *45
Defiance	65+
Hillsboro	*24+
Lima	35−, 44+, *57+
Lorain	43
Mansfield	*47+
Marion	68−
Newark	*31−, 52
Oxford	*14+
Portsmouth	30, 36, *42−
Sandusky	51−
Springfield	26+, *66
Steubenville	9+, *62+
Toledo	11−, 13, 24−, *30+, 54, 60−
Youngstown	21−, 27, 33, *58
Zanesville	18−

Oklahoma:

Ada	10+, *22
Altus	*19−
Ardmore	12−, *17[1], *28−
Bartlesville	17+
Cheyenne	*12+
Elk City	8+, *15−
Enid	20−, *26+
Eufaula	*3
Guymon	*16
Hugo	*15+[1], *48+
Hugo-Paris (Texas)	42+
Lawton	7+, *36−, 16−[1], 45
McAlester	*32−
Miami	*18−
Muskogee	19
Oklahoma City	4−, 5, 9−, *13+, 14−,
	25−, 34−, 43+
Tulsa	2+, 6+, 8−, *11−, 23, *35−, 41+, 47
Woodward	*17−

Oregon:

Astoria	*21
Bend	*15, 21+
Brookings	*14−
Burns	*18
Corvallis	*7−

Eugene	9+, 13, 16+, *28−
Klamath Falls	2−, *22+
LaGrande	13+, *16
Medford	5, 8+, 10+, *18+
North Bend	11, *17+
Portland	2, 6+, 8−, *10, 12, 24+, *30
Roseburg	4+
Salem	3+, *22, 32
The Dalles	*17−

Pennsylvania:

Allentown	*39, 69
Altoona	10−, 38−, 47, *57+
Bethlehem	60−
Clearfield	*3+
Erie	12, 24, 35+, *54+, 66+
Greensburg	40+
Harrisburg	21+, 27−, *33+
Hazleton	56
Johnstown	6, 19+, *28+
Lancaster	8−, 15+
Lebanon	59−
Philadelphia	3, 6−, 10, 17−, 29, *35−, 57
Pittsburgh	2−, 4+, 11, *13−, *16, 22, 53+
Reading	51
Scranton	16−, 22−, 38+, *44−, 64
State College	29+, *55+
Wilkes Barre	28
Williamsport	20−[1]
York	43, 49+

Rhode Island:

Providence	10+, 12+[1], 16, *36, 64+

South Carolina:

Aiken	*44
Allendale	*14
Anderson	40
Beaufort	*16−
Charleston	2+, 4, 5+, *7−
Columbia	10−, 19+, 25−, *35+, 57−
Conway	*23−
Florence	13+, 15−, 21, *33+
Georgetown	*41−
Greenville	4−, 16+, *29
Greenwood	*38
Myrtle Beach	43+
Rock Hill	30+, *55−
Spartanburg	7+, 49
Sumter	*27−

South Dakota:

Aberdeen	9−, *16−
Brookings	*8
Eagle Butte	*13
Huron	12+
Lead	5−, 11+
Lowry	*11−
Martin	*8−
Mitchell	5+
Pierre	4, *10+
Rapid City	3+, 7+, *9, 15−, 21−
Reliance	6−
Seneca	*2−

Sioux Falls	11, 13+, 17−, *23, 36+
Vermillion	*2+
Watertown	3−

Tennessee:

Athens	*24
Chattanooga	3+, 9, 12+, *45, 61−
Cookeville	*22, 28+
Crossville	*20+, 55+
Fayetteville	*52−
Greenville	39−
Jackson	7+, 16+, *32+
Johnson City	11−, *41
Kingsport	19
Knoxville	6, 10+, *15−, 26−, 43+
Lexington	*11
Memphis	3−, 5+, *10+, 13+, *14+, 24, 30
Murfreesboro	39+
Nashville	2−, 4+, 5, *8+, 17+, 30+, *42
Sneedville	*2+

Texas:

Abilene	9+, 15, *26+, 32+
Alpine	12−
Amarillo	*2−, 4, 7, 10, 14+
Austin	7+, *18+, 24, 36, 42−
Bay City	*43+
Beaumont	6−, 12−, 21, *34−
Big Spring	4−, *14
Boquillas	8−
Brady	13
Brownsville	23
Bryan	3, *15−
Childress	*21
Corpus Cristi	3−, 6, 10−, *16, 28−, 38+
Dallas	4+, 8, *13+, 27−, 33+, 39
Del Rio	10, *24+
Denton	*2
El Paso	4, *7, 9, 13, 14, 26+, *38−
Fort Stockton	5+
Fort Worth	5+, 11−, 21−, *31+
Galveston	*22, 47+
Harlingen	4+, *44, 60
Houston	2−, *8, 11+, 13−, *14, 20, 26, 39−
Laredo	8, 13, 27−, *39
Longview	16+[1], 51−
Lubbock	*5−, 11, 13−, 28, 34−
Lufkin	9
McAllen	48
Marfa	3
Marshall	*22−, 35+
Midland	2+, 18
Monahans	9−
Nacogdoches	19−, *32
Odessa	7−, 24−, 30, *36+
Paris–Hugo (Oklahoma)	42+
Port Arthur	4−
Presidio	7+
Richardson	23
Rosenberg	45
San Angelo	3−, 6, 8+, *21+
San Antonio	4, 5, *9−, 12+, *23−, 29+, 41+
Sherman	20−, *26
Sonora	11+

Sweetwater	12
Temple	6+, 46−
Texarkana	6, 17−, *34
Tyler	7, 14+, *38
Victoria	19+, 25
Waco	10+, 25+, *34+, 44−
Weslaco	5−
Wichita Falls	3+, 6−, 18−, *24

Utah:

Cedar City	4, *16+
Logan	12−, *22
Moab	*14+
Monticello	*16−
Ogden	*9+, *18−, 24, 30
Price	6, *15
Provo	*11+, 16
Richfield	8+, *19
Salt Lake City	2−, 4−, 5+, *7−, 14−, 20+, *26−
St. George	*18−
Vernal	3+, *17+

Vermont:

Burlington	3, 22+, *33−
Rutland	*28−
St. Johnsbury	*20−
Windsor	*41

Virginia:

Blacksburg	*43
Bluefield	*63+
Bristol	5+, *28−
Charlottesville	29−, *41−, 64+
Courtland	*52
Danville	24−, 44+, *56
Fredericksburg	*53, 69+
Front Royal	*42
Hampton	13−, *15
Harrisonburg	3−
Kenbridge	*31−
Lynchburg	13, 21−, *54+
Manassas	66+
Norfolk–Portsmouth–Newport News	3+, 10+, 27, 33, 49−, *55+
Norton	*47−
Onancock	*25+
Petersburg	8
Richmond	6+, 12−, *23, 35+, *57−, 63
Roanoke	7−, 10, *15+, 27+
Staunton	*51−
West Point	*46

Washington:

Anacortes	24
Bellingham	12+, *34, 64
Centralia	*15+
Everett	16−
Kennewick	42+
Pasco	19−
Pullman	*10−
Richland	25, *31
Seattle	4, 5+, 7, *9, 22+, *28+
Spokane	2−, 4−, 6−, *7+, 22, 28−

Tacoma	11+, 13−, 20, *56, *62
Vancouver	*14
Walla Walla	14−
Wenatchee	*18+, 27
Yakima	23+, 29+, 35, *47

West Virginia:

Beckley	4
Bluefield	6−, 40−
Charleston	8+, 23, 29, *49−
Clarksburg	12+, 46−
Fairmont	66−
Grandview	*9−
Huntington	3+, 13+, *33+
Keyser	*48+
Martinsburg	*44
Morgantown	*24−
Parkersburg	15−, 39+, *57
Weirton	*50+
Weston	5
Wheeling	7[1], 14, *41
Williamson	*31+

Wisconsin:

Appleton	32+
Colfax	*28−
Eau Claire	13+, 18
Fond du Lac	34+
Green Bay	2+, 5+, 11+, 26+, *38
Janesville	57+
Kenosha	55−
LaCrosse	8+, 19+ 25, *31
Madison	3, 15, *21−, 27−, 47+
Manitowoc	16+
Milwaukee	4−, 6, *10+, 12, 18−, 24+, 30, *36
Oshkosh	22+
Park Falls	*36+
Racine	49+
Rhinelander	12+
Sheboygan	28
Superior	6+, 40
Wausau	7−, 9, *20+, 33−

Wyoming:

Casper	2+, *6+, 14−, 20−
Cheyenne	5+, *17, 27−, 33−
Lander	4
Laramie	*8+
Rawlins	11−
Riverton	10+
Rock Springs	13
Sheridan	7, 12+

U.S. Territories and Possessions

Guam:

Agana	*4, 8, 10, *12

Puerto Rico:

Aguadilla	*32, 44
Arecibo–Aguadilla	12+
Arecibo	54, 80
Bayamon	36
Caguas	11−, *58
Carolina	52

Cayey	76
Fajardo	13+, *40
Guayama	46
Humacoa	68
Mayaguez	3+, 5−, 16, 22
Ponce	7+, 9−, 14, 20, *26, 48
San Juan	2+, 4−, *6+, 18, 24, 30, *76
San Sebastian	34
Utuado	*78
Vega Baja	64
Yauco	42

Virgin Islands:

Charlotte Amalie	10−, 17, *23, 43
Christiansted	8+, 15, *21, 27
Charlotte Amalie–Christiansted	*3, *12 [6]

[1] Following the decision in Docket No. 18261, channels so indicated will not be available for television use until further action by the commission.

[2] Operation on this channel is subject to the conditions, terms, and requirements set out in the Report and Order in Docket No. 19075, RM-1645, adopted January 5, 1972, released January 7, 1972, FCC 72-19.

[3] Channel 15 will not be available for television use until further action by the commission.

[4] This channel is not available for use at Elgin unless and until it is determined by the commission that it is not needed for use at Joliet, IL.

[5] This channel is not available for use at Asbury Park unless and until it is determined by the commission that it is not needed for educational use at New Brunswick, NJ.

[6] Stations using these assignments shall limit radiation toward stations on the same channel in Puerto Rico to no more than the effective radiated power that would be radiated by an omnidirectional station using maximum permissible effective radiated power, at the minimum distances from such stations specified in 73.610(b). The commission shall consider the status of the negotiations with the appropriate British authorities concerning these assignments when the applications for construction permits come before the commission.

73.607 *Availability of channels*

(*a*) Subject to the provisions of paragraph *b* of this section, applications may be filed to construct television broadcast stations only on the channels assigned in the "Table of Assignments" (73.606(*b*)) and only in communities listed therein. Applications that fail to comply with this requirement, whether or not accompanied by a petition to amend the table, will not be accepted for filing: provided, however, that applications specifying channels that accord with publicly announced commission orders changing the "Table of Assignments" will be accepted for filing even though such applications are tendered before the effective dates of such channel changes.

(*b*) A channel assigned to a community listed in the "Table of Assignments" is available upon application in any unlisted community that is located within 15 miles of the listed community. In addition, a channel assigned to a community listed in the "Table of Assignments" and not designated for use by noncommercial educational stations only is available upon application in any other community within 15 miles thereof which, although listed in the table, is assigned only a channel designated for use only by noncommercial educational stations. Where channels are assigned to two or more communities listed in combination in the "Table of Assignments" the provisions of this paragraph shall apply separately to each community so listed. The distance between communities shall be determined by the distance between the respective coordinates thereof as set forth in the publication of the United States Department of Commerce entitled "Air Line Distance between Cities in the United States." (This publication may be purchased from the Superintendent of Documents, Government Printing Office, Washington, DC, 20402.) If said publication does not contain the coordinates of either or both of such communities, the coordinates of the main post office in either or both of such communities shall be used.

73.609 *Zones*

(*a*) For the purpose of allocation and assignment, the United States is divided into three zones, as follows:

(1) Zone I consists of that portion of the United States located within the confines of the following lines drawn on the United States Albers Equal Area Projection Map (based on standard parallels 29½° and 45½°; North American datum): Beginning at the most easterly point on the state boundary line between North Carolina and Virginia; thence in a straight line to a point on the Virginia–West Virginia boundary line located at north latitude 37°49′ and west longitude 80°12′30″; thence westerly along the southern boundary lines of the states of West Virginia, Ohio, Indiana, and Illinois to a point at the junction of the Illinois, Kentucky, and Missouri state boundary lines; thence northerly along the western boundary line of the state of Illinois to a point at the junction of the Illinois, Iowa, and Wisconsin state boundary lines; thence easterly along the northern state boundary line of Illinois to the 90th meridian; thence north along this meridian to the 43.5° parallel; thence east along this parallel to the United States–Canada border; thence southerly and following that border until it again intersects the 43.5° parallel; thence east along this parallel to the 71st meridian; thence in a straight line to the intersection of the 69th meridian and the 45th parallel; thence east along the 45th parallel to the Atlantic Ocean. When any of the above lines pass through a city, the city shall be considered to be located in Zone I.

(2) Zone II consists of that portion of the United States which is not located in either Zone I or Zone III, and Puerto Rico, Alaska, the Hawaiian Islands, and the Virgin Islands.

(3) Zone III consists of that portion of the United States located south of a line, drawn on the United States Albers Equal Area Projection Map

(based on standard parallels 29½° and 45½°; North American datum), beginning at a point on the east coast of Georgia and the 31st parallel and ending at the United States–Mexican border, consisting of arcs drawn with a 150-mile radius to the north from the following specified points:

	North latitude	West longitude
(a)	29°40′00″	83°24′00″
(b)	30°07′00″	84°12′00″
(c)	30°31′00″	86°30′00″
(d)	30°48′00″	87°58′30″
(e)	30°00′00″	90°38′30″
(f)	30°04′30″	93°19′00″
(g)	29°46′00″	95°05′00″
(h)	28°43′00″	96°39′30″
(i)	27°52′30″	97°32′00″

When any of the above arcs pass through a city, the city shall be considered to be located in Zone III.

73.610 *Separations*

(*a*) The provisions of this section relate to assignment separations and station separations. Petitions to amend the "Table of Assignments" (73.606-(*b*))—other than those also expressly requesting amendment of this section or 73.609—will be dismissed and all applications for new television broadcast stations or for changes in the transmitter sites of existing stations will not be accepted for filing if they fail to comply with the requirements specified in paragraphs *b, c,* and *d* of this section.

Note: Licensees and permittees of television broadcast stations which were operating on April 14, 1952, pursuant to one or more separations below those set forth in 73.610 may continue to so operate, but in no event may they further reduce the separations below the minimum. As the existing separations of such stations are increased, the new separations will become the required minimum separations until separations are reached which comply with the requirements of 73.610. Thereafter, the provisions of said section shall be applicable.

(*b*) Minimum co-channel assignment and station separations:

(1)

Zone	Channels 2–13	Channels 14–83
	Miles	Miles
I	170	155
II	190	175
III	220	205

(2) The minimum co-channel mileage separation between a station in one zone and a station in another zone shall be that of the zone requiring the lower separation.

(*c*) Minimum assignment and station-adjacent-channel separations applicable to all zones:

(1) Channels 2–13: 60 miles; Channels 14–83: 55 miles

(2) Owing to the frequency spacing that exists between Channels 4 and 5, between Channels 6 and 7, and between Channels 13 and 14, the minimum adjacent-channel separations specified in the foregoing shall not be applicable to these pairs of channels (see 73.603(*a*)).

(*d*) In addition to the requirements of paragraphs *a, b,* and *c* of this section, the minimum assignment and station separations between stations on Channels 14–83, inclusive, must be met in either rule-making proceedings or in licensing proceedings. No channel will be assigned to any city, and no application for an authorization to operate on such a channel will be granted, unless the requisite mileage separations are met.

(*e*) The zone in which the transmitter of a television station is located or proposed to be located determines the applicable rules with respect to co-channel mileage separations where the transmitter is located in a different zone from that in which the channel to be employed is located.

73.613 *Main studio location*

(*a*) The main studio of a television broadcast station shall be located in the principal community to be served. Where the principal community to be served is a city, town, village or other political subdivision, the main studio shall be located within the corporate boundaries of such city, town, village or other political subdivisions. Where the principal community to be served does not have specifically defined political boundaries, applications will be considered on a case-to-case basis in the light of the particular facts involved to determine whether the main studio is located within the principal community to be served.

(*b*) Where an adequate showing is made that good cause exists for locating a main studio outside the principal community to be served and that to do so would be consistent with the operation of the station in the public interest, the commission will permit the use of a main studio location other than that specified in paragraph *a* of this section. No relocation of a main studio to a point outside the principal community to be served, or from one such point outside the community to another, may be made without first securing a modification of construction permit or license. The main studio may, however, be relocated within the principal community to be served or be moved from a location outside the commuunity to one within it without specific authority, but the commission shall be notified promptly of any such relocation.

73.614 *Power and antenna height requirements*

(*a*) Minimum requirements: Applications will not be accepted for filing if they specify less than −10dBk (100 watts) horizontally polarized visual effective radiated power in any horizontal direction. No minimum antenna height above average terrain is specified.

(*b*) Maximum power: Applications will not be accepted for filing if they specify a power in excess of that provided for in this paragraph. Except as provided in subparagraph 1 of this paragraph, the maximum horizontally polarized effective radiated powers of television broadcast stations operating on the channels set forth below with antenna heights not in excess of 2,000 feet above average terrain shall be as follows:

73.614(*a*) and (*b*) amended, effective May 20, 1977; III (76)–2

Channel Nos.	Maximum visual effective radiated power in dB above one kilowatt (dBk)
2–6	20 dBk (100 kW)
7–13	25 dBk (316 kW)
14–83	37 dBk (5000 kW)[1]

[1]The maximum visual effective radiated power of television broadcast stations operating on Channels 14–83 within 250 miles of the Canadian–United States border may not be in excess of 30 dBk (1000 kW).

(1) In Zone I, on Channels 2–13, inclusive, the maximum powers specified above for these channels may be used only with antenna heights not in excess of 1,000 feet above average terrain. Where antenna heights exceeding 1,000 feet above average terrain are used on Channels 2–13, or antenna heights exceeding 2,000 feet above average terrain are used on Channels 14–83, the maximum power shall be based on the chart designated as "Figure 3," of 73.699.

Note: This limitation shall not apply to any licensee or permittee in Zone I who received an authorization after March 22, 1951, to relocate its transmitter site and construct a new tower and antenna to a height in excess of 1,000 feet above average terrain and who constructed or who had substantially completed construction of said tower and antenna prior to April 14, 1952. In such case, maximum power may be utilized at the height above average terrain specified in the authorization. The limitation shall apply, however, where the tower or other principal supporting structure had been constructed prior to the date of such authorization.

(2) In Zones II and III, the maximum powers that may be used by television broadcast stations operating on the respective channels set forth in the preceding table with antenna heights exceeding 2,000 feet above average terrain shall be based on the chart designated as "Figure 4," of 73.699.

(3) The effective radiated power in any horizontal or vertical direction may not exceed the maximum values permitted by this section and Figures 3 and 4 of 73.699.

(4) The maximum effective radiated power in any direction above the horizontal plane shall be as low as the state of the art permits and may not exceed the effective radiated power in the horizontal direction in the same vertical plane.

(*c*) Determination of applicable rules: The zone in which the transmitter of a television station is located or proposed to be located determines the applicable rules with respect to maximum antenna heights and powers for VHF stations when the transmitter is located in Zone I and the channel to be employed is located in Zone II, or the transmitter is located in Zone II and the channel to be employed is located in Zone I.

73.621 *Noncommercial educational stations*

In addition to the other provisions of this subpart, the following shall be applicable to noncommercial educational television broadcast stations:

(*a*) Except as provided in paragraph *b* of this section, noncommercial educational broadcast stations will be licensed only to nonprofit educational organizations upon a showing that the proposed stations will be used primarily to serve the educational needs of the community; for the advancement of educational programs; and to furnish a nonprofit and noncommercial television broadcast service.

(1) In determining the eligibility of publicly supported educational organizations, the accreditation of their respective state departments of education shall be taken into consideration.

(2) In determining the eligibility of privately controlled educational organizations, the accreditation of state departments of education or recognized regional and national educational accrediting organizations shall be taken into consideration.

(*b*) Where a municipality or other political subdivision has no independently constituted educational organization such as, for example, a board of education having autonomy with respect to carrying out the municipality's educational program, such municipality shall be eligible for a noncommercial educational television broadcast station. In such circumstances, a full and detailed showing must be made that a grant of the application will be consistent with the intent and purpose of the commission's rules and regulations relating to such stations.

(*c*) Noncommercial educational television broadcast stations may transmit educational, cultural, and entertainment programs, and programs designed for use by schools and school systems in connection with regular school courses, as well as routine and administrative material pertaining thereto.

(*d*) A noncommercial educational television station may broadcast programs produced by or at the expense of, or furnished by persons other than, the licensee, if no other consideration than the furnishing of the program and the costs incidental to its production and broadcast are received by the licensee. The payment of line charges by another station or network, or someone other than the licensee of a noncommercial educational television station, or general contributions to the operating costs of a station, shall not be considered as being prohibited by this paragraph.

(*e*) Each station shall furnish a nonprofit and

noncommercial broadcast service. However, noncommercial educational television stations shall be subject to the provisions of 73.654 to the extent that they are applicable to the broadcast of programs produced by, or at the expense of, or furnished by others, except that no announcements (visual or aural) promoting the sale of a product or service shall be broadcast in connection with any program: provided, however, that where a sponsor's name or product appears on the visual image during the course of a simultaneous or rebroadcast program either on the backdrop or in similar form, the portions of the program showing such information need not be deleted.

Note 1: Announcements of the producing or furnishing of programs, or the provision of funds for their production, may be no more than twice, at the opening and at the close of any program, except that where a program lasts longer than 1 hour an announcement may be made at hourly intervals during the program if the last such announcement occurs at least 15 minutes before the announcement at the close of the program. The person or organization furnishing or producing the program or providing funds for its production, shall be identified by name only, except that in the case of a commercial company having bona fide operating divisions or subsidiaries which has furnished the program or funds, the division or subsidiary may be mentioned in addition to or instead of the commercial company. No material beyond the company (or division or subsidiary) name shall be included. Upon request for waiver of this provision, the commission may authorize the inclusion of brief additional descriptive material only when deemed necessary to avoid confusion with another company having the same or a similar name. No mention shall be made of any product or service with which a commercial enterprise being identified has a connection, except to the extent the name of the product or service is the same as that of the enterprise (or division or subsidiary) and is so included. A repeat broadcast of a particular program is considered a separate program for the purpose of this note.

Note 2: Announcements may be made of general contributions of a substantial nature which make possible the broadcast of programs for part, or all, of the day's schedule. Such announcements may be made at the opening and closing of the day or segment, including all of those persons or organizations whose substantial contributions are making possible the broadcast day or segment. In addition, one such general contributor may be identified once during each hour of the day or segment. The provisions of Note 1 of this section as to permissible contents apply to announcements under this note.

Note 3: The limitations on credit announcements imposed by Notes 1 and 2 of this section shall not apply to program material the production of which was completed before January 1, 1971, or to other announcements broadcast before January 1, 1971, pursuant to underwriting agreements entered into before November 30, 1970.

Note 4: The provisions of Notes 1 and 2 of this section shall not apply during the broadcast times in which "auctions" are held to finance station operation. Credit announcements during "auction" broadcasts may identify particular products or services, but shall not include promotion of such products or services beyond that necessary for the specific auction purpose. Visual exposure may be given to a display in the auction area including the underwriter's name and trademark, and product or service or a representation thereof.

Note 5: The numerical limitations on permissible announcements contained in Notes 1 and 2 of this section do not apply to announcements on behalf of noncommercial, nonprofit entities, such as the Corporation for Public Broadcasting, state or regional entities, or charitable foundations.

73.622 *Retention of audio recordings*

(*a*) Except as provided in paragraph *b* of this section, each licensee of a television broadcast station that, after August 6, 1973, receives assistance pursuant to Part IV of the Communications Act of 1934, as amended, shall retain an audio recording of each of its broadcasts of any public affairs program in which any issue of public importance is discussed. Each such recording shall be retained for a period of sixty days commencing from the date on which the program was last broadcast.

(1) As used in this regulation, *assistance* is defined to mean receipt from federally funded sources of (i) matching grants for the construction of noncommercial, educational broadcast facilities as provided for under Title III, Part IV of the Communications Act of 1934, as amended, (ii) grants for the production of educational television or radio programs for national or regional distribution as provided for under Title III, Part IV of the Communications Act of 1934, as amended, or (iii) payments to aid in the financing of either local programming or operational costs incurred by noncommercial, educational broadcast stations as provided for under Title III, Part IV of the Communications Act of 1934, as amended.

(*b*) The requirements of paragraph *a* of this section shall not apply with respect to a licensee's broadcast of a program if an entity designated by the licensee retains an audio recording of each of the licensee's broadcasts of such a program for the period prescribed by paragraph *a* of this section: provided that nothing within this paragraph shall be construed as absolving the licensee from responsibility for compliance with these rules in the event of an error or omission by a designated entity where the licensee has been involved in the access request and has failed to discharge that responsibility with reasonable diligence. A licensee shall record and retain audio recordings of all programs required to be retained by this regulation where an entity has not been delegated by the licensee to perform the requirements specified in paragraph *a* of this section.

(*c*) Each licensee or entity designated by a licensee under paragraph *b* which retains an audio recording pursuant to paragraphs *a* and *b* of this section shall, in the period during which the recordings are required under paragraph *a* of this section to be retained, make a copy of such recording available

(1) to the commission upon its request, and

(2) to any other person who requests such a copy and makes advance payment to the licensee or designated entity (as the case may be) of its reasonable costs of making such a copy.

(*d*) All requests for copies of audio recordings made pursuant to this section shall be made within 60 days of the date on which the program was last broadcast, and shall be in written form containing detail sufficient to identify the requested program with reasonable certainty. Requests may be made either to the licensee, for its action, or if the designated entity is known to the requesting party, to the designated entity. The written request, which shall be retained for a period of three years by the licensee or entity to which it is addressed, may be tendered in person or by correspondence at the licensee's main studio location or principal place of business, or at the principal place of business of the designated entity. The licensee or designated entity shall be accorded a reasonable time commencing upon receipt of both the request and the payment in which to satisfy the request: provided that

(1) where there is recording and retention by either a licensee or designated entity located within the licensee's community of license, a reasonable time shall not exceed seven days from the date on which the request is actually received, and

(2) where there has been recording and retention by a designated entity not located within the licensee's community of license, a reasonable time shall not exceed 21 days, commencing from the date the request is actually received.

Note 1: For purpose of this role, *copy* is defined as a mechanical or magnetic reproduction of sound transcribed upon reel-to-reel tapes, cassettes, cartridges, dictabelts, recording discs, or other similar devices. The definition of *copy* does not include written transcripts. Where the requested program is retained on film or video tape, a copy of the audio or sound track will suffice for purposes of this regulation.

Note 2: A request is not actually received until such time as both a written request and advance payment have been received by the licensee or entity.

(*e*) A licensee or designated entity that provides a copy of an audio recording to a member of the general public pursuant to a request made under these rules may, as a condition precedent, require the party making the request to disclose his or her name and address.

(*f*) Revenues derived by a licensee or designated entity from fees charged pursuant to paragraph *c*2 of this section shall not

(1) exceed the reasonable costs of complying with paragraph *c* of this section

(2) nor shall the revenue be used to subsidize other facets of the licensee's or entity's business operations.

(*g*) A party who requests the production of a recording pursuant to the provisions of paragraph *c* of this section may require the licensee or designated entity to

(1) provide a copy of an audio recording that is accurate, complete, intelligible, and capable of being audibly reviewed on playback devices commonly available to the general public, and

(2) provide an itemized statement of the reasonable costs of making a copy of the requested program.

73.623 *Applications for sharing of television channels*

Separate applications shall be filed by each applicant for the voluntary sharing of television channels. Such applications shall be accompanied by copies of the time-sharing agreement under which the applicants propose to operate.

73.624 *Notification of filing of applications*

(*a*) Radio astronomy and radio-research installations: In order to minimize harmful interference at the National Radio Astronomy Observatory site located at Green Bank, Pocahontas County, West Virginia, and at the Naval Radio Research Observatory at Sugar Grove, Pendleton County, West Virginia, an applicant for authority to construct a new television broadcast station or for authority to make changes in the frequency, power, antenna height, or antenna directivity of an existing station within the area bounded by 39°15' N on the north, 78°30' W on the east, 37°30' N on the south, and 80°30' W on the west shall, at the time of filing such application with the commission, simultaneously notify the Director, National Radio Astronomy Observatory, P.O. Box No. 2, Green Bank, WV 24944, in writing, of the technical particulars of the proposed station. Such notification shall include the geographical coordinates of the antenna, antenna height, antenna directivity, if any, proposed frequency, type of emission, and power. In addition, the applicant shall indicate in his application to the commission the date notification was made to the observatory. After receipt of such application, the commission will allow a period of 20 days for comments or objections in response to the notifications indicated. If an objection to the proposed operation is received during the 20-day period from the National Radio Astronomy Observatory for itself or on behalf of the Naval Radio Research Observatory, the commission will consider all aspects of the problem and take whatever action is deemed appropriate.

(*b*) [Reserved]

(*c*) Protection for Table Mountain Radio Receiving Zone, Boulder County, Colorado: Applicants for a station authorization to operate in the vicinity of Boulder County, Colorado, under this part are advised to give due consideration, prior to filing applications, to the need to protect the Table Mountain Radio Receiving Zone from harmful interference. These are the Research Laboratories of the Department of Commerce, Boulder County, Colorado. To prevent degradation of the present ambient radio-signal level at the site, the Department of Commerce seeks to ensure that field strengths at 40°07'50" north latitude, 105°14'40" west longitude, resulting from new assignments (other than mobile stations) or from the modifica- tion or relocation of existing facilities do not exceed the following values:

Frequency range	Field strength[1] (mV/m) in authorized bandwidth of service	Power-flux density[2] (dBW/m²) in authorized bandwidth of service
Below 540 kHz	10	−65.8
540–1600 kHz	20	−59.8
1.6–470 MHz	10	[2]65.8
470–890 MHz	30	[2]56.2
Above 800 MHz	1	[2]85.8

[1]Equivalent values of power-flux density are calculated assuming free-space characteristic impedance of $376.7 \approx 120 \pi$ ohms.

[2]Space stations shall conform to the power-flux density limits at the earth's surface specified in appropriate parts of the FCC rules, but in no case should exceed the above levels in any 4-kHz band for all angles of arrival.

(1) Advance consultation is recommended particularly for those applicants who have no reliable data that indicates whether the field strength or power-flux-density figures in the preceding table would be exceeded by their proposed radio facilities (except mobile stations). In such instances, the following is a suggested guide for determining whether coordination is recommended:

(i) all stations within 1.5 statute miles

(ii) stations within 3 statute miles with 50 watts or more effective radiated power (ERP) in the primary plane of polarization in the azimuthal direction of the Table Mountain Receiving Zone

(iii) stations within 10 statute miles with 1 kW or more ERP in the primary plane of polarization in the azimuthal direction of Table Mountain Receiving Zone

(iv) stations within 50 statute miles with 25 kW or more ERP in the primary plane of polarization in the azimuthal direction of Table Mountain Receiving Zone.

(2) Applicants concerned are urged to communicate with the Radio Frequency Management Coordinator, Department of Commerce, Research Support Services, NOAA/R5X3, Boulder Laboratories, Boulder, CO 80302 (tel. 303-499-1000, ext. 6548 or 6549) in advance of filing their applications with the commission.

(3) The commission will not screen applications to determine whether advance consultation has taken place. However, applicants are advised that such consultation can avoid objections from the Department of Commerce or proceedings to modify any authorization which may be granted which, in fact, delivers a signal at the reference point in excess of the field strength specified herein.

73.627 *Special field test authorization*

(*a*) Upon a showing that a need exists, a special test authorization to operate a portable or regularly authorized transmitter may be issued to persons desiring to make field-intensity surveys to determine factors influencing radio-wave propagation, in particular areas or paths for the period necessary to conduct the survey. Such authorizations may be granted upon the following conditions:

(1) No objectionable interference will result to the operation of other authorized radio services; in this connection, the power requested shall not exceed that necessary for the purposes of the test.

(2) The carriers will be unmodulated except for a visual test pattern and hourly voice identification.

(3) The output powers of the aural and visual transmitters shall not exceed the authorized test powers and the transmission line meter indications shall be maintained at constant values for each phase of the test.

(4) The output powers of the transmitters shall be logged at half-hour intervals and at any time that such power is changed. Certified copies of such log notations shall be submitted to the commission with the required report.

(5) The test equipment shall not be permanently installed, unless such installation has been separately authorized. Mobile units shall not be deemed permanent installations.

(6) The equipment must be operated by or under the personal direction of a licensed radio-telephone first-class operator.

(7) A report, containing the measurements, their analysis, and other results of the survey shall be filed with the commission within 60 days from the termination of the test authorization. The measurements shall be made and reported according to the procedures described in Section 73.686.

(*b*) The test equipment, installation, and operation thereof need not comply with the requirements of commission rules and standards except as specified in this section: provided, however, that the equipment, installation, and operation shall be consistent with good engineering principles and practices.

(*c*) No authorization shall be issued unless the applicant for such authorization is determined to be legally qualified. Requests for authorizations to operate a transmitter under this section shall be made in writing, signed by the applicant (with no special form provided, however), and shall set forth the following information:

(1) Purpose, duration, and need for the survey

(2) Frequency, transmitter-output powers, and time of operation

(3) A brief description of the test-antenna system, its estimated effective radiated field and height above average terrain, and the geographic coordinates of its proposed location

(4) In the case of a person who is not a licensee or permittee of this commission, the information required by section II of FCC Form 301.

(d) The authorization may be modified or terminated by notification from the commission if in its judgment such action will promote the public interest, convenience, or necessity.

73.630 *Normal license period*

(a) Initial licenses for television broadcast stations will ordinarily be issued for a period running until the date specified in this section for the state or territory in which the station is located or, if issued after such date, to the next triennial renewal date determined in accordance with this section; and, when renewed, will normally be renewed for three years: provided, however, that if the commission finds that the public interest, convenience, or necessity will be served thereby it may issue either an initial license or a renewal thereof for a lesser term. The time of expiration of normally issued initial and renewed licenses will be 3:00 A.M., local time, on the following dates, and at three-year intervals thereafter:

(1) For stations located in Iowa and Missouri, February 1, 1977

(2) For stations located in Minnesota, North Dakota, South Dakota, Montana, and Colorado, April 1, 1977

(3) For stations located in Kansas, Oklahoma, and Nebraska, June 1, 1977

(4) For stations located in Texas, August 1, 1977

(5) For stations located in Wyoming, Nevada, Arizona, Utah, New Mexico, and Idaho, October 1, 1977

(6) For stations located in California, December 1, 1977

(7) For stations located in Washington, Oregon, Alaska, Guam, and Hawaii, February 1, 1978

(8) For stations located in Connecticut, Maine, Massachusetts, New Hampshire, Rhode Island, and Vermont, April 1, 1978

(9) For stations located in New Jersey and New York, June 1, 1978

(10) For stations located in Delaware and Pennsylvania, August 1, 1978

(11) For stations located in Maryland, District of Columbia, Virginia, and West Virginia, October 1, 1978

(12) For stations located in North Carolina and South Carolina, December 1, 1978

(13) For stations located in Florida, Puerto Rico, and Virgin Islands, February 1, 1979

(14) For stations located in Alabama and Georgia, April 1, 1979

(15) For stations located in Arkansas, Louisiana, and Mississippi, June 1, 1979

(16) For stations located in Tennessee, Kentucky, and Indiana, August 1, 1979

(17) For stations located in Ohio and Michigan, October 1, 1979

(18) For stations located in Illinois and Wisconsin, December 1, 1979

73.640 *Acceptability of broadcast transmitters for licensing*

(a) In order to facilitate the filing of, and action on, applications for station authorizations, transmitters will be accepted for licensing by the commission under one of the following conditions:

(1) A transmitter may be type-accepted upon the request of any manufacturer of transmitters built in quantity, provided that the date and information submitted indicates that the transmitter meets the requirements of 73.687. If accepted, such transmitter will be included on the commission's "Radio Equipment List." Applicants specifying transmitters included on such a list need not submit detailed descriptions and diagrams where the correct type number is specified, if the equipment proposed is identical with that accepted. Copies of this list are available for inspection at the commisssion's office in Washington, DC, and at each of its field offices.

(2) An application specifying a transmitter not included on the "Radio Equipment List" may be accepted upon the request of a prospective licensee submitting with the application for construction permit a complete description of the transmitter, including the circuit diagram, a listing of all tubes used, the function of each, the multiplication in each stage, the plate current and voltage applied to each tube, a description of the oscillator circuit together with any devices installed for the purpose of frequency stabilization, and the means of varying output power to compensate for power-supply-voltage variations. However, if this data has been filed with the commission by a manufacturer in connection with a request for type acceptance, it need not be submitted with the application for construction permit but may be referred to as "on file." Measurement data for type acceptance made in accordance with subparagraph 1 of this paragraph shall be submitted with the license application.

(3) A transmitter shown on an instrument of authorization by manufacturer and type number, or as a composite, and which was in use prior to June 30, 1955, may continue to be used by the licensee, his successors or assigners, provided such transmitter continues to comply with the rules and regulations.

(4) A permittee may, without further authority, install and utilize a transmitter other than that specifically authorized in its construction permit if such transmitter is listed in the commission's "Radio Equipment List" as acceptable for the transmitter output power authorized.

(5) A licensee may, without further authority, install and utilize a transmitter other than that

specifically authorized in its station license if the transmitter so installed and utilized is listed in the commission's "Radio Equipment List" as acceptable for the transmitter-output power authorized. In the event of such a transmitter substitution, the commission and the engineer in charge of the radio district in which the station is located shall be notified within three days after the newly installed transmitter is placed in regular operation. Such notice shall specify the manufacturer and type number of the transmitter and shall include a certification by the licensee that the transmitter and overall station performance complies with the terms of its license and the technical requirements of this subpart. The certification shall also attest to the fact that transmitter and station performance measurements have been made and are on file with the station's records and that the data confirm that the transmitter and station performance are as certified.

(*b*) Additional rules with respect to withdrawal of type-acceptance, modification of type-accepted equipment, and limitations on the findings upon which type-acceptance is based are available from the FCC.

Over-the-Air Subscription Television Operations
73.641 *Definitions*

(*a*) Subscription television: a system whereby subscription television broadcast programs are transmitted and received.

(*b*) Subscription television broadcast program: a television broadcast program intended to be received in intelligible form by members of the public only for a fee or charge.

73.642 *Licensing policies*

(*a*) Subscription television service may be provided only upon specific authorization therefor by the commission. Such authorization will be issued only to

(1) the licensee of a commercial television broadcast station

(2) the holder of a construction permit for a new commercial television broadcast station, or

(3) an applicant for a construction permit for a new commercial television broadcast station: provided, however, that such authorization will not be issued prior to issuance of the construction permit for the new station. Moreover, such an authorization will be issued only for a station the principal community of which is located entirely within the grade-A contours of five or more commercial television broadcast stations (including the station of the applicant), whether the principal community each station is authorized to serve is the same as that of the applicant or is a nearby community. Only one such authorization will be granted in any community. No such authorization will be granted unless, not counting the station of the applicant, at least four of the stations which include the community of the applicant within their grade-A contours are operating nonsubscription stations.

(*b*) Application for such authorizations shall be made in the manner and form prescribed by the commission. If the commission, upon consideration of such application, finds that the public interest, convenience, and necessity would be served by the granting thereof, it will grant such application. In the event it is unable to make such a finding, the commission will then formally designate the application for subscription television authorization for hearing and proceed pursuant to the provisions of section 309 *e* of the Communications Act and the commission's rules and regulations applicable thereto. The commission may impose such conditions upon the grant as may be appropriate.

(*c*) Holders of subscription television authorizations shall complete construction of subscription television transmitting facilities within a period of eight months after issuance of the authorization unless otherwise determined by the commission upon proper showing in any particular case. During the process of construction of the subscription television facilities, the holder of the authorization, after notifying the commission and the engineer in charge of the radio district in which the station is located, may, without further authority of the commission, conduct equipment tests for the purpose of such adjustments and measurements as may be necessary to assure compliance with the terms of the authorization, the technical provisions of the application therefor, and the rules and regulations. The commission may notify the holder of the authorization not to conduct tests if such tests appear to be contrary to the public interest convenience, and necessity. Upon completion of the construction, the holder of the authorization shall submit a detailed showing that compliance with the terms of the authorization, the technical provisions of the application therefor, and the rules and regulations has been achieved. No subscription television operation shall commence until requirements of this paragraph have been fulfilled and operation has been specifically authorized by the commission.

(*d*) A subscription television authorization will not be issued or renewed for a period longer than the regular license period of the applicant's television broadcast authorization. Renewals of such authorizations will usually be considered together with renewals of the regular station authorizations.

(*e*) No subscription television authorization or renewal thereof shall be granted to a party having any contract, arrangement, or understanding, expressed or implied, which

(1) prevents or hinders it from rejecting or refusing any subscription television broadcast program which it reasonably believes to be unsatisfactory or unsuitable or contrary to the public interest, or substituting a subscription or conventional program which in its opinion is of greater local or national importance, or

(2) delegates to any other person the right to schedule the hours of transmission of subscription programs: provided, however, that this rule shall not prevent a licensee, permittee, or applicant from entering into an agreement or arrangement whereby it agrees to schedule a specific subscription television broadcast program at a specific time or to schedule a specific number of hours of sub-

scription programs during the broadcast day (or segments thereof) or week subject to commission approval, or

(3) prevents or hinders it from, or penalizes it for, making a free choice of subscription programs, whatever their source: provided, however, that upon making a satisfactory showing to the commission that the public interest would be served by permitting the licensee, permittee, or applicant to enter into an agreement or arrangement whereby it agrees to obtain all or a specified portion of its programming from one or more sources, this rule may be waived, or

(4) deprives it of the right of ultimate decision concerning the maximum amount of any subscription program charge or fee.

(*f*) No subscription television authorization or renewal thereof shall be granted to a party having any contract, arrangement, or understanding, expressed or implied, with other parties the provisions of which do not comply with the following policies of the commission:

(1) Unless a satisfactory signal is unavailable at the location where service is desired, subscription television service shall be provided to all persons desiring it within the grade-A contour of the nonsubscription television service provided by the station broadcasting subscription programs: provided, however, that geographic or other reasonable patterns of installation for new subscription services shall be permitted, and provided further that, for good cause, service may be terminated.

(2) Charges, terms, and conditions of service to subscribers shall be applied uniformly: provided, however, that subscribers may be divided into reasonable classifications approved by the commission, and the imposition of different sets of terms and conditions may be applied to subscribers in different classifications, and provided further that within such classifications deposits to assure payment may, for good cause, be required of some subscribers and not of others; and also for good cause, if a subscription system generally uses a credit-type decoder, cash-operated decoders may be installed for some subscribers.

(3) Subscription television decoders shall be leased, and not sold, to subscribers.

(*g*) All applications for subscription television authorization or renewal shall set forth, in such detail as the commission may require, the terms of agreements and arrangements the applicant has or intends to have with other parties concerning the supplying of subscription television programs, including specifically any provision that such programs shall be presented at a particular time or during a certain number of hours during the day (or segments thereof) or week, any arrangement or understanding that might hinder or prevent the presentation of programs from different sources, or penalize the applicant for so doing, and, as to any arrangement or understanding with a party other than the producer of the program, any other arrangement or understanding of which the applicant has knowledge, between such other party and third

parties, which prevents or hinders such other party from obtaining programs from different sources. The applicant shall use due diligence to ascertain the existence and nature of arrangements to which it is not a party.

73.643 *General operating requirements*

Subscription television broadcast programming shall comply with the following requirements:

(*a*) Feature films shall not be broadcast except as provided in this paragraph.

(1) A feature film may be broadcast if

(i) the film has been in general release in theaters anywhere in the United States for three years or less prior to its proposed broadcast;

(ii) a conventional television broadcast station licensed in the market of the subscription television broadcast station holds a present contractual right to exhibit the film—for purposes of this subdivision, a television station affiliated with a television network will be deemed to hold a present contractual right to exhibit a film if the network to which it is affiliated holds such a right;

Note: The manner in which the term *present contractual right* will be construed is explained in paragraphs 169 and 170, "First Report and Order in Docket 19554," FCC 75-369, 40 FR 15546.

(iii) the film has been in general release in theaters anywhere in the United States for more than ten years prior to its proposed subscription broadcast and the film has not been exhibited over conventional television in the market of the subscription television broadcast station for three years prior to its proposed subscription broadcast—once a film has been broadcast in the market pursuant to this subdivision or cablecast on a subscription basis pursuant to 76.225 *a*1iii, such film may thereafter be broadcast on a subscription basis in the market without regard to its subsequent exhibition over conventional television;

(iv) the film is in a foreign language.

(2) Feature films otherwise excluded by this paragraph may be broadcast upon a convincing showing to the commission that they are not desired for exhibition over conventional television in the market or that the owners of the broadcast rights to the films, even absent the existence of subscription television, would not make the films available to conventional television.

(3) Every subscription television broadcast station over which a feature film is broadcast pursuant to this paragraph shall maintain for public inspection a file listing the title of the film, the date on which it was broadcast, and the provision of this paragraph pursuant to which it was broadcast. When a feature film is broadcast pursuant to subparagraph 1ii of this paragraph, the station or network serving the market and holding a present contractual right to exhibit the film shall be specified. These files shall be retained for a period of two years.

(*b*) Sports events shall not be broadcast live except as provided in this paragraph.

(1) A specific event may be broadcast if the event has not been broadcast live over conventional

television in the market of the subscription television broadcast station during any one of the five seasons preceding the proposed subscription broadcast. If a regularly recurring event takes place at intervals of more than one year (e.g., summer Olympic games), the event shall not be broadcast on a subscription basis if it has been broadcast live over conventional television in the market of the subscription television broadcast station during any one of the ten years preceding the proposed subscription broadcast.

(2) New specific sports events that result from the restructuring of existing sports shall not be broadcast on a subscription basis until five seasons after their first occurrence. Thereafter, subscription broadcasts shall be governed by paragraph *b*1 of this section.

(3) The number of nonspecific events which may be broadcast on a subscription basis in any given season shall be determined as follows:

(i) If less than 25 percent of the events in a category of nonspecific events were broadcast live over conventional television in the market of the subscription television broadcast station during each of the five seasons preceding the proposed subscription broadcast, the number of events in the category broadcast on a subscription basis shall not exceed the number of events in the category not conventionally broadcast in that season among the preceding five seasons when the largest number of events in the category were broadcast over conventional television.

(ii) If 25 percent or more of the events in a category of nonspecific events were broadcast live over conventional television in the market of the subscription television broadcast station during any one of the five seasons preceding the proposed subscription broadcast, the number of events in the category broadcast on a subscription basis shall not exceed 50 percent of the number of events in the category not broadcast in that season among the preceding five seasons when the largest number of events in the category were broadcast over conventional television. However, if the number of events in the category to be broadcast over conventional television in the current season is a reduction from the number of events broadcast in that season among the preceding five seasons when the largest number of events in the category were broadcast, the number of events in the category which may be broadcast on a subscription basis pursuant to this subparagraph shall be reduced in proportion to the reduction in events broadcast over conventional television.

Note: The manner in which this paragraph will be administered and in which *sports events, new sports events, specific events, nonspecific events, live telecast* and *category* will be construed is explained in paragraphs 186–208 of the First Report and Order in Docket 19554, FCC 75-369, 40 FR 15546.

(*c*) No commercial advertising announcements shall be carried during subscription television operations except for promotion of subscription

television broadcast programs before and after such programs.

(*d*) Not more than 90 percent of the total subscription programming hours shall consist of feature films and sports events combined. The percentage calculations may be made on a yearly basis, but, absent a showing of good cause, the percentage of such programming hours may not exceed 95 percent of the total subscription programming hours in any calendar month.

(*e*) Any television broadcast station licensee or permittee authorized to broadcast subscription programs shall broadcast, in addition to its subscription broadcasts, at least the minimum hours of nonsubscription programming required by 73.651.

(*f*) Except as they may be otherwise waived by the commission in authorizations issued hereunder, the rules and policies applicable to regular television broadcast stations are applicable to subscription television operations.

Note: As referred to in this section, *the market* of a subscription broadcast station includes all commercial broadcast stations which place a grade-A contour over the entire community to which the subscription station is licensed.

73.644 *Equipment and technical system performance requirements*

(*a*) No subscription television authorization will be granted unless the technical system to be used has been approved in advance by the commission. Such advance approval may be applied for and granted in accordance with the following procedure, subject to the conditions and limitations set forth:

(1) A separate request for each different technical system shall be made by the applicant in writing.

(2) The applicant shall certify that the application was prepared by him or at his direction and that the facts set forth are true and correct to the best of his knowledge and belief.

(3) The applicant shall identify the technical system by a name or type number and shall define the system in terms of its technical characteristics; a functional block diagram shall be included. In addition, a complete description of the encoded transmitted signal and the encoding and decoding equipment used by the applicant shall be supplied. The description of this equipment shall include circuit diagrams and photographs.

(4) Preliminary test data shall be submitted to show system capability with regard to compliance with the criteria set forth in paragraph *b* of this section.

(5) The applicant shall supply any additional information and test data requested by the commission, to show to its satisfaction that the criteria set forth in paragraph *b* of this section are met.

(6) The information submitted by the applicant may be subject to check by field tests conducted without expense to the commission or by tests by commission personnel, if deemed necessary by the commission.

(7) No technical system will be deemed approved unless and until the commission has notified

the applicant in writing of the approval. Such notification of approval will be by letter to the applicant.

(8) Approval by the commission is limited to a determination that the particular technical system (the scheme for encoding and decoding the subscription television signal) is capable of meeting the criteria set forth in paragraph *b* of this section.

(9) The commission shall maintain a listing of approved technical systems.

(*b*) The criteria for approval of subscription television technical systems by the commission are as follows:

(1) The technical system shall be capable of operating by delivering a suitable signal to the antenna input terminals of receivers designed for reception of signals meeting the technical standards for color or monochrome television transmission and accompanying aural signal as set forth in this part. For the purpose of this requirement, a "suitable signal" shall be one which, except for distortion or attenuation occurring in the transmitting antenna, receiving antenna, or the propagation medium, complies with all technical standards for color or monochrome transmission and accompanying aural signal set forth in this part.

(2) Spectral energy in transmission shall not exceed limitations set forth in 73.687(i).

(3) No increase in width of the television broadcast channel (6MHz) shall be required.

(4) The technical system shall enable stations transmitting subscription television programs to produce visual and aural signal coverage and receive program quality not significantly inferior, in the judgment of the commission, to that produced by stations using the normal monochrome or color transmission standards set forth in this part without employing additional effective radiated power for either the visual or aural signals.

(5) The encoded visual and aural programs shall be recoverable without perceptible degradation as compared to the same programs transmitted in accordance with commission monochrome and color standards.

(6) Internal modifications to subscribers' receivers shall not be required.

(7) Interference to reception of conventional television and subscription television programs, co-channel and adjacent channel, monochrome and color shall not significantly, in the judgment of the commission, exceed that occurring from conventional television broadcasting conducted in compliance with the technical standards set forth in this part.

(8) Reception of subscription television programs shall not be, in the judgment of the commission, significantly more susceptible to interference of any kind than reception of conventional television programs transmitted in accordance with the technical standards set forth in this part.

General Operating Requirements
73.651 *Time of operation*

(*a*)

(1) All television broadcast stations will be licensed for unlimited time operation. Each such station shall maintain a regular program operating schedule as follows: Not less than two hours daily in any five broadcast days per week and not less than a total of 12 hours per week during the first 18 months of the station's operation; not less than two hours daily in any five broadcast days per week and not less than a total of 16 hours, 20 hours, and 24 hours per week for each successive six-month period of operation, respectively; and not less than two hours in each of the seven days of the week and not less than a total of 28 hours per week thereafter.

(2) "Operation" includes the period during which a station is operated pursuant to temporary authorization or during program tests, as well as during the license period. Time devoted to test patterns, or to aural presentations accompanied by the incidental use of fixed visual images which have no substantial relationship to the subject matter of such aural presentations, shall not be considered in computing periods of program service.

(3) In the event that causes beyond the control of a permittee or licensee make it impossible to adhere to the operating schedule in paragraph *a* of this section or to continue operating, the station may limit or discontinue operation for a period of not more than 30 days without further authority from the commission, provided that notification is sent to the commission in Washington, DC, no later than the tenth day of limited or discontinued operation. During such period, the permittee or licensee shall continue to adhere to the requirements of the station license pertaining to the lighting of antenna structures. In the event normal operation is restored prior to the expiration of the 30-day period, the permittee or licensee will so notify the commission in Washington, DC, of this date. If the causes beyond the control of the permittee or licensee make it impossible to comply within the allowed period, informal written request shall be made to the commission in Washington, DC, no later than the 30th day for such additional time as may be deemed necessary.

(*b*) Noncommercial educational television broadcast stations are not required to operate on a regular schedule and no minimum number of hours of operation is specified; but the hours of actual operation during a license period shall be taken into consideration in considering the renewal of noncommercial educational television broadcast licenses.

(*c*)

(1) The aural transmitter of a television station shall not be operated separately from the visual transmitter except for the following purposes:

(i) for actual tests of station equipment or actual experimentation in accordance with 73.666, and

(ii) for emergency "fills" in case of visual equipment failure or unscheduled and unavoidable delays in presenting visual programs. In such situations the aural transmitter may be used to advise the audience of difficulties and to transmit for a short period program material of such nature that the audience will be enabled to remain tuned to the station; for example, music or news accompanying a test pattern or other visual presentation.

(2) During periods of transmission of a test pattern on the visual transmitter of a television station, aural transmission shall consist only of a single tone or series of variable tones. During periods when still pictures or slides are employed to produce visual transmissions that are accompanied by aural transmissions, the aural and visual transmissions shall be integral parts of a program or announcement and shall have a substantial relationship to each other: provided that nothing herein shall preclude the transmission of a test pattern, still pictures, or slides for the following purposes and periods:

(i) to accompany aural announcements of the station's program schedule and aural news broadcasts or news commentaries, for a total period not to exceed one hour in any broadcast day,

(ii) to accompany aural transmissions for a period of time not to exceed 15 minutes immediately prior to the commencement of a programming schedule.

Examples: (1) Duplication of AM or FM programs on the aural transmitter of a television station while the same program is broadcast on the visual transmitter (i.e., a "simulcast") is consistent with this paragraph.

(2) Duplication of AM or FM programs on the aural transmitter of a television station while a test pattern is broadcast on the visual transmitter is not consistent with this paragraph, except for the specific purposes and periods specified in paragraph $c2$.

(3) A travel lecture in which the words of the lecturer are broadcast simultaneously with still pictures or slides of scenes illustrating the lecture, and a newscast in which the words of the newscaster are broadcast simultaneously with still pictures or slides of the news events, are examples of programs in which the aural and visual transmissions are integral parts of the same program having a substantial relationship to each other, within the meaning of paragraph $c2$. Mood music unrelated to the visual transmission is not consistent with this paragraph.

(4) The broadcast of a test pattern accompanied by a musical composition for the purpose of demonstration, sale, installation or orientation of television receivers, or receiving antennas is not consistent with this paragraph.

(5) Music accompanying the transmission of a test pattern upon which is visually imposed a moving text consisting of continuous program material, such as a running newscast or news commentary, is consistent with this paragraph.

(6) Music accompanying the transmission of a test pattern upon which is visually imposed a clock indicating the time of day, or a text that is changed at spaced intervals, is not consistent with this paragraph.

73.657 *Broadcasts by candidates for public office*

(*a*) Definitions: A *legally qualified candidate* means any person who has publicly announced that he is a candidate for nomination by a convention of a political party or for nomination or election in a primary, special, or general election, municipal, county, state, or national, and who meets the qualifications prescribed by the applicable laws to hold the office for which he is a candidate, so that he may be voted for by the electorate directly or by means of delegates or electors, and who either

(1) has qualified for a place on the ballot, or

(2) has publicly committed himself to seeking election by the write-in method, and is eligible under the applicable law to be voted for by sticker, by writing in his name on the ballot, or other method; and makes a substantial showing that he is a bona fide candidate for nomination or office.

(*b*) General requirements: No station licensee is required to permit the use of its facilities by any legally qualified candidate for public office, but if any licensee shall permit any such candidate to use its facilities, it shall afford equal opportunities to all other such candidates for that office to use such facilities: provided, that such licensee shall have no power of censorship over the material broadcast by any such candidate.

(*c*) Rates and practices:

(1) The rates, if any, charged all such candidates for the same office shall be uniform and shall not be rebated by any means direct or indirect. A candidate shall, in each case, be charged no more than the rate the station would charge if the candidate were a commercial advertiser whose advertising was directed to promoting its business within the same area as that encompassed by the particular office for which such person is a candidate. All discount privileges otherwise offered by a station to commercial advertisers shall be available upon equal terms to all candidates for public office.

(2) In making time available to candidates for public office no licensee shall make any discrimination between candidates in charges, practices, regulations, facilities, or services for or in connection with the service rendered pursuant to this part, or make or give any preference to any candidate for public office or subject any such candidate to any prejudice or disadvantage; nor shall any licensee make any contract or other agreement that shall have the effect of permitting any legally qualified candidate for any public office to broadcast to the exclusion of other legally qualified candidates for the same public office.

(*d*) Records, inspection: Every licensee shall keep and permit public inspection of a complete record (political file) of all requests for broadcast time made by or on behalf of candidates for public office, together with an appropriate notation showing the disposition made by the licensee of such requests, and the charges made, if any, if request is granted. In addition, where a license provides free time for use by or on behalf of such candidates within 72 hours prior to the day of the election, the licensee shall immediately place a record of any free time provided in the station's political file. All records required by this paragraph shall be retained for a period of two years.

(*e*) Time of request: A request for equal opportunities must be submitted to the licensee within one week of the day on which the first prior use, giving rise to the right to equal opportunities, occurred: provided, however, that where a person was not a candidate at the time of such first prior use, he shall submit his request within one week of the first subsequent use after he has become a legally qualified candidate for the office in question.

(*f*) Burden of proof: A candidate requesting such equal opportunities of the licensee, or complaining of non-compliance to the commission, shall have the burden of proving that he and his opponent are legally qualified candidates for the same public office (Sec. 315, 48 Stat. 1088, as amended; 47 U.S.C. 315).

73.658 *Affiliation agreements and network program practices; territorial exclusivity in non-network program arrangements*

(*a*) Exclusive affiliation of station: No license shall be granted to a television broadcast station having any contract, arrangement, or understanding, express or implied, with a network organization under which the station is prevented or hindered from, or penalized for, broadcasting the programs of any other network organization. (The term *network organization* as used in this section includes national and regional network organizations. See Chapter VII, J, of "Report on Chain Broadcasting.")

(*b*) Territorial exclusivity: No license shall be granted to a television broadcast station having any contract, arrangement, or understanding, express or implied, with a network organization that prevents or hinders another broadcast station located in the same community from broadcasting the network's programs not taken by the former station, or that prevents or hinders another broadcast station located in a different community from broadcasting any program of the network organization. This section shall not be construed to prohibit any contract, arrangement, or understanding between a station and a network organization pursuant to which the station is granted the first call in its community upon the programs of the network organization. As employed in this paragraph, the term *community* is defined as the community specified in the instrument of authorization as the location of the station.

(*c*) Term of affiliation: No license shall be granted to a television broadcast station having any contract, arrangement, or understanding, express or implied, with a network organization that provides, by original terms, provisions for renewal, or otherwise for the affiliation of the station with the network organization for a period longer than two years: provided that a contract, arrangement, or understanding for a period up to two years may be entered into within six months prior to the commencement of such period.

(*d*) Station commitment of broadcast time: No licenses shall be granted to a television broadcast station having any contract, arrangement, or understanding, express or implied, with any network organization, that provides for optioning of the station's time to the network organization, or that has

the same restraining effect as time optioning. As used in this section, *time optioning* is any contract, arrangement, or understanding, express or implied, between a station and a network organization that prevents or hinders the station from scheduling programs before the network agrees to utilize the time during which such programs are scheduled, or that requires the station to clear time already scheduled when the network organization seeks to utilize the time.

(*e*) Right to reject programs: No license shall be granted to a television broadcast station having any contract, arrangement, or understanding, express or implied, with a network organization that, with respect to programs offered or already contracted for pursuant to an affiliation contract, prevents or hinders the station from

(1) rejecting or refusing network programs that the station reasonably believes to be unsatisfactory or unsuitable or contrary to the public interest, or

(2) substituting a program that, in the station's opinion, is of greater local or national importance.

(*f*) Network ownership of stations: No license shall be granted to a network organization, or to any person directly or indirectly controlled by or under common control of a network organization, for a television broadcast station in any locality where the existing television broadcast stations are so few or of such unequal desirability (in terms of coverage, power, frequency, or other related matters) that competition would be substantially restrained by such licensing. (The word *control,* as used in this section, is not limited to full control but includes such a measure of control as would substantially affect the availability of the station to other networks.)

(*g*) Dual network operation: No license shall be issued to a television broadcast station affiliated with a network organization that maintains more than one network of television broadcast stations: provided that this section shall not be applicable if such networks are not operated simultaneously, or if there is no substantial overlap in the territory served by the group of stations comprising each such network.

(*h*) Control by networks of station rates: No license shall be granted to a television broadcast station having any contract, arrangement, or understanding, express or implied, with a network organization under which the station is prevented or hindered from, or penalized for, fixing or altering its rates for the sale of broadcast time for other than the network's programs.

(*i*) No license shall be granted to a television broadcast station that is represented for the sale of non-network time by a network organization or by an organization directly or indirectly controlled by or under common control with a network organization, if the station has any contract, arrangement or understanding, express or implied, that provides for the affiliation of the station with such network organization: provided, however, that this rule shall not be applicable to stations licensed to a network organization or to a subsidiary of a network organization.

(*j*) Network syndication and program practices:

(1) Except as provided in subparagraph 3 of this paragraph, no television network shall

(i) after June 1, 1973, sell, license, or distribute television programs to television station licensees within the United States for non-network television exhibition or otherwise engage in the business commonly known as syndication within the United States; or sell, license, or distribute television programs of which it is not the sole producer for exhibition outside the United States; or reserve any option or right to share in revenues or profits in connection with such domestic and/or foreign sale, license, or distribution; or

(ii) after August 1, 1972, acquire any financial or proprietary right or interest in the exhibition, distribution, or other commercial use of any television program produced wholly or in part by a person other than such television network, except the license or other exclusive right to network exhibition within the United States and on foreign stations regularly included within such television network: provided that if such network does not timely avail itself of such license or other exclusive right to network exhibition within the United States, the grantor of such license or right to network exhibition may, upon making a timely offer reasonably to compensate the network, reacquire such license or other exclusive right to exhibition of the program.

(2) Nothing contained in subparagraphs 1 and 2 of this paragraph shall prevent any television network from selling or distributing programs of which it is the sole producer for television exhibition outside the United States, or from selling or otherwise disposing of any program rights not acquired from another person, including the right to distribute programs for non-network exhibition (as in syndication) within the United States as long as it does not itself engage in such distribution within the United States or retain the right to share the revenues or profits therefrom.

(3) Nothing contained in this paragraph shall be construed to include any television network formed for the purpose of producing, distributing, or syndicating program materials for educational, noncommercial, or public broadcasting exhibition or uses.

(4) For the purposes of this paragraph and paragraph *k* of this section the term network means any person, entity, or corporation that offers an interconnected program service on a regular basis for 15 or more hours per week to at least 25 affiliated television licensees in ten or more States; and/or any person, entity, or corporation controlling, controlled by, or under common control with such person, entity, or corporation.

(*k*) Effective September 8, 1975, commercial television stations owned by or affiliated with a national television network in the 50 largest television markets (see Note 1 to this paragraph) shall devote, during the four hours of prime time (7–11

P.M. E.T. and P.T., 6–10 P.M. C.T. and M.T., no more than three hours to the presentation of programs from a national network, programs formerly on a national network (off-network programs), other than feature films, or, on Saturdays, provided, however, that the following categories of programs need not be counted toward the three-hour limitation:

(1) On nights other than Saturdays, network or off-network programs designed for children, public affairs programs, or documentary programs (see Note 2 to this paragraph for definitions).

(2) Special news programs dealing with fast-breaking news events, on-the-spot coverage of news events or other material related to such coverage, and political broadcasts by or on behalf of legally qualified candidates for public office.

(3) Regular network news broadcasts up to a half hour, when immediately adjacent to a full hour of continuous locally produced news or locally produced public affairs programming.

(4) Runovers of live network broadcasts of sporting events, where the event has been reasonably scheduled to conclude before prime time or occupy only a certain amount of prime time, but the event has gone beyond its expected duration due to circumstances not reasonably foreseeable by the networks or under their control (this exemption does not apply to post-game material).

(5) In the case of stations in the Mountain and Pacific time zones, on evenings when network prime-time programming consists of a sports event or other program broadcast live and simultaneously throughout the contiguous 48 states, such stations may assume that the network's schedule that evening occupies no more of prime time in these time zones than it does in the Eastern and Central time zones.

(6) Network broadcasts of an international sports event (such as the Olympic Games), New Year's Day college football games, or any other network programming of a special nature other than motion pictures or other sports events, when the network devotes all of its time on the same evening to the same programming, except brief incidental fill material.

Note 1. The top 50 markets to which this paragraph applies are the 50 largest markets in terms of prime time audience for all stations in the market, as listed each year in the Arbitron publication *Television Market Analysis*. This publication is currently issued each November, and shortly thereafter the commission will issue a list of markets to which the rule will apply for the year starting the following September.

Note 2. As used in this paragraph, the term *programs designed for children* means programs primarily designed for children aged 2 through 12. The term *documentary programs* means programs that are nonfictional and educational or informational, but not including programs where the information is used as part of a contest among participants in the program, and not including programs relating the visual entertainment arts (stage, motion pictures, or television) where more than 50 percent of the program is devoted to the presentation of entertainment material itself. The term *public affairs programs* means talks, commentaries, discussions, speeches, editorials, political programs, documentaries, forums, panels, roundtables, and similar programs primarily concerning local, national, and international public affairs.

(*l*) Broadcast of the programs of more than one network: The provisions of this paragraph govern and limit the extent to which, after October 1, 1971, commercial television stations in the 50 states of the United States, which are regular affiliates of one of the three national television networks, may broadcast programs of another network, in markets where there are two such affiliated stations and one or more operational VHF or UHF stations having reasonably comparable facilities that are not regular affiliates of any network. Whether or not the stations in a particular market come within the provisions of this paragraph is determined by whether, as of July 1 of each year with respect to programs beginning October 1, or as of January 1 of each year with respect to programs beginning April 1, there are in the market the stations specified in the last sentence.

(1) Definitions: As used in this paragraph, the following terms have the meanings given:

(i) *Station* means a commercial television station in the 50 States of the United States.

(ii) *Operational station* means a station authorized and operating as of June 10 (with respect to programs beginning October 1) or as of December 10 (with respect to programs beginning April 1), or a station authorized and that gives notice to the commission by such June 10 or December 10 date that it will be on the air by such October 1 or April 1 date (including request for program test authority if none has previously been given), and commits itself to remain on the air for six months after such October 1 or April 1 date. Such notice shall be received at the commission by the June 10 or December 10 date mentioned, and shall show that copies thereof have been sent to the three national networks and to the licensees of all operating television stations in the market.

(iii) *Affiliated station* means a station having a regular affiliation with one of the three national television networks, under which it serves as that network's primary outlet for the presentation of its programs in a market. It includes any arrangement under which the network looks primarily to this station rather than other stations for the presentation of its programs and the station chiefly presents the programs of this network rather than another network.

(iv) *Unaffiliated station* means a station not having an affiliation arrangement as defined in this subparagraph with a national television network, even though it may have other types of agreements or per-program arrangements with it.

(v) *Network* means a national organization distributing programs for a substantial part of each broadcast day to television stations in all parts of the United States, generally via interconnection facilities.

(vi) *Unaffiliated network* means a network not having an affiliated station (as defined in this paragraph) in a particular market, even though it may have other types of agreements or per-program arrangements.

(vii) *Market* means the television markets of the United States, and the stations in them, as identified in the latest publication of the American Research Bureau (ARB), together with any stations that have since become operational in the same communities.

(viii) *Evening programming* means programming (regular programs or "specials") starting and concluding on a network between the hours of 7:30 P.M. and 11 P.M. local time (except 6:30 P.M. and 10:00 P.M. in the Central time zone), plus all programs other than regular newscasts starting on the network between 7:00 and 7:30 P.M. local time (6:00 and 6:30 P.M. local time in the Central time zone). It does not include portions broadcast after 7:00 P.M. of programs starting earlier, or portions broadcast after 11:00 P.M. of programs starting earlier.

(ix) *Specials* means programs not carried on the network at least as often as once a week. It includes both programs scheduled well in advance and those scheduled very shortly before broadcast on the network.

(x) *Reasonably comparable facilities* means station transmitting facilities (effective radiated power and effective antenna height above average terrain) such that the station's grade-B coverage area is at least two-thirds as large (in square miles) as the smallest of the market affiliated stations' grade-B coverage areas. Where one or both of the affiliates is licensed to a city different from that of the unaffiliated station, the term *reasonably comparable facilities* also includes the requirement that the unaffiliated station must put a predicted grade-A or better signal over all of the city of license of the other regular (nonsatellite) station(s), except that where one of the affiliated stations is licensed to the same city as the unaffiliated station, and puts a grade-B but not a grade-A signal over the other city of license, the unaffiliated station will be considered as having reasonably comparable facilities if it too puts a predicted grade-B signal over all of the other city of license.

(2) Taking programs from unaffiliated networks: No affiliated station, in a market covered by this paragraph, shall take and broadcast, from an unaffiliated network, any programming of the times and types specified in this subparagraph, unless the conditions specified have first been met:

(i) any evening programming (as defined in this paragraph), unless and until the entire schedule of such programs has been offered by the unaffiliated network to the unaffiliated station as provided in subparagraph 4 of this paragraph, and the unaffiliated station has either accepted 15 hours per week of such programs, plus additional "special" hours when part of the "special" is included in the

15 hours, or has accepted a lesser amount and indicated that it does not wish to carry any more—such acceptance to be governed by the provisions of subparagraph 4 of this paragraph.

(ii) any programming beginning on the network between 12:00 noon and 7:00 P.M. on Saturdays, Sundays, and holidays, and consisting of sports events (including without limitation, college football and basketball, professional football, baseball, ice hockey, golf, tennis, horseracing, and autoracing), unless and until the program has first been offered to the unaffiliated station and that station has indicated that it does not wish to accept it

(iii) any programming broadcast after 11:00 P.M. local time (except 10:00 P.M. local time in the Central time zone) which is a continuation of programs starting earlier and carried by the unaffiliated station; or any material broadcast after 7:00 P.M. (6:00 P.M. in the Central time zone) which is a continuation of sports programs beginning earlier and carried by the unaffiliated station

(iv) any program presented in the same week by the unaffiliated station

(3) Carriage of programs of a network that has an affiliate: No affiliated station in a market covered by this paragraph shall broadcast, from another network that has an affiliated station in the market, any evening programming or Saturday, Sunday, or holiday sports programming, unless such programming has first been offered to the unaffiliated station in the market and the latter has indicated that it does not wish to carry it.

(4) Offer and acceptance:

(i) The *offer* by a network referred to in this paragraph means an offer to the unaffiliated station of the programs for broadcast. Programs so offered cannot be withdrawn by the network until the following April 1 or October 1, unless the station does not in fact broadcast the program as accepted, in which case the provisions of subdivision ii of this subparagraph shall apply, or unless the program is canceled on the network, in which case the replacement or substitute program shall be offered to the station as a new program under subparagraphs 2 or 3 of this paragraph. If a program accepted by the unaffiliated station is shifted in time, the station may exercise its right of "first call" either with respect to the program at its new time, or the previous time segment, at its option.

(ii) The acceptance referred to in subparagraphs 2 and 3 of this paragraph means that the unaffiliated station agrees to broadcast the program accepted, at its live network time or a delayed time acceptable to the network, unless in its judgment the program is not in the public interest or it wishes to substitute a local, or other live, program for it. The provisions of paragraph *a* of this section, prohibiting agreements that hinder the presentation of the programs of other networks, shall not apply to material covered by this paragraph. If a program is not presented in a particular week live or at a delayed time acceptable to the network, the network may place this particular broadcast of the program on another station; and if this occurs more than four times in any 13-week period the network may withdraw the program from the station without obligation to offer it any additional programming. The unaffiliated station is free to seek and obtain other terms of acceptance from the network; but the offer of programming by the network on the foregoing terms satisfies its obligations under this paragraph.

(iii) The offer by the network shall, to the extent possible, be on or before July 15 with respect to programs beginning in the fall season, and by January 15 with respect to programs presented after April 1, or otherwise as soon as possible. The unaffiliated station's acceptance or indication or nonacceptance shall be within two weeks after the date of the offer; where any negotiations between the network and the station concerning particular programs are involved, programs not accepted within 30 days of the date of the offer shall be deemed not accepted.

Note 1: If there are in a particular market two affiliated stations and two (or more) operational unaffiliated stations with reasonably comparable facilities the provisions of this paragraph (1) shall require an offer of programming to each; but the 15-hour-per-week "first call" provision applies to the total programming taken by all such stations.

Note 2: The provisions of this paragraph (1) do not apply to a market in which there are two VHF affiliated U.S. stations, and a foreign VHF station to which a national U.S. television network transmits programs pursuant to authority granted under section 325 of the Communications Act of 1934, as amended, and which serves as that network's primary affiliate in the market.

(*m*) Territorial exclusivity in non-network arrangements: No television station shall enter into any contract, arrangement, or understanding, express or implied, with a non-network program producer, distributor, or supplier, or other person that prevents or hinders another television station located in a community over 35 miles away, as determined by the reference points contained in 76.53 of this section (if reference points for a community are not listed in 76.53, the location of the main post office will be used) from broadcasting any program purchased by the former station from such non-network program producer, distributor, supplier, or other person, except that a television station may secure exclusivity against a television station licensed to another designated community in a hyphenated market specified in the market listing as contained in 76.51 of this section for those 100 markets listed, and for markets not listed in 76.51 of this section, the listing as contained in the ARB television market analysis for the most recent year at the time that the exclusivity contract, arrangement, or understanding is complete under practices of the industry. As used in this subsection, the term *community* is defined as the community specified in the instrument of authorization as the location of the station.

Note 1: Contracts, arrangements, or understandings that are complete under the practices of the industry prior to August 7, 1973, will not be disturbed. Extensions or renewals of such agreements are not permitted because they would in effect be new agreements without competitive bidding. However, such agreements that were based on the broadcaster's advancing "seed money" for the production of a specific program or series that specify two time periods—a tryout period and a period thereafter for general exhibition—may be extended or renewed as contemplated in the basis agreement.

(2) [Reserved]

Note 3: It is intended that the top 100 major television markets listed in 76.51 shall be used for the purposes of this rule and that the listing of the top 100 television markets appearing in the ARB television market analysis shall not be used. The reference in this rule to the listing of markets in the ARB television market analysis refers to hyphenated markets below the top-100 markets contained in the ARB television market analysis. If a community is listed in a hyphenated market in 76.51 and is also listed in one of the markets in the ARB listing, the listing in 76.51 shall govern.

Note 4: The provisions of this paragraph apply only to U.S. commercial television broadcast stations in the 50 states, and not to stations in Puerto Rico or the Virgin Islands, foreign stations or noncommercial educational television or "public" television stations (either by way of restrictions on their exclusivity or on exclusivity against them).

Note 5: New stations authorized in any community of hyphenated market listed in 76.51 of this chapter or in any community of a hyphenated market listed in the ARB Television Market Analysis (for markets below the top-100 markets) are subject to the same rules as previously existing stations therein. New stations authorized in other communities are considered stations in separate markets unless and until 76.51 is amended by commission action, or the ARB listing is changed.

73.660 *Station and operator licenses, posting of*

(a) The station license and any other instrument of station authorization shall be posted in a conspicuous place and in such manner that all terms are visible at the place the licensee considers to be the principal control point of the transmitter. At all other control points listed on the station authorization, a photocopy of the station license and other instruments of station authorization shall be posted.

(b) The operator license, or Form 759 (verification-of-operator license or permit), of each station operator employed full-time or part-time or via contract, shall be permanently posted and shall remain posted so long as the operator is employed by the licensee. The operator license shall be posted either

(1) at the transmitter or extension meter location or

(2) at the principal remote control point, if the station license authorizes operation by remote control.

(c) Posting of operator licenses and the station licenses and any other instrument of station authorization shall be accomplished by affixing the license to the wall at the posting location, or enclosing in a binder or inserting into a folder and retaining at the posting location so that the licenses will be readily available and easily accessible at that location.

[73.660(b) amended and par c effective July 8, 1976; III(76)-1]

73.665 *Station inspection*

The licensee of a television broadcast station shall make the station available for inspection by representatives of the commission at any reasonable hour.

73.666 *Experimental operation*

(a) Television broadcast stations may be used for experimental purposes in testing and maintaining apparatus on their assigned frequencies and not in excess of the authorized power at any time, without specific authorization from the commission.

(b) Television broadcast stations may obtain, upon informal application, authority to conduct technical experimentation directed to the improvement of technical phases of operation, and for such purposes may utilize a signal other than the standard television signal, subject to the following conditions:

(1) that the licensee complies with the provisions of 73.651 with regard to the minimum number of hours of transmission with a standard television signal

(2) that no transmissions are radiated outside the authorized channel and subject to the condition that no interference is caused to the transmission of a standard television signal by other television broadcast stations

(3) that no charges either direct or indirect shall be made by the licensee of a television broadcast station for the production or transmission of programs when conducting technical experimentation.

73.667 *Discontinuance of operation*

The licensee of each station shall notify the commission in Washington, DC, and the engineer in charge of the radio district where such station is located, of permanent discontinuance of operation at least two days before operation is discontinued. The licensee shall, in addition, immediately forward the station license and other instruments of authorization to the Washington, DC, office of the commission for cancelation.

73.669 *General requirements relating to logs*

(a) The licensee or permittee of each television broadcast station shall maintain program, operating, and maintenance logs as set forth in 73.670, 73.671, and 73.672. Each log shall be kept by the station employee or employees (or contract operator) competent to do so, having actual knowledge of the facts required, who in the case of program and operating logs shall sign the appropriate log when starting duty and again when going off duty and setting forth the time of each.

(b) The logs shall be kept in an orderly and legible manner, in suitable form, and in such detail that the data required for the particular class of station concerned is readily available. Key letters or abbreviations may be used if proper meaning or explanation is contained elsewhere in the log. Each sheet shall be numbered and dated. Time entries shall be made in local time and shall be indicated as advanced (e.g., EDT) or non-advanced time (e.g., EST).

(c) No log, or portion thereof, shall be erased, obliterated, or willfully destroyed within the period of retention provided by the provisions of this part. Any necessary correction shall be made only pursuant to 73.670, 73.671, and 73.672, and only by striking out the erroneous portion, or by making a corrective explanation on the log or attachment to it as provided in those sections.

(d) Entries shall be made in the logs as required by 73.670, 73.671, and 73.672. Additional information such as that needed for administrative or operational purposes may be entered on the logs. Such additional information, so entered, shall not be subject to the restrictions and limitations of the commission's rules on the making of corrections and changes in logs and may be physically removed, without otherwise altering the log in any way, before making the log a part of an application or available for public inspection.

(e) The operating log and the maintenance log may be kept individually on the same sheet in one common log, at the option of the permittee or licensee.

73.670 *Program log*

(a) A program log shall be kept in accordance with the provisions of 73.669 for each broadcast day, which, in this context, means from the station's sign-on to its sign-off, or from midnight to midnight for stations operating 24 hours a day. A station licensed or operating as noncommercial–educational shall maintain its program log in accordance with the provisions of 73.582, subpart C.

(b) Entries. The following entries shall be made in the program log:

(1) For each program—

(i) An entry identifying the program by name or title.

(ii) Entries that indicate the time each program begins and ends. If programs are broadcast during which separately identifiable program units of a different type or source are presented, and if the licensee wishes to count such units separately, the beginning and the ending time for the longer program need be entered only once for the entire program. The program units that the licensee wishes to count separately shall then be entered underneath the entry for a longer program, with the beginning and ending times of each such unit, and with the entry indented or otherwise distinguished so as to make it clear that the program unit referred to was broadcast within the longer program.

(iii) An entry classifying each program as to type, using the definitions set forth in Note 1 at the end of this section.

(iv) An entry classifying each program as to source, using the definitions set forth in Note 2 at the end of this section. (For network programs, also give name or initials of network; e.g., ABC, CBS, NBC, Mutual.)

(v) An entry for each program presenting a political candidate, showing the name and political affiliation of such candidate. See *j* of Note 1.

(2) For commercial matter—

(i) An entry identifying (a) the sponsor(s) of the program, (b) the person(s) who paid for the announcement, or (c) the person(s) who furnished materials or services; and the entry shall constitute a representation that identification was announced on the air as required by section 317 of the Communications Act and 73.1212 of the commission's rules. (See Note 3 at the end of this section for definition of commercial matter.)

(ii) An entry or entries showing the total duration of commercial matter in each hourly time segment (beginning on the hour) or the duration of each commercial message (commercial continuity in sponsored programs, or commercial announcements) in each hour. (See Note 5 at the end of this section for statement as to computation of commercial time.)

(3) For public service announcements—

(i) An entry showing that a public service announcement (PSA) has been broadcast, together with the name of the organization or interest on whose behalf it is made. (See Note 4 following this section for definition of a public service announcement.)

(4) For other announcements—

(i) An entry of the time that each required station identification announcement is made (call letters and licensed location, in accordance with the provisions of 73.1201).

(ii) An entry for each announcement presenting a political candidate showing the name and political affiliation of such candidate.

(iii) An entry for each announcement made pursuant to the local notice requirements of 1.580 (pre-grant), 1.594 (designation for hearing), and 73.1202 (licensee obligations), showing the time it was broadcast.

(iv) An entry showing that broadcast of taped or recorded material has been made in accordance with the provisions of 73.1208.

(5) A notation of tests of the emergency-broadcast-system procedures pursuant to the requirements of Subpart G of this Part and the appropriate station EBS checklist, unless such entries are consistently made in the station operating log.

(c) National network programming: A station broadcasting the programs of a national network that will supply it with all information as to such programs, commercial matter, and other announcements for the composite week need not log such data but shall record in its log the time when it joined the network, the name of each network program broadcast, the time it leaves the network, and any non-network matter broadcast required to be logged. The information supplied by the network, for the composite week that the station will use in its renewal application, shall be retained with the program logs and associated with the log pages to which it relates.

(d) Manually kept log:

(1) Entries on a manually kept log may be made either at the time of or prior to broadcast. The employee responsible for keeping the log shall sign the log when starting duty and when going off duty and enter the time of each. If entries are preprinted prior to broadcast and any deviation therefrom occurs in what was actually broadcast, an appropriate correction must be made on the log. When the employee keeping the log signs the log upon going off duty, that person attests to the fact that the log, with any corrections or additions made before he signed off, is an accurate representation of what was actually broadcast.

(e) Automatically kept log:

(1) Entries on an automatically kept program log may be made by automatic logging instruments with sequential language printouts corresponding to manually kept log entries.

(2) An employee on duty shall be responsible for the automatic logging process and the keeping of the log. In the event of failure or malfunctioning of the automatic logging process, the person responsible for the log shall make the required entries in the log manually.

(3) The employee responsible shall sign the log, or a separate page to be affixed to the log, when starting duty and when going off duty and enter the time of each. The signature when going off duty constitutes a certification that, as to the automatic printout part of the log, the employee checked the automatic logging equipment periodically throughout the tour and that to the best of his knowledge and belief at no time during his tour did it fail or malfunction, unless otherwise noted above the signature; and that, as to any part of the log that was kept manually with any corrections or additions made thereon before signing off duty, it was an accurate representation of what was actually broadcast.

(f) Automatic maintenance of logging data:

(1) An employee on duty shall be responsible for any automatic maintenance of data and the keeping of the log. In the event of failure or malfunctioning of the said automatic process, the employee responsible for the log shall make the required entries in the log manually at that time.

(2) The employee responsible shall sign, on a separate page to be affixed to the logging data, when starting duty and when going off duty and enter the time of each. The signature when going off duty constitutes a certification that, as to the automatic maintenance of data equipment, the employee checked it periodically throughout the tour and that to the best of his knowledge and belief, at no time during his tour, did it fail or malfunction, unless otherwise noted above the signature; and that, as to any part of the log which was kept manually, with any corrections or additions made thereon before signing off duty, it was an accurate representation of what was actually broadcast.

(3) The licensee shall extract any required information from automatically maintained program logging data for days specified by the commission or its duly authorized representative and submit it in writing log form, together with the underlying recording, tape, or other means employed, within such time as the commission may specify.

(g) Information required: The licensee, whether employing manual logging, automatic logging, or automatic maintenance of logging data, or any combination thereof, must be able accurately to furnish the commission with all information required to be logged.

(h) Corrections:

(1) Program logs shall be changed or corrected only in the manner prescribed in 73.669.

(2) If corrections or additions are made on the log after it has been signed, explanation must be made on the log or an amendment to it, dated and signed by either the person who kept the log, the station program director or manager, or an officer of the licensee.

Note 1. Program type definitions. The definitions of the first eight types of programs, *a* through *h,* are intended not to overlap each other and will normally include all the various programs broadcast. Definitions *i* through *k* are subcategories and the programs classified thereunder will also be classified under one of the appropriate first eight types. There may also be further duplication within types *i* through *k;* (e.g., a program presenting a candidate for public office, prepared by an educational institution, would be classified as *public affairs* (PA), *political* (POL), and *educational institution* (ED)).

(a) Agricultural programs (A) include market reports, farming, or other information specifically addressed, or primarily of interest, to the agricultural population.

(b) Entertainment programs (E) include all programs intended primarily as entertainment, such as music, drama, variety, comedy, quiz.

(c) News programs (N) include reports dealing with current local, national, and international events, including weather and stock-market reports; and, when an integral part of a news program, commentary, analysis, and sports news.

(d) Public affairs programs (PA) are programs dealing with local, state, regional, national, or international issues or problems, including, but not limited to, talks, commentaries, discussions, speeches, editorials, political programs, documentaries, mini-documentaries, panels, roundtables, vignettes, and extended coverage (whether live or recorded) of public events or proceedings, such as local council meetings, congressional hearings, and the like.

(e) Religous programs (R) include sermons or devotionals; religious news; and music, drama, and other types of programs designed primarily for religious purposes.

(f) Instructional programs (I) include programs (other than those classified under *agricultural, news, public affairs, religious* or *sports*) involving the discussion of, or primarily designed to further an appreciation or understanding of, literature, music, fine arts, history, geography, and the natural and social sciences; and programs devoted to occupational and vocational instruction, instruction with respect to hobbies, and similar programs intended primarily to instruct.

(g) Sports programs (S) include play-by-play and pre- or post-game related activities and separate programs of sports instruction, news, or information (e.g., fishing opportunities, golfing instructions).

(h) Other programs (O) include all programs not falling within definitions (a) through (g).

(i) Editorials (EDIT) include programs presented for the purpose of stating opinions of the licensee.

(j) Political programs (POL) include those that present candidates for public office or that give expressions (other than in station editorials) to views on such candidates or on issues subject to public ballot.

(k) Educational-institution programs (ED) include any program prepared by, in behalf of, or in cooperation with, educational institutions, educational organizations, libraries, museums, PTA's or similar organizations. Sports programs shall not be included.

Note 2. Program source definitions:

(a) A local program (L) is any program originated or produced by the station, or for the production of which the station is substantially responsible, and employing live talent more than 50 percent of the time. Such a program, taped, recorded, or filmed for later broadcast shall be classified by the station as local. A local program fed to a network shall be classified by the originating station as local. All non-network news programs may be classified as local. Programs primarily featuring syndicated or feature films or other nonlocally recorded programs shall be classified as *recorded* (REC) even though a station personality appears in connection with such material. However, identifiable units of such programs which are live and separately logged as such may be classified as local (e.g., if during the course of a feature film program, a non-network two-minute news report is given and logged as a news program, the report may be classified as local).

(b) A network program (NET) is any program furnished to the station by a network (national, regional, or special). Delayed broadcasts of programs originated by networks are classified as network.

(c) A recorded program (REC) is any program not defined in *a, b, c* above, including without limitation, syndicated programs, taped or transcribed programs, and feature films.

Note 3. The definition of commercial matter (CM) includes commercial continuity (network and non-network), commercial announcements (network and non-network), and announcements described in paragraph (c) of this note, as follows: (Distinction between continuity and announcements is made only for definition purposes. There is no need to distinguish the two types of commercial matters when logging.)

(a) Commercial continuity (CC) is the advertising message of a program sponsor.

(b) A commercial announcement (CA) is any other advertising message for which a charge is made or other consideration is received.

(1) Included are (i) "bonus spots"; (ii) trade-out spots, and (iii) promotional announcements of a future program where consideration is received for such an announcement or where such announcement identifies the sponsor of a future program beyond mention of the sponsor's name as an integral part of the title of the program (e.g., where the agreement for the sale of time provides that the sponsor will receive promotional announcements, or when the promotional announcement contains a statement such as "Listen tomorrow for _____ [name of program], brought to you by _____ [sponsor]").

(2) Other announcements including but not limited to the following are not commercial announcements:

(i) promotional announcements, except as heretofore defined in paragraph *b* of this note

(ii) station identification announcements for which no charge is made

(iii) broadcasts of taped, filmed, or recorded material announcements

(iv) public-service announcements

(v) announcements made pursuant to 73.1212(d) that materials or services have been furnished as an inducement to broadcast a political program or a program involving the discussion of controversial public issues

(vi) announcements made pursuant to local notice requirements of 1.580 (pre-grant), 1.594 (designation for hearing) and 73.1202 (licensee obligations) of this section

(c) promotional announcements broadcast by any AM, FM, or TV broadcast station for or on behalf of another commonly owned or controlled broadcast station serving the same community.

Note 4. Definition of a public-service announcement. A public-service announcement is an announcement for which no charge is made and which promotes programs, activities, or services of federal, state or local governments (e.g., recruiting, sales of government bonds) or the programs, activities or services of nonprofit organizations (e.g., Red Cross blood donations), and other announcements regarded as serving community interests, excluding time signals, routine weather announcements and promotional announcements.

Note 5. Computation of commercial time: Duration of commercial matter shall be as close an approximation to the time consumed as possible. The amount of commercial time scheduled will usually be sufficient. It is not necessary, for example, to correct an entry of a one-minute commercial to accommodate varying reading speeds even though the actual time consumed might be a few seconds more or less than the scheduled time. However, it is incumbent upon the licensee to ensure that the entry represents as close an approximation of the time actually consumed as possible.

73.674 *Availability of logs and records*

(a) The program, operating, and maintenance

logs shall be made available upon request by an authorized representative of the commission.

(*b*) Television station program logs shall be made available upon request for public inspection and reproduction at a location convenient and accessible to the residents of the community to which the station is licensed. All such requests for inspection shall be subject to the procedural requirements set forth in *c*. The licensee, however, may where good cause exists, as discussed in paragraph 64, the "Public and Broadcasting Procedural Manual," refuse to permit such inspection. Notwithstanding the provisions of this section, permitting inspection elsewhere than at the station, the licensee shall remain responsible for the safekeeping of the logs.

(*c*) In connection with requests for inspection the following procedural requirements shall govern:

(1) Parties wishing to inspect shall make a prior appointment with the licensee and, at that time, identify themselves by name and address; identify the organization they represent, if any; and state the general purpose of the examination.

(2) Inspection of the logs shall take place at the station or such other convenient and accessible location as may be specified by the licensee. At its option the licensee may make an exact copy available in lieu of the original program logs.

(3) Copies of logs shall be available to the party desiring to inspect the logs, provided such party shall pay the reasonable costs of reproduction.

(4) An inspecting party shall have a reasonable time to examine the program logs. If examination is requested beyond a reasonable time, the licensee may condition such further inspection upon the inspecting party's willingness to either duplicate such logs at the examiner's expense or reimburse the licensee for whatever reasonable expense is incurred if supervision is deemed necessary.

(5) No log need be made available for public inspection until 45 days have elapsed from the day covered by the log in question.

Note: In cases where the logging system employed does not provide for a written program log, the licensee shall retain, subject to the above provisions, copies of the station's pre-logs (operating schedules), updated and certified correct.

73.675 *Operation during emergency*

(*a*) Emergency situations with respect to which the broadcast of information is considered as furthering the safety of life and property include, but are not limited to, the following: tornadoes, hurricanes, floods, tidal waves, earthquakes, icing conditions, heavy snows, widespread fires, discharge of toxic gases, widespread power failures, industrial explosions, civil disorders, and school closings and changes in schoolbus schedules resulting from any of these conditions. If requested by responsible public officials, emergency point-to-point messages may be transmitted for the purposes of requesting or dispatching aid and assisting in rescue operations.

(*b*) Any emergency information transmitted in accordance with this section shall be transmitted both aurally and visually or only visually. Television broadcast stations may use any method of visual presentation that results in a legible message conveying the essential information. Methods that may be used include, but are not necessarily limited to, slides, electronic captioning, manual methods (e.g., hand printing) or mechanical printing processes. However, when emergency operation is being conducted under a national, state, or local-level Emergency Broadcast System (EBS) Plan, emergency announcements shall be transmitted both aurally and visually.

(*c*) When emergency operation is conducted under a state-level EBS operational plan, the attention signal (described in 73.906) may be employed.

(*d*) Emergency operation shall be confined to the hours, frequencies, powers, and modes of operation specified in the license documents of the stations concerned.

(*e*) Any emergency operation undertaken in accordance with this section may be terminated by the commission, if required in the public interest.

(*f*) Immediately upon cessation of an emergency during which broadcast facilities were used for the transmission of point-to-point messages under paragraph *a* of this section, a report in letter form shall be forwarded to the commission in Washington, DC, setting forth the nature of the emergency, the dates and hours of emergency operation, and a brief description of the material carried during the emergency period.

(*g*) If the Emergency Broadcast System (EBS) is activated at the national-level while a non-EBS emergency operation under this section is in progress, the EBS shall take precedence.

73.676 *Remote control operation*

(*a*) Television broadcast stations authorized to operate by remote control shall provide, as a minimum, the following telemetry, control, and test functions at the control point:

(1) Means for turning the transmitter on and off at will.

(2) Suitable instruments for indicating the operating parameters that are required by 73.671 to be entered in the operating log. The indicating instruments shall show the actual values of such parameters, or decimal multiples of those parameters and shall be calibrated to provide an indication within 2 percent of the corresponding instrument at the transmitter site.

(3) All remote control meters shall conform with specifications required for the regular transmitter, antenna, and monitor meters.

(4) Meters with arbitrary scale divisions may be used provided that calibration charts or curves are provided at the transmitter remote-control point showing the relationship between the arbitrary scales and the reading of the main meters.

(5) A sufficient number of control circuits to perform all transmitter adjustments normally required on a daily basis to insure strict compliance with the technical requirements of the rules.

(6) Apparatus designed to use the signal radiated from the antenna, or fed from the antenna circuit by

a coaxial link and suitable for continuously and accurately monitoring the waveform and other characteristics of the transmitted visual signal including the percentage of modulation of the signal (a vectorscope or other instrument designed to depict the instantaneous phase and amplitude relationships of color components shall be provided, if any portion of the transmissions are in color). The apparatus shall be capable of providing both full field displays, and displays of test signals inserted on selected lines in the vertical blanking interval (see 73.682(a)(21)); appropriate switching shall be provided so that either mode of presentation can be selected by the operator.

(7) A type-approved aural modulation monitor, equipped, where necessary, with a properly designed signal-frequency amplifier, which utilizes the signal radiated from the antenna, or obtained from the antenna circuit by a coaxial link, and is capable of continuously and accurately indicating the peak and quasi-peak percentages of modulation of the aural signal.

(8) Suitable instruments for generating special signals for the testing and adjustment of the entire transmission system from studio to antenna and the calibration of monitoring equipment, in accordance with paragraphs *f* and *g* of this section.

(9) Means for determining that any required obstruction lighting of the antenna and supporting tower is functioning properly.

(10) All stations, whether operating by remote control or direct control, shall be so equipped as to be able to follow the Emergency Action Notification procedures described in 73.911.

(*b*) The control point shall be under the immediate supervision and control of one or more operators meeting the requirements of 73.661 at all times when the station is operating by remote control. Such operators may perform other tasks that do not require absence from the remote control position, and do not otherwise impair necessary supervision of the TV transmitter.

(*c*) The control circuits from the control point to the transmitter and the return telemetry circuit shall be so designed and installed that open circuits, short circuits, accidental grounding or other line faults, where wire lines are used, or equipment failures, casual signals, or random-noise impulses, if other means are used, will not activate the transmitter. Any fault or failure that results in loss of control must cause the transmitter to cease operation. The loss of any telemetry function that provides information necessary to comply with the logging requirements of 73.671 shall result in the actuation of automatic circuitry that, not more than one hour from the time of telemetry failure, will terminate operation of the transmitter.

(*d*) The equipment at the control point and at the transmitter shall be so installed and protected as not to be accessible to or capable of being operated by persons other than those duly authorized to do so by the licensee.

(*e*) The waveform monitor at the remote control point shall be calibrated against a waveform monitor maintained at the transmitter during each inspection required by paragraph *g* of this section. Any calibration data found necessary to permit accurate interpretation of the indications of the remote monitor shall be posted at the remote control point in a position adjacent to the monitor.

(*f*) Test signals shall be generated and inserted in the vertical interval of the visual signal at the remote-control point, and shall be observed at the remote-control point after extraction from the radio-frequency signal at the output of the transmitter. Normally, the radiated signal is utilized after off-the-air reception, but the signal may be obtained by coupling to the output circuit of the transmitter at the point where the radio-frequency signal enters the antenna transmission line.

(1) The required test signals, and the place of insertion in the vertical interval shall be as follows:

(i) Multiburst, on field 1, line 17.

(ii) Color bars, on field 2, line 17. During monochrome transmission chrominance information shall not be included in this test signal.

(iii) Composite signal, on field 1, line 18 (see Figure 15 of 73.699).

(iv) Generally, a composite signal of characteristics identical to those prescribed in subdivision (iii) of this subparagraph, shall be inserted on field 2, line 18, at the remote-control point. However, to permit a separate determination to be made of the effects of the transmitter and the studio-transmitter link on system performance, the composite signal of field 2, line 18 may be inserted at the transmitter input. Alternatively, in lieu of the composite signal, a licensee may insert any suitable test signal on field 2 of line 18, either at the remote-control point or at the transmitter. When such signals are transmitted at the same time as the program material and/or the required test signals, the characteristics of the licensee-selected signals shall be such as to minimize the possibility that their transmission will result in interference with the required test signals, or in degradation of the picture or sound signals.

(2) The required test signals shall be transmitted continuously during all periods of regular station operation.

(3) The required test signals shall be observed immediately after commencement of operation, and thereafter at intervals not exceeding three hours. More frequent observations shall be made as necessary to insure proper performance of the transmitter and associated equipment.

(4) The date and time of each observation of the test signals shall be entered in the operating log, together with notations as to the results of these observations.

(5) Any signals or noise already existing on lines 17 and 18 (e.g., network test signals), shall be erased prior to the insertion in the vertical intervals of locally generated test signals.

Note: Stations authorized to operate by remote control, and which are transmitting test signals on lines 18 and 19 may continue to do so until November 15, 1975, after which date all test signal transmissions shall conform to the requirements of 73.676(f).

(g) The remote-control and monitoring equipment shall be calibrated and tested, and the television broadcast transmitter shall be inspected as often as necessary to insure operation in accordance with this Subpart E, and, in any event, at successive times no longer than one week apart.

(h) Upon completion of the calibration, testing, and inspection required by paragraphs e and g of this section, the inspecting operator shall enter a signed statement in the maintenance log that the required tests and inspection have been made, noting in detail the tests, adjustments, and repairs that were made to insure proper operation. If complete repair could not be effected, the statement shall set forth in detail the items of equipment concerned, the nature of the defect, and the reasons for failure to make the needed repairs.

73.677 *Remote control authorization*

(a) An application to operate a television broadcasting station by remote control, to add a remote-control point, or to change the location of a remote-control point shall be made on FCC Form 301-A. The application shall include the following information:

(1) the location of the control point, the reason for its choice if at other than the main studio, and the approximate airline distance from the control point to the television broadcast transmitter site

(2) the number and purpose of the control and telemetry functions that will be provided at the control point

(3) the method by which control functions will be transmitted to the television transmitter

(4) the method by which telemetry data required by the rules will be transmitted from the television transmitter to the control point

(5) a description of the fail-safe features of the remote control system that will insure that loss of either required control or telemetry will place the television transmitter in a nonradiating condition, pursuant to 73.676(c)

(6) measures taken to prevent tampering with or activation of transmitting and remote-control equipment by unauthorized persons

(7) a description of all apparatus maintained for off-the-air monitoring, with particular attention to features intended to insure that the demodulated visual signal is free from noise and interference, or from distortion introduced at the receiving point

(8) a description of apparatus that will be maintained at the control point for the generation and reception of test signals, and of the apparatus employed for their insertion in and extraction from the vertical-blanking interval

(9) a description of any features of the transmitting plant intended to insure continuity of operation in the event of malfunctioning or failure of the main transmitter, and of the automatic or remote-control switching arrangements to be utilized in connection therewith

(10) a description of means employed or proce-

dures that will be followed to make the daily frequency check required by 73.690(c)

(11) the method of determining, at the control point, that tower-obstruction lighting is functioning properly

(12) a description of the facilities maintained at the control point to permit compliance with 73.911

73.679 *Personal attacks; political editorials*

(a) When, during the presentation of views on a controversial issue of public importance, an attack is made upon the honesty, character, integrity, or like personal qualities of an identified person or group, the licensee shall, within a reasonable time and in no event later than one week after the attack, transmit to the person or group attacked

(1) notification of the date, time, and identification of the broadcast

(2) a script or tape (or an accurate summary if a script or tape is not available) of the attack

(3) an offer of a reasonable opportunity to respond over the licensee's facilities

(b) The provisions of paragraph a of this section shall not be applicable

(1) to attacks on foreign groups or foreign public figures

(2) to personal attacks that are made by legally qualified candidates, their authorized spokesmen, or those associated with them in the campaign, on other such candidates, their authorized spokesmen, or persons associated with the candidates in the campaign

(3) to bona fide newscasts, bona fide news interviews, and on-the-spot coverage of a bona fide news event (including commentary or analysis contained in the foregoing programs, but the provisions of paragraph a of this section shall be applicable to editorials of the licensee).

Note: The fairness doctrine is applicable to situations coming within b3, above, and, in a specific factual situation, may be applicable in the general area of political broadcasts b2, above. See section 315(a) of the Act, 47 U.S.C. 315(a); "Public Notice: Applicability of the Fairness Doctrine in the Handling of Controversial Issues of Public Importance, 29 F.R. 10415." The categories listed in b3 are the same as those specified in section 315(a) of the Act.

(c) Where a licensee, in an editorial, (1) endorses or (2) opposes a legally qualified candidate or candidates, the licensee shall, within 24 hours after the editorial, transmit to respectively (i) the other qualified candidate or candidates for the same office or (ii) the candidate opposed in the editorial (a) notification of the date and the time of the editorial; (b) a script or tape of the editorial; and (c) an offer of a reasonable opportunity for a candidate or a spokesman of the candidate to respond over the licensee's facilities: provided, however, that where such editorials are broadcast within 72 hours prior to the day of the election, the licensee shall comply with the provisions of this paragraph sufficiently far in advance of the broadcast to enable the candidate or candidates to have a reasonable opportunity to prepare a response and to present it in a timely fashion.

Note: Inasmuch as no noncommercial educational broadcasting station may engage in editorializing or may support or oppose any candidate for political office (Sec. 399(a) Communications Act), the provisions of subparagraph *b*3 referring to "editorials of the licensee" and paragraph *c* in its entirety do not apply to such stations.

73.680 *Equal employment opportunities*

(*a*) General policy: Equal opportunity in employment shall be afforded by all licensees or permittees of commercially or noncommercially operated standard, FM, television, or international broadcast stations (as defined in this part) to all qualified persons, and no person shall be discriminated against in employment because of race, color, religion, national origin, or sex.

(*b*) Equal employment opportunity program: Each station shall establish, maintain, and carry out, a positive continuing program of specific practices designed to insure equal opportunity in every aspect of station employment policy and practice. Under the terms of its program, a station shall:

(1) define the responsibility of each level of management to insure a positive application and vigorous enforcement of the policy of equal opportunity, and establish a procedure to review and control managerial and supervisory performance

(2) inform its employees and recognized employee organizations of the positive equal employment opportunity policy and program and enlist their cooperation

(3) communicate the station's equal employment opportunity policy and program and its employment needs to sources of qualified applicants without regard to race, color, religion, national origin, or sex, and solicit their recruitment assistance on a continuing basis

(4) conduct a continuing campaign to exclude every form of prejudice or discrimination based upon race, color, religion, national origin, or sex, from the station's personnel policies and practices and working conditions

(5) conduct a continuing review of job-structure and employment practices and adopt positive recruitment, training, job design, and other measures needed in order to insure genuine equality of opportunity to participate fully in all organizational units, occupations, and levels of responsibility in the station.

(*c*) Applicants for a construction permit for a new facility, for assignment of license or construction permit, or for transfer of control (other than pro forma or involuntary assignments and transfers), and applicants for renewal of license who have not previously done so, shall file with the commission programs designed to provide equal employment opportunities for Negroes, Orientals, American Indians, Spanish-surnamed Americans, and women, or amendments to such programs. Guidelines for the preparation of such programs are set forth in the commission's report and order "Nondiscrimination in the Employment Policies and Practices of Broadcast Licensees," FCC 76-426, adopted June 22, 1976. A program need not be filed by any station having ten or fewer full-time employees or with respect to any minority group that is represented in such insignificant numbers in the area that a program would not be meaningful. In the latter situation a statement of explanation should be filed.

History of Television

This brief chronology is meant to capture some of the newsworthy and interesting occurrences in the television industry since 1939. We are very grateful to the trade magazine, *Broadcasting,* for allowing us to use their magazine reports as our source for this information.

Note: All dates listed in this chronology represent the *week* the event occurred and not its exact date, which would have been difficult, if not impossible, to document in most cases.

1939

January 1: A patent for iconoscope–kinescope tubes, the basis of electronic television, is granted to Dr. Vladimir Zworykin after 15 years of litigation.

May 1: The telecast of the opening ceremonies of the New York World's Fair marks the start of a regular daily television schedule by RCA-NBC in New York. The first appearance of a President (Franklin Delano Roosevelt) is seen on TV.

1940

March 15: The Sun Oil Company becomes the first sponsor to have programs regularly telecast. The company's Monday–Friday Lowell Thomas newscasts on NBC-Blue are also carried on W2XBS, NBC's experimental TV station in New York.

RCA cuts the price of television sets and starts a sales drive to put a minimum of 25,000 into homes in the service area of NBC's New York video station.

April 1: The FCC suspends the order for "limited commercial" operation of TV, and censures RCA for sales efforts seen as an attempt to fix TV standards and calls a new hearing. Critics call the FCC move a "usurpation of power."

June 1: The FCC authorizes commercial operation for FM and assigns it 35 channels 200 kc wide between 43 and 50 mc. Commercial television must await an industry consensus on standards.

August 15: The National Television Systems Committee, representing TV manufacturers and broadcasters, organizes to establish standards for TV.

September 1: CBS demonstrates the system of color television developed by its chief TV engineer, Dr. Peter Goldmark.

1941

May 5: The FCC authorizes full commercial operation for TV as of July 1 and fixes standards at 525 lines, 30 frames, FM sound.

June 30: The Bulova Watch Company, the Sun Oil Company, the Lever Brothers Company, and Procter & Gamble sign as sponsors of the first commercial telecasts, on July 1, over NBC's WNBT-TV New York (until then W2XBS).

1942

April 13: The minimum program time required of TV stations is cut from 15 hours to 4 hours a week for the duration of the war.

1943

January 4: The Office of War Information asks stations to make available a quarter-hour, Monday–Friday segment of air time for important war-information broadcasts, which will be available for local sponsorship.

1944

February 7: The Television Broadcasters Association, organized in January, elects Allen B. Du-Mont its first president.

May 1: CBS proposes starting post-war TV with high-definition, full-color pictures.

May 22: Single network ownership of five TV stations is permitted by the FCC. The previous limit was three.

December 18: The first convention of the Television Broadcasters Association, with an attendance of 750, calls for a united effort to get TV started properly. J. R. Poppele, the chief engineer of WOR (AM), is elected president.

1945

April 23: The Philco Corporation establishes the world's first multirelay network between Philadelphia and Washington, a forerunner of nationwide television networks.

June 4: In joint request, FM Broadcasters, Inc., and the Television Broadcasters Association ask the FCC to allocate 44–108 megacycles (mc) immediately: FM to get 50–54 mc for educational use, 54–68 mc for commercial operation; and TV to get 68–74 mc and 78–108 mc.

July 2: The FCC assigns FM radio to an 88–106 mc band, TV Channel 1 to 44–50 mc, Channel 2–4 to 54–72 mc, and Channel 5–6 to 76–88 mc.

August 6: Westinghouse discloses a "stratovision" plan for airborne television transmitters to serve as relay stations for TV and FM programs as networks without wire connections.

September 17: The Associated Broadcasting Corporation starts a fifth national network.

September 24: The FCC issues a plan for the distribution of 13 VHF channels among 140 markets.

November 26: A new FCC television-allocations plan follows the proposals of the Television Broadcasters Association and assigns seven channels each to New York, Chicago and Los Angeles, additional channels to 33 other cities, and sets 28 hours a week as a minimum operating schedule.

1946

February 4: CBS demonstrates a color-television broadcast from its new UHF transmitter, and states that industry cooperation can result in color TV for the home within a year.

February 18: The first Washington–New York telecast through an AT&T coaxial cable is called a success by engineers and viewers.

April 22: A CBS color-television program is successfully transmitted over a 450-mile coaxial cable link from New York to Washington and back.

June 24: In a *Collier's* magazine article, E. F. McDonald, Jr., president of the Zenith Radio Corp., declares advertising alone cannot support television. The public, he says, must pay for TV programs as it does for movies, magazines and newspapers.

November 4: RCA demonstrates an all-electronic system of color TV.

November 11: Bristol-Myers is the first advertiser to sponsor a television-network program, *Geographically Speaking,* which began October 27 on NBC-TV's two-station network.

1947

March 24: The FCC denies a CBS petition for commercial color-TV operation because a "satisfactory" system must first be developed.

July 28: Both the House and the Senate approve appropriations of $6,240,000 for the FCC in 1948, the largest peacetime budget to date.

September 1: RCA offers to help other manufacturers begin the production of TV receivers by disclosing complete technical data of RCA's own new model.

October 13: The first telecast from the White House is made when President Truman addresses the nation on food conservation.

November 17: Television network service extends to Boston with the opening of an AT&T radio relay system between Boston and New York.

1948

January 12: It is announced that NBC plans an East Coast microwave relay system for network TV programs as an alternative to the AT&T coaxial cable.

February 2: RCA announces development of a 16-inch TV picture tube, the first metal kinescope, with a picture area of 125 square inches.

February 9: Western Union reveals plans to enter TV network service, starting with a microwave relay between New York and Philadelphia.

February 23: The FCC assigns a band for intercity TV relays to be operated by broadcasters for an interim period until permanent common-carrier facilities are available.

March 29: AT&T files new tariffs for intercity TV transmission, substantially lower than those proposed one year earlier.

May 10: The FCC orders into effect an earlier proposal assigning TV Channel 1 (44–50 mc) to nongovernment fixed and mobile services, denying FM spokesmen's pleas for the use of that channel in FM network relaying. FM stations in the 44–50 mc band are given until the end of the year to move to 88–108 mc. A proposed new, expanded TV allocation table is issued. A hearing is called on the feasibility of TV's use of frequencies above 475 mc. The FCC proposes that the required minimum hours of TV station operation be increased from 12 hours a week for the first 18 months to 28 hours a week after 36 months.

June 14: Texaco puts old-style vaudeville on TV by launching an hour series on NBC-TV starring Milton Berle and with commercials delivered by Sid Stone, a vaudeville pitchman.

June 28: TV coverage of the GOP convention reaches 10–12 million people and costs an estimated $200,000. It is transmitted to Midwest viewers by Stratovision.

September 27: NBC proposes new TV-affiliation contracts calling for each station to give NBC 30 hours of free time a month, the network to assume all connection costs. NBC sets an objective of 28 hours a week of network service.

Philco charges AT&T with insisting that its intercity facilities be used exclusively.

October 4: The FCC puts a freeze on TV licensing and hearing functions, pending a decision on changes in TV standards.

November 29: The Bulova Watch Company introduces a plan for combining time signals with TV station-identification announcements. The company's 1949 advertising budget includes $500,000 for TV, $3 million for radio.

December 6: Verdi's *Otello* is telecast in full from the stage of the Metropolitan Opera House in New York on ABC-TV, with Texaco as sponsor.

1949

January 10: Daytime stratovision tests deliver good pictures to some areas, but in others local-station interference mars reception.

The Admiral Corporation announces that it will sponsor an hour-long musical-revue series, *Friday Night Frolic,* on combined NBC and DuMont television networks, starring Sid Caesar, Imogene Coca, and the Marge and Gower Champion dance team.

January 17: An AT&T coaxial cable links East Coast and Midwest television stations.

January 24: CBS contracts Bing Crosby for both radio and television.

February 7: The Pennsylvania State Board of Censors of Motion Pictures orders censorship of TV films before they may be telecast by any Pennsylvania station.

March 21: Fred Allen signs a contract giving NBC exclusive rights to his services for radio and television.

May 9: Arthur Godfrey was reported as the top CBS wage-earner in 1948, with a salary of $258,450. Lowell Thomas was the top "independent contractor" on the network, receiving $402,300 for program services.

May 16: Don McNeill, host of ABC's *Breakfast Club,* was reportedly paid $180,229 by ABC in 1948, top payment by the network for a TV personality.

May 30: The longest direct TV pickup, 129 miles, is made by KFMB-TV, San Diego, when it receives and rebroadcasts a salute from KTLA-TV, Los Angeles, without any special equipment.

August 29: The FCC bans quiz show give-aways on television as a violation of criminal lottery laws.

September 26: The FCC suspends its ban on give-away programs until the matter is decided in court.

October 10: CBS demonstrates studio, film, and outside pickups in color to the FCC; observers find the quality generally good.

October 17: RCA's official demonstration of its color system to the FCC is disappointing; the later, informal showings are improved.

October 24: TV networks sign five-year contracts with the American Society of Composers, Authors, and Publishers (ASCAP), retroactive to January 1, 1949.

October 31: The U.S. District Court for the Eastern District of Pennsylvania rules that the attempt of the State Board of Censorship to require censorship of television films is invalid because it infringes on interstate commerce.

November 21: The Television Authority is launched as the AFL talent union for television, despite the opposition of the Screen Actors Guild and the Screen Extras Guild.

1950

January 16: CBS reports 90 percent of those seeing its half-hour public demonstration colorcasts in Washington say they find color more enjoyable than black and white.

April 17: The FCC, clarifying its decision on editorializing, declares that stations have "an affirmative duty to seek out, aid, and encourage the broadcast of opposing views on controversial questions of public importance."

May 15: According to a TV poll conducted by Jerry Jordan, television does not influence attendance at sports events after the first year of set ownership, when its novelty has worn off.

May 22: Color Television, Inc., demonstrates its color system to the FCC.

DuMont reveals its new three-color direct-view TV receiver tube.

May 29: Chromatic Television Labs and the Don Lee Broadcasting System both announce the development of new tri-color TV tubes.

June 19: ABC signs Don McNeill, conductor of "Breakfast Club," to a 20-year contract. ABC also purchases the Screen Guild Players. NBC signs Kate Smith to a five-year TV contract.

The Skiatron Corporation announces subscriber vision as its entry in the pay-television field.

July 24: Following the outbreak of hostilities in Korea, the White House calls for the formation of an all-inclusive Broadcasters Defense Council in order to organize radio–TV for instant availability to the government.

September 4: Color Television, Inc., announces a new "dash-sequential" system of color TV. They petition the FCC to reopen hearings on color TV.

September 11: Three TV networks—ABC, CBS, and NBC—agree to pay $50,000 apiece to the Gillette Safety Razor Company for a pooled telecast of the World Series, Gillette having paid $800,000 for TV rights. The stations are to be paid for one hour's time for each of the first four games. DuMont refuses to take part, denouncing the deal as "economically detrimental" to TV.

October 9: The FCC initiates a rulemaking proposal to equalize competition among the TV networks and eliminate the alleged domination of NBC-TV and, secondarily, of CBS-TV.

December 25: CBS asks all employees to sign loyalty oaths.

1951

January 1: The Gillette Safety Razor Company buys the TV rights to the World Series and All-Star baseball games for six years at $1 million a year.

February 12: In a report on the first four weeks of its pay-TV experiment, the Zenith Radio Corporation says that an average family sees movies at home approximately twice a week in the Phonevision test.

March 5: The Television Broadcasters Association dissolves.

March 26: Skiatron Electronics & Television, Inc., shows its Subscriber-Vision system of pay-TV to the FCC in a test broadcast from WOR-TV, New York.

July 2: Sixteen advertisers co-sponsor the first commercial colorcast, an hour-long program on a five-station East Coast CBS-TV hookup.

September 10: President Truman's address at the Japanese Peace-Treaty Conference in San Francisco is a pooled telecast to open the $40-million coast-to-coast television–network facilities of AT&T.

October 1: On completion of 45 years in radio, Brigadier General David Sarnoff, the RCA board chairman, asks RCA scientists for three "gifts" for his 59th anniversary: an electronic amplifier for light for television, a television picture recorder, and an electronic air-conditioner for home use.

October 15: RCA publicly shows its improved color system in New York and Washington; viewers agree that the quality is excellent.

October 22: The NARTB TV board approves a new and strict TV code with a seal that subscribing stations may show. The review board is to enforce advertising and program provisions and to check unfair competition within the industry. The seal may be withdrawn for code violations.

1952

January 7: The Philco Corporation buys the NBC radio–TV coverage of political conventions and election night for $3.8 million.

March 3: Speaker Sam Rayburn (D-Tex.) bars radio–television coverage of House committees.

July 28: President Truman signs the McFarland Bill, the first major overhaul of the Communications Act of 1934. The McFarland Bill permits the FCC to issue cease-and-desist orders, in addition to revoking licenses; it prohibits broadcasters from charging more for political advertising than for normal business ads; it requires the FCC to act on a case within three months of filing or six months after a hearing is concluded, or to explain its failure to do so to Congress.

September 22: KPTV-TV, Portland, goes on the air as the first commercial UHF TV station.

November 17: CBS opens its Television City in Hollywood.

1953

January 5: A *Broadcasting* survey discloses that BBDO (Batten, Barton, Durston and Osborne) has broadcast billings of $40 million in 1952, making it the top advertising agency of radio–TV for that year.

March 2: A special commission on educational TV in New York State finds "no justification" for a proposed ten-station educational TV network; for, it says, educators are not using all the time available on commercial stations.

June 29: RCA–NBC asks the FCC to approve compatible color standards for the RCA dot-sequential color-TV system on a commercial basis.

The FCC denies motion-picture theaters the allocation of special channels, ruling that theater-TV transmission should be a common-carrier operation.

July 27: The FCC proposes an extension of television-station licenses from one to three years.

August 31: A Kenyon & Eckhardt survey of merchandising services offered, free or for a fee, by nation's TV stations and networks is published in *Telecasting Yearbook*. It is the first such study ever made.

September 28: With the end of daylight saving time, CBS-TV and NBC-TV inaugurate new systems to put programs on the air on the West Coast at the same clock hour as in the East.

October 5: John L. Sinn, president of Ziv Television Programs, announces the sale of Spanish-language versions of five program series to advertisers for use in Mexico as the first step in a multilingual global-TV-program-distribution plan.

November 30: The FCC sets the maximum number of stations any one entity can own at five TV, seven AM radio and seven FM radio.

December 7: RCA demonstrates monochrome and color-TV programs recorded on magnetic tape. David Sarnoff, RCA–NBC board chairman, reports "principal elements tested and confirmed" and anticipates two years to be needed for finishing touches before the system is ready for marketing.

December 28: *Broadcasting*'s annual survey of agency time-and-talent expenditures shows that BBDO and Young & Rubicam are 1953's biggest agency spenders for TV and radio advertising.

1954

January 4: RCA announces the first all-electronic color tube and markets it as a commercial product available to set manufacturers.

March 29: RCA begins color-TV receiver production: the first 15-inch, open-face console, selling at $1,000, comes off the Bloomington, Indiana, factory line.

April 5: ABC and Walt Disney sign a long-term contract under which Disney studios will produce at least 26 hour-long programs a year for ABC-TV.

May 10: A new TV sales-promotion project, the Television Advertising Bureau, promises it will be operating in time to influence fall–winter planning by advertisers and agencies. Richard A. Moore, KTTV-TV Los Angeles, chairman of the organizing committee, announces that 38 stations have joined.

September 20: The FCC raises TV-station ownership limits to allow one entity to own seven TV stations: five VHF, two UHF.

November 1: President Eisenhower's cabinet becomes the first to be televised in session.

December 20: The FCC reports that the 1953 radio–TV gross income was $908 million: $475.3 million radio, $432.7 million TV.

1955

January 24: President Eisenhower opens a Presidential news conference to TV–film coverage for the first time.

March 21: NBC-TV opens its $3.7-million Color-Television City in Burbank, California.

March 28: The Simon video-film camera, capable of simultaneous motion-picture filming and live telecasting, is completed after four years of development.

April 11: The pay-TV controversy raises more public reaction than any issue since the hearing on color TV in 1950.

Zenith cancels its advertising on CBS-TV, charging network censorship of commercials, an accusation denied by CBS.

June 20: ABC-TV billings for 1955 are 68 percent above the toal gross in 1954, the major reasons being the success of Walt Disney and the decline of the DuMont network.

July 4: NBC-TV revamps daytime programming: it will present "service" shows in the morning, "entertainment" shows in the afternoon.

August 22: The U.S. Census Bureau finds that 32 million homes, 67 percent of all U.S. households, have TV.

August 29: TV proves its ability to cover court proceedings unobtrusively and decorously in a test performance at the American Bar Association meeting in Philadelphia.

October 17: According to an analysis prepared by Sidney S. Alexander, an economic adviser to CBS, 600 TV stations are the maximum number the nation can support.

November 21: A *Broadcasting* survey finds that almost 50 percent of television-broadcast time is taken up by movies.

1956

March 5: The Colorado Supreme Court decides in favor of those seeking permission for radio–TV court coverage.

July 16: CBS, Inc., discontinues its TV set-making division, CBS-Columbia.

November 5: The networks give Adlai Stevenson, the Democratic candidate for President, time to answer President Eisenhower's broadcast remarks on the Middle East crisis.

November 19: TvB research reveals that people devote more time to television than to newspapers.

1957

June 10: Tobacco advertisers assert that the report of the American Cancer Society, linking smoking with death, will have little effect on cigarette advertising.

Nikita Khrushchev is interviewed on CBS-TV.

August 19: An AT&T "scatter circuit" bridges 185 miles of the Atlantic to present American TV to Cuba.

September 9: A test of pay TV starts in Bartlesville, Oklahoma: a theater owner sends movies to a home audience by wire for a monthly fee.

A University of Michigan survey reveals that TV is the main source of the public's knowledge of politics. Newspapers rank second, radio third.

October 14: Sputnik inspires speculation about communications satellites.

October 21: Although networks don't want pay TV, they say if it comes they'll be amenable to it.

October 28: RCA reveals a new color video-tape recorder.

November 4: An American Bar Association committee recommends retention of Canon 35, barring cameras and microphones from courtrooms.

November 11: Subliminal communication—the presentation of messages at a subconscious level—interests advertisers and alarms congressmen.

1958

July 28: The world's first "telecopter," an airborne TV unit, is introduced at KTLA-TV, Los Angeles.

August 11: TV Q-Ratings are offered as a measure of program appeal.

October 13: CBS-TV broadcasts "The Plot to Kill Stalin"; the USSR closes the CBS News Moscow bureau.

October 20: NBC cancels the game show *Twenty-One* as its ratings drop and scandals involving quiz show frauds grow.

November 10: One of the producers of *Twenty-One* is indicted for perjury and admits the show was rigged.

1959

April 13: An Indiana study shows that subliminal advertising works, but not as well as direct ads.

June 22: NBC-TV broadcasts a news film sent from London through an undersea cable, using a "slow-scan" process.

September 21: The TV Code Review Board issues a guide for personal-products advertising.

October 12: Quiz contestants tell the House Legislative Oversight Subcommittee that they received answers in advance; CBS-TV drops the big-prize shows.

November 9: NBC and CBS move to eliminate all program practices that might deceive the public, as Charles Van Doren's confession that he had participated in the rigging of the game show *Twenty-One* causes public outrage and a House of Representatives investigation finds other quiz shows to have been fixed.

December 21: An Elmo Roper report indicates that despite the quiz show scandals the public has not lost faith in radio–TV.

1960

January 4: Fees from movies sold to TV are a major issue in Hollywood-union contract talks.

January 18: The FTC attacks TV commercials of Lever Brothers, Standard Brands, Colgate-Palmolive, and Alcoa, calling them "phony."

February 15: Telemeter puts coinboxes into 2,000 Canadian homes for a pay-TV test in a Toronto suburb.

May 16: A Cincinnati study finds that color commercials have 3.5 times the impact of black-and-white.

TV networks control 80 percent of shows for new season, an increase of 9 percent over 1959–60.

May 23: TV networks offer free time to major-party presidential candidates as the Senate considers a bill requiring the networks to do so.

September 12: Information programs move into network prime time.

October 3:   The opening Kennedy–Nixon debate gets the biggest TV audience ever.

1961

May 1:   A Campbell–Ewald study finds that the television audience is hard to please, demanding better programming.

CBS-TV signs a two-year, $9.3-million contract with the National Football League.

June 12:   Witnesses at Senate hearing seek to prove connection between televised crime and violence and juvenile delinquency.

June 19:   NAB bans prime-time triple-spotting, reduces commercial time in TV participation shows to four minutes per half-hour, and forbids personal-product ads on radio as well as TV.

July 3:   President Kennedy orders the Federal Space Council to study ways to develop a communications-satellite system.

July 24:   Game shows come back strong on TV networks, but are now strictly controlled and offer smaller prizes.

October 16:   Advertisers spent $10.03 per family on TV spot in 1960, a TVAR study shows. City expenditures vary from $12.76 (Chicago) to $2.73 (Evansville, IN–Henderson, KY).

November 20:   ABC-TV engineers develop processes for immediate playback of videotape recordings in slow motion.

December 11:   Nielsen reports that the average U.S. family has four TV and nine radio stations available to it.

1962

January 1:   Six European countries permit TV advertising.

January 8:   The FTC calls a Rapid Shave commercial involving sandpaper a "deliberate fraud" by Colgate-Palmolive and Ted Bates ad agency.

January 29:   Explicit violence in an episode of ABC-TV's prime-time series *Bus Stop* results in censure by the Senate Juvenile Delinquency Subcommittee.

February 5:   The cost of commercials rises, but profits fall. Producers blame union-scale wages and the agency bidding practice.

February 12:   The public has a higher opinion of TV now than it had two years earlier, a Roper survey shows.

President Kennedy proposes that a publicly held corporation own and operate a space-communications system.

February 19:   John Glenn's orbital space flight on February 20 is seen by 135 million TV viewers, at a cost of $3 million to networks.

March 5:   Young & Rubicam researchers find no evidence that program content influences the effectiveness of commercials.

March 12:   The Schwerin Research Corporation disputes Young & Rubicam's findings asserting that program mood does affect the viewing public's retention of commercial messages.

May 21:   Network heads deny that they present sex and violence in TV programs for their own sake, as the Senate Juvenile Delinquency Subcommittee hearings go on.

May 28:   Networks get seats on NAB TV code review board.

June 4:   Possible harm from smoking could endanger television's tobacco billings of $114.6 million a year.

June 25:   The American Cancer Society seeks to stop tobacco sponsorship of college sportscasts.

July 9:   Toll TV starts in Hartford, Connecticut.

July 16:   Telstar, AT&T's orbiting satellite, opens the era of global TV.

July 23:   The FCC dismisses protests against CBS-TV's "Biography of a Bookie Joint" and NBC-TV's "Battle of Newburgh," encouraging more controversial programming.

July 30:   Late-night television income has tripled in five years, accounting for 10 percent of all national TV billings.

September 3:   President Kennedy signs a bill creating the Communications Satellite Corporation.

October 1:   A Texas judge admits radio–TV to the Billy Sol Estes trial.

November 5:   Network news chiefs accuse the Pentagon of managing news in the Cuban crisis.

Networks deny bias against blacks as the Hollywood Race Relations Bureau prepares to picket Madison Avenue agencies.

December 17:   The Association for Competitive Television opens Washington office as a watchdog for member UHF stations.

1963

February 11: The American Bar Association votes to retain Canon 35, prohibiting broadcast and photography equipment in courtrooms.

February 18: "The People Look at Television" reports the key findings of a three-year, CBS-financed study: Everybody watches TV; some feel guilty about time "wasted"; commercials are resented chiefly for interrupting program mood.

March 25: The methodology of Pulse radio ratings and Nielsen TV ratings is probed at a House subcommittee hearing.

April 1: The FCC considers ways to limit the amount of time given to commercials.

May 20: Astronaut Gordon Cooper sends back the first TV pictures from space.

June 17: NBC-TV and MCA reveal plans to show feature films first on TV, then in theaters.

July 15: The Tobacco Institute advises its members not to sponsor shows appealing primarily to a youthful audience.

August 5: The Emergency Broadcasting System replaces Conelrad.

August 12: CORE starts a campaign to halt the discrimination against black actors in TV commercials.

September 2: A civil rights march on Washington gets full radio–TV coverage.

September 30: Screen Gems hires a black actor for its *Hazel* series, avoiding a clash with the NAACP.

October 21: California theater owners pledge $500,000 to fight pay TV.

November 18: President John F. Kennedy is assasinated in Dallas on November 22. Media coverage of the tragedy's aftermath is unprecedented. On the 24th, Jack Ruby kills Lee Harvey Oswald on national TV.

November 25: The first trans-Pacific broadcast via satellite previews live-TV coverage of the 1964 Olympics in Tokyo.

1964

January 20: The government, as well as tobacco companies and broadcasters, ponder their next moves after a report to the U.S. Surgeon General linking cigarette smoking to lung cancer.

January 27: A grand jury indicts the Drug Research Corporation and an advertising agency (Kastor, Hilton, Chesley, Clifford & Atherton) for fraudulent advertising of Regimen, a weight-reducing pill.

The NAB TV code board bans "piggybacks," involving cigarette commercials appealing to youngsters.

TV is now the nation's major news source, Roper researchers find in a study for the Television Information Office.

March 30: A Senate bill is submitted that would bar liquor advertising on radio–TV.

April 6: The Association of Motion Picture & Television Producers is formed by a merger of the two producers' groups.

May 18: ABC-TV and CBS-TV withdraw from the Emmy awards show because of a disagreement over the method of choosing winners.

June 15: ABC, CBS, and NBC set up a Network Election Service, a central vote-counting system. AP and UPI join the election-day pool.

June 22: The House gets a bill to prohibit broadcasting of early Eastern election returns while polls are still open in the West.

June 29: The FTC orders health warning on all cigarette packages as of January 1, 1965, and in all advertising as of July 1, 1965. The tobacco industry plans a court fight, if necessary.

July 20: Barry Goldwater, the Republican candidate for President, challenges President Johnson to TV debates, and is highly critical of CBS News' convention coverage.

August 3: Roger Mudd and Robert Trout replace Walter Cronkite as anchormen for CBS News at the Democratic convention.

August 10: Ranger 7 sends back close-up pictures of the moon.

August 17: More than 300 stations get fallout shelters, supplied by the federal government, for transmitter engineers.

August 24: The Senate votes down a bill to suspend the equal-time law.

October 5: The FCC rules that stations carrying presidential news conferences are subject to equal-time demands of other candidates.

October 26: A GOP campaign film, "Choice," depicting crime, mob violence, sex, and scandals in government, is scheduled for release on NBC-TV in many localities before candidate Barry Goldwater has it dropped as not "appropriate."

November 2: Costs for radio–TV campaign advertising are reportedly at $40 million.

A Dodd committee interim report calls the relationship between TV violence and juvenile delinquency "conclusively established."

November 9: The National Election Service works well: networks give fast returns and accurate predictions.

December 14: A Presidential commission recommends a massive antismoking drive, spearheaded by TV documentaries.

1965

January 25: Some 65 million watch President Lyndon B. Johnson inaugurated on TV.

February 8: The White House TV studio gets its first use for a live Presidential news conference.

April 5: An industry report indicates that films dominate network prime time, supplying 84.1 percent of scheduled shows.

April 12: Early Bird, the first commercial communications satellite, goes into a stationary orbit and opens trans-Atlantic circuits for TV use.

May 10: Early Bird sends TV shows both ways across the Atlantic.

June 14: The Supreme Court, in a five-to-four decision, rules that the presence of TV cameras in court prevented Billy Sol Estes from having a fair trial.

The Gemini 4 flight coverage costs networks $6 million.

July 19: A cigarette bill passed by Congress calls for health warnings on packages, but not in advertising.

August 23: Los Angeles broadcasters use helicopters to cover Watts riots, after mobile units were destroyed and newsmen beaten.

October 11: Pope Paul VI's historic visit to the U.S. is seen in 90 percent of the nation's homes. Dr. Carl McIntire, a radio evangelist, seeks free time to reply to what he calls "religious propaganda."

October 18: Color-set sales for the first nine months of 1965 double those of same period the year before.

The National Collegiate Athletic Association (NCAA) decides not to renew its contract with NBC-TV and signs a four-year $32 million contract with ABC-TV.

November 1: Nielsen reports that the TV nighttime audience is slightly smaller than it was in 1964.

November 22: Dr. Allen B. DuMont, pioneer TV inventor, manufacturer and broadcaster, dies at 64.

December 6: ABC-TV breaks with tradition, announcing a "new season" to start in January.

December 20: The Gemini 6 splashdown is covered live. The signal is relayed from the U.S.S. Wasp via Early Bird satellite to U.S. networks.

1966

January 10: CBS-TV reports the price of commercial minutes in football telecasts as $70,000 per minute.

January 31: The public's main news source is radio in the daytime and TV at night, a Radio Advertising Bureau (RAB) study shows.

March 7: Feature films are the best buy for advertisers, a BBDO study shows.

March 21: Network coverage of the Gemini 8 splashdown brings thousands of calls from angry viewers who missed their regular programs.

It is reported that there are 81 accredited radio–TV correspondents from the U.S. and about 30 from abroad in Vietnam.

April 18: ABC-TV gets the rights to the summer Olympics for $4.5 million, already having winter Olympics rights.

April 25: ABC-TV cites *Ben Casey* as an example in answering the FCC as to why shows are dropped: Ratings fell off and sponsor interest declined as well as live station clearance, and costs kept rising.

June 6: Live close-up pictures of the moon are sent back by Surveyor I.

July 4: Universal Studios makes two-hour color movies for first use on NBC-TV. MGM makes three features for ABC-TV.

October 3: TV buys $93-million worth of movies in a week: 63 MGM films go to CBS-TV, 17 to 20th Century-Fox pictures and 32 Paramount features to ABC-TV.

ABC-TV's three-hour broadcast of *The Bridge on the River Kwai* draws the largest audience of any movie ever shown on TV.

November 28: ABC-TV and Lani Bird, a Pacific satellite, take the Notre Dame–Michigan State football game to Hawaii.

December 19: The NFL and AFL complete a $9.5 million agreement with CBS-TV and NBC-TV for four-year rights to Super Bowl coverage. Both networks will broadcast the 1967 game, CBS-TV the 1968 and 1970 games and NBC-TV the 1969 game.

1967

January 23: The TvB challenges a Harris-poll claim that television is losing its appeal for better-educated, more-affluent viewers.

February 27: Technicolor shows new tape-to-film transfer method, claiming near perfection in broadcast quality.

April 10: Television is the major news source for 64 percent of adults, a Television Information Office-sponsored survey shows. The majority feel commercials are a fair price to pay for TV, but positive opinions of entertainment programming have noticeably declined in the past year.

May 8: The FCC rules that stations must make run-off-schedule announcements available to political candidates on request.

A Senate subcommittee approves a bill to subsidize educational radio and TV, and changes the name of the Corporation for Public Television to the Corporation for Public Broadcasting.

May 22: The Senate passes a bill establishing the Corporation for Public Broadcasting.

June 5: The FCC denies the request of John F. Banzhaf, III, for "roughly" proportional time to that used for cigarette spots on WCBS-TV, New York, but tells stations that antismoking proponents must be given a chance to rebut cigarette advertising on radio–TV. The FCC's General Counsel, Henry Geller, gives his personal view that a three-to-one ratio of cigarette commercials to antismoking messages would be acceptable.

July 10: The FCC adopts a fairness doctrine of personal attacks and editorials for or against political candidates.

August 7: An NAB study finds that the larger the revenue, the more likely a station is to editorialize.

Newscasts are exempt from the personal-attack provision of the fairness doctrine, the FCC notifies NBC after a complaint by a former employee of Senator Thomas Dodd (D-Conn.) that he was attacked by Senator Russel B. Long (D-La.) in a film clip used on the Huntley-Brinkley news program.

August 14: All three TV networks reject the recommendation of Senator Hugh Scott (R-Pa.) that networks and wire services adopt a "code of emergency procedure" to govern news coverage of racial riots.

August 21: President Johnson appoints a task force to study national and international communications policy.

October 9: The NAB television board revises its TV code: it divides broadcast material into program and nonprogram, limiting the latter to 10 minutes an hour in prime time and 16 minutes at other times, and restricts program interruptions to two per half-hour in prime time and four at other times.

November 13: President Johnson signs the Public Broadcasting Act into law, creating the Corporation for Public Broadcasting (Public Radio and Television).

1968

January 29: The NAB television board adopts new time standards for a maximum of four consecutive commercial announcements in any program interruption and a maximum of three in any station break. The radio board approves elimination of time standards for single sponsors of programs longer than 15 minutes; for a single-sponsored radio program five-minutes-long, the limit is one minute and a half; for shorter single-sponsored radio shows the approved commercial times are these: for a five-minute program, a one-and-a-half-minute commercial; for a ten-minute program, a two-and-a-half minute commercial; for a 15-minute program, a three-minute commercial.

March 25: The Children's Television Workshop, created by the Ford Foundation, Carnegie Corporation, and the Office of Education, is to develop a 26-week, hour-long color series for pre-school children.

House passes a bill authorizing HEW to set and enforce radiation standards for electronics. The action stems from last year's discovery that many color-TV receivers exceed maximum standards for X-radiation.

June 3: The murder of Senator Robert F. Kennedy in Los Angeles on June 5 is given the heaviest broadcast coverage since President Kennedy's assassination in 1963. Regular schedules are disregarded and commercials dropped.

The Senate suspends the equal-time requirement for presidential and vice-presidential campaigns.

June 17: Networks pledge cooperation with the new Commission on the Cause and Prevention of Violence.

July 29: General Foods tells agencies to steer clear of violence on TV and puts 57 syndicated programs off-limits for its patronage.

August 12: The networks give the GOP convention gavel-to-gavel coverage.

September 2: Battles inside the Democratic convention hall, battles in the Chicago streets outside and the feud between politicians and broadcast newsmen are all covered in detail by the media.

September 9: The President's Task Force on Telecommunications reports that cable systems are likely to supplement broadcast television, not supplant it.

October 14: The House votes to suspend equal time for presidential candidates. The Senate votes down the bill.

October 21: Pictures taken inside Apollo 7 in flight revive public interest in the space program.

November 25: An FCC rule that stations must carry antismoking spots is upheld by a Court of Appeals.

NBC-TV telecasts the movie *Heidi* on schedule and loses the Raiders' two-touchdowns-in-nine-seconds defeat of the Jets. The ire of football fans is aroused. A tape of the game ending is shown on the affiliates' late-news programs and on the next morning's *Today* show.

TV commercials are a prime source (40%) of actors' incomes, reports the Screen Actors Guild (SAG).

December 16: The President's Task Force on Communications Policy recommends a single carrier for all types of international communications and creates a federal agency to allocate portions of the radio spectrum to government and nongovernment users.

December 23: Television is accused of being a "corrosive force" at a hearing held by the President's Commission on the Causes and Prevention of Violence. ABC's Goldenson and CBS's Stanton report that steps are to be taken to reduce violence in programs and deny staging incidents for TV cameras during the Chicago disturbances.

A fifth global satellite, Intelsat III-A, is launched for synchronous orbit over the east coast of Brazil.

December 30: A Christmas broadcast from the Apollo space capsule orbiting the moon, followed by a successful splashdown, ends an eventful year.

Sales of U.S.-made color TV sets surpass those of black-and-white sets for the first time, Electronics Industry Association reports.

1969

January 20: The NAB code boards loosen personal-product advertising restrictions, approving feminine-spray ads on TV and tampon ads on radio.

February 10: The variety show *Turn On*, rejected by a number of ABC-TV affiliates after its first broadcast, because of the program's vulgar content, has its second show preempted by the network.

March 10: The top price for commercial minutes in prime-time TV network programs—$65,000—is asked by *Laugh-In, Mission: Impossible* and *Mayberry R.F.D.*

Apollo 9's intricate space maneuvers provide an exciting week for TV viewers.

March 24: Preplanned network coverage of the events following the death of former President Dwight D. Eisenhower on March 28 preempts regular programming.

March 31: A Roper survey shows that the public watches TV more, trusts it more as a news source, and likes its program mix better.

April 7: CBS-TV fires the Smothers brothers after disputes over the performers' failure to comply with the network's program standards and to meet deadlines for the delivery of program material to the network in time for preview by affiliates.

The TV rights to the 1972 Summer Olympics in Munich, Germany, go to ABC-TV for $12 million.

April 28: NBC-TV adds three 30-second antismoking spots to its weekly prime-time schedule.

May 19: NBC researchers state after an analysis of the 1964 and 1968 elections that election broadcasts have "no detectable influence on voting behavior."

June 2: Apollo 10 sends back the first color pictures of the moon and the earth from the moon.

June 9: The FCC orders broadcasters to establish programs "designed to insure equal opportunity in every aspect of station employment policy and practice."

July 13: U.S. astronaut Neil Armstrong becomes the first man to walk on the moon on July 20; TV viewers watch the historic event.

September 1: Politicians spent $59 million for radio–TV during 1968 campaign, up 70% from 1964.

September 22: The rising cost of TV programming is shown by the record of *Bonanza,* entering its 11th season on NBC-TV. Its 1969–70 production budget is nearly double that of 1959–60.

October 6: The Twentieth Century Fund proposes that prime-time half-hours be made available to presidential candidates for 35 days before an election, broadcast on all stations and CATV systems, and priced at 50 percent of the normal rate, with the government paying the bill.

November 17: Vice President Agnew charges networks with biased reporting. The new FCC chairman defends Agnew's right to "express views on the objectivity of network news coverage."

December 15: The Senate approves a ban on broadcast cigarette advertising by January 1, 1971.

1970

January 5: American Brands Corporation fails in an attempt to get a court order forcing TV networks to accept advertising for Silva Thins and Pall Mall Golds, which violate NAB code guidelines.

January 26: The Nixon administration recommends that the FCC establish an interim domestic satellite policy, permitting any one with the requisite financial and technical resources to own and operate his own system.

February 2: ABC, CBS and NBC agree to underwrite a study on the feasibility of jointly operating their own satellite system to distribute TV–radio programs. AT&T says it will seek the right to use satellites in its domestic-communications service.

An industry report indicates that 22.6 million U.S. homes have color TV sets.

Pro football contracts add up to a four-year, three-network total estimated at $184 million.

President Nixon uses TV to explain his veto of a controversial health-and-education bill, signing the veto during the broadcast.

TV set-makers offer to inspect color-TV sets in the homes of viewers after the National Commission on Product Safety reports that some sets have caused fires.

February 9: Stations and agencies question an ARB report of November 1969 showing a decline in the TV audience from 1968. ARB stands by its report.

February 16: The President asks Congress to let him establish a White House Office of Telecommunications Policy.

The "Frito Bandito" commercial is taken off the air after complaints from a Mexican-American group.

March 2: The asking prices for one-minute commercials on 1970–71 prime-time network shows have a wide range, with CBS-TV's *Mayberry R.F.D.* the highest ($69,000) and NBC-TV's *Laugh-In* the second highest ($68,000).

The Supreme Court refuses to review a lower court's ruling upholding the FCC's order authorizing pay-television service.

CBS News denies financing a plot to invade Haiti in 1966, but admits assigning a reporter–director to penetrate Caribbean exile groups for an investigation of their activities.

March 9: House and Senate conferees agree on legislation to outlaw cigarette advertising on radio–TV, but change the date from January 1, 1971, to January 2, to let commercials appear on New Year's Day football bowl games.

April 6: The Justice Department announces agreements with TV networks, motion picture producers and associated unions to insure that 20–25 percent of daily craft employment will be allotted to minority workers.

April 20: The Senate passes a bill repealing an equal-time requirement for Presidential and Vice Presidential candidates, enabling candidates to buy time at a lower rate than commercial advertisers for the same period, and limiting the amount any candidate for national office can spend for broadcast time.

May 4: The House Commerce Committee approves a bill to prohibit pay-TV stations from devoting more than 45 percent of broadcast time to movies and sports, from taking any programs from standard television, from broadcasting any commercials and from broadcasting any feature film that has had general release on a nonreserved-seat basis for more than a year. No station licensed before the enactment of the bill can engage in pay-TV operation. All pay-TV stations have to operate at least eight hours a day.

May 18: ARB reports that there are 59.3 million American homes with television, 25.3 million of them with color TV.

June 22: The FCC declares that if a station sells time to a political candidate, it must sell reply time to his opponents, but it doesn't have to give them free time to answer a paid announcement.

June 29: CBS president Frank Stanton announces that the political party not in office will be given several opportunities a year to present its views in free program time on CBS and agrees to paid political fund-raising appeals of up to one minute's length between campaigns.

August 10: The Food and Drug Administration acts to stop advertising of eight toothpastes and eight mouthwashes that claim to be medically effective in combating bad breath, germs, sore throats and common cold symptoms. The FDA says the claims are false. Cereal makers defend their products against "empty calorie" charges.

August 24: TV programs depict the dangers of drugs in response to the President's appeal for help in dealing with America's drug problem.

August 31: Feminist groups boycott Silva Thins, Ivory Liquid, Pristine, and *Cosmopolitan* magazine, calling their advertising offensive and insulting to women.

September 21: Industry sources reveal that twenty-three research projects, funded by HEW, probing the effect of televised violence on child behavior are at work.

September 28: The NAACP studies TV commercials, finding more black actors but still not enough.

October 5: The closed-circuit showing a Broadway sex-and-nudity show, *Oh! Calcutta!* is blocked in some cities.

1971

January 2: Cigarette advertising is off the air.

February 1: A report by the NAB and the Television Bureau of Advertising shows that there has been a notable increase in television viewing levels during 1970.

Twelve black Democratic members of the House who boycotted President Nixon's State of the Union message ask three TV networks and the Mutual Broadcasting System for equal time to reply to it.

February 22: The U.S. Army Recruiting Command and the Ayer agency plan a four-month, $10.6 million TV campaign to increase enlistments in the army.

Nutritionist Robert B. Choate and consumer advocate Ralph Nader seek separate action against food advertisements, Choate against breakfast cereals and Nader against Wonder Bread.

March 8: An estimated audience of 1.35 million U.S. and Canadian fight fans watch Joe Frazier and Muhammad Ali in battle on closed-circuit TV.

March 22: CBS-TV, in the most extensive prime-time schedule change in its history, cancels the long-running *Ed Sullivan Show,* along with 12 other programs.

March 29: A special study, ordered by the National Association of Broadcasters, reveals that newspaper ownership of broadcast stations is not increasing, as some have feared.

April 12: A. C. Neilsen figures show that 7.5 percent of all TV homes now use cable TV.

May 3: The FCC refuses to investigate allegations of distortion in CBS's "The Selling of Pentagon," an episode of *CBS Reports.* It tells the Staggers Subcommittee Commission that intervention would be inconsistent with the First Amendment.

Television Bureau of Advertising figures indicate the leading ($13.6 million) spender of spot TV in 1970 was Procter & Gamble.

A. C. Nielsen's profile of 1972 household TV viewing shows that the home set is on nearly six hours a day. Other data show that men watch TV less than women and 96 percent of all homes in the country have at least one TV set.

June 7: Vice President Agnew—though still carrying on his campaign against the press—tells the Mutual Affiliates Advisory Council that the U.S. has the world's "best, most professional" news fraternity.

June 14: The Supreme Court extends immunity from libel to include suits by private citizens (unless "malice" or "reckless disregard for truth" on the part of those bringing suit can be proved)—and in so doing, it explicitly treats broadcasting and print media as equals in this matter.

July 5: Industry findings indicate that nearly 80 percent of U.S. homes, or over 47.9 million, now receive UHF.

The Federal Trade Commission alleges false advertising in commercials for five products and two companies: Easy-Off window cleaner, Easy-On speed starch, Black Flag ant & roach killer, Aerowax floor wax, Vivarin, H&R Block, and the Beneficial Corporation.

July 19: Industry sources indicate that after 25 years of steady increases the price of broadcast rights to football games will decline slightly in 1971.

July 26: A Harvard Study funded by the National Institute of Mental Health finds preschoolers almost unable to distinguish programs from commercials. Teenagers, however, are found to be critical of commercials to the point of cynicism.

August 2: Network news organizations offer comprehensive coverage of Apollo 15 space mission, but viewing estimates indicate that Americans are becoming blasé about it all.

August 9: A U.S. Court of Appeals rules that licensees who sell time to commercial sponsors must do the same for proponents of controversial issues.

A Pennsylvania State University study on the influence of television reveals that young people react violently to violent shows and complacently to "pro-social" or neutral programs.

August 16: Nearly two dollars of every three spent on major media in 1970 by the top-100 national advertisers went to television, according to the Television Bureau of Advertising: TV has now been the chief recipient of advertising money for 16 years.

August 23: An NAB financial survey shows that while UHF broadcasters are still losing money, the loss ratio is declining: profit losses were reduced in 1970 from 34 percent to 5.9 percent.

August 30: The Federal Trade Commission, continuing its opposition to deceptive advertising, orders 11 air-conditioner and 4 electric-shaver manufacturers to document claims made in ads, including broadcast spots.

A U.S. Court of Appeals in Richmond, Virginia—rejecting a tobacco-industry appeal against the FCC—defends an FCC decision that licensees are not required to present prosmoking messages in reply to anti-smoking spots.

October 18: *Look* magazine goes out of business. Its demise is attributed by some sources to TV.

November 8: The FCC denies, for the first time in its history, the renewal application of a TV station on grounds of violation of technical rules.

December 13: A special report on cable television by the Sloan Commission recommends CATV "deregulation" to promote growth.

December 27: A decline of $3 million in network TV billings for November 1971 over the same period in 1970 is attributed by the TvB to the loss of cigarette advertising.

1972

January 17: Washington's nonprofit Urban Institute creates the Cable Television Information Center.

February 7: The Congressional Black Caucus asserts that under the separation of powers doctrine in the Constitution, all members of Congress have a right of access to broadcast facilities during primetime hours.

Commercials for little cigars are called into question by Senator Frank E. Moss (D-Utah). Are they cigarettes?

The FTC's "truth in advertising" campaign focuses on remedies for colds and coughs.

February 14: A Senate Consumer Subcommittee hears a Justice official express second thoughts on whether the ban on cigarette advertising was the best way to discourage smoking.

February 21: Bill Monroe of NBC News charges at a Senate hearing that the government is using its licensing power to control the broadcast press. Senator Ervin (D-North Carolina) agrees.

February 28: President Nixon's visit to mainland China has become a transglobal TV spectacular, with the three American networks providing unprecedented live coverage via satellite at a cost estimated at $3 million.

A public-opinion survey conducted in 1970 for the NAB but only now released finds a growing disenchantment with the media, particularly among blacks.

U.S. Surgeon General Jesse L. Steinfeld, vigorously denying that a recent report on TV violence was "rigged" in television's favor, impresses the FCC with his testimony in a two-hour session.

March 20: A joint NAB-TvB study indicates that TV viewing levels are higher in multiset homes and in homes with unlisted telephone numbers.

March 27: A congressional subcommittee concludes that an immediate and substantial reduction of violent material on TV is necessary.

April 3: Latest TvB figures show that TV's biggest spender last year was, again, Procter & Gamble, who outspent runner-up General Foods by $25 million.

April 17: The White House announces the President's appointment of Judge Benjamin Hooks, of Memphis, to serve on the FCC, the first black member of the FCC or any other federal agency.

April 24: The General Accounting Office says that under a new campaign law candidates for the Presidency may spend only $14.25 million, $8.55 million of it for broadcast campaigning. Ceilings for Senate and House candidates are also set.

May 1: All three networks have devoted more than 31 hours to special coverage of the Apollo 16 moon flight since its blast off from Earth on April 16th.

May 8: Color-TV penetration in U.S. has reached 55 percent or 34.5 million out of 63 million TV households, according to estimates of the American Research Bureau.

ABC and NBC program executives outline plans to forge ahead with the "mini-series" idea; CBS's Fred Silverman dissents.

NBC-TV's professional football coverage this year will be the most ambitious ever: a record 93 games.

May 22: 136 broadcast newsmen, plus many other journalists, take off to cover Nixon's mission to Moscow.

54.5% of TV homes are color-equipped, reports NBC.

July 3: President Nixon vetoes the Corporation for Public Broadcasting two-year extension bill. CPB fears it may run out of money.

The Supreme Court, faced for the first time with the question of whether newsmen occupy a special, privileged position in regard to grand-jury investigations, rules that they do not—that they must respond to subpoenas and answer questions as other citizens do.

July 10: The FTC says that the amount of tar and nicotine in little cigars exceeds the amount in cigarettes, but does not raise the question of whether TV commercials for them should be prohibited.

July 17: CBS brings game shows back to daytime television.

The networks cover the Democratic Convention in Miami, Florida.

July 31: An FTC appraisal of the first full year of prohibition of cigarette advertising on radio and TV indicates that people are nonetheless smoking more. The FTC calls for antismoking advertising.

An ABC news crew is ambushed in Saigon; two die, one escapes.

The sale of TV sets, both black and white and color, are up again in 1972.

August 7: J. B. Stoner, white supremacist and U.S. Senate aspirant from Georgia, having bought air time, rails against "niggers," as stations look on, legally powerless to stop him.

Time-Life video begins the marketing of cassettes.

August 14: 1970 census documents indicate that TV penetration of American homes now approaches "saturation"—between 90 and 100 percent.

August 21: The networks cover the Republican Convention. Ratings are the same as for the Democratic Convention.

FCC Commissioner Nicholas Johnson suggests that Congress hold full-scale hearings on what he sees as a Nixon administration plot to turn public broadcasting into "a domestic Voice of America."

Industry reports indicate that the Olympics may draw the biggest world-wide audience ever—possibly a billion viewers.

ABC gets exclusive on Ramsey Clark's Hanoi trip.

August 28: A. C. Nielsen's fast weekly TV Index is scheduled to start September 11.

September 4: Two University of California psychologists announce that they have found no evidence that watching TV violence increases aggression in young viewers.

Industry reports indicate that in the future networks will be presenting more specials.

Satellite transmission enables viewers around the world to witness Arab terrorists turn the Olympic games from a sports spectacle into a nightmare.

September 11: A controversy between station owners and unions over summer reruns evokes a response from President Nixon, who indicates that government regulation may be needed—a prospect favorable to the unions.

The first true attempt at pay-cable television is scheduled to start in San Diego.

September 25: *Goldfinger,* the James Bond box-office hit, is watched on half of the sets in use in Los Angeles and three out of five in New York, giving ABC hopes of good returns on its substantial investment in movies.

October 2: Industry reports indicate that reruns now occupy 41 percent of prime-time schedules. The average series is down to fewer than 23 new episodes.

October 9: Sports blackouts are attracting the concern of senators and representatives.

October 16: A Federal court refuses to overturn an FCC ruling denying Senator McGovern an automatic right of reply to President Nixon's televised messages.

November 20: A TIO survey shows that, notwithstanding criticism, the majority of people trust American journalism, especially television and radio journalism.

CPB's *Sesame Street* is reported as the biggest success of PBS to date.

December 4:   An estimated 90 million viewers watch on television as Apollo 17's blast off lights up the night skies over Cape Kennedy.

December 25:   *Life* magazine goes out of business, its demise attributed to TV by media analysts.

1973

January 8:   Feminine-product advertisers are reportedly still somewhat reluctant to advertise on television, despite the new NAB code.

January 15:   Dean Burch, Chairman of the FCC, declares that "the Commission has simply got to get out of the business of deciding which program may run in the prime-time period and which program may not."

January 22:   A Vietnam cease-fire agreement is reached and Nixon goes on TV to announce that fact.

Henry Kissinger holds a 95-minute briefing on the Vietnam agreement.

February 19:   Manufacturers of "little cigars" yield to pressure and cease to advertise their products on television.

February 26:   The NAB institutes strict and comprehensive guidelines for the advertising of drugs on television, in response to public concern.

March 5:   TV networks take in a record $1.8 billion in advertising revenues.

March 19:   Teleprompter breaks ground for projected cable network.

April 2:   The Television Information Office and the Roper rating service release their latest survey results: TV is still the top news medium.

April 30:   NBC research says that 77.5 million viewers watched President Nixon's speech on the Watergate scandal.

May 14:   The Watergate hearings begin on TV May 17.

June 18:   The networks provide live coverage of John Dean's testimony at the Watergate hearings.

Nielsen national ratings indicate that the first days of coverage of the Watergate hearings (May 17–18) drew larger audiences than had been expected.

July 9:   John Mitchell takes the stand at the Watergate hearings.

July 23:   John Ehrlichman takes the stand at the Watergate hearings.

August 13:   As the first series of Watergate hearings draws to a close, commercial networks, having provided 300 hours of coverage, have lost between seven and ten million dollars. But public broadcasters have collected more than one million dollars in contributions from viewers.

September 17:   Sports blackouts are lifted. Eight professional football games are locally telecast for the first time as a result of Congressional action and the signing by the President of legislation dealing with sports-blackout practices.

ABC gets exclusive rights to the winter Olympics, already having rights to the summer Olympics.

48 million tune in to see Billie Jean King beat Bobby Riggs at tennis.

September 24:   The decline in stadium attendance that NFL commissioner Pete Rozelle predicted if sports blackouts were lifted turns out to be real: 50,000 fans stay home on the first weekend of the new legislation.

October 8:   Vice President Agnew resigns on October 10, and President Nixon goes on TV to name Gerald Ford as Agnew's successor.

October 22:   Nixon goes on TV and castigates the networks for their treatment of his administration.

Colson, Magruder, Haldeman, and Higby memos show the depth of the administration's concern over the media and its attempts to control the networks.

November 5:   ABC will pay a record $3.3 million for one showing of 20th Century-Fox's film *The Poseidon Adventure.*

November 26:   President Nixon's proclamations that TV networks have given his administration an unfair shake have been unconvincing to the public, a conclusion of an Opinion Research poll.

December 3:   Gerald Ford is sworn in December 6 as the 40th Vice President, an event televised on all three networks.

1974

January 7:   According to a decision handed down by the U.S. Court of Appeals for the Third District, in Philadelphia, an FCC ruling that broadcast stations may not air winning numbers in state-run lotteries involves a violation of the First Amendment. In overruling the commission's order involving New Jersey's weekly lottery, the court said that such numbers are "hot news" and that their broadcast is "protected by the First Amendment."

January 14:   ABC, in an unprecedented legal action, asks a Los Angeles court to compel the White House to provide data and witnesses in a Justice Department antitrust suit. The request is part of ABC's attempt to demonstrate that the Justice Department's action amounts to retaliation on the part of the Nixon administration. CBS expects to take a similar step, NBC doesn't.

RCA becomes the first U.S. concern to enter the field of domestic satellite transmission with football transmissions to Alaska via Canadian satellite.

January 21:   *The Secret Storm,* a half-hour daytime drama on CBS-TV, is canceled after 20 years and is replaced with a game show, *Tattle-tales.* However, the series will continue on air via syndication.

February 4:   In an 11th-hour decision, ABC-TV cancels the broadcast of a *Dick Cavett Show* featuring political activists Abbie Hoffman, Tom Hayden, Jerry Rubin, and Rennie Davis—four of the Chicago Seven. ABC says that the program "contains discussions of controversial issues of public importance which ABC feels should be balanced on the same program by statements of opposing views."

March 4:   RCA demonstrates a 20-pound, portable color-TV camera—TRP-45-RCA. The camera is designed for indoor and outdoor shooting.

March 18:   Nixon and Dan Rather, CBS newscaster, clash head on at NAB annual meeting in Houston. Mr. Nixon to Dan Rather: "Are you running for something?" Dan Rather: "No, Mr. President. Are you?"

April 1:   The Justice Department, citing information obtained from the Watergate special prosecutor's office, maintains that politics played no part in its anti-trust suit against the networks.

April 8:   The Senate endorses legislation that would prohibit the broadcast of election tallies while they could still influence the outcome.

April 22:   CBS agrees to a large but unspecified payment to an employee in return for his dropping a suit claiming the network stole his idea for the series *The Beverly Hillbillies.* In another case, the network announces that it will fight a federal magistrate's decision in favor of a Rhode Island mechanic who claims to be the originator of *Have Gun Will Travel.*

April 29:   Howard Cosell, an ABC radio and TV sports reporter and commentator, receives the Broadcaster of the Year award of the International Radio and Television Society, for "providing new insights into the structures of the broad spectrum of both professional and amateur sports."

The House Judiciary Committee votes unanimously to allow live broadcast coverage of the impeachment hearings. The three major networks agree to rotate coverage, as they did for the previous summer's Senate Watergate hearings.

May 20:   NBC-TV pays a record price of $5 million to MGM for one showing of *Gone with the Wind* in the 1976–77 season. The previous record was ABC's $3.3 million to 20th Century-Fox for one showing of *The Poseidon Adventure.*

May 27:   The TvB says network-spot TV billings hit $2.6 billion in 1973.

June 3:   Dick Cavett, ABC-TV late-night star whose Emmy award went unmentioned during the presentations, announced he would reject the award. Robert Lewine, academy president, said Mr. Cavett's award was not the only one omitted.

June 10:   Television gets half of the $5 million advertising budget announced by officials of the U.S. Postal Service for what they called the first campaign by any governmental agency to sell a consumer product.

June 17:   A Phillips-Sindlinger survey finds general public acceptance of network-news personalities: Cronkite is the most trusted, Chancellor the best liked, and Sevareid the least conservative.

June 24:   CBS-TV has signed the Shell Oil Company (Ogilvy & Mather) as the sponsor for two years' of nightly "Bicentennial Minutes" (to be aired from July 4, 1974 to July 4, 1976). Shell gets a five-second identification tag at the end of each minute. Contract reportedly amounts to $10 million.

July 8:   CBS News correspondent Marvin Kalb was one of several network newsmen cut off the air by Soviet TV authorities. He was saying: "Tonight there are a couple of interesting developments at the TV studios here. The State Committee on Radio and Television, which controls all facili—" when the screen went blank and silent.

July 22:   According to survey results released by the Television Information Office, the number of adults who object to having commercials in children's TV programs declined from 32 percent to 23 percent between November, 1972, and May, 1974, while those considering such commercials acceptable rose from 60 percent to 66 percent.

Network coverage of impeachment proceedings against Nixon begins on July 24. For the first time, microphones and cameras for live coverage are admitted to a deliberative session of the House Committee.

August 5:   NBC pays a record $10 million for broadcasting rights to the movie *The Godfather.* The network will make some of that money back by charging $225,000 per minute for advertising—another record.

The House of Representatives decides to allow broadcast coverage of the impeachment debate on the House floor, scheduled to begin August 19. It is expected that there will be 55 hours of House debate on impeachment resolutions, followed by 32 hours of argument on floor motions. The final vote is expected to come before Labor Day.

The first national ratings of TV coverage of the House Judiciary Committee's impeachment deliberations show that evening sessions averaged 11.0; that is, more than seven million homes were watching each minute. The total-audience rating was 23.8; that is, nearly sixteen-million homes watched at some time for six minutes or more. Impeachment ratings trailed entertainment ratings by about five points. The daytime ratings that were available averaged around 7.1, or approximately four million homes per minute.

Up to 110 million persons watch some or all of President Nixon's resignation address on TV August 8—almost certainly a record for a single quarter hour. And up to 130 million watched portions of the full evening of special coverage the three networks devoted to it. One hundred and twenty-five million are estimated to have watched parts of the 31-hour coverage of the first moon-landing mission, in 1969.

August 26: A. C. Nielsen Co.'s tabulations are expected to show 46.9 million homes, or 70.9% of U.S. total, watched some segment of the network TV coverage of the three main events of the Aug. 8–9 presidential transition: President Nixon's resignation address, 9–9:15 P.M. NYT; his departure 9:30–10 A.M. and President Ford's inauguration, 11:55 A.M.–12:30 P.M. The actual viewing audience was undoubtedly higher; these figures do not count viewing on independent stations and the Public Broadcasting Service.

September 2: Broadcast coverage of Evel Knievel's leap over Idaho's Snake River canyon on Sunday, September 8, creates a stir in Congress and at the FCC. Representative John Murphy (D-N.Y.) enlisted 20 co-sponsors for a joint congressional resolution directing the FCC to prohibit any broadcast of the event. On August 30, FCC Chairman Richard E. Wiley told Murphy that Commission intervention would violate the anticensorship provisions of the Communications Act and was prohibited by the First Amendment. He also said that the Commission couldn't prevent closed-circuit pay-TV coverage, which a promoter, Top Rank, had booked into hundreds of public showplaces.

October 7: U.S. District Judge John J. Sirica turns down a request of three networks for permission to broadcast White House tapes that are to be played during the Watergate cover-up trial.

October 14: An FCC report indicates that TV stations devote 22.5 percent of their broadcast time, and 19.1 percent of prime time, to nonentertainment programs.

A first step in making TV cameras permanent fixtures in House and Senate chambers is taken when the Joint Committee on Congressional Operations issues a report to both Houses recommending a one-year trial for continuous live coverage of floor proceedings of the first session of the 94th Congress.

October 28: Leon Jaworski, former special Watergate prosecutor, declares that Congress can and should make 64 White House tapes available for broadcast, but that, because of obscenities in some of the conversations, not all of them can be put on the air.

November 4: An industry report estimates that the movie industry, which once regarded itself as imperiled by television, will spend $80 million in 1974 to promote its films on the airwaves.

November 11: Network news divisions announce that they will provide coverage, on a rotating basis, of Senate hearings on the nomination for the Vice Presidency of Nelson Rockefeller.

November 18: Federal Trade Commission chairman Lewis Engman reveals that the FTC has so far been unable to solve the practical problems involved in adding information on nutrition to food commercials—the chief one being that the commercials became unintelligible—but that the issue of disclosure of nutritional content will remain a live one.

CBS announces that it will make video cassettes of all regularly scheduled and special news broadcasts available to the public through an agreement with the National Archives and Records Service of the U.S. General Services Administration.

November 25: NBC-TV debut of *The Godfather* placed only fourth on the all-time Nielsen movie list, but network officials maintain they don't regret their $10 million investment.

December 9: A federal judge frees Nixon tapes for broadcast.

December 16: A Federal Trade Commission judge rules that advertising for Listerine mouthwash is misleading: the Warner-Lambert Company, which makes Listerine, announces that it will appeal the decision.

Former New York Governor Nelson A. Rockefeller is sworn in as the 41st Vice President on December 19, and the 15-minute ceremony is televised from the Senate chamber, the first time TV cameras are permitted inside. All three commercial networks carry the event live.

December 23: An Annenberg School of Communications study concludes that overall violence on television has declined but that the number of victims of violence portrayed on television have increased in number, and that audiences are getting an exaggerated picture of life's dangers.

1975

January 13: ABC's new show *AM America* enters the early morning ratings race. It receives mixed reviews and fair numbers, topping the *CBS Morning News* but falling far short of NBC's entrenched *Today* show.

February 3: President Ford and FCC member Charlotte T. Reid urge broadcasters of religious programs to promote a renewal of faith in America.

Norman Lear's controversial new show about the goings-on in a Baltimore hotel of ill-repute (*The Hot L Baltimore*) draws initial solid ratings and a few cancellations.

February 17: The House Ways and Means Committee votes to permit live radio and TV coverage of its hearings. Beginning March 3, cameras will be allowed for energy-tax sessions.

February 24: ABC and CBS each have four shows in the top ten of *McCall's* magazine survey of most-violent shows. *McCall's* explains that the survey was undertaken to test network claims that violence is what people want to watch, and found that none of the ten most-violent shows is in the top ten of the most recent Nielsen ratings.

Lawrence Spivak, moderator and producer of the longest-running network show, NBC-TV's *Meet the Press,* announces that he will retire in November.

March 3: The Tobacco Institute reports that cigarette advertising declined from $314.7 million in 1970—the last year such advertising was permitted in broadcast—to $256.2 million in 1974. Since cigarette advertising on TV and radio was estimated at $220 million in 1970, other media (magazines, newspapers, billboards) have benefited considerably from the broadcast ban.

March 17: It is announced that national broadcast coverage of major league baseball, an NBC exclusive for 28 years, will be divided between NBC and ABC.

March 24: MCA and Philips officials demonstrate their home video-disk systems, priced about the same as color TV sets.

March 31: A study by Arbitron conducted in 30 markets found that households equipped with cable TV average 11.5 percent more viewing hours than those without it.

ABC, CBS, and NBC each reject a proposal from supporters of former President Nixon for an exclusive interview with him, reportedly because of the high fee requested and the insistence on pre-screening all questions.

April 7: CBS broadcasts an interview with Robert Haldeman, former President Nixon's chief of staff.

Judge John Sirica turns down a request of networks and recording companies that the White House tapes be released for broadcast and reproduction.

April 14: According to a Roper study, the public again gives television high marks for believability, news, and entertainment.

Industry reports indicate that spot TV advertising for 1974 netted $1.6 billion—a new high.

April 21: The family-viewing standards of the National Association of Broadcasters code are adopted by all three major television networks. A *Wall Street Journal* story quotes an unidentified CBS official as saying of the family plan: "Coming out against it would have been like coming out against motherhood and apple pie."

May 5: According to FCC and Supreme Court rulings, internal memoranda are not subject to the provisions of the Freedom of Information Act.

Broadcasting's biggest and longest story of recent years—the war in Vietnam—draws to a close, with correspondents scrambling to file stories and then flee Saigon in the hectic final hours.

June 2: Figures from the Television Bureau of Advertising show that a record 516 advertisers spent a record $2.3 billion in 1974.

June 30: Bell Telephone's solid-state black-and-white TV camera, which is the size of a cigarette pack, meets resolution requirements for TV news coverage.

July 28: Television covers the joint Soviet–American space venture.

August 11: NBC's innovation in daytime programming, lengthening *Another World* and *Days of Our Lives* to full-hour dramas, has been a ratings success that may signal an important trend in network daytime TV.

August 18: According to a study by R. H. Bruskin Associates, television now attracts 22 million more adults daily than do newspapers.

David Frost and Richard Nixon agree on terms for a series of 90-minute interviews, although Frost won't reveal the figures.

September 15: President Ford, in marked contrast to his predecessors, finds local television much more to his liking than network TV. Stations in Providence, Milwaukee, Chicago, St. Louis, and Los Angeles are treated to interviews.

September 29: A Roper study finds that nearly two out of every three parents of youngsters under 12 feel that children's programming has improved.

October 6: Nielsen's first demographic studies of the fall season indicate a 7 percent increase in young viewers during the family hour and a 6 percent decrease in adult viewers.

The first pay-cable satellite transmission to systems in Florida and Mississippi begins.

The first black-owned television station, WGPR-TV Detroit, begins operations.

October 13: NAB's TV code board prohibits the advertisement of contraceptives on television and restricts commercials for feminine hygiene products to adult-viewing times.

October 20: ABC-TV overhauls its 7 A.M. show and renames it *Good Morning, America*. The new host will be David Hartman.

November 3: Sony's Betamax home video-recording-player, which can tape two shows at the same time, goes on the market, albeit at a high price.

December 22: The Federal Trade Commission declares that future Listerine advertisements must notify the public that the company's previous claims in behalf of its product as a remedy for colds and sore throats were false.

1976

January 26: Network executives dispute House Speaker Carl Albert's assertion that television time is arbitrarily granted to the President without fair treatment for the opposition.

At a conference of the Society of Motion Picture and Television Engineers, the Thomson–CSF Laboratories introduces a new, eight-pound color-TV camera.

February 23: The House votes to investigate a leak that led to the *Village Voice* publication of an Intelligence Committee investigation into the CIA. Part of the investigation will focus on CBS's Daniel Schorr. And the White House proposes legislation that would make it a crime to leak classified information.

March 1: CBS suspends indefinitely Daniel Schorr from all reporting, and announces that it will support his efforts to protect his source of the intelligence report but not his disclosure of information to the *Village Voice*.

March 8: A survey published in the *Columbia Journalism Review* finds a decrease in commitment to news and public affairs on network TV.

April 5: The Gerbner Report—the work of a University of Pennsylvania professor—concludes that a reduction of violence in prime-time programs was offset by its sharp increase in weekend children's programming.

April 26: It is announced that Barbara Walters will leave NBC's *Today* show and move to ABC as co-anchor of the evening news for a reported $1 million annually.

January 12: Ballyhoo over new NBC network logo strikes an embarrassing note when it's discovered that the Nebraska Educational Television Network has had identical logo for the past six months.

January 19: Industry sources reveal that pilots for the coming season include more comedies and Westerns and fewer violent police stories. There will also be more adaptations of motion-picture hits.

May 24: The TV movie *Eleanor and Franklin* wins 11 Emmys, a record number for one show.

House and Senate conferees agree on a bill to continue the antiblackout law.

May 31: The Supreme Court declares illegal the state of Virginia's ban on advertising the price of prescription drugs on television, on the grounds that commercials are disseminations of information and are in the public interest.

June 7: An NBC study finds no link between drug commercials on TV and the illicit use of drugs by the young.

June 14: The Supreme Court formally rules against prohibitions of prescription-drug advertising.

June 21: NBC celebrates its 50th anniversary as a commercial network.

July 19: The biggest news coverage ever accorded a national political convention is given by more than 3,600 news people from broadcast organizations to the Democratic Convention in New York.

August 9: Best Foods issues guidelines for its advertising that forbid buying time in or near programs with a "pervasive portrayal of violence."

August 16: A Gallup poll shows that most Americans would like to see televised debates this fall between the presidential candidates—Ford, Reagan, and Carter.

September 6: Ford, Carter, and representatives of the League of Women Voters agree to begin debates on September 23, with two more to follow for presidential candidates, and one for vice-presidential nominees.

October 4: Barbara Walters becomes the first anchorwoman of a network news program.

November 1: The Court of Appeals in Washington overrules District Judge Sirica's decision that the White House tapes in the Watergate trial should be withheld from the public for the time being. The networks are happy, and Warner Brothers is ready to release a two-record set of the tapes.

A Tunney subcommittee report determines that prior restraints on the press in covering trials are unjustifiable and that reporters should not be cited for contempt of court if they refuse to divulge their sources of information.

President Ford announces his support for a plan to include captions in programs in order to assist the deaf.

The FCC decides, by a vote of 6 to 0, that public stations must afford a reasonable degree of access to candidates for public office.

November 8: A federal judge in Los Angeles declares the concept of family-viewing time inconsonant with the rights of writers and producers as guaranteed by the First Amendment.

ABC, CBS, and NBC stay with the election-night drama until the early hours of the morning when a victory for Jimmy Carter is called, but without the expected number of viewers. Some 120 million, about the same number that watched the very predictable Nixon–McGovern race in 1972, made up the total audience.

A massive overhaul of the National Academy of Television Arts and Sciences and its Emmy award procedure is voted by the trustees.

November 15: The CPB board allocates its $103-million budget for 1977 to public television and radio.

CBS Chairman William Paley formally opens the Museum of Broadcasting in New York City. It is the first American museum dedicated to TV and radio broadcasting. Paley is to fund the first five years of its operation.

November 22: A home video-disk player system, developed by a German company and Decca of London and Germany, is demonstrated in New York.

December 6: A survey by Common Cause finds that House members are in favor of radio and television coverage of chamber proceedings.

Both the American Medical Association and the Parents-Teachers Association begin campaigns against TV violence.

December 13: The FCC approves the use of a portion of a station's TV signal for transmitting coded captioning for deaf viewers.

1977

February 7: The NBC network signs deal with the Russians for 1980 summer Olympic games, at an unprecedented price tag of $85 million.

ABC-TV's *Roots* breaks audience records, leading ABC to the highest rating—35.5—any network has achieved for one week.

February 28: It is announced that *The Tonight Show* is going live for the first time in 18 years. It's still strong in the ratings despite the late-night gains of ABC and CBS.

March 21: Actress Farrah Fawcett-Majors' planned defection from ABC-TV's *Charlie's Angels* results in a law suit from Spelling-Goldberg Productions.

April 4: A Roper study finds a slight decrease in the public's esteem for TV, but it remains far and away the dominant medium.

May 9: David Frost's interview of Richard Nixon is a sponsor sell-out. The ratings are excellent, and it is almost universally praised in the media.

June 6: A survey by the broadcast consulting firm of McHugh & Hoffman finds that TV programmers are failing to offer programs commensurate with their audience's maturity and expectations.

July 11: The New York black-out on July 13 sends networks and stations scrambling.

August 8: A Harris survey finds that 71 percent of those polled think there is too much violence on television. The figure is up 12 percent from a 1968 survey.

August 22: The Television Bureau of Advertising says that for the first time, television is taking in more ad revenues than newspapers, at least from advertisers for which TV and newspapers compete directly.

September 26: Georgia opens its Supreme Court to television and radio coverage.

October 17: More than 50 wives of senators and representatives, lead by Tipper Gore, enlist in a crusade against TV violence.

October 31: A study by the National Cancer Institute reveals that the number of anti-smoking public-service announcements has rapidly dwindled.

November 7: The erosion in homes-using-television (HUT) levels during daytime hours is 1977's ratings mystery of the year.

December 5: The Television Bureau of Advertising reports that although homes using TV have declined, the total number of homes with television has increased.

December 12: Nielsen's Ralph Clausen is quoted in *Broadcasting* as saying that TV viewing has peaked in the last few years and from now on will show only slight year-to-year changes.

1978

January 2: Nielsen finds only a 1 percent decline in HUT levels from December 1976 to December 1977. It could be a sign that the decrease in TV-viewing levels has stabilized.

Johnny Carson and NBC sign a new contract, which has the king of late-night TV working less and earning more.

February 13: ABC celebrates its 25th anniversary as a television network.

February 27: An FTC staff report calls for bans on the advertising of products aimed at children under the age of 8, a ban on advertising of highly sugared products, and a counteradvertising campaign against sugared products allowed on the air.

March 13: TvB releases a report that network television advertising amounted to $3.6 billion in 1977, 21 percent more than in 1976.

April 3: Carter signs a bill creating a new telecommunications agency.

April 10: CBS acquires exclusive TV rights to *Gone with the Wind* for 20 years at an unprecedented price of $35 million.

April 24: The Supreme Court reverses a lower court ruling on the release of the White House tapes in the Watergate trial. It stops immediate access by the public and requires that requests for permission to broadcast or reproduce them be processed through the General Services Administration.

May 1: A Supreme Court decision declares illegal a Massachusetts law prohibiting corporations from spending their own money to influence public referendums. The decision reinforces the free-speech rights of advertisers and, in Chief Justice Burger's opinion, gives "media conglomerates" some First Amendment protection against restrictions.

July 3: Television sales—both spot and network—are reported to be going higher than ever. Network executives estimate they've tallied close to $1 billion in prime-time sales for the upcoming season. Spot estimates for the third and fourth quarter also point toward sales above last year's.

August 28: It is announced that the first minority-owned VHF TV station, WHEC-TV, Rochester, NY, will be in operation soon.

September 18: A House–Senate conference committee advises the FTC that its proposed restrictions on advertising directed at children could pose constitutional problems.

October 30: The Children's Television Workshop announces it will launch a new program project in early 1980 designed to do for science what *Sesame Street* did for math and reading basics.

November 20: A study conducted by the Corporation for Public Broadcasting is highly critical of public broadcasting's treatment of minorities, both in employment and in programming.

November 27: Among the first to die in the bizarre events culminating in mass suicide at Jonestown, Guyana, are two NBC television newsmen—correspondent Don Harris and cameraman Robert Brown.

December 4: An FTC law judge advises the American Medical Association that doctors—like other professionals—must be allowed the freedom to advertise in the media.

1979

January 1: According to FCC figures, cable-Tv revenues exceed one billion dollars in 1977.

January 8: Advertiser investments in network television totaled $3.7 billion in the first 11 months of 1978, up 13 percent from the same 1977 period.

February 12: Industry reports on network plans and projects indicate a trend next season to programs based on blue-collar life styles, and in particular a return to stories about crime fighters.

February 19: Those seeking the admittance of cameras and microphones into courtrooms suffer a setback from the American Bar Association's house of delegates, which rejects a proposed relaxation of restrictions. In a related development, a test case involving television coverage of House of Representatives proceedings begins today on Capitol Hill.

March 12: It is disclosed that the major leagues will get $54.5 million for broadcast rights to play-by-play.

A Brief History of the Networks*

The American Broadcasting Company
1330 Ave. of the Americas
New York, NY 10019
(212) 581-7777

1313 N. Vine St.
Hollywood, CA 90038
(213) 663-3311

Executives and officers

Leonard H. Goldenson, chairman of the board and chief executive officer

Elton H. Rule, president and chief operating officer

Frederick S. Pierce, president, ABC-TV, and executive vice president, ABC Companies, Inc.

Anthony D. Thomopoulos, president, ABC Entertainment

Roone Arledge, president, ABC News and Sports

James E. Duffy, president, ABC-TV Network

Richard A. O'Leary, president, ABC-owned TV stations

Mark Cohen, senior vice president, affiliate services, ABC-TV

Edwin T. Vane, vice president, national program director, ABC-TV

Brandon Stoddard, senior vice president, dramatic programs, motion pictures, and novels for television

Ellis O. Moore, vice president, corporate relations

James L. Abernathy, vice president, corporate affairs

Richard J. Connelly, vice president, public relations

ABC

In the spring of 1941, the FCC issued a report on chain broadcasting which contained the sentence, "No license shall be issued to a station affiliated with a network organization maintaining more than one network." That sentence was the genesis of the American Broadcasting Company.

The FCC was referring to, and concerned about, NBC's Blue and Red networks. The government agency determined that the dual network was not in the public's interest; so NBC was required to divest itself of one of them.

Within eight months of the ruling, RCA, the parent company, incorporated the Blue network under the name of the American Broadcasting System and established it as an independent subsidiary

with 116 stations. (These were all radio stations. TV was not in operation until 1946.)

With all the paperwork done, RCA put the network up for sale. The buyer, with FCC approval, was Edward J. Noble, founder and chairman of the Life Savers Corporation. He paid $8 million for the network, the largest sum ever paid for any broadcasting entity up to that time. For a few years, 12½ percent of the network was owned by Time, Inc., and Chester LaRoche, but they divested themselves of their shares in its ownership by November of 1948.

Even the name American Broadcasting Company originally belonged to someone else—Radio Station WOL, in Washington, which sold the name for $10,000 on October 13, 1944.

The name became official in December, when a radio announcer said, "This is the Blue network of the American Broadcasting Company." The last change occurred on June 15, 1945, at 8:15 A.M., when James Gibbon announced to 197 affiliates, "This is the American Broadcasting Company."

ABC's first big-name star was Bing Crosby, who signed with the network in 1946. The fact that he had been turned down by the other two networks did not detract from the auspicious occasion.

The Age of TV for ABC began in April, 1948, with the signing of the first affiliate, WFIL, Philadelphia. On April 19, the network aired its first TV program, "On the Corner," with Henry Morgan. The program was carried in two markets, Philadelphia (WFIL) and Washington (WMAL). The sponsor was the Admiral Radio Corporation.

Two TV firsts occurred on ABC in 1948: a live broadcast of an opera, Verdi's *Otello,* from the Metropolitan Opera House in New York, and a TV documentary, "The Marshall Plan."

In 1949, Paramount Pictures was ordered under the Sherman Anti-Trust Act, to separate its film products from its theater operations, which it promptly did. It then formed United Paramount Theatres. A little over a year later, the new head of UPT, Leonard H. Goldenson, announced plans to merge with ABC. His board completely disapproved of the plan, because it felt ABC would operate at a loss for so long that it would destroy UPT. Goldenson, however, got the support of Harry Hagerty, vice chairman and chief financial officer of the Metropolitan Life Insurance Company, and a promise of Met Life financial backing. The UPT board then readily agreed to the merger.

On February 9, 1952, the FCC approved the merger, and the new company became American Broadcasting–Paramount Theatres, Inc.

Soon after the approval, ABC moved further uptown in New York, to the former New York

---

*Some of the information in this section was obtained from *Broadcasting* magazine and used with its permission, for which the authors are grateful.

Riding Club Arena, on West 66th Street. It had been originally headquartered in Rockefeller Center, but that location had proved somewhat awkward: To reach the ABC offices, visitors had to take NBC Studio elevators.

In 1954, ABC enjoyed its first notable TV commercial success. Walt Disney had laid plans to construct Disneyland and needed backing. Goldenson lent him $500,000 and received in return a 35 percent interest in the park and the Disney-produced TV programs. The Disney agreement also represented a break from the tradition according to which advertisers owned TV programs, and it gave ABC the power to buy other programs in later years.

In 1955, Warner Brothers signed an exclusive-rights contract with the network. The resulting show, *Cheyenne,* with Clint Walker, was the first of a series of Westerns that included *Bronco, Colt 45, Wyatt Earp, Maverick, Jim Bowie, The Rifleman, The Lawman, Sugarfoot,* and *The Rebel* on ABC alone.

Thanks to *The Mickey Mouse Club* and the Warner Brothers agreement, ABC was now operating at a profit. But it was still struggling to acquire affiliates. In 1956, ABC suggested to the FCC a plan of reallocation that would equally distribute the affiliates in the top 200 markets among the three networks. The FCC rejected the plan, and ABC's financial problems returned.

Up to this time, ABC had had no programming before 3 P.M. Then, in 1958, it began "Operation Daybreak" with the help of Young & Rubicam, the advertising agency, and several of its clients. The network began programming at 11:30 A.M., and Young & Rubicam financed the operation.

There was some sad news at ABC that year, too. Ed Noble, the original owner of ABC, died on December 28, at the age of 76.

In 1959, ABC began its commitment to sports coverage, by acquiring the rights to NCAA football and basketball, boxing, professional football, bowling, and major-league baseball. The network also acquired an independent sports production company, called Sports Programs, Inc., which produced the NCAA games. (One of the young sports producers with the company was Roone Arledge, destined to become the president of ABC Sports and News.)

1960 was a good year for ABC: For the first time the network was holding its own in the ratings race in markets where the three networks were in close competition.

In 1961, to the delight of sports fans everywhere, ABC introduced an electronic device developed by its engineers, called VTX (Video Tape Expander) or "instant replay." Moreover, *Wide World of Sports* and *The American Sportsman* debuted in 1961.

Color programming began in the fall season of 1962. And once again, ABC found itself in need of money to maintain respectable color operations. The prospect of abundant funds arose in 1965, when a proposed merger between ABC and ITT was announced. The FCC approved the merger, but the Justice Department prohibited it, because of the potential problems inherent in an international conglomerate's owning a powerful news medium. In 1968, ITT withdrew its offer—which would have meant more than $400 million to ABC stockholders.

Despite money troubles, ABC proceeded with costly changes, improvements, and innovations. In April of 1965, the company had changed its name from AB-PT to American Broadcasting Companies, Inc., and established its new corporate headquarters at 1330 Avenue of the Americas in New York City. In 1966, ABC broadcast *The Bridge on the River Kwai,* which (according to Nielsen) was viewed by 60 million. The blockbuster TV movie had arrived. This was also the year of full color broadcasting for the network.

In 1967, the ABC evening news was expanded to a half hour, and Joey Bishop inaugurated ABC's late-night programming with his talk show.

In July of 1968, Howard Hughes tried to gain control of ABC. Goldenson fought him tooth and nail in the courts but kept losing ground, and before long Hughes had the opportunity to buy 34 percent of ABC stock. However, he never bought it: He had relented, he explained, because of Goldenson's strong resistance to the takeover. Industry rumors offered a different interpretation. The FCC would have held a public hearing on the transference of the network and the network-owned stations, and would have required the new owner to attend. It was speculated that Hughes, an unflagging recluse, chose to savor his nominal victory in private rather than enjoy a substantial one at the intolerable cost of a public appearance.

In 1970, Harry Reasoner joined Howard K. Smith on the ABC evening news, and *Monday Night Football*—which was to be a great success—was inaugurated.

In 1972, with the Summer Olympics heading the list of profitable programs, ABC operated at a profit for the first time in ten years.

In 1976, Barbara Walters joined ABC, and became the first anchorwoman in TV history. Her salary—nearly $1 million a year—created considerable discomposure for Harry Reasoner and the anchormen at the other networks. This was also the year when ABC moved to the front in the ratings race: It was in first place for eight weeks with prime-time viewers.

In early 1977, the all-time highest-rated program, *Roots,* appeared on ABC. The network now had established a commanding lead in ratings over its competitors—much of the credit for which must go to Fred Silverman (who joined NBC in the summer of 1978 to become the new president of that network). But even with the loss of Fred Silverman, ABC still holds its lead in the entertainment area and becomes more entrenched in the number one spot each season.

The only area remaining for the network to conquer is news programming. Howard K. Smith has resigned and Harry Reasoner has returned to CBS and *60 Minutes,* leaving ABC News open to experimentation. This is exactly what Roone Arledge, president of ABC News and Sports, is doing, and in just a few short months, ABC News, with its Globetrotter-style pass-the-ball-around routine, has moved up in the ratings.

Looking back on ABC's past 25 years, it is apparent that the network's history has been characterized by a series of dramatic developments and notable innovations. If its next quarter century cannot be foreseen, television-industry buffs may nevertheless expect ABC to strive to maintain its current status.

Columbia Broadcasting System

51 W. 52nd St.
New York, NY 10019
(212) 975-4321

7800 Beverly Blvd.
Los Angeles, CA 90036
(213) 651-2345

Executives and officers

William S. Paley, chairman
John D. Bache, president
Robert A. Daly, president, CBS Entertainment Division
James H. Rosenfield, president, CBS Entertainment Division
B. Donald Grant, vice president, programs, CBS Entertainment Division
Robert L. Hosking, vice president, affiliate relations, CBS Entertainment Division
Bruce R. Bryant, vice president and director, affiliate relations, CBS Entertainment Division
Harvey Shephard, vice president, program planning, CBS Entertainment Division
Robert M. Silberling, vice president, dramatic program development, CBS Entertainment Division
Jerry Golod, vice president, children's programs, CBS Entertainment Division
William Self, vice president, programs, motion pictures for television, and mini-series, Hollywood, CBS Entertainment Division
Michael Gursey, vice president, variety programs, Hollywood, CBS Entertainment Division
Michael Ogiens, vice president, daytime programs, CBS Entertainment Division
Alan C. Wagner, vice president, nighttime programs, New York, CBS Entertainment Division
Andrew Siegel, vice president, comedy program development, CBS Entertainment Division
Barrie Richardson, vice president, press information, CBS Entertainment Division

CBS

In the early 1920s, Arthur Judson, a prominent concert-tour manager, formed a radio network, either because he could not convince NBC to buy a musical package he had put together or because he had become involved in a dispute with the American Society of Composers, Authors and Publishers. Whatever the causes and preliminary incidents may have been, Judson, in 1927, formed his network: United Independent Broadcasters, Inc.

Within a few months, money problems developed. UIB contracted 16 stations and bought from each ten hours of air time a week for $500. But advertising revenues were hard to come by. Eventually, however, the network got the backing of Louis Sterling, president of the Columbia Phonograph Company, who upon hearing that RCA was about to merge with the Victor Talking Machine Company decided that the time had come to advertise his products. He turned to UIB.

Shortly after Sterling's money went in, the network changed its name to the Columbia Phonograph Broadcasting System—at a cost to Sterling of about $163,000. An American opera, *The King's Henchman,* marked the debut of the network, on September 19, 1927. Since the network studios had not yet been completed, a make-shift control booth was established in the men's room of the WOR radio station in Newark, New Jersey.

Shortly thereafter, more money problems arose, and Columbia Phonograph abandoned the Columbia Phonograph Broadcasting System. Jerome H. Louchheim, a builder from Philadelphia, was the next to assume a controlling interest in the network. Two other men joined him in the venture: Dr. Leon Levy, the owner of radio station WCAU, in Philadelphia, and his brother Isaac. The network adopted a new name—a shortened version of its former name: the Columbia Broadcasting System. Toward the end of 1928, Louchheim, displeased that costs still exceeded earnings, got out. The Levys remained (Leon Levy was to remain a CBS director for 50 years, until his retirement, in 1977).

The next, and the best known, investor in CBS was William S. Paley, whose family paid between $250,000 and $450,000 for a controlling interest. Young Paley, as head of the advertising department of his father's company, Congress Cigars, had placed ads on WCAU and the CBS Network, and the ads had worked: thanks to them, Congress's sales had doubled. Hence, when an opportunity to buy into the network presented itself, the Paleys were quick to seize it.

On September 26, 1928, Paley, then 27, became president of CBS, and set about challenging NBC's predominance in radio. He set up headquarters at 485 Madison Avenue, in New York, in a building CBS would occupy for over 30 years, beginning in 1929. He commissioned a study by Price Waterhouse & Co. in 1930 to determine what radio station people listened to most. And the study revealed that NBC, which claimed to be the most-listened-to network, was the second-most-listened-to: CBS was the more popular.

One reason for CBS's ascendancy was the new talent it had booked—Bing Crosby, Kate Smith, and the Mills Brothers. Another was that CBS felt free to experiment and innovate, as NBC did not: The latter, with firm commitments from advertisers, felt it had to maintain the status quo or else aggravate its audience and so alienate the advertisers. Hence, the new things CBS was bringing to radio encountered few rivals from NBC.

In 1931, CBS completed an agreement with

Paramount whereby film stars were heard on radio for the first time. Between that year and 1935, the network signed such radio stars as Major Bowes, Will Rogers, Bob Hope, and Eddie Cantor—all formerly with NBC. And it acquired (also from NBC) the enormously successful series *The Shadow.* Such acquisitions enabled CBS to surpass its rival in sales, profits, and affiliates.

In 1938, Orson Welles made CBS radio history: In a Mercury Theatre presentation of "The War of the Worlds" he created such an illusion of reality as he "reported" an invasion of Martians that he scared the wits out of much of the country—even though the show opened with a disclaimer, much like those used today, to orient listeners to what they would hear.

CBS was in television from the outset of the industry. It demonstrated a new color system on August 27, 1940—a development of its chief television engineer, Peter G. Goldmark. RCA also had a color system and, after long legal battles, CBS had to yield to the RCA system. However, it was later learned that RCA had indeed used several pieces of equipment whose patents were held by CBS in its system.

During World War II, Paley was assigned overseas in the Office of War Information. Edward R. Murrow, in Europe as a CBS foreign correspondent, so influenced Paley that reportage was thereafter a significant element in the programming of CBS. Murrow put together such an excellent news staff that the network was to be regarded as more than a medium of entertainment.

After the war, CBS continued to search out and sign talent. As before, many of CBS's gains were NBC's losses. By January 1950, nearly every star of radio was under contract with CBS. Indeed, the network's ability to allure talent was such that Fred Allen closed one of his NBC shows by saying, "I'll be back next week, same time, same network—no other comedian can make that claim."

The idea behind building up a star-studded radio network was to prepare for success in TV. It was a good plan; however, many of CBS's stars approached television too conservatively, and it took a few years for CBS to catch and pass NBC in the ratings race.

Ed Sullivan went on the air in 1948. The viewers liked the show but Sullivan's peculiar postures caused a number of them to write in and ask what was wrong with his neck.

The big year for CBS turned out to be 1951, with the debut of *I Love Lucy.* Although the show from its inception looked to be a success, there was some question whether it would ever get on the air. Lucille Ball had to insist that CBS sign Desi Arnaz before the network would do so. Moreover, the couple wanted to do the show before a live audience, an idea that the network rejected. Ball and Arnaz produced the first show themselves to demonstrate their conception of *I Love Lucy* to the network. The upshot was that they invented the situation-comedy format.

Nineteen fifty-one was also the year that Bill

Gordon designed the CBS Eye, one of the most famous trademarks in the world. On September 3, 1951, CBS produced the first episode of *Search for Tomorrow,* which was destined to become the longest-running of all soap operas (the name *soap opera* derives from the kinds of products that generally sponsored the Monday through Friday series, and from their melodramatic—or "operatic"—plots). The second CBS soap opera, *Love of Life,* went on the air 21 days later, on September 24, 1951, and was followed by *The Guiding Light,* on June 30, 1952. All three were instant successes. The network in effect monopolized the soap-opera market for the next five years, until ABC introduced *The Edge of Night.* On April 2, 1956, CBS aired its fourth soap opera, *As the World Turns.*

By 1952, Arthur Godfrey had three shows on the air, two of them ranked second and third in the ratings. (In 1953, Godfrey stunned everyone by firing Julius LaRosa on the air.)

In the years to come, CBS maintained its top spot in the ratings with such long-running successes as *Gunsmoke* (1957), *The Defenders* (1961), *The Beverly Hillbillies* (1962), and *All in the Family* (1972). In 1965, the network moved into new headquarters—a 36-story dark-granite building sometimes called the "black rock"—at 51 West 52nd Street, New York City. In 1977, it slipped to the number two position in the ratings behind ABC.

If CBS does recapture the lead, it may hang on to it as hard and as long as it did in the past. A leader just gets used to leading.

National Broadcasting Company

30 Rockefeller Plaza
New York, NY 10020
(212) 664-4444

3000 W. Alameda Ave.
Burbank, CA 91504
(213) 845-7000

Executives and officers

Edgar H. Griffiths, president and chief executive officer, RCA Corp.

Kenneth W. Bilby, executive vice president, corporate affairs, RCA Corp.

Jane Cahill Pfeiffer, chairman of the board, NBC

David Adams, vice chairman of the board, NBC

Fred Silverman, president and chief executive officer, NBC

Robert Mulholland, president, NBC-TV

Lester Crystal, president, NBC news

Mike Weinblatt, president, NBC entertainment

Irwin Siegelstein, executive vice president, broadcasting, NBC-TV

Michael Brockman, vice president, daytime and children's programs, NBC entertainment

Joyce Burditt, vice president, comedy development, NBC entertainment

Peter Andrews, vice president, special projects

Donald J. Mercer, vice president, affiliate relations, NBC-TV

M. S. Rukeyser, executive vice president, public information, NBC

George Hoover, vice president, press and publicity

Robert C. Butler, executive vice president and chief financial officer, NBC

George D. Black, executive vice president, personnel and labor relations, NBC

NBC

The first radio station went on the air in 1921. By 1924, nearly 1400 stations were broadcasting. Most promoted one type of business or another, and all operated without any FCC sanctions. When the novelty of radio wore off, nearly half of the 1400 stations went out of business.

But radio was here to stay, and the fact that 21 million of the 26 million homes in America were without radios warranted the belief of radio manufacturers that their business was what we today call a growth industry. RCA was the first to act on its belief. With General Electric and Westinghouse as partners, the company bought a New York station, WEAF (soon to become WNBC), from AT&T. A month before the first NBC network program, RCA ran full-page newspaper ads declaring its intention to improve broadcasting and at the same time manufacture low-cost radio receivers with sharp reception. It did both expeditiously. From the onset, NBC's forte was organization. In fact, some historians believe that radio developed into a true industry largely because NBC impressed structure and purposefulness on it.

On November 15, 1926, from the Waldorf-Astoria, in New York, before 1,000 invited guests, at 8:00 P.M. NBC launched its network with a four-hour extravaganza broadcast over 25 stations from the Atlantic coast to the Mississippi River. Merlin H. Aylesworth, the network president, opened the program with a five-minute speech and then turned the mikes over to such stars as Weber and Fields and Will Rogers.

On January 1, 1927, NBC formed the Red and Blue networks, the Red having 25 stations, the Blue 6. (The network names derive from the colors used on coverage maps to indicate the areas of the country the networks served.) Eventually, the Blue Network was sold and became the ABC Network (See ABC). On the day the two networks were formed, NBC made the first coast-to-coast broadcast—of the Alabama–Stanford Rose Bowl game.

Nineteen twenty-seven was also the year three musical tones (G, E, C) became the famous NBC trademark.

NBC was the first network to use the studio audience. As some tell it, Will Rogers invited all those standing outside the studio to come inside and watch him work.

In 1929, *Amos 'n' Andy* became a hit across the country, as did *The Voice of Firestone* and *One Man's Family* later the same year.

Despite the onset of the Depression, things were going well enough at NBC for RCA to buy out its partners, General Electric and Westinghouse. On January 1, 1930, NBC became a wholly owned subsidiary of RCA.

In 1937, NBC became the first network to maintain a major symphony orchestra. The first concert, under the direction of Arturo Toscanini, who was to head the symphony for over 16 years, was heard on December 25, 1937. `

NBC television began in 1928. On April 4 of that year the FCC granted the network a permit to operate an experimental station, W2XBS, which began transmitting from the Empire State Building on October 30, 1931. Eight years later, the network started broadcasting on a regular basis, beginning with a broadcast of President Roosevelt at the opening of the New York World's Fair, April 30, 1939. For NBC, 1939 was a year of firsts:

On May 17, it broadcast a Princeton–Columbia baseball game and a fashion show—the first baseball game and the first fashion show to be seen on television. On May 20, it became the first network to use telephone lines as an element in a TV-relay system. On June 1, it became the first to broadcast a professional boxing match (between Max Baer and Lou Nova). On June 20, it broadcast the first full-hour dramatic production ("The Pirates of Penzance"). On June 29, it broadcast the first full-length television melodrama ("The Donovan Affair"). On July 5, it became the first network to broadcast a feature film ("The Heart of New York") as part of a regular-program schedule. On July 25, it became the first to broadcast an hour-long musical comedy ("Topsy and Eve"). On August 23, it began broadcasting the first TV series (*The Lost Jungle*). And on August 26, it introduced major-league baseball to televison (the game was between the Brooklyn Dodgers and the Cincinnati Redlegs).

NBC became a full-fledged TV network on January 12, 1940, when two stations, WNBC-TV, New York (formerly WNBT-TV), and WRGB-TV, Schenectady, New York, carried the first network programming (the occasion was witnessed by FCC members in Schenectady). In June of 1941, the FCC granted NBC the first commercial-TV license, and by July 1, the network had four advertisers signed up: Procter & Gamble, Lever Brothers, Sun Oil, and Bulova. (NBC's rate for TV advertising was $120 per hour for prime time and $60 per hour for daytime TV.)

Right after the war, NBC again jumped into the record books with two notable firsts. On June 19, 1946, Gillette become the first advertiser to sponsor a TV network show when Joe Louis defended his title against Billy Conn. Several months later on October 27, Bristol-Myers became the first sponsor of a network TV series, *Geographically Speaking*.

When the Japanese signed a peace treaty with the United States on September 4, 1951, in San Francisco, NBC-TV cameras were there. The broadcast marked the beginning of coast-to-coast network-television coverage.

The next year, NBC started early morning programming with the airing of *The Today Show*.

RCA's work on color TV manifested itself in 1954, when NBC broadcast *The Marriage*, the first regularly scheduled network color series. In the same year, NBC achieved the first west-to-east TV transmission with the televising of the "Tournament of Roses Parade," also in color. *The Tonight Show* debuted in 1954 also.

By the 1965–66 season, NBC was able to announce that it was the only "all-color network."

NBC also introduced new forms of TV programming with *The Name of the Game* in 1968, a series that incorporated feature-film elements in a 90-minute show. This developed into the *NBC Mystery Movie*—a series of programs, composed of *Columbo, Hec Ramsey, McMillan and Wife, McCloud, Amy Prentiss, McCoy,* and *Quincy, M.E.*

In 1973, the network demonstrated that the late hours of the night need not be barren of all programming other than reruns. It introduced *The Tomorrow Show* (1:00–2:00 A.M.), which during its first two seasons was viewed by about three million people each night. *Weekend*—another late-night show—appeared in 1974.

In 1976, NBC celebrated its 50th anniversary in broadcasting, with a four-hour, star-studded TV special.

Since 1978, NBC has fallen behind ABC and CBS in the ratings. But having entrusted its presidency to Fred Silverman, whose genius for programming enabled ABC to assume the number-one position in the ratings, the network has hopes of vanquishing its rivals.

How to Apply for a Broadcast Station*

Any qualified citizen, company, or group may apply to the Federal Communications Commission for authority to construct a standard (AM), frequency modulation (FM), or television (TV) broadcast station.

The licensing of these facilities is prescribed by the Communications Act of 1934, as amended, which sets up certain basic requirements. In general, applicants must satisfy the commission that they are legally, technically, and financially qualified, and that operation of the proposed station would be in the public interest.

Full details of the licensing procedure are in Part 1 of the commission's rules, "Practice and Procedure." Station operation is covered by Part 73 (formerly Part 3), "Radio Broadcast Services." This includes technical standards for AM, FM, and TV stations, and TV and FM channel (frequency) assignments by states and communities. Copies of the complete rules may be purchased from the Government Printing Office.

Most applicants employ engineering and legal services in preparing their applications. The commission does not make technical or other special studies for prospective applicants, nor does it recommend individual lawyers or engineers. Names of firms and individuals practicing before the commission are listed in various trade publications.

What follows is a summary of the consecutive steps to be followed in applying for authorization to build and operate a broadcast station. The application procedure is substantially the same whether the facility sought is AM, FM, or TV.

SELECTING A FACILITY

An AM applicant must make his own search for a frequency on which he can operate without causing or receiving interference from existing stations and stations proposed in pending applications. AM broadcast stations operate on "local," "regional," or "clear" channels. Stations of 250-watt power nighttime and up to 1-kilowatt power daytime serve small communities; stations of 500-watt to 5-kilowatt power cover centers of population and surrounding areas; stations of 10- to 50-kilowatt power are for large-area coverage, particularly at night.

An FM station applicant must request an FM channel assigned to the community in which he proposes to operate, or a place within a 10-mile radius (for Class A FM stations) or a 15-mile radius (for Class B or Class C FM stations), which has no FM channel assignment. Power, antenna height, and station separation are governed by the zone in which the station is located.

There are three classes of commercial FM stations and three zones. Class A stations use power of from 100 watts to 3 kilowatts to cover a radius of about 15 miles; Class B stations, 5 kilowatts to 50 kilowatts for 4-mile service; and Class C, 25 kilowatts to 100 kilowatts for a 65-mile range.

Noncommercial educational FM stations are in a separate category and may operate with power as low as 10 watts. Commercial and educational FM stations may apply for a "Subsidiary Communications Authorization" (Form 318) to furnish certain supplemental services. FM stations may engage in stereophonic broadcasting, for which no special application is required.

An applicant for a TV station must request a VHF (very high frequency) or a UHF (ultra high frequency) channel assignment to the community in which he proposes to operate, or a place having no channel assignment within 15 miles of that community. Power depends upon the kind of channel used (VHF or UHF) and station separation is determined by three zones. TV "translator" stations serve remote communities by picking up and rebroadcasting the programs of outside stations, with the latter's permission. They operate on any VHF channel or on any unassigned UHF channel between 55 and 69 or on any assigned channel. Certain channels are assigned for noncommercial educational-TV operation. There is a "Community Antenna Relay Service" for non-common-carrier microwave facilities to relay TV signals to cable TV systems.

APPLYING FOR A CONSTRUCTION PERMIT

After a prospective broadcaster has decided upon the type of station he desires, and the place where it is to be located, he should ascertain and plan to meet the programming needs of the locality he intends to serve through surveys of community leaders and the public.

The next step is to apply for a construction permit. This is done on FCC Form 301, "Application for Authority to Construct a New Broadcast Station or Make Changes in an Existing Station," which covers AM, FM, or TV broadcast, except educational applicants (who use FCC Form 340), FM and TV translators (Form 346), and FM booster stations (Form 349P). These forms require information about the citizenship and character of the applicant,

---

*Based on information provided by the FCC and reproduced with permission.

as well as his financial, technical, and other qualifications, plus details about the transmitting apparatus to be used, antenna and studio locations, and the service proposed.

Commercial broadcast applicants are required to show their financial ability to operate for one year after construction of the station. Triplicate copies of evidentiary matter are required. Nonprofit educational institutions apply for new or changed instructional-TV fixed stations on Form 330-P.

APPLICANTS MUST GIVE LOCAL NOTICE

Applicants for new broadcast stations, license renewals, station sales or major changes in existing stations must give local public notice of their plans and also of any subsequent designation of their applications for hearing. This is done over the applicant's local station (if any) and by advertising in the local newspaper. Such notice affords an opportunity for public comment on these applications to the commission. Applicants and stations also must maintain public reference files in their respective localities.

APPLICATION PROCESSING

All broadcast applications (except translators) are reported twice by the commission—when first tendered (received) and when formally accepted for filing. An application is not acted upon until at least 30 days after the commission gives public notice of its acceptance.

Competing AM-FM-TV applications may be filed up to a date in a notice of AM-FM-TV applications ready for processing. It usually is about 30 days following that notice. During that time objecting petitions may be filed.

Applications generally are processed in the order in which they are accepted. They are reviewed for engineering, legal, and financial data by the Broadcast Bureau, which, under delegated authority, acts on routine applications and reports to the commission those involving policy or other particular considerations. If an application has no engineering or other conflicts and no valid protests have been received, the applicant is found qualified. Assuming all other requirements are met, the application may be granted without a hearing and a construction permit issued. All such grants are announced by the commission. Petitions for reconsideration of grants made without a hearing can be filed within 30 days but must show good cause why objections were not raised before the grant.

HEARING PROCEDURE

Where it appears that an application does not conform to the FCC's rules and regulations, that serious interference with other frequencies would be caused, if there is protest of merit, or if there are other serious questions of a technical, legal, or financial character, a hearing is usually required. The FCC must accord a hearing to competing applications filed within specific time limits.

In designating an application for hearing, the commission gives public notice of the issues for the information of the applicant and others concerned. The hearing notice generally allows the applicant 60 days or more in which to prepare. Even after the hearing has been set, an applicant may amend his application to resolve engineering or other problems, if he so requests. (Commission approval is required for all mergers or situations in which a competing applicant withdraws on payment of expenses.)

Hearings on competing applications normally are held at the commission's Washington offices. Hearings on license revocations and renewals are held in the communities affected.

Hearings customarily are conducted by an administrative law judge. He has authority to administer oaths, examine witnesses, and rule upon the admission of evidence. A prehearing conference is held to reach agreement on procedural matters.

Within 20 days after the close of a record by the administrative law judge, each party and the chief of the FCC Broadcast Bureau can file proposed findings of fact and conclusions to support their contentions. After review of the evidence and statements, the judge issues an initial decision.

An applicant, or any other party in interest, wishing to contest the initial decision has 30 days from the date on which the initial decision was issued to file exceptions. In all cases heard by an administrative law judge, the commission or its review board may hear oral argument on timely request of any party. After oral argument, the commission or review board may adopt, modify, or reverse the judge's initial decision. In cases where the review board has acted on the exceptions, an appeal from its decision may be taken to the FCC within 30 days. However, the commission may deny an appeal for review without stating its reasons.

Court appeals can be taken within 30 days following release of the final decision, in which case the commission's action is stayed pending the court decision.

CONSTRUCTION PERMIT

When an application is granted, a construction permit is issued. The new permittee may then request call letters, which, if they are available and conform to the rules, are issued. A period of 60 days from the date of the construction permit is provided in which construction shall begin, and a maximum of 10 months (AM, FM, FM and TV translators, and ITFS) thereafter for completion (or 12 months in all) and a maximum of 16 months (commercial and educational television (UHF-VHF) thereafter for completion or 18 months in all).

Application to modify a broadcast-construction authorization or to modify a license is made on

Form 301-A for Remote Control Authority for transmitter.

If the permittee is unable to build his station within the time specified, he must apply for an extension of time on Form 701 ("Application for Additional Time to Construct a Radio Station"), giving reasons. Upon completion of construction, the permittee conducts equipment (not program) tests.

LICENSE

The final step is to apply for the actual license, on Form 302 ("Application for New Broadcast Station License") or on one of the following: Form 330-L (Instructional TV Fixed stations), Form 341 (Noncommercial Educational FM stations), Form 347 (TV and FM translators), or Form 349L (FM boosters). Applicants must show compliance with all terms, conditions, and obligations in the original application and the construction permit.

Not until he applies for a license can the holder of a construction permit request authorization to conduct program tests. The license application form provides a space for program-test requests, or they can be made separately. A station license and program-test authorization are issued if no new cause or circumstance has come to the attention of the commission that would make operation of the station contrary to the public interest.

RENEWALS

An applicant for renewal of a station license must show that he has operated according to the terms of his authorization and the promises made in obtaining it. Most renewal applications are made on Form 303 ("Application for Renewal of Broadcast Station License"). However, instructional-TV fixed stations use Form 330-R; noncommercial educational licensees use Form 342; TV and FM translators Form 348; and FM boosters Form 349R.

Pending the disposition of any commission hearing or other proceeding involving license renewal or revocation considerations, the station continues to operate even though its license term may have expired.

SALES AND TRANSFERS

If the holder of a construction permit or license desires to assign it to someone else, he makes application on Form 314 ("Application for Consent to Assignment of Radio Broadcast Station Construction Permit or License"). Should the permittee or licensee wish to transfer corporate control, he applies on Form 315 ("Application for Consent to Transfer Control of Corporation Holding Radio Broadcast Station Construction Permit or License"). Form 316 ("Application for Assignment or Transfer—Short Form") may be used when the transfer or assignment involves no substantial change in interest.

Sales of stations held less than three years are subject to hearing except in case of death, hardship, or other mitigating circumstances beyond the licensee's control.

CONSTRUCTION CHANGES

Applicants for authority to make construction changes in existing stations apply on the same form used for a construction permit for the type of station involved.

APPLICATION FEES

Since March 17, 1964, the commission has charged fees for most application filings, in compliance with a government policy to charge for certain federal services. On July 1, 1970, a new fee schedule was adopted for broadcast stations, covering three types of charges: (1) a filing fee (the only type of fee previously charged), payable when the application is tendered; (2) a grant fee, payable when the application is granted; and (3) an annual operating fee, paid by all commercial AM, FM, and TV stations, in lieu of the renewal-application fee previously charged.

Application filing fees for construction permits, generally considerably higher than those previously charged, vary with the type of station, from $50 (for a daytime-only 250-watt nondirectional AM station permit) and $200 (for a Class A FM) to $10,000 (for a VHF TV permit in the top-50 markets)—in TV, though not in radio, fees may vary with market size (top 50, next 50, and other); there is also a VHF-UHF differential.

Applications for major changes are charged the same fee as those for new stations. The grant fee is charged on the same varying schedule. For assignments of licenses and transfers of control, the filing fee is $200 (per license) and the grant fee, based on annual revenue (with certain exceptions), is payable on consummation.

The annual operating fee is based on a station's highest commercial announcement rate: in AM and FM, the highest one-minute rate multiplied by 8.5; and in TV, the highest half-minute rate multiplied by 4.25, with a minimum of $25 in radio and $100 in television.

Most "other" applications, such as those for covering licenses and minor changes, entail a filing fee of $100 and no grant fee; involuntary or voluntary assignments or transfers of control using Form 316 require a filing fee of $100 (per station, where more than one is involved) and no grant fee; and applications for subscription television authorizations entail a $700 filing fee, but no grant fee. Translators and noncommercial educational stations are exempt from fees.

March 1, 1975, was the generally effective date of the new schedule. The annual operating fee for broadcast stations is due each year on the anniversary of the station's license expiration date. The fee schedule is subject to continuing review to determine whether changes in over-all or comparative levels are in order.

PRINTED RULES

FCC rules may be obtained only through the Government Printing Office, Washington, DC, 20402. The rules on FCC practice and procedure are contained in volume I, which is available for $8.10 a copy; the broadcast rules are in volume III, for $13.00. Orders should be sent to the Government Printing Office direct (not through the FCC). The printed rules are sold on a subscription basis, which entitles the purchaser to receive subsequent amendments to the rule part purchased until an over-all-revised issue is printed.

Industrial Television

The use of television for communication in industry is increasing. Many organizations and companies are using television in sales work, personnel matters, staff training, and so on.

Even though there is a great deal of interest in the application of television to industry, there are few sources of centralized information. This is one of the reasons why the International Industrial Television Association was founded. A leading association in this field, it has established seminars, conferences, regular meetings, and local chapters to help everyone concerned with industrial TV to learn about new developments in the field—in equipment, in applications, in money-saving value.

The following, provided by the International Industrial Television Association and used with their permission, is a list of the local-chapter members and the regional directors of the IITA. Questions about any phase of industrial TV should be directed to the main office—

International Industrial Television Association
26 South St.
New Providence, NJ 07974
(201) 464-6747
Contact: Barbara Kandle

—or to the following:

Lane Smith
Bergen Brunswig Corp.
22351 S. Wilmington Ave.
Carson, CA 90250

Bob Laurence
Pacific Telephone, Rm. 700
116 New Montgomery St.
San Francisco, CA 94105

Thomas Cormier
Phoenix Mutual Life
1 American Row
Hartford, CT 06115

Deborah Harter
U.S. Gypsum Co.
101 S. Wacker Dr.
Chicago, IL 60606

Mortimer J. Roth
Evans Products Co.
Grossmans Div.
200 Union St.
Braintree, MA 02184

Jay Campbell
34 Lincoln Terrace
Hillsdale, NJ 07642

James Reynolds
Ohio Bell
100 Erieview Plaza
Cleveland, OH 44114

Tom Thompson
Smith Kline Corp.
1500 Spring Garden St.
Philadelphia, PA 19101

Donna Matrazzo
Fisher Scientific Co.
711 Forbes Ave.
Pittsburgh, PA 15219

Jean Nipper
Austin Independent School Dist.
8812 Mountain Path Circle
Austin, TX 78759

Bob Schiff
Tele-Image
2225 Beltline, Suite 321
Carrollton, TX 75006

Leonard M. Hart
V.A. Hospital
2002 Holcombe Blvd.
Houston, TX 77211

Dr. Dennis A. Harp
Box 4132
Lubbock, TX 79409

George Manno
American Red Cross
5816 Seminary Rd., A/V Ctr.
Falls Church, VA 22041

Richard Blackburn
Safeco Insurance Co.
Safeco Plaza
Seattle, WA 98185

Joy Shong
Memorial Hospital
791 E. Summit Ave.
Oconomowoc, WI 53066

(Canada)

Rodger Campbell
Steel Co. of Canada
100 King St., W. Stelco A/V
Hamilton, Ontario L8N 3T1

The Television Information Office

TELEVISION INFORMATION OFFICE
745 Fifth Ave.
New York, NY 10022
(212) 759-6800
Contact: James B. Poteat, librarian

The Television Information Office was established in October, 1959, to facilitate mutual understanding between the television industry and the public. It is supported by the three major television networks (ABC, CBS, NBC), individual commercial stations and groups, educational stations, and the National Association of Broadcasters. It provides an information service to meet the needs of educators, students, government agencies, the press, the clergy, librarians, allied communications professionals, and the general public, as well as broadcasters. TIO provides this service because of its belief that while television is an increasingly powerful social force in today's world, its cause–effect relationship with social phenomena is frequently unclear, even to communications professionals. TIO's purpose is to increase knowledge and understanding of the medium among those individuals and groups who have a direct interest in its impact upon our society. Nationwide, TIO maintains an extensive instructional program. Through mailings, speeches, interviews, conferences, and other activities, as well as through its research services, TIO serves individuals and groups representing a wide range of special interests.

RESEARCH AND PUBLICATIONS

Among the research projects TIO has originated and the more than 40 TIO publications currently available to the industry and the general public are the following:

- National surveys directed by The Roper Organization to measure changing public attitudes toward television and other mass media.
- Public opinion studies on the public's attitude toward violence on television, the primary sources for information on consumer, ecological, and energy matters, and the reliability of media.
- The *TV Mini-File,* a pocket summary of statistics, and opinions on television as a social force.
- *How Free TV Works,* a compendium of answers to questions about television's structure and function, how a station operates, who decides on programming, and who pays for it.
- A series of annotated bibliographies listing primary sources of information about television— *Television and Education; Television: Freedom, Re-* *sponsibility, Regulation; Television in Government and Politics; Television Careers;* and *Periodicals in Broadcasting and Communications.*
- *For the Young Viewer,* a study of worthwhile children's programming, which won a special George Foster Peabody Award.
- *Religious Television Programs: A Study of Relevance,* underwritten by TIO. The volume includes a comprehensive list of religious programs and offers guidelines to producers and broadcasters.
- An examination of broadcast editorial practices that resulted in *New Voices in a Democracy,* a study of the opinion-forming function of television.
- Reprints of speeches and articles dealing with television as a social force, such as Eric Sevareid's *The Quest for Objectivity* and *Why A Second-Class First Amendment for Broadcasting?,* Nat Hentoff's *How Fair Should TV Be?,* and Dr. Ner Littner's *A Psychiatrist Looks at Television and Violence.*

EDUCATION

To help teachers and students use television as an aid to schooling, TIO offers:

- *Teachers Guides to Television,* a twice-yearly magazine that offers teachers study aids for using commercial television in the classroom. It now includes regular features for parents.
- TIO-organized panels and TV festivals for national conferences of educational groups such as the National Council of Teachers of English and the Speech Association of America.
- Lectures by TIO personnel to college and university classes, as well as to service clubs and community organizations.
- *TV as Art,* a collection of ten essays by scholars and critics intended for teachers at every level of instruction, produced by the combined efforts of TIO and the National Council of Teachers of English to illustrate how principles of literary criticism can be applied to television.
- *Television and the Teaching of English,* a resource book and manual for teachers, prepared in collaboration with the National Council of Teachers of English to encourage greater instructional use of commercial television in classroom work.
- An article in *Social Education,* inspired by the TIO's work with the National Council for the Social Studies, which includes a resource unit for teachers on the study of television as a medium.
- Information distributed throughout the teaching profession concerning the relationship of the medium to children. *TV as a Teacher's Ally, TV Tie-ins as a Bridge to Books,* and excerpts from the Nuffield Foundation study, *Television and the Child,* are examples.

ADVANCE PROGRAM INFORMATION

TIO maintains a program-information service for many educational and religious publications, with a combined circulation of more than 7,000,000.

AUDIO-VISUAL SERVICES

- *Television in America,* a series of half-hour programs on issues such as media violence, children's television, and television journalism and the First Amendment, are distributed to help viewers gain a fuller picture of television's practices, policies, and problems.
- Spot announcements on such topics as television for children, the importance of television as a news medium, television's role in helping the community to deal with local problems, and its contribution to community organizations and causes, help inform viewers locally.

- Slide presentations inform the community on television issues and attitudes, including highlights of the continuing Roper research studies.

TIO INFORMATION CENTER AND LIBRARY

TIO maintains an extensive information center and library covering the social, cultural, and programming aspects of television. Since 1959 it has gathered and made available information about television from books, magazines, dissertations, speeches, debates, panel discussions, and government reports. Its file of clippings contains over 100,000 items, and nearly 200 periodicals are received regularly. An information retrieval system assists in storing and locating materials on the hundreds of television-related topics that are of interest to TIO and those who use its services.

Information reproduced through the courtesy of the Television Information Office.

Instructional Television

Listed here are the organizations that offer instructional films within the education market. Phone or write them for their catalogs if you are interested in utilizing such films in instructional-television programs. This information has been provided by the National Association of Educational Broadcasters, and used with their permission.

CALIFORNIA

The American Film Institute Center for Advanced Study (AFI-West)
501 Doheny Rd.
Beverly Hills, CA 90210
(213) 278-8777
Director, AFI-West: Martin Manulis

Public Service Satellite Consortium (PSSC)
4040 Sorrento Valley Blvd.
San Diego, CA 92121
(714) 452-1140
President: John P. Witherspoon

Western Educational Society for Telecommunications (WEST)
Solano Community College
P.O. Box 246
Suisun City, CA 94585
(707) 864-7000
President: Donald G. Kirkorian

COLORADO

Rocky Mountain Public Broadcasting Network (RMPBN)
Suite 50B, Diamond Hill
2480 W. 26th Ave.
Denver CO 80211
(303) 455-7161
Manager: Jon W. Cooper

DISTRICT OF COLUMBIA

American Film Institute (AFI)
John F. Kennedy Center for the Performing Arts
Washington, DC 20566
(202) 833-9300
Director: George Stevens, Jr.

Association for Education, Communications, and Technology (AECT)
1201 16th St. NW
Washington, DC 20036
(202) 833-4180
Executive Director: Howard B. Hitchens

Association of Public Radio Stations (APRS)
1050 17th St. NW, Suite 1040
Washington, DC 20036
(202) 785-4616
President: Matthew B. Coffey

Broadcast Education Association (BEA)
c/o National Association of Broadcasters
1771 N St. NW
Washington, DC 20036
(202) 293-3518
Executive Director: Harold Niven

Cable Television Information Center
The Urban Institute
2100 M St. NW
Washington, DC 20037
(202) 872-8888
Executive Director: Sheila Mahony

Citizens Communication Center (CCC)
1914 Sunderland Pl. NW
Washington, DC 20036
(202) 296-4238
Staff Attorney: Edwina Dowell

Congress
House Subcommittee on Communications
House Committee on Interstate and Foreign Commerce
Room B-331, Rayburn House Office Bldg.
Washington, DC 20515
(202) 225-9304
Chief Counsel: Harry M. Shooshan

Congress
Senate Subcommittee on Communications
Senate Commerce Committee
5202 Dirksen Senate Office Bldg.
Washington, DC 20510
(202) 224-9341
Communications Counsel: Nicholas P. Miller

Congress
Senate Subcommittee on Education
Senate Committee on Labor and Public Welfare
Room 4230 Dirksen Senate Office Bldg.
Washington, DC 20510
(202) 224-7666
Counsel: Jean S. Frohlicher

Corporation for Public Broadcasting (CPB)
1111 16th St. NW
Washington, DC 20036
(202) 293-6160
President: Henry Loomis

Council for UHF Broadcasting
P.O. Box 23640
L'Enfant Plaza Station
Washington, DC 20024
(202) 488-5211
Chairman: Richard Block

Federal Communications Commission
1919 M St. NW
Washington, DC 20026
(202) 655-4000
Chairman: Richard Wiley

Department of Health, Education and Welfare (HEW)
330 Independence Ave. SW
Washington, DC 20201
(202) 655-4000
Acting Director, Office of Telecommunications Policy (245-1891): Howard Hupe

Joint Council of Educational Telecommunications (JCET)
1126 16th St. NW
Washington, DC 20036
(202) 659-9740
Executive Director: Frank W. Norwood

National Association of Educational Broadcasters (NAEB)
1346 Connecticut Ave. NW
Washington, DC 20036
(202) 785-1100
President: James A. Fellows

National Cable Television Association
918 16th St. NW, Eighth Floor
Washington, DC 20006
(202) 457-6700
President: Robert L. Schmidt

National Education Association (NEA)
1201 16th St. NW
Washington, DC 20036
(202) 833-4120
Educational Telecommunications Specialist: Harold Wigren

National Endowment for the Arts (NEA)
Columbia Plaza
2401 E St. NW
Washington, DC 20506
(202) 634-6373
Chairman: Nancy Hanks

National Endowment for the Humanities
806 15th St. NW
Washington, DC 20506
(202) 382-7465
Chairman: Ronald Berman

National Institute of Education (NIE)
1200 19th St. NW
Washington, DC 20208
(202) 254-6050
Associate Director for Finance and Productivity: Arthur S. Melmed

National Public Radio (NPR)
2025 M St. NW
Washington DC 20036
(202) 785-5400
President: Lee C. Frischknecht

New York Office:
201 2nd Ave., Suite 701
New York, NY 10017
(212) 532-6066

San Francisco Office:
625 Market St.
San Francisco, CA 94105
(415) 495-4222

Office of Telecommunications Policy (OTP)
1800 G St. NW
Washington, DC 20504
(202) 395-5800
Director: Thomas J. Houser

Public Broadcasting Service (PBS)
475 L'Enfant Plaza West, SW
Washington, DC 20024
(202) 488-5000
President: Lawrence Grossman

New York Office:
15 W. 51st St.
New York, NY 10020
(212) 489-0945

Public Television Library (PTL)
475 L'Enfant Plaza NW
Washington, DC 20024
(202) 488-5220
Supervisor of Acquisitions: Alan Lewis

United States Office of Education (USOE)
400 Maryland Ave. SW
Washington, DC 20202
(202) 655-4000
Chief, Special Projects: Dr. Thomas Fagan

ILLINOIS

Central Educational Network (CEN)
5400 N. St. Louis Ave.
Chicago, IL 60625
(312) 463-3040
Executive Director: Raymond C. Giese

INDIANA

Agency for Instructional Televison (AIT)
Box A
Bloomington, IN 47401
(812) 339-2203
Executive Director: Edwin G. Cohen

MASSACHUSETTS

Eastern Educational Television Network (EEN)
1300 Soldiers Field Rd.
Boston, MA 02135
(617) 783-3660
Executive Director: John S. Porter

MINNESOTA

Midwestern Educational Television, Inc.
1640 Como Ave.
St. Paul, MN 55108
(612) 646-4611
General Manager: W. D. Donaldson

NEBRASKA

**Great Plains National Instructional Television
   Library (GPN)**
Box 80669
Lincoln, NB 68501
(402) 467-2502
Director: Paul H. Schupbach

NEW MEXICO

**Rocky Mountain Corporation for Public
   Broadcasting**
1603 Sigma Chi Rd. NE
Albuquerque, NM 87106
(505) 242-6930
Executive Director: Dr. E. W. Bundy

NEW YORK

Children's Television Workshop (CTW)
1 Lincoln Plaza
New York, NY 10023
(212) 595-3456
President: Joan Ganz Cooney

Ford Foundation
320 E. 43rd St.
New York, NY 10017
(212) 573-5263
Officer in Charge: David M. Davis

SOUTH CAROLINA

**Southern Educational Communications Associ-
ation (SECA)**
P.O. Box 5966
928 Woodrow St.
Columbia, SC 29250
(803) 799-5517
President: Robert C. Glazier

VIRGINIA

**International Instructional Television
   Cooperative, Inc. (ITV CO-OP)**
Skyline Center, Suite 1207
5205 Leesburg Pike
Falls Church, VA 22041
(703) 379-2707
President and Executive Director: Ray Gladfelter

Speech Communications Association
5205 Leesburg Pike
Falls Church, VA 22041
(703) 379-1888
Executive Secretary: William Work

INSTRUCTIONAL TELEVISION—FIXED
SERVICE

Instructional Television–Fixed Service (ITFS), a special band of television channels reserved for the exclusive use of educational institutions, was first established by the Federal Communications Commission in 1963 to respond to the needs of instructional television for multi-channel transmission capability at costs considerably lower than conventional VHF or UHF television. ITFS operates at frequencies higher than those used by standard television. For this reason special antennas and converters must be installed on each building which is to receive ITFS. This equipment converts the transmission to signals which can be received by ordinary television receivers. When viewed in the classroom, ITFS looks like any other kind of television.

ITFS offers an opportunity for low-cost multiple-channel television distribution. Each ITFS licensee may utilize up to four channels in the ITFS band, thus permitting the simultaneous transmission and reception of four different programs. Also available in the ITFS band is a special group of radio frequencies that may be utilized for audio or data response to the television program. This permits live interchange between teacher and student, and also offers the possibility of computer-managed television instruction.

In March, 1977, there were 376 ITFS channels reported in operation in the United States. These channels were operated by 89 different institutions holding a total of 186 ITFS licenses. At the same time, the FCC had granted construction permits for 13 additional ITFS systems, and was processing applications for eight more.

A survey conducted by the National Association of Educational Broadcasters (NAEB) in the spring of 1975 compiled data from 68 of the 83 institutions holding licenses. They reported reaching an audience of 1,750,000 students during the 1974–75 school year, with each system averaging 4,360 hours of programming. Public and parochial elementary, junior-high, and senior-high-school students constituted 92 percent of the viewing audience. Other significant groups using the service included medical professionals, business and industry executives, and engineers and scientists enrolled in continuing professional-education courses. Over half of the systems reported that they transmitted their programming in color.

The FCC is currently considering three proposed rulemakings relating to ITFS:

1. RM 2603, if adopted, would permit ITFS systems to utilize non-broadcast technical standards in certain production and transmission equipment. This would have the effect of lowering still further the capital expenditures necessary to construct new ITFS facilities, or to re-equip existing ones.
2. RM 2609, if adopted, would permit CATV systems to receive and retransmit ITFS signals on their cable. This would relieve cable-equipped schools and other reception points of the expense of acquiring and installing receiving antennas and convertors.
3. RM 2213, if adopted, would permit certain ITFS channels to be reallocated to Multipoint Distribution Service, a common carrier regulated by the FCC. MDS is presently used for pay television programming to hotels and apartment buildings. Reallocating ITFS channels to MDS would have the effect of limiting the availability of ITFS delivery systems to educational institutions in many major metropolitan areas.

Other news of interest to ITFS users comes from the U.S. Office of Education's Educational Broadcasting Facilities Program, which is now permitted to allocate some of its funding to non-broadcast services such as ITFS. Funding levels are generally low.

ITFS and the NAEB: The NAEB closely monitors ITFS development both in the field and in Washington, and cooperates with other national agencies in legislative and regulatory efforts that will preserve and foster this important area of instructional technology.

Representatives from ITFS systems have formed an interest group within the NAEB, and hold special meetings at each NAEB Convention. A six-person steering committee elcted by the field coordinates ITFS activities and concerns with designated NAEB staff. The members of the ITFS Steering Committee are the following:

Kenneth Down
Director, Stanford ITV Network
Stanford University
401 Durand Bldg.
Stanford, CA 94305

Don MacCullough (Chairman)
Director of Media Programs
Dade County Public Schools
1410 N.E. 2nd Ave.
Miami, FL 33137

Elmer Friman, Director
Medical Educational Resources Program
Indiana University School of Medicine
Indianapolis, IN 96206

Frances Forde Plude
Director of Development
Catholic Television Network
23 Catherine St.
Boston, MA 02131

John Hill
ITV Specialist
KLVX-TV
Las Vegas, NV 89120

Robert Suchy
Director of Instructional Resources
Milwaukee Public Schools
Drawer 10K
Milwaukee, WI 52308

Licensees

ALABAMA

Birmingham
Board of Education of Birmingham
KLC-77 Channels E-1-2-3-4
KZW-56 Channels G-1-4
W. Frank Martin, Facilities Director
2316 7th Ave. N, Room 225
Birmingham, AL 35202
(205) 934-3340

The Board of Education of Jefferson County
KIP-47 Channels A-1-4
A-400 Courthouse Bldg.
Birmingham, AL 35203

Operations also at:
Brownsville KIP-49 Channels C-1-4

Board of Trustees, The University of Alabama
WBN-31 Channels B-1-2
Ronald F. Johnson, Director
Telecommunications Center
University of Alabama in Birmingham
Box 436 University Sta.
Birmingham, AL 35294
(205) 394-3340

Gadsden
Board of Education of Etowah County
KCI-53 Channels A-1-2
KCO-38 Channels E-1-2
KVW-56 Channels A-1
Don Morton, Director of Instruction
Etowah County Board of Education
Etowah County Courthouse, Rm. 109
Gadsden, AL 35901
(201) 546-2821, Ext. 216

Huntsville
Board of Education, Huntsville
KHU-75 Channels D-1-4
David W. Marxer, Director of ETV Center
706 Read Dr. SE
Huntsville, AL 35801
(205) 539-6226

CALIFORNIA

Anaheim
Anaheim City School District
KUZ-56 Channels A-1-2-3-4
Dr. Helen Clower, Director of Instructional Systems
412 E. Broadway
Anaheim, CA 92805
(714) 535-6001

Operations also at
Fullerton KVP-26 Channels F-1-4

Berkeley
The Regents of the University of California
WAK-212 Channels A-1-2
WAC-273 Microwave
WAS-273 Channels A-1-2
John H. Oliphant, Coordinator of Service Programs
Office of the Vice President, Business and Finance
University of California
2200 University Ave.
Berkeley, CA 94720
(415) 642-1054

Davis
The Regents of the University of California
WAQ-325 Channel D-1
WSA-39 Channel G-1
WAW-457 Channel C-1
John H. Oliphant, Coordinator of Service Programs
Office of the Vice President, Business and Finance
University of California
2200 University Ave.
Berkeley, CA 94720
(415) 642-1054

Operations also at:
Berkeley WAS-273 Channels A-1-2
Chico WAP-562 Micro
Davis WAP-560 Micro

Livermore WBY-29 Channels B-4
Livermore WHP-58 Micro
Sacramento WAP-40 Channels B-1
Sacramento WBD-564 Micro
Sacramento WSA-40 Channels B-1
San Francisco KTB-97 Channels F-4
San Francisco KHU-89 Channels F-2
Goleta WAQ-323 Channel A-1
Point Mago WAG-324 Channel E-1
Vacaville WAW-457 Channel C-1
Yuba City WAQ-325 Channel D-1

Fresno
Fresno County Schools
Business:
Ernest A. Poore, Superintendent
Fresno County Schools
2314 Mariposa St.
Fresno, CA 93721
(209) 488-3337

Production and Technical:
Don Webster, Operations Manager
Fresno County Schools ITV Center
733 L. St.
Fresno, CA 93721
(209) 485-2643
KVK-21 Channels G-1-2
KYD-25 Channels B-1-2

Operations also at:
Auberry KZM-20 Channels C-1-2
Reedley KZM-21 Channels C-1-2
Tranquillity KZM-22 Channels C-1-2

Long Beach
Board of Education
Long Beach Unified School District
KZH-31 Channels D-1-4
Dr. Frank B. George, Director of Instructional Services
201 E. 8th St.
Long Beach, CA 90813
(213) 436-9931 Ext. 399

Los Angeles
Archdiocese of Los Angeles
Education and Welfare Corporation
KSW-92 Channels D-1-4
KSW-93 Channels G-1-4
David Moore, Director
Archdiocese of Los Angeles ITV
1520 W. 9th St.
Los Angeles, CA 90015

University of Southern California
KWE-33 Channels B-1-4
KWE-34 Channels F-1-4
Dr. Jack Munushian, Director of ITV
USC SSC 510
Los Angeles, CA 90007
(213) 746-5501

Pasadena
Pasadena Unified School District of Los Angeles
County
KQU-29 Channels E-1-4
Ramon C. Cortines, Superintendent of Schools
Education Center
351 S. Hudson Ave.
Pasadena, CA 91109
(213) 795-6981 Ext. 261

San Diego
Board of Trustees, California State University and
Colleges for San Diego State University
WBM-725 Channels A-1-2-3
WBM-726 Channels E-1-2-3
Dr. Donald R. Martin, Instructional Television
Coordinator
Instructional Television
San Diego State University
San Diego, CA 92182
(714) 286-6466

San Francisco
Roman Catholic Welfare Corporation of San Fran-
cisco
KZB-22 Channels G-1-4
KZB-23 Channels B-1-4
KZM-24 Channels D-1-4
KZB-25 Channels D-1-4
David Green, Station Manager, ETV Center
Archdiocese of San Francisco
324 Middlefield Rd.
Menlo Park, CA 95025
(415) 326-7850

Santa Ana
Santa Ana Unified School District
WSJ-69 Channels A-1-4
WSJ-70 Channels C-1-4
Robert Reed, Director, Television Center
1405 French St.
Santa Ana, CA 92701
(714) 558-5642

Santa Barbara
The Regents of the University of California
WAQ-323 Channels A-1-2
John H. Oliphant, Coordinator of Service Pro-
grams
Office of the Vice President, Business and Finance
University of California at Berkeley
Berkeley, CA 94720
(415) 642-1054

Operations also at:
Ventura WAQ-324 Channels E-1-2

Stanford
Board of Trustees, Stanford University
KGG-38 Channels E-1-4
Kenneth S. Down, Asst. Dean and Director

Stanford ITV Network
401 Durand Bldg.
Stanford University
Stanford, CA 94305
(415) 497-3616

Torrance
Board of Education of the Torrance Unified School
District
WAU-30 Channels C-1-4
Paul Barstow, Supervisor, ITV
2336 Plaza Del Amo
Torrance, CA 90509
(213) 328-8080

COLORADO

Boulder
Board of Regents, University of Colorado
WHA-72 Channels B-1-3
Billy D. Hillin, Senior Engineer
University of Colorado, Boulder
Stadium 365
Boulder, CO 80309
(303) 492-7341

FLORIDA

Boynton Beach:
School Board of Palm Beach County
KHU-90 Channels E-1-2-3-4
John H. Burger, General Manager, ITV/FM
505 S. Congress Ave.
Boynton Beach, FL 33435
(305) 737-7300

Operations also at:
Belle Glade KZB-28 Channels A-1-2-3-4
Riviera Beach KZB-29 Channels G-1-3-4
Loxahatchee KZB-30 Channels H-1-2-3

Daytona Beach
Volusia County School Board
WBE-795 Channels A-1
E. L. Phillips, Media Specialist
P.O. Box 1910, 729 Loomis Ave.
Daytona Beach, FL 32015
(904) 255-6475

Operations also at:
Deland WBK-225 Channels E-1

Ft. Lauderdale
School Board of Broward County
KZT-22 Channels G-1-4
KLC-80 Channels B-1-4
Mrs. Marion Bell, Coordinator
ITV Center
6600 SW Nova Dr.
Ft. Lauderdale, FL 33314
(305) 765-6067

Ft. Myers
School Board of Lee County
WBE-805 Channel B-1
Alden R. Tapio
Director of Media Services
2266 2nd St.
Ft. Myers, FL 33901
(813) 334-2446

Miami
School Board of Dade County
KTB-84 Channels F-1-2
KTB-85 Channels C-1-2
Don MacCullough, Director of Media Programs
1410 NE 2nd Ave.
Miami, FL 33142
(305) 350-3307

GEORGIA

Atlanta
Fulton-DeKalb Hospital Authority
KVI-65 Channels A-1-4
KVI-66 Channels A-1-4
Alan S. Kaminsky, Business Manager
69 Butler St. SE
Atlanta, GA 30303
(404) 659-5307

ILLINOIS

Chicago
Catholic Bishop of Chicago
WAC-262 Channels C-1-2-3-4
Rev. James F. Moriarty, Director
Catholic Television Network of Chicago
One North Wacker Dr.
Chicago, IL 60606
(312) 332-3860

Operations also at:
Westhaven WAH-801 Channels F-1-2-3-4
Schaumburg WAH-799 Channels F-1-2-3-4
Mundelein WAH-800 Channels C-1-2-3-4

Peoria
Bradley University
KTZ-30 Channels C-1-4
Philip Weinberg, Director
Center for Learning Resources
Bradley University
1501 W. Bradley Ave.
Peoria, IL 61625
(309) 676-7611, Ext. 209

Operations also at:
Metamore KVO-30 Channels E-1-2
Wyoming KVO-29 Channels A-1-2

Rock Falls
Board of Education of Rock Falls Township
WHA-62 Channels G-3
Tom Anderson, Director
101 12th Ave.
Rock Falls, IL 61071

Sterling
Board of Education of Sterling
Township High School, District 300
KVI-62 Channels D-3
1608 4th St.
Sterling, IL 61081
(815) 625-6800

Winnetka
Board of Education of Township
High School District 203
KGZ-66 Channels A-1-4
358 Winnetka Ave.
Northfield, IL 60094
(312) 466-9400

Operations also at:
Northfield AZB-26 Channels H-1

INDIANA

Indianapolis
Trustees of Indiana University
School of Medicine
WAT-21 Channels E-1-2
Elmer Friman, Director
Medical Educational Resources Program
Indiana University School of Medicine
1100 W. Michigan St.
Indianapolis, IN 46202
(317) 264-4083

Princeton
North Gibson School Corporation
WOX-84 Channels A-1
Robert H. Cloin, Television Director
Box 325
Princeton, IN 47670
(812) 385-2591

St. John
Indiana Higher Education Telecommunication System
KPD-40 Channels A-1-2
Dr. Jane G. Richards, Executive Director
1100 W. Michigan St.
Indianapolis, IN 46202
(317) 264-7945

KENTUCKY

Louisville
Jefferson County Board of Education
WAY-653 Channels B-1-4
WAY-655 Channels F-1-4

Bob Richardson, Administrative Director of ITV
4309 Bishop La.
Louisville, KY 40218
(502) 456-3181

Owensboro
Owensboro Vocational School
KBK-71 Channels A-1-2
Billy J. Stone, Chief Engineer
1501 Frederica St.
Owensboro, KY 42301
(502) 684-7225

Paducah
Board of Education of Paducah
KGA-28 Channels A-1-4
Bob J. Henson, Engineer
P.O. Box 1137
10th and Walter Jetton Blvd.
Paducah, KY 42001
(502) 442-6121

LOUISIANA

Lafayette
Louisiana State Board of Education
WBJ-81 Channel G-1
WBJ-82 Channel A-1
B. W. Crocker, Director of Broadcasting
University of Southwestern Louisiana
Box A-2091
Lafayette, LA 70504

MAINE

Portland
University of Maine
KVI-61 Channel D-1
Ed Winchester, Director
Maine Public Broadcasting Network
University of Maine
Alumni Hall
Orono, ME 04473
(207) 866-4493

MASSACHUSETTS

Boston
Boston Catholic Television Center
KVQ-24 Channels D-3-4
Joseph F. Sweeney, Operations Manager
Box 56
Newton, MA 02160
(617) 965-0050

Operations also at:
Andover KMA-57 Channels F-3-4
Danvers WAL-20 Channels G-3-4
Framington KLC-85 Channels G-1-4
Milton KQT-48 Channels F-3-4
Newton KQT-47 Channels F-3-4

President and Fellows of Harvard College
WBB-421 Channels C-3-4
Dr. A. Pandiscio, Associate Director O.I.T.
29 Oxford St.—Cruft Laboratory
Cambridge, MA 02138
(617) 495-2857

North Dartmouth
Southeastern Massachusetts University
WOG-94 Channel G-4
Ronald A. Magnant
Station Manager, WUSM-FM
SMU Old Westport Rd.
North Dartmouth, MA 02747
(617) 999-6459

MICHIGAN

Alpena
Alpena Public Schools
KVK-22 Channel A-1
Clifford Roberts, Director of IMC
3038 W. Washington Ave.
Alpena, MI 49707
(517) 354-5032

Detroit
Archdiocese of Detroit
KRX-65 Channels A-1-2
John B. Zwers, Consultant
305 Michigan Ave.
Detroit, MI 48226
(313) 237-5952

Board of Education of City of Detroit
KTB-98 Channels C-2-3
Dr. John McArthur, Acting Director
9345 Lawton St.
Detroit, MI 48206
(313) 494-1571

Regents of the University of Michigan
WDV-66 Channels G-1-2
Hal F. Schulte, Director of Instructional Television
College of Engineering
University of Michigan
Ann Arbor, MI 48109
(313) 763-1233

Wayne State University
KVP-20 Channels E-1-2
WAK-57 Channels B-1-2
James B. Tintera, Professor and Director
Center for Instructional Technology
Wayne State University
Detroit, MI 48202
(313) 577-4159

MINNESOTA

Minneapolis
Regents of the University of Minnesota
WIG-33 Channels C-1-2
WIG-35 Channels E-1-2
Frederick L. Street, Senior Engineer
Room 107 Lind Hall
207 Church St.
University of Minnesota
Minneapolis, MN 55455
(612) 376-5033

Operations also at:
Rochester WIG-34 Channels C-1-2

Osseo
Independent School District 279
KVI-64 Channel A-1
317 2nd Ave. N
Osseo, MN 55369
(612) 452-4131

MISSOURI

Columbia
Curators of the University of Missouri
KXY-61 Channels C-1-2
Don R. Mitchell, Director
Academic Support Center
University of Missouri
Columbia, MO 65201
(314) 882-3601

NEBRASKA

Omaha
School District of the City of Omaha
KWU-42 Channels A-1-2
KWU-43 Channels D-1-2
James Minear
Assistant Supervisor Radio/TV
Telecommunications Center
3219 Cummings St.
Omaha, NB 68131
(402) 556-2770

NEVADA

Las Vegas
Clark County School District
KZH-32 Channels C-1-4
KZH-33 Channels E-1-4
John K. Hill, ITV Coordinator
5700 Mountain Vista Ave.
Las Vegas, NV 89120
(702) 451-1026

NEW JERSEY

Trenton
Trenton Board of Education
WPA-57 Channel F-3
9 South Stockton St.
Trenton, NJ 08611

Union
Union Township Schools
WGM1-95 Channel C-1
Robert M. Petracco, Director of Media Services
Union High School
N. 3rd St.
Union, NJ 07083
(201) 688-1200, Ext. 326

West Windsor
Mercer County Community College
WOW-99 Channel B-1
Dr. James K. Carrol, Director Media Center
P.O. Box B
Trenton, NJ 08690
(609) 586-4800, Ext. 463

NEW YORK

Brooklyn
Roman Catholic Diocese of Brooklyn
KNZ-69 Channels B-1-4
KVS-31 Channels F-1-4
KZE-20 Channels B-1-4
Michael F. Hurley, Director of ETV
500 19th St.
Brooklyn, NY 11215
(212) 499-9705

Operations also at:
Jamaica KNZ-70 Channels F-1-4

Buffalo
State University of New York
WDG-55 Channel G-1
Ken Kavanagh, Jr., Chief Engineer
Room 22, Foster Annex
SUNY at Buffalo
Buffalo, NY 14214
(716) 831-2945

Fredonia
Chautauqua County Board of Cooperative Educational Services
WAQ-310 Channel C-1
Kenneth M. Wasmund, Divisional Director
Chautauqua County BOCES
9520 Fredonia-Stockton Rd.
Fredonia, NY 14063
(716) 672-4371

Hempstead
Sewanhaka Central High School
District of Elmont, Floral Park,
Franklin Square, and New Hyde Park
KHD-21 Channels A-1-2-3
Norman W. Hosler, District Director of ITV
230 Poppy Ave.
Franklin Square, NY 11010
(516) 328-4787

Kenmore
Union Free School District No. 1
Town of Tonawanda
KWE-21 Channels A-1-2
Owen Bliven, Supervisor
Instructional Resources Center
1500 Colvin Blvd.
Kenmore, NY 14223
(716) 877-6800, Ext. 44

Mineola
Mineola Union Free School District No. 10
Town of North Hempstead
KNZ-71 Channels G-1-4
John J. Collins, AV/TV Coordinator
Mineola High School
Armstron Rd.
Garden City Park, NY 11040
(516) 294-6125

Newburgh
City School District of Newburgh
KTN-66 Channels D-1-2
Hans R. Hansen, Director, ITV
Newburgh Free Academy
Fullerton Ave.
Newburgh, NY 12550
(914) 561-8500

New York
Archdiocese of New York
KRS-81 Channels A-1-3
Sister Irene Fugazy, Director of Instructional Television
Communications Center
Seminary Ave.
Yonkers, NY 10704

Operations also at:
Beacon KRS-85 Channels E-1-2-3
Kingston KRS-86 Channels A-1-3
Liberty KRW-67 Channels A-1-3
Peekskill KRS-84 Channels A-1-3
Staten Island KRS-82 Channels E-1-3
Yonkers KRS-83 Channels E-1-3

North Massapequa
Nassau Board of Cooperative Educational Services
KNU-43 Channels D-1-2
Dr. Dalton Levy, TV Administrator
County Center
Prospect Ave.
Westbury, NY 11590
(516) 997-8700

Olean
Board of Cooperative Educational Services
in Cattaraugus, Erie, and Wyoming Counties
WBB-433 Channel A-1
Frank J. Grates
Educational Television Coordinator
BOCES South Center
Windfall Rd.
Olean, NY 14760
(716) 372-8293, Ext. 13

Plainview
Plainview–Old Bethpage Central School District
KHC-94 Channels B-1-2
Dr. Louis Brown, Director
Educational Communications
Plainview–Old Bethpage Central School District
Washington and Kennedy Dr.
Plainview, NY 11803
(516) 938-5400, Ext. 301, 302

Rochester
Rochester Institute of Technology
WAX-30 Channel A-1
Jay Joseph Levine, Station Manager
Box 9969
Rochester, NY 14623
(716) 464-2000

Rockville Centre:
Roman Catholic Diocese of Rockville Centre
KNZ-65 Channels E-1-4
Dr. F. J. Ryan, Administrative Director
1345 Admiral La.
Uniondale, NY 11553
(516) 538-8700

Operations also at:
Central Islip KNZ-68 Channels B-1-4
Huntington KNZ-67 Channels A-1-4

NORTH CAROLINA

Durham
Duke University
KCO-86 Channels C-1-2
KCO-55 Channels G-1-2
Sam A. Agnello, Director of Audiovisual Education
Box 3163
Duke University Medical Center
Durham, NC 27710
(919) 684-2233

OHIO

Cincinnati
Board of Directors
University of Cincinnati
KHX-47 Channels A-1-2
C. J. Magrish, Chief Engineer
Dept. of Biomedical Communications
College of Medicine
231 Bethesda Ave.
Cincinnati, OH 45267
(513) 872-5652

Cleveland
ETV Association of Metropolitan Cleveland
KDX-68 Channels A-1-3
WAJ-20 Channels C-1-2-4
Dr. Alan Stephenson
Assistant Manager, WVIZ-TV
4300 Brookpark Rd.
Cleveland, OH 44134
(216) 398-2800

Mount Vernon
Mt. Vernon City Schools
KVT-69 Channel F-2
Tom Myser, AV Director
Mt. Vernon Senior High School
Mount Vernon, OH 43050
(614) 397-7422

Parma
Parma Board of Education
WGM-96 Channel F-3
KNZ-60 Channel A-1
James Bailey
Director, Instructional Services
2500 W. Pleasant Valley Rd.
Parma, OH 44129
(216) 842-5300, Ext. 470

OKLAHOMA

Oklahoma City
Oklahoma State Regents for Higher Education
WGM-93 Channels A-1-2-3
Jerry L. Hargis, Director
Division of Televised Instruction and Community
Service
500 Education Building—State Capitol Complex
Oklahoma City, OK 73105
(405) 521-2444

Operations also at:
Ada KHM-90 Channels A-1-2
Altus KGF-23 Channels A-1-2
Ardmore WAH-871 Channels A-3-4
Bartlesville WGM-91 Channels C-1-2
Duncan WAH-862 Channels A-1-2
Heavener KGF-24 Channels A-1-2
McAlester KGF-21 Channels A-1-2
Muskogee KGF-22 Channels A-1-2
Ponca WAH-861 Channels A-1-2
Tulsa WGM-92 Channels A-1-2-4

OREGON

Pendleton
Umatilla County Intermediate Education District
KYL-44 Channel A-1
C. McCullough, Media Director
Box 38
Pendleton, OR 97801
(503) 276-6616

Operations also at:
Coombs Canyon KYL-45 Channel F-1
Heppner KYL-46 Channel B-1
Milto-Freewater KMA-20 Channel E-1
Weston KYL-47 Channel E-1

PENNSYLVANIA

Altoona
Altoona Area School District
KVQ-25 Channels A-1-4
KCG-49 Channel G-1
KZC-21 Channels G-1-4
KZC-22 Channels G-1-4
Charles Baker
TV Systems Manager
6th Ave. and 15th St.
Altoona, PA 16603
(814) 944-8101

Hanover
Hanover Public School District
KZB-20 Channels F-1-2
KZB-21 Channels B-1-2
R. D. McCool, Asst. Superintendent
190 E. Walnut St.
Hanover, PA 17331
(717) 637-2261

Lewistown
Mifflin County Board of School Directors
KHU-20 Channels A-1-4
KHU-21 Channels E-1-4
34 S. Brown St.
Lewistown, PA 17044

Philadelphia
Temple University
WAU-29 Channels A-1-4
William H. Siebel
Director, Office of Television Services
Suite 18 Annenberg Hall
Temple University
Philadelphia, PA 19144
(215) 767-8497

Warminster
Tri-State Instructional Broadcasting Council
LOU-74 Channels G-1-4
David L. Barner, Director of ITFS Operations
William Tennent Intermediate High
Warminster, PA 18974
(215) 674-8020

Operations also at:
Quakertown WCX-20 Channels B-1-4

SOUTH CAROLINA

Columbia
South Carolina Educational Television Commission
KGF-20 Channels A-1-2-3-4
B. M. Roseborough, Director, Field Technical Services
P.O. Drawer L
Columbia, SC 29250
(803) 758-7244

Operations also at:
Lake City KGF-20 Channels A-1-4
Rock Hill WBX-216 Channels A-2-1
Rock Hill WBX-217 Channels G-1-2

TEXAS

Houston
Spring Branch Independent School District
KRZ-68 Channels D-1-4
Henry L. Thomas
Director of Televised Instruction
10670 Hammerly Rd.
Houston, TX 77043
(713) 461-8954

University of Texas Health Science Center, Houston
WAU-31 Channels B-1-2
Alan E. Potter, Manager
Room 1110
1100 Holcombe Blvd.
Houston, TX 77030
(713) 792-4671

Mesquite
Mesquite Independent School District
KHS-78 Channels D-1-3
Jim Frehner, Director
405 E. Davis
Mesquite, TX 75149
(241) 288-6411, Ext. 60

Richardson
Association for Graduate Education and Research of N. Texas (TAGER)
KWU-30 Channels F-1-4; C-4
Gilbert A. Peter, President
P.O. Box 688
Richardson, TX 75080
(214) 231-7211

Operations also at:
Fort Worth KWU-29 Channels E-1-2

Richardson Independent School District
WEF-69 Channels B-1-4
H. H. Bobele, TV Coordinator
8221 Towns St.
Dallas, TX 75231
(214) 235-7770

San Antonio
Edgewood Independent School District
KHS-77 Channels D-1-2-3-4
6458 W. Commerce St.
San Antonio, TX 78227

WISCONSIN

Milwaukee
Archdiocese of Milwaukee
KZH-34 Channels G-1-2-3-4
KZH-35 Channels C-1-2-3-4
KZH-36 Channels G-1-2-3-4
Steve Gorski, Program Director
Communications Center
12666 W. Beloit Rd.
Milwaukee, WI 53151
(414) 425-7820

Operations also at:
Kenosha KZH-35 Channels C-1-2-3-4
Elkhorn KZH-36 Channels G-1-2-3-4

Milwaukee Board of School Directors
KHF-80 Channels B-1-2-3-4
Robert Suchy, Director
Dept. of Instructional Resources
P.O. Drawer 10K
Milwaukee, WI 53201
(414) 475-8143

Milwaukee Regional Medical Instructional Television Station, Inc.
WAU-27 Channels E-1-2
George W. Spuda
Director of Network Operations
5000 W. National Ave.
Milwaukee, WI 53193
(414) 384-2000, Ext. 2391

Regents of the University of Wisconsin
WDG-56 Channels D-1-4
Theodore Steinke, Director
Instructional Media Laboratory
University of Wisconsin
P.O. Box 413
Milwaukee, WI 53201

Interesting TV Facts*

THE NUMBER OF TV STATIONS

FCC tabulations at the end of 1977 place the number of television stations at 986—727 commercial and 259 noncommercial. Nielsen figures show that 96% of all TV households can receive four or more stations, 66% can receive seven or more stations, and 33% can receive ten or more stations.

THE PERCENTAGE OF U.S. TV HOUSEHOLDS OWNING TV'S

According to Nielsen, as of September 1977, 72.9 million households or 98% of all households in the U.S. owned at least one television set. The number of TV households grew by more than three million since 1975. Almost 32 million households or 46% of the nation's TV households have two or more TV sets. Seventy-eight percent of the U.S. TV households have color sets.

TV POPULATION CHARACTERISTICS

From 1970 to 1977, the average size of the nation's TV households declined from 3.11 persons to 2.80 persons. Of the estimated 203,990,000 people in TV households, the majority live in cities or suburbs.

Fifty-seven percent (41.7 million) of all TV households do not have any children under 18 years of age. Forty-two percent (30.9 million) of the households have an income of $15,000 or more.

Households with five or more persons watched television substantially more than the average TV household. Those viewing the least were one- and two-person households with no children.

There were no dramatic differences by income level. Only those households with under $10,000 in

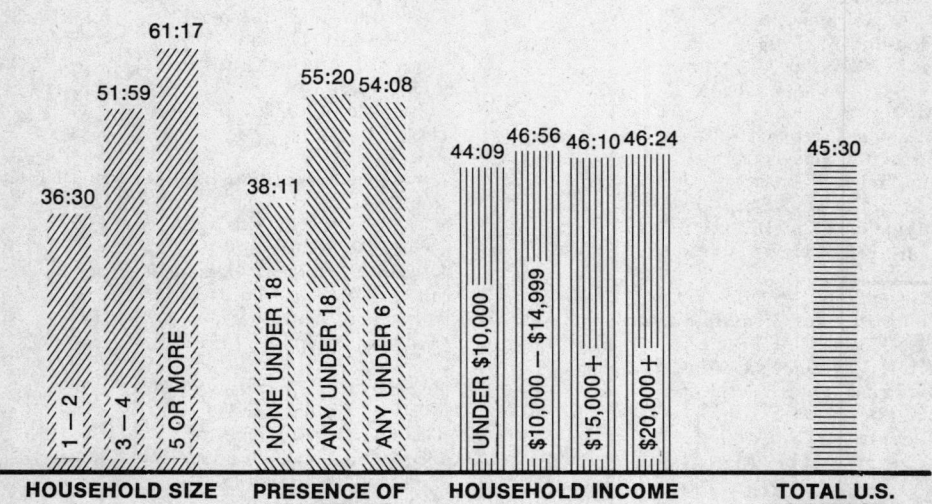

HOURS OF TV USAGE PER WEEK BY HOUSEHOLD CHARACTERISTICS

MONDAY — SUNDAY 24-HOUR TOTAL
HOURS:MINS.

HOUSEHOLD SIZE
- 1 – 2: 36:30
- 3 – 4: 51:59
- 5 OR MORE: 61:17

PRESENCE OF NON-ADULT
- NONE UNDER 18: 38:11
- ANY UNDER 18: 55:20
- ANY UNDER 6: 54:08

HOUSEHOLD INCOME
- UNDER $10,000: 44:09
- $10,000 – $14,999: 46:56
- $15,000 +: 46:10
- $20,000 +: 46:24

TOTAL U.S. AVERAGE: 45:30

NIELSEN ESTIMATES
NATIONAL AUDIENCE DEMOGRAPHICS REPORT
NOVEMBER 1977

*All information supplied by the A. C. Nielsen Company, Northbrook, IL 60062

annual income viewed below the U.S. average—possibly reflecting lower household size as much as income differences.

In general, women view TV more than men; older men and women view more than other age groups; and young children view more than older children and teenagers. This viewing activity is not in direct proportion to the hours available during the week, but instead takes place for the most part during each age group's available free time. For example, the heaviest viewing is during Monday–Sunday, 8:00–11:00 P.M. EST (prime time). The one exception is for preschoolers, who spend more time viewing Monday–Friday, 7:00 A.M.–4:30 P.M., and Monday–Sunday, 4:30–7:30 P.M.

TV VIEWING LEVELS

Television viewing levels increase throughout the day, reaching a peak between 8:00 and 10:00 P.M. By 11:00 P.M. there is a sharp decline. Levels vary from winter to summer. These variations are minor during the morning, early-afternoon, and late-evening hours, but are marked during the late-afternoon and early-evening hours of summer, when the level declines sharply.

DAILY TV USE

Daily TV use for 1977 was six hours and ten minutes per day for the average TV household. Even though there have been slight fluctuations from year to year in estimates of use, over the past 14 years the trend has been upward. As for seasonal variation, January TV use averaged seven hours and 15 minutes a day, and July use about five hours and 15 minutes a day.

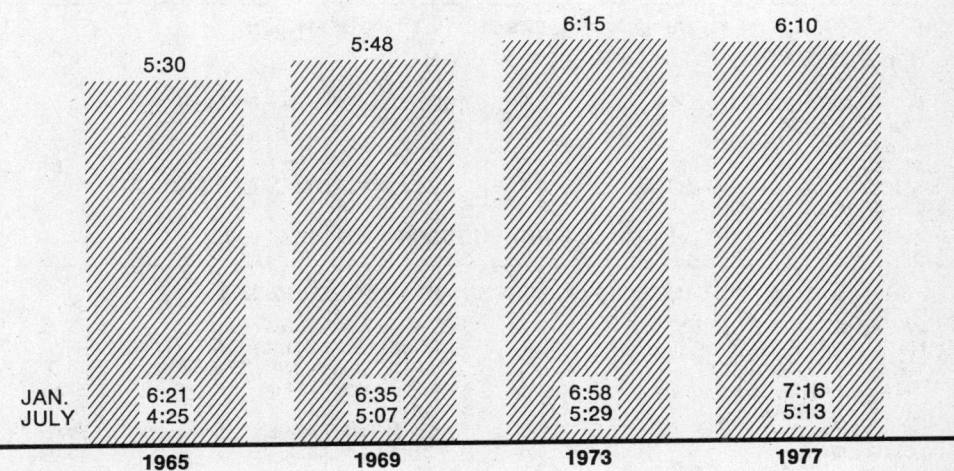

AVERAGE HOURS OF HOUSEHOLD TV USAGE PER DAY

HOURS:MINUTES PER DAY

	5:30	5:48	6:15	6:10
JAN.	6:21	6:35	6:58	7:16
JULY	4:25	5:07	5:29	5:13
	1965	**1969**	**1973**	**1977**

NIELSEN ESTIMATES
BASED ON TOTAL U.S. TV HOUSEHOLDS
EXCLUDING UNUSUAL DAYS
JAN.—DEC. AVG.

THE MOST POPULAR NIGHT FOR WATCHING TV

Sunday night attracts the largest TV audience during the week. Friday night has historically been the least-viewed night, but does register a large audience among children. During the fall of 1977, when these figures were gathered, over 88 million people watched TV between 8:00 and 11:00 P.M. on an average night.

THE MOST POPULAR KIND OF PROGRAM

Situation comedies attracted the largest TV audiences. They were also the most popular with children and teenagers. Women, however, gave equal preference to situation comedies and general drama. Among men, audiences were highest for feature films.

TOP 15 REGULARLY SCHEDULED NETWORK PRIME TIME PROGRAMS

(15 MINUTES OR LONGER)
OCTOBER—DECEMBER 1977
NIELSEN AVERAGE AUDIENCE ESTIMATES (4 OR MORE TELECASTS)

TOTAL U.S. (% TV HOUSEHOLDS)

LAVERNE AND SHIRLEY	32.1%	NBC MONDAY NIGHT MOVIES	22.8
HAPPY DAYS	31.4	LITTLE HOUSE ON THE PRAIRIE	22.8
THREE'S COMPANY	27.6	ON OUR OWN	22.4
ALL IN THE FAMILY	25.2	RHODA	21.9
CHARLIE'S ANGELS	24.6	SOAP	21.7
60 MINUTES	24.5	NFL MONDAY NIGHT FOOTBALL	21.7
ALICE	24.1	ONE DAY AT A TIME	21.6
EIGHT IS ENOUGH	22.9		

TOTAL U.S. TV HOUSEHOLDS 72,900,000

TOTAL WOMEN (% PERSONS IN TV HOUSEHOLDS)

LAVERNE AND SHIRLEY	24.9%	CHARLIE'S ANGELS	18.5
HAPPY DAYS	23.3	RHODA	18.5
THREE'S COMPANY	21.8	ON OUR OWN	18.4
ALL IN THE FAMILY	21.4	WALTONS, THE	18.1
ALICE	20.1	EIGHT IS ENOUGH	17.9
60 MINUTES	19.6	FAMILY	17.2
NBC MONDAY NIGHT MOVIES	19.5	BIG EVENT	17.1
LITTLE HOUSE ON THE PRAIRIE	19.4		

TOTAL WOMEN 18+ IN TV HOUSEHOLDS 77,060,000

TOTAL MEN (% PERSONS IN TV HOUSEHOLDS)

NFL MONDAY NIGHT FOOTBALL	20.6%	ON OUR OWN	16.0
60 MINUTES	20.5	BIG EVENT	15.6
LAVERNE AND SHIRLEY	18.8	SIX MILLION DOLLAR MAN	15.5
HAPPY DAYS	18.7	RHODA	15.3
ALL IN THE FAMILY	18.2	CHARLIE'S ANGELS	14.7
ALICE	17.3	M*A*S*H	14.6
ABC SUNDAY NIGHT MOVIE	16.7	NBC SATURDAY NIGHT MOVIES	14.2
THREE'S COMPANY	16.6		

TOTAL MEN 18+ IN TV HOUSEHOLDS 69,220,000

TOTAL TEENS (% PERSONS IN TV HOUSEHOLDS)

LAVERNE AND SHIRLEY	31.1%	STARSKY AND HUTCH	18.7
HAPPY DAYS	30.7	SIX MILLION DOLLAR MAN	18.3
THREE'S COMPANY	26.8	HARDY BOYS/NANCY DREW	18.0
CHARLIE'S ANGELS	22.4	ONE DAY AT A TIME	17.8
EIGHT IS ENOUGH	21.8	SOAP	16.0
WHAT'S HAPPENING	20.0	ALL IN THE FAMILY	15.6
LOVE BOAT	19.4	DONNY AND MARIE	15.0
WELCOME BACK, KOTTER	18.7		

TOTAL TEENS 12 — 17 IN TV HOUSEHOLDS 24,380,000

TOTAL CHILDREN (% PERSONS IN TV HOUSEHOLDS)

HAPPY DAYS	37.1%	WONDER WOMAN	20.7
LAVERNE AND SHIRLEY	35.2	WHAT'S HAPPENING	19.6
SIX MILLION DOLLAR MAN	26.0	WELCOME BACK, KOTTER	19.4
DONNY AND MARIE	24.0	STARSKY AND HUTCH	19.0
WONDERFUL WORLD/DISNEY	23.2	TABITHA	18.9
HARDY BOYS/NANCY DREW	21.7	BIONIC WOMAN	18.7
EIGHT IS ENOUGH	21.3	LOGAN'S RUN	18.1
THREE'S COMPANY	20.7		

TOTAL CHILDREN 2 — 11 IN TV HOUSEHOLDS 33,330,000

THE PERCENTAGE OF TV HOUSEHOLDS WATCHING EARLY-EVENING NETWORK NEWS

Nearly 84% of U.S. TV households viewed one or more of the three early-evening network news programs in a four-week November–December period. An average of 9.4 telecasts were viewed. Fourteen percent of the households viewed 17 or more telecasts. In a typical week an estimated 66% of U.S. TV households watched early-evening news an average of three times.

SYNDICATED PROGRAM RANKINGS

There are several hundred syndicated programs on television that are purchased from independent distributing organizations by local television stations. As a result, these stations can supplement network offerings with programs of special interest to local areas. The top 15 syndicated programs among households, women over 18, men over 18, teenagers, and children are listed here.

CABLE TV SUBSCRIPTIONS

Households subscribing to community-antenna systems are included in measurements of television audiences. In May of 1977, about 16% of the country's TV households subscribed to CATV service. CATV penetration (CATV households as a percentage of all TV households) tends to be higher in the smaller, non-metropolitan markets.

TV SPORTS COVERAGE

In the last six years, sports coverage has increased by more than 60%. Tennis, basketball, and multi-sports programs have had the greatest increase in coverage. Although football's share of telecasts has decreased by nine points since 1971, the actual number of games telecast has increased by ten.

The most widely-viewed sports event of all time was Superbowl XII, between the Dallas Cowboys and the Denver Broncos, telecast January 15, 1978.

PRESIDENT CARTER'S FIRST FIRESIDE CHAT

On Wednesday, February 2, 1977, President Jimmy Carter delivered his first "fireside chat." His remarks were carried by the combined facilities of the national television networks from 10:00 to 10:28 P.M., EST. Nielsen estimates of the audiences reached are as follows:

	Percent	Millions
Total audience households	62.3	44.4
Average audience households	59.5	42.4
Total persons	36.5	73.5
Total women	46.0	34.7
Women 18–49	43.0	20.1
Total men	40.8	27.6
Men 18–49	35.3	15.6
Total teens	24.4	6.0
Total children (those) under 2 yrs. of age excluded)	15.4	5.2

Lawyers

The following list, published by the Federal Communications Bar Association, consists of lawyers active in communications and communications law. All are members in good standing of a state bar and are eligible to practice before the FCC.

ALABAMA

Birmingham
FROST, Norman C.
P.O. Box 771
Birmingham, AL 35223
(205) 321-8205

Huntsville
HERRING, Harold F.
Lanier, Shaver & Herring
404 Madison St. S
Huntsville, AL 35801
(205) 553-5920

HUGHES, E. Cutter
Lanier, Shaver & Herring
404 Madison St. S
Huntsville, AL 35801
(205) 533-5920

ALASKA

SERDAHLEY, Douglas J.
Libbey & Serdahley
P.O. Box 1113
Anchorage, AK 99510
(907) 278-9551

ARIZONA

Phoenix
CHAUNCEY, Tom, II
KOOL Radio-TV, Inc.
511 W. Adams
Phoenix, AZ 85003
(602) 254-7457

McKNIGHT, Thomas K.
Combined Communications Corp.
P.O. Box 25518
Phoenix, AZ 85002
(602) 257-1333

SILVERMAN, Barry Q.
8204 N. 34th Dr.
Phoenix, AZ 85021
(602) 973-2782

Scottsdale
MOTT, Harold E.
3933 E. Rancho Dr.
Paradise Valley
Scottsdale, AZ 85253

CALIFORNIA

Encino
ROWELL, Russell
5718 Wish Ave.
Encino, CA 91316
(213) 705-1675

Fullerton
CHAFFEE, Walter B.
Launer, Chaffee & Hanna
131 W. Wilshire Ave.
P.O. Box 112
Fullerton, CA 92632
(714) 871-8600

La Jolla
PHILLIPS, Frank S.
Phillips & Phillips
P.O. Box 2907
La Jolla, CA 92038
(714) 454-6137

Los Angeles
COHEN, Harold J.
11937 Gorham Ave., Apt. 6
Los Angeles, CA 90049
(213) 826-8000

COLBY, Richard E.
10458 Wilkins Ave.
Los Angeles, CA 90024
(213) 475-4462

FIRESTONE, Charles M.
Communications Law Program
UCLA School of Law
405 Hilgard Ave.
Los Angeles, CA 90024
(213) 825-6211

KLEINBERG, Kenneth A.
Mitchell, Silberberg & Knupp
1800 Century Park E.
Los Angeles, CA 90067
(213) 553-5000

MILDER, Alvin S.
10880 Wilshire Blvd.
Suite 1900
Los Angeles, CA 90024
(213) 475-9777

PETRICH, Louis P.
Youngman, Hungate & Leopold
1801 Century Park E, Suite 1101
Los Angeles, CA 90067
(213) 277-3333

TAYLOR, Ray L.
11608 Chayote St.
Los Angeles, CA 90049
(213) 476-6493

WARNER, Harry P.
1900 Ave. of the Stars
Suite 2440
Los Angeles, CA 90067
(213) 277-3528

Menlo Park
MASON, Charles Perry, III
SRI International
383 Ravenswood Ave.
Menlo Park, CA 94025
(415) 326-6200

Pacific Palisades
HEARNE, John Patrick
15215 Sunset Blvd.
Pacific Palisades, CA 90272
(213) 454-7505

San Diego
HILLIARD, Carl B.
836 E. Washington St.
San Diego, CA 92103
(714) 241-0322

San Francisco
COOPER, Wayne B.
Farrand, Malti, Spillane & Cooper
555 California St.
Suite 2880
San Francisco, CA 94101
(415) 989-0680

FARRAND, Stephen R.
Farrand, Malti, Spillane & Cooper
29th Floor, Bank of America Center
555 California St.
San Francisco, CA 94104
(415) 989-0680

KOPF, Richard S.
Southern Pacific Communications Co.
Southern Pacific Bldg.
1 Market Plaza, Room 812
San Francisco, CA 94105
(415) 362-1212

MALTI, George M.
Farrand, Malti, Spillane & Cooper
555 California St., Suite 2985
San Francisco, CA 94104
(415) 989-0680

METZLER, Roger J.
Farrand, Malti, Spillane & Cooper
555 California St. Suite 2985
San Francisco, CA 94104
(415) 989-0680

MILLER, Thormund A.
Southern Pacific Communications Co.
1 Market St.
San Francisco, CA 94105
(415) 495-8515

PUTZ, C. Delos, Jr.
University of San Francisco
School of Law
San Francisco, CA 94117
(415) 666-6202

REED, Victor P.
300 Montgomery St.
Suite 1000
San Francisco, CA 94104
(415) 398-5212

SPILLANE, Lester W.
Farrand, Malti, Spillane & Cooper
555 California St. Suite 2985
San Francisco, CA 94101
(415) 989-0682

Universal City
HADL, Robert D.
MCA, Inc.
100 Universal City Plaza
Universal City, CA 91608
(213) 985-4321

TIGHE, M. Joan
MCA, Inc.
100 Universal City Plaza
Universal City, CA 91608
(213) 985-4321

COLORADO

Denver
SHIELDS, Daniel W.
Tele-Communications, Inc.
54 Denver Technological Center
P.O. Box 22595
Denver, CO 80222
(303) 771-8200

WAGNER, David J.
Wagner & D'Onofrio
University Bldg. - Suite 1020
910 16th St.
Denver, CO 80202
(303) 573-9236

Lakewood
HOLADAY, Donald F.
872 S Beech St.
Lakewood, CO 80228
(303) 985-8352

CONNECTICUT

Greenwich
HAWKINS, Howard R.
33 Meadow Croft La.
Greenwich, CT 06830
(203) 661-6116

Hartford
BLUME, Daniel
Blume, Elbaum & Fischman
United Bank & Trust Co. Bldg.
101 Pearl St.
Hartford, CT 06103
(203) 247-0300

New Haven
ULMAN, Lewis H.
Southern New England Telephone Co.
227 Church St.
P.O. Box 1562
New Haven, CT 06506
(203) 771-2191

Norwalk
POND, Walter
28 Gillis La.
Norwalk, CT 06854
(203) 853-2900

Southbury
QUISENBERRY, John T.
372-A Heritage Village
Southbury, CT 06488
(203) 264-8018

Stamford
BROPHY, Theodore F.
President
General Telephone & Electronics Corp.
1 Stamford Forum
Stamford, CT 06904
(203) 357-2000

GALLOGLY, Vincent
GTE Service Corp.
1 Stamford Forum
Stamford, CT 06904
(203) 357-2000

SHERTZER, George Edwin
GTE Service Corp.
1 Stamford Forum
Stamford, CT 06904
(203) 357-2000

DISTRICT OF COLUMBIA

ADAMS, Danny Eugene
Kirksland & Ellis
1776 K St. NW
Washington, DC 20006
(202) 857-5000

ALK, Isadore G.
Law Offices of Isadore G. Alk
4710 41st St. NW
Washington, DC 20016
(202) 362-6311

ANDERSON, David R.
Wilmer, Cutler & Pickering
1666 K St. NW
Washington, DC 20006
(202) 872-6032

ANDERSON, Howard C.
Dewey, Ballantine, Bushby, Palmer & Wood
1775 Pennsylvania Ave. NW
Washington, DC 20006
(202) 862-1050

ARAK, Sydney F.
Stein, Halpert & Miller
910 17th St. NW
Washington, DC 20006
(202) 785-3355

ARKIN, Russell E.
Schwartz & Woods
Suite 206 - The Palladium
1325 18th St. NW
Washington, DC 20036
(202) 833-2350

ARLOW, Allen J.
Central Telephone & Utilities Corp.
1140 Connecticut Ave. NW
Suite 603
Washington, DC. 20036
(202) 833-8700

ATTAWAY, Fritz
Motion Picture Association of America, Inc.
1600 Eye St. NW
Washington, DC 20006
(202) 293-1966

AUCKENTHALER, Alan
Arent, Fox, Kintner, Plotkin & Kahn
1815 H St. NW
Washington, DC 20006
(202) 857-6036

BADER, Michael H.
Haley, Bader & Potts
1730 M St. NW
Suite 700
Washington, DC 20036
(202) 331-0606

BAKER, Philip M.
4515 Willard Ave.
Washington, DC 20015
(301) 652-8919

BAKER, Ruth Smith
Cohn & Marks
1920 L St. NW
Washington, DC 20036
(202) 293-3860

BANKSON, John P., Jr.
Hamel, Park, McCabe & Saunders
1776 F St. NW
Washington, DC 20006
(202) 785-1234

BARAFF, B. Jay
Baraff, Koerner & Olender, P.C.
2033 M St. NW
Suite 293
Washington, DC 20036
(202) 452-8200

BARKER, Robert W.
Wilkinson, Cragun & Barker
1735 New York Ave. NW
Washington, DC 20006
(202) 833-9800

BARNARD, William
Miller & Schroeder
1220 19th St. NW
Washington, DC 20036
(202) 659-4400

BARRY, Thomas Michael
Shack & Mendenhall
1129 20th St. NW
Washington, DC 20036
(202) 293-5900

BARTLETT, John L
Kirkland & Ellis
1776 K St. NW
Suite 1100
Washington, DC 20006
(202) 857-5000

BAYES, James R. W.
Kirkland & Ellis
1776 K St. NW
Suite 1100
Washington, DC 20006
(202) 857-5000

BECHTEL, Gene A.
Arent, Fox, Kintner, Plotkin & Kahn
1815 H St. NW
Washington, DC 20006
(202) 857-6018

BECKER, Richard Sanford
1156 15th St. NW
Suite 516
Washington, DC 20005
(202) 872-0190

BEGLEY, Dennis F.
Midlen & Reddy
2033 M St. NW
Suite 500
Washington, DC 20036
(202) 659-5700

BEIZER, Robert A.
Schnader, Harrison, Segal & Lewis
1666 K St. NW
Suite 608
Washington, DC 20006
(202) 785-8866

BELL, Howard H.
American Advertising Federation
1225 Connecticut Ave. NW
Washington, DC 20036
(202) 659-1800

BELL, Stephen R.
Wilkinson, Cragun & Barker
1735 New York Ave. NW
Washington, DC 20006
(202) 833-9800

BENDER, Raymond G., Jr.
Dow, Lohnes & Albertson
1225 Connecticut Ave. NW
Washington, DC 20036
(202) 862-8072

BENTLEY, J. Geoffrey
Covington & Burling
888 16th St. NW
Washington, DC 20006
(202) 452-6282

BERFIELD, Morton L.
Cohen & Berfield
1129 20th St. NW
Washington, DC 20036
(202) 466-8565

BERG, Michael D.
Covington & Burling
888 16th St. NW
Washington, DC 20006
(202) 452-6194

BERGOLD, Laurel R.
Wilkinson, Cragun & Barker
1735 New York Ave. NW
Washington, DC 20006
(202) 833-9800

BERMAN, Paul Justin
Covington & Burling
888 16th St. NW
Washington, DC 20006
(202) 452-6194

BERMAN, William H.
Communication Satellite Corp.
950 L'Enfant Plaza South SW
Washington, DC 20024
(202) 554-6130

BERNARD, Lawrence J., Jr.
Greeley & Bernard
1990 M St. NW
Suite 660
Washington, DC 20036
(202) 785-2690

BERNSTEIN, Robert Alfred
Brown & Bernstein
1521 O St. NW
Washington, DC 20005
(202) 387-3100

BERNTHAL, Eric L
Arent, Fox, Kintner, Plotkin & Kahn
1815 H St. NW
Washington, DC 20006
(202) 857-6032

BERNTON, William P.
Glaser, Fletcher & Johnson, P.C.
1150 17th St. NW
Washington, DC 20036
(202) 872-0200

BILGER, Donald E.
Bilger & Blair
1730 M St. NW
Washington, DC 20036
(202) 659-4230

BLAIR, Forbes W.
Bilger & Blair
1730 M St. NW
Washington, DC 20036
(202) 659-4230

BLAKE, Jonathan Dewey
Covington & Burling
888 16th St. NW
Washington, DC 20006
(202) 452-6358

BLOOSTON, Arthur
2120 L St. NW
Washington, DC 20037
(202) 659-0830

BLUME, Jack P.
Fly, Shuebruk, Blume, Gaguine, Boros & Schulkind
1211 Connecticut Ave. NW
Washington, DC 20036
(202) 293-1280

BOARDMAN, Joan Therese
Pierson, Ball & Dowd
1200 18th St. NW
Washington, DC 20036
(202) 331-8566

BODORF, Richard J.
Fisher, Wayland, Southmayd & Cooper
1100 Connecticut Ave. NW
Suite 730
Washington, DC 20036
(202) 659-3494

BOOTH, Robert M., Jr.
Booth & Freret
1302 18th St. NW
Washington, DC 20036
(202) 296-9100

BORGHESANI, W. H., Jr.
Keller & Heckman
1150 17th St. NW
Suite 1000
Washington, DC 20036
(202) 296-2700

BORSARI, George R., Jr.
Daly, Joyce & Borsari
1830 Jefferson Pl. NW
Washington, DC 20036
(202) 296-8900

BORSARI, John A.
Daly, Joyce & Borsari
1830 Jefferson Pl. NW
Washington, DC 20036
(202) 296-8900

BOWERS, Jonathan S.
Gordon & Jacob
2000 L St. NW
Washington, DC 20036
(202) 293-2300

BOWIE, Nolan A.
Citizens Communications Center
1914 Sunderland Pl. NW
Washington, DC 20036
(202) 296-4238

BOYCE, Roy Walker
Cohen and Berfield
1129 20th St. NW
Washington, DC 20036
(202) 466-8565

BRADLEY, Samuel M.
Welch & Morgan
900 17th St. NW
Washington, DC 20006
(202) 296-5151

BRAUN, Howard Jay
Fly, Shuebruk, Blume, Gaguine, Boros & Schulkind
1211 Connecticut Ave. NW
Washington, DC 20036
(202) 293-1280

BROWN, Richard L.
Brown & Bernstein
1521 O St. NW
Washington, DC 20005
(202) 387-3100

BUENZLE, Robert J.
Smith & Pepper
1776 K St. NW
Washington, DC 20006
(202) 296-0600

BUFFONE, Samuel J.
Tigar & Buffone
1302 18th St. NW
Suite 201
Washington, DC 20036
(202) 466-5470

BURCH, Richard Kurt
National Association of Broadcasters
1771 N St. NW
Washington, DC 20036
(202) 293-3500

BURNS, George D.
Communications Resource Center
2000 K St. NW
Washington, DC 20006
(202) 857-4800

BUTCHER, Goler T.
White, Fine & Verville
1156 15th St. NW
Washington, DC 20005
(202) 659-2900

BYRNES, William J.
Haley, Bader & Potts
1730 M St. NW
Washington, DC 20036
(202) 331-0606

CAHILL, Robert Vincent
Glazer, Fletcher & Johnson, P.C.
1150 17th St. NW
Suite 1007
Washington, DC 20036
(202) 872-0200

CALLAGHAN, Richard L.
1828 L St. NW, Suite 1101
Washington, DC 20036
(202) 296-2360

CAMPBELL, Alan C.
Dow, Lohnes & Albertson
1225 Connecticut Ave. NW
Washington, DC 20036
(202) 862-8055

CARR, J. Richard
Dempsey & Koplovitz
938 Bowen Bldg.
Washington, DC 20005
(202) 737-6363

CARROCCIO, A. Thomas
Berliner, Maloney, Gimer & Muir
1100 Connecticut Ave. NW
Washington, DC 20036
(202) 293-1414

CARSON, Virginia S.
McKenna, Wilkinson & Kittner
1150 17th St. NW
Washington, DC 20036
(202) 296-1600

CASS, Ronald A.
Arent, Fox, Kintner, Plotkin & Kahn
1815 H St. NW
Washington, DC 20005
(202) 857-6036

CHASE, Seymour M.
1250 Connecticut Ave. NW
Suite 201
Washington, DC 20036
(202) 331-7373

CHRISTENSEN, Gary L.
Hogan & Hartson
815 Connecticut Ave. NW
Washington, DC 20006
(202) 331-4534

CHRISTOFFERSON, D. Todd
Dow, Lohnes & Albertson
1225 Connecticut Ave. NW
Washington, DC 20036
(202) 862-8070

CINCIOTTA, Linda A.
Arent, Fox, Kintner, Plotkin & Kahn
Federal Bar Bldg. W
1815 H St. NW
Washington, DC 20006
(202) 857-6029

COFFMAN, Gordon C.
Wilkinson, Cargun & Barker
1735 New York Ave. NW
Washington, DC 20006
(202) 833-9800

COHEN, Harold David
Pierson, Ball & Dowd
1000 Ring Bldg.
Washington, DC 20036
(202) 331-8566

COHEN, Lewis I.
Cohen & Berfield
1129 20th St. NW
Washington, DC 20036
(202) 466-8565

COHEN, Stanley B.
Cohn & Marks
1920 L St. NW
Washington, DC 20036
(202) 466-8565

COHEN, Wallace M.
Landis, Cohen, Singman & Rauh
1019 19th St. NW, Suite 500
Washington, DC 20036
(202) 785-2020

COHN, Lawrence N.
Cohn & Marks
1920 L St. NW
Washington, DC 20036
(202) 293-3860

COHN, Marcus
Cohn & Marks
1920 L St. NW
Washington, DC 20036
(202) 293-3860

COLE, Harry F.
Arent, Fox, Kintner, Plotkin & Kahn
1815 H St. NW
Washington, DC 20006
(202) 857-6033

COLE, John P., Jr.
Cole, Zylstra & Raywid
1919 Pennsylvania Ave. NW
Suite 200
Washington, DC 20006
(202) 659-9750

COLEMAN, Terry
Covington & Burling
888 16th St. NW
Washington, DC 20006
(202) 452-6084

COLL, Robert Wilson
McKenna, Wilkinson & Kittner
1150 17th St. NW
Washington, DC 20036
(202) 296-1600

CONNOR, J. Parker
Mullin, Connor & Rhyne, P.C.
Suite 1002
1000 Connecticut Ave. NW
Washington, DC 20036
(202) 659-4700

COOK, James A.
Fleischman & Walsh, P.C.
1150 Connecticut Ave. NW
Washington, DC 20036
(202) 296-7740

COOKE, James R.
McKenna, Wilkinson & Kittner
1150 17th St. NW
Washington, DC 20036
(202) 296-1600

COONEY, Bernard J.
Howrey & Simon
1730 Pennsylvania Ave. NW
Washington, DC 20006
(202) 872-8800

COOPER, Grover Collins
Fisher, Wayland, Southmayd & Cooper
1100 Connecticut Ave. NW
Washington, DC 20036
(202) 659-3494

COOPER, Samuel A., III
National Cable Television Association
918 16th St. NW
Washington, DC 20006
(202) 466-8111

CORDON, Alfred C., Jr.
Cordon & Jacob
2000 L St. NW
Washington, DC 20036
(202) 293-2300

CORRAZZINI, Robert F.
Smith & Pepper
1776 K St. NW
Washington, DC 20006
(202) 296-0600

COSSON, David
National Telephone Cooperative Association
2626 Pennsylvania Ave. NW
Washington, DC 20037
(202) 342-8200

COTTONE, Benedict P.
1730 M St. NW
Suite 910
Washington, DC 20036
(202) 296-1901

COULTER, William Kirk
Communications Satellite Corporation
950 L'Enfant Plaza SW
Washington, DC 20024
(202) 554-6140

COURSEN, Christopher Dennison
Dempsey & Koplovitz
938 Bower Bldg.
Washington, DC 20005
(202) 737-6363

COURTNEY, Jeremiah
2120 L St. NW
Washington, DC 20037
(202) 833-3050

COUZENS, Michael J.
1660 L St. NW
Suite 1100
Washington, DC 20036
(202) 452-7488

COX, Kenneth A.
Haley, Bader & Potts
1730 M St. NW
Washington, DC 20036
(202) 331-0606

COY, Wayne
Cohn & Marks
1920 L St. NW
Washington, DC 20006
(202) 293-3860

CREGAN, James R.
National Newspaper Association
491 National Press Bldg.
Washington, DC 20045
(202) 783-1651

CURTIS, Vincent J.
Fletcher, Heald & Hildreth
1225 Connecticut Ave. NW
Washington, DC 20036
(202) 659-9100

CUTLER, Charles R.
Kirkland & Ellis
1776 K St. NW
Suite 1100
Washington, DC 20036
(202) 857-5000

CUTLER, Lloyd N.
Wilmer, Cutler & Pickering
1666 K St. NW
Washington, DC 20006
(202) 872-6100

CZARRA, Edgar F., Jr.
Covington & Burling
888 16th St. NW
Washington, DC 20006
(202) 452-6066

DAVIS, John I.
Dow, Lohnes & Albertson
1225 Connecticut Ave. NW
Suite 500
Washington, DC 20036
(202) 862-8065

DAVISON, Calvin
Jones, Day, Reavis & Pogue
1100 Connecticut Ave. NW
Washington, DC 20036
(2)2) 452-5871

DeFRANCO, Joseph
CBS, Inc.
1800 M St. NW
Suite 300
Washington, DC 20036
(202) 457-4511

DEMPSEY, William J.
Dempsey & Koplovitz
938 Bowen Bldg.
Washington, DC 20005
(202) 737-6363

DENSLOW, L. Alton
Washington Bldg.
Washington, DC 20005
(202) 737-0727

DEUTSCH, Ellen S.
NTIA
1800 G St. NW
Washington, DC 20504
(202) 395-5616

DeVORE, Lawrence M.
Communications Satellite Corp.
950 L'Enfant Plaza South SW
Washington, DC 20024
(202) 554-6133

DIAMOND, Marvin J.
Hogan & Hartson
815 Connecticut Ave. NW
Washington, DC 20006
(202) 331-4523

DISENHAUS, Helen E.
Dow, Lohnes & Albertson
1225 Connecticut Ave. NW
Washington, DC 20036
(202) 862-8134

DOOLITTLE, J. William
Prather, Seeger, Doolittle & Farmer
1101 16th St. NW
Washington, DC 20036
(202) 296-0500

DOUGHERTY, Thomas J.
Metromedia, Inc.
5151 Wisconsin Ave. NW
Washington, DC 20016
(202) 244-5151

DOUGLAS, George R., Jr.
Misegades, Douglas & Levy
1126 16th St. NW
Suite 304
Washington, DC 20036
(202) 638-3833

DOWD, Thomas N.
Pierson, Ball & Dowd
Ring Bldg.
Washington, DC 20036
(202) 331-8566

DOWELL, Edwina Elizabeth
House Communications Subcommittee
B-333 Rayburn House Office Bldg.
Washington, DC 20515
(202) 225-9304

DUFFY, Gerard Joseph
Law Offices of John Tierney
1925 K St. NW, Suite 304
Washington, DC 20006
(202) 293-7979

DUNNE, Joseph E., III
James A. Gammon Law Offices
1925 K St. NW
Suite 304
Washington, DC 20006
(202) 293-7979

DYKE, James Webster, Jr.
Covington & Burling
888 16th St. NW
Washington, DC 20006
(202) 452-6000

EAGAN, R. Russell
Kirkland & Ellis
1776 K St. NW
Suite 1100
Washington, DC 20036
(202) 857-5020

EDGE, Joe Dixon
Hamel, Park, McCabe & Saunders
1776 F St. NW
Wash.ngton, DC 20006
(202) 785-1234

EDMUNDSON, James K., Jr.
Tepper & Edmundson
1150 Connecticut Ave. NW
Suite 1010
Washington, DC 20036
(202) 466-4455

EFFROS, Stephen R.
1100 17th St. NW
Washington, DC 20036
(202) 223-0486

EGER, John
Lamb, Halleck & Keats
1742 N St. NW
Washington, DC 20036
(202) 785-4822

EISEN, Bruce Alan
Stambler & Shrinsky, P.C.
1120 Connecticut Ave. NW
Washington, DC 20036
(202) 872-0010

EMMONS, Nathaniel F.
Mullin, Connor & Rhyne, P.C.
1000 Connecticut Ave. NW
Suite 1002
Washington, DC 20036
(202) 659-4700

ENDE, Asher H.
Fly, Shuebruk, Blume, Gaguine, Boros & Schulkind
1211 Connecticut Ave. NW
Washington, DC 20036
(202) 293-1282

ENNIS, James G.
Fletcher, Heald, & Hildreth
1225 Connecticut Ave. NW
Suite 400
Washington, DC 20036
(202) 659-9100

EPSTEIN, Gary M.
Arent, Fox, Kintner, Plotkin & Kahn
1815 H St. NW
Washington, DC 20006
(202) 857-6025

EVANS, Donald S.
Law Office of Leo I. George
900 17th St. NW
Suite 401
Washington, DC 20006
(202) 833-5678

FABER, Michael W.
Peabody, Rivlin, Lambert & Meyers
1150 Connecticut Ave. NW
12th Floor
Washington, DC 20036
(202) 457-1000

FAGER, Christopher B.
Reporters Committee for Freedom of the Press
1750 Pennsylvania Ave. NW
Room 1112
Washington, DC 20006
(202) 872-1620

FANELLI, Joseph A.
Corcoran, Youngman & Rowe
1511 K St. NW
Washington, DC 20005
(202) 783-7900

FELDSTEIN, Stuart F.
Wilner and Scheiner
2021 L St. NW
Washington, DC 20036
(202) 293-7800

FELS, Nicholas W.
Covington & Burling
888 16th St. NW
Washington, DC 20006
(202) 452-6186

FEORE, John R., Jr.
Dow, Lohnes & Albertson
1225 Connecticut Ave. NW
Suite 500
Washington, DC 20036
(202) 862-8069

FERRALL, Victor E., Jr.
Jones, Day, Reavis & Pogue
1100 Connecticut Ave. NW
Washington, DC 20036
(202) 452-5992

FIELD, John D., III
Dow, Lohnes & Albertson
1225 Connecticut Ave. NW
Suite 500
Washington, DC 20036
(202) 659-8200

FIELDS, Mark Edward
Miller & Fields
1901 Pennsylvania Ave. NW
Suite 400
Washington, DC 20006
(202) 785-2720

FIELSTRA, Carl John
James A. Gammon Law Offices
1925 K St. NW
Suite 304
Washington, DC 20006
(202) 293-7979

FINKELSTEIN, Michael
Boasberg, Hewes, Finkelstein & Klores
2101 L St. NW
Washington, DC 20037
(202) 466-8960

FINN, Frederick W.
National Cable TV Association
918 16th St. NW
Washington, DC 20006
(202) 457-6715

FIORINI, John Eugene, III
Smith & Pepper
1776 K St. NW
Washington, DC 20006
(202) 296-0600

FIRESTONE, Martin F.
Stein, Halpert & Miller
910 17th St. NW
Washington, DC 20006
(202) 785-3355

FISCHER, Henry G.
Pike & Fischer, Inc.
2000 L St. NW
Washington, DC 20036
(202) 223-4880

FISHER, Ben C.
Fisher, Wayland, Southmayd & Cooper
1100 Connecticut Ave. NW
Suite 730
Washington, DC 20036
(202) 659-3494

FITZ, William H.
Pierson, Ball & Dowd
1000 Ring Bldg.
Washington, DC 20036
(202) 331-8566

FLEISCHMAN, Aaron
Fleischman & Walsh, P.C.
1725 N St. NW
Washington, DC 20036
(202) 466-6250

FLEMING, David P.
Dow, Lohnes & Albertson
1225 Connecticut Ave. NW
Suite 500
Washington, DC 20036
(202) 862-8079

FLETCHER, Francis E., Jr.
Glaser, Fletcher & Johnson, P.C.
1150 17th St. NW
Washington, DC 20036
(202) 872-0200

FLETCHER, Frank U.
Fletcher, Heald & Hildreth
1225 Connecticut Ave. NW
Washington, DC 20036
(202) 659-9100

FLETCHER, Thomas W.
Cole, Zylstra & Raywid
1919 Pennsylvania Ave. NW
Suite 200
Washington, DC 20006
(202) 659-9750

FOLEY, Robert Matthew
Foley & Chhabra
1019 19th St. NW
Suite 800
Washington, DC 20036
(202) 659-9750

FORD, Frederick W.
Lovett, Ford & Hennessey
1901 L St. NW
Suite 200
Washington, DC 20036
(202) 293-7400

FORREST, Herbert E.
Steptoe & Johnson
1250 Connecticut Ave. NW
Washington, DC 20036
(202) 862-2219

FOULIS, Ronald J.
4432 Edmunds St. NW
Washington, DC 20007
(202) 338-1324

FOWLER, Mark Stapleton
Fowler & Meyers, P.C.
Suite 200, Mercury Bldg.
1015 20th St. NW
Washington, DC 20036
(202) 466-2272

FOX, Brenda Lee
National Association of Broadcasters
1771 N St. NW
Washington, DC 20036
(202) 293-3560

FRANK, Theodore David
Arent, Fox, Kintner, Plotkin, & Kahn
1815 H St. NW
Washington, DC 20006
(202) 857-6016

FREEMAN, James J.
Pierson, Ball & Dowd
1000 Ring Bldg.
Washington, DC 20036
(202) 331-8566

FRERET, Julian P.
Booth & Freret
1302 18th St. NW
Washington, DC 20036
(202) 296-9100

FRISCHKORN, Allen
General Telephone & Electronics
1120 Connecticut Ave. NW
Washington, DC 20036
(202) 293-2800

FRITZ, Karl H.
2120 L St. NW
Washington, DC 20037
(202) 833-3050

FROHOCK, Thomas N.
McKenna, Wilkinson & Kittner
1150 17th St. NW
Washington, DC 20036
(202) 296-1600

GAGUINE, Benito
Fly, Shuebruk, Blume, Gaguine, Boros & Schulkind
1211 Connecticut Ave. NW
Washington, DC 20036
(202) 293-1280

GAMMON, James A.
1925 K St. NW
Suite 304
Washington, DC 20006
(202) 293-7979

GARRETT, Robert A.
Arnold & Porter
1229 19th St. NW
Washington, DC 20036
(202) 872-3641

GASTFREUND, Irving
Fly, Shuebruk, Blume, Gaguine, Boros & Schulkind
1211 Connecticut Ave. NW
Washington, DC 20036
(202) 293-1280

GAYNES, Martin J.
Bonner, Thompson, O'Connell & Gaynes
900 17th St. NW
Washington, DC 20006
(202) 659-4660

GEORGE, Leo I.
Law Offices of Leo I. George
900 17th St. NW
Suite 401
Washington, DC 20006
(202) 833-5678

GILLESPIE, Gardner, F., III
Hogan & Hartson
815 Connecticut Ave. NW
Suite 600
Washington, DC 20006
(202) 331-4796

GILLMORE, Kathleen Cory
1523 L St. NW #500
Washington, DC 20005
(202) 347-1844

GLASER, Michael L.
Glaser, Fletcher & Johnson, P.C.
1150 17th St. NW
Washington, DC 20036
(202) 872-0200

GOLDBERG, Henry
Verner, Liipfert, Bernhard & McPherson
1660 L St. NW
Suite 1100
Washington, DC 20036
(202) 452-7440

GOLDSTEIN, Corinne Amy
Covington & Burling
888 16th St. NW
Washington, DC 20006
(202) 452-6490

GOLDSTEIN, Irving
COMSAT
950 L'Enfant Plaza SW
Washington, DC 20024
(202) 554-6433

GOODKIND, Arthur B.
Koteen & Burt
The Connecticut Bldg.
1150 Connecticut Ave. NW
Washington, DC 20036
(202) 467-5700

GRANGE, George R., II
James A. Gammon Law Offices
1925 K St. NW
Suite 304
Washington, DC 20006
(202) 293-7979

GRAWEY, Richard E.
Subcommittee on Manpower & Housing
U.S. House of Representatives
Rayburn Bldg. B-349A
Washington, DC 20515
(202) 225-6751

GRAY, John W., Jr.
American Telephone & Telegraph Co.
2000 L St. NW
Washington, DC 20036
(202) 457-3843

GREELEY, James E.
Greeley and Bernard
1990 M St. NW
Suite 660
Washington, DC 20036
(202) 785-2690

GREEN, Robert N.
Western Union Telegraph Co.
1828 L St. NW
Suite 1001
Washington, DC 20036
(202) 624-0145

GREEN, William S.
Pierson, Ball & Dowd
1000 Ring Bldg.
Washington, DC 20036
(202) 331-8566

GREGG, Donna Coleman
Dow, Lohnes & Albertson
1225 Connecticut Ave. NW
Suite 500
Washington, DC 20036
(202) 862-8075

GRENIER, Edward J., Jr.
Sutherland, Asbill & Brennan
1666 K St. NW
Suite 800
Washington, DC 20006
(202) 872-7827

GURMAN, Louis
Becker, Gurman & Lukar, P.C.
1156 15th St. NW
Suite 516
Washington, DC 20005
(202) 872-0190

HANKINS, Robert B.
Pierson, Ball & Dowd
1000 Ring Bldg.
Washington, DC 20036
(202) 331-8566

HANNON, John S., Jr.
Communications Satellite Corp.
950 L'Enfant Plaza SW
Washington, DC 20024
(202) 554-6000

HARDING, Arthur H.
National Cable TV Association
918 16th St. NW
Washington, DC 20006
(202) 457-6717

HARDMAN, Kenneth E.
Fortas & Koven
1200 29th St. NW
Washington, DC 20007
(202) 337-5700

HARDY, Ralph Williams, Jr.
Dow, Lohnes & Albertson
1225 Connecticut Ave. NW
Washington, DC 20036
(202) 862-8058

HARRINGTON, Clifford M.
Fisher, Wayland, Southmayd & Cooper
1100 Connecticut Ave. NW
Room 730
Washington, DC 20036
(202) 659-3494

HARRIS, Laurence E.
MCI Telecommunications Corporation
1150 17th St. NW
Washington, DC 20036
(202) 872-1600

HARTENBERGER, Werner K.
Dow, Lohnes & Albertson
1225 Connecticut Ave. NW
Suite 500
Washington, DC 20036
(202) 862-8101

HARVEY, Edmund E.
Chadbourne, Parke, Whiteside & Wolff
1150 17th St. NW
Washington, DC 20036
(202) 872-8050

HATHAWAY, Cynthia L.
Arent, Fox, Kintner, Plotkin & Kahn
1815 H St. NW, Suite 1200
Washington, DC 20006
(202) 857-6402

HAYES, Edward, Jr.
Hayes & White
1220 19th St. NW
Suite 203
Washington, DC 20036
(202) 452-1320

HEALD, Robert L.
Fletcher, Herald, & Hildreth
1225 Connecticut Ave. NW
Washington, DC 20036
(202) 659-9100

HEALY, Robert W.
Gordon & Healy
1821 Jefferson Pl. NW
Washington, DC 20036
(202) 785-5020

HEARNE, John Quinlan
Fisher, Wayland, Southmayd & Cooper
1100 Connecticut Ave. NW
Washington, DC 20036
(202) 659-3494

HECKMAN, Jerome H.
Keller and Heckman
1150 17th St. NW
Washington, DC 20036
(202) 296-2700

HELEIN, Charles H.
Dow, Lohnes & Albertson
1225 Connecticut Ave. NW
Suite 500
Washington, DC 20036
(202) 862-8054

HELMICK, Richard A.
Cohn & Marks
1920 L St. NW
Washington, DC 20036
(202) 293-3860

HENDRICKSON, Tom
National Cable Television Association
918 16th St. NW
Washington, DC 20006
(202) 457-6715

HENNESSEY, Joseph F.
Lovett, Ford & Hennessey
1901 L St. NW
Suite 200
Washington, DC 20036
(202) 293-7400

HENRY, E. William
Ginsburg, Feldman & Bress
1700 Pennsylvania Ave. NW
Room 300
Washington, DC 20006
(202) 223-3800

HILDEBRANDT, Stephen A.
Wilkinson, Cragun & Barker
1735 New York Ave. NW
Washington, DC 20006
(202) 833-9800

HILDRETH, Richard
Fletcher, Heald, & Hildreth
1225 Connecticut Ave. NW
Washington, DC 20036
(202) 659-9100

HILL, Carolyn C.
United Telecommunications, Inc.
1800 K St. NW
Suite 1102
Washington, DC 20006
(202) 659-4600

HILL, David L.
Keller & Heckman
1150 17th St. NW
Suite 1000
Washington, DC 20036
(202) 457-1146

HILLIARD, David E.
Kirkland & Ellis
1776 K St. NW
Washington, DC 20006
(202) 857-5058

HIRD, Frederick S., Jr.
Kaler, Worsley, Daniel & Hollman
710 Ring Bldg.
Washington, DC 20036
(202) 331-9100

HIRREL, Michael J.
Hamel, Park, McCabe & Saunders
1776 F St. NW
Suite 400
Washington, DC 20006
(202) 785-1234

HOBSON, James R.
GTE
1120 Connecticut Ave. NW
Suite 900
Washington, DC 20036
(202) 293-2815

HOCHBERG, Philip R.
O'Connor & Hannan
1747 Pennsylvania Ave. NW
6th Floor
Washington, DC 20006
(202) 785-8700

HOLT, Thaddeus
1700 Pennsylvania Ave. NW
Washington, DC 20006
(202) 785-5230

HOLTZ, Edgar W.
Hogan & Hartson
815 Connecticut Ave. NW
Washington, DC 20006
(202) 331-4520

HORNE, Michael S.
Covington & Burling
888 16th St. NW
Washington, DC 20006
(202) 452-6396

HOROWITZ, Richard M.
Fly, Shuebruk, Blume, Gaguine, Boros & Schulkind
1211 Connecticut Ave. NW
Washington, DC 20036
(202) 293-1282

HOUSER, Thomas J.
Weitzman and Houser
Suite 1200
1735 K St. NW
Washington, DC 20006
(202) 467-5424

HUBBARD, Alan C.
Western Union
1828 L St. NW
Suite 1001
Washington, DC 20036
(202) 862-4638

HUMMERS, Edward W., Jr.
Fletcher, Heald & Hildreth
1225 Connecticut Ave. NW
Washington, DC 20036
(202) 659-9100

HUMPHREY, Margot S.
Koteen & Burt
The Connecticut Bldg.
1150 Connecticut Ave. NW
Washington, DC 20036
(202) 467-5700

HYDE, Rosel H.
Wilkinson, Cragun & Barker
1735 New York Ave. NW
Washington, DC 20006
(202) 833-9800

ISAACS, Michael B.
National Cable Television Association
918 16th St. NW
Washington, DC 20036
(202) 457-6716

JACOB, John B.
Cordon & Jacob
2000 L St. NW, Suite 616
Washington, DC 20036
(202) 293-2300

JACOBI, Robert B.
Cohn & Marks
1920 L St. NW
Washington, DC 20036
(202) 293-3860

JAMES, Robert L.
Cole, Zylstra & Raywid
1919 Pennsylvania Ave. NW
Suite 200
Washington, DC 20006
(202) 659-9750

JATLOW, David C.
Fleischman & Walsh, P.C.
1725 St. NW
Washington, DC 20036
(202) 466-6250

JENCKS, Richard W.
1990 M St. NW
Washington, DC 20036
(202) 296-1234

JENKINS, Susan M.
Rowley, Green, Hochberg & Fairman
1990 M St. NW
Washington, DC 20036
(202) 293-2170

JENNES, Ernest W.
Covington & Burling
888 16th St. NW
Washington, DC 20006
(202) 452-6202

JOHNSON, Brian Allan
Pierson, Ball & Dowd
1000 Ring Bldg.
Washington, DC 20036
(202) 331-8566

JOHNSON, John Griffith, Jr.
Jorgensen, Johnson & Northrop
1926 Eye St. NW
Washington, DC 20006
(202) 331-9313

JOHNSON, Mark W.
CBS, Inc.
1800 M St. NW
Suite 300
Washington, DC 20036
(202) 457-4513

JOHNSON, M. Scott
Glaser, Fletcher & Johnson, P.C.
1150 17th St. NW
Washington, DC 20036
(202) 872-0200

JOHNSTON, Everett D.
1302 18th St. NW
Washington, DC 20036
(202) 296-9103

JOHNSTON, James H.
Cohn & Marks
1920 L St. NW
Washington, DC 20036
(202) 293-3860

JONES, Thomas L.
Continental Telephone Corp.
1800 K St. NW
Suite 629
Washington, DC 20006
(202) 872-1970

JORGENSEN, Norman E.
Jorgensen, Johnson & Northrop
1926 Eye St. NW
Washington, DC 20006
(202) 331-9313

JOYCE, Leonard S.
Daly, Joyce & Borsari
1830 Jefferson Pl. NW
Washington, DC 20036
(202) 296-8900

KATZEN, Sally
Wilmer, Cutler & Pickering
1666 K St. NW
Washington, DC 20006
(202) 872-6156

KEITHLEY, Carter E.
Smith, Bucklin & Associates
1730 Pennsylvania Ave. NW
Washington, DC 20006
(202) 785-0500

KELLEHER, John Michael
1710 H St. NW
Washington, DC 20006
(202) 637-9900

KELLER, Joseph E.
Keller & Heckman
1150 17th St. NW
Suite 1000
Washington, DC 20036
(202) 296-2700

KELLER, Lawrence
Ginsburg, Feldman and Bress
1700 Pennsylvania Ave. NW
Suite 300
Washington, DC 20006
(202) 637-9048

KELLER, Thomas J.
Verner, Liipfert, Bernhard & McPherson
1660 L St. NW
Suite 1100
Washington, DC. 20036
(202) 452-7407

KENEHAN, Edward F.
Fletcher, Heald & Hildreth
1225 Connecticut Ave. NW
Washington, DC 20036
(202) 659-9100

KENKEL, John Bonaventure
Miller & Schroeder
1220 19th St. NW
Washington, DC 20036
(202) 659-4400

KENNY, John V.
Southern Pacific Communications Co.
1801 K St. NW
Suite 221
Washington, DC 20006
(202) 293-1584

KIMBALL, Raymond J.
Shack & Mendenhall
1129 20th St. NW
Washington DC 20036
(202) 293-5900

KING, John W
Haley, Bader & Potts
1730 M St. NW
Suite 700
Washington, DC 20036
(202) 331-0606

KITTNER, Joseph M.
McKenna, Wilkinson & Kittner
1150 17th St. NW
Washington, DC 20036
(202) 296-1600

KNAUER, Leon Thomas
Wilkinson, Cragun & Barker
1735 New York Ave. NW
Washington, DC 20006
(202) 833-9800

KOERNER, James A.
Baraff, Koerner & Olender, P.C.
2033 M St. NW
Suite 203
Washington, DC 20036
(202) 452-8200

KOTEEN, Bernard
Koteen & Burt
The Connecticut Bldg.
1150 Connecticut Ave. NW
Washington, DC 20036
(202) 467-5700

KRASNOW, Erwin G.
General Counsel
National Association of Broadcasters
1771 N St. NW
Washington, DC 20036
(202) 293-3560

KRAUS, Rainer K.
Koteen & Burt
The Connecticut Bldg.
1150 Connecticut Ave. NW
Washington, DC 20036
(202) 467-5700

KRAVETZ, Eric S.
Law Offices of Donald E. Ward
1730 Rhode Island Ave. NW
Suite 512
Washington, DC 20036
(202) 466-3225

LANE, John D.
Hedrick and Lane
1211 Connecticut Ave. NW
Washington, DC 20036
(202) 628-5923

LEADER, Martin R.
Fisher, Wayland, Southmayd & Cooper
1100 Connecticut Ave. NW
Suite 730
Washington, DC 20036
(202) 659-3494

LEONARD, William L.
C & P Telephone Co.
1710 H St. NW
Washington, DC 20006
(202) 392-8653

LERMAN, Steven Alman
McKenna, Wilkinson & Kittner
1150 17th St. NW
Washington, DC 20036
(202) 296-1600

LEVENTHAL, Norman P.
McKenna, Wilkinson & Kittner
1150 17th St. NW
Washington, DC 20036
(202) 296-1600

LEVETOWN, Robert A.
C & P Telephone Co.
1710 H St. NW
Washington, DC 20006
(202) 392-5111

LEVINE, Robert E.
Gordon & Healy
1821 Jefferson Pl. NW
Washington, DC 20036
(202) 785-5020

LEVY, Joel H.
Cohn & Marks
1920 L St. NW
Washington, DC 20036
(202) 293-3860

LEVY, Sherman
Misegades, Douglas & Levy
633 Washington Bldg.
Washington, DC 20005
(202) 638-3833

LIBERMAN, Howard M.
Cohn & Marks
1920 L St. NW
Washington, DC 20036
(202) 293-3860

LITVIN, Fanney N.
2800 Quebec St. NW
Apt. 1022
Washington, DC 20008
(202) 362-6614

LLOYD, David H.
Arnold & Porter
1229 19th St. NW
Washington, DC 20036
(202) 872-6868

LOEFFLER, Robert H.
Isham, Lincoln & Beale
1050 17th St. NW
Suite 701
Washington, DC 20006
(202) 833-9730

LOEVINGER, Lee
Hogan & Hartson
815 Connecticut Ave. NW
Washington, DC 20006
(202) 331-4530

LOTHSCHUETZ, John M.
United Telecommunications, Inc.
1800 K St. NW
Suite 1102
Washington, DC 20006
(202) 659-4600

LOVETT, Lee G.
Lovett, Ford & Hennessey, P.C.
1901 L St. NW
Washington, DC 20036
(202) 293-7400

LUBIC, Robert Bennett
Baraff, Koerner & Olender, P.C.
2033 M St. NW
Suite 203
Washington, DC 20036
(202) 452-8200

LUTZKER, Arnold Paul
Dow, Lohnes & Albertson
1225 Connecticut Ave. NW
Washington, DC 20036
(202) 862-8066

MADDEN, Brian M.
Cohn & Marks
1920 L St. NW
Suite 700
Washington, DC 20036
(202) 293-3860

MAGEE, James E.
Wilkinson, Cragun & Barker
1735 New York Ave. NW
Washington, DC 20006
(202) 833-9800

MAILLOUX, Pierre E.
815 Bowen Bldg.
Washington, DC 20005
(202) 737-8154

MALLYCK, E. Theodore
Smith & Pepper
1776 K St. NW
Washington, DC 20006
(202) 296-0600

MALONE, William
1120 Connecticut Ave. NW
Suite 900
Washington, DC 20036
(202) 293-2837

MARKOWSKI, Joseph P.
Wilkinson, Cragun & Barker
1735 New York Ave. NW
Washington, DC 20006
(202) 833-9800

MARKS, Herbert E.
Wilkinson, Cragun & Barker
1735 New York Ave. NW
Washington, DC 20006
(202) 833-9800

MARKS, Leonard H.
Cohn & Marks
1920 L St. NW
Washington, DC 20036
(202) 293-3860

MARKS, Richard D.
Dow, Lohnes & Albertson
1225 Connecticut Ave. NW
Washington, DC 20036
(202) 862-8064

MARMET, Robert A.
Marmet Professional Corp.
1822 Jefferson Pl. NW
Washington, DC 20036
(202) 331-7300

MARTIN, Frank J., Jr.
Sutherland, Asbill & Brennan
1666 K St. NW
Washington, DC 20006
(202) 872-7833

MARTIN, Harry C.
Midlen & Reddy
2033 M St. NW
Washington, DC 20036
(202) 659-5700

MATTHEWS, John Duff
Dow, Lohnes & Albertson
1225 Connecticut Ave. NW
Washington, DC 20036
(202) 862-8047

MAURER, Phyllis Dobin
Swift & Swift, P.C.
1100 17th St. NW
Suite 710
Washington, DC 20036
(202) 833-3533

McCABE, Aloysius B.
Kirkland & Ellis
1776 K St. NW
Suite 1100
Washington, DC 20036
(202) 857-5000

McCABE, Carol J.
Corp. for Public Broadcasting
1111 16th St. NW
Washington, DC 20036
(202) 293-6160

McCABE, Thomas J.
2100 M St. NW
Suite 305
Washington, DC 20037
(202) 872-0440

McCARTHY, G. Daniel
Bilger & Blair
1730 M St. Nw
Washington, DC 20036
(202) 659-4230

McCARTHY, Michael J.
Dow, Lohnes & Albertson
1225 Connecticut Ave. NW
Washington, DC 20036
(202) 862-8068

McCOLLUM, Douglas J.
C&P Telephone Co.
1710 H St. NW
Washington, DC 20006
(202) 392-4456

McCOMBS, Harold, K., Jr.
Marmet Professional Corp.
1822 Jefferson Pl. NW
Washington, DC 20036
(202) 331-7300

McCOY, Craig S.
Cole, Zylstra & Raywid
1919 Pennsylvania Ave. NW
Suite 200
Washington, DC 20006
(202) 659-9750

McGILLAN, James J.
Smith & Pepper
1776 K St. NW
Suite 700
Washington, DC 20006
(202) 296-0600

McKEE, Clarence V.
Law, Murphey & McKee
1414 22nd St. NW, Suite 100
Washington, DC 20037
(202) 293-7886

McKENNA, James A., Jr.
McKenna, Wilkinson & Kittner
1150 17th St. NW
Washington, DC 20036
(202) 296-1600

McKENNA, Robert B.
Wilkinson, Cragun & Barker
1735 New York Ave. NW
Washington, DC 20006
(202) 833-9800

McKERNS, Charles J.
Dow, Lohnes & Albertson
1225 Connecticut Ave. NW
Washington, DC 20036
(202) 862-8000

McKETTA, John J., III
Covington & Burling
888 16th St. NW
Washington, DC 20006
(202) 452-6000

McLEOD, George R.
2000 N St. NW
Washington, DC 20036
(202) 223-2877

MENDENHALL, Gregory B.
Shack & Mendenhall
1129 20th St. NW
Washington, DC 20036
(202) 293-5900

METELSKI, John
AT&T Long Lines
2055 L St. NW
Washington, DC 20036
(202) 457-2121

MEYER, Suzanne
Dow, Lohnes & Albertson
1225 Connecticut Ave. NW
Washington, DC 20036
(202) 862-8062

MEYERS, David
Fowler & Meyers, P.C.
Suite 200—Mercury Bldg.
1015 20th St. NW
Washington, DC 20036
(202) 466-2272

MEYERS, Tedson J.
Peabody, Rivlin, Lambert & Meyers
1150 Connecticut Ave. NW
12th Floor
Washington, DC 20036
(202) 457-1000

MIDLEN, John H., Jr.
Midlen & Reddy
2033 M St. NW
Suite 500
Washington, DC 20036
(202) 659-5700

MILLER, Herbert D., Jr.
Koteen & Burt
The Connecticut Bldg.
1150 Connecticut Ave. NW
Washington, DC 20036
(202) 467-5700

MILLER, Lawrence M.
Schwartz & Woods
Suite 206—The Palladium
1325 18th St. NW
Washington, DC 20036
(202) 833-2350

MILLER, Nicholas P.
Preston, Thorgimson, Ellis, Holman & Fletcher
1776 F St. NW
Washington, DC 20006
(202) 331-1005

MILLER, Reed
Arnold & Porter
1229 19th St. NW
Washington, DC 20036
(202) 872-6826

MILLER, Samuel
Miller & Fields
1901 Pennsylvania Ave. NW
Suite 400
Washington, DC 20006
(202) 785-2720

MILLER, William E.
Steptoe & Johnson
1250 Connecticut Ave. NW
Washington, DC 20036
(202) 223-4800

MITCHELL, Lee M.
Sidley & Austin
1730 Pennsylvania Ave. NW
Suite 1100
Washington, DC 20006
(202) 624-9000

MITCHELL, Stuart B.
James A. Gammon Law Offices
1925 K St. NW
Suite 304
Washington, DC 20006
(202) 293-7979

MITTELBERGER, Ralph A.
Pierson, Ball & Dowd
1000 Ring Bldg.
1200 18th St. NW
Washington, DC 20036
(202) 331-8566

MOATES, G. Paul
Sidley & Austin
1730 Pennsylvania Ave. NW
Washington, DC 20006
(202) 624-9000

MONAHAN, James D.
Dow, Lohnes & Albertson
1225 Connecticut Ave. NW
Washington, DC 20036
(202) 862-8061

MONDERER, Howard
Vice President, Law
National Broadcasting Co.
1800 K St. NW
Suite 610
Washington, DC 20006
(202) 833-3600

MOORE, Richard A.
Wilner & Scheiner
2021 L St. NW
Washington, DC 20036
(202) 293-7800

MORDKOFSKY, Harold
2120 L St. NW
Washington, DC 20037
(202) 659-0830

MORGAN, Edward P.
Welch & Morgan
900 17th St. NW
300 Farragut Bldg.
Washington, DC 20006
(202) 296-5151

MORRISSEY, Michael J.
Welch & Morgan
900 17th St. NW
300 Farragut Bldg.
Washington, DC 20006
(202) 296-5151

MORRISSEY, Michael J.
C&P Telephone Co.
930 H St. NW
Washington, DC 20001
(202) 392-4456

MORSE, Walter Herbert
RCA Global Communications
2030 M St. NW
Washington, DC 20036
(202) 558-4422

MOTT, William C.
1101 17th St. NW
Suite 810
Washington, DC 20036
(202) 296-1683

MULLIN, Eugene F.
Mullin, Connor & Rhyne, P.C.
Suite 1002
1000 Connecticut Ave. NW
Washington, DC 20036
(202) 659-4700

MULVIHILL, Donald J.
Cahill, Gordon & Reindel
1819 H St. NW
Washington, DC 20006
(202) 223-3350

MUNTZING, L. Manning
LeBouef, Lamb, Leiby & MacRae
1757 N St. NW
Washington, DC 20036
(202) 872-8668

MUTINO, Paul A.
Corp. for Public Broadcasting
1111 16th St. NW
Washington, DC 20036
(202) 293-6160

NACE, David L.
2120 L St. NW
Washington, DC 20036
(202) 659-0830

NAFTALIN, Alan Y.
Koteen & Burt
The Connecticut Bldg.
1150 Connecticut Ave. NW
Washington, DC 20036
(202) 467-5700

NEUSTADT, Stanley S.
Cohn & Marks
1920 L St. NW
Washington, DC 20036
(202) 293-3860

NICHOLS, Willard R.
Kirkland & Ellis
1776 K St. NW
Washington, DC 20006
(202) 857-5000

NORTHROP, Carl Wooden
Jorgensen, Johnson & Northrop
1926 Eye St. NW
Washington, DC 20006
(202) 331-9313

NUSBAUM, William R.
NARUC
1102 ICC Bldg.
P.O. Box 684
Washington, DC 20044
(202) 628-7324

NUTTER, Guy B.
3010 Wisconsin Ave. NW
Apartment C-5
Washington, DC 20009
(202) 966-4048

OCKERSHAUSEN, Harry J.
Dempsey & Koplovitz
938 Bowen Bldg.
Washington, DC 20005
(202) 737-6363

O'CONNELL, Peter D.
Pierson, Ball & Dowd
1000 Ring Bldg.
Washington, DC 20036
(202) 331-8566

OLENDER, Robert L.
Baraff, Koerner & Olender, P.C.
2033 M St. NW, Suite 203
Washington, DC 20036
(202) 452-8200

OLSON, Jeffrey H.
Citizens Communications Center
1914 Sunderland Pl. NW
Washington, DC 20036
(202) 296-4238

O'NEILL, Edward S.
Wilner & Scheiner
2021 L St. NW
Washington, DC 20036
(202) 293-7800

OPPENHEIMER, Monroe
Surrey, Karasik & Moore
1156 15th St. NW
Washington, DC 20005
(202) 659-9050

O'REILLY, Thomas J.
Chadbourne, Parke, Whiteside & Wolff
1150 17th St. NW
Washington, DC 20036
(202) 872-8050

OWENS, Ella V.
Communications Satellite Corp.
950 L'Enfant Plaza SW
Washington, DC 20024
(202) 554-6168

OYSTER, James L.
Smith & Pepper
1776 K St. NW
Washington, DC 20006
(202) 296-0600

PADDEN, Preston R.
Metromedia, Inc.
5151 Wisconsin Ave. NW
Washington, DC 20016
(202) 244-5151

PAGLIN, Max D.
3001 Veazy Terr. NW
Washington, DC 20008
(202) 244-4525

PAIGE, L. Stanley
Vice President for Legal Affairs
Post–Newsweek Stations, Inc.
2139 Wisconsin Ave. NW
Suite 200
Washington, DC 20007
(202) 342-3820

PALCHICK, Mark J.
Fly, Schuebruk, Blume, Gaguine, Boros & Schulkind
1211 Connecticut Ave. NW
Washington, DC 20036
(202) 293-1280

PAULAS, Demetrios George, Jr.
Booth & Freret
1302 18th St. NW
Suite 401
Washington, DC 20036
(202) 296-9100

PELKEY, John
Haley, Bader & Potts
Suite 700
1730 M St. NW
Washington, DC 20036
(202) 331-0606

PEPPER, Vincent A.
Smith & Pepper
1776 K St. NW
Washington, DC 20006
(202) 296-0600

PERKINS, Roy F., Jr.
1400 20th St. NW
Suite 115
Washington, DC 20036
(202) 872-0234

PERRY, B. Dwight
Dow, Lohnes & Albertson
1225 Connecticut Ave. NW
Washington, DC 20036
(202) 862-8049

PETTIT, John W.
Hamel, Park, McCabe & Saunders
1776 F St. NW
Washington, DC 20006
(202) 785-1234

PETTIT, Robert L.
Fletcher, Heald & Hildreth
1225 Connecticut Ave. NW
Suite 400
Washington, DC 20036
(202) 659-9100

PIERSON, W. Theodore
Pierson, Ball & Dowd
1000 Ring Bldg.
1200 18th St. NW
Washington, DC 20036
(202) 331-8566

PIERSON, W. Theodore, Jr.
Pierson, Ball & Dowd
1000 Ring Bldg.
1200 18th St. NW
Washington, DC 20036
(202) 331-8566

PLOTKIN, Harry M.
Arent, Fox, Kintner, Plotkin & Kahn
1815 H St. NW
Washington, DC 20006
(202) 857-6015

POLIVY, Gail L.
General Telephone & Electronics
1120 Connecticut Ave. NW
Suite 900
Washington, DC 20036
(202) 293-2800

POLIVY, Margot
Renouf, McKenna & Polivy
1532 16th St. NW
Washington, DC 20036
(202) 265-1807

POLLOCK, James C.
Spiegel & McDiarmid
Watergate Office Bldg., Suite 310
2600 Virginia Ave. NW
Washington, DC 20036
(202) 333-4500

POPE, Robert J.
888 16th St. NW
Washington, DC 20006
(202) 452-6092

POPHAM, James J.
National Association of Broadcasters
1771 N St. NW
Washington, DC 20036
(202) 293-3560

PORTER, Roderick Kelvin
Fletcher, Heald & Hildreth
1225 Connecticut Ave. NW
Suite 400
Washington, DC 20036
(202) 659-9100

POTTS, William J., Jr.
Haley, Bader & Potts
1730 M St. NW
Washington, DC 20036
(202) 331-0606

PRICE, Ilene
Haley, Bader & Potts
Suite 700—Madison Nat'l. Bank Bldg.
1730 M St. NW
Washington, DC 20036
(202) 331-0606

QUALE, John C.
Kirkland & Ellis
1776 K St. NW
Washington, DC 20006
(202) 857-5032

RAFTER, John A.
Dow, Lohnes & Albertson
1225 Connecticut Ave. NW
Washington, DC 20036
(202) 862-8045

RAISH, Leonard Robert
1225 Connecticut Ave. NW
Suite 400
Washington, DC 20036
(202) 659-9100

RAMEY, Carl R.
McKenna, Wilkinson & Kittner
1150 17th St. NW
Washington, DC 20036
(202) 296-1600

RAWSON, Robert J.
Fletcher, Heald, & Hildreth
1225 Connecticut Ave. NW
Washington, DC 20036
(202) 659-9100

RAYWID, Alan
Cole, Zylstra & Raywid
1919 Pennsylvania Ave. NW
Suite 200
Washington, DC 20006
(202) 659-9750

REDDY, Edward B.
Midlen & Reddy
2033 M St. NW
Suite 500
Washington, DC 20036
(202) 659-5700

REDMOND, Daniel M.
Dow, Lohnes & Albertson
1225 Connecticut Ave. NW
Washington, DC 20036
(202) 862-8050

REED, Kevin F.
Dow, Lohnes & Albertson
1225 Connecticut Ave. NW
Washington, DC 20036
(202) 862-8076

REESE, Bruce T.
Wilkinson, Cragun & Barker
1735 New York Ave. NW
Washington, DC 20006
(202) 833-9800

REIFER, Joseph R.
Cole, Zylstra & Raywid
1919 Pennsylvania Ave. NW
Suite 200
Washington, DC 20006
(202) 659-9750

REIS, Harold F.
Newman, Reis & Axelrod
1025 Connecticut Ave. NW
Washington, DC 20036
(202) 833-8371

RESNICK, Leo
Board of Trade Bldg.
1129 20th St. NW
Washington, DC 20036
(202) 659-9636

REYNER, William S., Jr.
Hogan & Hartson
815 Connecticut Ave. NW
Washington, DC 20006
(202) 331-4510

REYNOLDS, Christopher J.
Dempsey & Koplovitz
938 Bowen Bldg.
Washington, DC 20005
(202) 737-6363

RHYNE, Charles S.
839 17th St. NW
Washington, DC 20006
(202) 347-1380

RHYNE, S. White, Jr.
Mullin, Connor & Rhyne, P.C.
Suite 1002
1000 Connecticut Ave. NW
Washington, DC 20036
(202) 659-4700

RICKLESS, David M.
Cohn & Marks
1920 L St. NW
Washington, DC 20036
(202) 293-3860

RICKS, Jay E.
Hogan & Hartson
815 Connecticut Ave. NW
Washington, DC 20006
(202) 331-4518

RIEHL, Alice T.
Storer Broadcasting Co.
1220 19th St. NW
Washington, DC 20036
(202) 296-3340

RIEHL, Richard M.
Haley, Bader & Potts
1730 M St. NW, Suite 200
Washington, DC 20036
(202) 331-0606

RILEY, James Patrick
Fletcher, Heald, & Hildreth
1225 Connecticut Ave. NW
Washington, DC 20036
(202) 659-9100

RIVLIN, Lewis A.
Peabody, Rivlin, Lambert & Meyers
1150 Connecticut Ave. NW
12th Floor
Washington, DC 20036
(202) 457-1000

ROBERTS, John C.
Senate Armed Services Committee
Old Senate Office Bldg.
Room 212
Washington, DC 20510
(202) 224-3871

ROBERTS, L. Adrian
Dow, Lohnes & Albertson
1225 Connecticut Ave. NW
Washington, DC 20036
(202) 862-8051

ROBERTSON, Larry S.
NTIA
1800 G St. NW
Washington, DC 20504
(202) 395-3122

ROBERTSON, Lawrence S.
Zuckert, Scoutt & Rasenberger
888 17th St. NW
Suite 600
Washington, DC 20007
(202) 298-8660

ROCHE, James T.
COMSAT General Corp.
950 L'Enfant Plaza SW
Washington, DC 20024
(202) 554-6445

RODGERS, William Paul, Jr.
General Counsel and Administrative Director
National Association of Regulatory Utility Commissioners
1102 ICC Bldg.
P.O. Box 684
Washington, DC 20044
(202) 628-7324

RODIN, Richard S.
Hogan & Hartson
815 Connecticut Ave. NW
Washington, DC 20006
(202) 331-4532

ROOT, Thomas Lawrence
Marmet Professional Corp.
1822 Jefferson Pl. NW
Washington, DC 20036
(202) 331-7300

ROSENBERG, Marvin
Fletcher, Heald, & Hildreth
1225 Connecticut Ave. NW
Washington, DC 20036
(202) 659-9100

ROSENBLOOM, Joel
Wilmer, Cutler & Pickering
1666 K St. NW
Washington, DC 20006
(202) 872-6216

ROSENBLOOM, Michael H.
Wilner & Scheiner
2021 L St. NW
Washington, DC 20036
(202) 293-7800

ROSS, Bradford
Ross, Marsh & Foster
730 15th St. NW
Washington, DC 20005
(202) 628-2623

ROSS, Robert W.
Southern Pacific Communications Co.
1801 K St. NW
Washington, DC 20006
(202) 293-1584

ROURKE, Gerald S.
Rourke & Bennett
2020 K St. NW
Washington, DC 20006
(202) 659-1080

ROWLENSON, Richard C.
Lovett, Ford & Hennessey, P.C.
1901 L St. NW
Suite 200
Washington, DC 20036
(202) 293-7400

ROYCROFT, Howard F.
Hogan & Hartson
815 Connecticut Ave. NW
Washington, DC 20006
(202) 331-4525

ROZZELLE, David G.
Fletcher, Heald, & Hildreth
1225 Connecticut Ave. NW
Suite 400
Washington, DC 20036
(202) 659-9100

RUSSO, Roy R.
Cohn & Marks
1920 L St. NW
Washington, DC 20036
(202) 293-3860

SANCHEZ, Ernest T.
National Public Radio
2025 M St. NW
Washington, DC 20036
(202) 785-5369

SANTARELLI, Donald E.
Santarelli & Gimer
2033 M St. NW
Suite 700
Washington, DC 20036
(202) 466-6800

SATTERFIELD, Lee A.
C&P Telephone Co.
930 H St. NW
Washington, DC 20001
(202) 392-5296

SAYPOL, Bruce P.
Cohn & Marks
1920 L St. NW
Washington, DC 20006
(202) 293-3860

SCHAFFER, Steven C.
Schwartz & Woods
1325 18th St. NW
The Palladium, Suite 206
Washington, DC 20036
(202) 833-2350

SCHANZER, Kenneth D.
Director, Government Relations
National Broadcasting Co.
1800 K St. NW, Suite 610
Washington, DC 20006
(202) 833-3600

SCHARFF, J. Laurent
Pierson, Ball & Dowd
1000 Ring Bldg.
1200 18th St. NW
Washington, DC 20036
(202) 331-8566

SCHATTENFIELD, Thomas
Arent, Fox, Kintner, Plotkin & Kahn
1815 H St. NW
Washington, DC 20006
(202) 857-6020

SCHATTMAN, Richard E.
Midlen & Reddy
2033 M St. NW
Washington, DC 20036
(202) 659-5700

SCHEINER, Arthur
Wilner & Scheiner
2021 L St. NW
Washington, DC 20036
(202) 293-7800

SCHER, Gerald
Sundlun, Tirana & Scher
Watergate 600 Bldg.
Washington, DC 20037
(202) 337-6800

SCHILDHAUSE, Sol
Farrow, Schildhause, Dent & Wilson
1705 DeSales St. NW, Suite 400
Washington, DC 20036
(202) 659-8746

SCHMELTZER, Kathryn
Fisher, Wayland, Southmayd & Cooper
1100 Connecticut Ave. NW
Suite 730
Washington, DC 20036
(202) 659-3494

SCHMIDT, Richard M., Jr.
Cohn & Marks
1920 L St. NW
Washington, DC 20036
(202) 293-3860

SCHULKIND, Herbert M.
Fly, Shuebruk, Blume, Gaguine, Boros & Schulkind
1211 Connecticut Ave. NW
Washington, DC 20036
(202) 293-1280

SCHWARTZ, Lois S.
Law Offices
Suite 200 - Mercury Bldg.
1015 20th St. NW
Washington DC 20036
(202) 296-3022

SCHWARTZ, Louis
Schwartz & Woods
Suite 206, The Palladium
1325 18th St. NW
Washington, DC 20036
(202) 833-2350

SCHWARTZMAN, Andrew Jay
Executive Director
Media Access Project
1609 Connecticut Ave. NW
Washington, DC 20009
(202) 232-4300

SCORCE, John M.
Western Union Telegraph Co.
Office of the General Counsel/Regulatory Division
Suite 1001
1828 L St. NW
Washington, DC 20036
(202) 862-4600

SEAKS, Robert G.
Wheeler & Wheeler
1729 H St. NW
Washington, DC 20006
(202) 337-6500

SECREST, Lawrence W., III
Kirkland & Ellis
1776 K St. NW
Washington, DC 20006
(202) 857-5074

SEDKY, Cherif
Hill, Christopher & Phillips
1900 M St. NW
Washington, DC 20036
(202) 833-3990

SELLS, Harry G.
Sells & Gregory
2000 L St. NW
Washington, DC 20036
(202) 659-3840

SEVERY, Richard B.
Fortas & Koven
1200 29th St. NW
Washington, DC 20007
(202) 337-5700

SHACK, Thomas G., Jr.
Shack & Mendenhall
1129 20th St. NW
Washington, DC 20036
(202) 293-5900

SHANNON, Charles V.
1700 K St. NW
Washington, DC 20006
(202) 296-4150

SHAPIRO, George H.
Arent, Fox, Kintner, Plotkin & Kahn
1815 H St. NW
Washington, DC 20006
(202) 857-6022

SHOOSHAN, Harry M., III
Subcommittee on Communications
U.S. House of Representatives
Rayburn Bldg., Room 331
Washington, DC 20515
(202) 225-9304

SHORENSTEIN, Stuart A.
Fly, Shuebruk, Blume, Gaguine, Boros & Schulkind
1211 Connecticut Ave. NW
Washington, DC 20036
(202) 293-1280

SHRINSKY, Jason L.
Stambler & Shrinsky, P.C.
1120 Connecticut Ave. NW
Suite 270
Washington, DC 20036
(202) 872-0010

SHUBERT, Lee W.
Bilger & Blair
1730 M St. NW
Washington, DC 20036
(202) 659-4230

SIEBERT, Thomas I.
Lovett, Ford & Hennessey, P.C.
1901 L St. NW
Suite 200
Washington, DC 20036
(202) 293-7400

SIEGEL, Ronald A.
Cohn & Marks
1920 L St. NW
Washington, DC 20036
(202) 293-3860

SIMS, William P., Jr.
Dow, Lohnes & Albertson
1225 Connecticut Ave. NW
Washington, DC 20036
(202) 862-8040

SINGER, Richard M.
Pierson, Ball & Dowd
1200 18th St. NW
Washington, DC 20036
(202) 331-8566

SKALL, Gregg P.
Chief Counsel
NTIA
1800 G St. NW
Washington, DC 20504
(202) 395-5616

SLATER, Terrence L.
ITT
1707 L St. NW
Washington, DC 20036
(202) 296-6000

SLAUGHTER, Harrison T.
Pierson, Ball & Dowd
1000 Ring Bldg.
Washington, DC 20036
(202) 331-8566

SMITH, Eric H.
Public Broadcasting Service
485 L'Enfant Plaza West SW
Washington, DC 20024
(202) 488-5057

SMITH, Jack R.
Law Offices of Jeremiah Courtney
2121 L St. NW
Washington, DC 20037
(202) 833-3050

SMITH, John J.
Senate Commerce Committee
Subcommittee on Communications
Washington, DC 20510
(202) 224-0411

SOLOMON, Henry A.
Haley, Bader & Potts
1730 M St. NW - Suite 700
Washington, DC 20036
(202) 331-0606

SOUTHMAYD, John P.
Fisher, Wayland, Southmayd & Cooper
1100 Connecticut Ave. NW
Suite 730
Washington, DC 20036
(202) 659-3494

SPARKS, Kenneth R.
Federal City Council
1155 15th St. NW
Washington, DC 20005
(202) 223-4560

SPELLMAN, John H.
Hamel, Park, McCabe & Saunders
1776 F St. NW
Washington, DC 20006
(202) 785-1234

SPEVAK, Arnold D.
Cohn & Marks
1920 L St. NW
Washington, DC 20036
(202) 293-3860

SPIEVACK, Edwin B.
Cohn & Marks
1920 L St. NW
Washington, DC 20036
(202) 293-3860

STAMBLER, Arthur
Stambler & Shrinsky, P.C.
1120 Connecticut Ave. NW
Suite 270
Washington, DC 20036
(202) 872-0010

STANLEY, Earl R.
Dow, Lohnes & Albertson
1225 Connecticut Ave. NW
Washington, DC 20036
(202) 862-8044

STEIN, Abe L.
1129 Munsey Bldg.
1329 E St. NW
Washington, DC 20004
(202) 737-7944

STEIN, Robert Jay
Eaton, Stein & Effroymson
1025 15th St. NW
Suite 600
Washington, DC 20005
(202) 347-6805

STERNLICHT, David N.
Fletcher, Heald & Hildreth
1225 Connecticut Ave. NW
Suite 400
Washington, DC 20036
(202) 659-9100

STEVENSON, Lisa J.
Koteen & Burt
1150 Connecticut Ave. NW
Suite 1000
Washington, DC 20036
(202) 467-5700

STRASSBURG, Bernard
1730 Rhode Island Ave. NW
Suite 512
Washington, DC 20036
(202) 466-3225

STRODEL, Richard H.
Wheeler & Wheeler
1729 H St. NW
Washington, DC 20006
(202) 337-6500

STURM, John F.
National Broadcasting Co.
1800 K St. NW
Suite 610
Washington, DC 20006
(202) 833-3600

SUMMERS, John B.
National Association of Broadcasters
1771 N St. NW
Washington, DC 20036
(202) 293-3511

SUNDERLAND, Louise A.
Hamel, Park, McCabe & Saunders
1776 F St. NW
Suite 400
Washington, DC 20006
(202) 785-1234

SUNDLUN, Bruce G.
Sundlun, Tirana & Scher
Watergate 600 Bldg.
Washington, DC 20037
(202) 337-6800

SWIFT, Richard F.
Dow, Lohnes & Albertson
1225 Connecticut Ave. NW
Suite 500
Washington, DC 20036
(202) 862-8056

TANNENWALD, Peter
Arent, Fox, Kintner, Plotkin & Kahn
1815 H St. NW
Washington, DC 20006
(202) 857-6024

TAPTICH, Edward P.
McKenna, Wilkinson, & Kittner
1150 17th St. NW
Washington, DC 20036
(202) 296-1600

TAUBER, Mark
Pierson, Ball & Dowd
1000 Ring Bldg.
1200 18th St. NW
Washington, DC 20036
(202) 331-8566

THOMPSON, Anthony J.
Hamel, Park, McCabe & Saunders
1776 F St. NW
Washington, DC 20006
(202) 785-1234

THROOP, Allen E.
Corcoran, Youngman & Rowe
1511 K St. NW
Investment Bldg., Suite 1100
Washington, DC 20005
(202) 783-7900

TIERNEY, John L.
Law Offices of John L. Tierney
1925 K St. NW
Suite 304
Washington, DC 20006
(202) 293-7979

TIFFANY, Curran C.
AT&T
2000 L St. NW
Washington, DC 20036
(202) 457-3845

TILLOTSON, David F.
Arent, Fox, Kintner, Plotkin & Kahn
1815 H St. NW
Washington, DC 20006
(202) 857-6027

TOOHEY, Daniel Weaver
Dow, Lohnes & Albertson
1225 Connecticut Ave. NW
Washington, DC 20036
(202) 862-8052

TOPEL, Howard A.
Mullin, Connor & Rhyne, P.C.
Suite 1002
1000 Connecticut Ave. NW
Washington, DC 20036
(202) 659-4700

TOWNLEY, Dennis Warren
Sidley & Austin
1730 Pennsylvania Ave. NW
Washington, DC 20006
(202) 624-9074

TRIMBLE, Joyce E.
Dow, Lohnes & Albertson
1225 Connecticut Ave. NW
Suite 500
Washington, DC 20036
(202) 862-8000

TUFT, Leonard W.
RCA Global Communications, Inc.
2030 M St. NW
Washington, DC 20036
(202) 558-4422

TURNER, John Alfred, Jr.
Assistant General Counsel
Privacy Protection Study Committee
2120 L St. NW, Suite 424
Washington, DC 20506
(202) 634-1477

VERRILL, Charles O. Jr.
1200 17th St. NW
Washington, DC 20036
(202) 223-4040

VOLNER, Ian David
Cohn & Marks
1920 L St. NW
Washington, DC 20036
(202) 293-3860

VOLPE, Joseph, III
Covington & Burling
888 16th St. NW
Washington, DC 20006
(202) 452-6294

WADLOW, Clark
Hogan & Hartson
815 Connecticut Ave. NW
Washington, DC 20006
(202) 331-4726

WALL, Thomas H.
Dow, Lohnes & Albertson
1225 Connecticut Ave. NW
Washington, DC 20036
(202) 862-8042

WALSH, Charles S.
Fleischman & Walsh
1725 N St. NW
Washington, DC 20036
(202) 466-6250

WALTON, Frederick H., Jr.
Dempsey & Koplovitz
938 Bowen Bldg.
Washington, DC 20005
(202) 737-6363

WARD, Donald E.
Law Offices of Donald E. Ward
1730 Rhode Island Ave. NW
Washington, DC 20036
(202) 466-3225

WARREN, Michael W.
1425 H St. NW
Suite 410
Washington, DC 20005
(202) 783-8150

WASHINGTON, Frank G.
Arnold and Porter
1229 19th St. NW
Washington, DC 20036
(202) 872-6998

WASILEWSKI, Vincent T.
1771 N St. NW
Washington, DC 20006
(202) 293-3500

WEIDENFELD, Edward L.
Hall, Estill, Hardwick, Gable, Collingsworth &
  Nelson
1701 Pennsylvania Ave. NW
Washington, DC 20006
(202) 965-2030

WEINBERG, Arthur V.
Smith & Pepper
1776 K St. NW
Washington, DC 20006
(202) 296-0600

WEINBERG, Richard M.
Arent, Fox, Kintner, Plotkin & Kahn
1200 Federal Bar Bldg.
Washington, DC 20006
(202) 857-6401

WEINSTEIN, Stanford B.
1015 20th St. NW
Suite 200
Washington, DC 20036
(202) 466-4500

WEISS, Howard M.
Mullin, Connor and Rhyne, P.C.
Suite 1002
1000 Connecticut Ave. NW
Washington, DC 20036
(202) 783-2454

WEISSMAN, William R.
Wald, Harkrader & Ross
1320 19th St. NW
Washington, DC 20036
(202) 296-2121

WEISWASSER, Stephen A.
Wilmer, Cutler & Pickering
1666 K St. NW
Washington, DC 20006
(202) 872-6153

WEITZMAN, James M.
Stambler & Shrinsky, P.C.
1120 Connecticut Ave. NW, Suite 270
Washington, DC 20036
(202) 872-0010

WERNER, Jack
Littman, Richter, Wright & Talisman, P.C.
1050 17th St. NW
Washington, DC 20036
(202) 331-1194

WEWER, William
Sutherland, Asbill & Brennan
1666 K St. NW
Suite 800
Washington, DC 20006
(202) 872-7800

WHEATLEY, Arthur P.
1863 Kalorama Rd. NW
Apt. 4-A
Washington, DC 20009
(202) 232-9181

WHEELER, George Y.
Koteen & Burt
The Connecticut Bldg.
1150 Connecticut Ave. NW
Washington, DC 20036
(202) 467-5700

WHITE, Curtis
Hayes & White
1220 19th St. NW
Suite 503
Washington, DC 20036
(202) 452-1320

WILEY, Richard E.
Kirkland & Ellis
1776 K St. NW
Suite 1100
Washington, DC 20006
(202) 857-5020

WILHELM, Michael J.
Corp. for Public Broadcasting
111 16th St. NW
Washington, DC 20036
(202) 293-6160

WILKINSON, Glen A.
Wilkinson, Cragun & Barker
1735 New York Ave. NW
Washington, DC 20006
(202) 833-9800

WILKINSON, Vernon L.
McKenna, Wilkinson & Kittner
1150 17th St. NW
Washington, DC 20036
(202) 296-1600

WILLIAMSON, Thomas S., Jr.
Covington & Burling
888 16th St. NW
Washington, DC 20006
(202) 293-3300

WILLIS, John W.
Pike & Fischer, Inc.
2000 L St. NW
Washington, DC 20036
(202) 223-4880

WILLIS, Robert M.
C&P Telephone Co.
1710 H St. NW
Suite 716
Washington, DC 20006
(202) 565-6082

WILNER, John R.
Wilner & Scheiner
2021 L St. NW
Washington, DC 20036
(202) 293-7800

WILNER, Morton H.
Wilner & Scheiner
2021 L St. NW
Washington, DC 20036
(202) 293-7800

WINKLER, Ronald L.
Sutherland, Asbill & Brennan
1666 K St. NW
Washington, DC 20006
(202) 872-7800

WOLLENBERG, J. Roger
Wilmer, Cutler & Pickering
1666 K St. NW
Washington, DC 20006
(202) 872-6220

WOODS, Robert A.
Schwartz & Woods
Suite 206, The Palladium
1325 18th St. NW
Washington, DC 20036
(202) 833-2350

WOODS, Warren
Wilson, Woods & Villalon
425 13th St. NW
Suite 1032, Pennsylvania Bldg.
Washington, DC 20004
(202) 628-4600

WOODWORTH, Ramsey L.
Hedrick & Lane
1211 Connecticut Ave. NW
Washington, DC 20036
(202) 628-5923

WYCKOFF, Richard E.
National Association of Broadcasters
1771 N St. NW
Washington, DC 20036
(202) 293-3500

YOUNG, Lloyd D.
Chadbourne, Parke, Whiteside & Wolff
1150 17th St. NW
Washington, DC 20036
(202) 872-8050

YOURSHAW, Michael
Kirkland & Ellis
1776 K St. NW
Washington, DC 20006
(202) 857-5028

ZARAGOZA, Richard R.
Fisher, Wayland, Southmayd & Cooper
1100 Connecticut Ave. NW
Washington, DC 20036
(202) 659-3494

ZEGER, Warren Yale
COMSAT General Corp.
950 L'Enfant Plaza SW
Washington, DC 20024
(202) 554-6133

ZEIFANG, Donald P.
National Association of Broadcasters
1771 N St. NW
Washington, DC 20036
(202) 293-2152

ZEVNIK, Paul A.
Covington & Burling
888 16th St. NW
Washington, DC 20006
(202) 452-6296

ZIEGLER, Arnold G.
2120 L St. NW
Washington, DC 20037
(202) 659-0830

ZWICKY, Warren C.
Storer Broadcasting Co.
1220 19th St. NW
Washington, DC 20036
(202) 296-3340

ZYLSTRA, Roger E.
Cole, Zylstra & Raywid
1919 Pennsylvania Ave. NW
Suite 200
Washington, DC 20006
(202) 659-9750

FLORIDA

Jensen Beach
SMITH, George S.
2556 N.E. Letitia
Jensen Beach, FL 33457
(305) 334-3892

Key Biscayne
ALBERTSON, Fred W.
310 Harbor Dr.
Key Biscayne, FL 33149
(305) 361-1614

Miami
BARFIELD, William B.
666 N.W. 79th Ave.
Room 630
Miami, FL 33126
(305) 263-3551

PILAFIAN, James
Pilafian Bldg.
200 S.W. 2nd Ave.
Miami, FL 33130
(305) 371-1773

Miami Beach
CHURCH, Abiah A.
Storer Broadcasting Co.
1177 Kane Concourse
Bay Harbor Island
Miami Beach, FL 33154
(305) 866-0211

McCOY, John E.
Storer Broadcasting Co.
1177 Kane Concourse
Bay Harbor Island
Miami Beach, FL 33154
(305) 866-0211

STRAIT, Loraine H.
Storer Broadcasting Co.
1177 Kane Concourse
Miami Beach. FL 33154
(305) 866-0211

Orlando
FONS, John P.
AT&T
6039 S. Rio Grande Ave.
Orlando, FL 32809
(305) 351-8108

MURRELL, Sam E., Jr.
Sam E. Murrell & Sons
1 N. Rosalind
P.O. Box 1748
Orlando, FL 32804
(305) 843-8500

MURRELL, William, Jr.
1904 W. Colonial Dr.
Orlando, FL 32804
(305) 841-4174

Palm Beach
BUCHER, H.I.
350 Royal Palm Way
Palm Beach, FL 33480
(305) 833-6110

Stuart
SCOTT, William Ralph
P.O. Box 2057
Stuart, FL 33494
(305) 287-3303

Tampa
CARIDEO, James V.
General Telephone Co. of Florida
P.O. Box 110
Tampa, FL 33601
(813) 224-4011

FOWLER, Cody
P.O. Box 1438
220 Madison St.
Tampa, FL 33601
(813) 228-7411

GEORGIA

Atlanta
FINE, Joseph J.
Fine & Block
100 Colony Sq.
Suite 1905
1175 Peachtree St.
Atlanta, GA 30361
(404) 892-7160

GORDON, Richard M.
Smith, Harman, Asbill, Roach & Nellis, P.C.
Suite 555, Day Bldg.
2751 Buford Hwy.
Atlanta, GA 30324
(404) 325-5555

MOELING, Walter G., IV
Powell, Goldstein, Frazer & Murphy
1100 Citizens & Southern National Bldg.
35 Broad St.
Atlanta, GA 30303
(404) 521-1900

ILLINOIS

Bloomington
MAULSON, Vernon C.
1312 E. Empire St.
Bloomington, IL 61701
(309) 829-8911

Chicago
COLLIAS, George A.
Century Broadcasting Corp.
875 N. Michigan Ave.
Chicago, IL 60611
(312) 922-1000

FAY, Raymond C.
Haley, Bader & Potts
77 W. Washington St.
Chicago, IL 60602
(312) 236-5335

FIFER, Samuel
Reuben & Procter
11 S. LaSalle St.
Chicago, IL 60603
(312) 558-5512

GRENARD, Frank M.
WBBN-AM
630 N. McClurg Ct.
Chicago, IL 60611
(312) 944-6000

HESTER, Thomas P.
Illinois Bell Telephone Co.
225 W. Randolph, Floor 27
Chicago, IL 60606
(312) 727-3513

LEHNER, Paul E.
Adams, Fox, Marcus, Adelstein & Gerding
208 S. LaSalle St.
Chicago, IL 60604
(312) 346-7731

MAHER, David W.
Reuben & Procter
11 S. LaSalle St.
Chicago, IL 60603
(312) 558-5510

MINOW, Newton N.
Sidney & Austin
1 First National Plaza
Chicago, IL 60603
(312) 329-5555

MOSER, John B.
Moser and Compere
875 N. Michigan Ave.
Suite 3653
Chicago, IL 60611
(312) 266-8140

OVERTON, George W.
105 W. Adams St.
Chicago, IL 60603
(312) 236-6945

REUBEN, Don H.
Reuben & Procter
11 S. LaSalle St.
Chicago, IL 60603
(312) 558-5555

SUJACK, Edwin T.
Kirkland & Ellis
200 E. Randolph Dr.
Chicago, IL 60601
(312) 726-2929

Clarendon Hills
DWYER, James, Jr.
5 Blodgett
Clarendon Hills, IL 60514
(312) 920-1169

Northlake
BAISLEY, James M.
GTE Automatic Electric, Inc.
400 N. Wolf Rd.
Northlake, IL 60164
(312) 562-7100

Schaumburg
SPENCER, Lewis D.
1303 E. Algonquin Rd.
Schaumburg, IL 60196

INDIANA

Indianapolis
BETLEY, Leonard J.
Ice, Miller, Donaldio & Ryan
111 Monument Circle
10th Floor
Indianapolis, IN 46204
(317) 635-1213

SMULVAN, Jeffrey Howard
S & M Broadcasting
4800 E. Raymond St.
Indianapolis, IN 46203
(317) 359-5591

IOWA

Des Moines
FISHER, Thomas George
Meredith Corp.
Des Moines, IA 50336
(515) 284-9166

GERLACH, Gary G.
Secretary & General Counsel
Des Moines Register & Tribune Co.
715 Locust St.
Des Moines, IA 50304
(515) 284-8112

Iowa Falls
WHITESELL, John P.
P.O. Box 1034
Iowa Falls, IA 50126
(515) 648-4646

KANSAS

Wichita
JONES, Charles E.
301 American Savings Bldg.
201 N. Main, P.O. Box 1034
Wichita, KS 67202
(316) 265-8591

LOUISIANA

Metairie
CARNEY, John
Jones, Walker, Waechter, Poitevent, Carrere &
   Denegre
3501 N. Causeway Blvd.
Metairie, LA 70002
(504) 837-5325

HARDY, Ashton R.
Jones, Walker, Waechter, Poitevent, Carrere &
   Denegre
3501 N. Causeway Blvd.
Metairie, LA 70002
(504) 837-5325

New Orleans
COLEMAN, James J.
321 St. Charles Ave.
10th Floor Suite
New Orleans, LA 70130
(504) 529-5652

DENECHAUD, Charles, I., Jr.
Denechaud & Denechaud
1412 Pere Marquette Bldg.
New Orleans, LA 70112
(504) 525-1344

VOELKER, Richard L., Jr.
Voelker & Jeffers
620 First National Bank of Commerce Bldg.
New Orleans, LA 70112
(504) 581-7471

WEGMANN, Edward F.
1047 National Bank of Commerce Bldg.
New Orleans, LA 70112
(504) 524-0732

MARYLAND

Baltimore
SARVER, James W.
C&P Telephone Co.
1 E. Pratt St.
8th Floor, East Wing
Baltimore, MD 21202
(301) 393-7725

Bethesda
HODSON, Robert E.
6204 Stardust La.
Bethesda, MD 20034
(301) 229-3225

SLOANE, A. Richard
8535 W. Howell Rd.
Bethesda, MD 20910

WILSON, Thomas W.
5315 Edgemoor La.
Bethesda, MD 20014
(301) 652-7082

Chevy Chase
BARNES, John Peter
3711 Cardiff Rd.
Chevy Chase, MD 20015
(301) 652-6868

HOUSE, Arthur G.
8401 Connecticut Ave. NW
Suite 1212
Chevy Chase, MD 20015
(301) 654-1181

Frederick
COLBY, Lauren A.
15 N. Court St.
Frederick, MD 21701
(301) 663-1086

Germantown
CAMPBELL, Michael D.
American Satellite Corp.
20301 Century Blvd.
Germantown, MD 20767
(301) 428-6338

DEALY, John Francis
Sherman Fairchild Technical Center
Germantown, MD 20767
(301) 948-9600

Rockville
SUTTON, George O.
10201 Grosvenor La.
Rockville, MD 20852
(301) 493-4142

Silver Spring
BELISLE, Joseph A.
#327, 1600 East-West Hwy.
Silver Spring, MD 20910
(301) 589-0160

Upper Marlboro
PARKER, Ellis, III
Taylor, Smith & Parker
14762 Main St.
Box 216
Upper Marlboro, MD 20870
(301) 627-5315

MASSACHUSETTS

Boston
ALDRICH, C. Duane
New England Telephone Co.
185 Franklin St.
Boston, MA 02107
(617) 743-5745

BLACKBURN, Richard
New England Telephone Co.
185 Franklin St.
Boston, MA 02107
(617) 743-7030

DAVENPORT, Harry A., III
New England Telephone Co.
185 Franklin St., Room 1600
Boston, MA 02107
(617) 743-2323

PIEMONTE, Gabriel F.
213 Hanover St.
Boston, MA 02113
(617) 227-8380

Cambridge
BRANSCOMB, Anne Wells
Chairman of the Board
Kalba Bowen Associates, Inc.
12 Arrow St.
Cambridge, MA 02138
(617) 661-2624

Woburn
BIGELOW, Robert P.
100 Tower Office Park
Woburn, MA 01801
(617) 935-9200

SALTZBERG, Edward C.
100 Tower Office Park
Woburn, MA 01801
(617) 935-9200

MINNESOTA

Minneapolis
GOLDMAN, David J.
2255 Dain Tower
Minneapolis, MN 55402
(612) 339-3700

JAEGAR, Hugh D.
1614 IDS Center
Minneapolis, MN 55402
(612) 339-8331

St. Paul
DIXON, William M.
Hubbard Broadcasting, Inc.
3415 University Ave.
St. Paul, MN 55114
(612) 645-2724

GECK, Donna D.
Hubbard Broadcasting, Inc.
3415 University Ave.
St. Paul, MN 55114
(612) 645-2724

MISSISSIPPI

Holly Springs
COLE, Ben Thomas, II
117 A College Ave.
Holly Springs, MS 38635
(601) 252-2278

Jackson
McCLENDON, B.B., Jr.
McClendon & McClendon
903 Deposit Guaranty Bank Bldg.
Jackson, MS 39201
(601) 948-5656

Oxford
CHAMBLISS, Alvin O.
N. Mississippi Rural Legal Services, Inc.
P.O. Box 826
Oxford, MS 38655
(601) 234-2918

JOSEPH, Wilhelm H.
N. Mississippi Rural Legal Services, Inc.
P.O. Box 826
Oxford, MS 38655
(601) 234-2918

McCLELLAN, Leonard
N. Mississippi Rural Legal Services, Inc.
P.O. Box 826
Oxford, MS 38655
(601) 234-2918

MYERS, Lewis, Jr.
N. Mississippi Rural Legal Services, Inc.
P.O. Box 826
Oxford, MS 38655
(601) 234-2918

West Point
OSBORNE, Solomon Curtis
P.O. Box 277
West Point, MS 39773
(601) 494-6122

MISSOURI

Kansas City
BAKER, Warren E.
United Telecommunications, Inc.
P.O. Box 11315
Kansas City, MO 64112
(913) 676-3308

CROKER, Richard J.
United Telecommunications, Inc.
P.O. Box 11315
Kansas City, MO 64112
(913) 676-3372

MARGOLIN, James S.
Margolin & Kirwan
1000 United Missouri Bank Bldg.
Kansas City, MO 64106
(816) 842-7080

St. Louis
BABLER, Wayne E.
1010 Pine St.
St. Louis, MO 63101
(314) 247-4492

JACOBS, Richard M.
Box 12705
St. Louis, MO 63141
(314) 721-5321

PARKER, Norman C.
c/o Flynn, Parker & Badaracco
319 N. 4th St.
St. Louis, MO 63102
(314) 231-8282

NEBRASKA

Omaha
McSHANE, James E.
2435 Fontenelle Blvd.
Omaha, NB 68104

MITCHELL, John G.
John C. Mitchell Law Offices
10407 Devonshire Circle
Suite 150
Omaha, NB 68114
(402) 397-9950

NEW HAMPSHIRE

Keene
CLOSE, Elmer Harry
P.O. Box 466
Keene, NH 03431
(603) 352-9230

Peterborough
SWEENEY, Walter H.
26A Concord St.
Peterborough, NH 03458
(603) 924-7153

Tilton
CIANELLI, Paul R.
New England Cable TV Association
P.O. Box 321
Tilton, NH 03276
(603) 286-4473

NEW JERSEY

Bedminster
BOONE, Robert E., Jr.
AT&T
Room 3C-165
Bedminster, NJ 07921
(201) 234-6317

FEIGENBAUM, Bennett
AT&T Long Lines
Bedminster, NJ 07921
(201) 234-6304

FISHER, Saul
AT&T Long Lines
P.O. Box 32
Bedminster, NJ 07921
(201) 234-6316

MAYFIELD, Edgar
AT&T Long Lines
Room 4B-112
Bedminster, NJ 07921
(201) 234-6300

RAFTIS, Edmund B.
AT&T
Room 3C-163
Bedminster, NJ 07921
(201) 234-6370

East Brunswick
MILEWSKI, Thomas J.
Greater Media, Inc.
197 Highway 18
East Brunswick, NJ 08816
(201) 247-6161

Piscataway
CANGELOSI, Carl J.
General Counsel
RCA American Communications, Inc.
201 Centennial Ave.
Piscataway, NJ 08854
(201) 855-4446

ELLIS, David R.
RCA American Communications, Inc.
201 Centennial Ave.
Piscataway, NJ 08854
(201) 885-4441

Short Hills
DREYER, Robert A.
6 Park Rd.
Short Hills, NJ 07078
(201) 376-7111

South Plainfield
SANTORO, Edward J.
304 Maple Ave.
South Plainfield, NJ 07080
(201) 756-0785

Tenafly
DWYER, Albert Hayden
188 Engle St.
Tenafly, NJ 07670
(201) 567-0335

Trenton
HAGGERTY, Daniel L., III
Stark & Stark, P.C.
Broad Bank St. Bldg.
Trenton, NJ 08608
(609) 989-7510

Voorhees Township
STRAUSS, Samuel W.
22 Alpha Ave.
Voorhees Township, NJ 08043
(609) 795-7878

NEW YORK

Armonk
WALTER, John Gordon
IBM Corp.
Old Orchard Rd.
Armonk, NY 10504
(914) 765-3640

Batavia
HOLLOWAY, Eugene C., III
Senior Counsel
GTE Consumer Electronics
Products Business
700 Ellicott St.
Batavia, NY 10420
(716) 343-3470

Buffalo
SWADOS, Robert
70 Niagara St.
Buffalo, NY 14202
(716) 856-4600

Larchmont
PARK, Robert J.
8 Oxford Rd.
Larchmont, NY 10538
(914) 834-1160

New York City
ABRAHAMS, Howard
Meredith Corp.
747 3rd Ave.
New York, NY 10017
(212) 688-7300

ABRAMS, Floyd
Cahill, Gordon & Reindel
80 Pine St.
New York, NY 10005
(212) 944-7400

AGRESS, Ellen Shaw
National Broadcasting Co.
30 Rockefeller Plaza
New York, NY 10020
(212) 664-3305

APPLEWHAITE, Eleanor S.
CBS, Inc.
Law Department
51 W. 52nd St.
New York, NY 10009
(212) 765-4321

ASHLEY, George E.
New York Telephone Co.
1095 Ave. of the Americas
New York, NY 10036
(212) 395-2311

BECKER, Mortimer
Becker and London
15 Columbus Circle
New York, NY 10023
(212) 541-7070

BERKMAN, Jack N.
22 E. 64th St.
New York, NY 10021
(212) 752-5532

BERKOWITZ, Morris
LIN Broadcasting Corp.
1370 Ave. of the Americas
New York, NY 10019
(212) 765-1902

BERLIN, Edward B.
Citibank, N.A.
399 Park Ave.
New York, NY 10022
(212) 559-7488

BILLINGSLEY, James R.
AT&T
195 Broadway
New York, NY 10007
(212) 393-4343

BLUMENFELD, Seth D.
Western Union International, Inc.
26 Broadway
New York, NY 10004
(212) 363-6400

BOROS, Jerome S.
Fly, Shuebruk, Blume, Gaguine, Boros & Schulkind
45 Rockefeller Plaza
New York, NY 10020
(212) 247-3040

BURKE, Raymond F.
New York Telephone Co.
1095 Ave. of the Americas
New York, NY 10036
(212) 394-4141

BURSTEIN, Herbert
1 World Trade Center
Suite 2373
New York, NY 10048
(212) 432-0940

BUSTARD, R. David
RKO General, Inc.
1440 Broadway
New York, NY 10018
(212) 764-7000

CHOPNICK, Max
9 E. 46th St.
New York, NY 10017
(212) 697-8130

CLANCY, Donald E.
51 W. 52nd St.
New York, NY 10019
(212) 765-4321

CODLIN, Dennis E.
Westinghouse Broadcasting Co., Inc.
90 Park Ave.
New York, NY 10016
(212) 983-6500

CONN, Robert E.
Western Union International, Inc.
26 Broadway
New York, NY 10004
(212) 363-6406

CUTCLIFF, Lee S.
AT&T
195 Broadway
New York, NY 10007
(212) 393-9800

DABNEY, Jean M.
AT&T
195 Broadway, Room 2514
New York, NY 10007
(212) 393-2217 or 4601

DAVIS, John R.
AT&T
Legal Dept., Room 2529
195 Broadway
New York, NY 10007
(212) 393-4246

DeROSA, Francis J.H.
RCA Global Communications, Inc.
60 Broad St.
New York, NY 10004
(212) 363-2070

EVANS, Robert V.
12 E. 41st Street
New York, NY 10017
(212) 685-0535

FRANKL, Kenneth R.
RKO General, Inc.
1440 Broadway
New York, NY 10018
(212) 564-8000

FREEDMAN, Robert I.
213 E. 49th St.
New York, NY 10017
(212) 560-3080

FRIEDMAN, Edward L
AT&T
195 Broadway, Room 2522
New York, NY 10007
(212) 393-5060

GERSON, Alan H.
NBC
30 Rockefeller Plaza
New York, NY 10020
(212) 247-8300

GODDARD, William D.
AT&T, Legal Dept.
195 Broadway
Room 2540
New York, NY 10007
(212) 393-3279

GOLDBERG, Ralph Elliot
CBS
51 W. 52nd St.
New York, NY 10019
(212) 765-4321

GOLDEY, Michael J.
AT&T
195 Broadway
New York, NY 10007
(212) 393-2220

GOLDFARB, Elisha
Regan, Goldfarb, Heller, Wetzler & Quinn
445 Park Ave.
New York, NY 10022
(212) 754-3000

GOLDSTEIN, Ira J.
1271 Ave. of the Americas
New York, NY 10020
(212) 246-3700

GREEN, Alfred A.
AT&T
195 Broadway, Room 2522
New York, NY 10007
(212) 393-9800

GREENE, William D.
Burns, Van Kirk, Green & Kafer
521 5th Ave.
New York, NY 10017
(212) 972-0500

HAMBURG, Morton I.
767 5th Ave.
Suite 3809
New York, NY 10022
(212) 838-0424

HARTGROVE, Richard C.
AT&T
195 Broadway, Room 2506
New York, NY 10017
(212) 393-3784

HECKER, Stuart
521 Fifth Ave.
New York, NY 10017
(212) 682-7070

HOKENSON, H. John
AT&T
195 Broadway, Room 2536
New York, NY 10007
(212) 393-4434

JANKLOW, Morton L.
Janklow & Traum
375 Park Ave.
New York, NY 10022
(212) 421-1700

JANNEY, Oliver J.
Law Department
RKO General, Inc.
1440 Broadway
New York, NY 10018
(212) 764-6729

KATKIN, Burton K.
AT&T
195 Broadway, Room 2555
New York, NY 10007
(212) 393-5380

KAUFMAN, Alan B.
Fly, Shuebruk, Blume, Gaguine, Boros & Schulkind
45 Rockefeller Plaza
New York, NY 10020
(212) 247-3040

KAYE, Sydney M.
Rosenman, Colin, Kaye, Petschek, Freund & Emil
575 Madison Ave.
New York, NY 10022
(212) 688-7800

KOLEVZON, Peter S.
919 3rd Ave.
New York, NY 10022
(212) 688-1100

KRETSCHMANN, Paul H.
567 81st St.
New York, NY 11209
(212) 748-7145

LANDAU, Sandra E.
Viacom Enterprises
1211 Ave. of the Americas
New York, NY 10036
(212) 575-5175

LEHRHAUPT, Charles M.
RCA Global Communications, Inc.
60 Broad St.
New York, NY 10004
(212) 363-2073

LEVY, Harold S.
AT&T
195 Broadway
New York, NY 10007
(212) 393-9800

LIGHTSTONE, Ronald
Viacom International, Inc.
1211 Ave. of the Americas
New York, NY 10036
(212) 575-5175

MAHONY, Sheila
Carnegie Commission on the Future of Public
  Broadcasting
1270 Avenue of the Americas
New York, NY 10020
(212) 245-2700

MARKEL, Robinson
Migrim, Thonajan & Jacobs
25 Broadway
New York, NY 10004
(212) 371-6000

McDOUGALD, Cornelia
AT&T
195 Broadway, Room 2538
New York, NY 10007
(212) 393-3526

McFADDEN, Douglas
AT&T
195 Broadway
New York, NY 10007
(212) 393-9800, ext. 3558

McGUIRE, Timothy S.
RCA Global Communications, Inc.
60 Broad St.
New York, NY 10004
(212) 363-2072

MOORE, Earle K.
Moore, Berson & Lifflander
555 Madison Ave.
New York, NY 10022
(212) 838-0600

MOULTON, Horace P.
195 Broadway
New York, NY 10807
(212) 785-1000

MURPHY, Eugene F.
RCA Global Communications, Inc.
60 Broad St.
New York, NY 10004
(212) 363-2071

MURRAY, Richard H.
c/o Touche, Ross & Co.
1633 Broadway
New York, NY 10019
(212) 489-1600

PARTOLL, Alfred C.
AT&T
195 Broadway, Room 2555
New York, NY 10007
(212) 393-4811

PRESTON, John F., Jr.
AT&T
195 Broadway, Room 2530
New York, NY 10007
(212) 393-5234

REDDICK, Melvin Lee
National Association of Broadcasters
30 W. 96th Street, Apt 4-H
New York, NY 10025
(212) 865-4138

REGAN, William M.
445 Park Ave.
New York, NY 10022
(212) 421-8800

ROBB, Scott Hall
Robb & Reukauf
655 Madison Ave.
New York, NY 10021
(212) PL2-5566

ROSE, Michael
CBS, Inc.
51 W. 52nd St.
New York, NY 10019
(212) 975-8422

SAFERIN, Steven Mark
Viacom International, Inc.
1211 Ave. of the Americas
New York, NY 10020
(212) 575-5175

SANDERS, Rodger M.
RCA Global Communications
60 Broad St.
New York, NY 10004
(212) 248-3451

SCHOEMER, John R., Jr.
Townley, Updike, Carter & Rodgers
200 E. 42nd St.
New York, NY 10017
(212) 682-4567

SCHOR, Edward
Meredith Corp.
747 3rd Ave.
New York, NY 10017
(212) 688-7300

SCHUMACHER, H. Richard
Cahill, Gordon & Reindel
80 Pine St.
New York, NY 10005
(212) 825-0100

SHAKLAN, Allen Yale
CBS Inc.
51 W. 52nd St.
New York, NY
(212) 765-4321

SHUEBRUK, Peter
Fly, Shuebruk, Blume, Gaguine, Boros & Schulkind
45 Rockefeller Plaza
New York, NY 10020
(212) 247-3040

SHUTE, John V.
NBC
30 Rockefeller Plaza
New York, NY 10020
(212) 664-4017

SOLINGER, David M.
Solinger & Gordon
250 Park Ave.
New York, NY 10017
(212) 687-1140

STEADMAN, Frank M., Jr.
AT&T
195 Broadway
New York, NY 10007
(212) 393-4894

STEIN, F. Robert
CBS, Inc., Law Department
52 W. 52nd St.
New York, NY 10019
(212) 765-4321

STERNBACH, Paul N.
Burns, Van Kirk, Greene & Kafer
521 5th Ave.
New York, NY 10017
(212) 972-0500

TAYLOR, Willis H., Jr.
330 Madison Ave.
New York, NY 10017
(212) 986-8686

TRAUM, Jerome S.
Janklow & Traum
375 Park Ave.
New York, NY 10022
(212) 421-1700

TRUNK, Carl F., Jr.
NBC
Legal Dept., Room 626
30 Rockefeller Center
New York, NY 10001
(212) 247-8300

VALENTINE, Franklin R., Jr.
SelecTVision, Inc.
1 Dag Hammarskjold Plaza
New York, NY 10017
(212) 572-5328

VAN WAGENEN, H. William
Westinghouse Broadcasting Co., Inc.
90 Park Ave.
New York, NY 10016
(212) 983-6500

WEAVER, Henry B., Jr.
Atlantic Richfield Co.
717 5th Ave.
New York, NY 10022
(212) 758-2345

WELS, Richard H.
18 E. 48th St.
New York, NY 10017
(212) 689-6450

WERNER, Robert L.
116 E. 68th St.
New York, NY 10020
(212) 661-3200

WHITE, Howard A.
ITT World Communications
67 Broad St.
New York, NY 10004
(212) 797-3300

WHOLL, Edward R.
New York Telephone Co.
1095 Ave. of the Americas
New York, NY 10036
(212) 395-2468

WILKERSON, Ernest
Center for Advanced Legal Training
Suite 432
11 W. 42nd St.
New York, NY 10036
(212) 221-1096

Rye
ESTES, Robert M.
66 Island Dr.
Rye, NY 10580
(212) 751-1311 X2508

NORTH CAROLINA

Albemarle
BLALOCK, Steven F.
Brown, Brown & Brown
P.O. Box 400
Albemarle, NC 28001
(704) 982-2141

Raleigh
HARGROVE, Wade H.
Tharrington, Smith & Hargrove
BB&T Bldg. Suite 300
Raleigh, NC 27602
(919) 821-4711

Winston-Salem
BINION, Emily Evelyn Helm
P.O. Box 5197
Winston-Salem, NC 27102
(919) 768-9437

BOND, Clifford, J., III
P.O. Box 5772
Winston-Salem, NC 27103
(919) 727-1255

SMITHWICK, Gary S.
First Center Bldg., Suite 409
Winston-Salem, NC 27104
(919) 724-3975

OHIO

Columbus
DUNBAR, Frank C., Jr.
250 E. Broad St.
Midland Bldg.
Columbus, OH 43215
(614) 228-4371

JONES, John Robert
100 E. Broad St.
Columbus, OH 43215
(614) 221-7863

McCONNAUGHEY, George C.
George, Greek, King, McMahon & McConnaughey
Columbus Center
100 E. Broad St.
Columbus, OH 43215
(614) 228-1541

OKLAHOMA

Oklahoma City
CLARO, John A.
Barefoot, Moler & Claro
3000 City National Bank Tower
Oklahoma City, OK 73102
(405) 232-3566

OREGON

Portland
BULLIVANT, Rupert R.
527 Pacific Bldg.
Portland, OR 97204
(503) 228-6351

DAY, Frank E.
1103 Georgia-Pacific Bldg.
Portland, OR 97204
(503) 221-1040

GARDNER, Alan Joel
Pacific Northwest & Bell Telephone Co.
421 S.W. Oak
Room 853
Portland, OR 97204
(503) 224-6261

PENNSYLVANIA

Erie
ENGLISH, John W.
English, Bowler & Jenks
162 W. 6th St.
P.O. Box 1560
Erie, PA 16501
(814) 454-4533

Philadelphia
CLARKE, Donald F.
Bell Telephone Co. of Pennsylvania
1 Pkwy.
Philadelphia, PA 19102
(215) 466-5481

CONNOLLY, Patrick M.
Dilworth, Paxson, Kalish, Levy & Kauffman
2600—The Fidelity Bldg.
Philadelphia, PA 19109
(215) 546-3000

McGONAGLE, John J., Jr.
c/o INA
1600 Arch St.
Philadelphia, PA 19101
(215) 241-2527

PUTNEY, Paul William
Dechert, Price & Rhoads
3400 Centre Square W.
1500 Market St.
Philadelphia, PA 19102
(215) 972-3629

SEGA, Bernard G.
Schnader, Harrison, Segal & Lewis
1719 Packard Bldg.
Philadelphia, PA 19102
(215) 491-0405

SEGAL, Irving R.
Schnader, Harrison, Segal & Lewis
1719 Packard Bldg.
Philadelphia, PA 19102
(215) 491-0405

SIMPKINS, John Paul
320 Robinson Bldg.
42 S. 15th St.
Philadelphia, PA 19102
(215) 103-2977

Pittsburgh
POLNER, Frederick A.
1203 Commonwealth Bldg.
Pittsburgh, PA 15222
(412) 261-2690

Pittston
BOLLER, Charles Albert
Channel 44, WVIA-TV/FM
The Public Broadcasting Center
Pittston, PA 18640
(717) 655-4561

PUERTO RICO

Humacao
ARCHILLA-ROIG, Efrain
Box C
Humacao, PR 00661
(809) 852-1230

SOUTH CAROLINA

Columbia
DUNBAR, James V., Jr.
Berry, Dunbar, Gibbes & Woods
1325 Laurel St.
P.O. Box 11645
Columbia, SC 29211
(803) 765-1030

Waterboro
McLEOD, W.J., Jr
Jefferies Blvd. & Washington St.
Waterboro, SC 29488
(803) 549-6811

SOUTH DAKOTA

Pierre
TOBIAS, Marc Weber
Box 941
Pierre, SD 57501
(605) 224-3215

TENNESSEE

Memphis
BAIRD, John Thomas
2714 Union Ave. Extended
Box 712
Memphis, TN 38112
(901) 320-4248

Oak Ridge
PERRY, Larry D.
Layton & Perry
101 E. Tennessee
P.O. Box 461
Oak Ridge, TN 37830
(615) 483-8474

STONE, Robert S.
Layton & Perry
101 E. Tennessee
P.O. Box 461
Oak Ridge, TN 37830
(615) 483-8474

TEXAS

Dallas
HOWARD, Gerald M.
P.O. Box 7689
Dallas, TX 75209
(214) 691-3608

Fort Worth
HERMAN, Morton L.
Brown, Herman, Scott, Dean & Miles
Forth Worth Club Bldg.
Suite 203
Fort Worth, TX 76102
(817) 332-1248

Houston
LOFTUS, William Robert
Vice Pres. & General Counsel
Taft Broadcasting Corp.
4808 San Felipe
Houston, TX 77056
(713) 622-1724

RUDDY, Francis S.
Exxon Company, U.S.A.
P.O. Box 2180
Houston, TX 77001
(713) 656-3636

SPAWN, Coy U., Jr.
733 Bankers Mortgage Bldg.
Houston, TX 77002
(713) 222-0105

San Antonio
SANDOVAL, Ruben
523 S. Main St.
San Antonio, TX 78204
(512) 224-1061

WELLS, J. Tullos
Law Offices of Les Mendelsohn, Inc.
711 Navarro St., Suite 255
San Antonio Bank & Trust Bldg.
San Antonio, TX 78205
(512) 222-2271

UTAH

Salt Lake City
AFFLECK, Gordon Burt
c/o KSL, Inc.
145 Social Hall Ave.
Salt Lake City, UT 84111
(801) 524-2500

VIRGINIA

Alexandria
BROWNSTEIN, Irving
124–126 S. Royal St.
Alexandria, VA 22314
(703) 548-8100

DELANEY, Paul L.
115 N. Fairfax
Alexandria, VA 22314
(703) 683-4200

KIMBALL, Clark
1337 Chetworth Ct.
Alexandria, VA 22314

PAUL, Ray R.
P.O. Box 11252
Alexandria, VA 22312
(703) 941-6501

Arlington
JACKSON, William P., Jr.
Jackson & Jessup
3426 N. Washington Blvd.
P.O. Box 267
Arlington, VA 22201
(703) 525-4050

JONES, Douglas N.
P.O. Box 582
Court House Station
Arlington, VA 22216
(703) 578-1346

KREUTZER, Arthur C.
National LP-Gas Association
1800 N. Kent St.
Arlington, VA 22209
(703) 525-5135

Fairfax
CHRISTENSEN, Thomas M.P.
3609 Prosperity Ave.
Fairfax, VA 22031
(703) 280-5558

SHELESKY, Raymond J.
Christensen & Shelesky
4084 University Dr.
Suite 102
Fairfax, VA 22030
(703) 273-0540

Falls Church
BURKE, Eugene L.
7777 Leesburg Pike
Falls Church, VA 22043
(703) 536-9200

Leesburg
SWEZEY, Robert D.
P.O. Box 1631
Leesburg, VA 22075
(703) 777-7277

Lynchburg
BAKER, Raymond E.
Communications Systems Div.
General Electric Co.
Lynchburg, VA 24505
(804) 846-7311

McLean
ELARDO, Donald J.
Satellite Business Systems
8003 Westpark Dr.
McLean, VA 22102
(703) 827-1713

ENGLISH, William de Shay
Satellite Business Systems
8003 Westpark Dr.
McLean, VA 22101
(703) 827-2000

HUNSAKER, David Malcolm
Putbrese & Kennedy
McLean House, Suite 100
6800 Fleetwood Rd.
McLean, VA 22101
(703) 790-8400

KENNEDY, Richard F.
Putbrese & Kennedy
6800 Fleetwood Dr.
Suite 100
McLean, VA 22101
(703) 790-8400

TUTTLE, Thomas F.
Satellite Business Systems
8003 Westpark Dr.
P.O. Box 908
McLean, VA 22101
(703) 827-2085

Reston
TOTH, Victor John
Toth & Mahn
11800 Sunrise Valley Dr.
Suite 1111
Reston, VA 22090
(703) 476-5515

Richmond
BRUNDAGE, Warner F., Jr.
C&P Telephone Co. of Virginia
703 E. Grace St.
Richmond, VA 23219
(804) 772-3104

FEELY, F. Joseph, III
C&P Telephone Co. of Virginia
703 E. Grace St.
Richmond, VA 23219
(804) 772-2473

Springfield
PELLEGRIN, John D.
6703 Bracken Ct.
Springfield, VA 22152
(703) 569-0029

Vienna
WALKER, Philip M.
Telenet Communications Corp.
8330 Old Courthouse Rd.
Vienna, VA 22180
(703) 827-9275

WASHINGTON

Everett
MARPLE, Jon
KRKO Radio
P.O. Box 1228
Everett, WA 98206
(206) 355-1144

Olympia
SILVA, James R.
Highways Licenses Bldg.
Olympia, WA 98504
(206) 491-6531

Seattle
GETZENDANER, Mark A.
17430 Ballinger Way NE
Seattle, WA 98155
(206) 363-7456

GOLDSTEIN, David Bennett
Davis, Wright, Todd, Riese & Jones
4200 Seattle First National Bank Bldg.
Seattle, WA 98154
(206) 622-3150

MURPHY, James A.
Ogden, Ogden & Murphy
1411 4th Avenue Bldg.
Seattle, WA 98101
(206) 622-2991

WEST VIRGINIA

SHOTT, Ned E.
412 Bland St.
Bluefield, WV 24701
(304) 327-6171

WISCONSIN

Green Bay
WELIN, Mark Sander
WBAY Television
115 S. Jefferson St.
Green Bay, WI 54301
(414) 432-3331

Milwaukee
BREIT, A. Thomas
722 N. Broadway
Milwaukee, WI 53202
(414) 393-2151

POSNER, Gene
152 W. Wisconsin Ave.
Milwaukee, WI 53203
(414) 276-7440

WYOMING

Torrington
JONES, Donald E.
Donald E. Jones Law Offices
108 E. 20th Ave.
Torrington, WY 82240
(307) 532-5523

Broadcast Libraries

Since libraries devoted to or specializing in communications and related fields differ in their holdings and their policies toward public use, patrons are advised to phone for information on what is available to them.

ARIZONA

University of Arizona
Main Library
Tucson, AZ 85721
(601) 626-2101

CALIFORNIA

American Film Institute
501 Doheny Rd.
Beverly Hills, CA 90210
(213) 278-8777

National Academy of Television Arts and Sciences
(NATAS)–UCLA Television Library
Melnitz Hall
University of California
Los Angeles, CA 90024
(213) 825-4480

University of California—Los Angeles
Research Library
405 Hilgard Ave.
Los Angeles, CA 90024
(213) 825-1323

University of California—Los Angeles
Theater Arts Library
22478 Research Library
Los Angeles, CA 90024
(213) 825-4880

California State University—Sacramento
Library of Science and Technology
Reference Dept.
2000 Jed Smith Dr.
Sacramento, CA 95819
(916) 454-6373

University of California—Santa Barbara
Santa Barbara Library
Santa Barbara, CA 93106
(805) 961-2674

Stanford University
Mendenhall Communications Library
Stanford, CA 94305
(415) 497-1789

University of Southern California
Edward L. Doheny Memorial Library
University Park, CA 90007
(213) 741-6050

Whittier College
Learning Resources Center
13406 E. Philadelphia St.
Whittier, CA 90608
(213) 693-0771

COLORADO

University of Denver
Penrose Library
2150 E. Evans
Denver, CO 80210
(303) 753-2212

DISTRICT OF COLUMBIA

American Film Institute
The John F. Kennedy Center for the Performing
  Arts
Washington, DC 20566
(202) 828-4088

American University
Battelle-Tompkins Memorial Library
Massachusetts & Nebraska Aves. NW
Washington, DC 20016
(202) 686-2323

Broadcast Pioneers Library
1771 N St. NW
Washington, DC 20036
(202) 223-0088

Library of Congress
Divisions for the Blind & Physically Handicapped
Taylor Annex
1291 Taylor St. NW
Washington, DC 20542
(202) 882-5500

National Association of Broadcasters
1771 N St. NW
Washington, DC 20036
(202) 293-3500

Public Broadcasting Service (PBS)
Public Television Library
475 L'Enfant Plaza SW
Washington, DC 20024
(202) 488-5000

U.S. National Archives
7th & Pennsylvania Aves. NW
Washington, DC 20409
(202) 655-4000

GEORGIA

University of Georgia
Ila Dunlap Little Memorial Library
Jackson St.
Athens, GA 30602
(404) 542-2716

Tri-County Regional Library
606 W. 1st St.
Rome, GA 30161
(404) 291-9360

ILLINOIS

WBBM-TV
630 N. McClurg Ct.
Chicago, IL 60611
(312) 944-6000

INDIANA

Indiana University
Journalism Library
Ernie Pyle Hall
Bloomington, IN 47401
(812) 337-3517

MASSACHUSETTS

Williams College
Sawyer Library
Williamstown, MA 01267
(413) 597-2501

NEBRASKA

Great Plains National Instructional Television
  (ITV) Library
P.O. Box 80669
Lincoln, NB 68501
(402) 472-2007

NEW JERSEY

New Jersey Public Television
1573 Parkside Ave.
Trenton, NJ 08638
(609) 882-5252

NEW YORK

Brooklyn College
Main Library
Bedford Ave. & Ave. H
Brooklyn, NY 11210
(212) 780-5342

ABC
1330 Ave. of the Americas
New York, NY 10019
(212) 581-7777

CBS
524 W. 57th St.
New York, NY 10019
(212) 975-4321

Columbia University
Oral History Office
Box 20
Butler Library
New York, NY 10027
(212) 280-2241

NBC
30 Rockefeller Plaza
New York, NY 10020
(212) 664-4444

New School for Social Research
Center for the Study of Television and Politics
Raymond Fogelman Library
65 5th Ave.
New York, NY 10003
(212) 741-7904

New York Public Library
General Library and Museum of the Performing
  Arts
111 Amsterdam Ave.
New York, NY 10023
(212) 799-2200

New York University
Elmer Holmes Bobst Library
70 Washington Square South
New York, NY 10012
(212) 598-2484

Television Information Office
745 5th Ave.
New York, NY 10022
(212) 759-6800

Eastman House
Eastman Kodak Company Engineering Division
Rochester, NY 14650
(716) 458-1000

OHIO

Ohio University
Vernon R. Alden Library
Park Place
Athens, OH 45701
(614) 594-5141

PENNSYLVANIA

Broadcasters Promotion Association
Broadcasters Promotion Library
P.O. Box 5102
Lancaster, PA 17601
(717) 626-4524

Drexel University
Drexel Library
32nd & Chestnut Sts.
Philadelphia, PA 19104
(215) 895-2750

United Church of Christ
Office for Audio-Visuals
1501 Race St.
Philadelphia, PA 19102
(215) 568-5750 ext. 78

TENNESSEE

Vanderbilt University
Vanderbilt Television News Archives
Joint University Library
Nashville, TN 37203
(615) 322-2927

TEXAS

North Texas State University
Oral History Collection
P.O. Box 13734
NTSU Station
Denton, TX 76203
(817) 788-2558

VIRGINIA

Union Theological Seminary
Reigner Library
3401 Brook Rd.
Richmond, VA 23227
(804) 355-0671

WISCONSIN

State Historical Society of Wisconsin
Mass Communications History Center
816 State St.
Madison, WI 53706
(608) 262-9561

WYOMING

University of Wyoming
William Robertson Coe Library
13th & Iverson
Laramie, WY 82071
(307) 766-3279

The Museum of Broadcasting

THE MUSEUM OF BROADCASTING
1 E. 53rd St.
New York, NY 10022
(212) 752-4690

The Museum of Broadcasting is the first American museum dedicated to the study and preservation of the more than 50-year history of radio and television broadcasting. Through the cooperation of all the networks and of public broadcasting, the museum maintains a collection of radio and television programs from the 1920s to the present. Patrons may view or hear them at one of the museum's broadcast consoles. The museum also maintains a library of rare radio and television scripts, as well as books and periodicals on broadcasting.

The Museum of Broadcasting is open between 12:00 noon and 5:00 P.M., Tuesdays through Saturdays. The public is invited to visit during these hours to see a videotape narrated by Alistair Cooke, which introduces the museum and includes selections from the collection. Visitors may then choose radio and television programs to monitor in the Broadcast Study Center—a $1.00 contribution is suggested. Annual memberships affording free, priority use of the Museum's facilities are also available.

During the morning hours, the museum is reserved for use by classes. It also offers lectures and holds seminars for colleges and universities and sponsors a number of special programs, bringing members together with people who have new insights into broadcasting's history, effects, and prospects.

Among the museum's acquisitions are some of the earliest broadcasts in existence. The collection contains speeches by each of the ten Presidents of the United States since Warren G. Harding.

Thirty-eight of Herbert Hoover's and Franklin D. Roosevelt's speeches from the 1932 campaign are included, as well as a full complement of Roosevelt's preserved statements, starting with one made in 1920. Rare musical, comedy, and dramatic material from the 1920's has also been acquired.

The museum has tapes of two entire days of broadcasting—one from the beginning of World War II (September 21, 1939) and one from V-J Day (August 14, 1945). Of special interest is a collection of propaganda broadcasts made by Americans and Englishmen working for the Axis powers—"Lord Haw Haw," "Paul Revere," "Axis Sally," "Tokyo Rose," and Ezra Pound. Other highlights of the radio collection include a full catalog of the *Columbia Workshop* and *One World Flight* series, examples of the 1937 "Shakespeare War" between the networks, the earliest version of *Amos 'n' Andy* (1926) radio coverage of Charles Lindbergh's triumphal return to the U.S. in 1927, and a sampling of the popular comedy and musical variety programs of the 1930s and 1940s.

Many of its television programs are from the first five years of large-scale television broadcasting (1948–1953). Among the items in this collection are the first transcontinental television broadcast (coverage of President Truman's signing of the Japanese Peace Treaty, 1951), the first Presidential tour of the White House (Truman, 1952), and the televised Kefauver Crime Hearings, of 1951. The pioneering dramatic series of the 1950s—*Studio One* and *Playhouse 90*—are represented, as are the classic comedy routines of Bert Lahr, Lucille Ball, Beatrice Lillie, Ernie Kovacs, and Jack Benny.

Information provided by The Museum of Broadcasting and reproduced with permission.

The National Academy of Television Arts and Sciences

FOUNDATIONS, HISTORY, AND PURPOSE

The National Academy of Television Arts and Sciences was begun a little over twenty years ago by Ed Sullivan and Don DeFore, with others. In 1956, it became a national organization with two chapters, one in New York City and the other in Hollywood.

The purpose of the National Academy is to promote excellence in all aspects of television.

HOW EMMY WINNERS ARE CHOSEN

Anyone who has been on national television is eligible for an Emmy. The voters must be members of the Academy, however, and voting is done according to each discipline; that is, actors vote for actors, directors for directors, and so forth. The names of panelists are always kept strictly confidential.

HIGHLIGHTS

The Academy does more than present the Emmy Awards; its work continues all year round, providing important platforms or speakers on national as well as local topics.

The Academy airs all viewpoints, rather than taking a unilateral position. It brings to light many concerns involving television and the public, through forums, symposia, and publications. It has a journal, *Television Quarterly,* and an international counsel concerned with television around the world. The Academy also sponsors social events for the purpose of fostering communication among the various disciplines of the media.

The New York chapter of the Academy provides about 30 different educational courses each year, the tuition from which goes into a scholarship fund.

Various workshops and special festivals, especially for writing and directing, are also offered by the Academy. These range from large-scale functions to those on the high-school level. The Academy also maintains a television library at UCLA.

THE VARIOUS ACADEMY CHAPTERS

The National Academy has active chapters in 15 major television markets. On the West Coast, Seattle, San Francisco, San Diego, and Phoenix have their own chapters; St. Louis, Chicago, Cleveland, Columbus, Dayton–Cincinnati, and Detroit in the midwest have theirs; Miami. Atlanta, and Washington DC in the south have theirs; and New York City and Boston in the northeast have theirs. There is also an international council, which meets on an average of every two years.

NEW MEMBERSHIP

The Academy maintains high standards for membership. There are two groups of new members of the Academy to help keep the organization youthful and growing: students and associates, the latter being those not in television but rather in a related field.

Those wishing to learn more about the various activities of the Academy or interested in applying for a scholarship, should phone or write a local chapter or the main office:

The National Academy of Television Arts and Sciences
110 W. 57th St.
New York, NY 10019
(212) 369-4880
Contact: John Cannon, president

Chapter Roster 1978–1979

President

Atlanta
Danny Royal
WETV, Senior Producer
740 Bismark Rd., NE
(404) 873-4471
(404) 633-5851

Executive Administrator

Joanna Ryder
WAGA-TV
1551 Briarcliff Rd., NE
Atlanta, GA 30306
(404) 875-5551

President	Executive Administrator

Boston
Charles Dutcher, III
WNAC-TV Channel 7
RKO General Bldg.
Government Center
Boston, MA 02114
(617) 725-2700

Leo Palmer
NATAS—Boston Chapter
P.O. Box 332
Lincoln, MA 01773
(617) 259-8656
(617) 259-8801

Chicago
James Ruddle
NBC News
Merchandise Mart
Chicago, IL 60654
(312) 583-5000

Nick Aronson
Consulting Director
2930 W. Catalpa
Chicago, IL 60625
(312) 753-4371
(312) 334-7686

Cleveland
Jack Moffitt
WUAB-TV
8443 Day Dr.
Parma, OH 44129
(216) 845-6043

Ms. Alice Kuhar
NATAS—Cleveland Chapter
1380 E. 6th St.
Cleveland, OH 44114
(216) 696-2929 Ext. 280

Columbus, Dayton, Cincinnati
Mrs. Jo Subler
WDTN-TV 2
4595 South Dixie Dr.
P.O. Box 741
Dayton, OH 45401
(513) 293-2101

Mrs. Barbara Fryman
3150 Sudbury Dr.
Kettering, OH 45420
(513) 293-8411

Detroit
Rod Burton
Burton Advertising Agency
1400 Penobscot Bldg.
Detroit, MI 48226
(313) 961-1166

(Mrs.) Fran Nicholson
Burton Advertising Agency
1400 Penobscot Bldg.
Detroit, MI 48226
(313) 961-1166

Miami
Robert A. Behrens
c/o The Behrens Company, Inc.
2451 Brickell Ave.
Miami, FL 33129
(305) 854-4935

(Mrs.) Betsy Behrens
c/o The Behrens Company, Inc.
2451 Brickell Ave.
Miami, FL 33129
(305) 854-4935

New York
Lee Polk
c/o King Features Syndicate
235 E. 45th St.
New York, NY 10017
(212) 682-5600

Kenneth Leedom
NATAS—NY Chapter Executive Director
110 W. 57th St.
New York, NY 10019
(212) 765-2450

Phoenix
Bill Stull
KTAR-TV
1101 N. Central
Phoenix, AZ 85001
(602) 257-1212
(602) 971-1459

Marquita Fancher
NATAS—Phoenix Chapter
6550 N. 11th Ave.
Phoenix, AZ 85013
(602) 242-4887

President	Executive Administrator

San Diego
D. Wayne Cyphert
Cyphert Creative Services
6343 Lake Albano
San Diego, CA 92119
(714) 292-0337
(714) 460-9761

Ms. Paula Sullivan
NATAS—San Diego Chapter
629 Home Tower Bldg.
707 Broadway
San Diego, CA 92101
(714) 232-1900

San Francisco
Jack A. Armstrong
NATAS—San Francisco Chapter
735 Montgomery St. #200
San Francisco, CA 94111
(415) 392-8002

Jack A. Armstrong
NATAS—San Francisco Chapter
735 Montgomery St. #200
San Francisco, CA 94111
(415) 392-8002

St. Louis
Harold Protter
KPLR-TV
4935 Lindell Blvd.
St. Louis, MO 63108
(314) 367-7211

Rev. Joseph O'Brien
Radio and TV Office
Archdiocese of St. Louis
4140 Lindell Blvd.
St. Louis, MO 63108
(314) 371-4980

Seattle
Art Pattison
KOMO-TV
100 4th Ave. N
Seattle, WA 98109
(206) 223-4044

Miss Marion Simpson
NATAS—Seattle Chapter
217 9th Ave. N
Seattle, WA 98109
(206) 682-3576
(206) 324-4189

Washington, DC
Dan O'Brien
WDCA-TV
5202 River Rd.
Washington, DC 20016
(301) 654-2600

Mrs. Jeanne O'Brien
P.O. Box 32425
Washington, DC 20007
(202) 337-3783

Information in this section provided by the National Academy of Television Arts & Sciences, and reproduced with their permission.

The National Association of Broadcasters*

The National Association of Broadcasters (NAB) represents an industry that touches the daily lives of every American who tunes in to any of the nation's more than 270 million radio receivers and 75 million television sets.

A nonprofit organization, the association was organized in 1922 to foster and promote the development of the arts and aural and visual broadcasting in all its forms; to protect its members in every lawful and proper manner from injustices and unjust exactions; to do all things necessary and proper to encourage and promote customs and practices that will strengthen and maintain the broadcasting industry to the end that it may best serve the public.

Working through their association, NAB members have accomplished many things that could not have been achieved individually. They have instituted voluntary codes for radio and television that provide broadcasters with guideposts in determining acceptable programming and advertising practices. They have upheld broadcasting's freedom from government censorship. They have opposed discriminatory legislation proposals, obtained more liberal acceptance of radio and television coverage of public proceedings, and improved the industry's relationship with public service groups. They have gained fair labor-relations laws and wage-hour regulations. The association also has enabled broadcasters to operate more efficiently by gaining FCC authorization for remote control for radio and TV stations, drafting engineering and recording standards universally accepted by the broadcasting industry, and introducing simplified program and engineering logs meeting FCC requirements.

NAB PURPOSES AND ACTIVITIES

The National Association of Broadcasters represents the industry before Congress, at the White House, and before administrative agencies. It has promoted industry action to acquaint the public with the effectiveness of radio and television, not only as informational and entertainment media but as channels for helping move the nation's goods and services.

It began the first department of radio advertising in 1941—the beginning of the independent organization now known as the Radio Advertising Bureau. It also helped set up the independent Television Bureau of Advertising. And it maintains a continual opposition to pay television.

MODE OF OPERATIONS

Members of the association set the policy and make the decisions on industry-wide matters through a board of directors, which is composed of representative radio and television broadcasters elected by their colleagues. This joint board is subdivided into a radio and a television board, each of the three with its own chairman.

NAB has an extensive committee structure enabling it to draw upon the specialized knowledge of its members in considering industry problems and in making recommendations to the board of directors. Fifteen standing committees and an average of four special committees guide the board and the staff in their work for the industry.

Every member of the association has an opportunity to gain a firsthand knowledge of NAB activities. Since 1923 the association has held annual spring conventions attended by the industry's top management. Later additions to the convention are the Broadcast Engineering Conference and the exposition of broadcast equipment.

Every fall six conferences are held throughout the country for management and for station executives.

The responsibility for carrying through NAB decisions rests with the association's staff of close to 100, headed by a president who devotes full time to NAB duties. In addition to its headquarters in Washington, NAB maintains a research office in New York City and code-authority offices in New York and Hollywood.

THEN AND NOW

Those who organized the NAB with the late Eugene F. McDonald, Jr., the first president, were concerned primarily with the growing pains that beset all fledgling industries. In the case of radio these growing pains were manifest in the undisciplined use of air waves. Without adequate channels or frequency separations, radio was becoming a hodge-podge of sounds in the night and appeared unlikely to fulfill its role as a medium of mass communication. Moreover, the laws pertaining to radio were inadequate because they were designed to cope only with the problems of safety of life at sea and ship-to-shore communication.

But the Radio Act of 1927—perhaps the beginning of the American system of broadcasting as it is known today—contained provisions to apportion

---

*Reproduced through the courtesy of the National Association of Broadcasters.

the radio spectrum through station licensing without incurring government control of business or programming.

The National Association of Broadcasters has grown with the broadcasting industry, incorporating other groups to give the industry unified strength. In 1945, the FM Broadcasters Association became a department of NAB. In 1951, the Television Broadcasters Association merged with the NAB and the name was changed to the National Association of Radio and Television Broadcasters. The association reverted to its former name in 1958. It now accepts associate members in fields allied to broadcasting.

In its early days, NAB maintained a small staff and its unpaid presidents devoted only part of their time to the activities of the association.

McDonald served until 1925 and was succeeded by Frank W. Elliott, 1925–26; Earle E. Anthony, 1926–28; William S. Hedges, 1928–30; Walter J. Damm, 1930–31; Harry Shaw, 1931–32; Alfred J. McCosker, 1932–34; Truman Ward, 1934–35; Leo J. Fitzpatrick, 1935–36; Charles W. Myers, 1936–37; John Elmer, 1937–38, and Mark Etheridge, 1938.

By 1938, the involvements of the association had grown to the extent that a full-time salaried president was necessary. Neville Miller was the first full-time president, serving from 1938 until 1944. His successors have been J. Harold Ryan, 1944–45; Justin Miller, 1945–51; Harold E. Fellows, 1951–60; LeRoy Collins, 1960–64, and Vincent T. Wasilewski, 1965–

NAB Television Code

Twentieth Edition, June 1978

Contents

Preamble

Broadcasters' responsibilities

Television is seen and heard in nearly every American home. These homes include children and adults of all ages, embrace all races and all varieties of philosophic or religious conviction and reach those of every educational background. Television broadcasters must take this pluralistic audience into account in programming their stations. They are obligated to bring their positive responsibility for professionalism and reasoned judgment to bear upon all those involved in the development, production, and selection of programs.

Advertisers' responsibilities

The free, competitive American system of broadcasting, which offers programs of entertainment, news, general information, education, and culture, is supported and made possible by revenues from advertising. While television broadcasters are responsible for the programming and advertising on their stations, the advertisers who use television to convey their commercial messages also have a responsibility to the viewing audience. Their advertising messages should be presented in an honest, responsible, and tasteful manner. Advertisers should also support the endeavors of broadcasters to offer a diversity of programs that meet the needs and expectations of the total viewing audience.

Viewers' responsibilities

The viewer also has a responsibility to help broadcasters serve the public. All viewers should make their criticisms and positive suggestions about programming and advertising known to the broadcast licensee. Parents particularly should oversee the viewing habits of their children, encouraging them to watch programs that will enrich their experience and broaden their intellectual horizons.

Program Standards

I. PRINCIPLES GOVERNING PROGRAM CONTENT

General goals

It is in the interest of television as a vital medium to encourage programs that are innovative, reflect a high degree of creative skill, deal with significant moral and social issues, and present challenging concepts and other subject matter that relate to the world in which the viewer lives.

Television programs should not only reflect the influence of the established institutions that shape our values and culture, but also expose the dynamics of social change which bear upon our lives.

Responsibly exercised artistic freedom

To achieve these goals, television broadcasters should be conversant with the general and specific needs, interests, and aspirations of all the segments of the communities they serve. They should affirmatively seek our responsible representatives of all parts of their communities so that they may structure a broad range of programs that will inform, enlighten, and entertain the total audience.

Broadcasters should also develop programs directed toward advancing the cultural and educational aspects of their communities.

To assure that broadcasters have the freedom to program fully and responsibly, none of the provisions of this code should be construed as preventing or impeding broadcast of the broad range of material necessary to help broadcasters fulfill their obligations to operate in the public interest.

The challenge to the broadcaster is to determine how suitably to present the complexities of human behavior. For television, this requires exceptional awareness of considerations peculiar to the medium.

Accordingly, in selecting program subjects and themes, great care must be exercised to be sure that treatment and presentation are made in good faith and not for the purpose of sensationalism or to shock or exploit the audience or appeal to prurient interests or morbid curiosity.

Family viewing considerations

Additionally, entertainment programming inappropriate for viewing by a general family audience should not be broadcast during the first hour of network entertainment programming in prime time and in the immediately preceding hour. In the occasional case when an entertainment program in this

time period is deemed to be inappropriate for such an audience, advisories should be used to alert viewers. Advisories should also be used when programs in later prime-time periods contain material that might be disturbing to significant segments of the audience.

These advisories should be presented in audio and video form at the beginning of the program and when deemed appropriate at a later point in the program. Advisories should also be used responsibly in promotional material in advance of the program. When using an advisory, the broadcaster should attempt to notify publishers of television-program listings.

Special care should be taken with respect to the content and treatment of audience advisories so that they do not disserve their intended purpose by containing material that is promotional, sensational, or exploitative. Promotional announcements for programs that include advisories should be scheduled on a basis consistent with the purpose of the advisory.

The scheduling provisions of Section I (Principles Governing Program Content) shall not apply to programs under contract to a station as of April 8, 1975, all episodes of which were then in existence, if such station is unable, despite reasonable good-faith efforts, to edit such programs to make them appropriate for family viewing or to reschedule them so as not to occupy family viewing periods. This exception shall in no event apply after September 1, 1977. Any such programs excepted from scheduling provisions shall, of course, bear the required advisory notices *(Interpretation No. 5)*.

II. RESPONSIBILITY TOWARD CHILDREN

Broadcasters have a special responsibility to children. Programs designed primarily for children should take into account the range of interests and needs of children from instructional and cultural material to a wide variety of entertainment material. In their totality, programs should contribute to the sound, balanced development of children to help them achieve a sense of the world at large and informed adjustments to their society.

In the course of a child's development, numerous social factors and forces, including television, affect the ability of the child to make the transition to adult society.

The child's training and experience during the formative years should include positive sets of values which will allow the child to become a responsible adult, capable of coping with the challenges of maturity.

Children should also be exposed, at the appropriate time, to a reasonable range of the realities which exist in the world sufficient to help them make the transition to adulthood.

Because children are allowed to watch programs designed primarily for adults, broadcasters should take this practice into account in the presentation of material in such programs when children may constitute a substantial segment of the audience.

All the standards set forth in this section apply to both program and commercial material designed and intended for viewing by children.

III. COMMUNITY RESPONSIBILITY

1. Television broadcasters and their staffs occupy positions of unique responsibility in their communities and should conscientiously endeavor to be acquainted fully with the community's needs and characteristics in order better to serve the welfare of its citizens.

2. Requests for time for the placement of public-service announcements or programs should be carefully reviewed with respect to the character and reputation of the group, campaign, or organization involved, the public-interest content of the message, and the manner of its presentation.

IV. SPECIAL PROGRAM STANDARDS

1. **Violence; conflict.**
   A. Violence, physical or psychological, may only be projected in responsibly handled contexts, not used exploitatively. Programs involving violence should present the consequences of it to its victims and perpetrators.

   Presentation of the details of violence should avoid the excessive, the gratuitous, and the instructional.

   The use of violence for its own sake and the detailed dwelling upon brutality or physical agony, by sight or by sound, are not permissible.
   B. **Conflict and children.** The depiction of conflict, when presented in programs designed primarily for children, should be handled with sensitivity.

2. **Anti-social behavior; crime.** The treatment of criminal activities should always convey their social and human effects.

   The presentation of techniques of crime in such detail as to be instructional or invite imitation shall be avoided.

3. **Self-destructive behavior: drugs; gambling; alcohol.**
   A. Narcotics addiction shall not be presented except as a destructive habit. The use of illegal drugs or the abuse of legal drugs shall not be encouraged or shown as socially acceptable.
   B. The use of gambling devices or scenes necessary to the development of plot or as appropriate background is acceptable only when presented with discretion and in moderation, and in a manner which would not excite interest in, or foster, betting nor be instructional in nature.
   C. The use of liquor and the depiction of smoking in program content should be deemphasized. When shown, they should be consistent with plot and character development.

4. **Sports programs.** Telecasts of actual sports programs at which on-the-scene betting is permit-

ted by law shall be presented in a manner in keeping with federal, state, and local laws, and should concentrate on the subject as a public sporting event.

5. **Mental/physical disadvantages.** Special precautions must be taken to avoid demeaning or ridiculing members of the audience who suffer from physical or mental afflictions or deformities.

6. **Human relationships; sex; costume.** The presentation of marriage, the family, and similarly important human relationships, and material with sexual connotations, shall not be treated exploitatively or irresponsibly, but with sensitivity. Costuming and movements of all performers shall be handled in a similar fashion.

7. **Pluralism; minorities.** Special sensitivity is necessary in the use of material relating to sex, race, color, age, creed, religious functionaries or rites, or national or ethnic derivation.

8. **Obscenity; profanity.** Subscribers shall not broadcast any material which they determine to be obscene, profane, or indecent.

Above and beyond the requirements of law, broadcasters must consider the family atmosphere in which many of their programs are viewed.

There shall be no graphic portrayal of sexual acts by sight or sound. The portrayal of implied sexual acts must be essential to the plot and presented in a responsible and tasteful manner.

Subscribers are obligated to bring positive responsibility and reasoned judgment to bear upon all those involved in the development, production, and selection of programs.

9. **Hypnosis.** The creation of a state of hypnosis by act or detailed demonstration on camera is prohibited, and hypnosis as a form of "parlor game" antics to create humorous situations within a comedy setting is forbidden.

10. **Superstition; pseudo-sciences.** Program material pertaining to fortune-telling, occultism, astrology, phrenology, palm-reading, numerology, mind-reading, character-reading, and the like is unacceptable if it encourages people to regard such fields as providing commonly accepted appraisals of life.

11. **Professional advice/diagnosis/treatment.** Professional advice, diagnosis, and treatment shall be presented in conformity with law and recognized professional standards.

12. **Subliminal perception.** Any technique whereby an attempt is made to convey information to the viewer by transmitting messages below the threshold of normal awareness is not permitted.

13. **Animals.** The use of animals, consistent with plot and character delineation, shall be in conformity with accepted standards of humane treatment.

14. **Game programs; contests.**
    A. Quiz and similar programs that are presented as contests of knowledge, information, skill or luck must, in fact, be genuine contests; and the results must not be controlled by collusion with or between contestants, or by any other action which will favor one contestant against any other.

B. Contests may not constitute a lottery.

15. **Prizes: credits, acknowledgements.** The broadcaster shall be constantly alert to prevent inclusion of elements within a program dictated by factors other than the requirements of the program itself. The acceptance of cash payments or other considerations in return for including scenic properties, the choice and identification of prizes, the selection of music and other creative program elements and inclusion of any identification of commercial products or services, their trade names, or advertising slogan within the program are prohibited except in accordance with Sections 317 and 508 of the Communications Act.

16. **Misrepresentation: deception.**

A. No program shall be presented in a manner which through artifice or simulation would mislead the audience as to any material fact. Each broadcaster must exercise reasonable judgment to determine whether a particular method of presentation would constitute a material deception, or would be accepted by the audience as normal theatrical illusion.

B. A television broadcaster should not present fictional events or other non-news material as authentic news telecasts or announcements, nor permit dramatizations in any program which would give the false impression that the dramatized material constitutes news.

17. **Applicability of Code standards.** The standards of this code covering program content are also understood to include, wherever applicable, the standards contained in the advertising section of the code.

V. TREATMENT OF NEWS AND PUBLIC EVENTS

General

Television code standards relating to the treatment of news and public events are, because of constitutional considerations, intended to be exhortatory. The standards set forth hereunder encourage high standards of professionalism in broadcast journalism. They are not to be interpreted as turning over to others the broadcaster's responsibility as to judgments necessary in news and public events programming.

News

1. A television station's news schedule should be adequate and well-balanced.

2. News reporting should be factual, fair and without bias.

3. A television broadcaster should exercise particular discrimination in the acceptance, placement, and presentation of advertising in news programs so that such advertising should be clearly distinguishable from the news content.

4. At all times, pictorial, and verbal material for both news and comment should conform to other sections of these standards, wherever such sections are reasonably applicable.

5. Good taste should prevail in the selection and handling of news:

Morbid, sensational, or alarming details not essential to the factual report, especially in connection with stories of crime or sex, should be avoided. News should be telecast in such a manner as to avoid panic and unnecessary alarm.

6. Commentary and analysis should be clearly identified as such.

7. Pictorial material should be chosen with care and not presented in a misleading manner.

8. All news-interview programs should be governed by accepted standards of ethical journalism, under which the interviewer selects the questions to be asked. Where there is advance agreement materially restricting an important or newsworthy area of questioning, the interviewer will state on the program that such limitation has been agreed upon. Such disclosure should be made if the person being interviewed requires that questions be submitted in advance or participates in editing a recording of the interview prior to its use on the air.

9. A television broadcaster should exercise due care in the supervision of content, format, and presentation of newscasts originated by his station, and in the selection of newscasters, commentators, and analysts.

Public Events

1. A television broadcaster has an affirmative responsibility at all times to be informed of public events, and to provide coverage consonant with the ends of an informed and enlightened citizenry.

2. The treatment of such events by a television broadcaster should provide adequate and informed coverage.

VI. CONTROVERSIAL PUBLIC ISSUES

1. Television provides a valuable forum for the expression of responsible views on public issues of a controversial nature. The television broadcaster should seek out and develop with accountable individuals, groups, and organizations programs relating to controversial public issues of import to his fellow citizens; and to give fair representation to opposing sides of issues which materially affect the life or welfare of a substantial segment of the public.

2. Requests by individuals, groups, or organizations for time to discuss their views on controversial public issues should be considered on the basis of their individual merits, and in the light of the contribution which the use requested would make to the public interest and to a well-balanced program structure.

3. Programs devoted to the discussion of controversial public issues should be identified as such. They should not be presented in a manner which would mislead listeners or viewers to believe that the program is purely of an entertainment, news, or other character.

4. Broadcasts in which stations express their own opinions about issues of general public interest should be clearly identified as editorials. They should be unmistakably identified as statements of station opinion and should be appropriately distinguished from news and other program material.

VII. POLITICAL TELECASTS

1. Political telecasts should be clearly identified as such. They should not be presented by a television broadcaster in a manner which would mislead listeners or viewers to believe that the program is of any other character. (Ref.: Communications Act of 1934, as amended, Secs 315 and 317, and FCC Rules and Regulations, Secs. 3.654, 3.657, 3.663, as discussed in NAB's "Political Broadcast Catechism & The Fairness Doctrine.")

VIII. RELIGIOUS PROGRAMS

1. It is the responsibility of a television broadcaster to make available to the community appropriate opportunity for religious presentations.
2. Programs reach audiences of all creeds simultaneously. Therefore, both the advocates of broad or ecumenical religious precepts and the exponents of specific doctrines are urged to present their positions in a manner conducive to viewer enlightenment on the role of religion in society.
3. In the allocation of time for telecasts of religious programs, the television station should use its best efforts to apportion such time fairly among responsible individuals, groups, and organizations.

Advertising Standards

IX. PRESENTATION OF ADVERTISING

1. **Applicability of Code Standards.**

A. This code establishes basic standards for all television broadcasting. The principles of acceptability and good taste within the Program Standards section govern the presentation of advertising where applicable. In addition, the code establishes in this section special standards which apply to television advertising.

B. Commercial television broadcasters make their facilities available for the advertising of products and services and accept commercial presentations for such advertising. However, television broadcasters should in recognition of their responsibility to the public, refuse the facilities of their stations to an advertiser where they have good reason to doubt the integrity of the advertiser, the truth of the advertising representations, or the compliance of the advertiser with the spirit and purpose of all applicable legal requirements.

C. Since advertising by television is a dynamic technique, a television broadcaster should keep under surveillance new advertising devices so that the spirit and purpose of these standards are fulfilled.

2. **Sponsor identification.** Identification of sponsorship must be made in all sponsored programs in accordance with the requirements of the Communications Act of 1934, as amended, and the Rules and Regulations of the Federal Communications Commission.

3. **Safety considerations.** Representations which disregard normal safety precautions shall be avoided.

Children shall not be represented, except under proper adult supervision, as being in contact with or demonstrating a product recognized as potentially dangerous to them.

4. **Audience sensibilities: general.**

A. In consideration of the customs and attitudes of the communities served, each television broadcaster should refuse his facilities to the advertisement of products and services, or the use of advertising scripts, which the station has good reason to believe would be objectionable to a substantial and responsible segment of the community. These standards should be applied with judgment and flexibility, taking into consideration the characteristics of the medium, its home and family audience, and the form and content of the particular presentation.

B. Advertising messages should be presented with courtesy and good taste; disturbing or annoying material should be avoided; every effort should be made to keep the advertising message in harmony with the content and general tone of the program in which it appears.

5. **Audience perceptions of clutter.** A multiple-product announcement is one in which two or more products or services are presented within the framework of a single announcement. A multiple-product announcement shall not be scheduled in a unit of time less than 60 seconds, except where integrated so as to appear to the viewer as a single message. A multiple-product announcement shall be considered integrated and counted as a single announcement if:

—the products or services are related and interwoven within the framework of the announcement (related products or services shall be defined as those having a common character, purpose, and use); and
—the voice(s), setting, background, and continuity are used consistently throughout so as to appear to the viewer as a single message.

Multiple-product announcements of 60 seconds in length or longer not meeting this definition of integration shall be counted as two or more announcements under this section of the code. This provision shall not apply to retail or service establishments.

6. **Audience sensibilities; children.**

A. The broadcaster and the advertiser should exercise special caution with the content and presentation of television commercials placed in or near programs designed for children. Exploitation of children should be avoided. Commercials directed to children should in no way mislead as to the product's performance and usefulness.

B. Commercials, whether live, filmed, or on tape, within programs initially designed primarily for children under 12 years of age shall be clearly separated from program material by an appropriate device.

C. Trade-name identification or other merchandising practices involving the gratuitous naming of products is discouraged in programs designed primarily for children.

D. Appeals involving matters of health which should be determined by physicians should not be directed primarily to children.

E. No children's program personality or cartoon character shall be utilized to deliver commercial messages within or adjacent to the programs in which such a personality or cartoon character regularly appears. This provision shall also apply to lead-ins to commercials when such lead-ins contain sell copy or imply endorsement of the product by program personalities or cartoon characters.

Restricted or unacceptable categories

7. **Alcoholic beverages.**
   A. The advertising of hard liquor (distilled spirits) is not acceptable.
   B. The advertising of beer and wines is acceptable only when presented in the best of good taste and discretion, and is acceptable only subject to federal and local laws.
   This requires that commercials involving beer and wine avoid any representation of on-camera drinking *(Interpretation No. 4)*.

8. **Vocational training.** Advertising by institutions or enterprises which in their offers of instruction imply promises of employment or make exaggerated claims for the opportunities awaiting those who enroll for courses is generally unacceptable.

9. **Ammunition; firearms; fireworks.** The advertising of firearms/ammunition is acceptable provided it promotes the product only as sporting equipment and conforms to recognized standards of safety as well as all applicable laws and regulations. Advertisements of firearms/ammunition by mail order are unacceptable. The advertising of fireworks is unacceptable.

10. **Astrology, etc.** The advertising of fortune-telling, occultism, astrology, phrenology, palm-reading, numerology, mind-reading, character-reading or subjects of a like nature is not permitted.

11. **Personal products.** Because all products of a personal nature create special problems, acceptability of such products should be determined with especial emphasis on ethics and the canons of good taste. Such advertising of personal products as is accepted must be presented in a restrained and obviously inoffensive manner.

12. **Betting/gambling.** The advertising of tip sheets and other publications seeking to advertise for the purpose of giving odds or promoting betting is unacceptable.

The lawful advertising of government organizations which conduct legalized lotteries and the advertising of private or governmental organizations which conduct legalized betting on sporting contests are acceptable provided such advertising does not unduly exhort the public to bet.

Restricted or unacceptable advertising techniques

13. **Indirect advertising.** An advertiser who markets more than one product should not be permitted to use advertising copy devoted to an acceptable product for purposes of publicizing the brand name or other identification of a product which is not acceptable.

14. **Bait and switch.** "Bait-switch" advertising, whereby goods or services which the advertiser has no intention of selling are offered merely to lure the customer into purchasing higher-priced substitutes, is not acceptable.

15. **Pitch techniques.** The "pitchman" technique of advertising on television is inconsistent with good broadcast practice and generally damages the reputation of the industry and the advertising profession.

Sponsored program-length segments consisting substantially of continuous demonstrations or sales presentation violate not only the time standards established in the code but the broad philosophy of improvement implicit in the voluntary code operation and are not acceptable *(Interpretation No. 1)*.

16. **Testimonials.** Personal endorsements (testimonials) shall be genuine and reflect personal experience. They shall contain no statement that cannot be supported if presented in the advertiser's own words.

17. **Policy regarding religious time sales.** A charge for television time to churches and religious bodies is not recommended.

X. CLAIMS: GENERAL

1. **False, misleading or deceptive advertising.** The role and capability of television to market sponsors' products are well recognized. In turn, this fact dictates that great care be exercised by the broadcaster to prevent the presentation of false, misleading, or deceptive advertising. While it is entirely appropriate to present a product in a favorable light and atmosphere, the presentation must not, by copy or demonstration, involve a material deception as to the characteristic, performance, or appearance of the product.

Broadcast advertisers are responsible for making available, at the request of the code authority, documentation adequate to support the validity and truthfulness of claims, demonstrations, and testimonials contained in their commercial messages.

2. **Use of research, surveys, or tests.** Reference to the results of bona fide research, surveys, or tests relating to the product to be advertised shall not be presented in a manner so as to create an impression of fact beyond that established by the work that has been conducted.

3. **Fictitious exploitations.** Appeals to help fictitious characters in television programs by purchasing the advertiser's product or service or sending for a premium should not be permitted, and such fictitious characters should not be introduced into the advertising message for such purposes.

4. **Competitive references.** Advertising should offer a product or service on its positive merits and refrain from discrediting, disparaging, or unfairly attacking competitors, competing products, other industries, professions, or institutions.

5. **Placement of advertising messages.** A sponsor's advertising messages should be confined within the framework of the sponsor's program structure. A television broadcaster should avoid the use of commercial announcements which are divorced from the program either by preceding the introduction of the program (as in the case of so-called "cow-catcher" announcements) or by following the apparent sign-off of the program (as in the case of so-called trailer or "hitch-hike" announcements). To this end, the program itself should be announced and clearly identified, both audio and video, before the sponsor's advertising material is first used, and should be signed off, both audio and video, after the sponsor's advertising material is last used.

XI. ADVERTISING OF MEDICAL PRODUCTS/SERVICES

1. The advertising of medical products presents considerations of intimate and far-reaching importance to consumers because of the direct bearing on their health.

2. Because of the personal nature of the advertising of medical products, claims that a product will effect a cure and the indiscriminate use of such words as *safe, without risk, harmless,* or terms of similar meaning should not be accepted in the advertising of medical products on television stations.

3. A television broadcaster should not accept advertising material which in his opinion offensively describes or dramatizes distress or morbid situations involving ailments, by spoken word, sound, or visual effects.

4. Commercials for services or over-the-counter products involving health considerations are of intimate and far-reaching importance to the consumer. The following principles should apply to such advertising:

A. Physicians, dentists, or nurses or actors representing physicians, dentists, or nurses shall not be employed directly or by implication. These restrictions also apply to persons professionally engaged in medical services (e.g., physical therapists, pharmacists, dental assistants, nurses' aides).

B. Visual representations of laboratory settings may be employed, provided they bear a direct relationship to bona fide research which has been conducted for the product or service *(see Television Code X-2).* In such cases, laboratory technicians shall be identified as such and shall not be employed as spokespersons or in any other way speak in behalf of the product.

C. Institutional announcements not intended to sell a specific product or service to the consumer and public-service announcements by non-profit organizations may be presented by accredited physicians, dentists, or nurses, subject to approval by the broadcaster. An accredited professional is one who has met required qualifications and has been licensed in his resident state.

XII. CONTESTS

1. Contests shall be conducted with fairness to all entrants, and shall comply with all pertinent laws and regulations. Care should be taken to avoid the concurrent use of the three elements which together constitute a lottery—prize, chance, and consideration.

2. All contest details, including rules, eligibility requirements, opening and termination dates should be clearly and completely announced and/or shown, or easily accessible to the viewing public, and the winners' names should be released and prizes awarded as soon as possible after the close of the contest.

3. When advertising is accepted which requests contestants to submit items of product identification or other evidence of purchase of products, reasonable facsimiles thereof should be made acceptable unless the award is based upon skill and not upon chance.

4. All copy pertaining to any contest (except that which is required by law) associated with the exploitation or sale of the sponsor's product or service, and all references to prizes or gifts offered in such connection should be considered a part of and included in the total time allowances as herein provided *(see Television Code XIV).*

XIII. PREMIUMS AND OFFERS

1. Full details of proposed offers should be required by the television broadcaster for investigation and approved before the first announcement of the offer is made to the public.

2. A final date for the termination of an offer should be announced as far in advance as possible.

3. Before accepting for telecast offers involving a monetary consideration, a television broadcaster should be satisfied as to the integrity of the advertiser and the advertiser's willingness to honor complaints, indicating dissatisfaction with the premium by returning the monetary consideration.

4. There should be no misleading descriptions or visual representations of any premiums or gifts

which would distort or enlarge their value in the minds of the viewers.

5. Assurances should be obtained from the advertiser that premiums offered are not harmful to person or property.

6. Premiums should not be approved which appeal to superstition on the basis of "luckbearing" powers or otherwise.

XIV. TIME STANDARDS FOR NETWORK-AFFILIATED STATIONS

In order that the time for non-program material and its placement shall best serve the viewer, the following standards are set forth in accordance with sound television practice:

1. **Non-Program Material Definition.** Non-program material, in both prime and all other time, includes billboards, commercials, and promotional announcements.

Non-program material also includes:

A. In programs of 90 minutes in length or less, credits in excess of 30 seconds per program, except in feature films, shall be counted against the allowable time for non-program material. In no event should credits exceed 40 seconds in such programs.

The 40 second limitation on credits shall not apply, however, in any situation governed by a contract entered into before October 1, 1971.

B. In programs longer than 90 minutes, credits in excess of 50 seconds per program, except in feature films, shall be counted against the allowable time for non-program material. In no event should credits exceed 60 seconds in such programs.

Public service announcements and promotional announcements for the same program are excluded from this definition.

2. **Allowable time for non-program material.**

A. In prime time on network affiliated stations, non-program material shall not exceed nine minutes 30 seconds in any 60-minute period.

Prime time is a continuous period of not less than three consecutive hours per broadcast day as designated by the station between the hours of 6:00 P.M. and midnight.

B. In all other time, non-program material shall not exceed 16 minutes in any 60-minute period.

C. **Children's programming time.** Defined as those hours other than prime time in which programs initially designed primarily for children under 12 years of age are scheduled.

Within this time period on Saturday and Sunday, non-program material shall not exceed nine minutes 30 seconds in any 60-minute period.

Within this time period on Monday through Friday, non-program material shall not exceed 12 minutes in any 60-minute time period.

3. **Program interruptions.**

A. Definition: A program interruption is any occurrence of non-program material within the main body of the program.

B. In prime time, the number of program interruptions shall not exceed two within any 30-minute program, or four within any 60-minute program.

Programs longer than 60 minutes shall be prorated at two interruptions per half-hour.

The number of interruptions in 60-minute variety shows shall not exceed five.

C. In all other time, the number of interruptions shall not exceed four within any 30-minute program period.

D. In children's weekend programming time, as defined in 2C, the number of program interruptions shall not exceed two within any 30-minute program or four within any 60-minute program.

E. In both prime time and all other time, the following interruption standard shall apply within programs of 15 minutes or less in length:

5-minute program—1 interruption;
10-minute program—2 interruptions;
15-minute program—2 interruptions.

F. News, weather, sports, and special-events programs are exempt from the interruption standard because of the nature of such programs.

4. **Consecutive announcements.** No more than four non-program material announcements shall be scheduled consecutively within programs, and no more than three non-program material announcements shall be scheduled consecutively during station breaks. The consecutive non-program material limitation shall not apply to a single sponsor who wishes to further reduce the number of interruptions in the program.

5. **Prize and donor identification.** Reasonable and limited identification of prizes and donors' names where the presentation of contest awards or prizes is a necessary part of program content shall not be included as non-program material as defined above.

Aural and/or visual prize identification of up to 10 seconds duration may be deemed "reasonable and limited." Where such identification is longer than 10 seconds, the entire announcement or visual presentation will be charged against the total commercial time for the program period *(Interpretation No. 3)*.

6. **Shopping guides/service formats.** Programs presenting women's/men's service features, shopping guides, fashion shows, demonstrations, and similar material provide a special service to the public in which certain material normally classified as non-program is an informative and necessary part of the program content. Because of this, the time standards may be waived by the code authority to a reasonable extent on a case-by-case basis.

7. **Product or service references.** Gratuitous references in a program to a non-sponsor's product or service should be avoided except for normal guest identification.

8. **Film promotion.** The presentation of commentary or film excerpts from current theatrical

releases in some instances may constitute commercial material under the Time Standards for Non-Program Material. Specifically, for example, when such presentation, directly or by inference, urges viewers to attend, it shall be counted against the commercial allowance for the program of which it is a part (*Interpretation No. 2*).

9. **Trade-name identification.** Stationary backdrops or properties in television presentations showing the sponsor's name or product, the name of the sponsor's product, trade-mark, or slogan should be used only incidentally and should not obtrude on program interest or entertainment.

XV. TIME STANDARDS FOR INDEPENDENT STATIONS

1. Non-program elements shall be considered as all-inclusive, with the exception of required credits, legally required station identifications, and "bumpers." Promotion spots and public-service announcements, as well as commercials, are to be considered non-program elements.

2. The allowed time for non-program elements, as defined above, shall not exceed seven minutes in a 30-minute period or multiples thereof in prime time (prime time is defined as any three contiguous hours between 6:00 P.M. and midnight, local time), or eight minutes in a 30-minute period or multiples thereof during all other times.

3. Where a station does not carry a commercial in a station break between programs, the number of program interruptions shall not exceed four within any 30-minute program, or seven within any 60-minute program, or 10 within any 90-minute program, or 13 in any 120-minute program. Stations which do carry commercials in station breaks between programs shall limit the number of program interruptions to three within any 30-minute program, or six within any 60-minute program, or nine within any 90-minute program, or 12 in any 120-minute program. News, weather, sports, and special events are exempted because of format.

4. Not more than four non-program material announcements, as defined above, shall be scheduled consecutively. An exception may be made only in the case of a program 60 minutes or more in length, when no more than seven non-program elements may be scheduled consecutively by stations who wish to reduce the number of program interruptions.

5. The conditions of paragraphs three and four shall not apply to live sports programs where the program format dictates and limits the number of program interruptions.

(*For children's time standards on independent stations see provisions XIV-2C, 3D under Time Standards for Network-Affiliated Stations.*)

GUIDELINES/INTERPRETATIONS BASED ON CODE STANDARDS

From time to time the code authority issues advertising guidelines and clarifications expanding on provi-

sions of the code. Among areas covered are acne, alcoholic beverages, arthritis and rheumatism remedies, bronchitis, comparative advertising, children's premiums and offers, children's TV advertising, disparagement, hallucinogens, hypnosis, lotteries, men-in-white, non-prescription medications, personal products, testimonials, time standards, toys, vegetable oils and margarines, and weight-reducing products/services. Copies may be obtained from any NAB Code Authority office.

Regulations and Procedures

The following regulations and procedures shall obtain as an integral part of the television code of the National Association of Broadcasters:

I. NAME

The name of this code shall be *The Television Code of the National Association of Broadcasters.**

II. PURPOSE OF THE CODE

The purpose of this code is cooperatively to maintain a level of television programming which gives full consideration to the educational, informational, cultural, economic, moral, and entertainment needs of the American public to the end that more and more people will be better served.

III. SUBSCRIBERS

Section 1. Eligibility

Any individual, firm, or corporation which is engaged in the operation of a television broadcast station or network, or which holds a construction permit for a television broadcast station within the United States or its dependencies, shall, subject to the approval of the Television Board of Directors as hereinafter provided, be eligible to subscribe to the television code of the NAB to the extent of one subscription for each such station and/or network which it operates or for which it holds a construction permit; provided, that a non-television member of NAB shall not become eligible via code subscription to receive any of the member services or to exercise any of the voting privileges of a member.

Section 2. Certification of Subscription

Upon subscribing to the code, subject to the approval of the Television Board of Directors, there shall be granted forthwith to each such subscribing station authority to use the "NAB

---

*By-Laws of the National Association of Broadcasters, Article VI. Section 8. C: "Television Board. The Television Board is hereby authorized:—(4) to enact, amend and promulgate standards of practice or codes for its Television members, and to establish such methods to secure observance thereof as it may deem advisable:—."

Television Seal of Good Practice," a copyrighted and registered seal to be provided in the form of a certificate, a slide, and/or a film, signifying that the recipient thereof is a subscriber in good standing to the television code of the NAB. The seal and its significance shall be appropriately publicized by the NAB.

Section 3. Duration of Subscription

Subscription shall continue in full force and effect until 30 days after the first of the month following receipt of notice of written resignation. Subscription to the code shall be effective from the date of application subject to the approval of the Television Board of Directors; provided, that the subscription of a television station going on the air for the first time shall, for the first six months of such subscription, be probationary, during which time its subscription can be summarily revoked by an affirmative two-thirds vote of the Television Board of Directors without the usual processes specified below.

Section 4. Suspension of Subscription

Any subscription, and/or the authority to utilize and show the above-noted seal, may be voided, revoked, or temporarily suspended for television programming, including commercial copy, which, by theme, treatment, or incident, in the judgment of the television board constitutes a continuing, willful, or gross violation of any of the provisions of the television code, by an affirmative two-thirds vote of the television Board of Directors at a regular or special meeting; provided, however, that the following conditions and procedures shall apply:

A. *Preferring of Charges—Conditions Precedent:*

Prior to the preferring of charges to the Television Board of Directors concerning violation of the code by a subscriber, the television code board (hereinafter provided for) (1) Shall have appropriately, and in good time, informed and advised such subscriber of any and all complaints and information coming to the attention of the television code board and relating to the programming of said subscriber, (2) Shall have reported to, and advised, said subscriber by analysis, interpretation, recommendation or otherwise, of the possibility of a violation or breach of the television code by the subscriber, and (3) Shall have served upon the subscriber, by registered mail a notice of intent to prefer charges, at least 20 days prior to the filing of any such charges with the Television Board of Directors. During this period the television code board may, within its sole discretion, reconsider its proposed action based upon such written reply as the subscriber may care to make, or upon such action as the subscriber may care to take programwise, in conformance with the analysis, interpretation, or recommendation of the television code board.

(i) Notice of Intent

The Notice of Intent shall include a statement of the grounds and reasons for the proposed charges, including appropriate references to the television code.

(ii) Time

In the event that the nature of the program in question is such that time is of the essence, the television code board may prefer charges within less than the 20 days above specified, provided that a time certain in which reply many be made is included in its notice of intent, and provided that its reasons therefor must be specified in its statement of charges preferred.

B. *The Charges:*

The subscriber shall be advised in writing by registered mail of the charges preferred. The charges preferred by the television code board to the Television Board of Directors shall include the grounds and reasons therefor, together with specific references to the television code. The charges shall contain a statement that the conditions precedent, herein before described, have been met.

C. *Hearing:*

The subscriber shall have the right to a hearing and may exercise same by filing an answer within 10 days of the date of such notification.

D. *Waiver:*

Failure to request a hearing shall be deemed a waiver of the subscriber's right thereto.

E. *Designation:*

If a hearing is requested by the subscriber, it shall be designated as promptly as possible and at such time and place as the television board may specify.

F. *Confidential Status:*

Hearings shall be closed; and all correspondence between a subscriber and the television code board and/or the Television Board of Directors concerning specific programming shall be confidential; provided, however, that the confidential status of these procedures may be waived by a subscriber.

G. *Presentation: Representation:*

A subscriber against whom charges have been preferred, and who has exercised his right to a hearing, shall be entitled to effect presentation of his case personally, by agent, by attorney, or by deposition and interrogatory.

H. *Intervention:*

Upon request by the subscriber-respondent or the television code board, the Television Board of Directors, in its discretion, may permit the intervention of one or more other subscribers as parties-in-interest.

I. *Transcript:*

A stenographic transcript record shall be taken and shall be certified by the chairperson of the Television Board of Directors to the office of the secretary of the National Association of Broadcasters, where it shall be maintained. The transcript shall not be open to inspection unless otherwise provided by the party respondent in the proceeding.

J. *Television Code Board; Counsel:*

The television code board may, at its discretion, utilize the services of an attorney from the staff of the NAB for the purpose of effecting its presentation in a hearing matter.

K. *Order of Procedure:*

At hearings the television code board shall open and close.

L. *Cross-Examination:*

The right of cross-examination shall specifically obtain. Where procedure has been by deposition or interrogatory, the use of cross-interrogatories shall satisfy this right.

M. *Presentation:*

Oral and written evidence may be introduced by the subscriber and by the television code board. Oral argument may be had at the hearing and written memoranda or briefs may be submitted by the subscriber and by the television code board. The Television Board of Directors may admit such evidence as it deems relevant, material, and competent, and may determine the nature and length of the oral argument and the written argument or briefs.

N. *Authority of Presiding Officer; of Television Board of Directors:*

The presiding officer shall rule upon all interlocutory matters, such as, but not limited to, the admissibility of evidence, the qualifications of witnesses, etc. On all other matters, authority to act shall be vested in a majority of the television board unless otherwise provided.

O. *Films, Transcriptions, etc.:*

Films, kinescopes, records, transcriptions, or other mechanical reproductions of television programs, properly identified, shall be accepted into evidence when relevant.

P. *Continuances and Extensions:*

Continuance and extension of any proceeding or for the time of filing or performing any act required or allowed to be done within a specific time may be granted upon request, for a good cause shown. The board or the presiding officer may recess or adjourn a hearing for such time as may be deemed necessary, and may change the place thereof.

Q. *Findings and Conclusions:*

The Television Board of Directors shall decide the case as expeditiously as possible and shall notify the subscriber and the television code board, in writing, of the decision. The decision of the Television Board of Directors shall contain findings of fact with conclusions, as well as the reasons or bases therefor. Findings of fact shall set out in detail and with particularity all basic evidentiary facts developed on the record (with appropriate citations to the transcript of record or exhibit relied on for each evidentiary fact) supporting the conclusion reached.

R. *Reconsideration or Rehearing:*

A request for reconsideration or rehearing may be filed by parties to the hearing. Requests for reconsideration or rehearing shall state with particularity in what respect the decision or any matter determined therein is claimed to be unjust, unwarranted, or erroneous, and with respect to any finding of fact shall specify the pages of record relied on. If the existence of any newly discovered evidence is claimed, the request shall be accompanied by a verified statement of the facts together with the facts relied on to show that the party, with due diligence, could not have known or discovered such facts at the time of the hearing.

The request for rehearing may seek:

a. Reconsideration
b. Additional oral argument
c. Reopening of the proceedings
d. Amendment of any findings, or
e. Other relief.

S. *Time for Filing:*

Requests for reconsideration or rehearing shall be filed within 10 days after receipt by the respondent of the decision. Opposition thereto may be filed within five days after the filing of the request.

T. *Penalty, Suspension of:*

At the discretion of the television board, application of any penalty provided for in the decision may be suspended until the board makes final disposition of the request for reconsideration or rehearing.

U. *Disqualification:*

Any member of the television board may disqualify himself or, upon good cause shown by any interested party, may be disqualified by a majority vote of the television board.

Section 5. *Additional Procedures*

When necessary to the proper administration of the code, additional rules of procedure will be established from time to time as authorized by the by-laws of the NAB; in keeping therewith, special consideration shall be given to the procedures for receipt and processing of complaints and to necessary rules to be adopted from time to time, taking into account the source and nature of such complaints; such rules to include precautionary measures such as the posting of bonds to cover costs and expenses of processing same; and further provided that special consideration will be given to procedures insuring the confidential status of proceedings relating to code observance.

Section 6. *Amendment and Review*

Because of the new and dynamic aspects inherent in television broadcast, the television code, as a living, flexible, and continuing document, may be amended from time to time by the Television Board of Directors; provided that said board is specifically charged with review and reconsideration of the entire code, its appendices and procedures, at least once each year.

Section 7. *Termination of Contracts*

All subscribers on the air at the time subscription to the code shall be permitted that period prior to and including the earliest legal cancellation date to terminate any contracts, then outstanding, calling for program presentations which would not be in conformity with the television code, provided, however, that in no event shall such period be longer than 52 weeks.

IV. AFFILIATE SUBSCRIBERS

Section 1. *Eligibility*

Any individual, firm or corporation which is engaged in the production or distribution, lease, or sale of recorded programs for television presentation, subject to the approval of the television code board as hereinafter provided, shall be eligible to become an affiliate subscriber to the television code of the NAB.

Section 2. Cerification of Subscription

Upon becoming an affiliate subscriber to the code, subject to the approval of the television code board, there shall be granted forthwith to each such affiliate subscriber authority to use a copyrighted and registered seal and declaration, in a manner approved by the television code board, identifying the individual firm or corporation as an affiliate subscriber to the television code of the NAB. Such authority shall not constitute formal clearance or approval by the television code board of specific film programs or other recorded material.

Section 3. Duration of Affiliate Subscription

The affiliate subscription shall continue in full force and effect until 30 days after the first of the month following receipt of a written notice of resignation. The affiliate subscription of the code shall be effective from the date of application subject to the approval of the television code board.

Section 4. Suspension of Affiliate Subscription

Any affiliate subscription and the authority to utilize and show the seal may be voided, revoked, or temporarily suspended for the sale or distribution for television presentation of any film or other recorded material which by theme, treatment, or incident, in the judgment of the television code board, constitutes a continuing, willful, or gross violation of any of the provisions of the television code, by a majority vote of the television code board at any regular or special meeting. The conditions and procedures applicable to subscribers shall not apply to affiliate subscribers.

Section 5. Representation of Affiliate Subscribers

Any affiliate subscriber or group of affiliate subscribers may authorize an individual or association to act for them in connection with their relations with the television code board by filing a written notice of such representation with the board. Such representation, however, in no way will limit the right of the television code board to suspend individual affiliate subscribers in accordance with the provisions of Section 4.

V. RATES

Each subscriber and affiliate subscriber shall pay "administrative" rates in accordance with such schedule, at such time, and under such conditions as may be determined from time to time by the television board *(see Article VI, Section 8, C. Television Board (3) and (4), By-Laws of the NAB);* provided, that appropriate credit shall be afforded to a television member of the NAB against the regular dues paid to NAB.

VI. THE TELEVISION CODE BOARD

Section 1. Composition

There shall be a continuing committee entitled the television code board to be composed of not more than nine members, all of whom shall be from subscribers to the television code. They shall be appointed by the president of NAB, subject to confirmation by the television board, and may include one member from each of the subscribing nationwide television networks. Members of the television board shall not be eligible to serve on the board. Due consideration shall be given, in making the appointments, to factors of diversification of geographical location, market size, company representation, and network affiliation.

No person shall continue as a member of the television code board if the station or entity he represents ceases to subscribe to the television code. In such case a vacancy occurs in the office immediately, and a successor may be appointed to serve out the unexpired term.

The first term shall be for three years. The second term shall be for two years. Each new term shall commence at the close of the annual meeting of membership following appointment.

A. *Limitation of Service:*

No person shall serve for more than two terms, consecutively, as a member of the television code board; provided, however, this limitation shall not apply to network representatives.

Serving out the unexpired term of a former member shall not constitute a term within the meaning of this section.

B. *Meetings:*

The television code board shall meet at least twice in each calendar year on a date to be determined by the chairperson. The chairperson, or the code authority general manager, may, at any time, on at least five days written notice, call a special meeting of the board.

C. *Quorum:*

For all purposes, a majority of the members of the television code board shall constitute a quorum.

Section 2. Authority and Responsibilities

The television code board is authorized and directed:

(1) To recommend to the Television Board of Directors amendments to the television code; (2) to consider, in its discretion, any appeal from any decision made by the code authority general manager with respect to any matter which has arisen under the code, and to suspend, reverse, or modify any such decision; (3) to prefer formal charges, looking toward the suspension or revocation of the authority to show the code seal, to the Television Board of Directors concerning violations and breaches of the television code by a subscriber; (4) to be available to the code authority general manager for consultation on any and all matters affecting the television code.

VII. CODE AUTHORITY GENERAL MANAGER

Section 1. Code Authority General Manager

There shall be a position designated as the code authority general manager. This position shall be filled by appointment of the president of NAB, subject to the approval of the board of directors.

Section 2. Authority and Responsibilities

The code authority general manager is authorized and directed: (1) to maintain a continuing review of all programming and advertising material presented over television, especially that of subscribers to the television code of NAB; (2) to receive, screen, and clear complaints concerning television programming; (3) to define and interpret words and phrases in the television code; (4) to develop and maintain appropriate liaison with governmental agencies and with responsible and accountable organizations and institutions; (5) to inform, expeditiously and properly, a subscriber to the television code of complaints or commendations, as well as to advise all subscribers concerning the attitudes and desires program-wise of accountable organizations and institutions, and of the American public in general; (6) to review and monitor, if necessary, any certain series of programs, daily programming or any other program presentations of a subscriber, as well as to request recorded material, or script and copy, with regard to any certain program presented by a subscriber; (7) to reach conclusions and make recommendations or prefer charges to the television code board concerning violations and breaches of the television code by a subscriber; (8) to recommend to the code board amendments to the television code.

A. *Delegation of Powers and
Responsibilities:*

The code authority general manager shall appoint such executive staff as is needed, consistent with resources, to carry out the above described functions, and may delegate to this staff such responsibilities as he may deem necessary.

Politics and TV

Presidents on TV

The following is a brief chronology of the most significant TV appearances of the Presidents of the United States, beginning with Franklin D. Roosevelt. Almost all the speeches were broadcast from either the White House or the Senate Building.

FRANKLIN DELANO ROOSEVELT

April 30, 1939 President Roosevelt spoke for about two minutes at the opening of the New York World's Fair, the first President to appear on television.

February 23, 1942 (Fireside Chat from White House: voice only with stills shown on New York screen) The President spoke about the necessity of our men and ships fighting in other parts of the world, and talked about the number of men killed and wounded at Pearl Harbor and the ships destroyed. He urged uninterrupted production from the American people.

April 28, 1942 (Fireside Chat from White House) He asked the public to help win the war by sacrificing on the home front and pledged executive power to ensure "total war" on elements in the U.S. who were hampering the war effort.

October 12, 1942 He praised the spirit of the people he met on his tour of war production and armed forces establishments, and said he would lower the age for armed-forces service to 18.

HARRY S TRUMAN

October 27, 1945 At a Navy Day program from Central Park in New York, the President spoke about foreign policy.

October 5, 1947 In his first address from the Oval Office in the White House, he spoke about food prices.

January 7, 1948 He delivered a State of the Nation address before a joint session of Congress.

March 17, 1948 He spoke before a joint session of Congress on the threat to world peace posed by the Soviet Union.

July 14, 1948 At the Democratic convention in Philadelphia, the President made his acceptance speech as the Democratic nominee for the Presidency.

July 27, 1948 He spoke before a joint session of Congress and urged immediate legislation to remedy the high cost of living, and advocated low-rental housing.

January 5, 1949 In a State of the Union address before a joint session of Congress (this was his "Fair Deal" speech), he asked for the repeal of the Taft-Hartley labor law, the raising of the minimum wage to 75 cents, federal aid to local schools, control of certain prices and wages, and initiated his civil-rights program.

January 20, 1949 In the first Presidential inauguration on TV, Truman delivered his "four point" inaugural address.

April 4, 1949 At the signing of the North Atlantic Treaty at the Departmental Auditorium in Washington, he spoke for ten minutes on the importance of the document and the organization of nations for peaceful purposes.

July 13, 1949 In the first fireside chat to be covered by National TV, the President talked about the government budget and the reason for returning to deficit spending.

January 1, 1950 In a State of the Union address before a joint session of Congress, he spoke about tax-law revisions, and estimated that by the year 2000 the average American income would be $12,000 per year.

July 19, 1950 For the first time a President was seen and heard during a period of national emergency—the Korean War. Truman asked for $10 billion for defense.

September 1, 1950 Speaking from the motion-picture room in the White House, the President described conditions arising out of Korean War.

September 9, 1950 Speaking from the Oval Office, the President talked about three problems: producing material for defense, raising money, and preventing inflation.

Information provided by the National Broadcasting Company, Inc.

December 15, 1950   From the Oval Office, the President said he would declare a state of emergency the next day, and announced the appointment of Charles E. Wilson, president of General Electric, as the head of the Office of Defense Mobilization, a new agency.

January 8, 1951   In a State of the Union address before a joint session of Congress, he spoke of the possibility of full mobilization for the war in Korea.

April 11, 1951   He spoke about foreign policy in the Far East and the dismissal of General MacArthur.

May 7, 1951   In a speech before a civil-defense conference at the Hotel Statler in Washington, the President argued against General MacArthur's recommendations regarding the war.

June 14, 1951   From the Oval Office, he talked about inflation and high prices.

July 28, 1951   From Detroit's Cadillac Square, the President pleaded against a let-down in defense mobilization.

September 4, 1951   Speaking at the Japanese Peace Conference in San Francisco, he complimented the Japanese on their recovery but said that they would have to regain the friendship of other nations.

November 7, 1951   From the White House, the President asked the Soviet Union to accept a new, "foolproof" disarmament plan to preclude World War III.

January 5, 1952   He greeted Winston Churchill at the Washington airport.

January 9, 1952   In a State of the Union address, he said that national politics must not be allowed to hurt national interests, and expressed the hope that Congress would ratify the Japanese Peace Treaty. He added that he wanted to initiate federal aid to education and national health insurance.

March 6, 1952   From the White House, the President spoke on the Mutual Security Program.

April 8, 1952   From the White House, he announced that he had directed Secretary of Commerce Charles Sawyer to take over and operate the steel mills.

May 3, 1952   After the White House had been renovated, Truman conducted a tour of the building for representatives of the three networks. During the tour, he commented on the renovations and spoke about the history and events that had occurred in various rooms. In the East Room, he played several measures of Mozart's "9th Sonata" on the gold Steinway and a few measures on the

Baldwin at the opposite end of the room. When thanked by one of the network representatives for conducting the tour, he said, "Not at all. Glad to do it."

June 10, 1952   From the House chamber, the President asked Congress to act quickly on the matter of the Federal Government's operating the steel mills.

January 1, 1953   From the Executive Wing of the White House, he delivered his informal farewell address.

DWIGHT D. EISENHOWER

January 20, 1953   The inaugural address by President Eisenhower began with an unscheduled prayer. He then stated that war was not "a chosen way" to end the threat of international communism.

February 2, 1953   In a State of the Union address, the President spoke of recommendations he would make to Congress which included elimination of waste in government, a balanced budget before any tax reductions, an amended Taft-Hartley law, and decontrol of prices and wages.

December 8, 1953   Upon his return from the Bermuda Conference, the President addressed the United Nations General Assembly in New York, and spoke on the "atomic perils" that existed in the world.

January 4, 1954   In his report to the nation, the President tried to allay some of the anxieties of the economic recession by looking forward to a "new year more fruitful to the security of the nation and the welfare of its people."

January 7, 1954   In a State of the Union address, he spoke of a stronger America prepared to meet any renewed aggression in Korea.

October 25, 1954   In the first White House cabinet meeting to be televised, the President stated that the purpose of the meeting was to hear Secretary of State John Foster Dulles report on the Paris Agreement.

January 6, 1955   In a State of the Union address, he asked for more cooperation from the Democratic-controlled Congress.

January 19, 1955   He held the first Presidental news conference covered by TV.

April 25, 1955   At an American Newspaper Association luncheon at the Waldorf Astoria, in New York, the President announced plans to build an atomic-powered merchant ship to demonstrate a peaceful use for atomic energy.

July 15, 1955   From the broadcast room in the White House, President Eisenhower expressed his hopes for the Big-Four Conference in Geneva.

July 25, 1955   From the Oval Office, he reported on the results of the Geneva Conference.

November 11, 1955   He delivered his first public speech since his heart attack, on September 9, 1955.

January 5, 1956   His State of the Union message was delivered to Congress by a clerk. The President was not well enough to give the speech himself.

February 29, 1956   He spoke to the American people about his decision to run for re-election.

October 31, 1956   From the White House, the President spoke about the Middle East Crisis.

January 5, 1957   Before a joint session of Congress, the President requested special powers to deploy troops. The request was based on the Middle East Crisis and the Hungarian Revolt against Soviet occupation.

January 10, 1957   In a State of the Union address, the President discussed inflation, civil rights, and the international situation.

January 21, 1957   His second inaugural address covered the Middle East Crisis and Israel's refusal to withdraw her troops behind the armistice lines.

May 14, 1957   From the White House, the President talked about the federal budget.

May 21, 1957   From the White House, he discussed why it was necessary to provide foreign aid in the form of arms, economic and technical assistance, and propaganda.

September 24, 1957   From the Oval Office he explained that he mustered federal troops in Little Rock, Arkansas, to enforce school integration.

November 7, 1957   From the Oval Office, he talked about science and national security. He said America was well ahead of the Soviets in nuclear science. On one side of his desk, a rocket nose-cone was on display.

January 9, 1958   In a State of the Union, the President presented an eight-point program dealing with atomic missiles, economic cold war, and the "brush-fire war" in the Pentagon—the last referring to interservice rivalries.

May 22, 1958   At the dedication ceremonies of NBC's new color studios in Washington, he spoke briefly about the importance of the communications industry. This was the first time a President appeared on color TV.

January 3, 1959   From the Cabinet Room of the White House, the President spoke briefly following the signing of the documents proclaiming Alaska the 49th State of the Union. He displayed a 49-star flag.

January 9, 1959   In a State of the Union address, he discussed foreign aid, civil rights, foreign relations, and labor problems.

March 16, 1959   From the Oval Office, the President spoke about Soviet–American relations and suggested a meeting between the two super powers if such a meeting could be meaningful.

September 10, 1959   Speaking from the White House, the President discussed his recent trip to Europe and Khrushchev's forthcoming visit to the U.S.

January 7, 1960   In a State of the Union address, he spoke about Russia, missiles, inflation, and civil rights.

May 20, 1960   On his arrival at Andrews Air Force Base, the President spoke about the failure of his summit meeting.

May 25, 1960   From the White House, the President said that in spite of the collapse of the summit conference, "we must continue businesslike dealings with the Soviet leaders."

January 17, 1961   He delivered his farewell address to the nation.

JOHN F. KENNEDY

January 20, 1961   Kennedy's inaugural address focused on world politics.

May 25, 1961   Before Congress, the President called for an increased budget for the space program, foreign aid, and defense.

June 2, 1961   In Paris, when addressing the Anglo-American Diplomatic Association, the President commented on the trip by saying "I am the man who accompanied Jacqueline Kennedy to Paris."

June 6, 1961   In his first address from the White House, he spoke about his trip to Europe and his meetings with DeGaulle, Khrushchev, and Macmillan.

July 25, 1961   From the White House, the President addressed the nation on the Berlin Crisis.

January 11, 1962   He delivered a State of the Union address before a joint session of Congress.

February 23, 1962   The President presented a medal to John Glenn, America's first astronaut to orbit the earth, at Cape Canaveral (later Cape Kennedy).

May 2, 1962   From the Oval Office, he spoke about plans to resume atmospheric nuclear testing.

August 13, 1962   From Washington, the President said he would not recommend reducing taxes to stimulate the economy.

September 30, 1962   From the White House, the President, speaking on integration in Mississippi, urged the university students and the people of the state to obey the law.

October 22, 1962   He informed the American people of Cuba's intent to install nuclear missiles on the island. He announced an embargo on shipping to Cuba and promised close surveillance of the island.

November 2, 1962   Speaking from the White House, he told the nation that Cuba was dismantling the Soviet missile bases it had installed.

December 29, 1962   He addressed freed Cuban prisoners and accepted the brigade's flag, saying one day it would be returned to a free Cuba.

January 14, 1963   He delivered a State of the Union address.

June 10, 1963   From the American University in Washington, DC, the President spoke on a strategy of peace for easing cold-war tensions.

June 11, 1963   From Washington, he spoke to the nation about civil-rights in Alabama.

June 26, 1963   The President addressed the people of Berlin, remarking "Ich bin ein Berliner" (I am a Berliner). His speech was transmitted by satellite.

June 27, 1963   In Dunganstown, Ireland, his ancestral birthplace, he spoke with relatives outside a farm house. The occasion was transmitted by satellite.

July 26, 1963   From the Oval Office, he urged Congress to ratify a limited nuclear-test-ban treaty.

September 18, 1963   From the Oval Office, he requested support for his program of tax reduction to boost the economy.

September 20, 1963   In an address before the UN General Assembly in New York, the President suggested a joint USA–USSR expedition to the moon.

LYNDON BAINES JOHNSON

November 22, 1963   At Andrews Air Base, the new President addressed the nation for the first time following the assassination of John F. Kennedy in Dallas. "This is a sad time for all people. We have suffered a loss that cannot be weighed. For me it is a deep personal tragedy. I know the world shares the sorrow that Mrs. Kennedy and her family bear. I will do my best. That is all I can do. I ask your help, and God's."

November 26, 1963   From the East Room, before the Latin American delegations who attended the Kennedy funeral, the President discussed the Alliance for Progress.

November 27, 1963   Before a joint session of Congress, the President asked for quick passage of civil-rights and tax legislation.

November 28, 1963   Delivering a Thanksgiving Day message from the Oval Office, he announced that Cape Canaveral would be renamed Cape Kennedy.

December 17, 1963   In his first address before the UN General Assembly in New York, the President pledged continuing support of the UN by the United States.

January 8, 1964   In a State of the Union address, he declared war on poverty and announced a budget below $100 billion. The speech was interrupted 80 times by applause.

January 21, 1964   From the White House, the President offered to negotiate with the Soviet Union to halt the arms race.

April 9, 1964   From the White House, the President announced a 15-day postponement of a threatened railroad strike.

August 4, 1964   From the White House, he stated that U.S. aircraft had been ordered to attack North Vietnamese gunboats and support facilities after the second attack by the Viet Cong in international waters.

August 5, 1964   The President discussed the Vietnam crisis at the dedication ceremonies for the Newhouse Communications Center, at Syracuse University.

October 16, 1964   From the White House, the President announced that Khrushchev had been ousted as Premier of the Soviet Union and China had entered the nuclear age with the testing of its first nuclear bomb.

October 18, 1964   From the White House, he discussed at length the ousting of Khrushchev and China's newly acquired nuclear ability.

January 4, 1965   In a State of the Union address, he outlined his Great Society program.

January 20, 1965   He delivered his inaugural address.

March 13, 1965   At a Presidential news conference, he made a lengthy statement about civil rights and said he would send a voting rights bill to Congress.

March 15, 1965   In the House Chamber before a joint session of Congress, the President demanded immediate action on the voting-rights measure. He wanted every barrier of discrimination against Negro citizens trying to vote or register removed.

March 23, 1965   From the Oval Office, the President offered his congratulations to Astronauts Grissom and Young via telephone.

March 26, 1965   From the White House, he spoke about the murder of Mrs. Liuzzo, a civil-rights worker, and declared war on the Ku Klux Klan.

April 7, 1965   From Shriver Hall, at Johns Hopkins University, in Baltimore, he delivered a foreign-policy statement regarding the United States' position on the war in Vietnam.

April 28, 1965   From the White House, the President announced that he had ordered troops into the Dominican Republic to protect and evacuate Americans.

May 7, 1965   From the TV Theatre in the White House, the President addressed the nation and Europe, via satellite, on the 20th Anniversary of V-E Day. He contrasted the 20 years of prosperity which followed WW II to those following WW I.

May 13, 1965   From the East Room of the White House, the President spoke to the Association of American Editorial Cartoonists about the Vietnam War.

May 15, 1965   From the White House, he announced that he would ask Congress to cut excise taxes.

June 7, 1965   From the Fish Room of the White House, the President spoke to Astronauts McDivit and White, who had just completed the successful flight of Gemini 4.

June 21, 1965   From the White House, he spoke briefly and then signed the Excise Tax Reduction Act of 1965.

June 25, 1965   At the War Memorial Opera House, in San Francisco, he addressed the UN on its 20th anniversary. He asked the UN to influence and lead North Vietnam to the conference table for a negotiated peace.

July 28, 1965   At a Presidential news conference, he delivered a lengthy statement on Vietnam and announced the appointment of Abe Fortas to succeed Arthur Goldberg on the Supreme Court.

July 29, 1965   From the White House, the President announced that agreement had been reached in the airline strike, but that ratification by the union was still needed.

July 30, 1965   From the Harry S Truman Memorial Library, in Independence, Missouri, the President signed the Medicare bill. He signed the bill in the presence of Mr. Truman, the first President to propose such a federal program.

August 6, 1965   From the Capitol Rotunda, President Johnson signed the Voting Rights Act of 1965. A brief speech was made and souvenir pens were passed out.

September 24, 1965   From the White House, the President reported on a new treaty for the Panama Canal, one to replace the 1903 agreement. He spoke of those points upon which agreement had been reached.

October 3, 1965   From Liberty Island, in New York, the President briefly spoke and then signed the Immigration Bill.

January 12, 1966   In a State of the Union address, the President asked continued support of the war effort and his Great Society programs. This was the first time the State of the Union speech was televised in color.

January 31, 1966   From the East Wing of the White House, he announced renewed bombing of North Vietnam, after a 37-day pause.

February 4, 1966   From the White House, he announced he would go to Honolulu to meet with South Vietnamese leaders.

July 12, 1966   From the White House, the President delivered his first major speech on Red China.

August 6, 1966   At the White House, on the day of the wedding of Luci Baines Johnson and Patrick Nugent, he did not speak except to say a word to Nancy Dickerson, a newswoman whose father had died a week earlier.

September 21, 1966   He held a news conference—the first televised in color.

October 24, 1966   He spoke briefly upon arriving in Manila.

October 27, 1966   The President, visiting Cam Ranh Bay in South Vietnam, spoke to American troops.

January 10, 1967　In a State of the Union address, he asked Congress for a 10 percent surcharge on personal and corporate income taxes to pay for the Vietnam War, the surcharge to be in effect for two years.

June 6, 1967　From the White House, he made a statement on the cease-fire vote in the U.N. Security Council concerning the Middle East Crisis.

June 19, 1967　From the State Department auditorium, the President discussed the Middle East Crisis.

June 23, 1967　From Glassboro, New Jersey, the President talked about his conference with Russia's Premier Kosygin.

July 24, 1967　From the White House, the President addressed the nation on the riots in Detroit and told of authorizing federal troops to be deployed there.

July 27, 1967　From the Oval Office, he announced the formation of a committee to investigate the riots and said rioters should be prosecuted as criminals.

September 29, 1967　Before the National Legislative Conference in San Antonio, Texas, the President delivered a policy address on Vietnam, answering those critical of America's war efforts.

December 9, 1967　TV cameras covered the President escorting his daughter Lynda Bird to the White House chapel to be wed.

January 17, 1968　He delivered a State of the Union address.

January 26, 1968　From the White House, the President discussed the Korean crisis that resulted from the Pueblo incident.

March 31, 1968　From the White House, he announced he would not run for re-election and that he would de-escalate the Vietnam War.

April 5, 1968　From the White House, the President made a statement on the Reverend Martin Luther King's death, which had occurred the day before, and proclaimed a national day of mourning.

April 11, 1968　From the White House, President Johnson spoke about the Civil Rights Act of 1968 and signed it into law.

May 3, 1968　At a Presidential news conference held in the East Room of the White House, the President announced that the United States and Hanoi had agreed to hold preliminary peace talks in Paris.

July 1, 1968　From the White House, the President discussed a nuclear anti-proliferation treaty.

RICHARD M. NIXON

January 20, 1969　President Nixon delivered his inaugural address.

May 14, 1969　From the White House, he reported on the situation in Vietnam.

September 9, 1969　From the Rotunda, in Washington, he delivered the eulogy for Senator Everett Dirksen.

September 18, 1969　From the UN in New York, he spoke on foreign policy.

November 3, 1969　From the Oval Office, he discussed Vietnam matters.

November 14, 1969　From Cape Kennedy, he witnessed his first space launch. He spoke to the crew of Apollo XII and the firing room crew and praised them for their efforts.

November 24, 1969　From the White House, by telephone, he talked to the returning astronauts and invited them to the White House.

December 8, 1969　At a news conference, he talked about the My Lai incident.

December 15, 1969　From the Oval Office, he discussed the Vietnam situation and announced forthcoming troop withdrawal.

January 22, 1970　He delivered a State of the Union address.

January 26, 1970　From the White House, he vetoed the HEW Bill. This was the first veto on TV.

March 23, 1970　From the White House, the President discussed the postal-workers strike.

April 18, 1970　From the Spacecraft Center, in Houston, the President spoke briefly to the ground crew of Apollo XIII before awarding them medals.

April 20, 1970　From San Clemente, the President announced that he would withdraw 150,000 ground troops from South Vietnam within the next year.

April 30, 1970　From the White House, he stated that he had decided to send U.S. troops into Cambodia to eliminate communist-troop sanctuaries.

June 3, 1970　From the White House, he reassured the American people that American troops would be out of Cambodia by June 30.

June 17, 1970　From the Oval Office, the President reported on the state of the nation's economy.

July 1, 1970 From the ABC-TV studios in Washington was broadcast "A Conversation with the President." The President was interviewed by Eric Sevareid, Howard K. Smith, and John Chancellor. He began by announcing the appointment of David Bruce as the US Ambassador to the Paris peace talks.

October 7, 1970 From the White House, he discussed his five-point peace plan for Indochina.

October 23, 1970 From the United Nations, he addressed the General Assembly on the 25th Anniversary of the UN.

January 4, 1971 From the Presidential library in the White House, "A Conversation with the President": The President was interviewed by Eric Sevareid, Howard K. Smith, John Chancellor and Nancy Dickerson.

January 22, 1971 He delivered a State of the Union address, in which he spoke only of domestic policies and issues.

March 17, 1971 He delivered a eulogy at the funeral of Whitney M. Young, Jr.

March 22, 1971 At the White House, he was interviewed by Howard K. Smith.

April 7, 1971 From the White House, the President spoke about his plans on troop withdrawal from Vietnam and the end of American involvement in the war.

May 20, 1971 From the White House, he discussed a pact with Russia to limit AMBs and ICBMs.

July 15, 1971 From NBC Studio 2 in Burbank, the President announced he would visit China in May, 1972.

August 15, 1971 From the White House, he announced a new economic policy that included a 90-day freeze on wages and prices and a 10 percent surcharge on imports.

September 9, 1971 Before a joint session of Congress, he asked for cooperation and legislation to implement his new economic policies.

October 7, 1971 From the White House, he announced Phase II of his economic program, which involved close government supervision of prices and wages once the freeze was lifted.

October 21, 1971 From the White House, he explained the criteria he used to select the newest Supreme Court judges.

January 25, 1972 From the White House, he revealed to the nation that secret peace talks with North Vietnam had been in progress since August 4, 1969. It was an eight-point peace plan which included withdrawal of all U.S. troops within six months of the agreement date, release of all U.S. POW's in the same time period, and the resignation of President Thieu of South Vietnam.

January 20, 1972 In a State of the Union address, he asked Congress to support him and said 1972 could be the year the country made significant progress toward peace.

February 17, 1972 From Andrews Air Force Base, the President briefly addressed the group seeing him off on his trip to China.

February 28, 1972 From Andrews Air Force Base, the President made a brief speech on his return from China.

March 16, 1972 From the White House, he discussed the legislation he was sending to Congress that would place a moratorium on new busing of school children, and the Equal Education Opportunities Act of 1972.

April 26, 1972 From the White House, he talked about the bombing of North Vietnam. He said there would be continued troop withdrawal but air support would be made available to the South Vietnamese ground forces.

May 8, 1972 From the White House, he announced he would mine the North Vietnamese harbors and continue naval and air strikes until all American POW's were released and a cease-fire declared throughout Indochina.

May 22, 1972 He arrived in Russia for a summit conference.

May 29, 1972 He signed a "declaration of principles."

June 1, 1972 Before Congress, the President reported on his summit talks in Russia.

November 7, 1972 From the Oval Office, he made a brief statement upon being re-elected.

December 27, 1972 President Nixon traveled to Independence, Missouri, to attend the funeral of President Truman.

January 23, 1973 From the White House, he announced the signing of a cease-fire agreement in Viet Nam.

March 29, 1973 From the White House, he spoke to the Nation on the eve of the completion of the troop withdrawal from Viet Nam and the relase of the POW's.

April 30, 1973   From the White House, he announced Watergate-related changes in the White House staff, and the appointment of Elliot Richardson as Attorney General. Though he knew nothing about Watergate, he accepted the blame for what had happened, he said.

June 13, 1973   From the Oval Office, he discussed new economic measures to combat inflation.

August 15, 1973   From the Oval Office, he said he would not turn over his tapes to the Senate Select Committee and again protested his innocence with respect to the break-in and the cover-up. He said the affair should be left up to the courts and that the nation should get on with its business.

October 12, 1973   From the East Room in the White House, President Nixon named Gerald R. Ford Vice President designate, upon the resignation of Vice President Agnew.

November 7, 1973   From the White House, the President addressed the nation on the Middle East oil embargo. He introduced a plan called Project Independence, which was to make the country, in respect of energy, self-sufficient by 1980. He closed the talk with an indication that he would not resign.

November 25, 1973   From the Oval Office, he again addressed the nation on the energy crisis.

January 17, 1974   From the White House, he announced that Egypt and Israel had reached agreement on troop disengagement.

April 29, 1974   From the Oval Office, the President, in response to a subpoena from the House Judiciary Committee for the White House tapes, outlined his compromise proposal of turning over a printed transcript of the tapes.

May 29, 1974   From the White House, he announced an agreement between Syria and Israel on a separation of forces.

July 2, 1974   From a room in the Kremlin, President Nixon addressed the people of the Soviet Union and America simultaneously. He said that the relationship between the U.S. and the U.S.S.R. had progressed from confrontation to negotiation.

July 3, 1974   From Loring Air Base in Maine, he addressed the nation upon returning from Russia.

July 25, 1974   From the Century Plaza Hotel in Los Angeles, the President spoke on the problem of inflation, and introduced new policies to stabilize the economy.

August 8, 1974   From the Oval Office, the President resigned from office. At 9:04 P.M., EST, he became the first President to do so.

August 9, 1974   From the White House, the President said farewell to the White House Staff.

GERALD R. FORD

August 9, 1974   President Ford delivered his inaugural address.

August 12, 1974   Before Congress, he discussed inflation and asked for more cooperation between Congress and the Executive branch.

August 20, 1974   From the Oval Office, he announced that Nelson A. Rockefeller was his choice as Vice President.

September 8, 1974   He granted former President Nixon a "full, free, and absolute pardon for any and all criminal offenses he committed or may have committed while in office."

September 16, 1974   From the Cabinet Room in the White House, the President announced his program for conditional amnesty for Viet Nam draft evaders and military deserters, and created a nine-man clemency review board.

September 18, 1974   Before the UN General Assembly, he delivered his first foreign policy address.

September 28, 1974   From the Hilton Hotel in Washington, he addressed the 800 representatives to his economic summit meeting.

October 8, 1974   Before Congress, he proposed a ten-point program to combat inflation.

January 13, 1975   From the library in the White House, he announced his proposals to fight inflation and conserve energy. For this particular talk, he used a prompter, which allowed him to look directly into the camera throughout the broadcast.

March 29, 1975   From the Oval Office, the President discussed a tax-cut bill recently signed into law.

May 27, 1975   From the Oval Office, he accused Congress of dragging its feet on energy conservation and a national energy policy.

May 28, 1975   Before his departure to Europe, he made a statement regarding the importance of the trip.

July 15, 1975   From the White House, he discussed the significance of the Apollo–Soyuz docking mission.

July 17, 1975   From the White House, by telephone, he talked to the astronauts in space.

July 25, 1975   After the splashdown of the Apollo flight, the President spoke about the successful mission.

July 28, 1975   On his arrival in Warsaw, Poland, the President spoke about his reasons for going to Eastern Europe.

September 22, 1975   An assassination attempt was made in San Francisco on President Ford's life, but the gun did not fire.

October 6, 1975   From the White House, he discussed the economy and a proposed tax cut.

December 1, 1975   He arrived in China for official talks.

January 5, 1976   In the White House, he was interviewed by NBC. He discussed foreign policy.

January 5, 1976   He delivered a State of the Union address.

February 17, 1976   He held a news conference, and made a statement on control of intelligence agencies.

August 19, 1976   At the Republican convention, in Kansas City, President Ford announced that Robert Dole would be his running mate.

September 9, 1976   From the White House, he eulogized Mao Tse-tung.

September 23, 1976   From the Walnut Street Theatre, in Philadelphia, he debated Democratic Presidential candidate Jimmy Carter.

October 6, 1976   From the Palace of Fine Arts Theatre, in San Francisco, he debated Carter.

October 14, 1976   At a news conference, he made a brief statement that he was glad a special prosecutor had found no misuse of his campaign funds while he was a representative from Michigan.

October 22, 1976   From the Phi Beta Kappa Hall at the College of William and Mary, in Williamsburg, Virginia, he debated Carter.

November 3, 1976   From the White House, he conceded the election to Carter. He being unable to speak, Mrs. Ford read the concession speech.

January 12, 1977   He delivered a State of the Union address before a joint session of Congress.

JIMMY CARTER

January 20, 1977   President Carter delivered his inaugural address.

March 17, 1977   Before the General Assembly of the UN, he spoke about America's foreign policy.

February 2, 1977   From the White House, he announced the signing of the Emergency National Gas Act. He also spoke of long-term energy legislation.

April 18, 1977   From the Oval Office, he spoke to the nation about the energy crisis.

April 20, 1977   Before a joint session of Congress, he discussed energy legislation.

September 7, 1977   In Washington, he signed the Panama Canal Treaty.

January 15, 1978   He delivered a eulogy at the memorial services for Senator Hubert Humphrey, in Washington, DC.

January 19, 1978   In a State of the Union address, he talked about the economy, energy, and the Panama Canal Treaty.

February 1, 1978   At the White House, the President discussed the Panama Canal Treaty.

February 24, 1978   From the Oval Office, he talked about a coal-strike settlement. His remarks were carried live on the nightly news of all three major networks.

March 6, 1978   In the Oval Office, he discussed invoking the Taft-Hartley Act in the lingering coal strike.

June 7, 1978   At Annapolis, he discussed detente.

September 18, 1978   Before Congress, the President, with Messrs. Begin, of Israel, and Sadat, of Egypt, signed an initial peace accord and pledged to continue peace negotiations.

October 24, 1978   From the White House, he discussed his antiinflation program.

January 23, 1979   In a State of the Union Address, he talked about effective government, controlling inflation, and the new strategic arms accord with Russia.

January 29, 1979   From the White House, President Carter welcomed Vice Premier Deng, of China.

March 8, 1979   President Carter traveled to the Mideast to negotiate the final peace agreement.

July 22, 1979   Carter gives major turning-point speech centering on energy and the "poor confidence of the American public."

Political Campaigning on TV

The Communications Act of 1934:
FACILITIES FOR CANDIDATES FOR PUBLIC OFFICE

Sec. 315. (a) If any licensee shall permit any person who is a legally qualified candidate for any public office to use a broadcasting station, he shall afford equal opportunities to all other such candidates for that office in the use of such broadcasting station: provided, that such licensee shall have no power of censorship over the material broadcast under the provisions of this section. No obligation is hereby imposed upon any licensee to allow the use of its station by any such candidate. Appearance by a legally qualified candidate on any

(1) bona fide newscast,
(2) bona fide news interview,
(3) bona fide news documentary (if the appearance of the candidate is incidental to the presentation of the subject or subjects covered by the news documentary), or
(4) on-the-spot coverage of bona fide news events (including but not limited to political conventions and activities incidental thereto)

shall not be deemed to be use of a broadcasting station within the meaning of this subsection. Nothing in the foregoing sentence shall be construed as relieving broadcasters, in connection with the presentation of newscasts, news interviews, news documentaries, and on-the-spot coverage of news events, from the obligation imposed upon them under this act to operate in the public interest and to afford reasonable opportunity for the discussion of conflicting views on issues of public importance.

(b) The charges made for the use of any broadcasting station for any of the purposes set forth in this section shall not exceed the charges made for comparable use of such station for other purposes.

(c) The commission shall prescribe appropriate rules and regulations to carry out the provisions of this section.

EXCERPTS FROM FEDERAL COMMUNICATIONS COMMISSION RULES AND REGULATIONS

Broadcasts by candidates for public office (following supplements Sec. 315 of the Communications Act)

3.657(TV) Broadcasts by candidates for public office.

(a) **Definitions.** A "legally qualified candidate" means any person who has publicly announced that he is a candidate for nomination by a convention of a political party or for nomination or election in a primary, special, or general election, municipal, county, state, or national, and who meets the qualifications prescribed by the applicable laws to hold the office for which he is a candidate, so that he may be voted for by the electorate directly or by means of delegates or electors, and who

(1) has qualified for a place on the ballot, or

(2) is eligible under the applicable law to be voted for by sticker, by writing in his name on the ballot, or other method, and

(i) has been duly nominated by a political party which is commonly known and regarded as such, or

(ii) makes a substantial showing that he is a bona fide candidate for nomination for office, as the case may be.

(b) **General requirements.** No station licensee is required to permit the use of its facilities by any legally qualified candidate for public office, but if any licensee shall permit any such candidate to use its facilities, it shall afford equal opportunities to all other such candidates for that office to use such facilities: Provided, that such licensee shall have no power of censorship over the material broadcast by any such candidate.

(c) **Rates and practices.** (1) The rates, if any, charged all such candidates for the same office shall be uniform and shall not be rebated by any means, direct or indirect. A candidate shall, in each case, be charged no more than the rate the station would charge if the candidate were a commercial advertiser whose advertising was directed to promoting its business within the same area as that encompassed by the particular office for which such person is a candidate. All discount privileges otherwise offered by a station to commercial advertisers shall be available upon equal terms to all candidates for public office.

(2) In making time available to candidates for public office no licensee shall make any discrimination between candidates in charges, practices, regulations, facilities, or services for or in connection with the service rendered pursuant to this part, or make or give any preference to any candidate for public office or subject any such candidate to any prejudice or disadvantage; nor shall any licensee make any contract or other agreement which shall have the effect of permitting any legally qualified candidate for any public office to broadcast to the exclusion of other legally qualified candidates for the same public office.

(d) **Records; inspection.** Every licensee shall keep and permit public inspection of a complete record of all requests for broadcast time made by or on behalf of candidates for public office, together with an appropriate notation showing the disposition made by the licensee of such requests, and the charges made, if any, if request is granted. Such records shall be retained for a period of two years.

(e) A request for equal opportunities must be submitted to the licensee within one week of the day on which the prior use occurred.

(f) A candidate requesting such equal opportunities of the licensee or complaining of noncompliance to the commission shall have the burden of proving that he and his opponent are legally qualified candidates for the same public office.

Major TV Production Companies

Avco Embassy Pictures
6601 Romaine
Los Angeles, CA 90038
(213) 462-7211

Chuck Barris Productions
6430 Sunset Blvd.
Hollywood, CA 90028
(213) 469-9080

Barry & Enright Productions
1888 Century Park East
Los Angeles, CA 90067
(213) 277-3414

The Bryna Company (Kirk Douglas)
141 El Camino Dr. #205
Beverly Hills, CA 90212
(213) 274-5294

Columbia Pictures
Col-Gems Sq.
Burbank, CA 91505
(213) 843-7280

Ralph Edwards Productions
5746 Sunset Blvd.
Hollywood, CA 90028
(213) 462-7111

Charles Fries Productions, Inc.
Alpine Productions
4024 N. Radford Ave.
Studio City, CA 91604
(213) 763-8411

Goodson-Todman Productions
6430 W. Sunset Blvd.
Hollywood, CA 90028
(213) 461-8211

Merv Griffin Productions
1541 N. Vine St.
Hollywood, CA 90028
(213) 461-4701

Hatos-Hall Productions
7833 W. Sunset Blvd.
Los Angeles, CA 90028
(213) 874-3000

Heatter Quigley Production
9255 Sunset Blvd.
Los Angeles, CA 90067
(213) 278-8870

Jerry Lewis Films, Inc.
1888 Century Park East #830
Los Angeles, CA 90067
(213) 552-2200

Lorimar Productions
4000 Warner Blvd.
Burbank, CA 91505
(213) 843-6000

Lyn Productions, Inc. (Michael Landon)
3700 Wilshire Blvd. #900
Los Angeles, CA 90010
(213) 381-5393

Metro-Goldwyn-Mayer, Inc.
10202 W. Washington Blvd.
Culver City, CA 90230
(213) 836-3000

MTM Enterprises, Inc.
CBS Studio Center
4024 Radford Ave.
Studio City, CA 91604
(213) 763-8411

Paramount Pictures Corp.
5451 Marathon St.
Hollywood, CA 90038
(213) 463-0100

Quinn Martin Productions
9595 Wilshire Blvd.
Beverly Hills, CA 90024
(213) 273-2330

Bob Stewart Productions
250 W. 57th St.
New York, NY 10019
(212) 730-4515

United Artists
10202 W. Washington Blvd.
Culver City, CA 90230
(213) 559-3450

Universal Studios
100 Universal City Plaza
Universal City, CA 91608
(213) 985-4321

Warner Bros.
4000 Warner Blvd.
Burbank, CA 91505
(213) 843-6000

The Zanuck/Brown Company
100 Universal City Plaza
Universal City, CA 91608
(213) 985-4321

Public and Educational Television

The term *educational television* reflects its use in the FCC Rules and Regulations (Subpart E, Sec. 73.621, noncommercial educational television stations) and includes all television stations licensed for noncommercial operation, whether the programming is cultural, instructional, public affairs or otherwise.

The term *public television* came into use with the passage of the Public Broadcasting Act of 1967. Most noncommercial television stations use *public* to describe themselves. The abbreviation P/ETV is sometimes used to designate public–educational television.

Virtually the entire country, including Puerto Rico, Guam, and the Virgin Islands, is served by noncommercial television.

Noncommercial television is an integral part of both formal and informal education. It brings into the home cultural events, public-affairs presentations, and a variety of other programs previously available only to those who had the means and the opportunities to seek them out in areas such as concert halls, opera houses, etc.

About one-fifth of noncommercial television time is devoted to programs for the classroom, where it presents instructors, demonstrations, and visual and aural materials that greatly increase the value of students' learning experiences.

The first noncommercial educational television station went on the air in May, 1953. By June, 1976, the number of educational stations had grown to 160 UHF and 100 VHF outlets. Moreover, by May, 1976, 169 instructional-television-fixed-service (ITFS) systems, with approximately 450 channels, had begun operation since that service was established by the Federal Communications Commission, in 1963.

HISTORY

Noncommercial educational broadcasting dates back to the beginning of broadcasting as a public-communications service. Educational institutions were among the pioneers in experimental radios, which led to the establishment of regular AM broadcasting following World War I.

In 1941, the FCC allocated five channels for noncommercial FM broadcasting and in 1945 increased the number to 20. By May, 1976, there were 856 educational FM stations and 30 noncommercial AM stations on the air.

In 1949, the FCC invited comments on the advisability of providing channels for noncommercial educational television, and on March 22, 1951, as part of a general review of television, the Commission proposed establishing reserved educational-TV channels.

On April 14, 1952, after extensive proceedings, the Commission opened UHF channels for expanding TV needs and at the same time reserved 242 channel assignments (80 UHF and 162 VHF) for noncommercial educational use. These reserved channels constituted about 12 percent of the total allocations at that time. The FCC said the following:

We conclude that the record shows the desire and ability of education to make a substantial contribution to the use of television. There is much evidence in the record concerning the activities of educational organizations in AM and FM broadcasting. It is true and was to be expected that education has not utilized these media to the full extent that commercial broadcasters have, in terms of number of stations and number of hours in operation. However, it has also been shown that many of the educational institutions which are engaged in aural broadcasting are doing an outstanding job in the presentation of high-quality programming, and have been getting excellent public response.

And most important in this connection, it is agreed that the potential of television for education is much greater and more readily apparent than that of aural broadcasting, and that the interest of the educational community in the field is much greater than it was in aural broadcasting. . . .

The public interest will clearly be served if these stations are used to contribute significantly to the educational process of the nation. The type of programs which have been broadcast by educational organizations, and those which the record indicated can and would be televised by educators, will provide a valuable complement to commercial programming.

GROWTH AND DEVELOPMENT

The first ETV station to go on the air was KUHT, University of Houston, Texas, on May 12, 1953.

The table of channel allocations, including noncommercial educational reservations, has been revised several times since it was first issued. A major revision, issued in June, 1965, and corrected in March, 1966, provided for 107 VHF and 508 UHF ETV reservations, an increase of more than two-thirds over the previous total, providing for 20 percent of total reservations.

This allocations plan was designed to permit future selection and assignment of unallocated channels to places where at that time noncommercial TV was not anticipated. As of June, 1976, 130 VHF and 537 UHF allocations were reserved for educational television. Nine of the P/ETV stations on the air, however, were operating on nonreserved channels.

The steady growth of ETV is illustrated in the following table of stations on the air at the end of each calendar year:

Year	Number
1953	1
1954	10
1955	17
1956	21
1957	27
1958	35
1959	44
1960	51
1961	62
1962	75
1963	84
1964	100
1965	113
1966	125
1967	151
1968	179
1969	187
1970	200
1971	212
1972	232
1973	240
1974	248
1975	258
1976 (June)	260

Seventy-eight percent of the American population, 162 million Americans, lives within range of a noncommercial television signal. A study in 1975 showed 49.2 percent monthly and 31.4 percent weekly viewing of public television by the nation's households.

The commission also licenses translators and boosters for relaying P/ETV broadcast signals and has jurisdiction over microwaving such signals.

On July 25, 1963, the FCC established the Instructional Television Fixed Service for the transmission of instructional and cultural materials to schools and other selected receiving locations, following an experiment in the 2000 megacycle (1990–2110) band in the Plainedge, Long Island, N.Y., school district. The Plainview–Old Bethpage Schools system was the first on the air, on March 2, 1964, in the 2500–2690 MHz ITFS band.

In early 1967, after almost two years of study of the technical, organizational, financial, and programming considerations of noncommercial television, the Carnegie Commission on Educational Television published a report, *Public Television: A Program for Action*. Its recommendations for P/ETV's future support and development were the bases for the initiation of the Public Broadcasting Act of 1967.

Title I of the act extended the matching-grant concept of the Educational Television Facilities Act of 1962 and included educational radio in the grants for the first time. In subsequent extensions of the Public Broadcasting Act of 1967, Congress provided for a federal share of facilities costs as high as 75 percent and for liberal use of funds for interconnection.

Title II of the act authorized establishment of a Corporation for Public Broadcasting (CPB), to function as a nonprofit enterprise, rather than as a U.S. government agency. The mission of the CPB is to foster the development of public broadcasting by supporting the production of program materials for noncommercial television and radio stations, station operation, interconnection of stations, and research and training in educational broadcasting, and to serve film-and-tape library and clearinghouse functions. A major CPB effort was the establishment of the Public Broadcasting Service (PBS) to manage the national distribution of TV programs.

Through the 1974–75 fiscal year, CPB and the Educational Broadcasting Facilities received annual appropriations for their matching-grant program operated by the U.S. Office of Education. In 1975, Congress passed a long-range, five-year funding bill.

NONCOMMERCIAL TV BROADCAST STATIONS

Of the 260 stations on the air in June, 1976, about 10 percent were licensed to local public-school systems, 30 percent to colleges and universities, 25 percent to community organizations, and 35 percent to states and municipal authorities.

At first, virtually all of the ETV stations were VHF. Since 1960, however, most of the construction permit (CP) grants and applications have been in the UHF part of the spectrum, and, in late 1967, the number of UHF stations on the air for the first time exceeded the number of VHF. (All-channel receiver legislation passed by Congress required that all TV sets sold after April 30, 1964, be capable of receiving UHF as well as VHF signals.)

Wtih the number of VHF unused reservations continually diminishing, the continued growth of UHF ETV stations seems likely. Technological advances have resulted in markedly improved UHF television receivers, diminishing the disparity between VHF and UHF reception, although much remains to be done.

P/ETV-station programming ranges from in-school instructional materials to performing arts for the home audience. Materials are obtained from many sources, including individual stations, private producing organizations, and instructional-television libraries.

Local in-school programs, sometimes locally produced, may be entire series, individual lessons, or part of a lesson, such as a demonstration. Supporting material, such as civic tours, visits to cultural sites, and interviews with prominent people, are frequent.

Cultural and public programming is broad in scope and includes programs of a probing and controversial nature, interviews with people in all areas of life, presentations of the performing and plastic arts, and programs for special groups or on special subjects. Noncommercial educational stations are prohibited by Section 399 of the Communications Act from editorializing or from supporting or opposing any candidate for public office.

Noncommercial programming purposes vary.

Some practitioners believe that P/ETV should reach the largest possible general audience with general-interest programs not usually available on commercial television. Others believe P/ETV should reach a large spectrum of viewing groups with special, including minority, interest programs.

INSTRUCTIONAL TELEVISION FIXED SERVICE

Instructional Television Fixed Service (ITFS) was established by the FCC in 1963 to provide multiple frequencies in the 2500–2690 MHz band for in-school educational television use. It was regularized by the FCC in 1971 with 28 channels.

It is not a broadcast service intended for reception by the general public. A single ITFS system can provide up to four simultaneous channels for in-school service, plus audio systems to permit two-way communications. ITFS is serving about 8,000 schools, with about 5 million pupils. In several areas it is being used for distributing materials for continuing education and educational-data exchange, and improving communication among governmental entities.

It has two-way communication capabilities, providing instantaneous feedback from students to instructors.

ITFS includes both voice and data-response stations. Systems in several states transmit informational programs from university campuses to surrounding industrial installations and medical centers as well as from industry and medical centers back to students on campus.

ITFS transmitting equipment operates with very low power, with a useful service range of about 20 miles, and is less costly than television-broadcast equipment. Although the 2500 MHz signal is transmitted openly, the cost of special receiving antennas and converters removes the system, for practical purposes, from home use. Special receiving devices convert the signals to regular TV channels so that programs may be seen on conventional TV receivers.

Because ITFS differs technically from standard VHF and UHF broadcasting, it operates under separate rules and regulations. Requirements for eligibility to be a licensee of an ITFS station are the same as those for a noncommercial educational television station. Transmitter engineers must be technically qualified; but routine operations may be performed by third-class radiotelephone permit holders; remote control and unattended operation of some equipment are provided for; and permission to utilize the signal must be obtained by the potential user from the transmitting licensee.

A booklet, *ITFS: What It Is . . . How to Plan,* was developed by the FCC's Committee for the ITFS, and was published in 1967 by the National Education Association. It can be ordered from the N.E.A. (1201 16th St. NW, Washington, DC 20005). Rules governing ITFS are contained in Part 74, Subpart I, "Instructional Television Fixed Service," of the FCC Rules and Regulations.

MICROWAVE

Microwave relay stystems use narrow, concentrated beams for efficient short-range transmission. P/ETV stations may use microwave equipment to provide program circuits between studio and transmitter (TV-STL), to relay programs between TV broadcast stations (TV intercity relay), and to pick up programs outside regular studios (TV pickup). The rules governing such TV auxiliaries are contained in Part 74, Subpart F of the FCC Rules, "Television Auxiliary Broadcast Stations."

TV program-relay facilities for closed-circuit TV systems may be authorized on certain microwave channels in the Business Radio Service, under Part 91, Section 91.554, of the FCC rules. Such stations may also be used in connection with ITFS systems. ITFS stations as well as studio-transmitter program circuits may be used for relaying programs between ITFS systems in adjacent areas, for delivering ITFS programs to TV broadcast stations, and for relaying TV broadcast programs to ITFS systems.

TRANSLATORS

Translators are used to provide coverage in weak signal areas of a station's signal zone and to extend TV service where the signal does not reach. They are called translators because in picking up and retransmitting the TV signal, they change, or "translate," the signal, strengthening it and retransmitting it on a different channel.

Many school districts and educational stations construct and operate translators for both school and community programming. TV translators may not operate as independent broadcast stations.

CABLE

Cable television systems pick up television broadcast signals, including those of noncommercial television stations, and distribute them by cable to subscribing members of the public and frequently to public buildings including schools.

Cable systems operate in areas where, because of terrain or obstructions from buildings, television reception is poor or the number of signals available is limited. Cable is also expanding to areas of good over-the-air reception to provide more channels than would otherwise be available for public and instructional services.

Under the Commission's rules, a cable system is required, on request, to carry the signals of all P/ETV stations and translators within whose grade-B contour service area the system operates. With the approval of the State ETV authorities, P/ETV signals may also be carried into other areas.

Cable systems may also distribute educational and instructional programs within the community on channels not used for broadcast signals; FCC cable TV rules require that every cable system of more than 3,500 subscribers dedicate at least one channel for educational and instructional purposes, one for government use, and one for public-access purposes, if channel capacity permits.

These channels are to be available without charge

from the time subscriber service is inaugurated until five years after the channel is made available.

SATELLITES

Although by mid-1976, noncommercial television had only experimented with satellite transmission, it had already planned to use satellites on a regular basis within the next decade. In January, 1976, the Corporation for Public Broadcasting committed up to $110 million over the subsequent ten-year period for a satellite-distribution system.

In 1975, a number of public-broadcasting, telecommunications, and educational organizations formed the Public Service Satellite Consortium, to plan for, encourage, and implement satellite use. In early 1976, the Public Broadcasting Service and CPB presented a proposal to the FCC to develop a network of ground terminals to receive signals from satellites already operated by The Western Union Telegraph Company.

Funded by PBS stations and CPB and with long-term loan financing, the proposal anticipated multi-channel public-broadcasting satellite transmissions within two years.

The most comprehensive experiment in satellite communications up to 1976 was the use of the ATS-6 in 1974 and 1975 for health, education, and other public-service applications in Appalachia, the Rocky Mountain states, and Alaska. A 1976 joint U.S.–Canada Communications Technology Satellite project was developed to provide similar services on a more extensive basis.

In early 1975 the FCC issued a Notice of Inquiry and in early 1976 a Second Notice of Inquiry on preparation of United States proposals for the World Administrative Radio Conference (WARC) of the International Telecommunications Union (ITU) scheduled for January 1, 1977, to plan the use of the 11.7–12.2 GHz frequency band for a Broadcasting-Satellite Service.

The principal U.S. recommendations were expected to relate to the sharing of the frequencies with other services to which the bands are allocated, including the Fixed Service, the Mobile Service, the Broadcasting Service, and the Fixed-Satellite (Space-to-Earth) Service.

A number of organizations interested in educational, medical, and other social programming advocated satellite reception by and distribution from surface complexes located at universities, schools, hospitals, and similar community centers. A principal concern was whether this ground-station approach was most advisable or whether there should be direct satellite-to-home broadcasting.

FINANCING

Financial support for P/ETV stations comes primarily from state and local government sources, from contributions from business, and from viewer subscriptions. Foundations, principally the Ford Foundation, have over the years contributed substantial sums to P/ETV.

P/ETV stations operated by colleges, univer-

sities, and school systems obtain about 75 percent of their income from direct budgeted support. Stations operated by state agencies receive about 80 percent of their funds from state and local appropriations. Community stations, on the other hand, receive about 60 percent of their support from gifts, grants, and services—the services provided primarily for the production of in-school programs. ITFS systems are supported by the local institutional licensee.

Some funding comes from Congress. The Public Broadcast Financing Act of 1975 provided, for the first time, long-term funding for public broadcasting, with amounts ranging from $88 million for fiscal year 1977 to $160 million in fiscal year 1981.

The act contains a matching-grant formula of $1 for every $2.50 in non-federal contributions raised by public broadcasting. For fiscal year 1977, $30 million for facilities and $1 million for experimental demonstration was authorized for the educational-broadcasting-facilities program. In fiscal year 1975, the U.S. Office of Education provided $10.8 million in matching grants for educational-television facilities, $7.5 million for programming under the Emergency School Aid Act, and $7 million for programming under the Special Project Act of the Elementary and Secondary Education Amendments of 1974. These amounts are relatively small compared with the ETV stations' non-federal income of about $230 million in fiscal year 1975.

Funds for P/ETV are included in the Elementary and Secondary Education Act of 1965, especially Title I, which provides for assistance to educationally deprived children; Title II, which provides printed and audiovisual materials; Title III, which provides for supplementary educational centers and services.

The Higher Education Act of 1965, especially Title VI, provides for the acquisition of closed-circuit instructional-television equipment, materials, and the minor remodeling of TV facilities. Funds may also be available for student training from the Vocational Education Act of 1963, as amended; the Appalachian Regional Development Act of 1965, especially Title I, "Special Appalachian Programs"; the Economic Opportunity Act of 1964, particularly Title I, "Youth Programs," and Title II, "Urban and Rural Community Action Programs"; and the Public Health Service, for research, demonstrations, and programming, particularly from the National Institute of Health, the National Institute of Mental Health, and the Division of Nursing of the Bureau of Health Manpower.

RULES

The rules and regulations pertaining to noncommercial educational television may be found in various sections of Subpart E of the FCC regulations. The basic information on applications and authorizations, however, is contained in Sec. 73.621, as follows:

73.621 Noncommercial educational stations
  In addition to the other provisions of this sub-

part, the following shall be applicable to noncommercial educational-television broadcast stations:

(*a*) Except as provided in paragraph *b* of this section, noncommercial educational broadcast stations will be licensed only to nonprofit educational organizations upon a showing that the proposed stations will be used primarily to serve the educational needs of the community; for the advancement of educational programs; and to furnish a nonprofit and noncommercial television broadcast service.

(1) In determining the eligibility of publicly supported educational organizations, the accreditation of their state departments of education shall be taken into consideration.

(2) In determining the eligibility of privately controlled educational organizations, the accreditation of state departments of education or recognized regional and national educational accrediting organizations shall be taken into consideration.

(*b*) Where a municipality or other political subdivision has no independently constituted educational organizations, such as, for example, a board of education having autonomy with respect to carrying out the municipality's educational program, such municipality shall be eligible for a noncommercial educational-television broadcasting station. In such circumstances, a full and detailed showing must be made that a grant of the application will be consistent with the intent and purpose of the commission's rules and regulations relating to such stations.

(*c*) Noncommercial educational-television broadcast stations may transmit educational, cultural, and entertainment programs, and programs designed for use by schools and school systems in connection with regular school courses, as well as routine and administrative material pertaining thereto.

(*d*) A noncommercial educational television station may broadcast programs produced by or at the expense of, or furnished by, persons other than the licensee, if no other consideration than the furnishing of the program and the costs incidental to its production and broadcast are received by the licensee. The payment of line charges by another station or network, or by someone other than the licensee of a noncommercial educational television station, or general contributions to the operating costs of a station, shall not be considered as being prohibited by this paragraph.

(*e*) Each station shall furnish a nonprofit and noncommercial broadcast service. However, noncommercial educational television stations shall be subject to the provisions of Section 73.654, to the extent that they are applicable to the broadcast of programs produced by, or at the expense of, or furnished by others, except that no announcements (visual or aural) promoting the sale of a product or service shall be broadcast in connection with any program: provided, however, that where a sponsor's name or product appears on the visual image during the course of a simultaneous or rebroadcast program either on the backdrop or in similar form, the portions of the program showing such information need not be deleted.

Note 1: Announcements of the producing or furnishing of programs, or the provision of funds for their production, may be made no more than twice, at the opening and the close of any program, except that when a program lasts longer than one hour, an announcement may be made at hourly intervals during the program if the last such announcement occurs at least 15 minutes before the announcement at the close of the program. The person or organization furnishing or producing the program, or providing funds for its production, shall be identified by name only, except that in the case of a commercial company having bona fide operating divisions or subsidiaries one of which has furnished the program or funds, the division or subsidiary may be mentioned in addition to or instead of the commercial company. No material beyond the company (or division or subsidiary) name shall be included. Upon request for waiver of this provision, the commission may authorize the inclusion of brief additional descriptive material only when deemed necessary to avoid confusion with another company having the same or a similar name. No mention shall be made of any product or service with which a commercial enterprise being identified has a connection except to the extent that the name of the product or service is the same as that of the enterprise (or division or subsidiary) and is so included. A repeat broadcast of a particular program is considered a separate program for the purpose of this note;

Note 2: Announcements may be made of general contributions of a substantial nature that make possible the broadcast of programs for part, or all, of the day's schedule. Such announcements may be made at the opening and the closing of the day or segment, and may include all those persons or organizations whose substantial contributions have made possible the broadcast day or segment. In addition, one such general contributor may be identified once during each hour of the day or segment. The provisions of Note 1 of this section as to permissible contents apply to announcements under this note.

Note 3: The limitations on credit announcements imposed by Notes 1 and 2 of this section shall not apply to program material the production of which was completed before January 1, 1971, or to other announcements broadcast before January 1, 1971, pursuant to underwriting agreements entered into before November 30, 1970.

Note 4: The provision of Notes 1 and 2 of this section shall not apply during the broadcast times in which auctions are held to finance station operation. Credit announcements during auction broadcasts may identify particular products or services, but shall not include promotion of such products or services beyond that necessary for the specific auction purpose. Visual exposure may be given to a display in the action area including the underwriter's name and trademark, and product or service or a representation thereof.

Note 5: The numerical limitations on permissible announcements contained in Notes 1 and 2 of this section do not apply to announcements on behalf of noncommercial, nonprofit entities, such as the Corporation for Public Broadcasting, state or regional entities, or charitable foundations.

Volume III of the FCC Rules and Regulations, which includes Part 73, Radio Broadcast Services, may be obtained from the Superintendent of Documents, U.S. Government Printing Office, Washington, DC 20402.

APPLICATION PROCEDURES

The Commission's table of TV assignments, Section 73.606 of the Rules and Regulations, contains the educational reservation status and frequencies of TV broadcast channels allocated to a given city. An educational organization or institution may apply for a reserved or nonreserved channel.

If there is no allocated channel in a given community, a qualified group may petition for reservation of an unused assigned channel, for the "drop-in" assignment of a channel, or for the reallocation of an unoccupied channel from another city. The petition must clearly delineate the purpose of the proposal and show why it would be in the public interest. If the Commission determines that the proposal warrants consideration, it will institute a rulemaking proceeding, and if the assignment is subsequently made, an application may then be made to activate the channel.

Many prospective applicants obtain legal and engineering counsel to assist in supplying required and accurate information to the Commission. Expeditious processing frequently is dependent upon the good order of the application and complete, specific, and precise information.

Applicants for new broadcast stations or for major changes in existing facilities must give public notice of the filing as specified in Section 1.580 of the Rules and Regulations. All broadcast applications must be submitted in triplicate to: The Secretary, Federal Communications Commission, Washington, DC 20554.

After they are tendered, if complete and in conformity with the rules, they are formally accepted for filing and assigned a file number. An application is not acted upon until at least 30 days following public notice of its acceptance. During this period it may be subject to objecting petitions. The application requires information on the applicant's legal qualifications and ownership, engineering, finances, proposed programming, and equal-employment opportunity.

Processing

The processing of applications involves three major areas of examination and review: engineering, financial, and legal.

The engineering examination verifies the coordinates and calculations to determine that they conform to FCC technical requirements. The Antenna Survey Branch determines whether the proposed antenna structure meets Federal Aviation Administration regulations.

The financial examination checks the applicant's financial qualifications, including adequacy of resources and matters such as discrepancies between estimated and potential actual operating costs, and total costs balanced against particular costs. The financial examination is particularly concerned with verification of the source of funds—whether the applicant has the necessary funds, available or committed, to construct and operate the station for one year or has been given the authority to use the money, bonds, securities, or other finances described in the application.

The legal examination determines whether the applicant is qualified under the Communications Act to become a licensee. Attorneys review technical and economic findings, check the corporate structure, determine if there are any matters before the FCC that might affect the applicant, and analyze the Statement of Program Service.

Construction Permit

When an application for a new station or for changes in an existing facility is approved, a Construction Permit (CP) is issued. The permittee has 18 months in which to complete the project. If the station cannot be constructed in the specified time, the extension may be applied for. Following issuance of the CP, the permittee may request call letters, with the first available preference assigned.

Within 30 days from the time the CP is issued the permittee must submit an Ownership Report. Subsequently, this report also must be filed every three years (most stations file with each license renewal), and within 30 days of a change of officers or ownership of the station.

When construction of the facility is complete, in accordance with the CP, the permittee may, following notification to the Commission, conduct equipment tests. Application for the license may be submitted, accompanied by measurements of equipment performance.

Program Test Authority

At the same time—but at least 10 days before regular programming is scheduled to begin—Program Test Authority (PTA) may be requested. PTA is contingent upon approval by the FCC of performance data as detailed in the license application. In effect, PTA entitles the permittee to begin regular station operation and programming, although the license itself is not granted until the license application receives final approval.

Renewal

A periodic license renewal is necessary. Renewal dates vary by geographic region. A first renewal must be filed at the first date specified for the licensee's state; therefore, licenses normally are for three years.

The renewal application contains information on the licensee's legal qualifications, engineering, finances, programming, and equal-employment-opportunity policy and practice. In addition a licensee must file an annual employment report (Form 395) showing its total employees and the number of women and specified minorities grouped into several job categories, to assist the FCC in determining whether it complies with the commission's equal-employment-opportunity rules.

Those wishing more information on the renewal process or wishing to make a complaint on any aspect of a station's operation are referred to *The Public and Broadcasting,* a procedural manual that can be obtained from the Public Information Office, the Federal Communications Commission, Washington, DC 20554.

Ascertainment

In 1976, the FCC issued a Report and Order requiring noncommercial TV stations to conduct a formal ascertainment survey of community problems in connection with their programming, similar to that required of commercial broadcasters, with filings beginning April 1, 1977 (August for renewals). The ascertainment must be conducted throughout the license term by renewal applicants or within six months of filing an application for a transfer, assignment, or construction permit. (The less formal procedures for radio applicants require only a narrative statement of the methods, content, and results of the community ascertainment; 10-watt stations are exempt.)

The educational-television applicant must place in its public file, available for public inspection, a statement of the demographic composition of its community of license, including a breakdown by sex, race, and age. In determining community problems, it must interview leaders representative of the different groups in the community and conduct a random survey of members of the general public. P/ETV renewal applicants may substitute public meetings or call-in programs for the random survey.

The public file must include information concerning these interviews and surveys and an annual list of ten problems ascertained and programs broadcast (by renewal applicants) or proposed (by other than renewal applicants) to meet the problems. A P/ETV station that presents only instructional programming is except from formal ascertainment requirements.

ITFS

ITFS channels are selected on a case-by-case basis. There is no preplanned assignment table in the rules, although community preplanning is desirable.

The Commission welcomes comments from local ITFS committees on applications received by the FCC. Licensing procedures for ITFS systems are similar to those for noncommercial television stations, except that when the ITFS system is ready to begin operation, the permittee is free to do so after notification to the FCC.

Forms

Noncommercial educational-television applications, requests, and reports are submitted on the following forms:

FCC Form 313: Application for Authorization in the Auxiliary Broadcast Services.

FCC Form 314: Application for Consent to Assignment of Broadcast Station Construction Permit or License.

FCC Form 315: Application for Consent to Transfer of Control of Corporation Holding Radio Broadcast Station Construction Permit or License.

FCC Form 316: Application for Consent to Assignment of Radio Broadcast Station Construction Permit or License or Transfer of Control of Corporation Holding Radio Broadcast Station Construction Permit or License (short form).

FCC Form 318: Request for Subsidiary Communications Authorizations.

FCC Form 321: Application for Construction Permit to Replace Expired Permit.

FCC Form 323E: Ownership Report for Noncommercial Educational-TV, FM, or Standard-Broadcast Station.

FCC Form 330L: Application for Instructional Television Fixed Station License.

FCC Form 330P: Application for Authority to Construct or Make Changes in an Instructional Television Fixed Station.

FCC Form 330R: Application for Renewal of an ITFS License.

FCC Form 340: Application for Authority to Construct or Make Changes in a Noncommercial Educational-TV, FM, or Standard-Broadcast Station.

FCC Form 341: Application for Noncommercial Educational-TV, FM, or Standard-Broadcast Station.

FCC Form 342: Application for Renewal of Noncommercial Educational-TV, FM, or Standard-Broadcast Station License.

FCC Form 345: Consent to Assignment of Broadcast Translator Station Construction Permit or License.

FCC Form 346: Application for Authority to Construct or Make Changes in the TV or FM Broadcast Translator Station.

FCC Form 347: Application for TV or FM Broadcast Translator Station License.

FCC Form 348: Application for Renewal of TV or FM Broadcast Translator Station License.

FCC Form 701: Application for Additional Time to Construct Radio Station.

NETWORKS AND PROGRAMS

The Public Broadcasting Service (PBS), 475 L'Enfant Plaza West SW, Washington, DC 20024, is the member organization of the nation's public television stations. Although it is not a television network in the usual sense, PBS manages and schedules the interconnection system that in early 1976 was providing about 70 hours of programming weekly to 251 PTV stations.

Program distribution from PBS is through AT&T long lines, microwaves, and its videotape library. PBS administers the Station Program Cooperative, a system through which stations select and collectively purchase many of the individual programs on their schedules. PBS also provides support services, including representation in Washington, research, promotion, and legal and engineering counsel to the stations.

PBS policies are established by a 25-member Lay Board of Governors, elected by the member stations, which in turn is advised by a 25-member Board of Managers representing station personnel. PBS is funded through annual member service fees from the stations, with its technical distribution facilities financed by the Corporation for Public Broadcasting.

The production of programs is primarily the responsibility of individual public television stations within the system, but some programs are obtained from independent producers and from a variety of international sources.

In 1975, the National Public Affairs Center for Television merged with station WETA-TV, in Washington, DC and became a production division of WETA. Located at 995 L'Enfant Plaza North SW, Washington, DC 20024, this production division concentrates on national events originating in Washington, usually for distribution over the PBS facilities. It offers special program coverage of such news events as Presidential speeches and press conferences, Presidential primaries, conventions, and Congressional hearings.

In 1970, National Educational Television, once the principal source of national ETV programming, merged with television station WNET, New York City, and became its production arm. It provides programming related to special news events in New York and produces cultural and artistic programs for PBS distribution. The WNET production division is located at 10 Columbus Circle, New York, NY 10023.

The Eastern Educational Television Network (31 Elliot St., Newton Upper Falls, MA 02164 (617) 783-3660) provides live interconnection and tape-distribution services to 40 stations in 12 states. Evening programming via tape distribution is available to ETV stations outside the eastern region via subscription to the Program Service Membership. The EETN provides approximately 20 hours of instructional television and 10 hours of evening programming per week to its interconnected members. For more information, phone or write John S. Porter, executive director.

The Southern Educational Communications Association (928 Woodrow St., Columbia, SC 29250 (803) 799-5517) provides programming and production assistance to TV and radio stations, educational institutions, and industry; grant-application, copyright-clearance, and utilization assistance; engineering consultation; and it has a library of aural and visual materials. It also produces and distributes original programming. For more information, phone or write Robert C. Glazier, president.

The Western Educational Network (c/o KWSU-TV, Murrow Communications Center, University of Washington, Pullman, WA 99163 (707) 864-7000) is a voluntary organization of ETV stations in the states of Alaska, California, Hawaii, Nevada, Oregon, and Washington, organized for the purpose of producing and exchanging original programming. For more information, phone or write Donald G. Kirkorian, president.

The Central Educational Network (5400 N. Saint Louis Ave., Chicago, IL 60625 (312) 463-3040) is a voluntary organization of ETV stations in 12 states in the central Midwest that provides both instructional and general-audience programming for its members by tape distribution and interconnection. For more information, phone or write Raymond C. Giese, director.

The Midwestern Educational Television, Inc. (1640 Como Ave., St. Paul, MN 55108 (612) 646-4611) consists of 17 ETV stations in Minnesota, North Dakota, South Dakota, and Wisconsin that are interconnected by microwave for program distribution. For more information, phone or write W. O. Donaldson, general manager.

The Rocky Mountain Corporation for Public Broadcasting (1603 Sigma Chi Rd. NW, Albuquerque, NM 87106 (505) 242-6930) serves seven states from the Mexican to the Canadian border through its operating division, the Rocky Mountain Public Broadcasting Network, and the Rocky Mountain regional distribution center. For more information, phone or write Dr. E. W. Bundy, executive director.

INSTRUCTIONAL TV SOURCES

There are two major sources of programs for instructional television. One is the Agency for Instructional Television (AIT) (Indiana University, Bloomington, IN 47405). Composed of members from the United States and Canada, it develops joint projects involving agencies from states and provinces and acquires, adapts, and distributes television, audiovisual, and print material for use as learning resources. AIT was established in 1973 through reorganization of the National Instructional Television Center, which had been in operation since 1962. The other is the National Great Plains Instructional Television Library (P.O. Box 80669, Lincoln, NB 68501). It serves as a distribution center of instructional TV courses for all academic levels and content areas, and in all forms, including tapes, cassettes, and films. In 1971, it acquired the assets of the Midwest Program for Airborne Television, which had ceased operations in 1968.

Almost every state is in the planning or active stage of an interconnected network and many states are developing multi-media networks that include a variety of television-delivery services, such as broadcasting, cable, ITFS, closed-circuit, micro-wave, and satellite. A number of groups, such as the Association of Media Producers and the National Audio-Visual Association, represent commercial producers and distributors of programs and equipment applicable to educational television needs. (See the section on instructional TV for further information)

ORGANIZATIONS

Almost all of the organizations listed under "Networks and Programs" provide additional services, such as conferences, workshops, information distribution, and legal and engineering assistance. A regional group not listed above that provides such services is the Western Educational Society for Telecommunications (P.O. Box 5346, Tacoma, WA 78405)

The Corporation for Public Broadcasting (CPB) (1111 16th St. NW, Washington, DC 20036) is a private nonprofit corporation that receives and dispenses private and public funds, pursuant to Title II of the Public Broadcasting Act of 1967, to support the production, acquisition, and distribution of high-quality radio and television programs and otherwise assist noncommercial broadcasting stations. Under specific criteria established by CPB, community-service grants are available to educational television stations upon application. The Corporation for Public Broadcasting also provides funds to the Public Broadcasting Service for station-interconnection activities, including support for the Station Program Cooperative. CPB is governed by a 15-member board appointed by the President and confirmed by the Senate.

The National Association of Educational Broadcasters (1346 Connecticut Ave. NW, Washington, DC 20036), founded in 1924, is a professional society of individuals and their institutions concerned with electronic-communications media for educational and social purposes. Its services include convention and conference programs, a bimonthly professional journal, a personnel-placement service, research and development activities, the Educational Broadcasting Institute program of seminars and workshops, a list of special publications, a biweekly newsletter, and consulting services.

The Association for Educational Communications and Technology (1201 16th St. NW, Washington, DC 20005) holds conferences, conducts research projects, publishes reports, and provides consultation on educational media for its member schools and teachers.

The Joint Council on Educational Telecommunications (1126 16th St. NW, Washington, DC 20005), is composed of national and regional educational and communications organizations and acts as a channel of communication among educational interests; broadcasting, cable, and satellite interests; federal offices; and Congress on issues affecting educational telecommunications.

The National Education Association (1201 16th St. NW, Washington, DC 20005) furnishes consultative services in educational telecommunications to schools and organizations throughout the country through its telecommunications office. It has issued publications on ITFS, CCTV, cable TV, satellite transmission, and other telecommunications services, and provides coordination for Public-Cable, Inc., a consortium of national organizations concerned with representing the public interest in cable development.

The Educational Media Council (1346 Connecticut Ave. NW, Washington, DC 20036) is composed of representatives of national educational and business organizations. It conducts research and develops project plans for the effective use of specialized interests and skills in educational communications.

The Broadcast Education Association (1771 N St. NW, Washington, DC 20036) is an organization of broadcast educators, principally on the college and university level, who prepare students for entry into broadcasting.

The development of satellite transmission for public broadcasting has led to the establishment of organizations such as the Public Service Satellite Consortium (San Diego, CA 92182), which is composed of broadcasters, health services, state telecommunications commissions, and national and regional educational associations interested in planning, promoting, and implementing satellite use, and the Public Interest Satellite Association (55 W. 42nd St., New York, NY 10036), which seeks ways to meet the needs of nonprofit organizations, including public broadcasting, in telephony, telex, radio, data transmission, and other narrowband uses.

The increasing use of cable TV by educators led to the establishment of Public-Cable, Inc. (Kutztown State College, Kutztown, PA 19530), a consortium of national organizations and individuals, which provides information on state and municipal actions and on the legislative and regulatory fields, publishes papers on national cable-TV issues, and holds an annual cable-TV conference.

Other groups on the national level, such as the International Radio and Television Society, the Speech Communications Association, the American Theatre Association, the American Association of School Administrators, the American Federation of Teachers, the Catholic Education Association, the American Council on Education, the American Library Association, and a number of organizations on the regional and state levels are involved to greater or lesser degrees in educational-television activities.

GOVERNMENT AGENCIES

The Educational Broadcasting Branch of the FCC studies educational-broadcasting services, develops policy recommendations on educational-communications matters, serves as a liaison between the FCC and other groups, provides consultation on educational communications to the public and to various commission offices, and serves as a clearinghouse of information.

The Office of Telecommunications Policy in the Department of Health, Education, and Welfare (330 Independence Ave. SW, Washington, DC 20201) coordinates HEW's involvements in communications technology.

The Office of Libraries and Learning Resources of the U.S. Office of Education includes an Educational Technology Division. One of its two subdivisions is the Educational Broadcasting Facilities Program Branch, which provides matching grants for facilities. Forms and guidelines for applying for such grants may be obtained directly from it: c/o the Division and Office, 400 Maryland Ave. SW, Washington, DC 20202. The other is the Educational Television Development Branch, which is concerned with innovative programming. Information about this may be obtained from the same address. (Additional information about these matters and U.S. Office of Education programs may be found under "Financing.")

The National Institute of Education (1200 19th St. NW, Washington, DC 20202) is the research-and-development arm of the Department of Health, Education, and Welfare. The Technological Applications Divison is responsible for the development and demonstration of technology for education.

The National Foundation on the Arts and the Humanities (806 15th St. NW, Washington, DC 20006) is composed of two groups. One is the National Council on the Arts, which administers grants for projects relating to the presentation, performance, execution, and enhancement of public understanding of major art forms, including television, radio, motion pictures, and videotape and sound recordings. The other is the National Council on the Humanities, the policy-making body for the Endowment of the Humanities. It promotes the humanities, including television and radio, through research and grants.

The General Services Administration (18th and F Sts. NW, Washington, DC 20405) administers the Federal Property Act, which authorizes donations of surplus property, equipment, and land. These may be applied for by some nonprofit educational institutions and organizations, such as educational-television and -radio stations.

The Federal Interagency Committee on Education (Office of the Assistant Secretary for HEW, Washington, DC 20202) consists of subcommittees dealing with significant areas of education, coordinating the efforts of a number of different federal agencies, and includes a Subcommittee on Educational Technology.

The National Audiovisual Center (General Services Administration, Washington, DC 20409) serves as a central bibliographic source and as a center of distribution for program materials available from a number of federal agencies.

Many other federal agencies offer grants, program materials, and production contracts to noncommercial television stations. Most states have established educational-telecommunications or -broadcasting offices or commissions, principally to coordinate activities for the development of state networks. Instructional-television offices are found in many departments of education or of public instruction. Moreover, many school systems, and even individual schools, have educational-television coordinators, and many colleges and universities, public and private, have persons responsible for ETV development and use. State and local ETV councils and citizens organizations are sometimes quasi-official in that many of their members and directors hold public office.

Information for this section was provided by the FCC and reproduced with their permission.

Public Television Station Directory*

ALABAMA

WAIQ-TV Channel 26 (Montgomery)
WBIQ-TV Channel 10 (Birmingham)
WCIQ-TV Channel 7 (Mt. Cheaha)
WDIQ-TV Channel 2 (Dozier)
WEIQ-TV Channel 42 (Mobile)
WFIQ-TV Channel 36 (Florence)
WGIQ-TV Channel 43 (Louisville)
WHIQ-TV Channel 25 (Huntsville)
WIIQ-TV Channel 41 (Demopolis)

Alabama ETV Commission
2101 Magnolia Ave.
Birmingham, AL 35205
(205) 328-8756
Contact: Denis N. Stork

ALASKA

KAKA-TV Channel 7
3211 Providence Dr.
Anchorage, AK 99504
(907) 276-7070
Contact: Elmo Sackett

KYUK-TV Channel 4
P.O. Box 468
Bethel, AK 99559
(907) 543-3131
Contact: Charles Schatz

*Reproduced through the courtesy of the Corporation or Public Broadcasting.

KUAC-TV Channel 9
University of Alaska
Fairbanks, AK 99701
(907) 479-7491
Contact: Donald B. Upham

ARIZONA

KAET-TV Channel 8 (Phoenix)
Arizona State University
Tempe, AZ 85281
(602) 965-3506
Contact: Robert H. Ellis

KUAT-TV Channel 6
Modern Languages Bldg.
University of Arizona
Tucson, AZ 85721
(602) 884-1434
Contact: Frank Barreca

ARKANSAS

KETS-TV Channel 2 (Little Rock)
KETG-TV Channel 09 (Arkadelphia)
KAFT-TV Channel 13 (Fayetteville)
KTEJ-TV Channel 19 (Jonesboro)

Arkansas Educational TV Commission
350 S. Donaghey St.
Conway, AR 72032
(501) 329-3887
Contact: Lee Reaves

CALIFORNIA

KEET-TV Channel 13
P.O. Box 13
Eureka, CA 95501
(707) 445-0813
Contact: James H. Turk

KMTF-TV Channel 18
733 L St.
Fresno, CA 93721
(209) 488-3018
Contact: Colin Dougherty

KOCE-TV Channel 50
15744 Golden West St.
Huntington Beach, CA 92647
(714) 897-0302
Contact: William A. Furniss

KCET-TV Channel 28
4401 Sunset Blvd.
Los Angeles, CA 90027
(213) 666-6500
Contact: James L. Loper

KLCS-TV Channel 58
1061 W. Temple St.
Los Angeles, CA 90012
(213) 625-6958
Contact: Tom Mossman

KIXE-TV Channel 9
825 Industrial St.
P.O. Box 9
Redding, CA 96001
(916) 241-7900
Contact: Robert P. Casey

KVIE-TV Channel 6
P.O. Box 6
Sacramento, CA 95801
(916) 929-5843
Contact: Arthur A. Paul

KVCR-TV Channel 24
701 S. Mt. Vernon Ave.
San Bernardino, CA 92403
(714) 885-0231
Contact: Fred R. Burgess

KPBS-TV Channel 15
San Diego State University
San Diego, CA 92182
(714) 286-6415
Contact: Paul J. Steen

KQED-TV Channel 9 (San Francisco)
KQEC-TV Channel 32 (San Francisco)
500 8th St.
San Francisco, CA 94103
(415) 864-2000
Contact: Anthony Tiano

KTEH-TV Channel 54
100 Skyport Dr.
San Jose, CA 95110
(408) 299-2754
Contact: Maynard E. Orme

KCSM-TV Channel 14
1700 W. Hillsdale Blvd.
San Mateo, CA 94402
(415) 574-6586
Contact: Douglas B. Montgomery

COLORADO

KRMA-TV Channel 6
1261 Glenarm Pl.
Denver, CO 80204
(303) 572-8218
Contact: Donald Holcomb

KTSC-TV Channel 8
900 W. Orman Ave.
Pueblo, CO 81004
(303) 549-3220
Contact: John Crabbe

CONNECTICUT

WEDH-TV Channel 24 (Hartford)
WEDW-TV Channel 49 (Bridgeport)
WEDN-TV Channel 53 (Norwich)
WEDY-TV Channel 65 (New Haven)

Connecticut ETV Corporation
24 Summit St.
Hartford, CT 06106
(203) 278-5310
Contact: Paul K. Taff

DISTRICT OF COLUMBIA

WETA-TV Channel 26
Box 2626
Washington, DC 20013
(703) 998-2600
Contact: Ward B. Chamberlin, Jr.

FLORIDA

WUFT-TV Channel 5
University of Florida
Room 234, Stadium Bldg.
Gainesville, FL 32611
(904) 392-0471
Contact: David T. Brugger

WJCT-TV Channel 7
2037 Main St.
Jacksonville, FL 32206
(904) 354-2806
Contact: Fred J. Rebman

WPBT-TV Channel 2
P.O. Box 610001
Miami, FL 33161
(305) 949-8321
Contact: George Dooley

WTHS-TV Channel 2 (Miami)
WLRN-TV Channel 17 (Miami)
1410 N.E. 2nd Ave.
Rm 210
Miami, FL 33132
(305) 350-3307
Contact: Don MacCullough

WMFE-TV Channel 24
2908 W. Oak Ridge Rd.
Orlando, FL 32809
(305) 855-3691
Contact: Stephen M. Steck

WSRE-TV Channel 23
1000 College Blvd.
Pensacola, FL 32504
(904) 476-5418
Contact: Donald Dorin

WFSU-TV Channel 11
Florida State University
202 Dodd Hall
Tallahassee, FL 32306
(904) 644-1736
Contact: Edward L. Herp

WEDU-TV Channel 3
908 S. 20th St.
Tampa, FL 33605
(813) 248-5751
Contact: P. Leroy Lastinger

WUSF-TV Channel 16
University of South Florida
4202 Fowler Ave.
Tampa, FL 33620
(813) 974-4000
Contact: William G. Mitchell

GEORGIA

WGTV-TV Channel 8 (Athens/Atlanta)
The Georgia Center
University of Georgia
Athens, GA 30602
(404) 542-3554
Contact: William H. Hale, Jr.

WETV-TV Channel 30
740 Bismark Rd. NE
Atlanta, GA 30324
(404) 873-4471
Contact: Larry Watkins

WCLP-TV Channel 18 (Chatsworth)
WDCO-TV Channel 15 (Cochran)
WJSP-TV Channel 28 (Columbus)
WACS-TV Channel 25 (Dawson)
WABW-TV Channel 14 (Pelham)
WVAN-TV Channel 9 (Savannah)
WXGA-TV Channel 8 (Waycross)
WCES-TV Channel 20 (Wrens)

Georgia ETV Network
1540 Stewart Ave. SW
Atlanta, GA 30310
(404) 656-5979
Contact: Richard E. Ottinger

HAWAII

KHET-TV Channel 11 (Hololulu)
KMEB-TV Channel 10 (Wailuku)
2350 Dole St.
Honolulu, HI 96822
(808) 955-7878
Contact: Mary G. F. Bitterman

IDAHO

KAID-TV Channel 4
Boise State University
1910 University Dr.
Boise, ID 83725
(208) 385-3344
Contact: Jack A. Schlaefle

KUID-TV Channel 12
University of Idaho
Radio–TV Center
Moscow, ID 83843
(208) 885-6723
Contact: Arthur Hook

KBGL-TV Channel 10
Idaho State University
Box 8111
Pocatello, ID 83201
(208) 236-2857
Contact: Herbert Everitt

ILLINOIS

WSIU-TV Channel　8 (Carbondale)
WUSI-TV Channel 16 (Olney)
Southern Illinois University
Communications Bldg., Room 1046
Carbondale, IL 62901
(618) 453-4343
Contact: Charles Lynch

WTTW-TV Channel 11 (Chicago)
WXXW-TV Channel 20 (Chicago)
5400 N. St. Louis Ave.
Chicago, IL 60625
(312) 583-5000
Contact: William J. McCarter

WTVP-TV Channel 47
1501 W. Bradley Ave.
Peoria, IL 61625
(309) 676-4747
Contact: Elwin Basquin

WILL-TV Channel 12
WILL-TV University of Illinois
1110 W. Main St.
Urbana, IL 61801
(217) 333-1070
Contact: Donald P. Mullally

INDIANA

WTIU-TV Channel 30
Indiana University
Radio–TV Bldg.
Bloomington, IN 47401
(812) 337-5900
Contact: Donely F. Feddersen

WNIN-TV Channel 9
9201 Petersburg Rd.
Evansville, IN 47711
(812) 867-6471
Contact: Vincent F. Saele

WFYI-TV Channel 20
1440 N. Meridian St.
Indianapolis, IN 46202
(317) 639-5591
Contact: Frank E. Meek

WIPB-TV Channel 49
246 Minnethrista Blvd.
Muncie, IN 47303
(317) 285-4771
Contact: James R. Needham

WCAE-TV Channel 50
123 Sesame St.
St. John, IN 46373
(219) 365-4041
Contact: John Nelson

WNIT-TV Channel 34
P.O. Box 34
South Bend, IN 46624
(219) 234-3434
Contact: Thomas E. Brubaker

WVUT-TV Channel 22
Vincennes University
1029 N. 4th St.
Vincennes, IN 47591
(812) 882-2237
Contact: Jim Jernigan

IOWA

KDIN-TV Channel 11 (Des Moines)
KIIN-TV Channel 12 (Iowa City)
KSIN-TV Channel 27 (Sioux City)
KRIN-TV Channel 32 (Waterloo)
KBIN-TV Channel 32 (Council Bluffs)
KHIN-TV Channel 36 (Red Oak)
KYIN-TV Channel 24 (Mason City)
KTIN-TV Channel 21 (Ft. Dodge)

Iowa Public Broadcast Network
P.O. Box 1758
Des Moines, Iowa 50306
(515) 281-4500
Contact: Rod Thole

KANSAS

KTWU-TV Channel 11
301 N. Wanamaker Rd.
Topeka, KS 66604
(913) 272-8181
Contact: Dale N. Anderson

KPTS-TV Channel 8
352 N. Broadway
P.O. Box 288
Wichita, KS 67202
(316) 262-4461
Contact: Zoel Parenteau

KENTUCKY

WKAS-TV Channel 25 (Ashland)
WKGB-TV Channel 53 (Bowling Green)
WCVN-TV Channel 54 (Covington)
WKZT-TV Channel 23 (Elizabethtown)
WKHA-TV Channel 35 (Hazard)
WKLE-TV Channel 46 (Lexington)
WKMJ-TV Channel 68 (Louisville)
WKMA-TV Channel 35 (Madisonville)
WKMR-TV Channel 38 (Morehead)
WKMU-TV Channel 21 (Murray)
WKON-TV Channel 52 (Owenton)
WKPI-TV Channel 22 (Pikeville)
WKSO-TV Channel 29 (Somerset)

Kentucky Authority for Educational TV
600 Cooper Dr.
Lexington, KY 40502
(606) 233-0666
Contact: O. Leonard Press

WKPC-TV Channel 15
P.O. Box 1515
Louisville, KY 40201
(502) 456-3286
Contact: Jerry D. Weaver

LOUISIANA

WLPB-TV Channel 27 (Baton Rouge)
KLTM-TV Channel 13 (Monroe)

Louisiana Educational-TV Authority
P.O. Box 44064
Education Bldg., Rm. B91
Baton Rouge, LA 70804
(504) 389-2131
Contact: A. Fred Frey

WYES-TV Channel 12
P.O. Box 24026
New Orleans, LA 70184
(505) 486-5511
Contact: William S. Hart

MAINE

WCBB-TV Channel 10 (Augusta)
1450 Lisbon St.
Lewiston, ME 04240
(207) 783-9101
Contact: H. Odell Skinner

WMEB-TV Channel 12 (Orono)
WMED-TV Channel 13 (Calais)
WMEM-TV Channel 10 (Presque Isle)
WMEG-TV Channel 26 (Biddeford)

Maine Public Broadcasting Network
University of Maine, Alumni Hall
Orono, ME 04473
(207) 866-4493
Contact: Edward Winchester

MARYLAND

WAPB-TV Channel 22 (Annapolis)
WMPB-TV Channel 67 (Baltimore)
WWPB-TV Channel 33 (Hagerstown)
WCPB-TV Channel 28 (Salisbury)

Maryland Center for Public Broadcasting
11767 Bonita Ave.
Owings Mills, MD 21117
(301) 356-5600
Contact: Frederick Breitenfeld, Jr.

MASSACHUSETTS

WGBH-TV Channel 2 (Boston)
WGBX-TV Channel 44 (Boston)

WGBH Educational Foundation
125 Western Ave.
Boston, MA 02134
(617) 492-2777
Contact: David O. Ives

WGBY-TV Channel 57
1 Armory Sq.
Springfield, MA 01105
(413) 781-2801
Contact: John T. Caldwell, Jr.

MICHIGAN

WGVC-TV Channel 35 (Grand Rapids)
Grand Valley State College
301 Manitou Hall
Allendale, MI 49401
(616) 895-6691
Contact: Gordon Lawrence

WTVS-TV Channel 56
7441 2nd Blvd.
Detroit, MI 48202
(313) 873-7200
Contact: James N. Christianson

WKAR-TV Channel 23
600 Kalamazoo St.
East Lansing, MI 48824
(517) 355-2300
Contact: Robert D. Page

WNMU-TV Channel 13
Learning Resources Center
Northern Michigan University
Marquette, MI 49855
(906) 227-1300
Contact: George E. Lott, Jr.

WCMU-TV Channel 14 (Mount Pleasant)
WCML-TV Channel   6 (Alpena)
Central Michigan University
Anspach Hall, Rm. 155
Mt. Pleasant, MI 48859
(517) 774-3105
Contact: William J. Grigaliunas

WUCM-TV Channel 19
Delta College
Delta Rd.
University Center, MI 48710
(517) 686-0400
Contact: William J. Ballard

MINNESOTA

KWCM-TV Channel 10
128 W. Sorenson
Appleton, MN 56208
(612) 289-1640
Contact: Ralph C. Schmidt

KAVT-TV Channel 15
1900 8th Ave., NW
Austin, MN 55912
(507) 433-6000
Contact: Donald C. Ingram

WDSE-TV Channel 8
210 Bradley Bldg.
Duluth, MN 55802
(218) 727-8734
Contact: George A. Beck

KTCA-TV Channel 2 (St. Paul–Minneapolis)
KTCI-TV Channel 17 (St. Paul–Minneapolis)
1640 Como Ave.
St. Paul, MN 55108
(612) 646-4611
Contact: William Kobin

MISSISSIPPI

WMAA-TV Channel 29 (Jackson)
WMAB-TV Channel 2 (State College)
WMAE-TV Channel 12 (Booneville)
WMAU-TV Channel 17 (Bude)
WMAO-TV Channel 23 (Greenwood)
WMAH-TV Channel 19 (Biloxi)
WMAV-TV Channel 18 (Oxford)
WMAW-TV Channel 14 (Meridian)

Mississippi Authority for ETV
P.O. Drawer 1101
Jackson, MS 39205
(601) 982-6565
Contact: Forrest L. Morris

MISSOURI

KCPT-TV Channel 19
2100 Stark
Kansas City, MO 64126
(816) 461-8100
Contact: Robert F. Fuzy

KETC-TV Channel 9
6996 Millbrook Blvd.
St. Louis, MO 63130
(314) 725-2460
Contact: Andy McMaster

KOZK-TV Channel 21
MPO Box 21
Springfield, MO 65801
(417) 865-2100
Contact: William T. Maynard

NEBRASKA

KTNE-TV Channel 13 (Alliance)
KMNE-TV Channel 7 (Bassett)
KHNE-TV Channel 29 (Hastings)
KINE-TV Channel 3 (Lexington)
KRNE-TV Channel 12 (Merriman)
KXNE-TV Channel 19 (Norfolk)
KPNE-TV Channel 9 (North Platte)
KYNE-TV Channel 26 (Omaha)

The Nebraska Educational-TV Commission
P.O. Box 83111
Lincoln, NB 68501
(402) 472-3611
Contact: Jack G. McBride

KUON-TV Channel 12
P.O. Box 83111
Lincoln, NB 68501
(402) 472-3611
Contact: Jack G. McBride

NEVADA

KLVX-TV Channel 10
5700 Mountain Vista St.
Las Vegas, NV 89120
(702) 451-1026
Contact: Ronald D. Hawley

NEW HAMPSHIRE

WEDB-TV Channel 40 (Berlin)
WENH-TV Channel 11 (Durham)
WHED-TV Channel 15 (Hanover)
WEKW-TV Channel 52 (Keene)
WLFD-TV Channel 49 (Littleton)

New Hampshire Network
Box 2
Durham, NH 03824
(603) 862-1047
Contact: Keith J. Nighbert

NEW JERSEY

WNJS-TV Channel 23 (Camden)
WNJM-TV Channel 50 (Montclair)
WNJB-TV Channel 58 (New Brunswick)
WNJT-TV Channel 52 (Trenton)

New Jersey Public Broadcasting Authority
1573 Parkside Ave.
Trenton, NJ 08638
(609) 882-5252
Contact: Lawrence T. Frymire

NEW MEXICO

KNME-TV Channel 5
1130 University Blvd.
Albuquerque, NM 87102
(505) 277-2121
Contact: Robert Gordon

KRWG-TV Channel 22
New Mexico State University
Milton Hall
Las Cruces, NM 88003
(505) 646-2212
Contact: James A. Dryden

KENW-TV Channel 3
Eastern New Mexico University
Portales, NM 88130
(505) 562-3112
Contact: Duane W. Ryan

NEW YORK

WYNE-TV Channel 25 (New York)
112 Tillary St.
Brooklyn, NY 11201
(212) 596-4425
Contact: Harold S. Marder

WNED-TV Channel 17
P.O. Box 1263
Buffalo, NY 14240
(716) 881-5000
Contact: J. Michael Collins

WSKG-TV Channel 46 (Binghamton)
P.O. Box 97
3311 E. Main St.
Endwell, NY 13760
(607) 754-4777
Contact: Arthur Dees

WLIW-TV Channel 21
Ellington Ave.
Garden City, NY 11530
(516) 222-2140
Contact: Charles R. Bell

WCNY-TV Channel 24 (Syracuse)
506 Old Liverpool Rd.
Liverpool, NY 13088
(315) 457-0440
Contact: Richard W. Russell

WNET-TV Channel 13
356 W. 58th St.
New York, NY 10019
(212) 262-4200
Contact: John J. Iselin

WNYC-TV Channel 31
2533 Municipal Bldg.
New York, NY 10007
(212) 566-3101
Contact: Mary Perot Nichols

WCFE-TV Channel 57
c/o State University College
Plattsburgh, NY 12901
(518) 564-2114
Contact: Paul C. Hassenplug

WXXI-TV Channel 21
Box 21
Rochester, NY 14601
(716) 325-7500
Contact: William J. Pearce

WMHT-TV Channel 17
Box 17
Schenectady, NY 12301
(518) 356-1700
Contact: Donald E. Schein

WNPI-TV Channel 18 (Norwood)
WNPE-TV Channel 16 (Watertown)
P.O. Box 114
Watertown, NY 13601
(315) 782-3142
Contact: Richard A. Jones

NORTH CAROLINA

WUNC-TV Channel 4 (Chapel Hill)
WUND-TV Channel 2 (Columbia)
WUNE-TV Channel 17 (Linville)
WUNF-TV Channel 33 (Asheville)
WUNG-TV Channel 58 (Concord)
WUNJ-TV Channel 39 (Wilmington)
WUNK-TV Channel 25 (Greenville)
WUNL-TV Channel 26 (Winston-Salem)

University of North Carolina TV Network
202 University Sq. W
Chapel Hill, NC 27514
(919) 933-8191
Contact: George E. Bair

WTVI-TV Channel 42
42 Coliseum Dr.
Charlotte, NC 28205
(704) 372-2442
Contact: Paul B. Marion

NORTH DAKOTA

KFME-TV Channel 13 (Fargo)
KGFE-TV Channel 2 (Grand Forks)

Prairie Public TV, Inc.
4500 South University Dr.
Fargo, ND 58102
(701) 232-8921
Contact: Dennis L. Falk

OHIO

WNEO-TV Channel 45 (Alliance)
WEAO-TV Channel 49 (Akron)
1640 Franklin Ave.
Kent, OH 44240
(216) 678-1656
Contact: John Hershberger

WOUB-TV Channel 20 (Athens)
WOUC-TV Channel 44 (Cambridge)
Radio–TV Communication Bldg.
Ohio University
College St.
Athens, OH 45701
(614) 594-6171
Contact: N. Joseph Welling

WBGU-TV Channel 57
Bowling Green State University
Troup Ave.
Bowling Green, OH 43403
(419) 372-0121
Contact: Duane E. Tucker

WCET-TV Channel 48
1223 Central Pkwy.
Cincinnati, OH 45214
(513) 381-4033
Contact: Charles W. Vaughan

WVIZ-TV Channel 25
4300 Brockpark Rd.
Cleveland, OH 44134
(216) 398-2800
Contact: Betty Cope

WOSU-TV Channel 34 (Columbus)
WPBO-TV Channel 42 (Portsmouth)
Ohio State University
2400 Olentangy River Rd.
Columbus, OH 43210
(614) 421-2540
Contact: Elizabeth L. Young

WPID-TV Channel 16 (Dayton)
WPTO-TV Channel 14 (Oxford)
3440 Office Park Dr.
Dayton, OH 45439
(513) 298-9500
Contact: Clair R. Tettemer

WGTE-TV Channel 30
415 N. St. Clair St.
Toledo, OH 43604
(419) 255-3330
Contact: Robert D. Smith

OKLAHOMA

KETA-TV Channel 13 (Oklahoma City)
KOED-TV Channel 11 (Tulsa)
KOET-TV Channel 3 (Eufaula)

The Oklahoma Educational TV Authority
7403 N. Kelly Ave.
Box 14190
Oklahoma City, OK 73114
(405) 848-8501
Contact: Bob Allen

KOKH-TV Channel 25
1801 N. Ellison St.
Oklahoma City, OK 73106
(405) 236-2661
Contact: Donna Hunter

OREGON

KSYS-TV Channel 8
34 S. Fir
Medford, OR 97501
(503) 772-3122
Contact: Edward P. Barnett

KOAP-TV Channel 10 (Portland)
KOAC-TV Channel 7 (Corvallis)
KVDO-TV Channel 3 (Salem)
KTVR-TV Channel 13 (La Grande)
2828 S.W. Front Ave.
Portland, OR 97201
(503) 229-4892
Contact: Donald S. Bryant

PENNSYLVANIA

WLVT-TV Channel 39 (Allentown)
South Mountain Dr., W
Bethlehem, PA 18015
(215) 867-4677
Contact: Sheldon P. Siegel

WQLN-TV Channel 54
8425 Peach St.
Erie, PA 16509
(814) 868-4654
Contact: Robert J. Chitester

WITF-TV Channel 33
P.O. Box Z
Hershey, PA 17033
(717) 534-3333
Contact: Robert F. Larson

WUAY-TV Channel 35 (Philadelphia)
WHYY-TV Channel 12 (Wilmington, Del.)
4548 Market St.
Philadelphia, PA 19139
(215) 243-2200
Contact: Jim Karayn

WQED-TV Channel 13 (Pittsburgh)
WQEX-TV Channel 16 (Pittsburgh)
4802 5th Ave.
Pittsburgh, PA 15213
(412) 622-1300
Contact: Lloyd Kaiser

WVIA-TV Channel 44 (Scranton)
Public Broadcasting Ctr.
Old Boston Rd.
Pittston, PA 18640
(717) 655-4561
Contact: George H. Strimel, Jr.

WPSX-TV Channel 3 (Clearfield)
Pennsylvania State University
Wagner Annex
University Park, PA 16802
(814) 865-9531
Contact: David L. Phillips

RHODE ISLAND

WSBE-TV Channel 36
24 Mason St.
Providence, RI 02903
(401) 831-2900
Contact: Warren Kraetzer

SOUTH CAROLINA

WJWJ-TV Channel 16
P.O. Box 4516
Beaufort, SC 29902
(803) 524-0808
Contact: Ronald L. Schoenherr

WEBA-TV Channel 14 (Allendale)
WITV-TV Channel 7 (Charleston)
WRLK-TV Channel 35 (Columbia)
WJPM-TV Channel 33 (Florence)
WNTV-TV Channel 29 (Greenville)

South Carolina ETV Commission
Drawer L
Columbia, SC 29250
(803) 758-7235
Contact: Henry J. Cauthen

WNSC-TV Channel 30
P.O. Box 11766
Rock Hill, SC 29730
(803) 324-3184
Contact: Robert Frierson

WRJA-TV Channel 27
15 N. Harvin St.
P.O. Box 1836
Sumter, SC 29150
(803) 773-5546
Contact: James Barnard

SOUTH DAKOTA

KESD-TV Channel 8
South Dakota State University
Pugsley Center
Brookings, SD 57006
(605) 688-4191
Contact: Eric F. Brown

KDSK-TV Channel 16 (Aberdeen)
KPSD-TV Channel 13 (Eagle Butte)
KTSD-TV Channel 10 (Pierre)
KBHE-TV Channel 9 (Rapid City)
KZSD-TV Channel 8 (Martin)

South Dakota ETV Board
310 E. Clark St.
Vermillion, SD 57069
(605) 624-4497
Contact: Martin P. Busch

KUSD-TV Channel 2
Old Union Bldg.
University of South Dakota
Vermillion, SD 57069
(605) 677-5277
Contact: Martin P. Busch

TENNESSEE

WTCI-TV Channel 45
4411 Amnicola Hwy.
Chattanooga, TN 37406
(615) 629-4368
Contact: Walter A. Alley

WLJT-TV Channel 11 (Lexington)
WSJK-TV Channel 2 (Knoxville-Sneedville)
WCTE-TV Channel 22 (Cookeville)
University of Tennessee
209 Communications Bldg.
Knoxville, TN 37916
(615) 974-5281
Contact: Ernest A. Curtis, Jr.

WKNO-TV Channel 10
Box 80000
Memphis, TN 38152
(901) 458-2521
Contact: Howard D. Holst

WDCN-TV Channel 8
P.O. Box 12555
Nashville, TN 37212
(615) 259-9325
Contact: Robert L. Shepherd

TEXAS

KLRN-TV Channel 9 (Austin–San Antonio)
P.O. Box 7158
Austin, TX 78712
(512) 471-4811
Contact: Harry Herbst

KAMU-TV Channel 15
Texas A&M University
New ETV Bldg.
College Station, TX 77843
(713) 845-5611
Contact: Mel Chastain

KEDT-TV Channel 16
P.O. Box 416
Corpus Christi, TX 78403
(512) 855-2213
Contact: Terrel L. Cass

KERA-TV Channel 13
3000 Harry Hines Blvd.
Dallas, TX 75201
(214) 744-1300
Contact: Ed Pfister

KUHT-TV Channel 8
4513 Cullen Blvd.
Houston, TX 77004
(713) 748-6814
Contact: James L. Bauer

KNCT-TV Channel 46
Central Texas College
U.S. Hwy. 190 W
Killeen, TX 76541
(817) 526-1182
Contact: P. Anthony Zeiss

KTXT-TV Channel 5
Texas Tech University
Tech Station Box 4359
Lubbock, TX 79409
(806) 742-2209
Contact: John W. Henson

UTAH

KBYU-TV Channel 11
Brigham Young University
C-306 Harris Fine Arts Center
Provo, UT 84602
(801) 374-1211
Contact: Bruce L. Christensen

KUED-TV Channel 7
University of Utah
101 Music Hall
Salt Lake City, UT 84112
(801) 581-7777
Contact: Milton L. Davis

VERMONT

WETK-TV Channel 33 (Burlington)
WVER-TV Channel 28 (Rutland)
WVTB-TV Channel 20 (St. Johnsbury)
WVTA-TV Channel 41 (Windsor)

Vermont Educational Television
Fort Ethan Allen Ave.
Winooski, VT 05404
(802) 656-3311
Contact: John W. Dunlop

VIRGINIA

WNVT-TV Channel 53
8325 Little River Tpke.
Annandale, VA 22003
(703) 323-7000
Contact: Daniel Ward

WVPT-TV Channel 51
Port Republic Rd.
Harrisonburg, VA 22801
(703) 434-5391
Contact: Richard L. Parker

WHRO-TV Channel 15
5200 Hampton Blvd.
Norfolk, VA 23508
(804) 489-9476
Contact: John R. Morison

WCVE-TV Channel 23 (Richmond)
WCVW-TV Channel 57 (Richmond)
23 Sesame St.
Richmond, VA 23235
(804) 320-1301
Contact: B. W. Spiller

WBRA-TV Channel 15 (Roanoke)
WSVN-TV Channel 47 (Norton)
P.O. Box 13246
Roanoke, VA 24032
(703) 344-0991
Contact: Ercil V. Rexrode, Jr.

WASHINGTON

KWSU-TV Channel 10
Washington State University
Edward R. Murrow Communications Center
Pullman, WA 99163
(509) 335-2681
Contact: Dennis Haarseger

KCTS-TV Channel 9
University of Washington
4045 Brooklyn Ave.
Seattle, WA 98105
(206) 543-2000
Contact: Richard J. Meyer

KSPS-TV Channel 7
South 3911 Regal St.
Spokane, WA 99203
(509) 455-3790
Contact: Walter J. Schaar

KCPQ-TV Channel 13 (Lakewood Center)
4400 Steilacocm Blvd.
Tacoma, WA 98499
(206) 552-5431
Contact: J. Albert Brevik

KTPS-TV Channel 62
P.O. Box 1357
Tacoma, WA 98401
(206) 572-6262
Contact: Robert P. Slingland

KYVE-TV Channel 47
1105 S. 15th Ave.
Yakima, WA 98902
(509) 575-3474
Contact: Frank E. Roberts

WEST VIRGINIA

WSWP-TV Channel 9 (Grandview)
P.O. Box AH
Beckley, WV 25801
(304) 255-1501
Contact: Arthur E. Albrecht

WMUL-TV Channel 33
3rd Ave.
Huntington, WV 25701
(304) 696-6630
Contact: Terry Hollinger

WWVU-TV Channel 24
P.O. Box TV 24
Morgantown, WV 26505
(304) 293-6511
Contact: C. Gregory Van Camp

WISCONSIN

WPNE-TV Channel 38 (Green Bay)
WHWC-TV Channel 28 (Colfax)
WHLA-TV Channel 31 (La Crosse)
WHRM-TV Channel 20 (Wausau)

Educational Communications Board
732 N. Midvale Blvd.
Madison, WI 53705
(608) 266-0036
Contact: Tony Moe

WHA-TV Channel 21
University of Wisconsin
Vilas Communications Hall
821 University Ave.
Madison, WI 53706
(608) 263-2121
Contact: Ronald C. Bornstein

WMVS-TV Channel 10 (Milwaukee)
WMVT-TV Channel 36 (Milwaukee)
1015 N. 6th St.
Milwaukee, WI 53203
(414) 271-1036
Contact: Otto F. Schlaak

AMERICAN SAMOA

KVZK-TV Channel 2
P.O. Box 2567
Pago Pago
American Samoa 96799
633-4191
Contact: Thomas Little

GUAM

KGTF-TV Channel 12
P.O. Box 3615
Agana, Guam 96910
(671) 734-2207
Contact: Iris Muna

PUERTO RICO

WIPR-TV Channel 6 (San Juan)
WIPM-TV Channel 3 (Mayaguez)
P.O. Box 909
Hato Rey, PR 00919
(809) 763-3666
Contact: Elsie Calero Demavtinez

VIRGIN ISLANDS

WTJX-TV Channel 12
P.O. Box 7077
St. Thomas, VI 00801
(809) 774-6255
Contact: Calvin F. Bastian

Publications

Advertising Age
740 N. Rush St.
Chicago, IL 60611
(312) 649-5200
Ed: Rance Crane
Circ: 69,000
Published: weekly
Subj: advertising industry
Price: $15.00

Advertising World
1718 Sherman Ave.
Evanston, IL 60201
(312) 491-0019
Ed: Albert Stridsberg
Circ: 4,000
Published: quarterly
Subj: international advertising
Price: $15.00

After Dark
10 Columbus Circle
New York, NY 10019
(212) 399-2400
Ed: William Como
Circ: 72,000
Published: monthly
Subj: entertainment, TV
Price: $14.00

American Film
The American Film Institute
The John F. Kennedy Center for the Performing Arts
Washington, DC 20566
(202) 828-4050
Ed: Hollis Alpert
Circ: 100,000
Published: monthly (except for combined December–January and July–August issues)
Subj: film, TV
Price: $15.00 (includes membership in AFI)

ANNY (Advertising News of New York)
230 Park Ave.
New York, NY 10017
(212) 661-8080
Ed: Val Cardinale
Circ: 18,000
Published: weekly
Subj: advertising
Price: $10.00

Audiovideo International
380 Madison Ave.
New York, NY 10017
(212) 867-0900
Ed: Richard Coccola
Circ: 33,000
Published: monthly
Subj: consumer electronics products
Price: $10.00

Audio-Visual Communications
750 3rd Ave.
New York, NY 10017
(212) 697-8300
Ed: Mike Yuhas
Circ: 29,000
Published: monthly
Subj: audiovisual techniques
Price: $18.00

Audio-Visual Equipment & Production Directory
750 3rd Ave.
New York, NY 10017
Ed: Mike Yuhas
Circ: 30,000
Published: annually
Subj: audiovisual materials
Price: $5.00

Audio-Visual Instructor
1126 16th St. NW
Washington, DC 20036
(202) 833-4180
Ed: Dr. H. B. Hitchens
Circ: 17,000
Published: monthly
Subj: telecommunications
Price: $9.00

Audio-Visual Guide Newsletter
434 S. Wabash Ave.
Chicago, IL 60605
(312) 922-8167
Ed: Joseph Ziemba
Circ: 3,000
Published: monthly
Subj: audiovisual products
Price: $6.00

Back Stage
165 W. 46th St.
New York, NY 10036
(212) 581-1080
Ed: Allen Zwerdling
Circ: 30,000
Published: weekly
Subj: communications/entertainment industry
Price: $18.00

Better Broadcasts News
423 N. Pinckney
Madison, WI 53703
(608) 255-2009
Ed: Leslie Spence
Circ: 12,000
Published: Five times a year
Subj: broadcasting industry
Price: $2.00

Black Stars
820 S. Michigan Ave.
Chicago, IL 60605
(312) 322-9200
Ed: John W. Johnson
Circ: figures not available
Published: monthly
Subj: TV and movie personalities
Price: $7.00

BM/E (Broadcast Management/Engineering)
295 Madison Ave.
New York, NY 10017
(212) 685-5320
Ed: James A. Lippke
Circ: 30,000
Published: monthly
Subj: communications mfg.
Price: $18.00

Broadcast Daily
18 E. 62nd St.
New York, NY 10021
(212) 751-3274
Ed: Charles Sinclair
Circ: 4,000
Published: three times a year
Subj: broadcast conventions
Price: free (controlled circulation)

Broadcast Engineering
9221 Quivira Rd.
P.O. Box 12901
Overland Park, KS 66212
(913) 888-4664
Ed: Ronald N. Merrell
Circ: 33,000
Published: monthly
Subj: broadcast–communications equipment
Price: $6.00

Broadcast Equipment Today
P.O. Box 423, Station J
Toronto, Ont., Canada M4J-4Y8
(416) 463-5304
Ed: Doug Loney
Circ: 13,000
Published: bimonthly
Subj: cable TV
Price: $9.00

Broadcasting
1735 De Sales St. NW
Washington, DC 20036
(202) 638-1022
Ed: Sol Taishoff
Circ: 34,000
Published: weekly
Subj: broadcasting industry
Price: $30.00

Broadcasting Cable Sourcebook
1735 De Sales St. NW
Washington, DC 20036
(202) 638-1022
Ed: Sol Taishoff
Circ: 4,000
Published: annually
Subj: cable-TV systems
Price: $25.00

Broadcasting Yearbook
1735 De Sales St. NW
Washington, DC 20036
(202) 638-1022
Ed: Sol Taishoff
Circ: 18,000
Published: annually (in March)
Subj: broadcasting
Price: $30.00

Broadcast Investor
100 Merrick Rd.
Rockville Centre, NY 11570
(516) 764-5516
Ed: Paul Kagan
Circ: figures not available
Published: bimonthly
Subj: TV financial and FCC information
Price: $235.00

Broadcast News
Front & Cooper Sts.
Camden, NJ 08102
(609) 963-8000
Ed: Miles Moon
Circ: controlled
Published: quarterly
Subj: broadcast industry
Price: free to industry

Broadcast Programming & Production
P.O. Box 2449
1850 N. Whitley Ave.
Hollywood, CA 90028
(213) 467-1111
Ed: Gary Kleinman
Circ: 1,400
Published: bimonthly
Subj: broadcasting
Price: $7.00

Cablecast
100 Merrick Rd.
Rockville Centre, NY 11570
(516) 764-5516
Ed: Paul Kagan
Circ: figures not available
Published: bimonthly
Subj: cable-TV financial information
Price: $295.00

Cable Communications
30 Bloor St. W
Toronto, Ont., Canada M4W-1A2
(416) 924-1214
Ed: Bill Pryde
Circ: 5,000
Published: monthly
Subj: cable-TV and telephone
Price: $20.00

Cablefile
1139 Delaware Plaza
P.O. Box 4305
Denver, CO 80204
(303) 573-1433
Ed: John Fitzpatrick
Circ: 3,500
Published: annually
Subj: cable-TV systems
Price: $24.95

Cable TV Regulations
100 Merrick Rd.
Rockville Centre, NY 11570
(516) 764-5516
Ed: John Mansell
Circ: figures not available
Published: biweekly
Subj: cable-TV regulations
Price: $175.00

Cablevision
1139 Delaware Plaza
P.O. Box 4305
Denver, CO 80204
(303) 573-1433
Ed: Paul Fitzpatrick
Circ: 5,000
Published: biweekly
Subj: CATV systems
Price: $21.50

CATJ (Community Antenna TV Journal)
4209 N.W. 23rd St.
Oklahoma City, OK 73107
(405) 947-4717
Ed: Robert B. Cooper
Circ: figures not available
Published: monthly
Subj: community antenna TV industry
Price: $12.00 regular; $9.00 for technicians

CATV Buyer's Guide
3900 S. Wadsworth Blvd.
Suite 560
Denver, CO 80235
(303) 988-4670
Ed: Barbara Ruger
Circ: 3,000
Published: annually
Subj: cable-TV equipment manufacturing
Price: $8.95 a copy

CATV/NCTA Convention Daily
3900 S. Wadsworth Blvd.
Suite 560
Denver, CO 80235
(303) 988-4670
Ed: Barbara Ruger
Circ: 2,000
Published: three times a year
Subj: National Cable TV Association convention
Price: distributed free at CATV conventions

CATV Systems Directory, Map Services and Handbook
3900 S. Wadsworth Blvd.
Suite 560
Denver, CO 80235
(303) 988-4670
Ed: Barbara Ruger
Circ: 3,000
Published: annually
Subj: the manufacture and distribution of CATV
Price: $14.98

Clio
30 E. 60th St.
New York, NY 10022
(212) 593-1900
Ed: Patrick Ferrara
Circ: 400
Published: quarterly
Subj: mass communications, advertising
Price: $9.00

Communications Arts
410 Sherman
P.O. Box 10300
Palo Alto, CA 94303
(415) 326-6040
Ed: Richard Coyne
Circ: 28,000
Published: bimonthly
Subj: advertising business
Price: $24.00

Communications/Engineering Digest
1139 Delaware Plaza
Denver, CO 80204
(303) 573-1433
Ed: Pat Gushman
Circ: 5,000
Published: monthly
Subj: cable TV
Price: $12.00

Communications
3900 S. Wadsworth Blvd.
Suite 560
Denver, CO 80235
(303) 988-4670
Ed: Robert A. Searle
Circ: 18,000
Published: monthly
Subj: communications industry
Price: $12.00

Communications Retailing
325 E. 75th St.
New York, NY 10021
(212) 794-0500
Ed: Mitch Ratliff
Circ: 23,500
Published: monthly
Subj: communications sales
Price: $20.00

Communications News
402 W. Liberty Dr.
Wheaton, IL 60187
(312) 653-4040
Ed: Kenneth M. Bourne
Circ: 34,000
Published: monthly
Subj: communications equipment
Price: $7.00

Communications World
229 Park Ave. South
New York, NY 10003
(202) 673-1300
Ed: Julian S. Martin
Circ: 48,000
Published: twice a year
Subj: radio and TV
Price: $1.35 a copy

Communicator
1730 Pennsylvania Ave. NW
Washington, DC 20006
(202) 785-0500
Ed: John Constable
Circ: 1,000
Published: monthly
Subj: radio–telephone industry
Price: $30.00

Consumer Electronics
325 E. 75th St.
New York, NY 10021
(212) 794-0500
Ed: Lois Whitman
Circ: 40,000
Published: monthly
Subj: consumer-electronics industry
Price: $10.00

Consumer Electronics Monthly
325 E. 75th St.
New York, NY 10021
(212) 794-0500
Ed: Lois Whitman
Circ: 40,000
Published: monthly
Subj: consumer-electronics industry
Price: $7.00

Consumer Electronics Product News
6 E. 43rd St.
New York, NY 10017
(212) 949-0800
Ed: Bryan Stanton
Circ: 36,000
Published: four times a year
Subj: consumer-electronics industry
Price: free to people in the field; all others $15.00

Consumer Electronics Show Daily
325 E. 75th St.
New York, NY 10021
(212) 794-0500
Ed: Lois Whitman
Circ: 25,000
Published: January and June, and daily during CES convention
Subj: consumer-electronics show
Price: $4.00

Consumer Electronics Show Daily News
310 Madison Ave.
New York, NY 10017
(212) 586-8333
Ed: W. Ross
Circ: 25,000 non-paid
Published: twice a year
Subj: consumer electronics industry
Price: free (controlled circulation)

Consumer Electronics Show Trade News
6 E. 43rd St.
New York, NY 10017
(212) 949-0800
Ed: Brian Stanton
Circ: 35,000, non-paid
Published: daily during the biennial consumer electronics show
Subj: consumer-electronics industry
Price: free (controlled circulation)

Cue
545 Madison Ave.
New York, NY 10022
(212) 371-7070
Ed: Nancy Love
Circ: 280,000
Published: biweekly
Subj: N.Y. entertainment, TV
Price: $12.00

Daily Variety
1400 N. Cahuenga Blvd.
Hollywood, CA 90023
(213) 469-1141
Ed: Thomas M. Pryor
Circ: 15,000
Published: daily except Sat., Sun., and holidays
Subj: entertainment business
Price: $40.00

Daylight TV
355 Lexington Ave.
New York, NY 10017
(212) 391-1400
Ed: Paul Dennis
Circ: figures not available
Published: monthly
Subj: daytime TV
Price: $.75 per issue

Daytime TV
355 Lexington Ave.
New York, NY 10017
(212) 391-1400
Ed: Paul Dennis
Circ: 323,000
Published: monthly
Subj: daytime TV, programs, and people
Price: $9.00

DB—The Sound Engineering Magazine
1120 Old Country Rd.
Plainview, NY 11803
(516) 433-6530
Ed: Larry Zide
Circ: 24,000
Published: monthly
Subj: audio industry—broadcasting
Price: $6.00

Educational and Industrial TV
P.O. Box 565
Ridgefield, CT 06877
(203) 438-3774
Ed: Mary M. Woolf
Circ: 26,000
Published: monthly
Subj: how to information about TV production and equipment
Price: $30.00

Electronic Distributing
33405 Aurora Rd.
Cleveland, OH 44139
(216) 248-4955
Ed: James C. Kinkaid
Circ: 15,000
Published: monthly
Subj: electronics
Price: $10.00

Electronic News
7 E. 12th St.
New York, NY 10003
(212) 741-4000
Ed: James J. Lydon
Circ: 70,000
Published: weekly
Subj: electronics-industry news
Price: $9.50

Electronic Products Magazine
645 Stewart Ave.
Garden City, NY 11530
(516) 222-2500
Ed: Frank T. Egan
Circ: 92,000
Published: 12 times a year
Subj: electronic products
Price: $15.00

Electronics
1221 Ave. of the Americas
New York, NY 10020
(212) 997-2645
Ed: Kemp Anderson
Circ: 90,000
Published: biweekly
Subj: electronics-industry news
Price: $12.00

Electronic Servicing
9221 Quivira Rd.
P.O. Box 12901
Overland Park, KS 66212
(913) 888-4664
Ed: Carl Babcoke
Circ: 66,000
Published: monthly
Subj: servicing electronics equipment
Price: $6.00

Electronics Journal
16 W. Downer Pl.
Aurora, IL 60506
(312) 897-4000
Ed: Bruce A. Dillon
Circ: 13,000,
Published: monthly
Subj: electronics products
Price: $6.00

Electronics Retailing
645 Stewart Ave.
Garden City, NY 11530
(516) 222-2500
Ed: Thomas Ewing
Circ: 33,500
Published: monthly
Subj: electronics-products sales
Price: $10.00

Electronic Technician/Dealer
757 3rd Ave.
New York, NY 10017
(212) 888-4405
Ed: Richard Lay
Circ: 68,000
Published: monthly
Subj: electronics products
Price: $9.00

Emmy Magazine
4605 Lankersham Blvd.
Suite 800
North Hollywood, CA 91602
(213) 506-7880
Ed: Stephen Zito
Circ: 35,000
Published: quarterly
Subj: television industry
Price: $12.00 USA, $15.00 foreign

Facts, Figures, Film
30 E. 42nd St.
New York, NY 10017
(212) 687-1668
Ed: Avra Fliegelman
Circ: figures not available
Published: monthly
Subj: TV industry
Price: $279.00, plus $10.00 postage and handling

Federal Communications Bar Journal
Communications Program
UCLA Law School
405 Hilgard Ave.
Los Angeles, CA 90024
(213) 825-6211
Ed: Charles Firestone
Circ: figures not available
Published: two issues a year
Subj: communications law
Price: price not available

Film Comment
Film Society of Lincoln Center
140 W. 65th St.
New York, NY 10023
(212) 877-1800
Ed: Richard Corliss
Circ: 20,000
Published: bimonthly
Subj: film, TV
Price: $10.00

Films in Review
210 E. 68th St.
New York, NY 10021
(212) 988-4916
Ed: Charles P. Reilly
Circ: 8,000
Published: monthly
Subj: motion pictures, TV
Price: $10.50

The Hollywood Reporter
6715 Sunset Blvd.
Hollywood, CA 90028
(213) 464-7411
Ed: Tichi W. Miles
Circ: 14,000
Published: daily except Sat., Sun., and holidays
Subj: entertainment, TV
Price: $48.00

IEEE Spectrum
345 E. 47th St.
New York, NY 10017
(212) 644-7555
Ed: Donald Christiansen
Circ: 170,000
Published: monthly
Subj: electrical–electronics engineering
Price: $4.00

Industrial Communications
National Press Bldg.
Washington, DC 20004
(202) 783-2482
Ed: Robert E. Tall
Circ: figures not available
Published: weekly
Subj: industrial communications
Price: $145.00

Journal of the Audio Engineering Society
60 E. 42nd St.
New York, NY 10017
(212) 661-2355
Ed: Robert O. Fehr
Circ: 9,000
Published: monthly
Subj: audio industry
Price: $35.00

Journal of Broadcasting
Communications Dept.
University of Georgia
Athens, GA 30602
(404) 542-3030
Ed: Dr. Joe Dominick
Circ: figures not available
Published: quarterly
Subj: broadcasting industry
Price: $17.50

Madison Avenue
750 3rd Ave.
New York, NY 10017
(212) 682-5250
Ed: Jenny Greenberg
Circ: 32,000
Published: monthly
Subj: advertising industry
Price: $20.00

Media and Methods
401 N. Broad St.
Philadelphia, PA 19108
(215) 574-9600
Ed: Anthony Prete
Circ: 45,000
Published: monthly during school year
Subj: multi-media and TV
Price: $9.00

Media Decisions
342 Madison Ave.
New York, NY 10017
(212) 954-1888
Ed: Norman R. Glenn
Circ: 26,000
Published: monthly
Subj: media monetary trends
Price: $20.00

Media Report to Women
3306 Ross Pl. NW
Washington, DC 20008
(202) 363-0812
Ed: Dr. Donna Allen
Circ: 1,000
Published: monthly
Subj: communications media
Price: $20.00

Millimeter
12 E. 46th St.
New York, NY 10017
(212) 867-3636
Ed: Alice Wolf
Circ: 17,740
Published: monthly
Subj: TV and cinema production
Price: $12.00

Modern Screen
355 Lexington Ave.
New York, NY 10017
(212) 391-1400
Ed: Joan Goldstein
Circ: 2,600
Published: monthly
Subj: TV and movie personalities
Price: $12.00

Movie Life
575 Madison Ave.
New York, NY 10022
(212) 759-9704
Ed: Seli Groves
Circ: 150,000
Published: monthly
Subj: TV and movie personalities
Price: $9.00

Multicast
100 Merrick Rd.
Rockville Centre, NY 11570
(516) 764-5516
Ed: George Eagle
Circ: figures not available
Published: biweekly
Subj: cable-TV industry
Price: $235.00

NAB Highlights
1771 N St. NW
Washington, DC 20036
(202) 293-3500
Ed: Marilyn O'Connor
Circ: 4,500 (members)
Published: weekly
Subj: communications industry
Price: $8.00

NAEB Newsletter
1346 Connecticut Ave. NW
Washington, DC 20036
(202) 785-1100
Ed: Olga Zabludoff
Circ: 4,000 (members)
Published: annually
Subj: educational communications
Price: $18.00

Narda News
2 N. Riverside Plaza
Suite 222
Chicago, IL 60606
(312) 454-0944
Ed: Martin Sheridan
Circ: 7,000
Published: monthly
Subj: retail dealers electronics
Price: $15.00

Natesa Scope
5908 S. Troy St.
Chicago, IL 60629
(312) 476-6363
Ed: Frank J. Moch
Circ: 7,500
Published: monthly
Subj: electronics industry
Price: $5.00

News and Views
111 W. Colorado Blvd.
Monrovia, CA 91016
(213) 358-1159
Ed: Janice Marugg
Circ: 500
Published: monthly
Subj: Chamber of Commerce, communications
Price: free

Notes from the Center
2100 M St. NW
Washington, DC 20037
(202) 872-8888
Ed: Marilynne R. Rudick
Circ: figures not available
Published: quarterly
Subj: cable-TV industry
Price: free (controlled circulation)

Pay TV Newsletter
100 Merrick Rd.
Rockville Centre, NY 11570
(516) 764-5516
Ed: Paul Kagan
Circ: figures not available
Published: biweekly
Subj: pay-TV industry
Price: $295.00

Photoplay
215 Lexington Ave.
New York, NY 10016
(212) 340-7500
Ed: Lynne Dorsey
Circ: 440,000
Published: monthly
Subj: TV and movie personalities
Price: $9.95

P.D. Cue
Box 5348
Lancaster, PA 17601
(717) 626-4824
Ed: Bob Bernstein
Circ: 1,000
Published: ten times a year
Subj: TV programming
Price: free to members; others $10.00 per copy

Popular Electronics
1 Park Ave.
New York, NY 10016
(212) 725-3516
Ed: Arthur Salsberg
Circ: 414,000
Published: monthly
Subj: electronics
Price: $6.00

Public Telecommunications Review
1346 Connecticut Ave. NW
Washington, DC 20036
(202) 785-1100
Ed: Eva Archer
Circ: figures not available
Published: bimonthly
Subj: telecommunications industry
Price: $18.00

Radio and TV Weekly
254 W. 31st St.
New York, NY 10001
(212) 594-4120
Ed: Ed Walter
Circ: 9,800
Published: weekly
Subj: electronics-distributing industry
Price: $10.00

Radio-Electronics
200 Park Ave. South
New York, NY 10003
(212) 777-6400
Ed: M. Harvey Gernsback
Circ: 173,000
Published: monthly
Subj: electronics
Price: $8.75

Satellite Communications
3900 S. Wadsworth Blvd.
Suite 560
Denver, CO 80235
(303) 988-4670
Ed: Dr. Delbert Smith
Circ: 12,500
Published: monthly
Subj: satellite-communications industry
Price: $14.95

Screen Actor
7750 Sunset Blvd.
Hollywood, CA 90046
(213) 876-3030
Ed: Judith Rheiner
Circ: 38,000
Published: quarterly
Subj: film
Price: $4.00

Series, Serials, Packages
30 E. 42nd St.
New York, NY 10017
(212) 687-1668
Ed: Avra Fliegelman
Circ: figures not available
Published: annually
Subj: TV, films
Price: $144.00, plus $5.00 postage and handling

Service Shop
1715 Expo La.
Indianapolis, IN 46224
(317) 241-8160
Ed: Steve Bernard
Circ: 8,000
Published: monthly
Subj: radio–TV service
Price: $5.00

Sight and Sound Marketing
51 E. 42nd St.
New York, NY 10017
Ed: Neil Spann
Circ: 21,000
Published: monthly
Subj: telecommunications equipment
Price: $7.00

Signal
12005 Chesterton Dr.
Upper Marlboro, MD 20870
(301) 249-7158
Ed: Judith H. Shreve
Circ: 12,000
Published: ten times a year
Subj: military communications
Price: $12.50 for nonmembers; $10.00 for members

SMPTE Journal
862 Scarsdale Ave.
Scarsdale, NY 10583
(914) 472-6606
Ed: Thomas E. King
Circ: 9,600
Published: monthly
Subj: engineering in movies and TV
Price: $35.00

Solid State Technology
14 Vanderventer Ave.
Port Washington, NY 10050
(516) 883-6200
Ed: Sam Marshall
Circ: 19,000
Published: monthly
Subj: solid-state manufacturing
Price: $15.00

Sound & Communications
150 E. 37th St.
New York, NY 10016
(212) 685-3480
Ed: Jerome J. Brookman
Circ: 7,000
Published: monthly
Subj: sound and telecommunications
Price: $10.00

Spectrum
345 E. 47th St.
New York, NY 10017
(212) 644-7900
Ed: Donald Christiansen
Circ: figures not available
Published: monthly
Subj: electronics industry
Price: $49.00

Telecommunications
610 Washington St.
Dedham, MA 02026
(617) 326-8220
Ed: James Hughes
Circ: 41,000
Published: monthly
Subj: telecommunications industry
Price: $25.00

Telecommunications Reports
National Press Bldg.
Washington, DC 20045
(202) 347-2654
Ed: Fred Henck
Circ: figures not available
Published: weekly
Subj: telecommunications industry
Price: $147.00

Television Digest
1836 Jefferson Pl. NW
Washington, DC 20036
(202) 872-9100
Ed: Albert Warren
Circ: figures not available
Published: weekly
Subj: TV industry
Price: $228.00

Television International
P.O. Box 2430
Hollywood, CA 90028
(213) 876-2219
Ed: Al Preiss
Circ: 12,000
Published: bimonthly
Subj: TV industry
Price: $10.00

Television/Radio Age
666 5th Ave.
New York, NY 10019
(212) 757-8400
Ed: S. J. Paul
Circ: 17,000
Published: biweekly
Subj: broadcast business
Price: $20.00

Thirteen (WNET/13)
356 W. 58th St.
New York, NY 10019
(212) 262-3064
Ed: Bonnie Lee Black
Circ: 300,000
Published: monthly
Subj: public-television listings
Price: $15.00

TV and Movie Screen
355 Lexington Ave.
New York, NY 10017
(212) 391-1400
Ed: Roseann Hirsch
Circ: 130,000
Published: monthly
Subj: TV and movies
Price: $9.00

TV Communications
3900 S. Wadsworth Blvd.
Suite 560
Denver, CO 80235
(303) 988-4670
Ed: R. Searle
Circ: 6,000
Published: monthly
Subj: CATV industry
Price: $17.00

TV Dawn To Dusk
575 Madison Ave.
New York, NY 10022
(212) 683-4200
Ed: Sherry Amentenstein
Circ: 103,700
Published: monthly
Subj: daytime TV
Price: $9.00

TV Digest and Consumer Electronics
1836 Jefferson Pl. NW
Washington, DC 20036
(202) 872-9200
Ed: Albert Warren
Circ: figures not available
Published: weekly
Subj: TV and electronics industry
Price: $245.00 (rates may vary with additional publications)

TV Fact Book
1836 Jefferson Pl. NW
Washington, DC 20036
(202) 872-9200
Ed: Albert Warren
Circ: 9,000
Published: annually
Subj: TV reference
Price: $74.50

TV Facts
131 Jericho Tpke.
Suite 401
Jericho, NY 11753
(516) 333-8866
Ed: Nick Gimple
Circ: 2,000,000
Published: weekly
Subj: television listings
Price: varies from one market to another

TV Film Source Book
30 E. 42nd St.
New York, NY 10017
(212) 687-1668
Ed: Avra Fliegelman
Circ: figures not available
Published: annually
Subj: TV-film industry
Price: $169.00, plus $5.00 postage and handling

TV Guide
250 King of Prussia Rd.
Radnor, PA 19088
(215) 688-7400
Ed: Roger Youman
Circ: 20,000,000
Published: weekly
Subj: news and reviews of television and TV listings
Price: $18.00

TV News
6330 Ferguson St.
Indianapolis, IN 46220
(317) 255-6362
Ed: Jack Carter
Circ: 38,000
Published: weekly
Subj: television listings
Price: $9.50

TV Picture Life
355 Lexington Ave.
New York, NY 10017
(212) 391-1400
Ed: Sanford Schwarz
Circ: 126,000
Published: monthly
Subj: TV entertainment
Price: $9.00

TV-Prevue
2548 S.E. Ankeny St.
Portland, OR 97214
(506) 235-4413
Ed: L. H. Imdieke
Circ: figures not available
Published: weekly
Subj: TV
Price: $3.50

TV Pro-Log
150 Fifth Ave.
New York, NY 10011
(212) 924-0320
Ed: Jerry Leichter
Circ: figures not available
Published: weekly
Subj: TV production
Price: $23.00

TV Radio Talk
575 Madison Ave.
New York, NY 10022
(212) 759-9704
Ed: John A. Scott
Circ: 114,000
Published: monthly
Subj: TV and radio
Price: $9.00

TV Star Parade
575 Madison Ave.
New York, NY 10022
(212) 759-9704
Ed: Kathy Loy
Circ: 129,000
Published: monthly
Subj: television listings
Price: $9.00

TV Time and Channel
203 E. Broad St.
Bethlehem, PA 18018
(215) 865-6600
Ed: Joseph A. Cunningham
Circ: figures not available
Published: weekly
Subj: television listings
Price: $9.00

T-V Times
Box 647
Baton Rouge, LA 70821
(504) 924-1575
Ed: Gerald Murray
Circ: 6,000
Published: weekly
Subj: television listings
Price: $6.96

TV Viewer
4214 Spenard Rd.
Anchorage, AL 99503
(907) 277-4012
Ed: Frank Martone
Circ: 13,000
Published: weekly
Subj: TV
Price: $14.95

Variety
154 W. 46th St.
New York, NY 10036
(212) 582-2700
Ed: Robert J. Landry
Circ: figures not available
Published: weekly
Subj: entertainment and broadcast advertising
Price: $30.00

Videography
750 3rd Ave.
New York, NY 10017
(212) 697-8300
Ed: Barry Ancona
Circ: figures not available
Published: monthly
Subj: video industry
Price: $10.00

The Video Handbook
750 3rd Ave.
New York, NY 10017
(212) 697-8300
Ed: Peter Caranicas
Circ: 10,000
Published: annually
Subj: video reference
Price: $12.75

Video News
8401 Connecticut Ave. NW
Washington, DC 20015
(301) 652-5522
Ed: Jerry Norton
Circ: figures not available
Published: biweekly
Subj: video industry
Price: $87.00

Video Publisher
2 Corporate Park Dr.
White Plains, NY 10604
(914) 694-8686
Ed: Seth Goldstein
Circ: figures not available
Published: biweekly
Subj: video-services industry
Price: $95.00

Video Systems
9221 Quivira Rd.
P.O. Box 12901
Overland Park, KS 66212
(913) 888-4464
Ed: George Laughead, Jr.
Circ: 15,500
Published: monthly
Subj: closed-circuit TV
Price: $20.00

Video Trade News
P.O. Box 565
Ridgefield, CT 06877
(203) 438-3774
Ed: Charles S. Tepfer
Circ: 2,000
Published: monthly
Subj: video equipment/programming
Price: $8.00

Vue
3900 S. Wadsworth Blvd.
Suite 560
Denver, CO 80235
(303) 988-4670
Ed: Mark Day
Circ: 2,000
Published: biweekly
Subj: CATV news
Price: $22.00

The World of AWRT (American Women In Radio and TV, Inc.)
1321 Connecticut Ave. N.W.
Washington, DC 20036
(202) 296-0009
Ed: Pat Ward
Circ: members
Published: ten times a year
Subj: women in the communications industry
Price: free to members

Syndicated TV Columns and Columnists

Column Name: Around Hollywood
Author: Luanne Murray
Subject: Movies and TV celebrities
Syndicate:
Trans-World News Service
767 National Press Bldg.
529 14th St. NW
Washington, DC 20045
(202) 638-5568
Contact: Bernard Blazes

Column Name: Ask TV Scout
Author: Joan Crosby
Subject: TV questions and answers
Syndicate:
Newspaper Enterprises Association
230 Park Ave.
New York, NY 10017
(212) 557-5870
Contact: David Hendin

Column Name: Assignment: Television
Author: Terrence O'Flaherty
Subject: Television criticism
Syndicate:
Chronical Features Syndicate
870 Market St.
San Francisco, CA 94102
(415) 777-1111
Contact: Stanleigh Arnold

Column Name: Better Living with the Stars
Author: Ruth E. Thompson
Subject: TV listings and inside looks at TV and movie
Syndicate:
Dickinson Newspaper Service, Inc.
271 Madison Ave.
New York, NY 10016
(212) 532-0170
Contact: Harry T. Dickinson

Column Name: Cecil Smith Column
Author: Cecil Smith
Subject: TV shows/personalities
Syndicate:
Los Angeles Times Syndicate
Times Mirror Square
Los Angeles, CA 90053
(213) 972-5000 Toll Free (800) 421-8800
Contact: Dan Byrne

Column Name: Channel Chatter
Author: Phyllis Maxwell
Subject: TV Commentary
Syndicate:
Trans-World News Service
767 National Press Bldg.
529 14th St. NW
Washington, DC 20045
(202) 638-5568
Contact: Bernard Blazes

Column Name: Curious Facts About TV
Author: Don Whitacre
Subject: Television facts
Syndicate:
Curious Facts Features
449 Glenview Dr.
Lebanon, OH 45036
(513) 932-1820
Contact: Don Whitacre

Column Name: Dateline America
Author: Jeffrey Blyth
Subject: TV personalities and shows; the business aspects of TV and motion pictures
Syndicate:
Interpress of London and New York
400 Madison Ave.
New York, NY 10017
(212) 832-2839
Contact: Jeffrey Blyth

Column Name: Daytime Dial
Author: Lynda Hirsch
Subject: TV soap operas
Syndicate:
Field Newspaper Syndicate
401 N. Wabash Ave.
Chicago, IL 60611
(312) 321-2795
Contact: Christian Chenoweth

Column Name: Entertainment Whirl
Author: Buddy Basch
Subject: Show business world
Syndicate:
Buddy Basch Feature Syndicate
771 West End Ave.
New York NY 10025
(212) 666-2300
Contact: Buddy Basch

Column Name: Entertainment World
Author: Damon Loy & Dart Anthony
Subject: World-wide coverage of TV, motion picture, and theatrical events
Syndicate:
Tu-Guy Enterprises
P.O. Box 14456
Las Vegas, NV 89114
(702) 734-2003
Contact: Dart Anthony

Column Name: Film Fare
Author: Laurie Lee
Subject: TV and film personalities, their lives and work
Syndicate:
World News Syndicate, Ltd.
6223 Selma Ave., Suite 201
Box 419
Hollywood, CA 90028
(213) 467-7024, 469-2333
Contact: William C. Lane

Column Name: Focus on Films
Author: Veronica Burke
Subject: Analysis of motion picture and television films
Syndicate:
Exclusive News Syndicate
P.O. Box 872
Santa Monica, CA 90406
(213) 451-4312
Contact: Wally Burke

Column Name: Footlights and Klieglights
Author: Ted Edwards
Subject: Films, TV, and general entertainment shows and personalities
Syndicate:
Trans-World News Service
767 National Press Bldg.
529 14th St. NW
Washington, DC 20045
(202) 638-5568
Contact: Bernard Blazes

Column Name: Hollywood Connection
Author: Wally Burke
Subject: Factual news about motion picture and television personalities
Syndicate:
Exclusive News Syndicate
P.O. Box 872
Santa Monica, CA 90406
(213) 451-4312
Contact: Wally Burke

Column Name: Hollywood Inside
Author: John Austin
Subject: Motion picture personalities
Syndicate:
Hollywood Inside Syndicate
P.O. Box 49957
Los Angeles, CA 90049
(213) 826-9602
Contact: John Austin

Column Name: Hollywood's Twilight Years
Author: Crosby L. Day
Subject: Motion picture and television happenings
Syndicate:
Trans-World News Service
767 National Press Bldg.
529 14th St. NW
Washington DC 20045
(202) 638-5568
Contact: Bernard Blazes

Column Name: International Adventures
Author: Julius Weiss
Subject: TV and radio stars who collect postage stamps and/or coins
Syndicate:
Weiss Philatelic & Numismatic Features
16000 Terrace Rd. (#208)
Cleveland, OH 44112
(216) 451-3331
Contact: Julius Weiss

Column Name: It Happened in Hollywood
Author: Scott Lawrence
Subject: Quizzes about TV and movies
Syndicate:
Los Angeles Times Syndicate
Times Mirror Square
Los Angeles, CA 90053
(213) 972-5000 Toll Free (800) 421-8800
Contact: Dan Byrne

Column Name: Jaundiced Eye
Author: Mark Deitch
Subject: Wrap-up of the entertainment industry
Syndicate:
Trans-World News Service
767 National Press Bldg.
529 14th St. NW
Washington, DC 20045
(202) 638-5568
Contact: Bernard Blazes

Column Name: John Austin's Hollywood
Author: John Austin
Subject: Entertainment
Syndicate:
 Hollywood Informer Syndicate
 P.O. Box 49321
 Los Angeles, CA 90049
 (213) 826-9602
 Contact: John Austin

Column Name: L'Annee Tele
Author: P. C. Haber
Subject: Survey of TV programs
Syndicate:
 Inter-Presse de France
 100 Beekman St.
 New York, NY 10038
 (212) 285-1872
 Contact: Pierre C. Haber

Column Name: L'Ecran Americain
Author: P. C. Haber
Subject: Television in the United States
Syndicate:
 Inter-Presse de France
 100 Beekman St.
 New York, NY 10038
 (212) 285-1872
 Contact: Pierre C. Haber

Column Name: Lifestyle
Author: Rita Harper
Subject: General commentary, including TV programming
Syndicate:
 Harper Communications
 2017 Marker Ave.
 Dayton, OH 45414
 (513) 274-2793
 Contact: Norma R. Harper

Column Name: Lookin' Around Hollywood
Author: Jerry M. Zalenka
Subject: Entertainment and television as it relates to film industry
Syndicate:
 Trans-World News Service
 767 National Press Bldg.
 529 14th St. NW
 Washington, DC 20045
 (202) 638-5568
 Contact: Bernard Blazes

Column Name: Look Who's Talking
Author: Alice Burke
Subject: Quotes and interviews from famous personalities in the entertainment field
Syndicate:
 Exclusive News Syndicate
 P.O. Box 872
 Santa Monica, CA 90406
 (213) 451-4312
 Contact: Wally Burke

Column Name: Lou Edman Describes
Author: Lou Edman
Subject: General commentary, including TV
Syndicate:
 The Edman Company
 P.O. Box 666
 Putnam, CT 06260
 (203) 928-3500
 Contact: Lou Edman

Column Name: Main Street
Author: Ted Green
Subject: General commentary on radio and TV personalities and shows
Syndicate:
 Press Wire Services/Press Wire Feature Services
 Box 2P, 144-45 35th Ave.
 Flushing, NY 11354
 (212) 539-6427
 Contact: Robert I. Queen

Column Name: Marilyn Beck's Hollywood
Author: Marilyn Beck
Subject: News about TV and movie celebrities or upcoming TV shows
Syndicate:
 United Feature Syndicate
 200 Park Ave.
 New York, NY 10017
 (212) 557-2333
 Contact: William C. Payette

Column Name: Marvin Kitman Column
Author: Marvin Kitman
Subject: TV criticism
Syndicate:
 Los Angeles Times Syndicate
 Times Mirror Square
 Los Angeles, CA 90053
 (213) 972-5000 Toll Free (800) 421-8800
 Contact: Dan Byrne

Column Name: Media Notebook
Author: U.S. Catholic Conference Film and Broadcasting Office, NY
Subject: General media criticism
Syndicate:
 National Catholic News Service
 1312 Massachusetts Ave. NW
 Washington, DC 20005
 (202) 659-6722
 Contact: Richard W. Daw

Column Name: More Than You Care to Know
Author: John Austin
Subject: Entertainment
Syndicate:
 Hollywood Informer Syndicate
 P.O. Box 49321
 Los Angeles, CA 90049
 (213) 826-9602
 Contact: John Austin

Column Name: Movie Memories
Author: Ruth Wucherer
Subject: Late night television
Syndicate:
  Trans-World News Service
  767 National Press Bldg.
  529 14th St. NW
  Washington, DC 20045
  (202) 638-5568
  Contact: Bernard Blazes

Column Name: On the Airwaves
Author: Tom Shales
Subject: TV criticism and previews
Syndicate:
  Washington Post Writers
  1150 15th St. NW
  Washington, DC 20007
  (202) 334-6375
  Contact: William B. Dickinson

Column Name: Pike Peeks
Author: Charles Pike
Subject: General entertainment, movies, and TV
Syndicate:
  Trans-World News Service
  767 National Press Bldg.
  529 14th St. NW
  Washington, DC 20045
  (202) 638-5568
  Contact: Bernard Blazes

Column Name: Postage Stamps and Coins Honoring
  TV and Radio
Author: Julius Weiss
Subject: see above
Syndicate:
  Weiss Philatelic & Numismatic Features
  16000 Terrace Rd. (#208)
  Cleveland, OH 44112
  (216) 451-3331
  Contact: Julius Weiss

Column Name: Prime Time Tips
Author: Paul Henniger
Subject: Upcoming TV shows
Syndicate:
  Los Angeles Times Syndicate
  Times Mirror Square
  Los Angeles, CA 90053
  (213) 972-5000 Toll Free (800) 421-8800
  Contact: Dan Byrne

Column Name: Private Eye
Author: David Handler
Subject: TV criticism
Syndicate:
  Newspaper Enterprise Assoc.
  200 Park Ave.
  New York, NY 10017
  (212) 557-5870
  Contact: David Hendin

Column Name: Profile
Author: Rita Harper
Subject: Commentary on TV actresses, actors, and
  writers
Syndicate:
  Harper Communications
  2017 Marker Ave.
  Dayton, OH 45414
  (513) 274-2793
  Contact: Norma Harper

Column Name: Publicite Televisee
Author: Gwendell McKoy
Subject: Commercials on TV
Syndicate:
  Inter-Presse de France
  100 Beekman St.
  New York, NY 10038
  (212) 285-1872
  Contact: Pierre C. Haber

Column Name: Radio Star of the Week
Author: John Austin
Subject: Interviews with motion picture and TV per-
  sonalities
Syndicate:
  Hollywood Inside Syndicate
  P.O. Box 49957
  Los Angeles, CA 90049
  (213) 826-9602
  Contact: John Austin

Column Name: Radio-TV News
Author: Jay Sharbutt
Subject: Interviews and personality sketches of fig-
  ures in the entertainment industry
Syndicate:
  AP Newfeatures
  50 Rockefeller Plaza
  New York, NY 10020
  (212) 262-4000
  Contact: Keith Fuller

Column Name: Radio and TV News Column
Author: Tom Shales
Subject: Radio and TV program listings
Syndicate:
  Washington Post Writers Group
  1150 15th St. NW
  Washington, DC 20007
  (202) 334-6375
  Contact: William B. Dickinson

Column Name: Radio-Television News Briefs
Author: Bob Queen
Subject: Noteworthy items related to a movie or TV
  personality
Syndicate:
  Press Wire Services/Press Wire Feature Services
  Box 2P, 144-45 35th Ave.
  Flushing, NY 11354
  (212) 539-6427
  Contact: Robert I. Queen

Column Name: Shows to Watch and Questions &
Answers
Author: Paul Henniger
Subject: TV show previews Q & A
Syndicate:
Los Angeles Times Syndicate
Times Mirror Square
Los Angeles, CA 90053
(213) 972-5000 Toll Free (800) 421-8800
Contact: Dan Byrne

Column Name: Tele-Log
Author: Staff
Subject: TV program listings
Syndicate:
Newspaper Enterprise Assoc., Inc.
230 Park Ave.
New York, NY 10017
(212) 557-5870
Contact: David Hendin

Column Name: Television
Author: Steve Casey
Subject: TV commentaries and interviews
Syndicate:
Copely News Service
350 Camino de la Rey
San Diego, CA 92112
(714) 299-3131
Contact: Charles Ohl

Column Name: Trivia Quiz
Author: Donald Saltz
Subject: TV trivia quizzes
Syndicate:
Trivia Quiz
4007 Connecticut Ave. NW
Washington, DC 20008
(202) 966-0025
Contact: Donald Saltz

Column Name: Tube Talk
Author: Various
Subject: TV personalities, shows, ratings, business
and corporate milieu
Syndicate:
AP Newsfeatures
50 Rockefeller Plaza
New York, NY 10020
(212) 262-4000
Contact: Keith Fuller

Column Name: TV Channels
Author: Various
Subject: TV programming
Syndicate:
Washington Post Writers
1150 15th St. NW
Washington, DC 20007
(202) 334-6375
Contact: William B. Dickinson

Column Name: TV Feature Reviews and Programs
of Note
Author: U.S. Catholic Conference Office of Film
and Broadcasting (NY)
Subject: TV program criticism
Syndicate:
Nat'l Catholic News Service
1312 Massachusetts Ave. NW
Washington, DC 20005
(202) 659-6722
Contact: Richard W. Daw

Column Name: TV From a Woman's Viewpoint
Author: Marcia Michels
Subject: Television shows and personalities
Syndicate:
Amusement Features Syndicate
218 West 47th St.
New York, NY 10036
(212) 586-4358
Contact: Joseph A. Kaliff

Column Name: TV Key
Author: Steve Scheuer and Staff
Subject: Television reviews and questions and an-
swers
Syndicate:
King Feature Syndicate
235 E. 45th St.
New York, NY 10017
(212) 682-5600
Contact: J. F. D'Angelo

Column Name: TV Mailbag
Author: Thom Mead
Subject: TV question and answer column
Syndicate:
Copley News Service
350 Camino del Rey
San Diego, CA 92112
(714) 299-3131
Contact: Charles Ohl

Column Name: TV to You
Author: Bill Lane
Subject: TV events and personalities in Hollywood
Syndicate:
World News Syndicate, Ltd.
6223 Selma Ave. Suite 201
P.O. Box 419
Hollywood, CA 90028
(213) 467-7024/469-2333
Contact: William C. Lane

Column Name: TV Scout Previews
Author: Joan Crosby, Dick Kleiner
Subject: Daily prime-time program previews
Syndicate:
Newspaper Enterprise Assoc., Inc.
230 Park Ave.
New York, NY 10017
(212) 557-5870
Contact: David Hendin

Column Name: TV Scout Reports
Author: Joan Crosby, Dick Kleiner
Subject: TV personalities and events
Syndicate:
Newspaper Enterprise Assoc., Inc.
230 Park Ave.
New York, NY 10017
(212) 557-5870
Contact: David Hendin

Column Name: TV Scout Sketches
Author: Joan Crosby, Dick Kleiner
Subject: In-depth interviews
Syndicate:
Newspaper Enterprise Assoc., Inc.
230 Park Ave.
New York, NY 10017
(212) 557-5870
Contact: David Hendin

Column Name: TV Table
Author: Various
Subject: TV personalities, shows, ratings, business
Syndicate:
AP Newsfeatures
50 Rockefeller Plaza
New York, NY 10020
(212) 262-4000
Contact: Keith Fuller

Column Name: You, Your Child, and Entertainment
Author: David Nydick
Subject: Children's entertainment (TV-radio)
Syndicate:
Dany News Service
22 Lesley Dr.
Syosset, NY 11791
(516) 681-4161/921-4611
Contact: David Nydick

Column Name: Video Every Day
Author: F. M. Knox
Subject: Television schedules plus editorial comments on programs
Syndicate:
Dickinson Newspaper Services, Inc.
271 Madison Ave.
New York, NY 10016
(212) 532-0170
Contact: Harry T. Dickinson

Column Name: View-TV
Author: F. M. Knox
Subject: Television schedules plus editorial comments on programs
Syndicate:
Dickinson Newspaper Services, Inc.
271 Madison Ave.
New York, NY 10016
(212) 532-0170
Contact: Harry T. Dickinson

Column Name: Weekend TV Preview
Author: F. M. Knox
Subject: Television schedules plus editorial comments on programs
Syndicate:
Dickinson Newspaper Services, Inc.
271 Madison Ave.
New York, NY 10016
(212) 532-0170
Contact: Harry T. Dickinson

Column Name: Where Are They Now
Author: Jess Hoaglin
Subject: Movie and television personalities of the past
Syndicate:
Trans-World News Service
767 National Press Bldg.
529 14th St. NW
Washington, DC 20045
(202) 638-5568
Contact: Bernard Blazes

Ratings

Top-rated shows since 1950

The following is a list of the top-rated shows, beginning with the 1950–51 television season. Until the end of the 1972–73 season the ratings are calculated for an October–April period. But the 1973–74 season gained a month when the new fall programs began to premiere in September. Therefore, beginning with the 1973–74 season, the ratings are calculated for a September-April period.

The list consists of yearly averages; hence, a new show with an initial large audience share can, and often does, appear high on the list. An example of this type of strong showing is seen in the case of *Angie*, which aired February 2, 1979, and earned more rating points than did *60 Minutes*, which had been on all season.

When a show appears for the first time in the Top 20, the on-air and off-air dates are given, along with the names of the main characters and the actors who played them. For variety shows, hosts and announcers are given. Since the cast credits of many television programs often change substantially from season to season, no attempt has been made here to document all of these changes. The reader interested in complete cast listings for their favorite programs should consult *The Complete Directory to Prime Time Network TV Shows, 1946–present* by Tim Brooks and Earle Marsh (Ballantine Books, 1979).

OCTOBER 1950–APRIL 1951

1. Texaco Star Theatre (NBC)
On air: June 8, 1948
Off air: June 9, 1953
Host: Milton Berle
Announcer: Jimmy Nelson (ventriloquist)

2. Fireside Theatre (NBC)
On air: July 3, 1951
Off air: June 25, 1957
Host: Jane Wyman

3. Your Show of Shows (Jack Carter Show–Saturday Night Review) (NBC)
On air: February 25, 1950
Off air: June 5, 1954
Host: Sid Caesar, Imogene Coca
Announcer: Vaughn Monroe

---

*Program rankings provided by the A.C. Nielsen Company. Specific program detail provided by the Program Analysis Department, National Broadcasting Company, Inc.

4. Philco Television Playhouse (NBC)
On air: October 3, 1948
Off air: October 2, 1955
Host: Bert Lytell

5. The Colgate Comedy Hour (NBC)
On air: September 10, 1950
Off air: December 25, 1955
Hosts: Eddie Cantor, Dean Martin, Jerry Lewis, Bud Abott, Lou Costello, Donald O'Connor, and Judy Canova

6. Gillette Cavalcade of Sports (Boxing) (NBC)
On air: September 29, 1944
Off air: June 24, 1960
Broadcaster: Jimmy Powers

7. Arthur Godfrey's Talent Scouts (CBS)
On air: December 6, 1948
Off air: July 21, 1958
Host: Arthur Godfrey
Substitute hosts: Joe E. Brown, Steve Allen, Guy Mitchell
Announcer: Tony Marvin

8. Mama (CBS)
On air: July 1, 1949
Off air: March 17, 1957
Cast:
Marta Hansen (Mama)—Peggy Wood
Lars Hansen (Papa)—Judson Laire
Nels—Dick Van Patten
Katrin—Rosemary Rice
Dagmar—Robin Morgan

9. Robert Montgomery Presents (NBC)
On air: January 30, 1950
Off air: June 24, 1957
Host: Robert Montgomery

10. Martin Kane, Private Eye (NBC)
On air: September 1, 1949
Off air: December 21, 1952
Cast:
Martin Kane—William Gargan
Happy McMann—Walter Kinsella

11. Man Against Crime (CBS)
On air: October 7, 1949
Off air: October 2, 1953
Cast:
Mike Barnett—Ralph Bellamy

12. Somerset Maugham Theatre (CBS)
On air: October 18, 1950
Off air: December 10, 1951
Host: Somerset Maugham

13. Kraft Television Theatre
On air: May 7, 1947 (NBC)
Off air: October 1, 1958
On air: October 15, 1953 (ABC)
Off air: January 6, 1955
Announcer: Ed Herlihy

14. Toast of the Town (CBS)
On air: June 20, 1948
Off air: September 18, 1955
Host: Ed Sullivan

15. The Aldrich Family (NBC)
On air: October 2, 1949
Off air: May 29, 1953
Cast:
  Henry Aldrich—Henry Girard
  Sam Aldrich—House Jameson
  Alice Aldrich—Barbara Robbin
  Mary Aldrich—Mary Malone
  Homer Brown—Robert Barry

16. You Bet Your Life (NBC)
On air: October 5, 1950
Off air: September 21, 1961
Host: Groucho Marx
Announcer: George Fenneman
Secret-word girl: Marilyn Burtis

17. The Armstrong Circle Theatre (NBC)
On air: June 6, 1950
Off air: June 25, 1957
Host: Nelson Case
Announcer: Kay Campbell

18. Big Town (NBC)
On air: October 5, 1950
Off air: September 23, 1956
Cast:
  Steve Wilson—Mark Stevens
  Lorelei Kilbourne—Trudy Wroe
  Charlie Anderson—Barry Kelly
  Lt. Tom Gregory—John Doucette

19. Lights Out (NBC)
On air: July 19, 1949
Off air: September 29, 1952
Host: Frank Gallop

20. The Alan Young Show (CBS)
On air: April 6, 1950
Off air: March 27, 1952
Host: Alan Young

OCTOBER 1951 - APRIL 1952

1. Arthur Godfrey's Talent Scouts
(*See* October 1950–April 1951)

2. Texaco Star Theater
(*See* October 1950–April 1951)

3. I Love Lucy (CBS)
On air: Oct. 15, 1951
Off air: June 24, 1957
Cast:
  Lucy Ricardo—Lucille Ball
  Ricky Ricardo—Desi Arnaz
  Fred Mertz—William Frawley
  Ethel Mertz—Vivian Vance

4. The Red Skelton Show
On air: September 30, 1953 (CBS)
Off air: June 23, 1970
On air: September 14, 1970 (NBC)
Off air: August 29, 1971
Host: Red Skelton
Announcer: Art Gilmore

5. The Colgate Comedy Hour
(*See* October 1950–April 1951)

6. Fireside Theatre
(*See* October 1950–April 1951)

7. The Jack Benny Show
On air: October 28, 1950 (CBS)
Off air: September 15, 1964
On air: September 25, 1964 (NBC)
Off air: September 10, 1965
Cast:
  Jack Benny
  Mary Livingston
  Rochester—Eddie Anderson
  Dennis Day
  Don Wilson
  Professor LeBlanc—Mel Blanc
  Harlow Wilson—Dale White
  Lois Wilson—Lois Corbett
  Schlepperman—Sam Hearn
Announcer: Don Wilson

8. Your Show of Shows (Saturday Night Review—Jack Carter Show)
(*See* October 1950–April 1951)

9. You Bet Your Life
(*See* October 1950–April 1951)

10. Arthur Godfrey and His Friends (CBS)
On air: January 12, 1949
Off Air: June 20, 1957
Host: Arthur Godfrey
Substitute Hosts: Herb Shriner, Robert Q. Lewis
Announcer: Tony Marvin

11. Mama
(*See* October 1950–April 1951)

12. Philco TV Playhouse (NBC)
On air: October 3, 1948
Off air: October 2, 1955
Host: Bert Lytell

13. Amos 'n' Andy (CBS)
On air: June 28, 1951
Off air: June 11, 1953
Cast:
  Andrew (Andy) Halt Brown—Spencer Williams, Jr.
  Amos Jones—Alvin Childress
  George "Kingfish" Stevens—Tim Moore
  Sapphire Stevens—Ernestine Wade
  Algonquin Calhoun—Johnny Lee
  Lightmis'—Horace Stewart
  Sapphire's Mama—Amanda Randolph
  Madame Queen—Lillian Randolph

14. Big Town
(See October 1950–April 1951)

15. Pabst Blue Ribbon Bouts (CBS)
On air: July 11, 1951
Off air: December 26, 1951
Broadcaster: Russ Hodges

16. Gillette Cavalcade of Sports (Boxing)
(See October 1950–April 1951)

17. The Alan Young Show
(See October 1950–April 1951)

18. All Star Review (NBC)
On air: September 8, 1951
Off air: April 18, 1953
Hosts: Jimmy Durante, Danny Thomas, Martha Raye, The Ritz Brothers, Ed Wynne, and Jack Carson

19. Dragnet (NBC)
On air: January 3, 1952
Off air: September 6, 1959
Cast:
  Sgt. Joe Friday—Jack Webb
  Sgt. Ed Jacobs—Barney Phillips
  Officer Frank Smith—Herb Ellis (1952); Ben Alexander (1953–59)

20. Kraft Television Theatre
(See October 1950–April 1951)

OCTOBER 1952–APRIL 1953

1. I Love Lucy
(See October 1951–April 1952)

2. Arthur Godfrey's Talent Scouts
(See October 1951–April 1952)

3. Arthur Godfrey and His Friends
(See October 1951–April 1952)

4. Dragnet
(See October 1951–April 1952)

5. Texaco Star Theater
(See October 1951–April 1952)

6. The Buick Circus Hour (NBC)
On air: October 7, 1952
Off air: June 16, 1953
Hosts: Joe E. Brown, Dolores Gray, John Raitt
Announcer: Frank Gallop

7. The Colgate Comedy Hour
(See October 1951–April 1952)

8. Gangbusters (NBC)
On air: March 20, 1952
Off air: Dec. 25, 1952
Host–narrators: Phillips H. Lord and guest police chiefs

9. You Bet Your Life
(See October 1951–April 1952)

10. Fireside Theatre
(See October 1951–April 1952)

11. The Red Buttons Show (CBS)
On air: October 14, 1952
Off air: June 14, 1954
Host: Red Buttons
Announcer: Nelson Case

12. The Jack Benny Show
(See October 1951–April 1952)

13. Life with Luigi (CBS)
On air: September 22, 1952
Off air: December 22, 1952
Cast:
  Luigi Basco—J. Carrol Naish
  Pasquale—Alan Reed
  Rosa—Jody Gilbert

14. Pabst Blue Ribbon Bouts
(See October 1951–April 1952)

15. Goodyear TV Playhouse (NBC)
On air: October 14, 1951
Off air: September 25, 1955
Announcer: Ed Herlihy

16. The Life of Riley
On air: October 4, 1949 (DuMont)
Off air: March 28, 1950
On air: January 2, 1953 (NBC)
Off air: August 22, 1958
Cast (NBC):
  Chester A. Riley—William Bendix
  Peggy Riley—Marjorie Reynolds
  Babs Riley—Lugene Saunders
  Chester Riley, Jr.—Wesley Morgan
  Jim Gillis—Tom D'Andrea
  Honeybee Gillis—Gloria Blondell

17. Mama
(See October 1951–April 1952)

18. **Your Show of Shows**
(*See* October 1951–April 1952)

19. **What's My Line? (CBS)**
On air: February 2, 1950
Off air: September 3, 1967
Host: John Daly
Announcers: John Briggs and Johnny Olsen

20. **Strike It Rich (CBS)**
On air: May 7, 1951
Off air: January 3, 1958
Host: Warren Hull
Substitute host: Monty Hall
Assistant: Jack Carson
Commercial spokesman: Virginia Graham

OCTOBER 1953–APRIL 1954

1. **I Love Lucy**
(*See* October 1951–April 1952)

2. **Dragnet**
(*See* October 1951–April 1952)

3. **Arthur Godfrey's Talent Scouts**
(*See* October 1951–April 1952)

4. **You Bet Your Life**
(*See* October 1951–April 1952)

5. **Bob Hope (NBC)**
On air: October 12, 1952
Off air: April 11, 1968
Host: Bob Hope
Announcer: Frank Barton

6. **The Milton Berle Show (NBC)**
On air: September 27, 1955
Off air: June 5, 1956
Host: Milton Berle
Announcer: Jack Lescoulie

7. **Arthur Godfrey and His Friends**
(*See* October 1951–April 1952)

8. **Ford Theatre (NBC)**
On air: October 2, 1952
Off air: September 27, 1956

9. **The Jackie Gleason Show (CBS)**
On air: September 20, 1952
Off air: June 18, 1955
Host: Jackie Gleason

10. **Fireside Theater**
(*See* October 1951–April 1952)

11. **The Colgate Comedy Hour**
(*See* October 1951–April 1952)

12. **This Is Your Life (NBC)**
On air: October 1, 1952
Off air: September 3, 1961
Host: Ralph Edwards
Announcer: Bob Warren

13. **The Red Buttons Show**
(*See* October 1952–April 1953)

14. **The Life of Riley**
(*See* October 1952–April 1953)

15. **Our Miss Brooks (CBS)**
On air: October 3, 1952
Off air: September 13, 1957
Cast:
   Connie Brooks—Eve Arden
   Osgood Conklin—Gale Gordon
   Philip Boynton—Robert Rockwell
   Walter Denton—Richard Crenna
   Mrs. Davis—Jane Morgan
   Harriet Conklin—Gloria McMillen

16. **Treasury Men in Action**
On air: September 11, 1950 (ABC)
Off air: December 4, 1950
On air: April 5, 1951 (NBC)
Off air: April 1, 1954
On air: October 7, 1954 (ABC)
Off air: June 4, 1955
Host: Walter Greaza
Announcer: Durward Kirby

17. **All Star Revue**
(*See* October 1951–April 1952)

18. **The Jack Benny Show**
(*See* October 1951–April 1952)

19. **Gillette Cavalcade of Sports**
(*See* October 1951–April 1952)

20. **Philco TV Playhouse**
(*See* October 1951–April 1952)

OCTOBER 1954–APRIL 1955

1. **I Love Lucy**
(*See* October 1951–April 1952)

2. **The Jackie Gleason Show**
(*See* October 1953–April 1954)

3. **Dragnet**
(*See* October 1951–April 1952)

4. **You Bet Your Life**
(*See* October 1951–April 1952)

5. The Toast of the Town (The Ed Sullivan Show) (CBS)
On air: June 20, 1948
Off air: September 18, 1955
On air: September 25, 1955
Off air: June 6, 1971
Host: Ed Sullivan
Commercial spokesman: Julia Meade
Announcer: Ralph Paul

6. Disneyland (ABC)
On air: October 27, 1954
Off air: September 3, 1958
Host: Walt Disney

7. The Bob Hope Show
(*See* October 1953–April 1954)

8. The Jack Benny Show
(*See* October 1951–April 1952)

9. The Martha Raye Show (NBC)
On air: December 26, 1953
Off air: May 29, 1956
Hostess: Martha Raye with Rocky Graziano

10. The George Gobel Show (NBC)
On air: October 2, 1954
Off air: June 29, 1957
On air: September 4, 1957
Off air: March 10, 1959
Host: George Gobel

11. Ford Theatre
(*See* October 1953–April 1954)

12. December Bride (CBS)
On air: October 4, 1954
Off air: September 24, 1959
Cast:
    Lily Ruskin—Spring Byington
    Matt Henshaw—Dean Miller
    Ruth Henshaw—Frances Rafferty
    Hilda Crocker—Verna Felton
    Peter Porter—Harry Morgan

13. The Buick–Berle Show
(*See* October 1952–April 1953, October 1953–April 1954)

14. This Is Your Life
(*See* October 1953–April 1954)

15. I've Got a Secret (CBS)
On air: June 19, 1952
Off air: April 3, 1967
Host: Garry Moore

16. Two for the Money (CBS)
On air: August 15, 1953
Off air: September 7, 1956
Hosts: Herb Shriner and Sam Levenson
Announcer: Dennis James

17. Your Hit Parade (NBC)
On air: July 10, 1950
Off air: June 17, 1958
Cast: Eileen Wilson, June Valli, Dorothy Collins, Snooky Lanson, Russell Arms, Gisele MacKenzie, Tommy Leonetti, Jill Corey, Alan Copeland, Virginia Gibson, and Polly Bergen
Announcer: Andre Baruch

18. The Millionaire (CBS)
On air: January 19, 1955
Off air: September 28, 1960
Cast:
    Michael Anthony—Marvin Miller
    John Beresford Tipton—Paul Frees
    Andrew V. McMahon—Roy Gordon
Announcer: Ed Herlihy

19. General Electric Theater (CBS)
On air: February 1, 1953
Off air: September 16, 1962
Host: Ronald Reagan

20. Arthur Godfrey's Talent Scouts
(*See* October 1951–April 1952)

OCTOBER 1955–APRIL 1956

1. The $64,000 Question (CBS)
On air: June 7, 1955
Off air: October 26, 1958
Host: Hal March
Announcer: Wayne Howell
Judge: Dr. Bergen Evans

2. I Love Lucy
(*See* October 1951–April 1952)

3. The Ed Sullivan Show
(*See* October 1954–April 1955)

4. Disneyland
(*See* October 1954–April 1955)

5. The Jack Benny Show
(*See* October 1951–April 1952)

6. December Bride
(*See* October 1954–April 1955)

7. You Bet Your Life
(*See* October 1951–April 1952)

8. Dragnet
(*See* October 1951–April 1952)

9. I've Got a Secret
(*See* October 1954–April 1955)

10. General Electric Theater
(*See* October 1954–April 1955)

11. **Private Secretary (CBS)**
On air: February 1, 1953
Off air: September 10, 1957
Cast:
  Susie McNamara—Ann Sothern
  Peter Sands—Don Porter
  Vi Praskins—Ann Tyrrell
  Cagey Calhoun—Jesse White
  Sylvia—Joan Banks

12. **Ford Theatre**
(*See* October 1953–April 1954)

13. **The Red Skelton Show**
(*See* October 1951–April 1952)

14. **The George Gobel Show**
(*See* October 1954–April 1955)

15. **The $64,000 Challenge (CBS)**
On air: April 8, 1956
Off air: September 31, 1958
Hosts: Sonny Fox and Ralph Story
Announcer: Bill Rogers

16. **Arthur Godfrey's Talent Scouts**
(*See* October 1951–April 1952)

17. **The Lineup (CBS)**
On air: October 1, 1954
Off air: January 20, 1960
Cast:
  Det. Lt. Ben Guthrie—Warner Anderson
  Inspector Matt Grebb—Tom Tully
  Sandy McAllister—Rachel Ames
  Officer Pete Larkin—Skip Ward

18. **Shower of Stars (CBS)**
On air: September 30, 1954
Off air: June 9, 1955
Host: Jack Barry

19. **The Perry Como Show (CBS)**
On air: October 2, 1950
Off air: June 24, 1955
On air: September 17, 1955
Off air: June 6, 1959
Host: Perry Como
Announcer: Frank Gallop

20. **The Honeymooners (CBS)**
On air: October 1, 1955
Off air: September 22, 1956
Cast:
  Ralph Kramden—Jackie Gleason
  Alice Kramden—Audrey Meadows
  Ed Norton—Art Carney
  Trixie Norton—Joyce Randolph
Announcer: Jack Lescoulie

OCTOBER 1956–APRIL 1957

1. **I Love Lucy**
(*See* October 1951–April 1952)

2. **The Ed Sullivan Show**
(*See* October 1954–April 1955)

3. **General Electric Theater**
(*See* October 1954–April 1955)

4. **The $64,000 Question**
(*See* October 1955–April 1956)

5. **December Bride**
(*See* October 1954–April 1955)

6. **Alfred Hitchcock Presents**
On air: October 2, 1955 (CBS)
Off air: September 25, 1960
On air: September 27, 1960 (NBC)
Off air: September 18, 1962
Host: Alfred Hitchcock

7. **I've Got a Secret**
(*See* October 1954–April 1955)

8. **Gunsmoke (CBS)**
On air: September 10, 1955
Off air: September 1, 1975
Cast:
  Marshal Matt Dillon—James Arness
  Kitty Russell—Amanda Blake
  Dr. Galen Adams (Doc)—Milburn Stone
  Quint Asper—Burt Reynolds
  Chester Goode—Dennis Weaver
  Festus Haggen—Ken Curtis

9. **The Perry Como Show**
(*See* October 1955–April 1956)

10. **The Jack Benny Show**
(*See* October 1951–April 1952)

11. **Dragnet**
(*See* October 1951–April 1952)

12. **Arthur Godfrey's Talent Scouts**
(*See* October 1951–April 1952)

13. **The Millionaire**
(*See* October 1954–April 1955)

14. **Disneyland**
(*See* October 1954–April 1955)

14. **Shower of Stars**
(*See* October 1955–April 1956)

16. **The Lineup**
(*See* October 1955–April 1956)

17. **The Red Skelton Show**
(*See* October 1951–April 1952)

18. **You Bet Your Life**
(*See* October 1951–April 1952)

19. **The Life and Legend of Wyatt Earp (ABC)**
On air: September 6, 1955
Off air: September 26, 1961
Cast:

    Wyatt Earp—Hugh O'Brian
    Bat Masterson—Alan Dinehart III

20. **Private Secretary**
(See October 1955–April 1956)

OCTOBER 1957–APRIL 1958

1. **Gunsmoke**
(See October 1956–April 1957)

2. **The Danny Thomas Show**
On air: September 29, 1953 (ABC)
Off air: July 17, 1957
On air: October 7, 1957 (CBS)
Off air: September 14, 1964
Cast:

    Danny Williams—Danny Thomas
    Margaret Williams—Jean Hagen
    Kathy Williams (Clancey)—Marjorie Lord
    Teresa (Terry) Williams—Sherry Jackson
    Russell (Rusty) Williams—Rusty Hamer
    Linda Williams—Angela Cartright
    Louise—Amanda Randolph

3. **Tales of Wells Fargo (NBC)**
On air: March 18, 1957
Off air: September 8, 1962
Cast:

    Jim Hardie—Dale Robertson

4. **Have Gun Will Travel (CBS)**
On air: September 14, 1957
Off air: September 21, 1963
Cast:

    Paladin—Richard Boone
    Hey Boy—Kam Tong

5. **I've Got a Secret**
(See October 1954–April 1955)

6. **The Life and Legend of Wyatt Earp**
(See October 1956–April 1957)

7. **General Electric Theater**
(See October 1954–April 1955)

8. **The Restless Gun**
On air: September 23, 1957 (NBC)
Off air: September 14, 1959
On air: October 12, 1959 (ABC)
Off air: September 30, 1960
Cast:

    Vint Bonner—John Payne

9. **December Bride**
(See October 1954–April 1955)

10. **You Bet Your Life**
(See October 1951–April 1952)

11. **Alfred Hitchcock Presents**
(See October 1956–April 1957)

12. **Cheyenne (ABC)**
On air: September 25, 1955
Off air: September 13, 1963
Cast:

    Cheyenne Bodie—Clint Walker

13. **Tennessee Ernie Ford Show**
On air: January 3, 1955 (NBC)
Off air: June 28, 1957
On air: April 2, 1962 (ABC)
Off air: March 26, 1965
Host: Tennessee Ernie Ford, Molly Bee, Doris
    Drew, Dick Williams, Jack Fascinato
Announcers: Skip Farrell

14. **The Red Skelton Show**
(See October 1951–April 1952)

15. **Wagon Train**
On air: September 18, 1957 (NBC)
Off air: September 12, 1962
On air: January 6, 1963 (ABC)
Off air: September 18, 1963
Cast:

    Seth Adams—Ward Bond
    Chris Hale—John McIntire
    Flint McCullough—Robert Horton
    Charlie Wooster—Frank McGrath
    Bill Hawks—Terry Wilson

16. **Sugarfoot (ABC)**
On air: September 17, 1957
Off air: September 13, 1960
Cast:

    Tom Brewster—Will Hutchins

17. **Father Knows Best**
On air: October 3, 1954 (CBS)
Off air: March 27, 1955
On air: August 31, 1955 (NBC)
Off air: September 17, 1958
On air: September 22, 1958 (CBS)
Off air: September 17, 1962
On air: September 30, 1962 (ABC)
Off air: February 3, 1967
Cast:

    Jim Anderson—Robert Young
    Margaret Anderson—Jane Wyatt
    Betty Anderson—Elinor Donahue
    Bud Anderson—Billy Gray
    Kathy Anderson—Lauren Chapin

18. **Twenty-One (NBC)**
On air: September 12, 1956
Off air: October 16, 1958
Host: Jack Barry

19. **The Ed Sullivan Show**
(See October 1954–April 1955)

20. **The Jack Benny Show**
(See October 1951–April 1952)

OCTOBER 1958–APRIL 1959

1. Gunsmoke
(*See* October 1956–April 1957)

2. Wagon Train
(*See* October 1957–April 1958)

3. Have Gun Will Travel
(*See* October 1957–April 1958)

4. The Rifleman (ABC)
On air: September 30, 1958
Off air: July 1, 1963
Cast:
   Lucas McCain—Chuck Connors
   Mark McCain—Johnny Crawford
   Marshall Micah Torrance—Paul Fix

5. The Danny Thomas Show
(*See* October 1957–April 1958)

6. Maverick (ABC)
On air: September 22, 1957
Off air: July 15, 1962
Cast:
   Bret Maverick—James Garner
   Bart Maverick—Jack Kelly

7. Tales of Wells Fargo
(*See* October 1957–April 1958)

8. The Real McCoys (ABC)
On air: October 3, 1957
Off air: September 20, 1962
Cast:
   Amos McCoy—Walter Brennan
   Luke McCoy—Richard Crenna
   Kate McCoy—Kathleen Nolan
   Hassie McCoy—Lydia Reed
   Little Luke McCoy—Michael Winkleman

9. I've Got a Secret
(*See* October 1954–April 1955)

10. The Life and Legend of Wyatt Earp
(*See* October 1956–April 1957)

11. The Price Is Right
On air: September 26, 1956 (NBC)
Off air: September 6, 1963
On air: September 9, 1963 (ABC)
Off air: September 3, 1965
Host: Bill Cullen
Announcer: Don Pardo

12. The Red Skelton Show
(*See* October 1951–April 1952)

13. Zane Grey Theater
On air: October 5, 1956
Off air: July 27, 1961
Host: Robert Taylor

14. Father Knows Best
(*See* October 1957–April 1958)

15. The Texan
On air: March 3, 1957 (CBS)
Off air: September 5, 1960
On air: October 3, 1960 (ABC)
Off air: January 6, 1961
On air: September 4, 1961 (ABC)
Off air: May 12, 1962
Cast:
   Bill Longley—Rory Calhoun

16. Wanted: Dead or Alive (CBS)
On air: September 6, 1958
Off air: March 29, 1961
Cast:
   Josh Randall—Steve McQueen
   Jason Nichols—Wright King

17. Peter Gunn
On air: September 22, 1958 (NBC)
Off air: September 26, 1960
On air: October 3, 1960 (ABC)
Off air: September 21, 1961
Cast:
   Peter Gunn—Craig Stevens
   Edie Hart—Lola Albright
   Lt. Jacoby—Herschel Bernardi
   Mother—Hope Emerson

18. Cheyenne
(*See* October 1957–April 1958)

19. Perry Mason
On air: September 21, 1957 (CBS)
Off air: September 4, 1966
Cast:
   Perry Mason—Raymond Burr
   Della Street—Barbara Hale
   Paul Drake—William Hopper
   Lt. Arthur Tragg—Ray Collins
   Hamilton Burger—William Talman

20. The Tennessee Ernie Ford Show
(*See* October 1957–April 1958)

OCTOBER 1959–APRIL 1960

1. Gunsmoke
(*See* October 1956–April 1957)

2. Wagon Train
(*See* October 1957–April 1958)

3. Have Gun Will Travel
(*See* October 1957–April 1958)

4. The Danny Thomas Show
(*See* October 1957–April 1958)

5. The Red Skelton Show
(*See* October 1951–April 1952)

6. Father Knows Best
(*See* October 1957–April 1958)

7. 77 Sunset Strip (ABC)
On air: October 3, 1958
Off air: February 7, 1964
Cast:
   Stuart Bailey—Efrem Zimbalist, Jr.
   Jeff Spencer—Roger Smith
   Gerald Lloyd Kookson III (Kookie)—Edward
   Byrnes

8. The Price Is Right
(*See* October 1958–April 1959)

9. Wanted: Dead or Alive
(*See* October 1958–April 1959)

10. Perry Mason
(*See* October 1958–April 1959)

11. The Real McCoys
(*See* October 1959–April 1959)

12. The Ed Sullivan Show
(*See* October 1957–April 1958)

13. The Bing Crosby Show (ABC)
On air: September 14, 1964
Off air: June 14, 1965
Cast:
   Bing Collins—Bing Crosby
   Ellie Collins—Beverly Garland
   Joyce Collins—Carol Faylen
   Janice Collins—Diane Sherry
   Willie Walters—Frank McHugh

14. The Rifleman
(*See* October 1958–April 1959)

15. The Ford Show Starring Tennessee Ernie Ford
(*See* October 1957–April 1958)

16. The Lawman (ABC)
On air: October 5, 1958
Off air: October 9, 1962
Cast:
   Marshal Dan Troop—John Russell
   Deputy Johnny McKay—Peter Brown
   Lily Merrill—Peggy Castle

17. Dennis the Menace (CBS)
On air: October 4, 1959
Off air: September 22, 1963
Cast:
   Dennis Mitchell—Jay North
   Henry Mitchell—Herbert Anderson
   Alice Mitchell—Gloria Henry
   George Wilson—Joseph Kearns
   Martha Wilson—Sylvia Field
   John Wilson—Gale Gordon

18. Cheyenne
(*See* October 1957–April 1958)

19. Rawhide (CBS)
On air: January 9, 1959
Off air: January 4, 1966
Cast:
   Gil Favor—Eric Fleming
   Rowdy Yates—Clint Eastwood
   Pete Nolan—Sheb Wooley
   Wishbone—Paul Brinegar
   Jim Quince—Steve Raines
   Joe Scarlett—Rocky Shahan
   Mushy—James Murdock

20. Maverick
(*See* October 1958–April 1959)

OCTOBER 1960–April 1961

1. Gunsmoke
(*See* October 1956–April 1957)

2. Wagon Train
(*See* October 1957–April 1958)

3. Have Gun Will Travel
(*See* October 1957–April 1958)

4. The Andy Griffith Show (CBS)
On air: October 3, 1960
Off air: September 16, 1968
Cast:
   Andy Taylor—Andy Griffith
   Barney Fife—Don Knotts
   Opie Taylor—Ronny Howard
   Bee Taylor—Frances Bavier
   Ellie Walker—Elinor Donahue

5. The Real McCoys
(*See* October 1958–April 1959)

6. Rawhide
(*See* October 1959–April 1960)

7. Candid Camera (CBS)
On air: October 2, 1960
Off air: September 1, 1967
Host: Alan Funt
Co-hosts: Durward Kirby, Bess Myerson
Announcer: Ken Roberts

8. The Untouchables (ABC)
On air: October 15, 1959
Off air: September 10, 1963
Cast:
   Eliot Ness—Robert Stack
   Agent Martin Flaherty—Jerry Paris
   Agent William Youngfellow—Abel Fernandez
   Agent Enrico Rossi—Nick Georgiade
   Agent Cam Allison—Anthony George
   Agent Lee Hobson—Paul Picerni
   Agent Rossman—Steve London
   Frank Nitti—Bruce Gordon

9. The Price Is Right
(*See* October 1958–April 1959)

10. **The Jack Benny Show**
(*See* October 1951–April 1952)

11. **Dennis the Menace**
(*See* October 1959–April 1960)

12. **The Danny Thomas Show**
(*See* October 1957–April 1958)

13. **My Three Sons (ABC)**
On air: September 29, 1960
Off air: September 2, 1965
Cast:
    Steve Douglas—Fred MacMurray
    Michael Francis "Bub" O'Casey—William Frawley
    Charley O'Casey—William Demarest
    Mike Douglas—Tim Considine
    Robbie Douglas—Don Grady
    Chip (Richard) Douglas—Stanley Livingston

14. **77 Sunset Strip**
(*See* October 1959–April 1960)

15. **The Ed Sullivan Show**
(*See* October 1957–April 1958)

16. **Perry Mason**
(*See* October 1958–April 1959)

17. **Bonanza (NBC)**
On air: September 12, 1959
Off air: January 16, 1973
Cast:
    Ben Cartwright—Lorne Greene
    Adam Cartwright—Pernell Roberts
    Hoss (Eric) Cartwright—Dan Blocker
    Little Joe Cartwright—Michael Landon
    Hop Sing—Victor Sen Yung

18. **The Flintstones (ABC)**
On air: September 30, 1960
Off air: September 2, 1966
Voices:
    Fred Flintstone—Alan Reed
    Wilma Flintstone—Jean Vander Pyl
    Barney Rubble—Mel Blanc
    Betty Rubble—Bea Benaderet
    Dino the Dinosaur—Mel Blanc

19. **The Red Skelton Show**
(*See* October 1951–April 1952)

20. **Alfred Hitchcock Presents**
(*See* October 1956–April 1957)

OCTOBER 1961–APRIL 1962

1. **Wagon Train**
(*See* October 1957–April 1958)

2. **Bonanza**
(*See* October 1960–April 1961)

3. **Gunsmoke**
(*See* October 1956–April 1957)

4. **Hazel**
On air: September 28, 1961 (NBC)
Off air: September 6, 1965
On air: September 13, 1965 (CBS)
Off air: September 5, 1966
Cast:
    Hazel Burke—Shirley Booth
    George Baxter—Don DeFore
    Dorothy Baxter—Whitney Blake
    Harold Baxter—Bobby Buntrock
    Harriet Johnson—Norma Varden
    Herbert Johnson—Donald Foster

5. **Perry Mason**
(*See* October 1958–April 1959)

6. **The Red Skelton Show**
(*See* October 1951–April 1952)

7. **The Andy Griffith Show**
(*See* October 1960–April 1961)

8. **The Danny Thomas Show**
(*See* October 1957–April 1958)

9. **Dr. Kildare (NBC)**
On air: September 28, 1961
Off air: August 30, 1966
Cast:
    Dr. James Kildare—Richard Chamberlain
    Dr. Leonard Gillespie—Raymond Massey
    Dr. Gerson—Jud Taylor
    Dr. Agurski—Eddie Ryder

10. **Candid Camera**
(*See* October 1960–April 1961)

11. **My Three Sons**
(*See* October 1960–April 1961)

12. **The Garry Moore Variety Show (CBS)**
On air: September 30, 1958
Off air: June 16, 1964
Host: Garry Moore
Announcer: Durward Kirby

13. **Rawhide**
(*See* October 1959–April 1960)

14. **The Real McCoys**
(*See* October 1958–April 1959)

15. **Lassie (CBS)**
On air: September 18, 1954
Off air: September 12, 1971
Cast:
    Timmy Martin—Jon Provost
    Ruth Martin—June Lockhart
    Paul Martin—Hugh Riley
    Doc Weaver—Arthur Space
    Lassie

16. Sing Along with Mitch (NBC)
On air: September 28, 1961
Off air: September 21, 1964
Host: Mitch Miller

17. Dennis the Menace
(*See* October 1959–April 1960)

18. Gunsmoke
(*See* October 1956–April 1957)

19. Ben Casey (ABC)
On air: October 21, 1961
Off air: March 21, 1966
Cast:
   Dr. Ben Casey—Vincent Edwards
   Dr. David Zorba—Sam Jaffe
   Dr. Maggie Graham—Bettye Ackerman
   Dr. Ted Hoffman—Harry Landers
   Nick Kanavaras—Nick Dennis
   Nurse Wills—Jeanne Bates

20. The Ed Sullivan Show
(*See* October 1957–April 1958)

OCTOBER 1962–APRIL 1963

1. The Beverly Hillbillies (CBS)
On air: September 26, 1962
Off air: September 7, 1971
Cast:
   Jed Clampett—Buddy Ebsen
   Daisy Moses (Granny)—Irene Ryan
   Elly May Clampett—Donna Douglas
   Jethro Bodine—Max Baer, Jr.
   Milton Drysdale—Raymond Bailey
   Jane Hathaway—Nancy Kulp

2. Candid Camera
(*See* October 1960–April 1961)

3. The Red Skelton Show
(*See* October 1951–April 1952)

4. Bonanza
(*See* October 1960–April 1961)

5. The Lucy Show (CBS)
On air: October 1, 1961
Off air: September 16, 1968
Cast:
   Lucy Carmichael—Lucille Ball
   Vivian Bagley—Vivian Vance
   Theodore J. Mooney—Gale Gordon
   Chris Carmichael—Candy Moore
   Jerry Carmichael—Jimmy Garrett
   Sherman Bagley—Ralph Hart
   Mr. Barnsdahl—Charles Lane
   Harry Connors—Dick Martin

6. The Andy Griffith Show
(*See* October 1960–April 1961)

7. Ben Casey
(*See* October 1961–April 1962)

8. The Danny Thomas Show
(*See* October 1957–April 1958)

9. The Dick Van Dyke Show (CBS)
On air: October 3, 1961
Off air: September 7, 1966
Cast:
   Rob Petrie—Dick Van Dyke
   Laura Petrie—Mary Tyler Moore
   Buddy Sorrell—Morey Amsterdam
   Sally Rogers—Rose Marie
   Ritchie Petrie—Larry Mathews
   Melvin Cooley—Richard Deacon
   Jerry Helper—Jerry Paris
   Millie Helper—Ann Morgan Guilbert
   Alan Brady—Carl Reiner

10. Gunsmoke
(*See* October 1956–April 1957)

11. Dr. Kildare
(*See* October 1961–April 1962)

12. The Jack Benny Show
(*See* October 1951–April 1952)

13. What's My Line (CBS)
On air: February 2, 1950
Off air: September 3, 1967
Host: John Daly
Announcers: John Briggs and Johnny Olsen

14. The Ed Sullivan Show
(*See* October 1957–April 1958)

15. Hazel
(*See* October 1961–April 1962)

16. I've Got a Secret
(*See* October 1954–April 1955)

17. The Jackie Gleason Show
(*See* October 1953–April 1954)

18. The Defenders (CBS)
On air: September 16, 1961
Off air: September 9, 1965
Cast:
   Lawrence Preston—E. G. Marshall
   Kenneth Preston—Robert Reed
   Helen Donaldson—Polly Rowles
   Joan Miller—Joan Hackett

19. The Garry Moore Show
(*See* October 1961–April 1962)

20. To Tell the Truth (CBS)
On air: December 18, 1956
Off air: May 22, 1967
Moderators: Bud Collyer
Announcers: Johnny Olsen and Bill Wendell

OCTOBER 1963–APRIL 1964

1. The Beverly Hillbillies
(*See* October 1962–April 1963)

2. Bonanza
(*See* October 1960–April 1961)

3. The Dick Van Dyke Show
(*See* October 1962–April 1963)

4. Petticoat Junction (CBS)
On air: September 24, 1963
Off air: September 12, 1970
Cast:
   Kate Bradley—Bea Benaderet
   Joe Carson—Edgar Buchanan
   Billie Jo Bradley—Jeannine Riley
   Bobbie Jo Bradley—Pat Woodell
   Betty Jo Bradley—Linda Kaye Henning
   Charley Pratt—Smiley Burnette
   Floyd Smoot—Rufe Davis
   Homer Bedloe—Charles Lane
   Sam Drucker—Frank Cady

5. The Andy Griffith Show
(*See* October 1960–April 1961)

6. The Lucy Show
(*See* October 1962–April 1963)

7. Candid Camera
(*See* October 1960–April 1961)

8. The Ed Sullivan Show
(*See* October 1957–April 1958)

9. The Danny Thomas Show
(*See* October 1957–April 1958)

10. My Favorite Martian (CBS)
On air: September 29, 1963
Off air: September 4, 1966
Cast:
   Martin O'Hara (Uncle Martin)—Ray Walston
   Tim O'Hara—Bill Bixby
   Mrs. Lorelei Brown—Pamela Britton
   Angela Brown—Ann Marshall
   Mr. Harry Burns—J. Pat O'Malley

11. The Red Skelton Show
(*See* October 1951–April 1952)

12. I've Got a Secret
(*See* October 1954–April 1955)

13. Lassie
(*See* October 1961–April 1962)

14. The Jack Benny Show
(*See* October 1951–April 1952)

15. The Jackie Gleason Show
(*See* October 1953–April 1954)

16. The Donna Reed Show (ABC)
On air: September 24, 1958
Off air: September 3, 1966
Cast:
   Donna Stone—Donna Reed
   Alex Stone—Carl Betz
   Mary Stone—Shelley Fabares
   Jeff Stone—Paul Petersen
   Trisha Stone—Patty Petersen
   Midge Kelsey—Ann McCrea
   Dr. David Kelsey—Bob Crane

17. The Virginian (NBC)
On air: September 19, 1962
Off air: September 8, 1971
Cast:
   The Virginian (Jim)—James Drury
   Judge Henry Garth—Lee J. Cobb
   Trampas—Doug McClure
   Steve—Gary Clarke
   Molly Wood—Pippa Scott
   Betsy—Roberta Shore
   Randy—Randy Boone

18. The Patty Duke Show (ABC)
On air: September 18, 1963
Off air: August 31, 1966
Cast:
   Patty/Cathy Lane—Patty Duke
   Martin Lane—William Schallert
   Natalie Lane—Jean Byron
   Ross Lane—Paul O'Keefe
   Richard—Eddie Applegate

19. Dr. Kildare
(*See* October 1961–April 1962)

20. Gunsmoke
(*See* October 1956–April 1957)

OCTOBER 1964–APRIL 1965

1. Bonanza
(*See* October 1960–April 1961)

2. Bewitched (ABC)
On air: September 17, 1964
Off air: July 1, 1972
Cast:
   Samantha Stevens/Serena—Elizabeth Montgomery
   Darrin Stevens—Dick York
   Endora—Agnes Moorehead
   Maurice—Maurice Evans
   Larry Tate—David White
   Louise Tate—Irene Vernon
   Abner Kravitz—George Tobias
   Gladys Kravitz—Alice Pearce
   Aunt Clara—Marion Lorne

3. **Gomer Pyle, U.S.M.C. (CBS)**
On air: September 25, 1964
Off air: September 19, 1969
Cast:
   Pvt. Gomer Pyle—Jim Nabors
   Sgt. Vincent Carter—Frank Sutton
   Duke Slater—Ronnie Schell
   Bunny—Barbara Stuart

4. **The Andy Griffith Show**
(*See* October 1960–April 1961)

5. **The Fugitive (ABC)**
On air: September 17, 1963
Off air: August 29, 1967
Cast:
   Richard Kimble—David Janssen
   Lt. Philip Gerard—Barry Morse
   Donna Taft—Jacqueline Scott
   Fred Johnson, the one-armed man—Bill Raisch

6. **The Red Skelton Hour**
(*See* October 1951–April 1952)

7. **The Dick Van Dyke Show**
(*See* October 1962–April 1963)

8. **The Lucy Show**
(*See* October 1962–April 1963)

9. **Peyton Place (Tuesday time slot) (ABC)**
On air: September 15, 1964
Off air: June 2, 1969
Cast:
   Dr. Michael Rossi—Ed Nelson
   Constance Mackenzie—Dorothy Malone
   Alison MacKenzie—Mia Farrow
   Rodney Harrington—Ryan O'Neal
   Betty Anderson—Barbara Parkins
   Matthew Swain—Warner Anderson
   Leslie Harrington—Paul Langton
   Norman Harrington—Christopher Connelly
   Steven Cord—James Douglas

10. **Combat (ABC)**
On air: October 2, 1962
Off air: August 29, 1967
Cast:
   Lt. Gil Hanley—Rick Jason
   Sgt. Chip Saunders—Vic Morrow
   Caje—Pierre Jalbert
   Kirby—Jack Hogan
   Littlejohn—Dick Peabody
   Doc—Conlon Carter

11. **Walt Disney's Wonderful World of Color (NBC)**
(*See* October 1954–April 1955)

12. **The Beverly Hillbillies**
(*See* October 1962–April 1963)

13. **My Three Sons**
(*See* October 1960–April 1961)

14. **Branded (NBC)**
On air: January 24, 1965
Off air: September 4, 1966
Cast:
   Jason McCord—Chuck Connors

15. **Petticoat Junction**
(*See* October 1963–April 1964)

16. **The Ed Sullivan Show**
(*See* October 1957–April 1958)

17. **Lassie**
(*See* October 1961–April 1962)

18. **The Munsters (CBS)**
On air: September 24, 1964
Off air: September 1, 1966
Cast:
   Herman Munster—Fred Gwynne
   Lily Munster—Yvonne DeCarlo
   Grandpa—Al Lewis
   Edward Wolfgang Munster—Butch Patrick
   Marilyn Munster—Pat Priest

19. **Gilligan's Island (CBS)**
On air: September 26, 1964
Off air: September 4, 1967
Cast:
   Jonas Grumby (Skipper)—Alan Hale, Jr.
   Gilligan—Bob Denver
   Ginger Grant—Tina Louise
   Thurston Howell III—Jim Backus
   Mrs. Lovey Howell III—Natalie Schafer
   Ray Hinkley (The Professor)—Russell Johnson
   Mary Ann Summers—Dawn Wells

20. **Peyton Place (Thursday time slot)**
(*See* 9, this section)

OCTOBER 1965–APRIL 1966

1. **Bonanza**
(*See* October 1960–April 1961)

2. **Gomer Pyle, U.S.M.C.**
(*See* October 1964–April 1965)

3. **The Lucy Show**
(*See* October 1962–April 1963)

4. **The Red Skelton Show**
(*See* October 1951–April 1952)

5. **Batman (ABC)**
On air: January 12, 1966
Off air: March 14, 1968
Cast:
   Bruce Wayne (Batman)—Adam West
   Dick Grayson (Robin)—Burt Ward
   Alfred—Alan Napier
   Aunt Harriet Cooper—Madge Blake
   Police Commissioner Gordon—Neil Hampton
   Chief O'Hara—Stafford Repp

6. **The Andy Griffith Show**
(*See* October 1960–April 1961)

7. **Bewitched**
(*See* October 1964–April 1965)

8. **The Beverly Hillbillies**
(*See* October 1962–April 1963)

9. **Hogan's Heroes (CBS)**
On air: September 17, 1965
Off air: July 4, 1971
Cast:
   Col. Robert Hogan—Bob Crane
   Col. Wilhelm Klink—Werner Klemperer
   Sgt. Hans Schultz—John Banner
   Louis LeBeau—Robert Clary
   Peter Newkirk—Richard Dawson
   Sgt. Kinchloe—Ivan Dixon
   Lt. Carter—Larry Hovis
   Helga—Cynthia Lynn

10. **Batman**
(*See* October 1965–April 1966)

11. **Green Acres (CBS)**
On air: September 15, 1965
Off air: September 7, 1971
Cast:
   Oliver Wendell Douglas—Eddie Albert
   Lisa Douglas—Eva Gabor
   Mr. Haney—Pat Buttram
   Ed Dawson—Tom Lester
   Hank Kimball—Alvy Moore
   Fred Ziffel—Hank Patterson
   Doris Ziffel—Barbara Pepper
   Sam Drucker—Frank Cady
   Newt Kiley—Kay E. Kuter
   Alf Monroe—Sid Melton
   Ralph Monroe—Mary Grace Canfield

12. **Get Smart**
On air: September 18, 1965 (NBC)
Off air: September 13, 1969
On air: September 26, 1969 (CBS)
Off air: September 11, 1970
Cast:
   Maxwell Smart—Don Adams
   Agent 99—Barbara Feldon
   Thaddeus, the Chief—Edward Platt

13. **The Man from U.N.C.L.E. (NBC)**
On air: September 22, 1964
Off air: January 15, 1968
Cast:
   Napoleon Solo—Robert Vaughn
   Illya Kuryakin—David McCallum
   Alexander Waverly—Leo G. Carroll

14. **Daktari (CBS)**
On air: January 11, 1966
Off air: January 15, 1969
Cast:
   Dr. Marsh Tracy—Marshall Thompson
   Paula Tracy—Cheryl Miller
   Jack Dane—Yale Summers
   Hedley—Hedley Mattingly
   Mike—Hari Rhodes

15. **My Three Sons**
(*See* October 1960–April 1961)

16. **The Dick Van Dyke Show**
(*See* October 1962–April 1963)

17. **Walt Disney's Wonderful World of Color**
(*See* October 1964–April 1965)

18. **The Ed Sullivan Show**
(*See* October 1957–April 1958)

19. **The Lawrence Welk Show (ABC)**
On air: July 2, 1955
Off air: September 3, 1971
On air: October 8, 1956
Off air: June 2, 1958
On air: September 10, 1958
Off air: June 3, 1959
Host: Lawrence Welk
Announcer: Bob Orrin

20. **I've Got a Secret**
(*See* October 1951–April 1952)

OCTOBER 1966–APRIL 1967

1. **Bonanza**
(*See* October 1960–April 1961)

2. **The Red Skelton Show**
(*See* October 1951–April 1952)

3. **The Andy Griffith Show**
(*See* October 1960–April 1961)

4. **The Lucy Show**
(*See* October 1962–April 1963)

5. **The Jackie Gleason Show**
(*See* October 1953–April 1954)

6. **Green Acres**
(*See* October 1965–April 1966)

7. **Daktari**
(*See* October 1965–April 1966)

8. **Bewitched**
(*See* October 1964–April 1965)

9. **The Beverly Hillbillies**
(*See* October 1962–April 1963)

10. Gomer Pyle, U.S.M.C.
(*See* October 1964–April 1965)

11. The Virginian
(*See* October 1963–April 1964)

12. The Lawrence Welk Show
(*See* October 1965–April 1966)

13. The Ed Sullivan Show
(*See* October 1957–April 1958)

14. The Dean Martin Show (NBC)
On air: September 16, 1965
Off air: August 15, 1974
Host: Dean Martin

15. Family Affair (CBS)
On air: September 12, 1966
Off air: September 9, 1971
Cast:
Bill Davis—Brian Keith
Giles French—Sebastian Cabot
Cissy Davis—Kathy Garver
Jody Davis—Johnnie Whitaker
Buffy Davis—Anissa Jones

16. The Smothers Brothers Comedy Hour (CBS)
On air: February 5, 1967
Off air: June 8, 1969
Hosts: Tom and Dick Smothers
Announcer: Roger Carroll

17. Friday Night Movie (CBS)
On air: September 17, 1965
Off air: March 3, 1978

18. Hogan's Heroes
(*See* October 1965–April 1966)

19. Walt Disney's Wonderful World of Color
(*See* October 1964–April 1965)

20. Saturday Night at the Movies (NBC)
On air: September 23, 1961

OCTOBER 1967–APRIL 1968

1. The Andy Griffith Show
(*See* October 1960–April 1961)

2. The Lucy Show
(*See* October 1962–April 1963)

3. Gomer Pyle, U.S.M.C.
(*See* October 1964–April 1965)

4. Gunsmoke
(*See* October 1956–April 1957)

5. Family Affair
(*See* October 1966–April 1967)

6. Bonanza
(*See* October 1960–April 1961)

7. The Red Skelton Show
(*See* October 1951–April 1952)

8. The Dean Martin Show
(*See* October 1966–April 1967)

9. The Jackie Gleason Show
(*See* October 1953–April 1954)

10. Saturday Night at the Movies
(*See* October 1966–April 1967)

11. Bewitched
(*See* October 1964–April 1965)

12. The Beverly Hillbillies
(*See* October 1962–April 1963)

13. The Ed Sullivan Show
(*See* October 1957–April 1958)

14. The Virginian
(*See* October 1963–April 1964)

15. Friday Night Movie
(*See* October 1966–April 1967)

16. Green Acres
(*See* October 1965–April 1966)

17. The Lawrence Welk Show
(*See* October 1965–April 1966)

18. The Smothers Brothers Comedy Hour
(*See* October 1966–April 1967)

19. Gentle Ben (CBS)
On air: September 10, 1967
Off air: August 31, 1969
Cast:
Tom Wedloe—Dennis Weaver
Ellen Wedloe—Beth Brickell
Mark Wedloe—Clint Howard
Boomhauer—Rance Howard

20. Tuesday Night at the Movies (NBC)
On air: September 14, 1965
Off air: August 31, 1971

OCTOBER 1968–APRIL 1969

1. Rowan & Martin's Laugh-In (NBC)
On air: January 22, 1968
Off air: May 7, 1973
Hosts: Dan Rowan and Dick Martin
Announcer: Gary Owens

2. Gomer Pyle, U.S.M.C.
(*See* October 1964–April 1965)

3. Bonanza
(*See* October 1960–April 1961)

4. Mayberry R.F.D. (CBS)
On air: September 23, 1968
Off air: September 6, 1971
Cast:
 Sam Jones—Ken Berry
 Mike Jones—Buddy Foster
 Millie Swanson—Arlene Golonka
 Goober Pyle—George Lindsey
 Bee Taylor—Frances Bavier
 Howard Sprague—Jack Dodson
 Emmett Clark—Paul Hartman

5. Family Affair
(*See* October 1966–April 1967)

6. Gunsmoke
(*See* October 1956–April 1957)

7. Julia (NBC)
On air: September 17, 1968
Off air: May 23, 1971
Cast:
 Julia Baker—Diahann Carroll
 Dr. Morton Chegley—Lloyd Nolan
 Corey Baker—Marc Capage
 Hannah Yarby—Lurene Tuttle

8. The Dean Martin Show
(*See* October 1966–April 1967)

9. Here's Lucy (CBS)
On air: September 23, 1968
Off air: September 2, 1974
Cast:
 Lucille Carter—Lucille Ball
 Harrison Otis Carter—Gale Gordon
 Kim Carter—Lucie Arnaz
 Craig Carter—Desi Arnaz, Jr.
 Mary Jane Lewis—Mary Jane Croft

10. The Beverly Hillbillies
(*See* October 1962–April 1963)

11. Mission: Impossible (CBS)
On air: September 17, 1966
Off air: September 8, 1973
Cast:
 Jim Phelps—Peter Graves
 Dan Briggs—Steven Hill
 Cinnamon Carter—Barbara Bain
 Rollin Hand—Martin Landau
 Barney Collier—Greg Morris
 Willie Armitage—Peter Lupus
 Paris—Leonard Nimoy

12. Bewitched
(*See* October 1964–April 1965)

13. The Red Skelton Hour
(*See* October 1951–April 1952)

14. My Three Sons
(*See* October 1960–April 1961)

15. The Glen Campbell Goodtime Hour (CBS)
On air: January 24, 1969
Off air: June 13, 1972
Host: Glen Campbell

16. Ironside (NBC)
On air: September 14, 1967
Off air: January 16, 1975
Cast:
 Robert Ironside—Raymond Burr
 Eve Whitefield—Barbara Anderson
 Det. Sgt. Ed Brown—Don Galloway
 Mark Sanger—Don Mitchell
 Commissioner Randall—Gene Lyons

17. The Virginian
(*See* October 1963–April 1964)

18. The F.B.I. (ABC)
On air: September 19, 1965
Off air: September 8, 1974
Cast:
 Inspector Lewis Erskine—Efrem Zimbalist, Jr.
 Arthur Ward—Philip Abbott
 Jim Rhodes—Stephen Brooks
 Special Agent Tom Colby—William Reynolds

19. Green Acres
(*See* October 1965–April 1966)

20. Dragnet
(*See* October 1951–April 1952)

OCTOBER 1969–APRIL 1970

1. Rowan & Martin's Laugh-In
(*See* October 1968–April 1969)

2. Gunsmoke
(*See* October 1956–April 1957)

3. Bonanza
(*See* October 1960–April 1961)

4. Mayberry R.F.D.
(*See* October 1968–April 1969)

5. Family Affair
(*See* October 1966–April 1967)

6. Here's Lucy
(*See* October 1968–April 1969)

7. The Red Skelton Hour
(*See* October 1951–April 1952)

8. Marcus Welby, M.D. (ABC)
On air: September 23, 1969
Off air: May 11, 1976
Cast:
  Dr. Marcus Welby—Robert Young
  Dr. Steven Kiley—James Brolin
  Consuelo Lopez—Elena Verdugo
  Myra Sherwood—Anne Baxter

9. Walt Disney's Wonderful World of Color
(See October 1964–April 1965)

10. The Doris Day Show (CBS)
On air: September 24, 1968
Off air: September 3, 1973
Cast:
  Doris Martin—Doris Day
  Buck Webb—Denver Pyle
  Billy Martin—Philip Brown
  Toby Martin—Tod Starke

11. The Bill Cosby Show (NBC)
On air: September 14, 1969
Off air: August 31, 1971
Cast:
  Chet Kincaid—Bill Cosby
  Marsha Patterson—Joyce Bulifant
  Brian Kincaid—Lee Weaver
  Verna Kincaid—Olga James
  Roger Kincaid—Donald Livingston
  Rose Kincaid—Lillian Randolph (1969-70);
    Beah Richards (1970-71)

12. The Jim Nabors Hour (CBS)
On air: September 25, 1969
Off air: May 20, 1971
Host: Jim Nabors

13. The Carol Burnett Show (CBS)
On air: September 11, 1967
Off air: March 29, 1978
Hostess: Carol Burnett
Regulars: Lyle Waggoner, Harvey Korman, Vicki
  Lawrence

14. The Dean Martin Show
(See October 1966–April 1967)

15. My Three Sons
(See October 1960–April 1961)

16. Ironside
(See October 1968–April 1969)

17. The Johnny Cash Show (ABC)
On air: June 7, 1969
Off air: September 6, 1969
On air: January 21, 1970
Off air: May 21, 1971
Host: Johnny Cash
Announcer: Mike Lawrence

18. The Beverly Hillbillies
(See October 1962–April 1963)

19. Hawaii Five-O (CBS)
On air: September 26, 1968
Cast:
  Det. Steve McGarrett—Jack Lord
  Det. Danny Williams—James MacArthur
  Det. Chin Ho Kelly—Kam Fong
  Det. Kono—Zulu
  Governor Philip Grey—Richard Denning
  Wo Fat—Khigh Dhiegh

20. The Glen Campbell Goodtime Hour
(See October 1968–April 1969)

OCTOBER 1970–APRIL 1971

1. Marcus Welby, M.D.
(See October 1969–April 1970)

2. The Flip Wilson Show (NBC)
On air: September 17, 1970
Off air: June 27, 1974
Host: Flip Wilson

3. Here's Lucy
(See October 1968–April 1969)

4. Ironside
(See October 1968–April 1969)

5. Gunsmoke
(See October 1956–April 1957)

6. ABC Movie of the Week (ABC)
On air: September 23, 1969
Off air: August 8, 1972

7. Hawaii Five-O
(See October 1969–April 1970)

8. Medical Center (CBS)
On air: September 24, 1969
Off air: September 13, 1976
Cast:
  Dr. Paul Lochner—James Daly
  Dr. Joe Gannon—Chad Everett

9. Bonanza
(See October 1960–April 1961)

10. The F.B.I.
(See October 1968–April 1969)

11. Mod Squad (ABC)
On air: September 24, 1968
Off air: August 23, 1973
Cast:
  Pete Cochran—Michael Cole
  Julie Barnes—Peggy Lipton
  Linc Hayes—Clarence Williams III
  Capt. Adam Greer—Tige Andrews

12. **Adam 12 (NBC)**
On air: September 21, 1968
Off air: August 26, 1975
Cast:
    Officer Pete Malloy—Martin Milner
    Officer Jim Reed—Kent McCord
    Sgt. MacDonald—William Boyett
    Officer Ed Wells—Gary Crosby

13. **Rowan & Martin's Laugh-In**
(*See* October 1968–April 1969)

14. **The Wonderful World of Disney**
(*See* October 1964–April 1965)

15. **Mayberry R.F.D.**
(*See* October 1968–April 1969)

16. **Hee Haw (CBS)**
On air: June 15, 1969
Off air: July 13, 1971
Hosts: Buck Owens and Roy Clark

17. **Mannix (CBS)**
On air: September 7, 1967
Off air: August 27, 1975
Cast:
    Joe Mannix—Michael Connors
    Peggy Fair—Gail Fisher
    Lt. Adam Tobias—Robert Reed

18. **The Men from Shiloh (The Virginian)**
(*See* October 1963–April 1964)

19. **My Three Sons**
(*See* October 1960–April 1961)

20. **The Doris Day Show**
(*See* October 1969–April 1970)

OCTOBER 1971–APRIL 1972

1. **All in the Family (CBS)**
On air: January 12, 1971
Cast:
    Archie Bunker—Carroll O'Connor
    Edith Bunker—Jean Stapleton
    Gloria Stivic—Sally Struthers
    Mike Stivic—Rob Reiner
    Lionel Jefferson—Mike Evans
    Louise Jefferson—Isabel Sanford
    Henry Jefferson—Mel Stewart

2. **The Flip Wilson Show**
(*See* October 1970–April 1971)

3. **Marcus Welby, M.D.**
(*See* October 1969–April 1970)

4. **Gunsmoke**
(*See* October 1956–April 1957)

5. **ABC Movie of the Week**
(*See* October 1970–April 1971)

6. **Sanford and Son (NBC)**
On air: January 14, 1972
Off air: September 2, 1977
Cast:
    Fred Sanford—Redd Foxx
    Lamont Sanford—Demond Wilson
    Melvin—Slappy White
    Bubba—Don Bexley
    Officer Swanhauser—Noam Pitlik
    Officer Smith—Hal Williams
    Rollo Larson—Nathaniel Taylor
    Donna Harris—Lynn Hamilton

7. **Mannix**
(*See* October 1970–April 1971)

8. **Funny Face (CBS)**
On air: September 18, 1971
Off air: December 11, 1971
Cast:
    Sandy Stockton—Sandy Duncan
    Alice McRaven—Valorie Armstrong
    Kate Harwell—Kathleen Freeman
    Pat Harwell—Henry Beckman

9. **Adam 12**
(*See* October 1970–April 1971)

10. **The Mary Tyler Moore Show (CBS)**
On air: September 1970
Off air: September 3, 1977
Cast:
    Mary Richards—Mary Tyler Moore
    Rhoda Morgenstern—Valerie Harper
    Lou Grant—Edward Asner
    Ted Baxter—Ted Knight
    Murray Slaughter—Gavin MacLeod
    Phyllis Lindstrom—Cloris Leachman
    Bess Lindstrom—Lisa Gerritsen
    Gordon Howard—John Amos

11. **Here's Lucy**
(*See* October 1968–April 1969)

12. **Hawaii Five-O**
(*See* October 1969–April 1971)

13. **Medical Center**
(*See* October 1970–April 1971)

14. **The NBC Mystery Movie (NBC Sunday Mystery Movie) (NBC)**
On air: September 15, 1971
Off air: September 4, 1977
Columbo: September 17, 1972–August 14, 1977
McMillan and Wife: September 24, 1972–August 14, 1977
McCloud: October 1, 1972–August 28, 1977
Hec Ramsey: October 8, 1972–August 25, 1974
Amy Prentiss: December 1, 1974–July 6, 1975
McCoy: October 5, 1975–March 28, 1976
Quincy: October 3, 1976–January 2, 1977

15. Ironside
(*See* October 1968–April 1969)

16. The Partridge Family (ABC)
On air: September 25, 1970
Off air: September 31, 1974
Cast:
  Shirley Partridge—Shirley Jones
  Keith Partridge—David Cassidy
  Laurie Partridge—Susan Dey
  Danny Partridge—Danny Bonaduce
  Tracy Partridge—Suzanne Crough
  Reuben Kinkaid—David Madden

17. The F.B.I.
(*See* October 1968–April 1969)

18. The New Dick Van Dyke Show (CBS)
On air: September 18, 1971
Off air: September 2, 1974
Cast:
  Dick Preston—Dick Van Dyke
  Jenny Preston—Hope Lange
  Bernie Davis—Marty Brill
  "Mike" Preston—Fannie Flagg
  Carol Davis—Nancy Dussault
  Annie Preston—Angela Powell

19. The Wonderful World of Disney
(*See* October 1964–April 1965)

20. Bonanza
(*See* October 1960–April 1961)

OCTOBER 1972–APRIL 1973

1. All in the Family
(*See* October 1971–April 1972)

2. Sanford and Son
(*See* October 1971–April 1972)

3. Hawaii Five-O
(*See* October 1969–April 1970)

4. Maude (CBS)
On air: September 12, 1972
Off air: April 29, 1978
Cast:
  Maude Findlay—Beatrice Arthur
  Walter Findlay—Bill Macy
  Carol—Adrienne Barbeau
  Phillip—Brian Morrison
  Dr. Arthur Harmon—Conrad Bain
  Vivian Cavender Harmon—Rue McClanahan
  Florida Evans—Esther Rolle

5. Bridget Loves Bernie (CBS)
On air: September 16, 1972
Off air: September 8, 1973
Cast:
  Bridget Fitzgerald Steinberg—Meredith Baxter
  Bernie Steinberg—David Birney
  Sam Steinberg—Harold J. Stone
  Sophie Steinberg—Bibi Osterwald
  Amy Fitzgerald—Audra Lindley
  Walt Fitzgerald—David Doyle

6. NBC Sunday Mystery Movie
(*See* October 1971–April 1972)

7. The Mary Tyler Moore Show
(*See* October 1971–April 1972)

8. Gunsmoke
(*See* October 1956–April 1957)

9. The Wonderful World of Disney
(*See* October 1964–April 1965)

10. Ironside
(*See* October 1968–April 1969)

11. Adam 12
(*See* October 1970–April 1971)

12. The Flip Wilson Show
(*See* October 1970–April 1971)

13. Marcus Welby, M.D.
(*See* October 1969–April 1970)

14. Cannon (CBS)
On air: September 14, 1971
Off air: September 19, 1976
Cast:
  Frank Cannon—William Conrad

15. Here's Lucy
(*See* October 1968–April 1969)

16. The Bob Newhart Show (CBS)
On air: September 16, 1972
Off air: September 2, 1978
Cast:
  Robert Hartley—Bob Newhart
  Emily Hartley—Suzanne Pleshette
  Howard Border—Bill Daily
  Jerry Robinson—Peter Bonerz
  Carol Kester Bondurant—Marcia Wallace

17. Tuesday Movie of the Week (ABC)
On air: Sepember 21, 1976

18. ABC NFL Monday Night Football
On air: September 21, 1970
Hosts:
  Howard Cosell
  Frank Gifford
  Don Meredith
  Alex Karras

19. The Partridge Family
(*See* October 1971–April 1972)

20. The Waltons (CBS)
On air: September 14, 1972
Cast:
John Walton—Ralph Waite
Olivia Walton—Michael Learned
Zeb (Grandpa) Walton—Will Geer
Esther (Grandma) Walton—Ellen Corby
John Boy Walton—Richard Thomas
Mary Ellen Walton—Judy Norton-Taylor
Jim-Bob Walton—David S. Harper
Elizabeth Walton—Kami Cotler
Jason Walton—Jon Warmsley
Erin Walton—Mary Elizabeth McDonough
Ben Walton—Eric Scott

SEPTEMBER 1973–APRIL 1974

1. All in the Family
(*See* October 1971–April 1972)

2. The Waltons
(*See* October 1972–April 1973)

3. Sanford and Son
(*See* October 1971–April 1972)

4. M*A*S*H (CBS)
On air: September 17, 1972
Cast:
Capt. Benjamin Franklin Pierce (Hawkeye)—
Alan Alda
Capt. John McIntyre (Trapper John)—Wayne
Rogers
Lt. Col. Henry Blake—McLean Stevenson
Maj. Margaret Houlihan (Hot Lips)—Loretta
Swit
Corporal Radar O'Reilly—Gary Burghoff
Maj. Frank Burns—Larry Linville
Col. Sherman Potter—Harry Morgan
Capt. B. J. Hunnicutt—Mike Farrell
Father John Mulcahy—William Christopher
Corporal Maxwell Klinger—Jamie Farr

5. Hawaii Five-O
(*See* October 1969–April 1970)

6. Maude
(*See* October 1972–April 1973)

7. Kojak (CBS)
On air: October 24, 1975
Off air: April 15, 1978
Cast:
Lt. Theo Kojak—Telly Savalas
Frank McNeil—Dan Frazer
Lt. Bobby Crocker—Kevin Dobson
Det. Stavros—George Savalas

8. The Sonny and Cher Comedy Hour (CBS)
On air: August 1, 1971
Off air: May 29, 1974
Hosts: Sonny and Cher Bono
Announcer: Peter Cullen

9. The Mary Tyler Moore Show
(*See* October 1971–April 1972)

10. Cannon
(*See* October 1972–April 1973)

11. The Six Million Dollar Man (ABC)
On air: October 20, 1973
Off air: March 6, 1978
Cast:
Steve Austin—Lee Majors
Dr. Rudy Wells—Alan Oppenheimer
Oscar Goldman—Richard Anderson

12. The Bob Newhart Show
(*See* October 1972–April 1973)

13. The Wonderful World of Disney
(*See* October 1964–April 1965)

14. NBC Sunday Mystery Movie
(*See* October 1971–April 1972)

15. Gunsmoke
(*See* October 1956–April 1957)

16. Happy Days (ABC)
On air: January 15, 1974
Cast:
Richie Cunningham—Ron Howard
Howard Cunningham—Tom Bosley
Marion Cunningham—Marion Ross
Arthur Fonzerelli (Fonzie)—Henry Winkler
Potsie Weber—Anson Williams
Ralph Malph—Donny Most
Joanie Cunningham—Erin Moran

17. Good Times (CBS)
On air: February 8, 1974
Cast:
James Evans—John Amos
Florida Evans—Esther Rolle
James Evans, Jr. —Jimmie Walker
Willona Woods—Ja'net DuBois
Michael Evans—Ralph Carter
Thelma Evans Anderson—BerNadette Stanis

18. Barnaby Jones (CBS)
On air: January 28, 1973
Cast:
Barnaby Jones—Buddy Ebsen
Betty Jones—Lee Meriwether

19. ABC NFL Monday Night Football
(*See* October 1972–April 1973)

20. CBS Friday Night Movie
On air: September 16, 1966
Off air: March 3, 1978

SEPTEMBER 1974–APRIL 1975

1. All in the Family
(*See* October 1971–April 1972)

2. Sanford and Son
(*See* October 1971–April 1972)

3. Chico and the Man (NBC)
On air: September 13, 1974
Off air: July 2, 1978
Cast:
  Ed Brown—Jack Albertson
  Chico Rodriguez—Freddie Prinze
  Louie—Scatman Crothers

4. The Jeffersons (CBS)
On air: January 18, 1975
Cast:
  George Jefferson—Sherman Hensley
  Louise Jefferson—Isabel Sanford
  Lionel Jefferson—Mike Evans
  Helen Willis—Roxie Roker
  Tom Willis—Franklin Cover
  Jenny Willis Jefferson—Berlinda Tolbert
  Harry Bentley—Paul Benedict

5. M*A*S*H
(*See* September 1973–April 1974

6. Rhoda (CBS)
On air: September 9, 1974
Off air: December 9, 1978
Cast:
  Rhoda Morgenstern Gerard—Valerie Harper
  Joe Gerard—David Groh
  Brenda Morgenstern—Julie Kavner
  Ida Morgenstern—Nancy Walker
  Martin Morgenstern—Harold J. Gould

7. Good Times
(*See* September 1973–April 1974)

8. The Waltons
(*See* October 1972–April 1973)

9. Maude
(*See* October 1972–April 1973)

10. Hawaii Five-O
(*See* October 1969–April 1970)

11. The Mary Tyler Moore Show
(*See* October 1971–April 1972)

12. The Rockford Files (NBC)
On air: September 13, 1974
Cast:
  Jim Rockford—James Garner
  Joseph Rockford—Noah Beery
  Det. Dennis Becker—Joe Santos
  Beth Davenport—Gretchen Corbett
  Angel Martin—Stuart Margolin

13. Little House on the Prairie (NBC)
On air: September 11, 1974
Cast:
  Charles Ingalls—Michael Landon
  Caroline Ingalls—Karen Grassle
  Laura Ingalls—Melissa Gilbert
  Mary Ingalls—Melissa Sue Anderson
  Carrie Ingalls—Lindsay and Sidney Greenbush

14. Kojak
(*See* September 1973–April 1974)

15. Police Woman (NBC)
On air: September 13, 1974
Off air: August 30, 1978
Cast:
  Sgt. Suzanne "Pepper" Anderson—Angie Dickinson
  Lt. William Crowley—Earl Holliman
  Det. Pete Royster—Charles Dierkop
  Det. Joe Styles—Ed Bernard
  Lt. Paul Marsh—Val Bisoglio

16. S.W.A.T. (ABC)
On air: February 24, 1975
Off air: June 29, 1975
Cast:
  Lt. Dan "Hondo" Harrelson—Steve Forrest
  Sgt. David "Deacon" Kay—Rod Perry
  Officer James Street—Robert Urich
  Officer T. J. McCabe—James Coleman
  Officer Dominic Luca—Mark Shera

17. The Bob Newhart Show
(*See* October 1972–April 1973)

18. The Wonderful World of Disney
(*See* October 1964–April 1965)

19. The Rookies (ABC)
On air: September 11, 1972
Off air: June 29, 1976
Cast:
  Lt. Edward Ryker—Gerald S. O'Loughlin
  Officer William Gillis—Michael Ontkean
  Officer Terry Webster—Georg Stanford Brown
  Officer Michael Danko—Sam Melville
  Jill Danko—Kate Jackson

20. Mannix
(*See* October 1970–April 1971)

SEPTEMBER 1975–APRIL 1976

1. All in the Family
(*See* October 1971–April 1972)

2. Rich Man, Poor Man (ABC)
On air: February 1, 1976
Off air: March 15, 1976
Cast:
  Rudy Jordache—Peter Strauss
  Tom Jordache—Nick Nolte
  Julie Prescott—Susan Blakely

3. Laverne & Shirley (ABC)
On air: January 27, 1976
Cast:
  Laverne De Fazio—Penny Marshall
  Shirley Feeney—Cindy Williams
  Carmine Ragusa—Eddie Mekka
  Frank De Fazio—Phil Foster
  Lenny Kolowski—Michael McKean
  Andrew "Squiggy" Squiggman—David Lander

4. Maude
(See October 1972–April 1973)

5. The Bionic Woman
On air: January 14, 1976 (ABC)
Off air: May 6, 1977
On air: September 10, 1977 (NBC)
Off air: May 4, 1978
Cast:
  Jamie Sommers—Lindsay Wagner
  Oscar Goldman—Richard Anderson
  Dr. Rudy Wells—Martin E. Brooks

6. Phyllis (CBS)
On air: September 8, 1975
Off air: August 30, 1977
Cast:
  Phyllis Lindstrom—Cloris Leachman
  Bess Lindstrom—Lisa Gerritsen
  Audrey Dexter—Jane Rose
  Judge Jonathan Dexter—Henry Jones
  Mother Dexter—Judith Lowry

7. Sanford and Son
(See October 1971–April 1972)

8. Rhoda
(See September 1974–August 1975)

9. The Six Million Dollar Man
(See September 1973–April 1974)

10. ABC Monday Night Movie (ABC)
On air: January 1, 1973

11. Happy Days
(See September 1973–April 1974

12. One Day at a Time (CBS)
On air: December 16, 1975
Cast:
  Ann Romano—Bonnie Franklin
  Julie Cooper—Mackenzie Phillips
  Barbara Cooper—Valerie Bertinelli
  Dwayne Schneider—Pat Harrington
  David Kane—Richard Masur

13. ABC Sunday Night Movie (ABC)
On air: April 8, 1962

14. The Waltons
(See October 1972–April 1973)

15. M*A*S*H
(See September 1973–April 1974)

16. Starsky and Hutch (ABC)
On air: September 10, 1975
Cast:
  Det. Dave Starsky—Paul Michael Glaser
  Det. Ken Hutchinson—David Soul
  Capt. Harold Dobey—Bernie Hamilton
  Huggy Bear—Antonio Fargas

17. Good Heavens (ABC)
On air: March 8, 1976
Off air: June 26, 1976
Cast:
  Mr. Angel—Carl Reiner

18. Welcome Back, Kotter (ABC)
On air: September 9, 1975
Cast:
  Gabe Kotter—Gabriel Kaplan
  Julie Kotter—Marcia Strassman
  Michael Woodman—John Sylvester White
  Vinnie Barbarino—John Travolta
  Juan Epstein—Robert Hegyes
  Freddie "Boom-Boom" Washington—
    Lawrence- Hilton Jacobs
  Arnold Horshack—Ron Palillo

19. The Mary Tyler Moore Show
(See October 1971–April 1972)

20. Kojak
(See September 1973–April 1974)

SEPTEMBER 1976–APRIL 1977

1. Happy Days
(See September 1973–April 1974)

2. Laverne & Shirley
(See September 1975–April 1976)

3. ABC Monday Night Movie
(See September 1975–April 1976)

4. M*A*S*H
(See September 1973–April 1974)

5. Charlie's Angels (ABC)
On air: September 22, 1976
Cast:
  Sabrina Duncan—Kate Jackson
  Jill Munroe—Farrah Fawcett-Majors
  Kelly Garrett—Jaclyn Smith
  Kris Munroe—Cheryl Ladd
  John Bosley—David Doyle
  Charlie Townsend (voice only)—John Forsythe

6. The Big Event (NBC)
On air: September 26, 1976

7. The Six Million Dollar Man
(See September 1973–April 1974)

8. ABC Sunday Night Movie
(*See* September 1975–April 1976)

9. Baretta (ABC)
On air: January 17, 1975
Off air: August 25, 1978
Cast:
  Tony Baretta—Robert Blake
  Billy Truman—Tom Ewell
  Inspector Schiller—Dana Elcar
  Lt. Hal Brubaker—Edward Grover
  Rooster—Michael D. Roberts

10. One Day at a Time
(*See* September 1975–April 1976)

11. Three's Company (ABC)
On air: March 24, 1977
Cast:
  Jack Tripper—John Ritter
  Janet Wood—Joyce DeWitt
  Chrissy Snow—Suzanne Somers
  Helen Roper—Audra Lindley
  Stanley Roper—Norman Fell

12. All in the Family
(*See* October 1971–April 1972)

13. Welcome Back, Kotter
(*See* September 1975–March 1976)

14. The Bionic Woman
(*See* September 1975–April 1976)

15. The Waltons
(*See* October 1972–April 1973)

16. Little House on the Prairie
(*See* September 1974–April 1975)

17. Barney Miller (ABC)
On air: January 23, 1975
Cast:
  Capt. Barney Miller—Hal Linden
  Det. Phil Fish—Abe Vigoda
  Det. Nick Yemana—Jack Soo
  Det. Wojohowicz—Maxwell Gail
  Det. Ron Harris—Ron Glass
  Det. Arthur Dietrich—Steve Landesberg

18. 60 Minutes (CBS)
On air: September 24, 1968
Correspondents: Harry Reasoner, Morley Safer, Dan Rather, Mike Wallace

19. Hawaii Five-O
(*See* October 1969–April 1970)

20. NBC Monday Night Movie (NBC)
On air: February 4, 1963
Off air: May 17, 1977

SEPTEMBER 1977–APRIL 1978

1. Laverne & Shirley
(*See* September 1975–April 1976)

2. Happy Days
(*See* September 1973–April 1974)

3. Three's Company
(*See* September 1976–April 1977)

4. 60 Minutes
(*See* September 1976–April 1977)

5. Charlie's Angels
(*See* September 1976–April 1977)

6. All in the Family
(*See* October 1971–April 1972)

7. Little House on the Prairie
(*See* September 1974–April 1975)

8. Alice (CBS)
On air: September 29, 1976
Cast:
  Alice Hyatt—Linda Lavin
  Mel—Vic Tayback
  Flo—Polly Holliday
  Vera—Beth Howland
  Tommy Hyatt—Philip McKeon

9. M*A*S*H
(*See* September 1973–April 1974)

10. One Day at a Time
(*See* September 1975–April 1976)

11. How the West Was Won (ABC)
On air: February 12, 1978
Off air: August 27, 1978
Cast:
  Zeg Macahan—James Arness
  Aunt Molly Macahan—Fionnula Flanagan
  Luke Macahan—Bruce Boxleitner
  Laura Macahan—Kathryn Holcomb
  Josh Macahan—William Kirby Cullen
  Jessie Macahan—Vicki Schreck

12. Eight Is Enough (ABC)
On air: March 22, 1977
Cast:
  Tom Bradford—Dick Van Patten
  Joan Bradford—Diana Hyland
  Abby Bradford—Betty Buckley
  David Bradford—Grant Goodeve
  Elizabeth Bradford—Connie Newton
  Nicholas Bradford—Adam Rich
  Tommy Bradford—Willie Aames
  Nancy Bradford—Dianne Kay
  Susan Bradford—Susan Richardson
  Mary Bradford—Lani O'Grady
  Joanie Bradford—Laurie Walters

13. Soap (ABC)
On air: September 13, 1977
Cast:
  Chester Tate—Robert Mandan
  Jessica Tate—Katherine Helmond
  Mary Dallas Campbell—Cathryn Damon
  Burt Campbell—Richard Mulligan

14. **The Love Boat (ABC)**
On air: September 24, 1977
Cast:
  Capt. Merrill Stubing—Gavin MacLeod
  Julie McCoy—Lauren Tewes
  Dr. Adam Bricker—Bernie Kopell
  Burl "Gopher" Smith—Fred Grandy
  Isaac Washington—Ted Lange

15. **NBC Monday Night Movie**
(*See* September 1976–April 1977)

16. **ABC NFL Monday Night Football**
(*See* October 1972–April 1973)

17. **Fantasy Island (ABC)**
On air: January 28, 1978
Cast:
  Mr. Roarke—Ricardo Montalban
  Tattoo—Herve Villechaize

18. **Barney Miller**
(*See* September 1976–April 1977)

19. **The Amazing Spider-Man (CBS)**
On air: April 5, 1978
Off air: May 3, 1978
Cast:
  Peter Parker/Spider-Man—Nicholas Hammand
  J. Jonah Jameson—Robert F. Simon
  Rita—Chip Fields

20. **Project U.F.O. (NBC)**
On air: February 19, 1978
Off air: January 4, 1979
Cast:
  Maj. Jake Gatlin—William Jordan
  S/Sgt. Harry Fitz—Caskey Swaim
  Capt. Ben Ryan—Edward Winter

SEPTEMBER 1978–APRIL 1979

1. **Laverne & Shirley**
(*See* September 1976–April 1977)

2. **Three's Company**
(*See* September 1977–April 1978)

3. **Mork & Mindy (ABC)**
On air: September 14, 1978
Cast:
  Mork—Robin Williams
  Mindy McConnell—Pam Dawber
  Frederick McConnell—Conrad Janis
  Cora Hudson—Elizabeth Kerr

4. **Happy Days**
(*See* September 1973–April 1974))

5. **Angie (ABC)**
On air: February 2, 1979
Cast:
  Angie Falco Benson—Donna Pescow
  Brad Benson—Robert Hays
  Joyce Benson—Sharon Spelman
  Theresa Falco—Doris Roberts
  Marie Falco—Debralee Scott

6. **60 Minutes**
(*See* September 1976–April 1977)

7. **M*A*S*H**
(*See* September 1973–April 1974)

8. **The Ropers (ABC)**
On air: March 13, 1979
Cast:
  Helen Roper—Audra Lindley
  Stanley Roper—Norman Fell

9. **All in the Family**
(*See* October 1971–April 1972)

10. **Taxi (ABC)**
On air: September 12, 1978
Cast:
  Alex Reigner—Judd Hirsch
  Bobby Wheeler—Jeff Conaway
  Latka Gravas—Andy Kaufman
  Louis DePalma—Danny DeVito
  Elaine Nardo—Marilu Henner
  Tony Banta—Tony Danza
  John Burns—Randall Carver

11. **Eight Is Enough**
(*See* September 1977–April 1978)

12. **Charlie's Angels**
(*See* September 1976–April 1977)

13. **Alice**
(*See* September 1977–April 1978)

14. **Little House on the Prairie**
(*See* September 1974–April 1975)

15. **ABC Sunday Night Movie**
(*See* September 1975–April 1976)

16. **Barney Miller**
(*See* September 1976–April 1977)

17. **The Love Boat**
(*See* September 1977–April 1978)

18. **One Day at a Time**
(*See* September 1975–April 1976)

19. **Soap**
(*See* September 1977–April 1978)

20. **The Dukes of Hazzard (CBS)**
On air: January 26, 1979
Cast:
  Luke—Tom Wopat
  Bo—John Schneider
  Boss Hogg—Sorrell Booke
  Sheriff Rosco—James Best
  Daisy—Katherine Bach
  Uncle Jessie—Denver Pyle
  Cotter—Ben Jones

Top 50 Programs of All Time

Rank	Program Name	Telecast Date	Network	Duration Min	Average Audience (%)
1	*Roots*—Pt. 8	Jan. 30, 1977	ABC	115	51.1
2	"Gone with the Wind"—Pt. 1 (*Big Event*, Pt. 1)	Nov. 7, 1976	NBC	179	47.7
3	"Gone with the Wind"—Pt. 2 (*NBC Mon. Movie*)	Nov. 8, 1976	NBC	119	47.4
4	Super Bowl XII	Jan. 15, 1978	CBS	218	47.2
5	Super Bowl XIII	Jan. 21, 1979	NBC	230	47.1
6	"Bob Hope Christmas Show"	Jan. 15, 1970	NBC	90	46.6
7	*Roots*—Pt. 6 tie	Jan. 28, 1977	ABC	120	45.9
	The Fugitive	Aug. 29, 1967	ABC	60	45.9
9	*Roots*—Pt. 5	Jan. 27, 1977	ABC	60	45.7
10	"Bob Hope Christmas Show"	Jan. 14, 1971	NBC	90	45.0
11	*Roots*—Pt. 3	Jan. 25, 1977	ABC	60	44.8
12	*Ed Sullivan Show*	Feb. 9, 1964	CBS	60	44.6
13	Super Bowl XI	Jan. 9, 1977	NBC	204	44.4
14	Super Bowl VI	Jan. 16, 1972	CBS	170	44.2
15	*Roots*—Pt. 2	Jan. 24, 1977	ABC	120	44.1
16	*Beverly Hillbillies*	Jan. 8, 1964	CBS	30	44.0
17	*Roots*—Pt. 4	Jan. 26, 1977	ABC	60	43.8
18	Academy Awards	Apr. 7, 1970	ABC	145	43.4
19	*Ed Sullivan Show*	Feb. 16, 1964	CBS	60	43.2
20	*Beverly Hillbillies*	Jan. 15, 1964	CBS	30	42.8
21	Super Bowl VII	Jan. 14, 1973	NBC	185	42.7
22	Super Bowl IX tie	Jan. 12, 1975	NBC	190	42.4
	Beverly Hillbillies	Feb. 26, 1964	CBS	30	42.4
24	Super Bowl X	Jan. 18, 1976	CBS	200	42.3
	"Airport" (*Movie Special*)	Nov. 11, 1973	ABC	170	42.3
	"Love Story" (*ABC Sunday Movie*) tie	Oct. 1, 1972	ABC	120	42.3
	"Cinderella"	Feb. 22, 1965	CBS	90	42.3
	Roots—Pt. 7	Jan. 29, 1977	ABC	60	42.3
29	*Beverly Hillbillies*	Mar. 25, 1964	CBS	30	42.2
30	Super Bowl XII—"Kickoff"	Jan. 15, 1978	CBS	15	42.1
31	*Beverly Hillbillies*	Feb. 5, 1964	CBS	30	42.0
32	*Beverly Hillbillies*	Jan. 29, 1964	CBS	30	41.9
33	Miss America Pageant tie	Sep. 9, 1961	CBS	150	41.8
	Beverly Hillbillies	Jan. 1, 1964	CBS	30	41.8
35	Super Bowl VIII tie	Jan. 13, 1974	CBS	160	41.6
	Bonanza	Mar. 8, 1964	NBC	60	41.6
37	*Beverly Hillbillies*	Jan. 22, 1964	CBS	30	41.5
38	*Bonanza*	Feb. 16, 1964	NBC	60	41.4
39	Academy Awards	Apr. 10, 1967	ABC	150	41.2
40	*Bonanza*	Feb. 9, 1964	NBC	60	41.0
41	*Gunsmoke*	Jan. 28, 1961	CBS	30	40.9
42	*Bonanza*	Mar. 28, 1965	NBC	60	40.8
43	*Bonanza* tie	Mar. 7, 1965	NBC	60	40.7
	All in the Family	Jan. 8, 1972	CBS	30	40.7
45	*Roots*—Pt. 1	Jan. 23, 1977	ABC	120	40.5
	Bonanza	Feb. 2, 1964	NBC	60	40.5
	Beverly Hillbillies tie	May 1, 1963	CBS	30	40.5
	Gunsmoke	Feb. 25, 1961	CBS	30	40.5
49	*Bonanza* tie	Feb. 21, 1965	NBC	60	40.4
	Gunsmoke	Dec. 17, 1960	CBS	30	40.4

Note:
- The above figures are average-audience % rankings based on the reports of July 1960 through February 25, 1979.
- These data represent sponsored programs, telecast on individual networks; i.e., no unsponsored or joint-network telecasts are reflected in the listings.
- Programs of under five minutes duration are excluded from the listing.

Information furnished by the A. C. Nielson Company

Satellite Communications

INTELSAT

International Telecommunications Satellite Organization
490 L'Enfant Plaza
Washington, DC 20024
(202) 488-2300

Telephone, telex, facsimile, and data messages, which represent over 95 percent of all international overseas telecommunications traffic, travel from homes and offices until they pass through a central switching facility, where they are "bundled" together into multiplexed frequencies and then transmitted from an earth station antenna to a satellite in outer space. [Huge dish antennae (most of them ten stories in height) to transmit and receive telecommunications signals are continuously automatically locked on a satellite 22,300 miles out in space within a fraction of a degree.] Such accuracy is necessary because often the signal received from the satellite is no stronger than several millionths of a watt. This tiny signal is amplified by the receiving earth station and instantly relayed by land lines to the user.

The process for transmitting international television is similar, except that each television channel, which requires a significant share of the satellite's capacity, is sent on a separate wideband channel. Television today represents only about three percent of the international telecommunications traffic carried by the global satellite system, which is operated by the 101-member International Telecommunications Satellite Organization (INTELSAT). Yet, live international satellite communications, which allowed a billion people to watch the Montreal Olympics, is an important part of today's world and the world of modern telecommunications.

The International Telecommunications Satellite Organization (INTELSAT), headquarters in Washington, DC, was created in August, 1964, through the adoption of interim agreements, signed by eleven countries, for the establishment of a global commercial communications satellite system.

Since February 12, 1973, INTELSAT has operated under definitive agreements, with an organizational structure consisting of (a) an Assembly of Parties (governments that are parties to the INTELSAT Agreement); (b) a Meeting of Signatories (governments or their designated telecommunications entities that have signed the Operating Agreement); (c) a board of governors; and (d) an executive organ headed by a Director General, Mr. Santiago Astrain, of Chile.

The board of governors, which has overall responsibility for the decisions relating to the design, development, construction, establishment, operation, and maintenance of the INTELSAT space segment, is currently composed of 26 governors representing 78 signatories.

Technical and operational services are provided by the Communications Satellite Corporation (Comsat) under a management services contract.

The INTELSAT global satellite system is composed of two essential elements: the space segment, consisting of satellites owned by INTELSAT, and the ground segment, consisting of the earth stations, owned by telecommunications entities in the countries in which they are located.

At present the space segment consists of five satellites in synchronous orbit at an altitude of approximately 35,780 km (22,240 miles). Global service is provided through a combination of INTELSAT IV-A and INTELSAT IV satellites over the Atlantic, Indian, and Pacific ocean regions.

The INTELSAT IV-A has a capacity of 6,000 voice circuits and two television channels, while the INTELSAT IV has a capacity of 4,000 voice circuits plus two television channels. The future generation of satellites—the INTELSAT V—which is expected to be in operation in late 1979, is designed for a capacity of 12,000 voice circuits plus two television channels.

The ground segment of the global system consists of 189 communications antennas at 152 earth station sites in 86 countries.

The combined system of satellites and earth stations provides approximately 500 earth station-to-earth station communications pathways.

In addition to the international voice circuits in full-time use (now approaching 10,000), INTELSAT provides a wide variety of telecommunications services, including telegraph, telex, data, and television to more than 100 countries, territories, and possessions.

INTELSAT currently has two standards for earth stations that operate with its satellites: Standard A, with 30-meter (100 ft.), or larger, dish antenna, 10 stories tall, which can be rotated one degree per second and which can track to within a fraction of a degree a satellite stationed in synchronous orbit; and Standard B, which, at 10 meters (33 ft.) is much less expensive to construct, yet operates at a utilization charge only 1-1/2 times that of the Standard A station.

571

SIGNATORIES TO THE OPERATING AGREEMENT*

Afghanistan
Ministry of Communications of the Royal Government of Afghanistan

Algeria
Government of the Democratic and Popular Republic of Algeria

Angola
Empresa Publica de Telecomunicacoes (PPTEL)

Argentina
Empresa Nacional de Telecomunicaciones de la Republica Argentina (ENTEL)

Australia
Overseas Telecommunications Commission (Australia)

Austria
Government of Austria

Bangladesh
The Telegraph and Telephone Board of Bangladesh

Barbados
Cable and Wireless (West Indies) Limited

Belgium
Regie des Telegraphes et des Telephones

Bolivia
Empresa Nacional de Telecomunicaciones (ENTEL)

Brazil
Empresa Brasileira de Telecomunicacoes (EMBRATEL)

Cameroon
Government of the United Republic of Cameroon

Canada
Teleglobe Canada

Central African Empire
Government of the Central African Empire

Chad
Societe des Telecommunications Internationales du Tchad

Chile
Empresa Nacional de Telecomunicaciones S.A. (ENTEL)

China, People's Republic of
Peking Administration of Long Distance Telecommunications

Colombia
Empresa Nacional de Telecomunicaciones de Colombia (TELECOM)

Costa Rica
Instituto Costarricense de Electricidad

Cyprus
Cyprus Telecommunications Authority

Denmark
Generaldirektoratet for Post-og Telegrafvaesenet

Dominican Republic
Compania Dominicana de Telefonos, C. por A.

Ecuador
Instituto Ecuatoriano de Telecomunicaciones (ETEL)

Egypt, Arab Republic of
Government of the Arab Republic of Egypt

El Salvador
Administracion Nacional de Telecomunicaciones (ANTEL)

Ethiopia
Imperial Board of Telecommunications

Fiji Islands
Fiji International Telecommunications Limited (FINTEL)

Finland
Administration of Posts and Telegraphs of Finland

France
Government of France

Gabon
Societe des Telecommunications Internationales Gabonaises (TIG)

Germany, Federal Republic of
Federal Ministry for Post and Telecommunication

Ghana
Ministry of Transport and Communications

Greece
Hellenic Telecommunications Organization (OTE) S.A.

Guatemala
Government of Guatemala

Haiti
Telecommunications d'Haiti S.A.

Iceland
Government of Iceland

------

*As of October 28, 1977.

India
Overseas Communications Service, Ministry of Communications, Government of India

Indonesia
Government of the Republic of Indonesia

Iran
Telecommunication Company of Iran

Iraq
Government of the Republic of Iraq

Ireland
Department of Posts and Telegraphs

Israel
Government of the State of Israel

Italy
Societa Telespazio

Ivory Coast
Government of the Republic of Ivory Coast

Jamaica
Jamaica International Telecommunications Limited (JAMINTEL)

Japan
Kokusai Denshin Denwa Company, Ltd.

Jordan
Government of the Hashemite Kingdom of Jordan

Kenya
East African External Telecommunications Company, Limited

Korea, Republic of
Government of the Republic of Korea

Kuwait
The Ministry of Communications, the State of Kuwait

Lebanon
Government of Lebanon

Libyan Arab Republic
Government of the Libyan Arab Republic

Liechtenstein
Government of the Principality of Liechtenstein

Luxembourg
Government of Luxembourg

Madagascar
Societe des Telecommunications Internationales de la Republique Malgache (STIMAD)

Malaysia
Telecommunications Department, Malaysia

Mali
Telecommunications Internationales du Mali (T.I.M.)

Mauritania
Government of the Islamic Republic of Mauritania

Mexico
Government of Mexico

Monaco
Government of the Principality of Monaco

Morocco
Government of Morocco

Netherlands
Government of the Kingdom of the Netherlands

New Zealand
Postmaster-General of New Zealand

Nicaragua
Compania Nicaraguense de Telecomunicaciones por Satelite

Nigeria
Nigerian External Telecommunications, Limited

Norway
Norwegian Telecommunications Administration (Teledirektoratet)

Oman
Sultanate of Oman

Pakistan
Government of the Islamic Republic of Pakistan

Panama
Intercontinental de Comunicaciones por Satelite, S.A. (INTERCOMSA)

Paraguay
Administracion Nacional de Telecomunicaciones (ANTELCO)

People's Republic of the Congo
Government of the People's Republic of the Congo

Peru
Empresa Nacional de Telecomunicaciones del Peru (ENTEL PERU)

Philippines
Philippine Communications Satellite Corporation (PHILCOMSAT)

Portugal
Companhia Portuguesa Radio Marconi

Qatar
Government of the State of Qatar

Saudi Arabia
Government of Saudi Arabia

Senegal
Government of the Republic of Senegal

Singapore
Telecommunication Authority of Singapore

South Africa
Department of Posts and Telecommunications of the Republic of South Africa

Spain
Compania Teletonica Nacional de Espana

Sri Lanka
Government of Sri Lanka

Sudan
Government of the Democratic Republic of the Sudan

Sweden
Swedish Telecommunications Administration

Switzerland
Direction Generale de l'Entreprise des Postes, Telephones des Telegraphes Suisses

Syrian Arab Republic
Government of the Syrian Arab Republic

Tanzania
East African External Telecommunications Company, Limited

Thailand
Government of Thailand

Trinidad and Tobago
Trinidad and Tobago External Telecommunications Company Limited (TEXTEL)

Tunisia
Administration for Post, Telegraph and Telephone of Tunisia

Turkey
Government of Turkey

Uganda
East African External Telecommunications Company, Limited

United Arab Emirates
Ministry of Communications of the Government of the United Arab Emirates

United Kingdom
Post Office

United States
Communications Satellite Corporation

Upper Volta
Office des Postes et Telecommunications de Haute-Volta

Vatican City State
Government of the Vatican City State

Venezuela
Venezuelan Telelphone Company (Compania Anonima Nacional Telefonos de Venezuela)

Viet Nam
Government of the Republic of Viet Nam

Yemen Arab Republic
Government of Yemen Arab Republic

Yugoslavia
Community of the Yugoslav Posts, Telegraphs, and Telephone

Zaire
Office National des Postes et Telecommunications du Zaire (ONPTZ)

Zambia
Government of the Republic of Zambia

INTELSAT NON-SIGNATORY USERS

Bahrain
Liberia
Malawi
Maldives
Mauritius
Mozambique
Nauru, Republic of
Niger
Roumania
Seychelles
U.S.S.R.

THE INTELSAT GLOBAL SATELLITE SYSTEM

The INTELSAT global system consists of high-capacity communications satellites stationed in synchronous orbits over the equator 22,240 miles above the Atlantic, Pacific, and Indian oceans. From these positions, each of the satellites serves an area larger than one-third of the earth's surface, thereby providing global coverage.

The satellites in the global system and the more than 200 earth station antennas operating with them provide over 550 pathways, or direct communication links, among more than 85 countries, territories, or possessions. Since satellite services are extended to still other countries through terrestrial connections, about 120 countries, territories, and possessions are using satellite services full time. It is expected that there will be as many as

225 antennas in 100 countries operating in the global system by 1980.

A growing number of countries are also building earth stations within their boundaries and using global system satellites to improve their domestic communications systems. This is making it possible to reach heretofore remote points in countries of increasing importance to U.S. business and industry. Among the countries using global system satellites for domestic communications are Algeria, Brazil, Chile, France, Malaysia, Nigeria, Norway, Oman, Saudi Arabia, Spain, Sudan, and Uganda. In a little over a decade, the INTELSAT global satellite system has established itself as the dominant carrier of all international communications. The system currently handles more than two-thirds of all transoceanic traffic.

Over 95 percent of all traffic carried by the INTELSAT global system consists of telephone calls, teletypewriter messages, and a growing variety of high-speed data services, including computer-to-computer connections. And through transoceanic television, it is now possible for more than a billion people, one out of every four on earth, to see an important international event "live, via satellite."

U.S.–Overseas
Full-time Services
via Satellite

Abu Dhabi
Algeria
Angola
Antigua
Argentina
Ascension Island
Australia
Austria
Bahrain
Bangladesh
Barbados
Belgium
Bolivia
Brazil
Bulgaria
Cameroon
Canary Islands
Chad
Chile
China, Peking
China, Taipei
Colombia
Costa Rica
Cyprus
Czechoslovakia
Denmark
Dominican Republic
Dubai
East Africa
Ecuador
Egypt
El Salvador
Ethiopia
Fiji Islands
Finland
France
French Guiana
French Polynesia
Gabon
Germany
Ghana
Greece
Guam
Guatemala
Guyana
Haiti
Honduras
Hong Kong
Hungary
India
Indonesia
Iran
Iraq
Ireland
Israel
Italy
Ivory Coast
Jamaica
Japan
Jordan
Korea
Kuwait
Lebanon
Liberia
Libya
Luxembourg
Madagascar
Malaysia
Mali
Martinique
Mauritius
Morocco
Netherlands
Netherlands Antilles
New Caledonia
New Zealand
Nigeria
Norway
Oman
Pakistan
Panama
Paraguay
Peru
Philippines
Poland
Portugal
Puerto Rico
Qatar
Ras-Al Khaimah
Rhodesia
Romania
Saudi Arabia
Senegal
Seychelles
Singapore
South Africa
Spain

Sri Lanka
Surinam
Sweden
Switzerland
Syria
Thailand
Trinidad
Tunisia
Turkey
United Kingdom
Upper Volta
Uruguay
U.S.S.R.
Venezuela
Yugoslavia
Zaire
Zambia

TELEVISION VIA SATELLITE

The transmission of live TV across the oceans, little more than a technological promise in the early 1960s, is commonplace today. Countries with more than one-half the world's population now routinely send and receive TV, live and in color, over a satellite system that is global in scale. Telecasts have by satellite reached millions of viewers with news of events from remote places as diverse as the site of an earthquake to the desolate surface of the moon.

Broadcasters have been prompt to explore and develop the new possibilities opened by satellite communications, and the use of satellites for television has shown remarkable growth, from an average of about five transmissions a month in 1965, to more than 650 transmissions per month today. Major news and sports events now often have global audiences; the words *via satellite* appear almost daily on TV screens during major news programs of both the U.S. and overseas TV networks.

Unlimited Reception Points. One of the unique benefits of satellite communications is the ability to transmit TV signals to a large number of receiving points. A single satellite "sees" more than one-third of the earth's surface, and satellites stationed over the Atlantic, Pacific, and Indian oceans provide global coverage. As a result, satellites are a highly efficient method for worldwide-TV-program distribution. This capability is responsible for the rapid growth of multidestination telecasts—telecasts that are received simultaneously at a number of earth stations.

Special-purpose Television. Satellite transmission has expanded the horizons of closed-circuit television, as well as broadcast TV. A variety of dramatic special-purpose telecasts by satellite has demonstrated a large potential for public and commercial applications in the financial, industrial, scientific, educational, and governmental communities. This has drawn new attention to closed-circuit TV for sales and promotion purposes, especially in introducing new projects, facilities, or services, and for training programs, briefings, consultations, or conferences. For example, highly successful international auctions of both art and industrial equipment

have been held by satellite transmission, thereby expanding the audience from room-size to international proportions. A major raw-materials company has telecast dedication ceremonies at its new iron-ore mine from Sydney, Australia, to simultaneous meetings in Tokyo, New York, and London, where potential customers had been assembled as part of a coordinated worldwide sales program. Companies with shareholders in many countries are using satellite closed-circuit TV in conjunction with their annual shareholder meetings. Physicians and medical scientists have been assembled simultaneously in several different European countries to participate in an international closed-circuit TV conference on aerospace medicine and cancer and tuberculosis research. And a live transatlantic press conference has been held, enabling reporters in Los Angeles to ask questions of a motion-picture director and his cast in Madrid.

Economics. One of the factors contributing to the rapid growth in the use of satellite television has been the dramatic reduction in charges since the introduction of commercial service.

EARTH STATIONS IN THE INTELSAT SYSTEM

Earth stations are owned and operated by designated telecommunications entities in the countries where they are located. The stations process all forms of long-distance communications. Thousands of telephone calls, telegraph messages, high-speed data, facsimile, and television signals are both transmitted and received at the same time. Incoming signals, only a fraction of a watt in power, are received from the satellite in the four-gigahertz range (four billion cycles per second), amplified by an antenna, funneled into supersensitive receiver-amplifiers, again boosted in power, and then further processed through the station. Outgoing signals are sent at the same time in the six-gigahertz range.

The flexibility of the system permits instantaneous direct communications between one station and another or among many stations simultaneously.

Each successive generation of stations has been characterized by better performance, lower cost, and simplified operation and maintenance.

Year	Antennas	Stations	Countries
1965	5	5	5
1966	8	8	6
1967	15	14	11
1968	20	19	13
1969	41	36	24
1970	51	43	30
1971	63	52	39
1972	79	65	49
1973	85	68	52
1974	104	83	60
1975	123	97	71
1976	157	126	82
1977	201	163	88
1978	231	199	93
1979	245	201	97

Atlantic Ocean Region

Algeria—Lakhdaria (LK): located in northern Algeria near the Mediterranean Sea and the capital city of Alger. Operated by the Ministry of Posts and Telecommunications. Domestic stations are located at Adrar (AD), Bechar (BE), Beni-Abbes (BN), Djanet (DA), El-Golea (EG), El-Oued (EO), Ghardaia (GR), In-Salah (IS), Lakhdaria (LK), Ourgla (OU), Tamanrasset (TS), Timinoun (TO), and Tindouf (TD).

Angola—Cacuaco (CC): located approximately 20 miles from Luanda, the capital city. Operated by the Companhia Portuguesa Radio Marconi.

Argentina—Balcarce (BA): located approximately 250 miles south of Buenos Aires. Operated by Empresa Nacional de Telecomunicaciones (ENTEL).

Barbados—Barbados (BB): located on the northeast coast approximately 10 miles from Bridgetown. Operated by Cable & Wireless (West Indies), Ltd.

Belgium—Lessive (LI): located approximately 70 miles from Brussels. Operated by the Belgian Telegraph and Telephone Administration.

Brazil—Tangua (TN): located approximately 20 miles northeast of Rio de Janeiro. Operated by Empresa Brasileira de Telecomunicacoes (EMBRATEL). Station also serves tracking, telemetry, and command (TT&C) function. Domestic stations are located at Cuiaba (CU), Manaus (MU), and Boa Vista (BV).

Cameroon—Zamengoe (ZA): located approximately 40 miles west of Yaounde. Operated by Societe des Telecommunications Internationales de Cameroun (INTELCAM). Station also serves tracking, telemetry, and command (TT&C) function.

Canada—Mill Village (MV): located approximately 80 miles southeast of Halifax, Nova Scotia. Operated by TELEGLOBE.

Chile—Longovilo (LO): located approximately 30 miles southwest of Santiago. Operated by Empresa Nacional de Telecomunicaciones S.A. (ENTEL). Domestic stations are located at Longovilo (LO) and Punta Arenas (PA).

Colombia—Choconta (CH): located approximately 50 miles north of Bogota. Operated by Empresa Nacional de Telecomunicaciones (TELECOM).

Dominican Republic—Cambita (CB): located near the village of Cambita Garabitas, Province of San Cristobal. Operated by Compania Dominicana de Telefonos.

Ecuador—Quito (QU): located approximately six miles from Quito, the capital city. Operated by Empresa de Telecomunicaciones del Norte (ETN).

Egypt—Cairo (CI): located in the capital city near the juncture of the Nile River and the Mediterranean Sea. Operated by the Telecommunications Organization, Radio Communications Administration.

El Salvador—Izalco (IZ): located approximately 25 miles west of San Miguel. Operated by Administracion Nacional de Telecomunicaciones (ANTEL).

Ethiopia: Operated by Telecommunications Service Provisional Military Government of Socialist Ethiopia.

Fiji: operated by Fiji International Telecommunications Limited (FINTEL).

France—Pleumeur-Bodou (PB): located in Brittany. Operated by the Ministry of Posts and Telecommunications.

French Guiana—Trou-Biran (TB): located in Cayenne on the coast of the Atlantic Ocean north of the equator. Operated by the Ministry of Posts and Telecommunications.

Martinique—Trois-Ilets (TR): located near Fort-de-France in the Caribbean. Operated by the Ministry of Posts and Telecommunications. Domestic stations are located at Pleumeur-Bodou (PB) and Saint Denis de la Reunion (SD).

Gabon—Nkoltang (NK): located approximately 20 miles southeast of Libreville. Operated by Societe des Telecommunications Internationales Gabonaises (TIG).

Germany—Raisting (RA): located approximately 20 miles southwest of Munich. Operated by Deutsche Bundespost.

Greece—Thermopylae (TH): located approximately 115 miles northwest of Athens. Operated by the Hellenic Telecommunications Organization (OTE).

Haiti—J-C Duvalier (DV): located near the capital city of Port-au-Prince. Operated by Telecommunications d'Haiti.

Iran—Asadabad (AA): located approximately 30 miles southwest of Hamadan. Operated by the Post, Telegraph and Telephone Ministry.

Iraq—Dujail (DL): located approximately 10 miles south of Baghdad. Operated by the Post and Telephone Administration (PTT).

Israel—Emeq Ha'ela (EH): located approximately 35 miles southeast of Tel Aviv. Operated by the Ministry of Communications.

Italy—Fucino (FO): located approximately 75 miles east of Rome. Operated by Societa Telespazio. Station also serves tracking, telemetry, and command (TT&C) function.

Italy—Lario (LR): located on Lake Como about 25 miles north of Milan. Operated by Societa Telespazio.

Ivory Coast—Abidjan (AI): located approximately 15 miles from Abidjan. Operated by Societe de Telecommunications Internationales (INTELCI).

Jamaica—Prospect Pen (PP): located in St. Thomas Parish approximately 15 miles from Kingston. Operated by Jamaica International Telecommunications, Ltd. (JAMINTEL).

Jordan—Baqa (BQ): located approximately 15 miles north of Amman. Operated by the Ministry of Communications.

Kuwait—Umm Al-Aish (UM): located approximately 35 miles northwest of the city of Kuwait.

Operated by the Ministry of Posts, Telegraphs, and Telephone.

Liberia—Sinkor (SK): located in the western part of the country on the Atlantic Ocean. Operated by Liberian Telecommunications Corporation.

Mali—Sullymanbougou (SL): located south of the capital city of Bamako. Operated by Post et Telecommunications Internationales du Mali.

Mexico—Tulancingo (TU): located approximately 80 miles northeast of Mexico City. Operated by the Department of Communications and Transportation.

Morocco—Sehouls (SE): located approximately 12 miles northeast of Rabat. Operated by the Ministry of Posts, Telegraphs, and Telephones.

Mozambique—Boane (BO): located approximately 20 miles from Lourenco Marques, the capital of Mozambique, in southeast Africa. Operated by the Companhia Portuguesa Radio Marconi.

Netherlands—Burum (BM): located approximately 80 miles northeast of Amsterdam. Operated by the Post Telegraph and Telephone Administration (PTT).

Nicaragua—Managua (MN): located approximately five miles southwest of Managua. Operated by NICATELSAT, a company jointly owned by the Nicaraguan government and COMSAT General.

Nigeria—Lanlate (LA): located approximately 75 miles north of Lagos. Operated by Nigerian External Telecommunications, Ltd. Domestic stations are located at Abeokuta (AE), Akure (AU), Bauchi (BH), Benin (BX), Calabar (CL), Enugu (EN), Ibadan (IA), Ilorin (IL), Jos (JO), Kaduna (KA), Kano (KN), Lagos (LS), Maiduguri (MI), Makurdi (MK), Minna (MO), Owerri (OW), Port Harcourt (PH), Sokota (SO), and Yola (YO).

Norway—Eik (EI), Ekofisk (EK), and Frigg (FI): domestic stations operated by the Norwegian Telecommunications Administration.

Oman—Al Hajar (AL) and Salalah (SZ): domestic stations operated by Oman Telecommunications Company, S.A.D.

Panama—Utibe (UT): located approximately 30 miles northeast of Panama City. Operated by Intercontinental de Comunicaciones por Satelites (INTERCOMSA) and jointly owned by INTERCOMSA and COMSAT General.

Paraguay—Aregua (AR): located approximately 50 miles east of the capital city of Asuncion. Operated by ANTELCO, Paraguay.

Peru—Lurin (LU): located approximately 20 miles south of Lima. Operated by the Empresa Nacional de Telecomunicaciones (ENTEL).

Portugal—Ponta Delgada (PN): located in the Azores. Operated by Companhia Portugesa Radio Marconi.

Portugal—Sintra (SI): located west of the Portuguese capital of Lisbon near the Atlantic Ocean. Operated by the Companhia Portuguesa Radio Marconi.

Romania—Cheia (CZ): located approximately 85 miles northwest of Bucharest. Operated by the

Ministry of Transportation and Telecommunications.

Saudi Arabia—Taif (TF): located approximately 25 miles east of Mecca. Operated by the Ministry of Communications.

Senegal—Gandoul (GA): located near Dakar. Operated by Telecommunications Internationales du Senegal (TELESENGAL).

South Africa—Pretoria (PR): located approximately 35 miles north of Johannesburg. Operated by the Department of Posts and Telecommunications of the Republic of South Africa.

Spain—Buitrago (BU): located approximately 50 miles north of Madrid. Operated by Compania Telefonica Nacional de Espana (CTNE). Domestic station is located at Aguimes-Canary Islands (AG).

Sudan—Umm Haraz (UH): located approximately 15 miles south of Khartoum on the east bank of the White Nile. Operated by The Department of Telecommunications. Domestic stations are located at Juba (JZ), Nyala (NY) and Khartoum (KH).

Sweden—Tanum (TM): located approximately 100 miles north of Goteborg in southwest Sweden. Operated by the Swedish Telecommunications Administration and jointly owned by Denmark, Finland, Norway and Sweden.

Switzerland—Leuk (LE): located approximately 25 miles from Montreux. Operated by Swiss PT&T.

Trinidad & Tobago—Matura Point (MA): located on the eastern coast of Trinidad, approximately 35 miles from Port of Spain. Operated by the Trinidad-Tobago External Telecommunications Co., Ltd.

Uganda—Ombachi (OM): located on the west coast near Lake Albert. Operated by the Ministry of Transport and Communications. Domestic stations are located at Arua (AX) and Kampala (KM).

United Kingdom—Goonhilly (GH): located in Cornwall, England. Operated by the Post Office Corporation.

Ascension Island (AS): located on Donkey Island. Operated by Cable & Wireless, Ltd.

United States—Andover (AN): located approximately 90 miles northwest of Portland, Maine. Operated by COMSAT. Station also serves tracking, telemetry, and command (TT&C) function.

Cayey (CY): located approximately 35 miles south of San Juan in east-central Puerto Rico. Operated by COMSAT.

Etam (ET): located in West Virginia approximately 200 miles west of Washington, DC. Operated by COMSAT.

U.S.S.R.—Moscow (MS): located in the capital city. Operated by the Ministry of Posts and Telecommunications of the U.S.S.R.

Lvov (LV): located in the Western Ukraine approximately 40 miles from the Polish border. Operated by the Ministry of Posts and Telecommunications of the U.S.S.R.

Venezuela—Camatagua (CM): located approximately 80 miles southwest of Caracas. Operated by CANTV-Compania Anonima Nacional Telefonos de Venezuela.

Yugoslavia—Jugoslavija (JU): located in the former city of Ivanjica approximately 100 miles south of the capital city of Belgrade. Operated by the community of Yugoslav Posts, Telegraphs, and Telephones.

Zaire—Nsele (NS): located approximately 25 miles from Kinshasa. Operated by the Office des Ports et Telecommunications.

Indian Ocean Region

Afghanistan—Kabul: operated by the Ministry of Information of the Democratic Republic of Afghanistan.

Australia—Ceduna (CE): located approximately 350 miles northwest of Adelaide in South Australia. Operated by Australian OTC.

Bahrain—Ras Abu Jarjur (RJ): located approximately 20 miles south of the city of Manama. Operated by Cable & Wireless, Ltd.

Bangladesh—Betbunia (BI): located in the Chittagong Hill Tracts District near the Bay of Bengal. Operated by Bangladesh Telegraph and Telephone (BT&T).

China—Peking (PE): located northeast of Peking. Operated by the Bureau of Long Distance Communications.

China—Taipei (TI): located near Taipei on Taiwan. Operated by the Ministry of Communications.

Germany—Raisting (RA): located approximately 20 miles southwest of Munich. Operated by Deutsche Bundespost.

Greece—Thermopylae (TH): located approximately 115 miles northwest of Athens. Operated by the Hellenic Telecommunications Organization (OTE).

India—Vikram (VI): located near Arvi approximately 150 miles from Bombay in the western part of India. Operated by the Government of India Overseas Communications Service.

Ahmed (AY): located approximately 150 miles northeast of New Delhi. Operated by the Government of India Overseas Communications Service.

Indonesia—Djatiluhur (DJ): located approximately 55 miles from Djakarta. Operated by the Indonesian Satellite Communications Corp. (INDOSAT).

Iran—Asadabad (AA): located in northwestern Iran approximately 30 miles west of Hamadan. Operated by the Post, Telegraph, and Telephone Ministry.

Iraq—Dujail (DL): located approximately 10 miles south of Baghdad. Operated by the Post and Telephone Administration (PTT).

Italy—Fucino (FO): located approximately 75 miles east of Rome. Operated by Societa Telespazio. Station also serves tracking, telemetry, and command (TT&C) function.

Japan—Yamaguchi (YA): located approximately 250 miles southwest of Kyoto. Operated by Kokusai Denshin Denwa Co., Ltd.

Kenya—Longonot (LG): located in the Rift Valley of Kenya near Nairobi. Operated by the East African External Telecommunications Company, Ltd.

Korea, Republic of—Kum San (KS): located approximately 75 miles south of Seoul. Operated by the Ministry of Communications.

Kuwait—Umm Al-Aish (UM): located approximately 35 miles northwest of the city of Kuwait. Operated by the Ministry of Posts, Telegraphs, and Telephone.

Lebanon—Arbaniyeh (AB): located approximately 20 miles northwest of Beirut. Operated by the Ministry of Posts, Telegraph, and Telephone.

Madagascar—Philibert Tsiranana (PT): located approximately 60 miles from Tananarive. Operated by Societe des Telecommunications Internationales de la Republique Malgache.

Malawi—Kanjedza (KJ): located approximately 15 miles from the capital city of Zomba. Operated by Cable & Wireless, Ltd.

Malaysia—Kuantan (KU): located approximately 100 miles east of Kuala Lumpur. Operated by the Ministry of Works, Posts, and Telecommunications.

Maldives—Male (ME): located on the southern tip of the island. Operated by the Telecommunications Department, Republic of Maldives.

Mali—Sullymanbougou (SL): located south of the capital city of Bamako. Operated by Post et Telecommunications Internationales du Mali.

Mauritius—Cassis (CS): located near Port Louis, the capital of Mauritius, an island off the east coast of Africa. Operated by Cable & Wireless, Ltd.

Niger—Niamey (NI): located in the capital city of Niamey on the Niger River. Operated by the Office of Post and Telecommunications.

Nigeria—Lanlate (LA): located approximately 75 miles north of Lagos. Operated by Nigerian External Telecommunications, Ltd.

Oman—Al Hajar (AL): located near the capital city of Muscat on the southeast Arabian peninsula. Operated by Cable & Wireless, Ltd.

Pakistan—Deh Mandro (DM): located approximately 30 miles north of Karachi. Operated by the Ministry of Communications.

Philippines—Pinugay (PG): located approximately 30 miles east of Manila. Operated by the Philippines Communications Satellite Corp. (PHILCOMSAT).

Qatar—Doha (DO): located in the capital city on the Persian Gulf. Operated by the Ministry of Communications and Transportation.

Saudi Arabia—Riyadh (RI): located in the capital city in the country's interior. Operated by the Ministry of Communications. Domestic stations are located at Abha (AH) and Buraida (BD).

Seychelles—Bon Espoir (BS): located near the capital city of Victoria. Operated by Cable & Wireless, Ltd.

Singapore—Sentosa (SN): located approximately three miles from downtown Singapore on the Island of Sentosa. Operated by the Telecommunication Authority of Singapore.

South Africa—Pretoria (PR): located approximately 35 miles north of Johannesburg. Operated by the Department of Post and Telecommunications of the Republic of South Africa.

Spain—Buitrago (BU): located approximately 50 miles north of Madrid. Operated by Compania Telefonica Nacional de Espana (CTNE).

Sri Lanka—Padukka (PD): located near the capital city of Colombo. Operated by Overseas Telecommunications Service.

Thailand—Si Racha (SR): located approximately 50 miles from Bangkok. Operated by the Post and Telegraph Department of the Kingdom of Thailand.

United Arab Emirates—Ras Al-Khaimah (RK): located in the city of Ras Al-Khaimah on the Persian Gulf. Operated by the Ministry of Communications, Ras Al-Khaimah Telecommunications Authority.

United Kingdom—Goonhilly (GH): located in Cornwall, England. Operated by the Post Office Corporation.

Hong Kong (HK): located on Stanley Peninsula. Operated by Cable & Wireless, Ltd.

Yemen—Sanaa (SX): located in the capital city in the interior of the country. Operated by Cable & Wireless, Ltd.

Zambia—Mwembeshi (MW): located in the center of Zambia near the capital city of Lusaka. Operated by the General Post Office, General Telecommunications Division.

Pacific Ocean Region

Australia—Carnarvon (CA): located north of Perth. Operated by Australian Overseas Telecommunications Commission (OTC). Station also serves tracking, telemetry, and command (TT&C) function.

Moree (MO): located near Moree north of Sydney in East Australia. Operated by Australian OTC.

Canada—Lake Cowichan (LC): located in western Canada on Vancouver Island. Operated by TELEGLOBE.

China—Peking (PE): located northwest of Peking. Operated by the Bureau of Long Distance Communications.

Shanghai (SH): located near the city of Shanghai. Operated by the Bureau of Long Distance Communications.

China—Taipei (TI): located near Taipei on Taiwan. Operated by the Ministry of Communications.

Fiji Islands—Suva (SV): located in the capital city on the Koro Sea. Operated by Cable & Wireless, Ltd.

France—New Caledonia, I'lle Nou (LL): located on the southern tip of the island on the Coral Sea.

Operated by the Ministry of Post and Telecommunications.

Japan—Ibaraki (IB): located approximately 90 miles north of Tokyo. Operated by Kakusai Denshin Denwa Co., Ltd.

Korea, Republic of—Kum San (KS): located approximately 75 miles south of Seoul. Operated by the Ministry of Communications.

Malaysia—Kota Kinabalu (KK) and Kuantan (KU): domestic stations. Operated by the Ministry of Works, Posts, and Telecommunications.

Nauru, Republic of—Nauru Island (NZ): located in the southwest Pacific, 33 miles south of the equator. Operated by the Government of Nauru.

New Zealand—Warkworth (WA): located approximately 75 miles north of Auckland on the North Island. Operated by New Zealand Post Office.

Philippines—Pinugay (PG): located approximately 30 miles east of Manila. Operated by the Philippines Communications Satellite Corp. (PHILCOMSAT).

Singapore—Sentosa (SN): located approximately three miles from downtown Singapore on the island of Sentosa. Operated by the Telecommunication Authority of Singapore.

Thailand—Si Racha (SR): located approximately 50 miles from Bangkok. Operated by the Post and Telegraph Department of the Kingdom of Thailand.

United Kingdom—Hong Kong (HK): located on Stanley Peninsula. Operated by Cable & Wireless, Ltd.

United States—Jamesburg (JB): located in the Carmel Valley approximately 35 miles southwest of Monterey in the central part of California. Operated by COMSAT.

Pulantat (PL): located approximately four miles from the capital city of Agana on the island of Guam. Operated by RCA Global Communications.

Paumalu (PA): located approximately 40 miles north of Honolulu, Hawaii. Operated by COMSAT. Station also serves tracking, telemetry, and command (TT&C) function.

Brewster (BR): located approximately halfway between Spokane and Seattle, Washington. Operated by COMSAT.

COMSAT

Communications Satellite Corporation
950 L'Enfant Plaza SW
Washington, DC 20024
Phone: (202) 554-6000
Telex: 89-2343
TWX: 710-822-9242

COMSAT is the privately owned U.S. corporation formed in February 1963 to carry out a mandate of the Congress under the Communications Satellite Act of 1962. The Act directed COMSAT to establish a global commercial communications satellite system in cooperation with other countries as quickly as practical.

COMSAT derives most of its revenues from the satellite services it provides to the U.S. communications common carriers serving the public between the U.S. and foreign points.

COMSAT offers U.S. users a wide variety of satellite services for message and private-line telephone, telegraph, low-, medium-, and high-speed data, television, and facsimile communications. COMSAT provides its global system services through satellites of the International Telecommunications Satellite Organization (INTELSAT), in which COMSAT has an ownership interest of about 25 percent, and through U.S. earth stations, 50-percent-owned, operated, and managed by COMSAT.

COMSAT General Corporation, a wholly owned subsidiary, provides maritime satellite (MARISAT) communications services to the U.S. Navy and commercial shipping and offshore industries, and leases the capacity of its COMSTAR satellites to AT&T for U.S. domestic communications. COMSAT General is also participating in Satellite Business Systems, a partnership formed to establish an advanced U.S. domestic satellite communications system.

Extensive research and development programs are carried out at COMSAT Laboratories for INTELSAT, COMSAT, COMSAT General, and other organizations to advance satellite-communications technology.

_____

Information for the above was provided by INTELSTAT and COMSAT, and used with their permission.

Scripts

Where to Send, and How to Protect, Scripts and Ideas for TV shows

Thousands of people wish to sell their scripts or ideas for television shows, and yet few know where to start. Following is a script of an actual television show, which will provide you with a sample of how a script should be presented. Here are a few suggestions for where to submit your script:

1. *Production companies.* Listed in this book are the major production companies in the United States. Production companies find properties and then begin to put all the pieces together for a pilot or a complete movie or series. They are usually busy, so don't expect a quick answer or any lengthy analysis of your script. They give straightforward answers as to whether they can use the script or if they would like to see something further on your idea. If they can't use the script or the idea, they will tell you so.

2. *Producers.* Producers usually work independently, but some are linked with the networks or the major film companies. Their affiliations are loosely structured, so they are generally in control of their own destinies, and if they find a property they are sure of, they can sign contracts and make commitments. The producers in the film industry are the money men. They find the property, raise the money for the project, hire all the people, and then sell the idea to a film company or network once the project is completed. Contact the Producers Guild of America, 8201 Beverly Blvd., Los Angeles, CA 90048 for information on how to get in touch with specific producers.

3. *Directors.* Directors are constantly in touch with producers, production companies, film companies, and networks, because they are usually seeking their next assignments. If they are successful directors, they will have clout, and producers, production companies, film companies, and networks will listen when they say they have found an excellent property. Because the directors are the work horses of the industry, sending your script or idea for a TV show or movie to one of them may prove beneficial: if he or she finds the project challenging, exciting, and fresh, his or her enthusiasm and reputation may get you where other avenues may have failed to get you. For a comprehensive list of directors contact the Directors Guild of America, 7950 Sunset Blvd., Hollywood, CA 90046.

PROTECTING YOUR IDEA

There are basically three ways to protect your idea.
1. Put a complete script or explanation of your idea in an envelope and mail it to yourself, registered. (Do not open the envelope.) This will give you a good case for the date of your idea and for its exact contents.
2. The Writer's Guild-West in Los Angeles offers the second means of protecting your script or idea. The Writer's Guild-West has for decades helped creative people by allowing them to register their ideas, scripts, plays, etc. with them for a fee. For Guild members the fee is $4 for each registration, and for non-members it is $10 for each registration. A person may register as many ideas, scripts, plays, story ideas, etc. as he or she wishes. Naturally, the service is open to everyone. The Guild is located at 8955 Beverly Blvd., Los Angeles, CA 90048.
3. Another way of protecting your idea, script, story, play, etc. is to send it to your lawyer with a dated cover letter. It also helps if you put the date on each page of your presentation.

If we may add a bit of personal history: We have been selling ideas for books for years and have never lost an idea because someone stole it. The truth is that an idea is only as good as the people executing it. This means that you will have to worry more about the quality of the producer, director, or production company you deal with than whether you will have your idea stolen.

Another fact to keep in mind is that there are thousands of people trying to get into television with their ideas and scripts and the market itself is very competitive, with many, many professionals vying for attention for their ideas and scripts. So don't think it will be easy, but keep after it, and if you think you're good and your ideas are good, you'll break through in time.

HAPPY DAYS™

"Howard's 45th Fiasco"
#60533-049

Teleplay by
Frank Buxton

Produced by
Mark Rothman
Lowell Ganz
Tony Marshall

A MILLER/MILKIS PRODUCTION
In association with Garry Marshall
SHOOTING SCRIPT
September 24, 1975

CAST

RICHIE CUNNINGHAM ... RON HOWARD
HOWARD CUNNINGHAM .. TOM BOSLEY
MARION CUNNINGHAM .. MARION ROSS
JOANIE CUNNINGHAM .... ERIN MORAN
FONZIE .... HENRY WINKLER
POTSIE .... ANSON WILLIAMS
RALPH .... DONNY MOST
ARNOLD .... PAT MORITA

SETS

INTERIORS:
CUMMINGHAM LIVING ROOM
ARNOLD'S
ARNOLD'S BATHROOM
FONZIE'S ROOM

ACT ONE

A

FADE IN:

INT. CUNNINGHAM LIVING ROOM/KIT-CHEN - MORNING

MARION AND JOANIE ARE PUTTING CANDLES IN A BIRTHDAY CAKE. RICHIE HURRIES DOWNSTAIRS. ALL THREE ARE WEARING PARTY HATS.

RICHIE
Here he comes, get ready to embarrass him.

MARION AND JOANIE JOIN RICHIE IN FRONT OF THE STAIRS. HOWARD COMES BOUNCING DOWN THE STAIRS, THE FAMILY SINGS "HAPPY BIRTHDAY" TO HOWARD, AS HE BEAMS APPRECIATIVELY. AT THE FINISH OF THE SONG, JOANIE PRESENTS THE CAKE TO HOWARD, WHO SCOOPS SOME ICING WITH HIS FINGER AND LICKS IT OFF. MARION PUTS A LITTLE TOP HAT, PARTY HAT, ON HOWARD'S HEAD.

HOWARD
Thank you, loved ones, I really appreciate this. Would anybody be offended if I had cereal for breakfast instead? You know I'm a sucker for snap, crackle, and pop.

MARION TAKES THE CAKE.

MARION
Don't be silly, dear, the cake's for dinner.

JOANIE
How old are you now, Dad?

HOWARD
I'm forty-three years young, dear.

MARION
Excuse me dear, but you're forty-five.

HOWARD
(SMILING) Look at this, she took away two years in thirty seconds. I'm sure I'm forty-three, dear.

MARION
Excuse me Howard, you're forty-five.

HOWARD AND MARION SMILE THROUGH CLENCHED TEETH NOW.

HOWARD
Forty-three, Marion.

MARION
Forty-five.

JOANIE
Look, a birthday fight.

RICHIE
I've never seen a birthday fight. I remember their Thanksgiving fight when Dad broke the wishbone with his teeth.

MARION
We're not fighting children, just disagreeing. (TO HOWARD) Forty-five.

HOWARD
Wait a second, I can prove I'm forty-three.

RICHIE
You'd better quit while you're ahead.

HOWARD
Look, Marion, I was thirty-one when Joanie was born, right?

MARION
Right.

HOWARD
Okay, so Joanie is twelve, and thirty-one and twelve is forty-three, right?

JOANIE
But, Dad, I'm fourteen.

HOWARD
You're twelve. (TO RICHIE) Isn't she twelve?

JOANIE
(TO RICHIE) I'm fourteen.

RICHIE
You act ten.

JOANIE
Sit on it.

HOWARD
Hold it. You sure you're fourteen, Joanie?

JOANIE
Sure I'm sure. Last April every kid in my class punched my arm fourteen times. They all wore rings.

HOWARD
Where have the years gone!

MARION
See, dear, you are forty-five.

HOWARD
(CRESTFALLEN) I was sure I was forty-three.

HE SITS DEJECTEDLY IN HIS CHAIR.

MARION
It's not that big a difference, dear.

JOANIE
Our gym teacher told us once you're over the hill, what's the difference how far?

HOWARD SHOOTS HER A LOOK.

JOANIE (CONT'D)

She's not a good teacher. Well, I guess I'll go to school. 'Bye, everybody. (KISSES HOWARD ON THE CHEEK) Happy Birthday, Dad.

JOANIE EXITS, HOWARD LOOKS AFTER HER.

HOWARD
I wish I was forty-three again.

RICHIE
Why? Forty-five isn't old.

MARION
It certainly isn't. You do the same things today that you did twenty years ago.

HOWARD
I do.

MARION PICKS UP BIRTHDAY CARDS AND ATTEMPTS TO CHANGE THE SUBJECT.

MARION
Look at the beautiful card Aunt Bessie sent you, and here's one from Uncle George.

HOWARD
The same things.

MARION
Bessie sent a little Teddy Bear holding a four and a five. I wonder where she got that?

RICHIE
Do the bear's eyes move?

MARION
No, his tail does.

RICHIE
I got eyes when I was six.

HOWARD
I never realized it before but I do do the same things today I did twenty years ago . . . *exactly* the same.

MARION
No you don't.

HOWARD
Yes I do. What happens when I get tense?

MARION
Your back goes out.

HE STANDS UP, AND FREEZES IN A BENT-OVER POSITION.

HOWARD
It's out now. I can do this—(BENDS OVER) I can't do this—(TRIES TO STRAIGHTEN UP) Exactly like every other time.

FONZIE ENTERS FROM THE KITCHEN.

FONZIE
Hey, Mr. C. Lose something?

HOWARD
Yeah. Two years of my life.

FONZIE
You sure it's in the house? Happy Birthday.

HOWARD
Thanks, but did you know I'm in a rut, Fonz? (TO RICHIE AND MARION) If Ralph Edwards ever did, "This Is Your Life, Howard Cunningham," it would be the shortest, dullest half-hour on television.

FONZIE
I'll say.

RICHIE
Dad, everybody can't be a Mantle or a Gable, or a. . . .

FONZIE

A Fonz.

MARION

Tonight's birthday party will cheer you up. Don't forget to pick up the ice cream.

HOWARD

Why should I pick up ice cream? There's nothing to celebrate. Face it, Marion. Every year of my life is exactly the same.

MARION

Well, get another flavor.

FONZIE

This family is a million laughs. Hey, Mr. C. I hear what you're saying. Every year of *my* life is the same. I love it.

HOWARD

Well, I don't love mine. When I was your age I had dreams. I wanted to be a painter. I wanted to go to Tahiti, and paint like Gauguin.

MARION

Oh, Howard, you're not going to Tahiti. You know how you hate sand between your toes.

RICHIE

I didn't know you painted. Every time we paint anything around here you get nauseous from the fumes.

HOWARD

Thanks for the encouragement. I'm going to work. . . . Like I do *every* day. See you later.

HOWARD GOES TO THE DOOR AND OPENS IT.

MARION

What's it like out, Howard?

HOWARD

The same.

HE EXITS.

FONZIE

Who's Gauguin?

RICHIE

A painter.

FONZIE

Walls or pictures?

RICHIE

Pictures. I wish I could cheer him up. Mom, can I run Dad's birthday party tonight? I got a great idea.

MARION

I don't think he wants a party.

RICHIE

He's just saying that. I'll show him he's had an exciting life. I gotta go to school. (KISSES MARION)

FONZIE

Well, I gotta go to work. Goodbye. (KISSES MARION AND GOES TO DOOR) You know . . . I used to think my life was dull.

RICHIE

Really? What did you do?

FONZIE

Waited, and sure enough things picked up when I started kindergarten. (STARTS OUT) I checked out the chicks and we buried ourselves in the sand box. EEEEY.

FONZIE EXITS.

DISSOLVE TO:

B

INT. ARNOLD'S - NIGHT

IT'S DARK AND EMPTY, AS HOWARD ENTERS. HE'S STILL DEPRESSED, BUT NO LONGER HUNCHED OVER.

HOWARD

(YELLING) Anybody here? Arnold?

ARNOLD COMES TO THE BATHROOM DOOR.

ARNOLD

Who is it? Oh, Mr. Cunningham. I'm closed.

HOWARD

How come?

ARNOLD

Today is Confucius' birthday. I always close.

HOWARD

I thought you were Japanese.

ARNOLD

On my father's side. My mother is Chinese. I speak Japanese, Chinese, Korean, and a little Hungarian.

HOWARD

What do you consider yourself?

ARNOLD

Good looking. Little short maybe but cute.

HOWARD

Oh. I need some ice cream for a birthday party tonight.

ARNOLD

No kidding. I thought I was only one in Milwaukee who celebrates Confucius' birthday.

HOWARD

No, it's *my* birthday.

ARNOLD

I'll get you the ice cream in a minute. I have to finish some work. (INDICATES MEN'S ROOM) You come in, we'll talk.

THEY START INTO THE BATHROOM.

HOWARD

You really close on Confucius' birthday?

ARNOLD

Sure. I'm surprised they don't close the schools.

HOWARD

Not many people in this country know it's Confucius' birthday.

ARNOLD

That's okay. No one in China knows it's your birthday.

CUT TO:

C

INT. BATHROOM - CONTINUOUS ACTION

ARNOLD

Where was I?

ARNOLD TAKES A MARKER AND STARTS WRITING GRAFITTI ON THE WALL. ARNOLD HAS TO STAND ON A CHAIR TO REACH HIGH ON THE WALL.

HOWARD

This is the "work" you had to do?

ARNOLD

Yes, but I'm on my last wall.

HOWARD

You write that stuff? I thought the kids did it.

ARNOLD

Kids not funny. I write good stuff. Brings in the crowds. (WRITES) "Want a good time, call Emma."

ARNOLD LAUGHS, BUT HOWARD DOESN'T.

For such a big day, you don't look happy.

HOWARD

Arnold, today I woke up and realized I'm forty-five years old and I've never done anything exciting.

ARNOLD

Whose life is exciting? Look at me, it's Confucius' birthday and I'm writing on a bathroom wall. I'm just like you—just another John Doe.

HOWARD

But my life has *always* been dull.

ARNOLD

Mine too.

HOWARD

Really?. . . I guess Richie was right. A lot of people lead dull lives.

ARNOLD

Sure. Mine the dullest . . . unless you count the time I got the Congressional Medal of Honor.

HOWARD

You're kidding.

ARNOLD

No. World War Two. I single-handedly captured a hundred-fifty Japanese.

HOWARD

How?

ARNOLD

No big deal. I dress up like Japanese general, cross the lines and say, "Hey, come on, you guys, let's surrender."

HOWARD

You won the Congressional Medal of Honor.

ARNOLD

So I win medal. So I have dinner with Roosevelt. Nice guy. We had a nice chat by the fireside. I petted his dog, Fala. Eleanor brought me cookies. It was years ago. Now I'm in the same rut as you.

HOWARD

At least you have memories. You know where I spent the war? Fort Dix, New Jersey. I was a cook. They called me Cookie Cunningham. The highlight of my career was the day General Patton tasted my meat loaf—and slapped my face. Why am I sitting here whining? My family is going to make me a nice party. I've got to go home. Get me my ice cream.

ARNOLD

What flavor you want? I got twenty-five flavors.

HOWARD

Vanilla.

ARNOLD

Vanilla. You are dull.

THEY EXIT.

DISSOLVE TO:

D

INT. CUNNINGHAM LIVING ROOM - NIGHT

JOANIE IS LOOKING OUT THE WINDOW.

JOANIE
He's here.

MARION
Does he still look sad?

JOANIE
He's getting out of the car. . . . He's dancing. No, he stepped in something. . . . Now he's coming and he looks all right.

MARION AND RICHIE RUSH IN FROM THE KITCHEN. THE FRONT DOOR OPENS AND HOWARD ENTERS, HAPPY.

HOWARD
Hi—I'm home.

MARION GRABS HIM AND PULLS HIM INTO THE EASY CHAIR.

MARION
Sit right down here, Howard. Make yourself comfortable.

HOWARD
I want to go up and wash my hands.

MARION
No you don't.

RICHIE
(SHOUTS) Let's watch television.

HOWARD
I'm not facing the TV.

RICHIE LOOKS AT TV GUIDE.

RICHIE
What luck! "This Is Your Life. . ." is on.

HOWARD
Isn't that on Sunday, Richard?

RICHIE
No it's tonight. This Is. . . Your. . . Life!!! Howard Cunningham!!!

HOWARD
Oh come on, *this is ridiculous!*

JOANIE
That's just what I told him. But who listens to me?

RICHIE STANDS UP AND RECITES. HE HAS A SPOON IN HIS HAND THAT HE USES AS A MICROPHONE.

RICHIE
Yes, Howard Cunningham . . . on the occasion of your forty-fifth birthday we proudly present *your* life, with my co-host and co-master of ceremonies, one of your best friends in the neighborhood.

HOWARD
You brought Warren from the lodge?

RICHIE
No.

HOWARD
You brought Jack from the store?

RICHIE
No.

HOWARD
Who did you bring?

RICHIE
Come on out Best Friend.

POTSIE ENTERS.

POTSIE
Hi, Mr. C.

HOWARD
Hi, Best Friend.

POTSIE
I'm glad to be here, Mr. C. I didn't know I was one of your close friends until Richie told me this afternoon.

HOWARD
It was a secret.

POTSIE
We can pal around together—go to a ball game.

HOWARD
Sure, Potsie.

POTSIE SITS DOWN.

RICHIE
Moving right along—

HOWARD
(SOTTO TO RICHIE) I'm not taking him to a ball game.

RICHIE
You don't have to. Now, on with (ANNOUNCES) "This Is Your Life, Howard Cunningham." Mom, get ready.

MARION AND JOANIE EXIT INTO KITCHEN.

RICHIE (CONT'D)
Howard Cunningham, now we look into the dim recesses of your life history.

HOWARD
You wrote all this yourself?

RICHIE
Yeah, Dad. The dim recesses of your life history. The life you think is the same thing over and over. You think your life is dull! Ha, ha, ha!

POTSIE
Dig this voice, Mr. C. . . . Does it remind you of anyone? Who's this lady?

FLORENCE PRISM (O.S.)
I remember Howard in the third grade spelling bee.

HOWARD
It's my mother. You flew my mother in from Florida. Ma . . .

RICHIE
It's not Grandma.

HOWARD
Oh.

RICHIE
(ANNOUNCING) But, here direct from some old teacher's home is Miss Florence Prism, your third grade teacher!

RICHIE OPENS DOOR.

PRISM (O.S.)
Oh—

RICHIE
Sorry.

POTSIE
How about that?

A VERY AGED AND DOTTERING MISS PRISM COMES OUT OF THE KITCHEN. SHE GOES UP TO RICHIE.

PRISM
Oh, Howard, how you've grown.

HOWARD
Miss Prism, I'm over here.

PRISM.
Boy, did you get fat.

RICHIE
(JUMPING IN) Miss Prism, tell us in your own words the exciting story of how Howard Cunningham won the annual third grade spelling contest.

PRISM
Where's Ralph Edwards?

RICHIE
He's not here.

PRISM
Why?

RICHIE
(PUSHES ON) Now what about this headline in his scrapbook, "Cunningham Wins Spelling Bee."

PRISM
He didn't win it. That was his smart cousin Lawrence. Howie went down the tubes in the first round.

HOWARD
(SAD) I couldn't spell "house."

RICHIE
Thank you for coming, Miss Prism.

PRISM
You're welcome. (TO HOWARD) I was expecting Ralph Edwards. You have a lot of nerve making me come out of my house for this. (SPELLS) H-O-U-S-E.

SHE EXITS.

RICHIE
Let's move on. And now, Howard Cunningham, we move from public school on to high school where you discovered a new talent. Here's another voice from your past.

O.S. WE HEAR A VOICE.

RALPH (O.S.)
(IN ITALIAN ACCENT) Howard, you played the horn so well. And who doesn't remember when it rained during half time and you threw yourself over the horn so it wouldn't rust.

POTSIE
Do you recognize that voice from your past?

HOWARD
It's Ralph.

RICHIE
But he's standing in for your old Bandmaster Wilheim Schmidt.

RALPH COMES CARRYING A BAND UNIFORM JACKET AND BAND HAT AND A BEAT-UP OLD TUBA. THE HAT IS SIMILAR TO A WEST POINT DRESS HAT. RALPH IS WEARING A HAT USUALLY WORN BY SOMEBODY'S GRANDFATHER.

RALPH

Buon giorno.

HOWARD

Schmidt was German.

RALPH

Sorry, I don't do German.

HOWARD

You don't do Italian either.

RICHIE

The real Bandmaster Schmidt was unavailable this evening. We went to his house and he sic'd his dogs on us.

HOWARD

That's how he got us to march.

THEY'RE PUTTING THE BAND UNIFORM ON HOWARD.

POTSIE

You look terrific in that, pal. We don't have to go to the ball game. We can go to the fights.

HOWARD

I'm busy.

POTSIE

When?

HOWARD

All the time.

RALPH

(IN ACCENT) Howard, show them why they nicknamed you "Magic Lips." (SHOVES HORN TO HOWARD)

HOWARD

Did I play this as a little kid?

HOWARD PLAYS "OOMPA, OOMPA, OOM-PA" ALL IN THE SAME NOTE.

RICHIE

He's just warming up.

HOWARD

No, that was it. (UPSET) I lost my lip.

RICHIE

The best is yet to come.

HOWARD

(STILL UPSET) I can't even button the jacket. Joanie's fourteen. I was in high school twenty-eight years ago.

RICHIE

And how about your lovely family which all started with this voice.

MARION (O.S.)

Howard, your first words to me were, "What is a nice girl like you doing in a place like this?"

HOWARD

Who is that?

RICHIE

That's right, Howard. That's your bride, the former Marion Kelp. Here to re-create the most important day of your life.

MARION ENTERS FROM THE KITCHEN WEARING A BRIDAL VEIL AND CARRYING A BOUQUET. RICHIE PLACES A TOP HAT OVER HOWARD'S BAND HAT. POTSIE ENTERS BEHIND MARION AND SINGS, "I LOVE YOU TRULY." WHEN POTSIE FINISHES SINGING, MARION IS NEXT TO HOWARD.

RICHIE (CONT'D)

Kiss the bride.

HOWARD

I'll try but I lost my lip.

RALPH

Thats'a nice.

RICHIE

Sit down, Schmidt. As the years went on your accomplishments grew. Yes it was just this past year when you took a stray lad off the streets. Here he is now a member of the Cunningham family. Do you recognize this voice?

FONZIE (O.S.)

Heyyy . . .

HOWARD

That one I know.

RICHIE

Yes! Here he is!

FONZIE

All the way from upstairs . . .

POTSIE

Arthur Fonzarelli . . . the Fonz!

FONZIE ENTERS. RICHIE HANDS HIM A PIECE OF PAPER.

FONZIE

He's got on a hat and everything. This family's so much fun.

POTSIE

We're going to the fights together.

RICHIE

Read, Fonz.

FONZIE
(READS OFF PAPER) Howard Cunningham . . . You took this Cool Cat off the street and put a roof over my head, not to mention an occasional warm meal in my tummy. (LOOKS AT RICHIE AGAIN) But more than just making a home for me, you befriended my bike. Gave it a beautiful home, a nice paved driveway. What did you ask for all this?

ALL
Nothing!

FONZIE
Nothing my kazoo, fifty bucks a month for a little walk-up room with a funny roof. Cheezzz . . .

RICHIE
Thank you, Fonz. And now let me read these other accomplishments. You almost made the basketball team in high school. You almost got your picture in the Hardware Journal. You were almost Grand PooPah of your lodge. And listen to this! You almost won the Irish Sweepstakes.

HOWARD
That's enough. Thank you for the lovely party. And you've helped make it clear to me that my life isn't worth looking back at.

HE STARTS OUT.

MARION
Where are you going, Howard?

HOWARD
I'm going to Tahiti.

POTSIE
Does that mean we're not going to the fights?

HOWARD EXITS UPSTAIRS.

FONZIE
He's right. I told you, you should have done "This Is Your Life, Fonz."

DISSOLVE TO:

E

INT. CUNNINGHAM LIVING ROOM - NIGHT

THE LIVING ROOM IS EMPTY FOR A MOMENT. THE FRONT DOOR OPENS AND RICHIE DRAGS IN.

MARION (O.S.)
(OFF, FROM THE KITCHEN) Howard?

RICHIE
No, it's me, Mom.

RICHIE FLOPS ON THE COUCH, GROANING. MARION ENTERS FROM THE KITCHEN. SHE'S STILL WEARING HER HAT AND GLOVES. SHE JUST CAME IN FROM SHOPPING AND IS CARRYING BAGS.

MARION
What's the matter, dear?

RICHIE
I never realized how hard Dad works. Those paint cans keep getting heavier.

MARION
Well, it was nice of you to help him out at the store today. This birthday business got him down. He didn't say a word this morning. Is your father with you?

RICHIE
He went home a couple of hours ago. He was depressed so I gave him the afternoon off.

A DOOR SLAM IS HEARD UPSTAIRS.

MARION
That's the bathroom door. He must be home.

RICHIE AND MARION LOOK EXPECTANTLY AT THE STAIRS. AFTER A MOMENT, JOANIE COMES DOWN, READING A MOVIE MAGAZINE AND EATING AN APPLE.

MARION (CONT'D)
Joanie!

JOANIE
(STARTLED) What?!

MARION
I thought you were your father.

JOANIE
No, he's the hefty man with the deep voice.

RICHIE
Is Dad upstairs?

JOANIE
No, I saw him about one o'clock. He took a bottle of suntan oil, said something about how hot it must be in Tahiti, and drove off.

RICHIE
Why didn't you stop him?

JOANIE
There's plenty more suntan oil.

RICHIE
Mom, where do you suppose he went?

MARION
(STARTING TO WORRY) I don't know.

JOANIE
Do you really think he went to Tahiti?

MARION
Of course not. Everything's just fine. There's got to be a reasonable explanation for this.

MARION GETS UP AND STARTS TO PACE FRANTICALLY BACK AND FORTH.

MARION (CONT'D)
The explanation is, children, your father has run away from home.

THEY REACT.

FADE OUT.

END OF ACT ONE

ACT TWO

H

RESET:

INT. CUNNINGHAM LIVING ROOM - NIGHT

MARION IS PACING AROUND THE ROOM.

MARION
Now let's just be sensible. Richie, you'll quit school and get a job. Joanie, you work in the shoe factory. I'll take in laundry.

RICHIE
(PUTTING AN ARM AROUND MARION)
Mom, settle down. Dad just went out for a while. Things aren't that bad.

JOANIE
Yet.

RICHIE
Joanie!

JOANIE
Just kidding.

RICHIE
Sit down, Mom.

MARION
(SITTING DOWN) Yes, I've got to remain calm. I'm sorry, children, things aren't good. Never in his life has your father not come home for dinner without phoning me.

JOANIE
Maybe he didn't have any change.

MARION SPRINGS FROM THE COUCH.

MARION
Why would he run off like this? Haven't I been a good wife?

RICHIE
Sure, Mom.

MARION
Couldn't be my cooking. He was thin when I married him. I never asked for a mink coat. I was happy with cloth. And when his ulcer bothers him, don't I rub his stomach . . . counterclockwise? (ON THE VERGE OF TEARS) Oh, where did I go wrong?

FONZIE ENTERS.

FONZIE
Hi, Mrs. C., I didn't get a chance to do any shopping today. Can I borrow a can of beans?

MARION CRIES HYSTERICALLY.

FONZIE (CONT'D)
It's all right, Mrs. C. I'll eat out.

RICHIE
Fonz, Dad hasn't come home yet, but he's bound to show up soon. It's probably nothing.

MARION
Nothing, Richard. Being deserted and left with two small children is not nothing.

JOANIE
We think Dad ran away from home.

FONZIE
Ain't he a little old for that?

MARION
It's my fault. I drove him out. I probably said, "Sit on it, Howard," once too often.

RICHIE
No, it's my fault. He's been mad at me ever since I got taller than him.

MARION
No, it's not your fault, Richard.

JOANIE
Well, it's not my fault. I'm still short.

FONZIE
(TAKING CHARGE) Okay, everybody, just cool it. Remain calm. Keep quiet. And don't panic.

MARION
Maybe we should call the police.

FONZIE
And tell 'em what?

MARION
That we've got a missing person.

FONZIE
You can't be an official missing person until you've been missing for at least twenty-four hours.

RICHIE
Are you sure, Fonz? Twenty-four hours?

FONZIE
I've made a study of these things. How else would I know when to bring my dates home? Heeyyy!

HE EXITS.

MARION
Don't worry. Everything is going to be all right. Fonzie will find your father. I'm just going to go upstairs and lie down. . . . And think.

SHE STOPS AND PICKS UP TUBA AND CARRIES IT UPSTAIRS. AS SHE EXITS:

MARION (CONT'D)
Just yesterday he was oompa pahing.

JOANIE
Do you think she's okay?

RICHIE
Yes.

FROM UPSTAIRS WE *HEAR* ONE NOTE ON THE TUBA.

CUT TO:

J

INT. *CUNNINGHAM LIVING ROOM - LATER THAT NIGHT*

IT'S FOUR O'CLOCK IN THE MORNING. RICHIE IS SOUND ASLEEP, SPRAWLED ON THE COUCH. JOANIE IS LYING ON THE FLOOR ASLEEP, OBVIOUSLY HAVING FALLEN ASLEEP THERE. MARION IS WIDE AWAKE TRYING BUT NOT SUCCEEDING AT READING. SHE IS SEATED, KEEPING ONE EYE ON THE PHONE, THE OTHER ON THE CLOCK. SHE SEEMS RESIGNED. THE DOORBELL RINGS. JOANIE AND RICHIE JUMP UP. THEY ALL GO TO THE DOOR.

MARION
Oh, maybe it's Howard.

THEY RUN TO FRONT DOOR. FONZIE POKES HIS HEAD IN THROUGH THE FRONT DOOR.

FONZIE
Oh, hi. I was hoping you'd be asleep.

MARION
You didn't find him. Did you, Arthur?

FONZIE COMES INTO THE LIVING ROOM.

FONZIE
Well, no. I checked all the likely spots . . . and found a lot of chubby little guys, but none of them answered to the name of Mr. C. I'm going to keep checking. If me and the boys don't find him tonight, I'll put my chicks on it. Hey, what a posse.

MARION
Fonzie, I think you should tell everybody to stop searching for Howard.

FONZIE
You don't want him back anymore?

MARION
Of course I do, I miss him already and we need him a lot. But he's made his decision and now we have to live with it. He's a grown man and I guess he'll come home when he wants to and not before. We all have lives to lead and the best thing for us is to get some sleep. I appreciate all you've done, Arthur, you've been a great comfort to us.

FONZIE
Mrs. C., you gotta lot of spunk. And don't worry. He'll be back. Believe me, he'll come back.

MARION NODS SADLY AND STARTS AWAY.

FONZIE (CONT'D)
And even if he don't, you still got your looks. You'll find somebody else.

MARION STARTS TO CRY.

FONZIE (CONT'D)
(TO RICHIE) What'd I say?

DISSOLVE TO:

K

INT. *FONZIE'S ROOM - SHORT TIME LATER*

AN EXHAUSTED FONZIE ENTERS.

FONZIE
(MUMBLES) You try . . . you try. . . . There's a lot of places to hide in Milwaukee.

HE SLUMPS IN A CHAIR AT THE TABLE. HE NOTICES SOME SLIPS OF PAPER, PICKS THEM UP AND READS.

FONZIE (CONT'D)
Jane called . . . couldn't sleep. . . . Mary Anne will call back. She loves me. I ought to call her. (PUTS NOTE IN POCKET) Jane: still can't sleep. . . . Trudy: look for my earring. . . . Who took these messages?

A BEAT, RISES AND GOES TO THE BATH-ROOM DOOR.

FONZIE (CONT'D)
Come on out, Mr. C.

THE CLOSET DOOR OPENS. HOWARD IS STANDING INSIDE.

HOWARD
Fonzie.

FONZIE TURNS.

HOWARD (CONT'D)
I guess you're surprised to see me here.

FONZIE
I'm surprised you could fit in the closet. What are you doing here?

HOWARD
I left your number with the airline. All the flights to Tahiti were booked full. I'm on standby. I guess a lot of men turned forty-five this week.

FONZIE
What were you doing in the closet?

HOWARD
I heard footsteps on the stairs. I thought it might be Marion or Richie. I couldn't face them.

FONZIE
So you're going to wait here for your phone call.

HOWARD
Yeah. You go about your business. I won't be in your way.

FONZIE REFERS TO MESSAGES.

FONZIE
Uh, about these messages. What's this "Mary Anne is dropping by tomorrow." I've already got a date.

HOWARD
She really wants to see you.

FONZIE
You fell for that?. . . Now, about this Cloris message. . . . (FURIOUS) What are you doing here? I've been looking for you all night. So have my friends. Your family's worried sick. (OPENS DOOR.) Get downstairs with your wife.

HOWARD
(ANGRY) Shhh. I don't want them to find me. (CLOSING DOOR) I told them I was going to Tahiti. They laughed at me.

FONZIE
What are you running away for?

HOWARD
Ahhh, you wouldn't understand.

FONZIE
The Fonz wouldn't understand? Fonz, the "Dear Abby" of Arnold's?

HOWARD
How would you understand a man who leads a dull life, a man with no dreams. You couldn't understand with your ten phone messages. The only one who ever called me more than once was Marion's mother screaming "She could have done better." What's the difference? You're the Fonz. I'm Cookie Cunningham. I'm forty-five years old and I've never done anything great. How could you understand that?

FONZIE
I understand and you're wrong. You do something great every day of your life. You take care of business. You take care of your wife and your kids.

HOWARD
Anybody can do that.

FONZIE
Poppycock. Not everybody, Mr. C. My old man split when I was four years old. All he left us was a strong box and no key. I had to ride over it three times with my tricycle before the lock sprung. You know what was inside? The strong box key, and that's all.

HOWARD
Well, *my* family isn't going to have that problem.

HOWARD TAKES AN ENVELOPE AND EMPTIES THE CONTENTS ON THE TABLE.

HOWARD (CONT'D)
Here are some things the family will need. (PICKS UP EACH ITEM AS HE MENTIONS IT) Here's the regular savings account, here's the emergency account, and here's the kids' college account. Here's my paid up life insurance and here's the home owner policy. And here's the key to the hardware store. Richie should open every morning at nine. And tell him to be sure to turn off the alarm first. Now, leave me alone while I wait for the call.

FONZIE SITS THINKING AS HE FINGERS THE KEYS. THEN. . .

FONZIE
Hey, Mr. C., they won't need the keys. Richie says he wants to go to college. They're selling the store.

HOWARD
Selling the store? It took me over twenty-five years to build up that business. I got my life, sweat, and blood in it.

FONZIE
Yeah, they think they can get four or five thousand for it.

HOWARD
Four or five thousand? That's not even a down payment. Marion won't permit it.

FONZIE
What does she care. She's going back to school. Says she wants to finish her studies.

HOWARD
In archeology? She's got rocks in her head. She's got to take care of Joanie.

FONZIE
Hey, don't worry about Joanie. She says she wants to quit school and get married in a couple of years.

HOWARD
Married! She's only twelve.

FONZIE
Fourteen.

HOWARD
What's the difference! Look at this: I'm not even gone yet and my family is falling to pieces.

FONZIE
It won't be so bad. Look at Gauguin, that picture painter. His family made out fine.

HOWARD
How do you know?

THE PHONE RINGS. HOWARD ANSWERS IT.

HOWARD (CONT'D)
Hello . . . Flight to Tahiti? . . . Are you crazy? I can't leave my family. They're nuts. They're giving away my store, my wife's digging ditches, and my daughter . . . What am I telling you this for? Give the ticket to another forty-five-year-old man.

HE HANGS UP AND STARTS TO STUFF KEYS, POLICIES, AND BANKBOOKS INTO ENVELOPE.

HOWARD (CONT'D)
Give me those things. I've go to go downstairs and straighten them out. I can't leave them alone for a minute.

HOWARD EXITS WITH THE ENVELOPE. FONZIE'S SCORED AND LAUGHS TO HIM-SELF. THE DOOR OPENS AND HOWARD SHAKES A FINGER AT FONZIE.

HOWARD (CONT'D)
You didn't fool me.

HOWARD EXITS. THE PHONE RINGS. FONZIE ANSWERS IT.

FONZIE
Whoa. Hello, airline girl. . . Yeah, the man was a little crazy but consider that your cancellation. Now, let's talk about more important things—you. What's a nice girl like you doing in a place like that, leading a dull, humdrum life. Throw down your pencil and hustle over to my place and have a cool time. . . . What did you say? What makes me think I'm so cool?

FONZIE HANGS UP. LOOKS AT WATCH AND COUNTS OFF SECONDS. A BEAT, THEN THE PHONE RINGS.

FONZIE (CONT'D)
That's what makes me think I'm so cool.

FADE OUT.

END OF ACT TWO

TAG

FADE IN:

INT. LIVING ROOM - NIGHT

MARION AND JOANIE ARE IN ROBES. THEY'RE SAYING GOODNIGHT TO HOW-ARD. HOWARD IS DRINKING COFFEE AT COUNTER. RICHIE IS STILL IN STREET CLOTHES.

JOANIE
(HUGGING AND KISSING HOWARD)
Daddy, if you promise you won't ever run away from home again, I'll try not to have such a fresh mouth.

HOWARD
I promise, and you don't have a fresh mouth. Now, run along to bed.

JOANIE KISSES HIM AND GOES UPSTAIRS.

MARION
(KISSING HOWARD) Goodnight, dear, it's nice to have you home.

HOWARD

Goodnight, sweetheart. I'll be right up. I just want to talk to Richie for a minute.

MARION

Don't be too long, dear. I heard so much about French artists. (GOING TO STAIRS) Ooo-la-la!

MARION EXITS. HOWARD CROSSES TO COUCH, AND HE MOTIONS RICHIE TO SIT IN HIS CHAIR.

RICHIE

You sure you want to talk, Dad? It's five-thirty in the morning. Couldn't we talk after lunch?

HOWARD

Richie, all I wanted to say is . . . I got a little carried away tonight. I really have a lot to be thankful for. I have a smart son who's about to go to college. A lovely daughter, who has a fresh mouth, but when she isn't talking is a doll. (THINKS) And maybe she'll need a fresh mouth one day. The way this world's changing, she just might choose to go out and work in this "man's" world.

RICHIE IS FAST ASLEEP. MARION COMES DOWN AND SITS AT FOOT OF STAIRS (OR WHERE SHE CAN BE SEEN).

HOWARD (CONT'D)

And I have a wife, who's more beautiful today, than when I met her. I hope I'm not boring you, Richard. . . .

HOWARD LOOKS AND SEES HE'S ASLEEP. MARION COMES FORWARD BUT HOWARD DOES NOT SEE HER.

MARION

More! More! (THEY KISS) It's nice to have you home, dear. (THEY KISS AGAIN)

HOWARD TURNS AROUND AND GIVES HER A HUG AND A KISS.

FADE OUT.

-THE END -

Studios

The NBC Studio Tour

(The only one of its kind)

Ten years ago NBC established a one-hour walking tour of its TV-studio facilities in Burbank. Since then, attendance has grown at such a rate that last year half a million people toured the giant broadcasting complex.

The tour consists of a behind-the-scenes look at the workings of TV: shows in progress, makeup work, set design and construction, wardrobe rooms, the sales department, engineering rooms, and perhaps even a star or two strolling through the halls.

The tour is in operation seven days a week from 10:00 A.M. to 5:00 P.M. Tickets, always on a first-come, first-served basis, are $2.25 for adults and $1.40 for children. Each touring group consists of no more than twenty-four people and a guide.

NBC also conducts special tours for student groups, clubs, organizations, etc. These tours must be booked two to four weeks in advance.

Other features offered by NBC include tours conducted in Spanish, French, Japanese, and sign language. These, too, must be scheduled in advance.

Because of the minimal amount of TV production now carried on in New York City, NBC's tour of its New York studios has been suspended.

For reservations or additional information, write or phone:

> NBC
> Group Services
> 3000 W. Alameda Ave.
> Burbank, CA 91523
> (213) 845-7000, ext. 2468

Tickets for TV Shows

Each network gives out complimentary tickets for those shows that tape before a live audience. To get them, write or phone any of the three networks and indicate when you are going to be in the Los Angeles area (the number of shows to be seen in New York is relatively small). You may also stop by the ticket office unannounced and pick up tickets.

A point to remember is that taping schedules for live-audience shows are often erratic, so you might not be able to see your favorite show or stars. Or the show could be booked solid for the season—popular shows sometimes are. However, you will be given a choice of several shows to attend when the show you request is not available.

After you phone or write a network for tickets,

you will be sent a letter or a guest card to be presented at the ticket office. Unfortunately, having a guest card or a letter is no guarantee you will get in to see the show: All tickets are on a first-come, first-served basis, and the networks always distribute more tickets than there are seats, in order to ensure a full house.

Depending on the show, you will have a numbered ticket, or a line will be formed outside the studio. If you have a low number or you arrive early and are near the front of the line, you will probably be admitted.

When there are seats available, ticket or not, you will be invited in.

If you are taking the family, be sure to check the age requirements. Unless otherwise posted, ABC does not permit children under 16 in the audience; CBS, 12; and NBC, 16 for game shows and 18 for talk shows.

Cameras and recorders are not allowed in studios.

When writing, it is recommended that you enclose a self-addressed envelope.

TICKET DEPARTMENTS

ABC
(Los Angeles)
ABC Ticket Department
4151 Prospect Ave.
Los Angeles, CA 90027
(213) 663-3311

(New York)
ABC Ticket Department
38 W. 66th St.
New York, NY 10023
(212) 581-7777

CBS
(Los Angeles)
CBS Ticket Department
7800 Beverly Blvd.
Los Angeles, CA 90036
(213) 651-2345

(New York)
CBS Ticket Department
524 W. 57th St.
New York, NY 10019
(212) 975-2476

NBC
(Los Angeles)
NBC Ticket Information
3000 W. Alameda Ave.
Burbank, CA 91504
(213) 849-3911

(New York)
NBC Ticket Information
30 Rockefeller Plaza
New York, NY 10020
(212) 664-3055

Syndicators and Service Companies

The following is a list of television syndicators and service companies, which has been supplied to us by the National Association of Television Program Executives. All are members of the Association. For further information, contact the Association's main office, Box 5272, Lancaster, PA 17601.

ABC Management/VIP Video
6311 Romaine
Hollywood, CA 90038
(213) 461-4061
William J. Griffiths, president

Series
Roller Superstars
Good Time America
Eyewitness to the Past
Champions: The Competitive Edge
Stanley's Smog-Less Steamer

Advanswers Media/Programming, Inc.
(Subsidiary of Gardner Advertising Company)
600 Madison Ave.
New York, NY 10022
(212) 752-0205
Kelly O'Neill, president

10 Broadway
St. Louis, MO 63102
(314) 444-2100

1717 N. Highland Ave.
Los Angeles, CA 90028
(213) 466-8539

Features
Bill Dance Outdoors
That Nashville Music
St. Louis Cardinals Regional Baseball Network

Air Time International, Inc.
919 3rd Ave.
New York, NY 10022
(212) 371-4570
Fred Weiner, president

Series
The Unknown War
Jerry Lewis . . . Looks at the Movies
The Race for the White House
The New Soupy Sales Show
World Championship Tennis

Specials
"The World's Largest Indoor Country Music Show"
"Rod McKuen's Christmas in New England"
"Giselle"

Alan Enterprises, Inc.
26170 Pacific Coast Hwy.
Malibu, CA 90265
(213) 456-3676
Alan L. Gleitsman, president

Features
Contemporary Cinema
Cinema Classics
Fine Arts Cinema
The Edward Small Package
High Adventure
Happy Plays
Matinee Playhouse
War and Peace

Series
The Abbott and Costello Show
Speed Racer
Felix the Cat
The Mighty Hercules

Alan Landsburg Productions
110 N. Doheny Dr.
Beverly Hills, CA 90211
(213) 273-7400
Alan Landsburg, chairman of the board

Features
"Fear on Trial"
"The Outer Space Connection"
"The Savage Bees"
"Ants: It Happened at Lake Wood Manor"
"Tarantulas: The Deadly Cargo"
"Ruby and Oswald"
"The Triangle Factory Fire Scandal"
"Torn Between Two Lovers"
"Terror Out of the Sky"
"The Mysterious Two"
"And Baby Makes Six"
"Chariot of the Gods"
"Manbeast, Myth or Monster"
"The White Lions"
"Secrets of the Bermuda Triangle"

Series
The Chisholms
In Search Of. . .
Between the Wars
It Was a Very Good Year

Specials
Health:
"How to Stay Alive"
"Life, Health and the American Woman"
"The Fragile Mind"
"The Fat of the Land"

Adventure:
"Still at Large"
"The Blue Edge"
"In Search of Ancient Astronauts"
"In Search of Ancient Mysteries"
"It Takes a lot of Love"
"Alaska Wilderness Lake"
"Armies of the Ant"
"Conquista"
"Are You a Missing Heir?"

Documentary:
"The Land"
"My Father Gave Me America"
"Glory Road West"
"Crime Watch"
"Unsolved Mysteries: The Investigators"
"The Starlets: Making it in Hollywood"
"Has Marriage Had It?"

Dramatic:
"Fawn"
"Death in Space"
"Murder Impossible"
"Murder in the First Person Singular"
"Oh Baby, Baby, Baby..."
"Rock-a-Die Baby"
"Song of the Succubus"

Alcare Communications Inc.
1503-05 Walnut St.
Philadelphia, PA 19102
(215) 546-7515
Frank Beazley, chairman of the board

Short Program Inserts
"Buyer Beware"
"Corner Drugstore"
"Maintenance Ms."
"Making Ends Meet"
"Medical Report"
"Movie Reviews"
"National Television Sports Quiz"
"One Great Moment in Sports"
"One Moment Please with Mort Crim"
"Senior Report"
"Star News"

Children Series:
Pixanne

Feature Packages
Classic Features

Music
Invitation to Dance

Mini-Series
Great American Men

Graphic Service
Network Graphics

Alfred Haber, Inc.
321 Commercial Ave.
Palisades Park, NJ 07650
(201) 224-8000
Alfred Haber, president

U.S. & International Television Rights
"Bing Crosby: His Life and Legend"
Disco Magic
"Marvin Gaye in Concert"
"Anne Murray in Concert"
"Charley Pride in Concert"
"Charlie Rich in Concert"

International Television Rights Only—Musical Variety Specials
"A Country Christmas"
"A Special Sesame Street Christmas"
"All Star Salute . . . Pearl Bailey"
"All Star Tribute to Jimmy Stewart"
"All Star Tribute to Elizabeth Taylor"
"All Star Tribute to John Wayne"
"Bing Crosby: The Christmas Years"
Glenn Campbell Music Shows
"Circus of the Stars"
"Easter by the Sea—Perry Como"
"General Electric All Star Anniversary"
"Lady Love In: Night & Day"
"Music from Hollywood—Perry Como"
The Other Broadway
"Paul Anka in Monte Carlo"
"People's Command Performance"
"Perry Como's Christmas in Early America from Colonial Williamsburg"
"Helen Reddy in Concert"
"Rockette: A Tribute to the Radio City Music Hall"
"Rockin in the USA"
"Sinatra and Friends"
Soap Factory
"Springtime Special—Perry Como"
"20th Anniversary of Rock and Roll"

Features
In Search of Eden

Allied Artists Television Corporation
15 Columbus Circle
New York, NY 10023
Andrew P. Jaeger, president

Features
Golden Seventies—Group VIII
    "The Betsy," "The Man Who Would Be King," "Gold," etc.
Golden Seventies—Group VII
    "Caberet," "Papillon," etc.
Golden Sixties—Group VI
    "A Man and a Woman," "Hunchback of Notre Dame," etc.
Cavalcade of 60's—Group V
    "Tickle Me," "Young Dillinger," "Thin Red Line," etc.
Cavalcade of 60's—Group IV
    "Soldier in the Rain," etc.

Cavalcade of 60's—Group III
  "Billy Budd," "Convicts Four," etc.
Cavalcade of 60's—Group II
  "Love in the Afternoon," "Big Circus," etc.
Cavalcade of 60's—Group I
  "Friendly Persuasion," "Al Capone," etc.
Cavalcade of 50's
  "Babe Ruth Story," "Bob Mathias Story," etc.
Dial "AA" for Action
Science Fiction
Charlie Chans
Bomba
Special "42"
Camp & Classic
Westerns

Series
Topper
The Evil Touch

Allworld Telefilm Sales Corporation
60 W. 57th St.
New York, NY 10019
(212) 541-8619
Gustave Nathan, president

Series, Mini-Series, Programs
Bozo the Clown
Celebrity Cabaret
Danceworld
Good for You
Great Adventure
Little Stars
Strike It Rich
The Adventure Man

Feature Packages
Allnight at the Movies
120 Half-Hour Mystery Package

Cartoons
Bozo the Clown
Laurel & Hardy

Short Program Inserts
"The Mind Matters"
"The Stars Who Made the Magic"
"Very Personally Yours"
"Watching Your Money"

American International Television, Inc.
9033 Wilshire Blvd.
Beverly Hills, CA 90211
(213) 278-8118
Hal Brown, president AI-TV

770 Lexington Ave.
New York, NY 10022
(212) 246-0107

Features
Films for the 80's
Ghoul-a-Rama II
Special Action Features
A Winning Hand
World of Macabre
Films for the 70's
Ghoul-a-Rama I
Startime Theatre
Fantastic Sci-Fi Theatre
Children's Showtime
Young Adult Theatre
New Science Fiction
Amazing Sci-Fi I–III
Top Secret Adventures
Dominant 10
Holiday Storybook of Fables
Real Life Adventures
Adventure Package
Strongmen of the World New Color Adventure
A.I.P.
Selma
A.I.P./Selma Science Fiction

Programs
Jukebox
Comeback
The Racers
Sports Challenge
Miss National Teenager Pageant
Daytime Star
The Night Before Christmas
Lorne Greene's Last of the Wild
Flipper
The Avengers
Adventures of Ozzie & Harriet
Johnny Sokko & His Flying Robot
Prince Planet
Touch of Music
Sinbad Jr.

American Television Syndication (ATS)
2 Lincoln Sq., Suite 18A
New York, NY 10023
(212) 874-0800
Lawrence P. O'Daly, president

Mini-series
Michael Strogoff
King's Adventure

Features
Feature Packages
The New Ed Allen Show

Arp Films, Inc.
342 Madison Ave.
New York, NY 10017
(212) 867-1700
Claude S. Hill, president

Cartoon Series
Marvel Superheroes
Spiderman

Artmedia, Inc.
430 N. Rodeo Dr., Suite 200
Beverly Hills, CA 90210
(213) 550-7371
Guus Jansen, Jr., president

Heidi
Crazy World of Sport
Don Quixote
Winnetou

Association Films, Inc.
866 3rd Ave.
New York, NY 10022
(212) 935-4210
Warren B. Smith, president

Distributors of free, public service programs to
television stations nationally. Five regional TV
centers service the broadcast industry within
their geographic territories. Catalog available.

5797 New Peachtree Rd.
Atlanta, GA 30340
(404) 458-6253

600 Grand Ave.
Ridgefield, NJ 07657
(201) 943-3855

512 Burlington Ave.
La Grange, IL 60525
(312) 354-7422

8615 Director's Row
Dallas, TX 75247
(214) 638-6799

7838 San Fernando Rd.
Sun Valley, CA 91352
(213) 767-0200

Astral Television Films Limited
720 King St. W
Toronto, Ontario M5V 2T3 Canada
(416) 364-3894
Lyell Sheilds, president

Series
Carol Burnett and Friends
Kidsworld
Hammy Hamster's Adventures on the Riverbank
The Forest Rangers
The Joyce Davidson Show
Shulman File
The Swiss Family Robinson
The Galloping Gourmet
Take Kerr
The Cisco Kid
The New Candid Camera
The Harold Lloyd Show
The Adventures of Black Beauty
Ryan's Hope
Mitch Miller
Southern 500
The Challenging Sea
Sandokan

Mini-series
A Man Called Intrepid

Feature Packages
American International Pictures
American Leisure Corporation
Anglo Amalgamated
Anglo EMI
Astral Commonwealth
Avco Embassy Pictures Corporation
Cinema Shares International
Heritage International
Mundis
RKO
Teleworld Inc.
Rank Film Distributors

Specials
Family Hour Festival
"Really Rosie"
"Tiny Three"
"Family Circus: Valentine & Christmas"
"The Nutcracker"

Avco Embassy Pictures Corporation
3460 Wilshire Blvd., Suite 903
Los Angeles, CA 90010
(213) 386-3920
Robert M. Newgard, vice-president television

300 E. 42nd St.
New York, NY 10017
(212) 949-8900

Features
The New Ones II
The New Ones
V.I.P. Group
Plus Twelve
28 for '68
Top Time
Nightmare Theatre

Series
Pete 'n Gladys
Ports of Call
Witness to Yesterday

Specials
"Years of Lightning, Day of Drums"

Bandera Enterprises, Inc.
P.O. Box 1107
Studio City, CA 91604
(213) 985-5050
Don Flagg, president

Sports

Baron Enterprises, Inc.
999 N. Doheny Dr.
Los Angeles, CA 90069
Barry Bergsman, president

Program Inserts
"Nature's Window"

Specials
Hallmark Hall of Fame

Music
The Country Club

Sports
Olympic Games 1948–1976

Series
City Lights—Brian Linehan Show

B D Productions, Inc.
14001 Palawan Way
Marina del Rey, CA 90291
(213) 823-5637
William J. Dobbins, president

Inserts
" 'How About' with Mister Wizard"

Specials
"King of the Channel"
"Nothing Great Is Easy"

The Behrens Company, Inc.
2451 Brickell Ave.
Miami, FL 33129
(305) 854-4935
Bob Behrens, representative
Betsy Behrens, representative

Kidsworld

Bill Burrud Productions, Inc.
1100 S. La Brea Ave.
Los Angeles, CA 90019
(213) 937-0300
Bill Burrud, president

Documentary-Features
"The Secret World of Reptiles"
"Vanishing Africa"
"The Great American Wilderness"
"Predators of the Sea"
"Amazing Apes"
"Devil's Mountain"

Docu-dramas-Features
"Curse of the Mayan Temple"
"Montezuma's Lost Gold"
"The Treasure Chase"
"Creatures of the Amazon"
"Man Against the Sea"

Series
Animal World
World of the Sea
Safari to Adventure

Blackwell Enterprises
7350 Lankersham Blvd., C-149
North Hollywood, CA 91605
(213) 982-4634
Ridge Blackwell, president

Program Inserts
The Short Classics Collection

Children's Specials
"Sleeping Beauty"
"Nobi"
"A Very Special Christmas"

Adult Special
"The Secret Paris"

Children's Features
"Rumpelstiltskin"
"The Adventures of Pinocchio"
"Pinocchio Saves the Show"
"Pinocchio and the Phantom"

The Bloom Film Group
1680 Vine St.
Hollywood, CA 90028
(213) 464-0030
David Bloom, president

Features
Adventure Quadrangle Features
American Film Features
Edgar Wallace Mystery Thrillers

Cartoons
The Funny Company
Roger Ramjet and the American Eagles

Documentary Series
It's a Small World
Four Winds to Adventure

The Blue Marble Company/Telemontage, Inc.
40 W. 57th St.
New York, NY 10019
(212) 541-8305
Robert Weimer, executive producer

Series
The Big Blue Marble

Specials
"My Seventeenth Summer"
"Treasure Island"
"My Name Is Lisa"

Bob Neece Associates
7711 Carondelet
St. Louis, MO 63105
(314) 726-6096
Robert F. Neece, president

The Mitch Miller Show
A New Zoo Revue
Life of Riley
Lone Ranger
Best of Groucho
Jeff's Collie
Timmy & Lassie
Sergeant Preston of the Yukon
Alexander Korda Features
Lone Ranger Features
Cheryl Features
Children's Film Classic
Your Choice for the Oscars
Bogart
Hollywood: The Selznick Years
Greatest Headlines of the Century
Sportfolio
RKO Shorts

Boston Broadcasters, Inc.
5 TV Pl.
Boston (Needham), MA 02192
(617) 449-0400
Robert M. Bennett, executive vice-president

Program Insert
"Update on Health News Inserts"

Series
House Call
The Baxters

Documentary
"Why Do I Feel This Way?"
"Just Hold My Hand"
This Was America
"Rheumatoid Factor"
The Body Works
(All above programs distributed on barter through
   J. Walter Thompson.)

Children
Catch a Rainbow
Jabberwocky
Drawing from Nature with Captain Bob

Brookville Marketing Corporation
420 Lexington Ave.
New York, NY 10017
(212) 687-3377
Jerome Shapiro, president

Soap Factory Disco

Bruce A. Raymond Company Limited
63 Huntley St.
Toronto, Ontario M4Y 2L2 Canada
(416) 923-9654
Bruce Raymond, president

Series
Alcohol Problem (Series A)
Alcohol Problem (Series C) .
Alphabet Soup
Changing Worlds
Concert for Earl Scruggs
Enjoy Being Beautiful
Superstars of Wrestling
Thacker's World
The Young Chefs

Program Insert
"One Day"

The Burt Rosen Company
8489 W. 3rd St.
Los Angeles, CA 90048
Burt Rosen, president

David Horowitz Consumer Buyline
David Horowitz Consumer Guideline
The Dream Thing

Capital Cities Television Productions
(A service of Capital Cities Communications, Inc.)
4100 City Line Ave.
Philadelphia, PA 10131
(215) 878-9700
Charles Keller, vice-president & general manager

Documentaries
"Inflation: The Fire That Won't Go Out"
"America, They Loved You Madly: The Civil
   Rights Years"
"Buffy St. Marie: National North American Child"

Specials
Capital Cities Family Specials
Auto Racing Specials
"Let's Eat Food"

Carter-Grant Productions, Inc.
17915 Ventura Blvd., Suite 208
Encino, CA 91316
Sherry Grant, president, Los Angeles office

545 Madison Ave.
New York, NY 10022
(212) 832-2242
Sandy Carter, president, New York office

Specials
The Women of Russia

Program Inserts
"The 21 Days of America"
"The 24 Days of Christmas"
"Eight Days of Chanukah"
"The Traditions of Easter"
"The Quality of Life"
"Star Scope with Arlene Dahl"
"Dr. Ari Kiev"
"Safety Trek"

Series
East Meets West
Charles Dickens

Catalena Productions Incorporated
P.O. Box 91728
West Vancouver, British Columbia V7V 4S1
  Canada
(604) 925-1334
Ian Maclennan, president

The "Stan Kann??" Show
"Pitfall" Game Show

Champlain Productions Ltd.
405 Ogilvy Ave.
Montreal, Quebec H3N 1M4 Canada
(514) 273-2865
John Krug, president

Video tape production house

The Christophers
12 E. 48th St.
New York, NY 10017
(212) 759-4050
Rev. John T. Catoir, director

Christopher Close-Up

Cinema Shares International Television Ltd.
450 Park Ave.
New York, NY 10022
(212) 421-3161
Ken Israel, president

Feature Film Packages I–VI

Cineworld Corporation
P.O. Box 276
North Miami, FL 33161
(305) 891-1181
John F. Rickert, president

Series
Rachel Copelan Show

Feature Films

Claster Television Productions
200 E. Joppa Rd., Suite 400
Towson, MD 21204
(301) 825-4576
John H. Claster, president

Star Force
Romper Room
Bowling for Dollars

Coe Film Associates, Inc.
70 E. 96th St.
New York, NY 10028
(212) 831-5355
Bernice Coe, president

The Children's Package
The Shorts Collection
Children's Features
Family Specials
Children's Specials
Children's Serials
Hour Documentaries

Colbert Television Sales
1888 Century Park East 1100
Los Angeles, CA 90067
(213) 277-7751
Dick Colbert, president

King World Productions, Inc. sales agent

Series
Tic Tac Dough
The Joker's Wild
Joker, Joker, Joker
People Watchers
Hollywood Connection
Break the Bank
Lassie
Rifleman

Movies
Charlie Chan
Lassie
East Side Kids
Mr. Motto
Sherlock Holmes

Columbia Pictures Television
15250 Ventura Blvd.
Sherman Oaks, CA 91403
(213) 995-1300
Joe Abruscato, vice-president, Western division

Feature Films
Television Movies
Series
Specials
Cartoon Series
First-Run Production

COMPRO
Communications Projects Incorporated
2080 Peachtree Industrial Ct., Suite 114
Atlanta, GA 30341
(404) 455-1943
Nels Anderson, president

Series
The Countryside
Active America
Here, There & Everywhere

Program Inserts
"Talkback"
"The Country Traveler"
"A Christmas Sampler"

Con Hartsock & Company
1100 Glendon Ave., Suite 941
Los Angeles, CA 90024
Con Hartsock, owner

Series
The Jerry Lewis Show
Mr. Wizard
Watch Mr. Wizard

Features
"The Littlest Angel"
"Alice Cooper's Welcome to My Nightmare"

Cori & Orient
2049 Century Park East, Suite 1200, South Tower
Century City
Los Angeles, CA 90067

Documentary Series
The Human Experience
Great Adventures
Welcome Tomorrow
Wild Country

Documentary Movies
Dead Birds
Rivers of Sand
Paul Robeson—The Tallest Tree in the Forest
Return to the Edge of the World

Documentary Specials
"Ileksen"
"Shadow Sister"
"Pacific, Pacific"
"Living Goddess"
"Island of the Spirits"
"Elusive Geisha"
"What Have You Done with My Country"
"Lalai Dreamtime"
"Floating"
"Iran, LA and the Mideast Connection"
"Behind the Revolution"
"Europe's Volcanoes"
Bird Films
Package of High Quality Nature Shorts
"Land Divers of Melanesia"
"Rhino Rescue"
"Woman of Toubou"
"Fat Tuesday"
"Garneel Gamal"
"The Hollow"
"Chatsworth Catalogue"

Features
Package of Six Movies
Return to the Edge of the World
Symptoms
Digby the Biggest Dog in the World
A City's Child
The Anna Contract

Music and Light Entertainment
Country Disco
Las Vegas Variety
British Hustle
"Me and Stella"
"Garneel Gamal"
"Martha Graham"
"Cruisin'/Shutdown"
"Guys and Dolls"
"Kiri Te Kanawa"

Sports
Thrillmaker Sports
Shutdown
"London Skateboards"
"Rodeo"

Children
"Ponies of Miklaeji"
"Legend of Paramo"
"Boy and His Boa"
"Elizabeth and the Marsh Mystery"
"Mandy's Grandmother"
"Red Pony"

Cartoons
Yupi

Docu-dramas
"Prisoners of Conscience"
"Children of Icarus"

Crystal Pictures, Inc.
1560 Broadway
New York, NY 10036
(212) 757-5130
F. Feinstein, president

Features
The African Queen
Charlie's Big Romance
Destination Moon
Flirting with Fate
The Gladiator
The Great Ruport
Heartbeat
Her Bridal Night
High Lonesome
Loving Couples
Melba
The Prowler
Riding on Air
Schweitzer—Jungle Doctor
The Southerner
The Sundowners
To Love
The Torch
When I Grow Up
When's Your Birthday
Wide Open Faces
Buck Rogers

Dave Bell Associates, Inc.
3211 Cahuenga Blvd. W
Hollywood, CA 90068
(213) 851-7801
David L. Bell, president

Series
Whitney and the Robot
Human Relations and School Discipline
Teaching Children to Read
Dealing with Classroom Problems
Values and Morality in School
The William Glaser Approach
Mainstreaming the Exceptional Child
Survival Skills for the Classroom Teacher

Specials
"Angel Death"
"The Feminine Mistake"
"The Real Rookies"

Short Program Inserts
"Medix"

DFS Program Exchange
405 Lexington Ave.
New York, NY 10017
(212) 661-0800
Wallace R. Chateauvert, manager

Animated Children's Programs
Scooby-Doo
Bullwinkle
Rocky & His Friends
Underdog
Tennessee Tuxedo and His Tales
Uncle Waldo
Dudley Do-Right & His Friends
Young Samson
Space Kidettes
Korg—70,000 B.C.
Inch High, Private Eye
Wheelie & the Chopper Bunch
Roman Holidays
Devlin
Around the World in 80 Days
Mission Magic
Valley of the Dinosaurs
The Jetsons

Program Inserts
"Olympic Champions"

D. L. Taffner/Limited
1370 Ave. of the Americas
New York, NY 10019
(212) 245-4680
Donald L. Taffner, president

5900 Wilshire Blvd.
Los Angeles, CA 90036
(213) 937-1144

Representative of Thames TV of London, CBC of
Canada, and ABC of Australia

The Benny Hill Show
World at War
Children's Animated Classics
Hollywood: The Silent Years
World at War
The Christians
Destination America

Don Fedderson Productions, Inc.
4024 Radford Ave.
Studio City, CA 91604
(213) 763-4325
Don Fedderson, chairman of the board

1626 N. Vine St.
Hollywood, CA 90028
(213) 461-4537
Irving Ross, syndication manager

The Lawrence Welk Show

Don L. Higley & Associates
610 N. Milpas St.
Santa Barbara, CA 93103
(805) 963-3305
Don L. Higley, president

Series
America's Wildlife
The American Outdoors

Sports, Other
Computer Football Forecast

Special
"Fred Bear: The Restless Spirit"

Feature
The Curse of Kilimanjaro

Edward Shaw Productions, Inc.
9465 Wilshire Blvd., Suite 501
Beverly Hills, CA 90212
(213) 274-5123
Edward S. Shaw, president

Documentaries
"Hard Look at New Cuba"

Features
Blood and Guns

Faith for Today
1100 Rancho Conejo Blvd.
Newbury Park, CA 91320
(805) 498-6661
William A. Fagal, director

Series
Westbrook Hospital
The Harvest

Filmvideo Releasing Corporation
37 W. 57th St.
New York, NY 10019
(212) 371-7828
Maurice H. Zouary, president

National Sales Office
3518 W. Cahuenga, Suite 301
Hollywood, CA 90068
(213) 851-5811

Features International
Features Sci-Fic/Action/Horror
Features Mystery/Drama/Comedy
Joe Franklin's Hollywood Memories
Princess Knight, Princess Knight
Laff-Movies
Guns of the Golden West Classics
Shirley Temple Comedy Theatre
Kiddie Camera
Toffsy Cartoon Theatre
History Machine
Felix the Cat Cartoon Theatre
Your Daily Horoscope
Victor & Horace
Les Onyx

Firestone Program Syndication Company
1200 W. Broadway
Hewlett, NY 11557
(516) 569-6900
Len Firestone, president

Series
Three's a Crowd
The Dating Game
The Gong Show

First American Films
4265 Marina City Dr., Suite 203
Marina del Rey, CA 90291
(213) 821-4444
John B. Kelly, president and chairman of the board

Feature Motion Pictures

Fish Communications, Inc.
515 Madison Ave.
New York, NY 10022
(212) 759-7340
Sanford H. Fisher, president

Marlo and the Magic Movie Machine

Four Star Entertainment Corporation
400 S. Beverly Dr.
Beverly Hills, CA 90212
(213) 277-7444
David B. Charnay, president and chairman of the
board, Four Star International

Series
The Big Valley
Target: The Impossible
The Lohman and Barkley
The Wonderful World of Magic
Thrillseekers
Can You Top This
Here Come the Stars
Monty Nash
Toward the Year 2000
Rogues
Burke's Law
Dick Powell Theater
Detectives
Target: The Corruptors
Honey West
Ensign O'Toole
Law and Mr. Jones
Richard Diamond
McKeever and the Colonel
Tom Ewell Show
Stagecoach West
Wanted: Dead or Alive
Westerners

Specials
James Whitmore—One-Man Specials
Blackstone Jr.—"Magic, Magic, Magic"
San Francisco Special
Portrait of a Star
"All Things Bright and Beautiful"
Musical Specials
"Seals & Crofts"
"Alice Cooper & His Friends"
"20 Years of Rock & Roll"
"Ferrante & Teicher"
"Sound Factors"

Children
Pippi Longstocking
Pippi in the South Seas
Pippi Goes on Board
Pippi on the Run
Once Upon a Time
Boy of Two Worlds

Features
Madron
Man Against the Organization
Funeral for an Assassin
Mary, Mary, Bloody Mary
Cagliostro
Secret Agent, Super Dragon
Last of the Mohicans
Tyrant of Castile
The Violent Patriot
Della

Franciscan Communications
1229 S. Santee St.
Los Angeles, CA 90015
Anthony Scannell, president

TeleSPOTS

Fremantle International, Inc.
555 Madison Ave.
New York, NY 10022
Paul Talbot, president

Fremantle International Prod. Pty. Ltd.
283 Alfred St.
North Sydney 2060 Australia
Russ Becker, manager director

Talbot Television, Ltd.
30 Dean St.
London W1V 5AN England
Tony Gruner, manager director

Fremantle of Canada, Ltd.
c/o Astral Television Films, Ltd.
720 King St. W
Toronto, Ontario M5V 2T3 Canada

Series
Adventures of Black Beauty
Swiss Family Robinson
Woobinda Animal Doctor
The New Candid Camera
Who's Afraid of Opera?
The Killiam Collection
The Galloping Gourmet
Take Kerr
It's Fun to Be Fooled
Romper Room
Kidsworld
Diana
Hopalong Cassidy
The Cisco Kid
Ryan's Hope
As the World Turns

Family Hour Festival"
"Bridge of Adam Rush"
"Secret Life of T.K. Dearing"
"Cosmic Awareness of Duffy Moon"
"Me and Dad's New Wife"
"Rookie of the Year"
"P. J. and the President's Son"
"Follow the North Star"
"Blind Sunday"
"Fawn Story"
"Mighty Moose and the Quarterback Kid"
"My Mom's Having a Baby"
"Michel's Mixed-Up Musical Bird"
"It's a Brand New World"
"The Horrible Honchos"
"Hewitt's Just Different"
"A Piece of Cake"
"One of a Kind"
"The Skating Rink"
"Psst! Hammerman's After You"
"Sara's Summer of the Swans"
"Francesca Baby"
"Very Good Friends"
"Gaucho"

"It's a Mile from Here to Glory"
"Trouble River"
"The Pinballs"
"Dear Lovey Heart I Am Desperate"
"A Home Run for Love"

Specials
"Really Rosie"
"Free to Be . . .You and Me"
"Tiny Tree"
"A Special Valentine with the Family Circus"
"Christmas with the Family Circus"
"Little Brown Burro"
National Geographic Specials (Far East only)
"The Nutcracker"
"The Life of Eric Von Stroheim"
"The National Crime Prevention Test"
"The Laff Boat"

General Foods Corporation
230 Park Ave.
New York, NY 10017
(212) 490-2237
Bob Gillespie, manager, local media services

Series
The Guinness Game

Gerber/Carter Communications
488 Madison Ave.
New York, NY 10022
(212) 688-7274
Charles S. Gerber, president

For You . . . Black Woman
"Black Broadway"

The Gillespie Company
101 Ocean Ave.
Santa Monica, CA 90402
(213) 459-5804
Henry A. Gillespie, president

Globo TV of Brazil
909 3rd Ave.
New York, NY 10022
(212) 754-0400
Joseph Wallach, president
Felipe Rodrigues, U.S. representative
Documentaries, music specials, soccer games, and
   mini-series

Golden TV
3716 Barham Pl., Suite B-110
Los Angeles, CA 90068
(213) 874-5400
Hal Golden, president

Series
Disaster
World Series of Tennis
Sue Dorn

Specials
"Tenth Annual Senior Olympics"
"Mid-Life Crisis"
"Parent Test"
"Stress"

Gold Key Entertainment
(A division of The Vidronics Company, Inc.)
159 W. 53rd St., Tower 53
New York, NY 10019
(212) 486-9116
Jerry Kurtz, president, The Vidronics Company, Inc.

Offices in Hollywood, CA; Toronto, Ontario; Tokyo, Japan

Series
Krofft Super Stars
Popeye Cartoons
Beatles Cartoons
Cool McCool
Krazy Kat
Barney Google
Beetle Bailey
Perspective on Greatness
TV Time Capsule

Features
The Neptune Journals
Galaxy One
The Beta Chronicles
The Alpha Chronicles
Bill Burrud Features
Rainbow I–IV Outdoor Adventures
Thirteen Television Premieres
Scream Theater
Awards Theatre
Action Theater I, II
Astor Classic Features
Astor Sci-Fi Features
The Late Show
Blondie Features
Cisco Kid Features

Specials
Alice's Adventures in Wonderland
"The Two Kennedys—A View from Europe"
"In Search of Ancient Astronauts"
"Loggins and Messina 'In the Attic' "
"Walt Wagner Show with Peggy Fleming"
A Christmas Carol by Charles Dickens
Dick Tracy Serials
Flash Gordon Serials

Granada Television International
1221 Ave. of the Americas
New York, NY 10010
(212) 869-9858
Haidee Granger, manager (U.S.)

Family at War
Victorian Scandals
Crown Court
Persuasion
Shabby Tiger
Stars Look Down
Once Upon a Time
Fallen Hero
House of Caradus
Laurence Olivier Presents
Single Plays
Disappearing World
The Christians
The Outsiders
World in Action
Flowers of Gloster
Ghosts of Motley Hall
The Intruder
Soldier & Me
International Pop Proms
Barenboim on Beethoven

Gray-Schwartz Enterprises, Inc.
425 S. Beverly Dr.
Beverly Hills, CA 90212
(213) 556-1628
Marv Gray, president and treasurer

The Lone Ranger
Jeff's Collie
Timmy & Lassie
Sergeant Preston of the Yukon
"Your Choice for the Oscars"
"Bogart"
"America's Sweetheart—The Mary Pickford Story"
"The Golden Era of the Silents"
Feature Films
Footage Series
Treasure Unlimited
Paramount Newsreels

Group IV Distributors, Inc.
150 E. 58th St
New York, NY 10022
Mort Zimmerman, president

Series
Upstairs, Downstairs

Features
Sci-Fi
General Entertainment
Block of Shock
Terror

Specials
"Santa and the Three Bears"

Group W Productions
7800 Beverly Blvd.
Los Angeles, CA 90036
(213) 852-4024
William F. Baker, president, Group W Television Group (NY)

Series
The Mike Douglas Show
PM Magazine
Marlo and the Magic Movie Machine
News/Test
Impact 27
The Coral Jungle
Playmates-Schoolmates
Call It Macaroni
Black African Heritage

Grundy Organization Pty. Ltd.
Grundy House, 448 Pacific Hwy.
Artarmon N.S.W. 2064 Australia
(02) 428-0666
Reg Grundy, chairman

425 E. 63rd St.
New York, NY 10021
(212) 935-0012

146 S. Spaulding Dr.
Beverly Hills, CA 90212
(213) 273-8343

Series
The Prisoner
The Restless Years
The Young Doctors

Features
The Alternative
Confessions of Ronald Biggs
The Death Train
Demolition
Gone to Ground
Image of Death
Mama's Gone a-Hunting
The Newman Shame
The Night Nurse
Plunge into Darkness
Roses Bloom Twice
The Scalp Merchant

Docudramas
"Poor Fella Me"
"The Wreck of the Batavia"

H.I.S. Marketing and Advertising
2690 State Rd.
Cuyahoga Falls, OH 44223
(216) 923-0434
Gary L. Taylor, general manager

Rex Humbard Program

Hoelscher Teleshows
1600 N. La Brea Ave., Suite 118
Los Angeles, CA 90028
(213) 462-5910
Jean Hoelscher, general partner
Clifford Hoelscher, general partner

Series
Millions to Inherit

Documentary
"The Great Depression: A Human Diary"

HTV Wales, Television Centre
Cardiff CF1 9XL Wales
The Rt. Hon. Lord Harlech, PC, KCMG, chairman

HTV West, Television Centre
Bath Rd.
Bristol BS4 3HG England

HTV Limited
99 Baker St.
London W1M 2AJ England

Family Drama
Kidnapped
The Doombolt Chase
The Clifton House Mystery
Children of the Stones
Follow Me
The Georgian House
Westway
Sky
King of the Castle
Pretenders

Drama
Murder at the Wedding
Our Little Town
Border Country
Darkness & Danger
Fadeout
The Inheritors

Exploration and Adventure
"Everest Unmasked"
"Dudh Kosi"
"Matterhorn"
"Land of Mist and Fire"
"Sailing Above the Alps"
"The Cerro Torre Enigma"
"High and Wild"

Music
"Don Pasquale"
"A Christmas Carol"
"The Mozart Requiem"
"Haydn's Creation"
"Brahm's Requiem"
"Cherubini's Requiem in D Minor"
"Murder the Magician"
"Stuart Burrows in Concert"
"Celebration"

Documentaries
"The World of Frank Letch"
"The Hebrides"
"Dylan Thomas"
"Fat Man on a Beach"

"Scars"
"Earth Magic"
"Annigoni"
"The Splendour Falls"
"Countryside"

Image Audio
P.O. Box 2153
Hollywood, CA 90028
(213) 464-5262
Eleanor Bingham, producer
Leslie Shatz, producer

Documentaries/Specials
"Mudhouse"
"The New Klan"
"Scientology: Religious Freedom in the Twentieth
   Century"

Interamerican Entertainment Company Ltd.
6055 E. Washington Blvd., Suite 633
Los Angeles, CA 90040
(213) 721-0102
Julio Gonzalez-Reyes, president

Series
The Professionals
The Frighteners
The New Avengers
Dick Turpin
Elephant Boy
Lucky Feller
Doctor
Bayley's Bird
The Top Secret Life of Edgar Briggs

Mini-Series
Lillie
Enemy at the Door
The Golden Soak
People Like Us
Bouquet of Barbed Wire

Documentaries
Untamed Frontiers

Animation
Petrus, Petro, Petrole
The Adventures of Energy

Musical Specials
Feature Films

Intercontinental Communications, Inc.
10 Rockefeller Plaza
New York, NY 10020
Donald W. Coyle, president

Last of the Pharoahs
The Friend of My Friends
The Revolutionaries
Primitive Man
Beany & Cecil
"The Wit and World of George Bernard Shaw"

**International Communications Consultants
   Corporation**
129 E. Hawthorne St.
Fallbrook, CA 92028
(714) 728-2364
John F. Bowman, president

Series
Eyewitness to the Past
Magic, Magic, Magic
Sari Celebrity Brunch
For Goodness Sake!
New Filmmakers
The Hollywood Experience
The Good Life
Fun and Fitness

Series——Children
The Toymaker
Stanley's Smogless Steamer & Traveling Library
Miss Phoebe's Garden
Nutz & Boltz Theater
Teego, The Star Traveler
Cosmic Frontiers
Open House Theater

Music
Nashville Country Fare
Music Country

Sports
Tee Off
Champions: The Competitive Edge
Tennis, The Name & the Game

Specials
"Disco Sketches"
"Salute"
"Trini Lopez"

Investor's Management Services, Inc.
366 N. Broadway
Jericho, NY 11753
(516) 935-5567
Jason A. Starr, president

Series
All properties are represented exclusively by Television Syndication Group, Inc.

ITC Entertainment
The Gallerie, 115 E. 57th St.
New York, NY 10022
(212) 371-6660
Abe Mandell, president

Series
The Muppet Show
Edward the King
Space: 1999
When Havoc Struck

Features
The Thriller
Entertainment, Volume One

Specials
Superlative Seven
"Julie & Sammy"
"From This Moment On . . . Cole Porter"
"The Beatles Forever"
"The Entertainers"
"Merry Christmas . . . With Love, Julie"
"Come Hear the Music Play"
"Heart and Soul"
Super Six
"Elton John and Bernie Taupin Say Goodbye
    Norma Jean and Other Things"
"Steve and Eydie: Our Love Is Here to Stay"
"Julie—A Salute to Hollywood"
"The Magical Musical World of Julie Andrews"
"Julie Andrews and Robert Goulet in Concert"
"James Paul McCartney"
Extraordinary 8
"Bravo Julie!"
"The Julie Andrews Christmas Special"
"Julie and Dick in Covent Garden"
"Julie Andrews & Jackie Gleason—How Sweet It
    Is"
"Julie—My Favorite Thing"
"Herb Alpert and the TJB"
"The Sandy Duncan Special"

Series
Crimes of Passion
The Protectors
My Partner the Ghost
Departments
UFO
The Persuaders
The Adventurer
The Champions
The Baron
Man in a Suitcase
The Prisoner
Secret Agent
Dangerman
The Gale Storm Show
Fury
Captain Scarlett and the Mysterons
Thunderbirds
Stingray
Fireball XL5
Mr. Piper

Features
Action 7
Magnificent 15

Janus Films
745 5th Ave.
New York, NY 10022
(212) 753-7100
Saul J. Turell, president

Laurel and Hardy

Features
Classic Mystery Theatre
Action 99
Janus Gold

J.E.D. Productions Corporation
140 E. 56th St.
New York, NY 10022
(212) 751-5758
Jackson E. Dube, president

Features
The Alexander Korda Classic Film Library
Children's Film Foundation/Rank Productions
Children's Feature Package

Shorts
RKO Shorts Library

Docu-specials

Jerry Dexter Program Syndication
139 S. Beverly Dr.
Beverly Hills, CA 90212
(213) 278-9510

Specials
"Johnny Cash Ridin' the Rails"
"The Little River Band"
"Bachman-Turner Overdrive"

Series
The Wolfman Jack Show

J. Morris Anderson Productions
24 W. Chelten Ave.
Philadelphia, PA 19144
(215) 844-8872
J. Morris Anderson, executive director

The Miss Black America Pageant

Joseph Green Pictures Company
200 W. 58th St.
New York, NY 10019
(212) 246-9343
Joseph Green, president

Features
International Theatre, Volume I
International Theatre, Volume II

JWT Syndication
420 Lexington Ave.
New York, NY 10017
(212) 867-1000
Robert E. (Buck) Buchanan, senior vice-president
    in charge of media

Series
Comedy Shop
Magic of Mark Wilson
Miss Peach
Roald Dahl's Tales of the Unexpected
World of Survival
Update on Health

Program Inserts
"Cartoon-a-torial"
"Kenneth and Company"
"Magic of Mark Wilson"
"Take Five with Stiller and Meara"
Newsweek Broadcasting Service
"Today's Woman"
"Update on Health"

Specials
"A Gorey Halloween"
"All in the Castle"
"For a Better World"
"Gold Coast"
"Spotlight"
"Update on Health"
"Watch Me"

Music Specials
All You Need Is Love
Billboard's Disco Party
"Vic on Campus"
"Wayne Newton's Country Portraits & Lynn Anderson's Country Welcome"
"Words & Music—Sammy Cahn"

King Features/Hearst Metrotone Television and Motion Pictures
235 E. 45th St.
New York, NY 10017
(212) 682-5600
J. F. D'Angelo, president

Properties
Syndicated domestically by Gold Key Entertainment
Blondie
Popeye
Beatles
Flash Gordon
Beetle Bailey
Barney Google & Snuffy Smith
Krazy Kat
Cool McCool
TV Time Capsule

The Laurel Group, Inc.
150 E. 58th St., Suite 2104
New York, NY 10022
(212) 753-1003
George A. Romero, chairman

Properties
The Winners
"To Be a Winner"
"Basketball: Fists or Finesse?"

Leo A. Gutman, Inc.
230 Park Ave.
New York, NY 10017
(212) 682-5652
Leo A. Gutman, president
Esther Balenz, vice-president

Features
Sherlock Holmes
Charlie Chan
Mr. Moto
East Side Kids
The International 3
The Hollywood 7
The Spectacular 5
The Cliffhangers 5

Lexington Broadcast Services Company
800 3rd Ave.
New York, NY 10022
(212) 838-1185
Harry Siegel, president

Sha Na Na
Health Field
Hot Fudge
Health Watch

Specials
"Fleetwood Mac"
"Sports Extra"

Lutheran Film Associates
360 Park Ave. South
New York, NY 10010
(212) 532-6350
Robert E.A. Lee, executive secretary

Special
"The Joy of Bach"

Features
Martin Luther
Question 7

Documentary
"Cinema Verite"

Lutheran Television
2185 Hampton Ave.
St. Louis, MO 63139
Janet R. Naji, manager, marketing/promotion

Series
This Is the Life
Pattern for Living
Esta Es la Vida

Specials
"Miles to Go"
"Christmas Is"
"The City That Forgot About Christmas"
"Easter Is"
"Freedom Is"

Other
Tension Point

M. A. Kempner, Inc.
2455 E. Sunrise Blvd., Suite 703
Fort Lauderdale, FL 33304
(305) 569-9419
Marv Kempner, president

TV Powww!

Marathon Entertainment
110 E. 59th St.
New York, NY 10022
(212) 753-3860
Alan Lubell, president
Patricia Gay, distribution manager

Greatest Sports Legends

Marvin Goodman Associates, Inc.
40 E. 62nd St.
New York, NY 10021
(212) 688-3344
Marvin Goodman, president

Masscasting—Neal P. Cortell
18 Newbury St.
Boston, MA 02116
(617) 247-0400
Neal P. Cortell, president

"Turn On"
"Wonderful World"
"Set Your Sights"
"The Look You Like"
"You're Right On"

MCA TV
445 Park Ave.
New York, NY 10022
(212) 759-7500
Lou Friedland, chairman of the board

Series
The Rockford Files
Kojak
Emergency +4
Holmes & Yoyo
Adam-12
Alias Smith & Jones
The Bionic Woman
The Bold Ones
Boris Karloff Presents
Dragnet
Don Adams Screen Test
Emergency!
Ironside
It Takes a Thief
The Jack Benny Show
Leave It to Beaver
Marcus Welby, M.D.
McHale's Navy
The Munsters
The Name of the Game
Rod Serling's Night Gallery
Run for Your Life
The Six Million Dollar Man
Suspense Theatre
The Virginian

Mini-series
Novels II
Operation Prime Time 1979, 1978, 1977
Novels I
Rich Man, Poor Man Book I

Sports, Music, Education, Themes, Other
The Road to Moscow 1980

Cartoons
Woody Woodpecker & Friends

Features
Champagne Movies
Ninety Minute Movies
Comedy Festival I, II
77 Horror Greats
29 Abbott & Costello
Universal Grand 50
Universal World Premiere
Universal Star-Spangled 33
Universal 40
Universal 49
Universal 50
Universal 52
Universal 53
Universal Color One Hundred
Universal 102
Universal 123
Universal 260 Select List
Universal 36 Black and White Elite
Western Round

Media Corporation of America
711 3rd Ave.
New York, NY 10017
(212) 867-3700
Albert Shepard, president

Curious George
"Sunshine Porcupine"
"Little Brown Burro"
"Why the Bears Dance on Christmas Eve"
"Miss World 1978"

Metromedia Producers Corporation
485 Lexington Ave.
New York, NY 10017
(212) 682-9100
Lennart Ringquist, president

Series, Mini-series, Programs
The Cross-Wits
David Frost Presents the Guiness Book of World Records
The Ice Palace
Living Together
Mayberry R.F.D.
The Merv Griffin Show
My Favorite Martian
That Girl
Vaudeville

Features
Premium I
Premium II
Premium Plus

Specials
"Future Shock"
"The First Annual Mother/Daughter Beauty
  Pageant"
The Jackie Gleason Specials
"Then and Now, Filmmakers Salute Oscar"

Documentaries, Docu-dramas, True Stories
Jane Goodall and the World of Animal Behavior
National Geographic Society Specials
"Natural History of Our World: The Time of Man"
The Undersea World of Jacques Cousteau
The Untamed World

Cartoons
Groovie Goolies and Friends

Sports, Music, Education, Themes, Others
Die Fledermaus
The Sleeping Beauty
"The Royal Ballet Salutes the U.S.A."

Metro Productions, Inc.
1 Century Plaza, 25th Floor
2029 Century Park East
Los Angeles, CA 90067
Michael Miller, president

The Melting Pot
Sky's the Limit
Down Home USA
America Sings
Sew What's New
Eat Yourself Healthy
Coping
The Sacred Space
Master Bridge
America Still
Country Serenade
The Sam Diego Show
Funny Man
Imagine That!
Success
Up for Grabs
Remarkable

MG Films, Inc.
400 E. 54th St.
New York, NY 10022
(212) 371-1622
Marvin M. Grieve, president

Hot Fudge
"Spirit of Independence"
"The Wonderful Stories of Professor Kitzel"
The Hilarious House of Frightenstein

MGM Television
(A division of Metro-Goldwyn-Mayer, Inc.)
10202 W. Washington Blvd.
Culver City, CA 90230
(213) 836-3000
Edward A. Montanus

1350 Ave. of the Americas
New York, NY 10019
(212) 977-3400

Series, Mini-series, Programs
Courtship of Eddie's Father
Daktari
Hawkins
How the West Was Won
Man from U.N.C.L.E.
Medical Center
Please Don't Eat the Daisies
Then Came Bronson

Feature Packages
Extra Extra Movies
Thirteen Tailor Mades

Specials
"An Evening with Gene Kelly"
"Conquest"
"Pre-Shows from MGM"
"The Rise and Fall of the Third Reich"
"Sports Previews from MGM"

Cartoons
Tom and Jerry

Mighty Minute Programs
840 Battery St.
San Francisco, CA 94111
(415) 788-1211

Program Inserts
"Joe Carcione—The Greengrocer"
"Greg Dumas 'Going to the Movies' "
"The Tipsters"
"On the Move with Charlie Coane"
"Celebrity Signature"
"Action Report"
"Instant Interviews"
"Money Talks"

Documentaries
"In Celebration of King Tutankhamun"

Special
"Pickle Family Circus"

Series
Magazine Television for the 80's

Multimedia Program Productions, Inc.
140 W. 9th St.
Cincinnati, OH 45202
Donald L. Dahlman, executive vice-president

Donahue
Donahue Access ½ Hour
Young People's Specials
Archie Campbell Presents
"The 13th Annual Music City News Country Awards"

Muscular Dystrophy Association
810 7th Ave.
New York, NY 10019
(212) 586-0808
Sylvester L. (Pat) Weaver, president

The Jerry Lewis Labor Day Telethon

National Association of Broadcasters
1771 N St., NW
Washington, DC 20036
(202) 293-3500
Jane E. Cohen, vice-president, television

National Filmboard of Canada
1251 Ave. of the Americas, 16th Floor
New York, NY 10020
(212) 586-2400
Kenneth Share, U.S. general manager

National Telefilm Associates, Inc.
12636 Beatrice St.
Los Angeles, CA 90066
Aubrey (Bud) Groskopf, chief operating officer

141 E. 56th St., Suite 3-G
New York, NY 10022
(212) 752-4982

Series
Search and Rescue
Bonanza
Get Smart
High Chaparral
Laramie
Laredo
Boots and Saddles
Californians
Cameo Theatre
Captured
Car 54, Where Are You?
Continental Classroom
Falcon
Great Gildersleeve
Roy Roger's Great Movie Cowboys
Jim Backus Show
Loretta Young Show
Not for Hire
Outlaws
Panic
People Are Funny
Pony Express
Richard Boone Show
Seven Greatest
Silent Service
Steve Donovan, Western Marshal

Theatre of Stars
Theatre Macabre
T.H.E. Cat
Uncommon Valor
Victory at Sea
Funny Manns
TVI Acts

Features
Best of NTA
Cary Grant Theatre
Bob Hope Theatre
John Wayne Theatre
John Wayne Classic Theatre
Phoenix Features
Storybook Theatre
Horror Features
Science Fiction Theatre
Mystery-Suspense Theatre

Cartoons
Betty Boop
George Pal Puppetoons
Max Fleischer Color Classics
Noveltoons

Serials
Republic Cliffhanger Serials
Captain America
Commando Cody

Short Subjects

Needham, Harper & Steers Advertising, Inc.
401 N. Michigan Ave.
Chicago, IL 60611
(312) 527-3400
Blair Vedder, president

10889 Wilshire Blvd.
Los Angeles, CA 90024
(213) 478-6526
Brad Roberts, vice-chairman

909 3rd Ave.
New York, NY 10022
(212) 758-7600
Paul Harper, chairman of the board

Nelvana Limited
207 Queen's Quay W
Toronto, Ontario M5J 1A7 Canada
(416) 863-0091
Patrick Loubert, producer

Producers of animated specials

The New York Times Syndication Sales Company
200 Park Ave.
New York, NY 10017
(212) 972-1070
Sam Summerlin, assistant general manager

Series
Portraits of Power: Those Who Shaped the 20th Century

Sports
Torch of Champions

Special
"50 Fabulous Years: Filmmakers Salute Oscar"

Newsweek Broadcasting
(A division of Newsweek, Inc.)
444 Madison Ave.
New York, NY 10022
(212) 350-2176
Bernard J. Shusman, vice-president, Newsweek, Inc. and executive producer, Newsweek Broadcasting

Cartoon-a-torial
Feature Service
Today's Woman
What's Cookin' with Burt Wolf

New York Communications, Inc.
207 S. State Rd.
Upper Darby, PA 19082
(215) 352-7472
Michael Davis, president

Full service research, marketing, creative, and production company, specializing in television news advertising and promotion.

New Zoo Revue Corporation
9401 Wilshire Blvd., #620
Beverly Hills, CA 90212
(213) 278-5325
Barbara Atlas, executive vice-president, chief operating officer

The New Zoo Revue

Nicholas Laboratories
P.O. Box 334
New Berlin, WI 53151
(414) 784-5600
Carey P. Cox, president

New York Production Office
1000 Clove Rd., #8-R
Staten Island, NY 10301
(212) 273-3852

For You . . . Black Woman

Nicholson-Muir Productions, Inc.
1890 Palmer Ave.
Larchmont, NY 10538
(914) 834-3005
E. Roger Muir, President

Bluffingame
Definition
Headline Hunters

Second Honeymoon
Supermates
Super Pay Cards

Nielsen-Ferns International Ltd.
55 University Ave., Suite 1100
Toronto, Ontario M5J 2H7 Canada
(416) 361-0306
Richard Nielsen, president

Series
Portraits of Power
Cities
Al Oeming—Man of the North
The Stationary Ark
A Third Testament

Drama/Adventure
The Newcomers/Les Arrivants
The New Avengers

Specials
"Lynn Seymour: In a Class of Her Own"
"Karen Kain—Ballerina"
"From Russia with Bruno Gerussi"
"Dostoevsky"
"An Ark for Our Time"

NTN Entertainment, Inc.
295 Madison Ave.
New York, NY 10017
(212) 532-6167
Edward P. Noyes, president

Series
Rockworld
Miss U.S.A. State Beauty Pageants

Mini-series
Classic World

Specials
"Hobbs' Choice"

Cartoons
Children's Insert Programming

Odin Corporation
225 Santa Monica Blvd., #506
Santa Monica, CA 90401
(213) 394-9606
Mia Beard, president

Series
Super Satellite Concerts
Smalltime
Comedy Cheerleaders
The Radio Show

Ogilvy & Mather, Inc.
2 E. 48th St.
New York, NY 10017
(212) 688-6100
Charles Bachrach, senior vice-president

The Guinness Game

Paramount Television Distribution
1 Gulf & Western Plaza
New York, NY 10023
(212) 333-4600
W. Randolph Reiss, senior vice-president, domestic syndication, NY

5451 Marathon St.
Los Angeles, CA 90038
(213) 468-5000
Richard Frank, president, Paramount Television Distribution, CA

Features
Portfolio I-VIII
Marquee I
Paramount Action Theatre

Series
Make Me Laugh
Laverne & Shirley
Happy Days
The Odd Couple
The Brady Bunch
The Brady Kids Animated
Star Trek
Star Trek Animated
Mission: Impossible
Love, American Style
The Untouchables
The Lucy Show
Premiere Fever

Pennzoil Film Center
1630 W. Olympic Blvd.
Los Angeles, CA 90015
(800) 421-8393
(213) 385-0311
Fred Williams, vice-president

Sports, Action, Outdoor & Adventure Specials

The Peter Rodgers Organization Ltd.
Park Westwood Tower, Penthouse 4
969 Hilgard Ave.
Los Angeles, CA 90024
(213) 851-3812
Peter S. Rodgers, president

Features
Science Fiction Feature Package
Horror Feature Package
Pro Feature Group 1 and 2
Intercontinental Feature Group 1
Yordan Feature Package
"P-M" Feature Group
Crystal Feature Group
Special Feature Group
Alexander Korda Feature Library
Masterpiece Feature Classics
Nostalgia Nine
Eleven First-Run Features
101 Feature Group
Children's Feature Film Package
RKO Shorts Library—Laugh Classics

Specials
Buck Rogers
"Kennedy's Ireland"
"The Man from Button Willow"
"Freddie the Football"
"Johnny Cash"
"How the West Was Lost"
"The Middle East—A View from the Inside"
"The American Song Festival"
"Wild Wonderful Winter"
"A Christmas Visit"
"Always Another Wave"

Series
Hollywood Memories
Wyatt Earp
Bill Cosby Show
Flip Side
High and Wild
The White Escape
Wide World of People
Luck Jim Adventure Show
Kenny Rogers—Rollin' on the River
The Barbara McNair Show
Story Theatre
The George Kirby Show

Cartoons
The New Three Stooges
Space Angel
Captain Fathom
Clutch Cargo
Roger Ramjet
Funny Company
Spunky & Tadpole
Nutty Squirrels

Phoenix Productions, Inc.
P.O. Box 88332
Seattle, WA 98188
(206) 747-0985
Mike Lynch, general manager/executive producer

The Amazing Flash

Picturmedia Limited
1775 Broadway, Suite 2120
New York, NY 10019
(212) 757-3573
Teodor Hreljanovic, president

Series
The Mischief Makers
The Comedy Capers

Features
Picturmedia Features I
14 Action Dramas
Togai
Picturmedia Classic Horrors
King, A Filmed Record: Montgomery to Memphis

Specials
"King: Legacy of a Dream"

Post-Newsweek Programs
(A division of Post-Newsweek Stations)
2139 Wisconsin Ave., NW
Washington, DC 20007
(202) 342-3800
Joel Chaseman, president

Specials
Go Tell It . . . Ben Hooks Reports
The Presidents: 80 Years on Camera
The American Documents

Prime TV Films, Inc.
527 Madison Ave.
New York, NY 10022
(212) 421-2170
E.J. Campbell, president

Features
Theft of the Mona Lisa
Stars Look Down
Redneck
D'Jango
Day the Sky Exploded
Incredible Petrified World
Teenage Zombies
Ape Man
Corpse Vanishes
Thirsty Dead
Limping Man
Orient Express
Memory of Love
White Fire

Feature Series
East Side Kids

Classic Family Fare
March of the Wooden Soldiers
When Comedy Was King
Golden Age of Comedy
Days of Thrills & Laughter
Lady Takes a Chance
Spotlight Scandals

Documentaries
"September 1939"

Series
The East Side Kids
Charlie Chaplin Comedy Theatre
Sherlock Holmes
The Goldbergs
Drugs: A to Z
Nutrition: A to Z
Courageous Cat

Productions Associates (U.K.) Ltd.
40 George St.
London W1H 5RE England
(01) 486-9921
Michael Baumohl, managing director

3682 Barham Blvd.
Los Angeles, CA 90068
(213) 874-0366
Margaret Hotham, director, American sales

Series
Parkinson

Documentaries
"Journey to the Moon"
"Naked Yoga"

Sports
World Senior Tennis Championships

Program Syndication Service, Inc.
405 Lexington Ave.
New York, NY 10017
(212) 532-1560
Peggy Green, president

Mini-series
Women of Russia
Unicorn Tales

Short Program Inserts
"21 Days of America"
"The 24 Days of Christmas"
"Quality of Life"

Specials
"Peanuts to the Presidency"
"Jerusalem, Jerusalem"
"Journey of Jesus"
"Gift of Winter"
"The Twelve Gifts"
"The Christmas Star"
"Sumthin' Good"
"Up Country, Down Under"
"The Eternal Tramp"
"Magic at the Roxy"

Series
Topper

Pro Sports Entertainment
154 E. 46th St.
New York, NY 10017
(212) 682-5390
Mike Vaughan, president

Series
NFL Great Teams/Great Years/Great Games
This Is the NFL
NFL Game of the Week
I Hope You're Bluffing!

Specials
"NFL Super Bowl XIII"

Program Inserts
"Big Buck Bingo"

Raymond Horn Productions
245 E. 63rd St.
New York, NY 10021
Raymond Horn, president

Series
Soap Factory Disco
Soap Opera Digest
Racing Fever

Specials
"American Image Awards"

R.D. Citron Associates, Inc.
17831 S.W. 108th Ct.
Miami, FL 33157
(305) 235-6600
Richard Citron, president

Series
Great Adventure

Production Consultation

Richard Feiner and Company, Inc.
230 Park Ave.
New York, NY 10017
(212) 687-5444
Richard Feiner, president

Laurel & Hardy Laughtoons

Robert Schuller Televangelism Association, Inc.
4201 W. Chapman Ave.
Orange, CA 92668
(714) 750-6969
Michael C. Nason, president

Robert Schuller with the Hour of Power

Roger B. Fransecky and Associates, Inc.
20 Nassau St., Suite 215
Princeton, NJ 08540
(609) 921-3696
Roger B. Francesky, president

515 Madison Ave.
New York, NY 10022
(212) 421-4030

Series
Hangin' Out
The Fable Company

Samuel Goldwyn Televison Company
1041 N. Formosa Ave.
Los Angeles, CA 90046
(213) 650-2400
Tom Seehof, vice-president

Best of Goldwin
Samuel Goldwyn Library of Feature Films
Hollywood: The Goldwyn Years
Snipets

Sandy Frank Film Syndication
635 Madison Ave.
New York, NY 10022
(212) 628-2770
Sandy Frank, president

Series
Battle of the Planets
$1.98 Beauty Show
Liars Club
$100,000 Name that Tune
Lee Mendelson Star Specials

Satori Productions, Inc.
250 W. 57th St., Suite 2105
New York, NY 10019
(212) 581-8450
Ernest G. Sauer, president

Features
Unknown Powers
The Great Gundown
Get Charlie Tully
Aliens from Spaceship Earth
The Hiding Place

Series
Celebration
Leslie the Shreve
Celebrity

SFM Media Service Corporation
6 E. 43rd St.
New York, NY 10017
(212) 682-0760
Stan Moger, president/programming

The SFM Holiday Network
Edward and Mrs. Simpson
The SFM Documentary Network
Television Annual

Show Biz, Inc.
110 21st Ave. S
Nashville, TN 37203
(615) 327-2532
J. Reginald Dunlap, president

Series
The $128,000 Question
Dolly
Gospel Singing Jubilee
Marty Robbins's Spotlight
Nashville on the Road
Pop! Goes the Country
The Porter Wagoner Show
Tony Brown's Special

Specials
"Anne Murray's Ladies' Night"

Sive Associates, Inc.
Broadway at 8th
Cincinnati, OH 45202
(513) 421-3000
Jack Thinnes, executive vice-president

Famous Classic Tales
A Cricket in Times Square
Yankee Doodle Cricket
Would You Believe. . .?

Solaris International Pictures, Inc.
2525 Ocean Park Blvd.
Santa Monica, CA 90405
(213) 450-6227
Les Lagoni, president

Mini-series
Shake a Leg
Enchanted Story Book
Magic Star Traveler
Fantasy Theater
The Hollywood Experience
Teego the Star Traveler
Cosmic Frontiers
Miss Phoebe's Garden
The New Filmmakers
For Goodness' Sake
Fun and Fitness
The Transformation of Rumpelstiltzkin
Blarney the Leprechaun
Heavenly Days
Memories of a Fairy Godmother
Noah and Son
Geppetto's Music Shop
Cosmic Junction
The Sandman
Sherlock and Me
Solarbration

Southern Baptist Radio and Television Commission
6350 West Freeway
Fort Worth, TX 76150
(817) 737-4011
Harold E. Martin, executive vice-president

Series
The Human Dimension
Jot
The Athletes
Listen

Starquest Productions, Inc.
1857 Taft Ave.
Hollywood, CA 90028
(213) 467-8277
Fred G. Thorne, president

Stanley's Smogless Steamer and Traveling Library
Champions: The Competitive Edge
Eyewitness to the Past
Nutz & Boltz Theatre
The Emerging Woman
The All-American Male Beauty Pageant
Stars of the Future
Race in Space

Program Inserts
"The Sum & Substance"

Sullivan Productions, Inc.
2029 Century Park East, Suite 1940
Los Angeles, CA 90067
(213) 552-6962
Robert Precht, president

Series
The Best of Sullivan
Calucci's Department

Specials
"AGVA 'Entertainer of the Year' Awards"

Survival Anglia Ltd.
420 Lexington Ave.
New York, NY 10017
(212) 867-6978
John F. Ball, president

Series
Roald Dahl's Tales of the Unexpected
World of Survival
For a Better World II

Syndicast Services, Inc.
919 3rd Ave.
New York, NY 10022
(212) 751-3394
Mitchell Johnson, president

Series
Don Kirshner's Rock Concert
Whitney & the Robot
At Home with Family Circle
Weigh in America

Sports
NASL Soccer
Spartakiade 79
NCAA Football Highlights

Specials
To America with Love
"Rhythm & Blues Awards"
"David Sheehan's Oscar Hopefuls"
"David Sheehan's Grammy Hopefuls"
Las Vegas Tonight
Readers' Digest Animated Classics
Readers' Digest "I Am Joe's . . ."

Taft H. B. Program Sales
1 E. 57th St.
New York, NY 10022
(212) 838-1225
Sam Johnston, president

Mini-series
Against the Wind

Animated Shows
Banana Splits & Friends
Fun World of Hanna-Barbera
After School Specials
Top Cat

Wait Till Your Father Gets Home
Captain Inventory
Josie & the Pussycats
"Energy: A National Issue"

Specials
"Elvis: Love Him Tender"

Program Inserts
"Loving Free"

T.A.T./Tandem/P.I.T.S.
1901 Ave. of the Stars, Suite 666
Los Angeles, CA 90067
(213) 553-3600
Robin French, president, syndication

Series
Sanford & Son
Maude
Good Times
The Baxters
America 2Night
Fernwood 2Night
Forever Fernwood
All that Glitters
Mary Hartman, Mary Hartman

Telecast International, Inc.
447 Lakeside Dr.
Burbank, CA 91505
(213) 846-9527
John F. Feeney, president

The Fourth Dimension
Spectreman
The Daring Breed
The Patsy Awards
"Reach for the Stars"

Telcom Associates, Inc.
1901 Ave. of the Stars, Suite 1030
Century City
Los Angeles, CA 90067
(213) 277-1691
Herb Jacobs, President

Programming and news consulting service

Telefilm Sales
35 Rowley Circle
Tiburon, CA 94920
(415) 435-9113
Ben Okulski, president

An independent western representative covering
14 states for Alan Enterprises, Inc., Gray-
Schwartz Enterprises, Inc., and Jim Victory Television, Inc.

Telepictures Corporation
1 Dag Hammarskjold Plaza
New York, NY 10017
(212) 838-1122
Michael J. Solomon, president

West Coast Offices
8732 Sunset Blvd.
Los Angeles, CA 90069
(213) 855-0975
Zane Bair, general manager-West Coast operations

The Sacketts
An Appointment with Dr. Joyce Brothers
Peter Lupus Body Shop
American Film Theatre
Who's #1
Canada Jam
Pet Vet

Features
American Film Theater
All the Kind Strangers

Television Business, Inc.
400 N. Michigan Ave.
Chicago, IL 60611
(312) 828-9422
Walter Schwimmer, president

News Program Inserts
"Wall Street Journal Television Business Report"
"Weekend Wall Street Journal Television Business
   Report"
"Today's News Flashbacks"
"Gallup TV Report"

Mini-series
The Jesus Trial

Television Representatives International, Inc.
9911 W. Pico Blvd.
Los Angeles, CA 90035
(213) 552-2660
Alan Silverbach, representative

Series
Carol Burnett and Friends
Laugh-In
Biography II
Sonny and Cher
The New Dick Van Dyke Show

Specials
The Word
The Martian Chronicles
"Scared Straight"
"The National Disaster Survival Test"
"The National Love, Sex and Marriage Test"
"Psychic Phenomenon: Exploring the Unknown"

Features
The Crash of Flight 401
The House on Garibaldi Street
The Winds of Kitty Hawk

Television Syndication Group, Inc.
366 N. Broadway, Suite 209
Jericho, NY 11753
(516) 935-9024
Jeffrey P. Smith, president

Series
Up for Grabs
The Melting Pot
Success
Country Serenade
Imagine That!
Coping
Eat Yourself Healthy
The Sam Diego Show
Remarkable
America Still
Sky's the Limit
Sew What's New
Down Home USA
America Sings
Master Bridge
Funny Man
Sacred Space

Teleworld, Inc.
10 Columbus Circle
New York, NY 10019
(212) 489-9310
Robert Seidelman, president

Specials
Prestige I
Entertainment Specials

Series
The Great Ones
The Laurel and Hardy Laughtoons
Star Maidens
Castaway

Features
Tele 20 Volume II
Chiller Package
Action Adventure Classics

Time-Life Television
(A division of Time-Life Films, Inc.)
Time-Life Bldg.
New York, NY 10020
(212) 841-2275
Bruce L. Paisner, president

Series
The Real McCoys
Wild, Wild World of Animals
A Horseman Riding By
All Creatures Great and Small
The Good Life
Joyce Davidson Show
Food, Wine and Friends
World War II: G.I. Diary
Doctor Who
The Harold Lloyd World of Comedy
Monty Python's Flying Circus
Murder Most English
Vision On
America
The Goodies
The Onedin Line

Features
Time-Life Volume 1 and 2
Harold Lloyd Film Classics

Specials and Mini-series
An Englishman's Castle
Moll Flanders
The Africans
Americans
Ten Who Dared
Europe, The Mighty Continent
Fall of Eagles
Glittering Prizes
BBC Outlook
  "A Blind Eye to Murder?"
  "The Bull's Eye War"
  "The Deep Cold War"
The Shirley Bassey Show
The Fight Against Slavery
The Search for the Nile
The Commanders
Family Classics
Ripping Yarns
Fawlty Towers
When the Boat Comes In
Window on the World
Civilization
The Ascent of Man
Wodehouse Playhouse
War and Peace
Billy Smart's Circus
The Six Wives of Henry VIII
The Fall and Rise of Reginald Perrin
Premiere
  "The Leo Sayer Show"
  "The Dick Van Dyke Harold Lloyd Special"

TM Productions, Inc.
1349 Regal Row
Dallas, TX 75247
(214) 634-8511
Jim Long, president

Packages
Where You Belong
Take a Good Look
Get to Know Us
Welcome to the World
You Can Count on Us
The Best Things in Life

Traco, Inc.
P.O. Box 3286
Tulsa, OK 74101
(918) 492-4094
Peggy George, general manager

Series
Oral Roberts and You

Specials
"Oral Roberts' Quarterly Specials"

Transda Advertising, Inc.
P.O. Box 0
Thousand Oakes, CA 91360
(805) 498-2133
Connie LaJoie, manager

It Is Written
Faith for Today
Breath of Life

TRC Productions/Israel Television Enterprises
21 Balfour St.
Jerusalem, Israel
(02) 630716
Yale Roe, president

Series
Israel Report
Holy Land Report

Specials
"Jerusalem, Jerusalem"
"The Journey of Jesus"
"The Dream Lives On"

Trois Amis Productions, Inc.
P.O. Box 414084
Miami Beach, FL 33141
(305) 891-5843
Leonard H. Schwartz, president

Medical Specialities
South Florida Locations
Aruba, Netherlands Antilles Locations

TV Sports Scene, Inc.
8200 Normandale Blvd.
Minneapolis, MN 55437
(612) 835-4716
Donald L. Herrick, president

"Always a New Beginning"
America Sings
American Ski Scene
"Benjamin"
Coping
"Dangerous Relations
"Douglas Stevens Special Delivery"
Down Home USA
Eat Yourself Healthy
"Fishing the Last Frontier"
High Adventure
"Holiday in Mazatland"
Magnum Package
"Marco Polo's Afganistan
"Miracle at City Hall"
"Pieces of Eight"
"Rescue Squad"
Sew What's New
"Ski Instructors Holiday"
Ski-Vision
Sky's the Limit
"Snow Dream"
"The Back-Packer"

The Green Scene
The Johnny Morris Ski Scene
The Melting Pot
The Roundhouse Show
The Sacred Space
"To Catch a Thrill"
"Trail to Alaska"
"New Star Over Hollywood"
"Israel—The Pressure Cooker"
Master Bridge

Features from China (limited to top 25 markets)
Witty Hand Sword
The 18 Bronze Girls of Shaolin
Little Hero Wins the Masks
The Lantern Street
The Rachel Copelan Show
Stampee Wrestling
You're Beautiful!
The Designery

TVS Television Network
280 Park Ave.
New York, NY 10017
(212) 949-3939
George H. Gallup, president

Series
The Supersatellite Concert Show
The Radio Show
A Joke's a Joke
Portraits of Power

Special
"The Edge"

Twentieth Century-Fox Television
10201 W. Pico Blvd.
Beverly Hills, CA 90213
(213) 277-2211
W. Russell Barry, president

Series
Dinah!
M*A*S*H
That's Hollywood
Dance Fever with Deney Terrio
Peyton Place '79
The Guinness Game
All Star Secrets
The Jackie Gleason Show
The National Enquirer
Smart Alecks
In the Madd House
T.H.E. Hospital
Batman
Circus
The Ghost and Mrs. Muir
Nanny and the Professor
Room 222
Land of the Giants
Lost in Space
Planet of the Apes
Voyage to the Bottom of the Sea

Feature Packages
Century Ten
Premiere 1
Fox Three
Laurel & Hardy
Century 5,6,7,8,9
Golden Century
Fox One and Two
Shriley Temple Theater

Sports
Numero Uno
The Olympiad

Cartoons
The Adventures of Mohammud Ali
Baggy Pants and the Nitwits

United Artists Television, Inc.
729 7th Ave.
New York, NY 10019
(212) 575-3000
Martin J. Robinson, president and chief executive
    officer
UA Showcase 6–10
UA Prime-Time Showcase 1 and 2
UA Showcase 12 and 13 Canada
Warner Brothers Features/Superstars
Charlie Chan/Mr. Wong
RKO Features
MG 8,10,11
MGM Pre-48 Movie Greats
Warner Brothers Cartoons
Popeye Cartoons
MGM Cartoons
MGM Shorts
Rat Patrol
Outer Limits
Gilligan's Island
Hollywood and the Stars
Mothers-in-Law
Patty Duke Show
Science Fiction Theatre

UPA Productions of America
4440 Lakeside Dr., P.O. Box 1546
Burbank, CA 91507
(213) 849-6666
Henry G. Saperstein, president

Features
High Seas Hijack
Atom Age Vampire
The Evil of Dracula
The Lake of Dracula
Espy
Project Doom
Battle of the Worlds
OSS-117 Double Agent
Island of the Burning Doomed
Deadly Companions
Bedelia
Paradise Alley
The Sicilians

Retreat from Kiska
Jackpot
Danger on My Side
Crosstrap
Jailbreak
Freedom to Die
Touch of Death
Ambush in Leopard Street

Series
What's New Mr. Magoo
Mr. Magoo Color Cartoons
Famous Adventures of Mr. Magoo
Roy Rogers Show
Dick Tracy Color Cartoons
Grenoble

Specials
"Mr. Magoo's Christmas Carol"
"Uncle Sam Magoo"
"Mr. Magoo's Snow White"
All Star Golf

Viacom Enterprises
1211 Ave. of the Americas
New York, NY 10036
(212) 575-5175
Kenneth Gorman, president, Viacom Entertain-
    ment Group (corporate)

Series, First-Run
Circus
The Price Is Right
$25,000 Pyramid
Family Feud

Series, Off-Network
All in the Family
Bob Newhart Show
Mary Tyler Moore Show
Hawaii Five-O
Grizzly Adams
Cannon
The Rookies
The Honeymooners
Family Affair
I Love Lucy
Beverly Hillbillies
Gunsmoke
Perry Mason
Hogan's Heroes
My Three Sons
Andy Griffith Show
Gomer Pyle
Dick Van Dyke Show
Wild Wild West
The Twilight Zone
Phil Silvers Show
Petticoat Junction

Feature Film Packages
Viacom Features I–VI
Viacom Movie Greats

Cartoons
Terrytoons

Programs (Animated)
"Cosmic Christmas"
"Devil and Daniel Mouse"
"Romie-O and Julie-8"

Victory Television
45 E. 45th St.
New York, NY 10017
(212) 687-1516
Jim Victory, president

Series
Streets of San Francisco
Match Game
Rhoda

Vipro, Inc.
645 N. Michigan Ave.
Chicago, IL 60611
(312) 664-7111
Donald J. Frehe, president

Series, Mini-series, Programs
Winner's Circle
Paul Harvey Comments
The Fisherman
Kup's Show
Celebrities on the Couch
The Gigglesnort Hotel
Computer Roulette
Let's Go to the Races
Harness Racing Sweepstakes

Specials
"The Gigglesnort Hotel Halloween Special"

Visual Productions (TV) Ltd.
118 Peter St.
Toronto, Ontario M5V 2G7 Canada
(416) 868-1563
Lionel Shenken, president

Series
Sounds Good
Lively Country
Lively Specials
The Wayne Thomas Comedy Show
Trip Tactics
Yesterday's Glitter

Vitt Media International
1114 Ave. of the Americas
New York, NY 10036
(212) 921-0500
Richard Olsen, vice-chairman

Regional Office
5900 Wilshire Blvd.
Los Angeles, CA 90036
(213) 938-2805

Cartoons
The Archies

Educational
Big Blue Marble

Specials
"My Seventeenth Summer"
"My Name Is Lisa"

Warner Brothers Television Distribution, Inc.
400 Warner Blvd.
Burbank, CA 91522
(213) 843-6000
Charles D. McGregor, president

Kung Fu
Wonder Woman
Roots: The Next Generation
The Phenomenon of Roots
Roots
The David L. Wolper Specials of the Seventies
The Waltons
Welcome Back, Kotter
Chico and the Man
The FBI Story
Volume 1-A and 2-A
Volume 11–21
13 Classic Thrillers
Tarzan Features
The Bowery Boys
Charlie Chan Film Festival
Starlite 1–6
The FBI
Maverick
Tarzan
F Troop
Superman
Batman/Superman/Aquaman
Porky Pig & Friends
Bugs Bunny & Friends

Weiss Global Enterprises
333 S. Beverly Dr.
Beverly Hills, CA 90212
(213) 553-5806
Adrian Weiss, president

Features
Galaxy "15"
Golden Showmanship "9"
Parade "4"
Impact "120"
English Classics
Westerns
Vintage Flicks

Documentaries
Custer's Last Stand
The Black Coin
The Clutching Hand

Series
Make Room for Daddy
My Little Margie
The Funny Farm
Voyages of a Queen
The Traveler/Northwest Traveler
Ski West
Craig Kennedy, Criminologist
Thrill of Your Life
Canine Comments

Comedy Shorts
The Chuckle Heads

Cartoons
Alice
Krazy Kid Kartunes
Nursery Rhymes

West Glen Communications, Inc.
565 5th Ave.
New York, NY 10017
(212) 986-5330
Stan S. Zeitlin, president

Producers and distributors of free-loan films

Public Affairs
Silent Countdown
If Only It Hurts a Little
Seeing
A Gift, an Obligation
The Prevention Factor
A House in the Woods
The Waiting Room

Sports
"Hockey: Where the Action Is"
"Heisman Trophy: The Possible Dream"
"25 Years: The NBA Story"

Series
Good Ideas for Decorating

Worldvision Enterprises, Inc.
660 Madison Ave.
New York, NY 10021
(212) 832-3838
Kevin O'Sullivan, president and chief executive officer

Features
Prime I–VI

Series
Little House on the Prairie
Stars on Ice
The Newlywed Game
The Doris Day Show
The Next Step Beyond
Dark Shadows
Let's Make a Deal
Casper, the Friendly Ghost
Wonders of the Wild
Great Adventure
FDR
The Irish Rovers
Come Along
The Wonderful Stories of Professor Kitzel
The Mod Squad
It Pays to Be Ignorant
The Jackson Five
Discovery
Specially for Kids
Ben Casey
Combat

Specials
Holocaust
Fabulous Sixties
"Bay City Rollers"
"Roberta Flack"
"Billy Paul & the Staple Singers"
"Raphael"

Y&R Program Services (Young & Rubicam, Inc.)
285 Madison Ave.
New York, NY 10017
(212) 953-6087
Joseph Schrier, vice-president, group supervisor

"Night Flight"

Talent Agencies

American Federation of Television and Radio Artists (AFTRA) Roster of Franchised Agents*

AB Services Associates, Inc.
(Althea Knowles)
738 N. LaSalle, Suite 300
Chicago, IL 60610
(312) 337-2726

Abrams-Rubaloff & Associates
9012 Beverly Blvd.
Los Angeles, CA 90048
(213) 273-5711

Act I Casting Agency
(Stella Freed)
1460 Brickell Ave., Suite 208
Miami, FL 33131
(305) 371-1371

Act 48 Management, Inc.
1501 Broadway, Rm. 1713
New York, NY 10036
(212) 354-4250

Rose Adair Agency
250 W. 57th St., Suite 1527
New York, NY 10019
(212) 582-1957

Bret Adams, Ltd.
36 E. 61st St., 2nd Fl.
New York, NY 10021
(212) 752-7864

Bret Adams, Ltd.
8282 Sunset Blvd., Suite F
Los Angeles, CA 90046
(213) 656-6420

William Adrian Agency
520 S. Lake Ave.
Pasadena, CA 91101
(213) 681-5750

Advertiser's Casting Agency
9205 W. Center
Milwaukee, WI 53222
(414) 259-1611

Advertiser's Casting Service
15324 E. Jefferson Ave., Suite 2-4
Grosse Pointe, MI 48230
(313) 823-1880

Affiliated Models, Inc.
28860 Southfield Rd., Suite 100
Southfield, MI 48076
(313) 559-3110

Agency for Artists
9200 Sunset Blvd., Suite 531
Los Angeles, CA 90069
(213) 278-6243

The Agency
512 Nicollet Mall, Suite 409
Minneapolis, MN 55402
(612) 339-3661

Agency for the Performing Arts, Inc.
120 W. 57th St.
New York, NY 10019
(212) 582-1500

Agency for the Performing Arts, Inc.
203 N. Wabash Ave.
Chicago, IL 60601
(312) 664-7703

Agency for the Performing Arts, Inc.
9000 Sunset Blvd., Suite 315
Los Angeles, CA 90069
(213) 273-0744

Agents for the Arts, Inc.
1650 Broadway, Suite 306
New York, NY 10019
(212) 247-3220

Aimee Entertainment Association
(Joyce Aimee)
14241 Ventura Blvd., Suite 104
Sherman Oaks, CA 91423
(213) 872-0374

*Reprinted with permission of the American Federation of Television and Radio Artists, AFL-CIO, 1350 Ave. of the Americas, New York, NY 10019, (212) 265-7700. Sanford I. Wolff National Executive Secretary — Constance McDowell, National Administrator, AFTRA Agents.

Willard Alexander, Inc.
660 Madison Ave.
New York, NY 10021
(212) 751-7070

Willard Alexander, Inc.
333 N. Michigan Ave.
Chicago, IL 60601
(312) 236-2460

Carlos Alvarado Agency
8820 Sunset Blvd.
Hollywood, CA 90069
(213) 652-0272

The Amaral Agency
10000 Riverside Dr., Suite 11
Toluca Lake, CA 91602
(213) 980-1013

Velvet Amber Agency
6515 Sunset Blvd., Suite 200A
Hollywood, CA 90028
(213) 464-8184

Ambrose, Nani & Associates, Inc.
60 E. 42nd St., Suite 610
New York, NY 10017
(212) 953-1910

American International Talent Agency
166 W. 125th St., Rm. 6
New York, NY 10027
(212) 663-4626

Fred Amsel & Associates
215 La Cienga Blvd., Suite 200
Beverly Hills, CA 90211
(213) 855-1201

Beverly Anderson Agency
1472 Broadway, Suite 806
New York, NY 10036
(212) 279-5553, 279-5554

A-Plus Talent Agency Corp.
666 N. Lake Shore Dr., Suite 1725
Chicago, IL 60611
(312) 642-8151

Arcara, Bauman & Hiller
250 W. 57th St.
New York, NY 10019
(212) 757-0098

Arcara, Bauman & Hiller
9220 Sunset Blvd.
Los Angeles, CA 90069
(213) 271-5601

Sam H. Armstrong, Inc.
8235 Santa Monica Blvd.
Los Angeles, CA 90048
(213) 656-4753

Arnold Agency, Inc.
1252 W. Peachtree St.
Atlanta, GA 30309
(404) 873-2001

Irvin Arthur Associates, Ltd.
9615 Brighton Way, Suite 212
Beverly Hills, CA 90210
(213) 278-5934

Artists Career Management (ACM)
9157 Sunset Blvd., Suite 206
Los Angeles, CA 90069
(213) 278-9157

Associated Booking Corp.
1995 Broadway
New York, NY 10023
(212) 874-2400

Associated Booking Corp.
2700 North River Rd.
Des Plaines, IL 60018
(312) 296-0930

Associated Booking Corp.
3511 Hall St.
Dallas, TX 75219
(214) 528-8296

Associated Booking Corp.
2925 La Cienga Blvd.
Beverly Hills, CA 90211
(213) 855-8051

Associated Booking Corp.
4055 S. Spencer St., #204
Las Vegas, NV 89109
(702) 734-8155

Associated Talent Agency, Inc.
56 W. 45th St.
New York, NY 10036
(212) 840-1909

Richard Astor Agency
119 W. 57th St., Suite 1111
New York, NY 10019
(212) 581-1970

Atlanta Models & Talent, Inc.
3030 Peachtree Rd. NW, Suite 308
Atlanta, GA 30305
(404) 261-9627

Miles Bohm Auer Agency
8344 Melrose Ave., Suite 29
Hollywood, CA 90069
(213) 462-6416

B B & A Talent Placement Agency
3098 Piedmont Rd. NE, Suite 307
Atlanta, GA 30305
(404) 231-9369

Backstages Workshop Talent Agency
8025 Ward Pkwy. Plaza
Kansas City, MO 64114
(816) 363-8088

Baldwin-Scully, Inc.
501 5th Ave., Suite 1012
New York, NY 10017
(212) 682-5335

Barbizon Agency of Colorado
(John Urquhart)
Cinderella City
Englewood, CO 80110
(303) 781-7828

Barbizon-Monza Model & Talent Agency
Garden Level Commerce Tower
Kansas City, MO 64105
(816) 421-0222

Barr/Wilder & Associates
8721 Sunset Blvd., Suite 205
Los Angeles, CA 90069
(213) 652-7994

Barry Agency
165 W. 46th St., Suite 810
New York, NY 10036
(212) 869-9310

The Barskin Agency
8730 Sunset Blvd., Suite 501
Los Angeles, CA 90069
(213) 657-5740

Larry Bastian Agency
2580 Crestwood La.
Deerfield, IL 60015
(312) 945-9283, 945-9284

Beakel & Jennings Agency
427 N. Canon Dr., Suite 205
Beverly Hills, CA 90210
(213) 274-5418

The Beckman Agency
8489 W. 3rd St., Suite 28
Los Angeles, CA 90048
(213) 653-5600

Peter Beilin Agency
Artists' Representatives
230 Park Ave., Suite 1223
New York, NY 10017
(212) 949-9119

Belson & Klass Associates
211 S. Beverly Dr., #107
Beverly Hills, CA 90212
(213) 274-9169

David Bendett Agency, Inc.
2431 Briarcrest Rd.
Beverly Hills, CA 90210
(213) 278-5657

N. S. Bienstock, Inc.
10 Columbus Circle, Suite 1270
New York, NY 10019
(212) 765-3040

Lola Bishop Agency
200 W. 51st St.
New York, NY 10019
(212) 245-4775

Tanya Blair Agency
2320 N. Griffin
Dallas, TX 75202
(214) 748-8353

The Blake Agency, Ltd.
(Merritt Blake)
409 N. Camden Dr., Suite 200
Beverly Hills, CA 90210
(213) 278-6885

Nina Blanchard Enterprises, Inc.
1717 N. Highland Ave., Suite 901
Los Angeles, CA 90028
(213) 462-7341

J. Michael Bloom, Ltd.
400 Madison Ave., Suite 1705
New York, NY 10017
(212) 832-6900

J. Michael Bloom, Ltd.
9220 Sunset Blvd., Suite 302
Los Angeles, CA 90069
(213) 275-6800

Bonnie Kid, Inc.
250 W. 57th St.
New York, NY 10019
(212) 246-0223

Brandon & Rogers Associates
9046 Sunset Blvd., Suite 201
Los Angeles, CA 90069
(213) 273-6173

Sonjia Warren Brandon's Commercials Unlimited,
    Inc.
(*see* Commercials Unlimited, Inc.)

Brebner Agencies, Inc.
China Basin Bldg.
161 Berry St., Suite 1248
San Francisco, CA 94107
(415) 495-6700

Bresler, Wolff, Cota & Livingston
190 N. Canon Dr.
Beverly Hills, CA 90210
(213) 278-3200

Alex Brewis Agency
8721 Sunset Blvd., Suite 104
Los Angeles, CA 90069
(213) 274-9874

Rosemary Brian Agency
50 E. Palisade Ave., Suite 203
Englewood, NJ 07631
(212) 564-8616

The Bruce Agency
1022 16th Ave. S
Nashville, TN 37212
(615) 255-5711

Don Buchwald & Associates, Inc.
10 E. 44th St.
New York, NY 10017
(212) 867-1070

Dott Burns Model & Talent Agency
478 Severn
Tampa, FL 33606
(813) 251-5882

Iris Burton Agency
1450 Belfast Dr.
Los Angeles, CA 90069
(213) 652-0954

The Calder Agency
8749 Sunset Blvd.
Hollywood, CA 90069
(213) 652-3380

Carey-Phelps-Colvin Agency, Inc.
1407 N. LaBrea Blvd.
Los Angeles, CA 90028
(213) 874-7780, 652-2137

William Carroll Agency
2321 W. Olive Ave., Unit C
Burbank, CA 91506
(213) 848-9948

The Nancy Carter Agency
1801 Ave. of the Stars, Suite 640
Los Angeles, CA 90067
(213) 277-2683

Bertha Case
42 W. 53rd St.
New York, NY 10019
(212) 581-6280

The Richard Cataldi Agency
250 W. 57th St., Suite 1527
New York, NY 10019
(212) 245-6660

Central Casting, Inc.
1000 Connecticut Ave. NW, Suite 804
Washington, DC 20006
(202) 659-8272

Century Artists, Ltd.
9744 Wilshire Blvd., Suite 206
Beverly Hills, CA 90212
(213) 273-4366

Rita Chandler Agency, Inc.
8833 Sunset Blvd., Suite 311
Los Angeles, CA 90069
(213) 855-0641

Charter Management
(Michael Greenfield)
9000 Sunset Blvd., Suite 1112
Los Angeles, CA 90069
(213) 278-1690

Chasin-Park-Citron Agency
9255 Sunset Blvd.
Los Angeles, CA 90069
(213) 273-7190

The Chez Agency
225 Peachtree St., Suite 705
Atlanta, GA 30303
(404) 588-1215

Clark-Boyd Agency
6210 Wilshire Blvd., Suite 201-203
Los Angeles, CA 90048
(213) 939-3503

David J. Cogan Management Co.
350 5th Ave., Rm. 7920
New York, NY 10001
(212) 563-9555, 563-9562

Coleman-Rosenberg
667 Madison Ave.
New York, NY 10021
(212) 838-0734

Kingsley Colton & Associates, Inc.
321 S. Beverly Dr.
Beverly Hills, CA 90212
(213) 277-5491

Columbia Artists Management, Inc.
165 W. 57th St.
New York, NY 10019
(212) 397-6900

Commercial Actors Agency
8500 Wilshire Blvd., Suite 604
Beverly Hills, CA 90025
(213) 855-0422

Commercial Artist Management Agency
2232 5th Ave.
San Diego, CA 92101
(714) 233-6655

Commercials Unlimited, Inc.
7461 Beverly Blvd.
Los Angeles, CA 90036
(213) 937-2220

Allen Connor-Alexis Corfino Associates, Inc.
14241 Ventura Blvd.
Sherman Oaks, CA 91403
(213) 981-1133

Contemporary-Korman Artists, Ltd.
Contemporary Artists Bldg.
132 Lasky Dr.
Beverly Hills, CA 90212
(213) 278-8250

Bill Cooper Associates, Inc.
16 E. 52nd St., Suite 1504
New York, NY 10022
(212) 758-6491

Coralie Jr., Theatrical Agency
4789 Vineland Ave., Suite 100
N. Hollywood, CA 91602
(213) 766-9501

The Craig Agency
8732 Sunset Blvd., Suite 256
Los Angeles, CA 90069
(213) 855-1448

Creative Artists Agency, Inc.
1888 Century Park E, Suite 1400
Los Angeles, CA 90067
(213) 277-4545

Creative Casting, Inc.
Talent Management
430 Oak Grove
Minneapolis, MN 55403
(612) 871-7866

Creative Enterprises Talent Agency, Inc.
(Gayle Hames)
2863 1st Ave. S
St. Petersburg, FL 33712
(813) 823-3700

Creative Expressions Agency
(Gloria Greene)
439 S. La Cienega Blvd., Suite 110
Los Angeles, CA 90048
(213) 278-5121

John Crosby & Associates
9046 Sunset Blvd., Suite 210
Los Angeles, CA 90069
(213) 278-5121

Mary Crosby Talent Agency
2130 4th Ave.
San Diego, CA 92101
(714) 234-7911

Lil Cumber Attractions Agency
6515 Sunset Blvd., Suite 408
Hollywood, CA 90028
(213) 469-1919

William D. Cunningham & Associates
919 3rd Ave.
New York, NY 10022
(212) 832-2700

William D. Cunningham & Associates
261 S. Robertson Blvd.
Beverly Hills, CA 90211
(213) 855-1700

Cup Stars, Inc.
527 Madison Ave., Suite 1201
New York, NY 10022
(212) 838-1163

D.M.I. Talent Associates, Ltd.
250 W. 57th St., Suite 713
New York, N.Y. 10019
(212) 246-4650

Dade/Rosen Associates
999 N. Doheny Dr., #102
Los Angeles, CA 90069
(213) 278-7077

Harrise Davidson & Associates, Inc.
230 N. Michigan Ave., Suite 1325
Chicago, IL 60601
(312) 782-4480

Kim Dawson Agency
1143 Apparel Mart
2300 Stemmons Freeway
Dallas, TX 75207
(214) 638-2414

Jane Deacy Agency, Inc.
119 E. 54th St.
New York, NY 10022
(212) 752-4865

Del Valle, Franklin, Levine Agency
2049 Century Park E, Suite 1330
Los Angeles, CA 90067
(213) 552-7852

Demeter & Reed, Ltd.
Pier 26, The Embarcadero
San Francisco, CA 94105
(415) 777-1337

Lew Deuser Agency
449 S. Beverly Dr.
Beverly Hills, CA 90212
(213) 553-8611

Diamond Artists, Ltd. Agency
(Abner J. Greshler, Pres.)
9200 Sunset Blvd., Suite 909
Hollywood, CA 90069
(213) 278-8146

Richard Dickens & Company
5550 Wilshire Blvd., Suite 306
Los Angeles, CA 90036
(213) 937-3080

The Dietrich Agency
10850 Riverside Dr., Suite 501
N. Hollywood, CA 91602
(213) 985-4824

Frances Dilworth Agency
Oradell Plaza
496 Kinderkamack Rd.
Oradell, NJ 07649
(212) 661-0070, (201) 265-4020

Gloria Dolan Management, Ltd.
850 7th Ave., Suite 1004
New York, NY 10019
(212) 581-7040

Stephen Draper Agency
37 W. 57th St.
New York, NY 10019
(212) 421-5780

Dryden-MacArthur-Randall & Associates
6430 Sunset Blvd., Suite 916
Los Angeles, CA 90028
(213) 461-2727

Ebony Talent Associates, Inc.
7558 S. Chicago
Chicago, IL 60619
(312) 752-3955

Dulcina Eisen Associates
346 E. 50th St., 2nd Fl.
New York, NY 10022
(212) 355-6617

The Steve Ellis Agency, Inc.
250 W. 57th St.
New York, NY 10019
(212) 757-5800

Entertainment Enterprises
Hollywood Taft Bldg.
Hollywood & Vine
Hollywood, CA 90028
(213) 462-6001

Travis Falcon Theatrical Agency
17070 Collins Ave., Suite 231
Miami Beach, FL 33160
(305) 947-7957

Leslie Fargo Agency
280 N. Woodward, Suite 200
Birmingham, MI 48011
(313) 647-7171

William Felber Agency
2126 Cahuenga Blvd.
Hollywood, CA 90068
(213) 466-7629

Jack Fields & Associates
9255 Sunset Blvd., Suite 1105
Hollywood, CA 90069
(213) 278-1333

Marje Fields, Inc.
250 W. 57th St., Suite 1518
New York, NY 10019
(212) 581-7240

Film Artists Associates
8730 Sunset Blvd., Suite 401
Los Angeles, CA 90069
(213) 652-6230

Film Artists Management Enterprises
8278 Sunset Blvd.
Los Angeles, CA 90046
(213) 656-7590

Filor Talent Agency, Inc.
110 E. 55th St.
New York, NY 10022
(212) 832-1636

Florida Talent Agency, Inc.
2631 E. Oakland Pk. Blvd., Suite 206
Ft. Lauderdale, FL 33317
(305) 563-3552 (FtL)
(305) 947-1931 (Miami)

Judith Fontaine Agency
6565 W. Sunset Blvd., Suite 512
Hollywood, CA 90028
(213) 467-6288

Ford-Talent Group, Inc.
344 E. 59th St.
New York, NY 10022
(212) 688-8628

Kurt Frings Agency, Inc.
9440 Santa Monica Blvd., Suite 400
Beverly Hills, CA 90210
(213) 274-8881

Fugate Agency for Models
Division of House of Charms
157 Maiden La. at Union Sq.
San Francisco, CA 94108
(415) 421-0968

The Gage Group, Inc.
(Martin Gage)
1650 Broadway, Suite 406
New York, N.Y. 10019
(212) 541-5250

The Gage Group, Inc.
8732 Sunset Blvd., Suite 750
Los Angeles, CA 90069
(213) 652-8833

Gail & Rice Talent
11845 Mayfield
Livonia, MI 48150
(313) 427-9300, 427-9315

Dale Garrick International Agency
8831 Sunset Blvd.
Hollywood, CA 90069
(213) 657-2661

Ann Geddes, Inc.
2444 Hancock Center
Chicago, IL 60611
(312) 664-9890 (Producers), 664-9892 (Talent)

Gem Model & Talent Agency
920 Nicollet Mall, Suite 210
Minneapolis, MN 55402
(612) 338-4442

Gerritsen International
8721 W. Sunset Blvd., Suite 205
Los Angeles, CA 90069
(213) 659-8414

Phil Gersh Agency, Inc.
222 N. Canon Dr., Suite 201
Beverly Hills, CA 90210
(213) 274-6611

J. Carter Gibson
9000 Sunset Blvd., Suite 811
Los Angeles, CA 90069
(213) 274-8813

Georgia Gilly/Sidney Levee
8721 Sunset Blvd., Suite 103
Los Angeles, CA 90069
(213) 657-5660, 652-0012

Goldin-Dennis & Associates
470 S. San Vicente Blvd., Suite 104
Los Angeles, CA 90048
(213) 651-1700

Allen Goldstein & Associates
201 N. Robertson Blvd.
Beverly Hills, CA 90211
(213) 278-5005

The Gordean-Friedman Agency, Inc.
9570 Wilshire Blvd., Suite 400
Beverly Hills, CA 90212
(213) 273-4195

Mary Grady Agency
10850 Riverside Dr., Suite 504
N. Hollywood, CA 91602
(213) 985-9800

The Granite Agency
1920 S. La Cienega Blvd., Suite 205
Los Angeles, CA 90034
(213) 934-8383

Greenevine Agency
9021 Melrose Ave., Suite 304
Los Angeles, CA 90069
(213) 278-5800

Grimme Agency
214 Grant Ave., Suite 302
San Francisco, CA 94115
(415) 421-8715

Grossman-Stalmaster Agency
8730 Sunset Blvd.
Los Angeles, CA 90069
(213) 657-3040

H. A. Artists & Associates, Inc.
575 Lexington Ave., Suite 2601
New York, NY 10022
(212) 935-8980

Peggy Hadley Enterprises, Ltd.
250 W. 57th St., Suite 2317
New York, NY 10019
(212) 246-2166, 246-2293

Jeanne Halliburton Agency
5205 Hollywood Blvd., Suite 203
Los Angeles, CA 90027
(213) 466-6138

Lola Hallowell Model & Talent Agency
158 Thomas St., Suite 14
Seattle, WA 98109
(206) 623-7311

Gerri Halpin Agency
911 Kipling
Houston, TX 77006
(713) 526-5749

Mitchell J. Hamilburg Agency
292 S. La Cienega Blvd., Suite 212
Beverly Hills, CA 90211
(213) 657-1501

Shirley Hamilton, Inc.
620 N. Michigan Ave.
Chicago, IL 60611
(312) 644-0300

The Carolyn Hansen Agency
1516 6th Ave.
Seattle, WA 98101
(206) 622-4992

Ellen Harth, Inc.
515 Madison Ave., Suite 1902
New York, NY 10022
(212) 593-2332

Hartig-Josephson Agency, Ltd.
527 Madison Ave., Suite 308
New York, NY 10022
(212) 759-9163

Beverly Hecht Agency
8949 Sunset Blvd.
Los Angeles, CA 90069
(213) 278-3544

Henderson/Hogan Agency, Inc.
200 W. 57th St., Rm. 304
New York, NY 10019
(212) 765-5190

Henderson/Hogan Agency, Inc.
247 S. Beverly Dr., Suite 102
Beverly Hills, CA 90212
(213) 274-7815

June Henry, Inc.
119 W. 57th St.
New York, NY 10019
(212) 582-8140

Hesseltine-Baker Associates, Ltd.
119 W. 57th St.
New York, NY 10019
(212) 489-0966

The House of Talent of Cain, Inc.
996 Lindridge Dr. NE
Atlanta, GA 30324
(404) 261-5543

Eric W. Howard
2 Century Plaza, Suite 1100
2049 Century Park E
Los Angeles, CA 90067
(213) 552-1540

The Hughes Agency
9100 Sunset Blvd., Suite 360
Los Angeles, CA 90069
(213) 550-7166

Diana Hunt Management
246 W. 44th St., Suite 807
New York, NY 10036
(212) 391-4971

George B. Hunt & Associates Theatrical Agency
8350 Santa Monica Blvd., Suite 104
Los Angeles, CA 90069
(213) 654-6600

Jeff Hunter Management
119 W. 57th St.
New York, NY 10019
(212) 245-1919

Ray Hunter & Associates
132 Lasky Dr.
Beverly Hills, CA 90212
(213) 276-1137

Robert G. Hussong Agency
8271 Melrose Ave., Suite 108
Los Angeles, CA 90046
(213) 655-2534

Hutto Management, Inc.
110 W. 57th St.
New York, NY 10019
(212) 531-5610

J. F. Images, Inc.
(Mary Jo Farrell)
1776 S. Jackson St., Suite 702
Denver, CO 80210
(303) 758-7777

George Ingersoll Agency
6513 Hollywood Blvd., Suite 217
Hollywood, CA 90028
(213) 874-6434

International Creative Management
A Division of Marvin Josephson Associates, Inc.
40 W. 57th St.
New York, NY 10019
(212) 556-5600

International Creative Management
A Division of Marvin Josephson Associates, Inc.
8899 Beverly Blvd.
Los Angeles, CA 90048
(213) 550-4000

International Creative Management
A Division of Marvin Josephson Associates, Inc.
111 N.W. 183rd St.
Miami, FL 33169
(305) 652-9111

Jacobson/Wilder, Inc.
400 Madison Ave., Suite 1408
New York, NY 10017
(212) 759-0860

Jan J. Agency
(Robert Jarrett)
222 E. 46th St.
New York, NY 10017
(212) 490-1875

Joe Jordan Talent Agency, Inc.
400 Madison Ave.
New York, NY 10017
(212) 838-4910

Junior Artists Unlimited
4914 Lankersham Blvd.
North Hollywood, CA 91601
(213) 763-9000, 786-1684

Jerry Kahn, Inc.
853 7th Ave.
New York, NY 10019
(212) 582-1280

Toni Kelman Agency
7813 Sunset Blvd.
Los Angeles, CA 90046
(213) 851-8822

Sharon Kemp
8601 Wilshire Blvd., Suite 601
Beverly Hills, CA 90211
(213) 553-9486

The Gregory Kerr Agency
4372 Woodman Ave.
Sherman Oaks, CA 91423
(213) 995-4317

Archer King, Ltd.
777 7th Ave., Suite M-93-94
New York, NY 10019
(212) 581-8513

The Tyler Kjar Agency
9229 Sunset Blvd., Suite 408
Los Angeles, CA 90069
(213) 278-0912

Kolmar-Luth Entertainment, Inc.
1776 Broadway
New York, NY 10019
(212) 581-5833

Lucy Kroll Agency
390 West End Ave.
New York, NY 10024
(212) 877-0627, 0556, 0557

LBH Associates, Inc.
20 W. 64th St., 30V
New York, NY 10023
(212) 787-2609

The Lantz Office, Inc.
114 E. 55th St.
New York, NY 10022
(212) 751-2107

Lionel Larner, Ltd.
850 7th Ave.
New York, NY 10019
(212) 246-3105

John LaRocca & Associates
3907 W. Alameda Ave.
Burbank, CA 91505
(213) 841-0031

Joanne Lawrence Agency
82 Patrick Rd.
Westport, CT 06880
(203) 226-7239

Irving Paul Lazar Agency
211 S. Beverly Dr., Suite 100
Beverly Hills, CA 90212
(213) 275-6153

Leaverton Associates, Ltd.
1650 Broadway, Suite 1113
New York, NY 10019
(212) 541-9640

Buddy Lee Attractions, Inc.
38 Music Sq. E, Suite 300
Nashville, TN 37203
(615) 244-4336

Buddy Lee Attractions, Inc.
1775 Broadway, Suite 632
New York, NY 10019
(212) 247-5216

David Lee Models Central Casting
936 N. Michigan Ave., Suite 201
Chicago, IL 60611
(312) 649-0500

David Lee Models Central Casting
325 Cleveland Plaza
Cleveland, OH 44115
(216) 522-1300

Dorian Leigh Model Agency
1001 Euclid Ave., Suite 400
Cleveland, OH 44115
(216) 579-1188

Sanford Leigh Enterprises, Ltd.
527 Madison Ave.
New York, N.Y. 10022
(212) 752-4450

Caroline Leonetti, Ltd.
6526 Sunset Blvd.
Hollywood, CA 90028
(213) 462-2345

Mark Levin Associates
328 S. Beverly Dr., Suite E
Beverly Hills, CA 90212
(213) 277-8881

Lester Lewis Associates, Inc.
156 E. 52nd St.
New York, NY 10022
(212) 753-5082

David Libert Agency
1108 N. Sherbourne Dr.
Los Angeles, CA 90069
(213) 659-6776

Terry Lichtman Company
9301 Wilshire Blvd., Suite 508
Beverly Hills, CA 90210
(213) 550-4550

Robert Longenecker Agency
11704 Wilshire Blvd., Suite 200
Los Angeles, CA 90025
(213) 477-0039

Bessie Loo Agency
8746 Sunset Blvd.
Los Angeles, CA 90069
(213) 657-5888

Lordly & Dame, Inc.
51 Church St.
Boston, MA 02116
(617) 482-3593

Emilia Lorence, Ltd.
619 N. Wabash
Chicago, IL 60611
(312) 787-2033

Love Artists, Ltd.
1900 Ave. of the Stars, Suite 560
Los Angeles, CA 90067
(213) 553-5117

Lovell & Associates
812 N. Highland Ave.
Los Angeles, CA 90038
(213) 659-8476

Lynn & Reilly Agency
Sunset-Vine Tower
6290 W. Sunset Blvd.
Hollywood, CA 90028
(213) 461-2828

M.E.W. Company
(*see* Mary Ellen White, Inc.
New York and California)

M-M-C Agency
(Mildred M. Claussen)
5400 Hollywood Blvd., Rm. 302
Hollywood, CA 90028
(213) 467-7278

MMG Enterprises, Ltd.
'Marcia's Kids'
250 W. 57th St., Suite 1815
New York, NY 10019
(212) 246-4360

Ernestine McClendon Enterprises, Inc.
8440 Sunset Blvd., M-5
Hollywood, CA 90069
(213) 654-4425

Beverly McDermott Talent Agency
923 N. Golf Dr.
Hollywood, FL 33021
(305) 947-6798

Marge McDermott Enterprises
214 E. 39th St.
New York, NY 10016
(212) 889-1583

James McHugh Agency
8150 Beverly Blvd., Suite 206
Los Angeles, CA 90048
(213) 651-2770

Jess Mack Theatrical Agency
1111 Las Vegas Blvd. S, Suite 209
Las Vegas, NV 89104
(702) 382-2193

The Mad Hatter, Inc.
(Mary Anne Duffy)
1400 S. Post Oak, Suite 1501
Houston, TX 77056
(713) 621-3720

Magna Artists Corp.
595 Madison Ave., Suite 901
New York, NY 10022
(212) 752-0363

Magna Artists Corp.
9200 Sunset Blvd.
Los Angeles, CA 90069
(213) 273-3177

Main Line Models Guild
1315 Walnut St., Room 1002
Philadelphia, PA 19107
(215) 546-5919

Mannequin Fashion Models Agency, Inc.
730 5th Ave.
New York, NY 10019
(212) 586-7716

MarBea Talent Agency
Key Executive Bldg.
104 Crandon Blvd., Suite 305
Key Biscayne, FL 33149
(305) 361-1144

Tina Marie's Talent Agency
1823 N. Western Ave.
Hollywood, CA 90027
(213) 469-9270, 464-2894

Herbert Marks Talent Agency
600 Lincoln Rd. Bldg.
Miami Beach, FL 33139
(305) 534-2119, 534-2110

Alese Marshall Model Agency
24050 Vista Montana
Torrance, CA 90505
(213) 378-1223

John Martinelli Attractions, Inc.
888 8th Ave.
New York, NY 10019
(212) 586-0963

Media Enterprises
(Regina N. Penner)
3459 Cahuenga Blvd. W, Suite 106
Los Angeles, CA 90068
(213) 851-2221

William Meiklejohn Associates
9250 Wilshire Blvd., Suite 412
Beverly Hills, Calif. 90212
(213) 273-2566

Fred Messenger Agency
8265 Sunset Blvd.
Hollywood, CA 90046
(213) 654-3800

George Michaud Agency
4950 Densmore, Suite 1
Encino, CA 91436
(213) 981-6680

Michele Unlimited
8060 Melrose Ave., Suite 225
Los Angeles, CA 90046
(213) 653-9610

Midiri Models, Inc.
1920 Chestnut St.
Philadelphia, PA 19103
(215) 561-5028

The Gilbert Miller Agency
8350 N. Kimball Ave.
Skokie, IL 60076
(312) 674-3630

The Mishkin Agency, Inc.
9255 Sunset Blvd.,
Los Angeles, CA 90069
(213) 274-5261

Models Guild of Philadelphia, Inc.
The Drake Hotel
1512 Spruce St., Suite 412
Philadelphia, PA 19102
(215) 735-4067

Eleanor Moore Model & Talent Agency, Inc.
1610-B W. Lake St.
Minneapolis, MN 55408
(612) 827-3823

William Morris Agency, Inc.
1350 Ave. of the Americas
New York, NY 10019
(212) 586-5100

William Morris Agency, Inc.
151 El Camino
Beverly Hills, CA 90212
(213) 274-7451

William Morris Agency, Inc.
2325 Crestmoor Rd., P.O. Box 15245
Nashville, TN 37215
(615) 385-0310

The Burton Moss Agency
113 N. San Vicente Blvd., Suite 202
Beverly Hills, CA 90211
(213) 655-1156

H. David Moss & Associates
113 N. San Vicente Blvd., Suite 302
Beverly Hills, CA 90211
(213) 653-2900

Marvin Moss, Inc.
9200 Sunset Blvd., Suite 601
Los Angeles, CA 90069
(213) 274-8483

Mary Murphy Agency
10701 Riverside Dr.
Toluca Lake, CA 91602
(213) 985-4241

New Faces
(Diane L. Kubat)
310 Groveland Ave.
Minneapolis, MN 55403
(612) 871-6000

Norton Agency, Inc.
European Crossroads
2829 W.N.W. Highway, Suite 701
Dallas, TX 75220
(214) 357-6439

Novel Models, Inc.
1204 Wisconsin Ave. NW
Washington, DC 20007
(202) 296-1570

The Oliver Agency
(Maurine Oliver)
8746 Sunset Blvd.
Los Angeles, CA 90069
(213) 657-1250

Oppenheim-Christie Associates, Ltd.
565 5th Ave.
New York, NY 10017
(212) 661-4330

Fifi Oscard Associates, Inc.
19 W. 44th St.
New York, NY 10036
(212) 764-1100

Barna Ostertag
501 5th Ave., Suite 1410
New York, NY 10017
(212) 697-6339

Dorothy Day Otis Agency
6430 Sunset Blvd.,
Hollywood, CA 90028
(213) 461-4911

Pacific Artists, Ltd.
515 N. La Cienega Blvd.
Los Angeles, CA 90048
(213) 657-5990

Dorothy Palmer Talent Agency, Inc.
250 W. 57th St., Rm. 1527
New York, NY 10019
(212) 765-4280, 765-4295

Patricia Parker Agency
2221 W. Olive Ave., Suite H
Burbank, CA 91506
(213) 271-0644

Ben Pearson Agency, Inc.,
606 Wilshire Blvd., #614
Santa Monica, CA 90401
(213) 451-8414

The Perkins Agency
156 E. 52nd St.
New York, NY 10022
(212) 752-4488

Judy Pfaff Modeling Agency
4017 Morningside Rd.
Edina, MN 55416
(612) 927-4445

Philbin Talent Agency
2323 W. Devon Ave.
Chicago, IL 60614
(312) 465-2839, 465-2490

Richard Pitman Agency
229 W. 42nd St.
New York, NY 10036
(212) 947-5555

Joel Pitt Agency
250 W. 57th St., Suite 725
New York, NY 10019
(212) 765-6373

Jerry Plantz Productions, Inc.
1703 Wyandotte, Suite 203
Kansas City, MO 64108
(816) 471-1501

Playboy Model Agency
8560 Sunset Blvd., Suite 500
Los Angeles, CA 90069
(213) 659-4080

Playboy Models, Inc.
919 N. Michigan Ave.
Chicago, IL 60614
(312) 664-9024

The Plaza Agency
(Chris Barry)
205 E. Joppa Rd., Suite 503
Towson, MD 21204
(301) 321-1611

Marian Polan Talent Agency
2451 Brickell Ave., Suite 4-E
Miami, FL 33129
(305) 379-7526

Premier Talent Agency
3 E. 54th St.
New York, NY 10022
(212) 758-4900

Premiere Artists & Productions Agency
6399 Wilshire Blvd., Suite 506
Los Angeles, CA 90048
(213) 651-3545

Professional Artists Management
9441 Wilshire Blvd., Penthouse Suite
Beverly Hills, CA 90212
(213) 275-4270

Professional Models & Actor Talent Agency
2975 Headland Dr.
Atlanta, GA 30311
(404) 346-1210, 763-2122

Progressive Artists Agency
400 S. Beverly Dr., Suite 216
Beverly Hills, CA 90212
(213) 553-8561

Quinn Casting & Theatrical Agency
518 Colorado Bldg.
1341 G St. NW
Washington, DC 20005
(202) 347-1611, 347-7412

Raglyn-Shamsky
Talent Representatives, Ltd.
60 E. 42nd St., Suite 1330
New York, NY 10017
(212) 661-6690

Robert Raison Agency
9575 Lime Orchard Rd.
Beverly Hills, CA 90210
(213) 274-7217

Raper Enterprises Agency
6311 Yucca St.
Hollywood, CA 90028
(213) 461-5033

Ray Rappa Agency
2018 Rosilla Pl.
Los Angeles, CA 90046
(213) 650-1190

Tina Real Agency
3108 5th Ave., Suite B
San Diego, CA 92103
(714) 298-0544

Regency Artists, Ltd.
9200 Sunset Blvd., Suite 823
Los Angeles, CA 90069
(213) 273-7103

Rice-McHugh Agency, Inc.
445 Park Ave.
New York, NY 10022
(212) 752-0222

Elaine Rich & Associates
8533 Sunset Blvd., Suite 203
Los Angeles, CA 90069
(213) 652-3951

Rifkin-David
9301 Wilshire Blvd., Suite 306
Beverly Hills, CA 90212
(213) 550-0359

Right Face, Inc.
12429 Cedar Rd.
Cleveland Heights, OH 44106
(216) 231-0505

Roberts/Shiffrin Artists, Ltd.
8833 Sunset Blvd., Suite 406
Hollywood, CA 90069
(213) 659-9396

Robinson-Weintraub & Associates, Inc.
554 S. San Vicente Blvd., Suite 3
Los Angeles, CA 90048
(213) 653-5802

Dick Romaine Agency
1900 Ave. of the Stars, #2350
Los Angeles, CA 90067
(213) 277-2987, night: 279-1364

Gilla Roos, Ltd.
501 Madison Ave.
New York, NY 10022
(212) 758-5480

Lewis Maxwell Rosen, Ltd.
1650 Broadway, Suite 601
New York, NY 10019
(212) 582-6762

Lynn Rosselli Agency
1650 Broadway, Suite 606
New York, NY 10019
(212) 489-7227, 489-7228, 489-7229

Sandy Roth Ruben
9418 Wilshire Blvd.
Beverly Hills, CA 90212
(213) 274-9448

Bernard Rubenstein Agency
342 Madison Ave.
New York, NY 10017
(212) 986-1317

Rush/Flaherty Agency, Inc.
10889 Wilshire Blvd., Suite 1130
Los Angeles, CA 90024
(213) 479-6591

Art Rush, Inc.
10221 Riverside Dr., Suite 219
North Hollywood, CA 91602
(213) 985-3033

Bennie Russell Talent Agent
11030 Ventura Blvd., #2
Studio City, CA 91604
(213) 980-3805

Jack Russell & Associates
244 Constance La.
Chicago Heights, IL 60411
(312) 756-7060

Charles V. Ryan Agency
200 W. 57th St., Suite 205
New York, NY 10019
(212) 245-2225

Ryden-Frazer Agency
Pruneyard Towers I, Suite 344
1901 S. Bascom Ave.
Campbell, CA 95008
(408) 371-1973, 371-1975

Sabina Talent, Inc.
Division of Sabina Models, Inc.
415 Merchant St.
San Francisco, CA 94111
(415) 788-3920

The Sackheim Agency
9301 Wilshire Blvd., Suite 606
Beverly Hills, CA 90210
(213) 858-0606

Gloria Safier, Inc.
667 Madison Ave.
New York, NY 10021
(212) 838-4868

Norah Sanders Agency
4737 Lankersham Blvd.
N. Hollywood, CA 91602
(213) 769-2162

Norah Sanders Agency
4467 Morrell St.
San Diego, CA 92109
(714) 270-9891

Peggy Schaefer Agency
10850 Riverside Dr., Suite 500-A
N. Hollywood, CA 91602
(213) 985-5547

The Irv Schechter Company
404 N. Roxbury Dr., Suite 800
Beverly Hills, CA 90210
(213) 278-8070

Norman Schucart Enterprises
1417 Green Bay Rd.
Highland Park, IL 60035
(312) 433-1113

The William Schuller Agency, Inc.
667 Madison Ave.
New York, NY 10021
(212) 758-1919

Howard W. Schultz Theatrical Agency
2525 W. Peterson Ave.
Chicago, IL 60659
(312) 769-2244

Don Schwartz & Associates
8721 Sunset Blvd.
Los Angeles, CA 90069
(213) 657-8910

Seattle Models Guild
1610 6th Ave.
Seattle, WA 98101
(206) 622-1406

Jack Segal Enterprises, Inc.
850 7th Ave., Suite 605
New York, NY 10019
(212) 265-7489

David Shapira & Associates, Inc.
9100 Wilshire E. Tower
Beverly Hills, CA 90212
(213) 278-2742

Seymour Shapiro Agency
(Seymour and Gertrude Shapiro)
307 N. Michigan Ave.
Chicago, IL 60601
(312) 236-9596

Glenn Shaw Agency
3330 Barham Blvd., Suite 103
Hollywood, CA 90068
(213) 851-6262

Lew Sherrell Agency, Ltd.
7060 Hollywood Blvd., Suite 210
Hollywood, CA 90028
(213) 461-9955

Shipley-Ishimoto Agency
9163 Sunset Blvd.
Los Angeles, CA 90069
(213) 276-6251, 276-6252

Dorothy Shreve Agency
13444 Ventura Blvd.
Sherman Oaks, CA 91423
(213) 783-1128

Monty Silver Agency, Ltd.
200 W. 57th St., Suite 1303
New York, NY 10019
(212) 765-4040

Susan Smith & Associates
850 7th Avenue, Suite 1003
New York, NY 10019
(212) 581-4490

Susan Smith & Associates
9869 Santa Monica Blvd., #207
Beverly Hills, CA 90212
(213) 277-8464

Anthony Soglio Agency
423 Madison Ave.
New York, NY 10017
(212) 751-1850

Arnold Soloway Associates
118 S. Beverly Dr., Suite 226
Beverly Hills, CA 90212
(213) 550-1300

The Starkman Agency, Inc.
1501 Broadway
New York, NY 10036
(212) 921-9191

STE Representation, Ltd.
888 7th Ave., 18th Fl.
New York, NY 10019
(212) 246-1030

STE Representation, Ltd.
211 S. Beverly Dr., Suite 201
Beverly Hills, CA 90212
(213) 550-3982

Lillian Stein Agency
1501 Broadway, Suite 2007
New York, NY 10036
(212) 840-8299

Charles H. Stern Agency, Inc.
9220 Sunset Blvd., Suite 218
Los Angeles, CA 90069
(213) 273-6890

Stevens-Gray Agency
8733 Sunset Blvd., Suite 206
Los Angeles, CA 90069
(213) 657-8955

Patricia Stevens Casting Agency
1900 W. Big Beaver Rd.
Troy, MI 48084
(313) 643-1900

Stewart Artists Corporation
140 E. 63rd St., 19th Fl.
New York, NY 10021
(212) 752-0944

Stewart Personal Management Corp.
140 E. 63rd St., 19th Fl.
New York, NY 10021
(212) 753-4610

The Stiefel Office, Ltd.
9255 Sunset Blvd., Suite 510
Los Angeles, CA 90069
(213) 274-7333

Stix & Gude
6 E. 45th St.
New York, NY 10017
(212) 986-8990

Stroud Management
18 E. 48th St., Rm. 1103
New York, NY 10017
(212) 688-0226

Summit Artists
8833 Sunset Blvd., Suite 301
Los Angeles, CA 90069
(213) 659-6211

Sutton Artists Corporation
505 Park Ave.
New York, NY 10022
(212) 832-8302

Sutton, Barth & Vennari Agency, Inc.
8322 Beverly Blvd.
Los Angeles, CA 90048
(213) 653-8322

Take One, Talent
3330 Peachtree Rd. NE, Suite 456
Atlanta, GA 30326
(404) 231-2315

Talent, Inc., Agency
1418 N. Highland Ave., Suite 111
Hollywood, CA 90028
(213) 462-0913

The Talent Agency
(Cam Rippinger)
16 W. 13th Ave., Suite 201
Denver, CO 80204
(303) 893-1383

Talent Central, Ltd.
1845 N. Farwell
Milwaukee, WI 53202
(414) 278-8811

Talent Enterprises, Inc.
1603 N.E. 123rd St.
Miami, FL 33181
(305) 891-1832

Talent Group, Inc.
8831 Sunset Blvd. E, Penthouse A
Los Angeles, CA 90069
(213) 659-8072

Talent & Model Land
1443 12th Ave. S
Nashville, TN 37203
(615) 385-2725

Talent Plus, Inc.
7525 Forsyth
St. Louis, MO 63105
(314) 721-3355

Talent Representatives, Inc.
20 E. 53rd St.
New York, NY 10022
(212) 752-1835

The Talent Shop
550 Pharr Rd. NE, Suite 210
Atlanta, GA 30305
(404) 261-0770

Herb Tannen & Associates
6640 Sunset Blvd., Suite 203
Los Angeles, CA 90028
(213) 466-6191

Taylor Artists Management
(Donna M. Taylor)
2035 LaVante Ave.
Las Vegas, NV 89109
(702) 735-5596, 734-6278

Peggy Taylor Talent, Inc.
3616 Howell, Suite 212
Dallas, TX 75204
(214) 526-4800

Peggy Taylor Talent, Inc.
3777 S. Gessner, 908
Houston, TX 77063
(713) 789-6835

Taylor Royall Casting
(Cory Taylor)
2308 South Rd.
Baltimore, MD 21209
(301) 466-5959, (202) 621-1769

Lyle Thayer Agency
510 Hillgreen Dr.
Beverly Hills, CA 90212
(213) 553-8918

Jean Thomas Agency, Inc.
342 Madison Ave., Suite 1126
New York, NY 10017
(212) 490-3954

Michael Thomas Agency, Inc.
22 E. 60th St.
New York, NY 10022
(212) 755-2616

Herb Tobias & Associates, Inc.
1901 Ave. of the Stars, Suite 840
Los Angeles, CA 90067
(213) 277-6211

Total Talent
3727 Broadway
Kansas City, MO 64111
(816) 931-9243

Tranum, Robertson & Hughes, Inc.
2 Hammarskjold Plaza
New York, NY 10017
(212) 371-7500

Trenda Artists
(Charles Trenda)
14755 Ventura Blvd.
Sherman Oaks, CA 91403
(213) 788-4521

Gloria Troy Talent Agency, Inc.
1790 Broadway
New York, NY 10019
(212) 582-0260

Twentieth Century Artists, Inc.
13273 Ventura Blvd., Suite 211
Studio City, CA 91604
(213) 990-8580

U. K. Management, Inc.
1052 Carol Dr.
Los Angeles, CA 90069
(213) 275-9599

The Ufland Agency, Inc.
190 N. Canon Dr.
Beverly Hills, CA 90210
(213) 273-9441

Universal Attractions, Inc.
888 7th Ave., Suite 401
New York, NY 10019
(212) 582-7575

La Vonne Valentine
Talent & Modeling Agency
2113 Van Ness Ave.
San Francisco, CA 94109
(415) 673-7965, 885-9604

Vannoy Talent Agency
1100 E. 16th Ave.
Denver, CO 80218
(303) 832-7177

Marge Van Ostrand & Associates
13437 Ventura Blvd., Suite 221
Sherman Oaks, CA 91423
(213) 995-0702

Angie Vitt Agency
6117 Reseda Blvd.
Reseda, CA 91335
(213) 276-1646

Bob Waters Agency, Inc.
510 Madison Ave.
New York, NY 10022
(212) 593-0543

Ruth Webb, Ltd.
9229 Sunset Blvd., Suite 509
Los Angeles, CA 90069
(213) 274-4311, 874-1700

Jack Weiner Agency
8721 Sunset Blvd.
Hollywood, CA 90069
(213) 652-1140

Murray Weintraub Agency
8230 Beverly Blvd., Suite 23
Los Angeles, CA 90048
(213) 653-5640

Wender & Associates
30 E. 60th St., Suite 903
New York, NY 10022
(212) 832-8330

Warren Wever Artists' Management
1104 S. Robertson Blvd.
Los Angeles, Calif 90035
(213) 276-7065

Mary Ellen White, Inc.
370 Lexington Ave.
New York, NY 10017
(212) 889-7272

Mary Ellen White, Inc.
151 N. San Vicente Blvd.
Beverly Hills, CA 90211
(213) 653-4731

Wilhelmina Model Agency, Inc.
9 E. 37th St.
New York, NY 10016
(212) 532-7141 (Genl. #), 889-9450 (TV)

Wilhelmina West, Inc.
1800 Century Park E, Suite 504
Los Angeles, CA 90067
(213) 553-9525

Ted Wilk Agency
9172 Sunset Blvd.
Hollywood, CA 90069
(213) 273-0801

Williamson & Associates
932 N. La Brea Blvd.
Los Angeles, CA 90038
(213) 851-1881

The Francine Witkin Agency
6430 Sunset Blvd., Suite 1010-B
Hollywood, CA 90028
(213) 461-3726

Ted Witzer Agency
1900 Ave. of the Stars, Suite 2850
Los Angeles, CA 90067
(213) 552-9521

Wormser, Heldfond & Joseph, Inc.
1717 N. Highland Ave.
Hollywood, CA 90028
(213) 466-9111

Sylvia Wosk Agency
439 S. La Cienega Blvd.
Los Angeles, CA 90048
(213) 274-8063

Ann Wright Associates, Ltd.
8422 Melrose Pl.
Los Angeles, CA 90069
(213) 655-5040

Ann Wright Representatives, Inc.
136 E. 57th St.
New York, NY 10022
(212) 832-0110

Writers & Artists Agency
162 W. 56th St., Suite 404
New York, NY 10019
(212) 246-9029

Writers & Artists Agency
450 N. Roxbury Dr., Suite 200
Beverly Hills, CA 90210
(213) 550-8030

Joy Wyse's Professional Talent Agency
6318 Gaston Ave.
Dallas, TX 75214
(214) 826-0330

Babs Zimmerman Productions, Inc.
101 W. 57th St.
New York, NY 10019
(212) 757-9735

Zoli Management, Inc.
121 E. 62nd St.
New York, NY 10021
(212) 758-5959

Video Recorders

There are many kinds of videocassette recorders, but the two leading types of home videocassette recorders sold in the United States are Beta and VHS (Video Home System). The basic differences between these two types of machines are the sizes of the cassettes (the VHS uses a bigger tape), the speed at which the tape moves, and the way in which the tape is drawn from the cassette. In the Beta system, the tape is drawn from the cassette in the machine and then wrapped around a rotating drum by the use of a swinging arm. In the VHS, the tape is drawn out and wrapped around a rotating drum by two parallel arms.

There are many machines on the market, but the difference between them, other than the basic differences between Beta and VHS, stem from the unique facilities each firm wishes built into their product. The company that manufactures most of the VHS machines is Matsushita of Japan.

The suggested list price of most current-model home videocassette recorders ranges from $1,000 to $1,500. The newer VHS machines are presently offering six hours of recording time (to be increased to nine with a new cassette containing more and thinner tape). The recording time for new Beta machines (using a thinner tape) is five hours. The more complex recorders of both the Beta and the VHS systems have a programmable timer that allows the owner to record various programs at various times over a period of a week or more. Most have a built-in timer that will automatically turn on and record a specific program and then shut off. Battery-operated portable recorders with color or black-and-white cameras are also available for making "electronic home movies." All videocassette recorders record in color.

Listed below are the major American manufacturers and importers now in the VCR business.

Curtis Mathes Co.
1 Curtis Mathes Pkwy.
Athens, TX 75751
(214) 675-2294

General Electric
3135 Easton Turnpike
Fairfield, CT 06431
(203) 373-2211

GTE Sylvania
700 Ellicott St.
Batavia, NY 14020
(716) 347-3470

Hitachi Sales Corp. of America
401 W. Artesia
Compton, CA 90220
(213) 537-8383

JVC America, Inc.
58-75 Queens Midtown Expwy.
Maspeth, NY 11378
(212) 476-8300

Magnavox Consumer Electronics Co.
1700 Magnavox Way
Fort Wayne, IN 46804
(219) 432-6411

Melco Sales, Inc. (MGA brand)
Subsidiary of Mitsubishi Electric Corp.
3030 E. Victoria St.
Compton, CA 90221
(213) 537-7132

Panasonic
Subsidiary of Matsushita Electric Corp. of America
1 Panasonic Way
Secaucus, NJ 07940
(201) 248-7000

Philco
700 Ellicott St.
Batavia, NY 14020
(716) 343-3470

Quasar Electronics Corp.
Subsidiary of Matsushita Electric Corp. of America
9401 W. Grand Ave.
Franklin Park, IL 60131

RCA Corp.
30 Rockefeller Plaza
New York, NY 10020
(212) 598-5900

Sanyo Electric, Inc.
1200 W. Artesia
Compton, CA 90220
(213) 537-5830

Sears Roebuck & Co.
Sears Tower
Chicago, IL 60684
(312) 875-2500

Sony Corp. of America
9 W. 57th St.
New York, New York 10019
(212) 371-5800

Toshiba America, Inc.
280 Park Ave.
New York, NY 10017

Zenith Radio Corp.
1000 Milwaukee Ave.
Glenview, IL 60025
(312) 391-7000

(The authors are most grateful to David Lachen-
bruch of *TV Digest* for his assistance with the information provided above.)

Index